Intermediate Financial Management

Intermediate Financial Management

EUGENE F. BRIGHAM
University of Florida

PHILLIP R. DAVES
University of Tennessee

CENGAGE
Learning·

Australia • Brazil • Mexico • Singapore • United Kingdom • United States

Intermediate Financial Management,
12th Edition

Eugene F. Brigham and Phillip R. Daves

Vice President, General Manager:
   Vice President, General Manager, Science,
Math & Quantitative Business: Balraj Kalsi

Product Director: Joe Sabatino

Sr. Product Manager: Mike Reynolds

Sr. Content Developer: Kendra Brown

Sr. Product Assistant: Adele Scholtz

Marketing Manager: Heather Mooney

Sr. Marketing Coordinator: Eileen Corcoran

Content Project Manager: Jana Lewis

Media Developer: Jessica Robbe

Manufacturing Planner: Kevin Kluck

Production Service: MPS Limited

Sr. Art Director: Michelle Kunkler

Internal Designer: Lou Ann Thesing

Cover Designer: Lou Ann Thesing

Cover Image:
   Dimitris Kolyris/Dreamstime.com

Intellectual Property

   Analyst: Christina Ciaramella

   Project Manager: Betsy Hathaway

For product information and technology assistance, contact us at
Cengage Learning Customer & Sales Support, 1-800-354-9706

For permission to use material from this text or product,
submit all requests online at **www.cengage.com/permissions**
Further permissions questions can be emailed to
permissionrequest@cengage.com

Unless otherwise noted, figures and tables © Cengage Learning.

Library of Congress Control Number: 2014946238

ISBN: 978-1-285-85003-0

Cengage Learning
20 Channel Center Street
Boston, MA 02210
USA

Cengage Learning is a leading provider of customized learning solutions with office locations around the globe, including Singapore, the United Kingdom, Australia, Mexico, Brazil, and Japan. Locate your local office at: **www.cengage.com/global**

Cengage Learning products are represented in Canada by Nelson Education Ltd.

To learn more about Cengage Learning Solutions, visit **www.cengage.com**

Purchase any of our products at your local college store or at our preferred online store **www.cengagebrain.com**

Printed in Canada
Print Number: 01   Print Year: 2014

Brief Contents

WEB CHAPTERS & WEB EXTENSIONS

Students: Access the Web Chapters and Web Extensions by visiting **www.cengagebrain.com**, searching ISBN 9781285850030, and clicking "Access Now" under "Study Tools" to go to the student textbook companion site.

Instructors: Access the Web Chapters, Web Extensions, and other instructor resources by going to **www.cengage.com/login**, logging in with your faculty account username and password, and using ISBN 9781285850030 to search for and to add resources to your account "Bookshelf."

WEB CHAPTERS

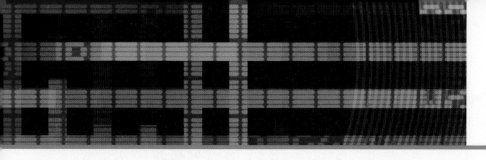

Contents

APPENDIXES

WEB CHAPTERS & WEB EXTENSIONS

Students: Access the Web Chapters and Web Extensions by visiting **www.cengagebrain.com**, searching ISBN 9781285850030, and clicking "Access Now" under "Study Tools" to go to the student textbook companion site.

Instructors: Access the Web Chapters, Web Extensions, and other instructor resources by going to **www.cengage.com/login**, logging in with your faculty account username and password, and using ISBN 9781285850030 to search for and to add resources to your account "Bookshelf."

Web Chapters

Web Extensions

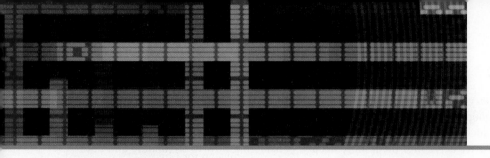

Much has happened in finance recently. Years ago, when the body of knowledge was smaller, the fundamental principles could be covered in a one-term lecture course and then reinforced in a subsequent case course. This approach is no longer feasible. There is simply too much material to cover in one lecture course.

As the body of knowledge expanded, we and other instructors experienced increasing difficulties. Eventually, we reached these conclusions:

- The introductory course should be designed for all business students, not just for finance majors, and it should provide a broad overview of finance. Therefore, a text designed for the first course should cover key concepts but avoid confusing students by going beyond basic principles.
- Finance majors need a second course that provides not only greater depth on the core issues of valuation, capital budgeting, capital structure, cost of capital, and working capital management but also covers such special topics as mergers, multinational finance, leasing, risk management, and bankruptcy.
- This second course should also utilize cases that show how finance theory is used in practice to help make better financial decisions.

When we began teaching under the two-course structure, we tried two types of existing books, but neither worked well. First, there were books that emphasized theory, but they were unsatisfactory because students had difficulty seeing the usefulness of the theory and consequently were not motivated to learn it. Moreover, these books were of limited value in helping students deal with cases. Second, there were books designed primarily for the introductory MBA course that contained the required material, but they also contained too much introductory material. We eventually concluded that a new text was needed, one designed specifically for the second financial management course, and that led to the creation of *Intermediate Financial Management*, or *IFM* for short.

The Next Level: *Intermediate Financial Management*

In your introductory finance course you learned a number of terms and concepts. However, an intro course cannot make you "operational" in the sense of actually "doing" financial management. For one thing, introductory courses necessarily focus on individual chapters and even sections of chapters, and first-course exams generally consist of relatively simple problems plus short-answer questions. As a result, it is hard to get a good sense of how the various parts of financial management interact with one another. Second, there is not enough time in the intro course to allow students to set up and work out realistic problems, nor is there time to delve into actual cases that illustrate how finance theory is applied in practice.

Now it is time to move on. In *Intermediate Financial Management*, we first review materials that were covered in the introductory course, then take up new material. The review is absolutely essential, because no one can remember everything

WEB

Students: Access the *Intermediate Financial Management 12e* companion site and online student resources by visiting **www.cengagebrain .com**, searching for ISBN 9781285850030 and clicking "Access Now" under "Study Tools" to go to the student textbook companion site.

Instructors: Access the *Intermediate Financial Management 12e* companion site and instructor resources by going to **www .cengage.com /login**, logging in with your faculty account username and password, and using ISBN 9781285850030 to reach the site through your account "Bookshelf."

that was covered in the first course, yet all of the introductory material is essential for a good understanding of the more advanced material. Accordingly, we revisit topics such as the net present value (NPV) and internal rate of return (IRR) methods, but now we delve into them more deeply, considering how to streamline and automate the calculations, how to obtain the necessary data, and how errors in the data might affect the outcome. We also relate the topics covered in different chapters to one another, showing, for example, how cost of capital, capital structure, dividend policy, and capital budgeting combine forces to affect the firm's value.

Also, because spreadsheets such as *Excel*, not financial calculators, are used for most real-world calculations, students need to be proficient with spreadsheets so that they will be more marketable after graduation. Therefore, we explain how to do various types of financial analysis with *Excel*. Working with *Excel* actually has two important benefits: (1) a knowledge of *Excel* is important in the workplace and the job market, and (2) setting up spreadsheet models and analyzing the results also provide useful insights into the implications of financial decisions.

Corporate Valuation as a Unifying Theme

Management's goal is to maximize firm value. Job candidates who understand the theoretical underpinning for value maximization and have the practical skills to analyze business decisions within this context make better, more valuable employees. Our goal is to provide you with both this theoretical underpinning and a practical skill set. To this end, we have developed several integrating features that will help you keep the big picture of value maximization in mind while you are honing your analytical skills:

- Every chapter starts off with a series of integrating *Beginning-of-Chapter Questions* that will help you place the material in the broader context of financial management.
- Most chapters have a valuation graphic and description that show exactly how the material relates to corporate valuation.
- Each chapter has a *Mini Case* that provides a business context for the material.
- Each chapter has an *Excel* spreadsheet *Tool Kit* that steps through all of the calculations in the chapter.
- Each chapter has a spreadsheet *Build-a-Model* that steps you through constructing an *Excel* model to work problems. We've designed these features and tools so that you'll finish your course with the skills to analyze business decisions and the understanding of how these decisions impact corporate value.

Design of the Book

Based on more than 30 years working on *Intermediate Financial Management* and teaching the advanced undergraduate financial management course, we have concluded that the book should include the following features:

- *Completeness.* Because *IFM* is designed for finance majors, it should be self-contained and suitable for reference purposes. Therefore, we specifically and purposely included: (a) some material that overlaps with introductory finance texts and (b) more material than can realistically be covered in a single course. We included in Chapters 2 through 5 some fundamental materials borrowed directly from other Cengage Learning texts. If an instructor chooses to cover this material, or if an individual student feels a need to cover it on his or her own, it is available. In other chapters, we included relatively brief reviews of first-course topics. This was necessary both to put *IFM* on a stand-alone basis and to help students who have a delay between their introductory and second financial management courses get up to speed before tackling new material. This review is particularly important for working capital management and such "special topics" as mergers, lease analysis, and convertibles—all of which are often either touched on only lightly or skipped in the introductory course. Thus, the variety of topics covered in the text provides adopters with a choice of materials for the second course, and students can use materials that were not covered for reference purposes. We note, though, that instructors must be careful not to bite off more than their students can chew.

- *Theory and applications*. Financial theory is useful to financial decision makers, both for the insights it provides and for direct application in several important decision areas. However, theory can seem sterile and pointless unless its usefulness is made clear. Therefore, in *IFM*, we present theory in a decision-making context, which motivates students by showing them how theory can lead to better decisions. The combination of theory and applications also makes the text more usable as a reference for case courses as well as for real-world decision making.

- *Computer orientation*. Today, a business that does not use computers in its financial planning is about as competitive as a student who tries to take a finance exam without a financial calculator. Throughout the text, we provide computer spreadsheet examples for the calculations and spreadsheet problems for the students to work. This emphasis on spreadsheets both orients students to the business environment they will face upon graduation and helps them understand key financial concepts better.

- *Global perspective*. Successful businesses know that the world's economies are rapidly converging, that business is becoming globalized, and that it is difficult to remain competitive without being a global player. Even purely domestic firms cannot escape the influence of the global economy, because international events have a significant effect on domestic interest rates and economic activity. All of this means that today's finance students—who are tomorrow's financial executives—must develop a global perspective. To this end, *IFM* also contains an entire chapter on multinational financial management. In addition, to help students "think global," we provide examples throughout the text that focus on the types of global problems companies face. Of course, we cannot make multinational finance experts out of students in a conventional corporate finance course, but we can help them recognize that insular decision making is insufficient in today's world.

Beginning-of-Chapter Questions

We start each chapter with several Beginning-of-Chapter (BOC) questions. You will be able to answer some of the questions before you even read the chapter, and you will be able to give better answers after you have read it. Other questions are harder, and you won't feel truly comfortable answering them until after they have been discussed in class. We considered putting the questions at the ends of the chapters, but we concluded that they would best serve our purposes if placed at the beginning. Here is a summary of our thinking as we wrote the questions:

- The questions indicate to you the key issues covered in the chapter and the things you should know when you complete the chapter.
- Some of the questions were designed to help you remember terms and concepts that were covered in the introductory course. Others indicate where we will be going beyond the intro course.
- You need to be able to relate different parts of financial management to one another, so some of the BOC questions were designed to get you to think about how the various chapters are related to one another. These questions tend to be harder, and they can be answered more completely after a classroom discussion.
- You also need to think about how financial concepts are applied in the real world, so some of the BOC questions focus on the application of theories to the decision process. Again, complete answers to these questions require a good bit of thought and discussion.
- Some of the BOC questions are designed to help you see how *Excel* can be used to make better financial decisions. These questions have accompanying models that provide tutorials on *Excel* functions and commands. The completed models are available on the textbook's Web site. Going through them will help you learn how to use *Excel* as well as give you valuable insights into the financial issues covered in the chapter. We have also provided an "*Excel* Tool Locater," which is an index of all of the *Excel* skills that the BOC models go over. This index is in the *Excel* file, *Excel Locations.xls*. Because recruiters like students who are good with *Excel*, this will also help you as you look for a good job. It will also help you succeed once you are in the workplace.

We personally have used the BOC questions in several different ways:

- In some classes we simply told students to use the BOC questions or not, as they wished. Some students did study them and retrieve the *Excel* models from the Web, but many just ignored them.
- We have also assigned selected BOC questions and then used them, along with the related *Excel* models, as the basis for some of our lectures.
- Most recently, we literally built our course around the BOC questions.[1] Here we informed students on day one that we would start each class by calling on them randomly and grading them on their answers.[2] We also informed them that our exams would be taken verbatim from the BOC questions. They complained a bit about the quizzes, but the students' course evaluations stated that the quizzes should be continued because without them they would have come to class less well prepared and hence would have learned much less than they did.
- The best way to prepare for the course as we taught it was by first reading the questions, then reading the chapter, and then writing out notes outlining

---

1. Actually, we broke our course into two segments, one where we covered selected text chapters and another where we covered cases that were related to and illustrated the text chapters. For the case portion of the course, students made presentations and discussed the cases. All of the cases required them to use *Excel*.

2. Most of our students were graduating seniors who were interviewing for jobs. We excused them from class (and the quizzes) if they informed us by e-mail before class that they were interviewing.

answers to the questions in preparation for the oral quiz. We expected students to give complete answers to "easy" questions, but we gave them good grades if they could say enough about the harder questions to demonstrate that they had thought about how to answer them. We would then discuss the harder questions in lieu of a straight lecture, going into the related *Excel* models both to explain *Excel* features and to provide insights into different issues.

• Our midterm and final exams consisted of five of the harder BOC questions, of which three had to be answered in 2 hours in an essay format. It took a much more complete answer to earn a good grade than would have been required on the oral quizzes. We also allowed students to use a four-page "cheat sheet" on the exams.[3] That reduced time spent trying to memorize things as opposed to understanding them. Also, students told us that making up the cheat sheets was a great way to study.

Major Changes in the Twelfth Edition

As in every revision, we updated and clarified sections throughout the text. Specifically, we also made the following changes in content:

References to, implications of, and explanations for the global economic crisis. Last edition we began using the global economic crisis to illustrate important learning points, and we have continued that in this edition with new examples and tie-ins to the chapters' topics.

Additional integration of the textbook and the accompanying Excel Tool Kit spreadsheet models for each chapter. Many figures in the textbook come directly from the chapter's *Excel Tool Kit* model. This serves two purposes. First, it makes the analysis more transparent to the student; the student or instructor can go to the *Tool Kit* and see exactly how all of the numbers in a figure were calculated. Second, it provides an additional resource for students and instructors to use in learning *Excel*.

Improvements in the MicroDrive Examples. For many editions, we have used a hypothetical company, MicroDrive, as a running example. This provides continuity in the examples from chapter to chapter and helps students apply the material more quickly. We have improved the integration in this edition and have made some changes to the financial statements to accommodate our changes. First, the financial statement values are now all integers and in most cases end with a zero, which simplifies calculations. Second, we have separated operating costs into three categories: cost of goods sold (excluding depreciation), other operating costs, and depreciation. This allows for added flexibility when defining ratios and forecasting financial statements. Third, we have modified the financial statements to allow MicroDrive to be the illustrative company for more chapters and more topics than in previous editions. This has been especially important in the systematic risk topic and the free cash flow valuation topic.

---

3. We did require that students make up their own "cheat sheets," and we required them to turn their sheets in with their exams so we could check for independence.

Significant Changes in Selected Chapters

We made many small improvements within each chapter; some of the more notable ones are discussed below.

Chapter 1: An Overview of Financial Management and the Financial Environment We added a box on high-frequency trading—"Life in the Fast Lane: High-Frequency Trading!"—and a box on mortgage-backed securities, "Anatomy of a Toxic Asset." We also increased our coverage of the global economic crisis to reflect changes in the past 3 years, including a section on the Dodd-Frank Act.

Chapter 2: Risk and Return: Part I As a part of our effort to integrate the illustrative company MicroDrive throughout the book, we made significant changes in this chapter. We begin with a discussion of discrete probability distributions involving different market scenarios and then segue into continuous distributions and estimating means and standard deviations using historical data for MicroDrive. We discuss two-stock portfolios and the impact of diversification by using data for MicroDrive and another company. This sets the stage for a discussion of market risk versus diversifiable risk and the appropriate measure of market risk, beta. We then describe the risk-return relationship defined by the CAPM and the basic concept of market equilibrium. This provides a natural transition into the efficient market hypothesis. We also added optional sections covering the Fama-French three-factor model and behavioral finance. These optional sections can be omitted without loss of continuity, or they can be covered to provide more depth on the topic of market efficiency and asset pricing. This new organization consolidates our treatment of risk and return and also illustrates these concepts with MicroDrive, providing a more effective learning experience for students.

Chapter 4: Bond Valuation We updated the box "Betting With or Against the U.S. Government: The Case of Treasury Bond Credit Default Swaps" to reflect the debt-ceiling crisis of July 2011. We added another new box describing the handful of AAA-rated companies, "The Few, the Proud, the..... AAA-Rated Companies!" We revised another box, "Fear and Rationality," to include the TED spread as well as the Hi-Yield bond spread. We also added a brief discussion of duration and its use as a measure of risk. MicroDrive is the company used as a running example throughout the book. We changed its example bond offering to be consistent with MicroDrive's revised financial statements.

Chapter 6: Accounting for Financial Management We reorganized and better integrated the sections on the statement of cash flows, operating cash flow, and free cash flow. We now have a single section focusing on the use of free cash flow and its components as performance measures. We added two new boxes. "Filling in the GAAP" describes the planned convergence of GAAP and IFRS; "When It Comes to Taxes, History Repeats and Repeals Itself!" discusses the actual taxes (or lack thereof) paid by many corporations. MicroDrive is the company used as a running example throughout the book. We changed its financial statements so that MicroDrive would provide additional learning points when we cover valuation and forecasting in Chapters 8 and 9.

Chapter 7: Analysis of Financial Statements In previous editions, we defined the inventory turnover ratio using sales instead of COGS because some compilers of financial ratio statistics, such as Dun & Bradstreet, use the ratio of sales to inventories. However, most sources now report the turnover ratio using COGS, so we have changed our definition to conform to the majority of reporting organizations and now define the inventory turnover ratio as COGS/Inventories. Also, to be more consistent with many Web-based reporting organizations, we now define the debt ratio as total debt divided by total assets, the market debt ratio as total debt divided by total debt plus the market value of equity, and the debt-to-equity ratio as total debt divided by total common equity. MicroDrive is the company used as a running example throughout the book, and we changed its financial statements (which change its ratios) so that MicroDrive would offer additional learning points when we cover valuation and forecasting in Chapters 8 and 9.

Chapter 8: Basic Stock Valuation We have substantially restructured the chapter on stock valuation. Rather than starting with the constant growth dividend growth model, we begin with the constant growth free cash flow valuation model and progress to the nonconstant growth version. The dividend growth model is presented as a special case of the free cash flow model. This change serves two purposes. First, it makes more sense to begin with a model that has broad application, unlike the constant growth dividend model, which can be applied successfully to only a small minority of companies. Second, it allows the chapter to tie in better with the earlier and financial statement chapters and the later valuation chapters. We have re-written the examples to work with MicroDrive, with free cash flows calculated as in the earlier financial statements chapter. We have also added sections on identifying value drivers, stock price volatility, and the long-run nature of stock prices.

Chapter 9: Corporate Valuation and Financial Planning We restructured this chapter to better integrate with the basic stock valuation chapter and with later chapters that use stock valuation techniques. We separated financial statement forecasting into two parts—forecasting operations first, and then forecasting the remaining parts of the financial statements. Additional funds needed (AFN) calculations are now an integral part of this step.

Chapter 10: Corporate Governance We moved the valuation material from the previous edition to the stock valuation chapter (Chapter 8) and to the financial forecasting chapter (Chapter 9). In addition to better integrating the topics in those chapters, the move allows us to focus on agency conflicts and corporate governance in this chapter.

Chapter 11: Determining the Cost of Capital We added a new box, "How Effective Is the Effective Corporate Tax Rate?" This box shows the differences between the statutory rate and the effective rate over time; it also compares the U.S. statutory and effective rate with those of other developed economies. For better integration, we now use the company in our running example, MicroDrive, to illustrate cost of capital estimation. We streamlined the chapter's coverage of the forward-looking risk premium by moving the discussion of the relatively complex multistage model to a Web Extension. This allows the text's coverage of the forward-looking premium focus on the concepts all MBA students need to understand, while at the same time letting the Web Extension address additional issues in more detail, such as the application of multistage models and the impact of stock repurchases. We now cover the own-bond-yield-plus-judgmental-risk-premium approach in the section on privately held companies, because this approach is used more often for such companies.

Chapter 12: Capital Budgeting: Decision Criteria We improved the integration with Chapter 13 by revising the numerical example in Chapter 12 so that the cash flows for Project L are now the cash flows that we estimate in Chapter 13. We put all the material related to IRR (such as the possibility of multiple IRRs) in a single section to make our coverage of IRR more cohesive.

Chapter 13: Capital Budgeting: Estimating Cash Flow and Analyzing Risk We revised the numerical example so that the cash flows we estimate in this chapter are the same cash flows we use in Chapter 12 for Project L.

Chapter 16: Capital Structure Decisions While updating Section 16-4 to include results from the latest empirical tests, we also reorganized the material and added subheadings to make it easier for students to synthesize. We moved the current valuation of Strausburg, the illustrative company, so that it immediately precedes Strausburg's recapitalization, which provides a better segue into the valuation effects of recapitalizations.

Chapter 17: Dynamic Capital Structures and Corporate Valuation We rewrote the chapter and organized it around the fundamental concept that a levered firm's value is equal to its unlevered value plus any side effects due to leverage. From this general concept, we examine special cases, including the MM models and the compressed adjusted present value (APV) model. In addition to the static case of a constant capital structure and constant growth, we apply the APV model to situations with dynamic capital structures that vary from year to year before becoming constant. We retained the MM proofs and put them in a separate section, which provides flexibility to instructors in selecting topics to cover.

Chapter 18: Initial Public Offerings, Investment Banking, and Financial Restructuring We added a section describing how the offer price is set in an IPO.

Chapter 19: Lease Financing We changed the definition of the net advantage of leasing (NAL) to "NAL = Present value of leasing − Present value of owning." Both present values are negative, so a positive NAL means that leasing should be preferred. The results from using this definition of NAL are unchanged from previous editions, but our students find this definition more intuitive.

Chapter 20: Hybrid Financing: Preferred Stock, Warrants, and Convertibles We added a new box describing the deductibility of preferred dividends by Section 521 cooperatives entitled "Hybrids Aren't Only for Corporations."

Chapter 21: Supply Chains and Working Capital Management We added two new boxes, "Your Check Isn't in the Mail" and "A Wag of the Finger or Tip of the Hat? The Colbert Report and Small Business Payment Terms." We rewrote the first section in the chapter to better distinguish between cash (including cash equivalents and marketable securities) used to support current operations and short-term investments (including marketable securities) held for possible future uses. We continued this distinction throughout the chapter in our discussions of cash management and managing short-term investments. Recall that in Chapter 6 we updated our definition of inventory turnover ratio to COGS/Inventories to be consistent with the majority of reporting, so we followed through with that definition in Chapter 21.

Chapter 24: Enterprise Risk Management We rewrote much of the chapter, changing it from a chapter about derivatives with applications in risk management to a chapter about enterprise risk management with applications of derivatives as one of several tools in managing risk. We adapted the general enterprise risk management framework of the Treadway Commission's Committee of Sponsoring Organizations (COSO) because it satisfies the requirements of the Sarbanes-Oxley Act and the Foreign Corrupt Practices Act (FCPA). We now include the use of Monte Carlo simulation as a technique for identifying risk. We use the results of a simulation example to illustrate VaR and the expected shortfall (ES) measures that is recommended by Basel III.

Chapter 25: Bankruptcy, Reorganization, and Liquidation We added a new section describing the events leading to GM's government bailout, bankruptcy, and IPO.

Chapter 26: Mergers and Corporate Control We added a section explaining how the stock-swap ratio is determined for mergers where the payment is in the form of the acquiring company's stock.

Chapter 27: Multinational Financial Management We added a section on foreign exchange notation to ensure that all readers will better understand the relative values of currencies as reported by the financial press. We added a new figure showing the growth in employment by U.S. multinational corporations, including the mix of domestic and international employment. We added a new figure showing the value of the dollar index relative to major currencies to show how demand for the dollar and its relative value has changed over time. We added a new section on sovereign debt, including a brief discussion of the current Greek debt crisis.

Test Bank The instructor's test bank has been updated and revised with many new questions and problems.

OTHER WAYS THE BOOK CAN BE USED

The second corporate finance course can be taught in a variety of other ways, depending on a school's curriculum structure and the instructor's personal preferences. We have been focusing on the BOC questions and discussions, but we have used alternative formats, and all can work out very nicely. Therefore, we designed the book so that it can be flexible.

Mini Cases as a framework for lectures.
We originally wrote the Mini Cases specifically for use in class. We had students read the chapter and the Mini Case, and then we systematically went through it in class to "explain" the chapter. (See the section titled "The Instructional Package" later in this Preface for a discussion of lecture aids available from Cengage Learning.) Here we use a *PowerPoint* slide show, which is located on the instructor's Web site, and which we make available to students on our own course Web site. Students bring a printout of the slides to class, which makes it easier to take good notes.

Generally, it takes us about two hours to frame the issues with the opening questions and then go through a Mini Case, so we allocate that much time. We want to facilitate questions and class discussion, and the Mini Case format stimulates both.

The Mini Cases themselves provide case content, so it is not as necessary to use regular cases as it would be if we used lectures based entirely on text chapters. Still, we like to use a number of the free-standing cases that are available from Cengage-Compose, Cengage Learning's online case library, at **http://compose.cengage.com**, and we have teams of students present their findings in class. The presenters play the role of consultants teaching newly hired corporate staff members (the rest of the class) how to analyze a particular problem, and we as instructors play the role of "chief consultant"—normally silent but available to answer questions if the student "consultants" don't know the answers (which is rare). We use this format because it is more realistic to have students think about *how to analyze* problems than to focus on the final decision, which is really the job of corporate executives with far more experience than undergraduate students.

To ensure that nonpresenting students actually study the case, we call on them randomly before the presentation begins, we grade them on class participation, and our exams are patterned closely after the material in the cases. Therefore, nonpresenting students have an incentive to study and understand the cases and to participate when the cases are discussed in class. This format has worked well, and we have obtained excellent results with a relatively small amount of preparation time. Indeed, some of our Ph.D. students with no previous teaching experience have taught the course entirely on their own, following our outline and format, and also obtained excellent results.

An emphasis on basic material.

If students have not gained a thorough understanding of the basic concepts from their earlier finance courses, instructors may want to place more emphasis on the basics and thus cover Chapters 2 through 5 in detail rather than merely as a review. We even provide a chapter (Web Chapter 28) on time value of money skills on the text-book's Web site for students who need an even more complete review. Then, Chapters 6 through 17 can be covered in detail, and any remaining time can be used to cover some of the other chapters. This approach gives students a sound background on the core of financial management, but it does not leave sufficient time to cover a number of interesting and important topics. However, because the book is written in a modular format, if students understand the fundamental core topics they should be able to cover the remaining chapters on their own, if and when the need arises.

A case-based course.

At the other extreme, where students have an exceptionally good background, hence little need to review topics that were covered in the basic finance course, instructors can spend less time on the early chapters and concentrate on advanced topics. When we take this approach, we assign Web Chapter 29 as a quick review and then assign cases that deal with the topics covered in the early chapters. We tell students to review the other relevant chapters on their own to the extent necessary to work the cases, thus freeing up class time for the more advanced material. This approach works best with relatively mature students, including evening students with some business experience.

COMPREHENSIVE LEARNING SOLUTIONS

Intermediate Financial Management includes a broad range of ancillary materials designed both to enhance students' learning and to help instructors prepare for and conduct classes.

Supplemental Student Resources

Students: Access all of the below resources by visiting **www.cengagebrain.com**, searching ISBN 9781285850030, and clicking "Access Now" under "Study Tools" to go to the student textbook companion site.

Beginning of chapter (BOC) spreadsheets. Many of the integrative questions that appear at the start of each chapter have a spreadsheet model that illustrates the topic. There is also an index of the *Excel* techniques covered in the BOC *Excel* models. This index is in the *Excel* file, *Excel Locations.xls*, and it provides a quick way to locate examples of *Excel* programming techniques

End of chapter Build-a-Model spreadsheet problems. In addition to the Tool Kits and Beginning of Chapter models, most chapters have a "Build a Model" spread-sheet problem. These spreadsheets contain financial data plus instructions for solving a particular problem. The model is partially completed, with headings but no formulas, so the models must literally be built. The partially completed spreadsheets for these "Build a Model" problems are on the student companion Web site, with the completed versions available to instructors.

Mini Case spreadsheets. These *Excel* spreadsheets do all the calculations required in the Mini Cases. They are similar to the Tool Kits for the chapter, except: (a) the numbers in the examples correspond to the Mini Case rather than to the chapter per se, and (b) there are some features that make it possible to do "what-if" analyses on a real-time basis in class.

Web Chapters and Web Extensions. Web chapters provide a chapter-length dis-cussion of specialized topics that are not of sufficient general interest to warrant inclusion in the printed version of the text. Web extensions provide additional dis-cussion or examples pertaining to material that is in the text.

Instructor Resources

Instructors: Access the above chapter resources and the following instructor ancil-laries by going to **www.cengage.com/login**, logging in with your faculty account username and password, and using ISBN 9781285850030 to search for and to add resources to your account "Bookshelf."

- *Instructor's Manual.* This comprehensive manual contains answers to all the Beginning-of-Chapter Questions, end-of-chapter questions and problems, and Mini Cases.
- *PowerPoint® slides.* Created by the authors, the PowerPoint® slides cover essen-tial topics for each chapter. Graphs, tables, and lists are developed sequentially for your convenience and can be easily modified for your needs. There are also slides that are specifically based on each chapter's Mini Case and in which graphs, tables, lists, and calculations are developed sequentially.

- **Test Bank.** The *Test Bank* contains more than 1,200 class-tested questions and problems. Information regarding the topic and degree of difficulty, along with the complete solution for all numerical problems, is provided with each question.
- **Cognero™ *Test Bank.*** Cengage Learning Testing Powered by Cognero™ is a flexible online system that allows you to: author, edit, and manage test bank content from multiple Cengage Learning solutions; create multiple test versions in an instant; deliver tests from your Learning Management System, your classroom, or wherever you want. The Cognero™ Test Bank contains the same questions that are in the Microsoft® Word Test Bank. All question content is now tagged according to Tier I (Business Program Interdisciplinary Learning Outcomes) and Tier II (Finance-specific) standards topic, Bloom's Taxonomy, and difficulty level.

ADDITIONAL COURSE TOOLS

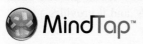 New! MindTap™ for *Intermediate Financial Management*. MindTap™, Cengage Learning's fully online, highly personalized learning experience, combines readings, multimedia, activities, and assessments into a singular Learning Path, MindTap™ guides students through their course with ease and engagement. Instructors can personalize the Learning Path for their students by customizing the robust suite of the Brigham/Daves 12e resources and adding their own content via apps that integrate into the MindTap™ framework seamlessly with Learning Management Systems.

Aplia for *Intermediate Financial Management*. **Engage, prepare, and educate** your students with this ideal online learning solution. Aplia™ Finance improves comprehension and outcomes by increasing student effort and engagement. Students stay on top of coursework with regularly scheduled homework assignments while automatic grading provides detailed, immediate feedback. Aplia™ assignments match the language, style, and structure of the text which allows your students to apply what they learn directly to homework. Find out more at **www.aplia.com/finance**.

- Grade It Now
- End-of-Chapter Problems
- Auto-Graded Problem Sets
- Preparing for Finance Tutorials

- News Analyses
- Course Management System
- Digital Textbook

 CengageNOW™ for *Intermediate Financial Management*. Designed by instructors for instructors, CengageNOW™ mirrors your natural workflow and provides time-saving, performance-enhancing tools for you and your students—all in one program!

CengageNOW™ takes the best of current technology tools including online homework management; fully customizable algorithmic end-of-chapter problems and test bank; and course support materials such as online quizzing, videos, and tutorials to support your course goals and save you significant preparation and grading time!

- **Plan** student assignments with an easy online homework management component
- **Manage** your grade book with ease
- **Teach** today's student using valuable course support materials
- **Reinforce** student comprehension with Personalized Study
- **Test** with customizable algorithmic end of chapter problems and test bank
- **Grade** automatically for seamless, immediate results

CengageCompose. More than 100 cases written by Eugene F. Brigham, Linda Klein, and Chris Buzzard are now available via CengageCompose, Cengage Learning's online case library, and new cases are added every year. These cases are in a customized case database that allows instructors to select cases and create their own customized casebooks. Most of the cases have accompanying spreadsheet models that, while not essential for working the case, do reduce number crunching and thus leave more time for students to consider conceptual issues. The models also show students how computers can be used to make better financial decisions. Cases that we have found particularly useful for the different chapters are listed in the end-of-chapter references. The cases, case solutions, and spreadsheet models can be previewed and ordered by professors at **http://compose.cengage.com**.

Cengage Learning Custom Solutions. Whether you need print, digital, or hybrid course materials, Cengage Learning Custom Solutions can help you create your perfect learning solution. Draw from Cengage Learning's extensive library of texts and collections, add your own original work, and/or create customized media and technology to match your learning and course objectives. Our editorial team will work with you through each step, allowing you to concentrate on the most important thing—your students. Learn more about all our services at **www.cengage.com/custom**.

The Cengage Global Economic Watch (GEW) Resource Center. This is your source for turning today's challenges into tomorrow's solutions. This online portal houses the most current and up-to-date content concerning the economic crisis. Organized by discipline, the GEW Resource Center offers the solutions that instructors and students need in an easy-to-use format. Included are an overview and timeline of the historical events leading up to the crisis, links to the latest news and resources, discussion and testing content, an instructor feedback forum, and global issues database. Visit **www.cengage.com/thewatch** for more information.

Acknowledgments

This book reflects the efforts of a great many people over a number of years. First, we would like to thank Fred Weston, Joel Houston, Mike Ehrhardt, and Scott Besley, who worked with us on other books published by Cengage Learning from which we borrowed liberally to create *IFM*. We also owe Lou Gapenski special thanks for his many past contributions to earlier editions of this text.

The following professors and professionals, who are experts on specific topics, provided extensive feedback on this edition. We are grateful for their insights.

Steven Beach	Melissa Hart	Alicia Rodriguez de Rubio
Sara Bennett	James Haskins	Camelia Rotaru
Julie Cagle	Xiankui Hu	Diane Suhler
Karen Denning	Stephen Lacewell	John Thornton
Ted Eschenbach	Alex Meisami	Ruoyang Wang
John Griffith	Shane Moser	Rustin Yerkes
Axel Grossmann	Ivelina Pavlova	

In addition, we would like to thank the following people, whose reviews and comments on prior editions and companion books have contributed to this edition: Mike Adler, Syed Ahmad, Sadhana M. Alangar, Z. Ayca Altintig, Onur Arugaslan, Edward I. Altman, Mary Schary Amram, Bruce Anderson, Ron Anderson, Bob

Angell, Vince Apilado, Henry Arnold, Nasser Arshadi, Bob Aubey, Abdul Aziz, Gil Babcock, Peter Bacon, Kent Baker, Tom Bankston, Les Barenbaum, Charles Barngrover, Steve Beach, John R. Becker-Blease, Bill Beedles, Moshe Ben-Horim, William (Bill) Beranek, Tom Berry, Bill Bertin, Roger Bey, Dalton Bigbee, John Bildersee, Lloyd P. Blenman, Kevin K. Boeh, Russ Boisjoly, Keith Boles, Gordon R. Bonner, Geof Booth, Kenneth Boudreaux, Helen Bowers, Lyle Bowlin, Oswald Bowlin, Don Boyd, G. Michael Boyd, Pat Boyer, Ben S. Branch, Joe Brandt, Elizabeth Brannigan, Greg Brauer, Mary Broske, Dave Brown, David T. Brown, Kate Brown, Mary R. Brown, Bill Brueggeman, Kirt Butler, Robert Button, Julie Cagle, Bill (B. J.) Campsey, Bob Carleson, Severin Carlson, David Cary, Steve Celec, Don Chance, Antony Chang, Susan Chaplinsky, Jay Choi, S. K. Choudhury, Lal Chugh, Maclyn Clouse, Margaret Considine, Phil Cooley, Joe Copeland, James J. Cordeiro, David Cordell, John Cotner, Charles Cox, David Crary, Tony Crawford, John Crockett, Roy Crum, Brent Dalrymple, Bill Damon, William H. Dare, Joel Dauten, Steve Dawson, Sankar De, Miles Delano, Fred Dellva, Anand Desai, Ross Dickens, Bernard Dill, Greg Dimkoff, Les Dlabay, Mark Dorfman, Gene Drycimski, Dean Dudley, David A. Dumpe, David Durst, Ed Dyl, Dick Edelman, Charles Edwards, John Ellis, Theodore Engel, Dave Ewert, John Ezzell, Richard Fendler, Michael Ferri, Jim Filkins, John Finnerty, Susan Fischer, Mark Flannery, Steven Flint, Russ Fogler, Jennifer Foo, E. Bruce Frederickson, Dan French, Tina Galloway, Phil Gardial, Michael Garlington, Jim Garvin, Adam Gehr, Jim Gentry, Philip Glasgo, Rudyard Goode, Myron Gordon, Walt Goulet, Bernie Grablowsky, Theoharry Grammatikos, John Griffith, Axel Grossmann, Ed Grossnickle, John Groth, Alan Grunewald, Manak Gupta, George Hachey, Sam Hadaway, Thomas Hall, Don Hakala, Sally Hamilton, Gerald Hamsmith, William Hardin, Joel Harper, John Harris, Paul Hastings, Bob Haugen, Steve Hawke, Del Hawley, Hal Heaton, Robert Hehre, John Helmuth, K. L. Henebry, George Hettenhouse, Hans Heymann, Kendall Hill, Roger Hill, Tom Hindelang, Linda Hittle, Ralph Hocking, J. Ronald Hoffmeister, Jim Horrigan, John Houston, John Howe, Keith Howe, Jim Hsieh, Hugh Hunter, Steve Isberg, James E. Jackson, Jim Jackson, Vahan Janjigian, Tim Jares, Kose John, Craig Johnson, Keith H. Johnson, Ramon Johnson, Ken Johnston, Ray Jones, Manuel Jose, Tejendra Kalia, Gus Kalogeras, Mike Keenan, Bill Kennedy, Joe Kiernan, Robert Kieschnick, Young Kim, Rick Kish, Linda Klein, Don Knight, Dorothy Koehl, Raj K. Kohli, Jaroslaw Komarynsky, Duncan Kretovich, Harold Krogh, Charles Kroncke, Merouane Lakehal-Ayat, Joan Lamm, P. Lange, Howard Lanser, Martin Laurence, Ed Lawrence, Richard LeCompte, Wayne Lee, Jim LePage, Ilene Levin, Jules Levine, John Lewis, Kartono Liano, Yingchou Lin, James T. Lindley, Chuck Linke, Bill Lloyd, Susan Long, Judy Maese, Bob Magee, Ileen Malitz, Phil Malone, Terry Maness, Chris Manning, Terry Martell, D. J. Masson, John Mathys, John McAlhany, Andy McCollough, Bill McDaniel, Robin McLaughlin, Tom McCue, Jamshid Mehran, Ilhan Meric, Larry Merville, Rick Meyer, Stuart Michelson, Jim Millar, Ed Miller, John Mitchell, Carol Moerdyk, Bob Moore, Barry Morris, Gene Morris, Fred Morrissey, Chris Muscarella, David Nachman, Tim Nantell, Don Nast, Bill Nelson, Bob Nelson, Bob Niendorf, Tom O'Brien, Dennis O'Connor, John O'Donnell, Jim Olsen, Robert Olsen, R. Daniel Pace, Coleen Pantalone, Jim Pappas, Stephen Parrish, Ohaness Paskelian, Glenn Petry, Jim Pettijohn, Rich Pettit, Dick Pettway, Hugo Phillips, John Pinkerton, Gerald Pogue, Ralph A. Pope, R. Potter, Franklin Potts, R. Powell, Chris Prestopino, Jerry Prock, Howard Puckett, Edward Pyatt, Herbert Quigley, George Racette, Bob

Radcliffe, Allen Rappaport, Bill Rentz, Ken Riener, Charles Rini, John Ritchie, Jay Ritter, Pietra Rivoli, Fiona Robertson, Alicia Rodriguez, Antonio Rodriguez, Kenneth Roskelley, E. M. Roussakis, Dexter Rowell, Michael Ryngaert, Jim Sachlis, Abdul Sadik, Atul Saxena, Thomas Scampini, Kevin Scanlon, Frederick Schadler, James Schallheim, Mary Jane Scheuer, Carl Schweser, John Settle, Alan Severn, Sol Shalit, Frederic Shipley, Dilip Shome, Ron Shrieves, Neil Sicherman, J. B. Silvers, Clay Singleton, Joe Sinkey, Mark Sipper, Stacy Sirmans, Jaye Smith, Steve Smith, Don Sorenson, David Speairs, Andrew Spieler, Ken Stanly, Ed Stendardi, Alan Stephens, Don Stevens, Jerry Stevens, G. Bennett Stewart, Glen Strasburg, Robert Strong, Tom Stuckey, Denver Swaby, Philip Swensen, Ernie Swift, Paul Swink, Eugene Swinnerton, Robert Taggart, Gary Tallman, Dennis Tanner, Russ Taussig, A. Tessmer, Manish Tewari, Richard Teweles, Ted Teweles, Andrew Thompson, Jonathan Tiemann, Sheridan Titman, George Trivoli, George Tsetsekos, Alan L. Tucker, Mel Tysseland, David Upton, Howard Van Auken, Pretorious Van den Dool, Pieter Vanderburg, Paul Vanderheiden, David Vang, Jim Verbrugge, Patrick Vincent, Steve Vinson, Susan Visscher, John Wachowicz, Joe Walker, Mike Walker, Sam Weaver, Kuo Chiang Wei, Bill Welch, Gary R. Wells, Fred Weston, Norm Williams, Tony Wingler, Ed Wolfe, Larry Wolken, Annie Wong, Bob G. Wood, Jr., Don Woods, Thomas Wright, Michael Yonan, Miranda Zhang, Zhong-guo Zhou, David Ziebart, Dennis Zocco, and Kent Zumwalt.

Special thanks are due to Fred Weston, Myron Gordon, Merton Miller, and Franco Modigliani, who have done much to help develop the field of financial management and who provided us with instruction and inspiration; to Roy Crum, who coauthored the multinational finance chapter; to Jay Ritter, who helped us with the materials on financial markets and IPOs; to Larry Wolken, who offered his hard work and advice for the development of the *PowerPoint* slides; to Dana Aberwald Clark, Susan Ball, and Chris Buzzard, who helped us develop the spreadsheet models; and to Susan Whitman, Amelia Bell, and Kirsten Benson, who provided editorial support.

Both our colleagues and our students at the Universities of Florida and Tennessee gave us many useful suggestions, and the Cengage Learning staff—especially Mike Reynolds, Kendra Brown, Jana Lewis, Heather Mooney, Adele Scholtz, Michelle Kunkler, Jessica Robbe, and Eileen Corcoran—helped greatly with all phases of text development, production, and marketing.

Errors in the Text

At this point, authors generally say something like this: "We appreciate all the help we received from the people listed above, but any remaining errors are, of course, our own responsibility." And in many books, there are plenty of remaining errors. Having experienced difficulties with errors ourselves, both as students and as instructors, we resolved to avoid this problem in *Intermediate Financial Management*. As a result of our error detection procedures, we are convinced that the book is relatively free of mistakes.

Partly because of our confidence that few such errors remain, but primarily because we want very much to detect those errors that may have slipped by to correct them in subsequent printings, we decided to offer a reward of $10 per error to the first person who reports it to us. For purposes of this reward, errors are defined as misspelled words, nonrounding numerical errors, incorrect statements, and any other error that inhibits comprehension. Typesetting problems such as irregular spacing and differences in opinion regarding grammatical or punctuation conventions do not qualify for this reward. Finally, any qualifying error that has follow-through effects is counted as two errors only. Please report any errors to Phillip Daves at the following email address: pdaves@utk.edu.

Conclusion

Finance is, in a real sense, the cornerstone of the free enterprise system. Good financial management is therefore vitally important to the economic health of business firms, hence to the nation and the world. Because of its importance, financial management should be thoroughly understood. However, this is easier said than done. The field is relatively complex, and it is undergoing constant change in response to shifts in economic conditions. All of this makes financial management stimulating and exciting, but also challenging and sometimes perplexing. We sincerely hope that the Twelfth Edition of *Intermediate Financial Management* will help you understand the financial problems faced by businesses today, as well as the best ways to solve those problems.

Eugene F. Brigham
College of Business Administration
University of Florida
Gainesville, Florida 32611-7167
gene.brigham@cba.ufl.edu

Phillip R. Daves
Haslam College of Business
University of Tennessee
Knoxville, Tennessee 37996-0540
pdaves@utk.edu
March, 2015

Fundamental Concepts of Corporate Finance

An Overview of Financial Management and the Financial Environment

This book is designed to explain what "financial management" is all about and to show how it can be used to help increase the value of a firm. It is intended for use in a second-level finance course, following the introductory course. Only the basic course is prerequisite, so if students have taken other finance courses, especially on investments or capital markets, they will find some of the material a review.

The book is often used in a "capstone" course taken during the last term before graduation. This is an exhilarating time for students, with graduation looming and a job search under way. It is also a good time to step back from the technical skills developed in the classroom and to look at the big picture of why financial management is so important. Spending the time now to develop a good overview of financial management can be tremendously valuable to your career. Why is financial management so valuable? In a nutshell, because it explains both how managers can increase their firms' value and why it is essential for them to do so.

Today's business environment is more complicated than ever. Investors are increasingly forcing managers to focus on value maximization, but events ranging from the scandals at Enron, WorldCom, Tyco, and a host of other companies during the early 2000s to the global financial meltdown and recession at the end of that decade have shown that ethical behavior and managerial accountability are crucial prerequisites. Mastering the technical details of financial management and understanding its role within the firm is important to graduating students because companies want to hire people who can make decisions with the broad corporate goal of value maximization in mind. Therefore, students who understand the principles of value maximization have a major advantage in the job market over students who do not. Demonstrating that you understand all this can make a big difference in both the quality of your initial job and your subsequent career path.

Beginning-of-Chapter Questions

As you read the chapter, consider how you would answer the following questions. You *should not* necessarily be able to answer the questions before you read the chapter. Rather, you should use them to get a sense of the issues covered in the chapter. After reading the chapter, you should be able to give at least partial answers to the questions, and you should be able to give better answers after the chapter has been discussed in class. Note, too, that it is often useful, when answering conceptual questions, to use hypothetical data to illustrate your answer. For example, your answer to Question 2 would probably be better if it were illustrated with numbers. We have done this, using *Excel*; our model is available on the textbook's Web site. Accessing the model and working through it is a useful exercise.

1. What is presumed to be the **primary goal** of financial management? How is this goal related to other societal goals and considerations? Is this goal consistent with the basic assumptions of microeconomics? Are managers' actions always consistent with this goal?

2. Finance is all about **valuation**—how to estimate asset values and what to do to increase them. We develop and use *Excel* models throughout the book. We start that process in this chapter with simple models used to value bonds, stocks, and capital budgeting projects. Working through the model will give you a refresher in valuation plus a refresher on (or preview of) *Excel*. The model can be accessed on the textbook's Web site under the "Chapter Models" section. If you have never used *Excel* at all, then you should not attempt to use it to help answer this question, or if you do, you should not get frustrated if you have trouble.

   a. Explain how to find the value of a bond given the rate of interest it pays (its coupon rate), its par value (assume $1,000), and the going rate of interest on bonds with the same risk and maturity.

   b. Explain how to find the value of a stock given its last dividend, its expected growth rate, and its required rate of return.

   c. Explain how to find the value of a capital budgeting project given its cost, its expected annual net cash flows, its life, and its cost of capital.

   d. In each of the above cases, discuss how changes in the inputs would affect the output. Would it matter if the outputs were highly sensitive to changes in the inputs?

3. What are the advantages of the corporate form over a sole proprietorship or a partnership? What are the disadvantages of this form?

4. What are the various factors that affect the cost of money and hence interest rates? How will changes in these components affect asset prices?

5. What is securitization? How is securitization supposed to help banks and S&Ls manage risks and increase homeowners' access to capital?

6. What was the global economic crisis? This is a really big question, so specifically, explain how in our interconnected global economy a decrease in housing prices in large U.S. cities ended up bankrupting Norwegian retirees.

1-1 **How to Use this Text**

In your introductory finance course you learned a number of terms and concepts, and you now have an idea of what financial management is all about. However, you probably focused on individual chapters, or sections of chapters, and you probably prepared for exams that consisted of relatively simple problems and short-answer questions, often given in a multiple-choice format. That was a necessary part of the learning process, but now it is time to move on.

In *Intermediate Financial Management*, we go back over much of what you covered in the introductory course, plus introduce new material. However, our focus now is different. At this point we want you to learn how to *apply* the concepts, how to obtain the data necessary to implement the various decision models, and how to relate the various parts of finance to one another. So, while we revisit topics such as the net present value (NPV) and internal rate of return (IRR) methods, we delve into them more deeply, considering how to streamline and automate the calculations, how to obtain the necessary data, and how errors in the data affect the outcome. We also spend more time comparing the topics covered in different chapters to one

Visit the textbook's Web site. This ever-evolving site, for students and instructors, is a tool for teaching, learning, financial research, and job searches.

THE GLOBAL ECONOMIC CRISIS

The global economic crisis is like a guest at a party who has one drink and is very interesting and entertaining but who then has many more drinks, gets sick, and lingers on after everyone else has left. At the risk of oversimplification, this is what happened during the past decade: Many of the world's individuals, financial institutions, and governments borrowed too much money and used those borrowed funds to make speculative investments. Those investments turned out to be worth less than the amounts owed by the borrowers, forcing widespread bankruptcies, buyouts, and restructurings for both borrowers and lenders. This in turn reduced the supply of available funds that financial institutions normally lent to creditworthy individuals, manufacturers, and retailers. Without access to credit, consumers bought less, manufacturers produced less, and retailers sold less—all of which led to layoffs. According to the National Bureau of Economic Research, the resulting recession in the United States lasted from December 2007 through June 2009. But as we write this chapter in 2014, the U.S. and global economies are still not growing very quickly. As we progress through this chapter and the rest of the book, we will discuss different aspects of the crisis. For real-time updates, go to the Global Economic Watch (GEW) Resource Center at **www.cengage.com/thewatch**.

Consult **www .careers-in-finance .com** for an excellent site containing information on a variety of business career areas, listings of current jobs, and other reference materials.

another. For example, you probably did not spend much time considering how the cost of capital, capital structure, dividend policy, and capital budgeting are related to one another, but we now discuss these critically important relationships.

Also, since spreadsheets such as *Excel*, not financial calculators, are used to analyze actual business decisions, you need to be proficient with spreadsheets to get many good jobs and certainly to succeed in those jobs. Therefore, we explain how to do the most common types of financial analyses using *Excel*. This focus has two benefits: Knowledge of *Excel* is useful per se, and setting up and analyzing the output from spreadsheet models will also teach you a lot about financial concepts.

To help sharpen your focus, we start each chapter with several *Beginning-of-Chapter Questions*. Some of these questions are designed to help you see how the chapter ties in with other chapters, while others will help you think about how the concepts are applied in the real world. You probably won't be able to answer all of the questions when you start working through the chapter, but that's fine! The questions aren't a pre-test. Their purpose is to help guide you through the material, and having them in mind when you read will help you understand the chapter in a more integrative and relevant way.

Most of the chapters have two spreadsheet models, which are available on the textbook's Web site. The first is a "Tool Kit," which contains the *Excel* models used to generate most of the tables and examples in the chapter. The second is a model that deals with specific Beginning-of-Chapter Questions. Both models contain notes and comments that explain the *Excel* procedures we used, so they can be used as a tutorial for learning more about both *Excel* and finance. Again, since recruiters prefer students who are good with *Excel*, learning more about it will help you get a better job and then succeed in it.

COLUMBUS WAS WRONG—THE WORLD *IS* FLAT! AND HOT! AND CROWDED!

In his best-selling book *The World Is Flat*, Thomas L. Friedman argues that many of the barriers that long protected businesses and employees from global competition have been broken down by dramatic improvements in communication and transportation technologies. The result is a level playing field that spans the entire world. As we move into the information age, any work that can be digitized will flow to those able to do it at the lowest cost, whether they live in San Jose's Silicon Valley or Bangalore, India. For physical products, supply chains now span the world. For example, raw materials might be extracted in South America, fabricated into electronic components in Asia, and then used in computers assembled in the United States, with the final product being sold in Europe.

Similar changes are occurring in the financial markets, as capital flows across the globe to those who can best use it. Indeed, the combined China and Hong Kong IPO market is comparable in size to the combined Europe and U.S. IPO market.

Unfortunately, a dynamic world can bring runaway growth, which can lead to significant environmental problems and energy shortages. Friedman describes these problems in another bestseller, *Hot, Flat, and Crowded*. In a flat world, the keys to success are knowledge, skills, and a great work ethic. In a flat, hot, and crowded world, these factors must be combined with innovation and creativity to deal with truly global problems.

1-2 The Corporate Life Cycle

Many major corporations, including Apple and Hewlett-Packard, began life in a garage or basement. How is it possible for such companies to grow into the giants we see today? No two companies develop in exactly the same way, but the following sections describe some typical stages in the corporate life cycle.

1-2a Starting Up as a Proprietorship

Many companies begin as a **proprietorship**, which is an unincorporated business owned by one individual. Starting a business as a proprietor is easy—one merely begins business operations after obtaining any required city or state business licenses. The proprietorship has three important advantages: (1) it is easily and inexpensively formed, (2) it is subject to few government regulations, and (3) its income is not subject to corporate taxation but is taxed as part of the proprietor's personal income.

However, the proprietorship also has three important limitations: (1) It may be difficult for a proprietorship to obtain the capital needed for growth. (2) The proprietor has unlimited personal liability for the business's debts, which can result in losses that exceed the money invested in the company (creditors may even be able to seize a proprietor's house or other personal property!). (3) The life of a proprietorship is limited to the life of its founder. For these three reasons, sole proprietorships are used primarily for small businesses. In fact, proprietorships account for only about 4% of all sales, based on dollar values, even though about 72% of all companies are proprietorships.

1-2b **More Than One Owner: A Partnership**

Some companies start with more than one owner, and some proprietors decide to add a partner as the business grows. A **partnership** exists whenever two or more persons or entities associate to conduct a noncorporate business for profit. Partnerships may operate under different degrees of formality, ranging from informal, oral understandings to formal agreements filed with the secretary of the state in which the partnership was formed. Partnership agreements define the ways any profits and losses are shared between partners. A partnership's advantages and disadvantages are generally similar to those of a proprietorship.

Regarding liability, the partners potentially can lose all of their personal assets, even assets not invested in the business, because under partnership law, each partner is liable for the business's debts. Therefore, in the event the partnership goes bankrupt, if any partner is unable to meet his or her pro rata liability then the remaining partners must make good on the unsatisfied claims, drawing on their personal assets to the extent necessary. To avoid this, it is possible to limit the liabilities of some of the partners by establishing a **limited partnership**, wherein certain partners are designated **general partners** and others **limited partners**. In a limited partnership, the limited partners can lose only the amount of their investment in the partnership, while the general partners have unlimited liability. However, the limited partners typically have no control—it rests solely with the general partners—and their returns are likewise limited. Limited partnerships are common in real estate, oil, equipment-leasing ventures, and venture capital. However, they are not widely used in general business situations, because usually no partner is willing to be the general partner and thus accept the majority of the business's risk, and no partners are willing to be limited partners and give up all control.

In both regular and limited partnerships, at least one partner is liable for the debts of the partnership. However, in a **limited liability partnership (LLP)**, sometimes called a **limited liability company (LLC)**, all partners enjoy limited liability with regard to the business's liabilities, and their potential losses are limited to their investment in the LLP. Of course, this arrangement increases the risk faced by an LLP's lenders, customers, and suppliers.

1-2c **Many Owners: A Corporation**

Most partnerships have difficulty attracting substantial amounts of capital. This is generally not a problem for a slow-growing business, but if a business's products or services really catch on, and if it needs to raise large sums of money to capitalize on its opportunities, then the difficulty in attracting capital becomes a real drawback. Thus, many growth companies, such as Hewlett-Packard and Microsoft, began life as a proprietorship or partnership, and at some point their founders decided to convert to a corporation. On the other hand, some companies, in anticipation of growth, actually begin as corporations. A **corporation** is a legal entity created under state laws, and it is separate and distinct from its owners and managers. This separation gives the corporation three major advantages: (1) *unlimited life*—a corporation can continue after its original owners and managers are deceased; (2) *easy transferability of ownership interest*—ownership interests are divided into shares of stock, which can be transferred far more easily than can proprietorship or partnership interests; and (3) *limited liability*—losses are limited to the actual funds invested.

To illustrate limited liability, suppose you invested $10,000 in a partnership that then went bankrupt and owed $1 million. Because the owners are liable for the debts of a partnership, you could be assessed for a share of the company's debt, and you could be held liable for the entire $1 million if your partners could not pay their shares. On the other hand, if you invested $10,000 in the stock of a corporation that went bankrupt, your potential loss on the investment would be limited to your $10,000 investment.[1] Unlimited life, easy transferability of ownership interest, and limited liability make it much easier for corporations than proprietorships or partnerships to raise money in the financial markets and grow into large companies.

The corporate form offers significant advantages over proprietorships and partnerships, but it also has two disadvantages: (1) Corporate earnings may be subject to double taxation—the earnings of the corporation are taxed at the corporate level, and then earnings paid out as dividends are taxed again as income to the stockholders. (2) Setting up a corporation involves preparing a charter, writing a set of bylaws, and filing the many required state and federal reports, which is more complex and time-consuming than creating a proprietorship or a partnership.

The **charter** includes the following information: (1) name of the proposed corporation, (2) types of activities it will pursue, (3) amount of capital stock, (4) number of directors, and (5) names and addresses of directors. The charter is filed with the secretary of the state in which the firm will be incorporated, and when it is approved, the corporation is officially in existence.[2] After the corporation begins operating, quarterly and annual employment, financial, and tax reports must be filed with state and federal authorities.

The **bylaws** are a set of rules drawn up by the founders of the corporation. Included are such points as: (1) how directors are to be elected (all elected each year or perhaps one-third each year for 3-year terms), (2) whether the existing stockholders will have the first right to buy any new shares the firm issues, and (3) procedures for changing the bylaws themselves, should conditions require it.

There are several different types of corporations. Professionals such as doctors, lawyers, and accountants often form a **professional corporation (PC)** or a **professional association (PA)**. These types of corporations do not relieve the participants of professional (malpractice) liability. Indeed, the primary motivation behind the professional corporation was to provide a way for groups of professionals to incorporate in order to avoid certain types of unlimited liability yet still be held responsible for professional liability.

Finally, if certain requirements are met, particularly with regard to size and number of stockholders, owners can establish a corporation but elect to be taxed as if the business were a proprietorship or partnership. Such firms, which differ not in organizational form but only in how their owners are taxed, are called **S corporations**.

---

1. In the case of very small corporations, the limited liability may be fiction because lenders frequently require personal guarantees from the stockholders.

2. More than 60% of major U.S. corporations are chartered in Delaware, which has, over the years, provided a favorable legal environment for corporations. It is not necessary for a firm to be headquartered, or even to conduct operations, in its state of incorporation, or even in its country of incorporation.

1-2d **Growing and Managing a Corporation**

Once a corporation has been established, how does it evolve? When entrepreneurs start a company, they usually provide all the financing from their personal resources, which may include savings, home equity loans, or even credit cards. As the corporation grows, it will need factories, equipment, inventory, and other resources to support its growth. In time, the entrepreneurs usually deplete their own resources and must turn to external financing. Many young companies are too risky for banks, so the founders must sell stock to outsiders, including friends, family, private investors (often called angels), or venture capitalists. If the corporation continues to grow, it may become successful enough to attract lending from banks, or it may even raise additional funds through an **initial public offering (IPO)** by selling stock to the public at large. After an IPO, corporations support their growth by borrowing from banks, issuing debt, or selling additional shares of stock. In short, a corporation's ability to grow depends on its interactions with the financial markets, which we describe in much more detail later in this chapter.

For proprietorships, partnerships, and small corporations, the firm's owners are also its managers. This is usually not true for a large corporation, which means that large firms' stockholders, who are its owners, face a serious problem. What is to prevent managers from acting in their own best interests, rather than in the best interests of the stockholder/owners? This is called an **agency problem**, because managers are hired as agents to act on behalf of the owners. Agency problems can be addressed by a company's **corporate governance**, which is the set of rules that control the company's behavior toward its directors, managers, employees, shareholders, creditors, customers, competitors, and community. We will have much more to say about agency problems and corporate governance throughout the book, especially in Chapters 10, 15, and 16.

> **SELF TEST**
>
> What are the key differences between proprietorships, partnerships, and corporations?
>
> Describe some special types of partnerships and corporations, and explain the differences among them.

1-3 **The Primary Objective of the Corporation: Value Maximization**

Shareholders are the owners of a corporation, and they purchase stocks because they want to earn a good return on their investment without undue risk exposure. In most cases, shareholders elect directors, who then hire managers to run the corporation on a day-to-day basis. Because managers are supposed to be working on behalf of shareholders, they should pursue policies that enhance shareholder value. Consequently, throughout this book we operate on the assumption that management's primary objective should be *stockholder wealth maximization*.

The **market price** is the stock price that we observe in the financial markets. We later explain in detail how stock prices are determined, but for now it is enough to say that a company's market price incorporates the information available to

ETHICS FOR INDIVIDUALS AND BUSINESSES

A firm's commitment to business ethics can be measured by the tendency of its employees, from the top down, to adhere to laws, regulations, and moral standards relating to product safety and quality, fair employment practices, fair marketing and selling practices, the use of confidential information for personal gain, community involvement, and illegal payments to obtain business.

Ethical Dilemmas. When conflicts arise between profits and ethics, sometimes legal and ethical considerations make the choice obvious. At other times the right choice isn't clear. For example, suppose Norfolk Southern's managers know that its trains are polluting the air, but the amount of pollution is within legal limits and further reduction would be costly, causing harm to their shareholders. Are the managers ethically bound to reduce pollution? Aren't they also ethically bound to act in their shareholders' best interests? This is clearly a dilemma.

Ethical Responsibility. Over the past few years, illegal ethical lapses have led to a number of bankruptcies, which have raised this question: Were the *companies* unethical, or was it just a few of their *employees*? Arthur Andersen, an accounting firm, audited Enron, WorldCom, and several other companies that committed accounting fraud.

The U.S. Justice Department concluded that Andersen itself was guilty because it fostered a climate in which unethical behavior was permitted and built an incentive system that made such behavior profitable to both the perpetrators and the firm itself. As a result, Andersen went out of business. Anderson was later judged to be not guilty, but by the time the judgment was rendered the company was already out of business. People simply did not want to deal with a tainted accounting firm.

Protecting Ethical Employees. If employees discover questionable activities or are given questionable orders, should they obey their bosses' orders, refuse to obey those orders, or report the situation to a higher authority, such as the company's board of directors, its auditors, or a federal prosecutor? In 2002 Congress passed the Sarbanes-Oxley Act, with a provision designed to protect "whistle-blowers." If an employee reports corporate wrongdoing and later is penalized, he or she can ask the Occupational Safety and Health Administration to investigate the situation. If the employee was improperly penalized, the company can be required to reinstate the person, along with back pay and a sizable penalty award. Several big awards have been handed out since the act was passed.

investors. If the market price reflects all *relevant* information, then the observed price is the **intrinsic price**, also called the **fundamental price**.

However, investors rarely have all relevant information. Companies report most major decisions, but they may withhold selected information to prevent competitors from gaining strategic advantages. In addition, managers may take actions that boost bonuses linked to higher current earnings yet actually decrease future cash flows, such as reducing scheduled maintenance. As we show in Chapter 8, short-term focus can reduce the intrinsic price but might actually increase the market price if such actions are difficult for investors to discern immediately. Thus, the market price can deviate from the intrinsic price. In this example, the market price initially would go up relative to the intrinsic price, but it would then fall in the future as the company experienced production problems due to poorly maintained equipment.

Therefore, when we say management's objective should be to maximize stock-holder wealth, we really mean it is to *maximize the fundamental price of the firm's common stock*, not just the current market price. Firms do, of course, have other objectives; in particular, the managers who make the actual decisions are interested in their own personal satisfaction, in their employees' welfare, and in the good of their communities and society at large. Still, for the reasons set forth in the following sections, *maximizing intrinsic stock value should be the most important objective for most corporations.*

1-3a Intrinsic Stock Value Maximization and Social Welfare

The Investment Company Institute is a great source of information. For updates on mutual fund ownership, see **www.ici.org /research#fact_books**.

If a firm attempts to maximize its intrinsic stock value, is this good or bad for society? In general, it is good. Aside from such illegal actions as fraudulent accounting, exploiting monopoly power, violating safety codes, and failing to meet environmental standards, *the same actions that maximize intrinsic stock values also benefit society.* Here are some of the reasons:

1. **Most individuals have a stake in the stock market.** Seventy-five years ago this was not true, because most stock ownership was concentrated in the hands of a relatively small segment of society consisting of the wealthiest individuals. More than 44% of all U.S. households now own mutual funds, as compared with only 4.6% in 1980. When direct stock ownership and indirect ownership through pension funds are also considered, many members of society now have an important stake in the stock market, either directly or indirectly. Therefore, when a manager takes actions to maximize the stock price, this improves the quality of life for millions of ordinary citizens.

2. **Consumers benefit.** Stock price maximization requires efficient, low-cost businesses that produce high-quality goods and services at the lowest possible cost. This means that companies must develop products and services that consumers want and need, which leads to new technology and new products. Also, companies that maximize their stock price must generate growth in sales by creating value for customers in the form of efficient and courteous service, adequate stocks of merchandise, and well-located business establishments.

    People sometimes argue that firms, in their efforts to raise profits and stock prices, increase product prices and gouge the public. In a reasonably competitive economy, which we have, prices are constrained by competition and consumer resistance. If a firm raises its prices beyond reasonable levels, it will simply lose market share. Even giant firms such as Dell and Coca-Cola lose business to domestic and foreign competitors if they set prices above the level necessary to cover production costs plus a "normal" profit. Of course, firms *want* to earn more, and they constantly try to cut costs, develop new products, and so on, and thereby earn above-normal profits. Note, though, that if they are indeed successful and do earn above-normal profits, those very profits will attract competition, which will eventually drive prices down. So again, the main long-term beneficiary is the consumer.

3. **Employees benefit.** In some situations a stock increases when a company announces plans to lay off employees, but viewed over time this is the exception rather than the rule. In general, companies that successfully increase stock prices also grow and add more employees, thus benefiting society. Note, too, that many governments across the world, including U.S. federal and state governments, are privatizing some of their state-owned activities by selling these operations to investors. Perhaps not surprisingly, the sales and cash flows of recently privatized companies generally improve. Moreover, studies show that newly privatized companies tend to grow and thus require more employees when they are managed with the goal of stock price maximization.

1-3b **Managerial Actions to Maximize Shareholder Wealth**

What types of actions can managers take to maximize shareholder wealth? To answer this question, we first need to ask, "What determines a firm's value?" In a nutshell, it is *a company's ability to generate cash flows now and in the future.*

We address different aspects of this in detail throughout the book, but we can lay out three basic facts now: (1) Any financial asset, including a company's stock, is valuable only to the extent that it generates cash flows. (2) The timing of cash flows matters—cash received sooner is better. (3) Investors are averse to risk, so all else equal, they will pay more for a stock whose cash flows are relatively certain than for one whose cash flows are more risky. Therefore, managers can increase their firm's value by increasing the size of the expected cash flows, by speeding up their receipt, and by reducing their risk.

The cash flows that matter are called **free cash flows (FCF)**, not because they are free, but because they are available (or free) for distribution to all of the company's investors, including creditors and stockholders. You will learn how to calculate free cash flows in Chapter 6, but for now you should know that free cash flow is:

$$\text{FCF} = \frac{\text{Sales}}{\text{revenues}} - \frac{\text{Operating}}{\text{costs}} - \frac{\text{Operating}}{\text{taxes}} - \frac{\text{Required investments}}{\text{in new operating capital}}$$

CORPORATE SCANDALS AND MAXIMIZING STOCK PRICE

The list of corporate scandals seems to go on forever: Sunbeam, Enron, ImClone, WorldCom, Tyco, Adelphia. . . . At first glance, it's tempting to say, "Look what happens when managers care only about maximizing stock price." But a closer look reveals a much different story. In fact, if these managers were trying to maximize stock price, they failed dismally, given the resulting values of these companies.

Although details vary from company to company, a few common themes emerge. First, managerial compensation was linked to the *short-term* performance of the stock price via poorly designed stock option and stock grant programs. This provided managers with a powerful incentive to drive up the stock price at the option vesting date without worrying about the future. Second, it is virtually impossible to take *legal and ethical* actions that quickly drive up the stock price. The value of a company ultimately depends on all of its expected future cash flows, and making a substantive change in them requires the old-fashioned hard work of increasing sales, cutting costs, or reducing capital requirements.

Because legal and ethical actions to drive up the stock price quickly don't exist, some managers began bending a few rules. Third, as they initially got away with bending rules, it seems that their egos and hubris grew to such an extent that they felt they were above all rules, so they began breaking even more rules.

Stock prices did go up, at least temporarily, but as Abraham Lincoln said, "You can't fool all of the people all of the time." As the scandals became public, the stocks' prices plummeted, and in some cases the companies were ruined.

There are several important lessons to be learned from these examples. First, people respond to incentives, and poorly designed incentives can cause disastrous results. Second, ethical violations usually begin with small steps, so if stockholders want managers to avoid large ethical violations, then they shouldn't let them make the small ones. Third, there is no shortcut to creating lasting value. It takes hard work to increase sales, cut costs, and reduce capital requirements, but this is the formula for success.

Brand managers and marketing managers can increase sales (and prices) by truly understanding their customers and then designing goods and services that customers want. Human resource managers can improve productivity through training and employee retention. Production and logistics managers can improve profit margins, reduce inventory, and improve throughput at factories by implementing supply chain management, just-in-time inventory management, and lean manufacturing. In fact, all managers make decisions that can increase free cash flows.

One of the financial manager's roles is to help others see how their actions affect the company's ability to generate cash flow and, hence, its intrinsic value. Financial managers also must decide *how to finance the firm.* In particular, they must choose the mix of debt and equity to use and the specific types of debt and equity securities to issue. They also must decide what percentage of current earnings to retain and reinvest rather than pay out as dividends. Along with these financing decisions, the general level of interest rates in the economy, the risk of the firm's operations, and stock market investors' overall attitude toward risk determine the rate of return required to satisfy a firm's investors. This rate of return from an investor's perspective is a cost from the company's point of view. Therefore, the rate of return required by investors is called the **weighted average cost of capital (WACC)**.

The following equation defines the relationship between a firm's fundamental value, its free cash flows, and its cost of capital:

(1–1)

$$\text{Value} = \frac{\text{FCF}_1}{(1 + \text{WACC})^1} + \frac{\text{FCF}_2}{(1 + \text{WACC})^2} + \frac{\text{FCF}_3}{(1 + \text{WACC})^3} + \cdots + \frac{\text{FCF}_\infty}{(1 + \text{WACC})^\infty}$$

We will explain how to use this equation in later chapters, but for now note that: (1) a growing firm often needs to raise external funds in the financial markets, and (2) the actual price of a firm's stock is determined in those markets. The rest of this chapter focuses on financial markets.

SELF TEST

What should be management's primary objective?

How does maximizing the fundamental stock price benefit society?

Free cash flow depends on what three factors?

How is a firm's fundamental value related to its free cash flows and its cost of capital?

1-4 An Overview of the Capital Allocation Process

Businesses often need capital to implement growth plans; governments require funds to finance building projects; and individuals frequently want loans to purchase cars, homes, and education. Where can they get this money? Fortunately, there are some individuals and firms with incomes greater than their expenditures. In spite of William Shakespeare's advice, most individuals and firms are both borrowers and lenders. For example, an individual might borrow money with a car loan or a home mortgage but might also lend money through a bank savings account. In the aggregate, individuals are net savers and provide most of the funds ultimately used by nonfinancial corporations. Although most nonfinancial corporations own some financial securities, such as short-term Treasury bills, nonfinancial corporations are net borrowers in the aggregate. In the United States, federal, state, and local governments are also net borrowers in the aggregate, although many foreign governments, such as those of China and oil-producing countries, are actually net lenders. Banks and other financial corporations raise money with one hand and invest it with the other. For example, a bank might raise money from individuals in the form of a savings account and then lend most of that money to business customers. In the aggregate, financial corporations borrow slightly more than they lend.

Transfers of capital between savers and those who need capital take place in three different ways. Direct transfers of money and securities, as shown in Panel 1 of Figure 1-1, occur when a business (or government) sells its securities directly to savers. The business delivers its securities to savers, who in turn provide the firm with the money it needs. For example, a privately held company might sell shares of stock directly to a new shareholder, or the U.S. government might sell a Treasury bond directly to an individual investor.

As shown in Panel 2, indirect transfers may go through an **investment banking house** such as Goldman Sachs, which *underwrites* the issue. An underwriter serves as a middleman and facilitates the issuance of securities. The company

---

FIGURE 1-1   Diagram of the Capital Allocation Process

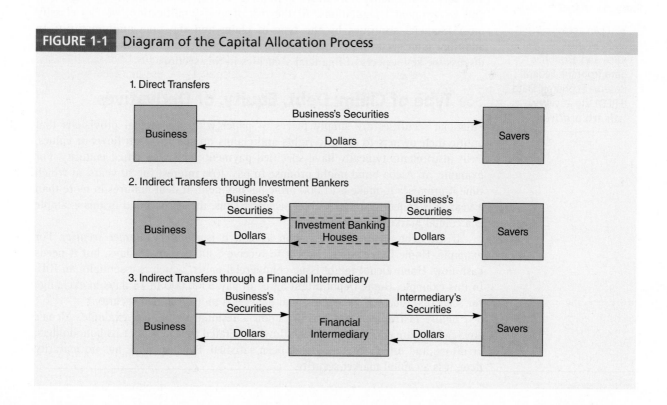

1. Direct Transfers

| Business | — Business's Securities → | Savers |
| | ← Dollars — | |

2. Indirect Transfers through Investment Bankers

| Business | Business's Securities → | Investment Banking Houses | Business's Securities → | Savers |
| | ← Dollars | | ← Dollars | |

3. Indirect Transfers through a Financial Intermediary

| Business | Business's Securities → | Financial Intermediary | Intermediary's Securities → | Savers |
| | ← Dollars | | ← Dollars | |

sells its stocks or bonds to the investment bank, which in turn sells these same securities to savers. Because new securities are involved and the corporation receives the proceeds of the sale, this is a "primary" market transaction.

Transfers also can be made through a **financial intermediary** such as a bank or mutual fund, as shown in Panel 3. Here the intermediary obtains funds from savers in exchange for its own securities. The intermediary then uses this money to purchase and then hold businesses' securities. For example, a saver might give dollars to a bank and receive a certificate of deposit, and then the bank might lend the money to a small business, receiving in exchange a signed loan. Thus, intermediaries literally create new types of securities.

There are three important characteristics of the capital allocation process. First, new financial securities are created. Second, financial institutions are often involved. Third, allocation between providers and users of funds occurs in financial markets.

> **SELF TEST**
>
> Identify three ways that capital is transferred between savers and borrowers.
>
> Distinguish between the roles played by investment banking houses and financial intermediaries.

1-5 **Financial Securities**

WWW

You can access current and historical interest rates and economic data from the Federal Reserve Economic Data (FRED) site at **www .stls.frb.org/fred**.

The variety of financial securities is limited only by human creativity, ingenuity, and governmental regulations. At the risk of oversimplification, we can classify most financial securities by the type of claim and the time until maturity. In addition, some securities actually are created from packages of other securities. We discuss the key aspects of financial securities in this section.

1-5a **Type of Claim: Debt, Equity, or Derivatives**

Financial securities are simply pieces of paper with contractual provisions that entitle their owners to specific rights and claims on specific cash flows or values. Debt instruments typically have specified payments and a specified maturity. For example, an Alcoa bond might promise to pay 10% interest for 30 years, at which time it promises to make a $1,000 principal payment. If debt matures in more than a year, it is called a *capital market security*. Thus, the Alcoa bond in this example is a capital market security.

If the debt matures in less than a year, it is a *money market security*. For example, Home Depot might expect to receive $300,000 in 75 days, but it needs cash now. Home Depot might issue commercial paper, which is essentially an IOU. In this example, Home Depot might agree to pay $300,000 in 75 days in exchange for $297,000 today. Thus, commercial paper is a money market security.

Equity instruments are a claim upon a residual value. For example, Alcoa's stockholders are entitled to the cash flows generated by Alcoa after its bondholders, creditors, and other claimants have been satisfied. Because stock has no maturity date, it is a capital market security.

Notice that debt and equity represent claims upon the cash flows generated by real assets, such as the cash flows generated by Alcoa's factories and operations. In contrast, **derivatives** are securities whose values depend on, or are *derived* from, the values of some other traded assets. For example, options and futures are two important types of derivatives, and their values depend on the prices of other assets. An option on Alcoa stock or a futures contract to buy pork bellies are examples of derivatives. We discuss options in Chapter 5 and in *Web Extension 1A*, which provides a brief overview of options and other derivatives.

Some securities are a mix of debt, equity, and derivatives. For example, preferred stock has some features like debt and some like equity, while convertible debt has both debt-like and option-like features.

We discuss these and other financial securities in detail later in the book, but Table 1-1 provides a summary of the most important conventional financial securities. We discuss rates of return later in this chapter, but notice now in Table 1-1 that interest rates tend to increase with the maturity and risk of the security.

Some securities are created from packages of other assets, a process called *securitization*. The misuse of securitized assets is one of the primary causes of the global financial crisis, so every manager needs to understand the process of securitization.

For an overview of derivatives, see **Web Extension 1A** on the textbook's Web site.

1-5b **The Process of Securitization**

Many types of assets can be securitized, but we will focus on mortgages because they played such an important role in the global financial crisis. At one time, most mortgages were made by **savings and loan associations (S&Ls)**, which took in the vast majority of their deposits from individuals who lived in nearby neighborhoods. The S&Ls pooled these deposits and then lent money to people in the neighborhood in the form of fixed-rate mortgages, which were pieces of paper signed by borrowers promising to make specified payments to the S&L. The new homeowners paid principal and interest to the S&L, which then paid interest to its depositors and reinvested the principal repayments in other mortgages. This was clearly better than having individuals lend directly to aspiring homeowners, because a single individual might not have enough money to finance an entire house or the expertise to know if the borrower was creditworthy.

Note that the S&Ls' assets consisted mainly of long-term, fixed-rate mortgages, but their liabilities were in the form of deposits that could be withdrawn immediately. The combination of long-term assets and short-term liabilities created a problem. If the overall level of interest rates increased, the S&Ls would have to increase the rates they paid on deposits or else savers would take their money elsewhere. However, the S&Ls couldn't increase the rates on their outstanding mortgages because these mortgages had fixed interest rates, which meant they couldn't increase the rates they paid on their deposits very much. This problem came to a head in the 1960s, when the Vietnam War led to inflation, which pushed up interest rates. At this point, the "money market fund" industry was born, and it literally sucked money out of the S&Ls, forcing many of them into bankruptcy.

This problem of long-term mortgages financed by short-term and unreliable deposits could be resolved if there were some way for the S&Ls and other mortgage lenders like banks to sell the mortgages to investors who wanted a long-term investment and lend out the resulting money again. The outcome was "mortgage

TABLE 1-1   Summary of Major Financial Instruments

Instrument	Major Participants	Risk	Original Maturity	Rates of Return on 6/30/13[a]
U.S. Treasury bills	Sold by U.S. Treasury	Default-free	91 days to 1 year	0.11%
Bankers' acceptances	A firm's promise to pay, guaranteed by a bank	Low if strong bank guarantees	Up to 180 days	0.28%
Commercial paper	Issued by financially secure firms to large investors	Low default risk	Up to 270 days	0.12%
Negotiable certificates of deposit (CDs)	Issued by major banks to large investors	Depends on strength of issuer	Up to 1 year	0.26%
Money market mutual funds	Invest in short-term debt; held by individuals and businesses	Low degree of risk	No specific maturity (instant liquidity)	0.42%
Eurodollar market time deposits	Issued by banks outside the United States	Depends on strength of issuer	Up to 1 year	0.22%
Consumer credit loans	Loans by banks/credit unions/finance companies	Risk is variable	Variable	Variable
Commercial loans	Loans by banks to corporations	Depends on borrower	Up to 7 years	Tied to prime rate (3.25%) or LIBOR (0.27%)[b]
U.S. Treasury notes and bonds	Issued by U.S. government	No default risk, but price falls if interest rates rise	2 to 30 years	3.40%
Mortgages	Loans secured by property	Risk is variable	Up to 30 years	4.50%
Municipal bonds	Issued by state and local governments to individuals and institutions	Riskier than U.S. government bonds, but exempt from most taxes	Up to 30 years	4.08%
Corporate bonds	Issued by corporations to individuals and institutions	Riskier than U.S. government debt; depends on strength of issuer	Up to 40 years[c]	4.37%
Leases	Similar to debt; firms lease assets rather than borrow and then buy them	Risk similar to corporate bonds	Generally 3 to 20 years	Similar to bond yields

Instrument	Major Participants	Risk	Original Maturity	Rates of Return on 6/30/13[a]
Preferred stocks	Issued by corporations to individuals and institutions	Riskier than corporate bonds	Unlimited	4% to 9%
Common stocks[d]	Issued by corporations to individuals and institutions	Riskier than preferred stocks	Unlimited	9% to 15%

[a]Data are from *The Wall Street Journal* (**online.wsj.com**) or the *Federal Reserve Statistical Release* (**www.federalreserve.gov/releases/H15/update**). Bankers' acceptances assume a 3-month maturity. Money market rates are for the Merrill Lynch Ready Assets Trust. The corporate bond rate is for AAA-rated bonds.

[b]The prime rate is the rate U.S. banks charge to good customers. LIBOR (London Interbank Offered Rate) is the rate that U.K. banks charge one another.

[c]A few corporations have issued 100-year bonds; however, most have issued bonds with maturities of less than 40 years.

[d]Common stocks are expected to provide a "return" in the form of dividends and capital gains rather than interest. Of course, if you buy a stock, your *actual* return may be considerably higher or lower than your *expected* return.

securitization," a process whereby banks, S&Ls, and specialized mortgage-originating firms would originate mortgages and then sell them to investment banks, which would bundle them into packages and then use these packages as collateral for bonds that could be sold to pension funds, insurance companies, and other institutional investors. Thus, individual mortgages were bundled and then used to back a bond—a "security"—that could be traded in the financial markets.

Congress facilitated this process by creating two stockholder-owned but government-sponsored entities, the Federal National Mortgage Association (Fannie Mae) and the Federal Home Loan Mortgage Corporation (Freddie Mac). Fannie Mae and Freddie Mac were financed by issuing a relatively small amount of stock and a huge amount of debt.

To illustrate the securitization process, suppose an S&L or bank is paying its depositors 5% but is charging its borrowers 8% on their mortgages. The S&L can take hundreds of these mortgages, put them in a pool, and then sell the pool to Fannie Mae. The mortgagees can still make their payments to the original S&L, which will then forward the payments (less a small handling fee) to Fannie Mae.

Consider the S&L's perspective. First, it can use the cash it receives from selling the mortgages to make additional loans to other aspiring homeowners. Second, the S&L is no longer exposed to the risk of owning mortgages. The risk hasn't disappeared—it has been transferred from the S&L (and its federal deposit insurers) to Fannie Mae. This is clearly a better situation for aspiring homeowners and, perhaps, also for taxpayers.

Fannie Mae can take the mortgages it just bought, put them into a very large pool, and sell bonds backed by the pool to investors. The homeowner will pay the S&L, the S&L will forward the payment to Fannie Mae, and Fannie Mae will use the funds to pay interest on the bonds it issued, to pay dividends on its stock, and to buy additional mortgages from S&Ls, which can then make additional loans to aspiring homeowners. Notice that the mortgage risk has been shifted from Fannie Mae to the investors who now own the mortgage-backed bonds.

How does the situation look from the perspective of the investors who own the bonds? In theory, they own a share in a large pool of mortgages from all over the country, so a problem in a particular region's real estate market or job market won't affect the whole pool. Therefore, their expected rate of return should be very close to the 8% rate paid by the home-owning mortgagees. (It will be a little less due to handling fees charged by the S&L and Fannie Mae and to the small amount of expected losses from the homeowners who could be expected to default on their mortgages.) These investors could have deposited their money at an S&L and earned a virtually risk-free 5%. Instead, they chose to accept more risk in hopes of the higher 8% return. Note, too, that mortgage-backed bonds are more liquid than individual mortgage loans, so the securitization process increases liquidity, which is desirable. The bottom line is that risk has been reduced by the pooling process and then allocated to those who are willing to accept it in return for a higher rate of return.

Thus, in theory it is a win–win–win situation: More money is available for aspiring homeowners, S&Ls (and taxpayers) have less risk, and there are opportunities for investors who are willing to take on more risk to obtain higher potential returns. Although the securitization process began with mortgages, it is now being used with car loans, student loans, credit card debt, and other loans. The details vary for different assets, but the processes and benefits are similar to those with mortgage securitization: (1) increased supplies of lendable funds, (2) transfer of risk to those who are willing to bear it, and (3) increased liquidity for holders of the debt.

Mortgage securitization was a win–win situation in theory, but as practiced in the last decade it has turned into a lose–lose situation. We will have more to say about securitization and the global economic crisis later in this chapter, but first let's take a look at the cost of money.

1-6 The Cost of Money

In a free economy, capital from those with available funds is allocated through the price system to users who have a need for funds. The interaction of the providers' supply and the users' demand determines the cost (or price) of money, which is the rate users pay to providers. For debt, we call this price the **interest rate**. For equity, we call it the **cost of equity**, and it consists of the dividends and capital gains stockholders expect. Keep in mind that the "price" of money is a cost from a user's perspective but a return from the provider's point of view.

Notice in Table 1-1 that a financial instrument's rate of return generally increases as its maturity and risk increase. We will have much more to say about the relationships among an individual security's features, risk, and return later in the book, but first we will examine some fundamental factors and economic conditions that affect all financial instruments.

1-6a Fundamental Factors That Affect the Cost of Money

The four most fundamental factors affecting the cost of money are: (1) **production opportunities**, (2) **time preferences for consumption**, (3) **risk**, and (4) **inflation**. By production opportunities, we mean the ability to turn capital into benefits. If a business raises capital, the benefits are determined by the expected rates of return on its production opportunities. If a student borrows to finance his or her education, the benefits are higher expected future salaries (and, of course, the sheer joy of learning!). If a homeowner borrows, the benefits are the pleasure from living in his or her own home, plus any expected appreciation in the value of the home. Observe that the expected rates of return on these "production opportunities" put an upper limit on how much users can pay to providers.

Providers can use their current funds for consumption or saving. By saving, they choose not to consume now, expecting to consume more in the future. If providers strongly prefer consumption now, then it takes high interest rates to induce them to trade current consumption for future consumption. Therefore, the time preference for consumption has a major impact on the cost of money. Notice that the time preference for consumption varies for different individuals, for different age groups, and for different cultures. For example, people in Japan have a lower time preference for consumption than those in the United States, which partially explains why Japanese families tend to save more than U.S. families even though interest rates are lower in Japan.

If the return on an investment is risky, then providers require a higher expected return to induce them to take the extra risk, which drives up the cost of money. As you will see later in this book, the risk of a security is determined by market conditions and the security's particular features.

Expected inflation also leads to a higher cost of money. For example, suppose you earned 10% one year on your investment but inflation caused prices to increase by 20%. This means you can't consume as much at the end of the year as when you originally invested your money. Obviously, if you had expected 20% inflation, you would have required a higher rate of return than 10%.

1-6b Economic Conditions and Policies That Affect the Cost of Money

Economic conditions and policies also affect the cost of money. These include: (1) Federal Reserve policy, (2) the federal budget deficit or surplus, (3) the level of business activity, and (4) international factors, including the foreign trade balance, the international business climate, and exchange rates.

Federal Reserve Policy

If the Federal Reserve Board wants to stimulate the economy, it most often uses open market operations to purchase Treasury securities held by banks. Because banks are selling some of their securities, the banks will have more cash, which increases their supply of loanable funds, which in turn makes banks willing to lend more money at lower interest rates. In addition, the Fed's purchases represent an increase in the demand for Treasury securities. As with anything for sale, increased demand causes Treasury securities' prices to go up and interest rates to go down. The net result is a reduction in interest rates, which stimulates the economy by making it less costly for companies to borrow for new projects or for individuals to borrow for major purchases or other expenditures.

When banks sell their holdings of Treasury securities to the Fed, the banks' reserves go up, which increases the money supply. A larger money supply ultimately leads to an increase in expected inflation, which eventually pushes interest rates up. Thus, the Fed can stimulate the economy in the short term by driving down interest rates and increasing the money supply, but this creates longer-term inflationary pressures. This was exactly the dilemma facing the Fed in mid-2013.

www

The home page for the Board of Governors of the Federal Reserve System can be found at **www.federalreserve .gov**. You can access general information about the Federal Reserve, including press releases, speeches, and monetary policy.

On the other hand, if the Fed wishes to slow down the economy and reduce inflation, the Fed reverses the process. Instead of purchasing Treasury securities, the Fed sells Treasury securities to banks, which reduces banking reserves and causes an increase in short-term interest rates but a decrease in long-term inflationary pressures.

Budget Deficits or Surpluses

www

For today's cumulative total federal debt (the total public debt), check out the *Current Daily Treasury Statement* at **www.fms.treas.gov /dts/index.html**.

If the federal government spends more than it takes in from tax revenues, then it runs a deficit, and that deficit must be covered either by borrowing or by printing money (increasing the money supply). The government borrows by issuing new Treasury securities. All else held equal, this creates a greater supply of Treasury securities, which leads to lower security prices and higher interest rates. Federal government actions that increase the money supply also increase expectations for future inflation, which drives up interest rates. Thus, the larger the federal deficit, other things held constant, the higher the level of interest rates. As shown in Figure 1-2, the federal government has run deficits in 15 of the past 19 years. Annual deficits in the mid-1990s were in the $250 billion range, but they have ballooned to well over a trillion dollars in recent years. These huge deficits have contributed to the cumulative federal debt, which in late 2013 stood at more than $17 trillion.

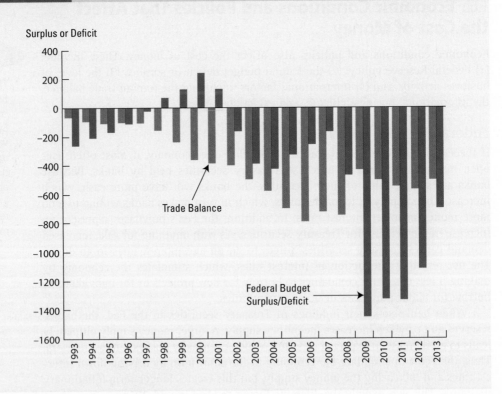

FIGURE 1-2   Federal Budget Surplus/Deficits and Trade Balances (Billions of Dollars)

Business Activity

Figure 1-3 shows interest rates, inflation, and recessions. Notice that interest rates and inflation typically rise prior to a recession and fall afterward. There are several reasons for this pattern.

Consumer demand slows during a recession, keeping companies from increasing prices, which reduces price inflation. Companies also cut back on hiring, which reduces wage inflation. Less disposable income causes consumers to reduce their purchases of homes and automobiles, reducing consumer demand for loans. Companies reduce investments in new operations, which reduces their demand for funds. The cumulative effect is downward pressure on inflation and interest rates. The Federal Reserve is also active during recessions, trying to stimulate the economy by driving down interest rates.

International Trade Deficits or Surpluses

Businesses and individuals in the United States buy from and sell to people and firms in other countries. If we buy more than we sell (that is, if we import more

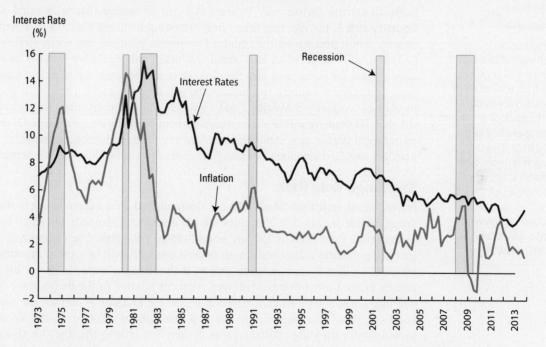

FIGURE 1-3   Business Activity, Interest Rates, and Inflation

Notes:

1. Tick marks represent January 1 of the year.
2. The shaded areas designate business recessions as defined by the National Bureau of Economic Research; see **www.nber.org/cycles**.
3. Interest rates are for AAA corporate bonds; see the St. Louis Federal Reserve Web site: **http://research.stlouisfed.org/fred**. These rates reflect the average rate during the month ending on the date shown.
4. Inflation is measured by the annual rate of change for the Consumer Price Index (CPI) for the preceding 12 months; see **http://research.stlouisfed.org/fred**.

than we export), we are said to be running a *foreign trade deficit*. When trade deficits occur, they must be financed, and the main source of financing is debt. In other words, if we import $200 billion of goods but export only $90 billion, we run a trade deficit of $110 billion, and we will probably borrow the $110 billion.[3] Therefore, the larger our trade deficit, the more we must borrow, and the increased borrowing drives up interest rates. Also, international investors are only willing to hold U.S. debt if the risk-adjusted rate paid on this debt is competitive with interest rates in other countries. Therefore, if the Federal Reserve attempts to lower interest rates in the United States, causing our rates to fall below rates abroad (after adjustments for expected changes in the exchange rate), then international investors will sell U.S. bonds, which will depress bond prices and result in higher U.S. rates. Thus, if the trade deficit is large relative to the size of the overall economy, it will hinder the Fed's ability to reduce interest rates and combat a recession.

The United States has been running annual trade deficits since the mid-1970s; see Figure 1-2 for recent years. The cumulative effect of trade deficits and budget deficits is that the United States has become the largest debtor nation of all time. As noted earlier, this federal debt exceeds *$17 trillion!* As a result, our interest rates are influenced by interest rates in other countries around the world.

International Country Risk

International risk factors may increase the cost of money that is invested abroad. **Country risk** is the risk that arises from investing or doing business in a particular country, and it depends on the country's economic, political, and social environment. Countries with stable economic, social, political, and regulatory systems provide a safer climate for investment and therefore have less country risk than less stable nations. Examples of country risk include the risk associated with changes in tax rates, regulations, currency conversion, and exchange rates. Country risk also includes the risk that: (1) property will be expropriated without adequate compensation, (2) the host country will impose new stipulations concerning local production, sourcing, or hiring practices, and (3) there might be damage or destruction of facilities due to internal strife.

Exchange Rate Risk

International securities frequently are denominated in a currency other than the dollar, which means that the value of an investment depends on what happens to exchange rates. This is known as **exchange rate risk**. For example, if a U.S. investor purchases a Japanese bond, interest probably will be paid in Japanese yen, which must then be converted to dollars if the investor wants to spend his or her money in the United States. If the yen weakens relative to the dollar, then the yen will buy fewer dollars when it comes time for the investor to convert the Japanese bond's payout. Alternatively, if the yen strengthens relative to the dollar, the investor will earn higher dollar returns. It therefore follows that the effective rate of return on a foreign investment will depend on both the performance of the foreign security in its home market and on what happens to exchange rates over the life of the investment. We discuss exchange rates in detail in Chapter 27.

www

Transparency International provides a ranking of countries based on their levels of perceived corruption. See **http://cpi .transparency.org /cpi2013/**. The U.S. Department of State provides thorough descriptions of countries' business climates at **www .state.gov/e/eb/rls /othr/ics/2014**.

---

3. The deficit could also be financed by selling assets, including gold, corporate stocks, entire companies, and real estate. The United States has financed its massive trade deficits through all of these means in recent years, but the primary method has been by borrowing from foreigners.

What four fundamental factors affect the cost of money?

Name some economic conditions that influence interest rates, and explain their effects.

SELF TEST

1-7 **The Global Economic Crisis**

Although the global economic crisis has many causes, mortgage securitization in the 2000s is certainly one culprit, so we begin with it.

1-7a **The Globalization of Mortgage Market Securitization**

A national TV program ran a documentary on the travails of Norwegian retirees resulting from defaults on Florida mortgages. Your first reaction might be to wonder how Norwegian retirees became financially involved with risky Florida mortgages. We will break the answer to that question into two parts. First, we will identify the different links in the financial chain between the retirees and mortgagees. Second, we will explain why there were so many weak links.

In the movie *Jerry Maguire*, Tom Cruise said, "Show me the money!" That's a good way to start identifying the financial links, starting with a single home purchase in Florida.

1. Home Purchase

In exchange for cash, a seller in Florida turned over ownership of a house to a buyer.

2. Mortgage Origination

To get the cash used to purchase the house, the buyer signed a mortgage loan agreement and gave it to an "originator." Years ago the originator would probably have been an S&L or a bank, but more recently the originators have been specialized mortgage brokers, as in this case. The broker gathered and examined the borrower's credit information, arranged for an independent appraisal of the house's value, handled the paperwork, and received a fee for these services.

3. Securitization and Resecuritization

In exchange for cash, the originator sold the mortgage to a securitizing firm. For example, Merrill Lynch's investment banking operation was a major player in securitizing loans. It would bundle large numbers of mortgages into pools and then create new securities that had claims on the pools' cash flows. Some claims were simple, such as a proportional share of a pool; some were more complex, such as a claim on all interest payments during the first 5 years or a claim on only principal payments. More complicated claims were entitled to a fixed payment, while other claims would receive payments only after the "senior" claimants had been paid. These slices of the pool were called "tranches," which comes from a French word for slice.

Some of the tranches were themselves recombined and then redivided into securities called collateralized debt obligations (CDOs), some of which were themselves combined and subdivided into other securities, commonly called CDOs-squared. For example, Lehman Brothers often bought different tranches, split them into CDOs of differing risk, and then had the different CDOs rated by an agency like Moody's or Standard & Poor's.

There are three very important points to notice. First, the process didn't change the *total amount of risk* embedded in the mortgages, but it did make it possible to create some securities that were less risky than average and some that were more risky. Second, the complexity of the CDOs spread a little bit of each mortgage's risk to many different investors, making it difficult for investors to determine the aggregate risk of a particular CDO. Third, each time a new security was created or rated, fees were being earned by the investment banks and rating agencies.

4. The Investors

In exchange for cash, the securitizing firms sold the newly created securities to individual investors, hedge funds, college endowments, insurance companies, and other financial institutions, including a pension fund in Norway. Keep in mind that financial institutions are funded by individuals, so cash begins with individuals and flows through the system until it is eventually received by the seller of the home. If all goes according to plan, payments on the mortgages eventually return to the individuals who originally provided the cash. But in this case, the chain was broken by a wave of mortgage defaults, resulting in problems for Norwegian retirees.

Students and managers often ask, "What happened to all the money?" The short answer is, "It went from investors to home sellers, with fees being skimmed off all along the way."

Although the process is complex, in theory there is nothing inherently wrong with it. In fact, it should, in theory, provide more funding for U.S. home purchasers, and it should allow risk to be shifted to those best able to bear it. Unfortunately, this isn't the end of the story.

1-7b The Dark Side of Securitization: The Sub-Prime Mortgage Meltdown

What caused the financial crisis? Entire books have been written on this subject, but we can identify a few of the culprits.

Regulators Approved Sub-Prime Standards

In the 1980s and early 1990s, regulations did not permit a nonqualifying mortgage to be securitized, so most originators mandated that borrowers meet certain requirements, including having at least a certain minimum level of income relative to the mortgage payments and a minimum down payment relative to the size of the mortgage. But in the mid-1990s, Washington politicians wanted to extend home ownership to groups that traditionally had difficulty obtaining mortgages. To accomplish this, regulations were relaxed so that nonqualifying mortgages could be securitized. Such loans are commonly called sub-prime or Alt-A mortgages. Thus, riskier mortgages were soon being securitized and sold to investors. Again, there was nothing inherently wrong, provided the two following questions were being answered in the affirmative: One, were home buyers making sound decisions regarding their ability to repay the loans? And two, did the ultimate investors recognize the additional risk? We now know that the answer to both questions is a resounding "No." Home-owners were signing mortgages that they could not hope to repay, and investors treated these mortgages as if they were much safer than they actually were.

The Fed Helped Fuel the Real Estate Bubble

With more people able to get a mortgage, including people who should not have obtained one, the demand for homes increased. This alone would have driven up house prices. However, the Fed also slashed interest rates to historic lows after the terrorist attacks of 9/11 to prevent a recession, and it kept them low for a long time. These low rates made mortgage payments lower, which made home ownership seem even more affordable, again contributing to an increase in the demand for housing. Figure 1-4 shows that the combination of lower mortgage qualifications and lower interest rates caused house prices to skyrocket. Thus, the Fed contributed to an artificial bubble in real estate.

FIGURE 1-4   The Real Estate Boom: Housing Prices and Mortgage Rates

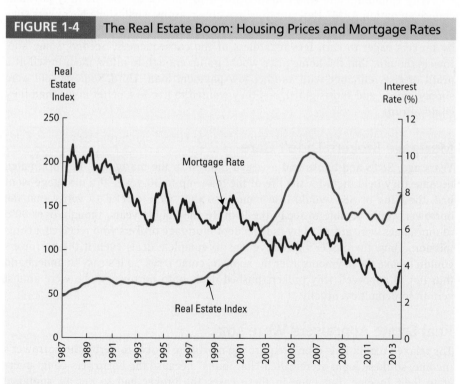

Notes:

1. The real estate index is the Case-Shiller composite index for house prices in 10 real estate markets, not seasonally adjusted, available at **www.standardandpoors.com/indices/sp-case-shiller-home-price-indices/en/us/?indexId=spusa-cashpidff--p-us----**.

2. Interest rates are for 30-year conventional fixed-rate mortgages, available from the St. Louis Federal Reserve: **http://research.stlouisfed.org/fred2/series/MORTG/downloaddata?cid=114**.

Home Buyers Wanted More for Less

Even with low interest rates, how could sub-prime borrowers afford the mortgage payments, especially with house prices rising? First, most sub-prime borrowers chose an adjustable rate mortgage (ARM) with an interest rate based on a short-term rate, such as that on 1-year Treasury bonds, to which the lender added a couple of percentage points. Because the Fed had pushed short-term rates so low, the initial rates on ARMs were very low.

With a traditional fixed-rate mortgage, the payments remain fixed over time. But with an ARM, an increase in market interest rates triggers higher monthly payments, so an ARM is riskier than a fixed-rate mortgage. However, many borrowers chose an *even riskier* mortgage, the "option ARM," where the borrower can choose to make such low payments during the first couple of years that they don't even cover the interest, causing the loan balance to actually increase each month! At a later date, the payments would be reset to reflect both the current market interest rate and the higher loan balance. For example, in some cases a monthly payment of $948 for the first 32 months was reset to $2,454 for the remaining 328 months. (We provide the calculations for this example in Web Chapter 28.)

Why would anyone who couldn't afford to make a $2,454 monthly payment choose an option ARM? Here are three possible reasons. First, some borrowers simply didn't understand the situation and were victims of predatory lending practices by brokers eager to earn fees regardless of the consequences. Second, some borrowers thought that the home price would go up enough to allow them to sell at a profit or else refinance with another low-payment loan. Third, some people were simply greedy and shortsighted, and they wanted to live in a better home than they could afford.

Mortgage Brokers Didn't Care

Years ago, S&Ls and banks had a vested interest in the mortgages they originated because they held them for the life of the loan—up to 30 years. If a mortgage went bad, the bank or S&L would lose money, so they were careful to verify that the borrower would be able to repay the loan. In the bubble years, though, over 80% of mortgages were arranged by independent mortgage brokers who received a commission. Thus, the broker's incentive was to complete deals even if the borrowers couldn't make the payments after the soon-to-come reset. So it's easy to understand (but not to approve!) why brokers pushed deals onto borrowers who were almost certain to default eventually.

Real Estate Appraisers Were Lax

The relaxed regulations didn't require the mortgage broker to verify the borrower's income, so these loans were called "liar loans" because the borrowers could over-state their income. But even in these cases the broker had to get an appraisal showing that the house's value was greater than the loan amount. Many real estate appraisers simply assumed that house prices would keep going up, so they were willing to appraise houses at unrealistically high values. Like the mortgage brokers, they were paid at the time of their service. Other than damage to their reputations, they weren't concerned if the borrower later defaulted and the value of the house turned out to be less than the remaining loan balance, causing a loss for the lender.

Originators and Securitizers Wanted Quantity, Not Quality

Originating institutions like Countrywide Financial and New Century Mortgage made money when they sold the mortgages, long before any of the mortgages defaulted. The same is true for securitizing firms such as Bear Stearns, Merrill Lynch, and Lehman Brothers. Their incentives were to generate volume through originating loans, not to ensure that the loans were safe investments. This started at the top—CEOs and other top executives received stock options and bonuses based on their firms' profits, and profits depended on volume. Thus, the top officers pushed their subordinates to generate volume, those subordinates pushed the originators to write more mortgages, and the originators pushed the appraisers to come up with high values.

Rating Agencies Were Lax

Investors who purchased the complicated mortgage-backed securities wanted to know how risky they were, so they insisted on seeing the bonds' "ratings." The securitizing firms paid rating agencies to investigate the details of each bond and to assign a rating that reflected the security's risk. For example, Lehman Brothers hired Moody's to rate some of its CDOs. Indeed, the investment banks would actually pay for advice from the rating agencies as they were designing the securities. The rating and consulting activities were extremely lucrative for the agencies, which ignored the obvious conflict of interest: The investment bank wanted a high rating, the rating agency got paid to help design securities that would qualify for a high rating, and high ratings led to continued business for the raters.

Insurance Wasn't Insurance

To provide a higher rating and make these mortgage-backed securities look even more attractive to investors, the issuers would frequently purchase a type of insurance policy on the security called a **credit default swap**. For example, suppose you had wanted to purchase a CDO from Lehman Brothers but worried about the risk. What if Lehman Brothers had agreed to pay an annual fee to an insurance company such as AIG, which would guarantee the CDO's payments if the underlying mortgages defaulted? You probably would have felt confident enough to buy the CDO.

But any similarity to a conventional insurance policy ends here. Unlike home insurance, where there is a single policyholder and a single insurer, totally uninvolved speculators can also make bets on your CDO by either selling or purchasing credit default swaps on the CDO. For example, a hedge fund could buy a credit default swap on your CDO if it thinks the CDO will default; or an investment bank like Bear Stearns could sell a swap, betting that the CDO won't default. In fact, the International Swaps and Derivatives Association estimates that in mid-2008 there was about $54 trillion in credit default swaps. This staggering amount was approximately 7 times the value of all U.S. mortgages, was over 4 times the level of the U.S. national debt, and was over twice the value of the entire U.S. stock market.

Another big difference is that home insurance companies are highly regulated, but there was virtually no regulation in the credit default swap market. The players traded directly among themselves, with no central clearinghouse. It was almost impossible to tell how much risk any of the players had taken on, making it impossible to know whether or not counterparties like AIG would be able to fulfill their obligations in the event of a CDO default. And that made it impossible to know the value of CDOs held by many banks, which in turn made it impossible to judge whether or not those banks were de facto bankrupt.

Rocket Scientists Had Poor Rearview Mirrors and Risk Managers Drove Blind

Brilliant financial experts, often trained in physics and hired from rocket science firms, built elegant models to determine the value of these new securities. Unfortunately, a model is only as good as its inputs. The experts looked at the high growth rates of recent real estate prices (see Figure 1-4) and assumed that future growth rates also would be high. These high growth rates caused models to calculate very high CDO prices. Perhaps more surprisingly, many risk managers simply did not insist on seeing scenarios in which housing prices fell.

Investors Wanted More for Less

In the early 2000s, low-rated debt (including mortgage-backed securities), hedge funds, and private equity funds produced great rates of return. Many investors jumped into this debt to keep up with the Joneses. As shown in Chapter 4 when we discuss bond ratings and bond spreads, investors began lowering the premium they required for taking on extra risk. Thus, investors focused primarily on returns and largely ignored risk. In fairness, some investors assumed the credit ratings were accurate, and they trusted the representatives of the investment banks selling the securities. In retrospect, however, Warren Buffett's maxim "I only invest in companies I understand" seems wiser than ever.

The Emperor Has No Clothes

In 2006, many of the option ARMs began to reset, borrowers began to default, and home prices first leveled off and then began to fall. Things got worse in 2007 and 2008, and by early 2009, almost 1 out of 10 mortgages was in default or foreclosure, resulting in displaced families and virtual ghost towns of new subdivisions. As homeowners defaulted on their mortgages, so did the CDOs backed by the mortgages. That brought down the counterparties like AIG who had insured the CDOs via credit default swaps. Virtually overnight, investors realized that mortgage-backed security default rates were headed higher and that the houses used as collateral were worth less than the mortgages. Mortgage-backed security prices plummeted, investors quit buying newly securitized mortgages, and liquidity in the secondary market disappeared. Thus, the investors who owned these securities were stuck with pieces of paper worth substantially less than the values reported on their balance sheets.

1-7c From Sub-Prime Meltdown to Liquidity Crisis to Economic Crisis

Like the Andromeda strain, the sub-prime meltdown went viral, and it ended up infecting almost all aspects of the economy. But why did a burst bubble in one market segment, sub-prime mortgages, spread across the globe?

First, securitization allocated the sub-prime risk to many investors and financial institutions. The huge amount of credit default swaps linked to sub-prime–backed securities spread the risk to even more institutions. Unlike previous downturns in a single market, such as the dot-com bubble in 2002, the decline in the sub-prime mortgage values affected many, if not most, financial institutions.

Second, banks were more vulnerable than at any time since the 1929 Depression. Congress had "repealed" the Glass–Steagall Act in 1999, allowing commercial banks and investment banks to be part of a single financial institution. The SEC compounded the problem in 2004 when it allowed large investment banks' brokerage operations to take on much higher leverage. Some, like Bear Stearns, ended up with $33 of debt for every dollar of its own equity. With such leverage, a small increase in the value of its investments would create enormous gains for the equity holders and large bonuses for the managers; conversely, a small decline would ruin the firm.

When the sub-prime market mortgages began defaulting, mortgage companies were the first to fall. Many originating firms had not sold all of their sub-prime mortgages, and they failed. For example, New Century declared bankruptcy in 2007, IndyMac was placed under FDIC control in 2008, and Countrywide was acquired by Bank of America in 2008 to avoid bankruptcy.

Securitizing firms also crashed, partly because they kept some of the new securities they created. For example, Fannie Mae and Freddie Mac had huge losses on their portfolio assets, causing them to be virtually taken over by the Federal Housing Finance Agency in 2008. In addition to big losses on their own sub-prime portfolios, many investment banks also had losses related to their positions in credit default swaps. Thus, Lehman Brothers was forced into bankruptcy, Bear Stearns was sold to JPMorgan Chase, and Merrill Lynch was sold to Bank of America, with huge losses to stockholders.

Because Lehman Brothers defaulted on some of its commercial paper, investors in the Reserve Primary Fund, a big money market mutual fund, saw the value of its investments "break the buck," dropping to less than a dollar per share. To avoid panic and a total lockdown in the money markets, the U.S. Treasury agreed to insure some investments in money market funds.

AIG was the largest backer of credit default swaps, and it operated worldwide. In 2008 it became obvious that AIG could not honor its commitments as a counterparty, so the Fed effectively nationalized AIG to avoid a domino effect in which AIG's failure would topple hundreds of other financial institutions.

In normal times, banks provide liquidity to the economy and funding for creditworthy businesses and individuals. These activities are crucial for a well-functioning economy. However, the financial contagion spread to commercial banks because some owned mortgage-backed securities, some owned commercial paper issued by failing institutions, and some had exposure to credit default swaps. As banks worried about their survival in the fall of 2008, they stopped providing credit to other banks and businesses. The market for commercial paper dried up to such an extent that the Fed began buying new commercial paper from issuing companies.

Prior to the sub-prime meltdown, many nonfinancial corporations had been rolling over short-term financing to take advantage of low interest rates on short-term lending. When the meltdown began, banks began calling in loans rather than renewing them. In response, many companies began throttling back their plans. Consumers and small businesses faced a similar situation: With credit harder to obtain, consumers cut back on spending and small businesses cut back on hiring. Plummeting real estate prices caused a major contraction in the construction industry, putting many builders and suppliers out of work.

What began as a slump in housing prices caused enormous distress for commercial banks, not just mortgage companies. Commercial banks cut back on lending, which caused difficulties for nonfinancial business and consumers. Similar scenarios played out all over the world, resulting in the worst recession in the United States since 1929.

GLOBAL ECONOMIC CRISIS

Anatomy of a Toxic Asset

Consider the dismal history of one particular toxic asset named "GSAMP TRUST 2006-NC2." This toxic asset began life as 3,949 individual mortgages issued by New Century in 2006 with a total principal of about $881 million. Almost all were adjustable rate mortgages, half were concentrated in just two states (California and Florida), and many of the borrowers had previous credit problems. Goldman Sachs bought the mortgages, pooled them into a trust, and divided the trust into 16 "debt" tranches called mortgage-backed securities (MBS). The tranches had different provisions regarding distribution of payments should there be any defaults, with senior tranches getting paid first and junior tranches getting paid only if funds were available. Despite the mortgages' poor quality and the pool's lack of diversification, Moody's and Standard & Poor's gave most tranches good ratings, with over 79% rated AAA.

Five years later, in July 2011, about 36% of the underlying mortgages were behind in payments, defaulted, or even foreclosed. Not surprisingly, the market prices of the mortgage-backed securities had plummeted. These were very toxic assets indeed!

The story doesn't end here. Fannie Mae and Freddie Mac had purchased some of these toxic assets and taken a beating. In September, 2011, the Federal Housing Finance Agency (now the conservator of Fannie Mae and Freddie Mac) sued Goldman Sachs, alleging that Goldman Sachs had knowingly overstated the value of the securities in the prospectuses. The FHFA also alleges that at the very same time Goldman Sachs was selling these and other mortgage-backed securities to Fannie and Freddie, Goldman was: (1) trying to get rid of the mortgages by "putting" them back to New Century, and (2) was "betting" against the mortgages in the credit default swap market. As of late 2013, this suit has not yet been settled, but it is safe to say that these toxic assets will continue to poison our economy for many more years.

Source: Adam B. Ashcraft and Til Schuermann, *Understanding the Securitization of Subprime Mortgage Credit*, Federal Reserve Bank of New York Staff Reports, no. 318, March 2008; John Cassidy, *How Markets Fail* (New York: Farrar, Straus and Giroux, 2009), pp. 260–272; and the Federal Housing Finance Agency, **www.fhfa.gov /webfiles/22589/FHFA%20v%20Goldman%20Sachs.pdf**.

1-7d **Responding to the Economic Crisis**

Unlike the beginning of the 1929 Depression, the U.S. government did not take a hands-off approach in the most recent crisis. In late 2008, Congress passed the Troubled Asset Relief Plan (TARP), which authorized the U.S. Treasury to purchase mortgage-related assets from financial institutions. The intent was to simultaneously inject cash into the banking system and get these toxic assets off banks' balance sheets. The Emergency Economic Stabilization Act of 2008 (EESA) allowed the Treasury to purchase preferred stock in banks (whether they wanted the investment or not). Again, this injected cash into the banking system. Most of the large banks have already paid back the funding they received from the TARP and EESA financing, although it is doubtful whether all recipients will be able to do so. It is almost certain that taxpayers will bear the burden of the Fannie Mae and Freddie Mac bailouts.

Although TARP and EESA were originally intended for financial institutions, they were subsequently modified so that the Treasury was able to make loans to GM and Chrysler in 2008 and early 2009 so that they could stave off immediate bankruptcy. Both GM and Chrysler went into bankruptcy in the summer of 2009 despite government loans, but they quickly emerged as stronger companies. The U.S. government has since sold all of the shares issued to it by Chrysler and plans to sell its remaining shares in GM by early 2014.

The government also used traditional measures, such as stimulus spending, tax cuts, and monetary policy: (1) The American Recovery and Reinvestment Act of 2009 provided over $700 billion in direct stimulus spending for a variety of federal projects and aid for state projects. (2) In 2010 the government also temporarily cut Social Security taxes from 6.2% to 4.2%. (3) The Federal Reserve has purchased around $2 trillion in assets, including long-term bonds, from financial institutions, a process called "quantitative easing."

Has the response worked? You will have a better answer at the time you read this than we had when we wrote this in late 2013, but here is our answer: The economy is better now than at the worst of the crisis, with the unemployment rate down to 7.2% from its 2009 high of 10%, and GDP is growing rather than contracting. Whether or not it was due to the government's response, it does not appear likely that the economy will soon fall into another Great Depression, something that we could not write in 2009. On the other hand, it is likely that it will take years, if not a full decade, for the economy and stock markets to fully recover.[4]

1-7e Preventing the Next Crisis

Can the next crisis be prevented? Congress passed the Dodd-Frank Wall Street Reform and Consumer Protection Act in 2010 as an attempt to do just that. As we write this in late 2013, many provisions have not yet been enacted. Following is a brief summary of some major elements in the Act.

Protect Consumers from Predators and Themselves

Dodd-Frank established the Consumer Financial Protection Bureau, whose objectives include ensuring that borrowers fully understand the terms and risks of the mortgage contracts, that mortgage originators verify borrower's ability to repay, and that originators maintain an interest in the borrowers by keeping some of the mortgages they originate. The Bureau will also oversee credit cards, debit cards, payday loans, and other areas in which consumers might have been targets of predatory lending practices. As of late 2013, the Bureau has been established, but it has done very little.

Separate Banking from Speculating

The act's "Volcker Rule," named after former Fed chairman Paul Volcker, would greatly limit a bank's proprietary trading, such as investing the banks' own funds into hedge funds. The basic idea is to prevent banks from making highly leveraged bets on risky assets. The Volcker Rule has not been implemented as of late 2013, but a final draft of the rule is expected at any time. In addition, Goldman Sachs and Morgan Stanley have already cut back their proprietary trading operations.

---

4. For a comparison of this crisis with 15 previous banking crises, see Serge Wind, "A Perspective on 2000's Illiquidity and Capital Crisis: Past Banking Crises and their Relevance to Today's Credit Crisis," *Review of Business*, Volume 31, Number 1, Fall 2010, pp. 68–83. Based on these previous crises, Professor Wind estimates it will take 10 years for equity markets to reach the pre-crisis high.

Increase Transparency

The act calls for regulation and transparency in the now-private derivatives markets, including the establishment of a trading exchange. It also provides for more oversight of hedge funds and credit rating agencies in an effort to spot potential landmines before they explode. Some progress has been made in establishing centralized clearing for standardized derivatives contracts, but much remains to be done as of mid-2014.

Head Off and Rein In Systemic Failures at Too-Big-to-Fail Banks

When a bank gets extremely large and has business connections with many other companies, it can be very dangerous to the rest of the economy if the institution fails and goes bankrupt, as the 2008 failure of Lehman Brothers illustrates. In other words, a bank or other financial institution can become "too big to fail." Systemic risk is defined as something that affects most companies. When there are a large number of too-big-to-fail institutions and systemic shock hits, the entire world can be dragged into a recession, as we saw in 2008.

Dodd-Frank gives regulators more oversight of too-big-to-fail institutions, including all banks with $50 billion in assets and any other financial institutions that regulators deem systemically important. This oversight includes authority to require additional capital or reductions in leverage if conditions warrant. In addition, these institutions must prepare "transition" plans that would make it easier for regulators to liquidate the institution should it fail. In other words, this provision seeks to reduce the likelihood that a giant financial institution will fail and to minimize the damage if it does fail. Not much has been implemented as of mid-2014.

> **SELF TEST** Briefly describe some of the mistakes that participants in the sub-prime mortgage process made.

1-8 The Big Picture

Finance has vocabulary and tools that might be new to you. To help you avoid getting bogged down in the trenches, Figure 1-5 presents the big picture. A manager's primary job is to increase the company's intrinsic value, but how exactly does one go about doing that? The equation in the center of Figure 1-5 shows that intrinsic value is the present value of the firm's expected free cash flows, discounted at the weighted average cost of capital. Thus, there are two approaches for increasing intrinsic value: improve FCF or reduce the WACC. Observe that several factors affect FCF and several factors affect the WACC. In the rest of the book's chapters, we will typically focus on only one of these factors, systematically building the vocabulary and tools that you will use after graduation to improve your company's intrinsic value. It is true that every manager needs to understand financial vocabulary and be able to apply financial tools, but successful managers also understand how their decisions affect the big picture. So as you read this book, keep in mind where each topic fits into the big picture.

FIGURE 1-5 The Determinants of Intrinsic Value: The Big Picture

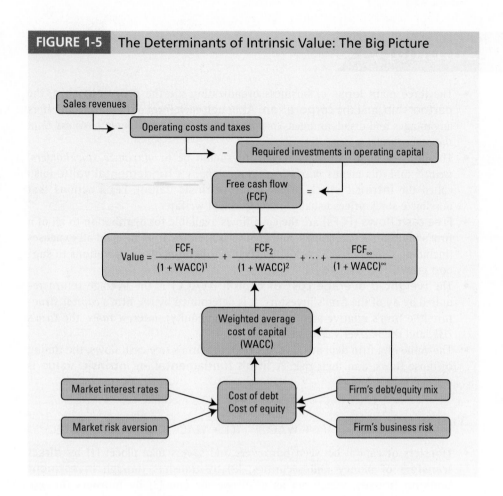

1-9 e-Resources

The textbook's Web site contains several types of files that will be helpful to you:

1. It contains *Excel* files, called **Tool Kits**, that provide well-documented models for almost all of the text's calculations. Not only will these **Tool Kits** help you with this finance course, they also will serve as tool kits for you in other courses and in your career.
2. Some of the beginning-of-chapter questions have spreadsheets to illustrate answers. The Web site contains these models.
3. There are problems at the end of the chapters that require spreadsheets, and the Web site contains the models you will need to begin work on these problems.

When we think it might be helpful for you to look at one of the Web site's files, we'll show an icon in the margin like the one shown here.

Other resources are also on the Web site, including an electronic library that contains Adobe PDF files for "extensions" to many chapters that cover additional useful material related to the chapter.

Summary

- The three main forms of business organization are the **proprietorship**, the **partnership**, and the **corporation**. Although each form of organization offers advantages and disadvantages, *corporations conduct much more business than the other forms.*
- The primary objective of management should be to *maximize stockholders' wealth,* and this means *maximizing the company's* **fundamental value** (also called the **intrinsic stock price** or the **intrinsic value**). Legal actions that maximize stock prices usually increase social welfare.
- **Free cash flows (FCFs)** are the cash flows available for distribution to all of a firm's investors (shareholders and creditors) after the firm has paid all expenses (including taxes) and has made the required investments in operations to support growth.
- The **weighted average cost of capital (WACC)** is the average return required by all of the firm's investors. It is determined by the firm's *capital structure* (the firm's relative amounts of debt and equity), *interest rates,* the firm's *risk,* and the *market's attitude toward risk.*
- The value of a firm depends on the size of the firm's free cash flows, the timing of those flows, and their risk. A **firm's fundamental**, or **intrinsic**, **value** is defined by:

$$\text{Value} = \frac{FCF_1}{(1 + WACC)^1} + \frac{FCF_2}{(1 + WACC)^2} + \frac{FCF_3}{(1 + WACC)^3} + \cdots + \frac{FCF_\infty}{(1 + WACC)^\infty}$$

- Transfers of capital between borrowers and savers take place: (1) by **direct transfers** of money and securities; (2) by transfers through **investment banking houses**, which act as go-betweens; and (3) by transfers through **financial intermediaries**, which create new securities.
- Four fundamental factors affect the cost of money: (1) **production opportunities**, (2) **time preferences for consumption**, (3) **risk**, and (4) **inflation**.
- **Derivatives**, such as options, are claims on other financial securities. In **securitization**, new securities are created from claims on packages of other securities.
- *Web Extension 1A* discusses derivatives, and *Web Extension 1B* provides additional coverage of stock markets.

Questions

1–1 Define each of the following terms:
    a. Proprietorship; partnership; corporation
    b. Limited partnership; limited liability partnership; professional corporation
    c. Stockholder wealth maximization
    d. Production opportunities; time preferences for consumption
    e. Foreign trade deficit

1-2 What are the three principal forms of business organization? What are the advantages and disadvantages of each?

1-3 What is a firm's fundamental, or intrinsic, value? What might cause a firm's intrinsic value to be different from its actual market value?

1-4 Edmund Enterprises recently made a large investment to upgrade its technology. Although these improvements won't have much of an impact on performance in the short run, they are expected to reduce future costs significantly. What impact will this investment have on Edmund Enterprises' earnings per share this year? What impact might this investment have on the company's intrinsic value and stock price?

1-5 Describe the ways in which capital can be transferred from suppliers of capital to those who are demanding capital.

MINI CASE

Assume that you recently graduated and have just reported to work as an investment advisor at the brokerage firm of Balik and Kiefer Inc. One of the firm's clients is Michelle DellaTorre, a professional tennis player who has just come to the United States from Chile. DellaTorre is a highly ranked tennis player who would like to start a company to produce and market apparel she designs. She also expects to invest substantial amounts of money through Balik and Kiefer. DellaTorre is very bright, and she would like to understand in general terms what will happen to her money. Your boss has developed the following set of questions you must answer to explain the U.S. financial system to DellaTorre.

a. Why is corporate finance important to all managers?

b. Describe the organizational forms a company might have as it evolves from a start-up to a major corporation. List the advantages and disadvantages of each form.

c. How do corporations go public and continue to grow? What are agency problems? What is corporate governance?

d. What should be the primary objective of managers?

   (1) Do firms have any responsibilities to society at large?

   (2) Is stock price maximization good or bad for society?

   (3) Should firms behave ethically?

e. What three aspects of cash flows affect the value of any investment?

f. What are free cash flows?

g. What is the weighted average cost of capital?

h. How do free cash flows and the weighted average cost of capital interact to determine a firm's value?

i. Who are the providers (savers) and users (borrowers) of capital? How is capital transferred between savers and borrowers?

j. What do we call the price that a borrower must pay for debt capital? What is the price of equity capital? What are the four most fundamental factors that affect the cost of money, or the general level of interest rates, in the economy?

k. What are some economic conditions (including international aspects) that affect the cost of money?

l. What are financial securities? Describe some financial instruments.

m. Briefly explain mortgage securitization and how it contributed to the global economic crisis.

Risk and Return: Part I

In this chapter, we start from the basic premise that investors like returns and dislike risk; this is called **risk aversion**. Therefore, people will invest in relatively risky assets only if they expect to receive relatively high returns—the higher the perceived risk, the higher the expected rate of return an investor will demand. In this chapter, we define exactly what the term risk means as it relates to investments, we examine procedures used to measure *risk*, and we discuss more precisely the relationship between risk and required returns. In later chapters, we extend these relationships to show how risk and return interact to determine security prices. Managers must understand and apply these concepts as they plan the actions that will shape their firms' futures, and investors must understand them in order to make appropriate investment decisions.

Beginning-of-Chapter Questions

As you read the chapter, consider how you would answer the following questions. You *should not* necessarily be able to answer the questions before you read the chapter. Rather, you should use them to get a sense of the issues covered in the chapter. After reading the chapter, you should be able to give at least partial answers to the questions, and you should be able to give better answers after the chapter has been discussed in class. Note, too, that it is often useful, when answering conceptual questions, to use hypothetical data to illustrate your answer. We illustrate the answers with an *Excel* model that is available on the textbook's Web site. Accessing the model and working through it is a useful exercise, and it provides insights that are useful when answering the questions.

1. Differentiate between (a) **stand-alone risk** and (b) **risk in a portfolio context**. How are they measured, and are both concepts relevant for investors?

2. Can an investor eliminate **market risk** from a portfolio of common stocks? How many stocks must a portfolio contain to be "reasonably well diversified"? Do all portfolios with, say, 50 stocks have about the same amount of risk?

3. a. Differentiate between the terms **expected rate of return**, **required rate of return**, and **historical rate of return** as they are applied to common stocks.

    b. If you found values for each of these returns for several different stocks, would the values for each stock most likely be the same or different? That is, would Stock A's expected, required, and historical rates of return be equal to one another? Why?

4. What does the term **risk aversion** mean, and how is risk aversion related to the expected return on a stock?

5. What is the **Capital Asset Pricing Model (CAPM)**? What are some of its key assumptions? Has it been empirically verified? What is the role of the **Security Market Line** in the CAPM? Suppose you had to estimate the required rate of return on a stock using the CAPM. What data would you need, where would you get the data, and how confident would you be of your estimate?

6. Suppose you have data that show the rates of return earned by Stock X, Stock Y, and the market over the last 5 years, along with the risk-free rate of return and the required return on the market. You also have estimates of the expected returns on X and Y.
   a. How could you decide, based on these expected returns, if Stocks X and Y are good deals, bad deals, or in equilibrium?
   b. Now suppose in Year 6 the market is quite strong. Stock X has a high positive return, but Stock Y's price falls because investors suddenly become quite concerned about its future prospects; that is, it becomes riskier, and like a bond that suddenly becomes risky, its price falls. Based on the CAPM and using the most recent 5 years of data, would Stock Y's required return as calculated just after the end of Year 6 rise or fall? What can you say about these results?

7. What does each of the three forms of the Efficient Markets Hypothesis say about each of the following?
   a. Technical trading rules—that is, rules based on past movements in the stock
   b. Fundamental analysis—that is, trying to identify undervalued or overvalued stocks based on publicly available financial information
   c. Insider trading
   d. Hot tips from: (1) Internet chat rooms, (2) close friends unconnected with the company, or (3) close friends who work for the company

2-1 Investment Returns and Risk

With most investments, an individual or business spends money today with the expectation of earning even more money in the future. However, most investments are risky. Following are brief definitions of return and risk.

2-1a Returns on Investments

The concept of *return* provides investors with a convenient way to express the financial performance of an investment. To illustrate, suppose you buy 10 shares of a stock for $1,000. The stock pays no dividends, but at the end of 1 year you sell the stock for $1,100. What is the return on your $1,000 investment?

One way to express an investment's return is in *dollar terms*:

$$\text{Dollar return} = \text{Amount to be received} - \text{Amount invested}$$
$$= \$1,100 - \$1,000$$
$$= \$100$$

If instead at the end of the year you sell the stock for only $900, your dollar return will be −$100.

Although expressing returns in dollars is easy, two problems arise: (1) To make a meaningful judgment about the return, you need to know the scale (size) of the investment; a $100 return on a $100 investment is a great return (assuming the investment is held for 1 year), but a $100 return on a $10,000 investment would be a poor return. (2) You also need to know the timing of the return; a $100 return on a

INTRINSIC VALUE, RISK, AND RETURN

The intrinsic value of a company is the present value of its expected future free cash flows (FCF) discounted at the weighted average cost of capital (WACC). This chapter shows you how to measure a firm's risk and the rate of return expected by shareholders, which affects the WACC. All else held equal, higher risk increases the WACC, which reduces the firm's value.

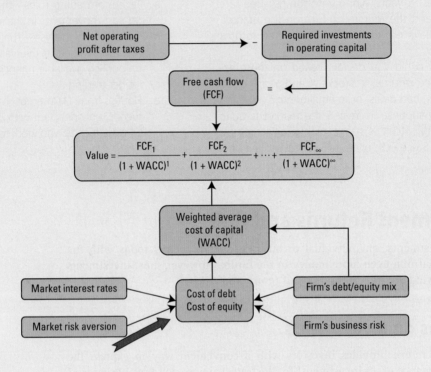

$100 investment is a great return if it occurs after 1 year, but the same dollar return after 20 years is not very good.

The solution to these scale and timing problems is to express investment results as *rates of return*, or *percentage returns*. For example, the rate of return on the 1-year stock investment, when $1,100 is received after 1 year, is 10%:

$$\text{Rate of return} = \frac{\text{Amount received} - \text{Amount invested}}{\text{Amount invested}}$$

$$= \frac{\text{Dollar return}}{\text{Amount invested}} = \frac{\$100}{\$1,000}$$

$$= 0.10 = 10\%$$

The rate of return calculation "standardizes" the dollar return by considering the annual return per unit of investment. Although this example has only one outflow and one inflow, the annualized rate of return can easily be calculated in situations where multiple cash flows occur over time by using time value of money concepts as discussed in Web Chapter 28.

2-1b Stand-Alone Risk versus Portfolio Risk

Risk is defined in *Webster's* as "a hazard; a peril; exposure to loss or injury." Thus, risk refers to the chance that some unfavorable event will occur. For an investment in financial assets or in new projects, the unfavorable event is ending up with a lower return than you expected. An asset's risk can be analyzed in two ways: (1) on a stand-alone basis, where the asset is considered in isolation; and (2) on a portfolio basis, where the asset is held as one of a number of assets in a portfolio. Thus, an asset's **stand-alone risk** is the risk an investor would face if she held only this one asset. Most assets are held in portfolios, but it is necessary to understand stand-alone risk in order to understand risk in a portfolio context.

Compare and contrast dollar returns and rates of return.

Why are rates of return superior to dollar returns when comparing different potential investments? (*Hint:* Think about size and timing.)

If you pay $500 for an investment that returns $600 in 1 year, what is your annual rate of return? **(20%)**

SELF TEST

2-2 Measuring Risk for Discrete Distributions

Political and economic uncertainty affect stock market risk. For example, in the summer of 2013, the market fell sharply when Ben Bernanke, the chairman of the Federal Reserve, indicated that the Fed's ongoing economic stimulus policies might end soon. If the economy picked up sufficiently (a good scenario), then the stimulus would be discontinued, but that would result in higher interest rates. If the economy did not pick up much (a bad scenario), then the stimulus would continue, which would keep interest rates low (a good scenario for investment). If the stimulus policies were discontinued too early, then the higher interest rates might further depress the economy (a very bad scenario). At the risk of oversimplification, these outcomes represented several distinct (or discrete) scenarios for the market, with each scenario having a very different market return.

Risk can be a complicated topic, so we begin with a simple example that has discrete possible outcomes.[1]

2-2a Probability Distributions for Discrete Outcomes

An event's *probability* is defined as the chance that the event will occur. For example, a weather forecaster might state: "There is a 40% chance of rain today and a 60% chance that it will not rain." If all possible events, or outcomes, are listed, and if a probability

---

1. The following discussion of risk applies to all random variables, not just stock returns.

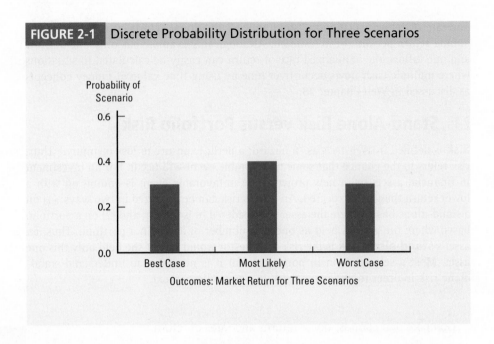

FIGURE 2-1   Discrete Probability Distribution for Three Scenarios

is assigned to each event, then the listing is called a **probability distribution**. (Keep in mind that the probabilities must sum to 1.0, or 100%.)

Suppose an investor is facing a situation similar to the debt ceiling crisis and believes there are three possible outcomes for the market as a whole: (1) Best case, with a 30% probability; (2) Most Likely case, with a 40% probability; and (3) Worst case, with a 30% probability. The investor also believes the market would go up by 37% in the Best scenario, go up by 11% in the Most Likely scenario, and go down by 15% in the Worst scenario.

Figure 2-1 shows the probability distribution for these three scenarios. Notice that the probabilities sum to 1.0 and that the possible returns are dispersed around the Most Likely scenario's return.

We can calculate expected return and risk using the probability distribution, as we illustrate in the next sections.

2-2b **Expected Rate of Return for Discrete Distributions**

The rate-of-return probability distribution is shown in the "Inputs" section of Figure 2-2; see Columns (1) and (2). This portion of the figure is called a *payoff matrix* when the outcomes are cash flows or returns.

If we multiply each possible outcome by its probability of occurrence and then sum these products, as in Column (3) of Figure 2-2, the result is a *weighted average* of outcomes. The weights are the probabilities, and the weighted average is the **expected rate of return**, $\hat{r}$, called "r-hat."[2] The expected rate of return is 11%, as shown in cell D66 in Figure 2-2.[3]

---

2. In other chapters, we will use $\hat{r}_d$ and $\hat{r}_s$ to signify expected returns on bonds and stocks, respectively. However, this distinction is unnecessary in this chapter, so we just use the general term $\hat{r}$ to signify the expected return on an investment.

3. Don't worry about why there is an 11% expected return for the market. We discuss the market return in more detail later in the chapter.

FIGURE 2-2 Calculating Expected Returns and Standard Deviations: Discrete Probabilities

	A	B	C	D	E	F	G
61	INPUTS:			**Expected Return**	**Standard Deviation**		
62	Scenario	**Probability of Scenario** **(1)**	**Market Rate of Return** **(2)**	**Product of Probability and Return** **(3) = (1) x (2)**	**Deviation from Expected Return** **(4) = (2) – D66**	**Squared Deviation** **(5) = (4)^2**	**Sq. Dev. × Prob.** **(6) = (1) x (5)**
63	Best Case	0.30	37%	11.1%	26%	6.8%	2.0%
64	Most Likely	0.40	11%	4.4%	0%	0.0%	0.0%
65	Worst Case	0.30	–15%	–4.5%	–26%	6.8%	2.0%
66		1.00	Exp. ret. =	Sum = 11.0%		Sum = Variance =	4.1%
67						Std. Dev. = Square root of variance =	20.1%
68	*Note:* Calculations in the model have been reported to one decimal, so rounding differences may occur.						

The calculation for expected rate of return can also be expressed as an equation that does the same thing as the payoff matrix table:

$$\text{Expected rate of return} = \hat{r} = p_1 r_1 + p_2 r_2 + \cdots + p_n r_n$$

$$= \sum_{i=1}^{n} p_i r_i$$

(2–1)

Here r_i is the return if outcome i occurs, p_i is the probability that outcome i occurs, and n is the number of possible outcomes. Thus, $\hat{r}$ is a weighted average of the possible outcomes (the r_i values), with each outcome's weight being its probability of occurrence. Using the data from Figure 2-2, we obtain the expected rate of return as follows:

$$\hat{r} = p_1(r_1) + p_2(r_2) + p_3(r_3)$$
$$= 0.3(37\%) + 0.4(11\%) + 0.3(-15\%)$$
$$= 11\%$$

2-2c Measuring Stand-Alone Risk: The Standard Deviation of a Discrete Distribution

For simple distributions, it is easy to assess risk by looking at the dispersion of possible outcomes—a distribution with widely dispersed possible outcomes is riskier than one with narrowly dispersed outcomes. For example, we can look at Figure 2-1 and see that the possible returns are widely dispersed. But when there are many possible outcomes and we are comparing many different investments, it isn't possible to assess risk simply by looking at the probability distribution—we need a quantitative measure of the tightness of the probability distribution. One such measure is the **standard deviation**, the symbol for which is σ, pronounced "sigma." A large standard deviation means that possible outcomes are widely dispersed, whereas a small standard deviation means that outcomes are more tightly clustered around the expected value.

To calculate the standard deviation, we proceed as shown in Figure 2-2, taking the following steps:

1. Calculate the expected value for the rate of return using Equation 2-1.
2. Subtract the expected rate of return ($\hat{r}$) from each possible outcome (r_i) to obtain a set of deviations about $\hat{r}$, as shown in Column (4) of Figure 2-2:

$$\text{Deviation}_i = r_i - \hat{r}$$

3. Square each deviation as shown in Column (5). Then multiply the squared deviations in Column (5) by the probability of occurrence for its related outcome; these products are shown in Column (6). Sum these products to obtain the **variance** of the probability distribution:

(2–2)

$$\text{Variance} = \sigma^2 = \sum_{i=1}^{n} (r_i - \hat{r})^2\, p_i$$

Thus, the variance is essentially a weighted average of the squared deviations from the expected value.

4. Finally, take the square root of the variance to obtain the standard deviation:

(2–3)

$$\text{Standard deviation} = \sigma = \sqrt{\sum_{i=1}^{n} (r_i - \hat{r})^2\, p_i}$$

WEB

See **Ch02 Tool Kit.xls** on the textbook's Web site for all calculations.

The standard deviation provides an idea of how far above or below the expected value the actual value is likely to be. Using this procedure in Figure 2-2, our hypothetical investor believes that the market return has a standard deviation of about 20%.

SELF TEST

What does "investment risk" mean?

Set up an illustrative probability distribution for an investment.

What is a payoff matrix?

How does one calculate the standard deviation?

An investment has a 20% chance of producing a 25% return, a 60% chance of producing a 10% return, and a 20% chance of producing a −15% return. What is its expected return? **(8%)** What is its standard deviation? **(12.9%)**

2-3 Risk in a Continuous Distribution

Investors usually don't estimate discrete outcomes in normal economic times but instead use the scenario approach during special situations, such as the debt ceiling crisis, the European bond crisis, oil supply threats, bank stress tests, and so on. Even in these situations, they would estimate more than three outcomes. For example, an investor might add more scenarios to our example; Figure 2-3 shows 15 scenarios for our original example (in blue) and for a situation (in brown) in which the expected return is the same but the standard deviation is much smaller.

We live in a complex world, with an infinite number of outcomes. But instead of adding more and more scenarios, most analysts turn to continuous distributions, with one of the most widely used being the **normal distribution**. With a normal distribution, the *actual* return will be within ± 1 standard deviation of the *expected* return 68.26% of the time. Figure 2-4 illustrates this point, and it also shows the situation for $\pm 2\sigma$ and $\pm 3\sigma$. For our 3-scenario example, $\hat{r} = 11\%$ and $\sigma = 20\%$. If returns come from a normal distribution with the same expected value and standard deviation rather than the discrete distribution, there would be a 68.26% probability that the actual return would be in the range of 11% $\pm$ 20%, or from -9% to 31%.

When using a continuous distribution, it is common to use historical data to estimate the standard deviation, as we explain in the next section.

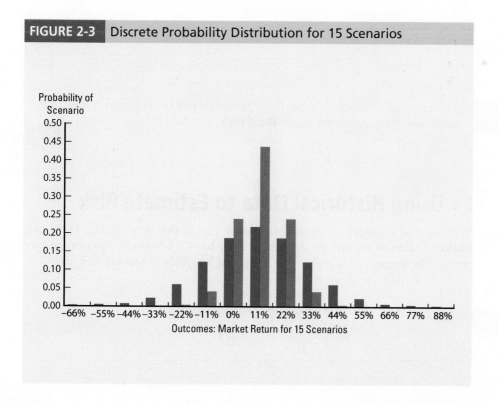

FIGURE 2-3   Discrete Probability Distribution for 15 Scenarios

Probability of
Scenario

Outcomes: Market Return for 15 Scenarios

WEB

For more discussion of probability distributions, see **Web Extension 2A,** available on the textbook's Web site.

FIGURE 2-4	Probability Ranges for a Normal Distribution

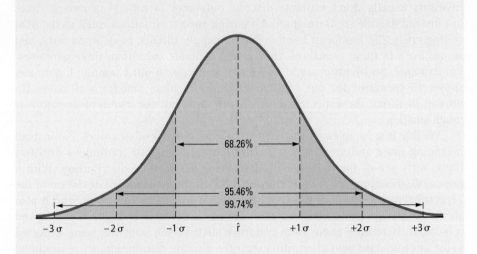

Notes:
1. The area under the normal curve always equals 1.0, or 100%. Thus, the areas under any pair of normal curves drawn on the same scale, whether they are peaked or flat, must be equal.
2. Half of the area under a normal curve is to the left of the mean, indicating that there is a 50% probability that the actual outcome will be less than the mean, and half is to the right of $\hat{r}$, indicating a 50% probability that it will be greater than the mean.
3. Of the area under the curve, 68.26% is within $\pm 1\sigma$ of the mean, indicating that the probability is 68.26% that the actual outcome will be within the range $\hat{r} - \sigma$ to $\hat{r} + \sigma$.

SELF TEST
For a normal distribution, what is the probability of being within 1 standard deviation of the expected value? **(68.26%)**

2-4 Using Historical Data to Estimate Risk

Suppose that a sample of returns over some past period is available. These past **realized rates of return** are denoted as $\bar{r}_t$ ("r bar t"), where t designates the time period. The average annual return over the last T periods is denoted as $\bar{r}_{Avg}$:

(2–4)

$$\bar{r}_{Avg} = \frac{\sum\limits_{t=1}^{T} \bar{r}_t}{T}$$

WHAT DOES RISK REALLY MEAN?

As explained in the text, the probability of being within 1 standard deviation of the expected return is 68.26%, so the probability of being further than 1 standard deviation from the mean is 100% − 68.26% = 31.74%. There is an equal probability of being above or below the range, so there is a 15.87% chance of being more than 1 standard deviation below the mean, which is roughly equal to a 1 in 6 chance (1 in 6 is 16.67%).

For the average firm listed on the New York Stock Exchange, σ has been in the range of 35% to 40% in recent years, with an expected return of around 8% to 12%. One standard deviation below this expected return is about 10% − 35% = −25%. This means that, for a typical stock in a typical year, there is about a 1 in 6 chance of having a 25% loss. You might be thinking that 1 in 6 is a pretty low probability, but what if your chance of getting hit by a car when you crossed a street were 1 in 6? When put that way, 1 in 6 sounds pretty scary.

You might also correctly be thinking that there would be a 1 in 6 chance of getting a return higher than 1 standard deviation above the mean, which would be about 45% for a typical stock. A 45% return is great, but human nature is such that most investors would dislike a 25% loss a whole lot more than they would enjoy a 45% gain.

You might also be thinking that you'll be OK if you hold stock long enough. But even if you buy and hold a diversified portfolio for 10 years, there is still roughly a 10% chance that you will lose money. If you hold it for 20 years, there is about a 4% chance of losing. Such odds wouldn't be worrisome if you were engaged in a game of chance that could be played multiple times, but you have only one life to live and just a few rolls of the dice.

We aren't suggesting that investors shouldn't buy stocks; indeed, we own stock ourselves. But we do believe investors should understand more clearly how much risk investing entails.

The standard deviation of a sample of returns can then be estimated using this formula:[4]

(2–5)

$$\text{Estimated } \sigma = S = \sqrt{\dfrac{\sum_{t=1}^{T}(\bar{r}_t - \bar{r}_{Avg})^2}{T-1}}$$

When estimated from past data, the standard deviation is often denoted by S.

2-4a Calculating the Historical Standard Deviation

To illustrate these calculations, consider the following historical returns for a company:

---

4. Because we are estimating the standard deviation from a sample of observations, the denominator in Equation 2-5 is "T − 1" and not just "T." Equations 2-4 and 2-5 are built into all financial calculators. For example, to find the sample standard deviation, enter the rates of return into the calculator and press the key marked S (or S_x) to get the standard deviation. See your calculator's manual for details.

Year	Return
2013	15%
2014	−5%
2015	20%

Using Equations 2-4 and 2-5, the estimated average and standard deviation, respectively, are:

$$\bar{r}_{Avg} = \frac{15\% - 5\% + 20\%}{3} = 10.0\%$$

$$\text{Estimated } \sigma \text{ (or S)} = \sqrt{\frac{(15\% - 10\%)^2 + (-5\% - 10\%)^2 + (20\% - 10\%)^2}{3 - 1}}$$

$$= 13.2\%$$

The average and standard deviation can also be calculated using *Excel's* built-in functions, shown below using numerical data rather than cell ranges as inputs:

$$=\text{AVERAGE}(0.15, -0.05, 0.20) = 10.0\%$$
$$=\text{STDEV}(0.15, -0.05, 0.20) = 13.2\%$$

The historical standard deviation is often used as an estimate of future variability. Because past variability is often repeated, past variability may be a reasonably good estimate of future risk. However, it is usually incorrect to use $\bar{r}_{Avg}$ based on a past period as an estimate of $\hat{r}$, the expected future return. For example, just because a stock had a 75% return in the past year, there is no reason to expect a 75% return this year.

2-4b Calculating MicroDrive's Historical Standard Deviation

Figure 2-5 shows 48 months of recent stock returns for two companies, MicroDrive and SnailDrive; the actual data are in the *Excel* file *Ch02 Tool Kit.xls.* A quick glance is enough to determine that MicroDrive's returns are more volatile.

We could use Equations 2-4 and 2-5 to calculate the average return and standard deviation, but that would be quite tedious. Instead, we use *Excel's* **AVERAGE** and **STDEV** functions and find that MicroDrive's monthly average return was 1.22% and its monthly standard deviation was 14.19%. SnailDrive had an average monthly return of 0.72% and a standard deviation of 7.45%. These calculations confirm the visual evidence in Figure 2-5: MicroDrive had greater stand-alone risk than SnailDrive.

We often use monthly data to estimate averages and standard deviations, but we normally present data in an annualized format. Multiply the monthly average return by 12 to get MicroDrive's annualized average return of 1.22%(12) = 14.6%. As noted earlier, the past average return isn't a good indicator of the future return.

To annualize the standard deviation, multiply the monthly standard deviation by the square root of 12. MicroDrive's annualized standard deviation was 14.19%($\sqrt{12}$) = 49.2%.[5] SnailDrive's average annual return was 8.6% and its annualized standard deviation was 25.8%.

---

5. If we had calculated the monthly variance, we would annualize it by multiplying it by 12, as intuition (and mathematics) suggests. Because standard deviation is the square root of variance, we annualize the monthly standard deviation by multiplying it by the square root of 12.

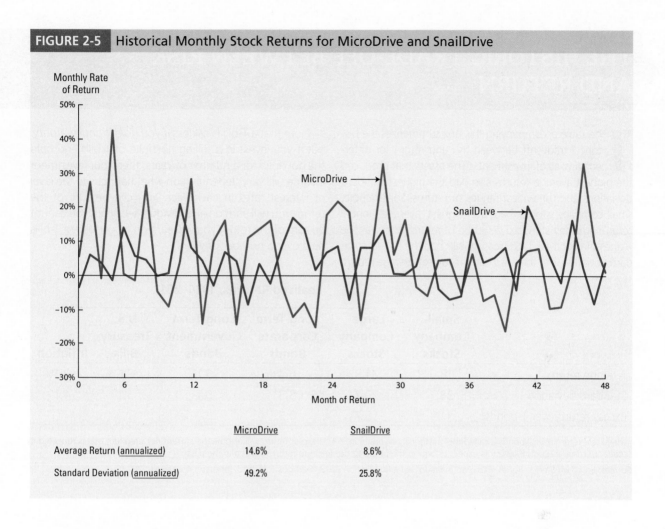

FIGURE 2-5 Historical Monthly Stock Returns for MicroDrive and SnailDrive

	MicroDrive	SnailDrive
Average Return (annualized)	14.6%	8.6%
Standard Deviation (annualized)	49.2%	25.8%

Notice that MicroDrive had higher risk than SnailDrive (a standard deviation of 49.2% versus 25.8%) and a higher average return (14.6% versus 8.6%) during the past 48 months. However, a higher return for undertaking more risk isn't guaranteed—if it were, then a riskier investment wouldn't really be risky!

The file *Ch02 Tool Kit.xls* calculates the annualized average return and standard deviation using just the most recent 12 months. Here are the results:

Results for Most Recent 12 Months	**MicroDrive**	**SnailDrive**
Average return (annual)	−29.3%	17.9%
Standard deviation (annual)	44.5%	28.8%

Even though MicroDrive's standard deviation remained well above that of Snail-Drive during the last 12 months of the sample period, MicroDrive experienced an annualized average loss of over 29%, while SnailDrive gained almost 18%.[6]

---

6. During the last 12 months, MicroDrive had an average monthly loss of 2.44%, but it had a compound loss for the year of over 30%. We discuss the difference between arithmetic averages and geometric averages (based on compound returns) in Chapter 11.

THE HISTORIC TRADE-OFF BETWEEN RISK AND RETURN

The table accompanying this box summarizes the historical trade-off between risk and return for different classes of investments. The assets that produced the highest average returns also had the highest standard deviations and the widest ranges of returns. For example, small-company stocks had the highest average annual return, but their standard deviation of returns also was the highest. In contrast, U.S. Treasury bills had the lowest standard deviation, but they also had the lowest average return.

Note that a T-bill is riskless *if you hold it until maturity,* but if you invest in a rolling portfolio of T-bills and hold the portfolio for a number of years, then your investment income will vary depending on what happens to the level of interest rates in each year. You can be sure of the return you will earn on an individual T-bill, but you cannot be sure of the return you will earn on a portfolio of T-bills held over a number of years.

Realized Returns, 1926–2012

	Small-Company Stocks	Large-Company Stocks	Long-Term Corporate Bonds	Long-Term Government Bonds	U.S. Treasury Bills	Inflation
Average return	18.0%	11.8%	6.4%	6.1%	3.6%	3.1%
Standard deviation	38.7	20.2	8.3	9.7	3.1	4.1
Excess return over T-bonds[a]	11.9	5.7	0.3			

[a] The excess return over T-bonds is called the "historical risk premium." This excess return will also be the current risk premium that is reflected in security prices if and only if investors expect returns in the future to be similar to returns earned in the past.

Source: Based on *Stocks, Bonds, Bills, and Inflation: Valuation Edition 2013 Yearbook* (Chicago: Ibbotson Associates, 2013).

MicroDrive's stockholders certainly learned that higher risk doesn't always lead to higher *actual* returns.

SELF TEST

A stock's returns for the past 3 years were 10%, −15%, and 35%. What is the historical average return? **(10%)** What is the historical sample standard deviation? **(25%)**

2-5 Risk in a Portfolio Context

Most financial assets are actually held as parts of portfolios. Banks, pension funds, insurance companies, mutual funds, and other financial institutions are required by law to hold diversified portfolios. Even individual investors—at least those whose security holdings constitute a significant part of their total wealth—generally hold portfolios, not the stock of only one firm.

2-5a Creating a Portfolio

A portfolio is a collection of assets. The weight of an asset in a portfolio is the percentage of the portfolio's total value that is invested in the asset. For example, if you invest $1,000 in each of 10 stocks, your portfolio has a value of $10,000, and each stock has a weight of $1,000/$10,000 = 10%. If instead you invest $5,000 in 1 stock and $1,000 apiece in 5 stocks, the first stock has a weight of $5,000/$10,000 = 50%, and each of the other 5 stocks has a weight of 10%. Usually it is more convenient to talk about an asset's weight in a portfolio rather than the dollars invested in the asset. Therefore, when we create a portfolio, we choose a weight (or a percentage) for each asset, with the weights summing to 1.0 (or the percentages summing to 100%).

Suppose we have a portfolio of n stocks. The actual return on a portfolio in a particular period is the weighted average of the actual returns of the stocks in the portfolio, with w_i denoting the weight invested in Stock i:

$$\bar{r}_p = w_1\bar{r}_1 + w_2\bar{r}_2 + \cdots + w_n\bar{r}_n$$
$$= \sum_{i=1}^{n} w_i\bar{r}_i$$

(2–6)

The average portfolio return over a number of periods is also equal to the weighted average of the stock's average returns:

$$\bar{r}_{Avg,p} = \sum_{i=1}^{n} w_i\bar{r}_{Avg,i}$$

Recall from the previous section that SnailDrive had an average annualized return of 8.6% during the past 48 months and MicroDrive had a 14.6% return. A portfolio with 75% invested in SnailDrive and 25% in MicroDrive would have had the following return:

$$\bar{r}_{Avg,p} = 0.75(8.6\%) + 0.25(14.6\%) = 10.1\%$$

Notice that the portfolio return of 10.1% is between the returns of SnailDrive (8.6%) and MicroDrive (14.6%), as you would expect.

Suppose an investor with stock only in SnailDrive came to you for advice, saying, "I would like more return, but I hate risk!" How do you think the investor would react if you suggested taking 25% of the investment in the low-risk SnailDrive (with a standard deviation of 25.8%) and putting it into the high-risk MicroDrive (with a standard deviation of 49.2%)? As shown above, the return during the 48-month period would have been 10.1%, well above the return on SnailDrive. But what would have happened to risk?

The file *Ch02 Tool Kit.xls* calculates the portfolio return for each month (using Equation 2-6) and calculates the portfolio's standard deviation by applying *Excel's* STDEV function to the portfolio's monthly returns. Imagine the investor's surprise in learning that the portfolio's standard deviation is 21.8%, which is *less than* that of SnailDrive's 25.8% standard deviation. In other words, adding a risky asset to a safer asset can reduce risk!

How can this happen? MicroDrive sells high-end memory storage, whereas SnailDrive sells low-end memory, including reconditioned hard drives. When the economy is doing well, MicroDrive has high sales and profits, but SnailDrive's sales lag because customers prefer faster memory. But when times are tough, customers resort to SnailDrive for low-cost memory storage. Take a look at Figure 2-5. Notice that SnailDrive's returns don't move in perfect lockstep with MicroDrive: Sometimes MicroDrive goes up and SnailDrive goes down, and vice versa.

2-5b **Correlation and Risk for a Two-Stock Portfolio**

The tendency of two variables to move together is called **correlation**, and the **correlation coefficient** measures this tendency. The symbol for the correlation coefficient is the Greek letter rho, ρ (pronounced "roe"). The correlation coefficient can range from $+1.0$, denoting that the two variables move up and down in perfect synchronization, to -1.0, denoting that the variables always move in exactly opposite directions. A correlation coefficient of zero indicates that the two variables are not related to each other at all—that is, changes in one variable are independent of changes in the other.

The estimate of correlation from a sample of historical data is often called "R." Here is the formula to estimate the correlation between stocks i and j ($\bar{r}_{i,t}$ is the actual return for Stock i in period t, and $\bar{r}_{i,Avg}$ is the average return during the T-period sample; similar notation is used for stock j):

(2–7)

$$\text{Estimated } \rho = R = \frac{\sum_{t=1}^{T} (\bar{r}_{i,t} - \bar{r}_{i,Avg})(\bar{r}_{j,t} - \bar{r}_{j,Avg})}{\sqrt{\left[\sum_{t=1}^{T} (\bar{r}_{i,t} - \bar{r}_{i,Avg})^2\right]\left[\sum_{t=1}^{T} (\bar{r}_{j,t} - \bar{r}_{j,Avg})^2\right]}}$$

Fortunately, it is easy to estimate the correlation coefficient with a financial calculator or *Excel*. With a calculator, simply enter the returns of the two stocks and then press a key labeled "r."[7] In *Excel*, use the **CORREL** function. See *Ch02 Tool Kit.xls*, where we calculate the correlation between the returns of MicroDrive and SnailDrive to be -0.10. The negative correlation means that when SnailDrive is having a poor return, MicroDrive tends to have a good return; when SnailDrive is having a good return, MicroDrive tends to have a poor return. In other words, adding some of MicroDrive's stock to a portfolio that only had SnailDrive's stock tends to reduce the volatility of the portfolio.

Here is a way to think about the possible benefit of diversification: *If a portfolio's standard deviation is less than the weighted average of the individual stocks' standard deviations, then diversification provides a benefit.* Does diversification

---

7. See your calculator manual for the exact steps. Also, note that the correlation coefficient is often denoted by the term "ρ." We use ρ here to avoid confusion with r, which is used to denote the rate of return.

always reduce risk? If so, by how much? And how does correlation affect diversification? Let's consider the full range of correlation coefficients, from -1 to $+1$.

If two stocks have a correlation of -1 (the lowest possible correlation), when one stock has a higher than expected return then the other stock has a lower than expected return, and vice versa. In fact, it would be possible to choose weights such that one stock's deviations from its mean return completely cancel out the other stock's deviations from its mean return.[8] Such a portfolio would have a zero standard deviation but would have an expected return equal to the weighted average of the stock's expected returns. In this situation, diversification can eliminate all risk: *For correlation of -1, the portfolio's standard deviation can be as low as zero if the portfolio weights are chosen appropriately.*

If the correlation were $+1$ (the highest possible correlation), the portfolio's standard deviation would be the weighted average of the stock's standard deviations. In this case, diversification doesn't help: *For correlation of $+1$, the portfolio's standard deviation is the weighted average of the stocks' standard deviations.*

For any other correlation, diversification reduces, but cannot eliminate, risk: *For correlation between -1 and $+1$, the portfolio's standard deviation is less than the weighted average of the stocks' standard deviations.*

The correlation between most pairs of companies is in the range of 0.2 to 0.3, so diversification reduces risk, but it doesn't completely eliminate risk.[9]

2-5c Diversification and Multi-Stock Portfolios

Figure 2-6 shows how portfolio risk is affected by forming larger and larger portfolios of randomly selected New York Stock Exchange (NYSE) stocks. Standard deviations are plotted for an average one-stock portfolio, an average two-stock portfolio, and so on, up to a portfolio consisting of all 2,000-plus common stocks that were listed on the NYSE at the time the data were plotted. The graph illustrates that, in general, the risk of a portfolio consisting of stocks tends to decline and to approach some limit as the number of stocks in the portfolio increases. According to data from recent years, σ_1, the standard deviation of a one-stock portfolio (or an average stock), is approximately 35%. However, a portfolio consisting of all stocks, which is called the **market portfolio**, would have a standard deviation, σ_M, of only about 20%, which is shown as the horizontal dashed line in Figure 2-6.

Thus, *almost half of the risk inherent in an average individual stock can be eliminated if the stock is held in a reasonably well-diversified portfolio, which is one containing 40 or more stocks in a number of different industries.* The part of a stock's risk that *cannot* be eliminated is called *market risk*, while the part that *can*

---

8. If the correlation between stocks 1 and 2 is equal to -1, then the weights for a zero-risk portfolio are $w_1 = \sigma_1/(\sigma_1 + \sigma_2)$ and $w_2 = \sigma_2/(\sigma_1 + \sigma_2)$.

9. During the period 1968–1998, the average correlation coefficient between two randomly selected stocks was 0.28, while the average correlation coefficient between two large-company stocks was 0.33; see Louis K. C. Chan, Jason Karceski, and Josef Lakonishok, "On Portfolio Optimization: Forecasting Covariance and Choosing the Risk Model," *The Review of Financial Studies*, Vol. 12, No. 5, Winter 1999, pp. 937–974. The average correlation fell from around 0.35 in the late 1970s to less than 0.10 by the late 1990s; see John Y. Campbell, Martin Lettau, Burton G. Malkiel, and YexiaoXu, "Have Individual Stocks Become More Volatile? An Empirical Exploration of Idiosyncratic Risk," *Journal of Finance*, February 2001, pp. 1–43.

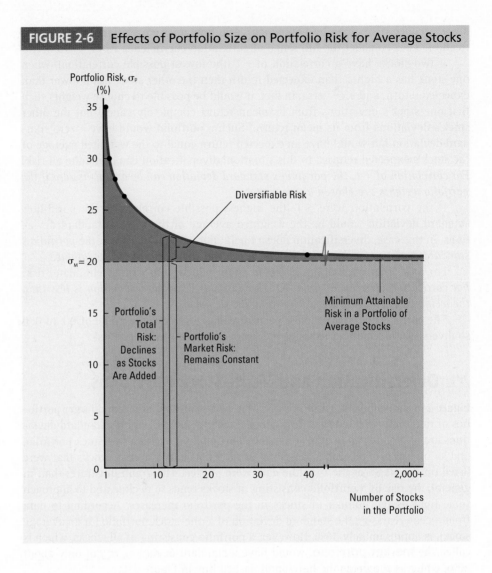

FIGURE 2-6 Effects of Portfolio Size on Portfolio Risk for Average Stocks

be eliminated is called *diversifiable risk*.[10] The fact that a large part of the risk of any individual stock can be eliminated is vitally important, because rational investors *will* eliminate it simply by holding many stocks in their portfolios and thus rendering it irrelevant.

Market risk stems from factors that systematically affect most firms: war, inflation, recessions, and high interest rates. Because most stocks are affected by these factors, market risk cannot be eliminated by diversification. **Diversifiable risk** is caused by such random events as lawsuits, strikes, successful and unsuccessful marketing programs, winning or losing a major contract, and other events that are unique to a particular firm. Because these events are random, their effects on a portfolio can be eliminated by diversification—bad events in one firm will be offset by good events in another.

---

10. Diversifiable risk is also known as *company-specific risk* or *unsystematic risk*. Market risk is also known as *nondiversifiable risk* or *systematic risk*; it is the risk that remains after diversification.

Explain the following statement: "An asset held as part of a portfolio is generally less risky than the same asset held in isolation."

What is meant by *perfect positive correlation, perfect negative correlation,* and *zero correlation?*

In general, can the risk of a portfolio be reduced to zero by increasing the number of stocks in the portfolio? Explain.

2-6 The Relevant Risk of a Stock: The Capital Asset Pricing Model (CAPM)

We assume that investors are risk averse and demand a premium for bearing risk; that is, the higher the risk of a security, the higher its expected return must be to induce investors to buy it or to hold it. All risk except that related to broad market movements can, and presumably will, be diversified away. After all, why accept risk that can be eliminated easily? This implies that investors are primarily concerned with the risk of their *portfolios* rather than the risk of the individual securities in the portfolio. How, then, should the risk of an individual stock be measured?

The **Capital Asset Pricing Model (CAPM)** provides one answer to that question. A stock might be quite risky if held by itself, but—because diversification eliminates about half of its risk—the stock's **relevant risk** is its *contribution to a well-diversified portfolio's risk*, which is much smaller than the stock's stand-alone risk.[11]

2-6a Contribution to Market Risk: Beta

A well-diversified portfolio has only market risk. Therefore, the CAPM defines the relevant risk of an individual stock as the amount of risk that the stock contributes to the market portfolio, which is a portfolio containing all stocks.[12] In CAPM terminology, ρ_{iM} is the correlation between Stock i's return and the market return, σ_i is the standard deviation of Stock i's return, and σ_M is the standard deviation of the market's return. The relevant measure of risk is called **beta**; the beta of Stock i, denoted by b_i, is calculated as:

$$b_i = \left(\frac{\sigma_i}{\sigma_M}\right)\rho_{iM}$$

(2–8)

This formula shows that a stock with a high standard deviation, σ_i, will tend to have a high beta, which means that, other things held constant, the stock contributes a lot of risk to a well-diversified portfolio. This makes sense, because a stock with high stand-alone risk will tend to destabilize a portfolio. Note too that a stock

---

11. Nobel Prizes were awarded to the developers of the CAPM, Professors Harry Markowitz and William F. Sharpe.

12. In theory, the market portfolio should contain all assets. In practice, it usually contains only stocks. Many analysts use returns on the S&P 500 Index to estimate the market return.

with a high correlation with the market, ρ_{iM}, will also tend to have a large beta and hence be risky. This also makes sense, because a high correlation means that diversification is not helping much, with the stock performing well when the portfolio is also performing well, and the stock performing poorly when the portfolio is also performing poorly.

Suppose a stock has a beta of 1.4. What does that mean? To answer that question, we begin with an important fact: The beta of a portfolio, b_p, is the weighted average of the betas of the stocks in the portfolio, with the weights equal to the same weights used to create the portfolio. This can be written as:

(2–9)

$$b_p = w_1 b_1 + w_2 b_2 + \ldots + w_n b_n$$
$$= \sum_{i=1}^{n} w_i b_i$$

For example, suppose an investor owns a $100,000 portfolio consisting of $25,000 invested in each of four stocks; the stocks have betas of 0.6, 1.2, 1.2, and 1.4. The weight of each stock in the portfolio is $25,000/$100,000 = 25%. The portfolio's beta will be $b_p = 1.1$:

$$b_p = 25\%(0.6) + 25\%(1.2) + 25\%(1.2) + 25\%(1.4) = 1.1$$

The second important fact is that the standard deviation of a well-diversified portfolio, σ_p, is approximately equal to the product of the portfolio's beta (or the absolute value if beta is negative) and the market standard deviation:

(2–10)

$$\sigma_p = b_p \sigma_M$$

Equation 2-10 shows that: (1) a portfolio with a beta greater than 1 will have a bigger standard deviation than the market portfolio; (2) a portfolio with a beta equal to 1 will have the same standard deviation as the market; and (3) a portfolio with a beta less than 1 will have a smaller standard deviation than the market. For example, suppose the market standard deviation is 20%. Using Equation 2-10, a well-diversified portfolio with a beta of 1.1 will have a standard deviation of 22%:

$$\sigma_p = 1.1(20\%) = 22\%$$

By substituting Equation 2-9 into Equation 2-10, we can see the impact that each individual stock beta has on the risk of a well-diversified portfolio:

(2–11)

$$\sigma_p = (w_1 b_1 + w_2 b_2 + \ldots + w_n b_n) \sigma_M$$
$$= \sum_{i=1}^{n} w_i b_i \sigma_M$$

FIGURE 2-7	The Contribution of Individual Stocks to Portfolio Risk: The Effect of Beta

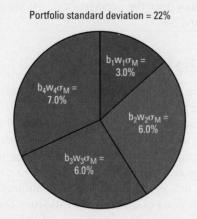

Portfolio standard deviation = 22%

Market standard deviation = σ_M = 20%

	Stock Beta: b_i	Weight in Portfolio: w_i	Contribution to Portfolio Beta: $b_i \times w_i$	Contribution to Portfolio Risk: $b_i \times w_i \times \sigma_M$
Stock 1	0.6	25.0%	0.150	3.0%
Stock 2	1.2	25.0%	0.300	6.0%
Stock 3	1.2	25.0%	0.300	6.0%
Stock 4	1.4	25.0%	0.350	7.0%
			b_p = 1.100	σ_p = 22.0%

A well-diversified portfolio would have more than four stocks, but for the sake of simplicity suppose that the four-stock portfolio in the previous example is well diversified. If that is the case, then Figure 2-7 shows how much risk each stock contributes to the portfolio.[13] Out of the total 22% standard deviation of the portfolio, Stock 1 contributes $w_1 b_1 \sigma_M$ = (25%)(0.6)(20%) = 3%. Stocks 2 and 3 have betas that are twice as big as Stock 1's beta, so Stocks 2 and 3 contribute twice as much risk as Stock 1. Stock 4 has the largest beta, and it contributes the most risk.

We demonstrate how to estimate beta in the next section, but here are some key points about beta. (1) Beta measures how much risk a stock contributes to a well-diversified portfolio. If all the stocks' weights in a portfolio are equal, then a stock with a beta that is twice as big as another stock's beta contributes twice as much risk. (2) The average of all stocks' betas is equal to 1; the beta of the market

---

13. If the portfolio isn't well diversified, then $b_p \sigma_M$ measures the part of the portfolio's standard deviation due to market risk, and $b_i w_i \sigma_M$ measures the amount of the portfolio's standard deviation that is due to the market risk of stock i.

also is equal to 1. Intuitively, this is because the market return is the average of all the stocks' returns. (3) A stock with a beta greater than 1 contributes more risk to a portfolio than does the average stock, and a stock with a beta less than 1 contributes less risk to a portfolio than does the average stock. (4) Most stocks have betas that are between about 0.4 and 1.6.

2-6b **Estimating Beta**

The CAPM is an *ex ante* model, which means that all of the variables represent before-the-fact, *expected* values. In particular, the beta coefficient used by investors should reflect the relationship between a stock's expected return and the market's expected return during some *future* period. However, people generally calculate betas using data from some *past* period and then assume that the stock's risk will be the same in the future as it was in the past.

Most analysts use 4 to 5 years of monthly data, although some use 52 weeks of weekly data. Using the 4 years of monthly returns from *Ch02 Tool Kit.xls*, we can calculate the betas of MicroDrive and SnailDrive using Equation 2-8:

	Market	MicroDrive	SnailDrive
Standard deviation (annual):	20.0%	49.2%	25.8%
Correlation with the market:		0.582	0.465
$b_i = \rho_{iM}(\sigma_i/\sigma_M)$		1.43	0.60

Table 2-1 shows the betas for some well-known companies as provided by two different financial organizations, Value Line and Yahoo!. Notice that their estimates of beta usually differ because they calculate it in slightly different ways. Given these differences, many analysts choose to calculate their own betas or else average the published betas.

W W W

To see updated estimates, go to **www.valueline.com** and enter the ticker symbol. Or go to **finance.yahoo.com** and enter the ticker symbol. When the results page comes up, select Key Statistics from the left panel to find beta.

TABLE 2-1	Beta Coefficients for Some Actual Companies	
Stock (Ticker Symbol)	**Value Line**	**Yahoo! Finance**
Amazon.com (AMZN)	1.05	0.78
Apple (AAPL)	1.00	0.76
Coca-Cola (KO)	0.65	0.30
Empire District Electric (EDE)	0.70	0.43
Energen Corp. (EGN)	1.25	1.66
General Electric (GE)	1.25	1.24
Google (GOOG)	0.90	1.09
Microsoft Corp. (MSFT)	0.85	0.77
Procter & Gamble (PG)	0.60	0.34

Sources: **www.valueline.com** and **finance.yahoo.com**, September 2013.

Calculators and spreadsheets can calculate the components of Equation 2-8 (ρ_{iM}, σ_i, and σ_M), which can then be used to calculate beta, but there is another way.[14] The **covariance between Stock i and the market, COV_{iM}**, is defined as:[15]

$$COV_{iM} = \rho_{iM}\sigma_i\sigma_M$$

(2–12)

Substituting Equation 2-12 into Equation 2-8 provides another frequently used expression for calculating beta:

$$b_i = \frac{COV_{iM}}{\sigma_M^2}$$

(2–13)

Suppose you plotted the stock's returns on the y-axis of a graph and the market portfolio's returns on the x-axis. The formula for the slope of a regression line is exactly equal to the formula for beta in Equation 2-13. Therefore, to estimate beta for a security, you can estimate a regression with the stock's returns on the y-axis and the market's returns on the x-axis. Figure 2-8 illustrates this approach. The blue dots represent each of the 48 data points, with the stock's returns on the y-axis and the market's returns on the x-axis. For reference purposes, the thick black line shows the plot of market versus market. Notice that MicroDrive's returns are generally above the market's returns (the black line) when the market is doing well but below the market when the market is doing poorly, suggesting that MicroDrive is risky.

We used the Trendline feature in *Excel* to show the regression equation and R^2 on the chart (these are colored red): MicroDrive has an estimated beta of 1.43, the same as we calculated earlier using Equation 2-8. It is also possible to use *Excel's* **SLOPE** function to estimate the slope from a regression: =**SLOPE**(known_y's,known_x's). The **SLOPE** function is more convenient if you are going to calculate betas for many different companies; see *Ch02 Tool Kit.xls* for more details.

2-6c **Interpreting the Estimated Beta**

First, always keep in mind that beta cannot be observed; it can only be estimated. The R^2 value shown in the chart measures the degree of dispersion about the regression line. Statistically speaking, it measures the proportion of the variation that is explained by the regression equation. An R^2 of 1.0 indicates that all points lie exactly on the regression line and hence that all of the variations in the y-variable are explained by the x-variable. MicroDrive's R^2 is about 0.34, which is similar

---

14. For an explanation of computing beta with a financial calculator, see *Web Extension 2B* on the textbook's Web site.

15. Using historical data, the sample covariance can be calculated as:

$$\text{Sample covariance from historical data} = COV_{iM} = \frac{\sum_{t=1}^{T}(\bar{r}_{i,t} - \bar{r}_{i,Avg})(\bar{r}_{M,t} - \bar{r}_{M,Avg})}{T - 1}$$

Calculating the covariance is somewhat easier than calculating the correlation. So if you have already calculated the standard deviations, it is easier to calculate the covariance and then calculate the correlation as $\rho_{iM} = COV_{iM}/(\rho_i\rho_M)$.

FIGURE 2-8 Stock Returns of MicroDrive and the Market: Estimating Beta

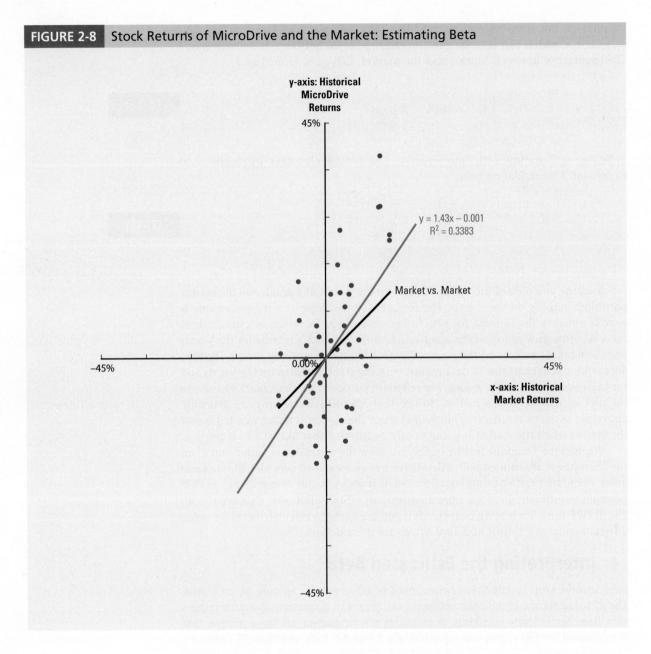

to the typical stock's R^2 of 0.32. This indicates that about 34% of the variation in MicroDrive's returns is explained by the market return; in other words, much of MicroDrive's volatility is due to factors other than market gyrations. If we had done a similar analysis for a portfolio of 40 randomly selected stocks, then the points would probably have been clustered tightly around the regression line and the R^2 probably would have exceeded 0.90. Almost 100% of a well-diversified portfolio's volatility is explained by the market.

Ch02 Tool Kit.xls demonstrates how to use the *Excel* function **LINEST** to calculate the confidence interval for MicroDrive's estimated beta and shows that the 95% confidence interval around MicroDrive's estimated beta ranges from about 0.8 to 2.0. This means that we can be 95% confident that MicroDrive's true beta is between 0.8 and 2.0. Notice that this is a fairly big range, which is also typical for most stocks. In other words, the estimated beta truly is an estimate!

MicroDrive's estimated beta is about 1.4. What does that mean? By definition, the average beta for all stocks is equal to 1, so MicroDrive contributes 40% more risk to a well-diversified portfolio than does a typical stock (assuming they have the same portfolio weight). Notice also from Figure 2-8 that the slope of the estimated line is about 1.4, which is steeper than a slope of 1. When the market is doing well, a high-beta stock like MicroDrive tends to do better than an average stock, and when the market does poorly, a high-beta stock also does worse than an average stock. The opposite is true for a low-beta stock: When the market soars, the low-beta stock tends to go up by a smaller amount; when the market falls, the low-beta stock tends to fall less than the market.

Finally, observe that the intercept shown in the regression equation on the chart is −0.001. This is a monthly return; the annualized value is 12(−0.1%) = −1.2%. This indicates that MicroDrive lost about 1.2% per year as a result of factors other than general market movements.

For more on calculating beta, take a look at *Ch02 Tool Kit.xls*, which shows how to download data for an actual company and calculate its beta.

THE BENEFITS OF DIVERSIFYING OVERSEAS

Figure 2-6 shows that an investor can significantly reduce portfolio risk by holding a large number of stocks. The figure accompanying this box suggests that investors may be able to reduce risk even further by holding stocks from all around the world, because the returns on domestic and international stocks are not perfectly correlated.

Source: For further reading, see Kenneth Kasa, "Measuring the Gains from International Portfolio Diversification," *Federal Reserve Bank of San Francisco Weekly Letter,* no. 94–14 (April 8, 1994).

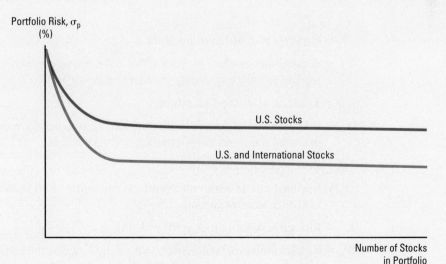

SELF TEST

What is the average beta? If a stock has a beta of 0.8, what does that imply about its risk relative to the market?

Why is beta the theoretically correct measure of a stock's risk?

If you plotted the returns on a particular stock versus those on the S&P 500 Index over the past 5 years, what would the slope of the regression line tell you about the stock's market risk?

What types of data are needed to calculate a beta coefficient for an actual company?

What does the R^2 measure? What is the R^2 for a typical company?

An investor has a three-stock portfolio with $25,000 invested in Dell, $50,000 invested in Ford, and $25,000 invested in Walmart. Dell's beta is estimated to be 1.20, Ford's beta is estimated to be 0.80, and Walmart's beta is estimated to be 1.0. What is the estimated beta of the investor's portfolio? **(0.95)**

2-7 The Relationship between Risk and Return in the Capital Asset Pricing Model

In the preceding section, we saw that beta measures a stock's contribution to the risk of a well-diversified portfolio. The CAPM assumes that the marginal investors (i.e., the investors with enough cash to move market prices) hold well-diversified portfolios. Therefore, beta is the proper measure of a stock's relevant risk. However, we need to quantify how risk affects required returns: For a given level of risk as measured by beta, what rate of expected return do investors require to compensate them for bearing that risk? To begin, we define the following terms:

$\hat{r}_i$ = *Expected* rate of return on Stock i.

r_i = *Required* rate of return on Stock i. This is the minimum expected return that is required to induce an average investor to purchase the stock.

$\bar{r}$ = Realized, after-the-fact return.

r_{RF} = Risk-free rate of return. In this context, r_{RF} is generally measured by the expected return on long-term U.S. Treasury bonds.

b_i = Beta coefficient of Stock i.

r_M = Required rate of return on a portfolio consisting of all stocks, which is called the *market portfolio*.

RP_i = Risk premium on Stock i: $RP_i = b_i (RP_M)$.

RP_M = Risk premium on "the market." $RP_M = (r_M - r_{RF})$ is the additional return over the risk-free rate required to induce an average investor to invest in the market portfolio.

2-7a **The Security Market Line (SML)**

In general, we can conceptualize the required return on an individual stock as the risk-free rate plus the extra return (i.e., the risk premium) needed to induce the investor to hold the stock. The CAPM's **Security Market Line (SML)** formalizes this general concept by showing that a stock's risk premium is equal to the product of the stock's beta and the market risk premium:

$$\text{Required return on Stock i} = \text{Risk-free rate} + \left(\begin{array}{c}\text{Risk premium} \\ \text{for Stock i}\end{array}\right)$$

(2–14)

$$\text{Required return on Stock i} = \text{Risk-free rate} + \left(\begin{array}{c}\text{Beta of} \\ \text{Stock i}\end{array}\right)\left(\begin{array}{c}\text{Market risk} \\ \text{premium}\end{array}\right)$$

$$r_i = r_{RF} + b_i (RP_M)$$
$$= r_{RF} + (r_M - r_{RF})b_i$$

Let's take a look at the three components of required return (the risk-free rate, the market risk premium, and beta) to see how they interact in determining a stock's required return.

The Risk-Free Rate

Notice that a stock's required return begins with the risk-free rate. To induce an investor to take on a risky investment, the investor will need a return that is at least as big as the risk-free rate. The yield on long-term Treasury bonds is often used to measure the risk-free rate.

The Market Risk Premium

The **market risk premium, RP$_M$**, is the extra rate of return that investors require to invest in the stock market rather than purchase risk-free securities. The size of the market risk premium depends on the degree of risk aversion that investors have on average. When investors are very risk averse, the market risk premium is high; when investors are less concerned about risk, the market risk premium is low. For example, suppose that investors (on average) need an extra return of 5% before they will take on the stock market's risk. If Treasury bonds yield r_{RF} = 6%, then the required return on the market, r_M, is 11%:

$$r_M = r_{RF} + RP_M = 6\% + 5\% = 11\%$$

If we had instead begun with an estimate of the required market return (perhaps through scenario analysis similar to the example in Section 2.2), then we can find the implied market risk premium. For example, if the required market return is estimated as 11%, then the market risk premium is:

$$RP_M = r_M - r_{RF} = 11\% - 6\% = 5\%$$

We discuss the market risk premium in detail in Chapter 11, but for now you should know now that most analysts use a market risk premium in the range of 4% to 7%.

The Risk Premium for an Individual Stock

The CAPM shows that the **risk premium for an individual stock, RP_i**, is equal to the product of the stock's beta and the market risk premium:

(2–15)

$$\text{Risk premium for Stock i} = RP_i = b_i (RP_M)$$

For example, consider a low-risk stock with $b_L = 0.5$. If the market risk premium is 5%, then the risk premium for the stock (RP_L) is 2.5%:

$$RP_L = (5\%)(0.5)$$
$$= 2.5\%$$

Using the SML in Equation 2-14, the required return for our illustrative low-risk stock is then found as follows:

$$r_L = 6\% + 5\%(0.5)$$
$$= 8.5\%$$

If a high-risk stock has $b_H = 2.0$, then its required rate of return is 16%:

$$r_H = 6\% + (5\%)2.0 = 16\%$$

An average stock, with $b_A = 1.0$, has a required return of 11%, the same as the market return:

$$r_A = 6\% + (5\%)1.0 = 11\% = r_M$$

Figure 2-9 shows the SML when $r_{RF} = 6\%$ and $RP_M = 5\%$. Note the following points:

1. Required rates of return are shown on the vertical axis, while risk as measured by beta is shown on the horizontal axis. This graph is quite different from the regression line shown in Figure 2-8, where the returns on individual stocks were plotted on the vertical axis and returns on the market index were shown on the horizontal axis. For the SML in Figure 2-9, the slope of the regression line from an analysis such as that conducted in Figure 2-8 is plotted as beta on the horizontal axis of Figure 2-9.
2. Riskless securities have $b_i = 0$; therefore, r_{RF} appears as the vertical axis intercept in Figure 2-9. If we could construct a portfolio that had a beta of zero, then it would have a required return equal to the risk-free rate.
3. The slope of the SML (5% in Figure 2-9) reflects the degree of risk aversion in the economy: The greater the average investor's aversion to risk, then (a) the steeper the slope of the line, (b) the greater the risk premium for all stocks, and (c) the higher the required rate of return on all stocks.[16]

---

16. Students sometimes confuse beta with the slope of the SML. The slope of any straight line is equal to the "rise" divided by the "run," or $(Y_1 - Y_0)/(X_1 - X_0)$. Consider Figure 2-9. If we let $Y = r$ and $X = $ beta, and if we go from the origin to $b = 1.0$, then we see that the slope is $(r_M - r_{RF})/(b_M - b_{RF}) = (11\% - 6\%)/(1 - 0) = 5\%$. Thus, the slope of the SML is equal to $(r_M - r_{RF})$, the market risk premium. In Figure 2-9, $r_i = 6\% + 5\%(b_i)$, so an increase of beta from 1.0 to 2.0 would produce a 5-percentage-point increase in r_i.

FIGURE 2-9	The Security Market Line (SML)

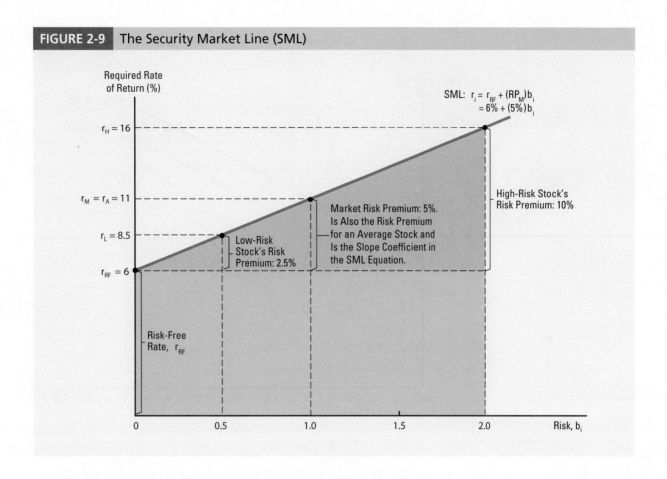

2-7b The Impact on Required Return Due to Changes in the Risk-Free Rate, Risk Aversion, and Beta

The required return depends on the risk-free rate, the market risk premium, and the stock's beta. The following sections illustrate the impact of changes in these inputs.

The Impact of Changes in the Risk-Free Rate

Suppose that some combination of an increase in real interest rates and in anticipated inflation causes the risk-free interest rate to increase from 6% to 8%. Such a change is shown in Figure 2-10. A key point to note is that a change in r_{RF} will not necessarily cause a change in the market risk premium. Thus, as r_{RF} changes, so will the required return on the market, and this will, other things held constant, keep the market risk premium stable.[17] Notice that, under the CAPM, the increase in r_{RF} leads

---

17. Think of a sailboat floating in a harbor. The distance from the ocean floor to the ocean surface is like the risk-free rate, and it moves up and down with the tides. The distance from the top of the ship's mast to the ocean floor is like the required market return: It too moves up and down with the tides. The distance from the mast-top to the ocean surface is like the market risk premium—it stays the same, even though tides move the ship up and down. Thus, other things held constant, a change in the risk-free rate also causes an identical change in the required market return, r_M, resulting in a relatively stable market risk premium, $r_M - r_{RF}$.

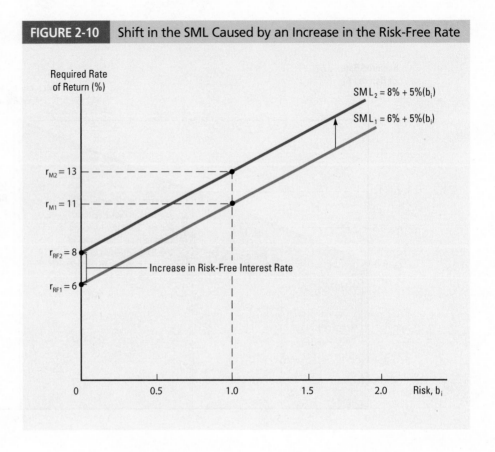

FIGURE 2-10   Shift in the SML Caused by an Increase in the Risk-Free Rate

to an *identical* increase in the required rate of return on all assets, because the same risk-free rate is built into the required rate of return on all assets. For example, the required rate of return on the market (and the average stock), r_M, increases from 11% to 13%. Other risky securities' returns also rise by 2 percentage points.

Changes in Risk Aversion

The slope of the Security Market Line reflects the extent to which investors are averse to risk: The steeper the slope of the line, the greater the average investor's aversion to risk. Suppose all investors were indifferent to risk—that is, suppose they were *not* risk averse. If r_{RF} were 6%, then risky assets would also provide an expected return of 6%, because if there were no risk aversion then there would be no risk premium, and the SML would be plotted as a horizontal line. As risk aversion increases, so does the risk premium, and this causes the slope of the SML to become steeper.

Figure 2-11 illustrates an increase in risk aversion. The market risk premium rises from 5% to 7.5%, causing r_M to rise from $r_{M1} = 11\%$ to $r_{M2} = 13.5\%$. The returns on other risky assets also rise, and the effect of this shift in risk aversion is greater for riskier securities. For example, the required return on a stock with $b_i = 0.5$ increases by only 1.25 percentage points, from 8.5% to 9.75%; that on a stock with $b_i = 1.0$ increases by 2.5 percentage points, from 11.0% to 13.5%; and that on a stock with $b_i = 1.5$ increases by 3.75 percentage points, from 13.5% to 17.25%.

FIGURE 2-11	Shift in the SML Caused by Increased Risk Aversion

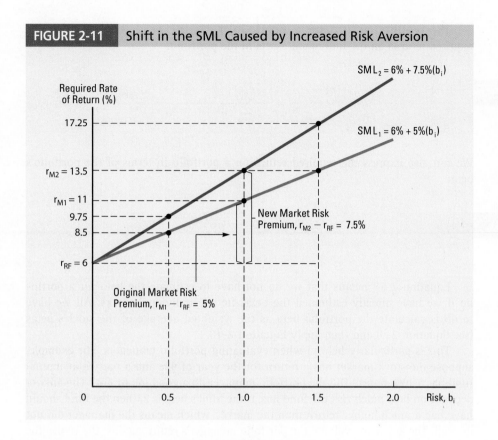

Changes in a Stock's Beta Coefficient

Given risk aversion and a positively sloped SML as in Figure 2-9, the higher a stock's beta, the higher its required rate of return. As we shall see later in the book, a firm can influence its beta through changes in the composition of its assets and also through its use of debt: Acquiring riskier assets will increase beta, as will a change in capital structure that calls for a higher debt ratio. A company's beta can also change as a result of external factors such as increased competition in its industry, the expiration of basic patents, and the like. When such changes lead to a higher or lower beta, the required rate of return will also change.

2-7c **Portfolio Returns and Portfolio Performance Evaluation**

The **expected return on a portfolio**, $\hat{r}_p$, is the weighted average of the expected returns on the individual assets in the portfolio. Suppose there are n stocks in the portfolio and the expected return on Stock i is $\hat{r}_i$. The expected return on the portfolio is:

$$\hat{r}_p = \sum_{i=1}^{n} w_i \hat{r}_i$$

(2–16)

The **required return on a portfolio, r_p**, is the weighted average of the required returns on the individual assets in the portfolio:

(2–17)

$$r_p = \sum_{i=1}^{n} w_i r_i$$

We can also express the required return on a portfolio in terms of the portfolio's beta:

(2–18)

$$r_p = r_{RF} + b_p RP_M$$

Equation 2-18 means that we do not have to estimate the beta for a portfolio if we have already estimated the betas for the individual stocks. All we have to do is calculate the portfolio beta as the weighted average of the stock's betas (see Equation 2-9) and then apply Equation 2-18.

This is particularly helpful when evaluating portfolio managers. For example, suppose the stock market has a return for the year of 9% and a particular mutual fund has a 10% return. Did the portfolio manager do a good job or not? The answer depends on how much risk the fund has. If the fund's beta is 2, then the fund should have had a much higher return than the market, which means the manager did not do well. The key is to evaluate the portfolio manager's return against the return the manager should have made given the risk of the investments.

2-7d Required Returns versus Expected Returns: Market Equilibrium

We explained in Chapter 1 that managers should seek to maximize the value of their firms' stocks. We also emphasized the difference between the market price and intrinsic value. Intrinsic value incorporates all *relevant available* information about expected cash flows and risk. This includes information about the company, the economic environment, and the political environment. In contrast to intrinsic value, market prices are based on investors' *selection and interpretation* of information. To the extent that investors don't select all relevant information and don't interpret it correctly, market prices can deviate from intrinsic values. Figure 2-12 illustrates this relationship between market prices and intrinsic value.

When market prices deviate from their intrinsic values, astute investors have profitable opportunities. For example, we will see in Chapter 4 that the value of a bond is the present value of its cash flows when discounted at the bond's required return, which reflects the bond's risk. This is the intrinsic value of the bond because it incorporates all relevant available information. Notice that the intrinsic value is "fair" in the sense that it incorporates the bond's risk and investors' required returns for bearing the risk.

What would happen if a bond's market price were lower than its intrinsic value? In this situation, an investor could purchase the bond and receive a rate of return in

FIGURE 2-12   Determinants of Intrinsic Values and Market Prices

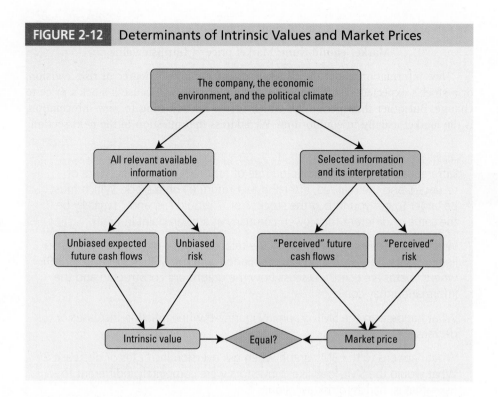

excess of the required return. In other words, the investor would get more compensation than justified by the bond's risk. If all investors felt this way, then demand for the bond would soar as investors tried to purchase it, driving the bond's price up. But as the price of a bond goes up, its yield goes down. This means that an increase in price would reduce the subsequent return for an investor purchasing (or holding) the bond at the new price.[18] It seems reasonable to expect that investors' actions would continue to drive the price up until the expected return on the bond equaled its required return. After that point, the bond would provide just enough return to compensate its owner for the bond's risk.

If the bond's price were too high compared to its intrinsic value, then investors would sell the bond, causing its price to fall and its yield to increase until its expected return equaled its required return.

A stock's future cash flows aren't as predictable as a bond's, but we show in Chapter 8 that a stock's intrinsic value is the present value of its expected future cash flows, just as a bond's intrinsic value is the present value of its cash flows. If the price of a stock is lower than its intrinsic value, then an investor would receive an expected return greater than the return required as compensation for risk. The same market forces we described for a mispriced bond would drive the mispriced stock's price up. If this process continues until its expected return equals its required return, then we say that there is **market equilibrium**:

Market equilibrium: Expected return = Required return

$$\hat{r} = r$$

---

18. The original owner of the bond when it was priced too low would reap a nice benefit as the price climbs, but the subsequent purchasers would only receive the now-lower yield.

We can also express market equilibrium in terms of prices:

Market equilibrium: Market price = Intrinsic value

New information about the risk-free rate, the market's degree of risk aversion, or a stock's expected cash flows (size, timing, or risk) will cause a stock's price to change. But other than periods in which prices are adjusting to new information, is the market usually in equilibrium? We address that question in the next section.

> **SELF TEST**
>
> Differentiate among the expected rate of return ($\hat{r}$), the required rate of return (r), and the realized, after-the-fact return ($\bar{r}$) on a stock. Which must be larger to get you to buy the stock, $\hat{r}$ or r? Would $\hat{r}$, r, and $\bar{r}$ typically be the same or different for a given company at a given point in time?
>
> What are the differences between the relative returns graph (the regression line in Figure 2-8), where "betas are made," and the SML graph (Figure 2-9), where "betas are used"? Discuss how the graphs are constructed and the information they convey.
>
> What happens to the SML graph in Figure 2-9 when inflation increases or decreases?
>
> What happens to the SML graph when risk aversion increases or decreases? What would the SML look like if investors were completely indifferent to risk—that is, had zero risk aversion?
>
> How can a firm's managers influence market risk as reflected in beta?
>
> A stock has a beta of 0.8. Assume that the risk-free rate is 5.5% and that the market risk premium is 6%. What is the stock's required rate of return? **(10.3%)**

2-8 The Efficient Markets Hypothesis

The **Efficient Markets Hypothesis (EMH)** asserts that: (1) stocks are always in equilibrium and (2) it is impossible for an investor to "beat the market" and consistently earn a higher rate of return than is justified by the stock's risk. In other words, a stock's market price is always equal to its intrinsic value. To put it a little more precisely, suppose a stock's market price is equal to the stock's intrinsic value but new information that changes the stock's intrinsic value arrives. The EMH asserts that the market price will adjust to the new intrinsic value so quickly that there isn't time for an investor to receive the new information, evaluate the information, take a position in the stock before the market price changes, and then profit from the subsequent change in price.

Here are three points to consider. First, almost every stock is under considerable scrutiny. With 100,000 or so full-time, highly trained, professional analysts and traders each following about 30 of the roughly 3,000 actively traded stocks (analysts tend to specialize in a specific industry), there are an average of about 1,000 analysts following each stock. Second, financial institutions, pension funds, money management firms, and hedge funds have billions of dollars available for

ANOTHER KIND OF RISK: THE BERNIE MADOFF STORY

In the fall of 2008, Bernard Madoff's massive Ponzi scheme was exposed, revealing an important type of risk that's not dealt with in this chapter. Madoff was a money manager in the 1960s, and apparently through good luck he produced above-average results for several years. Madoff's clients then told their friends about his success, and those friends sent in money for him to invest. Madoff's actual returns then dropped, but he didn't tell his clients that they were losing money. Rather, he told them that returns were holding up well, and he used new incoming money to pay dividends and meet withdrawal requests. The idea of using new money to pay off old investors is called a Ponzi scheme, named after Charles Ponzi, a Bostonian who set up the first widely publicized such scheme in the early 1900s.

Madoff perfected the system, ran his scheme for about 40 years, and attracted about $50 billion of investors' funds. His investors ranged from well-known billionaires to retirees who invested their entire life savings.

His advertising was strictly by word of mouth, and clients telling potential clients about the many wealthy and highly regarded people who invested with him certainly helped. All of his investors assumed that someone else had done the "due diligence" and found the operation to be clean. A few investors who actually did some due diligence were suspicious and didn't invest with him, but for the most part, people just blindly followed the others.

All Ponzi schemes crash when something occurs that causes some investors to seek to withdraw funds in amounts greater than the incoming funds from new investors. Someone tries to get out, can't do it, tells others who worry and try to get out too, and almost overnight the scam unravels. That happened to Madoff in 2008, when the stock market crash caused some of his investors to seek withdrawals and few new dollars were coming in. In the end, his investors lost billions; some lost their entire life savings, and several have committed suicide.

portfolio managers to use in taking advantage of mispriced stocks. Third, SEC disclosure requirements and electronic information networks cause new information about a stock to become available to all analysts virtually simultaneously and almost immediately. With so many analysts trying to take advantage of temporary mispricing due to new information, with so much money chasing the profits due to temporary mispricing, and with such widespread dispersal of information, a stock's market price should adjust quickly from its pre-news intrinsic value to its post-news intrinsic value, leaving only a very short amount of time that the stock is "mispriced" as it moves from one equilibrium price to another. That, in a nutshell, is the logic behind the efficient markets hypothesis.

The following sections discuss forms of the efficient markets hypothesis and empirical tests of the hypothesis.

2-8a **Forms of the Efficient Markets Hypothesis**

There are three forms of the efficient markets hypothesis, and each focuses on a different type of information availability.

Weak-Form Efficiency

The **weak form** of the EMH asserts that all information contained in past price movements is fully reflected in current market prices. If this were true, then information about recent trends in stock prices would be of no use in selecting stocks—the fact that a stock has risen for the past three days, for example, would give us no useful clues as to what it will do today or tomorrow. In contrast, **technical analysts**, also called "chartists," believe that past trends or patterns in stock prices can be used to predict future stock prices.

To illustrate the arguments supporting weak-form efficiency, suppose that after studying the past history of the stock market, a technical analyst identifies the following historical pattern: If a stock has fallen for three consecutive days, its price rose by 10% (on average) the following day. The technician would then conclude that investors could make money by purchasing a stock whose price has fallen three consecutive days.

Weak-form advocates argue that if this pattern truly existed then other investors would soon discover it, and if so, why would anyone be willing to sell a stock after it had fallen for three consecutive days? In other words, why sell if you know that the price is going to increase by 10% the next day? For example, suppose a stock had fallen three consecutive days to $40. If the stock were really likely to rise by 10% to $44 tomorrow, then its price *today, right now*, would actually rise to somewhere close to $44, thereby eliminating the trading opportunity. Consequently, weak-form efficiency implies that any information that comes from past stock prices is too rapidly incorporated into the current stock price for a profit opportunity to exist.

Semistrong-Form Efficiency

The **semistrong form** of the EMH states that current market prices reflect all *publicly available* information. Therefore, if semistrong-form efficiency exists, it would do no good to pore over annual reports or other published data because market prices would have adjusted to any good or bad news contained in such reports back when the news came out. With semistrong-form efficiency, investors should expect to earn returns commensurate with risk, but they should not expect to do any better or worse other than by chance.

Another implication of semistrong-form efficiency is that whenever information is released to the public, stock prices will respond only if the information is different from what had been expected. For example, if a company announces a 30% increase in earnings and if that increase is about what analysts had been expecting, then the announcement should have little or no effect on the company's stock price. On the other hand, the stock price would probably fall if analysts had expected earnings to increase by more than 30%, but it probably would rise if they had expected a smaller increase.

Strong-Form Efficiency

The **strong form** of the EMH states that current market prices reflect all pertinent information, whether publicly available or privately held. If this form holds, even insiders would find it impossible to earn consistently abnormal returns in the stock market.

2-8b **Is the Stock Market Efficient? The Empirical Evidence**

Empirical studies are joint tests of the EMH and an asset pricing model, such as the CAPM. They are joint tests in the sense that they examine whether a particular strategy can beat the market, where "beating the market" means earning a return higher than that predicted by the particular asset pricing model. Before addressing tests of the particular forms of the EMH, let's take a look at market bubbles.

Market Bubbles

The history of finance is marked by numerous instances in which: (1) prices climb rapidly to heights that would have been considered extremely unlikely before the run-up; (2) the volume of trading is much higher than past volume; (3) many new investors (or speculators?) eagerly enter the market; and (4) prices suddenly fall precipitously, leaving many of the new investors with huge losses. These instances are called market bubbles.

The stock market bubbles that burst in 2000 and 2008 suggest that, at the height of these booms, the stocks of many companies—especially in the technology sector in 2000 and the financial sector in 2008—vastly exceeded their intrinsic values, which should not happen if markets are always efficient. Two questions arise. First, how are bubbles formed? Behavioral finance, which we discuss in Section 2-10, provides some possible answers. Second, why do bubbles persist when it is possible to make a fortune when they burst? For example, hedge fund manager Mark Spitznagel reputedly made billions for his Universa funds by betting against the market in 2008. The logic underlying market equilibrium suggests that everyone would bet against an overvalued market, and that their actions would cause market prices to fall back to intrinsic values fairly quickly. To understand why this doesn't happen, let's examine the strategies for profiting from a falling market: (1) sell stocks (or the market index itself) short; (2) purchase a put option or write a call option; or (3) take a short position in a futures contract on the market index. Following is an explanation for how these strategies work (or fail).

Loosely speaking, selling a stock short means that you borrow a share from a broker and sell it. You get the cash (subject to collateral requirements required by the broker), but you owe a share of stock. For example, suppose you sell a share of Google short at a current price of $500. If the price falls to $400, you can buy a share of the stock at the now-lower $400 market price and return the share to the broker, pocketing the $100 difference between the higher price ($500) when you went short and the lower price ($400) when you closed the position. Of course, if the price goes up, say to $550, you lose $50 because you must replace the share you borrowed (at $500) with one that is now more costly ($550). Even if your broker doesn't require you to close out your position when the price goes up, your broker certainly will require that you put in more collateral.

Recall from Chapter 1 that a put option gives you the option to sell a share at a fixed strike price. For example, suppose you buy a put on Google for $60 with a strike price of $500. If the stock price falls below the strike price, say to $400, you can buy a share at the low price ($400) and sell it at the higher strike price ($500), making a net $40 profit from the decline in the stock price: $40 = −$60 −$400 + $500. However, if the put expires before the stock price falls below the strike price, you lose the $60 you spent buying the put. You can also use call options to bet on a decline. For example, if you write a call option, you receive cash in return for an obligation to sell a share at the strike price. Suppose you write a call option on Google with a strike price of $500 and receive $70. If Google's price stays below the $500 strike price, you keep the $70 cash you received from writing the call. But if Google goes up to $600 and the call you wrote is exercised, you must buy a share at the new high price ($600) and sell it at the lower strike price ($500), for a net loss of $30: $70 − $600 + $500 = −$30.[19]

With a short position in a futures contract on the market index (or a particular stock), you are obligated to sell a share at a fixed price. If the market price falls below the specified price in the futures contract, you make money because you can buy a share in the market and sell it at the higher price specified in the futures contract. But if the market price increases, you lose money because you must buy a share at the now higher price and sell it at the price fixed in the futures contract.[20]

Each of these strategies allows an investor to make a lot of money. And if all investors tried to capitalize on an overvalued market, their actions would soon drive the market back to equilibrium, preventing a bubble from forming. But here is the problem with these strategies. Even if the market is overvalued, it might takes months (or even years) before the market falls to its intrinsic value. During this period, an investor would have to spend a lot of cash maintaining the strategies described above, including margin calls, settling options, and daily marking to market for futures contracts. These negative cash flows could easily drive an investor into bankruptcy before the investor was eventually proven correct. Unfortunately, there aren't any low-risk strategies for puncturing a market bubble.

Notice that the problem of negative cash flows doesn't exist for the opposite situation of an undervalued market in which the intrinsic value is greater than the market price. Investors can simply buy stock at the too-low market price and hold it until the market price eventually increases to the intrinsic value. Even if the market price continues to go down before eventually rising, the investor experiences only paper losses and not actual negative cash flows. Thus, we would not expect "negative" bubbles to persist very long.

Tests of Weak-Form Efficiency

Most studies suggest that the stock market is highly efficient in the weak form, with two exceptions. The first exception is for long-term reversals, with studies showing that portfolios of stocks with poor past long-term performance (over the past 5 years, for example) tend to do slightly better in the long-term future than the CAPM predicts, and vice versa. The second is momentum, with studies showing that stocks with strong performance in the short-term past (over the past 6 to 9 months, for example) tend to do slightly better in the short-term future than the CAPM predicts, and likewise for weak performance.[21] Strategies based on taking advantage of long-term reversals or short-term momentum produce returns that are in excess of those predicted by the CAPM. However, the excess returns are small, especially when transaction costs are considered.

Tests of Semistrong-Form Efficiency

Most studies show that markets are reasonably efficient in the semistrong form: It is difficult to use publicly available information to create a trading strategy that

---

19. Options are usually settled by cash rather than by actually buying and selling shares of stock.
20. Recall from Chapter 1 that futures contracts are actually settled daily and that they are usually settled for cash rather than the actual shares.
21. For example, see N. Jegadeesh and S. Titman, "Returns to Buying Winners and Selling Losers: Implications for Stock Market Efficiency," *Journal of Finance*, March 1993, pp. 69–91; and W. F. M. DeBondt and R. H. Thaler, "Does the Stock Market Overreact?" *Journal of Finance*, July 1985, pp. 793–808.

consistently has returns greater than those predicted by the CAPM. In fact, the professionals who manage mutual fund portfolios, on average, do not outperform the overall stock market as measured by an index like the S&P 500 and tend to have returns lower than predicted by the CAPM, possibly because many mutual funds have high fees.[22]

However, there are two well-known exceptions to semistrong-form efficiency. The first is for small companies, which have had historical returns greater than predicted by the CAPM. The second is related to book-to-market ratios (B/M), defined as the book value of equity divided by the market value of equity (this is the inverse of the market/book ratio defined in Chapter 7). Companies with high B/M ratios have had higher returns than predicted by the CAPM. We discuss these exceptions in more detail in Section 2-9.

Tests of Strong-Form Efficiency

The evidence suggests that the strong form EMH does not hold, because those who possessed inside information could make and have (illegally) made abnormal profits. On the other hand, many insiders have gone to jail, so perhaps there is indeed a trade-off between risk and return!

What is the Efficient Markets Hypothesis (EMH)?

What are the differences among the three forms of the EMH?

Why is it difficult to puncture a market bubble?

What violations of the EMH have been demonstrated?

What is short-term momentum? What are long-term reversals?

SELF TEST

2-9 The Fama-French Three-Factor Model[23]

Take a look at Table 2-2, which reports the returns for 25 portfolios formed by Professors Eugene Fama and Kenneth French. The Fama-French portfolios are based on the company's size as measured by the market value of its equity (MVE) and the company's book-to-market (B/M) ratio, defined as the book value of equity divided by the market value of equity. Each row shows portfolios with similarly sized companies; each column shows portfolios whose companies have similar B/M ratios. Notice that if you look across each row, the average return tends to increase as the B/M ratio increases. In other words, stocks with high B/M ratios have higher returns. If you look up each column (except for the column with the lowest B/M ratios), stock returns tend to increase: Small companies have higher returns.

---

22. For a discussion of the performance of actively managed funds, see Jonathan Clements, "Resisting the Lure of Managed Funds," *The Wall Street Journal,* February 27, 2001, p. C1.

23. This section may be omitted with no loss in continuity.

TABLE 2-2	Average Annual Returns for the Fama-French Portfolios Based on Size and Book Equity to Market Equity, 1927–2013

| | Book Equity to Market Equity | | | | |
Size	Low	2	3	4	High
Small	12.8%	19.1%	21.6%	23.4%	30.1%
2	12.3	16.8	18.7	19.0	20.1
3	12.5	15.8	16.7	17.6	19.5
4	12.7	13.5	15.3	16.7	17.8
Big	11.1	12.6	13.3	14.0	16.2

Source: Professor Kenneth French, **mba.tuck.dartmouth.edu/pages/faculty/ken.french/data_library.html**. These are equal-weighted annual returns. Following is a description from Professor French's Web site describing the construction of the portfolios: "The portfolios, which are constructed at the end of each June, are the intersections of 5 portfolios formed on size (market equity, ME) and 5 portfolios formed on the ratio of book equity to market equity (BE/ME). The size breakpoints for year t are the NYSE market equity quintiles at the end of June of t. BE/ME for June of year t is the book equity for the last fiscal year end in t − 1 divided by ME for December of t − 1. The BE/ME breakpoints are NYSE quintiles. The portfolios for July of year t to June of t + 1 include all NYSE, AMEX, and NASDAQ stocks for which we have market equity data for December of t − 1 and June of t, and (positive) book equity data for t − 1."

This pattern alone would not be a challenge to the CAPM if small firms and high B/M firms had large betas (and thus higher returns). However, even after adjusting for their betas, the small-stock portfolios and the high B/M portfolios earned returns higher than predicted by the CAPM. This indicates that: (1) markets are inefficient or (2) the CAPM isn't the correct model to describe required returns.

In 1992, Fama and French published a study hypothesizing that the SML should have three factors rather than just beta as in the CAPM.[24] The first factor is the stock's CAPM beta, which measures the market risk of the stock. The second is the size of the company, measured by the market value of its equity (MVE). The third factor is the book-to-market (B/M) ratio.

When Fama and French tested their hypotheses, they found that small companies and companies with high B/M ratios had higher rates of return than the average stock, just as they hypothesized. Somewhat surprisingly, however, they found that beta was not useful in explaining returns. After taking into account the returns due to the company's size and B/M ratio, high-beta stocks did not have higher than average returns and low-beta stocks did not have lower than average returns.

In 1993, Fama and French developed a three-factor model based on their previous results.[25] The first factor in the **Fama-French three-factor model** is the market risk premium, which is the market return, $\bar{r}_M$, minus the risk-free rate, $\bar{r}_{RF}$. Thus, their model begins like the CAPM, but they go on to add a second and third factor.[26] To form the second factor, they ranked all actively traded stocks by size and then divided them into two portfolios, one consisting of small stocks and one consisting of big stocks. They calculated the return on each of these two portfolios and created

24. See Eugene F. Fama and Kenneth R. French, "The Cross-Section of Expected Stock Returns," *Journal of Finance,* Vol. 47, 1992, pp. 427–465. In 2013, Eugene Fama was awarded the Nobel Prize in Economics for this and his other work in asset pricing.

25. See Eugene F. Fama and Kenneth R. French, "Common Risk Factors in the Returns on Stocks and Bonds," *Journal of Financial Economics,* Vol. 33, 1993, pp. 3–56.

26. Although our description captures the essence of their process for forming factors, the actual procedure is a little more complicated. The interested reader should see their 1993 paper, cited in footnote 25.

a third portfolio by subtracting the return on the big portfolio from that of the small one. They called this the SMB (small minus big) portfolio. This portfolio is designed to measure the variation in stock returns that is caused by the size effect.

To form the third factor, they ranked all stocks according to their book-to-market (B/M) ratios. They placed the 30% of stocks with the highest ratios into a portfolio they called the H portfolio (for high B/M ratios) and placed the 30% of stocks with the lowest ratios into a portfolio called the L portfolio (for low B/M ratios). Then they subtracted the return of the L portfolio from that of the H portfolio to derive the HML (high minus low) portfolio. Their resulting model is shown here:

$$(\bar{r}_{i,t} - \bar{r}_{RF,t}) = a_i + b_i(\bar{r}_{M,t} - \bar{r}_{RF,t}) + c_i(\bar{r}_{SMB,t}) + d_i(\bar{r}_{HML,t}) + e_{i,t} \qquad \text{(2–19)}$$

where

$\bar{r}_{i,t}$ = Historical (realized) rate of return on Stock i in period t

$\bar{r}_{RF,t}$ = Historical (realized) rate of return on the risk-free rate in period t

$\bar{r}_{M,t}$ = Historical (realized) rate of return on the market in period t

$\bar{r}_{SMB,t}$ = Historical (realized) rate of return on the small-size portfolio minus the big-size portfolio in period t

$\bar{r}_{HML,t}$ = Historical (realized) rate of return on the high-B/M portfolio minus the low-B/M portfolio in period t

a_i = Vertical axis intercept term for Stock i

b_i, c_i, and d_i = Slope coefficients for Stock i

$e_{i,t}$ = Random error, reflecting the difference between the actual return on Stock i in period t and the return as predicted by the regression line

When this model is applied to actual stock returns, the "extra" return disappears for portfolios based on a company's size or B/M ratio. In fact, the extra returns for the long-term stock reversals that we discussed in Section 2-8 also disappear. Thus, the Fama-French model accounts for the many of the major violations of the EMH that we described earlier.

Because the Fama-French model explains so well a stock's actual return given the return on the market, the SMB portfolio, and the HML portfolio, the model is very useful in identifying the market's reaction to news about a company.[27] For example, suppose a company announces that it is going to include more outsiders on its board of directors. If the company's stock falls by 2% on the day of the

---

27. Because the Fama-French model doesn't seem to explain short-term momentum, many researchers also use the four-factor model, which includes a factor for momentum; see Mark Carhart, "On Persistence in Mutual Fund Performance," *Journal of Finance,* Vol. 52, No. 1. (Mar), pp. 57–82.

announcement, does that mean investors don't want outsiders on the board? We can answer that question by using the Fama-French model to decompose the actual return of the company on the announcement day into the portion that is explained by the environment (i.e., the market and the SMB and HML portfolios) and the portion due to the company's announcement.

To do this, we gather a sample of data ($\bar{r}_{i,t}$, $\bar{r}_{RF,t}$, $\bar{r}_{M,t}$, $\bar{r}_{SMB,t}$, and $\bar{r}_{HML,t}$) for T periods prior to the announcement date and then run a regression using Equation 2-20. (This is similar to the way in which we estimated beta in Section 2-6 except we are estimating more than one slope coefficient in a multiple regression.) Suppose the estimated coefficients are $a_i = 0.0$, $b_i = 0.9$, $c_i = 0.2$, and $d_i = 0.3$. On the day of the announcement, the stock market had a return of -3%, the r_{SMB} portfolio had a return of -1%, and the r_{HML} portfolio had a return of -2%. The annual risk-free rate was 6%, so the daily rate is 6%/365 = 0.01%, which is so small that it can be ignored. The predicted value of the error term in the Fama-French model, $e_{i,t}$, is by definition equal to zero. Based on these assumptions, the predicted return on the announcement day using the Fama-French three-factor model is:

$$
\begin{aligned}
\text{(2-20)} \qquad \text{Predicted return} &= a_i + b_i(\bar{r}_{M,t}) + c_i(\bar{r}_{SMB,t}) + d_i(\bar{r}_{HML,t}) \\
&= 0.0 + 0.9(-3\%) + 0.2(-1\%) + 0.3(-2\%) \\
&= -3.5\%
\end{aligned}
$$

The unexplained return is equal to the actual return less the predicted return:

$$\text{Unexplained return} = -2.0\% - (-3.5\%) = 1.5\%$$

Although the stock price went down by 2% on the announcement day, the Fama-French model predicted that the price should have gone down by 3.5%. Thus, the stock had a positive 1.5% reaction on the announcement day. This is just one company, but if we repeated this process for many companies that made similar announcements and calculated the average unexplained reaction, we could draw a conclusion regarding the market's reaction to adding more outside directors. As this example shows, the model is very useful in identifying actions that affect a company's value.

There is no question that the Fama-French three-factor model does a good job in explaining *actual* returns, but how well does it perform in explaining *required* returns? In other words, does the model define a relationship between risk and compensation for bearing risk?

Advocates of the model suggest that size and B/M are related to risk. Small companies have less access to capital markets than do large companies, which exposes small companies to greater risk in the event of a credit crunch—such as the one that occurred during the global economic crisis that began in 2007. With greater risk, investors would require a higher expected return to induce them to invest in small companies.

Similar arguments apply for companies with high B/M ratios. If a company's prospects are poor, then the company will have a low market value, which causes a high B/M ratio. Lenders usually are reluctant to extend credit to a company with poor prospects, so an economic downturn can cause such a company to experience financial distress. In other words, a stock with a high B/M ratio might be exposed to the risk of financial distress, in which case investors would require a higher expected return to induce them to invest in such a stock.

If a company's sensitivity to the size factor and the B/M factor are related to financial distress risk, then the Fama-French model would be an improvement on the CAPM regarding the relationship between risk and required return. However, the evidence is mixed as to whether financially distressed firms do indeed have higher expected returns as compensation for their risk. In fact, some studies show financially distressed firms actually have *lower* returns instead of higher returns.[28]

A number of other studies suggest that the size effect no longer influences stock returns, that there never was a size effect (the previous results were caused by peculiarities in the data sources), that the size effect doesn't apply to most companies, and that the book-to-market effect is not as significant as first supposed.[29]

In summary, the Fama-French model is very useful in identifying the unexplained component of a stock's return. However, the model is less useful when it comes to estimating the required return on a stock because the model does not provide a well-accepted link between risk and required return.

SELF TEST

What are the factors in the Fama-French model?

How can the model be used to estimate the predicted return on a stock?

Why isn't the model widely used by managers at actual companies?

An analyst has modeled the stock of a company using a Fama-French three-factor model and has estimate that $a_i = 0$, $b_i = 0.7$, $c_i = 1.2$, and $d_i = 0.7$. Suppose that the daily risk-free rate is approximately equal to zero, the market return is 11%, the return on the SMB portfolio is 3.2%, and the return on the HML portfolio is 4.8% on a particular day. The stock had an actual return of 16.9% on that day. What is the stock's predicted return for that day? **(14.9%)** What is the stock's unexplained return for the day? **(2%)**

---

28. For studies supporting the relationship between risk and return as related to size and the B/M ratio, see Nishad Kapadia, "Tracking Down Distress Risk," *Journal of Financial Economics*, Vol. 102, 2011, pp. 167–182; Thomas J. George, "A Resolution of the Distress Risk and Leverage Puzzles in the Cross Section of Stock Returns," *Journal of Financial Economics*, Vol. 96, 2010, pp. 56–79; and Lorenzo Garlappi and Hong Yan, "Financial Distress and the Cross-section of Equity Returns," *Journal of Finance*, June, 2011, pp. 789–822. For studies rejecting the relationship, see John Y. Campbell, Jens Hilscher, and Jan Szilagyi, "In Search of Distress Risk," *Journal of Finance*, December 2008, pp. 2899–2940; and Ilia D. Dichev, "Is the Risk of Bankruptcy a Systematic Risk?" *Journal of Finance*, June 1998, pp. 1131–1147.

29. See Peter J. Knez and Mark J. Ready, "On the Robustness of Size and Book-to-Market in the Cross-Sectional Regressions," *Journal of Finance*, September 1997, pp. 1355–1382; Dongcheol Kim, "A Reexamination of Firm Size, Book-to-Market, and Earnings Price in the Cross-Section of Expected Stock Returns," *Journal of Financial and Quantitative Analysis*, December 1997, pp. 463–489; Tyler Shumway and Vincent A. Warther, "The Delisting Bias in CRSP's Nasdaq Data and Its Implications for the Size Effect," *Journal of Finance*, December 1999, pp. 2361–2379; and Tim Loughran, "Book-to-Market across Firm Size, Exchange, and Seasonality: Is There an Effect?" *Journal of Financial and Quantitative Analysis*, September 1997, pp. 249–268.

2-10 **Behavioral Finance**[30]

A large body of evidence in the field of psychology shows that people often behave irrationally, but in predictable ways. The field of behavioral finance focuses on irrational, but predictable, financial decisions. The following sections examine applications of behavioral finance to market bubbles and to other financial decisions.

2-10a **Market Bubbles and Behavioral Finance**

We showed in Section 2.8 that strategies for profiting from a punctured bubble expose an investor to possible large negative cash flows if it takes a long time for the bubble to burst. That explains why a bubble can persist, but it doesn't explain how a bubble is created. There are no definitive explanations, but the field of behavioral finance offers some possible reasons, including overconfidence, anchoring bias, and herding.

Many psychological tests show that people are overconfident with respect to their own abilities relative to the abilities of others, which is the basis of Garrison Keillor's joke about a town where all the children are above average. Professor Richard Thaler and his colleague Nicholas Barberis address this phenomenon as it applies to finance:

> Overconfidence may in part stem from two other biases, self-attribution bias and hindsight bias. Self-attribution bias refers to people's tendency to ascribe any success they have in some activity to their own talents, while blaming failure on bad luck, rather than on their ineptitude. Doing this repeatedly will lead people to the pleasing but erroneous conclusion that they are very talented. For example, investors might become overconfident after several quarters of investing success [Gervais and Odean (2001)[31]]. Hindsight bias is the tendency of people to believe, after an event has occurred, that they predicted it before it happened. If people think they predicted the past better than they actually did, they may also believe that they can predict the future better than they actually can.[32]

Psychologists have learned that many people focus too closely on recent events when predicting future events, a phenomenon called **anchoring bias**. Therefore, when the market is performing better than average, people tend to think it will continue to perform better than average. When anchoring bias is coupled with overconfidence, investors can become convinced that their prediction of an increasing market is correct, thus creating even more demand for stocks. This demand drives stock prices up, which serves to reinforce the overconfidence and move the anchor even higher.

There is another way that an increasing market can reinforce itself. Studies have shown that gamblers who are ahead tend to take on more risks (i.e., they are playing with the house's money), whereas those who are behind tend to become more conservative. If this is true for investors, we can get a feedback loop: When

---

30. This section may be omitted with no loss of continuity.

31. See Terrance Odean and Simon Gervais, "Learning to Be Overconfident," *Review of Financial Studies*, Spring 2001, pp. 1–27.

32. See page 1066 in an excellent review of behavioral finance by Nicholas Barberis and Richard Thaler, "A Survey of Behavioral Finance," in *Handbook of the Economics of Finance*, George Constantinides, Milt Harris, and René Stulz, eds. (Amsterdam: Elsevier/North-Holland, 2003), Chapter 18.

the market goes up, investors have gains, which can make them less risk averse, which increases their demand for stock, which leads to higher prices, which starts the cycle again.

Herding behavior occurs when groups of investors emulate other successful investors and chase asset classes that are doing well. For example, high returns in mortgage-backed securities during 2004 and 2005 enticed other investors to move into that asset class. Herding behavior can create excess demand for asset classes that have done well, causing price increases which induce additional herding behavior. Thus, herding behavior can inflate rising markets.

Sometimes herding behavior occurs when a group of investors assumes that other investors are better informed—the herd chases the "smart" money. But in other cases herding can occur even when those in the herd suspect that prices are overinflated. For example, consider the situation of a portfolio manager who believes that bank stocks are overvalued even though many other portfolios are heavily invested in such stocks. If the manager moves out of bank stocks and they subsequently fall in price, then the manager will be rewarded for her judgment. But if the stocks continue to do well, the manager may well lose her job for missing out on the gains. If instead the manager follows the herd and invests in bank stocks, then the manager will do no better or worse than her peers. Thus, if the penalty for being wrong is bigger than the reward for being correct, it is rational for portfolio managers to herd even if they suspect the herd is wrong.

Researchers have shown that the combination of overconfidence and biased self-attribution can lead to overly volatile stock markets, short-term momentum, and long-term reversals.[33] We suspect that overconfidence, anchoring bias, and herding can contribute to market bubbles.

2-10b **Other Applications of Behavioral Finance**

Psychologists Daniel Kahneman and Amos Tversky show that individuals view potential losses and potential gains very differently.[34] If you ask an average person whether he or she would rather have $500 with certainty or flip a fair coin and receive $1,000 if it comes up heads and nothing if it comes up tails, most would prefer the certain $500 gain, which suggests an aversion to risk—a *sure* $500 gain is better than a risky *expected* $500 gain. However, if you ask the same person whether he or she would rather pay $500 with certainty or flip a coin and pay $1,000 if it's heads and nothing if it's tails, most would indicate that they prefer to flip the coin, which suggests a preference for risk—a risky *expected* $500 loss is better than a *sure* $500 loss. In other words, losses are so painful that people will make irrational choices to avoid sure losses. This phenomenon is called "loss aversion."

One way that people avoid a loss is by not admitting that they have actually had a loss. For example, in many people's mental bookkeeping, a loss isn't really a loss until the losing investment is actually sold. Therefore, they tend to hold risky losers instead of accepting a certain loss, which is a display of loss aversion.

---

33. See Terrance Odean, "Volume, Volatility, Price, and Profit When All Traders Are Above Average," *Journal of Finance,* December 1998, pp. 1887–1934; and Kent Daniel, David Hirshleifer, and Avanidhar Subrahmanyam, "Investor Psychology and Security Market Under- and Overreactions," *Journal of Finance,* December 1998, pp. 1839–1885.

34. Daniel Kahneman and Amos Tversky, "Prospect Theory: An Analysis of Decision under Risk," *Econometrica,* March 1979, pp. 263–292.

Of course, this leads investors to sell losers much less frequently than winners even though this is suboptimal for tax purposes.[35]

Many corporate projects and mergers fail to live up to their expectations. In fact, most mergers end up destroying value in the acquiring company. Because this is well known, why haven't companies responded by being more selective in their investments? There are many possible reasons, but research by Ulrike Malmendier and Geoffrey Tate suggests that overconfidence leads managers to overestimate their abilities and the quality of their projects.[36] In other words, managers might know that the average decision to merge destroys value, but they are certain that their decision is above average.

Finance is a quantitative field, but good managers in all disciplines must also understand human behavior.[37]

> **SELF TEST**
>
> What is behavioral finance?
>
> What is anchoring bias? What is herding behavior? How can these contribute to market bubbles?

2-11 The CAPM and Market Efficiency: Implications for Corporate Managers and Investors

A company is like a portfolio of projects: factories, retail outlets, R&D ventures, new product lines, and the like. Each project contributes to the size, timing, and risk of the company's cash flows, which directly affect the company's intrinsic value. This means that *the relevant risk and expected return of any project must be measured in terms of its effect on the stock's risk and return.* Therefore, all managers must understand how stockholders view risk and required return in order to evaluate potential projects.

Stockholders should not expect to be compensated for the risk they can eliminate through diversification, but only for the remaining market risk. The CAPM provides an important tool for measuring the remaining market risk and goes on to show how a stock's required return is related to the stock's market risk. It is for this reason that the CAPM is widely used to estimate the required return on a company's stock and, hence, the required returns that projects must generate to provide the stock's required return. We describe this process in more detail in Chapters 8 and 11, which cover stock valuation and the cost of capital. We apply these concepts to project analysis in Chapters 12 and 13.

---

35. See Terrance Odean, "Are Investors Reluctant to Realize Their Losses?" *Journal of Finance,* October 1998, pp. 1775–1798.

36. See Ulrike Malmendier and Geoffrey Tate, "CEO Overconfidence and Corporate Investment," *Journal of Finance,* December 2005, pp. 2661–2700.

37. Excellent reviews of behavioral finance are by Richard H. Thaler, Editor, *Advances in Behavioral Finance* (New York: Russell Sage Foundation, 1993); and Andrei Shleifer, *Inefficient Markets: An Introduction to Behavioral Finance* (New York: Oxford University Press, 2000).

Is the CAPM perfect? No. First, we cannot observe beta but must instead estimate beta. As we saw in Section 2-6, estimates of beta are not precise. Second, we saw that small stocks and stocks with high B/M ratios have returns higher than the CAPM predicts. This could mean that the CAPM is the wrong model, but there is another possible explanation. If the composition of a company's assets were changing over time with respect to the mix of physical assets and growth opportunities (involving, e.g., R&D or patents), then this would be enough to make it *appear* as though there were size and B/M effects. In other words, even if the returns on the individual assets conform to the CAPM, changes in the mix of assets would cause the firm's beta to change over time in such a way that the firm would appear to have size and book-to-market effects.[38] Recent research supports this hypothesis, and we will use the CAPM in subsequent chapters.[39]

Regarding market efficiency, our understanding of the empirical evidence suggests it is very difficult, if not impossible, to beat the market by earning a return that is higher than justified by the investment's risk. This suggests that markets are reasonably efficient for most assets for most of the time. However, we believe that market bubbles do occur and that it is very difficult to implement a low-risk strategy for profiting when they burst.

> Explain the following statement: "The stand-alone risk of an individual corporate project may be quite high, but viewed in the context of its effect on stockholders' risk, the project's true risk may be much lower."

SELF TEST

---

38. See Jonathan B. Berk, Richard C. Green, and Vasant Naik, "Optimal Investment, Growth Options, and Security Returns," *Journal of Finance,* October 1999, pp. 1553–1608.

39. See Zhi Da, Re-Jin Guo, and Ravi Jagannathan, "CAPM for Estimating the Cost of Equity Capital: Interpreting the Empirical Evidence," *Journal of Financial Economics,* Vol. 103, 2012, pp. 204–220.

Summary

This chapter focuses on the trade-off between risk and return. We began by discussing how to estimate risk and return for both individual assets and portfolios. In particular, we differentiated between stand-alone risk and risk in a portfolio context, and we explained the benefits of diversification. We introduced the CAPM, which describes how risk affects rates of return.

- **Risk** can be defined as exposure to the chance of an unfavorable event.
- The risk of an asset's cash flows can be considered on a **stand-alone basis** (each asset all by itself) or in a **portfolio context**, in which the investment is combined with other assets and its risk is reduced through **diversification**.
- Most rational investors hold **portfolios of assets**, and they are more concerned with the risk of their portfolios than with the risk of individual assets.

- The **expected return** on an investment is the mean value of its probability distribution of returns.
- The *greater the probability* that the actual return will be far below the expected return, the *greater the asset's stand-alone risk*.
- The average investor is **risk averse**, which means that he or she must be compensated for holding risky assets. Therefore, riskier assets have higher required returns than less risky assets.
- An asset's risk has two components: (1) **diversifiable risk**, which can be eliminated by diversification, and (2) **market risk**, which cannot be eliminated by diversification.
- Market risk is measured by the standard deviation of returns on a well-diversified portfolio, one that consists of all stocks traded in the market. Such a portfolio is called the **market portfolio**.
- The **CAPM** defines the **relevant risk** of an individual asset as its contribution to the risk of a well-diversified **portfolio**. Because market risk cannot be eliminated by diversification, investors must be compensated for bearing it.
- A stock's **beta coefficient, b,** measures how much risk a stock contributes to a well-diversified portfolio.
- A stock with a beta greater than 1 has stock returns that tend to be higher than the market when the market is up but tend to be below the market when the market is down. The opposite is true for a stock with a beta less than 1.
- The **beta of a portfolio** is a **weighted average** of the betas of the individual securities in the portfolio.
- The CAPM's **Security Market Line (SML)** equation shows the relationship between a security's market risk and its required rate of return. The return required for any security i is equal to the **risk-free rate** plus the **market risk premium** multiplied by the security's **beta**: $r_i = r_{RF} + (RP_M)b_i$.
- In equilibrium, the expected rate of return on a stock must equal its required return. However, a number of things can happen to cause the required rate of return to change: (1) *the risk-free rate can change* because of changes in either real rates or expected inflation, (2) *a stock's beta can change*, and (3) *investors' aversion to risk can change*.
- Because returns on assets in different countries are not perfectly correlated, *global diversification* may result in lower risk for multinational companies and globally diversified portfolios.
- The **intrinsic value** (also called the **fundamental value**) of a financial asset is the present value of an asset's expected future cash flows, discounted at the appropriate risk-adjusted rate. The intrinsic value incorporates all *relevant available* information about the asset's expected cash flows and risk.
- **Equilibrium** is the condition under which the expected return on a security as seen by the marginal investor is just equal to its required return, $\hat{r} = r$. Also, the stock's intrinsic value must be equal to its market price.
- The **Efficient Markets Hypothesis (EMH)** holds that: (1) stocks are always in equilibrium and (2) it is impossible for an investor who does not have inside information to consistently "beat the market." Therefore, according to the EMH, stocks are always fairly valued and have a required return equal to their expected return.

- The **Fama-French three-factor model** has one factor for the **market return**, a second factor for the **size effect**, and a third factor for the **book-to-market effect**.
- **Behavioral finance** assumes that investors don't always behave rationally. **Anchoring bias** is the human tendency to "anchor" too closely on recent events when predicting future events. **Herding** is the tendency of investors to follow the crowd. When combined with overconfidence, anchoring and herding can contribute to market bubbles.
- Two Web extensions accompany this chapter: *Web Extension 2A* provides a discussion of **continuous probability distributions**, and *Web Extension 2B* shows how to calculate beta with a financial calculator.

Questions

2–1 Define the following terms, using graphs or equations to illustrate your answers where feasible.

 a. Risk in general; stand-alone risk; probability distribution and its relation to risk

 b. Expected rate of return, $\hat{r}$

 c. Continuous probability distribution

 d. Standard deviation, σ; variance, σ^2

 e. Risk aversion; realized rate of return, $\bar{r}$

 f. Risk premium for Stock i, RP_i; market risk premium, RP_M

 g. Capital Asset Pricing Model (CAPM)

 h. Expected return on a portfolio, $\hat{r}p$; market portfolio

 i. Correlation as a concept; correlation coefficient, r

 j. Market risk; diversifiable risk; relevant risk

 k. Beta coefficient, b; average stock's beta

 l. Security Market Line (SML); SML equation

 m. Slope of SML and its relationship to risk aversion

 n. Equilibrium; Efficient Markets Hypothesis (EMH); three forms of EMH

 o. Fama-French three-factor model

 p. Behavioral finance; herding; anchoring

2–2 The probability distribution of a less risky return is more peaked than that of a riskier return. What shape would the probability distribution have for (a) completely certain returns and (b) completely uncertain returns?

2–3 Security A has an expected return of 7%, a standard deviation of returns of 35%, a correlation coefficient with the market of −0.3, and a beta coefficient of −1.5. Security B has an expected return of 12%, a standard deviation of returns of 10%, a correlation with the market of 0.7, and a beta coefficient of 1.0. Which security is riskier? Why?

2–4 If investors' aversion to risk *increased*, would the risk premium on a high-beta stock increase by more or less than that on a low-beta stock? Explain.

2–5 If a company's beta were to double, would its expected return double?

Problems

Answers Appear in Appendix B

Easy Problems 1–4

2–1 Portfolio Beta

Your investment club has only two stocks in its portfolio. $20,000 is invested in a stock with a beta of 0.7, and $35,000 is invested in a stock with a beta of 1.3. What is the portfolio's beta?

2–2 Required Rate of Return

AA Industries' stock has a beta of 0.8. The risk-free rate is 4% and the expected return on the market is 12%. What is the required rate of return on AA's stock?

2–3 Required Rates of Return

Suppose that the risk-free rate is 5% and that the market risk premium is 7%. What is the required return on (1) the market, (2) a stock with a beta of 1.0, and (3) a stock with a beta of 1.7?

2–4 Fama-French Three-Factor Model

An analyst has modeled the stock of a company using the Fama-French three-factor model. The risk-free rate is 5%, the market return is 10%, the return on the SMB portfolio (r_{SMB}) is 3.2%, and the return on the HML portfolio (r_{HML}) is 4.8%. If $a_i = 0$, $b_i = 1.2$, $c_i = -0.4$, and $d_i = 1.3$, what is the stock's predicted return?

Intermediate Problems 5–10

2–5 Expected Return: Discrete Distribution

A stock's return has the following distribution:

Demand for the Company's Products	Probability of This Demand Occurring	Rate of Return if This Demand Occurs (%)
Weak	0.1	−50%
Below average	0.2	−5
Average	0.4	16
Above average	0.2	25
Strong	0.1	60
	1.0	

Calculate the stock's expected return and standard deviation.

2–6 Expected Returns: Discrete Distribution

The market and Stock J have the following probability distributions:

Probability	r_M	r_J
0.3	15%	20%
0.4	9	5
0.3	18	12

a. Calculate the expected rates of return for the market and Stock J.

b. Calculate the standard deviations for the market and Stock J.

2-7 Required Rate of Return

Suppose r_{RF} = 5%, r_M = 10%, and r_A = 12%.

a. Calculate Stock A's beta.

b. If Stock A's beta were 2.0, then what would be A's new required rate of return?

2-8 Required Rate of Return

As an equity analyst you are concerned with what will happen to the required return to Universal Toddler Industries' stock as market conditions change. Suppose r_{RF} = 5%, r_M = 12%, and b_{UTI} = 1.4.

a. Under current conditions, what is r_{UTI}, the required rate of return on UTI stock?

b. Now suppose r_{RF} (1) increases to 6% or (2) decreases to 4%. The slope of the SML remains constant. How would this affect r_M and r_{UTI}?

c. Now assume r_{RF} remains at 5% but r_M (1) increases to 14% or (2) falls to 11%. The slope of the SML does not remain constant. How would these changes affect r_{UTI}?

2-9 Portfolio Beta

Your retirement fund consists of a $5,000 investment in each of 15 different common stocks. The portfolio's beta is 1.20. Suppose you sell one of the stocks with a beta of 0.8 for $5,000 and use the proceeds to buy another stock whose beta is 1.6. Calculate your portfolio's new beta.

2-10 Portfolio Required Return

Suppose you manage a $4 million fund that consists of four stocks with the following investments:

Stock	Investment	Beta
A	$ 400,000	1.50
B	600,000	−0.50
C	1,000,000	1.25
D	2,000,000	0.75

If the market's required rate of return is 14% and the risk-free rate is 6%, what is the fund's required rate of return?

Challenging Problems 11–14

2-11 Portfolio Beta

You have a $2 million portfolio consisting of a $100,000 investment in each of 20 different stocks. The portfolio has a beta of 1.1. You are considering selling $100,000 worth of one stock with a beta of 0.9 and using the proceeds to purchase another stock with a beta of 1.4. What will the portfolio's new beta be after these transactions?

2-12 Required Rate of Return

Stock R has a beta of 1.5, Stock S has a beta of 0.75, the expected rate of return on an average stock is 13%, and the risk-free rate is 7%. By how much does the required return on the riskier stock exceed that on the less risky stock?

2-13 Historical Realized Rates of Return

You are considering an investment in either individual stocks or a portfolio of stocks. The two stocks you are researching, Stock A and Stock B, have the following historical returns:

Year	$\bar{r}_A$	$\bar{r}_B$
2011	−20.00%	−5.00%
2012	42.00	15.00
2013	20.00	−13.00
2014	−8.00	50.00
2015	25.00	12.00

a. Calculate the average rate of return for each stock during the 5-year period.
b. Suppose you had held a portfolio consisting of 50% of Stock A and 50% of Stock B. What would have been the realized rate of return on the portfolio in each year? What would have been the average return on the portfolio during this period?
c. Calculate the standard deviation of returns for each stock and for the portfolio.
d. Suppose you are a risk-averse investor. Assuming Stocks A and B are your only choices, would you prefer to hold Stock A, Stock B, or the portfolio? Why?

2-14 Historical Returns: Expected and Required Rates of Return

You have observed the following returns over time:

Year	Stock X	Stock Y	Market
2011	14%	13%	12%
2012	19	7	10
2013	−16	−5	−12
2014	3	1	1
2015	20	11	15

Assume that the risk-free rate is 6% and the market risk premium is 5%.

a. What are the betas of Stocks X and Y?
b. What are the required rates of return on Stocks X and Y?
c. What is the required rate of return on a portfolio consisting of 80% of Stock X and 20% of Stock Y?

Spreadsheet Problem

2–15 **Evaluating Risk and Return**

Start with the partial model in the file *Ch02 P15 Build a Model.xls* on the textbook's Web site. The file contains hypothetical data for working this problem. Goodman Industries' and Landry Incorporated's stock prices and dividends, along with the Market Index, are shown below. Stock prices are reported for December 31 of each year, and dividends reflect those paid during the year. The market data are adjusted to include dividends.

	Goodman Industries		**Landry Incorporated**		**Market Index**
Year	**Stock Price**	**Dividend**	**Stock Price**	**Dividend**	**Includes Dividends**
2015	$25.88	$1.73	$73.13	$4.50	17,495.97
2014	22.13	1.59	78.45	4.35	13,178.55
2013	24.75	1.50	73.13	4.13	13,019.97
2012	16.13	1.43	85.88	3.75	9,651.05
2011	17.06	1.35	90.00	3.38	8,403.42
2010	11.44	1.28	83.63	3.00	7,058.96

a. Use the data given to calculate annual returns for Goodman, Landry, and the Market Index, and then calculate average annual returns for the two stocks and the index. (*Hint:* Remember, returns are calculated by subtracting the beginning price from the ending price to get the capital gain or loss, adding the dividend to the capital gain or loss, and then dividing the result by the beginning price. Assume that dividends are already included in the index. Also, you cannot calculate the rate of return for 2010 because you do not have 2009 data.)

b. Calculate the standard deviations of the returns for Goodman, Landry, and the Market Index. (*Hint:* Use the sample standard deviation formula given in the chapter, which corresponds to the **STDEV** function in *Excel.*)

c. Construct a scatter diagram graph that shows Goodman's returns on the vertical axis and the Market Index's returns on the horizontal axis. Construct a similar graph showing Landry's stock returns on the vertical axis.

d. Estimate Goodman's and Landry's betas as the slopes of regression lines with stock return on the vertical axis (y-axis) and market return on the horizontal axis (x-axis). (*Hint:* Use *Excel's* **SLOPE** function.) Are these betas consistent with your graph?

e. The risk-free rate on long-term Treasury bonds is 6.04%. Assume that the market risk premium is 5%. What is the required return on the market? Now use the SML equation to calculate the two companies' required returns.

f. If you formed a portfolio that consisted of 50% Goodman stock and 50% Landry stock, what would be its beta and its required return?

g. Suppose an investor wants to include some Goodman Industries stock in his portfolio. Stocks A, B, and C are currently in the portfolio, and their betas are 0.769, 0.985, and 1.423, respectively. Calculate the new portfolio's required return if it consists of 25% Goodman, 15% Stock A, 40% Stock B, and 20% Stock C.

MINI CASE

Assume that you recently graduated and landed a job as a financial planner with Cicero Services, an investment advisory company. Your first client recently inherited some assets and has asked you to evaluate them. The client owns a bond portfolio with $1 million invested in zero coupon Treasury bonds that mature in 10 years.[40] The client also has $2 million invested in the stock of Blandy, Inc., a company that produces meat-and-potatoes frozen dinners. Blandy's slogan is "Solid food for shaky times."

Unfortunately, Congress and the president are engaged in an acrimonious dispute over the budget and the debt ceiling. The outcome of the dispute, which will not be resolved until the end of the year, will have a big impact on interest rates one year from now. Your first task is to determine the risk of the client's bond portfolio. After consulting with the economists at your firm, you have specified five possible scenarios for the resolution of the dispute at the end of the year. For each scenario, you have estimated the probability of the scenario occurring and the impact on interest rates and bond prices if the scenario occurs. Given this information, you have calculated the rate of return on 10-year zero coupon Treasury bonds for each scenario. The probabilities and returns are shown below:

Scenario	Probability of Scenario	Return on a 10-Year Zero Coupon Treasury Bond During the Next Year
Worst Case	0.10	−14%
Poor Case	0.20	−4%
Most Likely	0.40	6%
Good Case	0.20	16%
Best Case	0.10	26%
	1.00	

You have also gathered historical returns for the past 10 years for Blandy, Gourmange Corporation (a producer of gourmet specialty foods), and the stock market.

---

40. The total par value at maturity is $1.79 million and yield to maturity is about 6%, but that information is not necessary for this mini case.

Historical Stock Returns

Year	Market	Blandy	Gourmange
1	30%	26%	47%
2	7	15	−54
3	18	−14	15
4	−22	−15	7
5	−14	2	−28
6	10	−18	40
7	26	42	17
8	−10	30	−23
9	−3	−32	−4
10	38	28	75
Average return:	8.0%	?	9.2%
Standard deviation:	20.1%	?	38.6%
Correlation with the market:	1.00	?	0.678
Beta:	1.00	?	1.30

The risk-free rate is 4% and the market risk premium is 5%.

a. What are investment returns? What is the return on an investment that costs $1,000 and is sold after 1 year for $1,060?

b. Graph the probability distribution for the bond returns based on the 5 scenarios. What might the graph of the probability distribution look like if there were an infinite number of scenarios (i.e., if it were a continuous distribution and not a discrete distribution)?

c. Use the scenario data to calculate the expected rate of return for the 10-year zero coupon Treasury bonds during the next year.

d. What is stand-alone risk? Use the scenario data to calculate the standard deviation of the bond's return for the next year.

e. Your client has decided that the risk of the bond portfolio is acceptable and wishes to leave it as it is. Now your client has asked you to use histori-

cal returns to estimate the standard deviation of Blandy's stock returns. (*Note:* Many analysts use 4 to 5 years of monthly returns to estimate risk and many use 52 weeks of weekly returns; some even use a year or less of daily returns. For the sake of simplicity, use Blandy's 10 annual returns.)

f. Your client is shocked at how much risk Blandy stock has and would like to reduce the level of risk. You suggest that the client sell 25% of the Blandy stock and create a portfolio with 75% Blandy stock and 25% in the high-risk Gourmange stock. How do you suppose the client will react to replacing some of the Blandy stock with high-risk stock? Show the client what the proposed portfolio return would have been in each of year of the sample. Then calculate the average return and standard deviation using the portfolio's annual returns. How does the risk of this two-stock portfolio compare with the risk of the individual stocks if they were held in isolation?

g. Explain correlation to your client. Calculate the estimated correlation between Blandy and Gourmange. Does this explain why the portfolio standard deviation was less than Blandy's standard deviation?

h. Suppose an investor starts with a portfolio consisting of one randomly selected stock. As more and more randomly selected stocks are added to the portfolio, what happens to the portfolio's risk?

i. (1) Should portfolio effects influence how investors think about the risk of individual stocks? (2) If you decided to hold a one-stock portfolio and consequently were exposed to more risk than diversified investors, could you expect to be compensated for all of your risk; that is, could you earn a risk premium on that part of your risk that you could have eliminated by diversifying?

j. According to the Capital Asset Pricing Model, what measures the amount of risk that an individual stock contributes to a well-diversified portfolio? Define this measurement.

k. What is the Security Market Line (SML)? How is beta related to a stock's required rate of return?

l. Calculate the correlation coefficient between Blandy and the market. Use this and the previously calculated (or given) standard deviations of Blandy and the market to estimate Blandy's beta. Does Blandy contribute more or less risk to a well-diversified portfolio than does the average stock? Use the SML to estimate Blandy's required return.

m. Show how to estimate beta using regression analysis.

n. (1) Suppose the risk-free rate goes up to 7%. What effect would higher interest rates have on the SML and on the returns required on high-risk and low-risk securities? (2) Suppose instead that investors' risk aversion increased enough to cause the market risk premium to increase to 8%. (Assume the risk-free rate remains constant.) What effect would this have on the SML and on returns of high- and low-risk securities?

o. Your client decides to invest $1.4 million in Blandy stock and $0.6 million in Gourmange stock. What are the weights for this portfolio?

What is the portfolio's beta? What is the required return for this portfolio?

p. Jordan Jones (JJ) and Casey Carter (CC) are portfolio managers at your firm. Each manages a well-diversified portfolio. Your boss has asked for your opinion regarding their performance in the past year. JJ's portfolio has a beta of 0.6 and had a return of 8.5%; CC's portfolio has a beta of 1.4 and had a return of 9.5%. Which manager had better performance? Why?

q. What does market equilibrium mean? If equilibrium does not exist, how will it be established?

r. What is the Efficient Markets Hypothesis (EMH) and what are its three forms? What evidence supports the EMH? What evidence casts doubt on the EMH?

SELECTED ADDITIONAL CASES

The following cases from CengageCompose cover many of the concepts discussed in this chapter and are available at compose.cengage.com.

Klein-Brigham Series:

Case 2, "Peachtree Securities, Inc. (A)."

Brigham-Buzzard Series:

Case 2, "Powerline Network Corporation (Risk and Return)."

CHAPTER 3

Risk and Return: Part II

In Chapter 2, we presented the key elements of risk and return analysis. There we saw that much of a stock's risk can be eliminated by diversification, so rational investors should hold portfolios of stocks rather than shares of a single stock. We also introduced the Capital Asset Pricing Model (CAPM), which links risk and required rates of return and uses a stock's beta coefficient as the relevant measure of risk. In this chapter, we extend these concepts and explain portfolio theory. We then present an in-depth treatment of the CAPM, including a more detailed look at how betas are calculated. We also describe the Arbitrage Pricing Theory model.

WEB

The textbook's Web site contains an *Excel* file that will guide you through the chapter's calculations. The file for this chapter is ***Ch03 Tool Kit.xls***, and we encourage you to open the file and follow along as you read the chapter.

Beginning-of-Chapter Questions

As you read the chapter, consider how you would answer the following questions. You *should not* necessarily be able to answer the questions before you read the chapter. Rather, you should use them to get a sense of the issues covered in the chapter. After reading the chapter, you should be able to give at least partial answers to the questions, and you should be able to give better answers after the chapter has been discussed in class. Note, too, that it is often useful, when answering conceptual questions, to use hypothetical data to illustrate your answer. We illustrate the answers with an *Excel* model that is available on the textbook's Web site. Accessing the model and working through it is a useful exercise, and it provides insights that are useful when answering the questions.

1. In general terms, what is the **Capital Asset Pricing Model (CAPM)**? What assumptions were made when it was derived?
2. Define the terms **covariance** and **correlation coefficient**. How are they related to one another, and how do they affect the required rate of return on a stock? Would correlation affect its required

rate of return if a stock were held (say, by the company's founder) in a one-asset portfolio?
3. What is an **efficient portfolio**? What is the **Capital Market Line (CML)**, how is it related to efficient portfolios, and how does it interface with an investor's indifference curve to determine the investor's optimal portfolio? Is it possible that two rational investors could agree as to the specifications of the Capital Market Line, but one would hold a portfolio heavily weighted with Treasury securities while the other held only risky stocks bought on margin?
4. What is the **Security Market Line (SML)**? What information is developed in the Capital Market Line analysis and then carried over and used to help specify the SML? For practical applications as opposed to theoretical considerations, which is more relevant, the CML or the SML?
5. What is the difference between a **historical beta**, an **adjusted beta**, and a **fundamental beta**? Does it matter which beta is used, and if so, which is best?

6. Has the validity of the CAPM been confirmed through empirical tests?

7. What is the difference between a **diversifiable risk** and a **nondiversifiable risk**? Should stock portfolio managers try to eliminate both types of risk?

8. If a publicly traded company has a large number of undiversified investors, along with some who are well diversified, can the undiversified investors earn a rate of return high enough to compensate them for the risk they bear? Does this affect the company's cost of capital?

INTRINSIC VALUE, RISK, AND RETURN

In Chapter 1, we told you that managers should strive to make their firms more valuable and that the value of a firm is determined by the size, timing, and risk of its free cash flows (FCF). In Chapter 2, we discussed risk, which affects WACC and value. Now we provide additional insights into how to manage a portfolio's risk and measure a firm's risk.

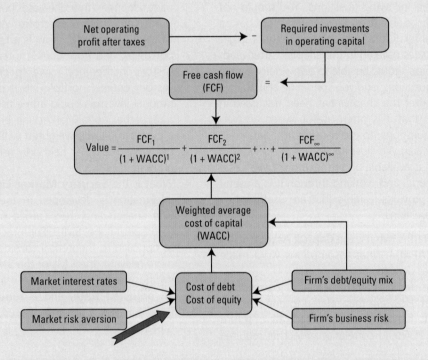

3-1 **Efficient Portfolios**

Recall from Chapter 2 the important role in portfolio risk that is played by the correlation between assets. One important use of portfolio risk concepts is to select **efficient portfolios**, defined as those portfolios that provide the highest expected return for any degree of risk—or the lowest degree of risk for any expected return. We begin with the two-asset case and then extend it to the general case of N assets.

3-1a **The Two-Asset Case**

Consider two assets, A and B. Suppose we have estimated the expected returns ($\hat{r}_A$ and $\hat{r}_B$), the standard deviations (σ_A and σ_B) of returns, and the correlation coefficient (ρ_{AB}) for returns.[1] The expected return and standard deviation (SD) for a portfolio containing these two assets are:

$$\hat{r}_p = w_A\hat{r}_A + (1 - w_A)\hat{r}_B \qquad \text{(3–1)}$$

and

$$\text{Portfolio SD} = \sigma_p = \sqrt{w_A^2\sigma_A^2 + (1 - w_A)^2\sigma_B^2 + 2w_A(1 - w_A)\rho_{AB}\sigma_A\sigma_B} \qquad \text{(3–2)}$$

Here w_A is the fraction of the portfolio invested in Security A, so $(1 - w_A)$ is the fraction invested in Security B.

To illustrate, suppose we can allocate our funds between A and B in any proportion. Suppose Security A has an expected rate of return of $\hat{r}_A = 5\%$ and a standard deviation of returns of $\sigma_A = 4\%$, while $\hat{r}_B = 8\%$ and $\sigma_B = 10\%$. Our first task is to determine the set of *attainable* portfolios and then, from this attainable set, to select the *efficient* subset.

To construct the attainable set, we need data on the degree of correlation between the two securities' expected returns, ρ_{AB}. Let us work with three different assumed degrees of correlation—namely, $\rho_{AB} = +1.0$, $\rho_{AB} = 0$, and $\rho_{AB} = -1.0$—and use them to develop the portfolios' expected returns, $\hat{r}_p$, and standard deviations, σ_p. (Of course, only one correlation can exist; our example simply shows three alternative situations that could occur.)

To calculate $\hat{r}_p$, we use Equation 3-1: Substitute the given values for $\hat{r}_A$ and $\hat{r}_B$, and then calculate $\hat{r}_p$ for different values of w_A. For example, if $w_A = 0.75$, then $\hat{r}_p = 5.75\%$:

$$\hat{r}_p = w_A\hat{r}_A + (1 - w_A)\hat{r}_B$$
$$= 0.75(5\%) + 0.25(8\%) = 5.75\%$$

---

1. See Chapter 2 for definitions using historical data to estimate the expected return, standard deviation, covariance, and correlation.

FIGURE 3-1 $\hat{r}_p$ and σ_p under Various Assumptions

	A	B	C	D	E	F
					σ_p	
	Proportion of	Proportion of				
144	Portfolio in	Portfolio in				
145	Security A	Security A		Case I	Case II	Case III
146	(Value of w_A)	(Value of $1 - w_A$)	$\hat{r}_p$	$\rho_{AB} = +1.0$	$\rho_{AB} = 0.0$	$\rho_{AB} = -1.0$
147						
148	1.00	0.00	5.00%	4.0%	4.0%	4.0%
149	0.75	0.25	5.75%	5.5%	3.9%	0.5%
150	0.50	0.50	6.50%	7.0%	5.4%	3.0%
151	0.25	0.75	7.25%	8.5%	7.6%	6.5%
152	0.00	1.00	8.00%	10.0%	10.0%	10.0%

See **Ch03 Tool Kit.xls** on the textbook's Web site for all calculations.

Other values of $\hat{r}_p$ are found similarly and are shown in the third column of Figure 3-1. Next, we use Equation 3-2 to find σ_p. Substitute the given values for σ_A, σ_B, and ρ_{AB}, and then calculate σ_p for different values of w_A. For example, if $\rho_{AB} = 0$ and $w_A = 0.75$, then $\sigma_p = 3.9\%$:

$$\sigma_p = \sqrt{w_A^2 \sigma_A^2 + (1 - w_A)^2 \sigma_B^2 + 2w_A(1 - w_A)\rho_{AB}\sigma_A\sigma_B}$$
$$= \sqrt{(0.75^2)(0.04^2) + (1 - 0.75)^2(0.10^2) + 2(0.75)(1 - 0.75)(0)(0.04)(0.10)}$$
$$= \sqrt{0.0009 + 0.000625 + 0} = \sqrt{0.001525} = 0.039 = 3.9\%$$

Figure 3-1 gives $\hat{r}_p$ and σ_p values for $w_A = 1.00, 0.75, 0.50, 0.25,$ and 0.00, and Figure 3-2 plots $\hat{r}_p$, σ_p, and the attainable set of portfolios for each correlation. In both the table and the graphs, note the following points:

1. The three graphs across the top row of Figure 3-2 designate Case I, where the two assets are perfectly positively correlated; that is, $\rho_{AB} = +1.0$. The three graphs in the middle row are for the case of zero correlation, and the three in the bottom row are for perfect negative correlation.

2. We rarely encounter $\rho_{AB} = -1.0, 0.0,$ or $+1.0$. Generally, ρ_{AB} is in the range of $+0.5$ to $+0.7$ for most stocks. Case II (zero correlation) produces graphs that, pictorially, most closely resemble real-world examples.

3. The left column of graphs shows how the *expected portfolio returns* vary with different combinations of A and B. We see that these graphs are identical in each of the three cases: The portfolio return, $\hat{r}_p$, is a linear function of w_A, and it does not depend on the correlation coefficients. This is also seen from the $\hat{r}_p$ column in Figure 3-1.

4. The middle column of graphs shows how risk is affected by the portfolio mix. Starting from the top, we see that portfolio risk, σ_p, increases linearly in Case I, where $\rho_{AB} = +1.0$; it is nonlinear in Case II; and Case III shows that risk can be completely diversified away if $\rho_{AB} = -1.0$. Thus, σ_p, unlike $\hat{r}_p$, *does* depend on correlation.

5. Note that in both Cases II and III, but not in Case I, someone holding only Stock A could sell some A and buy some B, thus increasing expected return and lowering risk as well.

6. The right column of graphs shows the attainable, or feasible, set of portfolios constructed with different mixes of Securities A and B. Unlike the other

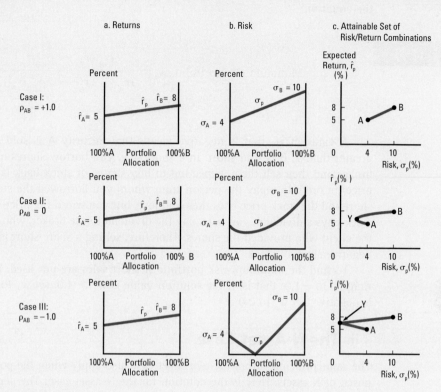

Source: *From Financial Management: Theory & Practice,* 2013, by Brigham and Ehrhardt. © Cengage Learning.

columns, which plotted return and risk versus the portfolio's composition, each of these three graphs was plotted from pairs of $\hat{r}_p$ and σ_p, as shown in Figure 3-1. For example, Point A in the upper-right graph is the point $\hat{r}_p = 5\%$, $\sigma_p = 4\%$ from the Case I data. All other points on the curves were plotted similarly. With only two securities in the portfolio, the attainable set is a curve or line, and we can achieve each risk/return combination on the relevant curve by some allocation of our investment funds between Securities A and B.

7. Are all combinations on the attainable set equally good? The answer is "no." Only that part of the attainable set from Y to B in Cases II and III is defined as *efficient.* The part from A to Y is inefficient because, for any degree of risk on the line segment AY, a higher return can be found on segment YB. Thus, no rational investor would hold a portfolio that lies on segment AY. In Case I, however, the entire feasible set is efficient—no combination of the securities can be ruled out.

From these examples we see that in one extreme case ($\rho = -1.0$), risk can be completely eliminated, while in the other extreme case ($\rho = +1.0$), diversification does no good whatsoever. In between these extremes, combining two stocks into a portfolio reduces but does not eliminate the risk inherent in the individual stocks. If we differentiate Equation 3-2 with respect to w_A, set the derivative equal to zero, and then solve for w_A, we obtain the fraction of the portfolio that should be invested in Security A if we wish to form the least-risky portfolio. Here is the equation:

(3–3)

$$\text{Minimum risk portfolio: } w_A = \frac{\sigma_B(\sigma_B - \rho_{AB}\sigma_A)}{\sigma_A^2 + \sigma_B^2 - 2\rho_{AB}\sigma_A\sigma_B}$$

A value of w_A that is negative means that Security A is sold short; if w_A is greater than 1, B is sold short. In a short sale, you borrow shares of stock from a broker and then sell them, expecting to buy shares of stock back later (at a lower price) in order to repay the person from whom you borrowed the stock. If you sell short and the stock price rises then you lose, but you win if the price declines. If the stock pays a dividend, you must pay the dividend to the broker, who passes it on to the client who provided the shares. Therefore, selling a share short is like owning a negative share of stock.

To find the minimum risk portfolio if short sales are not used, limit w_A to the range 0 to $+1.0$; that is, if the solution value is $w_A > 1.0$, set w_A to 1.0, and if w_A is negative, set w_A to 0.0.

3-1b The N-Asset Case

The same principles from the two-asset case also apply when the portfolio is composed of N assets. Here is the notation for the N-asset case: The percentage of the investment in asset i (the portfolio weight) is w_i, the expected return for asset i is $\hat{r}_i$, the standard deviation of asset i is σ_i, and the correlation between asset i and asset j is ρ_{ij}. The expected return for a portfolio with N assets is then:

(3–4)

$$\hat{r}_p = \sum_{i=1}^{N} w_i\hat{r}_i$$

And the variance of the portfolio is:

(3–5)

$$\sigma_p^2 = \sum_{i=1}^{N}\sum_{j=1}^{N} w_i w_j \sigma_i \sigma_j \rho_{ij}$$

For the case in which $i = j$, the correlation is $\rho_{ij} = \rho_{ii} = 1$. Notice also that when $i = j$, the product $\sigma_i\sigma_j = \sigma_i\sigma_i = \sigma_i^2$.

One way to apply Equation 3-5 is to set up a table with a row and column for each asset. Give the rows and columns labels showing the assets' weights and standard deviations. Then fill in each cell in the table by multiplying the values in the row and column headings by the correlation between the assets, as shown below:

	$w_1\sigma_1$ (1)	$w_2\sigma_2$ (2)	$w_3\sigma_3$ (3)
$w_1\sigma_1$ (1)	$w_1\sigma_1 w_1\sigma_1\rho_{11} = w_1^2\sigma_1^2$	$w_1\sigma_1 w_2\sigma_2\rho_{12}$	$w_1\sigma_1 w_3\sigma_3\rho_{13}$
$w_2\sigma_2$ (2)	$w_2\sigma_2 w_1\sigma_1\rho_{21}$	$w_2\sigma_2 w_2\sigma_2\rho_{22} = w_2^2\sigma_2^2$	$w_2\sigma_2 w_3\sigma_3\rho_{23}$
$w_3\sigma_3$ (3)	$w_3\sigma_3 w_1\sigma_1\rho_{31}$	$w_3\sigma_3 w_2\sigma_2\rho_{32}$	$w_3\sigma_3 w_3\sigma_3\rho_{33} = w_3^2\sigma_3^2$

The portfolio variance is the sum of the nine cells. For the diagonal, we have substituted the values for the case in which i = j. Notice that some of the cells have identical values. For example, the cell for Row 1 and Column 2 has the same value as the cell for Column 1 and Row 2. This suggests an alternative formula:

$$\sigma_p^2 = \sum_{i=1}^{N} w_i^2\sigma_i^2 + \sum_{i=1}^{N}\sum_{\substack{j=1 \\ j\neq i}}^{N} w_i\sigma_i w_j\sigma_j\rho_{ij}$$

(3–5a)

The main thing to remember when calculating portfolio standard deviations is simply this: Do not leave out any terms. Using a table like the one above can help.

What does the term "attainable set" mean?

Within the attainable set, which portfolios are "efficient"?

Stock A has an expected return of 10% and a standard deviation of 35%. Stock B has an expected return of 15% and a standard deviation of 45%. The correlation coefficient between Stocks A and B is 0.3. What are the expected return and the standard deviation of a portfolio invested 60% in Stock A and 40% in Stock B? **(12.0%; 31.5%)**

SELF TEST

3-2 Choosing the Optimal Portfolio

With only two assets, the feasible set of portfolios is a line or curve, as shown in the third column of graphs in Figure 3-2. However, by increasing the number of assets, we obtain an area, such as the shaded region in Figure 3-3. Points A, H, G, and E represent single securities (or portfolios containing only one security). All the other points in the shaded area and its boundaries, which comprise the feasible set, represent portfolios of two or more securities. Each point in this area represents a particular portfolio with a risk of σ_p and an expected return of $\hat{r}_p$. For example, Point X represents one such portfolio's risk and expected return, as do each of Points B, C, and D.

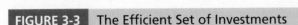

FIGURE 3-3   The Efficient Set of Investments

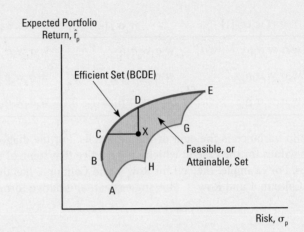

Source: From *Financial Management: Theory & Practice*, 2013, by Brigham and Ehrhardt.
© Cengage Learning.

Given the full set of potential portfolios that could be constructed from the available assets, which portfolio should actually be held? This choice involves two separate decisions: (1) determining the efficient set of portfolios and (2) choosing from the efficient set the single portfolio that is best for the specific investor.

3-2a **The Efficient Frontier**

In Figure 3-3, the boundary line BCDE defines the efficient set of portfolios, which is also called the **efficient frontier**.[2] Portfolios to the left of the efficient set are not possible because they lie outside the attainable set. Portfolios to the right of the boundary line (interior portfolios) are inefficient because some other portfolio would provide either a higher return for the same degree of risk or a lower risk for the same rate of return. For example, Portfolio X is *dominated* in this sense by all portfolios on the curve CD.

3-2b **Risk–Return Indifference Curves**

Given the efficient set of portfolios, which specific portfolio should an investor choose? To determine the optimal portfolio for a particular investor, we must know the investor's attitude toward risk as reflected in his or her risk–return trade-off function, or **indifference curve**.

An investor's risk–return trade-off function is based on the standard economic concepts of utility theory and indifference curves, which are illustrated in

---

2. A computational procedure for determining the efficient set of portfolios was developed by Harry Markowitz and first reported in his article "Portfolio Selection," *Journal of Finance*, March 1952, pp. 77–91. In this article, Markowitz developed the basic concepts of portfolio theory, and he later won the Nobel Prize in economics for his work.

FIGURE 3-4 | **Risk–Return Indifference Curves**

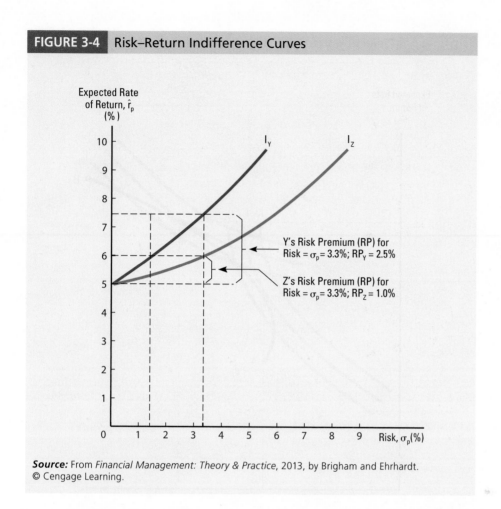

Source: From *Financial Management: Theory & Practice*, 2013, by Brigham and Ehrhardt. © Cengage Learning.

Figure 3-4. The curves labeled I_Y and I_Z represent the indifference curves of two individuals, Ms. Y and Mr. Z. Ms. Y's curve indicates indifference between the riskless 5% portfolio, a portfolio with an expected return of 6% but a risk of $\sigma_p = 1.4\%$, and so on. Mr. Z's curve indicates indifference between a riskless 5% return, an expected 6% return with risk of $\sigma_p = 3.3\%$, and so on.

Note that Ms. Y requires a higher expected rate of return as compensation for any given amount of risk; thus, Ms. Y is said to be more **risk averse** than Mr. Z. Her higher risk aversion causes Ms. Y to require a higher **risk premium**—defined here as the difference between the 5% riskless return and the expected return required to compensate for any specific amount of risk—than Mr. Z requires. Thus, Ms. Y requires a risk premium (RP_Y) of 2.5% to compensate for a risk of $\sigma_p = 3.3\%$, whereas Mr. Z's risk premium for this degree of risk is only $RP_Z = 1.0\%$. *As a generalization, the steeper the slope of an investor's indifference curve, the more risk averse the investor.* Thus, Ms. Y is more risk averse than Mr. Z.

Each individual has a "map" of indifference curves; the indifference maps for Ms. Y and Mr. Z are shown in Figure 3-5. The higher curves denote a greater level of satisfaction (or utility). Thus, I_{Z2} is better than I_{Z1} because, for any level of risk, Mr. Z has a higher expected return and hence greater utility. An infinite number of

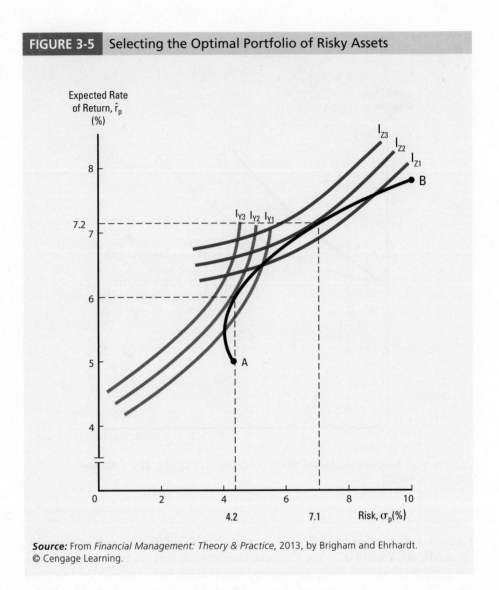

FIGURE 3-5   Selecting the Optimal Portfolio of Risky Assets

Source: From *Financial Management: Theory & Practice*, 2013, by Brigham and Ehrhardt. © Cengage Learning.

indifference curves could be drawn in the map for each individual, and each individual has a unique map.

3-2c The Optimal Portfolio for an Investor

Figure 3-5 also shows the feasible set of portfolios for the two-asset case, under the assumption that $\rho_{AB} = 0$, as it was developed in Figure 3-2. The optimal portfolio for each investor is found at the tangency point between the efficient set of portfolios and one of the investor's indifference curves. This tangency point marks the highest level of satisfaction the investor can attain. Ms. Y, who is more risk averse than Mr. Z, chooses a portfolio with a lower expected return (about 6%) but a risk of only $\sigma_p = 4.2\%$. Mr. Z picks a portfolio that provides an expected return of about 7.2% but has a risk of about $\sigma_p = 7.1\%$. Ms. Y's portfolio is more heavily weighted with the less risky security, while Mr. Z's portfolio contains a larger proportion of the more risky security.[3]

What is the efficient frontier?

What are indifference curves?

Conceptually, how does an investor choose his or her optimal portfolio?

3-3 The Basic Assumptions of the Capital Asset Pricing Model

The **Capital Asset Pricing Model (CAPM)**, which was introduced in Chapter 2, specifies the relationship between risk and required rates of return on assets when they are held in well-diversified portfolios. The assumptions underlying the CAPM's development are summarized in the following list.[4]

1. All investors focus on a single holding period, and they seek to maximize the expected utility of their terminal wealth by choosing among alternative portfolios on the basis of each portfolio's expected return and standard deviation.
2. All investors can borrow or lend an unlimited amount at a given risk-free rate of interest, r_{RF}, and there are no restrictions on short sales of any asset.
3. All investors have identical estimates of the expected returns, variances, and covariances among all assets (that is, investors have homogeneous expectations).
4. All assets are perfectly divisible and perfectly liquid (that is, marketable at the going price).
5. There are no transaction costs.
6. There are no taxes.
7. All investors are price takers (that is, all investors assume that their own buying and selling activity will not affect stock prices).
8. The quantities of all assets are given and fixed.

Theoretical extensions in the literature have relaxed some of these assumptions, and, in general, these extensions have led to conclusions that are reasonably consistent with the basic theory. However, the validity of any model can be established only through empirical tests, which we discuss later in the chapter.

---

3. Ms. Y's portfolio would contain 67% of Security A and 33% of Security B, whereas Mr. Z's portfolio would consist of 27% of Security A and 73% of Security B. These percentages can be determined with Equation 3-1 by simply seeing what percentage of the two securities is consistent with $\hat{r}_p = 6.0\%$ and 7.2%. For example, $w_A(5\%) + (1 - w_A)(8\%) = 7.2\%$, and solving for w_A, we obtain $w_A = 0.27$ and $(1 - w_A) = 0.73$.
4. The CAPM was originated by William F. Sharpe in his article "Capital Asset Prices: A Theory of Market Equilibrium under Conditions of Risk," *Journal of Finance*, September 1964, pp. 425–442. Professor Sharpe won the Nobel Prize in economics for his work on capital asset pricing. The assumptions inherent in Sharpe's model were spelled out by Michael C. Jensen in "Capital Markets: Theory and Evidence," *Bell Journal of Economics and Management Science*, Autumn 1972, pp. 357–398.

What are the key assumptions of the CAPM?

3-4 The Capital Market Line and the Security Market Line

Figure 3-5 showed the set of portfolio opportunities for the two-asset case, and it illustrated how indifference curves can be used to select the optimal portfolio from the feasible set. In Figure 3-6, we show a similar diagram for the many-asset case, but here we also include a risk-free asset with a return r_{RF}. The riskless asset by definition has zero risk, $\sigma = 0\%$, so it is plotted on the vertical axis.

The figure shows both the feasible set of portfolios of risky assets (the shaded area) and a set of indifference curves (I_1, I_2, I_3) for a particular investor. Point N, where indifference curve I_1 is tangent to the efficient set, represents a possible portfolio choice; it is the point on the efficient set of risky portfolios where the investor obtains the highest possible return for a given amount of risk and the smallest degree of risk for a given expected return.

However, the investor can do better than Portfolio N by reaching a higher indifference curve. In addition to the feasible set of risky portfolios, we now have a

---

FIGURE 3-6   Investor Equilibrium: Combining the Risk-Free Asset with the Market Portfolio

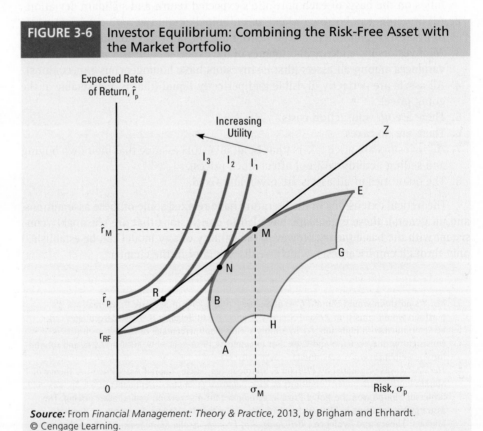

Source: From *Financial Management: Theory & Practice*, 2013, by Brigham and Ehrhardt. © Cengage Learning.

risk-free asset that provides a riskless return, r_{RF}. Given the risk-free asset, investors can create new portfolios that combine the risk-free asset with a portfolio of risky assets. This enables them to achieve any combination of risk and return on the straight line connecting r_{RF} with M, the point of tangency between that straight line and the efficient frontier of risky asset portfolios.[5] Some portfolios on the line r_{RF}MZ will be preferred to most risky portfolios on the efficient frontier BNME, so the points on the line r_{RF}MZ now represent the best attainable combinations of risk and return.

Given the new opportunities along line r_{RF}MZ, our investor will move from Point N to Point R, which is on her highest attainable risk–return indifference curve. Note that any point on the old efficient frontier BNME (except the point of tangency M) is dominated by some point along the line r_{RF}MZ. In general, because investors can purchase some of the risk-free security and some of the risky portfolio (M), it will be possible to move to a point such as R. In addition, if the investor can borrow as well as lend (lending is equivalent to buying risk-free debt securities) at the riskless rate r_{RF}, then it is possible to move out on the line segment MZ; an investor would do so if his or her indifference curve were tangent to r_{RF}MZ, to the right of Point M.[6]

---

5. The risk–return combinations between a risk-free asset and a risky asset (a single stock or a portfolio of stocks) will always be linear. To see this, consider the following equations, which were developed earlier, for return ($\hat{r}_p$) and risk (σ_p) for any combination w_{RF} and $(1 - w_{RF})$:

$$\hat{r}_p = w_{RF}r_{RF} + (1 - w_{RF})\hat{r}_M \qquad \text{(3–1a)}$$

and

$$\sigma_p = \sqrt{w_{RF}^2\sigma_{RF}^2 + (1 - w_{RF})^2\sigma_M^2 + 2w_{RF}(1 - w_{RF})\rho_{RF,M}\sigma_{RF}\sigma_M} \qquad \text{(3–2a)}$$

Equation 3-1a is linear. As for Equation 3-2a, we know that r_{RF} is the risk-free asset, so $\sigma_{RF} = 0$; hence, σ_{RF}^2 is also zero. Using this information, we can simplify Equation 3-2a as follows:

$$\sigma_p = \sqrt{(1 - w_{RF})^2\sigma_M^2} = (1 - w_{RF})\sigma_M \qquad \text{(3–2b)}$$

Thus, σ_p is also linear when a riskless asset is combined with a portfolio of risky assets.

If expected returns, as measured by $\hat{r}_p$, and risk, as measured by σ_p, are both linear functions of w_{RF}, then the relationship between $\hat{r}_p$ and σ_p, when graphed as in Figure 3-6, must also be linear. For example, if 100% of the portfolio is invested in r_{RF} with a return of 8%, then the portfolio return will be 8% and σ_p will be 0. If 100% is invested in M with $r_M = 12\%$ and $\sigma_M = 10\%$, then $\sigma_p = 1.0(10\%) = 10\%$ and $\hat{r}_p = 0(8\%) + 1.0(12\%) = 12\%$. If 50% of the portfolio is invested in M and 50% in the risk-free asset, then $\sigma_p = 0.5(10\%) = 5\%$ and $\hat{r}_p = 0.5(8\%) + 0.5(12\%) = 10\%$. Plotting these points will reveal the linear relationship given as r_{RF}MZ in Figure 3-6.

6. An investor who is highly risk averse will have a steep indifference curve and will end up holding only the riskless asset or perhaps a portfolio at a point such as R (i.e., holding some of the risky market portfolio and some of the riskless asset). An investor who is only slightly averse to risk will have a relatively flat indifference curve, which will cause her to move out beyond M toward Z, borrowing to do so. This investor might buy stocks on margin, which means borrowing and using the stocks as collateral. If individuals' borrowing rates are higher than r_{RF}, then the line r_{RF}MZ will tilt down (i.e., be less steep) beyond M. This condition would invalidate the basic CAPM, or at least require it to be modified. Therefore, the assumption of being able to borrow or lend at the same rate is crucial to CAPM theory.

All investors should hold portfolios lying on the line $r_{RF}MZ$ under the conditions assumed in the CAPM. This implies that they should hold portfolios that are combinations of the risk-free security and the risky Portfolio M. Thus, the addition of the risk-free asset totally changes the efficient set: The efficient set now lies along line $r_{RF}MZ$ rather than along the curve BNME. Note also that if the capital market is to be in equilibrium, then M must be a portfolio that contains every risky asset in exact proportion to that asset's fraction of the total market value of all assets. In other words, if Security i is X percent of the total market value of all securities, then X percent of the market portfolio M must consist of Security i. (That is, M is the market value–weighted portfolio of *all* risky assets in the economy.) Thus, all investors should hold portfolios that lie on the line $r_{RF}MZ$, with the particular location of a given individual's portfolio being determined by the point at which his indifference curve is tangent to the line.

The line $r_{RF}MZ$ in Figure 3-6 is called the **Capital Market Line (CML)**. It has an intercept of r_{RF} and a slope of $(\hat{r}_M - r_{RF})/\sigma_M$.[7] The equation for the Capital Market Line may be expressed as follows:

(3–6)

$$\text{CML: } \hat{r}_p = r_{RF} + \left(\frac{\hat{r}_M - r_{RF}}{\sigma_M}\right)\sigma_p$$

The expected rate of return *on an efficient portfolio* is equal to the riskless rate plus a risk premium that is equal to $(\hat{r}_M - r_{RF})/\sigma_M$ multiplied by the portfolio's standard deviation, σ_p. Thus, the CML specifies a linear relationship between an efficient portfolio's expected return and risk, where the slope of the CML is equal to the expected return on the market portfolio of risky stocks $(\hat{r}_M)$ *minus* the risk-free rate (r_{RF}), which is called the **market risk premium**, all divided by the standard deviation of returns on the market portfolio, σ_M:

$$\text{Slope of the CML} = (\hat{r}_M - r_{RF})/\sigma_M$$

For example, suppose $r_{RF} = 10\%$, $\hat{r}_M = 15\%$, and $\sigma_M = 15\%$. In this case, the slope of the CML would be $(15\% - 10\%)/15\% = 0.33$, and if a particular efficient portfolio had $\sigma_p = 10\%$, then its $\hat{r}_p$ would be:

$$\hat{r}_p = 10\% + 0.33(10\%) = 13.3\%$$

A (riskier) portfolio with $\sigma_p = 20\%$ would have $\hat{r}_p = 10\% + 0.33(20\%) = 16.6\%$.

The CML is graphed in Figure 3-7. It is a straight line with an intercept at r_{RF} and a slope equal to the market risk premium $(r_M - r_{RF})$ divided by σ_M. The slope of the CML reflects the aggregate attitude of investors toward risk.

Recall that an efficient portfolio is well diversified; hence all of its unsystematic risk has been eliminated and its only remaining risk is market risk. Therefore, unlike individual stocks, the risk of an efficient portfolio is measured by its standard deviation, σ_p. The CML equation specifies the relationship between risk and return

---

7. Recall that the slope of any line is measured as $\Delta Y/\Delta X$, or the change in height associated with a given change in horizontal distance. Here, r_{RF} is at 0 on the horizontal axis, so $\Delta X = \sigma_M - 0 = \sigma_M$. The vertical axis difference associated with a change from r_{RF} to $\hat{r}_M$ is $\hat{r}_M - r_{RF}$. Therefore, slope $= \Delta Y/\Delta X = (\hat{r}_M - r_{RF})/\sigma_M$.

FIGURE 3-7	The Capital Market Line (CML)

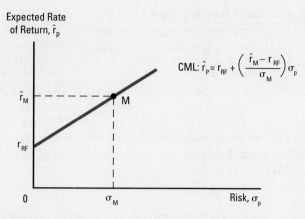

$$\text{CML: } \hat{r}_p = r_{RF} + \left(\frac{\hat{r}_M - r_{RF}}{\sigma_M} \right) \sigma_p$$

Source: From *Financial Management: Theory & Practice*, 2013, by Brigham and Ehrhardt. © Cengage Learning.

Note: We did not draw it in, but you can visualize the shaded space shown in Figure 3-6 in this graph and the CML as the line formed by connecting r_{RF} with the tangent to the shaded space.

for such efficient portfolios—that is, for portfolios that lie on the CML—and in the CML equation and graph risk is measured by portfolio standard deviation.

The CML specifies the relationship between risk and return for an efficient portfolio, but investors and managers are more concerned about the relationship between risk and return for *individual assets*. To develop the risk–return relationship for individual securities, note in Figure 3-6 that all investors are assumed to hold Portfolio M, so M must be the market portfolio (i.e., the one that contains all stocks). Note also that M is an *efficient* portfolio. Thus, the CML defines the relationship between the market portfolio's expected return and its standard deviation. Equations 3-4 and 3-5 show the formulas for the expected return and standard deviation for a multi-asset portfolio, including the market portfolio. It is possible to take the equations for the expected return and standard deviation of a multi-asset portfolio and show that the required return for each individual Stock i must conform to the following equation in order for the CML to hold for the market portfolio:[8]

$$r_i = r_{RF} + \frac{(r_M - r_{RF})}{\sigma_M} \left(\frac{\text{Cov}(r_i, r_M)}{\sigma_M} \right)$$

$$= r_{RF} + (r_M - r_{RF}) \left(\frac{\text{Cov}(r_i, r_M)}{\sigma_M^2} \right)$$

(3–7)

8. For consistency with most investment textbooks, we let $\text{Cov}(r_i, r_M)$ denote the covariance between the returns of assets i and M. Using the notation in Chapter 2, we would have denoted the covariance as $\text{COV}_{i,M}$.

The CAPM defines Company i's beta coefficient, b_i, as follows:

(3–8)

$$b_i = \frac{\text{Covariance between Stock i and the market}}{\text{Variance of market returns}} = \frac{\text{Cov}(r_i, r_M)}{\sigma_M^2}$$

$$= \frac{\rho_{iM}\sigma_i\sigma_M}{\sigma_M^2} = \rho_{iM}\left(\frac{\sigma_i}{\sigma_M}\right)$$

Recall that the risk premium for the market, RP_M, is $r_M - r_{RF}$. Using this definition and substituting Equation 3-8 into Equation 3-7 gives the **Security Market Line (SML):**

(3–9)

$$\text{SML: } r_i = r_{RF} + (r_M - r_{RF})b_i$$

$$= r_{RF} + (RP_M)b_i$$

The SML tells us that an individual stock's required return is equal to the risk-free rate plus a premium for bearing risk. The premium for risk is equal to the risk premium for the market, RP_M, multiplied by the risk of the individual stock, as measured by its beta coefficient. The beta coefficient measures the amount of risk that the stock contributes to the market portfolio.

Unlike the CML for a well-diversified portfolio, the SML tells us that the standard deviation (σ_i) of an individual stock should not be used to measure its risk, because some of the risk as reflected by σ_i can be eliminated by diversification. Beta reflects risk after taking diversification benefits into account, and so beta, rather than σ_i, is used to measure individual stocks' risks to investors. Be sure to keep in mind the distinction between the SML and the CML and why that distinction exists.

> **SELF TEST**
>
> Draw a graph showing the feasible set of risky assets, the efficient frontier, the risk-free asset, and the CML.
>
> Write out the equation for the CML and explain its meaning.
>
> Write out the equation for the SML and explain its meaning.
>
> What is the difference between the CML and the SML?
>
> The standard deviation of stock returns of Park Corporation is 60%. The standard deviation of the market return is 20%. If the correlation between Park and the market is 0.40, what is Park's beta? **(1.2)**

SKILL OR LUCK?

That's the question *The Wall Street Journal*'s Investment Dartboard Contest sought to answer by comparing the actual investment results of professional analysts against amateurs and dart throwers. Here's how the contest worked. First, *The Wall Street Journal (WSJ)* picked four professional analysts, and each of those pros formed a portfolio by picking four stocks. Second, amateurs could enter the contest by e-mailing their pick of a single stock to the *WSJ*, which then picked four amateurs at random and combined their choices to make a four-stock portfolio. Third, a group of *WSJ* editors formed a portfolio by throwing four darts at the stock tables. At the beginning of each contest, the *WSJ* announced the six resulting portfolios, and at the end of 6 months, the paper announced the results. The top two pros were invited back for the next contest.

Since 1990 the paper has completed 142 of these contests. The pros beat the darts 87 times and lost 55 times. The pros also beat the Dow Jones Industrial Average (DJIA) in 54% of the contests. The pros had an average 6-month portfolio return of 10.2%, much higher than either the DJIA 6-month average of 5.6% or the darts' return of only 3.5%. The amateurs lost an average of 4% versus a same-period gain of 7.2% for the pros.

Do these results mean that skill is more important than luck when it comes to investing in stocks? Not necessarily, according to Burton Malkiel, an economics professor at Princeton and the author of the widely read book *A Random Walk Down Wall Street*. Because the dart-selected portfolios consist of randomly chosen stocks, they should have average risk. However, the pros consistently picked high-risk stocks. Because there was a bull market during most of the contests, one would expect high-risk stocks to outperform the average stock. According to Malkiel, the pros' performance could be due as much to a rising market as to superior analytical skills. The *WSJ* discontinued that contest in 2002, so we can't know for sure whether Malkiel was right or wrong.

Until early 2013, *WSJ* ran a contest pitting six amateurs against six darts. In Contest No. 49, the readers averaged a 11% gain versus the darts' 17% gain (the Dow Jones Industrial Average was up 5.4%). Overall, readers won 19 contests and the darts won 30. *WSJ*'s more recent contest also pits investors against darts but allows frequent trading. To play, go to **www.marketwatch.com/game/dart**.

3-5 Calculating Beta Coefficients

Equation 3-8 defines beta, but recall from Chapter 2 that this equation for beta is also the formula for the slope coefficient in a regression of the stock return against the market return. Therefore, beta can be calculated by plotting the historical returns of a stock on the y-axis of a graph versus the historical returns of the market portfolio on the x-axis and then fitting the regression line. In his 1964 article that set forth the CAPM, Sharpe called this regression line the **characteristic line**. Thus, a stock's beta is the slope of its characteristic line. In Chapter 2, we used this approach to calculate the beta for General Electric. In this chapter, we perform a more detailed analysis of the calculation of beta for General Electric, and we also perform a similar analysis for a portfolio of stocks, Fidelity's Magellan Fund.

3-5a Calculating the Beta Coefficient for a Single Stock: General Electric

See *Ch03 Tool Kit.xls* on the textbook's Web site.

See *Ch03 ToolKit.xls* on the textbook's Web site for all calculations.

Table 3-1 shows a summary of the data used in this analysis; the full data set is in the file *Ch03 Tool Kit.xls* and has monthly returns for the 4-year period August 2009–July 2013. Table 3-1 shows the market returns (defined as the percentage price change of the S&P 500), the stock returns for GE, and the returns on the Magellan Fund (which is a well-diversified portfolio). The table also shows the risk-free rate, defined as the rate on a short-term (3-month) U.S. Treasury bill, which we will use later in this analysis.

As Table 3-1 shows, GE had an average annual return of 21.7% during this 4-year period, while the market had an average annual return of 14.4%. As we noted before, it is usually unreasonable to think that the future expected return for a stock will equal its average historical return over a relatively short period, such as 4 years. However, we might well expect past volatility to be a reasonable estimate of future volatility, at least during the next couple of years. Observe that the standard deviation for GE's return during this period was 27.0%, versus 14.1% for the market. Thus, the market's volatility is less than that of GE. This is what we would expect, because the market is a well-diversified portfolio and thus much of its risk has been diversified away. The correlation between GE's stock returns and the market returns is about 0.76, which is a little higher than the correlation for a typical stock.

Figure 3-8 shows a plot of GE's returns against the market's returns. We used the *Excel* regression analysis feature to estimate the regression. Table 3-2 reports some of the regression results for GE. Its estimated beta, which is the slope coefficient, is about 1.45.

As with all regression results, GM's estimated beta of 1.45 is just an estimate, not necessarily the true value of beta. Table 3-2 also shows the t-statistic and the probability that the true beta is zero. For GE, this probability is approximately equal to zero. This means that there is virtually a zero chance that the true beta is equal to zero. Because this probability is less than 5%, statisticians would say that the slope coefficient, beta, is "statistically significant." The output of the regression analysis also gives us the 95% confidence interval for the estimate of beta. For GE, the results tell us that we can be 95% confident that the true beta is between 1.08 and 1.82. This is an extremely wide range, but it is typical for most individual stocks. Therefore, the regression estimate for the beta of any single company is highly uncertain.

TABLE 3-1	Summary of Data for Calculating Beta (August 2009–July 2013)			
	r_M, **Market Return (S&P 500 Index)**	r_i, **GE Return**	r_p, **Fidelity Magellan Fund Return**	r_{RF}, **Risk-Free Rate (Monthly Return on 3-Month T-Bill)**
Average return (annual)	14.4%	21.7%	12.8%	1.1%
Standard deviation (annual)	14.1%	27.0%	16.9%	0.2%
Correlation with market return, ρ		0.76	0.97	0.14

FIGURE 3-8   Calculating a Beta Coefficient for General Electric

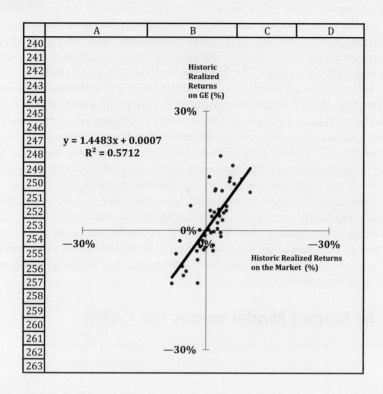

Microsoft Excel® is a registered trademark of Microsoft Corporation. © 2014 Microsoft.

TABLE 3-2   Regression Results for Calculating Beta

	Regression Coefficient	t-Statistic	Probability of t-Statistic	Lower 95% Confidence Interval	Upper 95% Confidence Interval
Panel A: General Electric (Market model)					
Intercept	0.0007	0.09	0.93	−0.01	0.02
Slope (beta)	1.4483	7.83	0.00	1.08	1.82
Panel B: Magellan Fund (Market model)					
Intercept	−0.0033	−1.82	0.08	−0.01	0.00
Slope (beta)	1.1624	26.76	0.00	1.07	1.25
Panel C: General Electric (CAPM: Excess returns)					
Intercept	0.0011	0.14	0.89	−0.01	0.02
Slope (beta)	1.4479	7.81	0.00	1.07	1.82

Note: The market model uses actual historical returns; the CAPM model uses returns in excess of the risk-free rate.

Observe also that the points in Figure 3-8 are not clustered very tightly around the regression line. Sometimes GE does much better than the market; other times it does much worse. The R^2 value shown in the chart measures the degree of dispersion about the regression line. Statistically speaking, it measures the proportion of variation that is explained by the regression equation. An R^2 of 1.0 indicates that all points lie exactly on the line; in this case, all of the variation in the y variable is explained by the x variable. The R^2 for GE is about 0.57, which is higher than the typical individual stocks, which usually is around 0.3. This indicates that about 57% of the variation in GE's returns is explained by the overall market return.

Finally, note that the intercept shown in the regression equation displayed on the chart is about 0.0007. Because the regression equation is based on monthly data, this means that GE had a 0.07% average annual return that was not explained by the CAPM model. However, the regression results in Table 3-2 also show that the probability of the t-statistic is much greater than 5%, meaning that the "true" intercept might be zero. Therefore, most statisticians would say that this intercept is not statistically significant—the returns of GE are so volatile that we cannot be sure the true intercept is not equal to zero. Translating statistician-speak into plain English, this means that the part of GE's average monthly return that is *not* explained by the CAPM could, in fact, be zero. Thus, the CAPM might very well explain all of GE's average monthly returns.

3-5b The Market Model versus the CAPM

When we estimated beta, we used the following regression equation:

(3-10)

$$\bar{r}_{i,t} = a_i + b_i \bar{r}_{M,t} + e_{i,t}$$

where

$\bar{r}_{i,t}$ = Historical (realized) rate of return on Stock i in period t

$\bar{r}_{M,t}$ = Historical (realized) rate of return on the market in period t

a_i = Vertical axis intercept term for Stock i

b_i = Slope, or beta coefficient, for Stock i

$e_{i,t}$ = Random error, reflecting the difference between the actual return on Stock i in a given period and the return as predicted by the regression line

Equation 3-10 is called the **market model**, because it regresses the stock's return against the market's return. However, the SML of the CAPM for realized returns is a little different from Equation 3-10:

(3-11)

$$\text{SML for realized returns: } \bar{r}_{i,t} = \bar{r}_{RF,t} + b_i(\bar{r}_{M,t} - \bar{r}_{RF,t}) + e_{i,t}$$

where $\bar{r}_{RF,t}$ is the historical (realized) risk-free rate in period t.

In order to use the CAPM to estimate beta, we must rewrite Equation 3-11 as a regression equation by adding an intercept, a_i. The result is:

$$(\bar{r}_i - \bar{r}_{RF,t}) = a_i + b_i(\bar{r}_{M,t} - \bar{r}_{RF,t}) + e_{i,t}$$

(3–12)

Therefore, to be theoretically correct when estimating beta, we should use the stock's return in excess of the risk-free rate as the y variable and use the market's return in excess of the risk-free rate as the x variable. We did this for GE using the data in Table 3-1, and the results were reported in Panel C of Table 3-2. Note that there are no appreciable differences between the results in Panel A, the market model, and in Panel C, the CAPM model. This typically is the case, so we will use the market model in the rest of the book.

3-5c Calculating the Beta Coefficient for a Portfolio: The Magellan Fund

Let's calculate beta for Fidelity's Magellan Fund, which is a well-diversified portfolio. Figure 3-9 shows the plot of Magellan's monthly returns versus the market's

FIGURE 3-9   Calculating a Beta Coefficient for Fidelity's Magellan Fund

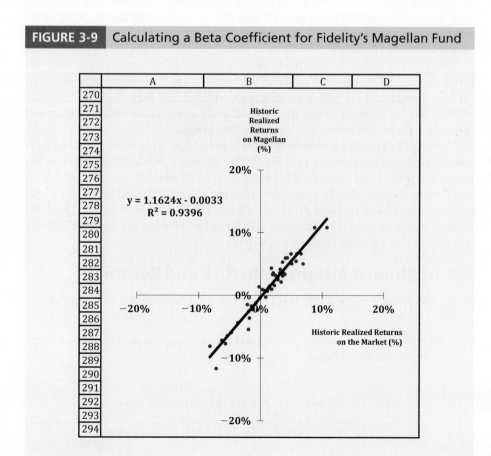

monthly returns. Note the differences between this chart and the one for GE shown in Figure 3-8. The points for Magellan are tightly clustered around the regression line, indicating that the vast majority of Magellan's variability is explained by the stock market. The R^2 of over 0.93 confirms this visual conclusion. We can also see from Table 3-1 that the Magellan Fund has a standard deviation of 16.9%, which is higher than the 14.1% standard deviation of the market.

As Table 3-2 shows, the estimated beta is 1.16 and the 95% confidence interval is from 1.07 to 1.25, which is much tighter than the one for GE. The intercept is virtually zero, and the probability of the intercept's t-statistic is greater than 5%. Therefore, the intercept is statistically insignificant, indicating that the CAPM explains the average monthly return of the Magellan Fund very well.

3-5d Performance Measures

WEB

See **Ch03 Tool Kit.xls** on the textbook's Web site for all calculations for these measures.

Mutual fund managers are often evaluated by their risk-adjusted performance. The three most widely used measures are *Jensen's alpha, Sharpe's reward-to-variability ratio,* and *Treynor's reward-to-volatility ratio.* **Jensen's alpha**, which is the intercept in a CAPM regression of excess returns, is −3.80% per year for Magellan, which seems to indicate that the Magellan Fund had slightly inferior performance (*see Ch03 Tool Kit.xls* for all calculations). However, statistically, this intercept was not significantly different from zero. Its t-statistic is −1.75, which is so low a value that it could happen about 9% of the time by chance even if the intercept were truly zero. When this probability is greater than 5%, as is the case for Magellan, then most statisticians would be reluctant to conclude that Magellan's *estimated* excess return of −3.80% is not *actually* equal to zero.

Sharpe's reward-to-variability ratio is defined as the portfolio's average return (in excess of the risk-free rate) divided by its standard deviation. Sharpe's ratio for Magellan during the past 4 years is 0.69, which is less than the S&P's measure of 0.95; both of these are larger than several years ago because both Magellan and the market performed rather well over this time period.

Treynor's reward-to-volatility ratio is defined as the portfolio's average return (in excess of the risk-free rate) divided by its beta. For Magellan, this is 10.1%, which is a little worse than the S&P 500's ratio of 13.4%. All in all, the Magellan Fund seems to have slightly underperformed the market, but perhaps not by a statistically significant amount. Although it's not clear whether Magellan "beat the market," it did dramatically reduce the risk faced by investors as compared with the risk inherent in a randomly chosen individual stock.

3-5e Additional Insights into Risk and Return

The CAPM provides some additional insights into the relationship between risk and return.

1. The relationship between a stock's total risk, market risk, and diversifiable risk can be expressed as follows:

(3–13)
$$\text{Total risk} = \text{Variance} = \text{Market risk} + \text{Diversifiable risk}$$
$$\sigma_i^2 = b_i^2 \sigma_M^2 + \sigma_{e_i}^2$$

Here, σ_i^2 is the variance (or total risk) of Stock i, σ_M^2 is the variance of the market, b_i is Stock i's beta coefficient, and $\sigma_{e_i}^2$ is the variance of Stock i's regression error term.

2. If all the points in Figure 3-8 had plotted exactly on the regression line, then the variance of the error term, $\sigma_{e_i}^2$, would have been zero, and all of the stock's total risk would have been market risk. On the other hand, if the points were widely scattered about the regression line, then much of the stock's total risk would be diversifiable. The shares of a large, well-diversified mutual fund will plot very close to the regression line.

3. Beta is a measure of relative market risk, but the *actual* market risk of Stock i is $b_i^2\sigma_M^2$. Market risk can also be expressed in standard deviation form, $b_i\sigma_M$. The higher a stock's beta, the higher its market risk. If beta were zero, the stock would have no market risk, whereas if beta were 1.0, then the stock would be exactly as risky as the market—assuming the stock is held in a diversified portfolio—and the stock's market risk would be σ_M.

3-5f Advanced Issues in Calculating Beta

Betas are generally estimated from the stock's characteristic line by running a linear regression between past returns on the stock in question and past returns on some market index. We define betas developed in this manner as **historical betas**. However, in most situations, it is the *future* beta that is needed. This has led to the development of two different types of betas: (1) adjusted betas and (2) fundamental betas.

Adjusted betas grew largely out of the work of Marshall E. Blume, who showed that true betas tend to move toward 1.0 over time.[9] Therefore, we can begin with a firm's pure historical statistical beta, make an adjustment for the expected future movement toward 1.0, and produce an adjusted beta that will, on average, be a better predictor of the future beta than the unadjusted historical beta would be. *Value Line* publishes betas based on approximately this formula:

$$\text{Adjusted beta} = 0.67(\text{Historical beta}) + 0.35(1.0)$$

Consider American Camping Corporation, a retailer of supplies for outdoor activities. ACC's historical beta is 1.2. Therefore, its adjusted beta is

$$\text{Adjusted beta} = 0.67(1.2) + 0.35(1.0) = 1.15$$

Other researchers have extended the adjustment process to include such fundamental risk variables as financial leverage, sales volatility, and the like. The end product here is a **fundamental beta**, which is constantly adjusted to reflect changes in a firm's operations and capital structure. In contrast, with historical betas (including adjusted ones), such changes might not be reflected until several years after the company's "true" beta had changed.

Adjusted betas obviously are heavily dependent on unadjusted historical betas, and so are fundamental betas as they are actually calculated. Therefore, the plain old historical beta, calculated as the slope of the characteristic line,

---

9. See Marshall E. Blume, "Betas and Their Regression Tendencies," *Journal of Finance*, June 1975, pp. 785–796; and Marshall E. Blume, "On the Assessment of Risk," *Journal of Finance*, March 1971, pp. 1–10.

is important even if one goes on to develop a more exotic version. With this in mind, it should be noted that several different sets of data can be used to calculate historical betas, and the different data sets produce different results. Here are some of the details:

1. Betas can be based on historical periods of different lengths. For example, data for the past 1 year, 3 years, 5 years, or even 10 years may be used. Many people who calculate betas today use 5 years of data; but this choice is arbitrary, and different lengths of time usually alter significantly the calculated beta for a given company.

2. Returns may be calculated over holding periods of different lengths—a day, a week, a month, a quarter, a year, and so on. For example, if data on NYSE stocks is analyzed over a 5-year period, then we might obtain 52(5) = 260 weekly returns on each stock and on the market index. We could also use 12(5) = 60 monthly returns, or 1(5) = 5 annual returns. The set of returns on each stock, however large the set turns out to be, would then be regressed on the corresponding market returns to obtain the stock's beta. In statistical analysis, it is generally better to have more rather than fewer observations, because using more observations generally leads to greater statistical confidence. This suggests the use of weekly returns and, say, 5 years of data for a sample size of 260, or even daily returns for a still larger sample size. However, the shorter the holding period, the more likely the data are to exhibit random "noise." Also, the greater the number of years of data, the more likely the company's basic risk position has changed. Thus, the choice of both the number of years of data and the length of the holding period for calculating rates of return involves trade-offs between the preference for many observations and a desire to rely on more recent and thus more relevant data.

3. The value used to represent "the market" is also an important consideration, because the index that is used can have a significant effect on the calculated beta. Many analysts today use the New York Stock Exchange Composite Index (based on more than 2,000 common stocks, weighted by the value of each company), but others use the S&P 500 Index. In theory, the broader the index, the better the beta. Indeed, the theoretical index should include returns on all stocks, bonds, leases, private businesses, real estate, and even "human capital." As a practical matter, however, we cannot get accurate returns data on most other types of assets, so measurement problems largely restrict us to stock indexes.

Where does this leave financial managers regarding the proper beta? Some managers calculate their own betas using whichever procedure seems most appropriate under the circumstances. Others use betas calculated by organizations such as Yahoo! Finance or *Value Line,* perhaps using one service or perhaps averaging the betas of several services. The choice is a matter of judgment and data availability, for there is no "right" beta. Generally, though, the betas derived from different sources will, for a given company, be reasonably close together. If they are not, then our confidence in using the CAPM will be diminished.

Explain the meaning and significance of a stock's beta coefficient. Illustrate your explanation by drawing, on one graph, the characteristic lines for stocks with low, average, and high risk. (*Hint:* Let your three characteristic lines intersect at $\bar{r}_i = \bar{r}_M = 6\%$, the assumed risk-free rate.)

What is a typical R^2 for the characteristic line of an individual stock? For a portfolio?

What is the market model? How is it different from the SML for the CAPM?

How are total risk, market risk, and diversifiable risk related?

3-6 Empirical Tests of the CAPM

Does the CAPM's SML produce reasonable estimates for a stock's required return? The literature dealing with empirical tests of the CAPM is quite extensive, so we can give here only a synopsis of some of the key work.

3-6a Tests of the Stability of Beta Coefficients

According to the CAPM, the beta used to estimate a stock's market risk should reflect investors' estimates of the stock's *future* variability in relation to that of the market. Obviously, we do not know now how a stock will be related to the market in the future, nor do we know how the average investor views this expected future relative variability. All we have are data on past variability, which we can use to plot the characteristic line and to calculate *historical betas*. If historical betas have been stable over time, then there would seem to be reason for investors to use past betas as estimators of future variability. For example, if Stock i's beta had been stable in the past, then its historical b_i would probably be a good proxy for its *ex ante*, or expected, beta. By "stable" we mean that if b_i were calculated with data from the period of, say, 2011 to 2015, then this same beta (approximately) should be found from 2016 to 2020.

Robert Levy, Marshall Blume, and others have studied in depth the question of beta stability.[10] Levy calculated betas for individual securities, as well as for portfolios of securities, over a range of time intervals. He concluded: (1) that the betas of individual stocks are unstable and hence past betas for *individual securities* are *not* good estimators of their future risk, but (2) that betas of portfolios of ten or more randomly selected stocks are reasonably stable and hence past *portfolio* betas are good estimators of future portfolio volatility. In effect, the errors in individual securities' betas tend to offset one another in a portfolio. The work of Blume and others supports this position.

---

10. See Robert A. Levy, "On the Short-Term Stationarity of Beta Coefficients," *Financial Analysts Journal*, November/December 1971, pp. 55–62; and Marshall E. Blume, "Betas and Their Regression Tendencies," *Journal of Finance*, June 1975, pp. 785–796.

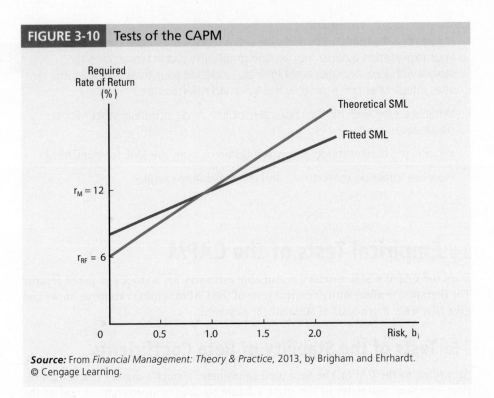

FIGURE 3-10   Tests of the CAPM

Source: From *Financial Management: Theory & Practice*, 2013, by Brigham and Ehrhardt. © Cengage Learning.

The conclusion that follows from the beta stability studies is that the CAPM is a better concept for structuring investment portfolios than it is for estimating the required return for individual securities.[11]

3-6b Tests of the CAPM Based on the Slope of the SML

The CAPM states that a linear relationship exists between a security's required rate of return and its beta. Moreover, when the SML is graphed, the vertical axis intercept should be r_{RF}, and the required rate of return for a stock (or portfolio) with b = 1.0 should be r_M, the required rate of return on the market. Various researchers have attempted to test the validity of the CAPM by calculating betas and realized rates of return, plotting these values in graphs such as that in Figure 3-10, and then observing whether or not: (1) the intercept is equal to r_{RF}, (2) the plot is linear, and (3) the line passes through the point b = 1.0, r_M. Monthly or daily historical rates of return are generally used for stocks, and both 30-day Treasury bill rates and long-term Treasury bond rates have been used to estimate the value of r_{RF}. Also, most of the studies actually analyzed portfolios rather than individual securities because security betas are so unstable.

Before discussing the results of the tests, it is critical to recognize that although the CAPM is an *ex ante*, or forward-looking, model, the data used to test it are

---

11. For more on beta stability, see Robert W. Kolb and Ricardo J. Rodriguez, "The Regression Tendencies of Betas: A Reappraisal," *The Financial Review*, May 1989, pp. 319–334. Also see Robert Kolb, "Is the Distribution of Betas Stationary?" *Journal of Financial Research*, Winter 1990, pp. 279–283.

entirely historical. This presents a problem, for there is no reason to believe that *realized* rates of return over past holding periods are necessarily equal to the rates of return to *expect* in the future. Also, historical betas may or may not reflect expected future risk. This lack of *ex ante* data makes it extremely difficult to test the CAPM, but for what it's worth, here is a summary of the key results.

1. The evidence generally shows a significant positive relationship between realized returns and beta. However, the slope of the relationship is usually less than that predicted by the CAPM.
2. The relationship between risk and return appears to be linear. Empirical studies give no evidence of significant curvature in the risk–return relationship.
3. Tests that attempt to assess the relative importance of market and company-specific risk do not yield conclusive results. The CAPM implies that company-specific risk should not be relevant, yet both kinds of risk appear to be positively related to security returns; that is, higher returns seem to be required to compensate for diversifiable as well as market risk. However, it may be that the observed relationships reflect statistical problems rather than the true nature of capital markets.
4. Richard Roll has questioned whether it is even conceptually possible to test the CAPM.[12] Roll showed that the linear relationship that prior researchers had observed in graphs like Figure 3-10 resulted from the mathematical properties of the models being tested; therefore, a finding of linearity would prove nothing whatsoever about the CAPM's validity. Roll's work did not disprove the CAPM, but it did demonstrate the virtual impossibility of proving that investors behave in accordance with its predictions.
5. If the CAPM were completely valid, then it should apply to all financial assets, including bonds. In fact, when bonds are introduced into the analysis, they do *not* plot on the SML. This is worrisome, to say the least.

3-6c **Current Status of the CAPM**

The CAPM is extremely appealing on an intellectual level: It is logical and rational, and once someone works through and understands the theory, his or her reaction is usually to accept it without question. However, doubts begin to arise when one thinks about the assumptions upon which the model is based, and these doubts are as much reinforced as reduced by the empirical tests. Our own views on the CAPM's current status are as follows.

1. The CAPM framework, with its focus on market as opposed to stand-alone risk, is clearly a useful way to think about the risk of assets. Thus, as a conceptual model, the CAPM is fundamentally important.
2. When applied in practice, the CAPM appears to provide neat, precise answers to important questions about risk and required rates of return. However, the answers are less clear than they seem. The simple truth is that we do not know precisely how to measure any of the inputs required to implement the CAPM. These inputs should all be *ex ante,* yet only *ex post* data are available. Furthermore, historical data on $\bar{r}_M$, r_{RF}, and betas vary greatly depending on the time

---

12. See Richard Roll, "A Critique of the Asset Pricing Theory's Tests," *Journal of Financial Economics,* March 1977, pp. 129–176.

period studied and the methods used to estimate them. Thus, even though the CAPM appears to be precise, estimates of r_i found through its use are subject to potentially large errors.[13]

3. Because the CAPM is logical in the sense that it represents the way risk-averse people ought to behave, the model is a useful conceptual tool.

4. It is appropriate to think about many financial problems in a CAPM framework. However, it is also important to recognize the limitations of the CAPM when using it in practice.

SELF TEST

What are the two major types of tests that have been performed to test the validity of the CAPM? **(Beta stability; slope of the SML)** Explain their results.

Are there any reasons to question the validity of the CAPM? Explain.

3-7 **Arbitrage Pricing Theory**

The CAPM is a single-factor model. That is, it specifies risk as a function of only one factor, the security's beta coefficient. Perhaps the risk–return relationship is more complex, with a stock's required return a function of more than one factor. For example, what if investors, because personal tax rates on capital gains are lower than those on dividends, value capital gains more highly than dividends? Then, if two stocks had the same market risk, the stock paying the higher dividend would have the higher required rate of return. In that case, required returns would be a function of two factors, market risk and dividend policy.

Further, what if many factors are required to specify the equilibrium risk–return relationship rather than just one or two? Stephen Ross has proposed an approach called the **Arbitrage Pricing Theory (APT)**.[14] The APT can include any number of risk factors, so the required return could be a function of two, three, four, or more factors. We should note at the outset that the APT is based on complex mathematical and statistical theory that goes far beyond the scope of this text. Also, although the APT model is widely discussed in academic literature, practical usage to date has been limited. However, such use may increase, so students should at least have an intuitive idea of what the APT is all about.

The SML states that each stock's required return is equal to the risk-free rate plus the product of the market risk premium times the stock's beta coefficient. If stocks are in equilibrium, then the required return will be equal to the expected return:

$$\hat{r}_i = r_i = r_{RF} + (r_M - r_{RF})b_i$$

---

13. For an article supporting a positive link between market risk and expected return, see Felicia Marston and Robert S. Harris, "Risk and Return: A Revisit Using Expected Returns," *The Financial Review*, February *1993*, pp. 117–137.

14. See Stephen A. Ross, "The Arbitrage Theory of Capital Asset Pricing," *Journal of Economic Theory*, December 1976, pp. 341–360.

The historical realized return, $\bar{r}_i$, which will generally be different from the expected return, can be expressed as follows:[15]

$$\bar{r}_i = \hat{r}_i + (\bar{r}_M - \hat{r}_M)b_i + e_i \qquad \textbf{(3–14)}$$

Thus, the realized return, $\bar{r}_i$, will be equal to the expected return, $\hat{r}_i$, plus a positive or negative increment, $(\bar{r}_M - \hat{r}_M)b_i$, which depends jointly on the stock's beta and on whether the market did better or worse than was expected, plus a random error term, e_i.

The market's realized return, $\bar{r}_M$, is in turn determined by a number of factors, including domestic economic activity as measured by gross domestic product (GDP), the strength of the world economy, the level of inflation, changes in tax laws, and so forth. Further, different groups of stocks are affected in different ways by these fundamental factors. So, rather than specifying a stock's return as a function of one factor (return on the market), one could specify required and realized returns on individual stocks as a function of various fundamental economic factors. If this were done, we would transform Equation 3-14 into 3-15:

$$\bar{r}_i = \hat{r}_i + (\bar{F}_1 - \hat{F}_1)b_{i1} + \cdots + (\bar{F}_j - \hat{F}_j)b_{ij} + e_i \qquad \textbf{(3–15)}$$

Here,

$\bar{r}_i$ = Realized rate of return on Stock i

$\hat{r}_i$ = Expected rate of return on Stock i

$\bar{F}_j$ = Realized value of economic Factor j

$\hat{F}_j$ = Expected value of Factor j

b_{ij} = Sensitivity of Stock i to economic Factor j

e_i = Effect of unique events on the realized return of Stock i

Equation 3-15 shows that the realized return on any stock is the sum of: (1) the stock's expected return; (2) increases or decreases that depend on unexpected changes in fundamental economic factors, multiplied by the sensitivity of the stock to these changes; and (3) a random term that reflects changes unique to the firm.

Certain stocks or groups of stocks are most sensitive to Factor 1, others to Factor 2, and so forth, and every portfolio's returns depend on what happened to the different fundamental factors. Theoretically, one could construct a portfolio such that: (1) the portfolio was riskless and (2) the net investment in it was zero (some stocks would be sold short, with the proceeds from the short sales being used to

---

15. To avoid cluttering the notation, we have dropped the subscript t to denote a particular time period.

buy the stocks held long). Such a zero-investment portfolio must have a zero expected return, or else arbitrage operations would occur and cause the prices of the underlying assets to change until the portfolio's expected return became zero. Using complex mathematics and a set of assumptions that include the possibility of short sales, the APT equivalent of the CAPM's Security Market Line can be developed from Equation 3-15 as follows:[16]

(3–16)

$$r_i = r_{RF} + (r_1 - r_{RF})b_{i1} + \cdots + (r_j - r_{RF})b_{ij}$$

Here, r_j is the required rate of return on a portfolio that is sensitive only to economic Factor j (b_{pj} = 1.0) and has zero sensitivity to all other factors. Thus, for example, ($r_2 - r_{RF}$) is the risk premium on a portfolio with b_{p2} = 1.0 and all other b_{pj} = 0.0. Note that Equation 3-16 is identical in form to the SML, but it permits a stock's required return to be a function of multiple factors.

To illustrate the APT concept, assume that all stocks' returns depend on only three risk factors: inflation, industrial production, and the aggregate degree of risk aversion (the cost of bearing risk, which we assume is reflected in the spread between the yields on Treasury and low-grade bonds). Further, suppose that: (1) the risk-free rate is 8.0%; (2) the required rate of return is 13% on a portfolio with unit sensitivity (b = 1.0) to inflation and zero sensitivities (b = 0.0) to industrial production and degree of risk aversion; (3) the required return is 10% on a portfolio with unit sensitivity to industrial production and zero sensitivities to inflation and degree of risk aversion; and (4) the required return is 6% on a portfolio (the risk-bearing portfolio) with unit sensitivity to the degree of risk aversion and zero sensitivities to inflation and industrial production. Finally, assume that Stock i has factor sensitivities (betas) of 0.9 to the inflation portfolio, 1.2 to the industrial production portfolio, and −0.7 to the risk-bearing portfolio. Stock i's required rate of return, according to the APT, would be 16.3%:

$$r_i = 8\% + (13\% - 8\%)0.9 + (10\% - 8\%)1.2 + (6\% - 8\%)(-0.7)$$
$$= 16.3\%$$

Note that if the required rate of return on the market were 15.0% and if Stock i had a CAPM beta of 1.1, then its required rate of return, according to the SML, would be 15.7%:

$$r_i = 8\% + (15\% - 8\%)1.1 = 15.7\%$$

The primary theoretical advantage of the APT is that it permits several economic factors to influence individual stock returns, whereas the CAPM assumes that the effect of all factors, except those that are unique to the firm, can be captured in a single measure: the variability of the stock with respect to the market portfolio. Also, the APT requires fewer assumptions than the CAPM and hence is more general. Finally, the APT does not assume that all investors hold the market portfolio, a CAPM requirement that is clearly not met in practice.

---

16. See Thomas E. Copeland, J. Fred Weston, and Kuldeep Shastri, *Financial Theory and Corporate Policy*, 4th ed. (Reading, MA: Addison-Wesley, 2005).

However, the APT faces several major hurdles in implementation, the most severe of which is that the theory does not actually identify the relevant factors. The APT does not tell us what factors influence returns, nor does it indicate how many factors should appear in the model. There is some empirical evidence that only three or four factors are relevant—perhaps inflation, industrial production, the spread between low- and high-grade bonds, and the term structure of interest rates—but no one knows for sure.

The APT's proponents argue that it is not necessary to identify the relevant factors. Researchers use a statistical procedure called **factor analysis** to develop the APT parameters. Basically, they start with hundreds, or even thousands, of stocks and then create several different portfolios, where the returns on each portfolio are not highly correlated with returns on the other portfolios. Thus, each portfolio is apparently more heavily influenced by one of the unknown factors than are the other portfolios. Then, the required rate of return on each portfolio becomes the estimate for that unknown economic factor, shown as r_j in Equation 3-16. The sensitivities of each individual stock's returns to the returns on that portfolio are the factor sensitivities (betas). Unfortunately, the results of factor analysis are not easily interpreted; hence it does not provide significant insights into the underlying economic determinants of risk.[17]

SELF TEST

What is the primary difference between the APT and the CAPM?

What are some disadvantages of the APT?

An analyst has modeled the stock of Brown Kitchen Supplies using a two-factor APT model. The risk-free rate is 5%, the required return on the first factor (r_1) is 10%, and the required return on the second factor (r_2) is 15%. If $b_{i1} = 0.5$ and $b_{i2} = 1.3$, what is Brown's required return? **(20.5%)**

---

17. For additional discussion of the APT, see Edward L. Bubnys, "Simulating and Forecasting Utility Stock Returns: Arbitrage Pricing Theory vs. Capital Asset Pricing Model," *The Financial Review*, February 1990, pp. 1–23; David H. Goldenberg and Ashok J. Robin, "The Arbitrage Pricing Theory and Cost-of-Capital Estimation: The Case of Electric Utilities," *Journal of Financial Research*, Fall 1991, pp. 181–196; and Ashok Robin and Ravi Shukla, "The Magnitude of Pricing Errors in the Arbitrage Pricing Theory," *Journal of Financial Research*, Spring 1991, pp. 65–82.

Summary

The primary goal of this chapter was to extend your knowledge of risk and return concepts. The key concepts covered are listed below.

- The **feasible set** of portfolios represents all portfolios that can be constructed from a given set of assets.
- An **efficient portfolio** is one that offers the most return for a given amount of risk or the least risk for a given amount of return.
- The **optimal portfolio** for an investor is defined by the investor's highest possible **indifference curve** that is tangent to the **efficient set** of portfolios.

- The **Capital Asset Pricing Model (CAPM)** describes the relationship between market risk and required rates of return.
- The **Capital Market Line (CML)** describes the risk–return relationship for efficient portfolios—that is, for portfolios consisting of a mix of the market portfolio and a riskless asset.
- The **Security Market Line (SML)** is an integral part of the CAPM, and it describes the risk–return relationship for individual assets. The required rate of return for any Stock i is equal to the **risk-free rate** plus the **market risk premium** multiplied by the stock's **beta coefficient**: $r_i = r_{RF} + (r_M - r_{RF})b_i$.
- Stock i's **beta coefficient, b_i**, is a measure of the stock's **market risk**. Beta measures the **variability** of returns on a security **relative to returns on the market**, which is the portfolio of all risky assets.
- The beta coefficient is measured by the slope of the stock's **characteristic line**, which is found by regressing historical returns on the stock versus historical returns on the market.
- Although the CAPM provides a convenient framework for thinking about risk and return issues, it *cannot be proven empirically* and its parameters are extremely difficult to estimate. Thus, the required rate of return for a stock as estimated by the CAPM may not be exactly equal to the true required rate of return.
- In contrast to the CAPM, the **Arbitrage Pricing Theory (APT)** hypothesizes that expected stock returns are due to more than one factor.

Questions

3-1 Define the following terms, using graphs or equations to illustrate your answers wherever feasible:
   a. Portfolio; feasible set; efficient portfolio; efficient frontier
   b. Indifference curve; optimal portfolio
   c. Capital Asset Pricing Model (CAPM); Capital Market Line (CML)
   d. Characteristic line; beta coefficient, b
   e. Arbitrage Pricing Theory (APT)

3-2 Security A has an expected rate of return of 6%, a standard deviation of returns of 30%, a correlation coefficient with the market of −0.25, and a beta coefficient of −0.5. Security B has an expected return of 11%, a standard deviation of returns of 10%, a correlation with the market of 0.75, and a beta coefficient of 0.5. Which security is more risky? Why?

Problems   Answers Appear in Appendix B

Easy Problems 1–2
3-1 Beta
The standard deviation of stock returns for Stock A is 40%. The standard deviation of the market return is 20%. If the correlation between Stock A and the market is 0.70, then what is Stock A's beta?

3-2 APT

An analyst has modeled the stock of Crisp Trucking using a two-factor APT model. The risk-free rate is 6%, the expected return on the first factor (r_1) is 12%, and the expected return on the second factor (r_2) is 8%. If $b_{i1} = 0.7$ and $b_{i2} = 0.9$, what is Crisp's required return?

Intermediate Problems 3-4

3-3 Two-Asset Portfolio

Stock A has an expected return of 12% and a standard deviation of 40%. Stock B has an expected return of 18% and a standard deviation of 60%. The correlation coefficient between Stocks A and B is 0.2. What are the expected return and standard deviation of a portfolio invested 30% in Stock A and 70% in Stock B?

3-4 SML and CML Comparison

The beta coefficient of an asset can be expressed as a function of the asset's correlation with the market as follows:

$$b_i = \frac{\rho_{iM} \sigma_i}{\sigma_M}$$

a. Substitute this expression for beta into the Security Market Line (SML), Equation 3-9. This results in an alternative form of the SML.

b. Compare your answer to part a with the Capital Market Line (CML), Equation 3-6. What similarities do you observe? What conclusions can you draw?

Challenging Problems 5-6

3-5 Characteristic Line and Security Market Line

You are given the following set of data:

	Historical Rates of Return	
Year	**NYSE**	**Stock X**
1	−26.5%	−14.0%
2	37.2	23.0
3	23.8	17.5
4	−7.2	2.0
5	6.6	8.1
6	20.5	19.4
7	30.6	18.2

a. Use a spreadsheet (or a calculator with a linear regression function) to determine Stock X's beta coefficient.

b. Determine the arithmetic average rates of return for Stock X and the NYSE over the period given. Calculate the standard deviations of returns for both Stock X and the NYSE.

c. Assume that the situation during Years 1 to 7 is expected to prevail in the future (i.e., $\hat{r}_X = \bar{r}_{X,Average}$, $\hat{r}_M = \bar{r}_{M,Average}$, and both σ_X and b_X in the future will equal their past values). Also assume that Stock X is in equilibrium—that is, it plots on the Security Market Line. What is the risk-free rate?

d. Plot the Security Market Line.

e. Suppose you hold a large, well-diversified portfolio and are considering adding to that portfolio either Stock X or another stock, Stock Y, which has the same beta as Stock X but a higher standard deviation of returns. Stocks X and Y have the same expected returns: $\hat{r}_X = \hat{r}_Y = 10.6\%$. Which stock should you choose?

3-6 Characteristic Line

You are given the following set of data:

	Historical Rates of Return	
Year	NYSE	Stock Y
1	4.0%	3.0%
2	14.3	18.2
3	19.0	9.1
4	−14.7	−6.0
5	−26.5	−15.3
6	37.2	33.1
7	23.8	6.1
8	−7.2	3.2
9	6.6	14.8
10	20.5	24.1
11	30.6	18.0
	Mean = 9.8%	9.8%
	σ = 19.6%	13.8%

a. Construct a scatter diagram showing the relationship between returns on Stock Y and the market. Use a spreadsheet or a calculator with a linear regression function to estimate beta.

b. Give a verbal interpretation of what the regression line and the beta coefficient show about Stock Y's volatility and relative risk as compared with those of other stocks.

c. Suppose the regression line were exactly as shown by your graph from part b but the scatter plot of points were more spread out. How would this affect: (1) the firm's risk if the stock is held in a one-asset portfolio, and (2) the actual risk premium on the stock if the CAPM holds exactly?

d. Suppose the regression line were downward sloping and the beta coefficient were negative. What would this imply about: (1) Stock Y's relative risk, (2) its correlation with the market, and (3) its probable risk premium?

Spreadsheet Problem

3-7 Feasible Portfolios

Start with the partial model in the file *Ch3 P07 Build a Model.xls* from the textbook's Web site. Following is information for the required returns and standard deviations of returns for A, B, and C:

Stock	r_i	σ_i
A	7.0%	33.11%
B	10.0	53.85
C	20.0	89.44

The correlation coefficients for each pair are shown below in a matrix, with each cell in the matrix giving the correlation between the stock in that row and column. For example, $\rho_{AB} = 0.1571$ is in the row for A and the column for B. Notice that the diagonal values are equal to 1 because a variable is always perfectly correlated with itself.

	A	B	C
A	1.0000	0.1571	0.1891
B	0.1571	1.0000	0.1661
C	0.1891	0.1661	1.0000

a. Suppose a portfolio has 30% invested in A, 50% in B, and 20% in C. What are the expected return and standard deviation of the portfolio?

b. The partial model lists six different combinations of portfolio weights. For each combination of weights, find the required return and standard deviation.

c. The partial model provides a scatter diagram showing the required returns and standard deviations already calculated. This provides a visual indicator of the feasible set. If you seek a return of 10.5%, then what is the smallest standard deviation that you must accept?

MINI CASE

Answer the following questions:

a. Suppose Asset A has an expected return of 10% and a standard deviation of 20%. Asset B has an expected return of 16% and a standard deviation of 40%. If the correlation between A and B is 0.35, what are the expected return and standard deviation for a portfolio consisting of 30% Asset A and 70% Asset B?

b. Plot the attainable portfolios for a correlation of 0.35. Now plot the attainable portfolios for correlations of +1.0 and −1.0.

c. Suppose a risk-free asset has an expected return of 5%. By definition, its standard deviation is zero, and its correlation with any other asset is also zero. Using only Asset A and the risk-free asset, plot the attainable portfolios.

d. Construct a plausible graph that shows risk (as measured by portfolio standard deviation) on the x-axis and expected rate of return on the y-axis. Now add an illustrative feasible (or attainable) set of portfolios and show what portion of the feasible set is efficient. What makes a particular portfolio efficient? Don't worry about specific values when constructing the graph—merely illustrate how things look with "reasonable" data.

e. Add a set of indifference curves to the graph created for part b. What do these curves represent? What is the optimal portfolio for this investor? Add a second set of indifference curves that leads to the selection of a different optimal portfolio. Why do the two investors choose different portfolios?

f. What is the Capital Asset Pricing Model (CAPM)? What are the assumptions that underlie the model?

g. Now add the risk-free asset. What impact does this have on the efficient frontier?

h. Write out the equation for the Capital Market Line (CML), and draw it on the graph. Interpret the plotted CML. Now add a set of indifference curves and illustrate how an investor's optimal portfolio is some combination of the risky portfolio and the risk-free asset. What is the composition of the risky portfolio?

i. What is a characteristic line? How is this line used to estimate a stock's beta coefficient? Write out and explain the formula that relates total risk, market risk, and diversifiable risk.

j. What are two potential tests that can be conducted to verify the CAPM? What are the results of such tests? What is Roll's critique of CAPM tests?

k. Briefly explain the difference between the CAPM and the Arbitrage Pricing Theory (APT).

SELECTED ADDITIONAL CASE

The following case from CengageCompose covers many of the concepts discussed in this chapter and is available at **http://compose.cengage.com.**

Klein-Brigham Series:

Case 2, "Peachtree Securities, Inc. (A)."

CHAPTER 4

Bond Valuation

Growing companies must acquire land, buildings, equipment, inventory, and other operating assets. The debt markets are a major source of funding for such purchases. Therefore, every manager should have a working knowledge of the types of bonds that companies and government agencies issue, the terms that are contained in bond contracts, the types of risks to which both bond investors and issuers are exposed, and procedures for determining the values of and rates of return on bonds.

Beginning-of-Chapter Questions

As you read the chapter, consider how you would answer the following questions. You *should not* necessarily be able to answer the questions before you read the chapter. Rather, you should use them to get a sense of the issues covered in the chapter. After reading the chapter, you should be able to give at least partial answers to the questions, and you should be able to give better answers after the chapter has been discussed in class. Note, too, that it is often useful, when answering conceptual questions, to use hypothetical data to illustrate your answer. We illustrate the answers with an *Excel* model that is available on the textbook's Web site. Accessing the model and working through it is a useful exercise, and it provides insights that are useful when answering the questions.

1. Define and discuss how to calculate a bond's **coupon rate, current yield, expected capital gains yield for the current year, yield to maturity (YTM)**, and **yield to call (YTC)**. What might be some representative numbers for a strong company like GE today? Are these rates fixed for the life of the bond, or do they change over time?

2. Define the terms **interest rate risk** and **reinvestment rate risk**. How are these risks affected by maturities, call provisions, and coupon rates? Why might different types of investors view these risks differently? How would they affect the yield curve? Illustrate your answers with bonds with different maturities and different coupon rates, but just discuss the effects of call provisions.

3. Would a bond be more or less desirable if you learned that it has a **sinking fund** that requires the company to redeem, say, 10% of the original issue each year beginning in 2019, either through open market purchases or by calling the redeemed bonds at par? How would it affect your answer if you learned that the bond was selling at a high premium, say, 130% of par, or at a large discount, say, 70% of par?

4. What is a **bond rating**, and how do ratings affect bonds' prices and yields? Who rates bonds, and what are some of the factors the rating agencies consider? Is it possible for a given company to have several different bonds outstanding that have different ratings? Explain.

5. Financial assets such as mortgages, credit card receivables, and auto loan receivables are often bundled up, placed in a bank trust department, and

then used as collateral for publicly traded bonds. Bond prices typically rise when interest rates decline, but bonds backed by mortgages frequently fall when rates decline. Why might this happen?

INTRINSIC VALUE AND THE COST OF DEBT

This chapter explains bond pricing and bond risk, which affect the return demanded by a firm's bondholders. A bondholder's return is a cost from the company's point of view. This cost of debt affects the firm's weighted average cost of capital (WACC), which in turn affects the company's intrinsic value. Therefore, it is important for all managers to understand the cost of debt, which we explain in this chapter.

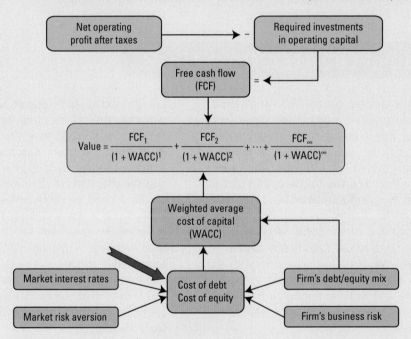

$$\text{Value} = \frac{FCF_1}{(1 + WACC)^1} + \frac{FCF_2}{(1 + WACC)^2} + \cdots + \frac{FCF_\infty}{(1 + WACC)^\infty}$$

Source: From *Financial Management: Theory & Practice*, 2013, by Brigham and Ehrhardt. © Cengage Learning.

4-1 Who Issues Bonds?

A **bond** is a long-term contract under which a borrower agrees to make payments of interest and principal, on specific dates, to the holders of the bond. For example, on January 5, 2015, MicroDrive Inc. issued $200 million of bonds. For convenience, we assume that MicroDrive sold 200,000 individual bonds for $1,000 each. Actually, it could have sold one $200 million bond, 10 bonds with a $20 million face value, or any other combination that totals to $200 million. In exchange for $200 million, MicroDrive promised to make annual interest payments and to repay the $200 million on a specified maturity date.

Investors have many choices when investing in bonds, but bonds are classified into four main types: Treasury, corporate, municipal, and foreign. Each type differs with respect to expected return and degree of risk.

Treasury bonds, sometimes referred to as *government bonds*, are issued by the U.S. federal government.[1] It is reasonable to assume that the federal government will make good on its promised payments, so these bonds have almost no default risk. However, Treasury bond prices decline when interest rates rise, so they are not free of all risks.

Federal agencies and other government-sponsored entities (GSEs) include the Tennessee Valley Authority, the Small Business Administration, Fannie Mae, Freddie Mac, and the Federal Home Loan Bank System, among others. **Agency debt** and **GSE debt** are not officially backed by the full faith and credit of the U.S. government, but investors assume that the government implicitly guarantees this debt, so these bonds carry interest rates only slightly higher than Treasury bonds. In 2008, the implicit guarantee became much more explicit as the government placed several GSEs into conservatorship, including Fannie Mae and Freddie Mac.

Corporate bonds, as the name implies, are issued by corporations. Unlike Treasury bonds, corporate bonds are exposed to default risk—if the issuing company gets into trouble, it may be unable to make the promised interest and principal payments. Different corporate bonds have different levels of default risk, depending on the issuing company's characteristics and the terms of the specific bond. Default risk is often referred to as "credit risk," and the larger the credit risk, the higher the interest rate the issuer must pay.

Municipal bonds, or "munis," are issued by state and local governments. Like corporate bonds, munis have default risk. However, munis offer one major advantage: The interest earned on most municipal bonds is exempt from federal taxes and also from state taxes if the holder is a resident of the issuing state. Consequently, municipal bonds carry interest rates that are considerably lower than those on corporate bonds with the same default risk.

Foreign bonds are issued by foreign governments or foreign corporations. Foreign corporate bonds are, of course, exposed to default risk, and so are some foreign government bonds, as became apparent in the spring of 2012 when Greece forced its bondholders into an exchange of securities that reduced the value of their holdings of Greek government debt by more than 50%. An additional risk exists if the bonds are denominated in a currency other than that of the investor's home currency. For example, if a U.S. investor purchases a corporate bond denominated in Japanese yen and if the yen subsequently falls relative to the dollar, then the investor will lose money even if the company does not default on its bonds.

The textbook's Web site contains an *Excel* file that will guide you through the chapter's calculations. The file for this chapter is ***Ch04 Tool Kit.xls***, and we encourage you to open the file and follow along as you read the chapter.

---

1. The U.S. Treasury actually issues three types of securities: bills, notes, and bonds. A bond makes an equal payment every 6 months until it matures, at which time it makes an additional lump-sum payment. If the maturity at the time of issue is less than 10 years, the security is called a note rather than a bond. A T-bill has a maturity of 52 weeks or less at the time of issue, and it makes no payments at all until it matures. Thus, T-bills are sold initially at a discount to their face, or maturity, value.

THE GLOBAL ECONOMIC CRISIS

Betting With or Against the U.S. Government: The Case of Treasury Bond Credit Default Swaps

It might be hard to believe, but there is actually a market for U.S. Treasury bond insurance. In July 2011, investors worried that Congress would not extend the debt ceiling, inducing defaults in Treasury securities. At that time a credit default swap (CDS) on a 5-year T-bond was selling for 63.5 basis points (a basis point is 1/100 of a percentage point). This means that you could pay $6.35 a year to a counterparty who would promise to insure $1,000 of T-bond principal against default. Considering that the T-bond was yielding an amount equal to about $15 a year, the insurance would eat up a lot of the annual return for an investor who owned the bond. However, most of the trading in this CDS is by speculators and hedgers who don't even own the T-bond but are simply betting for or against the financial soundness of the U.S. government.

But it does make you wonder: "If the United States fails, who will be around to pay off the CDS?"

Note: For updates on the 5-year CDS, go to **http://www.cnbc.com /id/38451750** and scroll down to US CDS 5YR.

SELF TEST

What is a bond?

What are the four main types of bonds?

Why are U.S. Treasury bonds not riskless?

To what types of risk are investors of foreign bonds exposed?

WWW

An excellent site for information on many types of bonds is the FINRA Web page, **http://cxa .marketwatch.com /finra/bondcenter /default.aspx**. The site has a great deal of information about corporates, municipals, Treasuries, and bond funds. It includes free bond searches, through which the user specifies the attributes desired in a bond and then the search returns the publicly traded bonds meeting the criteria.

4-2 Key Characteristics of Bonds

Although all bonds have some common characteristics, they do not always have identical contractual features, as described below.

4-2a Par Value

The **par value** is the stated face value of the bond; for illustrative purposes, we generally assume a par value of $1,000. In practice, some bonds have par values that are multiples of $1,000 (for example, $5,000) and some have par values of less than $1,000 (Treasury bonds can be purchased in multiples of $100). The par value generally represents the amount of money the firm borrows and promises to repay on the maturity date.

4-2b Coupon Interest Rate

MicroDrive's bonds require the company to pay a fixed number of dollars of interest every year (or, more typically, every 6 months). When this **coupon payment**, as it is called, is divided by the par value, the result is the **coupon interest rate**. For example, MicroDrive's bonds have a $1,000 par value, and they pay $90 in interest each year. The bond's coupon interest is $90, so its coupon interest rate is $90/$1,000 = 9%. The coupon payment, which is fixed at the time the bond is issued, remains in force during the life of the bond.[2] Typically, at the time a bond is issued, its coupon payment is set at a level that will enable the bond to be issued at or near its par value.

In some cases, a bond's coupon payment will vary over time. For these **floating-rate bonds**, the coupon rate is set for, say, the initial 6-month period, after which it is adjusted every 6 months based on some market rate. Some corporate issues are tied to the Treasury bond rate; other issues are tied to other rates, such as LIBOR (the London Interbank Offered Rate). Many additional provisions can be included in floating-rate issues. For example, some are convertible to fixed-rate debt, whereas others have upper and lower limits ("caps" and "floors") on how high or low the rate can go.

Floating-rate debt is popular with investors who are worried about the risk of rising interest rates, because the interest paid on such bonds increases whenever market rates rise. This stabilizes the market value of the debt, and it also provides institutional buyers, such as banks, with income that is better geared to their own obligations. Banks' deposit costs rise with interest rates, so the income on floating-rate loans they have made rises at the same time as their deposit costs rise. The savings and loan industry was almost destroyed as a result of its former practice of making fixed-rate mortgage loans but borrowing on floating-rate terms. If you earn 6% fixed but pay 10% floating (which they were), you will soon go bankrupt (which they did). Moreover, floating-rate debt appeals to corporations that want to issue long-term debt without committing themselves to paying a historically high interest rate for the entire life of the loan.

Some bonds pay no coupons at all but are offered at a substantial discount below their par values and hence provide capital appreciation rather than interest income. These securities are called **zero coupon bonds** ("zeros"). Most zero coupon bonds are Treasury bonds, although a few corporations, such as Coca-Cola, have zero coupon bonds outstanding. Some bonds are issued with a coupon rate too low for the bond to be issued at par, so the bond is issued at a price less than its par value. In general, any bond originally offered at a price significantly below its par value is called an **original issue discount (OID) bond**.

Some bonds don't pay cash coupons but pay coupons consisting of additional bonds (or a percentage of an additional bond). These are called **payment-in-kind bonds**, or just **PIK bonds**. PIK bonds are usually issued by companies with cash flow problems, which makes them risky.

Some bonds have a step-up provision: If the company's bond rating is downgraded, then it must increase the bond's coupon rate. Step-ups are more popular in

WEB

For more on zero coupon bonds, including U.S. Treasury STRIP bonds, see **Web Extension 4A** on the textbook's Web site.

---

2. At one time, bonds literally had a number of small coupons attached to them, and on each interest payment date the owner would clip off the coupon for that date and either cash it at the bank or mail it to the company's paying agent, who would then mail back a check for the interest. For example, a 30-year, semiannual bond would start with 60 coupons. Today, most new bonds are *registered*—no physical coupons are involved, and interest checks automatically are mailed to the registered owners or directly deposited in their bank accounts.

Europe than in the United States, but that is beginning to change. Note that a step-up is quite dangerous from the company's standpoint. The downgrade means that it is having trouble servicing its debt, and the step-up will exacerbate the problem. This combination has led to a number of bankruptcies.

4-2c **Maturity Date**

Bonds generally have a specified **maturity date** on which the par value must be repaid. MicroDrive bonds issued on January 5, 2015, will mature on January 5, 2030; thus, they have a 15-year maturity at the time they are issued. Most bonds have **original maturities** (the maturity at the time the bond is issued) ranging from 10 to 40 years, but any maturity is legally permissible.[3] Of course, the effective maturity of a bond declines each year after it has been issued. Thus, MicroDrive's bonds have a 15-year original maturity, but in 2016, a year later, they will have a 14-year maturity, and so on.

4-2d **Provisions to Call or Redeem Bonds**

Most corporate bonds contain a **call provision**, which gives the issuing corporation the right to call the bonds for redemption.[4] The call provision generally states that the company must pay the bondholders an amount greater than the par value if they are called. The additional sum, which is termed a **call premium**, is often set equal to 1 year's interest if the bonds are called during the first year, and the premium declines at a constant rate of INT/N each year thereafter (where INT = annual interest and N = original maturity in years). For example, the call premium on a $1,000 par value, 10-year, 10% bond would generally be $100 if it were called during the first year, $90 during the second year (calculated by reducing the $100, or 10%, premium by one-tenth), and so on. However, bonds are often not callable until several years (generally 5 to 10) after they are issued. This is known as a **deferred call**, and the bonds are said to have **call protection**.

Suppose a company sold bonds when interest rates were relatively high. Provided the issue is callable, the company could sell a new issue of low-yielding securities if and when interest rates drop. It could then use the proceeds of the new issue to retire the high-rate issue and thus reduce its interest expense. This process is called a **refunding operation**.

A call provision is valuable to the firm but potentially detrimental to investors. If interest rates go up, the company will not call the bond, and the investor will be stuck with the original coupon rate on the bond, even though interest rates in the economy have risen sharply. However, if interest rates fall, the company *will* call the bond and pay off investors, who then must reinvest the proceeds at the current market interest rate, which is lower than the rate they were getting on the original bond. In other words, the investor loses when interest rates go up but doesn't reap

---

3. In July 1993, Walt Disney Co., attempting to lock in a low interest rate, issued the first 100-year bonds to be sold by any borrower in modern times. Soon after, Coca-Cola became the second company to stretch the meaning of "long-term bond" by selling $150 million of 100-year bonds.
4. A majority of municipal bonds also contain call provisions. Although the U.S. Treasury no longer issues callable bonds, some past Treasury issues were callable.

the gains when rates fall. To induce an investor to take this type of risk, a new issue of callable bonds must provide a higher coupon rate than an otherwise similar issue of noncallable bonds.

Bonds that are **redeemable at par** at the holder's option protect investors against a rise in interest rates. If rates rise, the price of a fixed-rate bond declines. However, if holders have the option of turning their bonds in and having them redeemed at par, then they are protected against rising rates. If interest rates have risen, holders will turn in the bonds and reinvest the proceeds at a higher rate.

Event risk is the chance that some sudden event will occur and increase the credit risk of a company, hence lowering the firm's bond rating and the value of its outstanding bonds. Investors' concern over event risk means that those firms deemed most likely to face events that could harm bondholders must pay extremely high interest rates. To reduce this interest rate, some bonds have a covenant called a **super poison put**, which enables a bondholder to turn in, or "put," a bond back to the issuer at par in the event of a takeover, merger, or major recapitalization.

Some bonds have a **make-whole call provision**. This allows a company to call the bond, but it must pay a call price that is essentially equal to the market value of a similar noncallable bond. This provides companies with an easy way to repurchase bonds as part of a financial restructuring, such as a merger.

4-2e **Sinking Funds**

Some bonds include a **sinking fund provision** that facilitates the orderly retirement of the bond issue. On rare occasions the firm may be required to deposit money with a trustee, which invests the funds and then uses the accumulated sum to retire the bonds when they mature. Usually, though, the sinking fund is used to buy back a certain percentage of the issue each year. A failure to meet the sinking fund requirement puts the bond into default, which may force the company into bankruptcy.

In most cases, the firm is given the right to administer the sinking fund in either of two ways.

1. The company can call in for redemption (at par value) a certain percentage of the bonds each year; for example, it might be able to call 5% of the total original amount of the issue at a price of $1,000 per bond. The bonds are numbered serially, and those called for redemption are determined by a lottery administered by the trustee.
2. The company may buy the required number of bonds on the open market.

The firm will choose the least costly method. If interest rates have risen, causing bond prices to fall, then it will buy bonds in the open market at a discount; if interest rates have fallen, it will call the bonds. Note that a call for sinking fund purposes is quite different from a refunding call as discussed previously. A sinking fund call typically requires no call premium, but only a small percentage of the issue is normally callable in any one year.[5]

---

5. Some sinking funds require the issuer to pay a call premium.

Although sinking funds are designed to protect bondholders by ensuring that an issue is retired in an orderly fashion, you should recognize that sinking funds also can work to the detriment of bondholders. For example, suppose that the bond carries a 10% interest rate but that yields on similar bonds have fallen to 7.5%. A sinking fund call at par would require an investor to give up a bond that pays $100 of interest and then to reinvest in a bond that pays only $75 per year. This obviously harms those bondholders whose bonds are called. On balance, however, bonds that have a sinking fund are regarded as being safer than those without such a provision, so at the time they are issued sinking fund bonds have lower coupon rates than otherwise similar bonds without sinking funds.

4-2f Other Provisions and Features

Owners of **convertible bonds** have the option to convert the bonds into a fixed number of shares of common stock. Convertibles offer investors the chance to share in the upside if a company does well, so investors are willing to accept a lower coupon rate on convertibles than on an otherwise identical but nonconvertible bond.

Warrants are options that permit the holder to buy stock at a fixed price, thereby providing a gain if the price of the stock rises. Some bonds are issued with warrants. As with convertibles, bonds with warrants have lower coupon rates than straight bonds.

An **income bond** is required to pay interest only if earnings are high enough to cover the interest expense. If earnings are not sufficient, then the company is not required to pay interest and the bondholders do not have the right to force the company into bankruptcy. Therefore, from an investor's standpoint, income bonds are riskier than "regular" bonds.

Indexed bonds, also called **purchasing power bonds**, first became popular in Brazil, Israel, and a few other countries plagued by high inflation rates. The interest payments and maturity payment rise automatically when the inflation rate rises, thus protecting the bondholders against inflation. In January 1997, the U.S. Treasury began issuing indexed bonds called TIPS, short for Treasury Inflation-Protected Securities. Later in this chapter we show how TIPS can be used to estimate the risk-free rate.

4-2g Bond Markets

Corporate bonds are traded primarily in electronic/telephone markets rather than in organized exchanges. Most bonds are owned by and traded among a relatively small number of very large financial institutions, including banks, investment banks, life insurance companies, mutual funds, and pension funds. Although these institutions buy and sell very large blocks of bonds, it is relatively easy for bond dealers to arrange transactions because there are relatively few players in this market as compared with stock markets.

Information on bond trades is not widely published, but a representative group of bonds is listed and traded on the bond division of the NYSE and is reported on the bond market page of *The Wall Street Journal*. The most useful Web site (as of early 2014) is provided by the Financial Industry Regulatory Authority (FINRA) at **http://cxa.marketwatch.com/finra/bondcenter/default.aspx**.

Define "floating-rate bonds" and "zero coupon bonds."

Why is a call provision advantageous to a bond issuer?

What are the two ways a sinking fund can be handled? Which method will be chosen by the firm if interest rates have risen? If interest rates have fallen?

Are securities that provide for a sinking fund regarded as being riskier than those without this type of provision? Explain.

What are income bonds and indexed bonds?

Why do convertible bonds and bonds with warrants have lower coupons than similarly rated bonds that do not have these features?

4-3 Bond Valuation

The value of any financial asset—a stock, a bond, a lease, or even a physical asset such as an apartment building or a piece of machinery—is simply the present value of the cash flows the asset is expected to produce. The cash flows from a specific bond depend on its contractual features. The following section shows the time line and cash flows for a bond.

4-3a Time Line, Cash Flows, and Valuation Formulas for a Bond

For a standard coupon-bearing bond, the cash flows consist of interest payments during the life of the bond plus the amount borrowed when the bond matures (usually a $1,000 par value):

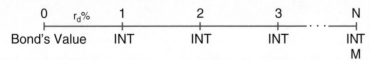

The notation in the time line is explained below.

r_d = The bond's required rate of return, which is the market rate of interest for that type of bond. This is the discount rate that is used to calculate the present value of the bond's cash flows. It is also called the "yield" or "going rate of interest." Note that r_d is *not* the coupon interest rate. It is equal to the coupon rate only if (as in this case) the bond is selling at par. Generally, most coupon bonds are issued at par, which implies that the coupon rate is set at r_d. Thereafter, interest rates, as measured by r_d, will fluctuate, but the coupon rate is fixed, so after issue r_d will equal the coupon rate only by chance. We use the term "i" or "I" to designate the interest rate for many calculations because those terms are used on financial calculators, but "r," with the subscript "d" to designate the rate on a debt security, is normally used in finance.

(Continued)

> N = Number of years until the bond matures. Note that N declines each year after the bond was issued, so a bond that had a maturity of 15 years when it was issued (original maturity = 15) will have N = 14 after 1 year, N = 13 after 2 years, and so on. Note also that for the sake of simplicity we assume the bond pays interest once a year, or annually, so N is measured in years. We consider bonds with semiannual payments later in the chapter.
>
> INT = Dollars of interest paid each year = (Coupon rate)(Par value). For a bond with a 9% coupon and a $1,000 par value, the annual interest is 0.09($1,000) = $90. In calculator terminology, INT = PMT = 90. If the bond had been a semiannual payment bond, the payment would have been $45 every 6 months.
>
> M = Par, or maturity, value of the bond. This amount must be paid off at maturity, and it is often equal to $1,000.

The following general equation, written in several forms, can be used to find the value of any bond, V_B:

(4–1)

$$V_B = \frac{INT}{(1 + r_d)^1} + \frac{INT}{(1 + r_d)^2} + \cdots + \frac{INT}{(1 + r_d)^N} + \frac{M}{(1 + r_d)^N}$$

$$= \sum_{t=1}^{N} \frac{INT}{(1 + r_d)^t} + \frac{M}{(1 + r_d)^N}$$

$$= INT \left[\frac{1}{r_d} - \frac{1}{r_d(1 + r_d)^N} \right] + \frac{M}{(1 + r_d)^N}$$

Observe that the cash flows consist of an annuity of N years plus a lump-sum payment at the end of Year N. Equation 4-1 can be solved by using: (1) a formula, (2) a financial calculator, or (3) a spreadsheet.

4-3b Solving for the Bond Price

Recall that MicroDrive issued a 15-year bond with an annual coupon rate of 9% and a par value of $1,000. To find the value of MicroDrive's bond by using a formula, insert values for MicroDrive's bond into Equation 4-1. You could use the first line of Equation 4-1 to discount each cash flow back to the present and then sum these PVs to find the bond's value of $1,000; see Figure 4-1 and Equation 4-1a:

(4–1a)

$$V_B = \sum_{t=1}^{15} \frac{\$90}{(1 + 0.09)^t} + \frac{\$1,000}{(1 + 0.09)^{15}} = \$1,000$$

FIGURE 4-1	Finding the Value of MicroDrive's Bond (V_B)

	A	B	C	D	E	F	G
19	INPUTS:						
20	Years to maturity = N =		15				
21	Coupon payment = INT =		$90				
22	Par value = M =		$1,000				
23	Required return = r_d =		9%				
24							
25	1. Step-by-Step: Divide each cash flow by $(1 + r_d)^t$						
26	Year (t)	Coupon Payment	PV of Coupon Payment	Par Value	PV of Par Value		
27	1	$90	$82.57				
28	2	$90	$75.75				
29	3	$90	$69.50				
30	4	$90	$63.76				
31	5	$90	$58.49				
32	6	$90	$53.66				
33	7	$90	$49.23				
34	8	$90	$45.17				
35	9	$90	$41.44				
36	10	$90	$38.02				
37	11	$90	$34.88				
38	12	$90	$32.00				
39	13	$90	$29.36				
40	14	$90	$26.93				
41	15	$90	$24.71	$1,000	$274.54		
42		Total =	$725.46				
43							
44	V_B = PV of all coupon payments + PV of par value =				$1,000.00		
45							
46	Inputs:	15	0		90		1,000
47	2. Financial Calculator:	N	I/YR	PV	PMT		FV
48	Output:			−$1,000.00			
49							
50	3. Excel:		PV function:	PV_N =	=PV(9%,15,90,1000)		
51			Fixed inputs:	PV_N =	=PV(9%,15,90,1000) =		−$1,000.00
52			Cell references:	PV_N =	=PV(C23,C20,C21,C22) =		−$1,000.00

Microsoft Excel® is a registered trademark of Microsoft Corporation. © 2014 Microsoft.

This procedure is not very efficient, especially if the bond has many years to maturity. Alternatively, you could use the formula in the second line of Equation 4-1 with a simple or scientific calculator:

See *Ch04 Tool Kit.xls* on the textbook's Web site.

(4–1b)

$$V_B = \$90 \left[\frac{1}{0.09} - \frac{1}{0.09(1 + 0.09)^{15}} \right] + \frac{\$1,000}{(1 + 0.09)^{15}}$$

$$= \$725.46 + \$274.54 = \$1,000$$

As shown in Equation 4-1b, the total bond value of $1,000 is the sum of the coupons' present values ($725.46) and the par value's present value ($274.54). This is easier than the step-by-step approach, but it is still somewhat cumbersome.

A financial calculator is ideally suited for finding bond values. Here is the setup for MicroDrive's bond:

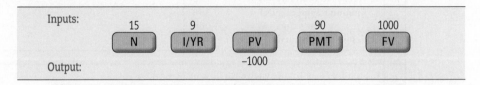

Input N = 15, I/YR = r_d = 9, INT = PMT = 90, and M = FV = 1000; then press the PV key to find the value of the bond, $1,000. Because the PV is an outflow to the investor, it is shown with a negative sign. The calculator is programmed to solve Equation 4-1: It finds the PV of an annuity of $100 per year for 15 years, discounted at 10%, then it finds the PV of the $1,000 maturity payment, and then it adds these two PVs to find the value of the bond. Notice that even though the bond has a total cash flow of $1,090 at Year 15, you should *not* enter FV = 1090! When you entered N = 15 and PMT = 90, you told the calculator that there is a $90 payment at Year 15. Thus, setting FV = 1000 accounts for any *extra* payment at Year 15, above and beyond the $90 payment.

With *Excel*, it is easiest to use the PV function: **=PV(I,N,PMT,FV,Type)**.[6] For MicroDrive's bond, the function is **=PV(0.09,15,90,1000,0)** with a result of −$1,000. Like the financial calculator solution, the bond value is negative because PMT and FV are positive.

Excel also provides specialized functions for bond prices based on actual dates. For example, in *Excel* you could find the MicroDrive bond value as of the date it was issued by using the function wizard to enter this formula:

$$=PRICE(DATE(2015,1,5),DATE(2030,1,5),9\%,9\%,100,1,1)$$

The first two arguments in the function are *Excel*'s DATE function. The DATE function takes the year, month, and day as inputs and converts them into a date. The first argument is the date on which you want to find the price, and the second argument is the maturity date. The third argument in the **PRICE** function is the bond's coupon rate, followed by the required return on the bond, r_d. The fifth argument, 100, is the redemption value of the bond at maturity per $100 of face value; entering "100" means that the bond pays 100% of its face value when it matures. The sixth argument is the number of payments per year. The last argument, 1, tells the program to base the price on the actual number of days in each month and year. This function produces a result based upon a face value of $100. In other words, if the bond pays $100 of face value at maturity, then the **PRICE** function result is the price of the bond. Because MicroDrive's bond pays $1,000 of face value at maturity, we must multiply the PRICE function's result by 10. In this example, the **PRICE** function returns a result of $100. When we multiply it by 10, we get the actual price of $1,000. This function is essential if a bond is

---

6. In Web Chapter 28 we note that Type is 0 (or omitted) for payments at the beginning of the period and 1 for payments at the end of the period.

being evaluated between coupon payment dates. See *Ch04 Tool Kit.xls* on the textbook's Web site for an example.[7]

4-3c **Interest Rate Changes and Bond Prices**

In this example, MicroDrive's bond is selling at a price equal to its par value. Whenever the going market rate of interest, r_d, is equal to the coupon rate, a *fixed-rate* bond will sell at its par value. Normally, the coupon rate is set at the going rate when a bond is issued, causing it to sell at par initially.

The coupon rate remains fixed after the bond is issued, but interest rates in the market move up and down. Looking at Equation 4-1, we see that an *increase* in the market interest rate (r_d) will cause the price of an outstanding bond to *fall*, whereas a *decrease* in rates will cause the bond's price to *rise*. For example, if the market interest rate on MicroDrive's bond increased by 5 percentage points to 14% immediately after it was issued, we would recalculate the price with the new market interest rate as follows:

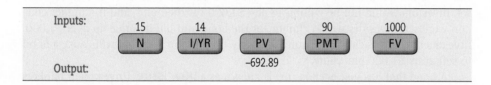

The price would fall to $692.89. Notice that the bond would then sell at a price below its par value. Whenever the going rate of interest *rises above* the coupon rate, a fixed-rate bond's price will *fall below* its par value, and it is called a **discount bond**.

On the other hand, bond prices rise when market interest rates fall. For example, if the market interest rate on MicroDrive's bond decreased by 5 percentage points to 4%, then we would once again recalculate its price:

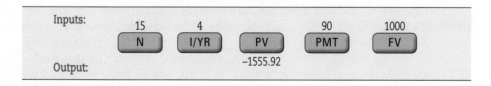

In this case, the price rises to $1,555.92. In general, whenever the going interest rate *falls below* the coupon rate, a fixed-rate bond's price will *rise above* its par value, and it is called a **premium bond**.

---

7. The bond prices quoted by brokers are calculated as described and are called "clean" prices. However, if you bought a bond between interest payment dates, the amount you would actually have to pay would be the basic price plus accrued interest, which is called the "dirty" price. Thus, if you purchased a MicroDrive bond 6 months after it was issued, your broker would send you an invoice stating that you must pay $1,000 as the basic price of the bond plus $45 interest, representing one-half the annual interest of $90, for a "dirty" price of $1,045. The seller of the bond would receive $1,045. If you bought the bond the day before its interest payment date, you would pay $1,000 + (364/365)($90) = $1,089.75. You would receive an interest payment of $90 at the end of the next day. Unless otherwise stated, all prices quoted in this text are "clean" prices.

SELF TEST

Why do the prices of fixed-rate bonds fall if expectations for inflation rise?

What is a discount bond? A premium bond?

A bond that matures in 6 years has a par value of $1,000, an annual coupon payment of $80, and a market interest rate of 9%. What is its price? **($955.14)**

A bond that matures in 18 years has a par value of $1,000, an annual coupon of 10%, and a market interest rate of 7%. What is its price? **($1,301.77)**

4-4 Changes in Bond Values Over Time

At the time a coupon bond is issued, the coupon is generally set at a level that will cause the market price of the bond to equal its par value. If a lower coupon were set, investors would not be willing to pay $1,000 for the bond, and if a higher coupon were set, investors would clamor for the bond and bid its price up over $1,000. Investment bankers can judge quite precisely the coupon rate that will cause a bond to sell at its $1,000 par value.

A bond that has just been issued is known as a **new issue**. (Investment bankers classify a bond as a new issue for about a month after it has first been issued. New issues are usually actively traded and are called "on-the-run" bonds.) Once the bond has been on the market for a while, it is classified as an **outstanding bond**, also called a **seasoned issue**. Newly issued bonds generally sell very close to par, but the prices of seasoned bonds vary widely from par. Except for floating-rate bonds, coupon payments are constant, so when economic conditions change, a 9% coupon bond with a $90 coupon that sold at par when it was issued will sell for more or less than $1,000 thereafter, and the annual coupon will remain at $90.

MicroDrive's bonds with a 9% coupon rate were originally issued at par. If r_d remained constant at 9%, what would the value of the bond be 1 year after it was issued? Now the term to maturity is only 14 years—that is, N = 14. With a financial calculator, just override N = 15 with N = 14, press the PV key, and you find a value of $1,000. If we continued, setting N = 13, N = 12, and so forth, we would see that the value of the bond will remain at $1,000 as long as the going interest rate remains equal to the coupon rate, 9%.

Now suppose interest rates in the economy fell drastically after the MicroDrive bonds were issued and, as a result, r_d *fell below the coupon rate*, decreasing from 9% to 4%. Both the coupon interest payments and the maturity value remain constant, but now 4% would have to be used for r_d in Equation 4-1. The value of the bond at the end of the first year would be $1,528.16:

$$V_B = \sum_{t=1}^{14} \frac{\$90}{(1 + 0.04)^t} + \frac{\$1,000}{(1 + 0.04)^{14}}$$

$$= \$90 \left[\frac{1}{0.04} - \frac{1}{0.04(1 + 0.04)^{14}} \right] + \frac{\$1,000}{(1 + 0.04)^{14}}$$

$$= \$1,528.16$$

With a financial calculator, just change r_d = I/YR from 9 to 4, and then press the PV key to get the answer, $1,528.16. Thus, if r_d fell *below* the coupon rate, the bond would sell *above* par, or at a **premium**.

The arithmetic of the bond value increase should be clear, but what is the logic behind it? Because r_d has fallen to 4%, with $1,000 to invest you could buy new bonds like MicroDrive's (every day some 10 to 12 companies sell new bonds), except that these new bonds would pay $40 of interest each year rather than $90. Naturally, you would prefer $90 to $40, so you would be willing to pay more than $1,000 for a MicroDrive bond to obtain its higher coupons. All investors would react similarly; as a result, the MicroDrive bonds would be bid up in price to $1,528.16, at which point they would provide the same 4% rate of return to a potential investor as the new bonds.

Assuming that interest rates remain constant at 4% for the next 14 years, what would happen to the value of a MicroDrive bond? It would fall gradually from $1,528.16 to $1,000 at maturity, when MicroDrive will redeem each bond for $1,000. This point can be illustrated by calculating the value of the bond 1 year later, when it has 13 years remaining to maturity. With a financial calculator, simply input the values for N, I/YR, PMT, and FV, now using N = 13, and press the PV key to find the value of the bond, $1,499.28. Thus, the value of the bond will have fallen from $1,528.16 to $1,499.28, or by $28.88. If you were to calculate the value of the bond at other future dates, the price would continue to fall as the maturity date approached.

Note that if you purchased the bond at a price of $1,528.16 and then sold it 1 year later with r_d still at 4%, you would have a capital loss of $28.88, or a total dollar return of $90.00 – $28.88 = $61.12. Your percentage rate of return would consist of the rate of return due to the interest payment (called the **current yield**) and the rate of return due to the price change (called the **capital gains yield**). This total rate of return is often called the bond yield, and it is calculated as follows:

Interest, or current, yield = $90/$1,528.16 = 0.0589 = 5.89%

Capital gains yield = −$28.88/$1,528.16 = −0.0189 = −1.89%

Total rate of return, or yield = $61.12/$1,528.16 = 0.0400 = 4.00%

Had interest rates risen from 9% to 14% during the first year after issue (rather than falling from 9% to 4%), then you would enter N = 14, I/YR = 14, PMT = 90, and FV = 1000, and then press the PV key to find the value of the bond, $699.90. In this case, the bond would sell below its par value, or at a **discount**. The total expected future return on the bond would again consist of an expected return due to interest and an expected return due to capital gains or capital losses. In this situation, the capital gains yield would be *positive*. The total return would be 14%. To see this, calculate the price of the bond with 13 years left to maturity, assuming that interest rates remain at 14%. With a calculator, enter N = 13, I/YR = 14, PMT = 90, and FV = 1000; then press PV to obtain the bond's value, $707.88.

Note that the capital gain for the year is the difference between the bond's value at Year 2 (with 13 years remaining) and the bond's value at Year 1 (with 14 years remaining), or $707.88 − $699.90 = $7.98. The interest yield, capital gains yield, and total yield are calculated as follows:

Interest, or current, yield = $90/$699.90 = 0.1286 = 12.86%

Capital gains yield = $7.98/$699.90 = 0.0114 = 1.14%

Total rate of return, or yield = $97.98/$699.90 = 0.1400 = 14.00%

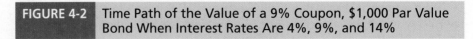

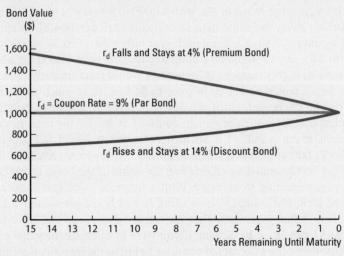

Note: The curves for 4% and 14% have a slight bow.

Source: From *Financial Management: Theory & Practice*, 2013, by Brigham and Ehrhardt.
© Cengage Learning.

See **Ch04 Tool Kit.xls** for all calculations.

Figure 4-2 graphs the value of the bond over time, assuming that interest rates in the economy: (1) remain constant at 9%, (2) fall to 4% and then remain constant at that level, or (3) rise to 14% and remain constant at that level. Of course, if interest rates do *not* remain constant, then the price of the bond will fluctuate. However, regardless of what future interest rates do, the bond's price will approach $1,000 as it nears the maturity date (barring bankruptcy, which might cause the bond's value to fall dramatically).

Figure 4-2 illustrates the following key points.

1. Whenever the going rate of interest, r_d, is equal to the coupon rate, a *fixed-rate* bond will sell at its par value. Normally, the coupon rate is set equal to the going rate when a bond is issued, causing it to sell at par initially.
2. Interest rates do change over time, but the coupon rate remains fixed after the bond has been issued. Whenever the going rate of interest *rises above* the coupon rate, a fixed-rate bond's price will *fall below* its par value. Such a bond is called a **discount bond**.
3. Whenever the going rate of interest *falls below* the coupon rate, a fixed-rate bond's price will *rise above* its par value. Such a bond is called a **premium bond**.
4. Thus, an *increase* in interest rates will cause the prices of outstanding bonds to *fall*, whereas a *decrease* in rates will cause bond prices to *rise*.
5. The market value of a bond will always approach its par value as its maturity date approaches, provided the firm does not go bankrupt.

These points are very important, for they show that bondholders may suffer capital losses or make capital gains depending on whether interest rates rise or fall after the bond is purchased.

> What is meant by the terms "new issue" and "seasoned issue"?
>
> Last year, a firm issued 30-year, 8% annual coupon bonds at a par value of $1,000. (1) Suppose that 1 year later the going rate drops to 6%. What is the new price of the bonds, assuming that they now have 29 years to maturity? **($1,271.81)** (2) Suppose instead that 1 year after issue the going interest rate increases to 10% (rather than dropping to 6%). What is the price? **($812.61)**

SELF TEST

DRINKING YOUR COUPONS

In 1996, Jonathan Maltus was looking for some cash to purchase additional vines and to modernize production facilities at Chateau Teyssier, a vineyard and winery in the Bordeaux region of France. The solution? With the assistance of a leading underwriter, Matrix Securities, the vineyard issued 375 bonds, each costing 2,650 British pounds. The issue raised nearly 1 million pounds, or roughly $1.5 million.

What makes these bonds interesting is that, instead of paying with something boring like money, they paid their investors back with wine. Each June until 2002, when the bond matured, investors received their "coupons." Between 1997 and 2001, each bond provided six cases of the vineyard's rosé or claret. Starting in 1998 and continuing through maturity in 2002, investors also received four cases of its prestigious Saint Emilion Grand Cru. Then, in 2002, they got their money back.

The bonds were not without risk. Maltus acknowledged that the quality of the wine "is at the mercy of the gods."

Source: Steven Irvine, "My Wine Is My Bond, and I Drink My Coupons," *Euromoney*, July 1996, p. 7.

4-5 Bonds with Semiannual Coupons

Although some bonds pay interest annually, the vast majority actually pay interest semiannually. To evaluate semiannual payment bonds, we must modify the valuation model as follows.

1. Divide the annual coupon interest payment by 2 to determine the dollars of interest paid every 6 months.
2. Multiply the years to maturity, N, by 2 to determine the number of semiannual periods.
3. Divide the nominal (quoted) interest rate, r_d, by 2 to determine the periodic (semiannual) interest rate.

By making these changes, we obtain the following equation for finding the value of a bond that pays interest semiannually:

$$V_B = \sum_{t=1}^{2N} \frac{INT/2}{(1 + r_d/2)^t} + \frac{M}{(1 + r_d/2)^{2N}}$$

(4–2)

To illustrate, assume now that MicroDrive's bonds pay $45 interest every 6 months rather than $90 at the end of each year. Each semiannual interest payment is only half as large, but there are twice as many of them. The nominal, or quoted, coupon rate is "9%, semiannual payments."[8]

When the going (nominal) rate of interest is 4% with semiannual compounding, the value of this 15-year bond is found as follows:

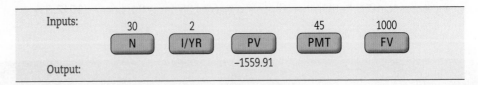

Enter N = 30, r_d = I/YR = 2, PMT = 45, FV = 1000, and then press the PV key to obtain the bond's value, $1,559.91. The value with semiannual interest payments is slightly larger than $1,552.92, the value when interest is paid annually. This higher value occurs because interest payments are received somewhat sooner under semiannual compounding.

Describe how the annual bond valuation formula is changed to evaluate semiannual coupon bonds. Write out the revised formula.

A bond has a 25-year maturity, an 8% annual coupon paid semiannually, and a face value of $1,000. The going nominal *annual* interest rate (r_d) is 6%. What is the bond's price? **($1,257.30)**

4-6 **Bond Yields**

Unlike the coupon interest rate, which is fixed, the bond's *yield* varies from day to day depending on current market conditions. Moreover, the yield can be calculated in three different ways, and three "answers" can be obtained. These different yields are described in the following sections.

4-6a **Yield to Maturity**

Suppose 1 year after it was issued, you could buy MicroDrive's 14-year, 9% annual coupon, $1,000 par value bond at a price of $1,528.16. What rate of interest would you earn on your investment if you bought the bond and held it to maturity? This rate is called the bond's **yield to maturity (YTM)**, and it is the interest rate

---

8. In this situation, the coupon rate of "9% paid semiannually" is the rate that bond dealers, corporate treasurers, and investors generally would discuss. Of course, if this bond were issued at par, then its *effective annual* rate would be higher than 9%:

$$\text{EAR} = \text{EFF\%} = \left(1 + \frac{r_{\text{NOM}}}{M}\right)^M - 1 = \left(1 + \frac{0.09}{2}\right)^2 - 1 = (1.045)^2 - 1 = 9.20\%$$

Because 9.20% with annual payments is quite different from 9% with semiannual payments, we have assumed a change in effective rates in this section from the situation described in the previous section, where we assumed 9% with annual payments.

generally discussed by investors when they talk about rates of return. The yield to maturity is usually the same as the market rate of interest, r_d. To find the YTM for a bond with annual interest payments, you must solve Equation 4-1 for r_d:[9]

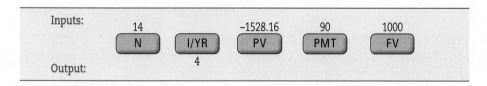

$$\text{Bond price} = \sum_{t=1}^{N} \frac{INT}{(1 + YTM)^t} + \frac{M}{(1 + YTM)^N}$$

(4–3)

For MicroDrive's yield, you must solve this equation:

$$\$1,528.16 = \frac{\$90}{(1 + r_d)^1} + \cdots + \frac{\$90}{(1 + r_d)^{14}} + \frac{\$1,000}{(1 + r_d)^{14}}$$

You could substitute values for r_d until you found a value that "works" and forces the sum of the PVs on the right side of the equal sign to equal $1,528.16, but this would be tedious and time-consuming.[10] As you might guess, it is much easier with a financial calculator. Here is the setup:

Inputs:	14		−1528.16	90	1000
	N	**I/YR**	**PV**	**PMT**	**FV**
Output:		4			

Simply enter N = 14, PV = −1,528.16, PMT = 90, and FV = 1000, and then press the I/YR key for the answer of 4%.

You could also find the YTM with a spreadsheet. In *Excel*, you would use the RATE function for this bond, inputting N = 14, PMT = 90, PV = −1528.16, FV = 1000, 0 for Type, and leave Guess blank: **=RATE(14,90,−1528.16,1000,0)**. The result is 4%. The RATE function works only if the current date is immediately after either the issue date or a coupon payment date. To find bond yields on other dates, use *Excel*'s YIELD function. See the *Ch04 Tool Kit.xls* file for an example.

See *Ch04 Tool Kit.xls* on the textbook's Web site.

The yield to maturity can be viewed as the bond's *promised rate of return*, which is the return that investors will receive if all the promised payments are made. However, the yield to maturity equals the *expected rate of return* only if: (1) the probability of default is zero and (2) the bond cannot be called. If there is some default risk or if the bond may be called, then there is some probability that the promised payments to maturity will not be received, in which case the calculated yield to maturity will differ from the expected return.

The YTM for a bond that sells at par consists entirely of an interest yield, but if the bond sells at a price other than its par value, then the YTM will consist of the interest yield plus a positive or negative capital gains yield. Note also that a bond's yield to maturity changes whenever interest rates in the economy change, and this is almost daily. If you purchase a bond and hold it until it matures, you will receive

---

9. If the bond has semiannual payments, you must solve Equation 4-2 for r_d.
10. Alternatively, you can substitute values of r_d into the third form of Equation 4-1 until you find a value that works.

the YTM that existed on the purchase date, but the bond's calculated YTM will change frequently between the purchase date and the maturity date.[11]

4-6b Yield to Call

If you purchased a bond that was callable and the company called it, you would not be able to hold the bond until it matured. Therefore, the yield to maturity would not be earned. For example, if MicroDrive's 9% coupon bonds were callable and if interest rates fell from 9% to 4%, then the company could call in the 9% bonds, replace them with 4% bonds, and save $90 − $40 = $50 interest per bond per year. This would be good for the company but not for the bondholders.

If current interest rates are well below an outstanding bond's coupon rate, then a callable bond is likely to be called, and investors will estimate its expected rate of return as the **yield to call (YTC)** rather than as the yield to maturity. To calculate the YTC, solve this equation for r_d:

(4–4)

$$\text{Price of callable bond} = \sum_{t=1}^{N} \frac{\text{INT}}{(1 + r_d)^t} + \frac{\text{Call price}}{(1 + r_d)^N}$$

Here N is the number of years until the company can call the bond, r_d is the YTC, and "Call price" is the price the company must pay in order to call the bond (it is often set equal to the par value plus 1 year's interest).

To illustrate, suppose MicroDrive's bonds had a provision that permitted the company, if it desired, to call the bonds 10 years after the issue date at a price of $1,100. Suppose further that 1 year after issuance the going interest rate had declined, causing the price of the bonds to rise to $1,528.16. Here is the time line and the setup for finding the bond's YTC with a financial calculator:

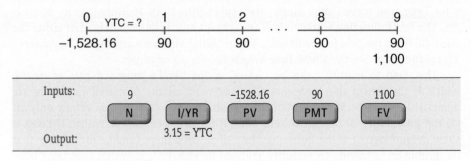

11. We often are asked by students if the purchaser of a bond will receive the YTM if interest rates subsequently change. The answer is definitely "yes" provided the question means "Is the realized rate of return on the investment in the bond equal to the YTM?" This is because the realized rate of return on an investment is by definition the rate that sets the present value of the realized cash flows equal to the price. If instead the question means "Is the realized rate of return on the investment in the bond and the subsequent reinvestment of the coupons equal to the YTM?" then the answer is definitely "no." Thus, the question really is one about strategy and timing. The bond, in combination with a reinvestment strategy, is really two investments, and clearly the realized rate on this combined strategy depends on the reinvestment rate. (See *Web Extension 4C* for more on investing for a target future value.) For the rest of the book, we assume that an investment in a bond is only an investment in the bond, and not a combination of the bond and a reinvestment strategy; this means the investor earns the expected YTM if the bond is held to maturity.

The YTC is 3.15%, which is the return you would earn if you bought the bond at a price of $1,528.16 and it was called 9 years from today. (The bond could not be called until 10 years after issuance, and 1 year has gone by, so there are 9 years left until the first call date.)

Do you think MicroDrive *will* call the bonds when they become callable? MicroDrive's actions will depend on the going interest rate when the bonds become callable. If the going rate remains at r_d = 4%, then MicroDrive could save 9% − 4% = 5%, or $50 per bond per year, by calling them and replacing the 9% bonds with a new 4% issue. There would be costs to the company to refund the issue, but the interest savings would probably be worth the cost, so MicroDrive would probably refund the bonds. Therefore, you would probably earn YTC = 3.15% rather than YTM = 4% if you bought the bonds under the indicated conditions.

In the balance of this chapter, we assume that bonds are not callable unless otherwise noted. However, some of the end-of-chapter problems deal with yield to call.

4-6c **Current Yield**

If you examine brokerage house reports on bonds, you will often see reference to a bond's **current yield**. The current yield is the annual interest payment divided by the bond's current price. For example, if MicroDrive's bonds with a 9% coupon were currently selling at $985, then the bond's current yield would be $90/$985 = 0.0914 = 9.14%.

Unlike the yield to maturity, the current yield does not represent the rate of return that investors should expect on the bond. The current yield provides information regarding the amount of cash income that a bond will generate in a given year, but it does not provide an accurate measure of the bond's total expected return, the yield to maturity. In fact, here is the relation between current yield, capital gains yield (which can be negative for a capital loss), and the yield to maturity:

$$\text{Current yield} + \text{Capital gains yield} = \text{Yield to maturity} \tag{4-5}$$

4-6d **The Cost of Debt and Intrinsic Value**

The "Intrinsic Value Box" at the beginning of this chapter highlights the cost of debt, which affects the weighted average cost of capital (WACC), which in turn affects the company's intrinsic value. The pre-tax cost of debt from the company's perspective is the required return from the debtholder's perspective. Therefore, the pre-tax cost of debt is the yield to maturity (or the yield to call if a call is likely). But why do different bonds have different yields to maturity? The following sections answer this question.

> Explain the difference between the yield to maturity and the yield to call.
>
> How does a bond's current yield differ from its total return?
>
> Could the current yield exceed the total return?

SELF TEST

(Continued)

> A bond currently sells for $850. It has an 8-year maturity, an annual coupon of $80, and a par value of $1,000. What is its yield to maturity? **(10.90%)** What is its current yield? **(9.41%)**
>
> A bond currently sells for $1,250. It pays a $110 annual coupon and has a 20-year maturity, but it can be called in 5 years at $1,110. What are its YTM and its YTC? **(8.38%, 6.85%)** Is the bond likely to be called if interest rates don't change?

4-7 The Pre-Tax Cost of Debt: Determinants of Market Interest Rates

Until now we have given you r_d, the going market rate. But as we showed in Chapter 1, different debt securities often have very different market rates. What explains these differences? In general, the quoted (or nominal) interest rate on a debt security, r_d, is composed of a real risk-free rate of interest, r^*, plus several premiums that reflect inflation, the risk of the security, and the security's marketability (or liquidity). A conceptual framework is shown below:

(4–6)

$$\text{Quoted market interest rate} = r_d = r^* + IP + DRP + LP + MRP$$
$$= r_{RF} + DRP + LP + MRP$$

Here are definitions of the variables in Equation 4-6:

See **www.bloomberg.com** and select MARKETS. Then select RATES AND BONDS for a partial listing of indexed Treasury bonds and their interest rates. See **http://online.wsj.com** for a complete set of Treasury quotes. See **www.treasurydirect.gov/indiv/products/products.htm** for a complete listing of all Treasury securities.

r_d = Quoted, or nominal, rate of interest on a given security.[12] There are many different securities and hence many different quoted interest rates.

r^* = Real risk-free rate of interest. Pronounced "r-star," r^* is the rate on a riskless security if zero inflation were expected.

IP = Inflation premium, which is equal to the average expected inflation rate over the life of the security. The expected future inflation rate is not necessarily equal to the current inflation rate, so IP is not necessarily equal to current inflation.

r_{RF} = $r^* + IP$, and it is the quoted risk-free rate of interest on a security such as a U.S. Treasury bill, which is very liquid and also free of most risks.

(Continued)

---

12. The term *nominal* as used here means the *stated* rate as opposed to the *real* rate, which is adjusted to remove inflation effects. Suppose you bought a 10-year Treasury bond with a quoted, or nominal, rate of about 4.6%. If inflation averages 2.5% over the next 10 years, then the real rate would be about $4.6\% - 2.5\% = 2.1\%$. To be technically correct, we should find the real rate by solving for r^* in the following equation: $(1 + r^*)(1 + 0.025) = (1 + 0.046)$. Solving the equation, we find $r^* = 2.05\%$. Because this is very close to the 2.1% just calculated, we will continue to approximate the real rate in this chapter by subtracting inflation from the nominal rate.

> Note that r_{RF} includes the premium for expected inflation because $r_{RF} = r^* + IP$.
>
> DRP = Default risk premium. This premium reflects the possibility that the issuer will not pay interest or principal at the stated time and in the stated amount. The DRP is zero for U.S. Treasury securities, but it rises as the riskiness of issuers increases.
>
> LP = Liquidity, or marketability, premium. This is a premium charged by lenders to reflect the fact that some securities cannot be converted to cash on short notice at a "reasonable" price. The LP is very low for Treasury securities and for securities issued by large, strong firms, but it is relatively high on securities issued by very small firms.
>
> MRP = Maturity risk premium. Changes in market interest rates can cause large changes in the prices of long-term bonds, even Treasury bonds. Lenders charge a maturity risk premium to reflect this risk.

We discuss the components whose sum makes up the quoted, or nominal, rate on a given security in the following sections.

Write out an equation for the nominal interest rate on any debt security.

SELF TEST

4-8 The Real Risk-Free Rate of Interest, r*

The **real risk-free rate of interest, r***, is defined as the interest rate that would exist on a riskless security if no inflation were expected, and it may be thought of as the rate of interest on *short-term* U.S. Treasury securities in an inflation-free world. The real risk-free rate is not static—it changes over time depending on economic conditions, especially: (1) the rate of return corporations and other borrowers expect to earn on productive assets, and (2) people's time preferences for current versus future consumption.[13]

In addition to its regular bond offerings, in 1997 the U.S. Treasury began issuing **indexed bonds**, with payments linked to inflation. These bonds are called **TIPS**, short for **Treasury Inflation-Protected Securities**. (For details on how TIPS are adjusted to protect against inflation, see *Web Extension 4B* on the textbook's Web site.) Because the payments (including the principal) are tied to inflation, the yield on a TIPS with 1 year until maturity is a good estimate of the real risk-free

---

13. The real rate of interest as discussed here is different from the *current* real rate as often discussed in the press. The current real rate is often estimated as the current interest rate minus the current (or most recent) inflation rate, whereas the real rate, as used here (and in the fields of finance and economics generally) without the word "current," is the current interest rate minus the *expected future* inflation rate over the life of the security. For example, suppose the current quoted rate for a 1-year Treasury bill is 5%, inflation during the previous year was 2%, and inflation expected for the coming year is 4%. Then the *current* real rate would be approximately 5% − 2% = 3%, but the *expected* real rate would be approximately 5% − 4% = 1%.

rate. In theory, we would like an even shorter maturity to estimate the real risk-free rate, but short-term TIPS are thinly traded and the reported yields are not as reliable.

Historically, the real interest rate has averaged around 1.5% to 2.5%. In December 2013, the TIPS with about 1 year remaining until maturity had a 2% yield while TIPS with slightly more time to maturity of 1.5 years had a −1.00% yield. Although unusual, negative real rates are possible. In spring 2008, the combination of stagnant economic growth, a high level of investor uncertainty, fears of inflation, and the Federal Reserve's reduction in nominal short-term interest rates caused the real rate to fall below zero, as measured by negative yields on several short-term TIPS. The yields on the shortest-term TIPS remained low until recently when the Federal Reserve indicated that it would begin to ease off on its policies that kept short-term rates low. Although the shortest-term TIPS rates have edged up, the slightly longer-term rates remain negative due to near-term fears of inflation. Negative real rates are possible, but negative nominal rates are impossible (or at least extraordinarily rare) because investors would just hold cash instead of investing in a negative-yield bond.

> **SELF TEST**   What security provides a good estimate of the real risk-free rate?

4-9 **The Inflation Premium (IP)**

Inflation has a major effect on interest rates because it erodes the purchasing power of the dollar and lowers the real rate of return on investments. To illustrate, suppose you invest $3,000 in a default-free zero coupon bond that matures in 1 year and pays a 5% interest rate. At the end of the year, you will receive $3,150—your original $3,000 plus $150 of interest. Now suppose that the inflation rate during the year is 10% and that it affects all items equally. If gas had cost $3 per gallon at the beginning of the year, it would cost $3.30 at the end of the year. Therefore, your $3,000 would have bought $3,000/$3 = 1,000 gallons at the beginning of the year but only $3,150/$3.30 = 955 gallons at the end. In *real terms*, you would be worse off—you would receive $150 of interest, but it would not be sufficient to offset inflation. You would thus be better off buying 1,000 gallons of gas (or some other storable asset) than buying the default-free bond.

Investors are well aware of inflation's effects on interest rates, so when they lend money, they build in an **inflation premium (IP)** equal to the average expected inflation rate over the life of the security. For a short-term, default-free U.S. Treasury bill, the actual interest rate charged, $r_{T\text{-bill}}$, would be the real risk-free rate, r^*, plus the inflation premium (IP):

$$r_{T\text{-bill}} = r_{RF} = r^* + IP$$

Therefore, if the real short-term risk-free rate of interest were $r^* = 0.6\%$ and if inflation were expected to be 1.0% (and hence IP = 1.0%) during the next year, then the quoted rate of interest on 1-year T-bills would be 0.6% + 1.0% = 1.6%.

It is important to note that the inflation rate built into interest rates is *the inflation rate expected in the future*, not the rate experienced in the past. Thus, the latest reported figures might show an annual inflation rate of 2%, but that is for the *past* year. But if people on average expect a 6% inflation rate in the future, then 6% would be built into the current interest rate.

Note also that the inflation rate reflected in the quoted interest rate on any security is the *average rate of inflation expected over the security's life.* Thus, the inflation rate built into a 1-year bond is the expected inflation rate for the next year, but the inflation rate built into a 30-year bond is the average rate of inflation expected over the next 30 years. If I_t is the expected inflation during year t, then the inflation premium for an N-year bond's yield (IP_N) can be approximated as:

$$IP_N = \frac{I_1 + I_2 + \cdots + I_N}{N}$$

(4–7)

For example, if investors expect inflation to average 3% during Year 1 and 5% during Year 2, then the inflation premium built into a 2-year bond's yield can be approximated by:[14]

$$IP_2 = \frac{I_1 + I_2}{2} = \frac{3\% + 5\%}{2} = 4\%$$

In the previous section, we saw that the yield on an inflation-indexed Treasury bond (TIPS) is a good estimate of the real interest rate. We can also use TIPS to estimate inflation premiums. For example, in late 2013 the yield on a 5-year nonindexed T-bond was 1.51% and the yield on a 5-year TIPS was -0.27%. Thus, the 5-year inflation premium was $1.51\% - (-0.27\%) = 1.78\%$, implying that investors expected inflation to average 1.78% over the next 5 years.[15] Similarly, the rate on a 20-year nonindexed T-bond was 3.60% and the rate on a 20-year indexed T-bond was 1.33%. Thus, the 20-year inflation premium was approximately $3.60\% - 1.33\% = 2.27\%$, implying that investors expected inflation to average 2.27% over the long term.[16] These calculations are summarized below:

Yields on:	Maturity		
	1 Year	5 Years	20 Years
Nonindexed U.S. Treasury Bond	0.15%	1.51%	3.60%
TIPS	−1.03%	−0.27%	1.33%
Inflation premium	1.18%	1.78%	2.27%

14. To be mathematically correct, we should take the *geometric average*: $(1 + IP_2)^2 = (1 + I_1)(1 + I_2)$. In this example, we have $(1 + IP_2)^2 = (1 + 0.03)(1 + 0.05)$. Solving for IP_2 yields 3.9952, which is close to our approximation of 4%.

15. As we noted in the previous footnote, the mathematically correct approach is to use a *geometric average* and solve the following equation: $(1 + IP)(1 + -0.0105) = 1 + .0121$. Solving for IP gives IP = 2.28%, which is very close to our approximation.

Note, though, that the difference in yield between a T-bond and a TIPS of the same maturity reflects both the expected inflation *and* any risk premium for bearing inflation risk. So the difference in yields is really an upper limit on the expected inflation.

16. There are several other sources for the estimated inflation premium. The Congressional Budget Office regularly updates the estimates of inflation that it uses in its forecasted budgets; see **www.cbo.gov**; select Economic Projections. A second source is the University of Michigan's Institute for Social Research, which regularly polls consumers regarding their expectations for price increases during the next year; see **www.sca.isr.umich.edu** for the survey.

We prefer using inflation premiums derived from indexed and nonindexed Treasury securities, as described in the text, because these are based on how investors actually spend their money, not on theoretical models or opinions.

Expectations for future inflation are closely, but not perfectly, correlated with rates experienced in the recent past. Therefore, if the inflation rate reported for last month increases, people often raise their expectations for future inflation, and this change in expectations will cause an increase in interest rates.

Note that Germany, Japan, and Switzerland have, over the past several years, had lower inflation rates than the United States, so their interest rates have generally been lower than ours. South Africa, Brazil, and most South American countries have experienced higher inflation, which is reflected in their interest rates.

> **SELF TEST**
>
> Explain how a TIPS and a nonindexed Treasury security can be used to estimate the inflation premium.
>
> The yield on a 15-year TIPS is 3% and the yield on a 15-year Treasury bond is 5%. What is the inflation premium for a 15-year security? **(2%)**

4-10 The Nominal, or Quoted, Risk-Free Rate of Interest, r_{RF}

The **nominal**, or **quoted**, **risk-free rate**, r_{RF}, is the real risk-free rate plus a premium for expected inflation: $r_{RF} = r^* + IP$. To be strictly correct, the risk-free rate should mean the interest rate on a totally risk-free security—one that has no risk of default, no maturity risk, no liquidity risk, no risk of loss if inflation increases, and no risk of any other type. There is no such security, so there is no observable truly risk-free rate. When the term "risk-free rate" is used without either the modifier "real" or the modifier "nominal," people generally mean the quoted (nominal) rate, and we will follow that convention in this book. Therefore, when we use the term "risk-free rate, r_{RF}" we mean the nominal risk-free rate, which includes an inflation premium equal to the average expected inflation rate over the life of the security. In general, we use the T-bill rate to approximate the short-term risk-free rate and use the T-bond rate to approximate the long-term risk-free rate (even though it also includes a maturity premium). So, whenever you see the term "risk-free rate," assume that we are referring either to the quoted U.S. T-bill rate or to the quoted T-bond rate.

Because $r_{RF} = r^* + IP$, we can express the quoted rate as:

(4–8)
$$\text{Nominal, or quoted, rate} = r_d = r_{RF} + DRP + LP + MRP$$

> **SELF TEST**
>
> What security is a good approximation of the nominal risk-free rate?

4-11 **The Default Risk Premium (DRP)**

If the issuer defaults on a payment, investors receive less than the promised return on the bond. The quoted interest rate includes a default risk premium (DRP)—the greater the default risk, the higher the bond's yield to maturity.[17] The default risk on Treasury securities is virtually zero, but default risk can be substantial for corporate and municipal bonds. In this section, we consider some issues related to default risk.

4-11a **Bond Contract Provisions that Influence Default Risk**

Default risk is affected by both the financial strength of the issuer and the terms of the bond contract, especially whether collateral has been pledged to secure the bond. Several types of contract provisions are discussed next.

Bond Indentures

An **indenture** is a legal document that spells out the rights of both bondholders and the issuing corporation. A **trustee** is an official (usually a bank) who represents the bondholders and makes sure the terms of the indenture are carried out. The indenture may be several hundred pages in length, and it will include **restrictive covenants** that cover such points as the conditions under which the issuer can pay off the bonds prior to maturity, the levels at which certain ratios must be maintained if the company is to issue additional debt, and restrictions against the payment of dividends unless earnings meet certain specifications.

The Securities and Exchange Commission: (1) approves indentures and (2) makes sure that all indenture provisions are met before allowing a company to sell new securities to the public. A firm will have different indentures for each of the major types of bonds it issues, but a single indenture covers all bonds of the same type. For example, one indenture will cover a firm's first mortgage bonds, another its debentures, and a third its convertible bonds.

Mortgage Bonds

A corporation pledges certain assets as security for a **mortgage bond**. The company might also choose to issue *second-mortgage bonds* secured by the same assets that were secured by a previously issued mortgage bond. In the event of liquidation, the holders of these second mortgage bonds would have a claim against the property, but only after the first mortgage bondholders had been paid off in full. Thus, second mortgages are sometimes called *junior mortgages* because they are junior in priority to the claims of *senior mortgages*, or *first-mortgage bonds*. All mortgage bonds are subject to an indenture that usually limits the amount of new bonds that can be issued.

Debentures and Subordinated Debentures

A **debenture** is an unsecured bond, and as such it provides no lien against specific property as security for the obligation. Debenture holders are, therefore, general creditors whose claims are protected by property not otherwise pledged.

---

17. Suppose two bonds have the same promised cash flows, coupon rate, maturity, liquidity, and inflation exposure, but one bond has more default risk than the other. Investors will naturally pay less for the bond with the greater chance of default. As a result, bonds with higher default risk will have higher yields.

The term *subordinate* means "below," or "inferior to"; thus, in the event of bankruptcy, subordinated debt has claims on assets only after senior debt has been paid off. **Subordinated debentures** may be subordinated either to designated notes payable (usually bank loans) or to all other debt. In the event of liquidation or reorganization, holders of subordinated debentures cannot be paid until all senior debt, as named in the debentures' indentures, has been paid.

Development Bonds

Some companies may be in a position to benefit from the sale of either **development bonds** or **pollution control bonds**. State and local governments may set up both *industrial development agencies* and *pollution control agencies*. These agencies are allowed, under certain circumstances, to sell **tax-exempt bonds** and then make the proceeds available to corporations for specific uses deemed (by Congress) to be in the public interest. For example, a Detroit pollution control agency might sell bonds to provide Ford with funds for purchasing pollution control equipment. Because the income from the bonds would be tax exempt, the bonds would have relatively low interest rates. Note, however, that these bonds are guaranteed by the corporation that will use the funds, not by a governmental unit, so their rating reflects the credit strength of the corporation using the funds.

Municipal Bond Insurance

Municipalities can have their bonds insured, which means that an insurance company guarantees to pay the coupon and principal payments should the issuer default. This reduces risk to investors, who will thus accept a lower coupon rate for an insured bond than for a comparable but uninsured one. Even though the municipality must pay a fee to have its bonds insured, its savings due to the lower coupon rate often make insurance cost-effective. Keep in mind that the insurers are private companies, and the value added by the insurance depends on the creditworthiness of the insurer. The larger insurers are strong companies, and their own ratings are AAA.

THE GLOBAL ECONOMIC CRISIS

Insuring with Credit Default Swaps: Let the Buyer Beware!

A credit default swap (CDS) is like an insurance policy. The purchaser of the CDS agrees to make annual payments to a counterparty that agrees to pay if a particular bond defaults. During the 2000s, investment banks often would purchase CDS for the mortgage-backed securities (MBS) they were creating in order to make the securities more attractive to investors. But how good was this type of insurance? As it turned out, not very. For example, Lehman Brothers might have bought a CDS from AIG in order to sell a Lehman-created MBS to an investor. But when the MBS began defaulting, neither Lehman nor AIG was capable of making full restitution to the investor.

4-11b **Bond Ratings**

Since the early 1900s, bonds have been assigned quality ratings that reflect their probability of going into default. The three major rating agencies are Moody's Investors Service (Moody's), Standard & Poor's Corporation (S&P), and Fitch Ratings. As shown in Columns (3) and (4) of Table 4-1, triple-A and double-A bonds are extremely safe, rarely defaulting even within 5 years of being assigned a rating. Single-A and triple-B bonds are also strong enough to be called **investment-grade bonds**, and they are the lowest-rated bonds that many banks and other institutional investors are permitted by law to hold. Double-B and lower bonds are speculative bonds and are often called **junk bonds**. These bonds have a significant probability of defaulting.

TABLE 4-1	Bond Ratings, Default Risk, and Yields

Rating Agency[a]		Percent Defaulting Within:[b]		Median Ratios[c]		Percent Upgraded or Downgraded in 2012[b]		
S&P and Fitch (1)	Moody's (2)	1 year (3)	5 years (4)	Return on capital (5)	Total debt/ Total capital (6)	Down (7)	Up (8)	Yield[d] (9)
Investment-grade bonds								
AAA	Aaa	0.00%	0.00%	27.6%	12.4%	5.40%	NA	3.65%
AA	Aa	0.03	0.19	27.0	28.3	9.83	0.09	3.65
A	A	0.08	0.76	17.5	37.5	6.23	1.92	3.87
BBB	Baa	0.20	2.45	13.4	42.5	4.57	3.63	4.81
Junk bonds								
BB	Ba	1.05	6.91	11.3	53.7	9.58	8.75	5.87
B	B	2.02	10.52	8.7	75.9	6.50	9.86	6.26
CCC	Caa	24.88	36.84	3.2	113.5	28.07	21.19	7.40

Notes:
[a]The ratings agencies also use "modifiers" for bonds rated below triple-A. S&P and Fitch use a plus and minus system; thus, A+ designates the strongest A-rated bonds and A− the weakest. Moody's uses a 1, 2, or 3 designation, with 1 denoting the strongest and 3 the weakest; thus, within the double-A category, Aa1 is the best, Aa2 is average, and Aa3 is the weakest.
[b]Default data are from Fitch Ratings Global Corporate Finance 2012 Transition and Default Study, March 15, 2013: see **www .fitchratings.com/web_content/nrsro/nav/NRSRO_Exhibit-1.pdf**.
[c]Median ratios are from Standard & Poor's 2006 Corporate Ratings Criteria, April 23, 2007: see **www2.standardandpoors.com /spf/pdf/fixedincome/Corporate_Ratings_2006.pdf.**
[d]Composite yields for 10-year AAA, AA, and A bonds can be found at **www.bondsonline.com/Todays_Market/Composite _Bond_Yields_table.php.** Representative yields for 10-year BBB, BB, B, and CCC bonds can be found using the bond screener at **http://finra-markets.morningstar.com/BondCenter/Screener.jsp?type=advanced**. Thin markets caused the AAA rate to be unusually high.

4-11c Bond Rating Criteria, Upgrades, and Downgrades

Bond ratings are based on both quantitative and qualitative factors, as we describe below.

1. **Financial Ratios.** Many ratios potentially are important, but the return on invested capital, debt ratio, and interest coverage ratio are particularly valuable for predicting financial distress. For example, Columns (1), (5), and (6) in Table 4-1 show a strong relationship between ratings and the return on capital and the debt ratio.
2. **Bond Contract Terms.** Important provisions for determining the bond's rating include whether the bond is secured by a mortgage on specific assets, whether the bond is subordinated to other debt, any sinking fund provisions, guarantees by some other party with a high credit ranking, and *restrictive covenants* such as requirements that the firm keep its debt ratio below a given level or that it keep its times interest earned ratio above a given level.
3. **Qualitative Factors.** Included here would be such factors as sensitivity of the firm's earnings to the strength of the economy, how it is affected by inflation, whether it is having or is likely to have labor problems, the extent of its international operations (including the stability of the countries in which it operates), potential environmental problems, potential antitrust problems, and so on.

Rating agencies review outstanding bonds on a periodic basis and re-rate if necessary. Columns (7) and (8) in Table 4-1 show the percentages of companies in each rating category that were downgraded or upgraded in 2012 by Fitch Ratings. The year 2012 was a difficult one, as more bonds were downgraded than upgraded.

Over the long run, ratings agencies have done a reasonably good job of measuring the average credit risk of bonds and of changing ratings whenever there is a significant change in credit quality. However, it is important to understand that ratings do not adjust immediately to changes in credit quality, and in some cases there can be a considerable lag between a change in credit quality and a change in rating. For example, Enron's bonds still carried an investment-grade rating on a Friday in December 2001, but the company declared bankruptcy two days later, on Sunday. Many other abrupt downgrades occurred in 2007 and 2008, leading to calls by Congress and the SEC for changes in rating agencies and the way they rate bonds. Clearly, improvements can be made, but there will always be occasions when completely unexpected information about a company is released, leading to a sudden change in its rating.

4-11d Bond Ratings and the Default Risk Premium

Why are bond ratings so important? First, most bonds are purchased by institutional investors rather than individuals, and many institutions are restricted to investment-grade securities. Thus, if a firm's bonds fall below BBB, it will have a difficult time selling new bonds because many potential purchasers will not be allowed to buy them. Second, many bond covenants stipulate that the coupon rate on the bond automatically increases if the rating falls below a specified level. Third, because a bond's rating is an indicator of its default risk, the rating has a direct, measurable influence on the bond's yield. Column (9) of Table 4-1 shows that an AAA bond has a yield of 3.65% and that yields increase as the rating falls. In fact, an investor would earn 7.40% on a CCC bond if it didn't default.

A **bond spread** is the difference between a bond's yield and the yield on some other security of the same maturity. Unless specified differently, the term "spread"

THE GLOBAL ECONOMIC CRISIS

U.S. Treasury Bonds Downgraded!

The worsening recession that began at the end of 2007 led Congress to pass a huge economic stimulus package in early 2009. The combination of the stimulus package and the government's bailouts of financial institutions caused the U.S. government to increase its borrowing substantially. The current (December 2013) level of public debt is $17.3 trillion, about 107% of gross domestic product (GDP). Any way you look at it, this is a lot of money, even by Washington standards!

With so much debt outstanding and enormous annual deficits continuing, in mid-2011 Congress was faced with the need to increase the amount of debt the federal government is allowed to issue. Although Congress had increased the debt ceiling 74 times previously, and 10 times since 2001, partisan and heated debate seriously delayed approval of the measure and brought the federal government to the brink of default on its obligations by August. At the last minute, Congress approved a debt ceiling increase, narrowly avoiding a partial government shutdown. However, the deficit reduction package that accompanied the legislation was small, doing little to address the structural revenue and spending imbalance the federal government faces going forward.

On August 5, 2011, the combination of a dysfunctional political process apparently incapable of reliably performing basic financial housekeeping chores and the lack of a clear plan to address future deficits raised enough questions about the U.S. government's financial stability to induce Standard & Poor's (S&P), the credit rating agency, to downgrade U.S. public debt from AAA to AA+, effectively removing it from its list of risk-free investments. Financial markets quickly responded to this dark assessment, with the Dow Jones Industrial Average plunging some 13% over the next week. Moody's and Fitch, the other two major rating agencies, however, kept their ratings of U.S. public debt at their highest levels. With two out of three agencies rating U.S. debt at the highest level, is the yield on U.S. debt still a proxy for the riskless rate? Only time will tell, but since the initial downgrade in 2011, a bitterly divided Congress has brought the federal government to the brink of default on its debt obligations two more times as of the end of 2013. This behavior does not bode well for the prospect of maintaining a AAA rating.

generally means the difference between a bond's yield and the yield on a Treasury bond of similar maturity.

Figure 4-3 shows the spreads between an index of AAA bonds and a 20-year Treasury bond; it also shows spreads for an index of BBB bonds relative to the T-bond. Figure 4-3 illustrates three important points. First, the BAA spread always is greater than the AAA spread. This is because a BAA bond is riskier than an AAA bond, so BAA investors require extra compensation for their extra risk. The same is true for other ratings: Lower-rated bonds have higher yields.

Second, the spreads are not constant over time. For example, look at the AAA spread. It was exceptionally low during the boom years of 2005–2007 but rose dramatically as the economy declined in 2008 and 2009.

Third, the difference between the BAA spread and the AAA spread isn't constant over time. The two spreads were reasonably close to one another in 2005 but were very far apart in early 2009. In other words, BAA investors didn't require much extra return over that of an AAA bond to induce them to take on that extra risk most years, but in 2009 they required a very large risk premium.

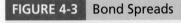

FIGURE 4-3 | Bond Spreads

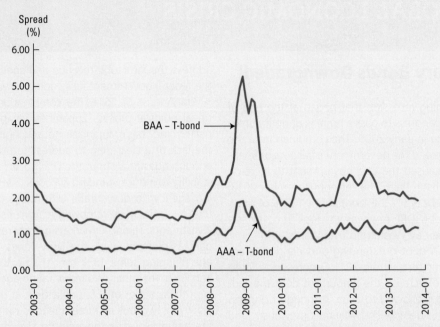

Note: All data are from the Federal Reserve Bank of St. Louis's Economic Database, FRED: **http://research.stlouisfed.org/fred2**. The spreads are defined as the yield on the risky bond (AAA or BAA) minus the yield on a 20-year Treasury bond.

THE FEW, THE PROUD, THE . . . AAA-RATED COMPANIES!

AAA-rated companies are members of an elite group. Over the last 20 years, this cream of the crop has included such powerhouses as 3M, Abbott Labs, BellSouth, ExxonMobil, GE, Kellogg, Microsoft, and UPS. Only large companies with stable cash flows make it into this group, and for years they guarded their AAA ratings vigilantly. In recent years, however, the nonfinancial AAA-rated corporation has become a vanishing breed. In December 2013, the major ratings agencies (Fitch, S&P, and Moody's) only agreed on the highest rating for one nonfinancial company without government backing: Johnson & Johnson.

Why do so few companies have AAA ratings? One reason may be that the recent financial crisis and recession have hurt the creditworthiness of even large, stable companies. Another reason is that many of the top companies are choosing to be rated by only one or two of the ratings agencies, rather than all three. A third likely explanation is that in recent years large, stable companies have increased their debt levels to take greater advantage of the tax savings that they afford. With higher debt levels, these companies are no longer eligible for the highest rating. In essence, they have sacrificed their AAA rating for lower taxes. Does this sound like a good trade-off to you? We will discuss how companies choose the level of debt in Chapter 16.

Source: **www.finra.org/Investors/InvestmentChoices/Bonds**.

Not only do spreads vary with the rating of the security, they also usually increase as maturity increases. This should make sense. If a bond matures soon, investors are able to forecast the company's performance fairly well. But if a bond has a long time until it matures, investors have a difficult time forecasting the likelihood that the company will fall into financial distress. This extra uncertainty creates additional risk, so investors demand a higher required return.

SELF TEST

Differentiate between mortgage bonds and debentures.

Name the major rating agencies, and list some factors that affect bond ratings.

What is a bond spread?

How do bond ratings affect the default risk premium?

A 10-year T-bond has a yield of 6%. A 10-year corporate bond with a rating of AA has a yield of 7.5%. If the corporate bond has excellent liquidity, what is an estimate of the corporate bond's default risk premium? **(1.5%)**

THE GLOBAL ECONOMIC CRISIS

Fear and Rationality

The graph below shows two measures of fear. One is the "Hi-Yield" spread between the yields on junk bonds and Treasury bonds. The second is the **TED spread**, which is the difference between the 3-month LIBOR rate and the 3-month T-bill rate. Both are measures of risk aversion. The Hi-Yield spread measures the amount of extra compensation investors need to induce them to take on risky junk bonds. The TED spread measures the extra compensation that banks require to induce them to lend to one another. Observe that the spreads were very low from mid-2003 through the end of 2007. During these boom years, investors and bankers had a voracious appetite for risk and simply didn't require much extra return for additional risk. But as the economy began to deteriorate in 2008, investors and bankers reversed course and became extremely risk averse, with spreads skyrocketing. Interestingly, the pre-financial crisis appetite for risk has returned seems to have returned, with spreads again very low. It is hard to

reconcile such drastic changes in risk aversion with careful, deliberate, and rational behavior!

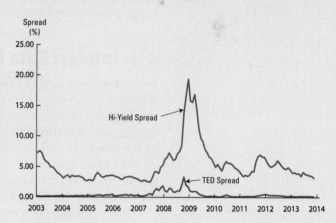

Note: The Hi-Yield spread is the average monthly value of the BofA Merrill Lynch US High Yield Master II Effective Yield minus the 10-year T-bond yield. TED is the difference between the 3-month LIBOR rate and the 3-month T-bill rate. All data are from the Federal Reserve Bank of St. Louis's Economic Database, FRED: **http://research.stlouisfed.org/fred2**.

4-12 The Liquidity Premium (LP)

A "liquid" asset can be converted to cash quickly and at a "fair market value." Financial assets are generally more liquid than real assets. Because liquidity is important, investors include **liquidity premiums (LPs)** when market rates of securities are established. Although liquidity premiums are difficult to measure accurately, a differential of at least 2 percentage points (and perhaps up to 4 or 5 percentage points) exists between the least liquid and the most liquid financial assets of similar default risk and maturity. Corporate bonds issued by small companies are traded less frequently than those issued by large companies, so small-company bonds tend to have a higher liquidity premium.

For example, liquidity in the market for mortgage-backed securities evaporated in 2008 and early 2009. The few transactions that occurred were priced so low that the yields on these MBS were extremely high, which was partially due to a much higher liquidity premium caused by the extremely low liquidity of MBS.

> **SELF TEST**   Which bond usually will have a higher liquidity premium: one issued by a large company or one issued by a small company?

4-13 The Maturity Risk Premium (MRP)

All bonds, even Treasury bonds, are exposed to two additional sources of risk: interest rate risk and reinvestment risk. The net effect of these two sources of risk upon a bond's yield is called the **maturity risk premium, MRP**. The following sections explain how interest rate risk and reinvestment risk affect a bond's yield.

4-13a Interest Rate Risk

Interest rates go up and down over time, and an increase in interest rates leads to a decline in the value of outstanding bonds. This risk of a decline in bond values due to rising interest rates is called **interest rate risk**. To illustrate, suppose you bought some 9% MicroDrive bonds at a price of $1,000, and then interest rates rose in the following year to 14%. As we saw earlier, the price of the bonds would fall to $692.89, so you would have a loss of $307.11 per bond.[18] Interest rates can and do rise, and rising rates cause a loss of value for bondholders. Thus, bond investors are exposed to risk from changing interest rates.

This point can be demonstrated by showing how the value of a 1-year bond with a 10% annual coupon fluctuates with changes in r_d and then comparing these

---

18. You would have an *accounting* (and tax) loss only if you sold the bond; if you held it to maturity, you would not have such a loss. However, even if you did not sell, you would still have suffered a *real economic loss in an opportunity cost sense* because you would have lost the opportunity to invest at 14% and would be stuck with a 9% bond in a 14% market. In an economic sense, "paper losses" are just as bad as realized accounting losses.

changes with those on a 25-year bond. The 1-year bond's value for r_d = 5% is shown below:

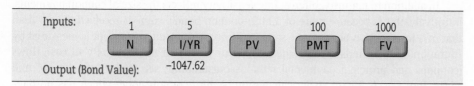

Inputs:

1	5	100	1000
N	I/YR	PV	PMT	FV

Output (Bond Value):   −1047.62

Using either a calculator or a spreadsheet, you could calculate the bond values for a 1-year and a 25-year bond at several current market interest rates; these results are plotted in Figure 4-4. Note how much more sensitive the price of the 25-year bond is to changes in interest rates. At a 10% interest rate, both the 25-year and the 1-year bonds are valued at $1,000. When rates rise to 15%, the 25-year bond falls to $676.79 but the 1-year bond falls only to $956.52.

For bonds with similar coupons, this differential sensitivity to changes in interest rates always holds true: The longer the maturity of the bond, the more its price changes in response to a given change in interest rates. Thus, even if the risk of default on two bonds is exactly the same, the one with the longer maturity is exposed to more risk from a rise in interest rates.

The explanation for this difference in interest rate risk is simple. Suppose you bought a 25-year bond that yielded 10%, or $100 a year. Now suppose interest rates on bonds of comparable risk rose to 15%. You would be stuck with only $100 of interest for the next 25 years. On the other hand, had you bought a 1-year bond, you would have a low return for only 1 year. At the end of the year, you would get your $1,000 back, and you could then reinvest it and receive a 15% return ($150)

See *Ch04 Tool Kit.xls.*

FIGURE 4-4 **Value of Long- and Short-Term 10% Annual Coupon Bonds at Different Market Interest Rates**

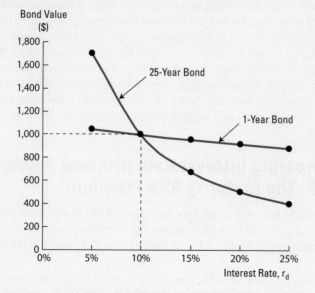

Source: From *Financial Management: Theory & Practice*, 2013, by Brigham and Ehrhardt.
© Cengage Learning.

for the next year. Thus, interest rate risk reflects the length of time one is committed to a given investment.

In addition to maturity, interest rate sensitivity reflects the size of coupon payments. Intuitively, this is because more of a high-coupon bond's value is received sooner than that of a low-coupon bond of the same maturity. This intuitive concept is measured by "duration," which finds the average number of years that the bond's PV of cash flows (coupons and principal payments) remains outstanding; see *Web Extension 4C* and *Ch04 Tool Kit.xls* for the exact calculation. A zero coupon bond, which has no payments until maturity, has a duration equal to its maturity. Coupon bonds have durations that are shorter than maturity, and the higher the coupon rate, the shorter the duration.

Duration measures a bond's sensitivity to interest rates in the following sense: Given a change in interest rates, the percentage change in a bond's price is proportional to its duration:[19]

$$\% \text{ change in } V_B = (\% \text{ change in } 1 + r_d)(-\text{Duration})$$

Excel's **DURATION** function provides an easy way to calculate a bond's duration. See Web *Extension 4C* and *Ch04 Tool Kit.xls* for more discussion of duration and its use in measuring and managing interest rate risk.

4-13b **Reinvestment Rate Risk**

As we saw in the preceding section, an *increase* in interest rates will hurt bondholders because it will lead to a decline in the value of a bond portfolio. But can a *decrease* in interest rates also hurt bondholders? The answer is "yes," because if interest rates fall, then a bondholder may suffer a reduction in his or her income. For example, consider a retiree who has a portfolio of bonds and lives off the income they produce. The bonds, on average, have a coupon rate of 10%. Now suppose that interest rates decline to 5%. The short-term bonds will mature, and when they do, they will have to be replaced with lower-yielding bonds. In addition, many of the remaining long-term bonds may be called, and as calls occur, the bondholder will have to replace 10% bonds with 5% bonds. Thus, our retiree will suffer a reduction of income.

The risk of an income decline due to a drop in interest rates is called **reinvestment rate risk**. Reinvestment rate risk is obviously high on callable bonds. It is also high on short-maturity bonds, because the shorter the maturity of a bond, the fewer the years when the relatively high old interest rate will be earned and the sooner the funds will have to be reinvested at the new low rate. Thus, retirees whose primary holdings are short-term securities, such as bank CDs and short-term bonds, are hurt badly by a decline in rates, but holders of long-term bonds continue to enjoy their old high rates.

4-13c **Comparing Interest Rate Risk and Reinvestment Rate Risk: The Maturity Risk Premium**

Note that interest rate risk relates to the *value* of the bonds in a portfolio, while reinvestment rate risk relates to the *income* the portfolio produces. If you hold long-term bonds then you will face a lot of interest rate risk, because the value of your

---

19. This is true for the case in which the term structure (which we discuss in Section 4.14) is flat and can only shift up and down. However, other duration measures can be developed for other term structure assumptions.

bonds will decline if interest rates rise; however, you will not face much reinvestment rate risk, so your income will be stable. On the other hand, if you hold short-term bonds, you will not be exposed to much interest rate risk, because the value of your portfolio will be stable, but you will be exposed to considerable reinvestment rate risk because your income will fluctuate with changes in interest rates. We see, then, that no fixed-rate bond can be considered totally riskless—even most Treasury bonds are exposed to both interest rate risk and reinvestment rate risk.[20]

Bond prices reflect the trading activities of the marginal investors, defined as those who trade often enough and with large enough sums to determine bond prices. Although one particular investor might be more averse to reinvestment risk than to interest rate risk, the data suggest that the marginal investor is more averse to interest rate risk than to reinvestment risk. To induce the marginal investor to take on interest rate risk, long-term bonds must have a higher expected rate of return than short-term bonds. Holding all else equal, this additional return is the maturity risk premium (MRP).

4-14 The Term Structure of Interest Rates

The **term structure of interest rates** describes the relationship between long-term and short-term rates. The term structure is important both to corporate treasurers deciding whether to borrow by issuing long-term or short-term debt and to investors who are deciding whether to buy long-term or short-term bonds.

Interest rates for bonds with different maturities can be found in a variety of publications, including *The Wall Street Journal* and the *Federal Reserve Bulletin*, as well as on a number of Web sites, including Bloomberg, Yahoo!, CNN Financial, and the Federal Reserve Board. Using interest rate data from these sources, we can determine the term structure at any given point in time. For example, Figure 4-5 presents interest rates for different maturities on three different dates. The set of data for a given date, when plotted on a graph such as Figure 4-5, is called the **yield curve** for that date.

As the figure shows, the yield curve changes both in position and in slope over time. In March 1980, all rates were quite high because high inflation was expected. However, the rate of inflation was expected to decline, so the inflation premium (IP) was larger for short-term bonds than for long-term bonds. This caused

20. Although indexed Treasury bonds are almost riskless, they pay a relatively low real rate. Note also that risks have not disappeared—they have simply been transferred from bondholders to taxpayers.

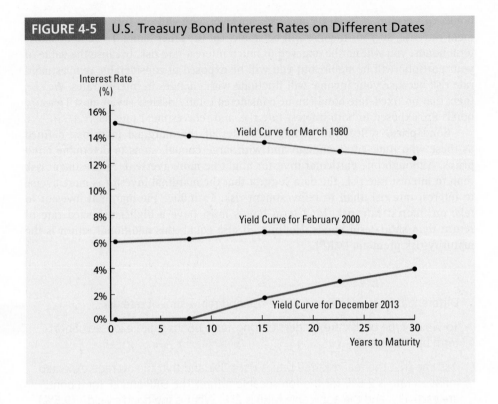

FIGURE 4-5   U.S. Treasury Bond Interest Rates on Different Dates

short-term yields to be higher than long-term yields, resulting in a *downward-sloping* yield curve. By February 2000, inflation had indeed declined and thus all rates were lower. The yield curve had become **humped**—medium-term rates were higher than either short- or long-term rates. In December 2013, all rates were below the 2000 levels. Because short-term rates had dropped below long-term rates, the yield curve was *upward sloping.*

Historically, long-term rates are generally higher than short-term rates owing to the maturity risk premium, so the yield curve usually slopes upward. For this reason, people often call an upward-sloping yield curve a **"normal" yield curve** and a yield curve that slopes downward an **inverted**, or **"abnormal," curve**. Thus, in Figure 4-5 the yield curve for March 1980 was inverted, whereas the yield curve in December 2013 was normal. As stated above, the February 2000 curve was humped.

A few academics and practitioners contend that large bond traders who buy and sell securities of different maturities each day dominate the market. According to this view, a bond trader is just as willing to buy a 30-year bond to pick up a short-term profit as to buy a 3-month security. Strict proponents of this view argue that the shape of the yield curve is therefore determined only by market expectations about future interest rates, a position that is called the **pure expectations theory**, or sometimes just the **expectations theory**. If this were true, then the maturity risk premium (MRP) would be zero and long-term interest rates would simply be a weighted average of current and expected future short-term interest rates. See *Web Extension 4D* for a more detailed discussion of the expectations theory.

WEB

For a discussion of the expectations theory, see **Web Extension 4D** on the textbook's Web site.

What is a yield curve, and what information would you need to draw this curve?

Distinguish among the shapes of a "normal" yield curve, an "abnormal" curve, and a "humped" curve.

If the interest rates on 1-, 5-, 20-, and 30-year bonds are (respectively) 4%, 5%, 6%, and 7%, then how would you describe the yield curve? How would you describe it if the rates were reversed?

4-15 **Financing with Junk Bonds**

Recall that bonds rated less than BBB are noninvestment-grade debt, also called junk bonds or high-yield debt. There are two ways that a bond can become a junk bond. First, the bond might have been investment-grade debt when it was issued but its rating subsequently was cut because the issuing corporation had fallen on hard times. Such bonds are called "fallen angels," and there are many such bonds as we write this in 2013.

Some bonds are junk bonds at the time they are issued, but this was not always true. Prior to the 1980s, fixed-income investors such as pension funds and insurance companies were generally unwilling to buy risky bonds, so it was almost impossible for risky companies to raise capital in the public bond markets. Then, in the late 1970s, Michael Milken of the investment banking firm Drexel Burnham Lambert, relying on historical studies that showed risky bonds yielded more than enough to compensate for their risk, convinced institutional investors that junk bond yields were worth their risk. Thus was born the junk bond market.

In the 1980s, large investors like T. Boone Pickens and Henry Kravis thought that certain old-line, established companies were run inefficiently and were financed too conservatively. These corporate raiders were able to invest some of their own money, borrow the rest via junk bonds, and take over the target company, usually taking the company private. The fact that interest on the bonds was tax deductible, combined with the much higher debt ratios of the restructured firms, increased after-tax cash flows and helped make the deals feasible. Because these deals used lots of debt, they were called **leveraged buyouts (LBOs)**.

In recent years, private equity firms have conducted transactions similar to the LBOs of the 1980s, taking advantage of historically low junk-bond rates to help finance their purchases. For example, in 2007 the private equity firm Kohlberg Kravis Roberts and Company (KKR) took the discount retailer Dollar General private in a $6.9 billion deal. As part of the transaction, Dollar General issued $1.9 billion in junk bonds. So KKR financed approximately 73% of the deal with its own cash (coming from its own equity and from money it had borrowed on its own account) and about 27% of the deal with money that Dollar General raised, for a net investment of about $5 billion. In late 2009, KKR took Dollar General public again at $21 per share with a resulting market value of equity of $7.1 billion and a very tidy gain!

What are junk bonds?

4-16 **Bankruptcy and Reorganization**

A business is *insolvent* when it does not have enough cash to meet its interest and principal payments. When this occurs, either the creditors or the company may file for bankruptcy in the United States Bankruptcy Court. After hearing from the creditors and the company's managers, a federal bankruptcy court judge decides whether to dissolve the firm through *liquidation* or to permit it to *reorganize* and thus stay alive. Chapter 7 of the federal bankruptcy statutes addresses liquidation, and Chapter 11 addresses reorganization.

The decision to force a firm to liquidate versus permit it to reorganize depends on whether the value of the reorganized firm is likely to be greater than the value of the firm's assets if they are sold off piecemeal. In a reorganization, the firm's creditors negotiate with management on the terms of a potential reorganization. The reorganization plan may call for a *restructuring* of the firm's debt, in which case the interest rate may be reduced, the term to maturity may be lengthened, or some of the debt may be exchanged for equity. The point of the restructuring is to reduce the financial charges to a level that the firm's cash flows can support. Of course, the common stockholders also have to give up something: They often see their position diluted as a result of additional shares being given to debtholders in exchange for accepting a reduced amount of debt principal and interest. In fact, the original common stockholders often end up with nothing. The court may appoint a trustee to oversee the reorganization, but usually the existing management is allowed to retain control.

Liquidation occurs if the company is deemed to be too far gone to be saved—if it is worth more dead than alive. If the bankruptcy court orders liquidation, then assets are sold off and the cash obtained is distributed as specified in Chapter 7 of the Bankruptcy Act. Here is the priority of claims: (1) past-due property tax liens; (2) secured creditors who are entitled to the proceeds from the sale of collateral; (3) the trustee's costs of administering and operating the bankrupt firm; (4) expenses incurred after bankruptcy was filed; (5) wages due workers, up to a limit of $10,000 per worker; (6) claims for unpaid contributions to employee benefit plans (with wages and claims not to exceed $10,000 per worker); (7) unsecured claims for customer deposits up to $1,800 per customer; (8) federal, state, and local taxes due; (9) unfunded pension plan liabilities (although some limitations exist); (10) general unsecured creditors; (11) preferred stockholders (up to the par value of their stock); and (12) common stockholders (although usually nothing is left for them).

The key points for you to know are: (1) the federal bankruptcy statutes govern both reorganization and liquidation, (2) bankruptcies occur frequently, and (3) a priority of the specified claims must be followed when distributing the assets of a liquidated firm. More information about bankruptcy can be found in Chapter 25.

> **SELF TEST**
>
> Differentiate between a Chapter 7 liquidation and a Chapter 11 reorganization.
>
> List the priority of claims for the distribution of a liquidated firm's assets.

Summary

This chapter described the different types of bonds that governments and corporations issue, explained how bond prices are established, and discussed how investors estimate the rates of return they can expect to earn. The rate of return required by debtholders is the company's pre-tax cost of debt, and this rate depends on the risk that investors face when they buy bonds.

- A **bond** is a long-term promissory note issued by a business or governmental unit. The issuer receives money in exchange for promising to make interest payments and to repay the principal on a specified future date.
- Some special types of long-term financing include **zero coupon bonds**, which pay no annual interest but are issued at a discount; see *Web Extension 4A* for more on zero coupon bonds. Other types are **floating-rate debt**, whose interest payments fluctuate with changes in the general level of interest rates; and **junk bonds**, which are high-risk, high-yield instruments issued by firms that use a great deal of financial leverage.
- A **call provision** gives the issuing corporation the right to redeem the bonds prior to maturity under specified terms, usually at a price greater than the maturity value (the difference is a **call premium**). A firm will typically call a bond if interest rates fall substantially below the coupon rate.
- A **sinking fund** is a provision that requires the corporation to retire a portion of the bond issue each year. The purpose of the sinking fund is to provide for the orderly retirement of the issue. A sinking fund typically requires no call premium.
- The **value of a bond** is found as the present value of an **annuity** (the interest payments) plus the present value of a lump sum (the **principal**). The bond is evaluated at the appropriate periodic interest rate over the number of periods for which interest payments are made.
- The equation used to find the value of an annual coupon bond is

$$V_B = \sum_{t=1}^{N} \frac{INT}{(1 + r_d)^t} + \frac{M}{(1 + r_d)^N}$$

- An adjustment to the formula must be made if the bond pays interest **semiannually**: divide INT and r_d by 2, and multiply N by 2.
- The expected rate of return on a bond held to maturity is defined as the bond's **yield to maturity (YTM)**:

$$\text{Bond price} = \sum_{t=1}^{N} \frac{INT}{(1 + YTM)^t} + \frac{M}{(1 + YTM)^N}$$

- The expected rate of return on a callable bond held to its call date is defined as the **yield to call (YTC)**.
- The **nominal** (or **quoted**) **interest rate** on a debt security, r_d, is composed of the real risk-free rate, r*, plus premiums that reflect inflation (IP), default risk (DRP), liquidity (LP), and maturity risk (MRP):

$$r_d = r^* + IP + DRP + LP + MRP$$

- The **risk-free rate of interest**, r_{RF}, is defined as the real risk-free rate, r^*, plus an inflation premium, IP: $r_{RF} = r^* + IP$.
- **Treasury Inflation-Protected Securities (TIPS)** are U.S. Treasury bonds that have no inflation risk. See *Web Extension 4B* for more discussion of TIPS.
- The longer the maturity of a bond, the more its price will change in response to a given change in interest rates; this is called **interest rate risk**. However, bonds with short maturities expose investors to high **reinvestment rate risk**, which is the risk that income from a bond portfolio will decline because cash flows received from bonds will be rolled over at lower interest rates.
- **Duration** is a measure of interest rate risk. See *Web Extension 4C* for a discussion of duration.
- Corporate and municipal bonds have **default risk**. If an issuer defaults, investors receive less than the promised return on the bond. Therefore, investors should evaluate a bond's default risk before making a purchase.
- Bonds are assigned **ratings** that reflect the probability of their going into default. The highest rating is AAA, and they go down to D. The higher a bond's rating, the lower its risk and therefore its interest rate.
- The relationship between the yields on securities and the securities' maturities is known as the **term structure of interest rates**, and the **yield curve** is a graph of this relationship.
- The shape of the yield curve depends on two key factors: (1) *expectations about future inflation* and (2) *perceptions about the relative risk of securities with different maturities.*
- The yield curve is normally **upward sloping**—this is called a **normal yield curve**. However, the curve can slope downward (an **inverted yield curve**) if the inflation rate is expected to decline. The yield curve also can be **humped**, which means that interest rates on medium-term maturities are higher than rates on both short- and long-term maturities.
- The **expectations theory** states that yields on long-term bonds reflect expected future interest rates. *Web Extension 4D* discusses this theory.

Questions

4-1 Define each of the following terms:
   a. Bond; Treasury bond; corporate bond; municipal bond; foreign bond
   b. Par value; maturity date; coupon payment; coupon interest rate
   c. Floating-rate bond; zero coupon bond; original issue discount bond (OID)
   d. Call provision; redeemable bond; sinking fund
   e. Convertible bond; warrant; income bond; indexed bond (also called a purchasing power bond)
   f. Premium bond; discount bond
   g. Current yield (on a bond); yield to maturity (YTM); yield to call (YTC)
   h. Indentures; mortgage bond; debenture; subordinated debenture
   i. Development bond; municipal bond insurance; junk bond; investment-grade bond
   j. Real risk-free rate of interest, r^*; nominal risk-free rate of interest, r_{RF}

k. Inflation premium (IP); default risk premium (DRP); liquidity; liquidity premium (LP)

l. Interest rate risk; maturity risk premium (MRP); reinvestment rate risk

m. Term structure of interest rates; yield curve

n. "Normal" yield curve; inverted ("abnormal") yield curve

4-2 "Short-term interest rates are more volatile than long-term interest rates, so short-term bond prices are more sensitive to interest rate changes than are long-term bond prices." Is this statement true or false? Explain.

4-3 The rate of return on a bond held to its maturity date is called the bond's yield to maturity. If interest rates in the economy rise after a bond has been issued, what will happen to the bond's price and to its YTM? Does the length of time to maturity affect the extent to which a given change in interest rates will affect the bond's price? Why or why not?

4-4 If you buy a *callable* bond and interest rates decline, will the value of your bond rise by as much as it would have risen if the bond had not been callable? Explain.

4-5 A sinking fund can be set up in one of two ways. Discuss the advantages and disadvantages of each procedure from the viewpoint of both the firm and its bondholders.

Problems

Answers Appear in Appendix B

Easy Problems 1–6

4-1 Bond Valuation with Annual Payments
Jackson Corporation's bonds have 12 years remaining to maturity. Interest is paid annually, the bonds have a $1,000 par value, and the coupon interest rate is 8%. The bonds have a yield to maturity of 9%. What is the current market price of these bonds?

4-2 Yield to Maturity for Annual Payments
Wilson Wonders' bonds have 12 years remaining to maturity. Interest is paid annually, the bonds have a $1,000 par value, and the coupon interest rate is 10%. The bonds sell at a price of $850. What is their yield to maturity?

4-3 Current Yield for Annual Payments
Heath Foods' bonds have 7 years remaining to maturity. The bonds have a face value of $1,000 and a yield to maturity of 8%. They pay interest annually and have a 9% coupon rate. What is their current yield?

4-4 Determinant of Interest Rates
The real risk-free rate of interest is 4%. Inflation is expected to be 2% this year and 4% during the next 2 years. Assume that the maturity risk premium is zero. What is the yield on 2-year Treasury securities? What is the yield on 3-year Treasury securities?

4-5 Default Risk Premium
A Treasury bond that matures in 10 years has a yield of 6%. A 10-year corporate bond has a yield of 9%. Assume that the liquidity premium

on the corporate bond is 0.5%. What is the default risk premium on the corporate bond?

4-6 Maturity Risk Premium
The real risk-free rate is 3%, and inflation is expected to be 3% for the next 2 years. A 2-year Treasury security yields 6.3%. What is the maturity risk premium for the 2-year security?

Intermediate Problems 7–20

4-7 Bond Valuation with Semiannual Payments
Renfro Rentals has issued bonds that have a 10% coupon rate, payable semi-annually. The bonds mature in 8 years, have a face value of $1,000, and a yield to maturity of 8.5%. What is the price of the bonds?

4-8 Yield to Maturity and Call with Semiannual Payments
Thatcher Corporation's bonds will mature in 10 years. The bonds have a face value of $1,000 and an 8% coupon rate, paid semiannually. The price of the bonds is $1,100. The bonds are callable in 5 years at a call price of $1,050. What is their yield to maturity? What is their yield to call?

4-9 Bond Valuation and Interest Rate Risk
The Garraty Company has two bond issues outstanding. Both bonds pay $100 annual interest plus $1,000 at maturity. Bond L has a maturity of 15 years, and Bond S has a maturity of 1 year.
a. What will be the value of each of these bonds when the going rate of interest is: (1) 5%, (2) 8%, and (3) 12%? Assume that there is only one more interest payment to be made on Bond S.
b. Why does the longer-term (15-year) bond fluctuate more when interest rates change than does the shorter-term bond (1 year)?

4-10 Yield to Maturity and Required Returns
The Brownstone Corporation's bonds have 5 years remaining to maturity. Interest is paid annually, the bonds have a $1,000 par value, and the coupon interest rate is 9%.
a. What is the yield to maturity at a current market price of: (1) $829 or (2) $1,104?
b. Would you pay $829 for one of these bonds if you thought that the appropriate rate of interest was 12%—that is, if $r_d = 12\%$? Explain your answer.

4-11 Yield to Call and Realized Rates of Return
Seven years ago, Goodwynn & Wolf Incorporated sold a 20-year bond issue with a 14% annual coupon rate and a 9% call premium. Today, G&W called the bonds. The bonds originally were sold at their face value of $1,000. Compute the realized rate of return for investors who purchased the bonds when they were issued and who surrender them today in exchange for the call price.

4-12 Bond Yields and Rates of Return
A 10-year, 12% semiannual coupon bond with a par value of $1,000 may be called in 4 years at a call price of $1,060. The bond sells for $1,100. (Assume that the bond has just been issued.)
a. What is the bond's yield to maturity?
b. What is the bond's current yield?

c. What is the bond's capital gain or loss yield?

d. What is the bond's yield to call?

4–13 Yield to Maturity and Current Yield

You just purchased a bond that matures in 5 years. The bond has a face value of $1,000 and has an 8% annual coupon. The bond has a current yield of 8.21%. What is the bond's yield to maturity?

4–14 Current Yield with Semiannual Payments

A bond that matures in 7 years sells for $1,020. The bond has a face value of $1,000 and a yield to maturity of 10.5883%. The bond pays coupons semiannually. What is the bond's current yield?

4–15 Yield to Call, Yield to Maturity, and Market Rates

Absalom Motors' 14% coupon rate, semiannual payment, $1,000 par value bonds that mature in 30 years are callable 5 years from now at a price of $1,050. The bonds sell at a price of $1,353.54, and the yield curve is flat. Assuming that interest rates in the economy are expected to remain at their current level, what is the best estimate of the nominal interest rate on new bonds?

4–16 Interest Rate Sensitivity

A bond trader purchased each of the following bonds at a yield to maturity of 8%. Immediately after she purchased the bonds, interest rates fell to 7%. What is the percentage change in the price of each bond after the decline in interest rates? Fill in the following table:

	Price @ 8%	Price @ 7%	Percentage Change
10-year, 10% annual coupon	_____	_____	_____
10-year zero	_____	_____	_____
5-year zero	_____	_____	_____
30-year zero	_____	_____	_____
Perpetuity, $100 annual coupon	_____	_____	_____

4–17 Bond Value as Maturity Approaches

An investor has two bonds in his portfolio. Each bond matures in 4 years, has a face value of $1,000, and has a yield to maturity equal to 9.6%. One bond, Bond C, pays an annual coupon of 10%; the other bond, Bond Z, is a zero coupon bond. Assuming that the yield to maturity of each bond remains at 9.6% over the next 4 years, what will be the price of each of the bonds at the following time periods? Fill in the following table:

t	Price of Bond C	Price of Bond Z
0	_____	_____
1	_____	_____
2	_____	_____
3	_____	_____
4	_____	_____

4–18 Determinants of Interest Rates

The real risk-free rate is 2%. Inflation is expected to be 3% this year, 4% next year, and then 3.5% thereafter. The maturity risk premium is estimated to be $0.0005 \times (t - 1)$, where t = number of years to maturity. What is the nominal interest rate on a 7-year Treasury security?

4-19 Maturity Risk Premiums

Assume that the real risk-free rate, r^*, is 3% and that inflation is expected to be 8% in Year 1, 5% in Year 2, and 4% thereafter. Assume also that all Treasury securities are highly liquid and free of default risk. If 2-year and 5-year Treasury notes both yield 10%, what is the difference in the maturity risk premiums (MRPs) on the two notes; that is, what is MRP_5 minus MRP_2?

4-20 Inflation Risk Premiums

Because of a recession, the inflation rate expected for the coming year is only 3%. However, the inflation rate in Year 2 and thereafter is expected to be constant at some level above 3%. Assume that the real risk-free rate is $r^* = 2\%$ for all maturities and that there are no maturity premiums. If 3-year Treasury notes yield 2 percentage points more than 1-year notes, what inflation rate is expected after Year 1?

Challenging Problems 21–23

4-21 Bond Valuation and Changes in Maturity and Required Returns

Suppose Hillard Manufacturing sold an issue of bonds with a 10-year maturity, a $1,000 par value, a 10% coupon rate, and semiannual interest payments.

a. Two years after the bonds were issued, the going rate of interest on bonds such as these fell to 6%. At what price would the bonds sell?

b. Suppose that 2 years after the initial offering, the going interest rate had risen to 12%. At what price would the bonds sell?

c. Suppose that 2 years after the issue date (as in part a) interest rates fell to 6%. Suppose further that the interest rate remained at 6% for the next 8 years. What would happen to the price of the bonds over time?

4-22 Yield to Maturity and Yield to Call

Arnot International's bonds have a current market price of $1,200. The bonds have an 11% annual coupon payment, a $1,000 face value, and 10 years left until maturity. The bonds may be called in 5 years at 109% of face value (call price = $1,090).

a. What is the yield to maturity?

b. What is the yield to call if they are called in 5 years?

c. Which yield might investors expect to earn on these bonds, and why?

d. The bond's indenture indicates that the call provision gives the firm the right to call them at the end of each year beginning in Year 5. In Year 5, they may be called at 109% of face value, but in each of the next 4 years the call percentage will decline by 1 percentage point. Thus, in Year 6 they may be called at 108% of face value, in Year 7 they may be called at 107% of face value, and so on. If the yield curve is horizontal and interest rates remain at their current level, when is the latest that investors might expect the firm to call the bonds?

4-23 Determinants of Interest Rates

Suppose you and most other investors expect the inflation rate to be 7% next year, to fall to 5% during the following year, and then to remain at a rate of 3% thereafter. Assume that the real risk-free rate, r^*, will remain at

2% and that maturity risk premiums on Treasury securities rise from zero on very short-term securities (those that mature in a few days) to a level of 0.2 percentage points for 1-year securities. Furthermore, maturity risk premiums increase 0.2 percentage points for each year to maturity, up to a limit of 1.0 percentage point on 5-year or longer-term T-notes and T-bonds.

a. Calculate the interest rate on 1-, 2-, 3-, 4-, 5-, 10-, and 20-year Treasury securities, and plot the yield curve.

b. Now suppose ExxonMobil's bonds, rated AAA, have the same maturities as the Treasury bonds. As an approximation, plot an ExxonMobil yield curve on the same graph with the Treasury bond yield curve. (*Hint:* Think about the default risk premium on ExxonMobil's long-term versus short-term bonds.)

c. Now plot the approximate yield curve of Long Island Lighting Company, a risky nuclear utility.

Spreadsheet Problem

4-24 Build a Model: Bond Valuation

Start with the partial model in the file *Ch04 P24 Build a Model.xls* on the textbook's Web site. A 20-year, 8% semiannual coupon bond with a par value of $1,000 may be called in 5 years at a call price of $1,040. The bond sells for $1,100. (Assume that the bond has just been issued.)

a. What is the bond's yield to maturity?

b. What is the bond's current yield?

c. What is the bond's capital gain or loss yield?

d. What is the bond's yield to call?

e. How would the price of the bond be affected by a change in the going market interest rate? (*Hint:* Conduct a sensitivity analysis of price to changes in the going market interest rate for the bond. Assume that the bond will be called if and only if the going rate of interest *falls below* the coupon rate. This is an oversimplification, but assume it for purposes of this problem.)

f. Now assume the date is October 25, 2016. Assume further that a 12%, 10-year bond was issued on July 1, 2016, pays interest semiannually (on January 1 and July 1) and sells for $1,100. Use your spreadsheet to find the bond's yield.

MINI CASE

Sam Strother and Shawna Tibbs are vice presidents of Mutual of Seattle Insurance Company and co-directors of the company's pension fund management division. An important new client, the North-Western Municipal Alliance, has requested that Mutual of Seattle present an investment seminar to the mayors of the represented cities, and Strother and Tibbs, who will make the actual presentation, have asked you to help them by answering the following questions.

a. What are the key features of a bond?

b. What are call provisions and sinking fund provisions? Do these provisions make bonds more or less risky?

c. How does one determine the value of any asset whose value is based on expected future cash flows?

d. How is the value of a bond determined? What is the value of a 10-year, $1,000 par value bond with a 10% annual coupon if its required rate of return is 10%?

e. (1) What would be the value of the bond described in part d if, just after it had been issued, the expected inflation rate rose by 3 percentage points, causing investors to require a 13% return? Would we now have a discount or a premium bond?

  (2) What would happen to the bond's value if inflation fell and r_d declined to 7%? Would we now have a premium or a discount bond?

  (3) What would happen to the value of the 10-year bond over time if the required rate of return remained at 13%? If it remained at 7%? (*Hint:* With a financial calculator, enter PMT, I/YR, FV, and N, and then change N to see what happens to the PV as the bond approaches maturity.)

f. (1) What is the yield to maturity on a 10-year, 9% annual coupon, $1,000 par value bond that sells for $887.00? That sells for $1,134.20? What does the fact that a bond sells at a discount or at a premium tell you about the relationship between r_d and the bond's coupon rate?

  (2) What are the total return, the current yield, and the capital gains yield for the discount bond? (Assume the bond is held to maturity and the company does not default on the bond.)

g. How does the equation for valuing a bond change if semiannual payments are made? Find the value of a 10-year, semiannual payment, 10% coupon bond if the nominal $r_d = 13\%$.

h. Suppose a 10-year, 10% semiannual coupon bond with a par value of $1,000 is currently selling for $1,135.90, producing a nominal yield to maturity of 8%. However, the bond can be called after 5 years for a price of $1,050.

  (1) What is the bond's *nominal* yield to call (YTC)?

  (2) If you bought this bond, do you think you would be more likely to earn the YTM or the YTC? Why?

i. Write a general expression for the yield on any debt security (r_d) and define these terms: real risk-free rate of interest (r^*), inflation premium (IP), default risk premium (DRP), liquidity premium (LP), and maturity risk premium (MRP).

j. Define the nominal risk-free rate (r_{RF}). What security can be used as an estimate of r_{RF}?

k. Describe a way to estimate the inflation premium (IP) for a t-year bond.

l. What is a *bond spread* and how is it related to the default risk premium? How are bond ratings related to default risk? What factors affect a company's bond rating?

m. What is *interest rate* (or *price*) *risk?* Which bond has more interest rate risk: an annual payment 1-year bond or a 10-year bond? Why?

n. What is *reinvestment rate risk?* Which has more reinvestment rate risk: a 1-year bond or a 10-year bond?

o. How are interest rate risk and reinvestment rate risk related to the maturity risk premium?

p. What is the term structure of interest rates? What is a yield curve?

q. Briefly describe bankruptcy law. If a firm were to default on its bonds, would the company be liquidated immediately? Would the bondholders be assured of receiving all of their promised payments?

SELECTED ADDITIONAL CASES

The following cases from CengageCompose cover many of the concepts discussed in this chapter and are available at http://compose.cengage.com.

Klein-Brigham Series:

Case 3, "Peachtree Securities, Inc. (B)"; Case 72, "Swan Davis"; and Case 78, "Beatrice Peabody."

Brigham-Buzzard Series:

Case 3, "Powerline Network Corporation (Bonds and Preferred Stock)."

Financial Options

There are two fundamental approaches to valuing assets. The first is the *discounted cash flow (DCF)* approach, which we covered in previous chapters: An asset's value is the present value of its cash flows. The second is the *option pricing* approach. It is important that all managers understand the basic principles of option pricing for the following reasons. First, many projects allow managers to make strategic or tactical changes in plans as market conditions change. The existence of these "embedded options" often means the difference between a successful project and a failure. Understanding basic financial options can help you manage the value inherent in these real options. Second, many companies use derivatives to manage risk; many derivatives are types of financial options, so an understanding of basic financial options is necessary before tackling derivatives. Third, option pricing theory provides insights into the optimal debt/equity choice, especially when convertible securities are involved. And fourth, knowing about financial options will help you understand any employee stock options that you receive.

WEB

The textbook's Web site contains an *Excel* file that will guide you through the chapter's calculations. The file for this chapter is ***Ch05 Tool Kit.xls***, and we encourage you to open the file and follow along as you read the chapter.

Beginning-of-Chapter Questions

As you read the chapter, consider how you would answer the following questions. You *should not* necessarily be able to answer the questions before you read the chapter. Rather, you should use them to get a sense of the issues covered in the chapter. After reading the chapter, you should be able to give at least partial answers to the questions, and you should be able to give better answers after the chapter has been discussed in class. Note, too, that it is often useful, when answering conceptual questions, to use hypothetical data to illustrate your answer. We illustrate the answers with an *Excel* model that is available on the textbook's Web site. Accessing the model and working through it is a useful exercise, and it provides insights that are useful when answering the questions.

1. How is the value of a financial option affected by: (a) the current price of the underlying asset, (b) the exercise (or strike) price, (c) the risk-free rate, (d) the time until expiration (or maturity), and (e) the variance of returns on the asset?

2. Should options given as part of compensation packages be reported on the income statement as an expense? What are some pros and cons relating to this issue?

3. The rationale behind granting stock options is to induce employees to work harder and be more productive. As the stock price increases (presumably due to their hard work), the employees share in this added wealth. Another way to share this wealth would be to grant shares of stock, rather

than options. What are the advantages and disadvantages of using stock options rather than shares of stock as employee incentives?

4. The stockholders' claim in a levered firm can be viewed as a call option; stockholders have the option to purchase the firm's assets by paying off its debt. What incentives does this provide to stockholders and managers in choosing investment projects?

THE INTRINSIC VALUE OF STOCK OPTIONS

In previous chapters we showed that the intrinsic value of an asset is the present value of its cash flows. This "time value of money" approach works well for stocks and bonds, but we must use another approach for options and derivatives. If we can find a portfolio of stocks and risk-free bonds that replicates an option's cash flows, then the intrinsic value of the option must be identical to the value of the replicating portfolio.

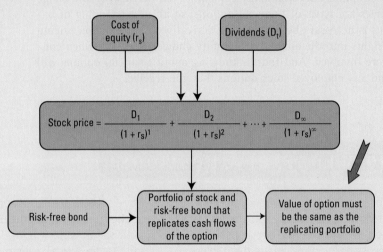

Source: From *Financial Management: Theory & Practice*, 2013, by Brigham and Ehrhardt. © Cengage Learning.

5-1 Overview of Financial Options

In general, an **option** is a contract that gives its owner the right to buy (or sell) an asset at some predetermined price within a specified period of time. However, there are many types of options and option markets.[1] Consider the options reported in Table 5-1,

---

1. For an in-depth treatment of options, see Don M. Chance and Robert Brooks, *An Introduction to Derivatives and Risk Management*, 9th ed. (Mason, OH: South-Western, Cengage Learning, 2013); or John C. Hull, *Options, Futures, and Other Derivatives*, 9th ed. (Upper Saddle River, NJ: Prentice-Hall, 2015).

TABLE 5-1	Listed Options Quotations for General Computer Corporation (GCC) on January 7, 2015						
		CALLS—LAST QUOTE			**PUTS—LAST QUOTE**		
Closing Price	**Strike Price**	**February**	**March**	**May**	**February**	**March**	**May**
53.50	50	4.25	4.75	5.50	0.65	1.40	2.20
53.50	55	1.30	2.05	3.15	2.65	r	4.50
53.50	60	0.30	0.70	1.50	6.65	r	8.00

Note: r means not traded on January 7.

which is an extract from a Listed Options Quotations table as it might appear on a Web site or in a daily newspaper. The first column reports the closing stock price. For example, the table shows that General Computer Corporation's (GCC) stock price closed at $53.50 on January 7, 2015.

A **call option** gives its owner the right to *buy* a share of stock at a fixed price, which is called the **strike price** (sometimes called the **exercise price** because it is the price at which you exercise the option). A **put option** gives its owner the right to *sell* a share of stock at a fixed strike price. For example, the first row in Table 5-1 is for GCC's options that have a $50 strike price. Observe that the table has columns for call options and for put options with this strike price.

Each option has an **expiration date**, after which the option may not be exercised. Table 5-1 reports data for options that expire in February, March, and May.[2] If the option can be exercised any time before the expiration, it is called an **American option**; if it can be exercised only on its expiration date, it is a **European option**. All of GCC's options are American options. The first row shows that GCC has a call option with a strike price of $50 that expires on Saturday, May 16 (the third Friday in May 2015 is the 15th). The quoted price for this option is $5.50.[3]

When the current stock price is greater than the strike price, the option is **in-the-money**. For example, GCC's $50 (strike) May call option is in-the-money by $53.50 − $50 = $3.50. Thus, if the option were immediately exercised, it would have a payoff of $3.50. On the other hand, GCC's $55 (strike) May call is **out-of-the-money** because the current $53.50 stock price is below the $55 strike price. Obviously, you currently would not want to exercise this option by paying the $55 strike price for a share of stock selling for $53.50. Therefore, the

2. At its Web site, **www.cboe.com/learncenter/glossary.aspx**, the CBOE defines the expiration date as follows: "The day on which an option contract becomes void. The expiration date for listed stock options is the Saturday after the third Friday of the expiration month. Holders of options should indicate their desire to exercise, if they wish to do so, by this date." The CBOE also defines the expiration time as: "The time of day by which all exercise notices must be received on the expiration date. Technically, the expiration time is currently 5:00PM on the expiration date, but public holders of option contracts must indicate their desire to exercise no later than 5:30PM on the business day preceding the expiration date. The times are Eastern Time."

3. Option contracts are generally written in 100-share multiples, but to reduce confusion we focus on the cost and payoffs of a single option.

exercise value, which is any profit (ignoring the initial cost of the option) from immediately exercising an option, is:[4]

| (5–1) | Exercise value = MAX[Current price of the stock − Strike price, 0] |

An American option's price always will be greater than (or equal to) its exercise value. If the option's price were less, you could buy the option and immediately exercise it, reaping a sure gain. For example, GCC's May call with a $50 strike price sells for $5.50, which is greater than its exercise value of $3.50. Also, GCC's out-of-the-money May call with a strike price of $55 sells for $3.15 even though it would be worthless if it had to be exercised immediately. An option always will be worth more than zero as long as there is still any chance it will end up in-the-money: Where there is life, there is hope! The difference between the option's price and its exercise value is called the **time value** because it represents the extra amount over the option's immediate exercise value that a purchaser will pay for the chance the stock price will appreciate over time.[5] For example, GCC's May call with a $50 strike price sells for $5.50 and has an exercise value of $3.50, so its time value is $5.50 − $3.50 = $2.00.

Suppose you bought GCC's $50 (strike) May call option for $5.50 and then the stock price increased to $60. If you exercised the option by purchasing the stock for the $50 strike price, you could immediately sell the share of stock at its market price of $60, resulting in a payoff of $60 − $50 = $10. Notice that the stock itself had a return of 12.1% = ($60 − $53.50)/$53.50, but the option's return was 81.8% = ($10 − $5.50)/$5.50. Thus, the option offers the possibility of a higher return.

However, if the stock price fell to $50 and stayed there until the option expired, the stock would have a return of −6.5% = ($50.00 − $53.50)/$53.50, but the option would have a 100% loss (it would expire worthless). As this example shows, call options are a lot riskier than stocks. This works to your advantage if the stock price goes up but to your disadvantage if the stock price falls.

Suppose you bought GCC's May put option (with a strike price of $50) for $2.20 and then the stock price fell to $45. The put option gives you the right to sell one share of GCC stock at the strike price, or $50, so you could buy a share of stock for $45 and exercise the put option. This would allow you to use the option to sell the share of stock for $50, and your payoff from exercising the put would be $5 = $50 − $45. Stockholders would lose money because the stock price fell, but a put holder would make money. In this example, your rate of return would be 127.3% = ($5 − $2.20)/$2.20. So if you think a stock price is going to fall, you can make money by purchasing a put option. On the other hand, if the stock price doesn't fall below the strike price of $50 before the put expires, you would lose 100% of your investment in the put option.[6]

---

4. MAX means choose the maximum. For example, MAX[15, 0] = 15 and MAX[−10, 0] = 0.
5. Among traders, an option's market price is also called its "premium." This is particularly confusing because for all other securities the word *premium* means the excess of the market price over some base price. To avoid confusion, we will not use the word *premium* to refer to the option price.
6. Most investors don't actually exercise an option prior to expiration. If they want to cash in the option's profit or cut its losses, they sell the option to some other investor. As you will see later in the chapter, the cash flow from selling an American option before its expiration is always greater than (or equal to) the profit from exercising the option.

Options are traded on a number of exchanges, with the Chicago Board Options Exchange (CBOE) being the oldest and the largest. Existing options can be traded in the secondary market in much the same way that existing shares of stock are traded in secondary markets. But unlike new shares of stock that are issued by corporations, new options can be "issued" by investors. This is called **writing** an option.

For example, you could write a call option and sell it to some other investor. You would receive cash from the option buyer at the time you wrote the option, but you would be obligated to sell a share of stock at the strike price if the option buyer later decided to exercise the option.[7] Thus, each option has two parties, the writer and the buyer, with the CBOE (or some other exchange) acting as an intermediary. Other than commissions, the writer's profits are exactly opposite those of the buyer. An investor who writes call options against stock held in his or her portfolio is said to be selling **covered options**. Call options sold without the stock to back them up are called **naked options**.

In addition to options on individual stocks, options are also available on several stock indexes such as the NYSE Index and the S&P 100 Index. Index options permit one to hedge (or bet) on a rise or fall in the general market as well as on individual stocks.

The leverage involved in option trading makes it possible for speculators with just a few dollars to make a fortune almost overnight. Also, investors with sizable portfolios can sell options against their stocks and earn the value of the option (less brokerage commissions) even if the stock's price remains constant. Most important, though, options can be used to create *hedges* that protect the value of an individual stock or portfolio.[8]

Conventional options are generally written for 6 months or less, but a type of option called a **Long-Term Equity AnticiPation Security (LEAPS)** is different. Like conventional options, LEAPS are listed on exchanges and are available on both individual stocks and stock indexes. The major difference is that LEAPS are long-term options, having maturities of up to almost 3 years. One-year LEAPS cost about twice as much as the matching 3-month option, but because of their much longer time to expiration, LEAPS provide buyers with more potential for gains and offer better long-term protection for a portfolio.

Corporations on whose stocks the options are written have nothing to do with the option market. Corporations do not raise money in the option market, nor do they have any direct transactions in it. Moreover, option holders do not vote for corporate directors or receive dividends. There have been studies by the SEC and others as to whether option trading stabilizes or destabilizes the stock market and whether this activity helps or hinders corporations seeking to raise new capital. The studies have not been conclusive, but research on the impact of option trading is ongoing.

www

The Chicago Board Options Exchange provides 20-minute delayed quotes for equity, index, and LEAPS options at *www.cboe.com*.

---

7. Your broker would require collateral to ensure that you kept this obligation.
8. Insiders who trade illegally generally buy options rather than stock because the leverage inherent in options increases the profit potential. However, it is illegal to use insider information for personal gain, and an insider using such information would be taking advantage of the option seller. Insider trading, in addition to being unfair and essentially equivalent to stealing, hurts the economy: Investors lose confidence in the capital markets and raise their required returns because of an increased element of risk, and this raises the cost of capital and thus reduces the level of real investment.

FINANCIAL REPORTING FOR EMPLOYEE STOCK OPTIONS

When granted to executives and other employees, options are a "hybrid" form of compensation. At some companies, especially small ones, option grants may be a substitute for cash wages: Employees are willing to take lower cash salaries if they have options. Options also provide an incentive for employees to work harder. Whether issued to motivate employees or to conserve cash, options clearly have value at the time they are granted, and they transfer wealth from existing shareholders to employees to the extent that they do not reduce cash expenditures or increase employee productivity enough to offset their value at the time of issue.

Companies like the fact that an option grant requires no immediate cash expenditure, although it might dilute shareholder wealth if it is exercised later. Employees, and especially CEOs, like the potential wealth they receive when they are granted options. When option grants were relatively small, they didn't show up on investors' radar screens. However, as the high-tech sector began making mega-grants in the 1990s, and as other industries followed suit, stockholders began to realize that large grants were making some CEOs filthy rich at the stockholders' expense.

Before 2005, option grants were barely visible in companies' financial reports. Even though such grants are clearly a wealth transfer to employees, companies were required only to footnote the grants and could ignore them when reporting their income statements and balance sheets. The Financial Accounting Standards Board now requires companies to show option grants as an expense on the income statement. To do this, the value of the options is estimated at the time of the grant and then expensed during the vesting period, which is the amount of time the employee must wait before being allowed to exercise the options. For example, if the initial value is $100 million and the vesting period is 2 years, the company would report a $50 million expense for each of the next 2 years. This approach isn't perfect, because the grant is not a cash expense. Nor does the approach take into account changes in the option's value after the initial grant. However, it does make the option grant more visible to investors, which is a good thing.

SELF TEST

What is an option? A call option? A put option?

Define a call option's exercise value. Why is the market price of a call option usually above its exercise value?

Brighton Memory's stock is currently trading at $50 a share. A call option on the stock with a $35 strike price currently sells for $21. What is the exercise value of the call option? **($15.00)** What is the time value? **($6.00)**

5-2 The Single-Period Binomial Option Pricing Approach

We can use a model like the Capital Asset Pricing Model (CAPM) to calculate the required return on a stock and then use that required return to discount its expected future cash flows to find its value. No such model exists for the required return on options, so we must use a different approach to find an option's value. In Section 5-5 we describe the Black-Scholes option pricing model, but in this section we explain the binomial option pricing model. The idea behind this model is different from that of the DCF model used for stock valuation. Instead of discounting cash flows at a required return to obtain a price, as we did with the stock valuation model, we will use the option, shares of stock, and the risk-free rate to construct a portfolio whose value we already know and then deduce the option's price from this portfolio's value.

The following sections describe and apply the binomial option pricing model to Western Cellular, a manufacturer of cell phones. Call options exist that permit the holder to buy 1 share of Western at a strike price, X, of $35. Western's options will expire at the end of 6 months (t is the number of years until expiration, so t = 0.5 for Western's options). Western's stock price, P, is currently $40 per share. Given this background information, we will use the binomial model to determine the call option's value. The first step is to determine the option's possible payoffs, as described in the next section.

5-2a **Payoffs in a Single-Period Binomial Model**

In general, the time until expiration can be divided into many periods, with n denoting the number of periods. But in a single-period model, which we describe in this section, there is only one period. We assume that, at the end of the period, the stock's price can take on only one of two possible values, so this is called the **binomial approach**. For this example, Western's stock will either go up (u) by a factor of 1.25 or go down (d) by a factor of 0.80. If we were considering a riskier stock, then we would have assumed a wider range of ending prices; we will show how to estimate this range later in the chapter. If we let u = 1.25 and d = 0.80, then the ending stock price will be either P(u) = $40(1.25) = $50 or P(d) = $40(0.80) = $32. Figure 5-1 illustrates the stock's possible price paths and contains additional information about the call option that is explained in the text that follows.

When the option expires at the end of the period, Western's stock will sell for either $50 or $32. As shown in Figure 5-1, if the stock goes up to $50, then the option will have a payoff, C_u, of $15 at expiration because the option is in-the-money: $50 − $35 = $15. If the stock price goes down to $32, then the option's payoff, C_d, will be zero because the option is out-of-the-money.

See **Ch05 Tool Kit.xls** on the textbook's Web site.

5-2b **The Hedge Portfolio Approach**

Suppose we created a portfolio by writing 1 call option and purchasing 1 share of stock. As Figure 5-1 shows, if the stock price goes up then our portfolio's stock will be worth $50 but we will owe $15 on the option, so our portfolio's net payoff is $35 = $50 − $15. If the stock price goes down, then our portfolio's stock will be worth only $32, but the amount we owe on the written option also will fall to zero, leaving the portfolio's net payoff at $32. The portfolio's end-of-period price range is smaller than if we had just owned the stock, so writing the call option reduces the portfolio's price risk. Taking this further: Is it possible for us to choose the number of shares held by our portfolio so that it will have the same net payoff whether the stock goes up or down? If so, then our portfolio is hedged and will have a riskless payoff when the option expires. Therefore, it is called a **hedge portfolio**.

We are not really interested in investing in the hedge portfolio, but we want to use it to help us determine the value of the option. The important thing to note is

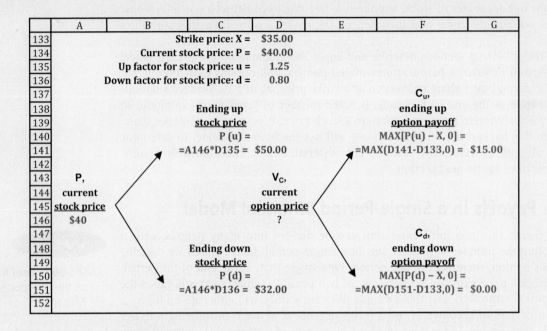

FIGURE 5-1   Binomial Payoffs from Holding Western Cellular's Stock or Call Option

Microsoft Excel® is a registered trademark of Microsoft Corporation. © 2014 Microsoft.

that if the hedge portfolio has a riskless net payoff when the option expires, then we can find the present value of this payoff by discounting it at the risk-free rate. Our current portfolio value must equal this present value, which allows us to determine the option's value. The following example illustrates the steps in this approach.

1. Find N_s, the Number of Shares of Stock in the Hedge Portfolio

We want the portfolio's payoff to be the same whether the stock goes up or down. If we write 1 call option and buy N_s shares of stock, then the portfolio's stock will be worth $N_s(P)(u)$ should the stock price go up, so its net payoff will be $N_s(P)(u) - C_u$. The portfolio's stock will be worth $N_s(P)(d)$ if the stock price goes down, so its net payoff will be $N_s(P)(d) - C_d$. Setting these portfolio payoffs equal to one another (since we want the portfolio to have the same ending value whether the stock goes up or down) and then solving for N_s yields the number of shares of stock to buy for each call option in order to create the hedge portfolio:

(5–2)

$$N_s = \frac{C_u - C_d}{P(u) - P(d)} = \frac{C_u - C_d}{P(u - d)}$$

For Western, the hedge portfolio has 0.83333 share of stock:[9]

$$N_s = \frac{C_u - C_d}{P(u) - P(d)} = \frac{\$15 - \$0}{\$50 - \$32} = 0.83333$$

2. Find the Hedge Portfolio's Payoff

Our next step is to find the hedge portfolio's payoff. Recall that the hedge portfolio has N_s shares of stock and that we have written one call option, so the call option's payoff must be subtracted:

$$\text{Hedge portfolio's payoff if stock is up} = N_s P(u) - C_u$$
$$= 0.83333(\$50) - \$15$$
$$= \$26.6665$$

$$\text{Hedge portfolio's payoff if stock is down} = N_s P(d) - C_d$$
$$= 0.83333(\$32) - \$0$$
$$= \$26.6665$$

Figure 5-2 illustrates the payoffs of the hedge portfolio.

3. Find the Present Value of the Hedge Portfolio's Payoff

Because the hedge portfolio's payoff is riskless, the current value of the hedge portfolio must be equal to the present value of its riskless payoff. Suppose the nominal annual risk-free rate, r_{RF}, is 8%. What is the present value of the hedge portfolio's riskless payoff of $26.6665 in 6 months? Recall that the present value depends on how frequently interest is compounded. Let's assume that interest is compounded daily.[10] We can use a financial calculator to find the present value of the hedge portfolio's payoff by entering N = 0.5(365), because there are 365 days in a year and the contract expires in half a year; I/YR = 8/365, because we want a daily interest rate; PMT = 0; and FV = −$26.6665, because we want to know the amount we would take today in exchange for giving up the payoff when the option expires. Using these inputs, we solve for PV = $25.6210, which is the present value of the hedge portfolio's payoff and which must also be the current value of the components of the hedge portfolio.[11]

4. Find the Option's Value

The current value of the hedge portfolio is the value of the stock, $N_s(P)$, less the value of the call option we wrote:

$$\text{Current value of hedge portfolio} = N_s(P) - V_C$$

Because the payoff is riskless, the current value of the hedge portfolio must also equal the present value of the riskless payoff:

$$\text{Current value of hedge portfolio} = \text{Present value of riskless payoff}$$

See **Ch05 Tool Kit.xls** on the textbook's Web site.

---

9. An easy way to remember this formula is to notice that N_s is equal to the range in possible option payoffs divided by the range in possible stock prices.

10. Option pricing models usually assume continuous compounding, which we discuss in **Web Extension 28C** on the textbook's Web site, but daily compounding works well. We will apply continuous compounding in Sections 5-3 and 5-4.

11. We could also solve for the present value using the present value equation with the daily periodic interest rate and the number of daily periods: PV = $26.6665/(1 + 0.08/365)^{0.5(365)} = $25.6210.

FIGURE 5-2	Hedge Portfolio with Riskless Payoffs

	A	B	C	D	E	F
180					Strike price: X =	$35.00
181					Current stock price: P =	$40.00
182					Up factor for stock price: u =	1.25
183					Down factor for stock price: d =	0.80
184					Up option payoff: C_u = MAX[0,P(u)-X] =	$15.00
185					Down option payoff: C_d =MAX[0,P(d)-X] =	$0.00
186				Number of shares of stock in portfolio: N_s = $(C_u - C_d)/P(u-d)$ =		0.83333
187						
188					Stock price = P (u) = $50.00	
189	P,				Portfolio's stock payoff: = $P(u)(N_s)$ =	$41.67
190	current				Subtract option's payoff: C_u =	$15.00
191	stock price				Portfolio's net payoff = $P(u)N_s - C_u$ =	$26.67
192	$40					
193						
194						
195						
196					Stock price = P (d) = $32.00	
197					Portfolio's stock payoff: = $P(d)(N_s)$ =	$26.67
198					Subtract option's payoff: C_d =	$0.00
199					Portfolio's net payoff = $P(d)N_s - C_d$ =	$26.67
200						

Microsoft Excel® is a registered trademark of Microsoft Corporation. © 2014 Microsoft.

Substituting for the current value of the hedge portfolio, we get:

$$N_s(P) - V_C = \text{Present value of riskless portfolio}$$

Solving for the call option's value, we get:

$$V_C = N_s(P) - \text{Present value of riskless portfolio}$$

For Western's option, this is:

$$V_C = 0.83333(\$40) - \$25.621$$
$$= \$7.71$$

5-2c Hedge Portfolios and Replicating Portfolios

In our previous derivation of the call option's value, we combined an investment in the stock with writing a call option to create a risk-free investment. We can modify this approach and, instead, create a portfolio that replicates the call option's payoffs. For example, suppose we formed a portfolio by purchasing 0.83333 shares of Western's stock and borrowing $25.621 at the risk-free rate (this is equivalent to selling a T-bill short). In 6 months, we would repay the future value of a $25.621, compounded daily at the risk-free rate. Using a financial calculator, input N = 0.5(365), I/YR = 8/365, PV = −$25.621, and solve for FV = $26.6665.[12] If the stock goes up, our net payoff would be 0.83333($50) − $26.6665 = $15.00. If the stock goes down, our net payoff would be 0.83333($32) − $26.6665 = $0. The portfolio's payoffs are exactly equal to the option's payoffs as shown in Figure 5-1, so our portfolio of 0.83333 shares of stock and the $25.621 that we borrowed would exactly replicate the option's payoffs. Therefore, this is called a **replicating portfolio**. Our cost to create this portfolio is the cost of the stock less the amount we borrowed:

$$\text{Cost of replicating portfolio} = 0.83333(\$40) - \$25.621 = \$7.71$$

If the call option did not sell for exactly $7.71, then a clever investor could make a sure profit. For example, suppose the option sold for $8. The investor would write an option, which would provide $8 of cash now but would obligate the investor to pay either $15 or $0 in 6 months when the option expires. However, the investor could use the $8 to create the replicating portfolio, leaving the investor with $8 − $7.71 = $0.29. In 6 months, the replicating portfolio will pay either $15 or $0. Thus, the investor isn't exposed to any risk—the payoffs received from the replicating portfolio exactly offset the payoffs owed on the option. The investor uses none of his own money, has no risk, has no net future obligations, but has $0.29 in cash. This is **arbitrage**, and if such an arbitrage opportunity existed then the investor would scale it up by writing thousands of options.[13]

Such arbitrage opportunities don't persist for long in a reasonably efficient economy because other investors will also see the opportunity and will try to do the same thing. With so many investors trying to write (i.e., sell) the option, its price will fall; with so many investors trying to purchase the stock, its price will increase. This will continue until the option and replicating portfolio have identical prices. And because our financial markets are really quite efficient, you would never observe the derivative security and the replicating portfolio trading for different prices—they would always have the same price and there would be no arbitrage opportunities. What this means is that, by finding the price of a portfolio that replicates a derivative security, we have also found the price of the derivative security itself!

Describe how a risk-free hedge portfolio can be created using stocks and options.

How can such a portfolio be used to help estimate a call option's value?

What is a replicating portfolio, and how is it used to find the value of a derivative security?

SELF TEST

(Continued)

---

12. Alternatively, use the present value equation with daily compounding: $25.621
    $(1 + 0.08/365)^{365(0.5/1)} = \$26.6665$.
13. If the option sold for less than the replicating portfolio, the investor would raise cash by shorting the portfolio and use the cash to purchase the option, again resulting in arbitrage profits.

What is arbitrage?

Lett Incorporated's stock price is now $50, but it is expected either to rise by a factor of 1.5 or fall by a factor of 0.7 by the end of the year. There is a call option on Lett's stock with a strike price of $55 and an expiration date 1 year from now. What are the stock's possible prices at the end of the year? **($75 or $35)** What is the call option's payoff if the stock price goes up? **($20)** If the stock price goes down? **($0)** If we sell 1 call option, how many shares of Lett's stock must we buy to create a riskless hedged portfolio consisting of the option position and the stock? **(0.5)** What is the payoff of this portfolio? **($17.50)** If the annual risk-free rate is 6%, then how much is the riskless portfolio worth today (assuming daily compounding)? **($16.48)** What is the current value of the call option? **($8.52)**

5-3 The Single-Period Binomial Option Pricing Formula[14]

The hedge portfolio approach works well if you only want to find the value of one type of option with one period until expiration. But in all other situations, the step-by-step approach becomes tedious very quickly. The following sections describe a formula that replaces the step-by-step approach.

5-3a The Binomial Option Pricing Formula

With a little (or a lot!) of algebra, we can derive a single formula for a call option. Instead of using daily compounding, we use continuous compounding to make the binomial formula consistent with the Black-Scholes formula (presented in Section 5-5).[15] Here is the resulting binomial option pricing formula:

(5–3)

$$V_C = \frac{C_u \left[\dfrac{e^{r_{RF}(t/n)} - d}{u - d} \right] + C_d \left[\dfrac{u - e^{r_{RF}(t/n)}}{u - d} \right]}{e^{r_{RF}(t/n)}}$$

After programming it into *Excel*, which we did for this chapter's *Tool Kit*, it is easy to change inputs and determine the new value of a call option.

---

14. The material in this section is relatively technical, and some instructors may choose to skip it with no loss in continuity.

15. With daily compounding, the present value is equal to the future value divided by $(1 + r_{RF}/365)^{365(0.5/1)}$. With continuous compounding, the present value is $e^{-r_{RF}(t/n)}$. See *Web Extension 28C* on the textbook's Web site for more discussion of continuous compounding.

We can apply this formula to Western's call option:

$$V_C = \frac{\$15\left[\dfrac{e^{0.08(0.5/1)} - 0.80}{1.25 - 0.80}\right] + \$0\left[\dfrac{1.25 - e^{0.08(0.5/1)}}{1.25 - 0.80}\right]}{e^{0.08(0.5/1)}}$$

$$= \frac{\$15(0.5351) + \$0(0.4649)}{1.04081} = \$7.71$$

Notice that this is the same value that resulted from the step-by-step process shown earlier.

The binomial option pricing formula in Equation 5-3 does not include the actual probabilities that the stock will go up or down, nor does it include the expected stock return, which is not what one might expect. After all, the higher the stock's expected return, the greater the chance that the call will be in-the-money at expiration. Note, however, that the stock's expected return is already indirectly incorporated into the stock price.

5-3b **Primitive Securities and the Binomial Option Pricing Formula**

If we want to value other Western call options or puts that expire in 6 months, then we can use Equation 5-3, but there is a time-saving approach. Notice that for options with the same time left until expiration, C_u and C_d are the only variables that depend on the option itself. The other variables depend only on the stock process (u and d), the risk-free rate, the time until expiration, and the number of periods until expiration. If we group these variables together, we can then define π_u and π_d as:

$$\pi_u = \frac{\left[\dfrac{e^{r_{RF}(t/n)} - d}{u - d}\right]}{e^{r_{RF}(t/n)}}$$

(5–4)

and

$$\pi_d = \frac{\left[\dfrac{u - e^{r_{RF}(t/n)}}{u - d}\right]}{e^{r_{RF}(t/n)}}$$

(5–5)

By substituting these values into Equation 5-3, we obtain an option pricing model that can be applied to all of Western's 6-month options:

$$V_C = C_u \pi_u + C_d \pi_d$$

(5–6)

In this example, π_u and π_d are:

$$\pi_u = \frac{\left[\dfrac{e^{0.08(0.5/1)} - 0.80}{1.25 - 0.80} \right]}{e^{0.08(0.5/1)}} = 0.5142$$

and

$$\pi_d = \frac{\left[\dfrac{1.25 - e^{0.08(0.5/1)}}{1.25 - 0.80} \right]}{e^{0.08(0.5/1)}} = 0.4466$$

Using Equation 5-6, the value of Western's 6-month call option with a strike price of $35 is:

$$\begin{aligned} V_C &= C_u\pi_u + C_d\pi_d \\ &= \$15(0.5142) + \$0(0.4466) \\ &= \$7.71 \end{aligned}$$

Sometimes π_u and π_d are called *primitive securities* because π_u is the price of a simple security that pays $1 if the stock goes up and nothing if it goes down; π_d is the opposite. This means that we can use π_u and π_d to find the price of any 6-month option on Western. For example, suppose we want to find the value of a 6-month call option on Western but with a strike price of $30. Rather than reinvent the wheel, all we have to do is find the payoffs of this option and use the same values of π_u and π_d in Equation 5-6. If the stock goes up to $50, the option will pay $50 − $30 = $20; if the stock falls to $32, the option will pay $32 − $30 = $2. The value of the call option is:

$$\begin{aligned} \text{Value of 6-month call with \$30 strike price} &= C_u\pi_u + C_d\pi_d \\ &= \$20(0.5142) + \$2(0.4466) \\ &= \$11.18 \end{aligned}$$

It is a bit tedious initially to calculate π_u and π_d, but once you save them, it is easy to find the value of any 6-month call or put option on the stock. In fact, you can use these values of π to find the value of any security with payoffs that depend on Western's 6-month stock prices, which makes them a very powerful tool.

SELF TEST

Yegi's Fine Phones has a current stock price of $30. You need to find the value of a call option with a strike price of $32 that expires in 3 months. Use the binomial model with one period until expiration. The factor for an increase in stock price is u = 1.15; the factor for a downward movement is d = 0.85. What are the possible stock prices at expiration? **($34.50 or $25.50)** What are the option's possible payoffs at expiration? **($2.50 or $0)** What are π_u and π_d? **(0.5422 and 0.4429)** What is the current value of the option (assume each month is 1/12 of a year)? **($1.36)**

5-4 **The Multi-Period Binomial Option Pricing Model**[16]

Clearly, the one-period example is simplified. Although you could duplicate buying 0.8333 share and writing 1 option by buying 8,333 shares and writing 10,000 options, the stock price assumptions are unrealistic—Western's stock price could be almost anything after 6 months, not just $50 or $32. However, if we allowed the stock to move up or down more often, then a more realistic distribution of ending prices would result. In other words, dividing the time until expiration into more periods would improve the realism of the resulting prices at expiration. The key to implementing a multi-period binomial model is to keep the stock return's annual standard deviation the same no matter how many periods you have during a year. In fact, analysts typically begin with an estimate of the annual standard deviation and use it to determine u and d. The derivation is beyond the scope of a financial management textbook, but the appropriate equations are:

$$u = e^{\sigma\sqrt{t/n}}$$ (5–7)

$$d = \frac{1}{u}$$ (5–8)

where σ is the annualized standard deviation of the stock's return, t is the time in years until expiration, and n is the number of periods until expiration.

The standard deviation of Western's stock returns is 31.5573%, and application of Equations 5-7 and 5-8 confirms the values of u and d that we used previously:

$$u = e^{0.315573\sqrt{0.5/1}} = 1.25 \quad \text{and} \quad d = \frac{1}{1.25} = 0.80$$

Now suppose we allow stock prices to change every 3 months (which is 0.25 years). Using Equations 5-7 and 5-8, we estimate u and d to be:

$$u = e^{0.31573\sqrt{0.5/2}} = 1.1709 \quad \text{and} \quad d = \frac{1}{1.1709} = 0.8540$$

At the end of the first 3 months, Western's price would either rise to $40(1.1709) = $46.84 or fall to $40(0.8540) = $34.16. If the price rises in the first 3 months to $46.84, then it would either go up to $46.84(1.1709) = $54.84 or go down to $46.84(0.8540) = $40 at expiration. If instead the price initially falls to $40(0.8540) = $34.16 during the first 3 months, then it would either go up to $34.16(1.1709) = $40 or go down to $34.16(0.8540) = $29.17 by expiration. This pattern of stock price movements is called a **binomial lattice** and is shown in Figure 5-3.

---

16. The material in this section is relatively technical, and some instructors may choose to skip it with no loss in continuity.

FIGURE 5-3	Two-Period Binomial Lattice and Option Valuation

	A	B	C	D	E	F	G	H	I
450	Standard deviation of stock return: σ =				31.5573%				
451	Current stock price: P =				$40.00				
452	Up factor for stock price: u =				1.1709				
453	Down factor for stock price: d =				0.8540				
454	Strike price: X =				$35.00				
455	Risk-free rate: r_{RF} =				8.00%				
456	Years to expiration: t =				0.50				
457	Number of periods until expiration: n =				2				
458	Price of $1 payoff if stock goes up: π_u =				0.51400				
459	Price of $1 payoff if stock goes down: π_d =				0.46620				
460									
461	**Now**					**3 months**		**6 months**	

Stock = P (u) (u) = $54.84
C_{uu} = Max[P(u)(u) − X, 0]
C_{uu} = $19.84

Stock = P (u) = $46.84
$C_u = C_{uu}\pi_u + C_{ud}\pi_d$
C_u = $12.53

Stock = P (u) (d) = P (d) (u)
Stock = $40.00
$C_{ud} = C_{du}$ = Max[P(u)(d) − X, 0]
C_{ud} = $5.00

P = $40.00
$V_C = C_u\pi_u + C_d\pi_d$
V_C = $7.64

Stock = P (d) = $34.16
$C_d = C_{ud}\pi_u + C_{dd}\pi_d$
C_u = $2.57

Stock = P (d) (d) = $29.17
C_{dd} = Max[P(d)(d) − X, 0]
C_{dd} = $0.00

Microsoft Excel ® is a registered trademark of Microsoft Corporation. © 2014 Microsoft.

See **Ch05 Tool Kit.xls** on the textbook's Web site.

Because the interest rate and the volatility (as defined by u and d) are constant for each period, we can calculate π_u and π_d for any period and apply these same values for each period:[17]

$$\pi_u = \frac{\left[\dfrac{e^{0.08(0.5/2)} - 0.80}{1.25 - 0.80}\right]}{e^{0.08(0.5/2)}} = 0.51400$$

$$\pi_d = \frac{\left[\dfrac{1.25 - e^{0.08(0.5/1)}}{1.25 - 0.80}\right]}{e^{0.08(0.5/1)}} = 0.46620$$

17. These values were calculated in *Excel*, so there may be small differences due to rounding in intermediate steps.

These values are shown in Figure 5-3.

The lattice shows the possible stock prices at the option's expiration, and we know the strike price, so we can calculate the option payoffs at expiration. Figure 5-3 also shows the option payoffs at expiration. If we focus only on the upper right portion of the lattice shown inside the dotted lines, then it is similar to the single-period problem we solved in Section 5-3. In fact, we can use the binomial option pricing model from Equation 5-6 to determine the value of the option in 3 months given that the stock price increased to $46.84. As shown in Figure 5-3, the option will be worth $12.53 in 3 months if the stock price goes up to $46.84. We can repeat this procedure on the lower right portion of Figure 5-3 to determine the call option's value in 3 months if the stock price falls to $34.16; in this case, the call's value would be $2.57. Finally, we can use Equation 5-6 and the 3-month option values just calculated to determine the current price of the option, which is $7.64. Thus, we are able to find the current option price by solving three simple binomial problems.

If we broke the year into smaller periods and allowed the stock price to move up or down more often, then the lattice would have an even more realistic range of possible ending stock prices. Of course, estimating the current option price would require solving lots of binomial problems within the lattice, but each problem is simple and computers can solve them rapidly. With more outcomes, the resulting estimated option price is more accurate. For example, if we divide the year into 15 periods, then the estimated price is $7.42. With 50 periods, the price is $7.39. With 100 periods it is still $7.39, which shows that the solution converges to its final value within a relatively small number of steps. In fact, as we break the time to expiration into smaller and smaller periods, the solution for the binomial approach converges to the Black-Scholes solution, which is described in the next section.

The binomial approach is widely used to value options with more complicated payoffs than the call option in our example, such as employee stock options. This is beyond the scope of a financial management textbook, but if you are interested in learning more about the binomial approach, you should take a look at the textbooks by Don Chance and John Hull cited in footnote 1.

SELF TEST

Ringling Cycle's stock price is now $20. You need to find the value of a call option with a strike price of $22 that expires in 2 months. You want to use the binomial model with 2 periods (each period is a month). Your assistant has calculated that u = 1.1553, d = 0.8656, π_u = 0.4838, and π_d = 0.5095. Draw the binomial lattice for stock prices. What are the possible stock prices after 1 month? **($23.11 or $17.31)** After 2 months? **($26.69, $20, or $14.99)** What are the option's possible payoffs at expiration? **($4.69, $0, or $0)** What will the option's value be in 1 month if the stock goes up? **($2.27)** What will the option's value be in 1 month if the stock price goes down? **($0)** If each month is 1/12 of a year, what is the current value of the option? **($1.10)**

5-5 The Black-Scholes Option Pricing Model (OPM)

The **Black-Scholes option pricing model (OPM)**, developed in 1973, helped give rise to the rapid growth in options trading. This model has been programmed into many handheld and Web-based calculators, and it is widely used by option traders.

5-5a **OPM Assumptions and Results**

In deriving their model to value call options, Fischer Black and Myron Scholes made the following assumptions.

For a Web-based option calculator, see **www.cboe .com/LearnCenter /OptionCalculator .aspx**.

1. The stock underlying the call option provides no dividends or other distributions during the life of the option.
2. There are no transaction costs for buying or selling either the stock or the option.
3. The short-term, risk-free interest rate is known and is constant during the life of the option.
4. Any purchaser of a security may borrow any fraction of the purchase price at the short-term, risk-free interest rate.
5. Short selling is permitted, and the short seller will receive immediately the full cash proceeds of today's price for a security sold short.
6. The call option can be exercised only on its expiration date.
7. Trading in all securities takes place continuously, and the stock price moves randomly.

The derivation of the Black-Scholes model rests on the same concepts as the binomial model, except time is divided into such small increments that stock prices change continuously. The Black-Scholes model for call options consists of the following three equations:

(5–9)
$$V_C = P[N(d_1)] - Xe^{-r_{RF}t}[N(d_2)]$$

(5–10)
$$d_1 = \frac{\ln(P/X) + [r_{RF} + (\sigma^2/2)]t}{\sigma\sqrt{t}}$$

(5–11)
$$d_2 = d_1 - \sigma\sqrt{t}$$

Robert's Online Option Pricer can be accessed at **www.intrepid .com/robertl/index .html**. The site provides a financial service over the Internet to small investors for option pricing, giving anyone a means to price option trades without having to buy expensive software and hardware.

The variables used in the Black-Scholes model are explained below.

V_C = Current value of the call option.

P = Current price of the underlying stock.

$N(d_i)$ = Probability that a deviation less than d_i will occur in a standard normal distribution. Thus, $N(d_1)$ and $N(d_2)$ represent areas under a standard normal distribution function.

X = Strike price of the option.

$e \approx 2.7183$.

r_{RF} = Risk-free interest rate.[18]

---

18. The correct process to estimate the risk-free rate for use in the Black-Scholes model for an option with 6 months to expiration is to find the annual nominal rate (compounded continuously) that has the same effective annual rate as a 6-month T-bill. For example, suppose a 6-month T-bill is yielding a 6-month periodic rate of 4.081%. The risk-free rate to use in the Black-Scholes model is $r_{RF} = \ln(1 + 0.0408)/0.5 = 8\%$. Under continuous compounding, a nominal rate of

t = Time until the option expires (the option period).

ln(P/X) = Natural logarithm of P/X.

σ = Standard deviation of the rate of return on the stock.

The value of the option is a function of five variables: (1) P, the stock's price; (2) t, the option's time to expiration; (3) X, the strike price; (4) σ, the standard deviation of the underlying stock; and (5) r_{RF}, the risk-free rate. We do not derive the Black-Scholes model—the derivation involves some extremely complicated mathematics that go far beyond the scope of this text. However, it is not difficult to use the model. Under the assumptions set forth previously, if the option price is different from the one found by Equation 5-9, then this would provide the opportunity for arbitrage profits, which would force the option price back to the value indicated by the model. As we noted earlier, the Black-Scholes model is widely used by traders because actual option prices conform reasonably well to values derived from the model.

5-5b **Application of the Black-Scholes Option Pricing Model to a Call Option**

The current stock price (P), the exercise price (X), and the time to maturity (t) can all be obtained from a newspaper, such as *The Wall Street Journal*, or from the Internet, such as the CBOE's Web site. The risk-free rate (r_{RF}) is the yield on a Treasury bill with a maturity equal to the option expiration date. The annualized standard deviation of stock returns (σ) can be estimated from daily stock prices. First, find the stock return for each trading day for a sample period, such as each trading day of the past year. Second, estimate the variance of the daily stock returns. Third, multiply this estimated daily variance by the number of trading days in a year, which is approximately 250.[19] Take the square root of the annualized variance, and the result is an estimate of the annualized standard deviation.

8% produces an effective rate of $e^{0.08} - 1 = 8.33\%$. This is the same effective rate yielded by the T-bill: $(1+0.0408)^2 - 1 = 8.33\%$. The same approach can be applied for options with different expiration periods. We will provide the appropriate risk-free rate for all problems and examples.

19. If stocks traded every day of the year, then each return covers a 24-hour period; you would simply estimate the variance of the 1-day returns with your sample of daily returns and then multiply this estimate by 365 for an estimate of the annual variance. However, stocks don't trade every day, because of weekends and holidays. If you measure returns from the close of one trading day until the close of the next trading day (called "trading-day returns"), then some returns are for 1 day (such as Thursday close to Friday close) and some are for longer periods, like the 3-day return from Friday close to Monday close. It might seem reasonable that the 3-day returns have 3 times the variance of a 1-day return and should be treated differently when estimating the daily return variance, but that is not the case. It turns out that the 3-day return over a weekend has only slightly higher variance than a 1- day return (perhaps because of less new information on non-weekdays), and so it is reasonable to treat all of the trading-day returns the same. With roughly 250 trading days in a year, most analysts take the estimate of the variance of daily returns and multiply by 250 (or 252, depending on the year, to be more precise) to obtain an estimate of the annual variance.

We will use the Black-Scholes model to estimate Western's call option that we discussed previously. Here are the inputs:

$$P = \$40$$
$$X = \$35$$
$$t = 6 \text{ months (0.5 years)}$$
$$r_{RF} = 8.0\% = 0.080$$
$$\sigma = 31.557\% = 0.31557$$

Given this information, we first estimate d_1 and d_2 from Equations 5-10 and 5-11:

$$d_1 = \frac{\ln(\$40/\$35) + [0.08 + ((0.31557^2)/2)](0.5)}{0.31557\sqrt{0.5}}$$

$$= \frac{0.13353 + 0.064896}{0.22314} = 0.8892$$

$$d_2 = d_1 - 0.31557\sqrt{0.5} = 0.6661$$

WEB

See **Ch05 Tool Kit.xls** on the textbook's Web site for all calculations.

Note that $N(d_1)$ and $N(d_2)$ represent areas under a standard normal distribution function. The easiest way to calculate this value is with *Excel*. For example, we can use the function =NORMSDIST(0.8892), which returns a value of $N(d_1) = N(0.8892) = 0.8131$. Similarly, the **NORMSDIST** function returns a value of $N(d_2) = 0.7473$.[20] We can use those values to solve Equation 5-9:

$$V_c = \$40[N(0.8892)] - \$35e^{-(0.08)(0.5)}[N(0.6661)]$$
$$= \$7.39$$

Thus, the value of the option is $7.39. This is the same value we found using the binomial approach with 100 periods in the year.

5-5c The Five Factors That Affect Call Option Prices

The Black-Scholes model has five inputs, so there are five factors that affect call option prices. As we will see in the next section, these five inputs also affect put option prices. Figure 5-4 shows how three of Western Cellular's call options are affected by Western's stock price. All three options have a strike price of $35. The first expires in 1 year, the second in 6 months (0.5 years, like the option in our example), and the third in 3 months (or 0.25 years).

WEB

See **Ch05 Tool Kit.xls** on the textbook's Web site.

Figure 5-4 offers several insights regarding option valuation. Notice that for all stock prices in the Figure, the call option prices are always above the exercise value. If this were not true, then an investor could purchase the call and immediately exercise it for a quick profit.[21]

---

20. If you do not have access to *Excel*, then you can use the table in Appendix A. For example, the table shows that the value for $d_1 = 0.88$ is $0.5000 + 0.3106 = 0.8106$ and that the value for $d_1 = 0.89$ is $0.5000 + 0.3133 = 0.8133$, so $N(0.8892)$ lies between 0.8106 and 0.8133. You could interpolate to find a closer value, but we suggest using *Excel* instead.

21. More precisely, this statement is true for all American call options (which can be exercised before expiration) and for European call options written on stocks that pay no dividends. Although European options may not be exercised prior to expiration, investors could earn a riskless profit if the call price were less than the exercise value by selling the stock short, purchasing the call, and investing at the risk-free rate an amount equal to the present value of the strike price. The vast majority of call options are American options, so the call price is almost always above the exercise value.

FIGURE 5-4	Western Cellular's Call Options with a Strike Price of $35

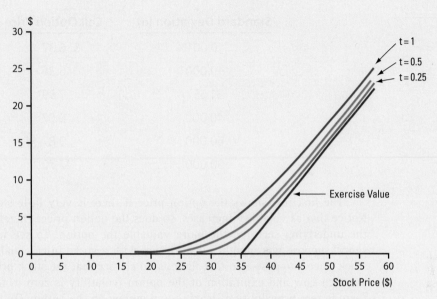

Source: From *Financial Management: Theory & Practice*, 2013, by Brigham and Ehrhardt. © Cengage Learning.

Also, when the stock price falls far below the strike price, call option prices fall toward zero. In other words, calls lose value as they become more and more out-of-the-money. When the stock price greatly exceeds the strike price, call option prices fall toward the exercise value. Thus, for very high stock prices, call options tend to move up and down by about the same amount as does the stock price.

Call option prices increase if the stock price increases. This is because the strike price is fixed, so an increase in stock price increases the chance that the option will be in-the-money at expiration. Although we don't show it in the figure, an increase in the strike price would obviously cause a decrease in the call option's value because higher strike prices mean a lower chance of being in-the-money at expiration.

The 1-year call option always has a greater value than the 6-month call option, which always has a greater value than the 3-month call option; thus, the longer a call option has until expiration, the greater its value. Here is the rationale for that result. With a long time until expiration, the stock price has a chance to increase well above the strike price by the expiration date. Of course, with a long time until expiration, there is also a chance that the stock price will fall far below the strike price by expiration. But there is a big difference in payoffs for being well in-the-money versus far out-of-the-money. Every dollar that the stock price is above the strike price means an extra dollar of payoff, but no matter how far the stock price is below the strike price, the payoff is zero. When it comes to a call option, the gain in value due to the chance of finishing well in-the-money with a big payoff more than compensates for the loss in value due to the chance of being far out-of-the money.

See **Ch05 Tool Kit.xls**
for all calculations.

How does volatility affect call options? Following are the Black-Scholes model prices for Western's call option with the original inputs except for different standard deviations:

Standard Deviation (σ)	Call Option Price
0.001%	$ 6.37
10.000	6.38
31.557	7.39
40.000	8.07
60.000	9.87
90.000	12.70

The first row shows the option price if there is very little stock volatility.[22] Notice that as volatility increases, so does the option price. Therefore, the riskier the underlying security, the more valuable the option. To see why this makes sense, suppose you bought a call option with a strike price equal to the current stock price. Suppose also that there is no chance that the stock price will change between now and expiration of the option (volatility is zero in this case). Then there is zero probability of making any money on the option. On the other hand, if you bought a call option on a higher-volatility stock, there would be a higher probability that the stock would increase well above the strike price by the expiration date. Of course, with higher volatility there also would be a higher probability that the stock price would fall far below the strike price. But as we previously explained, an increase in the price of the stock helps call option holders more than a decrease hurts them: The greater the stock's volatility, the greater the value of the option. This makes options on risky stocks more valuable than those on safer, low-risk stocks. For example, an option on Cisco should have a greater value than an otherwise identical option on Kroger, the grocery store chain.

The risk-free rate also has a relatively small impact on option prices. Shown below are the prices for Western's call option with the original inputs except for the risk-free rate, which is allowed to vary.

See **Ch05 Tool Kit.xls**
for all calculations.

---

22. With such a low standard deviation, the current stock price of $40 will with certainty increase at the risk-free rate until expiration, ending up at the future value of $40; let's call it FV($40). The option will therefore be in-the-money at expiration and the owner will certainly pay the strike price and exercise the option at that time, receiving FV(40) − $35. The present value of this payoff is PV(FV(40) − 35) = PV(FV(40)) − PV(35). The first part, PV(FV(40)), is just the current stock price, or $40. This is because the current stock price is always the present value of its expected future payoffs. So the value of the option today is approximately equal to the current stock price of $40 less the present value of the strike price that must be paid when the stock is exercised at expiration. If we assume daily compounding, then the current option price should be:

$$V_C \text{ (for } \sigma = 0.001\%) \approx \$40 - \frac{\$35}{\left(1 + \frac{0.08}{365}\right)^{365(0.5)}} = \$6.37$$

Observe that this is the same value given by the Black-Scholes model, even though we calculated it more directly. This approach only works if the volatility is almost zero.

Risk-free rate (r_{RF})	Call option price
0%	$6.41
4	6.89
8	7.39
12	7.90
20	8.93

As the risk-free rate increases, the value of the option increases. The principal effect of an increase in r_{RF} is to reduce the present value of the exercise price, which increases the current value of the option. Option prices in general are not very sensitive to interest rate changes, at least not to changes within the ranges normally encountered.

TAXES AND STOCK OPTIONS

If an employee stock option grant meets certain conditions, it is called a "tax-qualifying grant" or sometimes an "incentive stock option"; otherwise, it is a "nonqualifying grant." For example, suppose you receive a grant of 1,000 options with an exercise price of $50. If the stock price goes to $110 and you exercise the options, you must pay $50(1,000) = $50,000 for stock that is worth $110,000, which is a sweet deal. But what is your tax liability? If you receive a nonqualifying grant, then you are liable for ordinary income taxes on 1,000($110 − $50) = $60,000 when you exercise the option. But if it is a tax-qualified grant, you owe no regular taxes when exercised. By waiting at least a year and then selling the stock for, say, $150, you would have a long-term capital gain of 1,000($150 − $50) = $100,000, which would be taxed at the lower capital gains rate.

Before you gloat over your newfound wealth, you had better consult your accountant. Your "profit" when you exercise the tax-qualified options isn't taxable under the regular tax code, but it is under the Alternative Minimum Tax (AMT) code. With an AMT tax rate of up to 28%, you might owe as much as 0.28($110 − $50)(1,000) = $16,800. Here's where people get into trouble. The AMT tax isn't due until the following April, so you might think about waiting until then to sell some stock to pay your AMT tax (so that the sale will qualify as a long-term capital gain). But what happens if the stock price falls to $5 by next April? You can sell your stock, which raises only $5(1,000) = $5,000 in cash. Even though you will have a long-term capital loss of 1,000($50 − $5) = $45,000, IRS regulations limit your net capital loss in a single year to $3,000. In other words, the cash from the sale and the tax benefit from the capital loss aren't nearly enough to cover the AMT tax. You may be able to reduce your taxes in future years because of the AMT tax you pay this year and the carryforward of the remaining long-term capital loss, but that doesn't help right now. You lost $45,000 of your original $50,000 investment, you now have very little cash, and—adding insult to injury—the IRS will insist that you also pay the $16,800 AMT tax.

This is exactly what happened to many people who made paper fortunes in the dot-com boom only to see them evaporate in the ensuing bust. They were left with worthless stock but multimillion-dollar AMT tax obligations. In fact, many still have IRS liens garnishing their wages until they eventually pay their AMT tax. So if you receive stock options, we congratulate you. But unless you want to be the next poster child for poor financial planning, we advise you to settle your AMT tax when you incur it.

Myron Scholes and Robert Merton (who also was a pioneer in the field of options) were awarded the 1997 Nobel Prize in Economics, and Fischer Black would have been a co-recipient had he still been living. Their work provided analytical tools and methodologies that are widely used to solve many types of financial problems, not just option pricing. Indeed, the entire field of modern risk management is based primarily on their contributions. Although the Black-Scholes model was derived for a European option that can be exercised only on its maturity date, it also applies to American options that don't pay any dividends prior to expiration. The textbooks by Don Chance and John Hull (cited in footnote 1) show adjusted models for dividend-paying stocks.

> **SELF TEST**
>
> What is the purpose of the Black-Scholes option pricing model?
>
> Explain what a "riskless hedge" is and how the riskless hedge concept is used in the Black-Scholes OPM.
>
> Describe the effect of a change in each of the following factors on the value of a call option: (1) stock price, (2) exercise price, (3) option life, (4) risk-free rate, and (5) stock return standard deviation (i.e., risk of stock).
>
> Using an *Excel* worksheet, what is the value of a call option with these data: P = \$35, X = \$25, r_{RF} = 6%, t = 0.5 (6 months), and σ = 0.6? **(\$12.05)**

5-6 The Valuation of Put Options

A put option gives its owner the right to sell a share of stock. Suppose a stock pays no dividends and a put option written on the stock can be exercised only upon its expiration date. What is the put's value? Rather than reinventing the wheel, we can establish the price of a put relative to the price of a call.

5-6a Put–Call Parity

Consider the payoffs for two portfolios at expiration date T, as shown in Table 5-2. The first portfolio consists of a put option and a share of stock; the second has a call option (with the same strike price and expiration date as the put option) and some cash. The amount of cash is equal to the present value of the strike price discounted at the continuously compounded risk-free rate, which is $Xe^{-r_{RF}t}$. At expiration, the value of this cash will equal the strike price, X.

If P_T, the stock price at expiration date T, is less than X, the strike price, when the option expires, then the value of the put option at expiration is $X - P_T$. Therefore, the payoff of Portfolio 1, which contains the put and the stock, is equal to X minus P_T plus P_T, or just X. For Portfolio 2, the value of the call is zero at expiration (because the call option is out-of-the-money), and the value of the cash is X, for a total payoff of X. Notice that both portfolios have the same payoffs if the stock price is less than the strike price.

What if the stock price is greater than the strike price at expiration? In this case, the put is worth nothing, so the payoff of Portfolio 1 is equal to P_T, the stock price at

TABLE 5-2	Portfolio Payoffs	
	Payoff at Expiration If:	
	$P_T < X$	$P_T \geq X$
Put	$X - P_T$	0
Stock	$\underline{P_T}$	$\underline{P_T}$
Portfolio 1:	X	P_T
Call	0	$P_T - X$
Cash	$\underline{X}$	$\underline{X}$
Portfolio 2:	X	P_T

Source: From *Financial Management: Theory & Practice*, 2013, by Brigham and Ehrhardt. © Cengage Learning.

expiration. The call option is worth $P_T - X$, and the cash is worth X, so the payoff of Portfolio 2 is P_T. Hence, the payoffs of the two portfolios at expiration are equal regardless of whether the stock price is below or above the strike price.

If the two portfolios have identical payoffs, then they must have identical values. This is known as the **put–call parity relationship**:

Put option + Stock = Call option + PV of exercise price

If V_C is the Black-Scholes value of the call option, then the value of a put is:[23]

$$\text{Put option} = V_C - P + Xe^{-r_{RF}t} \qquad \text{(5–12)}$$

For example, consider a put option written on the stock discussed in the previous section. If the put option has the same exercise price and expiration date as the call, then its price is:

$$\text{Put option} = \$7.39 - \$40 + \$35\, e^{-0.08(0.5)}$$
$$= \$7.39 - \$40 + \$33.63 = \$1.02$$

It is also possible to modify the Black-Scholes call option formula to obtain a put option formula:

$$\text{Put option} = P[N(d_1) - 1] - Xe^{-r_{RF}t}\,[N(d_2) - 1] \qquad \text{(5–13)}$$

The only difference between this formula for puts and the formula for calls is the subtraction of 1 from $N(d_1)$ and $N(d_2)$ in the call option formula.

---

23. This model cannot be applied to an American put option or to a European option on a stock that pays a dividend prior to expiration. For an explanation of valuation approaches in these situations, see the books by Chance and Hull cited in footnote 1.

5-6b **The Five Factors That Affect Put Option Prices**

Just like with call options, the exercise price, the underlying stock price, the time to expiration, the stock's standard deviation, and the risk-free rate affect the price of a put option. Because a put pays off when the stock price declines below the exercise price, the impact on the put of the underlying stock price, exercise price, and risk-free rate are opposite that of the call option. That is, put prices are higher when the stock price is lower and when the exercise price is higher. Put prices are also lower when the risk-free rate is higher, mostly because a higher risk-free rate reduces the present value of the exercise price, which for a put is a payout to the option holder when the option is exercised.

On the other hand, put options are affected by the stock's standard deviation just like call options. Both put and call option prices are higher when the stock's standard deviation is higher. This is true for put options because the higher the standard deviation, the bigger the chance of a large stock price decline and a large put payoff.

The effect of the time to maturity on the put option price is indeterminate. A call option is more valuable the longer the maturity, but some puts are more valuable the longer to maturity, and some are less valuable. For example, consider an in-the-money put option (the stock price is below the exercise price) on a stock with a low standard deviation. In this case a longer maturity put option is less valuable than a shorter maturity put option because the longer the time to maturity, the more likely the stock is to grow and erode the put's payoff. But if the stock's standard deviation is high, then the longer maturity put option will be more valuable because the likelihood of the stock declining even more and resulting in a high payoff to the put is greater.

In words, what is put–call parity?

A put option written on the stock of Taylor Enterprises (TE) has an exercise price of $25 and 6 months remaining until expiration. The risk-free rate is 6%. A call option written on TE has the same exercise price and expiration date as the put option. TE's stock price is $35. If the call option has a price of $12.05, then what is the price (i.e., value) of the put option? **($1.31)**

Explain why both put and call options are worth more if the stock return standard deviation is higher, but put and call options are affected oppositely by the stock price.

5-7 **Applications of Option Pricing in Corporate Finance**

Option pricing is used in four major areas of corporate finance: (1) real options analysis for project evaluation and strategic decisions, (2) risk management, (3) capital structure decisions, and (4) compensation plans.

5-7a Real Options

Suppose a company has a 1-year proprietary license to develop a software application for use in a new generation of wireless cellular telephones. Hiring programmers and marketing consultants to complete the project will cost $30 million. The good news is that if consumers love the new cell phones, there will be a tremendous demand for the software. The bad news is that if sales of the new cell phones are low, the software project will be a disaster. Should the company spend the $30 million and develop the software?

Because the company has a license, it has the option of waiting for a year, at which time it might have a much better insight into market demand for the new cell phones. If demand is high in a year, then the company can spend the $30 million and develop the software. If demand is low, it can avoid losing the $30 million development cost by simply letting the license expire. Notice that the license is analogous to a call option: It gives the company the right to buy something (in this case, software for the new cell phones) at a fixed price ($30 million) at any time during the next year. The license gives the company a **real option**, because the underlying asset (the software) is a real asset and not a financial asset.

There are many other types of real options, including the option to increase capacity at a plant, to expand into new geographical regions, to introduce new products, to switch inputs (such as gas versus oil), to switch outputs (such as producing sedans versus SUVs), and to abandon a project. Many companies now evaluate real options with techniques that are similar to those described earlier in the chapter for pricing financial options.

5-7b Risk Management

Suppose a company plans to issue $400 million of bonds in 6 months to pay for a new plant now under construction. The plant will be profitable if interest rates remain at current levels, but if rates rise then it will be unprofitable. To hedge against rising rates, the company could purchase a put option on Treasury bonds. If interest rates go up, then the company would "lose" because its bonds would carry a high interest rate, but it would have an offsetting gain on its put options. Conversely, if rates fall, then the company would "win" when it issues its own low-rate bonds, but it would lose on the put options. By purchasing puts, the company has hedged the risk due to possible interest rate changes that it would otherwise face.

Another example of risk management is a firm that bids on a foreign contract. For example, suppose a winning bid means that the firm will receive a payment of 12 million euros in 9 months. At a current exchange rate of $1.57 per euro, the project would be profitable. But if the exchange rate falls to $1.10 per euro, the project would be a loser. To avoid exchange rate risk, the firm could take a short position in a forward contract that allows it to convert 12 million euros into dollars at a fixed rate of $1.50 per euro in 9 months, which would still ensure a profitable project. This eliminates exchange rate risk if the firm wins the contract, but what if the firm loses the contract? It would still be obligated to sell 12 million euros at a price of $1.50 per euro, which could be a disaster. For example, if the exchange rate rises to $1.75 per euro, then the firm would have to spend $21 million to purchase 12 million euros at a price of $1.75/€ and then sell the euros for $18 million = ($1.50/€)(€12 million), a loss of $3 million.

To eliminate this risk, the firm could instead purchase a currency put option that allows it to sell 12 million euros in 9 months at a fixed price of $1.50 per euro.

If the company wins the bid, it will exercise the put option and sell the 12 million euros for $1.50 per euro if the exchange rate has declined. If the exchange rate hasn't declined, then it will sell the euros on the open market for more than $1.50 and let the option expire. On the other hand, if the firm loses the bid, it has no reason to sell euros and could let the option contract expire. Note, however, that even if the firm doesn't win the contract, it still is gambling on the exchange rate because it owns the put; if the price of euros declines below $1.50, the firm will still make some money on the option. Thus, the company can lock in the future exchange rate if it wins the bid and can avoid any net payment at all if it loses the bid. The total cost in either scenario is equal to the initial cost of the option. In other words, the cost of the option is like insurance that guarantees the exchange rate if the company wins the bid and guarantees no net obligations if it loses the bid.

Many other applications of risk management involve futures contracts and other complex derivatives rather than calls and puts. However, the principles used in pricing derivatives are similar to those used earlier in this chapter for pricing options. Thus, financial options and their valuation techniques play key roles in risk management.

5-7c Capital Structure Decisions

Decisions regarding the mix of debt and equity used to finance operations are quite important. One interesting aspect of the capital structure decision is based on option pricing. For example, consider a firm with debt requiring a final principal payment of $60 million in 1 year. If the company's value 1 year from now is $61 million, then it can pay off the debt and have $1 million left for stockholders. If the firm's value is less than $60 million, then it may well file for bankruptcy and turn over its assets to creditors, resulting in stockholders' equity of zero. In other words, the value of the stockholders' equity is analogous to a call option: The equity holders have the right to buy the assets for $60 million (which is the face value of the debt) in 1 year (when the debt matures).

Suppose the firm's owner-managers are considering two projects. One project has very little risk, and it will result in an asset value of either $59 million or $61 million. The other has high risk, and it will result in an asset value of either $20 million or $100 million. Notice that the equity will be worth zero if the assets are worth less than $60 million, so the stockholders will be no worse off if the assets end up at $20 million than if they end up at $59 million. On the other hand, the stockholders would benefit much more if the assets were worth $100 million rather than $61 million. Thus, the owner-managers have an incentive to choose risky projects, which is consistent with an option's value rising with the risk of the underlying asset. Potential lenders recognize this situation, so they build covenants into loan agreements that restrict managers from making excessively risky investments.

Not only does option pricing theory help explain why managers might want to choose risky projects (consider, for example, the cases of Enron, Lehman Brothers, and AIG) and why debtholders might want restrictive covenants, but options also play a direct role in capital structure choices. For example, a firm could choose to issue convertible debt, which gives bondholders the option to convert their debt into stock if the value of the company turns out to be higher than expected. In exchange for this option, bondholders charge a lower interest rate than for nonconvertible debt. Because owner-managers must share the wealth with convertible-bond holders, they have a smaller incentive to gamble with high-risk projects.

5-7d **Compensation Plans**

Many companies use stock options as a part of their compensation plans. It is important for boards of directors to understand the value of these options before they grant them to employees. We discuss compensation issues associated with stock options in more detail in Chapter 10.

Describe four ways that option pricing is used in corporate finance.

SELF TEST

Summary

In this chapter we discussed option pricing topics, which included the following.

- **Financial options** are instruments that: (1) are created by exchanges rather than firms, (2) are bought and sold primarily by investors, and (3) are of importance to both investors and financial managers.
- The two primary types of financial options are: (1) **call options**, which give the holder the right to purchase a specified asset at a given price (the **exercise price**, which is also called the **strike price**) for a given period of time; and (2) **put options**, which give the holder the right to sell an asset at a given price for a given period of time.
- A call option's **exercise value** is defined as the maximum of zero or the current price of the stock less the strike price.
- The **Black-Scholes option pricing model (OPM)** or the **binomial model** can be used to estimate the value of a call option.
- The five inputs to the Black-Scholes model are: (1) P, the current stock price; (2) X, the strike price; (3) r_{RF}, the risk-free interest rate; (4) t, the remaining time until expiration; and (5) σ, the standard deviation of the stock's rate of return.
- A call option's value increases if P increases, X decreases, r_{RF} increases, t increases, or σ increases.
- The **put–call parity relationship** states that:

$$\text{Put option} + \text{Stock} = \text{Call option} + \text{PV of exercise price}$$

Questions

5-1 Define each of the following terms:
  a. Option; call option; put option
  b. Exercise value; strike price
  c. Black-Scholes option pricing model

5–2 Why do options sell at prices higher than their exercise values?

5–3 Describe the effect on a call option's price that results from an increase in each of the following factors: (1) stock price, (2) strike price, (3) time to expiration, (4) risk-free rate, and (5) standard deviation of stock return.

Problems   Answers Appear in Appendix B

Easy Problems 1–2

5–1 Options
A call option on the stock of Bedrock Boulders has a market price of $7. The stock sells for $30 a share, and the option has a strike price of $25 a share. What is the exercise value of the call option? What is the option's time value?

5–2 Options
The exercise price on one of Flanagan Company's options is $15, its exercise value is $22, and its time value is $5. What are the option's market value and the price of the stock?

Intermediate Problems 3–4

5–3 Black-Scholes Model
Assume that you have been given the following information on Purcell Industries:

Current stock price = $15	Strike price of option = $15
Time to maturity of option = 6 months	Risk-free rate = 6%
Variance of stock return = 0.12	
$d_1 = 0.24495$	$N(d_1) = 0.59675$
$d_2 = 0.00000$	$N(d_2) = 0.50000$

According to the Black-Scholes option pricing model, what is the option's value?

5–4 Put-Call Parity
The current price of a stock is $33, and the annual risk-free rate is 6%. A call option with a strike price of $32 and with 1 year until expiration has a current value of $6.56. What is the value of a put option written on the stock with the same exercise price and expiration date as the call option?

Challenging Problems 5–7

5–5 Black-Scholes Model
Use the Black-Scholes Model to find the price for a call option with the following inputs: (1) current stock price is $30, (2) strike price is $35, (3) time to expiration is 4 months, (4) annualized risk-free rate is 5%, and (5) variance of stock return is 0.25.

5–6 Binomial Model
The current price of a stock is $20. In 1 year, the price will be either $26 or $16. The annual risk-free rate is 5%. Find the price of a call option on the stock that has a strike price of $21 and that expires in 1 year. (*Hint:* Use daily compounding.)

5-7 Binomial Model

The current price of a stock is $15. In 6 months, the price will be either $18 or $13. The annual risk-free rate is 6%. Find the price of a call option on the stock that has a strike price of $14 and that expires in 6 months. (*Hint:* Use daily compounding.)

Spreadsheet Problem

5-8 Build a Model: Black-Scholes Model

Start with the partial model in the file *Ch05 P08 Build a Model.xls* on the textbook's Web site. You have been given the following information for a call option on the stock of Puckett Industries: P = $65.00, X = $70.00, t = 0.50, r_{RF} = 5.00%, and σ = 50.00%.

a. Use the Black-Scholes option pricing model to determine the value of the call option.

b. Suppose there is a put option on Puckett's stock with exactly the same inputs as the call option. What is the value of the put?

MINI CASE

Assume that you have just been hired as a financial analyst by Triple Play Inc., a mid-sized California company that specializes in creating high-fashion clothing. Because no one at Triple Play is familiar with the basics of financial options, you have been asked to prepare a brief report that the firm's executives can use to gain a cursory understanding of the topic.

To begin, you gathered some outside materials on the subject and used these materials to draft a list of pertinent questions that need to be answered. In fact, one possible approach to the report is to use a question-and-answer format. Now that the questions have been drafted, you have to develop the answers.

a. What is a financial option? What is the single most important characteristic of an option?

b. Options have a unique set of terminology. Define the following terms:
   (1) Call option
   (2) Put option
   (3) Strike price or exercise price
   (4) Expiration date

(5) Exercise value

(6) Option price

(7) Time value

(8) Writing an option

(9) Covered option

(10) Naked option

(11) In-the-money call

(12) Out-of-the-money call

(13) LEAPS

c. Consider Triple Play's call option with a $25 strike price. The following table contains historical values for this option at different stock prices:

Stock Price	Call Option Price
$25	$ 3.00
30	7.50
35	12.00
40	16.50
45	21.00
50	25.50

(1) Create a table that shows: (a) stock price, (b) strike price, (c) exercise value, (d) option price, and (e) the time value, which is the option's price less its exercise value.

(2) What happens to the time value as the stock price rises? Why?

d. Consider a stock with a current price of P = $27. Suppose that over the next 6 months the stock price will either go up by a factor of 1.41 or down by a factor of 0.71. Consider a call option on the stock with a strike price of $25 that expires in 6 months. The risk-free rate is 6%.

(1) Using the binomial model, what are the ending values of the stock price? What are the payoffs of the call option?

(2) Suppose you write one call option and buy N_s shares of stock. How many shares must you buy to create a portfolio with a riskless payoff (i.e., a hedge portfolio)? What is the payoff of the portfolio?

(3) What is the present value of the hedge portfolio? What is the value of the call option?

(4) What is a replicating portfolio? What is arbitrage?

e. In 1973, Fischer Black and Myron Scholes developed the Black-Scholes option pricing model (OPM).

(1) What assumptions underlie the OPM?

(2) Write out the three equations that constitute the model.

(3) According to the OPM, what is the value of a call option with the following characteristics?

Stock price = $27.00
Strike price = $25.00
Time to expiration = 6 months = 0.5 years
Risk-free rate = 6.0%
Stock return standard deviation = 0.49

f. What impact does each of the following parameters have on the value of a call option?
(1) Current stock price
(2) Strike price
(3) Option's term to maturity
(4) Risk-free rate
(5) Variability of the stock price

g. What is put–call parity?

Accounting for Financial Management

The stream of cash flows a firm is expected to generate in the future determines its fundamental value (also called intrinsic value). But how does an investor go about estimating future cash flows, and how does a manager decide which actions are most likely to increase cash flows? The first step is to understand the financial statements that publicly traded firms must provide to the public. Thus, we begin with a discussion of financial statements, including how to interpret them and how to use them. Value depends on *after-tax cash flows*, so we provide an overview of the federal income tax system and highlight differences between accounting income and cash flow.

WEB

The textbook's Web site contains an *Excel* file that will guide you through the chapter's calculations. The file for this chapter is ***Ch06 Tool Kit.xls***, and we encourage you to open the file and follow along as you read the chapter.

Beginning-of-Chapter Questions

As you read the chapter, consider how you would answer the following questions. You *should not* necessarily be able to answer the questions before you read the chapter. Rather, you should use them to get a sense of the issues covered in the chapter. After reading the chapter, you should be able to give at least partial answers to the questions, and you should be able to give better answers after the chapter has been discussed in class. Note, too, that it is often useful, when answering conceptual questions, to use hypothetical data to illustrate your answer. We illustrate the answers with an *Excel* model that is available on the textbook's Web site. Accessing the model and working through it is a useful exercise, and it provides insights that are useful when answering the questions.

1. How are the balance sheet and the income statement *related* to one another? How would you explain to a layperson the *primary purpose* of each of the statements? Which of the numbers in the income statement is considered to be most important?

2. WorldCom capitalized some costs that should, under standard accounting practices, have been expensed. Enron and some other companies took similar actions to inflate their reported income and to hide debts. (a) Explain how such improper and illegal actions would affect the firms' financial statements and stock prices. (b) What effect did the revelations about these actions have on the specific companies' stock prices and the prices of other stocks? (c) Could such actions affect the entire economy?

3. How could (accurate) balance sheet and income statement information be used, along with other information, to make a **statement of cash flows**? What is the primary purpose of this statement?

4. Differentiate between **net income**, **EPS**, **EBITDA**, **net cash flow**, **NOPAT**, **free cash flow**, **MVA**, and **EVA**. What is the primary purpose of each item; that is, when and how is it used?

5. How and why are regular accounting data *modified* for use in financial management? (*Hint:* Think about cash and operations.)

6. The **income statement** shows "flows" over a period of time, while the **balance sheet** shows accounts at a given point in time. Explain how these two concepts are combined when we calculate **free cash flow**.

7. **Taxes** affect many financial decisions. Explain how: (a) **interest and dividend payments** are treated for tax purposes, from both a company's and an investor's perspective, and (b) how **dividends and capital gains** are treated for tax

purposes by individuals. In your answers, explain how these tax treatments influence corporations' and investors' behavior.

8. If Congress wants to *stimulate* the economy, explain how it might alter each of the following: (a) **personal and corporate tax rates**, (b) **depreciation schedules**, and (c) the **differential between the tax rate on personal income and long-term capital gains**. How would these changes affect corporate profitability and free cash flow? How would they affect investors' choices regarding which securities to hold in their portfolios? Might any of these actions affect the general level of interest rates?

INTRINSIC VALUE, FREE CASH FLOW, AND FINANCIAL STATEMENTS

In Chapter 1, we told you that managers should strive to make their firms more valuable and that a firm's intrinsic value is determined by the present value of its free cash flows (FCF) discounted at the weighted average cost of capital (WACC). This chapter focuses on FCF, including its calculation from financial statements and its interpretation when evaluating a company and manager.

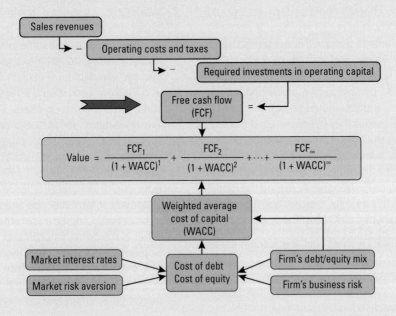

Source: From *Financial Management: Theory & Practice*, 2013, by Brigham and Ehrhardt. © Cengage Learning.

6-1 Financial Statements and Reports

A company's **annual report** usually begins with the chairperson's description of the firm's operating results during the past year and a discussion of new developments that will affect future operations. The annual report also presents four basic financial statements—the *balance sheet,* the *income statement,* the *statement of stockholders' equity,* and the *statement of cash flows.*

The quantitative and written materials are equally important. The financial statements report *what has actually happened* to assets, earnings, dividends, and cash flows during the past few years, whereas the written materials attempt to explain why things turned out the way they did.

WEB

See the Securities and Exchange Commission's (SEC) Web site for quarterly reports and more detailed annual reports that provide breakdowns for each major division or subsidiary. These reports, called *10-Q* and *10-K reports,* are available on the SEC's Web site at ***www.sec.gov*** under the heading "EDGAR."

> What is the annual report, and what two types of information does it present?
>
> What four types of financial statements does the annual report typically include?

SELF TEST

6-2 The Balance Sheet

For illustrative purposes, we use a hypothetical company, MicroDrive Inc., which produces memory components for computers and smartphones. Figure 6-1 shows MicroDrive's most recent **balance sheets**, which represent "snapshots" of its financial position on the last day of each year. Although most companies report their balance sheets only on the last day of a given period, the "snapshot" actually changes daily as inventories are bought and sold, as fixed assets are added or retired, or as loan balances are increased or paid down. Moreover, a retailer will have larger inventories before Christmas than later in the spring, so balance sheets for the same company can look quite different at different times during the year.

The balance sheet begins with assets, which are the "things" the company owns. Assets are listed in order of "liquidity," or length of time it typically takes to convert them to cash at fair market values. The balance sheet also lists the claims that various groups have against the company's value; these are listed in the order in which they must be paid. For example, suppliers may have claims called "accounts payable" that are due within 30 days, banks may have claims called "notes payable" that are due within 90 days, and bondholders may have claims that are not due for 20 years or more.

Stockholders' claims represent ownership (or equity) and need never be "paid off." These are residual claims in the sense that stockholders may receive payments only if there is value remaining after other claimants have been paid. The nonstockholder claims are liabilities from the stockholders' perspective. The amounts shown on the balance sheets are called **book values** because they are based on the amounts recorded by bookkeepers when assets are purchased or liabilities are issued. As you will see throughout this textbook, book values may be very different from **market values**, which are the current values as determined in the marketplace.

WEB

See ***Ch06 Tool Kit.xls*** for details.

FIGURE 6-1   MicroDrive Inc.: December 31 Balance Sheets (Millions of Dollars)

	A	B	C	D	E	F	G
						2015	2014
30	*Assets*						
31	Cash and equivalents					$ 50	$ 60
32	Short-term investments					-	40
33	Accounts receivable					500	380
34	Inventories					1,000	820
35	Total current assets					$ 1,550	$ 1,300
36	Net plant and equipment					2,000	1,700
37	Total assets					$ 3,550	$ 3,000
38							
39	*Liabilities and Equity*						
40	Accounts payable					$ 200	$ 190
41	Notes payable					280	130
42	Accruals					300	280
43	Total current liabilities					$ 780	$ 600
44	Long-term bonds					1,200	1,000
45	Total liabilities					$ 1,980	$ 1,600
46	Preferred stock (1,000,000 shares)					100	100
47	Common stock (50,000,000 shares)					500	500
48	Retained earnings					970	800
49	Total common equity					$ 1,470	$ 1,300
50	Total liabilities and equity					$ 3,550	$ 3,000

The following sections provide more information about specific asset, liability, and equity accounts.

6-2a Assets

Cash, short-term investments, accounts receivable, and inventories are listed as current assets because MicroDrive is expected to convert them into cash within a year. All assets are stated in dollars, but only cash represents actual money that can be spent. Some marketable securities mature very soon, and these can be converted quickly into cash at prices close to their book values. Such securities are called "cash equivalents" and are included with cash. Therefore, MicroDrive could write checks for a total of $50 million. Other types of marketable securities have a longer time until maturity, and their market values are less predictable. These securities are classified as "short-term investments." In addition, we distinguish between the component of cash that is used for operations (such as minimum required balances in checking accounts and cash required to be on hand for daily operations) and cash and other short-term investment balances that are held for purposes not related to the firm's operations, such as speculative balances or amounts held in anticipation of eventually distributing them as dividends or through stock repurchases. Accountants don't distinguish between operating and nonoperating components of cash or short-term investment balances, but we will find this distinction useful in later chapters.

When MicroDrive sells its products to a customer but doesn't demand immediate payment, the customer then has an obligation to make the payment, which MicroDrive reports as an "account receivable." The $500 million shown in accounts receivable is the amount of sales for which MicroDrive has not yet been paid.

Inventories show the dollars MicroDrive has invested in raw materials, work-in-process, and finished goods available for sale. MicroDrive uses the **FIFO (first-in, first-out)** method to determine the inventory value shown on its balance sheet ($1 billion). It could have used the **LIFO (last-in, first-out)** method. During a period of rising prices, by taking out old, low-cost inventory and leaving in new, high-cost items, FIFO will produce a higher balance sheet inventory value but a lower cost of goods sold on the income statement. (FIFO is strictly used for accounting purposes; companies actually use older items first.) Because MicroDrive uses FIFO and because inflation has been occurring: (1) its balance sheet inventories are higher than they would have been had it used LIFO, (2) its cost of goods sold is lower than it would have been under LIFO, and (3) its reported profits are therefore higher. In MicroDrive's case, if the company had elected to switch to LIFO, then its balance sheet would have had inventories of $850 million rather than $1 billion, and its pre-tax earnings (discussed in the next section) would have been reduced by $50 million. Thus, the inventory valuation method can have a significant effect on financial statements, which is important to know when comparing companies.

Rather than treat the entire purchase price of a long-term asset (such as a factory, plant, or equipment) as an expense in the purchase year, accountants "spread" the purchase cost over the asset's useful life.[1] The amount they charge each year is called the **depreciation** expense. Some companies report an amount called "gross plant and equipment," which is the total cost of the long-term assets they have in place, and another amount called "accumulated depreciation," which is the total amount of depreciation that has been charged on those assets. Some companies, such as MicroDrive, report only net plant and equipment, which is gross plant and equipment less accumulated depreciation. Chapter 13 provides a more detailed explanation of depreciation methods.

6-2b **Liabilities and Equity**

Accounts payable, notes payable, and accruals are listed as current liabilities because MicroDrive is expected to pay them within a year. When MicroDrive purchases supplies but doesn't immediately pay for them, it takes on an obligation called an account payable. Similarly, when MicroDrive takes out a loan that must be repaid within a year, it signs an IOU called a note payable. MicroDrive doesn't pay its taxes or its employees' wages daily, and the amount it owes on these items at any point in time is called an "accrual" or an "accrued expense." Long-term bonds are also liabilities because they, too, reflect a claim held by someone other than a stockholder.

Preferred stock is a hybrid, or a cross between common stock and debt. In the event of bankruptcy, preferred stock ranks below debt but above common stock. Also, the preferred dividend is fixed, so preferred stockholders do not benefit if the company's earnings grow. Most firms do not use much, if any, preferred stock, so "equity" usually means "common equity" unless the words "total" or "preferred" are included.

---

1. This is called *accrual accounting*, which attempts to match revenues to the periods in which they are earned and expenses to the periods in which the effort to generate income occurred.

When a company sells shares of stock, it records the proceeds in the common stock account.[2] Retained earnings are the cumulative amount of earnings that have not been paid out as dividends. The sum of common stock and retained earnings is called "common equity," or just "equity." If a company could actually sell its assets at their book value, and if the liabilities and preferred stock were actually worth their book values, then a company could sell its assets, pay off its liabilities and preferred stock, and the remaining cash would belong to common stockholders. Therefore, common equity is sometimes called **net worth**—it's the assets minus (or "net of") the liabilities.

SELF TEST

What is the balance sheet, and what information does it provide?

What determines the order of the information shown on the balance sheet?

Why might a company's December 31 balance sheet differ from its June 30 balance sheet?

A firm has $8 million in total assets. It has $3 million in current liabilities, $2 million in long-term debt, and $1 million in preferred stock. What is the total value of common equity? **($2 million)**

THE GLOBAL ECONOMIC CRISIS

Let's Play Hide-and-Seek!

In a shameful lapse of regulatory accountability, banks and other financial institutions were allowed to use "structured investment vehicles" (SIVs) to hide assets and liabilities and simply not report them on their balance sheets. Here's how SIVs worked and why they subsequently failed. The SIV was set up as a separate legal entity that the bank owned and managed. The SIV would borrow money in the short-term market (backed by the credit of the bank) and then invest in long-term securities. As you might guess, many SIVs invested in mortgage-backed securities. When the SIV paid only 3% on its borrowings but earned 10% on its investments, the managing bank was able to report fabulous earnings, especially if it also earned fees for creating the mortgage-backed securities that went into the SIV.

But this game of hide-and-seek didn't have a happy ending. Mortgage-backed securities began defaulting in 2007 and 2008, causing the SIVs to pass losses through to the banks. SunTrust, Citigroup, Bank of America, and Northern Rock are just a few of the many banks that reported enormous losses in the SIV game. Investors, depositors, and the government eventually found the hidden assets and liabilities, but by then the assets were worth a lot less than the liabilities.

In a case of too little and too late, regulators are closing these loopholes, and it doesn't look like there will be any more hidden SIVs in the near future. But the damage has been done, and the entire financial system was put at risk in large part because of this high-stakes game of hide-and-seek.

---

2. Companies sometimes break the total proceeds into two parts, one called "par" and the other called "paid-in capital" or "capital surplus." For example, if a company sells shares of stock for $10, it might record $1 of par and $9 of paid-in capital. For most purposes, the distinction between par and paid-in capital is not important, and most companies use no-par stock.

6-3 The Income Statement

See *Ch06 Tool Kit.xls* for details.

Figure 6-2 shows the **income statements** and selected additional information for Micro Drive. Income statements can cover any period of time, but they are usually prepared monthly, quarterly, and annually. Unlike the balance sheet, which is a snapshot of a firm at a point in time, the income statement reflects performance during the period.

Net sales are the revenues less any discounts or returns. Depreciation and amortization reflect the estimated costs of the assets that wear out in producing goods and services. To illustrate depreciation, suppose that in 2014 MicroDrive purchased a $100,000 machine with a life of 5 years and zero expected salvage value. This $100,000 cost is not expensed in the purchase year but is instead spread out over the

FIGURE 6-2	MicroDrive Inc.: Income Statements for Years Ending December 31 (Millions of Dollars, Except for Per Share Data)

	A	B	C	D	E	F	G
59						**2015**	**2014**
60	Net sales					$ 5,000	$ 4,760
61	Costs of goods sold except depreciation					3,800	3,560
62	Depreciation and amortization[a]					200	170
63	Other operating expenses					500	480
64	Earnings before interest and taxes (EBIT)					$ 500	$ 550
65	Less interest					120	100
66	Pre-tax earnings					$ 380	$ 450
67	Taxes					152	180
68	Net Income before preferred dividends					$ 228	$ 270
69	Preferred dividends					8	8
70	Net Income available to common stockholders					$ 220	$ 262
71							
72	*Additional Information*						
73	Common dividends					$ 50	$ 48
74	Addition to retained earnings					$ 170	$ 214
75	Number of common shares					50.00	50.00
76	Stock price per share					$27.00	$40.00
77							
78	*Per Share Data*						
79	Earnings per share, EPS[b]					**$4.40**	**$5.24**
80	Dividends per share, DPS[c]					**$1.00**	**$0.96**
81	Book value per share, BVPS[d]					**$29.40**	**$26.00**

Notes:

[a]MicroDrive has no amortization charges.

$$^{b}EPS = \frac{\text{Net income available to common stockholders}}{\text{Common shares outstanding}}$$

$$^{c}DPS = \frac{\text{Dividends paid to common stockholders}}{\text{Common shares outstanding}}$$

$$^{d}BVPS = \frac{\text{Total common equity}}{\text{Common shares outstanding}}$$

Microsoft Excel® is a registered trademark of Microsoft Corporation. © 2014 Microsoft.

machine's 5-year depreciable life. In straight-line depreciation, which we explain in Chapter 13, the depreciation charge for a full year would be $100,000/5 = $20,000. The reported depreciation expense on the income statement is the sum of all the assets' annual depreciation charges. Depreciation applies to tangible assets, such as plant and equipment, whereas amortization applies to intangible assets such as patents, copyrights, trademarks, and goodwill.[3]

The cost of goods sold (COGS) includes labor, raw materials, and other expenses directly related to the production or purchase of the items or services sold in that period. The COGS includes depreciation, but we report depreciation separately so that analysis later in the chapter will be more transparent. Subtracting COGS (including depreciation) and other operating expenses results in earnings before interest and taxes (EBIT).

Many analysts add back depreciation to EBIT to calculate **EBITDA**, which stands for earnings before interest, taxes, depreciation, and amortization. Because neither depreciation nor amortization is paid in cash, some analysts claim that EBITDA is a better measure of financial strength than is net income. MicroDrive's EBITDA is:

$$\text{EBITDA} = \text{EBIT} + \text{Depreciation}$$

$$= \$500 + \$200 + \$700 \text{ million}$$

Alternatively, EBITDA's calculation can begin with sales:

$$\text{EBITDA} = \text{Sales} - \text{COGS excluding depreciation} - \text{Other expenses}$$

$$= \$5,000 - \$3,800 - \$500 = \$700$$

However, as we show later in the chapter, EBITDA is not as useful to managers and analysts as free cash flow, so we usually focus on free cash flow instead of EBITDA.

The net income available to common shareholders, which equals revenues less expenses, taxes, and preferred dividends (but before paying common dividends), is generally referred to as **net income**. Net income is also called **accounting profit**, **profit**, or **earnings**, particularly in financial news reports. Dividing net income by the number of shares outstanding gives earnings per share (EPS), often called "the bottom line." Throughout this book, unless otherwise indicated, net income means net income available to common stockholders.[4]

---

3. The accounting treatment of goodwill resulting from mergers has changed in recent years. Rather than an annual charge, companies are required to periodically evaluate the value of goodwill and reduce net income only if the goodwill's value has decreased materially ("become impaired," in the language of accountants). For example, in 2002 AOL Time Warner wrote off almost $100 billion associated with the AOL merger. It doesn't take too many $100 billion expenses to really hurt net income!

4. Companies also report "comprehensive income," which is the sum of net income and any "comprehensive" income item, such as the change in market value of a financial asset. For example, a decline in a financial asset's value would be recorded as a loss even though the asset has not been sold. We assume that there are no comprehensive income items in our examples.

Some companies also choose to report "pro forma income." For example, if a company incurs an expense that it doesn't expect to recur, such as the closing of a plant, it might calculate pro forma income as though it had not incurred the one-time expense. There are no hard-and-fast rules for calculating pro forma income, so many companies find ingenious ways to make pro forma income higher than traditional income. The SEC and the Public Company Accounting Oversight Board (PCAOB) are taking steps to reduce deceptive uses of pro forma reporting.

What is an income statement, and what information does it provide?

What is often called "the bottom line?"

What is EBITDA?

How does the income statement differ from the balance sheet with regard to the time period reported?

A firm has $2 million in earnings before taxes. The firm has an interest expense of $300,000 and depreciation of $200,000; it has no amortization. What is its EBITDA? **($2.5 million)**

6-4 Statement of Stockholders' Equity

Changes in stockholders' equity during the accounting period are reported in the **statement of stockholders' equity.** Figure 6-3 shows that MicroDrive earned $220 million during 2015, paid out $50 million in common dividends, and plowed $170 million back into the business. Thus, the balance sheet item "Retained earnings" increased from $800 million at year-end 2014 to $970 million at year-end 2015.[5] The last column shows the beginning stockholders' equity, any changes, and the end-of-year stockholders' equity.

See **Ch06 Tool Kit.xls** for details.

Note that "retained earnings" is not a pile of money just waiting to be used; it does not represent assets but is instead a *claim against assets*. In 2015, MicroDrive's stockholders allowed it to reinvest $170 million instead of distributing the money as dividends, and management spent this money on new assets. Thus, retained

FIGURE 6-3   MicroDrive Inc.: Statement of Stockholders' Equity, December 31, 2015

	A	B	C	D	E	F	G	H
				Preferred Stock	Common Shares	Common Stock	Retained Earnings	Total Equity
103								
104	Balances, Dec. 31, 2014			$100	50	$500	$800	$1,400
105	Changes during year:							
106	Net income						$220	$220
107	Cash dividends						(50)	(50)
108	Issuance/repurchase of stock			0	0	0		
109	Balances, Dec. 31, 2015			$100	50	$500	$970	$1,570
110								
111	*Note:* In financial statements, parentheses denote a negative number.							

Microsoft Excel® is a registered trademark of Microsoft Corporation. © 2014 Microsoft.

5. If they had been applicable, then columns would have been used to show "Additional Paid-in Capital" and "Treasury Stock." Also, additional rows would have contained information on such items as new issues of stock, treasury stock acquired or reissued, stock options exercised, and unrealized foreign exchange gains or losses.

earnings, as reported on the balance sheet, does not represent cash and is not "available" for the payment of dividends or anything else.[6]

SELF TEST

What is the statement of stockholders' equity, and what information does it provide?

Why do changes in retained earnings occur?

Explain why the following statement is true: "The retained earnings reported on the balance sheet does not represent cash and is not available for the payment of dividends or anything else."

A firm had a retained earnings balance of $3 million in the previous year. In the current year, its net income is $2.5 million. If it pays $1 million in common dividends in the current year, what is its resulting retained earnings balance? **($4.5 million)**

FINANCIAL ANALYSIS ON THE WEB

A wide range of valuable financial information is available on the Web. With just a couple of clicks, an investor can easily find the key financial statements for most publicly traded companies. Here's a partial (by no means a complete) list of places you can go to get started.

- Try Yahoo! Finance's Web site, **http://finance.yahoo.com**. Here you will find updated market information along with links to a variety of interesting research sites. Enter a stock's ticker symbol, click Get Quotes, and you will see the stock's current price along with recent news about the company. The panel on the left has links to key statistics and to the company's income statement, balance sheet, statement of cash flows, and more. The Web site also has a list of insider transactions, so you can tell if a company's CEO and other key insiders are buying or selling their company's stock. In addition, there is a message board where investors share opinions about the company, and there is a link to the company's filings with the SEC. Note that, in most cases, a more complete list of the SEC filings can be found at **www.sec.gov**.

- Other sources for up-to-date market information are **http://money.cnn.com** and **www.zacks.com**. These sites also provide financial statements in standardized formats.

---

6. The amount reported in the retained earnings account is *not* an indication of the amount of cash the firm has. Cash (as of the balance sheet date) is found in the cash account, an asset account. A positive number in the retained earnings account indicates only that the firm earned some income in the past, but its dividends paid were less than its earnings. Even if a company reports record earnings and shows an increase in its retained earnings account, it still may be short of cash.

   The same situation holds for individuals. You might own a new BMW (no loan), lots of clothes, and an expensive stereo and hence have a high net worth. But if you have only 23 cents in your pocket plus $5 in your checking account, you will still be short of cash.

- Both **www.bloomberg.com** and **www.market watch.com** have areas where you can obtain stock quotes along with company financials, links to Wall Street research, and links to SEC filings.
- If you are looking for charts of key accounting variables (for example, sales, inventory, depreciation and amortization, and reported earnings) as well as financial statements, take a look at **www.smartmoney.com**.

- Another good place to look is **www.reuters.com**. Here you can find links to analysts' research reports along with the key financial statements.

In addition to this information, you may be looking for sites that provide opinions regarding the direction of the overall market and views regarding individual stocks. Two popular sites in this category are The Motley Fool's Web site, **www.fool.com**, and the Web site for The Street.com, **www.thestreet.com**.

6-5 **Statement of Cash Flows**

Even if a company reports a large net income during a year, the *amount of cash* reported on its year-end balance sheet may be the same or even lower than its beginning cash. The reason is that the company can use its net income in a variety of ways, not just keep it as cash in the bank. For example, the firm may use its net income to pay dividends, to increase inventories, to finance accounts receivable, to invest in fixed assets, to reduce debt, or to buy back common stock. Indeed, many factors affect a company's *cash position* as reported on its balance sheet. The **statement of cash flows** separates a company's activities into three categories—operating, investing, and financing—and summarizes the resulting cash balance.

6-5a **Operating Activities**

As the name implies, the section for operating activities focuses on the amount of cash generated (or lost) by the firm's operating activities. The section begins with the reported net income before paying preferred dividends and makes several adjustments, beginning with noncash activities.

Noncash Adjustments

Some revenues and expenses reported on the income statement are not received or paid in cash during the year. For example, depreciation and amortization reduce reported net income but are not cash payments.

Reported taxes often differ from the taxes that are paid, resulting in an account called deferred taxes, which is the cumulative difference between the taxes that are reported and those that are paid. Deferred taxes can occur in many ways, including the use of accelerated depreciation for tax purposes but straight-line depreciation for financial reporting. This increases reported taxes relative to actual tax payments in the early years of an asset's life, causing the resulting net income to be lower than the true cash flow. Therefore, increases in deferred taxes are added to net income when calculating cash flow, and decreases are subtracted from net income.

Another example of noncash reporting occurs if a customer purchases services or products that extend beyond the reporting date, such as a 3-year extended warranty for a computer. Even if the company collects the cash at the time of the purchase, it will spread the reported revenues over the life of the purchase. This causes income to be lower than cash flow in the first year and higher in subsequent years, so adjustments must be made when calculating cash flow.

Changes in Working Capital

Increases in current assets other than cash (such as inventories and accounts receivable) decrease cash, whereas decreases in these accounts increase cash. For example, if inventories are to increase, then the firm must use cash to acquire the additional inventory. Conversely, if inventories decrease, this generally means the firm is selling inventories and not replacing all of them, hence generating cash. Here's how we keep track of whether a change in assets increases or decreases cash flow: If the amount we own goes up (like getting a new laptop computer), it means we have spent money and our cash goes down. On the other hand, if something we own goes down (like selling a car), our cash goes up.

Now consider a current liability, such as accounts payable. If accounts payable increase then the firm has received additional credit from its suppliers, which saves cash; however, if payables decrease, this means it has used cash to pay off its suppliers. Therefore, increases in current liabilities such as accounts payable increase cash, whereas decreases in current liabilities decrease cash. To keep track of the cash flow's direction, think about the impact of getting a student loan. The amount you owe goes up and your cash goes up. Now think about paying off the loan: The amount you owe goes down, but so does your cash.

6-5b Investing Activities

Investing activities include transactions involving fixed assets or short-term financial investments. For example, if a company buys new IT infrastructure, its cash goes down at the time of the purchase. On the other hand, if it sells a building or T-bill, its cash goes up.

6-5c Financing Activities

Financing activities include raising cash by issuing short-term debt, long-term debt, or stock. Because dividend payments, stock repurchases, and principal payments on debt reduce a company's cash, such transactions are included here.

6-5d Putting the Pieces Together

The statement of cash flows is used to help answer questions such as these: Is the firm generating enough cash to purchase the additional assets required for growth? Is the firm generating any extra cash it can use to repay debt or to invest in new products? Such information is useful both for managers and investors, so the statement of cash flows is an important part of the annual report.

Figure 6-4 shows MicroDrive's statement of cash flows as it would appear in the company's annual report. The top section shows cash generated by and used in operations—for MicroDrive, operations provided net cash flows of $158 million. This subtotal is in many respects the most important figure in any of the financial statements. Profits as reported on the income statement can be "doctored" by such tactics as depreciating assets too slowly, not recognizing bad debts promptly, and the like. However, it is far more difficult to simultaneously doctor profits and the working capital accounts. Therefore, it is not uncommon for a company to report positive net income right up to the day it declares bankruptcy. In such cases, however, the net cash flow from operations almost always began to deteriorate much earlier, and analysts who kept an eye on cash flow could have predicted trouble. Therefore, if you are ever analyzing a company and are pressed for time, look first at the trend in net cash flow provided by operating activities, because it will tell you more than any other single number.

See **Ch06 Tool Kit.xls** for details.

The second section shows investing activities. MicroDrive purchased fixed assets totaling $500 million and sold $40 million of short-term investments, for a net cash flow from investing activities of *minus* $460 million.

FIGURE 6-4	MicroDrive Inc.: Statement of Cash Flows for 2015 (Millions of Dollars)

	A	B	C	D	E	F	
123	*Operating Activities*						**2015**
124	Net Income before preferred dividends					$	228
125	*Noncash adjustments*						
126	Depreciation[a]						200
127	*Working capital adjustments*						
128	Increase in accounts receivable[b]						(120)
129	Increase in inventories						(180)
130	Increase in accounts payable						10
131	Increase in accruals						20
132	Net cash provided (used) by operating activities					$	158
133							
134	*Investing Activities*						
135	Cash used to acquire fixed assets[c]					$	(500)
136	Sale of short-term investments						40
137	Net cash provided (used) by investing activities					$	(460)
138							
139	*Financing Activities*						
140	Increase in notes payable					$	150
141	Increase in bonds						200
142	Payment of common and preferred dividends						(58)
143	Net cash provided (used) by financing activities					$	292
144							
145	*Summary*						
146	Net change in cash and equivalents					$	(10)
147	Cash and securities at beginning of the year						60
148	Cash and securities at end of the year					$	50

Notes:

[a]Depreciation is a noncash expense that was deducted when calculating net income. It must be added back to show cash flow from operations.

[b]An increase in a current asset decreases cash. An increase in a current liability increases cash. For example, inventories increased by $180 million and therefore reduced cash by that amount.

[c]The net increase in fixed assets is $300 million; however, this net amount is after a deduction for the year's depreciation expense. Depreciation expense must be added back to find the increase in gross fixed assets. From the company's income statement, we see that the year's depreciation expense is $200 million; thus, expenditures on fixed assets were actually $500 million.

Microsoft Excel® is a registered trademark of Microsoft Corporation. © 2014 Microsoft.

The third section, financing activities, includes borrowing from banks (notes payable), selling new bonds, and paying dividends on common and preferred stock. MicroDrive raised $350 million by borrowing, but it paid $58 million in preferred and common dividends. Therefore, its net inflow of funds from financing activities was $292 million.

In the summary, when all of these sources and uses of cash are totaled, we see that MicroDrive's cash outflows exceeded its cash inflows by $10 million during 2015; that is, its net change in cash was a *negative* $10 million.

MicroDrive's statement of cash flows should be worrisome to its managers and to outside analysts. The company had $5 billion in sales but generated only $158 million from operations, not nearly enough to cover the $500 million it spent on fixed assets and the $58 million it paid in dividends. It covered these cash outlays by borrowing heavily and by liquidating short-term investments. Obviously, this situation cannot continue year after year, so MicroDrive managers will have to make changes. We will return to MicroDrive throughout the textbook to see what actions its managers are planning.

FILLING IN THE GAAP

While U.S. companies adhere to "generally accepted accounting principles," or GAAP, when preparing financial statements, most other developed countries use "International Financial Reporting Standards," or IFRS. The U.S. GAAP system is rules-based, with thousands of instructions, or "guidances," for how individual transactions should be reported in financial statements. IFRS, on the other hand, is a principles-based system in which detailed instructions are replaced by overall guiding principles.

For example, whereas GAAP provides extensive and detailed rules about when to recognize revenue from any conceivable activity, IFRS provides just four categories of revenue and two overall principles for timing recognition. This means that even the most basic accounting measure, revenue, is different under the two standards— Total Revenue, or Sales, under GAAP won't typically equal Total Revenue under IFRS. Thus, financial statements prepared under GAAP cannot be compared directly to IFRS financial statements, making comparative financial analysis of U.S. and international companies difficult. Perhaps more problematic is that the IFRS principles allow for more company discretion in recording transactions. This means that two companies may treat identical transactions differently when using IFRS, which makes company-to-company comparisons more difficult.

The U.S. Financial Accounting Standards Board (FASB) and the International Accounting Standards Board (IASB) have been working to merge the two sets of standards since 2002. As of the end of 2013, many of the joint standards are completed but with several important standards, such as revenue recognition, still not adopted. If the current timetable holds, adoption by U.S. firms could occur by 2015.

What does this mean for you? There will still be an income statement, a balance sheet, and an equivalent to the statement of cash flows. Line item summary measures may change a bit, and the technical details about how to record individual transactions will certainly change. Accounting systems will be reprogrammed, accounting texts will be rewritten, and CPAs will have to retrain. The end result, though, will be a better ability to compare U.S. and international companies' financial statements.

To keep abreast of developments in IFRS/GAAP convergence, visit the IASB Web site at **www.iasb.org** and the FASB Web site at **www.fasb.org**.

What types of questions does the statement of cash flows answer?

Identify and briefly explain the three categories of activities in the statement of cash flows.

A firm has inventories of $2 million for the previous year and $1.5 million for the current year. What impact does this have on net cash provided by operations? **(Increase of $500,000)**

6-6 Net Cash Flow

In addition to the cash flow from operations as defined in the statement of cash flows, many analysts also calculate **net cash flow**, which is defined as:

Net cash flow = Net income − Noncash revenues + Noncash expenses

$$\text{Net cash flow} = \text{Net income} - \text{Noncash revenues} + \text{Noncash expenses} \tag{6-1}$$

where net income is the net income available for distribution to common shareholders. Depreciation and amortization usually are the largest noncash items, and in many cases the other noncash items roughly net out to zero. For this reason, many analysts assume that net cash flow equals net income plus depreciation and amortization:

$$\text{Net cash flow} = \text{Net income} + \text{Depreciation and amortization} \tag{6-2}$$

We will generally assume that Equation 6-2 holds. However, you should remember that Equation 6-2 will not accurately reflect net cash flow when there are significant noncash items other than depreciation and amortization.

We can illustrate Equation 6-2 with 2015 data for MicroDrive taken from Figure 6-2:

$$\text{Net cash flow} = \$220 + \$200 = \$420 \text{ million}$$

You can think of net cash flow as the profit a company would have if it did not have to replace fixed assets as they wear out. This is similar to the net cash flow from operating activities shown on the statement of cash flows, except that the net cash flow from operating activities also includes the impact of working capital. Net income, net cash flow, and net cash flow from operating activities each provide insight into a company's financial health, but none is as useful as the measures we discuss in the next section.

Differentiate between net cash flow and accounting profit.

A firm has net income of $5 million. Assuming that depreciation of $1 million is its only noncash expense, what is the firm's net cash flow? **($6 million)**

6-7 Free Cash Flow: The Cash Flow Available for Distribution to Investors

So far in the chapter we have focused on financial statements as presented in the annual report. When you studied income statements in accounting, the emphasis was probably on the firm's net income. However, the intrinsic value of a company's operations is determined by the stream of cash flows that the operations will generate now and in the future. To be more specific, the value of operations depends on all the future expected **free cash flows (FCF)**, defined as after-tax operating profit minus the amount of new investment in working capital and fixed assets necessary to sustain the business. *Therefore, the way for managers to make their companies more valuable is to increase free cash flow now and in the future.*

Notice that FCF is the cash flow *available for distribution to all the company's investors after the company has made all investments necessary to sustain ongoing operations.* How successful were MicroDrive's managers in generating FCF? In this section, we will calculate MicroDrive's FCF and evaluate the performance of MicroDrive's managers.

Figure 6-5 shows the five steps in calculating free cash flow. As we explain each individual step in the following sections, refer back to Figure 6-5 to keep the big picture in mind.

6-7a Net Operating Profit after Taxes (NOPAT)

If two companies have different amounts of debt, thus different amounts of interest charges, they could have identical operating performances but different net

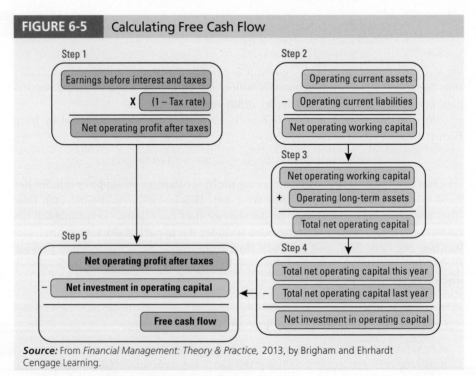

FIGURE 6-5   Calculating Free Cash Flow

Step 1

Earnings before interest and taxes

X (1 – Tax rate)

Net operating profit after taxes

Step 2

Operating current assets

– Operating current liabilities

Net operating working capital

Step 3

Net operating working capital

+ Operating long-term assets

Total net operating capital

Step 5

Net operating profit after taxes

– Net investment in operating capital

Free cash flow

Step 4

Total net operating capital this year

– Total net operating capital last year

Net investment in operating capital

Source: From *Financial Management: Theory & Practice,* 2013, by Brigham and Ehrhardt Cengage Learning.

Microsoft Excel® is a registered trademark of Microsoft Corporation. © 2014 Microsoft.

incomes—the one with more debt would have a lower net income. Net income is important, but it does not always reflect the true performance of a company's operations or the effectiveness of its managers. A better measure for comparing managers' performance is **net operating profit after taxes (NOPAT)**, which is the amount of profit a company would generate if it had no debt and held no financial assets. NOPAT is defined as follows:[7]

$$\text{NOPAT} = \text{EBIT}(1 - \text{Tax rate}) \qquad \textbf{(6–3)}$$

Using data from the income statements of Figure 6-2, MicroDrive's 2015 NOPAT is:

$$\text{NOPAT} = \$500(1 - 0.4) = \$500(0.6) = \$300 \text{ million}$$

This means MicroDrive generated an after-tax operating profit of $300 million, less than its previous NOPAT of $550(0.6) = $330 million.

6-7b Net Operating Working Capital

Most companies need some current assets to support their operating activities. For example, all companies must carry some cash to "grease the wheels" of their operations. Companies continuously receive checks from customers and write checks to suppliers, employees, and so on. Because inflows and outflows do not coincide perfectly, a company must keep some cash in its bank account. In other words, it must have some cash to conduct operations. The same is true for most other current assets, such as inventory and accounts receivable, which are required for normal operations. The short-term assets normally used in a company's operating activities are called **operating current assets**.

Not all current assets are operating current assets. For example, holdings of short-term marketable securities generally result from investment decisions made by the treasurer and not as a natural consequence of operating activities. Therefore, short-term investments are **nonoperating assets** and normally are excluded when calculating operating current assets. A useful rule of thumb is that if an asset pays interest, it should not be classified as an operating asset.

In this textbook we will always distinguish between the cash needed for operations and the marketable securities held as short-term investments. However, many companies don't make such a clean distinction. For example, Apple reported $14 billion in cash for the fiscal year end in September 2013, in addition to $26 billion in short-term investments. Apple certainly doesn't need $14 billion in cash to run its business operations. Therefore, if we were calculating operating current assets for Apple, we would classify about $2 billion as cash and the remainder as short-term investments: $14 − $2 + $26 = $38 billion. The reverse situation is possible, too, where a company reports very little cash but many short-term investments. In such a case we would classify some of the short-term investments as operating cash when calculating operating current assets.

---

7. For firms with a more complicated tax situation, it is better to define NOPAT as follows: NOPAT = (Net income before preferred dividends) + (Net interest expense)(1 − Tax rate). Also, if a firm is able to defer paying some taxes, perhaps by the use of accelerated depreciation, then it needs to adjust NOPAT to reflect the taxes it actually paid on operating income. See P. Daves, M. Ehrhardt, and R. Shrieves, *Corporate Valuation: A Guide for Managers and Investors* (Mason, OH: Thomson South-Western, 2004) for a detailed explanation of these and other adjustments.

Some current liabilities—especially accounts payable and accruals—arise in the normal course of operations. Such short-term liabilities are called **operating current liabilities**. Not all current liabilities are operating current liabilities. For example, consider the current liability shown as notes payable to banks. The company could have raised an equivalent amount as long-term debt or could have issued stock, so the choice to borrow from the bank was a financing decision and not a consequence of operations. Again, the rule of thumb is that if a liability charges interest, it is not an operating liability.

If you are ever uncertain about whether an item is an operating asset or operating liability, ask yourself whether the item is a natural consequence of operations or if it is a discretionary choice, such as a particular method of financing or an investment in a particular financial asset. If it is discretionary, then the item is not an operating asset or liability.

Notice that each dollar of operating current liabilities is a dollar that the company does not have to raise from investors in order to conduct its short-term operating activities. Therefore, we define **net operating working capital (NOWC)** as operating current assets minus operating current liabilities. In other words, net operating working capital is the working capital acquired with investor-supplied funds. Here is the definition in equation form:

(6–4)
$$\text{Net operating working capital} = \text{Operating current assets} - \text{Operating current liabilities}$$

We can apply these definitions to MicroDrive, using the balance sheet data given in Figure 6-1. Here is its net operating working capital at year-end 2015:

$$\begin{aligned}
\text{NOWC} &= \text{Operating current assets} - \text{Operating current liabilities} \\
&= (\text{Cash} + \text{Accounts receivable} + \text{Inventories}) \\
&\quad - (\text{Accounts payable} - \text{Accruals}) \\
&= (\$50 + \$500 + \$1{,}000) - (\$200 + \$300) \\
&= \$1{,}050 \text{ million}
\end{aligned}$$

For the previous year, net operating working capital was:

$$\begin{aligned}
\text{NOWC} &= (\$60 + \$380 + \$820) - (\$190 + \$280) \\
&= \$790 \text{ million}
\end{aligned}$$

6-7c Total Net Operating Capital

In addition to working capital, most companies also use long-term assets to support their operations. These include land, buildings, factories, equipment, and the like. **Total net operating capital** is the sum of NOWC and operating long-term assets:

(6–5)
$$\text{Total net operating capital} = \text{NOWC} + \text{Operating long-term assets}$$

Because MicroDrive's operating long-term assets consist only of net plant and equipment, its total net operating capital at year-end 2015 was:

$$\begin{aligned}
\text{Total net operating capital} &= \$1{,}050 + \$2{,}000 \\
&= \$3{,}050 \text{ million}
\end{aligned}$$

For the previous year, its total net operating capital was:

$$\text{Total net operating capital} = \$790 + \$1,700$$
$$= \$2,490 \text{ million}$$

Notice that we have defined total net operating capital as the sum of net operating working capital and operating long-term assets. In other words, our definition is in terms of operating assets and liabilities. However, we can also calculate total net operating capital by looking at the sources of funds. **Total investor-supplied capital** is defined as the total of funds provided by investors, such as notes payable, long-term bonds, preferred stock, and common equity. For most companies, total investor-supplied capital is:

$$\begin{matrix} \text{Total investor-supplied} \\ \text{capital} \end{matrix} = \begin{matrix} \text{Notes} \\ \text{payable} \end{matrix} + \begin{matrix} \text{Long-term} \\ \text{bonds} \end{matrix} + \begin{matrix} \text{Preferred} \\ \text{stock} \end{matrix} + \begin{matrix} \text{Common} \\ \text{equity} \end{matrix} \qquad \textbf{(6–6)}$$

For MicroDrive, the total capital provided by investors at year-end 2014 was $130 + $1,000 + $100 + $1,300 = $2,530 million. Of this amount, $40 million was tied up in short-term investments, which are not directly related to MicroDrive's operations. Therefore, we define **total investor-supplied operating capital** as:

$$\begin{matrix} \text{Total investor-supplied} \\ \text{operating capital} \end{matrix} = \begin{matrix} \text{Total investor-supplied} \\ \text{capital} \end{matrix} - \begin{matrix} \text{Short-term} \\ \text{investments} \end{matrix} \qquad \textbf{(6–7)}$$

MicroDrive had $2,530 − $40 = $2,490 million of investor-supplied operating capital in 2014. Notice that this is exactly the same value as calculated before. Therefore, we can calculate total net operating capital either from net operating working capital and operating long-term assets or from the investor-supplied funds. We usually base our calculations on operating data because this approach allows us to analyze a division, factory, or work center. In contrast, the approach based on investor-supplied capital is applicable only for the entire company.

The expression "total net operating capital" is a mouthful, so we often call it *operating capital* or even just *capital*. Also, unless we specifically say "investor-supplied capital," we are referring to total net operating capital.

6-7d Net Investment in Operating Capital

As calculated previously, MicroDrive had $2,490 million of total net operating capital at the end of 2014 and $3,050 million at the end of 2015. Therefore, during 2015, it made a **net investment in operating capital** of:

$$\text{Net investment in operating capital} = \$3,050 - \$2,490 = \$560 \text{ million}$$

Most of this investment was made in net operating working capital, which rose from $790 million to $1,050 million, or by $260 million. This 33% increase in net operating working capital, in view of a sales increase of only 5% (to $5 billion from $4.76 billion), should set off warning bells in your head: Why did MicroDrive tie up so much additional cash in working capital? Is the company gearing up for a big increase in sales, or are inventories not moving and receivables not being collected? We will address these questions in detail in Chapter 7, when we cover ratio analysis.

6-7e **Calculating Free Cash Flow**

Free cash flow is defined as:

(6–8)
$$FCF = NOPAT - \text{Net investment in operating capital}$$

MicroDrive's free cash flow in 2015 was:

$$\begin{aligned} FCF &= \$300 - (\$3,050 - \$2,490) \\ &= \$300 - \$560 \\ &= -\$260 \text{ million} \end{aligned}$$

Although we prefer this approach to calculating FCF, sometimes the financial press calculates FCF differently:

(6–9)
$$FCF = \begin{bmatrix} EBIT\ (1-T) \\ + \text{Depreciation} \end{bmatrix} - \begin{bmatrix} \text{Gross investment} \\ \text{in fixed assets} \end{bmatrix} - \begin{bmatrix} \text{Investment} \\ NOWC \end{bmatrix}$$

For MicroDrive, this calculation is:

$$FCF = (\$300 + \$200) - \$500 - (\$1,050 - \$790) = -\$260$$

Notice that the results are the same for either calculation. To see this, substitute NOPAT into the first bracket of Equation 6-9 and substitute the definition for net investment in fixed assets into the second bracket:

(6–9)a
$$FCF = \begin{bmatrix} NOPAT \\ + \text{Depreciation} \end{bmatrix} - \begin{bmatrix} \text{Net investment} \\ \text{in fixed assets} \\ + \text{Depreciation} \end{bmatrix} - \begin{bmatrix} \text{Investment} \\ \text{in NOWC} \end{bmatrix}$$

Both the first and second brackets have depreciation, so depreciation can be cancelled out, leaving:

(6–9)b
$$FCF = NOPAT - \begin{bmatrix} \text{Net investment} \\ \text{in fixed assets} \end{bmatrix} - \begin{bmatrix} \text{Investment} \\ \text{in NOWC} \end{bmatrix}$$

The last two bracketed terms are equal to the net investment in operating capital, so Equation 6-9b simplifies to Equation 6-8. We usually use Equation 6-8 because it saves us the step of adding depreciation both to NOPAT and to the net investment in fixed assets and also because frequently only net fixed assets and not gross fixed assets are reported on the firm's financial statements.

6-7f **The Uses of FCF**

Recall that free cash flow (FCF) is the amount of cash that is available for distribution to all investors, including shareholders and debtholders. There are five good uses for FCF:

1. Pay interest to debtholders, keeping in mind that the net cost to the company is the after-tax interest expense.

SARBANES-OXLEY AND FINANCIAL FRAUD

Investors need to be cautious when they review financial statements. Although companies are required to follow generally accepted accounting principles (GAAP), managers still use a lot of discretion in deciding how and when to report certain transactions. Consequently, two firms in the same operating situation may report financial statements that convey different impressions about their financial strength. Some variations may stem from legitimate differences of opinion about the correct way to record transactions. In other cases, managers may choose to report numbers in a way that helps them present either higher earnings in the current year or more stable earnings over time. As long as they follow GAAP, such actions are not illegal, but these differences make it harder for investors to compare companies and gauge their true performances.

Unfortunately, there have also been cases in which managers reported fraudulent statements. Indeed, a number of high-profile executives have faced criminal charges because of their misleading accounting practices. For example, in June 2002 it was discovered that WorldCom (now called MCI and is a subsidiary of Verizon Communications) had committed the most massive accounting fraud of all time by recording over $7 billion of ordinary operating costs as capital expenditures, thus overstating net income by the same amount.

WorldCom's published financial statements fooled most investors, who bid the stock price up to $64.50, and banks and other lenders provided the company with more than $30 billion of loans. Arthur Andersen, the firm's auditor, was faulted for not detecting the fraud. WorldCom's CFO and CEO were convicted, and Arthur Andersen went bankrupt. But these consequences didn't help the investors who relied on the published financial statements.

In response to these and other abuses, Congress passed the Sarbanes-Oxley Act of 2002. One of its provisions requires both the CEO and the CFO to sign a statement certifying that the "financial statements and disclosures fairly represent, in all material respects, the operations and financial condition" of the company. In principle, this should make it easier to haul off in handcuffs a CEO or CFO who has been misleading investors. In practice, as of the act's 10-year anniversary in 2012 only a handful of executives had ever been charged under the provision, and even fewer convictions were obtained.[a] It may be that the threat of prosecution has reduced the incidence of financial fraud; whether it will prevent future financial fraud remains to be seen.

[a]Alison Frankel, Reuters July 27, 2013, www.reuters.com/article/2012/07/27/us-financial-sarbox-idUSBRE86Q1BY20120727

2. Repay debtholders; that is, pay off some of the debt.
3. Pay dividends to shareholders.
4. Repurchase stock from shareholders.
5. Buy short-term investments or other nonoperating assets.

Consider MicroDrive, with its FCF of −$260 million in 2015. How did MicroDrive use the FCF?

MicroDrive's income statement shows an interest expense of $120 million. With a tax rate of 40%, the after-tax interest payment for the year is:

$$\text{After-tax interest payment} = \$120(1 - 40\%) = \$72 \text{ million}$$

The net amount of debt that is repaid is equal to the amount at the beginning of the year minus the amount at the end of the year. This includes notes payable and long-term debt. If the amount of ending debt is less than the beginning debt, the company paid down some of its debt. But if the ending debt is greater than the beginning debt, the company actually borrowed additional funds from creditors. In that case, it would be a negative use of FCF. For MicroDrive, the net debt repayment for 2015 is equal to the amount at the beginning of the year minus the amount at the end of the year:

Net debt repayment = ($130 + $1,000) − ($280 + $1,200) = −$350 million

This is a "negative use" of FCF because it increased the debt balance. This is typical of most companies because growing companies usually add debt each year.

MicroDrive paid $8 million in preferred dividends and $50 in common dividends for a total of:

Dividend payments = $8 + $50 = $58 million

The net amount of stock that is repurchased is equal to the amount at the beginning of the year minus the amount at the end of the year. This includes preferred stock and common stock. If the amount of ending stock is less than the beginning stock, then the company made net repurchases. But if the ending stock is greater than the beginning stock, the company actually made net issuances. In that case, it would be a negative use of FCF. Even though MicroDrive neither issued nor repurchased stock during the year, many companies use FCF to repurchase stocks as a replacement for or supplement to dividends, as we discuss in Chapter 15.

The amount of net purchases of short-term investments is equal to the amount at the end of the year minus the amount at the beginning of the year. If the amount of ending investments is greater than the beginning investments, then the company made net purchases. But if the ending investments are less than the beginning investments, the company actually sold investments. In that case, it would be a negative use of FCF. MicroDrive's net purchases of short-term investments in 2015 are:

Net purchases of short-term investments = $0 − $40 = −$40 million

Notice that this is a "negative use" because MicroDrive sold short-term investments instead of purchasing them.

We combine these individual uses of FCF to find the total uses.

1.	After-tax interest:	$ 72
2.	Net debt repayments:	−350
3.	Dividends:	58
4.	Net stock repurchases:	0
5.	Net purchases of ST investments:	−40
	Total uses of FCF:	−$260

As it should be, the −$260 total for uses of FCF is identical to the value of FCF from operations that we calculated previously.

Observe that a company does not use FCF to acquire operating assets, because the calculation of FCF already takes into account the purchase of operating assets needed to support growth. Unfortunately, there is evidence to suggest that some companies with high FCF tend to make unnecessary investments that don't add value, such as paying too much to acquire another company. Thus, high FCF can cause waste if managers fail to act in the best interests of shareholders. As discussed in Chapter 1, this is called an agency cost, because managers are hired as agents to act on behalf of stockholders. We discuss agency costs and ways to control them in Chapter 19, where we discuss value-based management and corporate governance, and in Chapter 16, where we discuss the choice of capital structure.

6-7g **FCF and Corporate Value**

Free cash flow is the amount of cash available for distribution to investors; so the fundamental value of a company to its investors depends on the present value of its expected future FCFs, discounted at the company's weighted average cost of capital (WACC). Subsequent chapters will develop the tools needed to forecast FCFs and evaluate their risk. Chapter 9 ties all this together with a model used to calculate the value of a company. Even though you do not yet have all the tools to apply the model, you must understand this basic concept: *FCF is the cash flow available for distribution to investors. Therefore, a company's fundamental value depends primarily on its expected future FCF.*

SELF TEST

What is net operating working capital? Why does it exclude most short-term investments and notes payable?

What is total net operating capital? Why is it important for managers to calculate a company's capital requirements?

Why is NOPAT a better performance measure than net income?

What is free cash flow? Why is it important?

A firm's total net operating capital for the previous year was $2 million. For the current year, its total net operating capital is $2.5 million and its NOPAT is $1.2 million. What is its free cash flow for the current year? **($700,000)**

6-8 **Performance Evaluation**

Because free cash flow has such a big impact on value, managers and investors can use FCF and its components to measure a company's performance. The following sections explain three performance measures: return on invested capital, market value added, and economic value added.

6-8a **The Return on Invested Capital**

Even though MicroDrive had a positive NOPAT, its very high investment in operating assets caused a negative FCF. Is a negative free cash flow always bad? The answer is, "Not necessarily; it depends on why the free cash flow is negative." It's a bad sign if FCF is negative because NOPAT is negative, which probably means the company is experiencing operating problems. However, many high-growth companies have positive NOPAT but negative FCF because they are making large investments in operating assets to support growth. For example, Buffalo Wild Wings' sales grew by 33% in 2012 and its NOPAT was stable compared to 2011 at $60 million; however, its FCF was *negative* $42 million, due largely to a $100 million investment in operating capital to support its high sales growth.

There is nothing wrong with value-adding growth, even if it causes negative free cash flows, but it is vital to determine whether growth is actually adding value. For this we use the **return on invested capital (ROIC)**, which shows how much NOPAT is generated by each dollar of operating capital:

(6–10)

$$\text{ROIC} = \frac{\text{NOPAT}}{\text{Operating capital}}$$

As shown in Figure 6-6, in 2015 MicroDrive's ROIC is $300/$3,050 = 9.84%. To determine whether this ROIC is high enough to add value, compare it to the weighted average cost of capital (WACC). Chapter 11 explains how to calculate the WACC; for now, accept that the WACC considers a company's individual risk as well as overall market conditions. Figure 6-6 shows that MicroDrive's 9.84% ROIC is less than its 11% WACC. Thus, MicroDrive did not generate a sufficient rate of return to compensate its investors for the risk they bore in 2015. This is markedly different from the previous year, in which MicroDrive's 13.25% ROIC was greater than its 10.5% WACC. Not only is the current ROIC too low, but the trend is in the wrong direction.

Although not the case for MicroDrive, in many situations a negative FCF is not necessarily bad. For example, Buffalo Wild Wings had a negative FCF in 2012, but its ROIC was about 18.3%. Because its WACC was only 12%, Buffalo Wild Wings' growth was adding value.[8] At some point Buffalo Wild Wings' growth will slow and it will not require such large capital investments. If it maintains a high ROIC, then its FCF will become positive and very large as growth slows.

Neither traditional accounting data nor return on invested capital incorporates stock prices, even though the primary goal of management should be to maximize the firm's intrinsic stock price. In contrast, Market Value Added (MVA) and Economic Value Added (EVA) do attempt to compare intrinsic measures with market measures.[9]

6-8b Market Value Added (MVA)

One measure of shareholder wealth is the *difference* between the market value of the firm's stock and the cumulative amount of equity capital that was supplied by shareholders. This difference is called the **Market Value Added (MVA)**:

(6–11)

MVA = Market value of stock − Equity capital supplied by shareholders
= (Shares outstanding)(Stock price) − Total common equity

---

8. If g is the growth rate in capital, then with a little (or a lot of!) algebra, free cash flow is:

$$\text{FCF} = \text{Captial}\left(\text{ROIC} - \frac{g}{1+g}\right)$$

This shows that when the growth rate gets almost as high as ROIC, then FCF will be negative.

9. The concepts of EVA and MVA were developed by Joel Stern and Bennett Stewart, co-founders of the consulting firm Stern Stewart & Company. Stern Stewart trademarked the term "EVA" so other consulting firms have given other names to this value, as they have to MVA. Still, EVA and MVA are the terms most commonly used in practice.

FIGURE 6-6	Calculating Performance Measures for MicroDrive Inc. (Millions of Dollars)

	A	B	C	D	E	F	G
374						2015	2014
375	*Calculating NOPAT*						
376	EBIT					$500	$550
377	x (1 – Tax rate)					60%	60%
378	NOPAT = EBIT(1 – T)					$300	$330
379							
380	*Calculating Net Operating Working Capital (NOWC)*						
381	Operating current assets					$1,550	$1,260
382	– Operating current liabilities					$500	$470
383	NOWC					$1,050	$790
384							
385	*Calculating Total Net Operating Capital*						
386	NOWC					$1,050	$790
387	+ Net plant and equipment					$2,000	$1,700
388	Total net operating capital					$3,050	$2,490
389							
390	*Calculating Return on Invested Capital (ROIC)*						
391	NOPAT					$300	$330
392	÷ Total net operating capital					$3,050	$2,490
393	ROIC = NOPAT/Total net operating capital					9.84%	13.25%
394	Weighted average cost of capital (WACC)					11.00%	10.50%
395							
396	*Calculating the Operating Profitability Ratio (OP)*						
397	NOPAT					$300	$330
398	÷ Sales					$5,000	$4,760
399	OP = NOPAT/Sales					6.00%	6.93%
400							
401	*Calculating Capital Requirement Ratio (CR)*						
402	Total net operating capital					$3,050	$2,490
403	÷ Sales					$5,000	$4,760
404	CR = Total net operating capital/Sales					61.00%	52.31%
405							
406	*Calculating Market Value Added (MVA)*						
407	Price per share					$27	$40
408	x Number of shares (millions)					50	50
409	Market value of equity = P x (# of shares)					$1,350	$2,000
410	– Book value of equity					$1,470	$1,300
411	MVA = Market value – Book value					–$120	$700
412							
413	*Calculating Economic Value Added (EVA)*						
414	Total net operating capital					$3,050.0	$2,490.0
415	x Weighted average cost of capital (WACC)					11.0%	10.5%
416	Dollar cost of capital					$335.5	$261.5
417							
418	NOPAT					$300.0	$330.0
419	– Dollar cost of capital					$335.5	$261.5
420	EVA = NOPAT – Dollar cost of capital					–$35.5	$68.6

Microsoft Excel® is a registered trademark of Microsoft Corporation. © 2014 Microsoft.

www

For an updated estimate of Coca-Cola's MVA, go to **http://finance .yahoo.com**, enter KO, and click GO. This shows the market value of equity, called Mkt Cap. To get the book value of equity, select Balance Sheet from the left panel.

To illustrate, consider Coca-Cola. In September 2013, its total market equity value, commonly called market capitalization, was $170 billion while its balance sheet showed that stockholders had put up only $33 billion. Thus, Coca-Cola's MVA was $170 − $33 = $137 billion. This $137 billion represents the difference between the money that Coca-Cola's stockholders have invested in the corporation since its founding—including indirect investment by retaining earnings—and the cash they could get if they sold the business. The higher its MVA, the better the job management is doing for the firm's shareholders.

Sometimes MVA is defined as the total market value of the company minus the total amount of investor-supplied capital:

(6–11a)

$$\text{MVA} = \text{Total market value} - \text{Total investor-supplied capital}$$
$$= (\text{Market value of stock} + \text{Market value of debt})$$
$$- \text{Total investor-supplied capital}$$

For most companies, the total amount of investor-supplied capital is the sum of equity, debt, and preferred stock. We can calculate the total amount of investor-supplied capital directly from their reported values in the financial statements. The total market value of a company is the sum of the market values of common equity, debt, and preferred stock. It is easy to find the market value of equity because stock prices are readily available, but it is not always easy to find the market value of debt. Hence, many analysts use the value of debt reported in the financial statements, which is the debt's book value, as an estimate of the debt's market value.

For Coca-Cola, the total amount of reported debt was about $31 billion; Coca-Cola had no preferred stock. Using the debt's book value as an estimate of the debt's market value, Coke's total market value was $170 + $31 = $201 billion. The total amount of investor-supplied funds was $33 + $31 = $64 billion. Using these total values, the MVA was $201 − $64 = $137 billion. Note that this is the same answer as when we used the previous definition of MVA. Both methods will give the same result if the market value of debt is approximately equal to its book value.

Figure 6-6 shows that MicroDrive has 50 million shares of stock and a stock price of $27, giving it a market value of equity equal to $1,350 million. MicroDrive has $1,470 in book equity, so its MVA is $1,350 − $1,470 = −$120. In other words, MicroDrive's current market value is less than the cumulative amount of equity that its shareholders have invested during the company's life.

6-8c Economic Value Added (EVA)

Whereas MVA measures the effects of managerial actions since the inception of a company, **Economic Value Added (EVA)** focuses on managerial effectiveness in a given year. The EVA formula is:

(6–12)

$$\text{EVA} = \frac{\text{Net operating profit}}{\text{after taxes}} - \frac{\text{After-tax dollar cost of capital}}{\text{used to support operations}}$$
$$= \text{NOPAT} - (\text{Total net operating capital})(\text{WACC})$$

Economic Value Added is an estimate of a business's true economic profit for the year, and it differs sharply from accounting profit.[10] EVA represents the residual income that remains after the cost of *all* capital, including equity capital, has been deducted, whereas accounting profit is determined without imposing a charge for equity capital. As we will discuss in Chapter 11, equity capital has a cost because shareholders give up the opportunity to invest and earn returns elsewhere when they provide capital to the firm. This cost is an *opportunity cost* rather than an *accounting cost,* but it is real nonetheless.

Note that when calculating EVA we do not add back depreciation. Although it is not a cash expense, depreciation is a cost because worn-out assets must be replaced, and it is therefore deducted when determining both net income and EVA. Our calculation of EVA assumes that the true economic depreciation of the company's fixed assets exactly equals the depreciation used for accounting and tax purposes. If this were not the case, adjustments would have to be made to obtain a more accurate measure of EVA.

Economic Value Added measures the extent to which the firm has increased shareholder value. Therefore, if managers focus on EVA, they will more likely operate in a manner consistent with maximizing shareholder wealth. Note too that EVA can be determined for divisions as well as for the company as a whole, so it provides a useful basis for determining managerial performance at all levels. Consequently, many firms include EVA as a component of compensation plans.

We can also calculate EVA in terms of ROIC:

$$\text{EVA} = (\text{Total net operating capital})(\text{ROIC} - \text{WACC}) \qquad \textbf{(6-13)}$$

As this equation shows, a firm adds value–that is, has a positive EVA–if its ROIC is greater than its WACC. If WACC exceeds ROIC, then growth can actually reduce a firm's value.

Using Equation 6-12, Figure 6-6 shows that MicroDrive's EVA is:

$$\text{EVA} = \$300 - (\$3,050)(11\%) = \$300 - \$335.5 = -\$35.5 \text{ million}$$

This negative EVA reinforces our earlier conclusions that MicroDrive lost value in 2015 due to an erosion in its operating performance. In Chapter 9, we will determine MicroDrive's intrinsic value and explore ways in which MicroDrive can reverse its downward trend.

6-8d Intrinsic Value, MVA, and EVA

We will have more to say about both MVA and EVA later in the book, but we can close this section with two observations. First, there is a relationship between MVA and EVA, but it is not a direct one. If a company has a history of negative EVAs, then its MVA will probably be negative; conversely, its MVA probably will be positive if

---

10. The most important reason EVA differs from accounting profit is that the cost of equity capital is deducted when EVA is calculated. Other factors that could lead to differences include adjustments that might be made to depreciation, to research and development costs, to inventory valuations, and so on. These other adjustments also can affect the calculation of investor-supplied capital, which affects both EVA and MVA. See G. Bennett Stewart, III, *The Quest for Value* (New York: HarperCollins Publishers, Inc., 1991).

the company has a history of positive EVAs. However, the stock price, which is the key ingredient in the MVA calculation, depends more on expected future performance than on historical performance. Therefore, a company with a history of negative EVAs could have a positive MVA, provided investors expect a turnaround in the future.

The second observation is that when EVAs or MVAs are used to evaluate managerial performance as part of an incentive compensation program, EVA is the measure that is typically used. The reasons are: (1) EVA shows the value added during a given year, whereas MVA reflects performance over the company's entire life, perhaps even including times before the current managers were born; and (2) EVA can be applied to individual divisions or other units of a large corporation, whereas MVA must be applied to the entire corporation.

A company's NOPAT is $12 million and its total net operating capital is $100 million. What is the ROIC? **(12%)**

Define Market Value Added (MVA) and Economic Value Added (EVA).

How does EVA differ from accounting profit?

A firm has $100 million in total net operating capital. Its return on invested capital is 14%, and its weighted average cost of capital is 10%. What is its EVA? **($4 million)**

6-9 The Federal Income Tax System

The value of any financial asset (including stocks, bonds, and mortgages), as well as most real assets such as plants or even entire firms, depends on the after-tax stream of cash flows produced by the asset. The following sections describe the key features of corporate and individual taxation.

6-9a Corporate Income Taxes

The corporate tax structure, shown in Table 6-1, is relatively simple. The **marginal tax rate** is the rate paid on the last dollar of income, while the **average tax rate** is the average rate paid on all income. To illustrate, if a firm had $65,000 of taxable income, its tax bill would be:

$$\text{Taxes} = \$7,500 + 0.25(\$65,000 - \$50,000)$$
$$= \$7,500 + \$3,750 = \$11,250$$

Its marginal rate would be 25%, and its average tax rate would be $11,250/$65,000 = 17.3%. Note that corporate income above $18,333,333 has an average and marginal tax rate of 35%.

Interest and Dividend Income Received by a Corporation

Interest income received by a corporation is taxed as ordinary income at regular corporate tax rates. However, *70% of the dividends received by one corporation from another are excluded from taxable income, while the remaining 30% are taxed*

TABLE 6-1	Corporate Tax Rates as of December 2013		
If a Corporation's Taxable Income Is	**It Pays This Amount on the Base of the Bracket**	**Plus This Percentage on the Excess Over the Base**	**Average Tax Rate at Top of Bracket**
Up to $50,000	$0	15%	15.0%
$50,000–$75,000	$7,500	25	18.3
$75,000–$100,000	$13,750	34	22.3
$100,000–$335,000	$22,250	39	34.0
$335,000–$10,000,000	$113,900	34	34.0
$10,000,000–$15,000,000	$3,400,000	35	34.3
$15,000,000–$18,333,333	$5,150,000	38	35.0
Over $18,333,333	$6,416,667	35	35.0

at the ordinary tax rate.[11] Thus, a corporation earning more than $18,333,333 and paying a 35% marginal tax rate would pay only (0.30)(0.35) = 0.105 = 10.5% of its dividend income as taxes, so its effective tax rate on dividends received would be 10.5%. If this firm had $10,000 in pre-tax dividend income, then its after-tax dividend income would be $8,950:

$$\text{After-tax income} = \text{Before-tax income} - \text{Taxes}$$
$$= (\text{Before-tax income}) - (\text{Before-tax income}) (\text{Effective tax rate})$$
$$= (\text{Before-tax income}) (1 - \text{Effective tax rate})$$
$$= \$10,000[1 - (0.30)(0.35)]$$
$$= \$10,000(1 - 0.105) = \$10,000(0.895) = \$8,950$$

If the corporation pays its own after-tax income out to stockholders as dividends, then the income is ultimately subject to *triple taxation:* (1) the original corporation is first taxed, (2) the second corporation is then taxed on the dividends it received, and (3) the individuals who receive the final dividends are taxed again. This is the reason for the 70% exclusion on intercorporate dividends.

If a corporation has surplus funds that can be invested in marketable securities, the tax treatment favors investment in stocks, which pay dividends, rather than in bonds, which pay interest. For example, suppose Microsoft had $1 million to invest, and suppose it could buy either bonds that paid interest of $80,000 per year or preferred stock that paid dividends of $70,000. Microsoft is in the 35% tax bracket; therefore, its tax on the interest, if it bought bonds, would be 0.35($80,000) = $28,000,

---

11. The size of the dividend exclusion actually depends on the degree of ownership. Corporations that own less than 20% of the stock of the dividend-paying company can exclude 70% of the dividends received; firms that own more than 20% but less than 80% can exclude 80% of the dividends; and firms that own more than 80% can exclude the entire dividend payment. We will, in general, assume a 70% dividend exclusion.

WHEN IT COMES TO TAXES, HISTORY REPEATS AND REPEALS ITSELF!

Prior to 1987, many large corporations such as General Electric and Boeing paid no federal income taxes even though they reported profits. How could this happen? Some expenses, especially depreciation, were defined differently for calculating taxable income than for reporting earnings to stockholders. So some companies reported positive profits to stockholders but losses—hence no taxes—to the Internal Revenue Service. Also, some companies that otherwise would have paid taxes were able to use various tax credits to avoid paying taxes.

The Tax Reform Act of 1986 eliminated many loopholes and tightened up provisions in the corporate Alternative Minimum Tax (AMT) code so that companies would not be able to utilize tax credits and accelerated depreciation to such an extent that their federal taxes fell below a certain minimum level.

Fast forward to the present. According to a report published in late 2011, General Electric and Boeing paid no federal income taxes in 2008, 2009, or 2010 even though they reported profits in each year. In fact, 30 companies with an average profit of over $1.7 billion per year paid no taxes during the 3-year study period. Of the 280 companies in the study, 97 paid 10% or less of their reported profit as federal income taxes. The average effective rate was less than 19%, much lower than the 35% rate shown in the corporate tax table. Only 25% of the companies in the study paid more than 30%. How did history repeat itself?

Over the years in response to corporate lobbying efforts Congress gradually repealed many of the 1986 tax reforms and weakened the AMT, adding more and more loopholes and credits. Some of these breaks were for all firms, such as the 2008 acceleration of depreciation intended to stimulate corporate investment in the wake of the global economic crisis. Others were for specific industries, such as tax breaks for ethanol production that might help reduce reliance on imported oil. However, some of the changes appear difficult to justify, such as the 2010 tax breaks given to NASCAR track owners.

The net result is a complicated tax system in which corporations with shrewd accountants and well-connected lobbyists pay substantially less than other companies. As we write this in 2014, President Obama and a few leaders in Congress are calling for corporate tax reform, although Congress as a whole continues to show little interest in rolling back the tax benefits they have granted their well-connected contributors!

Source: Adapted from Robert S. McIntyre, Matthew Gardner, Rebecca J. Wilkins, and Richard Phillips "Corporate Taxpayers & Corporate Tax Dodgers 2008–10," *Joint Project of Citizens for Tax Justice & the Institute on Taxation and Economic Policy*, November 2011; see **www.ctj.org/corporatetaxdodgers/CorporateTaxDodgersReport.pdf.**

and its after-tax income would be $52,000. If it bought preferred (or common) stock, its tax would be 0.35[(0.30)($70,000)] = $7,350, and its after-tax income would be $62,650. Other factors might lead Microsoft to invest in bonds, but the tax treatment certainly favors stock investments when the investor is a corporation.[12]

---

12. This illustration demonstrates why corporations favor investing in lower-yielding preferred stocks over higher-yielding bonds. When tax consequences are considered, the yield on the preferred stock, [1 − 0.35(0.30)](7.0%) = 6.265%, is higher than the yield on the bond, (1 − 0.35)(8.0%) = 5.2%. Also, note that corporations are restricted in their use of borrowed funds to purchase other firms' preferred or common stocks. Without such restrictions, firms could engage in *tax arbitrage*, whereby the interest on borrowed funds reduces taxable income on a dollar-for-dollar basis while taxable income is increased by only $0.30 per dollar of dividend income. Thus, current tax laws reduce the 70% dividend exclusion in proportion to the amount of borrowed funds used to purchase the stock.

Interest and Dividends Paid by a Corporation

A firm's operations can be financed with either debt or equity capital. If the firm uses debt then it must pay interest on this debt, but if the firm uses equity then it is expected to pay dividends to the equity investors (stockholders). The interest *paid* by a corporation is deducted from its operating income to obtain its taxable income, but dividends paid are not deductible. Therefore, a firm needs $1 of pre-tax income to pay $1 of interest, but if it is in the 40% federal-plus-state tax bracket, it must earn $1.67 of pre-tax income to pay $1 of dividends:

$$\frac{\text{Pre-tax income needed}}{\text{to pay \$1 of dividends}} = \frac{\$1}{1 - \text{Tax rate}} = \frac{\$1}{0.60} = \$1.67$$

Working backward, if a company has $1.67 in pre-tax income, it must pay $0.67 in taxes: (0.4)($1.67) = $0.67. This leaves the firm with after-tax income of $1.00.

Of course, it is generally not possible to finance exclusively with debt capital, and the risk of doing so would offset the benefits of the higher expected income. Still, *the fact that interest is a deductible expense has a profound effect on the way businesses are financed: Our corporate tax system favors debt financing over equity financing.* This point is discussed in more detail in Chapters 11 and 16.

Corporate Capital Gains

Before 1987 corporate long-term capital gains were taxed at lower rates than corporate ordinary income, so the situation was similar for corporations and individuals. Under current law, however, corporations' capital gains are taxed at the same rates as their operating income.

Corporate Loss Carryback and Carryforward

Ordinary corporate operating losses can be carried back (**carryback**) to each of the preceding 2 years and forward (**carryforward**) for the next 20 years and thus be used to offset taxable income in those years. For example, an operating loss in 2015 could be carried back and used to reduce taxable income in 2013 and 2014 as well as carried forward, if necessary, to reduce taxes in 2016, 2017, and so on, to the year 2035. After carrying back 2 years, any remaining loss is typically carried forward first to the next year, then to the one after that, and so on, until losses have been used up or the 20-year carryforward limit has been reached.

To illustrate, suppose Apex Corporation had $2 million of *pre-tax* profits (taxable income) in 2013 and 2014, and then, in 2015, Apex lost $12 million. Also, assume that Apex's federal-plus-state tax rate is 40%. As shown in Table 6-2, the company would use the carryback feature to recalculate its taxes for 2013, using $2 million of the 2015 operating losses to reduce the 2013 pre-tax profit to zero. This would permit it to recover the taxes paid in 2013. Therefore, in 2015 Apex would receive a refund of its 2013 taxes because of the loss experienced in 2015. Because $10 million of the unrecovered losses would still be available, Apex would repeat this procedure for 2014. Thus, in 2015 the company would pay zero taxes for 2015 and also would receive a refund for taxes paid in 2013 and 2014. Apex would still have $8 million of unrecovered losses to carry forward, subject to the 20-year limit. This $8 million could be used to offset future taxable income. The purpose of this loss treatment is to avoid penalizing corporations whose incomes fluctuate substantially from year to year.

TABLE 6-2	Apex Corporation: Calculation of $12 Million Loss Carryback and Amount Available for Carryforward		
	Past Year 2013	**Past Year 2014**	**Current Year 2015**
Original taxable income	$2,000,000	$2,000,000	−$12,000,000
Carryback credit	2,000,000	2,000,000	
Adjusted profit	$ 0	$ 0	
Taxes previously paid (40%)	800,000	800,000	
Difference = Tax refund due	$ 800,000	$ 800,000	
Total tax refund received			$ 1,600,000
Amount of loss carryforward available			
Current loss			−$12,000,000
Carryback losses used			4,000,000
Carryforward losses still available			−$ 8,000,000

See **Ch06 Tool Kit.xls** for details.

Improper Accumulation to Avoid Payment of Dividends

Corporations could refrain from paying dividends and thus permit their stockholders to avoid personal income taxes on dividends. To prevent this, the Tax Code contains an **improper accumulation** provision stating that earnings accumulated by a corporation are subject to penalty rates *if the purpose of the accumulation is to enable stockholders to avoid personal income taxes*. A cumulative total of $250,000 (the balance sheet item "retained earnings") is by law exempted from the improper accumulation tax for most corporations. This is a benefit primarily to small corporations.

The improper accumulation penalty applies only if the retained earnings in excess of $250,000 are *shown by the IRS to be unnecessary to meet the reasonable needs of the business*. A great many companies do indeed have legitimate reasons for retaining more than $250,000 of earnings. For example, firms may retain and use earnings to pay off debt, finance growth, or provide the corporation with a cushion against possible cash drains caused by losses. How much a firm should be allowed to accumulate for uncertain contingencies is a matter of judgment. We shall consider this matter again in Chapter 15, which deals with corporate dividend policy.

Consolidated Corporate Tax Returns

If a corporation owns 80% or more of another corporation's stock, then it can aggregate income and file one consolidated tax return; thus, the losses of one company can be used to offset the profits of another. (Similarly, one division's losses can be used to offset another division's profits.) No business ever wants to incur losses (you can go broke losing $1 to save 35¢ in taxes), but tax offsets do help make it more feasible for large, multidivisional corporations to undertake risky new ventures or ventures that will suffer losses during a developmental period.

Taxes on Overseas Income

Many U.S. corporations have overseas subsidiaries, and those subsidiaries must pay taxes in the countries where they operate. Often, foreign tax rates are lower than U.S. rates. As long as foreign earnings are reinvested overseas, no U.S. tax is due on those earnings. However, when foreign earnings are repatriated to the U.S. parent, they are taxed at the applicable U.S. rate, less a credit for taxes paid to the foreign country. As a result, U.S. corporations such as IBM, Coca-Cola, and Microsoft have been able to defer billions of dollars of taxes. This procedure has stimulated overseas investments by U.S. multinational firms—they can continue the deferral indefinitely, but only if they reinvest the earnings in their overseas operations.[13]

6-9b **Taxation of Small Businesses: S Corporations**

The Tax Code provides that small businesses that meet certain restrictions may be set up as corporations and thus receive the benefits of the corporate form of organization—especially limited liability—yet still be taxed as proprietorships or partnerships rather than as corporations. These corporations are called **S corporations**. ("Regular" corporations are called C corporations.) If a corporation elects S corporation status for tax purposes, then all of the business's income is reported as personal income by its stockholders, on a pro rata basis, and thus is taxed at the rates that apply to individuals. This is an important benefit to the owners of small corporations in which all or most of the income earned each year will be distributed as dividends, because then the income is taxed only once, at the individual level.

6-9c **Personal Taxes**

Web Extension 6A provides a more detailed treatment of individual taxation, but the key elements are presented here. **Ordinary income** consists primarily of wages or profits from a proprietorship or partnership, plus investment income. For the 2014 tax year, individuals with less than $9,075 of taxable income are subject to a federal income tax rate of 10%. For those with higher income, tax rates increase and go up to 39.6%, depending on the level of income. This is called a **progressive tax**, because the higher one's income, the larger the percentage paid in taxes.

As noted before, individuals are taxed on investment income as well as earned income, but with a few exceptions and modifications. For example, interest received from most state and local government bonds, called **municipals** or **munis**, is not subject to federal taxation. However, interest earned on most other bonds or lending is taxed as ordinary income. This means that a lower-yielding muni can provide the same after-tax return as a higher-yielding corporate bond. For a taxpayer in the

See *Web Extension 6A* on the textbook's Web site for details concerning personal taxation.

---

13. This is a contentious political issue. U.S. corporations argue that our tax system is similar to systems in the rest of the world, and if they were taxed immediately on all overseas earnings then they would be at a competitive disadvantage vis-à-vis their global competitors. Others argue that the tax treatment of foreign profits encourages overseas investments at the expense of domestic investments, contributing to the jobs-outsourcing problem and also to the federal budget deficit.

35% marginal tax bracket, a muni yielding 5.5% provides the same after-tax return as a corporate bond with a pre-tax yield of 8.46%: 8.46%(1 − 0.35) = 5.5%.

Assets such as stocks, bonds, and real estate are defined as capital assets. If you own a capital asset and its price goes up, then your wealth increases, but you are not liable for any taxes on your increased wealth until you sell the asset. If you sell the asset for more than you originally paid, the profit is called a **capital gain**; if you sell it for less, then you suffer a **capital loss**. The length of time you owned the asset determines the tax treatment. If held for less than 1 year, then your gain or loss is simply added to your other ordinary income. If held for more than a year, then gains are called *long-term capital gains* and are taxed at a lower rate. See *Web Extension 6A* for details, but the long-term capital gains rate is 15% for most situations.

Under the 2003 tax law changes, dividends are now taxed as though they are capital gains. As stated earlier, corporations may deduct interest payments but not dividends when computing their corporate tax liability, which means that dividends are taxed twice, once at the corporate level and again at the personal level. This differential treatment motivates corporations to use debt relatively heavily and to pay small (or even no) dividends. The 2003 tax law did not eliminate the differential treatment of dividends and interest payments from the corporate perspective, but it did make the tax treatment of dividends more similar to that of capital gains from investors' perspectives. To see this, consider a company that doesn't pay a dividend but instead reinvests the cash it could have paid. The company's stock price should increase, leading to a capital gain, which would be taxed at the same rate as the dividend. Of course, the stock price appreciation isn't actually taxed until the stock is sold, whereas the dividend is taxed in the year it is paid, so dividends will still be more costly than capital gains for many investors.

Finally, note that the income of S corporations *and* noncorporate businesses is reported as income by the firms' owners. Because there are far more S corporations, partnerships, and proprietorships than C corporations (which are subject to the corporate tax), individual tax considerations play an important role in business finance.

SELF TEST

Explain what is meant by this statement: "Our tax rates are progressive."

If a corporation has $85,000 in taxable income, what is its tax liability? **($17,150)**

Explain the difference between marginal tax rates and average tax rates.

What are municipal bonds, and how are these bonds taxed?

What are capital gains and losses, and how are they taxed?

How does the federal income tax system treat dividends received by a corporation versus those received by an individual?

What is the difference in the tax treatment of interest and dividends paid by a corporation? Does this factor favor debt or equity financing?

Briefly explain how tax loss carryback and carryforward procedures work.

Summary

- The four basic statements contained in the **annual report** are the balance sheet, the income statement, the statement of stockholders' equity, and the statement of cash flows.
- The **balance sheet** shows assets and liabilities and equity, or claims against assets. The balance sheet may be thought of as a snapshot of the firm's financial position at a particular point in time.
- The **income statement** reports the results of operations over a period of time, and it shows earnings per share as its "bottom line."
- The **statement of stockholders' equity** shows the change in stockholders' equity, including the change in retained earnings, between balance sheet dates. Retained earnings represent a claim against assets, not assets per se.
- The **statement of cash flows** reports the effect of operating, investing, and financing activities on cash flows over an accounting period.
- **Net cash flow** differs from **accounting profit** because some of the revenues and expenses reflected in accounting profits may not have been received or paid out in cash during the year. Depreciation is typically the largest noncash item, so net cash flow is often expressed as net income plus depreciation.
- **Operating current assets** are the current assets that are used to support operations, such as cash, inventory, and accounts receivable. They do not include short-term investments.
- **Operating current liabilities** are the current liabilities that occur as a natural consequence of operations, such as accounts payable and accruals. They do not include notes payable or any other short-term debts that charge interest.
- **Net operating working capital** is the difference between operating current assets and operating current liabilities. Thus, it is the working capital acquired with investor-supplied funds.
- **Operating long-term assets** are the long-term assets used to support operations, such as net plant and equipment. They do not include any long-term investments that pay interest or dividends.
- **Total net operating capital** (which means the same as **operating capital** and **net operating assets**) is the sum of net operating working capital and operating long-term assets. It is the total amount of capital needed to run the business.
- **NOPAT** is net operating profit after taxes. It is the after-tax profit a company would have if it had no debt and no investments in nonoperating assets. Because NOPAT excludes the effects of financial decisions, it is a better measure of operating performance than is net income.
- **Return on Invested Capital (ROIC)** is equal to NOPAT divided by total net operating capital. It measures the rate of return that the operations are generating. It is the best measure of operating performance.
- **Free cash flow (FCF)** is the amount of cash flow remaining after a company makes the asset investments necessary to support operations. In other words, FCF is the amount of cash flow available for distribution to investors, so *the value of a company is directly related to its ability to generate free cash flow.* FCF is defined as NOPAT minus the net investment in operating capital.

- **Market Value Added (MVA)** represents the difference between the total market value of a firm and the total amount of investor-supplied capital. If the market values of debt and preferred stock equal their values as reported on the financial statements, then MVA is the difference between the market value of a firm's stock and the amount of equity its shareholders have supplied.
- **Economic Value Added (EVA)** is the difference between after-tax operating profit and the total dollar cost of capital, including the cost of equity capital. EVA is an estimate of the value created by management during the year, and it differs substantially from accounting profit because no charge for the use of equity capital is reflected in accounting profit.
- Interest income received by a corporation is taxed as **ordinary income**; however, 70% of the dividends received by one corporation from another are excluded from **taxable income**.
- Because interest paid by a corporation is a **deductible expense** whereas dividends are not, our tax system favors debt over equity financing.
- Ordinary corporate operating losses can be **carried back** to each of the preceding 2 years and **carried forward** for the next 20 years in order to offset taxable income in those years.
- **S corporations** are small businesses that have the limited-liability benefits of the corporate form of organization yet are taxed as partnerships or proprietorships.
- In the United States, tax rates are **progressive**—the higher one's income, the larger the percentage paid in taxes.
- Assets such as stocks, bonds, and real estate are defined as **capital assets**. If a capital asset is sold for more than its cost, the profit is called a **capital gain**; if the asset is sold for a loss, it is called a **capital loss**. Assets held for more than a year provide **long-term gains** or **losses**.
- Dividends are taxed as though they were capital gains.
- **Personal taxes** are discussed in more detail in *Web Extension 6A*.

Questions

6–1 Define each of the following terms:
   a. Annual report; balance sheet; income statement
   b. Common stockholders' equity, or net worth; retained earnings
   c. Statement of stockholders' equity; statement of cash flows
   d. Depreciation; amortization; EBITDA
   e. Operating current assets; operating current liabilities; net operating working capital; total net operating capital
   f. Accounting profit; net cash flow; NOPAT; free cash flow; return on invested capital
   g. Market Value Added; Economic Value Added
   h. Progressive tax; taxable income; marginal and average tax rates
   i. Capital gain or loss; tax loss carryback and carryforward
   j. Improper accumulation; S corporation

6–2 What four statements are contained in most annual reports?

6–3 If a "typical" firm reports $20 million of retained earnings on its balance sheet, can the firm definitely pay a $20 million cash dividend?

6–4 Explain the following statement: "Whereas the balance sheet can be thought of as a snapshot of the firm's financial position *at a point in time,* the income statement reports on operations *over a period of time.*"

6–5 What is operating capital, and why is it important?

6–6 Explain the difference between NOPAT and net income. Which is a better measure of the performance of a company's operations?

6–7 What is free cash flow? Why is it the most important measure of cash flow?

6–8 If you were starting a business, what tax considerations might cause you to prefer to set it up as a proprietorship or a partnership rather than as a corporation?

Problems ◀ Answers Appear in Appendix B

Note: By the time this book is published, Congress may have changed rates and/or other provisions of current tax law. Work all problems on the assumption that the information in the chapter is applicable.

Easy Problems 1–6

6–1 Personal After-Tax Yield
An investor recently purchased a corporate bond that yields 9%. The investor is in the 36% combined federal and state tax bracket. What is the bond's after-tax yield?

6–2 Personal After-Tax Yield
Porporate bonds issued by Johnson Corporation currently yield 8%. Municipal bonds of equal risk currently yield 6%. At what tax rate would an investor be indifferent between these two bonds?

6–3 Income Statement
Molteni Motors Inc. recently reported $6 million of net income. Its EBIT was $13 million, and its tax rate was 40%. What was its interest expense? (*Hint:* Write out the headings for an income statement and then fill in the known values. Then divide $6 million net income by $1 - T = 0.6$ to find the pretax income. The difference between EBIT and taxable income must be the interest expense. Use this procedure to work some of the other problems.)

6–4 Income Statement
Talbot Enterprises recently reported an EBITDA of $8 million and net income of $2.4 million. It had $2.0 million of interest expense, and its corporate tax rate was 40%. What was its charge for depreciation and amortization?

6–5 Net Cash Flow
Kendall Corners Inc. recently reported net income of $3.1 million and depreciation of $500,000. What was its net cash flow? Assume it had no amortization expense.

6-6 Statement of Retained Earnings

In its most recent financial statements, Del-Castillo Inc. reported $70 million of net income and $900 million of retained earnings. The previous retained earnings were $855 million. How much in dividends did the firm pay to shareholders during the year?

Intermediate Problems 7–11

6-7 Corporate Tax Liability

The Talley Corporation had a taxable income of $365,000 from operations after all operating costs but before: (1) interest charges of $50,000, (2) dividends received of $15,000, (3) dividends paid of $25,000, and (4) income taxes. What are the firm's income tax liability and its after-tax income? What are the company's marginal and average tax rates on taxable income?

6-8 Corporate Tax Liability

The Wendt Corporation had $10.5 million of taxable income.
a. What is the company's federal income tax bill for the year?
b. Assume the firm receives an additional $1 million of interest income from some bonds it owns. What is the tax on this interest income?
c. Now assume that Wendt does not receive the interest income but does receive an additional $1 million as dividends on some stock it owns. What is the tax on this dividend income?

6-9 Corporate After-Tax Yield

The Shrieves Corporation has $10,000 that it plans to invest in marketable securities. It is choosing among AT&T bonds, which yield 7.5%, state of Florida muni bonds, which yield 5% (but are not taxable), and AT&T preferred stock, with a dividend yield of 6%. Shrieves' corporate tax rate is 35%, and 70% of the dividends received are tax exempt. Find the after-tax rates of return on all three securities.

6-10 Net Cash Flows

The Moore Corporation has operating income (EBIT) of $750,000. The company's depreciation expense is $200,000. Moore is 100% equity financed, and it faces a 40% tax rate. What is the company's net income? What is its net cash flow?

6-11 Income and Cash Flow Analysis

The Berndt Corporation expects to have sales of $12 million. Costs other than depreciation are expected to be 75% of sales, and depreciation is expected to be $1.5 million. All sales revenues will be collected in cash, and costs other than depreciation must be paid for during the year. Berndt's federal-plus-state tax rate is 40%. Berndt has no debt.
a. Set up an income statement. What is Berndt's expected net cash flow?
b. Suppose Congress changed the tax laws so that Berndt's depreciation expenses doubled. No changes in operations occurred. What would happen to reported profit and to net cash flow?
c. Now suppose that Congress changed the tax laws such that, instead of doubling Berndt's depreciation, it was reduced by 50%. How would profit and net cash flow be affected?
d. If this were your company, would you prefer Congress to cause your depreciation expense to be doubled or halved? Why?

Challenging Problems 12–13

6–12 Free Cash Flows

Using Rhodes Corporation's financial statements (shown below), answer the following questions.

a. What is the net operating profit after taxes (NOPAT) for 2015?

b. What are the amounts of net operating working capital for both years?

c. What are the amounts of total net operating capital for both years?

d. What is the free cash flow for 2015?

e. What is the ROIC for 2015?

f. How much of the FCF did Rhodes use for each of the following purposes: after-tax interest, net debt repayments, dividends, net stock repurchases, and net purchases of short-term investments? (*Hint:* Remember that a net use can be negative.)

Rhodes Corporation: Income Statements for Year Ending December 31 (Millions of Dollars)

	2015	2014
Sales	$11,000	$10,000
Operating costs excluding depreciation	9,360	8,500
Depreciation and amortization	380	360
Earnings before interest and taxes	$ 1,260	$ 1,140
Less interest	120	100
Pre-tax income	$ 1,140	$ 1,040
Taxes (40%)	456	416
Net income available to common stockholders	$ 684	$ 624
Common dividends	$ 220	$ 200

Rhodes Corporation: Balance Sheets as of December 31 (Millions of Dollars)

	2015	2014
Assets		
Cash	$ 550	$ 500
Short-term investments	110	100
Accounts receivable	2,750	2,500
Inventories	1,650	1,500
Total current assets	$5,060	$4,600
Net plant and equipment	3,850	3,500
Total assets	$8,910	$8,100

(*Continued*)

Liabilities and Equity

Accounts payable	$1,100	$1,000
Accruals	550	500
Notes payable	384	200
Total current liabilities	$2,034	$1,700
Long-term debt	1,100	1,000
Total liabilities	$3,134	$2,700
Common stock	4,312	4,400
Retained earnings	1,464	1,000
Total common equity	$5,776	$5,400
Total liabilities and equity	$8,910	$8,100

6–13 Loss Carryback and Carryforward

The Bookbinder Company has made $150,000 before taxes during each of the last 15 years, and it expects to make $150,000 a year before taxes in the future. However, in 2015 the firm incurred a loss of $650,000. The firm will claim a tax credit at the time it files its 2015 income tax return, and it will receive a check from the U.S. Treasury. Show how it calculates this credit, and then indicate the firm's tax liability for each of the next 5 years. Assume a 40% tax rate on *all* income to ease the calculations.

Spreadsheet Problems

6–14 Build a Model: Financial Statements, EVA, and MVA

Begin with the partial model in the file *Ch06 P14 Build a Model.xls* on the textbook's Web site.

a. The 2015 sales of Cumberland Industries were $455,000,000; operating costs (excluding depreciation) were equal to 85% of sales; net fixed assets were $67,000,000; depreciation amounted to 10% of net fixed assets; interest expenses were $8,550,000; the state-plus-federal corporate tax rate was 40%; and Cumberland paid 25% of its net income out in dividends. Given this information, construct Cumberland's 2015 income statement. Also calculate total dividends and the addition to retained earnings. (*Hint:* Start with the partial model in the file and report all dollar figures in thousands to reduce clutter.)

b. The partial balance sheets of Cumberland Industries are shown below. Cumberland issued $10,000,000 of new common stock in 2015. Using this information and the results from part a, fill in the missing values for common stock, retained earnings, total common equity, and total liabilities and equity.

Cumberland Industries: Balance Sheets as of December 31
(Thousands of Dollars)

	2015	2014
Assets		
Cash	$ 91,450	$ 74,625
Short-term investments	11,400	15,100
Accounts receivable	108,470	85,527
Inventories	38,450	34,982
Total current assets	$249,770	$210,234
Net fixed assets	67,000	42,436
Total assets	$316,770	$252,670
Liabilities and Equity		
Accounts payable	$ 30,761	$ 23,109
Accruals	30,405	22,656
Notes payable	12,717	14,217
Total current liabilities	$ 73,883	$ 59,982
Long-term debt	80,263	63,914
Total liabilities	$154,146	$123,896
Common stock	?	$ 90,000
Retained earnings	?	38,774
Total common equity	?	$128,774
Total liabilities and equity	?	$252,670

c. Construct the statement of cash flows for 2015.

6–15 **Build a Model: Free Cash Flows, EVA, and MVA**

Begin with the partial model in the file *Ch06 P15 Build a Model.xls* on the textbook's Web site.

a. Using the financial statements shown below for Lan & Chen Technologies, calculate net operating working capital, total net operating capital, net operating profit after taxes, free cash flow, and return on invested capital for 2015. (*Hint:* Start with the partial model in the file and report all dollar figures in thousands to reduce clutter.)

b. Assume there were 15 million shares outstanding at the end of 2015, the year-end closing stock price was $65 per share, and the after-tax cost of capital was 8%. Calculate EVA and MVA for 2015.

Lan & Chen Technologies: Income Statements for Year Ending December 31 (Thousands of Dollars)

	2015	2014
Sales	$945,000	$900,000
Expenses excluding depreciation and amortization	812,700	774,000
EBITDA	$132,300	$126,000
Depreciation and amortization	33,100	31,500
EBIT	$ 99,200	$ 94,500
Interest expense	10,470	8,600
Pre-tax earning	$ 88,730	$ 85,900
Taxes (40%)	35,492	34,360
Net income	$ 53,238	$ 51,540
Common dividends	$ 43,300	$ 41,230
Addition to retained earnings	$ 9,938	$ 10,310

Lan & Chen Technologies: December 31 Balance Sheets (Thousands of Dollars)

	2015	2014
Assets		
Cash and cash equivalents	$ 47,250	$ 45,000
Short-term investments	3,800	3,600
Accounts receivable	283,500	270,000
Inventories	141,750	135,000
Total current assets	$476,300	$453,600
Net fixed assets	330,750	315,000
Total assets	$807,050	$768,600
Liabilities and Equity		
Accounts payable	$ 94,500	$ 90,000
Accruals	47,250	45,000
Notes payable	26,262	9,000
Total current liabilities	$ 168,012	$144,000
Long-term debt	94,500	90,000
Total liabilities	$ 262,512	$234,000
Common stock	444,600	444,600
Retained earnings	99,938	90,000
Total common equity	$544,538	$534,600
Total liabilities and equity	$807,050	$768,600

MINI CASE

Jenny Cochran, a graduate of The University of Tennessee with 4 years of experience as an equities analyst, was recently brought in as assistant to the chairman of the board of Computron Industries, a manufacturer of computer components.

The company doubled its plant capacity, opened new sales offices outside its home territory, and launched an expensive advertising campaign. Computron's results were not satisfactory, to put it mildly. Its board of directors, which consisted of its president and vice president plus its major stockholders (who were all local businesspeople), was most upset when directors learned how the expansion was going. Suppliers were being paid late and were unhappy, and the bank was complaining about the deteriorating situation and threatening to cut off credit. As a result, Robert Edwards, Computron's president, was informed that changes would have to be made—and quickly—or he would be fired. At the board's insistence, Jenny Cochran was given the job of assistant to Gary Meissner, a retired banker who was Computron's chairman and largest stockholder. Meissner agreed to give up a few of his golfing days and to help nurse the company back to health, with Cochran's assistance.

Cochran began by gathering financial statements and other data. Note: these are available in the file *Ch06 Tool Kit.xls* in the *Mini Case* tab.

	2014	2015
Balance Sheets		
Assets		
Cash	$ 9,000	$ 7,282
Short-term investments	48,600	20,000
Accounts receivable	351,200	632,160
Inventories	715,200	1,287,360
Total current assets	$1,124,000	$1,946,802
Gross fixed assets	491,000	1,202,950
Less: Accumulated depreciation	146,200	263,160
Net fixed assets	$ 344,800	$ 939,790
Total assets	$1,468,800	$2,886,592
Liabilities and Equity		
Accounts payable	$ 145,600	$ 324,000
Notes payable	200,000	720,000
Accruals	136,000	284,960
Total current liabilities	$ 481,600	$1,328,960
Long-term debt	323,432	1,000,000
Common stock (100,000 shares)	460,000	460,000
Retained earnings	203,768	97,632
Total equity	$ 663,768	$ 557,632
Total liabilities and equity	$1,468,800	$2,886,592

	2014	2015
Income Statements		
Sales	$3,432,000	$ 5,834,400
Cost of goods sold	2,864,000	4,980,000
Other expenses	340,000	720,000
Depreciation and amortization	18,900	116,960
Total operating costs	$3,222,900	$ 5,816,960
EBIT	$ 209,100	$ 17,440
Interest expense	62,500	176,000
Pre-tax earnings	$ 146,600	($ 158,560)
Taxes (40%)	58,640	(63,424)
Net income	$ 87,960	($ 95,136)

Other Data	2014	2015
Stock price	$ 8.50	$ 6.00
Shares outstanding	100,000	100,000
EPS	$ 0.880	($ 0.951)
DPS	$ 0.220	$ 0.110
Tax rate	40%	40%

	2015
Statement of Cash Flows	
Operating Activities	
Net income	($ 95,136)
Adjustments:	
Noncash adjustments:	
Depreciation and amortization	116,960
Changes in working capital:	
Change in accounts receivable	(280,960)
Change in inventories	(572,160)
Change in accounts payable	178,400
Change in accruals	148,960
Net cash provided (used) by operating activities	($ 503,936)
Investing Activities	
Cash used to acquire fixed assets	($ 711,950)
Change in short-term investments	28,600
Net cash provided (used) by investing activities	($ 683,350)

(*Continued*)

Financing Activities

Change in notes payable	$ 520,000
Change in long-term debt	676,568
Change in common stock	—
Payment of cash dividends	(11,000)
Net cash provided (used) by financing activities	$1,185,568

Summary

Net change in cash	($ 1,718)
Cash at beginning of year	9,000
Cash at end of year	$ 7,282

Assume that you are Cochran's assistant and that you must help her answer the following questions for Meissner:

a. What effect did the expansion have on sales and net income? What effect did the expansion have on the asset side of the balance sheet? What effect did it have on liabilities and equity?

b. What do you conclude from the statement of cash flows?

c. What is free cash flow? Why is it important? What are the five uses of FCF?

d. What is Computron's net operating profit after taxes (NOPAT)? What are operating current assets? What are operating current liabilities? How much net operating working capital and total net operating capital does Computron have?

e. What is Computron's free cash flow (FCF)? What are Computron's "net uses" of its FCF?

f. Calculate Computron's return on invested capital. Computron has a 10% cost of capital (WACC). Do you think Computron's growth added value?

g. Cochran also has asked you to estimate Computron's EVA. She estimates that the after-tax cost of capital was 10% in both years.

h. What happened to Computron's Market Value Added (MVA)?

i. Assume that a corporation has $100,000 of taxable income from operations plus $5,000 of interest income and $10,000 of dividend income. What is the company's federal tax liability?

j. Assume that you are in the 25% marginal tax bracket and that you have $5,000 to invest. You have narrowed your investment choices down to California bonds with a yield of 7% or equally risky ExxonMobil bonds with a yield of 10%. Which one should you choose and why? At what marginal tax rate would you be indifferent to the choice between California and ExxonMobil bonds?

Analysis of Financial Statements

Financial statement analysis involves: (1) comparing a firm's performance with that of other firms in the same industry and (2) evaluating trends in the firm's financial position over time. Managers use financial analysis to identify situations needing attention, potential lenders use financial analysis to determine whether a company is creditworthy, and stockholders use financial analysis to help predict future earnings, dividends, and free cash flow. This chapter will explain the similarities and differences among these uses.

Beginning-of-Chapter Questions

As you read the chapter, consider how you would answer the following questions. You *should not* necessarily be able to answer the questions before you read the chapter. Rather, you should use them to get a sense of the issues covered in the chapter. After reading the chapter, you should be able to give at least partial answers to the questions, and you should be able to give better answers after the chapter has been discussed in class. Note, too, that it is often useful, when answering conceptual questions, to use hypothetical data to illustrate your answer. We illustrate the answers with an *Excel* model that is available on the textbook's Web site. Accessing the model and working through it is a useful exercise, and it provides insights that are useful when answering the questions.

1. Why are **financial ratios** used? Name five categories of ratios, and then list several ratios in each category. Would a bank loan officer, a bond analyst, a stock analyst, and a manager be likely to put the same emphasis and interpretation on each ratio?

2. Suppose a company has a DSO that is considerably higher than its industry average. If the company could reduce its accounts receivable to the point where its DSO was equal to the industry average *without affecting its sales or its operating costs,* how would this affect: (a) its **free cash flow**, (b) its **return on common equity**, (c) its **debt ratio**, (d) its **times-interest-earned ratio**, (e) its **loan/EBITDA ratio**, (f) its **price/earnings ratio**, and (g) its **market/book ratio**?

3. How do managers, bankers, and security analysts use: (a) **trend analysis**, (b) **benchmarking**, (c) **percent change analysis**, and (d) **common size analysis**?

4. Explain how **ratio analysis** in general, and the **DuPont system** in particular, can be used by managers to help maximize their firms' stock prices.

5. How would each of the following factors affect ratio analysis? (a) The firm's sales are highly seasonal. (b) The firm uses some type of window dressing. (c) The firm issues more debt and uses the proceeds

to repurchase stock. (d) The firm leases more of its fixed assets than most firms in its industry. (e) In an effort to stimulate sales, the firm eases its credit policy by offering 60-day credit terms rather than the current 30-day terms. How might one use sensitivity analysis to help quantify the answers?

6. How might one establish norms (or target values) for the financial ratios of a company that is just getting started? Where might data for this purpose be obtained? Could information of this type be used to help determine how much debt and equity capital a new firm would require?

INTRINSIC VALUE AND ANALYSIS OF FINANCIAL STATEMENTS

The intrinsic value of a firm is determined by the present value of the expected future free cash flows (FCF) when discounted at the weighted average cost of capital (WACC). This chapter explains how to use financial statements to evaluate a company's profitability, required capital investments, business risk, and mix of debt and equity.

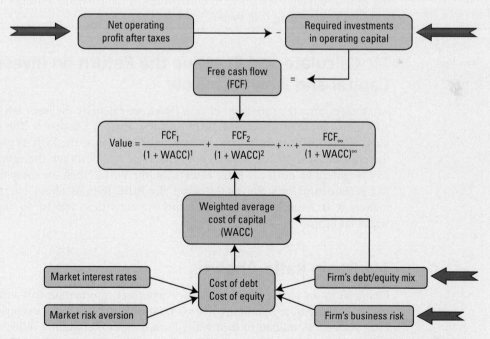

$$\text{Value} = \frac{\text{FCF}_1}{(1 + \text{WACC})^1} + \frac{\text{FCF}_2}{(1 + \text{WACC})^2} + \cdots + \frac{\text{FCF}_\infty}{(1 + \text{WACC})^\infty}$$

Source: From *Financial Management: Theory & Practice*, 2013, by Brigham and Ehrhardt. © Cengage Learning.

See **www.zacks .com** for a source of standardized financial statements.

7-1 **Financial Analysis**

When we perform a financial analysis, we conduct the following steps.

7-1a **Gather Data**

The first step in financial analysis is to gather data. As discussed in Chapter 6, financial statements can be downloaded from many different Web sites. One of our favorites is Zacks Investment Research, which provides financial statements in a standardized format. If you cut and paste financial statements from Zacks into a spreadsheet and then perform a financial analysis, you can quickly repeat the analysis on a different company by pasting that company's financial statements into the same cells of the spreadsheet. In other words, you do not need to reinvent the wheel each time you analyze a company.

7-1b **Examine the Statement of Cash Flows**

Some financial analysis can be done with virtually no calculations. For example, we always look to the statement of cash flows first, particularly the net cash provided by operating activities. Downward trends or negative net cash flow from operations almost always indicate problems. The statement of cash flows section on investing activities shows whether the company has made a big acquisition, especially when compared with the prior years' net cash flows from investing activities. A quick look at the section on financing activities also reveals whether a company is issuing debt or buying back stock; in other words, is the company raising capital from investors or returning it to them?

7-1c **Calculate and Examine the Return on Invested Capital and Free Cash Flow**

After examining the statement of cash flows, we calculate the free cash flow (FCF) and return on invested capital (ROIC) as described in Chapter 6. The ROIC provides a vital measure of a firm's overall performance. If the ROIC is greater than the company's weighted average cost of capital (WACC), then the company usually is adding value. If the ROIC is less than the WACC, then the company usually has serious problems. No matter what the ROIC tells us about overall performance, it is important to examine specific activities, and to do that we use financial ratios.

7-1d **Begin Ratio Analysis**

Financial ratios are designed to extract important information that might not be obvious simply from examining a firm's financial statements. For example, suppose Firm A owes $5 million in debt while Firm B owes $50 million. Which company is in a stronger financial position? It is impossible to answer this question without first standardizing each firm's debt relative to total assets, earnings, and interest. Such standardized comparisons are provided through *ratio analysis*.

FIGURE 7-1	MicroDrive Inc.: Balance Sheets and Income Statements for Years Ending December 31 (Millions of Dollars, Except for Per Share Data)

	A	B	C	D	E
23	*Balance Sheets*			**2015**	**2014**
24	*Assets*				
25	Cash and equivalents			$ 50	$ 60
26	Short-term investments			-	40
27	Accounts receivable			500	380
28	Inventories			1,000	820
29	Total current assets			$ 1,550	$ 1,300
30	Net plant and equipment			2,000	1,700
31	Total assets			$ 3,550	$ 3,000
32					
33	*Liabilities and Equity*				
34	Accounts payable			$ 200	$ 190
35	Notes payable			280	130
36	Accruals			300	280
37	Total current liabilities			$ 780	$ 600
38	Long-term bonds			1,200	1,000
39	Total liabilities			$ 1,980	$ 1,600
40	Preferred stock (400,000 shares)			100	100
41	Common stock (50,000,000 shares)			500	500
42	Retained earnings			970	800
43	Total common equity			$ 1,470	$ 1,300
44	Total liabilities and equity			$ 3,550	$ 3,000
45					
46	*Income Statements*			**2015**	**2014**
47	Net sales			$ 5,000	$ 4,760
48	Costs of goods sold except depreciation			3,800	3,560
49	Depreciation			200	170
50	Other operating expenses			500	480
51	Earnings before interest and taxes (EBIT)			$ 500	$ 550
52	Less interest			120	100
53	Pre-tax earnings			$ 380	$ 450
54	Taxes (40%)			152	180
55	Net income before preferred dividends			$ 228	$ 270
56	Preferred dividends			8	8
57	Net income available to common stockholders			$ 220	$ 262
58	*Other Data*				
59	Common dividends			$50	$48
60	Addition to retained earnings			$170	$214
61	Lease payments			$28	$28
62	Bonds' required sinking fund payments			$20	$20
63	Common stock price per share			$27	$40

Microsoft Excel® is a registered trademark of Microsoft Corporation. © 2014 Microsoft.

We will calculate the 2015 financial ratios for MicroDrive Inc. using data from the balance sheets and income statements given in Figure 7-1. We will also evaluate the ratios in relation to the industry averages. Note that dollar amounts are in millions.

7-2 **Liquidity Ratios**

See *Ch07 Tool Kit.xls* for all calculations.

As shown in Figure 7-1, MicroDrive has current liabilities of $780 million that it must pay off within the coming year. Will it have trouble satisfying those obligations? **Liquidity ratios** attempt to answer this type of question. We discuss two commonly used liquidity ratios in this section.

7-2a **The Current Ratio**

Calculate the **current ratio** by dividing current assets by current liabilities:

$$\text{Current ratio} = \frac{\text{Current assets}}{\text{Current liabilities}}$$

$$= \frac{\$1,550}{\$780} = 2.0$$

Industry average $= 2.2$

Current assets normally include cash, marketable securities, accounts receivable, and inventories. Current liabilities consist of accounts payable, short-term notes payable, current maturities of long-term debt, accrued taxes, and other accrued expenses.

MicroDrive has a slightly lower current ratio than the average for its industry. Is this good or bad? Sometimes the answer depends on who is asking the question. For example, suppose a supplier is trying to decide whether to extend credit to MicroDrive. In general, creditors like to see a high current ratio. If a company starts to experience financial difficulty, it will begin paying its bills (accounts payable) more slowly and borrowing more from its bank, so its current liabilities will be increasing. If current liabilities are rising faster than current assets then the current ratio will fall, and this could spell trouble. Because the current ratio provides the best single indicator of the extent to which the claims of short-term creditors are covered by assets that are expected to be converted to cash fairly quickly, it is the most commonly used measure of short-term solvency.

Now consider the current ratio from a shareholder's perspective. A high current ratio could mean that the company has a lot of money tied up in nonproductive assets, such as excess cash or marketable securities. Or perhaps the high current ratio is due to large inventory holdings, which might become obsolete before they can be sold. Thus, shareholders might not want a high current ratio.

An industry average is not a magic number that all firms should strive to maintain—in fact, some well-managed firms will be above the average, while other good firms will be below it. However, if a firm's ratios are far from the averages for its industry, this is a red flag, and analysts should be concerned about why the variance occurs. For example, suppose a low current ratio is traced to low inventories. Is this a competitive advantage resulting from the firm's mastery of just-in-time inventory management, or is it an Achilles' heel that is causing the firm to miss shipments and lose sales? Ratio analysis doesn't answer such questions, but it does point to areas of potential concern.

7-2b **The Quick, or Acid Test, Ratio**

The **quick ratio**, also called the **acid test ratio**, is calculated by deducting inventories from current assets and then dividing the remainder by current liabilities:

$$\text{Quick ratio} = \frac{\text{Current assets} - \text{Inventories}}{\text{Current liabilities}}$$

$$= \frac{\$1,550 - \$1,000}{\$780} = 0.7$$

$$\text{Industry average} = 0.8$$

A **liquid asset** is one that trades in an active market, so it can be converted quickly to cash at the going market price. Inventories are typically the least liquid of a firm's current assets; hence they are the current assets on which losses are most likely to occur in a bankruptcy. Therefore, a measure of the firm's ability to pay off short-term obligations without relying on the sale of inventories is important.

MicroDrive's quick ratio is close to the industry average. However, both are below 1.0, which means that inventories would have to be liquidated in order to pay off current liabilities should the need arise.

How does MicroDrive compare to S&P 500 companies? There has been a steady decline in the average liquidity ratios of S&P 500 companies during the past decade. As we write this in 2014, the average current and quick ratios are well below 1.0, so MicroDrive and its industry peers are more liquid than the typical S&P 500 company.

Identify two ratios to use to analyze a firm's liquidity position, and write out their equations.

What are the characteristics of a liquid asset? Give some examples.

Which current asset is typically the least liquid?

A company has current liabilities of $800 million, and its current ratio is 2.5. What is its level of current assets? **($2,000 million)** If this firm's quick ratio is 2, how much inventory does it have? **($400 million)**

SELF TEST

7-3 **Asset Management Ratios**

Asset management ratios measure how effectively a firm is managing its assets. If a company has excessive investments in assets, then its operating capital is unduly high, which reduces its free cash flow and ultimately its stock price. On the other hand, if a company does not have enough assets then it may lose sales, which would hurt profitability, free cash flow, and the stock price. Therefore, it is important to have the *right* amount invested in assets. Ratios that analyze the different types of assets are described in this section.

7-3a **Evaluating Total Assets: The Total Assets Turnover Ratio**

The **total assets turnover ratio** measures the dollars in sales that are generated for each dollar that is tied up in assets:

$$\text{Total assets turnover ratio} = \frac{\text{Sales}}{\text{Total assets}}$$

$$= \frac{\$5,000}{\$3,550} = 1.4$$

Industry average $= 1.8$

MicroDrive's ratio is somewhat below the industry average, indicating that the company is not generating as much business (relative to its peers) given its total asset investment. In other words, MicroDrive uses its assets relatively inefficiently. The following ratios can be used to identify the specific asset classes that are causing this problem.[1]

7-3b **Evaluating Fixed Assets: The Fixed Assets Turnover Ratio**

The **fixed assets turnover ratio** measures how effectively the firm uses its plant and equipment. It is the ratio of sales to net fixed assets:

$$\text{Fixed assets turnover ratio} = \frac{\text{Sales}}{\text{Net fixed assets}}$$

$$= \frac{\$5,000}{\$2,000} = 2.5$$

Industry average $= 3.0$

MicroDrive's ratio of 2.5 is a little below the industry average, indicating that the firm is not using its fixed assets as intensively as are other firms in its industry

Inflation can cause problems when interpreting the fixed assets turnover ratio because fixed assets are reported using the historical costs of the assets instead of current replacement costs that may be higher due to inflation. Therefore, a mature firm with fixed assets acquired years ago might well have a higher fixed assets turnover ratio than a younger company with newer fixed assets that are reported at inflated prices relative to the historical prices of the older assets. However, this would reflect the difficulty accountants have in dealing with inflation rather than

---

1. Sales occur throughout the year, but assets are reported at end of the period. For a growing company or a company with seasonal variation, it would be better to use *average* assets held during the year when calculating turnover ratios. However, we use year-end values for all turnover ratios so that we are more comparable with most reported industry averages.

inefficiency on the part of the new firm. You should be alert to this potential problem when evaluating the fixed assets turnover ratio.

7-3c Evaluating Receivables: The Days Sales Outstanding

Days sales outstanding (DSO), also called the "average collection period" (ACP), is used to appraise accounts receivable, and it is calculated by dividing accounts receivable by average daily sales to find the number of days' sales that are tied up in receivables. Thus, the DSO represents the average length of time that the firm must wait after making a sale before receiving cash, which is the average collection period. MicroDrive's DSO is 37, above the 30-day industry average:

$$\text{DSO} = \frac{\text{Days sales}}{\text{outstanding}} = \frac{\text{Receivables}}{\text{Average sales per day}} = \frac{\text{Receivables}}{\text{Annual sales}/365}$$

$$= \frac{\$500}{\$5,000/365} = \frac{\$500}{\$13.7} = 36.5 \text{ days} \approx 37 \text{ days}$$

$$\text{Industry average} = 30 \text{ days}$$

MicroDrive's sales terms call for payment within 30 days. The fact that 37 days of sales are outstanding indicates that customers, on average, are not paying their bills on time. As with inventory, high levels of accounts receivable cause high levels of NOWC, which hurts FCF and stock price.

A customer who is paying late may be in financial trouble, which means MicroDrive may have a hard time collecting the receivable. Therefore, if the trend in DSO has been rising unexpectedly, steps should be taken to review credit standards and to expedite the collection of accounts receivable.

7-3d Evaluating Inventories: The Inventory Turnover Ratio

The **inventory turnover ratio** is defined as costs of goods sold (COGS) divided by inventories.[2] The previous ratios use sales instead of COGS. However, sales revenues include costs and profits, whereas inventory usually is reported at cost. Therefore, it is better to compare inventory with costs rather than sales.

The income statement in Figure 7-1 separately reports depreciation and the portion of costs of goods sold that is not comprised of depreciation, which is helpful when calculating cash flows. However, we need the total COGS for calculating the inventory turnover ratio. For MicroDrive, virtually all depreciation is associated with producing its products, so its COGS is:

$$\text{COGS} = \text{Costs of goods sold except depreciation} + \text{Depreciation}$$
$$= \$3,800 + \$200 = \$4,000 \text{ million}$$

---

2. In previous editions, we defined the inventory turnover ratio using sales instead of COGS because some compilers of financial ratio statistics, such as Dun & Bradstreet, use the ratio of sales to inventories. However, most sources now report the turnover ratio using COGS, so we have changed our definition to conform to the majority of reporting organizations.

We can now calculate the inventory turnover:

$$\text{Inventory turnover ratio} = \frac{\text{COGS}}{\text{Inventories}}$$

$$= \frac{\$3,800 + \$200}{\$1,000} = 4.0$$

Industry average $= 5.0$

As a rough approximation, each item of MicroDrive's inventory is sold out and restocked, or "turned over," 4 times per year.[3]

MicroDrive's turnover of 4 is lower than the industry average of 5. This suggests that MicroDrive is holding too much inventory. High levels of inventory add to net operating working capital (NOWC), which reduces FCF, which leads to lower stock prices. In addition, MicroDrive's low inventory turnover ratio makes us wonder whether the firm is holding obsolete goods not worth their stated value.

In summary, MicroDrive's low fixed assets turnover ratio, high DSO, and low inventory turnover ratio each cause MicroDrive's total assets turnover ratio to be lower than the industry average.

THE GLOBAL ECONOMIC CRISIS

The Price Is Right! (Or Wrong!)

How much is an asset worth if no one is buying or selling? The answer to that question matters because an accounting practice called "mark to market" requires that some assets be adjusted on the balance sheet to reflect their "fair market value." The accounting rules are complicated, but the general idea is that if an asset is available for sale, then the balance sheet would be most accurate if it showed the asset's market value. For example, suppose a company purchased $100 million of Treasury bonds and the value of those bonds later fell to $90 million. With mark to market, the company would report the bonds' value on the balance sheet as $90 million, not the original purchase price of $100 million. Notice that marking to market can have a significant impact on financial ratios and thus on investors' perception of a firm's financial health.

But what if the assets are mortgage-backed securities that were originally purchased for $100 million? As defaults increased during 2008, the value of such securities fell rapidly, and then investors virtually stopped trading them. How should the company report them? At the $100 million original price? At a $60 million price that was observed before the market largely dried up? At $25 million when a hedge fund in desperate need for cash to avoid a costly default sold a few of these securities? At $0, because there are no current quotes? Or

---

3. "Turnover" is derived from the old Yankee peddler who would load up his wagon with goods and then go off to peddle his wares. If he made 10 trips per year, stocked 100 pans, and made a gross profit of $5 per pan, his annual gross profit would be (100)($5)(10) = $5,000. If he "turned over" (i.e., sold) his inventory faster and made 20 trips per year, then his gross profit would double, other things held constant. So, his turnover directly affected his profits.

should they be reported at a price generated by a computer model or in some other manner?

The answer to this is especially important during times of economic stress. Congress, the SEC, FASB, and the U.S. Treasury all are working to find the right answers. If they come up with a price that is too low, it could cause investors mistakenly to believe that some companies are worth much less than their intrinsic values, and this could trigger runs on banks and bankruptcies for companies that might otherwise survive. But if the price is too high, some "walking dead" or "zombie" companies could linger on and later cause even larger losses for investors, including the U.S. government, which is now the largest investor in many financial institutions. Either way, an error in pricing could perhaps trigger a domino effect that might topple the entire financial system. So let's hope the price is right!

SELF TEST

Identify four ratios that measure how effectively a firm is managing its assets, and write out their equations.

What problem might arise when comparing firms' fixed assets turnover ratios?

A firm has $200 million annual sales, $180 million costs of goods sold, $40 million of inventory, and $60 million of accounts receivable. What is its inventory turnover ratio? **(4.5)** What is its DSO based on a 365-day year? **(109.5 days)**

7-4 Debt Management Ratios

The extent to which a firm uses debt financing is called **financial leverage**. Here are three important implications: (1) Stockholders can control a firm with smaller investments of their own equity if they finance part of the firm with debt. (2) If the firm's assets generate a higher pre-tax return than the interest rate on debt, then the shareholders' returns are magnified, or "leveraged." Conversely, shareholders' losses are also magnified if assets generate a pre-tax return less than the interest rate. (3) If a company has high leverage, even a small decline in performance might cause the firm's value to fall below the amount it owes to creditors. Therefore, a creditor's position becomes riskier as leverage increases. Keep these three points in mind as you read the following sections.

7-4a How the Firm Is Financed: Leverage Ratios

MicroDrive's two primary types of debt are notes payable and long-term bonds, but more complicated companies also might report the portion of long-term debt due within a year, the value of capitalized leases, and other types of obligations that charge interest. For MicroDrive, total debt is:

$$\text{Total debt} = \text{Notes payable} + \text{Long-term bonds}$$

$$= \$280 + \$1,200 = \$1,480 \text{ million}$$

Is this too much debt, not enough, or the right amount? To answer this question, we begin by calculating the percentage of MicroDrive's assets that are financed by debt. The ratio of total debt to total assets is called the **debt-to-assets ratio**. It is sometimes shortened to the **debt ratio**.[4] Total debt is the sum of all short-term debt and long-term debt; it does not include other liabilities. MicroDrive's debt ratio is:

$$\text{Debt-to-assets ratio} = \text{Debt ratio} = \frac{\text{Total debt}}{\text{Total assets}}$$

$$= \frac{\$280 + \$1,200}{\$3,550} = \frac{\$1,480}{\$3,550} = 41.7\%$$

$$\text{Industry average} = 25.0\%$$

MicroDrive's debt ratio is 41.7%, which is substantially higher than the 25% industry average.

The debt-to-equity ratio is defined as:[5]

$$\text{Debt-to-equity ratio} = \frac{\text{Total debt}}{\text{Total common equity}}$$

$$= \frac{\$280 + \$1,200}{\$1,470} = \frac{\$1,480}{\$1,470} = 1.01$$

$$\text{Industry average} = 0.46$$

The debt-to-equity ratio shows that MicroDrive has $1.01 of debt for every dollar of equity, whereas the debt ratio shows that 41.7% of MicroDrive's assets are financed by debt. We find it more intuitive to think about the percentage of the firm that is financed with debt, so we usually use the debt ratio. However, the debt-to-equity ratio is also widely used, so you should know how to interpret it as well.

Be sure you know how a ratio is defined before you use it. Some sources define the debt ratio using only long-term debt instead of total debt; others use investor-supplied capital instead of total assets. Some sources make similar changes in the debt-to-equity ratio, so be sure to check your source's definition.

Sometimes it is useful to express debt ratios in terms of market values. It is easy to calculate the market value of equity, which is equal to the stock price multiplied by the number of shares. MicroDrive's market value of equity is $27(50) = $1,350. Often it is difficult to estimate the market value of debt, so many analysts use the debt reported in the financial statements. The market debt ratio is defined as:

---

4. In previous editions, we defined the debt ratio as total liabilities divided by total assets. For better comparability with Web-based reporting sources, we have changed our definition to total debt divided by total assets.

5. In previous editions we defined the debt-to-equity ratio as total liabilities divided by total common equity. For better comparability with Web-based reporting sources, we have changed our definition to total debt divided by total common equity.

$$\text{Market debt ratio} = \frac{\text{Total debt}}{\text{Total debt} + \text{Market value of equity}}$$

$$= \frac{\$280 + \$1,200}{(\$280 + \$1,200) + (\$27 \times 50)} = \frac{\$1,480}{\$1,480 + \$1,350}$$

$$= 52.3\%$$

Industry average $= 20.0\%$

MicroDrive's market debt ratio in the previous year was 36.1%. The big increase was due to two major factors: Debt increased and the stock price fell. The stock price reflects a company's prospects for generating future cash flows, so a decline in stock price indicates a likely decline in future cash flows. Thus, the market debt ratio reflects a source of risk that is not captured by the conventional debt ratio.

Finally, the ratio of total liabilities to total assets shows the extent to which a firm's assets are not financed by equity. The **liabilities-to-assets ratio** is defined as:

$$\text{Liabilities-to-assets ratio} = \frac{\text{Total liabilities}}{\text{Total assets}}$$

$$= \frac{\$1,980}{\$3,550} = 55.8\%$$

Industry average $= 45.0\%$

For all the ratios we examined, MicroDrive has more leverage than its industry peers. The next section shows how close MicroDrive might be to serious financial distress.

7-4b Ability to Pay Interest: Times-Interest-Earned Ratio

The **times-interest-earned (TIE) ratio**, also called the **interest coverage ratio**, is determined by dividing earnings before interest and taxes (EBIT in Figure 7-1) by the interest expense:

$$\text{Times-interest-earned (TIE) ratio} = \frac{\text{EBIT}}{\text{Interest expense}}$$

$$= \frac{\$500}{\$120} = 4.2$$

Industry average $= 10.0$

The TIE ratio measures the extent to which operating income can decline before the firm is unable to meet its annual interest costs. Failure to meet this obligation can bring legal action by the firm's creditors, possibly resulting in bankruptcy. Note that earnings before interest and taxes, rather than net income, is used in the numerator. Because interest is paid with pre-tax dollars, the firm's ability to pay current interest is not affected by taxes.

MicroDrive's interest is covered 4.2 times, which is well above 1, the point at which EBIT isn't sufficient to pay interest. The industry average is 10, so even though MicroDrive has enough EBIT to pay interest expenses, it has a relatively low margin of safety compared to its peers. Thus, the TIE ratio reinforces the conclusion from our analysis of the debt ratio that MicroDrive might face difficulties if it attempts to borrow additional funds.

7-4c **Ability to Service Debt: EBITDA Coverage Ratio**

The TIE ratio is useful for assessing a company's ability to meet interest charges on its debt, but this ratio has two shortcomings: (1) Interest is not the only fixed financial charge—companies must also reduce debt on schedule, and many firms lease assets and thus must make lease payments. Failure to repay debt or meet lease payments may force them into bankruptcy. (2) EBIT (earnings before interest and taxes) does not represent all the cash flow available to service debt, especially if a firm has high noncash expenses, like depreciation and/or amortization charges. A better coverage ratio would take all of the "cash" earnings into account in the numerator and the other financial charges in the denominator.

MicroDrive had $500 million of EBIT and $200 million in depreciation, for an EBITDA (earnings before interest, taxes, depreciation, and amortization) of $700 million. Also, lease payments of $28 million were deducted while calculating EBIT. That $28 million was available to meet financial charges; hence it must be added back, bringing the total available to cover fixed financial charges to $728 million. Fixed financial charges consisted of $120 million of interest, $20 million of sinking fund payments, and $28 million for lease payments, for a total of $168 million.[6]

MicroDrive's **EBITDA coverage ratio** is:[7]

$$\text{EBITDA coverage ratio} = \frac{\text{EBITDA} + \text{Lease payments}}{\text{Interest} + \text{Principal payments} + \text{Lease payments}}$$

$$= \frac{(\$500 + 200) + \$28}{\$120 + \$20 + \$28} = \frac{\$728}{\$168} = 4.3$$

$$\text{Industry average} = 12.0$$

MicroDrive covered its fixed financial charges by 4.3 times. MicroDrive's ratio is well below the industry average, so again the company seems to have a relatively high level of debt.

The EBITDA coverage ratio is most useful for relatively short-term lenders such as banks, which rarely make loans (except real estate-backed loans) for longer than

---

6. A sinking fund is a required annual payment designed to reduce the balance of a bond or preferred stock issue.

7. Different analysts define the EBITDA coverage ratio in different ways. For example, some omit the lease payment information; others "gross up" principal payments by dividing them by $1 - T$ because these payments are not tax deductions and so must be made with after-tax cash flows. We included lease payments because they are quite important for many firms, and failing to make them can lead to bankruptcy as surely as can failure to make payments on "regular" debt. We did not gross up principal payments because, if a company is in financial difficulty, then its tax rate will probably be zero; hence the gross up is not necessary whenever the ratio is really important.

about 5 years. Over a relatively short period, depreciation-generated funds can be used to service debt. Over a longer time, those funds must be reinvested to maintain the plant and equipment or else the company cannot remain in business. Therefore, banks and other relatively short-term lenders focus on the EBITDA coverage ratio, whereas long-term bondholders focus on the TIE ratio.

How does the use of financial leverage affect current stockholders' control position?

Name six ratios that are used to measure the extent to which a firm uses financial leverage, and write out their equations.

A company has EBITDA of $600 million, interest payments of $60 million, lease payments of $40 million, and required principal payments (due this year) of $30 million. What is its EBITDA coverage ratio? **(4.9)**

7-5 **Profitability Ratios**

Profitability is the net result of a number of policies and decisions. The ratios examined thus far provide useful clues as to the effectiveness of a firm's operations, but the **profitability ratios** go on to show the combined effects of liquidity, asset management, and debt on operating results.

7-5a **Net Profit Margin**

The **net profit margin**, also called the **profit margin on sales**, is calculated by dividing net income by sales. It gives the profit per dollar of sales:

$$\text{Net profit margin} = \frac{\text{Net income available to common stockholders}}{\text{Sales}}$$

$$= \frac{\$220}{\$5,000} = 4.4\%$$

$$\text{Industry average} = 6.2\%$$

MicroDrive's net profit margin is below the industry average of 6.2%, but why is this so? Is it due to inefficient operations, high interest expenses, or both?

Instead of just comparing net income to sales, many analysts also break the income statement into smaller parts to identify the sources of a low net profit margin. For example, the **operating profit margin** is defined as:

$$\text{Operating profit margin} = \frac{\text{EBIT}}{\text{Sales}}$$

The operating profit margin identifies how a company is performing with respect to its operations before the impact of interest expenses is considered.

Some analysts drill even deeper by breaking operating costs into their components. For example, the **gross profit margin** is defined as:

$$\text{Gross profit margin} = \frac{\text{Sales} - \text{Cost of goods sold}}{\text{Sales}}$$

The gross profit margin identifies the gross profit per dollar of sales before any other expenses are deducted.

Rather than calculate each type of profit margin here, later in the chapter we will use common size analysis and percent change analysis to focus on different parts of the income statement. In addition, we will use the DuPont equation to show how the ratios interact with one another.

Sometimes it is confusing to have so many different types of profit margins. To simplify the situation, we will focus primarily on the net profit margin throughout the book and call it the "profit margin."

7-5b Basic Earning Power (BEP) Ratio

The **basic earning power (BEP) ratio** is calculated by dividing earnings before interest and taxes (EBIT) by total assets:

THE WORLD MIGHT BE FLAT, BUT GLOBAL ACCOUNTING IS BUMPY! THE CASE OF IFRS VERSUS FASB

In a flat world, distance is no barrier. Work flows to where it can be done most efficiently, and capital flows to where it can be invested most profitably. If a radiologist in India is more efficient than one in the United States, then images will be e-mailed to India for diagnosis; if rates of return are higher in Brazil, then investors throughout the world will provide funding for Brazilian projects. One key to "flattening" the world is agreement on common standards. For example, there are common Internet standards so that users throughout the world are able to communicate.

A glaring exception to standardization is in accounting. The Securities and Exchange Commission (SEC) in the United States requires firms to comply with standards set by the Financial Accounting Standards Board (FASB). But the European Union requires all EU-listed companies to comply with the International Financial Reporting Standards (IFRS) as defined by the International Accounting Standards Board (IASB).

IFRS tends to rely on general principles, whereas FASB standards are rules-based. As the recent accounting scandals demonstrate, many U.S. companies have been able to comply with U.S. rules while violating the principle, or intent, underlying the rules. The United States is likely to adopt IFRS, or a slightly modified IFRS, but the question is, "When?" The SEC estimated that a large company is likely to incur costs of up to $32 million when switching to IFRS. So even though a survey by the accounting firm KPMG indicates that most investors and analysts favor adoption of IFRS, the path to adoption is likely to be bumpy.

Source: See the Web sites of the IASB and the FASB, **www.iasb.org.uk and www.fasb.org**. Also see David M. Katz and Sarah Johnson, "Top Obama Advisers Clash on Global Accounting Standards," January 15, 2009, at **www.cfo.com**; and "Survey Favors IFRS Adoption," February 3, 2009, at **www.webcpa.com**.

$$\text{Basic earning power (BEP) ratio} = \frac{\text{EBIT}}{\text{Total assets}}$$

$$= \frac{\$500}{\$3,550} = 14.1\%$$

Industry average $= 20.2\%$

This ratio shows the earning power of the firm's assets before the influence of taxes and leverage, and it is useful for comparing firms with different tax situations and different degrees of financial leverage. Because of its low turnover ratios and low profit margin on sales, MicroDrive is not getting as high a return on its assets as is the average company in its industry.

7-5c **Return on Total Assets**

The ratio of net income to total assets measures the **return on total assets (ROA)** after interest and taxes. This ratio is also called the **return on assets** and is defined as follows:

$$\text{Return on total assets} = \text{ROA} = \frac{\text{Net income available to common stockholders}}{\text{Total assets}}$$

$$= \frac{\$220}{\$3,550} = 6.2\%$$

Industry average $= 11.0\%$

MicroDrive's 6.2% return is well below the 11% average for the industry. This low return is due to: (1) the company's low basic earning power, and (2) high interest costs resulting from its above-average use of debt. Both of these factors cause MicroDrive's net income to be relatively low.

7-5d **Return on Common Equity**

The ratio of net income to common equity measures the **return on common equity (ROE)**:

$$\text{Return on common equity} = \text{ROE} = \frac{\text{Net income available to common stockholders}}{\text{Common equity}}$$

$$= \frac{\$220}{\$1,470} = 15.0\%$$

Industry average $= 19.0\%$

Stockholders invest to earn a return on their money, and this ratio tells how well they are doing in an accounting sense. MicroDrive's 15% return is below the 19% industry average, but not as far below as its return on total assets. This somewhat better result is due to the company's greater use of debt, a point that we explain in detail later in the chapter.

SELF TEST

Identify and write out the equations for four profitability ratios.

Why is the basic earning power ratio useful?

Why does the use of debt lower ROA?

What does ROE measure?

A company has $200 billion of sales and $10 billion of net income. Its total assets are $100 billion, financed half by debt and half by common equity. What is its profit margin? **(5%)** What is its ROA? **(10%)** What is its ROE? **(20%)** Would ROA increase if the firm used less leverage? **(Yes)** Would ROE increase? **(No)**

7-6 Market Value Ratios

Market value ratios relate a firm's stock price to its earnings, cash flow, and book value per share. Market value ratios are a way to measure the value of a company's stock relative to that of another company.

7-6a Price/Earnings Ratio

The **price/earnings (P/E) ratio** shows how much investors are willing to pay per dollar of reported profits. MicroDrive has $220 million in net income and 50 million shares, so its earnings per share (EPS) is $4.40 = $220/50. MicroDrive's stock sells for $27, so its P/E ratio is:

$$\text{Price/earnings (P/E) ratio} = \frac{\text{Price per share}}{\text{Earnings per share}}$$

$$= \frac{\$27.00}{\$4.40} = 6.1$$

Industry average = 10.5

Price/earnings ratios are higher for firms with strong growth prospects, other things held constant, but they are lower for riskier firms. Because MicroDrive's P/E ratio is below the average, this suggests that the company is regarded as being somewhat riskier than most, as having poorer growth prospects, or both. In early 2014, the average P/E ratio for firms in the S&P 500 was 18.98, indicating that investors were willing to pay $18.98 for every dollar of earnings.

7-6b **Price/Cash Flow Ratio**

Stock prices depend on a company's ability to generate cash flows. Consequently, investors often look at the **price/cash flow ratio**, where cash flow is defined as net income plus depreciation and amortization:

$$\text{Price/cash flow ratio} = \frac{\text{Price per share}}{\text{Cash flow per share}}$$

$$= \frac{\$27.00}{(\$220 + \$200)/50} = 3.2$$

$$\text{Industry average} = 6.8$$

MicroDrive's price/cash flow ratio is also below the industry average, once again suggesting that its growth prospects are below average, its risk is above average, or both.

The **price/EBITDA ratio** is similar to the price/cash flow ratio, except the price/EBITDA ratio measures performance before the impact of interest expenses and taxes, making it a better measure of operating performance. MicroDrive's EBITDA per share is $(\$500 + \$200)/50 = \$14$, so its price/EBITDA is $\$27/\$14 = 1.9$. The industry average price/EBITDA ratio is 4.0, so we see again that MicroDrive is below the industry average.

Note that some analysts look at other multiples as well. For example, depending on the industry, some may look at measures such as price/sales or price/customers. Ultimately, though, value depends on free cash flows, so if these "exotic" ratios do not forecast future free cash flow, they may turn out to be misleading. This was true in the case of the dot-com retailers before they crashed and burned in 2000, costing investors many billions.

7-6c **Market/Book Ratio**

The ratio of a stock's market price to its book value gives another indication of how investors regard the company. Companies with relatively high rates of return on equity generally sell at higher multiples of book value than those with low returns. First, we find MicroDrive's book value per share:

$$\text{Book value per share} = \frac{\text{Total common equity}}{\text{Shares outstanding}}$$

$$= \frac{\$1,470}{50} = \$29.4$$

Now we divide the market price by the book value to get a **market/book (M/B) ratio**:

$$\text{Market/book ratio} = \text{M/B} = \frac{\text{Market price per share}}{\text{Book value per share}}$$

$$= \frac{\$27.00}{\$29.40} = 0.9$$

Industry average $= 1.8$

Investors are willing to pay relatively little for a dollar of MicroDrive's book value.

The book value is a record of the past, showing the cumulative amount that stockholders have invested, either directly by purchasing newly issued shares or indirectly through retaining earnings. In contrast, the market price is forward looking, incorporating investors' expectations of future cash flows. For example, in early 2014 Bank of America had a market/book ratio of only 0.8, reflecting the financial services industry's problems, whereas Apple's market/book ratio was 4.0, indicating that investors expected Apple's past successes to continue.

Table 7-1 summarizes selected ratios for MicroDrive. As the table indicates, the company has many problems.

TABLE 7-1 MicroDrive Inc.: Summary of Selected Financial Ratios (Millions of Dollars)

Ratio	Formula	Calculation	Ratio	Industry Average	Comment
Liquidity					
Current	$\dfrac{\text{Current assets}}{\text{Current liabilities}}$	$\dfrac{\$1,550}{\$780} =$	2.0	2.2	Poor
Quick	$\dfrac{\text{Current assets} - \text{Inventories}}{\text{Current liabilities}}$	$\dfrac{\$550}{\$780} =$	0.7	0.8	Poor
Asset Management					
Total assets turnover	$\dfrac{\text{Sales}}{\text{Total assets}}$	$\dfrac{\$5,000}{\$3,550} =$	1.4	1.8	Poor
Fixed assets turnover	$\dfrac{\text{Sales}}{\text{Net fixed assets}}$	$\dfrac{\$5,000}{\$2,000} =$	2.5	3.0	Poor
Days sales outstanding (DSO)	$\dfrac{\text{Receivables}}{\text{Annual sales}/365}$	$\dfrac{\$500}{\$13.7} =$	36.5	30.0	Poor
Inventory turnover	$\dfrac{\text{COGS}}{\text{Inventories}}$	$\dfrac{\$4,000}{\$1,000} =$	4.0	5.0	Poor
Debt Management					
Debt-to-assets ratio	$\dfrac{\text{Total debt}}{\text{Total assets}}$	$\dfrac{\$1,480}{\$3,550} =$	41.7%	25.0%	High (risky)
Times-interest-earned (TIE)	$\dfrac{\text{Earnings before interest and taxes (EBIT)}}{\text{Interest charges}}$	$\dfrac{\$500}{\$120} =$	4.2	10.0	Low (risky)

Ratio	Formula	Calculation	Ratio	Industry Average	Comment
Profitability					
Profit margin on sales	$\dfrac{\text{Net income available to common stockholders}}{\text{Sales}}$	$\dfrac{\$220}{\$5,000} =$	4.4%	6.2%	Poor
Basic earning power (BEP)	$\dfrac{\text{Earnings before interest and taxes (EBIT)}}{\text{Total assets}}$	$\dfrac{\$500}{\$3,550} =$	14.1%	20.2%	Poor
Return on total assets (ROA)	$\dfrac{\text{Net income available to common stockholders}}{\text{Total assets}}$	$\dfrac{\$220}{\$3,550} =$	6.2%	11.0%	Poor
Return on common equity (ROE)	$\dfrac{\text{Net income available to common stockholders}}{\text{Common equity}}$	$\dfrac{\$220}{\$1,470} =$	15.0%	19.0%	Poor
Market Value					
Price/earnings (P/E)	$\dfrac{\text{Price per share}}{\text{Earnings per share}}$	$\dfrac{\$27.00}{\$4.40} =$	6.1	10.5	Low
Market/book (M/B)	$\dfrac{\text{Market price per share}}{\text{Book value per share}}$	$\dfrac{\$27.00}{\$29.40} =$	0.9	1.8	Low

SELF TEST

Describe three ratios that relate a firm's stock price to its earnings, cash flow, and book value per share, and write out their equations.

What does the price/earnings (P/E) ratio show? If one firm's P/E ratio is lower than that of another, what are some factors that might explain the difference?

How is book value per share calculated? Explain why book values often deviate from market values.

A company has $6 billion of net income, $2 billion of depreciation and amortization, $80 billion of common equity, and 1 billion shares of stock. If its stock price is $96 per share, what is its price/earnings ratio? **(16)** Its price/cash flow ratio? **(12)** Its market/book ratio? **(1.2)**

7-7 Trend Analysis, Common Size Analysis, and Percentage Change Analysis

Trends give clues as to whether a firm's financial condition is likely to improve or deteriorate. To do a **trend analysis,** you examine a ratio over time, as shown in Figure 7-2. This graph shows that MicroDrive's rate of return on common equity

| FIGURE 7-2 | MicroDrive Inc.: Trend Analysis of Rate of Return on Common Equity |

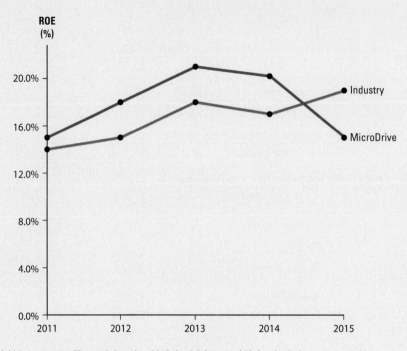

Source: From *Financial Management: Theory & Practice,* 2013, by Brigham and Ehrhardt. © Cengage Learning.

has been declining since 2013, in contrast to the industry average. All the other ratios could be analyzed similarly.

In a **common size analysis**, all income statement items are divided by sales and all balance sheet items are divided by total assets. Thus, a common size income statement shows each item as a percentage of sales, and a common size balance sheet shows each item as a percentage of total assets.[8] The advantage of common size analysis is that it facilitates comparisons of balance sheets and income statements over time and across companies.

Common size statements are easy to generate if the financial statements are in a spreadsheet. In fact, if you obtain your data from a source that uses standardized financial statements, then it is easy to cut and paste the data for a new company over your original company's data, and all of your spreadsheet formulas will be valid for the new company. We generated Figure 7-3 in the *Excel* file ***Ch07 Tool Kit.xls.*** Figure 7-3 shows MicroDrive's 2014 and 2015 common size income statements, along with the composite statement for the industry. (*Note:* Rounding may cause addition/subtraction differences in Figures 7-3, 7-4, and 7-5.) MicroDrive's EBIT is slightly below average, and its interest expenses are slightly above average. The net effect is a relatively low profit margin.

---

8. Some sources of industry data, such as Risk Management Associates (formerly known as Robert Morris Associates), are presented exclusively in common size form.

FIGURE 7-3	MicroDrive Inc.: Common Size Income Statement

	A	B	C	D	E	F
				Industry Composite	MicroDrive	
175						
176				2015	2015	2014
177	Net sales			100.0%	100.0%	100.0%
178	Costs of goods sold except depreciation			75.5%	76.0%	74.8%
179	Depreciation			3.0%	4.0%	3.6%
180	Other operating expenses			10.0%	10.0%	10.1%
181	Earnings before interest and taxes (EBIT)			11.5%	10.0%	11.6%
182	Less interest			1.2%	2.4%	2.1%
183	Pre-tax earnings			10.4%	7.6%	9.5%
184	Taxes (40%)			4.1%	3.0%	3.8%
185	Net income before preferred dividends			6.2%	4.6%	5.7%
186	Preferred dividends			0.0%	0.2%	0.2%
187	Net income available to common stockholders			6.2%	4.4%	5.5%

Microsoft Excel® is a registered trademark of Microsoft Corporation. © 2014 Microsoft.

Figure 7-4 shows MicroDrive's common size balance sheets along with the industry composite. Its accounts receivable are slightly higher than the industry average, its inventories are significantly higher, and it uses much more debt than the average firm.

FIGURE 7-4	MicroDrive Inc.: Common Size Balance Sheet

	A	B	C	D	E
			Industry Composite	MicroDrive	
195					
196			2015	2015	2014
197	*Assets*				
198	Cash and equivalents		1.8%	1.4%	2.0%
199	Short-term investments		0.0%	0.0%	1.3%
200	Accounts receivable		14.0%	14.1%	12.7%
201	Inventories		26.3%	28.2%	27.3%
202	Total current assets		42.1%	43.7%	43.3%
203	Net plant and equipment		57.9%	56.3%	56.7%
204	Total assets		100.0%	100.0%	100.0%
205					
206	*Liabilities and Equity*				
207	Accounts payable		7.0%	5.6%	6.3%
208	Notes payable		0.0%	7.9%	4.3%
209	Accruals		12.3%	8.5%	9.3%
210	Total current liabilities		19.3%	22.0%	20.0%
211	Long-term bonds		25.4%	33.8%	33.3%
212	Total liabilities		44.7%	55.8%	53.3%
213	Preferred stock		0.0%	2.8%	3.3%
214	Total common equity		55.3%	41.4%	43.3%
215	Total liabilities and equity		100.0%	100.0%	100.0%

Microsoft Excel® is a registered trademark of Microsoft Corporation. © 2014 Microsoft.

FIGURE 7-5 MicroDrive Inc.: Income Statement Percentage Change Analysis

	A	B	C	D
				Percent
225	**Base year = 2014**			**Change in**
226				**2015**
227	Net sales			5.0%
228	Costs of goods sold except depreciation			6.7%
229	Depreciation			17.6%
230	Other operating expenses			4.2%
231	Earnings before interest and taxes (EBIT)			(9.1%)
232	Less interest			20.0%
233	Pre-tax earnings			(15.6%)
234	Taxes (40%)			(15.6%)
235	Net Income before preferred dividends			(15.6%)
236	Preferred dividends			0.0%
237	Net income available to common stockholders			(16.0%)

Microsoft Excel® is a registered trademark of Microsoft Corporation. © 2014 Microsoft.

See *Ch07 Tool Kit.xls*
for details.

In **percentage change analysis**, growth rates are calculated for all income statement items and balance sheet accounts relative to a base year. To illustrate, Figure 7-5 contains MicroDrive's income statement percentage change analysis for 2015 relative to 2014. Sales increased at a 5% rate during 2015, but EBIT fell by 9.1%. Part of this decline was due to an increase in depreciation, which is a noncash expense, but the cost of goods sold also increased by a little more than the growth in sales. In addition, interest expenses grew by 20%. We apply the same type of analysis to the balance sheets (see the file *Ch07 Tool Kit.xls*), which shows that inventories grew at a whopping 22% rate and accounts receivable grew over 31%. With only a 5% growth in sales, the extreme growth in receivables and inventories should be of great concern to MicroDrive's managers.

SELF TEST

What is a trend analysis, and what information does it provide?

What is common size analysis?

What is percentage change analysis?

7-8 Tying the Ratios Together: The DuPont Equation

In ratio analysis, it is sometimes easy to miss the forest for all the trees. In particular, how do managerial actions affecting a firm's profitability, asset efficiency, and financial leverage interact to determine the return on equity, a performance measure that is important for investors? The extended **DuPont equation** provides just such a framework.

The DuPont equation uses two ratios we covered previously, the profit margin and the total asset turnover ratio, as measures of profitability and asset efficiency, but it uses a new measure of financial leverage, the **equity multiplier**, which is the ratio of assets to common equity:

$$\text{Equity multiplier} = \frac{\text{Total assets}}{\text{Common equity}} \qquad \textbf{(7–1)}$$

Using this new definition of financial leverage, the extended DuPont equation is:

$$\text{ROE} = \frac{\text{Net income}}{\text{Common equity}} = \frac{\text{Net income}}{\text{Sales}} \times \frac{\text{Sales}}{\text{Total assets}} \times \frac{\text{Total assets}}{\text{Common equity}} \qquad \textbf{(7–2)}$$
$$= (\text{Profit margin})\,(\text{Total assets turnover})\,(\text{Equity multiplier})$$

As calculated previously, MicroDrive's 2015 profit margin is 4.4% and its total assets turnover ratio is 1.41. MicroDrive's equity multiplier is:

$$\text{Equity multiplier} = \frac{\$3,550}{\$1,470} = 2.415$$

Applying the DuPont equation to MicroDrive, its return on equity is:

$$\text{ROE} = (4.4\%)(1.41)(2.415) = 15\%$$

Sometimes it is useful to focus just on asset profitability and financial leverage. Firms that have a lot of financial leverage (i.e., a lot of liabilities or preferred stock) have a high equity multiplier because the assets are financed with a relatively smaller amount of equity. Therefore, the return on equity (ROE) depends on the ROA and the use of leverage:

$$\text{ROE} = \text{ROA} \times \text{Equity multiplier} \qquad \textbf{(7–3)}$$
$$= \frac{\text{Net income}}{\text{Total assets}} \times \frac{\text{Total assets}}{\text{Common equity}}$$

Using Equation 7-3, we see that MicroDrive's ROE is 15.0%, the same value given by the DuPont equation:

$$\text{ROE} = 6.20\% \times 2.415 = 15\%$$

The insights provided by the DuPont model are valuable, and the model can be used for "quick and dirty" estimates of the impact that operating changes have on returns. For example, holding all else equal, if MicroDrive can implement lean production techniques and increase to 1.8 its ratio of sales to total assets, then its ROE will improve to (4.4%)(1.8)(2.415) = 19.1%.

For a more complete "what-if" analysis, most companies use a forecasting model such as the one described in Chapter 9.

SELF TEST

Explain how the extended, or modified, DuPont equation can be used to reveal the basic determinants of ROE.

What is the equity multiplier?

A company has a profit margin of 6%, a total asset turnover ratio of 2, and an equity multiplier of 1.5. What is its ROE? **(18%)**

7-9 Comparative Ratios and Benchmarking

Ratio analysis involves comparisons. A company's ratios are compared with those of other firms in the same industry—that is, with industry average figures. However, like most firms, MicroDrive's managers go one step further: They also compare their ratios with those of a smaller set of the leading computer companies. This technique is called **benchmarking**, and the companies used for the comparison are called **benchmark companies**. For example, MicroDrive benchmarks against five other firms that its management considers to be the best-managed companies with operations similar to its own.

Many companies also benchmark various parts of their overall operation against top companies, whether they are in the same industry or not. For example, MicroDrive has a division that sells hard drives directly to consumers through catalogs and the Internet. This division's shipping department benchmarks against Amazon, even though they are in different industries, because Amazon's shipping department is one of the best. MicroDrive wants its own shippers to strive to match Amazon's record for on-time shipments.

Comparative ratios are available from a number of sources, including *Value Line,* Dun and Bradstreet (D&B), and the *Annual Statement Studies* published by Risk Management Associates, which is the national association of bank loan officers. Table 7-2 reports selected ratios from Reuters for Apple and its industry, revealing that Apple has a much higher return on assets and a lower debt ratio than its peers.

Each data-supplying organization uses a somewhat different set of ratios designed for its own purposes. For example, D&B deals mainly with small firms, many of which are proprietorships, and it sells its services primarily to banks and other lenders. Therefore, D&B is concerned largely with the creditor's viewpoint, and its ratios emphasize current assets and liabilities, not market value ratios. So, when you select a comparative data source, you should be sure that your own emphasis is similar to that of the agency whose ratios you plan to use. Additionally, there are often definitional differences in the ratios presented by different sources, so before using a source, be sure to verify the exact definitions of the ratios to ensure consistency with your own work.

Compare and contrast trend analysis and comparative ratio analysis.

Explain benchmarking.

| TABLE 7-2 | Comparative Ratios for Apple Inc., the Computer Hardware Industry, and the Technology Sector |

Ratio	Apple	Computer Hardware Industry[a]	Technology Sector[b]
P/E ratio	12.31	15.25	24.24
Market to book	3.63	2.11	4.94
Net profit margin	22.28	5.46	5.80
Quick ratio	1.83	1.34	1.56
Current ratio	1.88	1.64	2.68
Total debt-to-equity	13.75	43.81	27.92
Interest coverage (TIE)[c]	—	9.36	200.39
Return on assets	20.81	6.65	12.52
Return on equity	32.11	14.93	18.53
Inventory turnover	74.19	19.14	140.93
Asset turnover	0.93	1.52	0.91

[a]The computer hardware industry includes such firms as Apple, Lexmark, Hewlett-Packard, EMC Corp., and Silicon Graphics.
[b]The technology sector contains 11 industries, including communications equipment, computer hardware, computer networks, semiconductors, and software and programming.
[c]Apple had more interest income than interest expense.

Source: Adapted from **www.reuters.com**, October 14, 2013. For updates, Select Market, Stocks, enter the ticker symbol for Apple (AAPL), and select Financials.

7-10 Uses and Limitations of Ratio Analysis

Ratio analysis provides useful information concerning a company's operations and financial condition, but it has limitations that necessitate care and judgment. Some potential problems include the following.

1. Many large firms operate different divisions in different industries, and for such companies it is difficult to develop a meaningful set of industry averages. Therefore, industry averages are more meaningful for small, narrowly focused firms than for large, multidivisional ones.
2. To set goals for high-level performance, it is best to benchmark on the industry *leaders'* ratios rather than the industry *average* ratios.

RATIO ANALYSIS ON THE WEB

A great source for comparative ratios is **www.reuters.com**. Enter a company's ticker at the top of the page. This brings up a table with the stock quote, company information, and additional links. Select Financials, which brings up a page with a detailed ratio analysis for the company and includes comparative ratios for other companies in the same sector and the same industry. (*Note:* You may have to register to get extra features, but registration is free.)

3. Inflation may badly distort firms' balance sheets—reported values are often substantially different from "true" values. Further, because inflation affects depreciation charges and inventory costs, reported profits are also affected. Thus, inflation can distort a ratio analysis for one firm over time or a comparative analysis of firms of different ages.

4. Seasonal factors can distort a ratio analysis. For example, the inventory turnover ratio for a food processor will be radically different if the balance sheet figure used for inventory is the one just before versus the one just after the close of the canning season. This problem can be minimized by using monthly averages for inventory (and receivables) when calculating turnover ratios.

5. Firms can employ **"window dressing" techniques** to make their financial statements look stronger. To illustrate, suppose a company takes out a 2-year loan in late December. Because the loan is for more than 1 year, it is not included in current liabilities even though the cash received through the loan is reported as a current asset. This improves the current and quick ratios and makes the year-end balance sheet look stronger. If the company pays the loan back in January, then the transaction was strictly window dressing.

6. Companies' choices of different accounting practices can distort comparisons. For example, choices of inventory valuation and depreciation methods affect financial statements differently, making comparisons among companies less meaningful. As another example, if one firm leases a substantial amount of its productive equipment, then its assets may appear low relative to sales (because leased assets often do not appear on the balance sheet) and its debt may appear low (because the liability associated with the lease obligation may not be shown as debt).[9]

In summary, conducting ratio analysis in a mechanical, unthinking manner is dangerous. But when ratio analysis is used intelligently and with good judgment, it can provide useful insights into a firm's operations and identify the right questions to ask.

---

9. This may change when FASB and IASB complete their joint project on leasing. As of early 2014, the estimated project completion date was not certain. For the current status of the project, go to **www.fasb.org**, and select the tab for Projects.

7-11 **Looking Beyond the Numbers**

Sound financial analysis involves more than just calculating and comparing ratios—qualitative factors must be considered. Here are some questions suggested by the American Association of Individual Investors (AAII).

1. To what extent are the company's revenues tied to one key customer or to one key product? To what extent does the company rely on a single supplier? Reliance on single customers, products, or suppliers increases risk.
2. What percentage of the company's business is generated overseas? Companies with a large percentage of overseas business are exposed to risk of currency exchange volatility and political instability.
3. What are the probable actions of current competitors and the likelihood of additional new competitors?
4. Do the company's future prospects depend critically on the success of products currently in the pipeline or on existing products?
5. How do the legal and regulatory environments affect the company?

Summary

This chapter explained techniques investors and managers use to analyze financial statements. The key concepts covered are listed below.

- **Liquidity ratios** show the relationship of a firm's current assets to its current liabilities and thus its ability to meet maturing debts. Two commonly used liquidity ratios are the **current ratio** and the **quick ratio** (also called the **acid test ratio**).
- **Asset management ratios** measure how effectively a firm is managing its assets. These ratios include **inventory turnover, days sales outstanding, fixed assets turnover,** and **total assets turnover**.
- **Debt management ratios** reveal: (1) the extent to which the firm is financed with debt, and (2) its likelihood of defaulting on its debt obligations. They include the **debt-to-assets ratio** (also called the **debt ratio**), the **debt-to-equity ratio,** the **times-interest-earned ratio,** and the **EBITDA coverage ratio**.
- **Profitability ratios** show the combined effects of liquidity, asset management, and debt management policies on operating results. They include the

net profit margin (also called the **profit margin on sales**), the **basic earning power ratio**, the **return on total assets**, and the **return on common equity**.

- **Market value ratios** relate the firm's stock price to its earnings, cash flow, and book value per share, thus giving management an indication of what investors think of the company's past performance and future prospects. These include the **price/earnings ratio**, the **price/cash flow ratio**, and the **market/book ratio**.
- **Trend analysis**, in which one plots a ratio over time, is important because it reveals whether the firm's condition has been improving or deteriorating over time.
- The **DuPont system** is designed to show how the profit margin on sales, the assets turnover ratio, and the use of debt all interact to determine the rate of return on equity. The firm's management can use the DuPont system to analyze ways of improving performance.
- **Benchmarking** is the process of comparing a particular company with a group of similar successful companies.

Ratio analysis has limitations, but when used with care and judgment it can be very helpful.

Questions

7-1 Define each of the following terms:
    a. *Liquidity ratios:* current ratio; quick, or acid test, ratio
    b. Asset management ratios: inventory turnover ratio; days sales outstanding (DSO); fixed assets turnover ratio; total assets turnover ratio
    c. *Financial leverage ratios:* debt ratio; times-interest-earned (TIE) ratio; coverage ratio
    d. *Profitability ratios:* profit margin on sales; basic earning power (BEP) ratio; return on total assets (ROA); return on common equity (ROE)
    e. Market value ratios: price/earnings (P/E) ratio; price/cash flow ratio; market/book (M/B) ratio; book value per share
    f. Trend analysis; comparative ratio analysis; benchmarking
    g. DuPont equation; window dressing; seasonal effects on ratios

7-2 Financial ratio analysis is conducted by managers, equity investors, long-term creditors, and short-term creditors. What is the primary emphasis of each of these groups in evaluating ratios?

7-3 Over the past year, M. D. Ryngaert & Co. has realized an increase in its current ratio and a drop in its total assets turnover ratio. However, the company's sales, quick ratio, and fixed assets turnover ratio have remained constant. What explains these changes?

7-4 Profit margins and turnover ratios vary from one industry to another. What differences would you expect to find between a grocery chain such as Safeway and a steel company? Think particularly about the turnover ratios, the profit margin, and the DuPont equation.

7-5 How might (a) seasonal factors and (b) different growth rates distort a comparative ratio analysis? Give some examples. How might these problems be alleviated?

7–6 Why is it sometimes misleading to compare a company's financial ratios with those of other firms that operate in the same industry?

Problems   Answers Appear in Appendix B

Easy Problems 1–5

7–1 Days Sales Outstanding
Greene Sisters has a DSO of 20 days. The company's average daily sales are $20,000. What is the level of its accounts receivable? Assume there are 365 days in a year.

7–2 Debt Ratio
Vigo Vacations has $200 million in total assets, $5 million in notes payable, and $25 million in long-term debt. What is the debt ratio?

7–3 Market/Book Ratio
Winston Washers's stock price is $75 per share. Winston has $10 billion in total assets. Its balance sheet shows $1 billion in current liabilities, $3 billion in long-term debt, and $6 billion in common equity. It has 800 million shares of common stock outstanding. What is Winston's market/book ratio?

7–4 Price/Earnings Ratio
Reno Revolvers has an EPS of $1.50, a cash flow per share of $3.00, and a price/cash flow ratio of 8.0. What is its P/E ratio?

7–5 ROE
Needham Pharmaceuticals has a profit margin of 3% and an equity multiplier of 2.0. Its sales are $100 million and it has total assets of $50 million. What is its ROE?

Intermediate Problems 6–10

7–6 DuPont Analysis
Gardial & Son has an ROA of 12%, a 5% profit margin, and a return on equity equal to 20%. What is the company's total assets turnover? What is the firm's equity multiplier?

7–7 Current and Quick Ratios
Ace Industries has current assets equal to $3 million. The company's current ratio is 1.5, and its quick ratio is 1.0. What is the firm's level of current liabilities? What is the firm's level of inventories?

7–8 Profit Margin and Debt Ratio
Assume you are given the following relationships for the Haslam Corporation:

Sales/total assets	1.2
Return on assets (ROA)	4%
Return on equity (ROE)	7%

Calculate Haslam's profit margin and liabilities-to-assets ratio. Suppose half its liabilities are in the form of debt. Calculate the debt-to-assets ratio.

7–9 Current and Quick Ratios

The Nelson Company has $1,312,500 in current assets and $525,000 in current liabilities. Its initial inventory level is $375,000, and it will raise funds as additional notes payable and use them to increase inventory. How much can Nelson's short-term debt (notes payable) increase without pushing its current ratio below 2.0? What will be the firm's quick ratio after Nelson has raised the maximum amount of short-term funds?

7–10 Times-Interest-Earned Ratio

The Morris Corporation has $600,000 of debt outstanding, and it pays an interest rate of 8% annually. Morris' annual sales are $3 million, its average tax rate is 40%, and its net profit margin on sales is 3%. If the company does not maintain a TIE ratio of at least 5 to 1, then its bank will refuse to renew the loan and bankruptcy will result. What is Morris' TIE ratio?

Challenging Problems 11–14

7–11 Balance Sheet Analysis

Complete the balance sheet and sales information in the table that follows for J. White Industries using the following financial data:

Total assets turnover: 1.5
Gross profit margin on sales: (Sales − Cost of goods sold)/Sales = 25%
Total liabilities-to-assets ratio: 40%
Quick ratio: 0.80
Days sales outstanding (based on 365-day year): 36.5 days
Inventory turnover ratio: 3.75

Partial Income	**Statement Information**		
Sales	_____		
Cost of goods sold	_____		
Balance Sheet			
Cash	_____	Accounts payable	_____
Accounts receivable	_____	Long-term debt	50,000
Inventories	_____	Common stock	_____
Fixed assets	_____	Retained earnings	100,000
Total assets	$400,000	Total liabilities and equity	_____

7–12 Comprehensive Ratio Calculations

The Kretovich Company had a quick ratio of 1.4, a current ratio of 3.0, a days sales outstanding of 36.5 days (based on a 365-day year), total current assets of $810,000, and cash and marketable securities of $120,000. What were Kretovich's annual sales?

7–13 Comprehensive Ratio Analysis

Data for Lozano Chip Company and its industry averages follow.

a. Calculate the indicated ratios for Lozano.
b. Construct the extended DuPont equation for both Lozano and the industry.
c. Outline Lozano's strengths and weaknesses as revealed by your analysis.

Lozano Chip Company: Balance Sheet as of December 31, 2015 (Thousands of Dollars)

Cash	$ 225,000	Accounts payable	$ 601,866
Receivables	1,575,000	Notes payable	326,634
Inventories	1,125,000	Other current liabilities	525,000
Total current assets	$2,950,000	Total current liabilities	$ 1,453,500
Net fixed assets	1,350,000	Long-term debt	1,068,750
		Common equity	1,752,750
Total assets	$4,275,000	Total liabilities and equity	$ 4,275,000

Lozano Chip Company: Income Statement for Year Ended December 31, 2015 (Thousands of Dollars)

Sales	$ 7,500,000
Cost of goods sold	6,375,000
Selling, general, and administrative expenses	825,000
Earnings before interest and taxes (EBIT)	$ 300,000
Interest expense	111,631
Earnings before taxes (EBT)	$ 188,369
Federal and state income taxes (40%)	75,348
Net income	$ 113,022

Ratio	Lozano	Industry Average
Current assets/Current liabilities	_____	2.0
Days sales outstanding (365-day year)	_____	35.0 days
COGS/Inventory	_____	6.7
Sales/Fixed assets	_____	12.1
Sales/Total assets	_____	3.0
Net income/Sales	_____	1.2%
Net income/Total assets	_____	3.6%
Net income/Common equity	_____	9.0%
Total debt/Total assets	_____	30.0%
Total liabilities/Total assets	_____	60.0%

7–14 **Comprehensive Ratio Analysis**

The Jimenez Corporation's forecasted 2016 financial statements follow, along with some industry average ratios. Calculate Jimenez's 2016 forecasted ratios, compare them with the industry average data, and comment briefly on Jimenez's projected strengths and weaknesses.

Jimenez Corporation: Forecasted Balance Sheet as of December 31, 2016

Assets

Cash	$ 72,000
Accounts receivable	439,000
Inventories	894,000
Total current assets	$1,405,000
Fixed assets	431,000
Total assets	$1,836,000

Liabilities and Equity

Accounts payable	$ 332,000
Notes payable	100,000
Accruals	170,000
Total current liabilities	$ 602,000
Long-term debt	404,290
Common stock	575,000
Retained earnings	254,710
Total liabilities and equity	$1,836,000

Jimenez Corporation: Forecasted Income Statement for 2016

Sales	$4,290,000
Cost of goods sold (excluding depreciation)	3,580,000
Selling, general, and administrative expenses	370,320
Depreciation	159,000
Earnings before taxes (EBT)	$ 180,680
Taxes (40%)	72,272
Net income	$ 108,408

Per Share Data

EPS	$ 4.71
Cash dividends per share	$ 0.95
P/E ratio	5.0
Market price (average)	$ 23.57
Number of shares outstanding	23,000

Industry Financial Ratios (2015)[a]

Quick ratio	1.0
Current ratio	2.7
Inventory turnover[b]	7.0
Days sales outstanding[c]	32.0 days
Fixed assets turnover[b]	13.0
Total assets turnover[b]	2.6
Return on assets	9.1%
Return on equity	18.2%
Profit margin on sales	3.5%
Debt-to-assets ratio	21.0%
Liabilities-to-assets ratio	50.0%
P/E ratio	6.0
Price/Cash flow ratio	3.5
Market/Book ratio	3.5

[a]Industry average ratios have been stable for the past 4 years.
[b]Based on year-end balance sheet figures.
[c]Calculation is based on a 365-day year.

Spreadsheet Problem

7–15 Build a Model: Ratio Analysis
Start with the partial model in the file *Ch07 P15 Build a Model.xls* from the textbook's Web site. Joshua & White (J&W) Technologies's financial statements

are also shown below. Answer the following questions. (*Note:* Industry average ratios are provided in *Ch07 P15 Build a Model.xls.*)

a. Has J&W's liquidity position improved or worsened? Explain.
b. Has J&W's ability to manage its assets improved or worsened? Explain.
c. How has J&W's profitability changed during the last year?
d. Perform an extended DuPont analysis for J&W for 2014 and 2015. What do these results tell you?
e. Perform a common size analysis. What has happened to the composition (that is, percentage in each category) of assets and liabilities?
f. Perform a percentage change analysis. What does this tell you about the change in profitability and asset utilization?

Joshua & White Technologies: December 31 Balance Sheets (Thousands of Dollars)

Assets	2015	2014	Liabilities & Equity	2015	2014
Cash	$ 21,000	$ 20,000	Accounts payable	$ 33,600	$ 32,000
Short-term investments	3,759	3,240	Accruals	12,600	12,000
Accounts receivable	52,500	48,000	Notes payable	19,929	6,480
Inventories	84,000	56,000	Total current liabilities	$ 66,129	$ 50,480
Total current assets	$ 161,259	$ 127,240	Long-term debt	67,662	58,320
Net fixed assets	218,400	200,000	Total liabilities	$ 133,791	$108,800
Total assets	$379,659	$327,240	Common stock	183,793	178,440
			Retained earnings	62,075	40,000
			Total common equity	$245,868	$218,440
			Total liabilities & equity	$379,659	$327,240

Joshua & White Technologies: December 31 Income Statements (Thousands of Dollars)

	2015	2014
Sales	$420,000	$400,000
COGS excluding depr. & amort.	300,000	298,000
Depreciation and amortization	19,660	18,000
Other operating expenses	27,600	22,000
EBIT	$ 72,740	$ 62,000
Interest expense	5,740	4,460
EBT	$ 67,000	$ 57,540
Taxes (40%)	26,800	23,016
Net income	$ 40,200	$ 34,524
Common dividends	$ 18,125	$ 17,262

Other Data	2014	2013
Year-end stock price	$ 90.00	$ 96.00
Number of shares (Thousands)	4,052	4,000
Lease payment (Thousands of Dollars)	$ 20,000	$ 20,000
Sinking fund payment (Thousands of Dollars)	$ 5,000	$ 5,000

MINI CASE

The first part of the case, presented in Chapter 6, discussed the situation of Computron Industries after an expansion program. A large loss occurred in 2015, rather than the expected profit. As a result, its managers, directors, and investors are concerned about the firm's survival.

Jenny Cochran was brought in as assistant to Gary Meissner, Computron's chairman, who had the task of getting the company back into a sound financial position. Computron's 2014 and 2015 balance sheets and income statements, together with projections for 2016, are shown in the following tables. The tables also show the 2014 and 2015 financial ratios, along with industry average data. The 2016 projected financial statement data represent Cochran's and Meissner's best guess for 2016 results, assuming that some new financing is arranged to get the company "over the hump."

Balance Sheets

	2014	2015	2016E
Assets			
Cash	$ 9,000	$ 7,282	$ 14,000
Short-term investments	48,600	20,000	71,632
Accounts receivable	351,200	632,160	878,000
Inventories	715,200	1,287,360	1,716,480
Total current assets	$ 1,124,000	$ 1,946,802	$ 2,680,112
Gross fixed assets	491,000	1,202,950	1,220,000
Less: Accumulated depreciation	146,200	263,160	383,160
Net fixed assets	$ 344,800	$ 939,790	$ 836,840
Total assets	$1,468,800	$2,886,592	$3,516,952
Liabilities and Equity			
Accounts payable	$ 145,600	$ 324,000	$ 359,800
Notes payable	200,000	720,000	300,000
Accruals	136,000	284,960	380,000
Total current liabilities	$ 481,600	$ 1,328,960	$1,039,800
Long-term debt	323,432	1,000,000	500,000
Common stock (100,000 shares)	460,000	460,000	1,680,936
Retained earnings	203,768	97,632	296,216
Total equity	$ 663,768	$ 557,632	$ 1,977,152
Total liabilities and equity	$1,468,800	$2,886,592	$3,516,952

Note: "E" denotes "estimated"; the 2016 data are forecasts.

Income Statements

	2014	2015	2016E
Sales	$3,432,000	$5,834,400	$7,035,600
Cost of goods sold except depr.	2,864,000	4,980,000	5,800,000
Depreciation and amortization	18,900	116,960	120,000
Other expenses	340,000	720,000	612,960
Total operating costs	$3,222,900	$5,816,960	$6,532,960
EBIT	$ 209,100	$ 17,440	$ 502,640
Interest expense	62,500	176,000	80,000
EBT	$ 146,600	($ 158,560)	$ 422,640
Taxes (40%)	58,640	(63,424)	169,056
Net income	$ 87,960	($ 95,136)	$ 253,584
Other Data			
Stock price	$ 8.50	$ 6.00	$ 12.17
Shares outstanding	100,000	100,000	250,000
EPS	$ 0.880	–$ 0.951	$ 1.014
DPS	$ 0.220	0.110	0.220
Tax rate	40%	40%	40%
Book value per share	$ 6.638	$ 5.576	$ 7.909
Lease payments	$ 40,000	$ 40,000	$ 40,000

Note: "E" denotes "estimated"; the 2016 data are forecasts.

Ratio Analysis

	2014	2015	2016E	Industry Average
Current	2.3	1.5	_____	2.7
Quick	0.8	0.5	_____	1.0
Inventory turnover	4.0	4.0	_____	6.1
Days sales outstanding	37.3	39.6	_____	32.0
Fixed assets turnover	10.0	6.2	_____	7.0
Total assets turnover	2.3	2.0	_____	2.5
Debt ratio	35.6%	59.6%	_____	32.0%
Liabilities-to-assets ratio	54.8%	80.7%	_____	50.0%
TIE	3.3	0.1	_____	6.2
EBITDA coverage	2.6	0.8	_____	8.0
Profit margin	2.6%	−1.6%	_____	3.6%
Basic earning power	14.2%	0.6%	_____	17.8%
ROA	6.0%	−3.3%	_____	9.0%
ROE	13.3%	−17.1%	_____	17.9%
Price/Earnings (P/E)	9.7	−6.3	_____	16.2
Price/Cash flow	8.0	27.5	_____	7.6
Market/Book	1.3	1.1	_____	2.9

Note: "E" denotes "estimated."

Cochran must prepare an analysis of where the company is now, what it must do to regain its financial health, and what actions to take. Your assignment is to help her answer the following questions. Provide clear explanations, not yes or no answers.

a. Why are ratios useful? What three groups use ratio analysis and for what reasons?

b. Calculate the 2016 current and quick ratios based on the projected balance sheet and income statement data. What can you say about the company's liquidity position in 2014, 2015, and as projected for 2016? We often think of ratios as being useful: (1) to managers to help run the business, (2) to bankers for credit analysis, and (3) to stockholders for stock valuation. Would these different types of analysts have an equal interest in the liquidity ratios?

c. Calculate the 2016 inventory turnover, days sales outstanding (DSO), fixed assets turnover, and total assets turnover. How does Computron's utilization of assets stack up against that of other firms in its industry?

d. Calculate the 2016 debt ratio, liabilities-to-assets ratio, times-interest-earned ratio, and EBITDA coverage ratios. How does Computron compare with the industry with respect to financial leverage? What can you conclude from these ratios?

e. Calculate the 2016 profit margin, basic earning power (BEP), return on assets (ROA), and return on equity (ROE). What can you say about these ratios?

f. Calculate the 2016 price/earnings ratio, price/cash flow ratio, and market/book ratio. Do these ratios indicate that investors are expected to have a high or low opinion of the company?

g. Perform a common size analysis and percentage change analysis. What do these analyses tell you about Computron?

h. Use the extended DuPont equation to provide a summary and overview of Computron's financial condition as projected for 2016. What are the firm's major strengths and weaknesses?

i. What are some potential problems and limitations of financial ratio analysis?

j. What are some qualitative factors that analysts should consider when evaluating a company's likely future financial performance?

SELECTED ADDITIONAL CASES

The following cases from CengageCompose cover many of the concepts discussed in this chapter and are available at http://compose.cengage.com.

Klein-Brigham Series:

Case 35, "Mark X Company (A)," illustrates the use of ratio analysis in the evaluation of a firm's existing and potential financial positions; Case 36, "Garden State Container Corporation," is similar in content to Case 35; Case 51, "Safe Packaging Corporation," updates Case 36; Case 68, "Sweet Dreams Inc.," also updates Case 36; and Case 71, "Swan-Davis, Inc.," illustrates how financial analysis—based on both historical statements and forecasted statements—is used for internal management and lending decisions.

Corporate Valuation

Basic Stock Valuation

How much is a company worth? What can managers do to make a company more valuable? Why are stock prices so volatile? This chapter addresses those questions through the application of two widely used valuation models: the free cash flow valuation model and the dividend growth model. But before plunging into stock valuation, we begin with a closer look at what it means to be a stockholder.

Beginning-of-Chapter Questions

As you read the chapter, consider how you would answer the following questions. You *should not* necessarily be able to answer the questions before you read the chapter. Rather, you should use them to get a sense of the issues covered in the chapter. After reading the chapter, you should be able to give at least partial answers to the questions, and you should be able to give better answers after the chapter has been discussed in class. Note, too, that it is often useful, when answering conceptual questions, to use hypothetical data to illustrate your answer. We illustrate the answers with an *Excel* model that is available on the textbook's Web site. Accessing the model and working through it is a useful exercise, and it provides insights that are useful when answering the questions.

1. Assuming that the required rate of return is determined by the CAPM, explain how you would use the dividend growth model to estimate the price for Stock i. Indicate what data you would need, and give an example of a "reasonable" value for each data input. How would this be different

if you used free cash flows as the basis for your evaluation?

2. How would the stock's calculated price be affected if g_L, r_{RF}, IP (the premium for inflation), r_M, and b_i each (a) "improved" or (b) "became worse" by some arbitrary but "reasonable" amount? "Improved" means caused the stock price to increase, and "became worse" means lowered the price. "Reasonable" means that the condition has existed in the recent past for the economy and/or some particular company. You can look at our model for examples.

3. How could you use the nonconstant growth model to find the value of the stock? Here you can assume that the expected growth rate starts at a high level, then declines for several years, and finally reaches a steady state where growth is constant.

4. Suppose you were offered a chance to buy a stock at a specified price. The stock paid a dividend last year, and the dividend is expected to grow at a very high rate for several years, at a moderate rate for several more years, and at a constant rate from

then on. How could you estimate the expected rate of return on the stock?

5. In general, what are some characteristics of stocks for which a dividend growth model is appropriate? What are some characteristics of stocks for which dividend growth is not appropriate but a FCF model is? How could you evaluate this second type of stock? Are there some stocks for which neither an FCF model nor a dividend growth model is appropriate?

CORPORATE VALUATION AND STOCK PRICES

Free cash flows (FCF) are the cash flows available for distribution to all of a company's investors; the weighted average cost of capital is the overall return required by all of a company's investors. So the present value of a company's expected free cash flows, discounted by the company's weighted average cost of capital, is the total value of the company to all its investors. It is called the value of operations because operating activities generate the FCF.

We can use this approach to estimate the stock price, but we can do this more directly in some circumstances. Recall that one use of FCF is to pay dividends, which are distributed to stockholders. Chapter 2 showed how to estimate stockholders' required return. Therefore, discounting the expected cash flows to stockholders (the dividends) at the rate required by stockholders determines the stock's value.

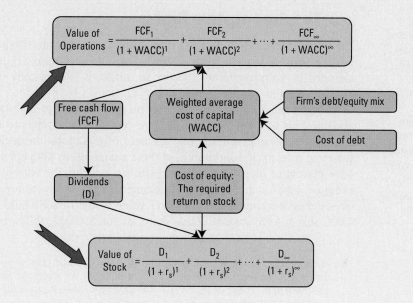

$$\text{Value of Operations} = \frac{FCF_1}{(1 + WACC)^1} + \frac{FCF_2}{(1 + WACC)^2} + \cdots + \frac{FCF_\infty}{(1 + WACC)^\infty}$$

Free cash flow (FCF)

Weighted average cost of capital (WACC)

Firm's debt/equity mix

Cost of debt

Dividends (D)

Cost of equity: The required return on stock

$$\text{Value of Stock} = \frac{D_1}{(1 + r_s)^1} + \frac{D_2}{(1 + r_s)^2} + \cdots + \frac{D_\infty}{(1 + r_s)^\infty}$$

8-1 Legal Rights and Privileges of Common Stockholders

Common stockholders are the *owners* of a corporation, and as such they have certain rights and privileges as discussed in this section.

8-1a Control of the Firm

A firm's common stockholders have the right to elect its directors, who, in turn, elect the officers who manage the business. In a small firm, the largest stockholder typically serves as president and chairperson of the board. In a large, publicly owned firm, the managers typically have some stock, but their personal holdings are generally insufficient to give them voting control. Thus, the managers of most publicly owned firms can be removed by the stockholders if the management team is not effective.

Corporations must hold periodic elections to select directors, usually once a year, with the vote taken at the annual meeting. At some companies, all directors are elected each year for a 1-year term. At other companies, the terms are staggered. For example, one-third of the directors might be elected each year for a 3-year term.

Each share of stock has one vote, so the owner of 1,000 shares has 1,000 votes for each director.[1] Stockholders can appear at the annual meeting and vote in person, but typically they transfer their right to vote to another party by means of a **proxy**. Management always solicits stockholders' proxies and usually gets them. However, if earnings are poor and stockholders are dissatisfied, an outside group may solicit the proxies in an effort to overthrow management and take control of the business. This is known as a **proxy fight**. Proxy fights are discussed in detail in Chapter 10.

8-1b The Preemptive Right

The **preemptive right** allows current common stockholders to purchase any additional shares sold by the firm. In some states, the preemptive right is automatically included in every corporate charter; in others, it is used only if it is specifically inserted into the charter.

The preemptive right enables current stockholders to maintain control, and it also prevents a transfer of wealth from current stockholders to new stockholders. If not for this safeguard, the management of a corporation could issue additional shares at a low price and purchase these shares itself. Management could thereby seize control of the corporation and steal value from the current stockholders. For example, suppose 1,000 shares of common stock, each with a price of $100, were outstanding, making the total market value of the firm $100,000. If an additional 1,000 shares were sold at $50 a share, or for $50,000, this would raise the total

---

1. In the situation described, a 1,000-share stockholder could cast 1,000 votes for each of three directors if there were three contested seats on the board. An alternative procedure that may be prescribed in the corporate charter calls for *cumulative voting*. Here the 1,000-share stockholder would get 3,000 votes if there were three vacancies, and he or she could cast all of them for one director. Cumulative voting helps minority stockholders (i.e., those who do not own a majority of the shares) get representation on the board.

market value to $150,000. When total market value is divided by new total shares outstanding, a value of $75 a share is obtained. The old stockholders thus lose $25 per share, and the new stockholders have an instant profit of $25 per share. Thus, selling common stock at a price below the market value would dilute its price and transfer wealth from the present stockholders to those who were allowed to purchase the new shares. The preemptive right prevents such occurrences.

8-2 Types of Common Stock

Although most firms have only one type of common stock, in some instances companies use **classified stock** to meet special needs. Generally, when special classifications are used, one type is designated *Class A,* another *Class B,* and so on. Small, new companies seeking funds from outside sources frequently use different types of common stock. For example, when Genetic Concepts went public, its Class A stock was sold to the public and paid a dividend, but this stock had no voting rights for 5 years. Its Class B stock, which the firm's organizers retained, had full voting rights for 5 years, but the legal terms stated that the company could not pay dividends on the Class B stock until it had established its earning power and built up retained earnings to a designated level. The use of classified stock thus enabled the public to take a position in a conservatively financed growth company without sacrificing income, while the founders retained absolute control during the crucial early stages of the firm's development. At the same time, outside investors were protected against excessive withdrawals of funds by the original owners. As is often the case in such situations, the Class B stock was called **founders' shares**.[2]

As these examples illustrate, the right to vote is often a distinguishing characteristic between different classes of stock. Suppose two classes of stock differ in only one respect: One class has voting rights but the other does not. As you would expect, the stock with voting rights would be more valuable. In the United States, which has a legal system with fairly strong protection for minority stockholders (that is, noncontrolling stockholders), voting stock typically sells at a price 4% to 6% above that of otherwise similar nonvoting stock. Thus, if a stock with no voting rights sold for $50, then one with voting rights would probably sell for $52 to $53. In countries with legal systems that provide less protection for minority stockholders, the right to vote is far more valuable. For example voting stock in Israel sells for 45% more on average than nonvoting stock, and voting stock in Italy has an 82% higher value than nonvoting stock.

Some companies have multiple lines of business, with each line having different growth prospects. Because cash flows for all business lines are mingled on financial

---

2. Note that the terms "Class A," "Class B," and so on have no standard meanings. Most firms have no classified shares, but a firm that does could designate its Class B shares as founders' shares and its Class A shares as those sold to the public; another firm might reverse these designations.

statements, some companies worry that investors are not able to value the high-growth business lines correctly. To separate the cash flows and to allow separate valuations, occasionally a company will have classes of stock with dividends tied to a particular part of a company. This is called **tracking stock**, or **target stock**. For example, in 2006 Liberty Media Corporation, a conglomerate that owned such entertainment assets as the Starz movie channel and investments in Time Warner, issued two different tracking stocks to track its two different business lines. One of these, Liberty Interactive tracking stock, was designed to track the performance of its QVC home shopping network and other high-growth Internet-based interactive assets. The other, Liberty Capital Group, comprised slower-growth holdings like the Starz Entertainment Group. The idea was that investors would assign a higher value to the high growth portion of the company if it traded separately.

However, many analysts are skeptical as to whether tracking stock increases a company's total market value. Companies still report consolidated financial statements for the entire company and have considerable leeway in allocating costs, deploying capital, and reporting the financial results for the various divisions, even those with tracking stock. Thus, a tracking stock is far from identical to the stock of an independent, stand-alone company. In fact, in 2014 Liberty scrapped plans to issue tracking stock for its cable business and, instead, made plans to create a separate publicly traded company to house that line of business.

> **SELF TEST**   What are some reasons why a company might use classified stock?

8-3 Stock Market Reporting

Stock price quotes and other information are readily available from Internet sources, including Zacks, Bloomberg, *The Wall Street Journal*, Google, and Yahoo.[3] Figure 8-1 shows a quote for MicroDrive. A typical quote shows the ticker symbol (MDVE), where the stock is traded (such as NASDAQ), and a time stamp. If the quote is during trading hours, then some sources report current information about the prices and volumes at which the stock could be bought (the Ask quote) or sold (the Bid quote). Otherwise, the reported quote is the last price at which the stock traded, which was $27.00 for MicroDrive. Most sources also show the change in the price ($0.50) and the percentage change (1.9%) from the previous day's closing price. This was a relatively slow day of trading for MicroDrive, as shown by the number of shares traded (830,000) versus the 30-day average of 1,356,539. Many sources provide "historical" price information. For example, MicroDrive closed the previous day at $26.50, opened the current day at $26.65 (implying there was positive news prior to the start of trading), went down to $26.15 during the day, increased to $27.40, and finally closed at $27.00. During the past 52 weeks, the price has been as high as $35.28 and as low as $20.30.

Most Web sites also report other data, such as the total market value of common stock (the Market Capitalization), the dividend, the dividend yield, and the

---

3. Most free sources actually provide quotes that are delayed by 20 minutes, but if you subscribe to a paid online service or have a brokerage account, you can generally get real-time quotes online.

FIGURE 8-1	Stock Quote for MicroDrive Inc.

MicroDrive, Inc. (MCDV)

27.00 (0.50, 1.9%) NASDAQ: 12/31/2015, 4:00 PM EST

Opening Price:	26.65	Dividends Per Share (Annual)	1.00
Ask Quote:	NA	Dividend Yield	3.70%
Bid Quote:	NA	Earnings Per Share (ttm)	4.40
Daily High:	27.40	Market Capitalization (Billions)	1.35
Daily Low:	26.15	Volume	830,000
Previous Closing Price:	26.50	30-Day Average Volume	1,356,539
52 Week High:	35.28		
52 Week Low:	20.30		

Note: For quotes of other companies, see **www.zacks.com/stocks**, **www.bloomberg.com**, **http://finance.yahoo.com**, or **http://quotes.wsj.com**.

most recent "ttm" ("trailing twelve months") of earnings per share. Some sites also provide a graph showing the stock's price over time and links to financial statements, research reports, historical ratios, analysts' forecasts of EPS and EPS growth rates, and a wealth of other data.

What information is provided on the Internet in addition to the stock's latest price?

SELF TEST

8-4 Valuing Common Stocks—Introducing the Free Cash Flow (FCF) Valuation Model

To make good decisions, a manager must be able to estimate the impact that possible strategies, tactics, and projects have on a company's value. In other words, a manager needs a tool that clearly shows the connections between managerial choices and firm value. This is exactly what the **free cash flow (FCF) valuation** model can do. The FCF valuation model defines the value of a company's operations as the present value of its expected free cash flows when discounted at the weighted average cost of capital (WACC). Managerial choices that change operating profitability, asset utilization, or growth also change FCF and, hence, the value of operations. Managerial choices that affect risk, such as implementing riskier strategies or changing the amount of debt financing, also affect the weighted average cost of capital, which affects the company's value. Therefore, the FCF valuation model is an important tool for managers.

Later in this chapter we describe two other valuation approaches, the dividend growth model and market multiples, but we begin with the FCF valuation model because it is applicable in more situations. For example, the FCF valuation model can be applied to all companies, whether or not they pay a dividend and whether they are publicly traded or privately held. It also can be applied to divisions within companies, and not just whole companies. The broad applicability and clear links between managerial decisions and value explain why the FCF model is the most widely used valuation model in merger and acquisition analysis.

8-4a Sources of Value and Claims on Value

Companies have two primary sources of value, the value of operations and the value of nonoperating assets. There are three major types of claims on this value: debt, preferred stock, and common stock. Following is a description of these sources and claims.

Sources of Value

Recall from Chapter 6 that free cash flow (FCF) is the cash flow available for distribution to *all* of a company's investors. The weighted average cost of capital (WACC) is the overall return required by *all* of a company's investors. Because FCF is generated by a company's operations, the present value of expected FCF when discounted by the WACC is equal to the company's **value of operations, V$_{op}$**:

(8–1)

$$V_{op} = \frac{FCF_1}{(1 + WACC)^1} + \frac{FCF_2}{(1 + WACC)^2} + \cdots + \frac{FCF_\infty}{(1 + WACC)^\infty}$$

$$= \sum_{t=1}^{\infty} \frac{FCF_t}{(1 + WACC)^t}$$

Even though the summation in Equation 8-1 goes to infinity, there are two situations in which we can calculate the value of this infinite sum: (1) the free cash flows are constant in each period, and (2) the free cash flows *eventually* grow at a constant rate. Virtually all companies fall into this second situation—free cash flows presently may be growing at nonconstant rates, but product maturation, competition, and market saturation eventually will cause the expected long-term growth rate to level off at a constant rate for all companies. We will apply this second, and more realistic, situation to several companies later in the chapter, but we start with the simplest situation because this provides a good overview of the valuation process.

Consider B&B Corporation, which owns and manages several bed and breakfast inns located in historic Philadelphia. B&B generated $10 million in free cash flow in the most recent year. B&B's stockholders have strong local ties and do not wish to expand. Therefore, B&B expects to have a constant free cash flow of $10 million each year for the foreseeable future.

B&B's estimated weighted average cost of capital is 10%, which is the rate B&B must earn on its investments to fairly compensate its investors, a combination of debtholders, preferred stockholders, and common stockholders. We will show how to estimate the WACC in Chapter 11, but for now will just accept 10% as B&B's estimated WACC.

The value of operations is the present value of all expected free cash flows discounted at the cost of capital. Because the FCFs are expected to be constant, the cash flow stream is a perpetuity (see Web Chapter 28 for a review of perpetuities). The present value of a perpetuity is the cash flow divided by the cost of capital:

$$V_{op} \text{ (for a perpetuity)} = \frac{FCF}{WACC} \qquad (8\text{--}2)$$

Therefore, B&B's value of operations is $100 million:

$$V_{op} \text{ (for a perpetuity)} = \frac{FCF}{WACC} = \frac{\$10}{0.10} = \$100 \qquad (8\text{--}2a)$$

The primary source of value for most companies is the value of operations. A secondary source of value comes from **nonoperating assets**, which are also called financial assets. There are two major types of nonoperating assets: (1) Short-term investments, which are very marketable short-term securities (like T-bills) that are temporarily held for future needs rather than to support current operations; (2) Other nonoperating assets, which often are investments in other businesses. For example, Ford Motor Company's automotive operation held about $20.7 billion in marketable securities at the end of March 2014, and this was in addition to $4.5 billion in cash. Second, Ford also had $3.8 billion of investments in other businesses, which were reported on the asset side of the balance sheet as "Equity in Net Assets of Affiliated Companies." In total, Ford had $20.7 + $3.8 = $24.5 billion of nonoperating assets, amounting to 26% of its $92.5 billion of total automotive assets. For most companies, the percentage is much lower. For example, as of the end of January 2014, Walmart's percentage of nonoperating assets was less than 1%, which is more typical.

We see, then, that for most companies, operating assets are far more important than nonoperating assets. Moreover, companies can influence the values of their operating assets, whereas market forces determine the values of short-term investments and other nonoperating assets.

A company's **total intrinsic value** is the value of operations plus the value of short-term investments (assuming the company owns no other nonoperating assets, which is true for most companies). This is called the intrinsic value (or fundamental value) to distinguish it from the market value—the market value is whatever price the market is willing to pay, but the intrinsic value is estimated from the expected cash flows:

$$\text{Total intrinsic value} = \text{Value of operations} + \text{Short-term investments} \qquad (8\text{--}3)$$

B&B has $2 million in bank certificates of deposit, earning a little interest while B&B decides how to use the funds. Because B&B does not need the $2 million to run its operations, these should be classified as short-term investments. Therefore, from Equation 8-3 the total intrinsic value of B&B is:

$$\text{Total intrinsic value} = \text{Value of operations} + \text{Short-term investments}$$
$$= \$100 + \$2 = \$102$$

Because the FCF valuation model determines the total value of the firm before estimating the per share stock price, it is called an **entity valuation model.** The following section explains how to use the estimated entity value (i.e., the total value of the firm) to estimate the value of common stock.

Claims on Value

For a company that is a going concern, debtholders have the first claim on value in the sense that interest and scheduled principal payments must be paid before any preferred or common dividends can be paid. Preferred stockholders have the next claim because preferred dividends must be paid before common dividends. Common shareholders come last in this pecking order and have a residual claim on the company's value.

The estimated **intrinsic value of equity** is the remaining value after subtracting the claims of debtholders and preferred stockholders from the total intrinsic value:

(8–4)

$$\text{Intrinsic value of equity} = \text{Total intrinsic value} - \text{All debt} - \text{Preferred stock}$$

B&B owes a total of $28 million in mortgages and bank loans. B&B also has $4 million of preferred stock outstanding which was issued to the founders' families early in the company's life. B&B's estimated intrinsic value of equity is:

$$\text{Intrinsic value of equity} = \text{Total intrinsic value} - \text{All debt} - \text{Preferred stock}$$
$$= \$102 - \$28 - \$4$$
$$= \$70$$

8-4b The Intrinsic Value per Share of Common Stock

The estimated **intrinsic stock price** is equal to the intrinsic value of equity divided by the number of shares:

(8–5)

$$\text{Intrinsic stock price} = \text{Intrinsic value of equity} / \text{Number of shares}$$

B&B has 5 million shares of common stock outstanding. Therefore, B&B's estimated intrinsic stock price is:

$$\text{Intrinsic stock price} = \text{Intrinsic value of equity} / \text{Number of shares}$$
$$= \$70 / 5 = \$14 \text{ dollars per share}$$

Figure 8-2 summarizes these calculations and shows B&B's two value "pies"—one pie shows the sources of value and the other pies shows the "pieces" belonging to debtholders, preferred stockholders, and common stockholders.

FIGURE 8-2	B&B Corporation's Sources of Value and Claims on Value (Millions of Dollars except Per Share Data)

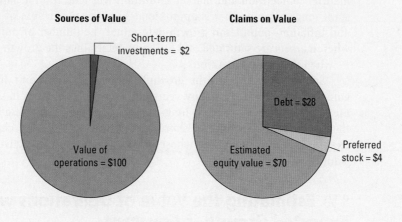

Why is the free cash flow valuation model so widely used?

Write out the equation for the value of operations.

Explain how to estimate the price per share using the free cash flow valuation model.

A company expects a constant FCF of $240 million per year forever. If the WACC is 12%, what is the value of operations? **($2,000 million)**

A company has a current value of operations of $800 million, and it holds $100 million in short-term investments. If the company has $400 million in debt and has 10 million common shares outstanding, what is the estimated price per share? **($50.00)**

8-5 The Constant Growth Model: Valuation When Expected Free Cash Flow Grows at a Constant Rate

The company in the previous section illustrates the FCF valuation model's steps, but the perpetuity approach is not applicable to most companies because their cash flows aren't constant. In fact, most companies expect to have growing cash flows, often with nonconstant growth rates in the near future. However, even if free cash flows currently are growing at nonconstant rates, the expected *long-term* free cash flows should eventually level off at a constant rate for all companies. To see this, think about the impact of competition and market saturation. For a firm to grow faster than the economy, either the industry must become a bigger part of the economy or the firm must take market share from its competitors. However, market saturation eventually limits the size of the industry and competition limits the ability to take market share while maintaining profits. This means that as markets mature, competition and market saturation will tend to limit FCF growth to a constant long-term rate that is approximately equal to the sum of population growth and inflation—population growth determines the number of units that can be sold when markets are saturated and inflation determines the growth in prices and profits when there is competition.

Some companies are in growing industries and won't hit their long-term constant growth rate for many years, but some mature firms in saturated industries are already at their constant long-term growth rate. We will address valuation in the presence of nonconstant short-term growth later in the chapter, but we now examine a mature company whose free cash flows are expected to grow at a constant rate.

8-5a Estimating the Value of Operations when Expected Growth is Constant

Recall that the value of operations is the present value of expected free cash flows discounted at the weighted average cost of capital. There is a simple formula to find the present value of cash flows growing at a constant rate, but it is easy to misapply the formula if you don't understand its logic. To help you avoid this mistake, we will proceed step-by-step.

Suppose we can estimate the first expected free cash flow (FCF_1) and it is expected to grow at a constant long-term growth rate of g_L. Since the growth rate is constant, we can write the value of a free cash flow for any year as the compounded free cash flow from the previous year:

(8–6)
$$FCF_t = FCF_{t-1}(1 + g_L)$$

For example, if the first expected free cash flow is \$105 (i.e., $FCF_1 = \$105$) and the expected growth rate thereafter is 5%, then the expected free cash flow at t = 2 is:

(8–6a)
$$FCF_2 = FCF_1(1 + g_L)$$

$$FCF_2 = \$105(1 + 0.05) = \$110.25$$

Using this result, we can reapply Equation 8-6 to estimate the free cash flow at t = 3:

(8–6b)
$$FCF_3 = FCF_2(1 + g_L)$$

$$= \$110.25(1 + 0.05) = \$115.7625$$

Rather than estimate future free cash flows using this sequential approach, we can express the free cash flow at any future date using the first expected free cash flow and the constant expected growth rate:

$$FCF_t = FCF_1 (1 + g_L)^{t-1}$$

(8–7)

For example, we can use Equation 8-7 to estimate the free cash flow at t = 3:

$$FCF_t = FCF_1 (1 + g_L)^{t-1}$$
$$FCF_3 = FCF_1 (1 + g_L)^{3-1}$$

(8–7a)

$$= \$105 (1 + 0.05)^2 = \$115.7625$$

Notice that this is the same value we found using Equation 8-7 in a sequential manner.

Now that we have an expression for future free cash flows, we can take Equation 8-1 (which shows the present value of all expected free cash flows) and substitute Equation 8-7 (which shows the value at time t of a constantly growing FCF), giving us the value of operations when FCF is expected to grow at a constant rate:

$$
\begin{aligned}
V_{op} \text{ (constant growth)} &= \frac{FCF_1}{(1 + WACC)^1} + \frac{FCF_2}{(1 + WACC)^2} + \cdots + \frac{FCF_\infty}{(1 + WACC)^\infty} \\
&= \frac{FCF_1}{(1 + WACC)^1} + \frac{FCF_1(1 + g_L)^1}{(1 + WACC)^2} + \cdots + \frac{FCF_1(1 + g_L)^{t-1}}{(1 + WACC)^t} \cdots + \frac{FCF_1(1 + g_L)^{\infty-1}}{(1 + WACC)^\infty} \\
&= \sum_{t=1}^{\infty} \frac{FCF_1(1 + g_L)^{t-1}}{(1 + WACC)^t} \\
&= \sum_{t=1}^{\infty} \left[\frac{FCF_1}{1 + g_L}\right]\left[\frac{1 + g_L}{1 + WACC}\right]^t \\
&= \frac{FCF_1}{1 + g_L} \sum_{t=1}^{\infty} \left[\frac{1 + g_L}{1 + WACC}\right]^t
\end{aligned}
$$

(8–8)

The last row of Equation 8-8 is a summation to infinity, but take a close look at the term in brackets. If the long-term growth rate of g_L is less than the WACC, then the term in brackets is less than 1. When you compound a number that is less than 1, you get a number that is even smaller, and the infinite summation of ever-shrinking numbers is not necessarily equal to infinity. To see this, let's pick a number that is less than 1, compound it, and look at its cumulative compounded sum for several years. The time line below shows the year (t), the compounded value of ½ (which is less than 1) at each year, and the cumulative sum. For example, at

Year 1, we have ½ compounded once, which is ½. The cumulative sum is just ½, too, because this is the first year. For Year 2 we have ½ squared, which is ¼. The cumulative sum is the previous sum of ½ plus ¼, which is ¾. The other entries are calculated similarly.

Year t =	1	2	3	4	5
$(1/2)^t$ =	1/2	1/4	1/8	1/16	1/32
Cumulative sum of $(1/2)^t$ =	1/2	3/4	7/8	15/16	31/32

We stopped after 5 years, but it appears as though the cumulative sum would not grow to infinity even if we continued adding years. In fact, it looks as though the cumulative sum is getting closer and closer to 1, but not exceeding 1. In other words, the cumulative sum is converging to 1.

The infinite sum of free cash flows in Equation 8-8 also converges if the growth rate is less than the WACC. The formula is:

(8–9)

$$V_{op}\text{(constant growth)} = \frac{FCF_1}{1 + g_L} \sum_{t=1}^{\infty} \left[\frac{1 + g_L}{1 + WACC} \right]^t$$

$$= \frac{FCF_1}{1 + g_L} \left[\frac{1 + g_L}{WACC - g_L} \right]$$

$$= \frac{FCF_1}{WACC - g_L}$$

WEB

The last term in Equation 8-8 is derived in **Web Extension 8A** on the textbook's Web site.

Equation 8-9 is called the **constant growth model**, and it provides a simple formula for the present value of an infinite stream of constantly growing free cash flows. However, be alert when using Equation 8-9, because we have seen many students try to apply it prematurely when the growth rate has not yet leveled off to a value less than WACC. They come up with a negative value, based on the third row of Equation 8-9. They overlooked the fact that the third row is valid only if the infinite summation converges, which only can happen if $g_L < $ WACC. In fact, if g_L is greater than or equal to WACC, the bracketed term in the first row of Equation 8-9 is greater than or equal to 1, so its infinite summation is equal to infinity. We really want students to avoid this mistake, so please don't use Equation 8-9 if $g_L \geq$ WACC!

There are two related cases for the constant growth model. The first is when constant growth begins at t = 1 and the second is when constant growth begins at t = 0.

Case 1: Application of the Constant Growth Model When Constant Growth Begins at t = 1

Let's apply the constant growth model to a company with an expected free cash flow of $105 at t = 1 and an expected constant growth rate of 5% thereafter.

Suppose the weighted average cost of capital is 9%. The growth rate is less than the cost of capital, so we can use Equation 8-9 to estimate the value of operations:

$$V_{op} \text{ (constant growth)} = \frac{FCF_1}{WACC - g_L} \quad \text{(8–9a)}$$

$$= \frac{\$105}{0.09 - 0.05}$$
$$= \$2,625$$

Case 2: Application of the Constant Growth Model When Constant Growth Begins at t = 0

Equation 8-9 is valid any time we have an estimate of the first cash flow and the expected growth is constant thereafter. But Equation 8-9 is also valid if constant growth begins immediately. In this situation, we can estimate the first expected free cash flow using the most recent actual free cash flow:

$$FCF_1 = FCF_0 (1 + g_L) \quad \text{(8–6c)}$$

Substituting this into Equation 8-9 provides a way to calculate the present value of future cash flows if growth begins immediately:

$$V_{op} \text{ (immediate constant growth)} = \frac{FCF_1}{WACC - g_L} = \frac{FCF_0(1 + g_L)}{WACC - g_L} \quad \text{(8–10)}$$

For example, suppose a company's most recent free cash flow was $200 and it expects FCF to begin growing immediately at a 7% constant growth rate and that the cost of capital is 12%. Again, noting that the growth rate is less than the cost of capital, we can apply the constant growth model in Equation 8-10 to find the value of operations to be:

$$V_{op} \text{ (immediate constant growth)} = \frac{FCF_0(1 + g_L)}{WACC - g_L}$$

$$= \frac{\$200(1 + 0.07)}{0.12 - 0.07}$$

$$= \$4,280$$

8-5b How to Avoid Common Mistakes When Applying the Constant Growth Model

Here are three mistakes to avoid when using the constant growth model. First, the model is applicable only if the expected growth rate is constant and is less than the weighted average cost of capital. If growth is greater than the cost of capital, you must use the multi-stage model that we describe in the next section.

Second, the constant growth models are calculating the present value of all future cash flows from t = 1 to infinity, *not from t = 0 to infinity!* The cash flow at t = 0 has just occurred, so it is in the past and is not included in the present value of *future* cash flows. Even though the numerator of Equation 8-10 shows FCF_0, it is shown there only because it is used to estimate FCF_1, not because FCF_0 is included in the present value of future free cash flows.

Third, don't use Equation 8-10 if constant growth doesn't begin immediately. For example, suppose FCF_0 = $963, FCF_1 is estimated to be $1,040, WACC is 9% and the expected growth rate from t = 1 and thereafter is 4%. Notice that the growth rate from t = 0 to t = 1 is 8% = ($1040 − $963)/$963. However, the value of operations is the present value of *future* free cash flows, and those future free cash flows beyond t = 1 are growing at a constant rate of 4% even though the current FCF is growing at 8%. Therefore, you must use Equation 8-9 instead of 8-10 to find the value of operations, as follows:

(8–9b)

$$V_{op} \text{ (constant growth)} = \frac{FCF_1}{WACC - g_L}$$

$$= \frac{\$1,040}{0.09 - 0.04}$$

$$= \$20,800$$

Now suppose that the current free cash flow is $1,000 and all the other inputs are the same as in the example. The current free cash flow is expected to grow by 4% = ($1,040 – $1,000)/$1,000 from t = 0 to t = 1, and then continue to grow at a constant rate of 4%. In this case, you could use either Equation 8-9 or 8-10 because $FCF_1 = FCF_0(1 + g_L)$.

SELF TEST

A company expects to have an FCF in 1 year of $300, which is expected to grow at a constant rate of 3% forever. If the WACC is 11%, what is the value of operations? **($3,750)**

A company's most recent free cash flow was $270. The company expects to have an FCF in 1 year of $300, which is expected to grow at a constant rate of 3% forever. If the WACC is 11%, what is the value of operations? **($3,750)**

A company's most recent free cash flow was $500 and is expected to grow at a constant rate of 4% forever. If the WACC is 10%, what is the value of operations? **($10,400)**

8-6 The Multi-Stage Model: Valuation When Expected Short-Term Free Cash Flow Grows at a Nonconstant Rate

The annual growth in expected free cash flows of most companies is nonconstant for years before eventually leveling off at a sustainable long-term constant growth rate. Because the short-term growth rates are nonconstant, we cannot immediately apply the constant growth model from the previous section. However, we can use the **multi-stage valuation model** to estimate the value of operations, as described in the following steps:

Step 1. Forecast expected free cash flows and calculate the annual growth rates for each year in the forecast. Continue forecasting additional years until the growth rate in FCF is expected to become constant. The last year in the forecast is called the **forecast horizon**. It is also called the **horizon date** or the **terminal date** (because it is at the end of the explicit forecast, not because the free cash flows terminate). For companies in mature, highly competitive markets, you may need to forecast only a few years. For companies in high-growth industries you may need to forecast 15 to 25 years.

Step 2. Because expected growth is constant after the horizon date, you can apply the constant growth model from the previous section to estimate the value of operations at the horizon year. This is called the **horizon value**, and it is the value of all free cash flows *beyond* the horizon discounted back to the horizon. In other words, it is how much the operations would be worth if they were sold immediately after receiving the FCF at the horizon date. This is also called the **terminal value** (because it is at the end of the explicit forecast) or the **continuing value** (because it is the value if operations continue to be used rather than be liquidated).

Step 3. Create a time line with the free cash flows for each year up to the horizon date. The time line should also include the horizon value at the horizon date. This means there will be two cash flows on the horizon date, the free cash flow for that year and the previously-calculated horizon value.

Step 4. Discount the cash flows in the time line using the weighted average cost of capital. The result is the estimated value of operations as of t = 0.

The following example illustrates this approach.

8-6a The Forecast Period and the Horizon Value

We will forecast MicroDrive's free cash flows later in the chapter, but for now let's focus on Thurman Corporation, a fast-growing company in the health care industry. Thurman's expected free cash flows (in millions) for the next 4 years are shown below:

Year	0	1	2	3	4
FCF		−$20	$80	$100	$110
Growth in FCF				25%	10%

Thurman expects to have a negative FCF in Year 1 due to the company's rapid expansion. Free cash flows become positive at Year 2 and grow rapidly for a couple of years. Thurman expects competition and market saturation to reduce its growth rate after Year 4 to 5% for all years in the foreseeable future. This is why Thurman ends its explicit forecast period at Year 4.

Because growth is constant after Year 4, we can apply the constant growth formula at Year 4 to find the present value of all the cash flows from Year 5 to infinity when discounted back to Year 4. This is result is the horizon value at Year 4, HV_4. If growth in FCF is expected to be constant after Year t, the general formula for the horizon value at Year t is:

(8–11)
$$HV_t = \frac{FCF_t(1 + g_L)}{WACC - g_L}$$

Thurman's cost of capital is 15%. We can apply Equation 8-11 to estimate Thurman's horizon value at Year 4:

(8–11a)
$$HV_4 = \frac{FCF_4(1 + g_L)}{WACC - g_L}$$

$$= \frac{\$110(1 + 0.05)}{0.15 - 0.05}$$

$$= \$1,155 \text{ million}$$

Figure 8-3 summarizes the calculation of the horizon value. We explain the other steps shown in the Figure 8-3 in the continuing description of the multi-stage model.

8-6b The Current Value of Operations

Now that we have estimated Thurman's horizon value, we can lay out a time line of the free cash flows and the horizon value:

Year	0	1	2	3	4
FCF		–$20	$80	$100	$110
Horizon value at Year 4, HV_4					$1,155

The current value of operations ($V_{op,0}$) is the present value of all future free cash flows discounted back to Year 0. We estimate the current value of operations in three steps: (1) estimate the present value of the free cash flows in the forecast period; (2) estimate the present value of the horizon value; (3) add the present value of the free cash flows to the present value of the horizon value. Here is the intuition—the

FIGURE 8-3 Thurman Corporation's Value of Operations (Millions of Dollars)

	A	B	C	D	E	F	G	H
228	INPUTS:							
229	g_L =	5%						
230	WACC =	15%		Projections				
231	Year	0	1	2	3	4		
232	FCF		−$20.00	$80.00	$100.00	$110.00	→→ →↴	↓
233			↓	↓	↓	↓		
234			FCF_1	FCF_2	FCF_3	FCF_4	HV = $V_{op(t=4)}$	
235			—	—	—	—	↓	
236			$(1+WACC)^1$	$(1+WACC)^2$	$(1+WACC)^3$	$(1+WACC)^4$	$FCF_4(1+g_L)$	
237			↓	↓	↓	↓	—	
238			↓	↓	↓	↓	$(WACC-g_L)$	
239			↓	↓	↓	↓	↓	
240			↓	↓	↓	↓	$115.500	
241		−$17.391 ←←↵	↓	↓	↓		10.00%	
242	PVs of FCFs	$60.491 ←←←←	←↵	↓	↓		↓	
243		$65.752 ←←←←	←←←←	←↵	↓		$1,155.000	
244		$62.893 ←←←←	←←←←	←←←←	←↵		↓	
245	PV of HV	$660.375 ←←←←	←←←←	←←←←	$1,155.000	←←←↵		
246		↓			= —			
247	V_{op} =	$832.12			$(1+WACC)^4$			

Note: Numbers in the figure are shown as rounded values for clarity in reporting. However, unrounded values are used for all calculations. See the *Excel Tool Kit* for this chapter.

Microsoft Excel® is a registered trademark of Microsoft Corporation. © 2014 Microsoft.

owner of the operations collects the FCF from Year 1 to Year 4 and then immediately sells the operations one second after collecting the FCF at Year 4. The purchaser pays a price at Year 4 equal to the present value of the FCF beyond Year 4 discounted back to Year 4. Therefore, the current value to the owner is the present value of the free cash flows and "sales" price that the owner expects to receive. Notice that this is similar to finding the value of a bond, which is equal to the present value of its coupons plus the present value of the par value paid at maturity.[4]

If the horizon date is Year T, then the current value of operations is:

$$V_{op,0} = \sum_{t=1}^{T} \frac{FCF_t}{(1+WACC)^t} + \frac{HV_T}{(1+WACC)^T}$$

(8–12)

Let's apply this to Thurman Corporation. The present value of the free cash flows from Years 1 through 4 is:

4. You may have noticed that we could have defined the horizon date at Year 3 because we have an estimate of the Year 4 free cash flow, which is expected to grow at a constant rate thereafter. However, we recommend defining the horizon date as the last date in the forecast period even if growth becomes constant at or prior to this date because we have found that doing so leads to fewer errors. We illustrate this approach in the *Excel Tool Kit* for the interested reader.

$$\text{PV of FCF} = \frac{\text{FCF}_1}{(1 + \text{WACC})^1} + \frac{\text{FCF}_2}{(1 + \text{WACC})^2} + \frac{\text{FCF}_3}{(1 + \text{WACC})^3} + \frac{\text{FCF}_4}{(1 + \text{WACC})^4}$$

$$= \frac{-\$20}{(1 + 0.15)^1} + \frac{\$80}{(1 + 0.15)^2} + \frac{\$100}{(1 + 0.15)^3} + \frac{\$110}{(1 + 0.15)^4}$$

$$= \$171.745$$

The present value of the horizon value is:

$$\text{Present value of HV}_4 = \frac{\text{HV}_4}{(1 + \text{WACC})^4}$$

$$= \frac{\$1,155}{(1 + 0.15)^4} = \$660.375$$

The value of operations at Year 0 is equal to the sum of the present value of the horizon value and the present value of the free cash flows:

(8–12a)

$$V_{op,0} = \sum_{t=1}^{4} \frac{\text{FCF}_t}{(1 + \text{WACC})^t} + \frac{\text{HV}_4}{(1 + \text{WACC})^4}$$

$$= \$171.745 + \$660.375$$
$$= \$832.12$$

We apply this approach in the next section to estimate MicroDrive's value.[5]

SELF TEST

What is the *horizon value*? Why is it also called the *terminal value* or *continuing value*?

A company expects to have an FCF at Year 10 of $600, which is expected to grow at a constant rate of 4% thereafter. If the WACC is 12%, what is the value of operations at Year 10, HV_{10}? **($15,600)**

A company expects FCF of −$10 million at Year 1 and FCF of $20 million at Year 2; after Year 2, FCF is expected to grow at a 5% rate. If the WACC is 10%, then what is the horizon value of operations, $V_{op(Year\ 2)}$? **($420 million)** What is the current value of operations, $V_{op(Year\ 0)}$? **($354.55 million)**

---

5. When using a financial calculator, it requires fewer steps if you combine the free cash flow in the last year and the horizon value into a single cash flow. For example, you could find Thurman's value of operations as:

$$V_{op,0} = \frac{\text{FCF}_1}{(1 + \text{WACC})^1} + \frac{\text{FCF}_2}{(1 + \text{WACC})^2} + \frac{\text{FCF}_3}{(1 + \text{WACC})^3} + \frac{(\text{FCF}_4 + \text{HV}_4)}{(1 + \text{WACC})^4}$$

$$= \frac{-\$20}{(1 + 0.15)^1} + \frac{\$80}{(1 + 0.15)^2} + \frac{\$100}{(1 + 0.15)^3} + \frac{(\$110 + \$1,155)}{(1 + 0.15)^4}$$

$$= \$832.12$$

This procedure saves a step in the calculations. However, combining cash flows makes it easier to make an error, so we recommend using this approach only if you are extremely careful and confident.

8-7 Application of the FCF Valuation Model to MicroDrive

We now apply the free cash flow valuation model to MicroDrive, beginning with a simple approach to estimate free cash flows.

8-7a Forecasting MicroDrive's Free Cash Flows

We will forecast MicroDrive's full set of financial statements in Chapter 9, but for purposes of valuation we need only forecast certain components of the financial statements, the ones that determine free cash flows. In particular, we will forecast sales, net operating profit after taxes, and total net operating capital. But before we plunge into the forecast, let's take a look at MicroDrive's current situation.

MicroDrive's Current Situation

Figure 8-4 shows MicroDrive's most recent financial statements and selected additional data. Chapters 6 and 7 explain ratio analyses in detail, but here we only focus on the items that are required to forecast free cash flows.

Figure 8-5 shows the calculation of free cash flow and other selected performance measures for the previous 2 years. We can see that MicroDrive's return on invested capital is much lower than that of its industry peers (9.84% versus 15.04%).

FIGURE 8-4   MicroDrive's Most Recent Financial Statements (Millions, Except for Per Share Data)

	A	B	C	D	E	F
260	INCOME STATEMENTS			BALANCE SHEETS		
261		2014	2015	*Assets*	2014	2015
262	Net sales	$ 4,760	$ 5,000	Cash	$ 60	$ 50
263	COGS (excl. depr.)	3,560	3,800	ST Investments	40	–
264	Depreciation	170	200	Accounts receivable	380	500
265	Other operating expense	480	500	Inventories	820	1,000
266	EBIT	$ 550	$ 500	Total CA	$ 1,300	$ 1,550
267	Interest expense	100	120	Net PP&E	1,700	2,000
268	Pre-tax earnings	$ 450	$ 380	Total assets	$ 3,000	$ 3,550
269	Taxes (40%)	180	152			
270	NI before pref. div.	$ 270	$ 228	*Liabilities and equity*		
271	Preferred div.	8	8	Accounts payable	$ 190	$ 200
272	Net income	$ 262	$ 220	Accruals	280	300
273				Notes payable	130	280
274	*Other Data*			Total CL	$ 600	$ 780
275	Common dividends	$48	$50	Long-term bonds	1,000	1,200
276	Addition to RE	$214	$170	Total liabilities	$ 1,600	$ 1,980
277	Tax rate	40%	40%	Preferred stock	100	100
278	Shares of common stock	50	50	Common stock	500	500
279	Price per share	$40.00	$27.00	Retained earnings	800	970
280				Total common equity	$ 1,300	$ 1,470
281	Weighted average cost			Total liabs. & equity	$ 3,000	$ 3,550
282	of capital (WACC)	10.50%	10.97%			

FIGURE 8-5 Key Performance Measures for MicroDrive (Millions, Except for Per Share Data)

	A	B	C	D	E	F	G
						MicroDrive	Industry
289							
290					2014	2015	2015
291	*Calculating Net Operating Profit After Taxes (NOPAT)*						
292	NOPAT = EBIT(1 − T)				$330	$300	
293	*Calculating Net Operating Working Capital (NOWC)*						
294	Operating current assets				$1,260	$1,550	
295	− Operating current liabilities				$470	$500	
296	NOWC				$790	$1,050	
297	*Calculating Total Net Operating Capital (OpCap)*						
298	NOWC				$790	$1,050	
299	+ Net PP&E				$1,700	$2,000	
300	OpCap				$2,490	$3,050	
301	Investment in operating capital					$560	
302	*Calculating Free Cash Flow (FCF)*						
303	FCF = NOPAT − Investment in operating capital					−$260	
304	*Calculating Return on Invested Capital (ROIC)*						
305	ROIC = NOPAT/Total net operating capital				13.25%	9.84%	15.04%
306	*Calculating the Operating Profitability Ratio (OP)*						
307	OP = NOPAT/Sales				6.93%	6.00%	6.92%
308	*Calculating Capital Requirement Ratio (CR)*						
309	CR = Total net operating capital/Sales				52.31%	61.00%	46.00%
310							

Note: Numbers in the figure are shown as rounded values for clarity in reporting. However, unrounded values are used for all calculations. See the *Excel Tool Kit* for this chapter.

Microsoft Excel® is a registered trademark of Microsoft Corporation. © 2014 Microsoft.

MicroDrive's operating profitability has fallen so that it is now lower than the industry average (6.00% versus 6.92%). MicroDrive's asset utilization efficiency has drastically worsened, as shown by the increase in its capital requirement ratio (which means that MicroDrive now requires more capital to generate a dollar of sales), and is significantly worse than the industry average (61% versus 46%). We first will forecast MicroDrive's free cash flows assuming that these ratios remain unchanged and then show how MicroDrive's value of operations would be affected by improvements in the ratios.

Forecasting Sales, Net Operating Profit after Taxes, and Total Net Operating Capital

The first step is to forecast sales. MicroDrive's managers estimate that sales will initially grow at a 10% rate but will decline to a sustainable long-term growth rate of 5% due to market saturation and competition; see Panel A in Figure 8-6 for the forecasted sales growth rates in each year of the 5-year forecast period. Had MicroDrive's managers projected nonconstant growth for more than 5 years, new columns for additional years would be added to Figure 8-6 until the growth rate does level out. Keep in mind that this is just a preliminary estimate and that it is easy to make changes in the *Excel* model (after doing the hard work to build the model!).

MicroDrive's managers initially assume that the operating profitability ratio (OP) and the capital requirement ratio (CR) will remain unchanged. We begin with

FIGURE 8-6	MicroDrive's Forecast of Operations for the Selected Scenario (Millions of Dollars, Except for Per Share Data)

	A	B	C	D	E	F	G	H	I
324	**Status Quo**	**Industry**	**MicroDrive**				**MicroDrive**		
325	**Panel A**	**Actual**	**Actual**				**Forecast**		
326	*Operating Ratios*	2015	2014	2015	2016	2017	2018	2019	2020
327	g = Sales growth rate		*15%*	*5%*	10%	8%	7%	5%	5%
328	OP = NOPAT/Sales	6.92%	*6.9%*	6%	6%	6%	6%	6%	6%
329	CR = OpCap/Sales	46.0%	*52.3%*	61%	61%	61%	61%	61%	61%
330	Tax rate	40%	*40%*	*40%*	40%	40%	40%	40%	40%
331	**Panel B**			**Actual**			**Forecast**		
332	*Operating Items*			*2015*	2016	2017	2018	2019	2020
333	Net sales			*$5,000*	$5,500	$5,940	$6,356	$6,674	$7,007.270
334	Net operating profit after taxes			*$300*	$330	$356	$381	$400	$420.436
335	Total net operating capital			*$3,050*	$3,355	$3,623	$3,877	$4,071	$4,274.434
336	FCF = NOPAT – Investment in OpCap			–$260	$25	$88	$128	$207	$216.892
337	Growth in FCF					252%	45.1%	61.7%	5.0%
338	ROIC = NOPAT/OpCap			9.84%	9.84%	9.84%	9.84%	9.84%	9.84%

Note: Numbers in the figure are shown as rounded values for clarity in reporting. However, unrounded values are used for all calculations. See the *Excel **Tool Kit*** for this chapter.

this Status Quo scenario, but we also will explore other scenarios later in the chapter. Panel A of Figure 8-6 shows the input ratios, including actual recent values of the ratios for industry peers (the silver section), actual values for MicroDrive's past 2 years, and forecasted values for MicroDrive's 5-year forecast. The blue section shows inputs for the first year and inputs for any subsequent years that differ from the previous year.

Panel B of Figure 8-6 begins with the forecast of net sales based on the previous year's sales and the forecasted growth rate in sales. For example, the forecast of net sales for 2017 is:

$$\text{Sales}_{2017} = (1 + g_{2016,2017})\,\text{Sales}_{2016}$$
$$= (1 + 0.10)(\$5{,}000) = \$5{,}500$$

The next row shows the forecast of net operating profit after taxes. We will forecast NOPAT's separate components in Chapter 9, but for now we assume that the NOPAT for a particular year will be proportional to the sales for that year. This means we can forecast NOPAT as the product of sales and the operating profitability ratio. For example, the forecast of NOPAT for 2017 is:

$$\text{NOPAT}_{2017} = (\text{Sales}_{2017})\,(\text{OP}_{2017})$$
$$= (\$5{,}500)(0.06) = \$330$$

To support additional sales, we assume that total net operating capital (OpCap) must grow. We forecast OpCap's individual components in Chapter 9, but for now we assume that OpCap will be proportional to sales, so the forecast is equal to sales multiplied by the capital requirement ratio. For example, the forecast of OpCap for 2017 is:

$$\text{OpCap}_{2017} = (\text{Sales}_{2017})\,(\text{CR}_{2017})$$
$$= (\$5,500)\,(0.61) = \$3,355$$

With forecasts of NOPAT and total net operating capital, it is straightforward to calculate the forecasted FCF. For example, the forecasted FCF for 2017 is:

$$\text{FCF}_{2017} = \text{NOPAT}_{2017} - (\text{OpCap}_{2017} - \text{OpCap}_{2016})$$
$$= \$330 - (\$3,355 - \$3,050)$$
$$= \$25$$

Figure 8-6 shows the estimated free cash flows for each year in the forecast period. Notice that FCF is growing at the same rate as sales by the last year in the forecast period and that the input ratios for operating profit and capital utilization have not changed in the 2 years prior to the end of the forecast period. Therefore, we can be sure that the growth in FCF has levelled off to the long-term growth rate of 5% and we don't need to forecast any additional years. Had the input ratios and growth rates not been stable by the end of 5 years, then we would have continued to forecast more years until they were stable.

Notice that the forecasted ROIC of 9.84% is identical to the most recent actual ROIC. This should make sense, because the forecasted inputs for the operations (i.e., the OP and CR ratios) are the same as those in the most recent year. In other words, if operations aren't changing, then the ROIC shouldn't change.

Now that we have a forecast of FCF, we can estimate the value of operations, beginning with the horizon value.

8-7b MicroDrive's Horizon Value

We apply the horizon value formula at the last year in the forecast (2021) because expected growth is constant afterwards for the foreseeable future.[6] Recall from Figure 8-4 that Microdrive's WACC for 2016 and years thereafter is 10.97%. For MicroDrive, the horizon value is the present value of all the cash flows from 2022 to infinity when discounted back to 2021, which is:

(8–11b)

$$\text{HV}_t = \frac{\text{FCF}_t(1 + g_L)}{\text{WACC} - g_L}$$

$$\text{HV}_{2021} = \frac{\text{FCF}_{2021}(1 + g_L)}{\text{WACC} - g_L}$$

$$= \frac{\$216.892(1 + 0.05)}{0.1097 - 0.05} = \$3,814.68$$

Figure 8-7 summarizes the calculation of the horizon value and the subsequent calculations needed to estimate the value of operations.

---

6. We could have defined the horizon date to be 2019 because we have an estimate of the 2020 free cash flow, which is expected to grow at a constant rate thereafter. But as we stated previously, we recommend defining the horizon date as the last date in the forecast period even if growth becomes constant at or prior to this date because we have found that doing so leads to fewer errors.

FIGURE 8-7   MicroDrive Inc.'s Value of Operations (Millions of Dollars)

	A	B	C	D	E	F	G	H	I
376	INPUTS:								
377	g_L =	5%							
378	WACC =	10.97%			Projections				
379	Year	2015	2016	2017	2018	2019	2020		
380	FCF		$25.000	$88.000	$127.710	$206.564	$216.892	→ ↴	
381			↓	↓	↓	↓	↓		↓
382			FCF_{2016}	FCF_{2017}	FCF_{2018}	FCF_{2019}	FCF_{2020}		↓
383			———	———	———	———	———	HV = $V_{op(2020)}$	
384			$(1+WACC)^1$	$(1+WACC)^2$	$(1+WACC)^3$	$(1+WACC)^4$	$(1+WACC)^5$	↓	
385			↓	↓	↓	↓	↓	$FCF_{2020}(1+g_L)$	
386			↓	↓	↓	↓	↓	———	
387			↓	↓	↓	↓	↓	$(WACC - g_L)$	
388			↓	↓	↓	↓	↓	↓	
389		$22.529 ←↵		↓	↓	↓	↓	$227.736	
390		$71.461 ←←←←	←↵		↓	↓	↓	0.0597	
391	PVs of FCFs	$93.456 ←←←←	←←←←	←↵	↓	↓	↓	
392		$136.217 ←←←←	←←←←	←←←←	←↵	↓	$3,814.678	
393		$128.889 ←←←←	←←←←	←←←←	←←←←	←↵	↓	
394	PV of HV	$2,266.887 ←←←←	←←←←	←←←←	←←←←	←←←←	$3,814.678	←←↵
395		↓						= ———	
396	V_{op} = $2,719.44							$(1+WACC)^5$	

Note: Numbers in the figure are shown as rounded values for clarity in reporting. However, unrounded values are used for all calculations. See the *Excel **Tool Kit*** for this chapter.

Microsoft Excel® is a registered trademark of Microsoft Corporation. © 2014 Microsoft.

8-7c **MicroDrive's Current Value of Operations**

The current value of operations is the present value of the FCF during the forecast period plus the present value of the horizon value: MicroDrive's current value of operations is shown below and in Figure 8-7:

$$V_{op} = \frac{FCF_1}{(1+WACC)^1} + \frac{FCF_2}{(1+WACC)^2} + \frac{FCF_3}{(1+WACC)^3} + \frac{FCF_4}{(1+WACC)^4}$$
$$+ \frac{FCF_5}{(1+WACC)^5} + \frac{HV_5}{(1+WACC)^5}$$

MicroDrive's current value of operations is shown below and in Figure 8-7:

$$V_{op} = \frac{\$25}{(1+0.1097)^1} + \frac{\$88.0}{(1+0.1097)^2} + \frac{\$127.71}{(1+0.1097)^3} + \frac{\$206.564}{(1+0.1097)^4}$$
$$+ \frac{\$216.892}{(1+0.1097)^5} + \frac{\$3,814.678}{(1+0.1097)^5}$$
$$= \$452.55 + \$2,266.89$$
$$= \$2,719.44$$

8-7d **MicroDrive's Intrinsic Value per Share of Common Stock**

MicroDrive's balance sheets in Figure 8-4 show that it has zero short-term invest-ments, $280 in notes payable, $1,200 in long-term bonds, and $100 in preferred stock. We can use these values, along with MicroDrive's value of operations, to estimate its intrinsic stock price:

Total Intrinsic Value

A company's total intrinsic value is the value of operations plus the value of short-term investments (assuming the company owns no other nonoperating assets). From Equation 8-3, MicroDrive's total intrinsic value is:

$$\text{Total intrinsic value} = \text{Value of operations} + \text{Short-term investments}$$
$$= \$2{,}719.44 + \$0 = \$2{,}719.44$$

Intrinsic Value of Equity

The estimated intrinsic value of equity, shown in Equation 8-4, is the remaining value after subtracting the claims of debtholders and preferred stockholders from the total intrinsic value:

$$\text{Intrinsic value of equity} = \text{Total intrinsic value} - \text{All debt} - \text{preferred stock}$$
$$= \$2{,}719.44 - (\$280 + \$1{,}200) - \$100$$
$$= \$1{,}139.44$$

Intrinsic Stock Price

From Equation 8-5, the estimated intrinsic stock price is equal to the intrinsic value of equity divided by the number of shares. MicroDrive has 50 million shares of common stock, so the estimated intrinsic stock price is:

$$\text{Intrinsic stock price} = \text{Intrinsic value of equity/Number of shares}$$
$$= \$1{,}139.44 \,/\, 50 = \$22.79 \text{ dollars per share}$$

Figure 8-8 summarizes these calculations.

MicroDrive's intrinsic stock price of $22.79 is close to the market value of $27.00 shown in Figure 8-4. This suggests that the investors aren't much more optimistic about MicroDrive's future performance than are our current projections. Specifi-cally, they don't appear to expect MicroDrive to improve its operations. We will use MicroDrive's free cash flow valuation model in the next sections to address three important questions. First, how much of a company's value is based on short-term cash flows versus long-term cash flows? Second, how can a company identify its most important value drivers (which are growth, operating profitability, and capital utilization)? Third, does high market volatility necessarily imply irrational investors?

SELF TEST

Cathey Corporation currently has sales of $1,000, which are expected to grow by 10% from Year 0 to Year 1 and by 4% from Year 1 to Year 2. The company currently has and operating profitability (OP) ratio of 7% and a capital requirement (CR) ratio of 50% and expects to maintain these ratios

(Continued)

FIGURE 8-8	MicroDrive Inc.'s Intrinsic Stock Price (Millions, Except for Per Share Data)

	A	B	C	D	E	F	G
447	INPUTS:						
448	g_L =	5%					
449	WACC =	10.97%					
450	Year =	2016	2017	2018	2019	2020	
451	Projected FCF =	$25	$88.0	$127.71	$206.564	$216.892	
452							
453	Horizon Value:				Value of operations		$2,719
454					+ ST investments		$0
455	$HV_{2020} = \dfrac{FCF_{2020}(1+g_L)}{(WACC - g_L)} =$		$3,815		Estimated total intrinsic value		$2,719
456					– All debt		$1,480
457	Value of Operations:				– Preferred stock		$100
458	Present value of HV		$2,267		Estimated intrinsic value of equity		$1,139
459	+ Present value of FCF		$453		÷ Number of shares		50
460	Value of operations =		$2,719		Estimated intrinsic stock price =		$22.79

Note: Numbers in the figure are shown as rounded values for clarity in reporting. However, unrounded values are used for all calculations. See the *Excel Tool Kit* for this chapter.

Microsoft Excel® is a registered trademark of Microsoft Corporation. © 2014 Microsoft.

at their current levels. The current level of operating capital is $510. Use these inputs to forecast free cash flow (FCF) for Years 1 and 2. (*Hint:* You must first forecast sales, net operating profit after taxes (NOPAT), and total net operating capital (OpCap) for each year.) **($37.00 and $58.08)**

Cathey Corporation has a 12% weighted average cost of capital. Cathey's free cash flows, estimated in the previous question, are expected to grow at 4% after Year 2 for the foreseeable future. What is the horizon value (use Year 2 for the horizon)? What is the current value of operations? **($755.04 and $681.25)**

Cathey Corporation has $80 in short-term investments, $20 in short-term debt, $140 in long-term debt, $30 in preferred stock, and 10 shares of common stock outstanding. Use the value of operations from the previous question to estimate the intrinsic common stock price per share. **($60.13)**

8-8 Do Stock Values Reflect Long-Term or Short-Term Cash Flows?

Managers often complain that the stock market is shortsighted and that investors care only about conditions over the next few years. Let's use MicroDrive's valuation to test this assertion. Previously we estimated MicroDrive's current value of operations to be $2,719.44 million, with $452.55 of the value due to free cash flows occurring in Years 1 to 5 and $2,266.89 due to free cash flows beyond Year 5 (i.e., the present value of the horizon value).

If we divide the present value due to cash flows beyond the horizon by the total value of operations, we can identify the percent of value due to long-term cash flows occurring more than 5 years in the future:

$$\text{Percent of value due to long-term cash flows} = \frac{\$2,266.89}{\$2,719.44}$$
$$= 0.83 = 83\%$$

This shows that 83% of MicroDrive's value is due to cash flows occurring more than 5 years in the future, which means that managers can affect stock values more by working to increase long-term cash flows than by focusing on short-term flows. This situation holds for most companies, not just MicroDrive. Indeed, a number of professors and consulting firms have used actual company data to show that more than 80% of a typical company's stock price is due to cash flows expected more than 5 years in the future.

This brings up an interesting question. If most of a stock's value is due to long-term cash flows, then why do managers and analysts pay so much attention to quarterly earnings? Part of the answer lies in the information conveyed by short-term earnings. For example, when actual quarterly earnings are lower than expected because a company has increased its research and development (R&D) expenditures and not because of operational problems, studies have shown that the stock price probably won't decline and may actually increase. This makes sense, because R&D should increase future cash flows. On the other hand, if quarterly earnings are lower than expected because customers don't like the company's new products, then this new information will have negative implications for future cash flows and the long-term growth rate. As we show later in this chapter, even small changes in expected long-term growth can lead to large changes in stock prices. Therefore, short-term quarterly earnings themselves might not contribute a large portion to a stock's price, but the information they convey about future prospects can be extremely important.

Another reason many managers focus on short-term earnings is that some firms pay managerial bonuses on the basis of current earnings rather than stock prices (which reflect future earnings). For these managers, the concern with quarterly earnings is not due to their effect on stock prices—it's due to their effect on bonuses!

Many apparent puzzles in finance can be explained either by managerial compensation systems or by peculiar features of the Tax Code. So, if you can't explain a firm's behavior in terms of economic logic, look to compensation procedures or taxes as possible explanations.

SELF TEST

Are stock values more affected by short-term cash flows or by long-term cash flows?

Describe two reasons why managers might focus on quarterly earnings.

8-9 Using the Free Cash Flow Valuation Model to Identify Value Drivers

The key inputs to the free cash flow valuation model are: (1) the most recent level of sales; (2) the most recent level of total net operating capital; (3) the projected sales growth rates; (4) the projected operating profitability ratios; (5) the projected capital requirement ratios; and (6) the weighted average cost of capital. Changes to any of these inputs will cause the intrinsic value of operations to change.

Value drivers are the subset of inputs that managers are able to influence through strategic choices and execution of the resulting business plans. Because managers can't change the past, the most recent level of sales and operating capital are *not* value drivers. This means that growth rates, operating profitability, capital requirements, and the cost of capital *are* the value drivers.

Each of these value drivers has an impact on the intrinsic value of operations and the intrinsic stock price. However, the degree of impact varies and depends on each company's particular situation. Therefore, managers must be able to identify the most important value drivers for their companies in order to make good strategic, operating, and financial decisions.

We can use the free cash flow valuation model we developed for MicroDrive to identify its most important value drivers by estimating how the inputs (sales growth, operating profitability, capital requirements, and cost of capital) affect the value of operations and intrinsic stock price. It is very easy to do this in *Excel* by using the Scenario Manager feature. The **Ch08 Tool Kit** provides a detailed explanation of the process, but we will only examine the results here.

Figure 8-9 shows seven scenarios. The first is the "Status Quo" scenario, which we used previously when estimating MicroDrive's value of operations and intrinsic stock price. Figure 8-9 shows the key inputs in the blue section: sales growth rates, operating profitability, capital requirements, and cost of capital. Any inputs that differ from those of the Status Quo Scenario are shown in orange. Figure 8-9 reports key results in the green section: the value of operations, the intrinsic stock price, and the return on invested capital that is expected for the long run (the inputs are stable by the end of the forecast period, so the ROIC in the forecast's last year is the ROIC that is expected to continue into the foreseeable future).

Recall that MicroDrive's stock price fell from $40 per share in the previous year to $27 in the current year, which is close to the estimated intrinsic stock price of $22.79. Some of MicroDrive's managers recommended that MicroDrive create a new marketing campaign to increase the sales growth rates, which would lead to higher FCF growth rates. This Higher Sales Growth scenario is shown next to the Status Quo in Figure 8-9. The managers were surprised to see that the value of operations and intrinsic stock price actually declined when sales growth increased![7]

The previous example demonstrates that growth doesn't add value for a particular set of ratios, but let's examine a more general case to better understand why this is so. Suppose Year T is the horizon, which means the company has stable ratios and constant expected growth. It is possible (with a lot of algebra!) to express the value of operations in terms of the value drivers:

---

7. To avoid unnecessarily complicating these examples, we ignore the cost of the changes. Obviously, additional costs must be taken into account before completing the analysis; see Chapter 9 for details.

FIGURE 8-9	Value Drivers for MicroDrive Inc. (Millions, Except for Per Share Data)

	A	B	C	D	E	F	G	H	I
538						Scenario			
539				(2)	(3)	(4)	(5)	(6)	(7)
540				Higher	Higher	Better	Improve	Improve	Improve
541			(1)	Sales	Operating	Capital	Growth and	Growth	Growth,
542			Status	Growth	Profitability	Utilization	Operating	and	OP, and
543			Quo	(Only)	(Only)	(Only)	Profitability	Capital	CR
544	**Inputs**								
545	Sales growth in 1st year		10%	11%	10%	10%	11%	11%	11%
546	Sales growth in 2nd year		8%	9%	8%	8%	9%	9%	9%
547	Sales growth in 3rd year		7%	8%	7%	7%	8%	8%	8%
548	Long-term sales growth (g_L)		5%	6%	5%	5%	6%	6%	6%
549	Operating profitability (OP)		6%	6%	7%	6%	7%	6%	7%
550	Capital requirement (CR)		61%	61%	61%	52%	61%	52%	52%
551	Weighted average cost of capital (WACC)		10.97%	10.97%	10.97%	10.97%	10.97%	10.97%	10.97%
552	**Results**								
553	Value of operations		$2,719	$2,713	$3,682	$3,576	$3,880	$3,751	$4,918
554	Intrinsic stock price		$22.79	$22.67	$42.04	$39.91	$46.00	$43.42	$66.76
555	Return on invested capital (ROIC)		9.84%	9.84%	11.48%	11.54%	11.48%	11.54%	13.46%

Note: Numbers in the figure are shown as rounded values for clarity in reporting. However, unrounded values are used for all calculations. See the *Excel Tool Kit* for this chapter.

Microsoft Excel® is a registered trademark of Microsoft Corporation. © 2014 Microsoft.

(8–13)

$$V_{\text{op(at Horizon Year T)}} = \text{OpCap}_T \left[1 + \frac{\left((1 + g_L) \dfrac{\text{OP}_T}{\text{CR}_T} - \text{WACC} \right)}{\text{WACC} - g_L} \right]$$

We can use Equation 8-13 to express the horizon value in terms of the return on invested capital as follows. First, notice that the operating profitability ratio divided by the capital requirement ratio is equal to the return on invested capital:

(8–14)

$$\frac{\text{OP}_T}{\text{CR}_T} = \frac{(\text{NOPAT}_T/\text{Sales}_T)}{(\text{OpCap}_T/\text{Sales}_T)} = \frac{\text{NOPAT}_T}{\text{OpCap}_T} = \text{ROIC}_T$$

Substituting Equation 8-14 into Equation 8-13 provides an expression for the horizon value in terms of the return on invested capital (ROIC) and the other inputs:

$$V_{\text{op(at Horizon Year T)}} = \text{OpCap}_T \left[1 + \frac{(1 + g_L)\,\text{ROIC}_T - \text{WACC}}{\text{WACC} - g_L} \right]$$

How do these drivers affect value? First, an increase in the ROIC, whether due to improvement in operating profitability or in capital utilization, always has a positive effect—the higher the ROIC, the higher the value of operations. Second, a reduction in the cost of capital always has a positive effect on the value of operations.

However, an increase in the growth rate can have a positive or negative effect. To see why, look at Equation 8-15 and focus on the numerator of the fraction in the brackets: $(1 + g_L)\,\text{ROIC}_T - \text{WACC}$. If this term is negative because $\text{ROIC}_T < \text{WACC}/(1 + g_L)$, then the fraction in Equation 8-15 will be negative, which means that value of operations will be less than the amount the company has spent on it through its investment in total net operating capital. And if ROIC_T is even lower so that $\text{ROIC}_T < \text{WACC}/(1 + \text{WACC})$, then an increase in growth will make the fraction in Equation 8-15 even more negative, which means that a higher growth rate makes the company *less* valuable.[8] Mathematically, this is because the denominator of the fraction, $\text{WACC} - g_L$, is getting smaller faster than the numerator, $(1 + g_L)\,\text{ROIC}_T - \text{WACC}$, is getting larger. Another way to look at it is if ROIC_T is sufficiently smaller than WACC, then each new dollar of investment to support growth is expected to earn a return that is less than the required return. As we will see in Chapter 12, earning a return less than the required return reduces the value of the firm.

The key point to remember is not to implement growth strategies if the return on invested capital is too low. In that situation, managers must improve operating profitability or capital utilization, which will increase the ROIC, before pursuing growth.

Returning to Figure 8-9, Scenarios 3 and 4 improve operating profitability and capital utilization. Notice that these improvements increase the ROIC, which leads to much higher estimates of the value of operations and the intrinsic stock price. Scenarios 5 and 6 show that when improvements in operations increase ROIC, growth adds even more value. Scenario 7 shows the very large increase in value if managers can improve operating profitability, capital utilization, and growth. We will discuss Micro-Drive's plans in more details when we forecast its full financial statements in Chapter 9.

The *Excel Ch08 Tool Kit* shows an 8th scenario in which the cost of capital is reduced. This increases value substantially, but we defer a discussion of the cost of capital until Chapter 11.

What are value drivers?

Does an increase in the operating profitability ratio always cause an increase in the value of operations?

Does a decrease in the capital requirement ratio always cause an increase in the value of operations?

Does an increase in the long-term growth rate of free cash flows always cause and increase in the value of operations? Explain your answer.

SELF TEST

---

8. To see why this is true, take the partial derivative of Equation 8-15 with respect to g_L. This partial derivative is negative for values of $\text{ROIC}_T < \text{WACC}/(1 + \text{WACC})$.

8-10 **Why Are Stock Prices so Volatile?**

Recall from Chapter 2 that a typical company's stock returns are very volatile. Because the average stock's standard deviation is about 30%, it should not be surprising that many stocks declined by 80% or more during 2014, and some enjoyed gains of over 100%. At the risk of understatement, the stock market is volatile!

To help understand why stock prices are volatile, look at Figure 8-9. Even though the changes in the value drivers were relatively small, the changes in MicroDrive's intrinsic stock price were very large, with the price ranging from $22.67 to $66.76. This shows that if investors change their expectations regarding future sales growth, operating profitability, capital utilization, or the cost of capital, then the stock price will change. As Figure 8-9 demonstrates, even small changes in the expected value drivers cause large changes in stock prices.

What might cause investors to change their expectations? It could be new information about the company, such as preliminary results for an R&D program, initial sales of a new product, or the discovery of harmful side effects from the use of an existing product. Or new information that will affect many companies could arrive, such as the collapse of the credit markets in 2008. Given the existence of computers and telecommunications networks, new information hits the market on an almost continuous basis, and it causes frequent and sometimes large changes in stock prices. In other words, *ready availability of information causes stock prices to be volatile.*

If a stock's price is stable, this probably means that little new information is arriving. But if you think it's risky to invest in a volatile stock, imagine how risky it would be to invest in a company that rarely releases new information about its sales or operations. It may be bad to see your stock's price jump around, but it would be a lot worse to see a stable quoted price most of the time and then to see huge moves on the rare days when new information is released.[9] Fortunately, in our economy timely information is readily available, and evidence suggests that stocks—especially those of large companies—adjust rapidly to new information.

> **SELF TEST**   Why doesn't a volatile stock price necessarily imply irrational pricing?

8-11 **Valuing Common Stocks with the Dividend Growth Model**

Free cash flows are the cash flows available for distribution to all of a company's investors (debtholders, preferred stockholders, and common stockholders). The FCF valuation model discounts the cash flows available to *all* investors by the overall rate of return required by *all* investors. This results in a company's primary source of value, the value of operations. Recall that *all* of a company's investors have a claim on this value, with common stockholders having the residual claim.

---

9. Note, however, that if information came out infrequently, stock prices would probably be stable for a time and then experience large price swings when news did come out. This would be a bit like not having a lot of little earthquakes (frequent new information) that relieve stress along the fault and instead building up stress for a number of years before a massive earthquake.

Rather than find the total entity value and then determining the residual share that belongs to common stockholders, we can find the intrinsic price per share more directly for companies that pay dividends. The dividends per share are the cash flows that go directly to the owner of a share of common stock, so if you discount dividends at the rate of return required by common stockholders, the result is the intrinsic stock price.

8-11a Definitions of Terms Used in Stock Valuation Models

We begin by defining key terms:

D_t = Dividend the stockholder *expects* to receive at the end of Year t. D_0 is the most recent dividend, which has already been paid; D_1 is the first dividend expected, which will be paid at the end of this year; D_2 is the dividend expected at the end of Year 2; and so forth. D_1 represents the first cash flow that a new purchaser of the stock will receive, because D_0 has just been paid. D_0 is known with certainty, but all future dividends are expected values.[10]

P_0 = Actual **market price** of the stock today.

$\hat{P}_t$ = Expected price of the stock at the end of each Year t (pronounced "P hat t"). $\hat{P}_0$ is the estimated value of the stock today as seen by the particular investor doing the analysis; $\hat{P}_1$ is the price expected at the end of 1 year; and so on.

D_1/P_0 = Expected **dividend yield** during the coming year. For example, if a stock is expected to pay a dividend of $D_1 = \$1$ during the next 12 months and if its current price is $P_0 = \$10$, then the expected dividend yield is $\$1/\$10 = 0.10 = 10\%$.

$\dfrac{\hat{P}_1 - P_0}{P_0}$ = Expected **capital gains yield** during the coming year. If the stock sells for $10 today and if it is expected to rise to $10.50 at the end of 1 year, then the expected capital gain is $\hat{P}_1 - P_0 = \$10.50 - \$10.00 = \$0.50$, and the expected capital gains yield is $\$0.50/\$10 = 0.05 = 5\%$.

g = Expected **growth rate** in dividends as predicted by a marginal investor. Constant expected long-term growth is denoted as g_L.

r_s = The **required rate of return**, on the stock. As shown in Chapter 2, the primary determinants of r_s include the risk-free rate and adjustments for the stock's risk.

(Continued)

---

10. Stocks generally pay dividends quarterly, so theoretically we should evaluate them on a quarterly basis. However, in stock valuation, most analysts work on an annual basis because the data generally are not precise enough to warrant refinement to a quarterly model. For additional information on the quarterly model, see Robert Brooks and Billy Helms, "An N-Stage, Fractional Period, Quarterly Dividend Discount Model," *Financial Review*, November 1990, pp. 651–657.

$\hat{r}_s$ = **Expected rate of return** that an investor who buys the stock expects to receive in the future. $\hat{r}_s$ (pronounced "r hat s") could be above or below r_s, but one would buy the stock only if $\hat{r}_s \geq r_s$. Note that the expected return ($\hat{r}_s$) is equal to the expected dividend yield (D_1/P_0) plus the expected capital gains yield ($[\hat{P}_1 - P_0]/P_0$). In our example, $\hat{r}_s = 10\% + 5\% = 15\%$.

$\bar{r}_s$ = **Actual**, or **realized**, *after-the-fact* **rate of return**, pronounced "r bar s." For a risky security, the actual return can differ considerably from the expected return.

8-11b Expected Dividends as the Basis for Stock Values

Like all financial assets, the value of a stock is estimated by finding the present value of a stream of expected future cash flows. What are the cash flows that corporations are expected to provide to their stockholders? First, think of yourself as an investor who buys a stock with the intention of holding it (in your family) forever. In this case, all that you (and your heirs) will receive is a stream of dividends, and the value of the stock today is calculated as the present value of an infinite stream of dividends:

(8–16)

$$\text{Value of stock} = \hat{P}_0 = \text{PV of expected future dividends}$$

$$= \frac{D_1}{(1 + r_s)^1} + \frac{D_2}{(1 + r_s)^2} + \cdots + \frac{D_\infty}{(1 + r_s)^\infty}$$

$$= \sum_{t=1}^{\infty} \frac{D_t}{(1 + r_s)^t}$$

What about the more typical case, where you expect to hold the stock for a finite period and then sell it—what is the value of $\hat{P}_0$ in this case? Unless the company is likely to be liquidated or sold and thus to disappear, *the value of the stock is again determined by Equation 8-16.* To see this, recognize that for any individual investor, the expected cash flows consist of expected dividends plus the expected sale price of the stock. However, the sale price a current investor receives will depend on the dividends the buyer expects. Therefore, for all present and future investors in total, expected cash flows must be based on expected future dividends. Put another way, unless a firm is liquidated or sold to another concern, the cash flows it provides to its stockholders will consist only of a stream of dividends. Therefore, the value of a share of its stock must be the present value of that expected dividend stream.

The general validity of Equation 8-16 can also be confirmed by solving the following problem. Suppose you buy a stock and expect to hold it for 1 year. You will receive dividends during the year plus the value $\hat{P}_1$ when you sell at the end of the year. But what will determine the value of $\hat{P}_1$? The answer is that it will be determined as the present value of the dividends expected during Year 2 plus the stock price at the end of that year, which, in turn, will be determined as the present value of another set of future dividends and an even more distant stock price. This process can be continued ad infinitum, and the ultimate result is Equation 8-16.[11]

8-11c **Valuing a Constant Growth Stock**

As we explained previously, market saturation and competition will eventually drive free cash flow growth to a constant level approximately equal to the long-term population growth rate plus the long-term inflation rate. Because free cash flows are the source of funds available for distribution to all investors, including dividends to stockholders, the long-term growth rate in dividends must be equal to the long-term growth rate in free cash flows.

We will address valuation of faster-growing firms later in the chapter, but for now we focus on a mature company whose dividends are growing at a constant rate, g_L. If the growth rate (g_L) is less than the rate of return required by common shareholders (r_s), then Equation 8-16 can be rewritten as follows:

$$\hat{P}_0 = \frac{D_0(1 + g_L)^1}{(1 + r_s)^1} + \frac{D_0(1 + g_L)^2}{(1 + r_s)^2} + \cdots + \frac{D_0(1 + g_L)^\infty}{(1 + r_s)^\infty}$$

$$= D_0 \sum_{t=1}^{\infty} \frac{(1 + g_L)^t}{(1 + r_s)^t}$$

$$= \frac{D_0(1 + g_L)}{r_s - g_L} = \frac{D_1}{r_s - g_L}$$

(8–17)

The last term of Equation 8-17 is called the **constant dividend growth model**, or the **Gordon model**, after Myron J. Gordon, who did much to develop and popularize it.

Notice that the last term in Equation 8-17 has the same form as the constant growth model for free cash flows in Equation 8-9: an expected cash flow at Year 1 (free cash flow or dividend) is divided by the difference between the required rate of return (WACC for FCF or r_s for dividends) and the constant growth rate. Similar to the constant growth model for FCF, a necessary condition for the validity of Equation 8-17 is that r_s must greater than g_L, otherwise, the first row of Equation 8-17 is equal to infinity. Always keep in mind that the last form of Equation 8-17 is valid only when g is less than r_s. *If g is greater than r_s then the constant growth model cannot be used, and the answer you would get from using Equation 8-17 would be wrong and misleading.*

---

11. It is ironic that investors periodically lose sight of the long-run nature of stocks as investments and forget that, in order to sell a stock at a profit, one must find a buyer who will pay the higher price. If you analyze a stock's value in accordance with Equation 8-16, conclude that the stock's market price exceeds a reasonable value, and then buy the stock anyway, then you would be following the "bigger fool" theory of investment—you think that you may be a fool to buy the stock at its excessive price, but you think that when you get ready to sell it, you can find someone who is an even bigger fool. Many investors might have been following the bigger fool theory during the big stock run-ups prior to the bursting bubbles in 2000 and 2007.

Illustration of a Constant Growth Stock

Assume that R&R Enterprises just paid a dividend of $1.15 (that is, $D_0 = \$1.15$). Its stock has a required rate of return, r_s, of 13.4%, and investors expect the dividend to grow at a constant 8% rate in the future. The estimated dividend 1 year hence would be $D_1 = \$1.15(1.08) = \$1.24$. We can use Equation 8-17 to estimate the intrinsic stock price:

$$\hat{P}_0 = \frac{D_0(1 + g_L)}{r_s - g_L} = \frac{D_1}{r_s - g_L}$$

$$= \frac{\$1.15(1.08)}{0.134 - 0.08} = \frac{\$1.242}{0.054} = \$23.00$$

Expected Rate of Return on a Constant Growth Stock

When using Equation 8-17, we first estimated D_1 and r_s, the *required* rate of return on the stock; then we solved for the stock's intrinsic value, which we compared to its actual market price. We can also reverse the process, observing the actual stock price, substituting it into Equation 8-17, and solving for the rate of return. In doing so, we are finding the *expected* rate of return (recall from Chapter 2 that if the market is in equilibrium, the expected return will equal the *required* rate of return, $\hat{r}_s = r_s$):

(8–18)

$$\hat{r}_s = \begin{matrix} \text{Expected rate} \\ \text{of return} \end{matrix} = \begin{matrix} \text{Expected} \\ \text{dividend yield} \end{matrix} + \begin{matrix} \text{Expected capital} \\ \text{gains yield} \end{matrix}$$

$$= \begin{matrix} \text{Expected} \\ \text{dividend yield} \end{matrix} + \begin{matrix} \text{Expected} \\ \text{growth rate} \end{matrix}$$

$$= \frac{D_1}{P_0} + g$$

Thus, if you buy a stock for a price $P_0 = \$23$, and if you expect the stock to pay a dividend $D_1 = \$1.242$ in a year and to grow at a constant rate $g = 8\%$ in the future, then your expected rate of return will be 13.4%:

$$\hat{r}_s = \frac{\$1.242}{\$23} + 8\% = 5.4\% + 8\% = 13.4\%$$

In this form, we see that $\hat{r}_s$ is the *expected total return* and that it consists of an *expected dividend yield*, $D_1/P_0 = 5.4\%$, plus an *expected growth rate* (which is also the *expected capital gains yield*) of $g = 8\%$.

Suppose that the current price, P_0, is equal to $23 and that the Year-1 expected dividend, D_1, is equal to $1.242. What is the expected price at the end of the first year, immediately after D_1 has been paid? First, we can estimate the expected Year-2 dividend as $D_2 = D_1(1 + g) = \$1.242(1.08) = \$1.3414$. Then we can apply a version of Equation 8-17 that is shifted ahead by 1 year, using D_2 instead of D_1 and solving for $\hat{P}_1$ instead of $\hat{P}_0$:

$$\hat{P}_1 = \frac{D_2}{r_s - g} = \frac{\$1.3414}{0.134 - 0.08} = \$24.84$$

Even easier, notice that $\hat{P}_1$ must be 8% larger than \$23, the price found 1 year earlier for P_0:

$$\$23(1.08) = \$24.84$$

Either way, we expect a capital gain of \$24.84 − \$23.00 = \$1.84 during the year, which is a capital gains yield of 8%:

$$\text{Capital gains yield} = \frac{\text{Capital gain}}{\text{Beginning price}} = \frac{\$1.84}{\$23.00} = 0.08 = 8\%$$

We could extend the analysis, and in each future year the expected capital gains yield would always equal g, the expected dividend growth rate.

The dividend yield during the year could be estimated as follows:

$$\text{Dividend yield} = \frac{D_2}{\hat{P}_1} = \frac{\$1.3414}{\$24.84} = 0.054 = 5.4\%$$

The dividend yield for the following year could also be calculated, and again it would be 5.4%. Thus, *for a constant growth stock*, the following conditions must hold:

1. The dividend is expected to grow forever at a constant rate, g.
2. The stock price will also grow at this same rate.
3. The expected dividend yield is constant.
4. The expected capital gains yield is also constant and is equal to g, the dividend (and stock price) growth rate.
5. The expected total rate of return, $\hat{r}_s$, is equal to the expected dividend yield plus the expected growth rate: $\hat{r}_s$ = dividend yield + g.

8-11d **Valuing Nonconstant Growth Stocks**

Suppose R&R, the company from the previous section, was not yet in its constant growth phase. Dividends are expected to grow at a 30% rate for the first year, 20% for the second year, 10% for the third year, after which the growth rate is expected to fall to 8% and remain there. Figure 8-10 illustrates this pattern of nonconstant growth and also compares it with normal growth, zero growth, and negative growth.[12]

The value of R&R is the present value of its expected future dividends as determined by Equation 8-16. When D_t is growing at a constant rate, we simplify Equation 8-16 to $\hat{P}_0 = D_1/(r_s − g)$. In the nonconstant case, however, the expected growth rate is not a constant during the first 3 years, so we cannot apply the constant growth formula during these years.

---

12. A negative growth rate indicates a declining company. A mining company whose profits are falling because of a declining ore body is an example. Someone buying such a company would expect its earnings, and consequently its dividends and stock price, to decline each year, and this would lead to capital losses rather than capital gains. Obviously, a declining company's stock price will be relatively low, and its dividend yield must be high enough to offset the expected capital loss and still produce a competitive total return. Students sometimes argue that they would never be willing to buy a stock whose price was expected to decline. However, if the annual dividends are large enough to *more than offset* the falling stock price, the stock could still provide a fair return.

FIGURE 8-10	Illustrative Dividend Growth at Different Rates

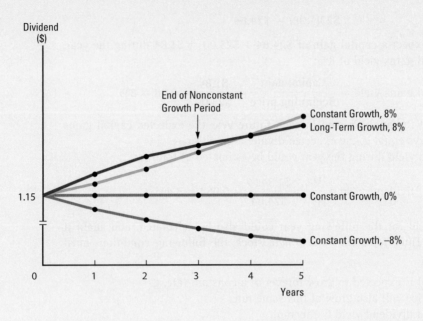

Because Equation 8-17 requires a constant growth rate, we obviously cannot use it at Year 0 to value stocks that subsequently have nonconstant growth. However, assuming a company currently experiencing nonconstant growth will eventually slow down and become a constant growth stock, we can use Equation 8-17 to help find the stock's value. First, we assume that the dividend will grow at nonconstant rates (generally at relatively high rates) for T periods, after which it will grow at a constant rate, g_L. Analogous to the previous examples with the FCF valuation model, T is called the horizon date or the terminal date.

Recall that a stock's current estimated value, $\hat{P}_0$, is the present value of all dividends after Time 0, discounted back to Time 0. Similarly, the estimated value of a stock at Time T is the present value of all dividends beyond Time T, discounted back to Time T. When dividends beyond Time T are expected to grow at a constant long-term rate of g_L, we can use a variation of the constant growth formula, Equation 8-17, to estimate the stock's intrinsic value at Time T. Analogous to the previous examples with the FCF valuation model, the estimated price at Time T is often called the horizon value, continuing value, or the terminal value. For stocks, $\hat{P}_T$ denotes the horizon value of the expected stock price at Time T:

(8–19)	

$$\text{Horizon value for stock} = \hat{P}_T = \frac{D_{T+1}}{r_s - g_L} = \frac{D_T(1 + g_L)}{r_s - g_L}$$

A stock's estimated value today, $\hat{P}_0$, is the present value of the dividends during the nonconstant growth period plus the present value of the dividends after the horizon date:

$$\hat{P}_0 = \frac{D_1}{(1+r_s)^1} + \frac{D_2}{(1+r_s)^2} + \cdots + \frac{D_T}{(1+r_s)^T} + \frac{D_{T+1}}{(1+r_s)^{T+1}} + \cdots + \frac{D_\infty}{(1+r_s)^\infty}$$

$$= \quad \underbrace{\text{PV of dividends during the nonconstant growth period } t = 1 \text{ to } T} \quad + \quad \underbrace{\text{PV of dividends during the constant growth period } t = T+1 \text{ to } \infty}$$

The horizon value is the value of all dividends beyond Time T discounted back to Time T. Discounting the horizon value from Time T to Time 0 provides an estimate of the present value of all dividends beyond the nonconstant growth period. Thus, the stock's current estimated value is the present value of all dividends during the nonconstant growth period plus the present value of the horizon value:

(8–20)

$$\hat{P}_0 = \left[\frac{D_1}{(1+r_s)^1} + \frac{D_2}{(1+r_s)^2} + \cdots + \frac{D_T}{(1+r_s)^T} \right] + \frac{\hat{P}_T}{(1+r_s)^T}$$

$$= \left[\frac{D_1}{(1+r_s)^1} + \frac{D_2}{(1+r_s)^2} + \cdots + \frac{D_T}{(1+r_s)^T} \right] + \frac{[(D_{T+1})/(r_s - g_L)]}{(1+r_s)^T}$$

To implement Equation 8-20, we go through the following three steps.

See **Ch08 Tool Kit.xls** on the textbook's Web site.

1. Estimate the expected dividends for each year during the period of nonconstant growth.
2. Find the expected price of the stock at the end of the nonconstant growth period, at which point it has become a constant growth stock.
3. Find the present values of the expected dividends during the nonconstant growth period and the present value of the expected stock price at the end of the nonconstant growth period. Their sum is the estimated value of the stock, $\hat{P}_0$.

Figure 8-11 illustrates the process for valuing a nonconstant growth stock. Notice that the dividends are projected using the appropriate growth rate for each year. The estimated horizon value, $\hat{P}_3$, is the value of all dividends from Year 4 through infinity, discounted back to Year 3 by application of the constant growth model at Year 3. The horizon value is actually the value a split-second after D_3 has been paid. Therefore, the estimated value at Time 0 is the present value of the first three dividends plus the present value of $\hat{P}_3$, for an estimate $\hat{P}_0$ of $31.13. A detailed explanation is set forth in the steps below the diagram.

FIGURE 8-11   Process for Finding the Value of a Nonconstant Growth Stock

	A	B	C	D	E	F	G
764	**INPUTS:**						
765	$D_0 =$	$1.15	Last dividend the company paid.				
766	$r_s =$	13.4%	Stockholders' required return.				
767	$g_{0,1} =$	30%	Growth rate for Year 1 only.				
768	$g_{1,2} =$	20%	Growth rate for Year 2 only.				
769	$g_{2,3} =$	10%	Growth rate for Year 3 only.				
770	$g_L =$	8%	Constant long-run growth rate for all years after Year 3.				
771				**Projections**			
772	**Year**	**0**	**1**	**2**	**3**	**→ ∞**	
773	**Growth rate**		30%	20%	10%	8%	
774	**Dividend**	D_0	$D_0(1+g_{0,1})$	$D_1(1+g_{1,2})$	$D_2(1+g_{1,2})$		
775	D_t	$1.15	$1.495	$1.794	$1.973		
776			↓	↓	↓		
777			D_1	D_2	D_3		
778			———	———	———	$HV_3 = \hat{P}_3$	
779			$(1+r_s)^1$	$(1+r_s)^2$	$(1+r_s)^3$	↓	
780			↓	↓	↓	$\hat{P}_3 = \dfrac{D_3(1+g_L)}{(r_s - g_L)}$	
781			↓	↓	↓		
782			↓	↓	↓		
783			↓	↓	↓		
784			↓	↓	↓	$\hat{P}_3 = \dfrac{\$2.131}{5.400\%}$	
785	**PVs of**	$1.318	←↵	↓	↓		
786	**Dividends**	$1.395	←←←←	←↵	↓	↓	
787		$1.353	←←←←	←←←←	←↵	$\hat{P}_3 = 39.468	
788						↓	
789	**PV of $\hat{P}_3$**	$27.065	←←←←	←←←←	$39.468		$\hat{P}_3$
790		↓			$= \dfrac{}{(1+0.134)^3}$	←←←←	$= \dfrac{}{(1+r_s)^3}$
791	$V_{op} =$	$31.13					

Notes: Numbers in the figure are shown as rounded values for clarity in reporting. However, unrounded values are used for all calculations. See the *Excel **Tool Kit*** for this chapter.

Following is an explanation of the steps in the figure.

Step 1. Calculate the dividends expected at the end of each year during the nonconstant growth period. Calculate the first dividend, $D_1 = D_0(1 + g_{0,1}) = \$1.15(1.30) = \$1.495$. Here $g_{0,1}$ is the growth rate (30%) during the first year of the nonconstant growth period. Show the $1.495 on the time line as the cash flow at Year 1. Then calculate $D_2 = D_1(1 + g_{1,2}) = \$1.495(1.20) = \$1.794$ and then $D_3 = D_2(1 + g_{2,3}) = \$1.794(1.10) = \$1.9734$. (The figure shows the values rounded to three decimal places, but all calculations used nonrounded values.) Show these values on the time line as the cash flows at Year 2 and Year 3. Note that D_0 is used only to calculate D_1.

Step 2. At Year 3, the stock becomes a constant growth stock. Therefore, we can use the constant growth formula to find $\hat{P}_3$, which is the PV of the dividends from Year 4 to infinity as evaluated at Year 3. First we determine $D_4 = \$1.9734(1.08) = \$2.1313$ for use in the formula, and then we calculate $\hat{P}_3$ as follows:

$$\hat{P}_3 = \frac{D_4}{r_s - g_L} = \frac{\$2.1313}{0.134 - 0.08} = \$39.468$$

We show this $39.468 on the time line as a second cash flow at Year 3. The $39.468 is a Year-3 cash flow in the sense that the owner of the stock could sell it for $39.468 at Year 3 immediately after receiving D_3 and also in the sense that $39.468 is the value at Year 3 of the dividend cash flows from Year 4 to infinity.

Step 3. Now that the cash flows have been placed on the time line, we can discount each cash flow at the required rate of return, $r_s = 13.4\%$. This produces the PVs shown to the left below the time line, and the sum of the PVs is the value of the nonconstant growth stock, $31.13.

In the figure we show the setup for an *Excel* solution. With a financial calculator, you could use the cash flow (CFLO) register of your calculator. Enter 0 for CF_0 because you get no cash flow at Time 0, $CF_1 = 1.495$, $CF_2 = 1.7940$, and $CF_3 = 1.973 + 39.468 = 41.441$. Then enter I/YR = 13.4 and press the NPV key to find the value of the stock, $31.131.

What are the two components of most stocks' expected total return?

How does one calculate the capital gains yield and the dividend yield of a stock?

Write out and explain the valuation formula for a constant growth stock.

Are stock prices affected more by long-term or short-term performance? Explain.

What conditions must hold in order for a stock to be evaluated using the constant growth model?

Explain how to find the value of a nonconstant growth stock.

If $D_1 = \$3.00$, $P_0 = \$50$, and $\hat{P}_1 = \$52$, what are the stock's expected dividend yield, expected capital gains yield, and expected total return for the coming year? **(6%, 4%, 10%)**

A stock is expected to pay a dividend of $2 at the end of the year. The required rate of return is $r_s = 12\%$. What would the stock's price be if the constant growth rate in dividends were 4%? **($25.00)** What would the price be if $g = 0\%$? **($16.67)**

If $D_0 = \$4.00$, $r_s = 9\%$, and $g = 5\%$ for a constant growth stock, what are the stock's expected dividend yield and capital gains yield for the coming year? **(4%, 5%)**

Suppose $D_0 = \$5.00$ and $r_s = 10\%$. The expected growth rate from Year 0 to Year 1 is $g_{0,1} = 20\%$, the expected growth rate from Year 1 to Year 2 is $g_{1,2} = 10\%$, and the constant growth rate beyond Year 2 is $g_L = 5\%$. What are the expected dividends for Year 1 and Year 2? **($6.00 and $6.60)** What is the expected horizon value price at Year 2 ($\hat{P}_3$)? **($138.60)** What is $\hat{P}_0$? **($125.45)**

8-12 Market Multiple Analysis

Some analysts use **market multiple analysis** to estimate a company's value. The analyst chooses a metric for the firm—say, its EPS—and then multiplies the company's EPS by a market-determined multiple such as the average P/E ratio for a sample of similar companies. This would give an estimate of the stock's intrinsic value. Market multiples can also be applied to total net income, to sales, to book value, or to number of subscribers for businesses such as cable TV or cellular telephone systems. Whereas the discounted dividend method applies valuation concepts by focusing on expected cash flows, market multiple analysis is more judgmental.

To illustrate the concept, suppose Tapley Products is a privately held firm whose forecasted earnings per share are $7.70, and suppose the average price/earnings (P/E) ratio for a set of similar publicly traded companies is 12. To estimate the intrinsic value of Tapley's stock, we would simply multiply its $7.70 EPS by the multiple 12, obtaining the value $7.70(12) = $92.40.

Another commonly used metric is *earnings before interest, taxes, deprecia-tion, and amortization (EBITDA)*. The EBITDA *multiple* is the total value of a company (the market value of its equity plus that of its debt) divided by EBITDA. This multiple is based on total value, since EBITDA is used to compensate the firm's stock-holders and bondholders. Therefore, it is called an **entity multiple**. The EBITDA market multiple is the average EBITDA multiple for a group of similar publicly traded companies. This procedure gives an estimate of the company's total value, and to find the estimated intrinsic value of the stock we would subtract the value of the debt from total value and then divide by the shares of stock outstanding.

As suggested previously, in some businesses, such as cable TV and cellular telephone, a critical factor is the number of customers the company has. For example, when a telephone company acquires a cellular operator, it might pay a price that is based on the number of customers. Managed care companies such as HMOs have applied similar logic in acquisitions, basing valuations primarily on the number of people insured. Some Internet companies have been valued by the number of "eye-balls," which is the number of hits on the site.

> **SELF TEST**
>
> What is market multiple analysis?
>
> What is an entity multiple?

8-13 **Preferred Stock**

Preferred stock is a *hybrid*—it's similar to bonds in some respects and to common stock in others. Like bonds, preferred stock has a par value, and a fixed amount of dividends must be paid on it before dividends can be paid on the common stock. However, if the preferred dividend is not earned, the directors can omit (or "pass") it without throwing the company into bankruptcy. So, although preferred stock has a fixed payment like bonds, a failure to make this payment will not lead to bank-ruptcy.

The dividends on preferred stock are fixed, and if they are scheduled to go on forever, the issue is a perpetuity whose value is found as follows:

(8–21)

$$V_{ps} = \frac{D_{ps}}{r_{ps}}$$

V_{ps} is the value of the preferred stock, D_{ps} is the preferred dividend, and r_{ps} is the re-quired rate of return. Notice that Equation 8-21 is just a special case of the constant dividend growth model for which growth is zero.

MicroDrive has preferred stock outstanding that pays a dividend of $8 per year. If the required rate of return on this preferred stock is 8%, then its value is $100:

$$V_{ps} = \frac{\$8.00}{0.08} = \$100.00$$

If we know the current price of a preferred stock and its dividend, we can transpose terms and solve for the expected rate of return as follows:

$$\hat{r}_{ps} = \frac{D_{ps}}{V_{ps}}$$

(8–22)

Some preferred stock has a stated maturity, say, 50 years. If a firm's preferred stock matures in 50 years, pays a $8 annual dividend, has a par value of $100, and has a required return of 6%, then we can find its price using a financial calculator: Enter N = 50, I/YR = 6, PMT = 8, and FV = 100. Then press PV to find the price, V_{ps} = $131.52. If you know the price of a share of preferred stock, you can solve for I/YR to find the expected rate of return, $\hat{r}_{ps}$.

Most preferred stock pays dividends quarterly. This is true for MicroDrive, so we could find the effective rate of return on its preferred stock as follows:

$$EFF\% = EAR = \left(1 + \frac{r_{NOM}}{M}\right)^M - 1 = \left(1 + \frac{0.08}{4}\right)^4 - 1 = 8.24\%$$

If an investor wanted to compare the returns on MicroDrive's bonds and its preferred stock, it would be best to convert the nominal rates on each security to effective rates and then compare these "equivalent annual rates."

> Explain the following statement: "Preferred stock is a hybrid security."
>
> Is the equation used to value preferred stock more like the one used to evaluate perpetual bonds or the one used for common stock? Explain.
>
> A preferred stock has an annual dividend of $5. The required return is 8%. What is the V_{ps}? **($62.50)**

SELF TEST

Summary

Corporate decisions should be analyzed in terms of how alternative courses of action are likely to affect a firm's value. However, it is necessary to know how stock prices are established before attempting to measure how a given decision will affect a firm's value. This chapter showed how stock values are determined and also how investors go about estimating the rates of return they expect to earn. The key concepts covered are listed below.

- A **proxy** is a document that gives one person the power to act for another, typically the power to vote shares of common stock. A **proxy fight** occurs when an outside group solicits stockholders' proxies in an effort to overthrow the current management.

- Stockholders often have the right to purchase any additional shares sold by the firm. This right, called the **preemptive right**, protects the present stockholders' control and prevents dilution of their value.
- Although most firms have only one type of common stock, in some instances **classified stock** is used to meet the special needs of the company. One type is **founders' shares**. This is stock owned by the firm's founders that carries sole voting rights but restricted dividends for a specified number of years.
- The **free cash flow model** estimates the total value of the firm before estimating the per share stock price, so it is called an **entity valuation model**.
- The **value of operations** is the present value of all the future free cash flows expected from operations when discounted at the weighted average cost of capital:

$$V_{op(at\ time\ 0)} = \sum_{t=1}^{\infty} \frac{FCF_t}{(1 + WACC)^t}$$

- **Nonoperating assets** include short-term investments in marketable securities and noncontrolling interests in the stock of other companies.
- The **value of nonoperating assets** is usually close to the figure reported on the balance sheet.
- The **total intrinsic value** is the sum of the value of operations and the nonoperating assets.
- The **horizon date** is the date when there is no need to make additional forecasts because the growth rate in sales, cash flows, and dividends is assumed to be constant thereafter. This is also called the **terminal date**.
- The **horizon value** of operations is the value of operations at the end of the explicit forecast period. It is also called the **terminal value** or **continuing value**, and it is equal to the present value of all free cash flows beyond the forecast period, discounted back to the end of the forecast period at the weighted average cost of capital:

$$\text{Horizon value} = V_{op(at\ time\ T)} = \frac{FCF_{T+1}}{WACC - g} = \frac{FCF_T(1 + g)}{WACC - g}$$

Web Extension 8A provides a derivation of this formula.

- The estimated **value of equity** is the total value of the company minus the value of the debt and preferred stock. The estimated **intrinsic price per share** is the total value of the equity divided by the number of shares.
- To estimate the **value of operations for a nonconstant growth stock**: (1) forecast the free cash flows expected during the nonconstant growth period, (2) estimate the horizon value of operations at the end of the nonconstant growth period, (3) discount the free cash flows and estimated horizon value of operations back to the present, and (4) sum these PVs to find the current estimated value of operations.
- The expected **dividend yield** is expected dividend divided by the current stock price.
- The expected **capital gains yield** is expected change in the stock price divided by the current stock price.

- The value of a share of stock is the present value of expected future dividends when discounted at the required return on common stock:

$$\hat{P}_0 = \sum_{t=1}^{\infty} \frac{D_t}{(1 + r_s)^t}$$

- The **constant dividend growth model**, which is also called the **Gordon growth model**, can be used when dividend growth is constant:

$$\hat{P}_0 = \frac{D_1}{r_s - g_L}$$

- The **horizon value** for a stock is the present value of all dividends *after* the horizon date discounted back to horizon date:

$$\hat{P}_T = \frac{D_{T+1}}{r_s - g_L}$$

- The **expected total rate of return** from a stock consists of an expected dividend yield plus an expected capital gains yield. For a constant growth firm, both the dividend yield and the capital gains yield are expected to remain constant in the future.

- The equation for $\hat{r}_s$, the **expected rate of return on a constant growth stock**, is

$$\hat{r}_s = \frac{D_1}{P_0} + g$$

- A **zero growth stock** is one whose future dividends are not expected to grow at all. A **nonconstant growth stock** is one whose earnings and dividends are expected to grow much faster than the economy as a whole over some specified time period and then to grow at a sustainable long-term rate.

- To estimate the **present value of a nonconstant growth stock**: (1) forecast the dividends expected during the nonconstant growth period, (2) estimate the projected price of the stock at the end of the nonconstant growth period, (3) discount the dividends and the projected price back to the present, and (4) sum these PVs to find the current estimated value of the stock, $\hat{P}_0$.

- **Preferred stock** is a hybrid security having some characteristics of debt and some of equity.

- The **value of a share of perpetual preferred stock** is found as the dividend divided by the required rate of return:

$$V_{ps} = \frac{D_{ps}}{r_{ps}}$$

- **Preferred stock** that has a finite maturity is evaluated with a formula that is identical in form to the bond value formula.

Questions

8–1 Define each of the following terms:
   a. Proxy; proxy fight; preemptive right; classified stock; founders' shares
   b. Estimated value ($\hat{P}_0$); market price (P_0)

c. Required rate of return, r_s; expected rate of return, $\hat{r}_s$; actual, or realized, rate of return, $\bar{r}_s$

d. Capital gains yield; dividend yield; expected total return

e. Constant growth; nonconstant growth; zero growth stock

f. Preferred stock

g. Nonoperating assets

h. Value of operations; horizon value; free cash flow valuation model

8-2 Two investors are evaluating General Electric's stock for possible purchase. They agree on the expected value of D_1 and also on the expected future dividend growth rate. Further, they agree on the risk of the stock. However, one investor normally holds stocks for 2 years and the other normally holds stocks for 10 years. On the basis of the type of analysis done in this chapter, they should both be willing to pay the same price for General Electric's stock. True or false? Explain.

8-3 A bond that pays interest forever and has no maturity date is a perpetual bond, also called a perpetuity or a consol. In what respect is a perpetual bond similar to: (1) a no-growth common stock and (2) a share of preferred stock?

8-4 Explain how to use the free cash flow valuation model to find the price per share of common equity.

Problems   Answers Appear in Appendix B

Easy Problems 1–7

8-1 DPS Calculation
Thress Industries just paid a dividend of $1.50 a share (i.e., $D_0 = \$1.50$). The dividend is expected to grow 5% a year for the next 3 years and then 10% a year thereafter. What is the expected dividend per share for each of the next 5 years?

8-2 Constant Growth Valuation
Boehm Incorporated is expected to pay a $1.50 per share dividend at the end of this year (i.e., $D_1 = \$1.50$). The dividend is expected to grow at a constant rate of 6% a year. The required rate of return on the stock, r_s, is 13%. What is the estimated value per share of Boehm's stock?

8-3 Constant Growth Valuation
Woidtke Manufacturing's stock currently sells for $22 a share. The stock just paid a dividend of $1.20 a share (i.e., $D_0 = \$1.20$), and the dividend is expected to grow forever at a constant rate of 10% a year. What stock price is expected 1 year from now? What is the estimated required rate of return on Woidtke's stock (assume the market is in equilibrium with the required return equal to the expected return)?

8-4 Preferred Stock Valuation
Nick's Enchiladas Incorporated has preferred stock outstanding that pays a dividend of $5 at the end of each year. The preferred sells for $50 a share. What is the stock's required rate of return (assume the market is in equilibrium with the required return equal to the expected return)?

8–5 **Nonconstant Growth Valuation**

A company currently pays a dividend of $2 per share ($D_0 = \$2$). It is estimated that the company's dividend will grow at a rate of 20% per year for the next 2 years, and then at a constant rate of 7% thereafter. The company's stock has a beta of 1.2, the risk-free rate is 7.5%, and the market risk premium is 4%. What is your estimate of the stock's current price?

8–6 **Value of Operations of Constant Growth Firm**

EMC Corporation has never paid a dividend. Its current free cash flow of $400,000 is expected to grow at a constant rate of 5%. The weighted average cost of capital is WACC = 12%. Calculate EMC's estimated value of operations.

8–7 **Horizon Value of Free Cash Flows**

Current and projected free cash flows for Radell Global Operations are shown below. Growth is expected to be constant after 2017, and the weighted average cost of capital is 11%. What is the horizon (continuing) value at 2018 if growth from 2017 remains constant?

	Actual	Projected		
	2015	2016	2017	2018
Free cash flow (millions of dollars)	$606.82	$667.50	$707.55	$750.00

Intermediate Problems 8–17

8–8 **Constant Growth Rate, g**

A stock is trading at $80 per share. The stock is expected to have a year-end dividend of $4 per share ($D_1 = \$4$), and it is expected to grow at some constant rate g throughout time. The stock's required rate of return is 14% (assume the market is in equilibrium with the required return equal to the expected return). What is your forecast of g?

8–9 **Constant Growth Valuation**

Crisp Cookware's common stock is expected to pay a dividend of $3 a share at the end of this year ($D_1 = \$3.00$); its beta is 0.8; the risk-free rate is 5.2%; and the market risk premium is 6%. The dividend is expected to grow at some constant rate g, and the stock currently sells for $40 a share. Assuming the market is in equilibrium, what does the market believe will be the stock's price at the end of 3 years (i.e., what is $\hat{P}_3$)?

8–10 **Preferred Stock Rate of Return**

What is the required rate of return on a preferred stock with a $50 par value, a stated annual dividend of 7% of par, and a current market price of (a) $30, (b) $40, (c) $50, and (d) $70 (assume the market is in equilibrium with the required return equal to the expected return)?

8–11 **Declining Growth Stock Valuation**

Brushy Mountain Mining Company's coal reserves are being depleted, so its sales are falling. Also, environmental costs increase each year, so its costs are rising. As a result, the company's earnings and dividends are declining at the constant rate of 4% per year. If $D_0 = \$6$ and $r_s = 14\%$, what is the estimated value of Brushy Mountain's stock?

8-12 Nonconstant Growth Stock Valuation

Assume that the average firm in your company's industry is expected to grow at a constant rate of 6% and that its dividend yield is 7%. Your company is about as risky as the average firm in the industry and just paid a dividend (D_0) of $1. You expect that the growth rate of dividends will be 50% during the first year $(g_{0,1} = 50\%)$ and 25% during the second year $(g_{1,2} = 25\%)$. After Year 2, dividend growth will be constant at 6%. What is the required rate of return on your company's stock? What is the estimated value per share of your firm's stock?

8-13 Nonconstant Growth Stock Valuation

Simpkins Corporation does not pay any dividends because it is expanding rapidly and needs to retain all of its earnings. However, investors expect Simpkins to begin paying dividends, with the first dividend of $0.50 coming 3 years from today. The dividend should grow rapidly—at a rate of 80% per year—during Years 4 and 5. After Year 5, the company should grow at a constant rate of 7% per year. If the required return on the stock is 16%, what is the value of the stock today (assume the market is in equilibrium with the required return equal to the expected return)?

8-14 Preferred Stock Valuation

Several years ago, Rolen Riders issued preferred stock with a stated annual dividend of 10% of its $100 par value. Preferred stock of this type currently yields 8%. Assume dividends are paid annually.

a. What is the estimated value of Rolen's preferred stock?

b. Suppose interest rate levels have risen to the point where the preferred stock now yields 12%. What would be the new estimated value of Rolen's preferred stock?

8-15 Return on Common Stock

You buy a share of The Ludwig Corporation stock for $21.40. You expect it to pay dividends of $1.07, $1.1449, and $1.2250 in Years 1, 2, and 3, respectively, and you expect to sell it at a price of $26.22 at the end of 3 years.

a. Calculate the growth rate in dividends.

b. Calculate the expected dividend yield.

c. Assuming that the calculated growth rate is expected to continue, you can add the dividend yield to the expected growth rate to obtain the expected total rate of return. What is this stock's expected total rate of return (assume the market is in equilibrium with the required return equal to the expected return)?

8-16 Constant Growth Stock Valuation

Investors require a 13% rate of return on Brooks Sisters's stock $(r_s = 13\%)$.

a. What would the estimated value of Brooks' stock be if the previous dividend were $D_0 = \$3.00$ and if investors expect dividends to grow at a constant annual rate of: (1) -5%, (2) 0%, (3) 5%, and (4) 10%?

b. Using data from part a, what is the constant growth model's estimated value for Brooks Sisters's stock if the required rate of return is 13% and the expected growth rate is: (1) 13% or (2) 15%? Are these reasonable results? Explain.

c. Is it reasonable to expect that a constant growth stock would have $g > r_s$?

8-17 **Value of Operations**

Kendra Enterprises has never paid a dividend. Free cash flow is projected to be $80,000 and $100,000 for the next 2 years, respectively; after the second year, FCF is expected to grow at a constant rate of 8%. The company's weighted average cost of capital is 12%.

a. What is the terminal, or horizon, value of operations? (*Hint:* Find the value of all free cash flows beyond Year 2 discounted back to Year 2.)

b. Calculate the value of Kendra's operations.

8-18 **Free Cash Flow Valuation**

Dozier Corporation is a fast-growing supplier of office products. Analysts project the following free cash flows (FCFs) during the next 3 years, after which FCF is expected to grow at a constant 7% rate. Dozier's weighted average cost of capital is WACC = 13%.

	Year		
	1	2	3
Free cash flow ($ millions)	−$20	$30	$40

a. What is Dozier's horizon value? (*Hint:* Find the value of all free cash flows beyond Year 3 discounted back to Year 3.)

b. What is the current value of operations for Dozier?

c. Suppose Dozier has $10 million in marketable securities, $100 million in debt, and 10 million shares of stock. What is the intrinsic price per share?

Challenging Problems 19–21

8-19 **Constant Growth Stock Valuation**

You are analyzing Jillian's Jewlery (JJ) stock for a possible purchase. JJ just paid a dividend of $1.50 *yesterday*. You expect the dividend to grow at the rate of 6% per year for the next 3 years; if you buy the stock, you plan to hold it for 3 years and then sell it.

a. What dividends do you expect for JJ stock over the next 3 years? In other words, calculate D_1, D_2, and D_3. Note that D_0 = $1.50.

b. JJ's stock has a required return of 13%, and so this is the rate you'll use to discount dividends. Find the present value of the dividend stream; that is, calculate the PV of D_1, D_2, and D_3, and then sum these PVs.

c. JJ stock should trade for $27.053 years from now (i.e., you expect $\hat{P}_3$ = $27.05). Discounted at a 13% rate, what is the present value of this expected future stock price? In other words, calculate the PV of $27.05.

d. If you plan to buy the stock, hold it for 3 years, and then sell it for $27.05, what is the most you should pay for it?

e. Use the constant growth model to calculate the present value of this stock. Assume that g = 6% and is constant.

f. Is the value of this stock dependent on how long you plan to hold it? In other words, if your planned holding period were 2 years or 5 years rather than 3 years, would this affect the value of the stock today, $\hat{P}_0$? Explain your answer.

8-20 **Nonconstant Growth Stock Valuation**

Reizenstein Technologies (RT) has just developed a solar panel capable of generating 200% more electricity than any solar panel currently on the market.

As a result, RT is expected to experience a 15% annual growth rate for the next 5 years. By the end of 5 years, other firms will have developed comparable technology, and RT's growth rate will slow to 5% per year indefinitely. Stockholders require a return of 12% on RT's stock. The most recent annual dividend (D_0), which was paid yesterday, was $1.75 per share.

a. Calculate RT's expected dividends for t = 1, t = 2, t = 3, t = 4, and t = 5.

b. Calculate the estimated intrinsic value of the stock today, $\hat{P}_0$. Proceed by finding the present value of the dividends expected at t = 1, t = 2, t = 3, t = 4, and t = 5 plus the present value of the stock price that should exist at t = 5, $\hat{P}_5$. The $\hat{P}_5$ stock price can be found by using the constant growth equation. Note that to find $\hat{P}_5$ you use the dividend expected at t = 6, which is 5% greater than the t = 5 dividend.

c. Calculate the expected dividend yield $(D_1/\hat{P}_0)$, the capital gains yield expected during the first year, and the expected total return (dividend yield plus capital gains yield) during the first year. (Assume that $\hat{P}_0 = P_0$, and recognize that the capital gains yield is equal to the total return minus the dividend yield.) Also calculate these same three yields for t = 5 (e.g., $D_6/\hat{P}_5$).

8-21 Nonconstant Growth Stock Valuation

Conroy Consulting Corporation (CCC) has been growing at a rate of 30% per year in recent years. This same nonconstant growth rate is expected to last for another 2 years $(g_{0,1} = g_{1,2} = 30\%)$.

a. If D_0 = $2.50, r_s = 12%, and g_L = 7%, then what is CCC's stock worth today? What is its expected dividend yield for the first year? What is the expected capital gains yield for the first year?

b. Now assume that CCC's period of nonconstant growth is to last another 5 years rather than 2 years $(g_{0,1} = g_{1,2} = g_{2,3} = g_{3,4} = g_{4,5} = 30\%)$. How would this affect its price, dividend yield, and capital gains yield? Answer in words only.

c. What will CCC's dividend yield and capital gains yield be once its period of nonconstant growth ends? (*Hint:* These values will be the same regardless of whether you examine the case of 2 or 5 years of nonconstant growth, and the calculations are very easy.)

d. Of what interest to investors is the relationship over time between dividend yield and capital gains yield?

Spreadsheet Problem

8-22 Build a Model: Free Cash Flow Valuation Model

Start with the partial model in the file *Ch08 P22 Build a Model.xlsx* on the textbook's Web site. Selected data for the Derby Corporation are shown below. Use the data to answer the following questions.

a. Calculate the estimated horizon value (i.e., the value of operations at the end of the forecast period immediately after the Year-4 free cash flow).

b. Calculate the present value of the horizon value, the present value of the free cash flows, and the estimated Year-0 value of operations.

c. Calculate the estimated Year-0 price per share of common equity.

INPUTS (In Millions)

	Current	Year			
			Projected		
	0	**1**	**2**	**3**	**4**
Free cash flow		−$20.0	$20.0	$80.0	$84.0
Marketable securities	$ 40				
Notes payable	$ 100				
Long-term bonds	$300				
Preferred stock	$ 50				
WACC	9.00%				
Number of shares of stock	40				

8–23 **Build a Model: Value Drivers in the Free Cash Flow Valuation Model**

Start with the partial model in *Ch08 Build a Model.xlsx* on the textbook's Web site. Traver-Dunlap Corporation has a 15% weighted average cost of capital (WACC). Its most recent sales were $980 million and its total net operating capital is $870 million. The following shows estimates of the forecasted growth rates, operating profitability ratios, and capital requirement ratios for the next three years. All of these ratios are expected to remain constant after the third year. Use this information to answer the following questions.

a. Use the data to forecast sales, net operating profit after taxes (NOPAT), total net operating capital (OpCap), free cash flow (FCF), growth rate in FCF, and return on invested capital (ROIC) for the next 3 years. What is the FCF growth rate for Year 3 and how does it compare with the growth rate in sales? What is the ROIC for Year 3 and how does it compare with the 15% WACC?

b. What is the value of operations at Year 3, $V_{op,3}$? What is the current value of operations, $V_{op,0}$? How does the value of operations at Year 0 compare with the total net operating working capital at Year 3, and what might explain this relationship?

c. Suppose the growth rates for Years 2, 3, and thereafter can be increased to 7%. What is the new value of operations? Did it go up or down? Why did it change in this manner?

d. Return the growth rates to the original values. Now suppose that the capital requirement ratio can be decreased to 60% for all 3 years and thereafter. What is the new value of operations? Did it go up or down relative to the original base case? Why did it change in this manner?

e. Leave the capital requirement ratios at 60% for all 3 years and thereafter, but increase the sales growth rates for Years 2, 3, and thereafter to 7%. What is the new value of operations? Did it go up or down relative to the other scenarios? Why did it change in this manner?

WEB

Estimated Data for Traver-Dunlap Corporation

	Forecast Year		
	1	2	3
Annual sales growth rate	20%	7%	7%
Operating profitability (NOPAT/Sales)	12%	10%	10%
Capital requirement (OpCap/Sales)	60%	60%	60%
Tax rate	35%	35%	35%

8–24 Build a Model: Dividend Growth Valuation Model

Start with the partial model in the file *Ch08 P24 Build a Model.xlsx* on the textbook's Web site. Hamilton Landscaping's dividend growth rate is expected to be 30% in the next year, drop to 15% from Year 1 to Year 2, and drop to a constant 5% for Year 2 and all subsequent years. Hamilton has just paid a dividend of $2.50, and its stock has a required return of 11%.

a. What is Hamilton's estimated stock price today?

b. If you bought the stock at Year 0, what are your expected dividend yield and capital gains for the upcoming year?

c. What are your expected dividend yield and capital gains for the second year (from Year 1 to Year 2)? Why aren't these the same as for the first year?

MINI CASE

Your employer, a mid-sized human resources management company, is considering expansion into related fields, including the acquisition of Temp Force Company, an employment agency that supplies word processor operators and computer programmers to businesses with temporary heavy workloads. Your employer is also considering the purchase of a Biggerstaff & McDonald (B&D), a privately held company owned by two friends, each with 5 million shares of stock. B&M currently has free cash flow of $24 million, which is expected to grow at a constant rate of 5%. B&M's financial statements report short-term investments of $100 million, debt of $200 million, and preferred stock of $50 million. B&M's weighted average cost of capital (WACC) is 11%. Answer the following questions.

a. Describe briefly the legal rights and privileges of common stockholders.

b. What is free cash flow (FCF)? What is the weighted average cost of capital? What is the free cash flow valuation model?

c. Use a pie chart to illustrate the sources that comprise a hypothetical company's total value. Using another pie chart, show the claims on a company's value. How is equity a residual claim?

d. Suppose the free cash flow at Time 1 is expected to grow at a constant rate of g_L forever. If $g_L < $ WACC, what is a formula for the present value of expected free cash flows when discounted at the WACC? If the most recent free cash flow is expected to grow at a constant rate of g_L forever (and $g_L < $ WACC), what is a formula for the present value of expected free cash flows when discounted at the WACC?

e. Use B&M's data and the free cash flow valuation model to answer the following questions.

  (1) What is its estimated value of operations?

  (2) What is its estimated total corporate value? (This is the entity value.)

  (3) What is its estimated intrinsic value of equity?

  (4) What is its estimated intrinsic stock price per share?

f. You have just learned that B&M has undertaken a major expansion that will change its expected free cash flows to –$10 million in 1 year, $20 million in 2 years, and $35 million in 3 years. After 3 years, free cash flow will grow at a rate of 5%. No new debt or preferred stock was added; the investment was financed by equity from the owners. Assume the WACC is unchanged at 11% and that there are still 10 million shares of stock outstanding.

(1) What is the company's horizon value (i.e., its value of operations at Year 3)? What is its current value of operations (i.e., at Time 0)?

(2) What is its estimated intrinsic value of equity on a price-per-share basis?

g. If B&M undertakes the expansion, what percent of B&M's value of operations at Year 0 is due to cash flows from Year 4 and beyond? (*Hint:* Use the horizon value at t = 3 to help answer this question.)

h. Based on your answer to the previous question, what are two reasons why managers often emphasize short-term earnings?

i. Your employer also is considering the acquisition of Hatfield Medical Supplies. You have gathered the following data regarding Hatfield, with all dollars reported in millions: (1) most recent sales of $2,000; (2) most recent total net operating capital, OpCap = $1,120; (3) most recent operating profitability ratio, OP = NOPAT/Sales = 4.5%; and (4) most recent capital requirement ratio, CR = OpCap/Sales = 56%. You estimate that the growth rate in sales from Year 0 to Year 1 will be 10%, from Year 1 to Year 2 will be 8%, from Year 2 to Year 3 will be 5%, and from Year 3 to Year 4 will be 5%. You also estimate that the long-term growth rate beyond Year 4 will be 5%. Assume the operating profitability and capital requirement ratios will not change. Use this information to forecast Hatfield's sales, net operating profit after taxes (NOPAT), OpCap, free cash flow, and return on invested capital (ROIC) for Years 1 through 4. Also estimate the annual growth in free cash flow for Years 2 through 4. The weighted average cost of capital (WACC) is 9%. How does the ROIC in Year 4 compare with the WACC?

j. What is the horizon value at Year 4? What is the value of operations at Year 4? Which is larger, and what can explain the difference? What is the value of operations at Year 0?

How does the value of operations compare with the current total net operating capital?

k. What are value drivers? What happens to the ROIC and current value of operations if expected growth increases by 1 percentage point relative to the original growth rates (including the long-term growth rate)? What can explain this? (*Hint:* Use Scenario Manager.)

l. Assume growth rates are at their original levels. What happens to the ROIC and current value of operations if the operating profitability ratio increases to 5.5%? Now assume growth rates and operating profitability ratios are at their original levels. What happens to the ROIC and current value of operations if the capital requirement ratio decreases to 51%? Assume growth rates are at their original levels. What is the impact of simultaneous improvements in operating profitability and capital requirements? What is the impact of simultaneous improvements in the growth rates, operating profitability, and capital requirements? (*Hint:* Use Scenario Manager.)

m. What insight does the free cash flow valuation model provide us about possible reasons for market volatility? (*Hint:* Look at the value of operations for the combinations of ROIC and g_L in the previous questions.)

n. (1) Write out a formula that can be used to value any dividend-paying stock, regardless of its dividend pattern.

(2) What is a constant growth stock? How are constant growth stocks valued?

(3) What happens if a company has a constant g_L that exceeds its r_s? Will many stocks have expected growth greater than the required rate of return in the short run (i.e., for the next few years)? In the long run (i.e., forever)?

o. Assume that Temp Force has a beta coefficient of 1.2, that the risk-free rate (the yield on T-bonds) is 7.0%, and that the market risk premium is 5%. What is the required rate of return on the firm's stock?

p. Assume that Temp Force is a constant growth company whose last dividend (D_0, which was paid yesterday) was $2.00 and whose dividend is expected to grow indefinitely at a 6% rate.

(1) What is the firm's current estimated intrinsic stock price?

(2) What is the stock's expected value 1 year from now?

(3) What are the expected dividend yield, the expected capital gains yield, and the expected total return during the first year?

q. Now assume that the stock is currently selling at $30.29. What is its expected rate of return?

r. Now assume that Temp Force's dividend is expected to experience nonconstant growth of 30% from Year 0 to Year 1, 25% from Year 1 to Year 2, and 15% from Year 2 to Year 3. After Year 3, dividends will grow at a constant rate of 6%. What is the stock's intrinsic value under these conditions? What are the expected dividend yield and capital gains yield during the first year? What are the expected dividend yield and capital gains yield during the fourth year (from Year 3 to Year 4)?

s. Compare and contrast the free cash flow valuation model and the dividend growth model.

t. What is market multiple analysis?

u. What is preferred stock? Suppose a share of preferred stock pays a dividend of $2.10 and investors require a return of 7%. What is the estimated value of the preferred stock?

SELECTED ADDITIONAL CASES

The following cases from CengageCompose cover many of the concepts discussed in this chapter and are available at http://compose.cengage.com.

Klein-Brigham Series:

Case 3, "Peachtree Securities, Inc. (B)"; Case 71, "Swan Davis"; Case 78, "Beatrice Peabody"; and Case 101, "TECO Energy."

Brigham-Buzzard Series:

Case 4, "Powerline Network Corporation (Stocks)."

CHAPTER 9

Corporate Valuation and Financial Planning

WEB

The textbook's Web site contains an *Excel* file that will guide you through the chapter's calculations. The file for this chapter is **Ch09 Tool Kit.xls**, and we encourage you to open the file and follow along as you read the chapter.

Our primary objective in this book is to explain how financial managers can make their companies more valuable. However, value creation is impossible unless the company has well-designed operating and financial plans. As Yogi Berra once said, "You've got to be careful if you don't know where you're going, because you might not get there."

A vital step in financial planning is to forecast financial statements, which are called **projected financial statements** or **pro forma financial statements**. Managers use projected financial statements in four ways: (1) By looking at projected statements, they can assess whether the firm's anticipated performance is in line with the firm's own general targets and with investors' expectations. (2) Pro forma statements can be used to estimate the effect of proposed operating changes, enabling managers to conduct "what-if" analyses. (3) Managers use pro forma statements to anticipate the firm's future financing needs. (4) Managers forecast free cash flows under different operating plans, forecast their capital requirements, and then choose the plan that maximizes shareholder value. Security analysts make the same types of projections, forecasting future earnings, cash flows, and stock prices.

Beginning-of-Chapter Questions

As you read the chapter, consider how you would answer the following questions. You *should not* necessarily be able to answer the questions before you read the chapter. Rather, you should use them to get a sense of the issues covered in the chapter. After reading the chapter, you should be able to give at least partial answers to the questions, and you should be able to give better answers after the chapter has been discussed in class. Note, too, that it is often useful, when answering conceptual questions, to use hypothetical data to illustrate your answer. We illustrate the answers with an *Excel* model that is available on the textbook's Web site. Accessing the model and working through it is a useful exercise, and it provides insights that are useful when answering the questions.

1. List and discuss briefly the major components of a firm's **financial plan**. What role do projections of financial statements play in the development of the financial plan?

2. A major component of financial planning is to forecast future financial statements. If you had a company's balance sheets and income statements for the past 5 years but no other information, how could you use the forecasted financial statement approach to forecast the following items for the coming year? (a) Its sales revenues. (b) Its financial statements. (c) Its funds requirements (AFN). (d) Its financial condition and profitability as shown by its ROE and other key ratios.

3. If you had a set of industry average ratios for the firm you were analyzing, how might you use these data?

4. All forecasts are subject to error. Do you think top managers would be concerned about the effects on the firm if sales revenues or unit costs, for example, turned out to be different from the forecasted level? How could you provide information on the effects of such errors?

5. Define the following terms and then explain the role they might play in your forecast. (a) **Economies of scale**. (b) **Lumpy assets**. (c) **Excess capacity**.

6. The funds requirement can be forecasted by the forecasted financial statement approach, but you could also use the **AFN formula**. What is this formula, and how does it operate? What are its advantages and disadvantages relative to the financial statement method?

7. For most firms, there is some sales growth rate at which they could grow without needing any external financing, that is, where AFN = $0. How could you determine that growth rate? What variables under management's control would affect this **sustainable growth rate**?

CORPORATE VALUATION AND FINANCIAL PLANNING

The value of a firm is determined by the size, timing, and risk of its expected future free cash flows (FCF). Managers use projected financial statements to estimate the impact that different operating plans have on intrinsic value. Managers also use projected statements to identify deficits that must be financed in order to implement the operating plans. This chapter explains how to project financial statements that incorporate operating assumptions and financial policies.

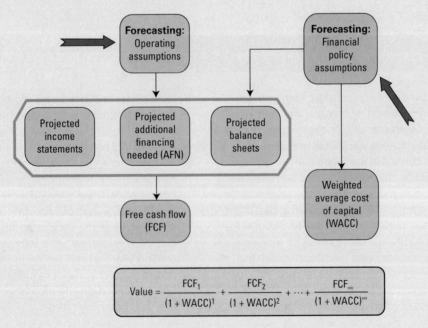

$$\text{Value} = \frac{FCF_1}{(1 + WACC)^1} + \frac{FCF_2}{(1 + WACC)^2} + \cdots + \frac{FCF_\infty}{(1 + WACC)^\infty}$$

9-1 **Overview of Financial Planning**

The two most important components of financial planning are the operating plan and the financial plan.

9-1a **The Operating Plan**

As its name suggests, an operating plan provides detailed implementation guidance for a firm's operations, including the firm's choice of market segments, product lines, sales and marketing strategies, production processes, and logistics. An operating plan can be developed for any time horizon, but most companies use a 5-year horizon, with the plan being quite detailed for the first year but less and less specific for each succeeding year. The plan explains who is responsible for each particular function and when specific tasks are to be accomplished.

An important part of the operating plan is the forecast of sales, production costs, inventories, and other operating items. In fact, this part of the operating plan actually is a forecast of the company's expected free cash flow. (Recall from Chapter 2 that free cash flow is defined as net operating profit after taxes (NOPAT) minus the investment in total operating capital.)

Free cash flow is the primary source of a company's value. Using what-if analysis, managers can analyze different operating plans to estimate their impact on value. In addition, managers can apply sensitivity analysis, scenario analysis, and simulation to estimate the risk of different operating plans, which is an important part of risk management.

9-1b **The Financial Plan**

By definition, a company's operating assets can grow only by the purchase of additional assets. Therefore, a growing company must continually obtain cash to purchase new assets. Some of this cash might be generated internally by its operations, but some might have to come externally from shareholders or debtholders. This is the essence of financial planning—forecasting the additional sources of financing required to fund the operating plan.

There is a strong connection between financial planning and free cash flow. A company's operations generate the free cash flow, but the financial plan determines how the company will use the free cash flow. Recall from Chapter 6 that free cash flow can be used in five ways: (1) pay dividends, (2) repurchase stock, (3) pay the net after-tax interest on debt, (4) repay debt, or (5) purchase financial assets such as marketable securities. A company's financial plan must use free cash flow differently if FCF is negative than if FCF is positive.

If free cash flow is positive, the financial plan must identify how much FCF to allocate among its investors (shareholders or debtholders) and how much to put aside for future needs by purchasing marketable securities. If free cash flow is negative, either because the company is growing rapidly (which requires large investments in operating capital) or because the company has low NOPAT, then the total uses of free cash flow must also be negative. For example, instead of repurchasing stock, the company might have to issue stock; instead of repaying debt, the company might have to issue debt.

Therefore, the financial plan must incorporate: (1) the company's dividend policy, which determines the targeted size and method of cash distributions to shareholders, and (2) the capital structure, which determines the targeted mix of debt and equity used to finance the firm, which in turn determines the relative mix of distributions to shareholders and payments to debtholders.

SELF TEST

Briefly describe the key elements of an operating plan.

Identify the five uses of free cash flow and how these uses are related to a financial plan.

9-2 Financial Planning at MicroDrive Inc.

As we described in Chapters 6, 7, and 8, MicroDrive's operating performance and stock price have declined in recent years. As a result, MicroDrive's board recently installed a new management team: A new CEO, CFO, marketing manager, sales manager, inventory manager, and credit manager—only the production manager was retained. The new team met for a 3-day retreat with the goal of developing a plan to improve the company's performance.

In preparation for the retreat, the new CFO developed a simple *Excel* model to forecast free cash flows and to identify the impacts that different value drivers (sales growth rates, operating profitability, and capital requirements) have on MicroDrive's value of operations and intrinsic stock price; see Chapter 8 for this analysis. The CFO then created a more detailed model to incorporate a complete operating plan and financial plan based on the status quo to give the management team a better idea of where the company is now and where it will be if they don't make changes; refer to *Ch09 Tool Kit.xls* as we explain MicroDrive's financial planning.

The CFO's first step was to examine the current and recent historical data. Figure 9-1 shows MicroDrive's most recent financial statements and selected additional data; see Chapters 6 and 7 for a full discussion of the process used to assess MicroDrive's current position and trends.

The CFO's second step was to choose a forecasting framework. Many companies, including MicroDrive, forecast their entire financial statements as part of the planning process. This approach is called **forecasted financial statements (FFS) method** of financial planning.

Figure 9-2 shows the inputs MicroDrive uses to forecast different scenarios for its operating plan and financial plan. The inputs are for the Status Quo scenario, which assumes most of MicroDrive's operating activities and financial policies remain unchanged. The figure shows actual values for industry peers (the silver section), actual values for MicroDrive's past 2 years, and forecasted values for MicroDrive's 5-year forecast. The blue section shows inputs for the first year and inputs for any subsequent years that differ from the previous year. Section 1 shows the ratios required to project the items required for an operating plan, Section 2 shows the inputs related to the capital structure, Section 3 shows the costs of the capital components, and Section 4 shows the target dividend policy. We will describe each of these sections as they are applied to the forecast, beginning with the forecast of operations.

FIGURE 9-1	MicroDrive's Most Recent Financial Statements (Millions, Except for Per Share Data)

	A	B	C		D	E	F	G
15	**INCOME STATEMENTS**				**BALANCE SHEETS**			
16		**2014**	**2015**		*Assets*		**2014**	**2015**
17	Net sales	$ 4,760	$ 5,000		Cash		$ 60	$ 50
18	COGS (excl. depr.)	3,560	3,800		ST Investments		40	–
19	Depreciation	170	200		Accounts receivable		380	500
20	Other operating expenses	480	500		Inventories		820	1,000
21	EBIT	$ 550	$ 500		Total CA		$ 1,300	$ 1,550
22	Interest expense	100	120		Net PP&E		1,700	2,000
23	Pre-tax earnings	$ 450	$ 380		Total assets		$ 3,000	$ 3,550
24	Taxes (40%)	180	152					
25	NI before pref. div.	$ 270	$ 228		*Liabilities and equity*			
26	Preferred div.	8	8		Accounts payable		$ 190	$ 200
27	Net income	$ 262	$ 220		Accruals		280	300
28					Notes payable		130	280
29	*Other Data*				Total CL		$ 600	$ 780
30	Common dividends	$48	$50		Long-term bonds		1,000	1,200
31	Addition to RE	$214	$170		Total liabilities		$ 1,600	$ 1,980
32	Tax rate	40%	40%		Preferred stock		100	100
33	Shares of common stock	50	50		Common stock		500	500
34	Earnings per share	$5.24	$4.40		Retained earnings		800	970
35	Dividends per share	$0.96	$1.00		Total common equity		$ 1,300	$ 1,470
36	Price per share	$40.00	$27.00		Total liabs. & equity		$ 3,000	$ 3,550
37								

Note: Numbers in the figure are shown as rounded values for clarity in reporting. However, unrounded values are used for all calculations. See the *Excel Tool Kit* for this chapter.

Microsoft Excel® is a registered trademark of Microsoft Corporation. © 2014 Microsoft.

9-3 Forecasting Operations

The first row in Section 1 of Figure 9-2 shows the forecast of the sales growth rate. After discussions with teams from marketing, sales, product development, and production, MicroDrive's CFO chose a growth rate of 10% for the next year. Keep in mind that this is just a preliminary estimate and that it is easy to make changes later in the *Excel* model. Notice that MicroDrive is forecasting sales growth to decline and level off by the end of the forecast. Recall from Chapter 8 that the growth rate for a company's sales and free cash flows must level off at some future date in order to apply the constant growth model at the forecast horizon. Had MicroDrive's managers projected nonconstant growth for more than 5 years, Figure 9-2 would need to be extended until growth does level out.

For operating items other than sales, MicroDrive's CFO included only the operating profitability ratio and the capital requirement ratio in Chapter 8. However, the CFO's comprehensive forecast described here includes the individual financial statement accounts that comprise operating profitability and capital requirements, as shown in Figure 9-2. MicroDrive's managers initially assumed that all the operating ratios other than growth would remain constant for the entire forecast period. However, it would be quite easy for them to make changes in the future ratios, with one caveat. The operating ratios must level off by the end of the forecast period,

MicroDrive's Forecast: Inputs for the Status Quo Scenario

	A	B	C	D	E	F	G	H	I
60	Status Quo	Industry	MicroDrive				MicroDrive		
61	Inputs	Actual	Actual				Forecast		
62	**1. Operating Ratios**	2015	2014	2015	2016	2017	2018	2019	2020
63	Sales growth rate	5%	15%	5%	10%	8%	7%	5%	5%
64	COGS (excl. depr.)/Sales	76%	75%	76%	76%	76%	76%	76%	76%
65	Depreciation/Net PP&E	9%	10%	10%	10%	10%	10%	10%	10%
66	Other op. exp./Sales	10%	10%	10%	10%	10%	10%	10%	10%
67	Cash/Sales	1%	1%	1%	1%	1%	1%	1%	1%
68	Acc. rec./Sales	8%	8%	10%	10%	10%	10%	10%	10%
69	Inventory/Sales	15%	17%	20%	20%	20%	20%	20%	20%
70	Net PP&E/Sales	33%	36%	40%	40%	40%	40%	40%	40%
71	Acc. pay./Sales	4%	4%	4%	4%	4%	4%	4%	4%
72	Accruals/Sales	7%	6%	6%	6%	6%	6%	6%	6%
73	Tax rate	40%	40%	40%	40%	40%	40%	40%	40%
74	**2. Capital Structure**	Actual Market Weights				Target Market Weights			
75	% Long-term debt	22%	31%	41%	28%	28%	28%	28%	28%
76	% Short-term debt	3%	4%	10%	2%	2%	2%	2%	2%
77	% Preferred stock	0%	3%	3%	3%	3%	3%	3%	3%
78	% Common stock	75%	62%	46%	67%	67%	67%	67%	67%
79	**3. Costs of Capital**						Forecast		
80	Rate on LT debt				9.0%	9%	9%	9%	9%
81	Rate on ST debt				10.0%	10%	10%	10%	10%
82	Rate on preferred stock (ignoring flotation costs)				8.0%	8%	8%	8%	8%
83	Cost of equity				13.58%	14%	14%	14%	14%
84	**4. Target Dividend Policy**		Actual						
85	Growth rate of dividends		11%	4.2%	5%	5%	5%	5%	5%

Note: Numbers in the figure are shown as rounded values for clarity in reporting. However, unrounded values are used for all calculations. See the *Excel Tool Kit* for this chapter.

or else the free cash flows *will not* be growing at a constant rate by the end of the forecast period even if sales *are* growing at a constant rate.

The following sections explain how MicroDrive uses the ratios in Figure 9-2 to forecast its operations. For convenience, the operating ratio inputs are repeated in Panel A of Figure 9-3; Panel B reports the resulting operating forecast.

9-3a Sales Revenues

Section B1 of Figure 9-3 shows the forecast of net sales based on the previous year's sales and the forecasted growth rate in sales. For example, the forecast of net sales for 2016 is $(1 + 0.10)(\$5,000) = \$5,500$.

9-3b Operating Assets

Section B2 of Figure 9-3 shows the forecast of operating assets. As noted earlier, MicroDrive's assets must increase if sales are to increase, and some types of assets grow proportionately to sales, including cash.

FIGURE 9-3 MicroDrive's Forecast of Operations for the Status Quo Scenario (Millions of Dollars, Except for Per Share Data)

	A	B	C	D	E	F	G	H	I
120	**Status Quo**	**Industry**	**MicroDrive**		**MicroDrive**				
121	**Panel A: Inputs**	**Actual**	**Actual**		**Forecast**				
122	*A1. Operating Ratios*	2015	2014	2015	2016	2017	2018	2019	2020
123	Sales growth rate	5%	15%	5%	10%	8%	7%	5%	5%
124	COGS (excl. depr.)/Sales	76%	75%	76%	76%	76%	76%	76%	76%
125	Depreciation/Net PP&E	9%	10%	10%	10%	10%	10%	10%	10%
126	Other op. exp./Sales	10%	10%	10%	10%	10%	10%	10%	10%
127	Cash/Sales	1%	1%	1%	1%	1%	1%	1%	1%
128	Acc. rec./Sales	8%	8%	10%	10%	10%	10%	10%	10%
129	Inventory/Sales	15%	17%	20%	20%	20%	20%	20%	20%
130	Net PP&E/Sales	33%	36%	40%	40%	40%	40%	40%	40%
131	Acc. pay./Sales	4%	4%	4%	4%	4%	4%	4%	4%
132	Accruals/Sales	7%	6%	6%	6%	6%	6%	6%	6%
133	Tax rate	40%	40%	40%	40%	40%	40%	40%	40%
134	**Panel B: Results**			**Actual**			**Forecast**		
135	*B1. Sales Revenues*			2015	2016	2017	2018	2019	2020
136	Net sales			$5,000	$5,500	$5,940	$6,356	$6,674	$7,007
137	*B2. Operating Assets and Operating Liabilities*								
138	Cash			$50	$55	$59	$64	$67	$70
139	Accounts receivable			$500	$550	$594	$636	$667	$701
140	Inventories			$1,000	$1,100	$1,188	$1,271	$1,335	$1,401
141	Net PP&E			$2,000	$2,200	$2,376	$2,542	$2,669	$2,803
142	Accounts payable			$200	$220	$238	$254	$267	$280
143	Accruals			$300	$330	$356	$381	$400	$420
144	*B3. Operating Income*								
145	COGS (excl. depr.)			$3,800	$4,180	$4,514	$4,830	$5,072	$5,326
146	Depreciation			$200	$220	$238	$254	$267	$280
147	Other operating expenses			$500	$550	$594	$636	$667	$701
148	EBIT			$500	$550	$594	$636	$667	$701
149	Net operating profit after taxes			$300	$330	$356	$381	$400	$420
150	*B4. Free Cash Flows*								
151	Net operating working capital			$1,050	$1,155	$1,247	$1,335	$1,401	$1,472
152	Total operating capital			$3,050	$3,355	$3,623	$3,877	$4,071	$4,274
153	FCF = NOPAT − Δ op capital			−$260	$25	$88	$128	$207	$217
154	*B5. Estimated Intrinsic Value*								
155	Target WACC				11.0%	11.0%	11.0%	11.0%	11.0%
156	Return on invested capital			9.8%	9.8%	9.8%	9.8%	9.8%	9.8%
157	Growth in FCF					252%	45.1%	61.7%	5.0%

159	**Horizon Value:**		Value of operations	$2,719
160			+ ST investments	$0
161	$HV_{2020} = \dfrac{FCF_{2020}(1+g_L)}{(WACC - g_L)}$ =	$3,814	Estimated total intrinsic value	$2,719
162			− All debt	$1,480
163	**Value of Operations:**		− Preferred stock	$100
164	Present value of HV	$2,267	Estimated intrinsic value of equity	$1,139
165	+ Present value of FCF	$453	÷ Number of shares	$50
166	Value of operations =	$2,719	Estimated intrinsic stock price =	$22.78

Note: Numbers in the figure are shown as rounded values for clarity in reporting. However, unrounded values are used for all calculations. See the *Excel **Tool Kit*** for this chapter.

MicroDrive writes and deposits checks every day. Because its managers don't know exactly when all of the checks will clear, they can't predict exactly what the balance in their checking accounts will be on any given day. Therefore, they must maintain a balance of cash and cash equivalents (such as very short-term marketable securities) to avoid overdrawing their accounts. We discuss the issue of cash management in Chapter 21, but MicroDrive's CFO assumed that the cash required to support MicroDrive's operations is proportional to its sales. For example, the forecasted cash in 2016 is 1%(2016 sales) = 1%($5,500) = $55. The CFO applied the same process to project cash in subsequent years.

Unless a company changes its credit policy or has a change in its customer base, accounts receivable should be proportional to sales. The CFO assumed that the credit policy and customers' paying patterns would remain constant and so projected accounts receivable as 10%($5,500) = $550.

As sales increase, firms generally must carry more inventories. The CFO assumed here that inventory would be proportional to sales. (Chapter 21 will discuss inventory management in detail). The projected inventory is 20%($5,500) = $1,100.

It might be reasonable to assume that cash, accounts receivable, and inventories will be proportional to sales, but will the amount of net property, plant, and equipment go up and down as sales go up and down? The correct answer could be either yes or no. When companies acquire PP&E, they often install more capacity than they currently need due to economies of scale in building capacity. Moreover, even if a plant is operating at its maximum-rated capacity, most companies can produce additional units by reducing downtime for scheduled maintenance, by running machinery at a higher than optimal speed, or by adding a second or third shift. Therefore, at least in the short run, sales and net PP&E may not have a close relationship.

However, some companies do have a close relationship between sales and net PP&E, even in the short term. For example, new stores in many retail chains achieve the same sales during their first year as the chain's existing stores. The only way such retailers can grow (beyond inflation) is by adding new stores. Such companies therefore have a strong proportional relationship between fixed assets and sales.

Finally, in the long term there is a close relationship between sales and net PP&E for virtually all companies: Few companies can continue to increase sales unless they also add capacity. Therefore, it is reasonable to assume that the long-term ratio of net PP&E to sales will be constant.

For the first years in a forecast, managers generally build in the actual planned expenditures on plant and equipment. If those estimates are not available, it is generally best to assume a constant ratio of net PP&E to sales.

MicroDrive is a relatively large company and makes capital expenditures every year, so the CFO forecast net PP&E as a percent of sales. The projected net PP&E is 40%($5,500) = $2,200.

9-3c **Operating Liabilities**

Section B2 of Figure 9-3 shows the forecast of operating liabilities. Some types of liabilities grow proportionately to sales; these are called **spontaneous liabilities**, as we explain next.

As sales increase, so will purchases of raw materials, and those additional purchases will spontaneously lead to a higher level of accounts payable. MicroDrive's forecast of accounts payable in 2016 is 4%($5,500) = $220.

Higher sales require more labor, and higher sales normally result in higher taxable income and thus taxes. Therefore, accrued wages and taxes both increase as sales increase. The projection of accruals is 6%($5,500) = $330.

9-3d Operating Income

For most companies, the cost of goods sold (COGS) is highly correlated with sales, and MicroDrive is no exception. As shown in Section B3 of Figure 9-3, MicroDrive's forecast of COGS for 2016 is 76%($5,500) = $4,180.

Because depreciation depends on an asset's depreciable basis, as described in Chapter 13, it is more reasonable to forecast depreciation as a percent of net plant and equipment rather than of sales. MicroDrive's projection of depreciation in 2016 is 10%(2016 Net PP&E) = 10%($2,200) = $220.

MicroDrive's other operating expenses include items such as salaries of executives, insurance fees, and marketing costs. These items tend to be related to a company's size, which is related to sales. MicroDrive's projection is 10%($5,500) = $550.

Subtracting the COGS, depreciation, and other operating expenses from net sales gives the earnings before interest and taxes (EBIT). Recall from Chapter 6 that the net operating profit after taxes (NOPAT) is defined as EBIT(1 − T), where T is the tax rate.

9-3e Free Cash Flow (FCF)

Section B4 in Figure 9-3 calculates free cash flow (FCF) using the process described in Chapter 6. The first row in Section B4 begins with a calculation of net operating capital (NOWC), which is defined as operating current assets minus operating current liabilities. Operating current assets is the sum of cash, accounts receivable, and inventories; operating current liabilities is the sum of accounts payable and accruals. The second row shows the forecast of total operating capital, which is NOWC plus net PP&E. All of the items required for these calculations were previously forecast in Section B2.

Recall from Chapter 6 that free cash flow is equal to NOPAT minus the investment in total operating capital; the forecast of NOPAT is in Section B3 and the forecast of total net operating capital is in the second row of Section B4.

9-3f Estimated Intrinsic Value

Section B5 begins with the estimated target WACC, calculated using the inputs from Sections 2 and 3 of Figure 9-2. These values are the same ones we will use in Chapter 11 to estimate MicroDrive's weighted average cost of capital, with the exception of the cost of preferred stock. To simplify the forecast of preferred dividends when projecting the income statement, MicroDrive's CFO decided to ignore flotation costs because they have a negligible impact on the WACC.

The weighted average cost of capital is calculated based on the target capital structure. MicroDrive's CFO decided to use the target capital structure for all scenarios, but to modify the projections later if the board decides to change the capital structure.

The second row in Section B5 of Figure 9-3 reports return on invested capital (ROIC) for easy comparison to the WACC. The third row shows the growth rate in

FCF. Notice that the growth rate is very high in the early years of the forecast but then levels out at the sustainable growth rate of sales, 5%. Had it not done so, the forecast period would need to be extended until the growth in FCF became constant.

Using the estimated FCF, WACC, and long-term constant growth rate in FCF, Section B5 shows the calculation of the value of operations using the constant growth horizon value formula from Chapter 8. To find the value of operations, it is necessary to find the present value of the horizon value and the present value of the forecasted free cash flows, and then sum them, as shown at the lower left corner of the figure.

The panel on the lower right of Section B5 estimates the intrinsic stock price using the approach in Chapter 8. For the Status Quo forecast, the estimated intrinsic value is $22.78. This estimate is about 16% lower than the price of $27 observed on December 31, 2015. What can account for this difference? First, keep in mind that MicroDrive's standard deviation of stock returns is about 49%, as estimated in Chapter 2. This high standard deviation makes the 16% difference between the estimated and actual stock price look pretty small. It could well be that the estimated intrinsic value would have been exactly equal to the actual stock price on a day during the week before or after December 31, 2015. Second, it could be that investors (who determine the price through their buying and selling activities) expect MicroDrive's performance in the future to be better than the Status Quo scenario.

We will have more to say about the operating forecast after completing the forecast of financial statements.

9-3g Enhancements to the Basic Model

Although the assumption that operating assets and operating liabilities grow proportionally to sales is a very good approximation for most companies, there are a few circumstances that might require more complicated modeling techniques. We describe four possible refinements in Section 9-7: economies of scale, nonlinear relationships, lumpy purchases of assets, and excess capacity adjustments. However, always keep in mind that additional complexity in a model might not be worth the incremental improvement in accuracy.

SELF TEST

Which items comprise operating current assets? Why is it reasonable to assume that they grow proportionally to sales?

What are some reasons that net PP&E might grow proportionally to sales, and what are some reasons that it might not?

What are spontaneous liabilities?

9-4 Projecting MicroDrive's Financial Statements

A key output of a financial plan is the set of projected financial statements. The basic approach in projecting statements is a simple, three-step process: (1) forecast the operating items, (2) forecast the amounts of debt, equity, and dividends that are determined by the company's preliminary short-term financial policy, and (3) ensure that the company has sufficient but not excess financing to fund the operating plan.

Despite the simple process, projecting financial statements can be similar to peeling onions—but not because it smells bad and brings tears to your eyes! Just as there are many different onions (white, purple, large, small, sweet, sour, etc.), there are many different variations on the basic approach. And just as onions have many layers, a financial plan can have many layers of complexity. It would be impossible for us to cover all the different methods and details used when projecting financial statements, so we are going to focus on the straightforward method MicroDrive's CFO used, which is applicable to most companies.

Here are the three steps in this method:

1. MicroDrive will project all the operating items that are part of the operating plan.
2. For the initial forecast, MicroDrive's CFO applied the following preliminary short-term financial policy: (1) MicroDrive will not issue any long-term bonds, preferred stock, or common stock in the upcoming year; (2) MicroDrive will not pay off or increase notes payable; and (3) MicroDrive will increase regular dividends at the sustainable long-term growth rate discussed previously in the sales forecast.
3. If the short-term financial policies described in the second step do not provide sufficient additional financing to fund the additional operating assets needed by the operating plan described in the first step, MicroDrive will draw on a special line of credit. If the financial policies provide surplus financing, MicroDrive will pay a special dividend.

9-4a **Forecast the Accounts from the Operating Plan**

Figure 9-4 shows MicroDrive's projected financial statements for the Status Quo scenario for the upcoming year. MicroDrive's CFO forecast the operating plan in Section 9-3, so it is an easy matter to replicate the process and forecast the corresponding operating items on the financial statement accounts. Column C shows the most recent year, Column D shows the inputs from Figure 9-2, Columns E and F describe how the inputs are applied, and Column G shows the forecast for the upcoming year. Notice that the forecasts for the operating items in Figure 9-4 are identical to those in Figure 9-3.

9-4b **Forecast Items Determined by the Preliminary Short-Term Financial Policy**

MicroDrive has a target capital structure and target dividend growth, shown in Figure 9-2, Sections 2–4. Like most companies, MicroDrive is willing to deviate from those targets in the short term. For the purpose of this initial forecast, MicroDrive has a preliminary short-term financial policy that sets the projected values for notes payable, long-term debt, preferred stock, and common stock equal to their previous values. In other words, the preliminary short-term financial policy does not call for any change in these items. Keep in mind that financial planning is an iterative process—specify a plan, look at the results, modify if needed, and repeat the process until the plan is acceptable and achievable.

FIGURE 9-4   MicroDrive's Projected Financial Statements (Millions of Dollars, Except for Per Share Data)

	A	B	C	D	E	F	G
210	Status Quo						
211	**1. Balance Sheets**		**Most Recent**				**Forecast**
212			**2015**	**Input**	**Basis for 2016 Forecast**		**2016**
213	*Assets*						
214	Cash		$50.0	1.00%	× 2016 Sales		$55.00
215	Accounts receivable		500.0	10.00%	× 2016 Sales		$550.00
216	Inventories		1,000.0	20.00%	× 2016 Sales		$1,100.00
217	Total current assets		$1,550.0				$1,705.00
218	Net PP&E		2,000.0	40.00%	× 2016 Sales		$2,200.00
219	Total assets (TA)		$3,550.0				$3,905.00
220	*Liabilities and equity*						
221	Accounts payable		$200.0	4.00%	× 2016 Sales		$220.00
222	Accruals		300.0	6.00%	× 2016 Sales		$330.00
223	Notes payable		280.0		Carry over from previous year		$280.00
224	Line of credit		0.0		Draw on LOC if financing deficit		$117.10
225	Total CL		$780.0				$947.10
226	Long-term bonds		1,200.0		Carry over from previous year		$1,200.00
227	Total liabilities		$1,980.0				$2,147.10
228	Preferred stock		$100.0		Carry over from previous year		$100.00
229	Common stock		500.0		Carry over from previous year		$500.00
230	Retained earnings		970.0		Old RE + Add. to RE		$1,158
231	Total common equity		$1,470.0				$1,658
232	Total liabs. & equity		$3,550.0				$3,905
233					**Check: TA – Total Liab. & Eq. =**		$0.00
234	**2. Income Statement**		**Most Recent**				**Forecast**
235			**2015**	**Input**	**Basis for 2016 Forecast**		**2016**
236	Net sales		$5,000.0	110%	× 2015 Sales		$5,500.00
237	COGS (excl. depr.)		3,800.0	76.00%	× 2016 Sales		$4,180.00
238	Depreciation		200.0	10.00%	× 2016 Net PP&E		$220.00
239	Other operating expenses		$500.0	10.00%	× 2016 Sales		$550.00
240	EBIT		$500.0				$550.00
241	Less: Interest on notes		20.0	10.00%	× Avg notes		$28.00
242	Interest on bonds		100.0	9.00%	× Avg bonds		$108.00
243	Interest on LOC		0.0	11.50%	× Beginning LOC		$0.00
244	Pre-tax earnings		$380.0				$414.00
245	Taxes (40%)		152.0	40.00%	× Pretax earnings		$165.60
246	NI before pref. div.		$228.0				$248.40
247	Preferred div.		8.0	8.00%	× Avg pref. stock		$8.00
248	Net income		$220.0				$240.40
249	Regular common dividends		$50.0	105%	× 2015 Dividend		$52.50
250	Special dividends		$0.0		Pay if financing surplus		$0.00
251	Addition to RE		$170.0		Net income – Dividends		$187.90
252							
253	**3. Elimination of the Financial Deficit or Surplus**						
254	Increase in spontaneous liabilities (accounts payable and accruals)						$50.00
255	+ Increase in notes payable, long-term bonds, preferred stock, and common stock						$0.00
256	+ Net income minus regular common dividends						$187.90
257	– Previous line of credit						$0.00
258	Increase in financing						$237.90
259	– Increase in total assets						$355.00
260	Amount of deficit or surplus financing:						–$117.10
261	If deficit in financing (negative), draw on line of credit				Line of credit		$117.10
262	If surplus in financing (positive), pay special dividend				Special dividend		$0.00

Note: Numbers in the figure are shown as rounded values for clarity in reporting. However, unrounded values are used for all calculations. See the *Excel **Tool Kit*** for this chapter.

The pale silver rows with blue print in Figure 9-4 show the items determined by the preliminary short-term financial policy. Section 1 shows the projected balance sheets, with the projected values for notes payable, long-term debt, preferred stock, and common stock unchanged from their previous values. The basic approach for projecting financial statements would remain unchanged if the preliminary short-term financial policy had called for changes in these items, such as issuing new debt or equity. In fact, MicroDrive's CFO plans on presenting long-term recommendations to the board regarding the possibility of issuing additional common stock, preferred stock, or long-term bonds after the preliminary forecast has been analyzed.

Section 2 shows the projected income statement. The interest expense on notes payable is projected as the interest rate on notes payable multiplied by the average value of the notes payable outstanding during the year. For example, MicroDrive's notes payable balance was $280 at the end of 2015 and was projected to be $280 at the end of 2016, so the average balance during the year is $280 = ($280 + $280)/2. If MicroDrive's plans had called for borrowing an additional $40 in notes payable during the year (resulting in an end-of-year balance of $320), the average balance would have been $300 = ($280+ $320)/2. The same process is applied to long-term bonds and preferred stock.

Basing interest expense on the average amount of debt outstanding during the year implies that the debt is added (or repaid) smoothly during the year. However, if debt is not added until the last day of the year, that year's interest expense should be based on just the debt at the beginning of the year (i.e., the debt at the end of the previous year), because virtually no interest would have accrued on the new debt. On the other hand, if the new debt is added on the first day of the year, interest would accrue all year, so the interest expense should be based on the amount of debt shown at the end of the year.

MicroDrive's preliminary short-term financial policy calls for dividend growth of 5%.

The only items on the projected statements that have not been forecast by the operating plan or the preliminary short-term financial plan are the line of credit (LOC), interest on the LOC, and the item for special dividends. These are shown in dark red ink in the pale gray rows, and we explain them in the following section.

9-4c **Identify and Eliminate the Financing Deficit or Surplus in the Projected Balance Sheets**

At this point in the projection, it would be extremely unlikely for the balance sheets to balance because the increase in assets required by the operating plan probably is not equal to the increase in liabilities and financing caused by the operating plan and the preliminary short-term financial policy. There will be a financing deficit if the additional financing is less than the additional assets, and a financing surplus if the additional financing is greater than the additional assets. If there is a financing deficit, MicroDrive will not be able to afford its operating plan; if there is a financing surplus, MicroDrive must use it in some manner. Therefore, a realistic projection requires balance sheets that balance.

How should a company handle a financing deficit or surplus? There are an infinite number of answers to that question, which is why financial modeling can be complicated. MicroDrive's CFO chose a simple but effective approach. If there is a deficit, draw on a line of credit even though it has a relatively high interest rate (the rate on the LOC is 1.5 percentage points higher than the rate on notes payable). If there is a surplus, pay a special dividend. Keep in mind that this is a preliminary plan and that MicroDrive might choose a different source of financing in its final plan.

The first step in implementing this approach is to identify the preliminary amounts of net additional financing. The second step is to identify the required additional assets. The third step is to identify the resulting financing deficit or surplus. The fourth step is to eliminate the financing deficit or surplus. We explain these steps below.

Identify the Net Additional Financing

Preliminary additional financing comes from three sources: (1) spontaneous liabilities, (2) external financing (such as issuing new long-term bonds or common equity), and (3) internal financing (which is the amount of earnings that are reinvested rather than paid out as dividends). In addition, the preliminary financial plan assumes no line of credit. Following is an explanation of how to calculate the additional financing for MicroDrive.

Section 3 in Figure 9-4 begins by adding up the additional financing in the forecast relative to the previous year. For example, MicroDrive's spontaneous liabilities (accounts payable and accruals) went from a total of $500 to $550, an increase of $50. Due to MicroDrive's preliminary short-term financial policy, there were no changes in the external financing provided by notes payable, long-term bonds, preferred stock, or common stock. MicroDrive's preliminary policy calls for no changes in external financing, but it would be easy to modify this assumption. In fact, the CFO did make changes in external financing in a final plan that we discuss later. The preliminary amount of internal financing available is the difference between net income and regular common dividends—this is the amount of earnings that are being reinvested.

The preliminary plan assumes that there is no line of credit. Therefore, if there is a balance on a line of credit for the previous year, this must be subtracted before estimating the net additional financing. In other words, it is as though MicroDrive must pay off any previous line of credit on the last day of the year before drawing on a new line of credit.

Based on the preliminary operating and financing plans, MicroDrive projects a total increase in financing of $237.9, as shown in Section 3 of Figure 9-4.

Identify the Required Additional Assets

The second step is to calculate the required additional assets. MicroDrive forecast calls for total assets to grow from $3,550 to $3,905, for a net increase in assets of $355: $3,905 − $3,550 = $355.

Identify the Financing Deficit or Surplus

The third step is to determine whether there is a financing deficit or surplus. The difference between MicroDrive's increase in financing and its increase in projected assets is $237.9 − $355 = −$117.1. This amount is negative because the increase in MicroDrive's projected assets is greater than the increase in MicroDrive's projected financing. Therefore, MicroDrive has a preliminary financing deficit—MicroDrive needs more financing to support its operating plan and will need to draw on a line of credit. Had this value been positive, MicroDrive would have had a financing surplus and would have had funds available to pay a special dividend. The last two rows in Section 3 of Figure 9-4 apply this logic, and show an amount for either a line of credit or a special dividend, but not both.

Eliminate the Financing Deficit or Surplus

The fourth step is to adjust the financial statements to eliminate the financing deficit or surplus. MicroDrive has a deficit, so it will need to draw on a line of credit (LOC). The cell for the LOC in the balance sheet in Section 1 (Cell G224) is linked to the cell for the necessary amount of the LOC that is identified in Section 3 (G261). Notice that this adjustment increases the total liabilities so that the balance sheets now balance.

MicroDrive's balance sheets now show $117.10 for the line of credit. Does this mean that MicroDrive needs to adjust the interest expense on its income statement? MicroDrive's CFO made a simplifying assumption for the preliminary projection: The LOC will be drawn upon on the last day of the year. Therefore, the LOC will not accrue interest, so the interest expense on the LOC is equal to the interest rate multiplied by the balance of the LOC at the beginning of the year rather than the end of the year.

The CFO realizes that the projected interest expense will understate the true interest expense if MicroDrive draws on the LOC earlier in the year. However, the CFO wanted to keep the model simple for the preliminary presentations at the retreat. The CFO actually made more realistic (but more complex) assumptions in another model, which we describe later in the chapter.

Now that the hard work of projecting the financial statements is done, it is time for MicroDrive's managers to discuss the projections and formulate their plans.

How are operating items projected on financial statements?

How are preliminary levels of debt, preferred stock, common stock, and dividends projected?

What is the financing surplus or deficit? How is it calculated?

SELF TEST

9-5 Analysis and Revision of the Preliminary Plan

After explaining the process used to forecast the statements in Figure 9-4, Micro-Drive's CFO constructed a 5-year forecast based on the methods and assumptions of the 1-year forecast. Important inputs and key results are shown in Figure 9-5; the full forecast is shown in *Ch09 Tool Kit.xls.*

9-5a Analysis of the Preliminary Plan

Section B1 of Figure 9-5 shows key results from the operating plan for the Status Quo scenario. The good news is that FCF becomes positive, but the bad news is that the return on invested capital is much lower than the industry average. Even worse, recall from Chapter 8 that if the ROIC < WACC/(1 + g_L), then the value of operations will be less than the total net operating working capital. In other words, the value

FIGURE 9-5	The Status Quo Scenario: Summary of Important Inputs and Key Results (Millions of Dollars, Except for Per Share Data)

	A	B	C	D	E	F	G	H
365	**Status Quo**	**Industry**		MicroDrive				
366	**Panel A: Inputs**	**Actual**	**Actual**			Forecast		
367	*A1. Operating Ratios*	**2015**	**2015**	**2016**	**2017**	**2018**	**2019**	**2020**
368	Sales growth rate	5%	5%	10%	8%	7%	5%	5%
369	COGS (excl. depr.)/Sales	76%	76%	76%	76%	76%	76%	76%
370	Inventory/Sales	15%	20%	20%	20%	20%	20%	20%
371	Net PP&E/Sales	33%	40%	40%	40%	40%	40%	40%
372	**Panel B: Key Results**	**Industry**		MicroDrive				
373		**Actual**	**Actual**			Forecast		
374	*B1. Operations*	**2015**	**2015**	**2016**	**2017**	**2018**	**2019**	**2020**
375	Total net operating capital		$3,050	$3,355	$3,623	$3,877	$4,071	$4,274
376	Free cash flow	NA	−$260	$25	$88	$128	$207	$217
377	Return on invested capital	15.0%	9.8%	9.8%	9.8%	9.8%	9.8%	9.8%
378	NOPAT/Sales	6.9%	6.0%	6.0%	6.0%	6.0%	6.0%	6.0%
379	Total op. capital/Sales	46.0%	61.0%	61.0%	61.0%	61.0%	61.0%	61.0%
380	Inventory turnover	5.0	4.0	4.0	4.0	4.0	4.0	4.0
381	Days sales outstanding	30.0	36.5	36.5	36.5	36.5	36.5	36.5
382	Fixed asset turnover	3.0	2.5	2.5	2.5	2.5	2.5	2.5
383	*B2. Financing*							
384	Total liabilities/TA	45.0%	55.8%	55.0%	53.5%	51.6%	49.0%	46.3%
385	Net income/Sales	6.2%	4.4%	4.4%	4.4%	4.4%	4.4%	4.6%
386	Return on assets (ROA)	11.0%	6.2%	6.2%	6.1%	6.2%	6.2%	6.4%
387	Return on equity (ROE)	19.0%	15.0%	14.5%	13.9%	13.4%	12.8%	12.4%
388	Times interest earned	10.0	4.2	4.0	4.0	4.1	4.2	4.5
389	Line of credit	NA	$0	$117	$182	$214	$173	$121
390	Payout ratio	35.0%	22.7%	21.8%	21.3%	20.7%	20.5%	20.0%
391	Regular dividends/share	NA	$1.00	$1.05	$1.10	$1.16	$1.22	$1.28
392	Special dividends/share	NA	$0.00	$0.00	$0.00	$0.00	$0.00	$0.00
393	Earnings per share	NA	$4.40	$4.81	$5.17	$5.58	$5.92	$6.38
394	*B3. Estimated intrinsic value*							
395			Weighted average cost of capital =		11%			
396	12/31/2015		Estimated value of operations =	$2,719				
397	12/31/2015		Estimated intrinsic stock price =	$22.78				

Note: Numbers in the figure are shown as rounded values for clarity in reporting. However, unrounded values are used for all calculations. See the *Excel Tool Kit* for this chapter.

of cash flows generated from the operating capital will be less than the amount invested in operating capital and investors would be better off if they had this capital back rather than invested in MicroDrive! For MicroDrive, the ROIC in the last year of the forecast is 9.8%, the WACC is 11%, and the long-term growth rate is 5%:

$$\text{ROIC} < \text{WACC}/(1 + g_L)$$

$$9.8\% < 0.11/(1 + 0.05) = 10.48\%$$

Because MicroDrive's ROIC is less than WACC/$(1 + g_L)$, it is not surprising that MicroDrive's current value of operations ($2,719 million) is less than the amount it currently has invested in operating capital ($3,050 million).

Recall from Chapter 8 that MicroDrive cannot "grow" out of its problems. Growth adds value only if ROIC > WACC/(1 + WACC). For MicroDrive, WACC/(1 + WACC) = 0.11/(1 + 0.11) = 9.91%. MicroDrive's ROIC of 9.8% is less, so MicroDrive must address its ROIC before seeking growth.

Why is MicroDrive's ROIC so low? Rows 378 and 379 show that MicroDrive has a lower NOPAT/Sales ratio and a higher Capital/Sales ratio than its peers. In other words, MicroDrive is less profitable *and* less efficient. Digging deeper, Rows 380–382 show that MicroDrive's poor capital utilization results from carrying too much inventory, collecting more slowly from its customers, and utilizing its factories inefficiently.

The Status Quo financial plan reflects this poor operating performance. The projected ratio of total liabilities to sales shows that MicroDrive will have more leverage than its peers and will need to borrow from the expensive line of credit. However, even higher leverage is not enough to boost MicroDrive's return on equity to the industry average.

The poor performance also is reflected in MicroDrive's estimated intrinsic stock value of $22.78, which is less than the current market price of $27. The management team concluded that unless they make changes soon, the market price will fall.

9-5b The Final Plan

Based on the analysis in Chapter 8, MicroDrive learned that its key value driver was operating profitability. After much discussion, the management team concluded that, because of licensing fees and other costs, it was not feasible for MicroDrive to reduce its COGS/Sales ratio in the next year. However, the director of R&D explained that the new products in the pipeline will have higher profit margins. If MicroDrive can fund some extra field tests, the new products can reach the market in a year and drive the ratio of COGS/Sales down to 75% from its current level of 76%.

The production, sales, and purchasing managers are jointly responsible for inventory in MicroDrive's supply chain. With some additional funding for technology to improve channels of information among suppliers and customers, MicroDrive can reduce inventory levels without hurting product availability. They estimated that the improved technology would push the Inventory/Sales ratio down to 17% from its current level of 20%.

The production and human resource managers stated that productivity could be increased with new training programs so that employees can better utilize the new production equipment that had been added the previous year. They estimated that the increased productivity would cause the ratio of PP&E/Sales to fall from its current level of 40% to 36% in the next 2 years.

Managers from accounting and finance estimated that the total cost for these improvement programs would be about $200 million.

The CFO entered these new inputs (except the cost to implement the new plans) into the model and named it the Final scenario. The results are shown in Figure 9-6. The value of operations increased from $2,719 million to $4,140 million. This is an increase of over $1.4 billion ($4,140 − $2,719 = $1.421), well above the $200 million cost to implement the plans. Although the Final plan from the management retreat does not include the costs to implement the improvement plans, the CFO included these costs upon returning to headquarters.

Figure 9-6 shows that the ROIC improves to 12.7% by the second year, well above the WACC of 11%. Free cash flow becomes much larger, causing the estimated

FIGURE 9-6	The Final Scenario: Summary of Important Inputs and Key Results (Millions of Dollars, Except for Per Share Data)

	A	B	C	D	E	F	G	H
365	Final	Industry	MicroDrive					
366	Panel A: Inputs	Actual	Actual	Forecast				
367	A1. Operating Ratios	2015	2015	2016	2017	2018	2019	2020
368	Sales growth rate	5%	5%	10%	8%	7%	5%	5%
369	COGS (excl. depr.)/Sales	76%	76%	76%	75%	75%	75%	75%
370	Inventory/Sales	15%	20%	17%	17%	17%	17%	17%
371	Net PP&E/Sales	33%	40%	39%	36%	36%	36%	36%
372	Panel B: Key Results	Industry	MicroDrive					
373		Actual	Actual	Forecast				
374	B1. Operations	2015	2015	2016	2017	2018	2019	2020
375	Total net operating capital		$3,050	$3,135	$3,208	$3,432	$3,604	$3,784
376	Free cash flow	NA	−$260	$248	$334	$210	$285	$299
377	Return on invested capital	15.0%	9.8%	10.6%	12.7%	12.7%	12.7%	12.7%
378	NOPAT/Sales	6.9%	6.0%	6.1%	6.8%	6.8%	6.8%	6.8%
379	Total op. capital/Sales	46.0%	61.0%	57.0%	54.0%	54.0%	54.0%	54.0%
380	Inventory turnover	5.0	4.0	4.7	4.6	4.6	4.6	4.6
381	Days sales outstanding	30.0	36.5	36.5	36.5	36.5	36.5	36.5
382	Fixed asset turnover	3.0	2.5	2.6	2.8	2.8	2.8	2.8
383	B2. Financing							
384	Total liabilities/TA	45.0%	55.8%	55.1%	54.6%	52.0%	50.3%	48.6%
385	Net income/Sales	6.2%	4.4%	4.4%	5.3%	5.4%	5.5%	5.6%
386	Return on assets (ROA)	11.0%	6.2%	6.6%	8.3%	8.5%	8.6%	8.7%
387	Return on equity (ROE)	19.0%	15.0%	15.7%	19.5%	18.6%	18.1%	17.7%
388	Times interest earned	10.0	4.2	4.1	5.0	5.3	5.6	5.9
389	Line of credit	NA	$0	$0	$0	$0	$0	$0
390	Payout ratio	35.0%	22.7%	65.1%	77.1%	34.9%	53.2%	53.8%
391	Regular dividends/share	NA	$1.00	$3.17	$4.88	$2.41	$3.91	$4.19
392	Special dividends/share	NA	$0.00	$2.12	$3.78	$1.25	$2.69	$2.91
393	Earnings per share	NA	$4.40	$4.87	$6.33	$6.90	$7.34	$7.79
394	B3. Estimated intrinsic value							
395			Weighted average cost of capital =		11%			
396	12/31/2015		Estimated value of operations =		$4,140			
397	12/31/2015		Estimated intrinsic stock price =		$51.20			

Note: Numbers in the figure are shown as rounded values for clarity in reporting. However, unrounded values are used for all calculations. See the *Excel **Tool Kit*** for this chapter.

Microsoft Excel® is a registered trademark of Microsoft Corporation. © 2014 Microsoft.

intrinsic stock price to increase to $51.20. With respect to financing, MicroDrive will not have to draw on its line of credit. In fact, the company will have extra cash available to distribute as a special dividend if the board chooses to do so.

9-5c The CFO's Model[1]

The CFO's final model, shown in the worksheet named *CFO Model* in the file *Ch09 Tool Kit.xls*, has several refinements to the basic model presented in the previous

---

1. This section is relatively technical, and some instructors may choose to skip it with no loss in continuity.

sections, including the incorporation of financing feedback and implementation of the target capital structure.

Financing Feedback

The basic model assumed that no interest would accrue on the line of credit because the LOC would be added at the end of the year. However, if interest is calculated on the LOC's average balance during the year, which is more realistic, here is what happens:

1. The line of credit required to make the balance sheets balance is added to the balance sheet.
2. Interest expense increases due to the LOC.
3. Net income decreases because interest expenses are higher.
4. Internally generated financing decreases because net income decreases.
5. The financing deficit increases because internally generated financing decreases.
6. An additional amount of the LOC is added to the balance sheets to make them balance.
7. Go to step 2 and repeat the loop.

This loop is called *financing feedback* because the additional financing feeds back and causes a need for more additional financing. If programmed into *Excel*, there will be a circular reference. Sometimes *Excel* can handle this (if the iteration feature is enabled), but sometimes *Excel* freezes up. Fortunately, there is a simple way to modify the required line of credit by scaling it up so that no iterations are required. If this piques your interest, take a look at the **CFO Model** in the **Tool Kit.**

Implementing the Target Capital Structure

The preliminary financial policy chosen by the CFO during the managers' retreat held external financing constant—with no additional borrowing or repayment of debt (other than the line of credit) and no new issues or repurchases of preferred stock or common stock. However, this ignores the target capital structure. Fortunately, there is a simple way to implement the target capital structure in the projected statements.

If MicroDrive implements its target capital structure, then it can find the current value of operations, as shown in Figure 9-3. Furthermore, MicroDrive also can estimate its value of operations for *each year* of the forecast, starting at the horizon and working backwards. For example, MicroDrive's horizon value from the final plan is $5,260 (to see this, select the Final scenario in the **Tool Kit** and look at the updated Figure 9-3). The value of operations at the horizon, 2020, is equal to the horizon value—this is the value of all FCF from 2021 and beyond discounted back to 2020. The value of operations at 2019, 1 year before the horizon, is equal to the value of all free cash flows beyond 2019, discounted at the WACC back to 2019. But we have already found the value of all FCF beyond 2020 discounted back to 2020 (which is equal to the value of operations at 2020) and we know the FCF of 2020. Therefore, we can discount the 2020 value of operations and the 2020 free cash flow back 1 year to get the 2019 value of operations: Value at 2019 = ($5,260 + $299)/(1 + 0.11) = $5,008. We can work our way back to the current date by repeating this process, providing estimates of the yearly values of operations.

We know the weights in the target capital structure for each year. For example, the target weight for long-term debt, w_d, is 28%. We can multiply this target weight by the value of operations each year to obtain the amount of long-term debt that conforms to the target capital structure. For example, in 2019 MicroDrive should have long-term debt of \$1,402: w_d, $(V_{op,2019})$ = 28%(\$5,008) = \$1,120. Repeating this process for all the capital components each year provides the amounts of external funding that match the target capital structure.

The CFO's model implements a modified version of this procedure. Instead of setting the actual capital structure weights equal to the target weights in the first year of the forecast, the CFO allows the actual weights in the capital structure each year to move smoothly from the actual current values to the target values at the horizon. See the *CFO Model* in the *Tool Kit* for details.

> **SELF TEST**
>
> Suppose a company's return on invested capital is less than its WACC. What happens to the value of operations if the sales growth rate increases? Explain your answer.

9-6 Additional Funds Needed (AFN) Equation Method

A complete financial plan includes projected financial statements, but the **additional funds needed (AFN) equation** method provides a simple way to get a ballpark estimate of the additional external financing that will be required. The AFN approach identifies the financing surplus or deficit in much the same way as we did in the previous sections: (1) Identify the amount of additional funding required by the additional assets due to growth in sales. (2) Identify the amount of spontaneous liabilities (which reduces the amount of external financing that is required to support the additional assets). (3) Identify the amount of funding generated internally from net income that will be available for reinvestment in the company after paying dividends. (4) Assume no new external financing (similar to the preliminary financial policy in the Status Quo scenario). The difference between the additional assets and the sum of spontaneous liabilities and reinvested net income is the amount of additional financing needed from external sources. Following are explanations and applications of these steps.

9-6a Required Increase in Assets

In a steady-state situation in which no excess capacity exists, the firm must have additional plant and equipment, more delivery trucks, higher inventories, and so forth if sales are to increase. In addition, more sales will lead to more accounts receivable, and those receivables must be financed from the time of the sale until they are collected. Therefore, both fixed and current assets must increase if sales are to increase. Of course, if assets are to increase, liabilities and equity must also increase by a like amount to make the balance sheet balance.

9-6b Spontaneous Liabilities

The first sources of expansion funding are the "spontaneous" increases that will occur in MicroDrive's accounts payable and accrued wages and taxes. The company's suppliers give it 10 days to pay for inventory purchases, and because purchases will increase with sales, accounts payable will automatically rise. For example, if sales rise by 10% then inventory purchases will also rise by 10%, and this will cause accounts payable to rise spontaneously by the same 10%. Similarly, because the company pays workers every 2 weeks, more workers and a larger payroll will mean more accrued wages payable. Finally, higher expected income will mean more accrued income taxes, and its higher wage bill will mean more accrued withholding taxes. Normally no interest is paid on these spontaneous funds, but their amount is limited by credit terms, contracts with workers, and tax laws. Therefore, *spontaneous funds will be used to the extent possible, but there is little flexibility in their usage.*

9-6c Addition to Retained Earnings

The second source of funds for expansion comes from net income. Part of Micro-Drive's profit will be paid out in dividends, but the remainder will be reinvested in operating assets, as shown in the Assets section of the balance sheet; a corresponding amount will be reported as an addition to retained earnings in the Liabilities and equity section of the balance sheet. There is some flexibility in the amount of funds that will be generated from new reinvested earnings because dividends can be increased or decreased, but if the firm plans to hold its dividend steady or to increase it at a target rate, as most do, then flexibility is limited.

9-6d Calculating Additional Funds Needed (AFN)

If we start with the required new assets and then subtract both spontaneous funds and additions to retained earnings, we are left with the additional funds needed, or AFN. The AFN must come from *external sources*; hence, it is sometimes called EFN. The typical sources of external funds are bank loans, new long-term bonds, new preferred stock, and newly issued common stock. The mix of the external funds used should be consistent with the firm's financial policies, especially its target debt ratio.

9-6e Using MicroDrive's Data to Implement the AFN Equation Method

Equation 9-1 summarizes the logic underlying the AFN equation method. Figure 9-7 defines the notation in Equation 9-1 and applies it to identify MicroDrive's AFN. The **additional funds needed (AFN) equation** is:

$$
\underset{\substack{\text{Required}\\ \text{increase}\\ \text{in assets}}}{} - \underset{\substack{\text{Increase in}\\ \text{spontaneous}\\ \text{liabilities}}}{} - \underset{\substack{\text{Increase in}\\ \text{retained}\\ \text{earnings}}}{} = \underset{\substack{\text{Additional}\\ \text{funds}\\ \text{needed}}}{}
$$

$$
(A_0^*/S_0)\Delta S \; - \; (L_0^*/S_0)\Delta S \; - \; S_1 \times M \times \left(1 - \frac{\text{Payout}}{\text{Ratio}}\right) \; = \; \text{AFN}
$$

(9–1)

We see from Part B of Figure 9-7 that for sales to increase by $500 million, Micro Drive must increase assets by $355 million. Therefore, liabilities and capital must also increase by $355 million. Of this total, $50 million will come from spontaneous

FIGURE 9-7	Additional Funds Needed (AFN) (Millions of Dollars)

	A	B	C	D	E	F	G	H	I
406	*Part A. Inputs and Definitions*								
407	S_0:		Most recent year's sales =						$5,000
408	g:		Forecasted growth rate in sales =						10.00%
409	S_1:		Next year's sales: $S_0 \times (1 + g)$ =						$5,500
410	gS_0:		Change in sales = $S_1 - S_0 = \Delta S$ =						$500
411	A_0^*:		Most recent year's operating assets =						$3,550
412	A_0^*/S_0:		Required assets per dollar of sales =						71.00%
413	L_0^*:		Most recent year's spontaneous liabilities i.e., payables + accruals =						$500
414	L_0^*/S_0:		Spontaneous liabilities per dollar of sales =						10.00%
415	Profit margin (M):		Most recent profit margin = net income/sales =						4.40%
416	Payout ratio (POR):		Most recent year's dividends/net income = % of income paid out =						22.73%
417	*Part B. Additional Funds Needed (AFN) to Support Growth*								
418									
419	Additional		Required		Increase in			Increase in	
420	funds =		increase	−	spontaneous	−		retained	
421	needed		in assets		liabilities			earnings	
422									
423	AFN =		$(A_0^*/S_0)\Delta S$	−	$(L_0^*/S_0)\Delta S$	−		$S_1 \times M \times (1 - POR)$	
424				−		−			
425	=		$(A_0^*/S_0)(gS_0)$	−	$(L_0^*/S_0)(gS_0)$	−		$(1+g)S_0 \times M \times (1 - POR)$	
426				−		−			
427	=		(0.710)($500)	−	(0.10)($500)	−		$5,500(0.044)(1 − 0.2273)	
428	=		$355	−	$50.00	−		$187.00	
429	AFN = $118.00								

Note: Numbers in the figure are shown as rounded values for clarity in reporting. However, unrounded values are used for all calculations. See the *Excel **Tool Kit*** for this chapter.

Microsoft Excel® is a registered trademark of Microsoft Corporation. © 2014 Microsoft.

liabilities, and another $187 million will come from new retained earnings. The remaining $118 million must be raised from external sources—probably some combination of short-term bank loans, long-term bonds, preferred stock, and common stock. Notice that the AFN from this model is very close to the surplus financing required in the Status Quo model for the projected financial statements because both methods assume that the operating ratios for MicroDrive will not change.

9-6f Key Factors in the AFN Equation

The AFN equation shows that external financing requirements depend on five key factors.

1. **Sales growth (g)**. Rapidly growing companies require large increases in assets and a corresponding large amount of external financing, other things held constant.
2. **Capital intensity (A_0^*/S_0),** The amount of assets required per dollar of sales, A_0^*/S_0, is the **capital intensity ratio**, which has a major effect on capital requirements. Companies with relatively high assets-to-sales ratios require a relatively large number of new assets for any given increase in sales; hence

they have a greater need for external financing. If a firm can find a way to lower this ratio—for instance, by adopting a just-in-time inventory system, by going to two shifts in its manufacturing plants, or by outsourcing rather than manufacturing parts—then it can achieve a given level of growth with fewer assets and thus less new external capital.

3. **Spontaneous liabilities-to-sales ratio (L_0^*/S_0).** If a company can increase its spontaneously generated liabilities, this will reduce its need for external financing. One way of raising this ratio is by paying suppliers in, say, 20 days rather than 10 days. Such a change may be possible but, as we shall see in Chapter 21, it would probably have serious adverse consequences.

4. **Profit margin (M = Net Income/Sales).** The higher the profit margin, the more net income is available to support increases in assets—and hence the less the need for external financing. A firms' profit margin is normally as high as management can get it, but sometimes a change in operations can boost the sales price or reduce costs, thus raising the margin further. If so, this will permit a faster growth rate with less external capital.

5. **Payout ratio (POR = DPS/EPS).** The less of its income a company distributes as dividends, the larger its addition to retained earnings—hence the less its need for external capital. Companies typically like to keep their dividends stable or to increase them at a steady rate—stockholders like stable, dependable dividends, so such a dividend policy will generally lower the cost of equity and thus maximize the stock price. So even though reducing the dividend is one way a company can reduce its need for external capital, companies generally resort to this method only if they are under financial duress.

9-6g **The Self-Supporting Growth Rate**

One useful question is, "What is the maximum growth rate the firm could achieve if it had no access to external capital?" This rate is called the *self-supporting growth rate*, and it can be found as the value of g that, when used in the AFN equation, results in an AFN of zero. We first replace ΔS in the AFN equation with gS_0 and S_1 with $(1+g)S_0$ so that the only unknown is g; we then solve for g to obtain the following equation for the self-supporting growth rate:

$$\text{Self-supporting } g = \frac{M(1 - POR)(S_0)}{A_0^* - L_0^* - M(1 - POR)(S_0)} \qquad \text{(9–2)}$$

The definitions of the terms used in this equation are shown in Figure 9-7.

If the firm has any positive earnings and pays out less than 100% in dividends, then it will have some additions to retained earnings, and those additions could be combined with spontaneous funds to enable the company to grow at some rate without having to raise external capital. As explained in the chapter's *Excel Tool Kit*, this value can be found either algebraically or with *Excel*'s Goal Seek function. For MicroDrive, the self-supporting growth rate is 5.9%; this means it could grow at that rate even if capital markets dried up completely, with everything else held constant.

See **Ch09 Tool Kit.xls** on the textbook's Web site for details.

If all ratios are expected to remain constant, an equation can be used to forecast AFN. Write out the equation and briefly explain it.

Describe how the following factors affect external capital requirements: (1) payout ratio, (2) capital intensity, (3) profit margin.

In what sense do accounts payable and accruals provide "spontaneous funds" to a growing firm?

Is it possible for the calculated AFN to be negative? If so, what would this imply?

Refer to data in the MicroDrive example presented, but now assume that MicroDrive's growth rate in sales is forecasted to be 15% rather than 10%. If all ratios remain constant, what would the AFN be? **($205.6 million)**

9-7 **Forecasting When the Ratios Change**

The versions of the percent of sales forecasting model and the AFN method assumed that the forecasted items could be estimated as a percent of sales. This implies that each of the accounts for assets, spontaneous liabilities, and operating costs is proportional to sales. In graph form, this implies the type of relationship shown in Panel A of Figure 9-8, a relationship whose graph: (1) is linear and (2) passes through the origin. Under those conditions, if the company's sales increase from $200 million to $400 million, or by 100%, then inventory will also increase by 100%, from $100 million to $200 million.

The assumption of constant ratios and identical growth rates is appropriate at times, but there are times when it is incorrect. We describe three such situations in the following sections.

9-7a **Economies of Scale**

There are economies of scale in the use of many kinds of assets, and when economies of scale occur, the ratios are likely to change over time as the size of the firm increases. For example, retailers often need to maintain base stocks of different inventory items even if current sales are quite low. As sales expand, inventories may then grow less rapidly than sales, so the ratio of inventory to sales (I/S) declines. This situation is depicted in Panel B of Figure 9-8. Here we see that the inventory/sales ratio is 1.5 (or 150%) when sales are $200 million but declines to 1.0 when sales climb to $400 million.

It is easy in *Excel* to incorporate this type of scale economy in the forecast. For example, the basic method forecasts inventory as Inventory = m(Sales), where m is a constant. With economies of scale, forecast Inventory as: Inventory = b + m(Sales), where m and b are constants.

9-7b **Nonlinear Relationships**

The relationship in Panel B is linear, but nonlinear relationships often exist. Indeed, if the firm uses one popular model for establishing inventory levels (the Economic

| FIGURE 9-8 | Four Possible Ratio Relationships (Millions of Dollars) |

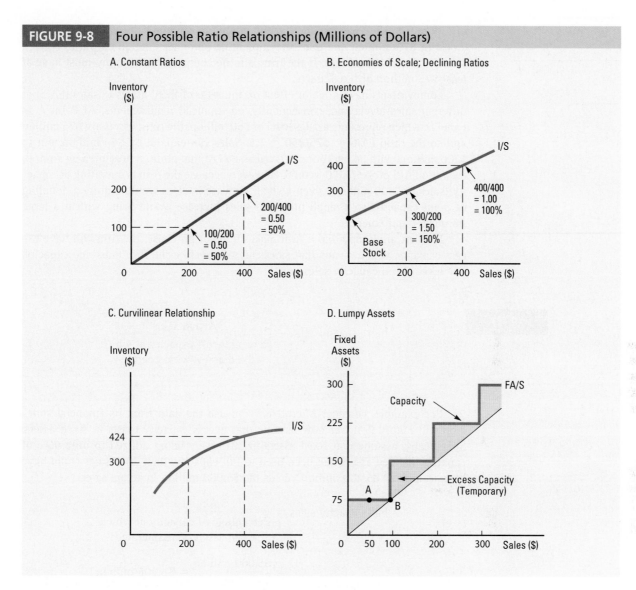

Ordering Quantity, or EOQ, model), its inventories will rise with the *square root* of sales. This situation is shown in Panel C of Figure 9-8, which shows a curved line whose slope decreases at higher sales levels. In this situation, very large increases in sales would require very little additional inventory. To incorporate this type of nonlinearity in *Excel*, for example, you could forecast inventory as a function of the square root of sales: Inventory $= m(\text{Sales}^{0.5})$.

9-7c **Lumpy Assets and Excess Capacity**

In many industries, technological considerations dictate that if a firm is to be competitive, it must add fixed assets in large, discrete units; such assets are often referred to as **lumpy assets**. In the paper industry, for example, there are strong economies of scale in basic paper mill equipment, so when a paper company expands capacity, it must do so in large, lumpy increments. This type of situation is depicted in Panel D of Figure 9-8. Here we assume that the minimum economically efficient plant has a cost of $75 million, and that such a plant can produce enough output to reach a sales level of $100 million. If the firm is to be competitive, it simply must have at least $75 million of fixed assets.

Lumpy assets have a major effect on the ratio of fixed assets to sales (FA/S) at different sales levels and, consequently, on financial requirements. At Point A in Panel D, which represents a sales level of $50 million, the fixed assets are $75 million and so the ratio FA/S = $75/$50 = 1.5. Sales can expand by $50 million, out to $100 million, with no additions to fixed assets. At that point, represented by Point B, the ratio FA/S = $75/$100 = 0.75. However, because the firm is operating at capacity (sales of $100 million), even a small increase in sales would require a doubling of plant capacity, so a small projected sales increase would bring with it a large financial requirement.[2]

If assets are lumpy and a firm makes a major purchase, the firm will have excess capacity, which means that sales can grow before the firm must add capacity. The level of full capacity sales is:

(9–3)

$$\text{Full capacity sales} = \frac{\text{Actual sales}}{\text{Percentage of capacity at which fixed assets were operated}}$$

For example, consider MicroDrive and use the data from its financial statements in Figure 9-1, but now assume that excess capacity exists in fixed assets. Specifically, assume that fixed assets in 2015 were being utilized to only 96% of capacity. If fixed assets had been used to full capacity, then 2015 sales could have been as high as $5,208 million versus the $5,000 million in actual sales:

$$\text{Full capacity sales} = \frac{\text{Actual sales}}{\text{Percentage of capacity at which fixed assets were operated}}$$

$$= \frac{\$5,000 \text{ million}}{0.96} = \$5,208 \text{ million}$$

The target fixed assets/sales ratio can be defined in terms of the full capacity sales:

---

2. Several other points should be noted about Panel D of Figure 9-8. First, if the firm is operating at a sales level of $100 million or less, then any expansion that calls for a sales increase of more than $100 million would require a *doubling* of the firm's fixed assets. A much smaller percentage increase would be involved if the firm were large enough to be operating a number of plants. Second, firms generally go to multiple shifts and take other actions to minimize the need for new fixed asset capacity as they approach Point B. However, these efforts can only go so far, and eventually a fixed asset expansion will be required. Third, firms often arrange to share excess capacity with other firms in their industry. For example, the situation in the electric utility industry is very much like that depicted in Panel D. However, electric companies often build plants jointly, or they "take turns" building plants. Then they buy power from or sell power to other utilities to avoid building new plants that would be underutilized.

$$\text{Target fixed assets/Sales} = \frac{\text{Actual fixed assets}}{\text{Full capacity sales}}$$

(9–4)

MicroDrive's target fixed assets/sales ratio should be 38.4% rather than 40%:

$$\text{Target fixed assets/Sales} = \frac{\text{Actual fixed assets}}{\text{Full capacity sales}}$$

$$= \frac{\$2,000}{\$5,208} = 0.384 = 38.4\%$$

The required level of fixed assets depends upon this target fixed assets/sales ratio:

$$\begin{pmatrix}\text{Required level} \\ \text{of fixed assets}\end{pmatrix} = \left(\frac{\text{Target fixed assets}}{\text{Sales}}\right)\begin{pmatrix}\text{Projected} \\ \text{sales}\end{pmatrix}$$

(9–5)

Therefore, if MicroDrive's sales increase to $5,500 million, its fixed assets would have to increase to $2,112 million:

$$\begin{pmatrix}\text{Required level} \\ \text{of fixed assets}\end{pmatrix} = \left(\frac{\text{Target fixed assets}}{\text{Sales}}\right)\begin{pmatrix}\text{Projected} \\ \text{sales}\end{pmatrix}$$

$$= 0.384(\$5,500) = \$2,112 \text{ million}$$

We previously forecasted that MicroDrive would need to increase fixed assets at the same rate as sales, or by 10%. That meant an increase of $200 million, from $2,000 million to $2,200 million under the old assumption of no excess capacity. Under the new assumption of excess capacity, the actual required increase in fixed assets is only from $2,000 million to $2,112 million, which is an increase of $112 million. Thus, the capacity-adjusted forecast is less than the earlier forecast: $200 − $112 = $88 million. With a smaller fixed asset requirement, the projected AFN would decline from an estimated $118 million to $118 − $88 = $30 million.

Note also that when excess capacity exists, sales can grow to the capacity sales as calculated above with no increase in fixed assets, but sales beyond that level would require additions of fixed assets as in our example. The same situation could occur with respect to inventories, and the required additions would be determined in exactly the same manner as for fixed assets. Theoretically, the same situation could occur with other types of assets, but as a practical matter excess capacity normally exists only with respect to fixed assets and inventories.

How do economies of scale and lumpy assets affect financial forecasting?   **SELF TEST**

Summary

- The **forecasted financial statements (FFS) method** of financial planning forecasts the entire set of financial statements. It usually begins with a forecast of the firm's sales and then projects many items on the financial statements as a percent of sales.
- The **additional funds needed (AFN) equation** can be used to forecast additional external financing requirements, but only for 1 year ahead and only if all asset-to-sales ratios are identical, all spontaneous liabilities-to-sales ratios are identical, and all cost-to-sales ratios are identical.
- A firm can determine its **AFN** by estimating the amount of new assets necessary to support the forecasted level of sales and then subtracting from this amount the spontaneous funds that will be generated from operations.
- The higher a firm's **sales growth rate** and the higher its **payout ratio**, the greater will be its need for additional financing.
- There are two major applications of forecasted financial statements. First, the forecasted free cash flows can be used to estimate the impact that changes in operating plans have on the firm's estimated intrinsic value of operations and stock price. Second, the forecasted financing surplus or deficit allows the firm to identify its future financing needs.
- Adjustments must be made if **economies of scale** exist in the use of assets, if **excess capacity** exists, or if growth must occur in large increments **(lumpy assets)**.
- **Excess capacity adjustments** can be used to forecast asset requirements in situations in which assets are not expected to grow at the same rate as sales.

Questions

9-1 Define each of the following terms:
    a. Operating plan; financial plan
    b. Spontaneous liabilities; profit margin; payout ratio
    c. Additional funds needed (AFN); AFN equation; capital intensity ratio; self-supporting growth rate
    d. Forecasted financial statement approach using percent of sales
    e. Excess capacity; lumpy assets; economies of scale
    f. Full capacity sales; target fixed assets/sales ratio; required level of fixed assets

9-2 Some liability and net worth items increase spontaneously with increases in sales. Put a check (✓) by those items listed below that typically increase spontaneously:

Accounts payable	_____	Mortgage bonds	_____
Notes payable to banks	_____	Common stock	_____
Accrued wages	_____	Retained earnings	_____
Accrued taxes	_____		

9–3 The following equation is sometimes used to forecast financial requirements:

$$AFN = (A_0^*/S_0)(\Delta S) - (L_0^*/S_0)(\Delta S) - MS_1(1 - POR)$$

What key assumption do we make when using this equation? Under what conditions might this assumption not hold true?

9–4 Name five key factors that affect a firm's external financing requirements.

9–5 What is meant by the term "self-supporting growth rate"? How is this rate related to the AFN equation, and how can that equation be used to calculate the self-supporting growth rate?

9–6 Suppose a firm makes the policy changes listed below. If a change means that external, nonspontaneous financial requirements (AFN) will increase, indicate this by a (+); indicate a decrease by a (−); and indicate no effect or an indeterminate effect by a (0). Think in terms of the immediate effect on funds requirements.
a. The dividend payout ratio is increased.   _____
b. The firm decides to pay all suppliers on delivery, rather than after a 30-day delay, to take advantage of discounts for rapid payment.   _____
c. The firm begins to offer credit to its customers, whereas previously all sales had been on a cash basis.   _____
d. The firm's profit margin is eroded by increased competition, although sales hold steady.   _____
e. The firm sells its manufacturing plants for cash to a contractor and simultaneously signs an outsourcing contract to purchase from that contractor goods that the firm formerly produced.   _____
f. The firm negotiates a new contract with its union that lowers its labor costs without affecting its output.   _____

Problems   Answers Appear in Appendix B

Easy Problems 1–3

9–1 AFN Equation

Broussard Skateboard's sales are expected to increase by 15% from $8 million in 2015 to $9.2 million in 2016. Its assets totaled $5 million at the end of 2015. Broussard is already at full capacity, so its assets must grow at the same rate as projected sales. At the end of 2015, current liabilities were $1.4 million, consisting of $450,000 of accounts payable, $500,000 of notes payable, and $450,000 of accruals. The after-tax profit margin is forecasted to be 6%, and the forecasted payout ratio is 40%. Use the AFN equation to forecast Broussard's additional funds needed for the coming year.

9–2 AFN Equation

Refer to Problem 9-1. What would be the additional funds needed if the company's year-end 2015 assets had been $7 million? Assume that all other numbers, including sales, are the same as in Problem 9-1 and that the company is operating at full capacity. Why is this AFN different from the one you found in Problem 9-1? Is the company's "capital intensity" ratio the same or different?

9–3 AFN Equation

Refer to Problem 9-1. Return to the assumption that the company had $5 million in assets at the end of 2015, but now assume that the company pays no dividends. Under these assumptions, what would be the additional funds needed for the coming year? Why is this AFN different from the one you found in Problem 9-1?

Intermediate Problems 4–6

9–4 Sales Increase

Maggie's Muffins Inc. generated $5,000,000 in sales during 2015, and its year-end total assets were $2,500,000. Also, at year-end 2015, current liabilities were $1,000,000, consisting of $300,000 of notes payable, $500,000 of accounts payable, and $200,000 of accruals. Looking ahead to 2016, the company estimates that its assets must increase at the same rate as sales, its spontaneous liabilities will increase at the same rate as sales, its profit margin will be 7%, and its payout ratio will be 80%. How large a sales increase can the company achieve without having to raise funds externally—that is, what is its self-supporting growth rate?

9–5 Long-Term Financing Needed

At year-end 2015, Wallace Landscaping's total assets were $2.17 million and its accounts payable were $560,000. Sales, which in 2015 were $3.5 million, are expected to increase by 35% in 2016. Total assets and accounts payable are proportional to sales, and that relationship will be maintained. Wallace typically uses no current liabilities other than accounts payable. Common stock amounted to $625,000 in 2015, and retained earnings were $395,000. Wallace has arranged to sell $195,000 of new common stock in 2016 to meet some of its financing needs. The remainder of its financing needs will be met by issuing new long-term debt at the end of 2016. (Because the debt is added at the end of the year, there will be no additional interest expense due to the new debt.) Its net profit margin on sales is 5%, and 45% of earnings will be paid out as dividends.

a. What were Wallace's total long-term debt and total liabilities in 2015?
b. How much new long-term debt financing will be needed in 2016?
   (*Hint:* AFN − New stock = New long-term debt.)

9–6 Additional Funds Needed

The Booth Company's sales are forecasted to double from $1,000 in 2015 to $2,000 in 2016. Here is the December 31, 2015, balance sheet:

Cash	$ 100	Accounts payable	$ 50
Accounts receivable	200	Notes payable	150
Inventories	200	Accruals	50
Net fixed assets	500	Long-term debt	400
		Common stock	100
		Retained earnings	250
Total assets	$1,000	Total liabilities and equity	$1,000

Booth's fixed assets were used to only 50% of capacity during 2015, but its current assets were at their proper levels in relation to sales. All assets except fixed assets must increase at the same rate as sales, and fixed assets would also have to increase at the same rate if the current excess capacity did not exist. Booth's after-tax profit margin is forecasted to be 5% and its payout ratio to be 60%. What is Booth's additional funds needed (AFN) for the coming year?

Challenging Problems 7–9

9–7 Forecasted Statements and Ratios

Upton Computers makes bulk purchases of small computers, stocks them in conveniently located warehouses, ships them to its chain of retail stores, and has a staff to advise customers and help them set up their new computers. Upton's balance sheet as of December 31, 2015, is shown here (millions of dollars):

Cash	$ 3.5	Accounts payable	$ 9.0
Receivables	26.0	Notes payable	18.0
Inventories	58.0	Line of credit	0
Total current assets	$ 87.5	Accruals	8.5
Net fixed assets	35.0	Total current liabilities	$ 35.5
		Mortgage loan	6.0
		Common stock	15.0
		Retained earnings	66.0
Total assets	$122.5	Total liabilities and equity	$122.5

Sales for 2015 were $350 million and net income for the year was $10.5 million, so the firm's profit margin was 3.0%. Upton paid dividends of $4.2 million to common stockholders, so its payout ratio was 40%. Its tax rate was 40%, and it operated at full capacity. Assume that all assets/sales ratios, spontaneous liabilities/sales ratios, the profit margin, and the payout ratio remain constant in 2016.

a. If sales are projected to increase by $70 million, or 20%, during 2016, use the AFN equation to determine Upton's projected external capital requirements.

b. Using the AFN equation, determine Upton's self-supporting growth rate. That is, what is the maximum growth rate the firm can achieve without having to employ nonspontaneous external funds?

c. Use the forecasted financial statement method to forecast Upton's balance sheet for December 31, 2016. Assume that all additional external capital is raised as a line of credit at the end of the year and is reflected (because the debt is added at the end of the year, there will be no additional interest expense due to the new debt). Assume Upton's profit margin and dividend payout ratio will be the same in 2016 as they were in 2015. What is the amount of the line of credit reported on the 2016 forecasted balance sheets? (*Hint:* You don't need to forecast the income statements because you are given the projected sales, profit margin, and dividend payout ratio; these figures allow you to calculate the 2016 addition to retained earnings for the balance sheet.)

9-8 Financing Deficit

Stevens Textiles' 2015 financial statements are shown below:

Balance Sheet as of December 31, 2015 (Thousands of Dollars)

Cash	$ 1,080	Accounts payable	$ 4,320
Receivables	6,480	Accruals	2,880
Inventories	9,000	Line of credit	0
Total current assets	$16,560	Notes payable	2,100
Net fixed assets	12,600	Total current liabilities	$ 9,300
		Mortgage bonds	3,500
		Common stock	3,500
		Retained earnings	12,860
Total assets	$29,160	Total liabilities and equity	$29,160

Income Statement for December 31, 2015 (Thousands of Dollars)

Sales	$36,000
Operating costs	32,440
Earnings before interest and taxes	$ 3,560
Interest	460
Pre-tax earnings	$ 3,100
Taxes (40%)	1,240
Net income	$ 1,860
Dividends (45%)	$ 837
Addition to retained earnings	$ 1,023

a. Suppose 2016 sales are projected to increase by 15% over 2015 sales. Use the forecasted financial statement method to forecast a balance sheet and income statement for December 31, 2016. The interest rate on all debt is 10%, and cash earns no interest income. Assume that all additional debt in the form of a line of credit is added at the end of the year, which means that you should base the forecasted interest expense on the balance of debt at the beginning of the year. Use the forecasted income statement to determine the addition to retained earnings. Assume that the company was operating at full capacity in 2015, that it cannot sell off any of its fixed assets, and that any required financing will be borrowed as notes payable. Also, assume that assets, spontaneous liabilities, and operating costs are expected to increase by the same percentage as sales. Determine the additional funds needed.

b. What is the resulting total forecasted amount of the line of credit?

c. In your answers to Parts a and b, you should not have charged any interest on the additional debt added during 2016 because it was assumed that the new debt was added at the end of the year. But now suppose that the new debt is added throughout the year. Don't do any calculations, but how would this change the answers to parts a and b?

9-9 Financing Deficit
Garlington Technologies Inc.'s 2015 financial statements are shown below:

Balance Sheet as of December 31, 2015

Cash	$ 180,000	Accounts payable	$ 360,000
Receivables	360,000	Notes payable	156,000
Inventories	720,000	Line of credit	0
Total current assets	$1,260,000	Accruals	180,000
Fixed assets	1,440,000	Total current liabilities	$ 696,000
		Common stock	1,800,000
		Retained earnings	204,000
Total assets	$2,700,000	Total liabilities and equity	$2,700,000

Income Statement for December 31, 2015

Sales	$3,600,000
Operating costs	3,279,720
EBIT	$ 320,280
Interest	18,280
Pre-tax earnings	$ 302,000
Taxes (40%)	120,800
Net income	$ 181,200
Dividends	$ 108,000

Suppose that in 2016 sales increase by 10% over 2015 sales and that 2016 dividends will increase to $112,000. Forecast the financial statements using the forecasted financial statement method. Assume the firm operated at full capacity in 2015. Use an interest rate of 13%, and assume that any new debt will be added at the end of the year (so forecast the interest expense based on the debt balance at the beginning of the year). Cash does not earn any interest income. Assume that the all new debt will be in the form of a line of credit.

Spreadsheet Problems

9–10 Build a Model: Forecasting Financial Statements

Start with the partial model in the file *Ch09 P10 Build a Model.xlsx* on the textbook's Web site, which contains the 2015 financial statements of Zieber Corporation. Forecast Zeiber's 2016 income statement and balance sheets. Use the following assumptions: (1) Sales grow by 6%. (2) The ratios of expenses to sales, depreciation to fixed assets, cash to sales, accounts receivable to sales, and inventories to sales will be the same in 2016 as in 2015. (3) Zeiber will not issue any new stock or new long-term bonds. (4) The interest rate is 11% for long-term debt and the interest expense on long-term debt is based on the average balance during the year. (5) No interest is earned on cash. (6) Regular dividends grow at an 8% rate. Calculate the additional funds needed (AFN). If new financing is required, assume it will be raised by drawing on a line of credit with an interest rate of 12%. Assume that any draw on the line of credit will be made on the last day of the year, so there will be no additional interest expense for the new line of credit. If surplus funds are available, pay a special dividend.

a. What are the forecasted levels of the line of credit and special dividends? (*Hints:* Create a column showing the ratios for the current year; then create a new column showing the ratios used in the forecast. Also, create a preliminary forecast that doesn't include any new line of credit or special dividends. Identify the financing deficit or surplus in this preliminary forecast and then add a new column that shows the final forecast that includes any new line of credit or special dividend.)

b. Now assume that the growth in sales is only 3%. What are the forecasted levels of the line of credit and special dividends?

9–11 Build a Model: Forecasting and Valuation

Start with the partial model in the file *Ch09 P11 Build a Model.xlsx* on the textbook's Web site, which contains Henley Corporation's most recent financial statements. Use the following ratios and other selected information for the current and projected years to answer the next questions.

	Actual	Projected			
	12/31/ 2015	12/31/ 2016	12/31/ 2017	12/31/ 2018	12/31/ 2019
Sales growth rate		15%	10%	6%	6%
Costs/Sales	72%	72	72	72	72
Depreciation/Net PPE	10	10	10	10	10
Cash/Sales	1	1	1	1	1
Accounts receivable/Sales	10	10	10	10	10
Inventories/Sales	20	20	20	20	20

Net PPE/Sales	75	75	75	75	75
Accounts payable/Sales	2	2	2	2	2
Accruals/Sales	5	5	5	5	5
Tax rate	40	40	40	40	40
Weighted average cost of capital (WACC)	10.5	10.5	10.5	10.5	10.5

a. Forecast the parts of the income statement and balance sheet that are necessary for calculating free cash flow.

b. Calculate free cash flow for each projected year. Also calculate the growth rates in free cash flow each year to ensure that there is constant growth (that is, the same as the constant growth rate in sales) by the end of the forecast period.

c. Calculate the return on invested capital (ROIC = NOPAT/Total net operating capital) and the growth rate in free cash flow. What is the ROIC in the last year of the forecast? What is the long-term constant growth rate in free cash flow (g_L is the growth rate in FCF in the last forecast period because all ratios are constant)? Do you think that Hensley's value would increase if it could add growth without reducing its ROIC? (*Hint:* Growth will add value if the ROIC > WACC/[1+WACC]). Do you think that the company will have a value of operations greater than its total net operating capital? (*Hint:* Is ROIC > WACC/[1 + g_L]?)

d. Calculate the current value of operations. (*Hint:* First calculate the horizon value at the end of the forecast period, which is equal to the value of operations at the end of the forecast period. Assume that the annual growth rate beyond the horizon is equal to the growth rate at the horizon.) How does the current value of operations compare with the current amount of total net operating capital?

e. Calculate the price per share of common equity as of 12/31/2015.

MINI CASE

Hatfield Medical Supplies' stock price had been lagging its industry averages, so its board of directors brought in a new CEO, Jaiden Lee. Lee had brought in Ashley Novak, a finance MBA who had been working for a consulting company, to replace the old CFO, and Lee asked Ashley to develop the financial planning section of the strategic plan. In her previous job, Novak's primary task had been to help clients develop financial forecasts, and that was one reason Lee hired her.

Novak began by comparing Hatfield's financial ratios to the industry averages. If any ratio was substandard, she discussed it with the responsible manager to see what could be done to improve the situation. The following data show Hatfield's latest financial statements plus some ratios and other data that Novak plans to use in her analysis.

Hatfield Medical Supplies (Millions of Dollars Except Per Share Data)

Balance Sheet, 12/31/2015

Cash	$ 20
Accts. rec.	280
Inventories	400
Total CA	$ 700
Net fixed assets	500
Total assets	$1,200
Accts. pay. & accruals	$ 80
Line of credit	$ 0
Total CL	$ 80
Long-term debt	500
Total liabilities	$ 580
Common stock	420
Retained earnings	200
Total common equ.	$ 620
Total liab. & equity	$1,200

Income Statement, Year Ending 2015

Sales	$2,000
Op. costs (excl. depr.)	1,800
Depreciation	50
EBIT	$ 150
Interest	40
Pre-tax earnings	$ 110
Taxes (40%)	44
Net income	$ 66
Dividends	$ 20.0
Add. to RE	$ 46.0
Common shares	10.0
EPS	$ 6.60
DPS	$ 2.00
Ending stock price	$52.80

Selected Additional Data for 2015

	Hatfield	Industry		Hatfield	Industry
Op. costs/Sales	90.0%	88.0%	Total liability/Total assets	48.3%	36.7%
Depr./FA	10.0%	12.0%	Times interest earned	3.8	8.9
Cash/Sales	1.0%	1.0%	Return on assets (ROA)	5.5%	10.2%
Receivables/Sales	14.0%	11.0%	Profit margin (M)	3.30%	4.99%
Inventories/Sales	20.0%	15.0%	Sales/Assets	1.67	2.04
Fixed assets/Sales	25.0%	22.0%	Assets/Equity	1.94	1.58
Acc. pay. & accr. / Sales	4.0%	4.0%	Return on equity (ROE)	10.6%	16.1%
Tax rate	40.0%	40.0%	P/E ratio	8.0	16.0
ROIC	8.0%	12.5%			
NOPAT/Sales	4.5%	5.6%			
Total op. capital/Sales	56.0%	45.0%			

a. Using Hatfield's data and its industry averages, how well run would you say Hatfield appears to be compared to other firms in its industry? What are its primary strengths and weaknesses? Be specific in your answer, and point to various ratios that support your position. Also, use the DuPont equation (see Chapter 7) as one part of your analysis.

b. Use the AFN equation to estimate Hatfield's required new external capital for 2016 if the sales growth rate is 10%. Assume that the firm's 2015 ratios will remain the same in 2016. (*Hint:* Hatfield was operating at full capacity in 2015.)

c. Define the term capital intensity. Explain how a decline in capital intensity would affect the AFN, other things held constant. Would economies of scale combined with rapid growth affect capital intensity, other things held constant? Also, explain how changes in each of the following would affect AFN, holding other things constant: the growth rate, the amount of accounts payable, the profit margin, and the payout ratio.

d. Define the term self-supporting growth rate. What is Hatfield's self-supporting growth rate? Would the self-supporting growth rate be affected by a change in the capital intensity ratio or the other factors mentioned in the previous question? Other things held constant, would the calculated capital intensity ratio change over time if the company were growing and were also subject to economies of scale and/or lumpy assets?

e. Use the following assumptions to answer the questions below: (1) Operating ratios remain unchanged. (2) Sales will grow by 10%, 8%, 5%, and 5% for the next 4 years. (3) The target weighted average cost of capital (WACC) is 9%. This is the *No Change* scenario because operations remain unchanged.

   (1) For each of the next 4 years, forecast the following items: sales, cash, accounts receivable, inventories, net fixed assets, accounts payable & accruals, operating costs (excluding depreciation), depreciation, and earnings before interest and taxes (EBIT).

   (2) Using the previously forecasted items, calculate for each of the next 4 years the net operating profit after taxes (NOPAT), net operating working capital, total operating capital, free cash flow, (FCF), annual growth rate in FCF, and return on invested capital. What does the forecasted free cash flow in the first year imply about the need for external financing? Compare the forecasted ROIC with the WACC. What does this imply about how well the company is performing?

   (3) Assume that FCF will continue to grow at the growth rate for the last year in the forecast horizon (*Hint:* $g_L = 5\%$). What is the horizon value at 2019? What is the present value of the horizon value? What is the present value of the forecasted FCF? (*Hint:* Use the free cash flows for 2016 through 2019.) What is the current value of operations? Using information from the 2015 financial statements, what is the current estimated intrinsic stock price?

f. Continue with the same assumptions for the *No Change* scenario from the previous question, but now forecast the balance sheet and income statements for 2016 (but not for the following 3 years) using the following preliminary financial policy. (1) Regular dividends will grow by 10%. (2) No additional long-term debt or common stock will be issued. (3) The interest rate on all debt is 8%. (4) Interest expense for long-term debt is based on the average balance during the year. (5) If the operating results and the preliminary financing plan cause a financing deficit, eliminate the deficit by drawing on a line of credit. The line of credit would be tapped on the last day of the year, so it would create no additional interest expenses for that year. (6) If there is a financing surplus, eliminate it by paying a special dividend. After forecasting the 2016 financial statements, answer the following questions.

   (1) How much will Hatfield need to draw on the line of credit?

   (2) What are some alternative ways than those in the preliminary financial policy that Hatfield might choose to eliminate the financing deficit?

g. Repeat the analysis performed the previous question, but now assume that Hatfield is able to improve the following inputs: (1) reduce operating costs (excluding depreciation)/sales to 89.5% at a cost of $40 million; and (2) reduce inventories/sales to 16% at a cost of $10 million. This is the Improve scenario.

   (1) Should Hatfield implement the plans? How much value would they add to the company?

   (2) How much can Hatfield pay as a special dividend in the Improve scenario? What else might Hatfield do with the financing surplus?

SELECTED ADDITIONAL CASES

The following cases from CengageCompose cover many of the concepts discussed in this chapter and are available at http://compose.cengage.com.

Klein-Brigham Series:

Case 37, "Space-Age Materials, Inc."; Case 38, "Automated Banking Management, Inc."; Case 52, "Expert Systems"; and Case 69, "Medical Management Systems, Inc."

Corporate Governance

There is no conflict at a one-person company—the owner makes all the decisions, does all the work, reaps all the rewards, and suffers all the losses. This situation changes as the owner begins hiring employees because the employees don't fully share in the owner's rewards and losses. The situation becomes more complicated if the owner sells some shares of the company to an outsider, and even more complicated if the owner hires someone else to run the company. In this situation, there are many potential conflicts between owners, managers, employees, and creditors. These **agency conflicts** occur whenever owners authorize someone else to act on their behalf as their agents. The degree to which agency problems are minimized often depends on a company's **corporate governance**, which is the set of laws, rules, and procedures that influence the company's operations and the decisions its managers make. This chapter addresses these topics, beginning with agency conflicts.

Beginning-of-Chapter Questions

As you read the chapter, consider how you would answer the following questions. You *should not* necessarily be able to answer the questions before you read the chapter. Rather, you should use them to get a sense of the issues covered in the chapter. After reading the chapter, you should be able to give at least partial answers to the questions, and you should be able to give better answers after the chapter has been discussed in class. Note, too, that it is often useful, when answering conceptual questions, to use hypothetical data to illustrate your answer. We illustrate the answers with an *Excel* model that is available on the textbook's Web site. Accessing the model and working through it is a useful exercise, and it provides insights that are useful when answering the questions.

1. What is an **agent** and what is a **principal**? What kinds of situations in companies give rise to conflicts between these two, called agency conflicts?

2. Managers of corporations don't always take actions that are in the best interest of the corporation's owners. What are some of those actions, and how can corporations structure the management contract to help control them?

3. What are some of the pros and cons of using stock options to compensate managers?

4. Why is **corporate governance** important to investors? Explain how each of the following is related to corporate governance: (a) management entrenchment, (b) hostile takeovers, (c) incentive compensation plans, (d) greenmail, (e) poison pills, (f) strong boards of directors, (g) vesting periods for options, and (h) ESOPs.

5. How have events such as the accounting frauds at AIG, Enron, WorldCom, and several other companies affected people's ideas about corporate governance, the government's role in corporate governance, and the use of options for management compensation?

CORPORATE GOVERNANCE AND CORPORATE VALUATION

A company's managers make decisions that affect operations, financing, corporate culture, and many other organizational characteristics. These decisions affect the operating and financing choices the company makes, which in turn affect free cash flow and risk.

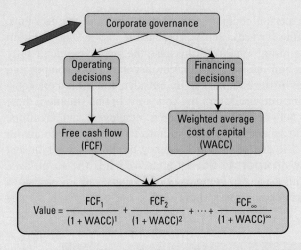

$$\text{Value} = \frac{\text{FCF}_1}{(1 + \text{WACC})^1} + \frac{\text{FCF}_2}{(1 + \text{WACC})^2} + \cdots + \frac{\text{FCF}_\infty}{(1 + \text{WACC})^\infty}$$

Source: From *Financial Management: Theory & Practice,* 2013, by Brigham and Ehrhardt. © Cengage Learning.

10-1 Agency Conflicts

An **agency relationship** arises whenever someone, called a **principal**, hires someone else, called an **agent**, to perform some service, and the principal delegates decision-making authority to the agent. In companies, the primary agency relationships are between: (1) stockholders and creditors, (2) inside owner/managers (managers who own a controlling interest in the company) and outside owners (who have no control), and (3) outside stockholders and hired managers.[1] These conflicts lead to **agency costs**, which are the reductions in a company's value due to agency conflicts. The following sections describe the agency conflicts, the costs, and methods to minimize the costs.

10-1a Conflicts Between Stockholders and Creditors

Creditors have a claim on the firm's earnings stream, and they have a claim on its assets in the event of bankruptcy. However, stockholders have control (through the

---

1. One of the first, and most important, papers in finance and economics to address agency conflicts was written by Michael Jensen and William Meckling and entitled "Theory of the Firm: Managerial Behavior, Agency Costs and Ownership Structure," *Journal of Financial Economics*, Vol. 3, 1976, pp. 305–360.

managers) of decisions that affect the firm's riskiness. Therefore, creditors allocate decision-making authority to someone else, creating a potential agency conflict.

Creditors lend funds at rates based on the firm's perceived risk at the time the credit is extended, which in turn is based on: (1) the risk of the firm's existing assets, (2) expectations concerning the risk of future asset additions, (3) the existing capital structure, and (4) expectations concerning future capital structure changes. These are the primary determinants of the risk of the firm's cash flows, and hence the safety of its debt.

Suppose the firm borrows money, then sells its relatively safe assets and invests the proceeds in assets for a large new project that is far riskier. The new project might be extremely profitable, but it also might lead to bankruptcy. If the risky project is successful, most of the benefits go to the stockholders, because creditors' returns are fixed at the original low-risk rate. However, if the project is unsuccessful, the bondholders take a loss. From the stockholders' point of view, this amounts to a game of "heads, I win; tails, you lose," which obviously is not good for the creditors. Thus, the increased risk due to the asset change will cause the required rate of return on the debt to increase, which in turn will cause the value of the outstanding debt to fall. This is called asset switching or "bait-and-switch."

A similar situation can occur if a company borrows and then issues additional debt, using the proceeds to repurchase some of its outstanding stock, thus increasing its financial leverage. If things go well, the stockholders will gain from the increased leverage. However, the value of the debt will probably decrease, because now there will be a larger amount of debt backed by the same amount of assets. In both the asset switch and the increased leverage situations, stockholders have the potential for gaining, but such gains are made at the expense of creditors.

There are two ways that lenders address the potential of asset switching or subsequent increases in leverage. First, creditors may charge a higher rate to protect themselves in case the company engages in activities which increase risk. However, if the company doesn't increase risk, then its weighted average cost of capital (WACC) will be higher than is justified by the company's risk. This higher WACC will reduce the company's intrinsic value (recall that intrinsic value is the present value of free cash flows discounted at the WACC). In addition, the company will reject projects that it otherwise would have accepted at the lower cost of capital. Therefore, this potential agency conflict has a cost, which is called an agency cost.

The second way that lenders address the potential agency problems is by writing detailed debt covenants specifying what actions the company can and cannot take. Many debt covenants have provisions that: (1) prevent the company from increasing its debt ratios beyond a specified level, (2) prevent the company from repurchasing stock or paying dividends unless profits and retained earnings are above a certain level, and (3) require the company to maintain liquidity ratios above a specified level. These covenants can cause agency costs if they restrict a company from value-adding activities. For example, a company may not be able to accept an unexpected but particularly good investment opportunity if it requires temporarily adding debt above the level specified in the bond covenant. In addition, the costs incurred to write the covenant and monitor the company to verify compliance also are agency costs.

10-1b Conflicts Between Inside Owner/Managers and Outside Owners

If a company's owner also runs the company, the owner/manager will presumably operate it so as to maximize his or her own welfare. This welfare obviously includes the increased wealth due to increasing the value of the company, but it also includes perquisites (or "perks") such as more leisure time, luxurious offices, executive assistants, expense accounts, limousines, corporate jets, and generous retirement plans. However, if the owner/manager incorporates the business and then sells some of the stock to outsiders, a potential conflict of interest immediately arises. Notice that the value of the perquisites still accrues to the owner/manager, but the cost of the perquisites is now partially born by the outsiders. This might even induce the owner/manager to increase consumption of the perquisites because they are relatively less expensive now that the outsider is sharing their costs.

This agency problem causes outsiders to pay less for a share of the company and require a higher rate of return. This is exactly why dual class stock (see Chapter 1) that doesn't have voting rights has a lower price per share than voting stock.

10-1c Conflicts Between Managers and Shareholders

Shareholders want companies to hire managers who are able and willing to take legal and ethical actions to maximize intrinsic stock prices.[2] This obviously requires managers with technical competence, but it also requires managers who are willing to put forth the extra effort necessary to identify and implement value-adding activities. However, managers are people, and people have both personal and corporate goals. Logically, therefore, managers can be expected to act in their own self-interests, and if their self-interests are not aligned with those of stockholders, then corporate value will not be maximized. There are six ways in which a manager's behavior might harm a firm's intrinsic value.

1. Managers might not expend the time and effort required to maximize firm value. Rather than focusing on corporate tasks, they might spend too much time on external activities, such as serving on boards of other companies, or on nonproductive activities, such as golf, gourmet meals, and travel.
2. Managers might use corporate resources on activities that benefit themselves rather than shareholders. For example, they might spend company money on such perquisites as lavish offices, memberships at country clubs, museum-quality art for corporate apartments, large personal staffs, and corporate jets. Because these perks are not actually cash payments to the managers, they are called **nonpecuniary benefits**.
3. Managers might avoid making difficult but value-enhancing decisions that harm friends in the company. For example, a manager might not close a plant or terminate a project if the manager has personal relationships with those who

---

2. Notice that we said both legal and ethical actions. The accounting frauds perpetrated by Enron, WorldCom, and others that were uncovered in 2002 raised stock prices in the short run, but only because investors were misled about the companies' financial positions. Then, when Enron finally revealed the correct financial information, the stocks tanked. Investors who bought shares based on the fraudulent financial statements lost tens of billions of dollars. Releasing false financial statements is illegal. Aggressive earnings management and the use of misleading accounting tricks to pump up reported earnings is unethical, and executives can go to jail as a result of their shenanigans. When we speak of taking actions to maximize stock prices, we mean making operational or financial changes designed to maximize intrinsic stock value, not fooling investors with false or misleading financial reports.

are adversely affected by such decisions, even if termination is the economically sound action.

4. Managers might take on too much risk or they might not take on enough risk. For example, a company might have the opportunity to undertake a risky project with a positive NPV. If the project turns out badly, then the manager's reputation will be harmed and the manager might even be fired. Thus, a manager might choose to avoid risky projects even if they are desirable from a shareholder's point of view. On the other hand, a manager might take on projects with too much risk. Consider a project that is not living up to expectations. A manager might be tempted to invest even more money in the project rather than admit that the project is a failure. Or a manager might be willing to take on a second project with a negative NPV if it has even a slight chance of a very positive outcome, because hitting a home run with this second project might cover up the first project's poor performance. In other words, the manager might throw good money after bad.

5. If a company is generating positive free cash flow, a manager might "stockpile" it in the form of marketable securities instead of returning FCF to investors. This potentially harms investors because it prevents them from allocating these funds to other companies with good growth opportunities. Even worse, positive FCF often tempts a manager into paying too much for the acquisition of another company. In fact, most mergers and acquisitions end up as break-even deals, at best, for the acquiring company because the premiums paid for the targets are often very large.

   Why would a manager be reluctant to return cash to investors? First, extra cash on hand reduces the company's risk, which appeals to many managers. Second, a large distribution of cash to investors is an admission that the company doesn't have enough good investment opportunities. Slow growth is normal for a maturing company, but this isn't very exciting for a manager to admit. Third, there is a lot of glamour associated with making a large acquisition, and this can provide a large boost to a manager's ego. Fourth, compensation usually is higher for executives at larger companies; cash distributions to investors make a company smaller, not larger.

6. Managers might not release all the information that investors desire. Sometimes, they might withhold information to prevent competitors from gaining an advantage. Other times, they might try to avoid releasing bad news. For example, they might "massage" the data or "manage the earnings" so that the news doesn't look so bad. If investors are unsure about the quality of information managers provide, they tend to discount the company's expected free cash flows at a higher cost of capital, which reduces the company's intrinsic value.

If senior managers believe there is little chance they will be removed, we say that they are *entrenched*. Such a company faces a high risk of being poorly run, because entrenched managers are able to act in their own interests rather than in the interests of shareholders.

What are agency conflicts? What groups can have agency conflicts?

Name six types of managerial behaviors that can reduce a firm's intrinsic value.

SELF TEST

w w w

For excellent discussions of corporate governance, see the Web pages of CalPERS (the California Public Employees' Retirement System), **www.calpers.org**, and TIAA-CREF (Teachers Insurance and Annuity Association College Retirement Equity Fund), **www.tiaacref.org**.

10-2 Corporate Governance

Agency conflicts can decrease the value of stock owned by outside shareholders. Corporate governance can mitigate this loss in value. Corporate governance can be defined as the set of laws, rules, and procedures that influence a company's operations and the decisions its managers make. At the risk of oversimplification, most corporate governance provisions come in two forms, sticks and carrots. The primary stick is the *threat of removal*, either as a decision by the board of directors or as the result of a hostile takeover. If a firm's managers are maximizing the value of the resources entrusted to them, they need not fear the loss of their jobs. On the other hand, if managers are not maximizing value, they should be removed by their own boards of directors, by dissident stockholders, or by other companies seeking to profit by installing a better management team. The main carrot is *compensation*. Managers have greater incentives to maximize intrinsic stock value if their compensation is linked to the firm's performance rather than being strictly in the form of salary.

Almost all corporate governance provisions affect either the threat of removal or compensation. Some provisions are internal to a firm and are under its control.[3] These internal provisions and features can be divided into five areas: (1) monitoring and discipline by the board of directors, (2) charter provisions and bylaws that affect the likelihood of hostile takeovers, (3) compensation plans, (4) capital structure choices, and (5) accounting control systems. In addition to the corporate governance provisions that are under a firm's control, there are also environmental factors outside of a firm's control, such as the regulatory environment, block ownership patterns, competition in the product markets, the media, and litigation. Our discussion begins with the internal provisions.

10-2a Monitoring and Discipline by the Board of Directors

Shareholders are a corporation's owners, and they elect the board of directors to act as agents on their behalf. In the United States, it is the board's duty to monitor senior managers and discipline them if they do not act in the interests of shareholders, either by removal or by a reduction in compensation.[4] This is not necessarily the case outside the United States. For example, many companies in Europe are required to have employee representatives on the board. Also, many European and Asian companies have bank representatives on the board. But even in the United States, many boards fail to act in the shareholders' best interests. How can this be?

Consider the election process. The board of directors has a nominating committee. These directors choose the candidates for the open director positions, and the ballot for a board position usually lists only one candidate. Although outside

---

3. We have adapted this framework from the one provided by Stuart L. Gillan, "Recent Developments in Corporate Governance: An Overview," *Journal of Corporate Finance*, June 2006, pp. 381–402. Gillan provides an excellent discussion of the issues associated with corporate governance, and we highly recommend this article to the reader who is interested in an expanded discussion of the issues in this section.

4. There are a few exceptions to this rule. For example, some states have laws allowing the board to consider the interests of other stakeholders, such as employees and members of the community.

candidates can run a "write-in" campaign, only those candidates named by the board's nominating committee are on the ballot.[5] At many companies, the CEO is also the chairman of the board and has considerable influence on this nominating committee. This means that in practice it often is the CEO who, in effect, nominates candidates for the board. High compensation and prestige go with a position on the board of a major company, so board seats are prized possessions. Board members typically want to retain their positions, and they are grateful to whoever helped get them on the board. Thus, the nominating process often results in a board that is favorably disposed to the CEO.

At most companies, a candidate is elected simply by having a majority of votes cast. The proxy ballot usually lists all candidates, with a box for each candidate to check if the shareholder votes "For" the candidate and a box to check if the shareholder "Withholds" a vote on the candidate—you can't actually vote "No"; you can only withhold your vote. In theory, a candidate could be elected with a single "For" vote if all other votes were withheld. In practice, though, most shareholders either vote "For" or assign to management their right to vote (proxy is defined as the authority to act for another, which is why it is called a proxy statement). In practice, then, the nominated candidates virtually always receive a majority of votes and are thus elected.

Occasionally there is a "Just vote no" campaign in which a large investor (usually an institution such as a pension fund) urges stockholders to withhold their votes for one or more directors. Although such campaigns do not directly affect the director's election, they do provide a visible way for investors to express their dissatisfaction. Recent evidence shows that "Just vote no" campaigns at poorly performing firms lead to better performance and a greater probability that the CEO will be dismissed.[6]

Voting procedures also affect the ability of outsiders to gain positions on the board. If the charter specifies cumulative voting, then each shareholder is given a number of votes equal to his or her shares multiplied by the number of board seats up for election. For example, the holder of 100 shares of stock will receive 1,000 votes if 10 seats are to be filled. Then, the shareholder can distribute those votes however he or she sees fit. One hundred votes could be cast for each of 10 candidates, or all 1,000 votes could be cast for one candidate. If noncumulative voting is used, the hypothetical stockholder cannot concentrate votes in this way—no more than 100 votes can be cast for any candidate, and the stockholder may do this for as many seats as there are to be filled.

With noncumulative voting, if management controls 51% of the shares then they can fill every seat on the board, leaving dissident stockholders without any representation on the board. With cumulative voting, however, if 10 seats are to be filled then dissidents could elect a representative, provided they have 10% plus 1 additional share of the stock.

Note also that bylaws specify whether the entire board is to be elected annually or if directors are to have staggered terms with, say, one-third of the seats to be filled each year and directors to serve 3-year terms. With staggered terms, fewer seats come up each year, making it harder for dissidents to gain representation on the board. Staggered boards are also called **classified boards**.

---

5. There is currently (early 2014) a movement under way to allow shareholders to nominate candidates for the board, but only time will tell whether this movement is successful.

6. See Diane Del Guercio, Laura Seery, and Tracie Woidtke, "Do Boards Pay Attention When Institutional Investor Activists 'Just Vote No'?" *Journal of Financial Economics*, October 2008, pp. 84–103.

Many board members are "insiders"—that is, people who hold managerial positions within the company, such as the CFO. Because insiders report to the CEO, it may be difficult for them to oppose the CEO at a board meeting. To help mitigate this problem, several exchanges, such as the NYSE and NASDAQ, now require that listed companies have a majority of outside directors.

Some "outside" board members often have strong connections with the CEO through professional relationships, personal friendships, and consulting or other fee-generating activities. In fact, outsiders sometimes have very little expert business knowledge but have "celebrity" status from nonbusiness activities. Some companies also have **interlocking boards of directors**, where Company A's CEO sits on Company B's board and B's CEO sits on A's board. In these situations, even the outside directors are not truly independent and impartial.

Large boards (those with more than about 10 members) often are less effective than smaller boards. As anyone who has been on a committee can attest, individual participation tends to fall as committee size increases. Thus, there is a greater likelihood that members of a large board will be less active than those on smaller boards.

The compensation of board members has an impact on the board's effectiveness. When board members have exceptionally high compensation, the CEO also tends to have exceptionally high compensation. This suggests that such boards tend to be too lenient with the CEO.[7] The form of board compensation also affects board performance. Rather than compensating board members with only salary, many companies now include restricted stock grants or stock options in an effort to better align board members with stockholders.

Studies show that corporate governance usually improves if: (1) the CEO is not also the chairman of the board, (2) the board has a majority of true outsiders who bring some type of business expertise to the board and are not too busy with other activities, (3) the board is not too large, and (4) board members are compensated appropriately (not too high and not all cash, but including exposure to equity risk through options or stock). The good news for the shareholder is that the boards at many companies have made significant improvements in these directions during the past decade. Fewer CEOs are also board chairmen and, as power has shifted from CEOs to boards as a whole, there has been a tendency to replace insiders with strong, independent outsiders. Today, the typical board has about one-third insiders and two-thirds outsiders, and most outsiders are truly independent. Moreover, board members are compensated primarily with stock or options rather than a straight salary. These changes clearly have decreased the patience of boards with poorly performing CEOs. Within the past several years, the CEOs of Wachovia, Sprint Nextel, Hewlett-Packard, Home Depot, Citigroup, Pfizer, Groupon, Siemens, J.C. Penney, and Men's Warehouse, to name just a few, have been removed by their boards. This would not have occurred 30 years ago.

10-2b Charter Provisions and Bylaws That Affect the Likelihood of Hostile Takeovers

Hostile takeovers usually occur when managers have not been willing or able to maximize the profit potential of the resources under their control. In such a

---

7. See I. E. Brick, O. Palmon, and J. Wald, "CEO Compensation, Director Compensation, and Firm Performance: Evidence of Cronyism?" *Journal of Corporate Finance*, June 2006, pp. 403–423.

situation, another company can acquire the poorly performing firm, replace its managers, increase free cash flow, and improve MVA. The following paragraphs describe some provisions that can be included in a corporate charter to make it harder for poorly performing managers to remain in control.[8]

A shareholder-friendly charter should ban **targeted share repurchases**, also known as **greenmail**. For example, suppose a company's stock is selling for $20 per share. Now a hostile bidder, or raider, who plans to replace management if the takeover is successful, buys 5% of the company's stock at the $20 price.[9] The raider then makes an offer to purchase the remainder of the stock for $30 per share. The company might offer to buy back the raider's stock at a price of, say, $35 per share. This is called a targeted share repurchase because the stock will be purchased only from the raider and not from any other shareholders. A raider who paid only $20 per share for the stock would be making a quick profit of $15 per share, which could easily total several hundred million dollars. As a part of the deal, the raider would sign a document promising not to attempt to take over the company for a specified number of years; hence the buyback also is called greenmail. Greenmail hurts shareholders in two ways. First, they are left with $20 stock when they could have received $30 per share. Second, the company purchased stock from the bidder at $35 per share, which represents a direct loss by the remaining shareholders of $15 for each repurchased share.

Managers who buy back stock in targeted repurchases typically argue that their firms are worth more than the raiders offered and that, in time, the "true value" will be revealed in the form of a much higher stock price. This situation might be true if a company were in the process of restructuring itself, or if new products with high potential were in the pipeline. But if the old management had been in power for a long time and had a history of making empty promises, then one should question whether the true purpose of the buyback was to protect stockholders or management.

Another characteristic of a stockholder-friendly charter is that it does not contain a **shareholder rights provision**, better described as a **poison pill**. These provisions give the shareholders of target firms the right to buy a specified number of shares in the company at a very low price if an outside group or firm acquires a specified percentage of the firm's stock. Therefore, if a potential acquirer tries to take over a company, its other shareholders will be entitled to purchase additional shares of stock at a bargain price, thus seriously diluting the holdings of the raider. For this reason, these clauses are called poison pills, because if they are in the charter, the acquirer will end up swallowing a poison pill if the acquisition is successful. Obviously, the existence of a poison pill makes a takeover more difficult, and this helps to entrench management.

---

8. Some states have laws that go further than others to protect management. This is one reason that many companies are incorporated in manager-friendly Delaware. Some companies have even shifted their state of incorporation to Delaware because their managers felt that a hostile takeover attempt was likely. Note that a "shareholder-friendly charter" could and would waive the company's right to strong anti-takeover protection, even if the state allowed it.

9. Someone can, under the law, acquire up to 5% of a firm's stock without announcing the acquisition. Once the 5% limit has been hit, the acquirer has 10 days to "announce" the acquisition by filing Schedule 13D with the SEC. Schedule 13D reports not only the acquirer's number of shares but also his or her intentions, such as a passive investment or a takeover. These reports are monitored closely, so as soon as one is filed, management is alerted to the possibility of an imminent takeover.

THE GLOBAL ECONOMIC CRISIS

Would the U.S. Government Be an Effective Board Director?

In response to the global economic crisis that began with the recession of 2007, many governments are becoming major stakeholders in companies that had been publicly traded. For example, the U.S. government has invested billions in Fannie Mae and Freddie Mac, taking them into conservatorship and having a direct say in their leadership and operations, including the dismissal of former Fannie Mae CEO Daniel Mudd in 2008.

The U.S. government also made multibillion-dollar investments in banks (among them, Citigroup, Bank of America, JPMorgan Chase, and Wells Fargo), insurance companies, AIG (spectacularly), and auto companies (GM and Chrysler). Much of this has been in the form of preferred stock, which does not give the government any direct voting or decision-making authority. However, the government has certainly applied moral suasion, as evidenced by the removal of GM's former CEO Rick Wagoner. The government also imposed limits on executive compensation at firms receiving additional government funds.

For the most part, however, the government does not have voting rights with bailout recipients, nor does it have representation on their boards of directors. It will be interesting to see if this changes and if the government takes a more direct role in corporate governance.

Many large banks, including Citigroup, Goldman Sachs, and JPMorgan Chase, have repaid the government's investments. In fact, as of early 2014, when dividends and other payments are included the TARP funds have returned a small profit to the Treasury, although $228 billion of the original $609 billion disbursed has not been repaid.

Sources: See **http://projects.nytimes.com/creditcrisis/recipients /table** for updates on TARP recipients. See **http://projects.propublica .org/bailout/list** for a more comprehensive list that includes the bailouts funded through other programs, such as the bailout of Fannie Mae.

A third management entrenchment tool is a **restricted voting rights** provision, which automatically cancels the voting rights of any shareholder who owns more than a specified amount of the company's stock. The board can grant voting rights to such a shareholder, but this is unlikely if that shareholder plans to take over the company.

10-2c Using Compensation to Align Managerial and Shareholder Interests

The typical CEO today receives a fixed salary, a cash bonus based on the firm's performance, and stock-based compensation, either in the form of stock grants or option grants. Cash bonuses often are based upon short-term operating factors, such as this year's growth in earnings per share, or medium-term operating performance, such as earnings growth over the past 3 years.

Stock-based compensation is often in the form of options. Chapter 5 explains option valuation in detail, but here we discuss how a standard **stock option compensation plan** works. Suppose IBM decides to grant an option to an employee, allowing her to purchase a specified number of IBM shares at a fixed price, called the **strike price** (or **exercise price**), regardless of the actual price of the stock. The strike price is usually set equal to the current stock price at the time the option is granted. Thus, if IBM's current price were $100, then the option would have an exercise price of $100. Options usually cannot be exercised until after some specified period (the **vesting period**), which is usually 1 to 5 years. Some grants have **cliff vesting**, which means that all the granted options vest at the same date, such as 3 years after the grant. Other grants have **annual vesting**, which means that a certain percentage vests each year. For example, one-third of the options in the grant might vest each year. The options have an **expiration date**, usually 10 years after issue. For our IBM example, assume that the options have cliff vesting in 3 years and have an expiration date in 10 years. Thus, the employee can exercise the option 3 years after issue or wait as long as 10 years. Of course, the employee would not exercise unless IBM's stock is above the $100 exercise price, and if the price never rose above $100, the option would expire unexercised. However, if the stock price were above $100 on the expiration date, the option would surely be exercised.

Suppose the stock price had grown to $134 after 5 years, at which point the employee decided to exercise the option. She would buy stock from IBM for $100, so IBM would get only $100 for stock worth $134. The employee would (probably) sell the stock the same day she exercised the option and hence would receive in cash the $34 difference between the $134 stock price and the $100 exercise price. There are two important points to note in this example. First, most employees sell stock soon after exercising the option. Thus, the incentive effects of an option grant typically end when the option is exercised. Second, option pricing theory shows that it is not optimal to exercise a conventional call option on stock that does not pay dividends before the option expires: An investor is always better off selling the option in the marketplace rather than exercising it. But because employee stock options are not tradable, grantees often exercise the options well before they expire. For example, people often time the exercise of options to the purchase of a new home or some other large expenditure. But early exercise occurs not just for liquidity reasons, such as needing cash to purchase a house, but also because of behavioral reasons. For example, exercises occur more frequently after stock run-ups, which suggests that grantees view the stock as overpriced.

In theory, stock options should align a manager's interests with those of shareholders, influencing the manager to behave in a way that maximizes the company's value. But in practice, there are two reasons why this does not always occur.

First, suppose a CEO granted options on 1 million shares. If we use the same stock prices as in our previous example then the grantee would receive $34 for each option, or a total of $34 million. Keep in mind that this is in addition to an annual salary and cash bonuses. The logic behind employee options is that they motivate people to work harder and smarter, thus making the company more valuable and benefiting shareholders. But take a closer look at this example. If the risk-free rate is 5.5%, the market risk premium is 6%, and IBM's beta is 1.19, then the expected return, based on the CAPM, is 5.5% + 1.19(6%) = 12.64%. IBM's dividend yield is only 0.8%, so the expected annual price appreciation must be about 11.84% (12.64% − 0.8% = 11.84%). Now note that if IBM's stock price grew from $100 to $134 over 5 years, this would translate to an annual growth rate of only 6%, not the 11.84% shareholders expected. Thus, the executive would receive $34 million for helping run a company that performed below shareholders' expectations. As this example illustrates, standard stock options do not necessarily link executives' wealth with that of shareholders.

Second, and even worse, the events of the early 2000s showed that some executives were willing to illegally falsify financial statements in order to drive up stock prices just prior to exercising their stock options.[10] In some notable cases, the subsequent stock price drop and loss of investor confidence have forced firms into bankruptcy. Such behavior is certainly not in shareholders' best interests!

As a result, companies today are experimenting with different types of compensation plans that involve different vesting periods and different measures of performance. For example, from a legal standpoint it is more difficult to manipulate EVA (Economic Value Added) than earnings per share.[11] Therefore, many companies incorporate EVA-type measures in their compensation systems. Also, many companies have quit granting options and instead are granting restricted stock that cannot be sold until it has vested.

Just as "all ships rise in a rising tide," so too do most stocks rise in a bull market such as that of 2003–2007. In a strong market, even the stocks of companies whose performance ranks in the bottom 10% of their peer group can rise and thus trigger handsome executive bonuses. This situation is leading to compensation plans that are based on *relative* as opposed to *absolute* stock price performance. For example, some compensation plans have indexed options whose exercise prices depend on the performance of the market or a subset of competitors.

Finally, the empirical results from academic studies show that the correlation between executive compensation and corporate performance is mixed. Some studies suggest that the type of compensation plan used affects company performance, while others find little effect, if any. But we can say with certainty that managerial compensation plans will continue to receive lots of attention from researchers, the popular press, and boards of directors.

THE DODD-FRANK ACT AND "SAY ON PAY"

The Dodd-Frank Act requires corporations to hold a nonbinding vote to approve or reject the company's executive compensation plan. During 2011, the first proxy season in which the vote was required, shareholders approved about 92% of the proposals. As we write this in early 2014, it is too early to say for sure, but already there are a number of companies whose shareholders have rejected the compensation plans, including Navistar International, RadioShack, Abercrombie & Fitch, and Big Lots.

In addition to say on pay, shareholders are also concerned with other issues, including political lobbying. The table at right shows selected shareholder proposals in 2013.

---

10. Several academic studies show that option-based compensation leads to a greater likelihood of earnings restatements (which means having to refile financial statements with the SEC because there was a material error) and outright fraud. See A. Agrawal and S. Chadha, "Corporate Governance and Accounting Scandals," *Journal of Law and Economics*, 2006, pp. 371–406; N. Burns and S. Kedia, "The Impact of Performance-Based Compensation on Misreporting," *Journal of Financial Economics*, January 2006, pp. 35–67; and D. J. Denis, P. Hanouna, and A. Sarin, "Is There a Dark Side to Incentive Compensation?" *Journal of Corporate Finance*, June 2006, pp. 467–488.

11. For a discussion of EVA, see Al Ehrbar, *EVA: The Real Key to Creating Wealth* (New York: John Wiley & Sons, 1998); and Pamela P. Peterson and David R. Peterson, *Company Performance and Measures of Value Added* (The Research Foundation of the Institute of Chartered Financial Analysts, 1996).

	Number of Proposals		Number of Proposals
Board Issues		**Social Responsibility**	
Equal access to the proxy	11	Review political spending/lobbying	102
Independent board chairman	58	Climate change	16
Takeover Defenses/Other		Report on impact of fracturing	6
Right to call special meeting	10	Report on sustainability	38
Allow for written consent	26	Board diversity	24
End supermajority vote requirement	17		
Repeal classified board	29		

Source: Institutional Shareholder Services, http://www.issgovernance.com/2013postseasonreportus.

10-2d Capital Structure and Internal Control Systems

Capital structure decisions can affect managerial behavior. As the debt level increases, so does the probability of bankruptcy. This increased threat of bankruptcy affects managerial behavior in two ways. First, as discussed earlier in this chapter, managers may waste money on unnecessary expenditures and perquisites. This behavior is more likely when times are good and firms are flush with cash; it is less likely in the face of high debt levels and possible bankruptcy. Thus high levels of debt tend to reduce managerial waste. Second, however, high levels of debt may also reduce a manager's willingness to undertake positive-NPV but risky projects. Most managers have their personal reputation and wealth tied to a single company. If that company has a lot of debt, then a particularly risky project, even if it has a positive NPV, may be just too risky for the manager to tolerate because a bad outcome could lead to bankruptcy and loss of the manager's job. Stockholders, on the other hand, are diversified and would want the manager to invest in positive-NPV projects even if they are risky. When managers forgo risky but value-adding projects, the resulting **underinvestment problem** reduces firm value. So increasing debt might increase firm value by reducing wasteful expenditures, but it also might reduce value by inducing underinvestment by managers. Empirical tests have not been able to establish exactly which effect dominates.

Internal control systems have become an increasingly important issue since the passage of the Sarbanes-Oxley Act of 2002. Section 404 of the act requires companies to establish effective internal control systems. The Securities and Exchange Commission, which is charged with the implementation of Sarbanes-Oxley, defines an effective internal control system as one that provides "reasonable assurance regarding the reliability of financial reporting and the preparation of financial statements for external purposes in accordance with generally accepted accounting principles." In other words, investors should be able to trust a company's reported financial statements.

THE SARBANES-OXLEY ACT OF 2002 AND CORPORATE GOVERNANCE

In 2002, Congress passed the Sarbanes-Oxley Act, known in the industry as SOX, as a measure to improve transparency in financial accounting and to prevent fraud. SOX consists of eleven chapters, or *titles*, which establish wide-ranging new regulations for auditors, CEOs and CFOs, boards of directors, investment analysts, and investment banks. These regulations are designed to ensure that: (a) companies that perform audits are sufficiently independent of the companies that they audit, (b) a key executive in each company *personally* certifies that the financial statements are complete and accurate, (c) the board of directors' audit committee is relatively independent of management, (d) financial analysts are relatively independent of the companies they analyze, and (e) companies publicly and promptly release all important information about their financial condition. The individual titles are briefly summarized below.

Title I establishes the Public Company Accounting Oversight Board, whose charge is to oversee auditors and establish quality control and ethical standards for audits.

Title II requires that auditors be independent of the companies that they audit. Basically this means they can't provide consulting services to the companies they audit. The purpose is to remove financial incentives for auditors to help management cook the books.

Title III requires that the board of directors' audit committee must be composed of "independent" members. Section 302 requires that the CEO and CFO must review the annual and quarterly financial statements and reports and personally certify that they are complete and accurate. Penalties for certifying reports that executives know are false range up to a $5 million fine, 20 years in prison, or both. Under Section 304, if the financial statements turn out to be false and must be *restated*, then certain bonuses and equity-based compensation that executives earn must be reimbursed to the company.

Title IV's Section 401(a) requires prompt disclosure and more extensive reporting on off–balance sheet transactions. Section 404 requires that management evaluate its internal financial controls and report whether they are "effective." The external auditing firm must also indicate whether it agrees with management's evaluation of its internal controls. Section 409 requires that a company disclose to the public promptly and *in plain English* any material changes to its financial condition. Title IV also places restrictions on the loans that a company can make to its executives.

Title V addresses the relationship between financial analysts, the investment banks they work for, and the companies they cover. It requires that analysts and brokers who make stock recommendations disclose any conflicts of interest they might have concerning the stocks they recommend.

Titles VI and VII are technical in nature, dealing with the SEC's budget and powers and requiring that several studies be undertaken by the SEC.

Title VIII establishes penalties for destroying or falsifying audit records. It also provides "whistle-blower protection" for employees who report fraud.

Title IX increases the penalties for a variety of white-collar crimes associated with securities fraud, such as mail and wire fraud. Section 902 also makes it a crime to alter, destroy, or hide documents that might be used in an investigation. It also makes it a crime to conspire to do so.

Title X requires that the CEO sign the company's federal income tax return.

Title XI provides penalties for obstructing an investigation and grants the SEC authority to remove officers or directors from a company if they have committed fraud.

10-2e Environmental Factors Outside of a Firm's Control

As noted earlier, corporate governance is also affected by environmental factors that are outside of a firm's control, including the regulatory/legal environment, block ownership patterns, competition in the product markets, the media, and litigation.

Regulations and Laws

The regulatory/legal environment includes the agencies that regulate financial markets, such as the SEC. Even though the fines and penalties levied on firms for financial misrepresentation by the SEC are relatively small, the damage to a firm's reputation can have significant costs, leading to extremely large reductions in the firm's value.[12] Thus, the regulatory system has an enormous impact on corporate governance and firm value.

The regulatory/legal environment also includes the laws and legal system under which a company operates. These vary greatly from country to country. Studies show that firms located in countries with strong legal protection for investors have stronger corporate governance and that this is reflected in better access to financial markets, a lower cost of equity, increases in market liquidity, and less nonsystematic volatility in stock returns.[13]

Block Ownership Patterns

Prior to the 1960s, most U.S. stock was owned by a large number of individual investors, each of whom owned a diversified portfolio of stocks. Because each individual owned a small amount of any given company's stock, there was little that he or she could do to influence its operations. Also, with such a small investment, it was not cost effective for the investor to monitor companies closely. Indeed, dissatisfied stockholders would typically just "vote with their feet" by selling the stock. This situation began to change as institutional investors such as pension funds and mutual funds gained control of larger and larger shares of investment capital—and as they then acquired larger and larger percentages of all outstanding stock. Given their large block holdings, it now makes sense for institutional investors to monitor management, and they have the clout to influence the board. In some cases, they have actually elected their own representatives to the board. For example, when TIAA-CREF, a huge private pension fund, became frustrated with the performance and leadership of Furr's/Bishop, a cafeteria chain, the fund led a fight that ousted the entire board and then elected a new board consisting only of outsiders.

In general, activist investors with large blocks in companies have been good for all shareholders. They have searched for firms with poor profitability and then replaced management with new teams that are well versed in value-based management techniques, thereby improving profitability. Not surprisingly, stock prices usually rise on the news that a well-known activist investor has taken a major position in an underperforming company.

Note that activist investors can improve performance even if they don't go so far as to take over a firm. More often, they either elect their own representatives to the board or simply point out the firm's problems to other board members. In such

---

12. For example, see Jonathan M. Karpoff, D. Scott Lee, and Gerald S. Martin, "The Cost to Firms of Cooking the Books," *Journal of Financial and Quantitative Analysis*, September 2008, pp. 581–612.

13. For example, see R. La Porta, F. Lopez-de-Silanes, A. Shleifer, and R. Vishny, "Legal Determinants of External Finance," *Journal of Finance*, January 1997, pp. 1131–1150; Hazem Daouk, Charles M. C. Lee, and David Ng, "Capital Market Governance: How Do Security Laws Affect Market Performance?" *Journal of Corporate Finance*, June 2006, pp. 560–593; and Li Jin and Stewart C. Myers, "R^2 Around the World: New Theory and New Tests," *Journal of Financial Economics*, February 2006, pp. 257–292.

cases, boards become less tolerant of management behavior when they realize that the management team is not acting to increase shareholder value. Moreover, the firm's top managers recognize what will happen if they don't whip the company into shape, and they go about doing just that.

Competition in Product Markets

The degree of competition in a firm's product market has an impact on its corporate governance. For example, companies in industries with lots of competition don't have the luxury of tolerating poorly performing CEOs. As might be expected, CEO turnover is higher in competitive industries than in those with less competition.[14] When most firms in an industry are similar, you might expect it to be easier to find a qualified replacement from another firm for a poorly performing CEO. This is exactly what the evidence shows: As industry homogeneity increases, so does the incidence of CEO turnover.[15]

The Media and Litigation

Corporate governance, especially compensation, is a hot topic in the media. The media can have a positive impact by discovering or reporting corporate problems,

INTERNATIONAL CORPORATE GOVERNANCE

Corporate governance includes the following factors: (1) the likelihood that a poorly performing firm can be taken over; (2) whether the board of directors is dominated by insiders or outsiders, (3) the extent to which most of the stock is held by a few large "blockholders" versus many small shareholders, and (4) the size and form of executive compensation. An interesting study compared corporate governance in Germany, Japan, and the United States.

First, note from the accompanying table that the threat of a takeover serves as a stick in the United States but not in Japan or Germany. This threat, which reduces management entrenchment, should benefit shareholders in the United States relative to the other two countries. Second, German and Japanese boards are

larger than those in the United States. Japanese boards consist primarily of insiders, unlike German and American boards, which have similar inside/outside mixes. It should be noted, though, that the boards of most large German corporations include representatives of labor, whereas U.S. boards represent only shareholders. Thus, it would appear that U.S. boards, with a higher percentage of outsiders, would have interests most closely aligned with those of shareholders.

German and Japanese firms are also more likely to be controlled by large blocks of stock than those in the United States. Although institutional investors such as pension and mutual funds are increasingly important in the United States, block ownership is still less prevalent than in Germany and Japan. In both Germany and Japan, banks often own

---

14. See M. De Fond and C. Park, "The Effect of Competition on CEO Turnover," *Journal of Accounting and Economics*, Vol. 27, 1999, pp. 35–56; and T. Fee and C. Hadlock, "Management Turnover and Product Market Competition: Empirical Evidence from the U.S. Newspaper Industry," *Journal of Business*, April 2000, pp. 205–243.

15. See R. Parrino, "CEO Turnover and Outside Succession: A Cross-Sectional Analysis," *Journal of Financial Economics*, Vol. 46, 1997, pp. 165–197.

large blocks of stock, something that is not permitted by law in the United States, and corporations also own large blocks of stock in other corporations. In Japan, combinations of companies, called **keiretsus**, have cross-ownership of stock among the member companies, and these interlocking blocks distort the definition of an outside board member. For example, when the performance of a company in a keiretsu deteriorates, new directors are often appointed from the staffs of other members of the keiretsu. Such appointees might be classified officially as insiders, but they represent interests other than those of the troubled company's CEO.

In general, large blockholders are better able to monitor management than are small investors, so one might expect the blockholder factor to favor German and Japanese shareholders. However, these blockholders have other relationships with the company that might be detrimental to outside shareholders. For example, if one company buys from another, transfer pricing might be used to shift wealth to a favored company, or a company might be forced to buy from a sister company in spite of the availability of lower-cost resources from outside the group.

Executive compensation packages differ dramatically across the three countries, with U.S. executives receiving by far the highest compensation. However, compensation plans are remarkably similar in terms of how sensitive total compensation is to corporate performance.

Which country's system of corporate governance is best from the standpoint of a shareholder whose goal is stock price maximization? There is no definitive answer. U.S. stocks have had the best performance in recent years. Moreover, German and Japanese companies are slowly moving toward the U.S. system with respect to size of compensation, and compensation plans in all three countries are being linked ever more closely to performance. At the same time, however, U.S. companies are moving toward the others in the sense of having larger ownership blocks; because those blocks are primarily held by pension and mutual funds (rather than banks and related corporations), they better represent the interests of shareholders.

Source: Steven N. Kaplan, "Top Executive Incentives in Germany, Japan, and the USA: A Comparison," in *Executive Compensation and Shareholder Value*, Jennifer Carpenter and David Yermack, eds. (Boston: Kluwer Academic Publishers, 1999), pp. 3–12.

International Characteristics of Corporate Governance

	Germany	Japan	United States
Threat of a takeover	Moderate	Low	High
Board of directors			
Size of board	26	21	14
Percent insiders	27%	91%	33%
Percent outsiders	73%	9%	67%
Are large blocks of stock typically owned by			
A controlling family?	Yes	No	No
Another corporation?	Yes	Yes	No
A bank?	Yes	Yes	No
Executive compensation			
Amount of compensation	Moderate	Low	High
Sensitivity to performance	Low to moderate	Low to moderate	Low to moderate

such as the Enron scandal. Another example is the extensive coverage that was given to option backdating, in which the exercise prices of executive stock options were set *after* the options officially were granted. Because the exercise prices were set at the lowest stock price during the quarter in which the options were granted, the options were in-the-money and more valuable when their "official" lives began. Several CEOs lost their jobs over this practice.

However, the media can also hurt corporate governance by focusing too much attention on a CEO. Such "superstar" CEOs often command excessive compensation packages and spend too much time on activities outside the company, resulting in too much pay for too little performance.[16]

In addition to penalties and fines from regulatory bodies such as the SEC, civil litigation also occurs when companies are suspected of fraud. Research indicates that such suits lead to improvements in corporate governance.[17]

SELF TEST

What are the two primary forms of corporate governance provisions that correspond to the stick and the carrot?

What factors improve the effectiveness of a board of directors?

What are three provisions in many corporate charters that deter takeovers?

Describe how a typical stock option plan works. What are some problems with a typical stock option plan?

10-3 Employee Stock Ownership Plans (ESOPs)

See **www
.esopassociation.org**
for updates on ESOP
statistics.

Studies show that 90% of the employees who receive stock under option plans sell the stock as soon as they exercise their options, so the plans motivate employees only for a limited period.[18] Moreover, many companies limit their stock option plans to key managers and executives. To help provide long-term productivity gains and improve retirement incomes for all employees, Congress authorized the use of **Employee Stock Ownership Plans (ESOPs)**. Today over 10,000 privately held companies and about 330 publicly held firms have ESOPs, accounting for almost 13 million workers. Typically, the ESOP's major asset is shares of the common stock of the company that created it, and of the 10,000 total ESOPs, about half of them actually own a majority of their company's stock.[19]

---

16. See U. Malmendier and G. A. Tate, "Superstar CEOs," *Quarterly Journal of Economics*, November 2009, pp. 1593–1638.

17. For example, see D. B. Farber, "Restoring Trust after Fraud: Does Corporate Governance Matter?" *Accounting Review*, April 2005, pp. 539–561; and Stephen P. Ferris, Tomas Jandik, Robert M. Lawless, and Anil Makhija, "Derivative Lawsuits as a Corporate Governance Mechanism: Empirical Evidence on Board Changes Surrounding Filings," *Journal of Financial and Quantitative Analysis*, March 2007, pp. 143–166.

18. See Gary Laufman, "To Have and Have Not," *CFO*, March 1998, pp. 58–66.

19. For current information on ESOPs and other equity-based compensation, see The National Center for Employee Ownership's Web page at **www.nceo.org**.

To illustrate how an ESOP works, consider Gallagher & Abbott Inc. (G&A), a construction company located in Knoxville, Tennessee. G&A's simplified balance sheet is shown below:

G&A's Balance Sheet Prior to ESOP (Millions of Dollars)			
Assets		**Liabilities and Equity**	
Cash	$ 10	Debt	$100
Other	190	Equity (1 million shares)	100
Total	$200	Total	$200

Now G&A creates an ESOP, which is a new legal entity. The company issues 500,000 shares of new stock at $100 per share, or $50 million in total, which it sells to the ESOP. The company's employees are the ESOP's stockholders, and each employee receives an ownership interest based on the size of his or her salary and years of service. The ESOP borrows the $50 million to buy the newly issued stock.[20] Financial institutions are willing to lend the ESOP the money because G&A signs a guarantee for the loan. Here is the company's new balance sheet:

G&A's Balance Sheet after the ESOP (Millions of Dollars)			
Assets		**Liabilities and Equity**	
Cash	$ 60	Debt[a]	$100
Other	190	Equity (1.5 million shares)	150
Total	$250	Total	$250

[a]The company has guaranteed the ESOP's loan, and it has promised to make payments to the ESOP sufficient to retire the loan, but this does not show up on the balance sheet.

The company now has an additional $50 million of cash and $50 million more of book equity, but it has a de facto liability owing to its guarantee of the ESOP's debt. It could use the cash to finance an expansion, but many companies use the cash to repurchase their own common stock, so we assume that G&A will do likewise. The company's new balance sheets, and that of the ESOP, are shown on the next page:

20. Our description is simplified. Technically, the stock would be placed in a suspense account and then be allocated to employees as the debt is repaid.

G&A's Balance Sheet after the ESOP and Share Repurchase (Millions of Dollars)			
Assets		**Liabilities and Equity**	
Cash	$ 10	Debt	$100
Other	190	Equity (1 million shares)	150
		Treasury stock	(50)
Total	$200	Total	$200

ESOP's Initial Balance Sheet (Millions of Dollars)			
Assets		**Liabilities and Equity**	
G&A stock	$ 50	Debt	$50
		Equity	0
Total	$ 50	Total	$50

Note that although the company's balance sheet looks exactly as it did initially, there is actually a huge difference—the company has guaranteed the ESOP's debt, and hence it has an off–balance sheet liability of $50 million. Moreover, because the ESOP has no equity, the guarantee is very real indeed. Finally, observe that operating assets have not been increased at all, but the total debt outstanding supported by those assets has increased by $50 million.[21]

If this were the whole story, then there would be no reason to have an ESOP. However, G&A has promised to make payments to the ESOP in sufficient amounts to enable the ESOP to pay interest and principal charges on the debt, amortizing it over 15 years. Thus, after 15 years, the debt will be paid off and the ESOP's equity holders (the employees) will have equity with a book value of $50 million and a market value that could be much higher if G&A's stock increases, as it should over time. Then, as employees retire, the ESOP will distribute a pro rata amount of the G&A stock to each employee, who can then use it as a part of his or her retirement plan.

---

21. We assumed that the company used the $50 million paid to it by the ESOP to repurchase common stock and thus to increase its de facto debt. It could have used the $50 million to retire debt, in which case its true debt ratio would remain unchanged, or it could have used the money to support an expansion.

An ESOP is clearly beneficial for employees, but why would a company want to establish one? There are five primary reasons.

1. Congress passed the enabling legislation in hopes of enhancing employees' productivity and thus making the economy more efficient. In theory, employees who have equity in the enterprise will work harder and smarter. Note too that if employees are more productive and creative then this will benefit outside shareholders, because productivity enhancements that benefit ESOP shareholders also benefit outside shareholders.

2. The ESOP represents additional compensation to employees: In our example, there is a $50 million (or more) transfer of wealth from existing shareholders to employees over the 15-year period. Presumably, if the ESOP were not created then some other form of compensation would have been required, and that alternative compensation might not have the secondary benefit of enhancing productivity. Also note that the ESOP's payments to employees (as opposed to the payment by the company) come primarily at retirement, and Congress wanted to boost retirement incomes.

3. Depending on when an employee's rights to the ESOP are vested, the ESOP may help the firm retain employees.

4. There are strong tax incentives that encourage a company to form an ESOP. First, Congress decreed that when the ESOP owns 50% or more of the company's common stock, financial institutions that lend money to ESOPs can exclude from taxable income 50% of the interest they receive on the loan. This improves the financial institutions' after-tax returns, which allows them to lend to ESOPs at below-market rates. Therefore, a company that establishes an ESOP can borrow through the ESOP at a lower rate than would otherwise be available—in our example, the $50 million of debt would be at a reduced rate.

   There is also a second tax advantage. If the company were to borrow directly, it could deduct interest but not principal payments from its taxable income. However, companies typically make the required payments to their ESOPs in the form of cash dividends. Dividends are not normally deductible from taxable income, but *cash dividends paid on ESOP stock are deductible if the dividends are paid to plan participants or are used to repay the loan.* Thus, companies whose ESOPs own 50% of their stock can in effect borrow on ESOP loans at subsidized rates and then deduct both the interest and principal payments made on the loans. American Airlines and Publix Supermarkets are two of the many firms that have used ESOPs to obtain this benefit, along with motivating employees by giving them an equity interest in the enterprise.

5. A less desirable use of ESOPs is to help companies avoid being acquired by another company. The company's CEO, or someone appointed by the CEO, typically acts as trustee for its ESOP, and the trustee is supposed to vote the ESOP's shares according to the will of the plan participants. Moreover, the participants, who are the company's employees, usually oppose takeovers because they frequently involve labor cutbacks. Therefore, if an ESOP owns a significant percentage of the company's shares, then management has a powerful tool for warding off takeovers. This is not good for outside stockholders.

Are ESOPs good for a company's shareholders? In theory, ESOPs motivate employees by providing them with an ownership interest. That should increase productivity and thereby enhance stock values. Moreover, tax incentives mitigate the costs associated with some ESOPs. However, an ESOP can be used to help entrench management, and that could hurt stockholders. How do the pros and cons balance out? The empirical evidence is not entirely clear, but certain findings are worth noting. First, if an ESOP is established to help defend against a takeover, then the firm's stock price typically falls when plans for the ESOP are announced. The market does not like the prospect of entrenching management and having to give up the premium normally associated with a takeover. However, if the ESOP is established for tax purposes and/or to motivate employees, the stock price generally goes up at the time of the announcement. In these cases, the company typically has a subsequent improvement in sales per employee and other long-term performance measures, which stimulates the stock price. Indeed, a study showed that companies with ESOPs enjoyed a 26% average annual stock return compared to a return of only 19% for peer companies without ESOPs.[22] It thus appears that ESOPs, if used appropriately, can be a powerful tool for creating shareholder value.

SELF TEST   What are ESOPs? What are some of their advantages and disadvantages?

---

22. See Daniel Eisenberg, "No ESOP Fable," *Time*, May 10, 1999, p. 95.

Summary

- An **agency relationship** arises whenever an individual or group, called a **principal**, hires someone called an **agent** to perform some service and the principal delegates decision-making power to the agent.
- Important agency relationships include those between stockholders and creditors, owner/managers and outside shareholders, and stockholders and managers.
- An **agency conflict** refers to a conflict between principals and agents. For example, managers, as agents, may pay themselves excessive salaries, obtain unreasonably large stock options, and the like, at the expense of the principals, the stockholders.
- **Agency costs** are the reductions in a company's value due to actions by agents, including the costs principals incur (such as monitoring costs) trying to modify their agents' behaviors.
- **Corporate governance** involves the manner in which shareholders' objectives are implemented, and it is reflected in a company's policies and actions.
- The two primary mechanisms used in corporate governance are: (1) the threat of removal of a poorly performing CEO and (2) the type of plan used to compensate executives and managers.
- Poorly performing managers can be removed either by a takeover or by the company's own board of directors. Provisions in the corporate charter affect

the difficulty of a successful takeover, and the composition of the board of directors affects the likelihood of a manager being removed by the board.

- **Managerial entrenchment** is most likely when a company has a weak board of directors coupled with strong anti-takeover provisions in its corporate charter. In this situation, the likelihood that badly performing senior managers will be fired is low.

- **Nonpecuniary benefits** are noncash perks such as lavish offices, memberships at country clubs, corporate jets, foreign junkets, and the like. Some of these expenditures may be cost effective, but others are wasteful and simply reduce profits. Such fat is almost always cut after a hostile takeover.

- **Targeted share repurchases**, also known as **greenmail**, occur when a company buys back stock from a potential acquirer at a price higher than the market price. In return, the potential acquirer agrees not to attempt to take over the company.

- **Shareholder rights provisions**, also known as **poison pills**, allow existing shareholders to purchase additional shares of stock at a price lower than the market value if a potential acquirer purchases a controlling stake in the company.

- A **restricted voting rights** provision automatically deprives a shareholder of voting rights if he or she owns more than a specified amount of stock.

- **Interlocking boards of directors** occur when the CEO of Company A sits on the board of Company B and B's CEO sits on A's board.

- A **stock option** provides for the purchase of a share of stock at a fixed price, called the **exercise price**, no matter what the actual price of the stock is. Stock options have an **expiration date**, after which they cannot be exercised.

- An **Employee Stock Ownership Plan (ESOP)** is a plan that facilitates employees' ownership of stock in the company for which they work.

Questions

10-1 Define each of the following terms:
   a. Agent; principal; agency relationship
   b. Agency cost
   c. Basic types of agency conflicts
   d. Managerial entrenchment; nonpecuniary benefits
   e. Greenmail; poison pills; restricted voting rights
   f. Stock option; ESOP

10-2 What is the possible agency conflict between inside owner/managers and outside shareholders?

10-3 What are some possible agency conflicts between borrowers and lenders?

10-4 What are some actions an entrenched management might take that would harm shareholders?

10-5 How is it possible for an employee stock option to be valuable even if the firm's stock price fails to meet shareholders' expectations?

MINI CASE

Suppose you decide (as did Steve Jobs and Mark Zuckerberg) to start a company. Your product is a software platform that integrates a wide range of media devices, including laptop computers, desktop computers, digital video recorders, and cell phones. Your initial market is the student body at your university. Once you have established your company and set up procedures for operating it, you plan to expand to other colleges in the area and eventually to go nationwide. At some point, hopefully sooner rather than later, you plan to go public with an IPO and then to buy a yacht and take off for the South Pacific to indulge in your passion for underwater photography. With these issues in mind, you need to answer for yourself, and potential investors, the following questions.

a. What is an agency relationship? When you first begin operations, assuming you are the only employee and only your money is invested in the business, would any agency conflicts exist? Explain your answer.

b. If you expanded and hired additional people to help you, might that give rise to agency problems?

c. Suppose you need additional capital to expand and you sell some stock to outside investors. If you maintain enough stock to control the company, what type of agency conflict might occur?

d. Suppose your company raises funds from outside lenders. What type of agency costs might occur? How might lenders mitigate the agency costs?

e. Suppose your company is very successful and you cash out most of your stock and turn the company over to an elected board of directors. Neither you nor any other stockholders own a controlling interest (this is the situation at most public companies). List six potential managerial behaviors that can harm a firm's value.

f. What is corporate governance? List five corporate governance provisions that are internal to a firm and are under its control.

g. What characteristics of the board of directors usually lead to effective corporate governance?

h. List three provisions in the corporate charter that affect takeovers.

i. Briefly describe the use of stock options in a compensation plan. What are some potential problems with stock options as a form of compensation?

j. What is block ownership? How does it affect corporate governance?

k. Briefly explain how regulatory agencies and legal systems affect corporate governance.

CHAPTER 11

Determining the Cost of Capital

Businesses require capital to develop new products, build factories and distribution centers, install information technology, expand internationally, and acquire other companies. For each of these actions, a company must estimate the total investment required and then decide whether the expected rate of return exceeds the cost of the capital. The cost of capital is also a factor in compensation plans, with bonuses dependent on whether the company's return on invested capital exceeds the cost of that capital. This cost is also a key factor in choosing the firm's mixture of debt and equity and in decisions to lease rather than buy assets. As these examples illustrate, the cost of capital is a critical element in many business decisions.[1]

WEB

The textbook's Web site contains an *Excel* file that will guide you through the chapter's calculations. The file for this chapter is **Ch11 Tool Kit.xls**, and we encourage you to open the file and follow along as you read the chapter.

Beginning-of-Chapter Questions

As you read the chapter, consider how you would answer the following questions. You *should not* necessarily be able to answer the questions before you read the chapter. Rather, you should use them to get a sense of the issues covered in the chapter. After reading the chapter, you should be able to give at least partial answers to the questions, and you should be able to give better answers after the chapter has been discussed in class. Note, too, that it is often useful, when answering conceptual questions, to use hypothetical data to illustrate your answer. We illustrate the answers with an *Excel* model that is available on the textbook's Web site. Accessing the model and working through it is a useful exercise, and it provides insights that are useful when answering the questions.

1. What are the main components of a company's cost of capital? Rank these components from lowest to highest cost (a) on a before-tax and (b) on an after-tax cost basis, and explain why these differences exist.

2. How are the component costs combined to form a **weighted average cost of capital (WACC)**, and why is it necessary to use the WACC in capital budgeting?

3. What weights should be used when you calculate the WACC? Discuss the choice between book value and market value weights, and the role of the "target" capital structure for a firm whose actual capital structure is far removed from the target.

---

1. The cost of capital is also an important factor in the regulation of electric, gas, and water companies. These utilities are natural monopolies in the sense that one firm can supply service at a lower cost than could two or more firms. Because it has a monopoly, an unregulated electric or water company could exploit its customers. Therefore, regulators: (1) determine the cost of the capital investors have provided the utility and then (2) set rates designed to permit the company to earn its cost of capital, no more and no less.

4. Describe each of the following methods for estimating the cost of equity: (a) the **CAPM**, (b) **DCF**, and (c) the **bond-yield-plus-risk-premium**. Where can you obtain inputs for each of these methods, and how accurate are estimates based on each procedure? Can you state categorically that one method is better than the others, or does the "best" method depend on the circumstances?

5. How do **flotation costs** affect the cost of capital? Are these costs about the same for each of the three capital components? How do they change as the firm raises larger and larger amounts of capital, and how do flotation costs affect the way a company raises capital from year to year?

6. For a given firm, **why does WACC change over time**? Can the firm control the factors that lead to changes in the WACC and thus determine its WACC?

7. At any one time, should the **same WACC** be used to evaluate each of a company's capital budgeting projects? If not, how should the WACC be adjusted for the different projects?

CORPORATE VALUATION AND THE COST OF CAPITAL

In Chapter 1, we told you that managers should strive to make their firms more valuable and that the value of a firm is determined by the size, timing, and risk of its free cash flows (FCF). Indeed, a firm's intrinsic value is estimated as the present value of its FCFs, discounted at the weighted average cost of capital (WACC). In previous chapters, we examined the major sources of financing (stocks, bonds, and preferred stock) and the costs of those instruments. In this chapter, we put those pieces together and estimate the WACC that is used to determine intrinsic value.

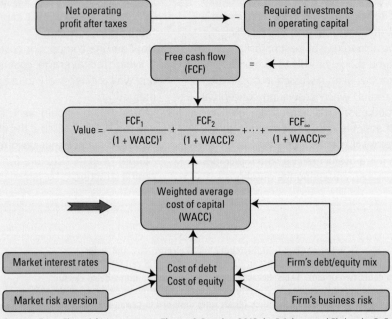

Source: From *Financial Management: Theory & Practice*, 2013, by Brigham and Ehrhardt. © Cengage Learning.

11-1 **The Weighted Average Cost of Capital**

The value of a company's operations is the present value of the expected free cash flows (FCF) discounted at the weighted average cost of capital (WACC):

$$V_{op} = \sum_{t=1}^{\infty} \frac{FCF_t}{(1 + WACC)^t}$$

(11–1)

We defined free cash flows (FCF) in Chapter 6, explained how to find present values in Web Chapter 28, and used the valuation equation in Chapter 8. Now we define the **weighted average cost of capital (WACC)**:

$$WACC = w_d r_d(1 - T) + w_{std} r_{std}(1 - T) + w_{ps} r_{ps} + w_s r_s$$

(11–2)

Some of these variables should be familiar to you from previous chapters, but some are new. All are defined as follows:

r_d = Coupon rate on new long-term debt being issued by the firm. Recall from Chapter 4 that r_d is the required return on a bond; for previously issued bonds, r_d is equal to the bond's yield to maturity.

T = The firm's effective marginal tax rate.

r_{std} = Interest rate on short-term debt, such as notes payable.

r_{ps} = Required return on preferred stock, as defined in Chapter 8.

r_s = Required return on common stock, as defined in Chapter 8.

w = w_d, w_{std}, w_{ps}, and w_s are weights of long-term debt, short-term debt, preferred stock, and common stock in the firm's target capital structure. The weights are the percentages of the different sources of capital the firm plans to use on a regular basis, with the percentages based on the market values of those sources of capital in the target capital structure.

In the following sections we explain how to estimate the WACC of a specific company, MicroDrive Inc., but let's begin with a few general concepts. First, companies are financed by several sources of investor-supplied capital, which are called **capital components**. We have included short-term debt and preferred stock because some companies use them as sources of funding, but most companies only use two major sources of investor-supplied capital, long-term debt, and common stock.

Second, investors providing the capital components require rates of return (r_d, r_{std}, r_{ps}, and r_s) commensurate with the risks of the components in order to induce them to make the investments. Previous chapters defined those required returns from an investor's view, but those returns are costs from a company's viewpoint. This is why we call the WACC a *cost* of capital.

Third, recall that FCF is the cash flow available for distribution to all investors. Therefore, the free cash flows must provide an overall rate of return sufficient to compensate investors for their exposure to risk. Intuitively, it makes sense that this overall return should be a weighted average of the capital components' required returns. This intuition is confirmed by applying algebra to the definitions of required returns, free cash flow, and the value of operations: The discount rate used in Equation 11-1 is equal to the WACC as defined in Equation 11-2. In other words, the correct rate for estimating the present value of a company's (or project's) cash flows is the *weighted* average cost of capital.

> **SELF TEST**
>
> Identify a firm's major capital structure components and give the symbols for their respective costs and weights.
>
> What is a component cost?

11-2 Choosing Weights for the Weighted Average Cost of Capital

Figure 11-1 reports selected data for MicroDrive Inc. including: (1) liabilities and equity (L&E) from the balance sheets, (2) percentages of total L&E comprised by each liability or equity account, (3) book values (as reported on the balance sheets) and percentages of financing from investor-supplied capital, (4) current market values and percentages of financing from investor-supplied capital, and (5) target capital structure weights.

Notice that we exclude accounts payable and accruals from capital structure weights. Capital is provided by *investors*—interest-bearing debt, preferred stock, and common equity. Accounts payable and accruals arise from operating decisions, not from financing decisions. Recall that the impact of payables and accruals is incorporated into a firm's free cash flows and a project's cash flows rather than into the cost of capital. Therefore, we consider only investor-supplied capital when discussing capital structure weights.

Figure 11-1 reports percentages of financing based on book values, market values, and target weights. Book values are a record of the cumulative amounts of capital supplied by investors over the life of the company. For equity, stockholders have supplied capital directly when MicroDrive issued stock, but they have also supplied capital indirectly when MicroDrive retained earnings instead of paying bigger dividends. The WACC is used to find the present value of *future* cash flows, so it would be inconsistent to use weights based on the *past* history of the company.

Stock prices are volatile, so current market values of total common equity often change dramatically from day to day. Companies certainly don't try to maintain the weights in their capital structures daily by issuing stock, repurchasing stock, issuing debt, or repaying debt in response to changes in their stock price. Therefore, the capital structure weights based on the current market values

FIGURE 11-1	MicroDrive Inc.: Selected Capital Structure Data (Millions of Dollars, December 31, 2015)

	A	B	C	D	E	F	G	H	I	J
					Investor-Supplied Capital				Target Capital Structure	
30					**Investor-Supplied Capital**					
31					**Book**		**Market**		**Target**	
32				**Percent**	**Book**	**Percent**	**Market**	**Percent**	**Capital**	
33	_**Liabilities and Equity**_			of Total	Value	of Total	Value	of Total	Structure	
34	Accounts payable		$ 200	5.6%						
35	Notes payable		280	7.9%	$ 280	9.2%	$ 280	9.9%	w_{std} =	2%
36	Accruals		300	8.5%						
37	Total C.L.		$ 780	22.0%						
38	Long-term debt		1,200	33.8%	1,200	39.3%	1,200	42.4%	w_d =	28%
39	Total liabilities		$1,980	55.8%						
40	Preferred stock		100	2.8%	100	3.3%	100	3.5%	w_{ps} =	3%
41	Common stock		500	14.1%						
42	Retained earnings		970	27.3%						
43	Total common equity		$1,470	41.4%	$1,470	48.2%	$1,250	44.2%	w_s =	67%
44	Total L&E		$3,550	100.0%	$3,050	100.0%	$2,830	100.0%		100%
45										
46	Other Data (Millions, except per share data):									
47	Number of common shares outstanding =				50					
48	Price per share of common stock =				$25.00					
49	Number of preferred shares outstanding =				1					
50	Price per share of preferred stock =				$100.00					

Notes:

1. The market value of the notes payable is equal to the book value. Some of the long-term bonds sell at a discount and some sell at a premium, but their aggregate market value is approximately equal to their aggregate book value.
2. The common stock price is $25 per share. There are 50 million shares outstanding, for a total market value of equity of $25(50) = $1,250 million.
3. The preferred stock price is $100 per share. There are 1 million shares outstanding, for a total market value of preferred stock of $100(1) = $100 million.

Microsoft Excel® is a registered trademark of Microsoft Corporation. © 2014 Microsoft.

might not be a good estimate of the capital structure that the company will have on average during the future.

The target capital structure is defined as the average capital structure weights (based on market values) that a company will have during the future. MicroDrive has chosen a target capital structure composed of 2% short-term debt, 28% long-term debt, 3% preferred stock, and 67% common equity. MicroDrive presently has more debt in its actual capital structure (using either book values or market values), but it intends to move toward its target capital structure in the near future. We explain how firms choose their capital structures in Chapter 16, but for now just accept the given target weights for MicroDrive.

The following sections explain how to estimate the required returns for the capital structure components.

11-3 After-Tax Cost of Debt: $r_d(1 - T)$ and $r_{std}(1 - T)$

The first step in estimating the cost of debt is to determine the rate of return lenders require.

11-3a The Before-Tax Cost of Short-Term Debt: r_{std}

Short-term debt should be included in the capital structure only if it is a permanent source of financing in the sense that the company plans to continually repay and refinance the short-term debt. This is the case for MicroDrive, whose bankers charge 10% on notes payable. Therefore, MicroDrive's short-term lenders have a required return of $r_{std} = 10\%$, which is MicroDrive's before-tax cost of short-term debt.

Some large companies use commercial paper as a source of short-term financing. We discuss this in Chapter 21.

11-3b The Before-Tax Cost of Long-Term Debt: r_d

For long-term debt, estimating r_d is conceptually straightforward, but some problems arise in practice. Companies use both fixed-rate and floating-rate debt, both straight debt and convertible debt, as well as debt with and without sinking funds. Each type of debt may have a somewhat different cost.

It is unlikely that the financial manager will know at the beginning of a planning period the exact types and amounts of debt that will be used during the period. The type or types used will depend on the specific assets to be financed and on capital market conditions as they develop over time. Even so, managers do know what types of debt are typical for their firms. For example, MicroDrive typically issues 15-year bonds to raise long-term debt used to help finance its capital budgeting projects. Because the WACC is used primarily in capital budgeting, MicroDrive's treasurer uses the cost of 15-year bonds in her WACC estimate.

Assume that it is January 2016 and that MicroDrive's treasurer is estimating the WACC for the coming year. How should she calculate the component cost of debt? Most financial managers begin by discussing current and prospective interest rates with their investment bankers. Assume MicroDrive's bankers believe that a new, 15-year, noncallable, straight bond issue would require a 9% coupon rate with semiannual payments. It can be offered to the public at its $1,000 par value. Therefore, their estimate of r_d is 9%.[2]

Note that 9% is the cost of new debt, so it is often called the **marginal rate**. The rate on new debt probably will not be the same as the average rate on MicroDrive's previously issued debt, which is called the **historical rate** or the **embedded rate**. The embedded cost is important for some decisions but not for

---

2. Because it is a semiannual bond, the effective annual rate is $(1 + 0.09/2)^2 - 1 = 9.2\%$, but MicroDrive and most other companies use nominal rates for all component costs.

others. For example, the average cost of all the capital raised in the past and still outstanding is used by regulators when they determine the rate of return that a public utility should be allowed to earn. However, in financial management the WACC is used primarily to make investment decisions, and these decisions hinge on projects' expected future returns versus the cost of the new capital that will be used to finance those projects. *Thus, for our purposes, the relevant cost is the marginal cost of new debt to be raised during the planning period.*

MicroDrive has issued debt in the past and the bonds are publicly traded. The financial staff can use the market price of the bonds to find the yield to maturity (or yield to call, if the bonds sell at a premium and are likely to be called). This yield is the rate of return that current bondholders expect to receive, and it is also a good estimate of r_d, the rate of return that new bondholders will require.

MicroDrive's outstanding bonds were recently issued and have a 9% coupon, paid semiannually. The bonds mature in 15 years and have a par value of $1,000. Since interest rates in the economy haven't changed much since the bonds were issued, they are still trading at $1,000. We can find the yield to maturity by using a financial calculator with these inputs: N = 30, PV = −1000, PMT = 45, and FV = 1000. Solving for the rate, we find I/YR = 4.5%. This is a semiannual periodic rate, so the nominal annual rate is 9.0%. This is consistent with the investment bankers' estimated rate, so 9% is a reasonable estimate for r_d.

MicroDrive's outstanding bonds are trading at par, so the yield is equal to the coupon rate. But consider a hypothetical example in which interest rates in the economy have changed since the bonds were issued so the market price isn't par but instead is $923.14. We can find the yield to maturity by using a financial calculator with these inputs: N = 30, PV = −923.14, PMT = 45, and FV = 1000. Solving for the rate, we find I/YR = 5%, which implies a hypothetical nominal annual rate of 10%. As this hypothetical example illustrates, it is not necessary for the bond to trade at par in order to estimate the cost of debt.

Even if MicroDrive had no publicly traded debt, its staff could still look at the yields on publicly traded debt of similar firms for a reasonable estimate of r_d.

Although the yield to maturity is most frequently used to estimate the investor's required rate of return and firm's capital cost, this isn't appropriate when there is a significant probability that the company will default on its debt. In such a case, the yield to maturity (whether calculated from market prices of an outstanding bond or taken as the coupon rate on a newly issued bond) overstates the investor's expected return and hence the company's expected cost. For example, let's reconsider MicroDrive's 15-year semiannual bonds that can be issued at par if the coupon rate is 9%. As shown previously, the nominal annual yield to maturity is 9%. But suppose investors believe there is a significant chance that MicroDrive will default. To keep the example simple, suppose investors believe that the bonds will default in 14 years and that the recovery rate on the par value will be 70%. Here are the new inputs: N = 2(14) = 28, PV = −1000, PMT = 45, and FV = 0.70(1000) = 700. Solving for the rate, we find I/YR = 3.9%, implying an annual expected return of 7.8%. This is an extremely simple example, but it illustrates that the expected return on a bond is less than the yield to maturity as it is normally calculated. For bonds with a relatively low expected default rate, we recommend using the yield to maturity. But for bonds with high expected default rates, it would be necessary to do a scenario analysis (such as the one in Section 2.2) to estimate the bond's expected return.

11-3c The After-Tax Cost of Debt: $r_d(1 - T)$ and $r_{std}(1 - T)$

The required return to debtholders, r_d, is not equal to the company's cost of debt, because interest payments are deductible, which means the government in effect pays part of the total cost. As a result, the weighted average cost of capital is calculated using the **after-tax cost of debt, $r_d(1 - T)$**, which is the interest rate on debt, r_d, less the tax savings that result because interest is deductible. Here T is the firm's marginal tax rate:[3]

(11–3)

$$\text{After-tax component cost of debt} = \text{Interest rate} - \text{Tax savings}$$
$$= r_d - r_d T$$
$$= r_d(1 - T)$$

If we assume that MicroDrive's marginal federal-plus-state tax rate is 40%, then its after-tax cost of debt is 5.4%:[4]

$$r_d(1 - T) = 9\%(1.0 - 0.4)$$
$$= 9\%(0.6)$$
$$= 5.4\%$$

For MicroDrive's short-term debt, the after-tax cost is 6%:

$$r_{std}(1 - T) = 10\%(1.0 - 0.4)$$
$$= 6.0\%$$

11-3d Flotation Costs and the Cost of Debt

Most debt offerings have very low flotation costs, especially for privately placed debt. Because flotation costs are usually low, most analysts ignore them when estimating the after-tax cost of debt. However, the following example illustrates the procedure for incorporating flotation costs as well as their impact on the after-tax cost of debt.

Suppose MicroDrive can issue 30-year debt with an annual coupon rate of 9%, with coupons paid semiannually. The flotation costs, F, are equal to 1% of the value of the issue. Instead of finding the pre-tax yield based upon pre-tax cash flows and then adjusting it to reflect taxes, as we did before, we can find the after-tax, flotation-adjusted cost by using this formula:

---

3. The federal tax rate for most corporations is 35%. However, most corporations are also subject to state income taxes, so the marginal tax rate on most corporate income is about 40%. For illustrative purposes, we assume that the effective federal-plus-state tax rate on marginal income is 40%. The effective tax rate is *zero* for a firm with such large current or past losses that it does not pay taxes. In this situation, the after-tax cost of debt is equal to the pre-tax interest rate.

4. Strictly speaking, the after-tax cost of debt should reflect the *expected* cost of debt. Although MicroDrive's bonds have a promised return of 9%, there is some chance of default and so its bondholders' expected return (and consequently MicroDrive's cost) is a bit less than 9%. However, for a relatively strong company such as MicroDrive, this difference is quite small.

HOW EFFECTIVE IS THE EFFECTIVE CORPORATE TAX RATE?

The statutory U.S. federal corporate tax rate is 35%. With Japan cutting its tax rate in 2012, U.S. corporations face the highest combined federal and state taxes in the world. Or do they? The following chart shows the actual federal corporate tax receipts as a percentage of domestic economic profits. Notice that the effective tax rate averaged around 25% for about 15 years after the tax reforms of 1986, but that it has gyrated wildly since 2000, dropping to an all-time low of 12.1% in 2011, probably due to temporary changes in the tax code made to stimulate the economy in response to the recession. International comparisons are difficult due to data availability and complexity (and due to the analysts' political leanings), but the average effective tax rate on corporations in developed countries usually is around 25%.

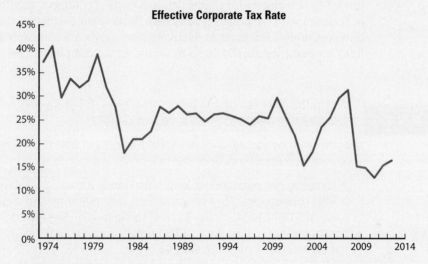

Source: Adapted from the Congressional Budget Office report on February 4, 2014, *The Budget and Economic Outlook: Fiscal Years 2014 to 2024*. To see the report, go to **www.cbo.gov /publication/45010**. To get the data in an *Excel* workbook, select Data Underlying Figures.

$$M(1 - F) = \sum_{t=1}^{N} \frac{INT(1 - T)}{[1 + r_d(1 - T)]^t} + \frac{M}{[1 + r_d(1 - T)]^N}$$

(11–4)

Here M is the bond's maturity (or par) value, F is the **percentage flotation cost** (i.e., the percentage of proceeds paid to the investment bankers), N is the number of payments, T is the firm's tax rate, INT is the dollars of interest per period, and $r_d(1 - T)$ is the after-tax cost of debt adjusted for flotation costs. With a financial calculator, enter N = 60, PV = −1000(1 − 0.01) = −990, PMT = 45(1 − 0.40) = 27, and FV = 1000. Solving for I/YR, we find I/YR = $r_d(1 - T)$ = 2.73%, which is the semiannual after-tax component cost of debt. The nominal after-tax cost of debt is 5.46%. Note that this is quite close to the original 5.40% after-tax cost, so in this instance adjusting for flotation costs doesn't make much difference.[5]

However, the flotation adjustment would be higher if F were larger or if the bond's life were shorter. For example, if F were 10% rather than 1%, then the nominal annual flotation-adjusted $r_d(1 - T)$ would be 6.13%. With N at 1 year rather than 30 years and F still equal to 1%, the nominal annual $r_d(1 - T) = 6.45\%$. Finally, if $F = 10\%$ and $N = 1$, then the nominal annual $r_d(1 - T) = 16.67\%$. In all of these cases, the effect of flotation costs would be too large to ignore.

As an alternative to adjusting the cost of debt for flotation costs, in some situations it makes sense to instead adjust the project's cash flows. For example, **project financing** is a special situation in which a large project, such as an oil refinery, is financed with debt plus other securities that have a specific claim on the project's cash flows. This is different from the usual debt offering, in which the debt has a claim on all of the corporation's cash flows. Because project financing is funded by securities with claims tied to a particular project, the flotation costs can be included with the project's other cash flows when evaluating the project's value. However, project financing is relatively rare, so when we incorporate the impact of flotation costs, we usually do so by adjusting the component cost of the new debt.

> **SELF TEST**
>
> Why is the after-tax cost of debt, rather than its before-tax cost, used to calculate the weighted average cost of capital?
>
> Is the relevant cost of debt when calculating the WACC the interest rate on already *outstanding* debt or the rate on *new* debt? Why?
>
> A company has outstanding long-term bonds with a face value of $1,000, a 10% coupon rate, 25 years remaining until maturity, and a current market value of $1,214.82. If it pays interest semiannually, then what is the nominal annual pre-tax cost of debt? **(8%)** If the company's tax rate is 40%, what is the after-tax cost of debt? **(4.8%)**

11-4 Cost of Preferred Stock, r_{ps}

Many firms (including MicroDrive) use, or plan to use, preferred stock as part of their financing mix. Preferred dividends are not tax deductible, so the company bears their full cost. Therefore, *no tax adjustment is used when calculating the cost of preferred stock.* Some preferred stocks are issued without a stated maturity date, but today most have a sinking fund that effectively limits their life. Finally, although it is not mandatory that preferred dividends be paid, firms generally have every intention of doing so, because otherwise: (1) they cannot pay dividends on their common stock, (2) they

---

5. Equation 11-4 produces the correct after-tax cost of debt only for bonds issued at par. For bonds with a price other than par, the after-tax cash flows must be adjusted to take into account the actual taxation of the discount or premium. See *Web Extension 4A* on the textbook's Web site for a discussion of the taxation of original issue discount bonds. Also, we ignored the tax shield due to amortization of flotation costs because it has very little effect on the cost of debt; see *Ch11 Tool Kit.xls* for an example that incorporates the amortization tax shield.

will find it difficult to raise additional funds in the capital markets, and (3) in some cases preferred stockholders can take control of the firm.

The **component cost of preferred stock, r$_{ps}$,** is the cost used in the WACC calculation. For preferred stock with a stated maturity date, we use the same approach as in the previous section for the cost of debt, keeping in mind that a firm has no tax savings with preferred stock. For preferred stock without a stated maturity date, r$_{ps}$ is:

$$\text{Component cost of preferred stock} = r_{ps} = \frac{D_{ps}}{P_{ps}(1 - F)}$$

(11–5)

Here D$_{ps}$ is the preferred dividend, P$_{ps}$ is the preferred stock price, and F is the flotation cost as a percentage of proceeds.

To illustrate the calculation, assume MicroDrive has preferred stock that pays an $8 dividend per share and sells for $100 per share. If MicroDrive issued new shares of preferred stock, it would incur an underwriting (or flotation) cost of 2.5%, or $2.50 per share, so it would net $97.50 per share. Therefore, MicroDrive's cost of preferred stock is 8.2%:

$$r_{ps} = \$8/\$97.50 = 8.2\%$$

If we had not incorporated flotation costs, we would have incorrectly estimated r$_{ps}$ = $8/$100 = 8.0%, which is too big a difference to ignore. Therefore, analysts usually include flotation costs when estimating the firm's cost of preferred stock.

Although preferred stock is riskier than debt, MicroDrive's preferred stock has a lower return to investors than does its debt: 8% versus 9%. However, recall that most preferred stock is held by other companies, which are allowed to exclude at least 70% of preferred stocks' dividends from taxation. Thus, the after-tax return to these investors is higher for preferred stock than for debt, which is consistent with preferred stock being riskier than debt.

SELF TEST

Does the component cost of preferred stock include or exclude flotation costs? Explain.

Why is no tax adjustment made to the cost of preferred stock?

A company's preferred stock currently trades for $50 per share and pays a $3 annual dividend. Flotation costs are equal to 3% of the gross proceeds. If the company issues preferred stock, what is the cost of that stock? **(6.19%)**

11-5 Cost of Common Stock: The Market Risk Premium, RP$_M$

Before addressing the required return for an individual stock, let's start with the big picture, which is the required return for the entire stock market. In other words, how much return do investors require to induce them to invest in stocks? It often is more convenient to focus on the extra return that investors require to induce them to invest in risky equities over and above the return on a Treasury bond. As Chapter 2 explained, this extra return is called the market risk premium, RP_M. Sometimes this is called the **equity risk premium**, or just the **equity premium**.

Unfortunately, the required return on the market, and hence the equity premium, is not directly observable. Three approaches may be used to estimate the market risk premium: (1) calculate historical premiums and use them to estimate the current premium; (2) survey experts; and (3) use the current value of the market to estimate forward-looking premiums. Following are descriptions of each approach.

11-5a **Historical Risk Premium**

Historical risk premium data for U.S. securities, updated annually, are available from many sources, including Ibbotson Associates.[6] Using data from 1926 through the most recent year, Ibbotson calculates the actual realized rate of return each year for the stock market and for long-term government bonds. Ibbotson defines the annual equity risk premium as the difference between the historical realized returns on stocks and the historical yields to maturity on long-term T-bonds.[7] Ibbotson recently reported a 6.6% arithmetic average historical risk premium.[8] How should these data be used?

First, stock returns are quite volatile, which leads to low statistical confidence in estimated averages. For example, the estimated historical average premium is 5.7%, but based on the market return's standard deviation of around 20%, the 95% confidence interval ranges about plus or minus 3% from 5.7%. In other words, the historical average is helpful in deciding whether the risk premium is on the order of 6% or 20%, but it isn't very helpful in deciding whether the premium should be 4% or 6%.

Second, the historical average is extremely sensitive to the period over which it is calculated. For example, we provide annual data for the period 1968–2013 in the file *Ch11 Tool Kit.xls*. For this period, the estimated historic risk premium is just 4.7%.

Third, changes in the risk premium can occur if investors' tolerance for risk changes. This causes problems in interpreting historical returns because a change in the required risk premium causes an *opposite change in the observed* premium. For example, an increase in the required premium means that investors have become more risk averse and require a higher return on stocks. But applying a higher discount rate to a stock's future cash flows causes a decline in stock price. Thus, an *increase* in the required premium causes a simultaneous *decrease* in the observed premium. Part of the market's precipitous decline in 2008 and 2009 surely was due to investors' increased risk aversion.

---

6. See *Ibbotson Stocks, Bonds, Bills, and Inflation: 2013 Valuation Yearbook* (Chicago: Morningstar, Inc., 2013) for the most recent estimates.

7. The risk premium should be defined using the yield on T-bonds. As a proxy for yield, Ibbotson uses the return on 20-year T-bonds that is due to coupons. This underestimates yield for discount bonds and overstates yield for premium bonds, but the error probably averages out to zero in most years.

8. The arithmetic average often is used as an estimate of next year's risk premium; this is most appropriate if investor risk aversion had actually been constant during the sample period. On the other hand, the geometric average would be most appropriate to estimate the longer-term risk premium, say, for the next 20 years. The geometric average for this time period is 4.7%, which is less than the arithmetic average.

11-5b Surveys of Experts

What do the experts think about the market risk premium? Two professors at Duke University, John Graham and Campbell Harvey (working in conjunction with *CFO* magazine), have surveyed CFOs quarterly beginning in 2000.[9] One survey question asks CFOs what they expect the S&P 500 return to be over the next 10 years; the CFOs are also given the yield on a 10-year T-bond. Their average response in the December 2013 survey implied an average expected risk premium of about 3.73%.

Professor Pablo Fernández of the IESE Business School regularly surveys professors, analysts, and companies.[10] For 2013, based on the average U.S. responses, professors recommend a premium of 5.8%, analysts recommend 5.7%, and companies recommend 5.7%.

In summary, in 2013, experts predicted a premium within the range of about 3.73% to 5.8%.

11-5c Forward-Looking Risk Premiums

An alternative to the historical risk premium is the forward-looking, or ex ante, risk premium. As shown in Chapter 8, if we assume that: (1) the market dividend will grow at a constant rate and (2) all distributions are as dividends (i.e., the firms make no stock repurchases or purchases of short-term investments), then the expected market rate of return, $\hat{r}_M$ is:

$$\hat{r}_M = \frac{D_1}{P_0} + g$$

(11–6)

If we also assume that the market is in equilibrium, then required return on the market, r_M, is equal to the expected return, $\hat{r}_M$, found by using Equation 11-6. Thus, the required return on the market can be estimated as the sum of the market's expected dividend yield plus the expected constant growth rate in dividends.

Simplified Illustration of Estimating a Forward-Looking Risk Premium

Following is an illustration for how to use Equation 11-6 to estimate the required return on the market. First, you need an estimate of the expected dividend. In February 2014, Standard & Poor's Web site reported a projected dividend yield of 2.08% for the S&P 500 for all of 2014, based on declared dividends. Second, you need an estimate of the constant dividend growth rate, g. One approach is to use the historical average growth rate in dividends for the S&P 500, which is

For current estimates, see instructions in **Ch11 Tool Kit.xls**.

9. See John Graham and Campbell Harvey, "The Equity Risk Premium in 2014," Working Paper, Duke University, 2014. For periodic updates, see Professor Graham's Web site, **http://faculty .fuqua.duke.edu/~jgraham/resume.html**, and look for the section on Permanent Working Papers.
10. See Pablo Fernández, "Market Risk Premium and Risk Free Rate Used for 51 Countries in 2013: A Survey with 6,237 Answers," at SSRN: **ssrncom/abstract = 914160**.

about 4.37% (for 1988–2013). Using these estimates produces an estimate of the required market return:

$$r_M = \hat{r}_M = \frac{D_1}{P_0} + g$$

$$= 2.08\% + 4.37\%$$

$$= 6.45\%$$

At the time we estimated r_M, the 10-year T-bond yield was 2.73%. Using the previously estimated r_M of 6.45%, the estimated forward-looking market risk premium is:

$$RP_M = r_M - r_{RF}$$

$$= 6.45\% - 2.73\%$$

$$= 3.72\%$$

Complications when Estimating a Forward-Looking Risk Premium

We made numerous simplifying assumptions in the previous example regarding three complications that arise in practice. First, the growth rate in dividends probably will not be constant in the near future but might instead take many years before leveling out. Second, the historical average growth rate in dividends might not be a good estimate of the expected long-term dividend growth rate. Long-term growth in dividends is probably related to long-term sales and profits, which in turn depend on inflation (which affects reported dollar value of sales), population growth (which affects the unit volume of sales), and productivity (which affects profits). Third, the model is based on dividends per share, but it ignores the impact of stock repurchases on the number of outstanding shares (which then changes the growth rate of dividends per share).

Fortunately, there are ways to address these technical issues, including the use of a multistage growth model. The interested reader should see *Web Extension 11A* and the corresponding worksheet, *Web 11A*, in *Ch11 Tool Kit.xls*.

11-5d Our View on the Market Risk Premium

After reading the previous sections, you might well be confused about the best way to estimate the market risk premium. Here's our opinion: The risk premium is driven primarily by investors' attitudes toward risk, and there are good reasons to believe that investors' risk aversion changes over time. The introduction of pension plans, Social Security, health insurance, and disability insurance over the last 50 years means that people today can take more chances with their investments, which should make them less risk averse. Moreover, many households have dual earners, allowing households to take more chances. Therefore, we think the risk premium is lower now than it was 50 years ago.

In our consulting, we currently (winter 2014) use a risk premium of about 5% to 6%, but we would have a hard time arguing with someone who used a risk premium anywhere in the range of 3% to 7%. We believe that investors' aversion to risk is relatively stable much of the time, but it is not absolutely constant from year to year and is certainly not constant during periods of great stress, such as during the 2008–2009 financial crisis. When stock prices are relatively high, investors feel less risk averse, so we use a risk premium at the low end of our range. Conversely, when prices are depressed, we use a premium at the high end of the range. The bottom line is that there is no way to prove that a particular risk premium is either right or wrong, though we'd be suspicious of an estimated market premium that is less than 3% or greater than 7%.

11-6 Using the CAPM to Estimate the Cost of Common Stock, r_s

Before estimating the return required by MicroDrive's shareholders, r_s, it is worth considering the two ways that a company can raise common equity: (1) Sell newly issued shares to the public. (2) Reinvest (retain) earnings by not paying out all net income as dividends.

Does new equity capital raised by reinvesting earnings have a cost? The answer is a resounding "yes!" If earnings are reinvested, then stockholders will incur an **opportunity cost**—the earnings could have been paid out as dividends or used to repurchase stock, and in either case stockholders would have received funds that they could reinvest in other securities. *Thus, the firm should earn on its reinvested earnings at least as much as its stockholders could earn on alternative investments of equivalent risk.*

What rate of return could stockholders expect to earn on equivalent-risk investments? The answer is r_s, because they could presumably earn that return by simply buying the stock of the firm in question or that of a similar firm. *Therefore, r_s is the cost of common equity raised internally as reinvested earnings.* If a company can't earn at least r_s on reinvested earnings, then it should pass those earnings on to its stockholders as dividends and let them invest the money themselves in assets that do yield r_s.

11-6a The Capital Asset Pricing Model

To estimate the cost of common stock using the Capital Asset Pricing Model as discussed in Chapter 2, we proceed as follows.

1. Estimate the risk-free rate, r_{RF}.
2. Estimate the current market risk premium, RP_M, which is the required market return in excess of the risk-free rate.
3. Estimate the stock's beta coefficient, b_i, which measures the stock's relative risk. The subscript i signifies Stock i's beta.
4. Use these three values to estimate the stock's required rate of return:

$$r_s = r_{RF} + (RP_M)b_i$$

(11–7)

Equation 11-7 shows that the CAPM estimate of r_s begins with the risk-free rate, r_{RF}. We then add a risk premium that is equal to the risk premium on the market,

RP_M, scaled up or down to reflect the particular stock's risk as measured by its beta coefficient. The following sections explain how to implement this four-step process.

11-6b Estimating the Risk-Free Rate, r_{RF}

WWW

To find the rate on a T-bond, go to **www.federalreserve.gov**. Select "Economic Research & Data" and then select "Statistical Releases and Historical Data." Click on "Daily" for "H.15: Selected Interest Rates."

The starting point for the CAPM cost-of-equity estimate is r_{RF}, the risk-free rate. There is no such thing as a truly riskless asset in the U.S. economy. Treasury securities are essentially free of default risk; however, nonindexed long-term T-bonds will suffer capital losses if interest rates rise, indexed long-term bonds will decline if the real rate rises, and a portfolio of short-term T-bills will provide a volatile earnings stream because the rate earned on T-bills varies over time.

Because we cannot, in practice, find a truly riskless rate upon which to base the CAPM, what rate should we use? Keep in mind that our objective is to estimate the cost of capital, which will be used to discount a company's free cash flows or a project's cash flows. Free cash flows occur over the life of the company and many projects last for many years. Because the cost of capital will be used to discount relatively long-term cash flows, it seems appropriate to use a relatively long-term risk-free rate, such as the yield on a 10-year Treasury bond. Indeed, a survey of highly regarded companies shows that about two-thirds of them use the rate on 10-year Treasury bonds.[11]

T-bond rates can be found in *The Wall Street Journal*, the *Federal Reserve Bulletin*, or on the Internet. Although most analysts use the yield on a 10-year T-bond as a proxy for the risk-free rate, yields on 20-year or 30-year T-bonds are also reasonable proxies.

11-6c Estimating the Market Risk Premium, RP_M

WWW

To find an estimate of beta, go to **www.valueline.com** and then enter the ticker symbol for a stock quote.

We described three approaches for estimating the market risk premium, RP_M, in Section 11.5: (1) use historical averages, (2) survey experts, and (3) estimate forward-looking expected market returns. All three approaches provide estimates in the same ballpark, around 3% to 7%. The final choice really boils down to judgment informed by the current state of the market and the estimates provided by the three approaches. We will use a market risk premium of 6% in this example.

11-6d Estimating Beta, b_i

Recall from Chapter 2 that a stock's beta, b_i, can be estimated as:

(11–8)

$$b_i = \left(\frac{\sigma_i}{\sigma_M}\right)\rho_{iM}$$

where ρ_{iM} is the correlation between Stock i's return and the market return, σ_i is the standard deviation of Stock i's return, and σ_M is the standard deviation of the

---

11. See Robert E. Bruner, Kenneth M. Eades, Robert S. Harris, and Robert C. Higgins, "Best Practices in Estimating the Cost of Capital: Survey and Synthesis," *Financial Practice and Education*, Spring/Summer 1998, pp. 13–28.

market's return. This definition is also equal to the estimated slope coefficient in a regression, with the company's stock returns on the y-axis and market returns on the x-axis.

It is easy to gather historical returns from the Web and then estimate your own beta, as we show in the *Tool Kit* for Chapter 2. Also, many Web sources provide estimates of beta. The good news is that there is no shortage of beta estimates; the bad news is that many estimates differ from one another. We will discuss this in the next section.

11-6e An Illustration of the CAPM Approach: MicroDrive's Cost of Equity, r_s

Following is an application of the CAPM approach to MicroDrive. As estimated in Chapter 2, MicroDrive's beta, b_i, is 1.43. We assume that the market risk premium, RP_M, is about 6%. For this example, assume that the risk-free rate, r_{RF}, is 5%. Using Equation 11-7, we estimate MicroDrive's required return as about 13.6%:

$$r_s = 5\% + (6\%)(1.43)$$
$$= 5\% + 8.58\%$$
$$= 13.58\% \approx 13.6\%$$

This estimate of 13.6% is a required return from an investor's point of view, but it is a cost of equity from a company's perspective.

Always keep in mind that the estimated cost of equity is indeed an estimate, for several reasons. First, the yield on any long-term T-bond would be an appropriate estimate of the risk-free rate, and different yields would lead to different estimates of r_s. Second, no one truly knows the correct market risk premium. We can narrow the estimated RP_M down to a fairly small range, but different estimates in this range would lead to different estimates of r_s. Third, estimates of beta are inexact. In addition to a large range of the confidence interval around an estimated beta, using slightly different time periods to estimate beta can lead to rather large differences in the estimated beta.

Still, in our judgment, it is possible to develop "reasonable" estimates of the required inputs, and we believe that the CAPM can be used to obtain reasonable estimates of the cost of equity. Indeed, despite the difficulties we have noted, surveys indicate that the CAPM is by far the most widely used method. Although most firms use more than one method, almost 74% of respondents in one survey (and 85% in another) used the CAPM.[12] This is in sharp contrast to a 1982 survey, which found that only 30% of respondents used the CAPM.[13]

---

12. See John R. Graham and Campbell Harvey, "The Theory and Practice of Corporate Finance: Evidence from the Field," *Journal of Financial Economics*, 2001, pp. 187–243, and the paper cited in footnote 10. It is interesting that a growing number of firms (about 34%) also are using CAPM-type models with more than one factor. Of these firms, over 40% include factors for interest rate risk, foreign exchange risk, and business cycle risk (proxied by gross domestic product). More than 20% of these firms include a factor for inflation, size, and exposure to particular commodity prices. Less than 20% of these firms make adjustments due to distress factors, book-to-market ratios, or momentum factors.

13. See Lawrence J. Gitman and Vincent Mercurio, "Cost of Capital Techniques Used by Major U.S. Firms: Survey Analysis of *Fortune's* 1000," *Financial Management*, 1982, pp. 21–29.

What are the two primary sources of equity capital?

Explain why there is a cost to using reinvested earnings; that is, why aren't reinvested earnings a free source of capital?

Which is generally considered the more appropriate estimate of the risk-free rate: the yield on a short-term T-bill or the yield on a 10-year T-bond?

A company's beta is 1.4, the yield on a 10-year T-bond is 4%, and the market risk premium is 4.5%. What is r_s? **(10.3%)**

11-7 Dividend-Yield-Plus-Growth-Rate, or Discounted Cash Flow (DCF), Approach

In Chapter 8, we saw that if an investor expects dividends to grow at a constant rate and if the company makes all payouts in the form of dividends (the company does not repurchase stock), then the price of a stock can be found as follows:

(11–9)

$$\hat{P}_0 = \frac{D_1}{r_s - g}$$

Here $\hat{P}_0$ is the intrinsic value of the stock for the investor, D_1 is the dividend expected to be paid at the end of Year 1, g is the expected growth rate in dividends, and r_s is the required rate of return. For the marginal investor, the required return is equal to the expected return. If this investor is the marginal investor then $\hat{P}_0 = P_0$, the market price of the stock, and we can solve for r_s to obtain the required rate of return on common equity:

(11–10)

$$\hat{r}_s = r_s = \frac{D_1}{P_0} + \text{Expected g}$$

Thus, investors expect to receive a dividend yield, D_1/P_0, plus a capital gain, g, for a total expected return of $\hat{r}_s$. In equilibrium, this expected return is also equal to the required return, r_s. This method of estimating the cost of equity is called the **discounted cash flow (DCF) approach**. Henceforth, we will assume that markets are at equilibrium (which means that $r_s = \hat{r}_s$), and this permits us to use the terms r_s and $\hat{r}_s$ interchangeably.

11-7a Estimating Inputs for the DCF Approach

Three inputs are required to use the DCF approach: the current stock price, the current dividend, and the marginal investor's expected dividend growth rate. The stock price and the dividend are easy to obtain, but the expected growth rate is difficult to estimate, as we will see in the following sections.

Historical Growth Rates

If earnings and dividend growth rates have been relatively stable in the past, and if investors expect these trends to continue, then the past realized growth rate may be used as an estimate of the expected future growth rate. Unfortunately, such situations occur only at a handful of very mature, slow-growing companies, which precludes the usefulness of historical growth rates as predictors of future growth rates for most companies.

Retention Growth Model

Most firms pay out some of their net income as dividends and reinvest, or retain, the rest. The more they retain, and the higher the earned rate of return on those retained earnings, the larger their growth rate. This is the idea behind the retention growth model.

The **payout ratio** is the percent of net income that the firm pays out in dividends, and the **retention ratio** is the complement of the payout ratio: Retention ratio = (1 − Payout ratio). Intuitively, the retention ratio represents how much of each dollar of earnings the company reinvests back into the company for growth. To illustrate, consider Aldabra Corporation, a mature company. Aldabra's payout ratio has averaged 63% over the past 15 years, so its retention rate has averaged 1.0 − 0.63 = 0.37 = 37%. Also, Aldabra's return on equity (ROE) has averaged 14.5% over the past 15 years. We know that, other things held constant, the earnings growth rate depends on the amount of reinvestment in the firm, which comes from the income the firm retains, and from the rate of return it earns on those retained earnings. The **retention growth equation** shows how growth is related to reinvestment and is expressed as follows:

$$g = \text{ROE(Retention ratio)} \qquad \textbf{(11–11)}$$

Using Aldabra's 14.5% average ROE and its 37% retention rate, we can use Equation 11-11 to find the estimated g:

$$g = 14.5\%(0.37) = 5.365 \approx 5.4\%$$

Although easy to implement, this approach requires four major assumptions: (1) The payout rate and therefore the retention rate remain constant. (2) The ROE on new investments remains constant and equal to the ROE on existing assets. (3) The firm is not expected to repurchase or issue new common stock, or, if it does, this new stock will be sold at a price equal to its book value. (4) Future projects are expected to have the same degree of risk as the firm's existing assets. Unfortunately, these assumptions apply in very few situations, limiting the usefulness of the retention growth model.

Analysts' Forecasts

A third technique calls for using security analysts' forecasts. As we discussed earlier, analysts publish earnings' growth rate estimates for most of the larger publicly owned companies. For example, *Value Line* provides such dividend forecasts on about 1,700 companies. Several sources compile analysts' earnings forecasts on a regular basis, and these earnings growth rates can be used as proxies for dividend growth rates.

However, analysts usually forecast nonconstant growth in earnings, which limits the usefulness of the constant growth model. Instead, a multi-stage model must be used. See *Web Extension 11A* on the textbook's Web site for an explanation of how to calculate a required return on equity using the multi-stage approach; all calculations are in the worksheet *Web 11A* in the file *Ch11 Tool Kit.xls*.

11-7b **An Illustration of the DCF Approach**

To illustrate the DCF approach, suppose Aldabra's stock sells for $32, its next expected dividend is $1.82, and its expected constant growth rate is 5.4%. Aldabra is not expected to repurchase any stock. Aldabra's stock is thought to be in equilibrium, so its expected and required rates of return are equal. Based on these assumptions, its estimated DCF cost of common equity is 11.1%:

$$\hat{r}_s = r_s = \frac{\$1.82}{\$32.00} + 5.4\%$$
$$= 5.7\% + 5.4\%$$
$$= 11.1\%$$

As previously noted, it is difficult to apply the DCF approach because dividends do not grow at a constant rate for most companies. Surveys show that 16% of responding firms use the DCF approach, down from 31% in 1982.[14]

> **SELF TEST**
>
> What inputs are required for the DCF method?
>
> What are three ways to estimate the expected dividend growth rate?
>
> A company's estimated growth rate in dividends is 6%, its current stock price is $40, and its expected annual dividend is $2. Using the DCF approach, what is the firm's r_s? **(11%)**

11-8 **The Weighted Average Cost of Capital (WACC)**

As we mentioned earlier in this chapter (and as we discuss in more detail in Chapter 15), each firm has an optimal capital structure, which is defined as the mix of debt, preferred stock, and common equity that maximizes its stock price. Therefore, a value-maximizing firm must attempt to find its *target (or optimal) capital structure* and then raise new capital in a manner that will keep the actual capital structure on target over time. In this chapter, we assume that the firm has identified its optimal capital structure, that it uses this optimum as the target, and that it finances so as to remain constantly on target. How the target is established is examined in Chapter 16.

---

14. See the sources cited in footnotes 12 and 13.

The target proportions of debt, preferred stock, and common equity, along with the component costs of capital, are used to calculate the WACC, as shown previously in Equation 11-2:

$$\text{WACC} = w_d r_d (1 - T) + w_{std} r_{std} (1 - T) + w_{ps} r_{ps} + w_s r_s \tag{11–2}$$

Here w_d, w_{std}, w_{ps}, and w_s are the target weights for long-term debt, short-term debt, preferred stock, and common equity, respectively.

To illustrate, we first note that MicroDrive has a target capital structure calling for 28% long-term debt, 2% short-term debt, 3% preferred stock, and 67% common equity. MicroDrive's before-tax cost of long-term debt, r_d, is 9%; its before-tax cost of short-term debt, r_{std}, is 10%; its cost of preferred stock, r_{ps}, is 8.16%; its cost of common equity, r_s, is 13.58%; and its marginal tax rate is 40%. We can now calculate MicroDrive's weighted average cost of capital as follows:

$$\text{WACC} = 0.28(9.0\%)(1 - 0.4) + 0.02(10.0\%)(1 - 0.4) + 0.03(8.16\%) + 0.67(13.58\%)$$
$$= 11\%$$

Three points should be noted. First, the WACC is the cost the company would incur to raise each new, or *marginal*, dollar of capital—it is not the average cost of dollars raised in the past. Second, the percentages of each capital component, called *weights*, should be based on management's target capital structure, not on the particular sources of financing in any single year. Third, the target weights should be based on market values and not on book values. The following sections explain these points.

11-8a **Marginal Rates versus Historical Rates**

The required rates of return for a company's investors, whether they are new or old, are always marginal rates. For example, a stockholder might have invested in a company last year when the risk-free interest rate was 6% and the required return on equity was 12%. If the risk-free rate subsequently falls and is now 4%, then the investor's required return on equity is now 10% (holding all else constant). This is the same required rate of return that a new equity holder would have, whether the new investor bought stock in the secondary market or through a new equity offering. In other words, whether the shareholders are already equity holders or are brand-new equity holders, they all have the same required rate of return, which is the current required rate of return on equity. The same reasoning applies for the firm's bondholders. All bondholders, whether old or new, have a required rate of return equal to today's yield on the firm's debt, which is based on current market conditions.

Because investors' required rates of return are based on *current* market conditions, not on market conditions when they purchased their securities, it follows that the cost of capital depends on current conditions and not on past market conditions.

11-8b **Target Weights versus Annual Financing Choices**

We have heard managers (and students!) say, "Our debt has a 5% after-tax cost versus a 10% WACC and a 14% cost of equity. Therefore, because we will finance only with debt this year, we should evaluate this year's projects at a 5% cost." There are two flaws in this line of reasoning.

First, suppose the firm exhausts its capacity to issue low-cost debt this year to take on projects with after-tax returns as low as 5.1% (which is slightly higher than the after-tax cost of debt). Then next year, when the firm must finance with common equity, it will have to turn down projects with returns as high as 13.9% (which is slightly lower than the cost of equity). It doesn't make any economic sense for the order in which projects are considered to matter this much, so to avoid this problem, a firm that plans to remain in business indefinitely should evaluate all projects using the 10% WACC.

Second, both existing and new investors have claims on *all* future cash flows. For example, if a company raises debt and also invests in a new project that same year, the new debtholders don't have a specific claim on that specific project's cash flows (assuming it is not non-recourse project financing). In fact, new debtholders receive a claim on the cash flows being generated by existing as well as new projects, while old debtholders (and equity holders) have claims on both new and existing projects. Thus, the decision to take on a new project should depend on the project's ability to satisfy all of the company's investors, not just the new debtholders, even if only debt is being raised that year.

11-8c Weights for Component Costs: Book Values versus Market Values versus Targets

Our primary reason for calculating the WACC is to use it in capital budgeting or corporate valuation. In particular, we need to compare the expected returns on projects and stocks with investors' required returns to determine whether investors are compensated fairly for the risk they bear. The total amount of required compensation depends both on the *rate of return required* by investors and the *amount* they have at stake.

Regarding the rate of return required by investors, the previous sections showed that investors require a rate of return equal to the current rate they could get on alternative investments of equivalent risk. In other words, the required rate is the opportunity cost.

Regarding the amount that investors have at stake, we again apply the "opportunity" concept. Investors have the opportunity to sell their investment at the market value, so this is the amount that investors have at stake. Notice that the amount at stake is not equal to the book values as reported on the financial statements. Book values are a record of historical investments, not the current market value of the investment. Because the WACC is used to discount future cash flows, the weights should be based on the market value weights expected on average in the future, not necessarily the current weights based on current market values.

In summary, the weights should not be based on book values but instead should be based on the market-value weights in the target capital structure. Obviously, the target capital structure must be realistic—companies can't take on so much debt that they will almost certainly go bankrupt. Also, a company must try to adjust its market value weights toward the target weights; otherwise the average weights over time might differ significantly from those in the target capital structure. We discuss capital structures, including how fast companies adjust their weights, in Chapter 16.

GLOBAL VARIATIONS IN THE COST OF CAPITAL

For U.S. firms to be competitive with foreign companies, they must have a cost of capital no greater than that faced by their international competitors. In the past, many experts argued that U.S. firms were at a disadvantage. In particular, Japanese firms enjoyed a very low cost of capital, which lowered their total costs and thus made it hard for U.S. firms to compete with them. Recent events, however, have considerably narrowed cost-of-capital differences between U.S. and Japanese firms. In particular, the U.S. stock market has outperformed the Japanese market in recent years, which has made it easier and cheaper for U.S. firms to raise equity capital.

As capital markets become increasingly integrated, cross-country differences in the cost of capital are declining. Today, most large corporations raise capital throughout the world; hence, we are moving toward one global capital market instead of distinct capital markets in each country. Government policies and market conditions can affect the cost of capital within a given country, but this primarily affects smaller firms that do not have access to global capital markets, and even these differences are becoming less important as time passes. What matters most is the risk of the individual firm, not the market in which it raises capital.

SELF TEST

How is the weighted average cost of capital calculated? Write out the equation.

Should the weights used to calculate the WACC be based on book values, market values, or something else? Explain.

A firm has the following data: target capital structure of 25% debt, 10% preferred stock, and 65% common equity; tax rate = 40%; r_d = 7%; r_{ps} = 7.5%; and r_s = 11.5%. Assume the firm will not issue new stock. What is this firm's WACC? **(9.28%)**

11-9 Adjusting the Cost of Equity for Flotation Costs

Few firms with moderate or slow growth issue new shares of common stock through public offerings.[15] In fact, less than 2% of all new corporate funds come from the external public equity market, for two very good reasons: (1) negative signaling and (2) direct costs. We discuss signaling in Chapter 16, but we address direct costs here.

The direct costs of new issuance are called **flotation costs**. Table 11-1 shows the average flotation costs for debt and equity U.S. corporations issued in the 1990s. Notice that flotation costs, as a *percentage* of capital raised, fall as the *amount* of capital raised increases. The common stock flotation costs are for non-IPO issues. For IPOs, flotation costs are higher—about 17% higher if less than $10 million is

---

15. A few companies issue new shares through new-stock dividend reinvestment plans, which we discuss in Chapter 15. Many companies sell stock to their employees, and companies occasionally issue stock to finance huge projects or mergers. Also, some utilities regularly issue common stock.

| TABLE 11-1 | Average Flotation Costs for Debt and Equity |

Amount of Capital Raised (Millions of Dollars)	Average Flotation Cost for Common Stock (% of Total Capital Raised)	Average Flotation Cost for New Debt (% of Total Capital Raised)
2–9.99	13.28%	4.39%
10–19.99	8.72	2.76
20–39.99	6.93	2.42
40–59.99	5.87	2.32
60–79.99	5.18	2.34
80–99.99	4.73	2.16
100–199.99	4.22	2.31
200– 499.99	3.47	2.19
500 and up	3.15	1.64

Source: Inmoo Lee, Scott Lochhead, Jay Ritter, and Quanshui Zhao, "The Costs of Raising Capital," *The Journal of Financial Research*, Spring 1996, pp. 59–74.

raised and higher still as issue size increases. The data in Table 11-1 include both utility and nonutility companies; if utilities had been excluded, the reported flotation costs would have been higher. Table 11-1 shows that flotation costs are significantly higher for equity than for debt. One reason for higher equity flotation costs is that corporate debt is sold mainly in large blocks to institutional investors, whereas common stock is sold in smaller amounts to many different investors; this imposes higher costs on the investment banks, which pass these costs on to the issuing company. Also, stock values are harder to estimate than debt values, which make selling stock more difficult, again leading to higher costs for the investment banks.

For companies that do issue new common stock, the **cost of new common equity, r_e,** or external equity, is higher than the cost of equity raised internally by reinvesting earnings, r_s, because of the flotation costs involved in issuing new common stock. What rate of return must be earned on new investments to make issuing stock worthwhile? Put another way, what is the cost of new common stock?

r_e = component cost of *external equity*, or common equity raised by issuing new stock. As we will see, r_e is equal to r_s plus a factor that reflects the cost of issuing new stock.

The answer, for a constant growth firm, is found by applying this formula:

(11–12)

$$r_e = \hat{r}_e = \frac{D_1}{P_0(1 - F)} + g$$

In Equation 11-12, F is the percentage flotation cost incurred in selling the new stock, so $P_0(1 - F)$ is the net price per share received by the company.

Here is an example. In Section 11.7b, we estimated Aldabra's cost of common equity using the DCF approach as 11.1%, assuming Aldabra didn't issue new equity. Now assume that Aldabra must issue new equity with a flotation cost of 12.5%. The cost of new outside equity is calculated as follows:

$$r_e = \frac{\$1.82}{\$32(1 - 0.125)} + 5.4\%$$

$$= 6.5\% + 5.4\% = 11.9\%$$

Because of flotation costs, Aldabra must earn 11.9% on the new equity capital in order to provide shareholders the 11.1% they require.

As we noted previously, most analysts use the CAPM to estimate the cost of equity. How would the analyst incorporate flotation costs into a CAPM cost estimate? If application of the DCF methodology gives a cost of internally generated equity of 11.1% but a cost of 11.9% when flotation costs are involved, then the flotation costs add 0.8 percentage points to the cost of equity. To incorporate flotation costs into the CAPM estimate, we would simply add 0.8% to the CAPM estimate.

As an alternative to adjusting the cost of equity for flotation costs, many companies simply include the flotation costs as a negative cash flow when they perform project analysis. See Chapter 13 for a description of cash flow estimation for projects.

What are flotation costs?

Why are flotation costs higher for stock than for debt?

A firm has common stock with $D_1 = \$3.00$; $P_0 = \$30$; $g = 5\%$; and $F = 4\%$. If the firm must issue new stock, what is its cost of external equity, r_e? **(15.42%)**

SELF TEST

11-10 Privately Owned Firms and Small Businesses

So far our discussion of the cost of capital has been focused on publicly owned corporations. Privately owned firms and small businesses have different situations calling for slightly different approaches.

11-10a Estimating the Cost of Stock by the Comparison Approach

When we estimated the rate of return required by public stockholders, we use stock returns to estimate beta as an input for the CAPM approach and stock prices as input data for the DCF method. But how can one measure the cost of equity for a firm whose stock is not traded? Most analysts begin by identifying one or more publicly traded firms that are in the same industry and that are approximately the same size as the privately owned firm.[16] The analyst then estimates the betas for these publicly traded firms and uses their average beta as an estimate of the beta of the privately owned firm.

11-10b Own-Bond-Yield-Plus-Judgmental-Risk-Premium Approach

From Chapter 4, we know that a company's cost of debt is above the risk-free rate due to the default risk premium. We also know that a company's cost of stock should be greater than its cost of debt because equity is riskier than debt. Therefore, some analysts use a subjective, ad hoc procedure to estimate a firm's cost of common equity: They simply add a judgmental risk premium of 3% to 5% to the cost of debt. In this approach:

(11–13)

$$r_s = r_d + \text{Judgmental risk premium}$$

For example, consider a privately held company with a 10% cost of debt. Using 4% as the judgmental risk premium (because it is the mid-point of the 3%–5% range), the estimated cost of equity is 14%:

$$r_s = 10\% + 4\% = 14\%$$

11-10c Adjusting for Lack of Liquidity

The stock of a privately held firm is less liquid than that of a publicly held firm. As we explained in Chapter 4, investors require a liquidity premium on thinly traded bonds. Therefore, many analysts make an ad hoc adjustment to reflect this lack of liquidity by adding 1 to 3 percentage points to the firm's cost of equity. This rule of thumb is not theoretically satisfying because we don't know exactly how large the liquidity premium should be, but it is logical and is also a common practice.

11-10d Estimating Consistent Weights in the Capital Structure

Suppose a privately held firm is concerned about whether its current capital structure weights are appropriate. The first step for a publicly traded company would be to estimate the capital structure weights based on current market values. However, a privately held firm can't directly observe its market value, so it can't directly observe its market value weights.

To resolve this problem, many analysts begin by making a trial guess about the value of the firm's equity. The analysts then use this estimated value of equity to estimate the cost of capital. They then use this cost of capital to estimate the value of the firm. Finally, they complete the circle by using the estimated value of the firm

---

16. In Chapter 16, we show how to adjust if these comparison firms have differences in capital structures.

to estimate the value of its equity. If this newly estimated equity value is different from their trial guess, analysts repeat the process but start the iteration with the newly estimated equity value as the trial value of equity. After several iterations, the trial value of equity and the resulting estimated equity value usually converge. Although somewhat tedious, this process provides consistent estimates of the weights, the cost of capital, and the value of the firm.

Identify problems that occur when estimating the cost of capital for a privately held firm. What are some solutions to these problems?

Explain the reasoning behind the bond-yield-plus-judgmental-risk-premium approach.

A company's bond yield is 7%. If the appropriate own-bond-yield risk premium is 3.5%, then what is r_s? **(10.5%)**

SELF TEST

11-11 Managerial Issues and the Cost of Capital

We describe several managerial issues in this section, starting with how managerial decisions affect the cost of capital.

11-11a How Managerial Decisions Affect the Cost of Capital

The cost of capital is affected by some factors that are under a firm's control and some that are not.

Four Factors the Firm Cannot Control

Four factors are beyond managerial control: (1) interest rates, (2) credit crises, (3) the market risk premium, and (4) tax rates.

Interest Rates. Interest rates in the economy affect the costs of both debt and equity, but they are beyond a manager's control. Even the Fed can't control interest rates indefinitely. For example, interest rates are heavily influenced by inflation, and when inflation hit historic highs in the early 1980s, interest rates followed. Rates trended mostly down for 25 years through the recession accompanying the 2008 financial crisis. Strong actions by the federal government in the spring of 2009 brought rates even lower, which contributed to the official ending of the recession in June 2009. Since then, rates have trended up a bit as the economy has slowly recovered. These actions encouraged investment, and there is little doubt that they will eventually lead to stronger growth. However, many observers fear that the government's actions will also reignite long-run inflation, which would lead to substantially higher interest rates.

Credit Crisis. Although rare, sometimes credit markets are so disrupted that it is virtually impossible for a firm to raise capital at reasonable rates. This happened in 2008 and 2009, before the U.S. Treasury and the Federal Reserve intervened to open up the capital markets. During such times, firms tend to cut back on growth plans; if they must raise capital, its cost can be extraordinarily high.

Market Risk Premium. Investors' aversion to risk determines the market risk premium. Individual firms have no control over the RP_M, which affects the cost of equity and thus the WACC.

Tax Rates. Tax rates, which are influenced by the president and set by Congress, have an important effect on the cost of capital. They are used when we calculate the after-tax cost of debt for use in the WACC. In addition, the lower tax rate on dividends and capital gains than on interest income favors financing with stock rather than bonds, as we discuss in detail in Chapter 16.

Three Factors the Firm Can Control

A firm can affect its cost of capital through: (1) its capital structure policy, (2) its dividend policy, and (3) its investment (capital budgeting) policy.

Capital Structure Policy. In this chapter, we assume the firm has a given target capital structure, and we use weights based on that target to calculate its WACC. However, a firm can change its capital structure, and such a change can affect the cost of capital. For example, the after-tax cost of debt is lower than the cost of equity, so if the firm decides to use more debt and less common equity, then this increase in debt will tend to lower the WACC. However, an increased use of debt will increase the risk of debt and the equity, offsetting to some extent the effect due to a greater weighting of debt. In Chapter 16, we discuss this in more depth, and we demonstrate that the optimal capital structure is the one that minimizes the WACC, which maximizes the intrinsic value of the stock.

Dividend Policy. As we will see in Chapter 15, the percentage of earnings paid out in dividends may affect a stock's required rate of return, r_s. Also, if the payout ratio is so high that the firm must issue new stock to fund its capital budget, then the resulting flotation costs will also affect the WACC.

Investment Policy. When we estimate the cost of capital, we use as the starting point the required rates of return on the firm's outstanding stocks and bonds, which reflect the risks inherent in the existing assets. Therefore, we are implicitly assuming that new capital will be invested in assets with the same degree of risk as existing assets. This assumption is generally correct, because most firms invest in assets similar to those they currently use. However, the equal risk assumption is incorrect if a firm dramatically changes its investment policy. For example, if a company invests in an entirely new line of business, then its marginal cost of capital should reflect the risk of that new business. For example, we can see with hindsight that GE's huge investments in the TV and movie businesses, as well as its investment in mortgages, increased its risk and thus its cost of capital.

The following section explains how to adjust the cost of capital to reflect the risk of individual divisions and projects.

11-11b Adjusting the Cost of Capital for Risk: Divisions and Projects

As we have calculated it, the weighted average cost of capital reflects the average risk and overall capital structure of the entire firm. No adjustments are needed when using the WACC as the discount rate when estimating the value of a company by discounting its cash flows. However, adjustments for risk are often needed when evaluating a division or project. For example, what if a firm has divisions in several business lines that differ in risk? Or what if a company is considering a project that is much riskier than its typical project? It is not logical to use the overall cost of capital to discount divisional or project-specific cash flows that don't have the same risk as the company's average cash flows. The following sections explain how to adjust the cost of capital for divisions and for specific projects.

Divisional Costs of Capital

Consider Starlight Sandwich Shops, a company with two divisions—a bakery operation and a chain of cafes. The bakery division is low-risk and has a 10% WACC. The cafe division is riskier and has a 14% WACC. Each division is approximately the same size, so Starlight's overall cost of capital is 12%. The bakery manager has a project with an 11% expected rate of return, and the cafe division manager has a project with a 13% expected return. Should these projects be accepted or rejected? Starlight will create value if it accepts the bakery's project, because its rate of return is greater than its cost of capital (11% > 10%), but the cafe project's rate of return is less than its cost of capital (13% < 14%), so it should reject that project. However, if management simply compared the two projects' returns with Starlight's 12% overall cost of capital, then the bakery's value-adding project would be rejected while the cafe's value-destroying project would be accepted.

Many firms use the CAPM to estimate the cost of capital for specific divisions. To begin, recall that the Security Market Line (SML) equation expresses the risk–return relationship as follows:

$$r_s = r_{RF} + (RP_M)b_i$$

As an example, consider the case of Huron Steel Company, an integrated steel producer operating in the Great Lakes region. For simplicity, assume that Huron has only one division and uses only equity capital, so its cost of equity is also its corporate cost of capital, or WACC. Huron's beta = b = 1.1, r_{RF} = 5%, and RP_M = 6%. Thus, Huron's cost of equity (and WACC) is 11.6%:

$$r_s = 5\% + (6\%)1.1 = 11.6\%$$

This suggests that investors should be willing to give Huron money to invest in new, average-risk projects if the company expects to earn 11.6% or more on this money. By "average risk" we mean projects having risk similar to the firm's existing division.

Now suppose Huron creates a new transportation division consisting of a fleet of barges to haul iron ore, and suppose barge operations typically have betas of 1.5 rather than 1.1. The barge division, with b = 1.5, has a 14.0% cost of capital:

$$r_{Barge} = 5\% + (6\%)1.5 = 14.0\%$$

On the other hand, if Huron adds a low-risk division, such as a new distribution center with a beta of only 0.5, then that division's cost of capital would be 8%:

$$r_{Center} = 5\% + (6\%)0.5 = 8.0\%$$

A firm itself may be regarded as a "portfolio of assets," and because the beta of a portfolio is a weighted average of the betas of its individual assets, adding the barge and distribution center divisions will change Huron's overall beta. The exact value of the new corporate beta would depend on the size of the investments in the new divisions relative to Huron's original steel operations. If 70% of Huron's total value ends up in the steel division, 20% in the barge division, and 10% in the distribution center, then its new corporate beta would be calculated as follows:

$$\text{New beta} = 0.7(1.1) + 0.2(1.5) + 0.1(0.5) = 1.12$$

Thus, investors in Huron's stock would require a return of:

$$r_{\text{Huron}} = 5\% + (6\%)1.12 = 11.72\%$$

Even though investors require an overall return of 11.72%, they should expect a rate of return on projects in each division at least as high as the division's required return based on the SML. In particular, they should expect a return of at least 11.6% from the steel division, 14.0% from the barge division, and 8.0% from the distribution center.

Our example suggests a level of precision that is much higher than firms can obtain in the real world. Still, managers should be aware of this example's logic, and they should strive to measure the required inputs as accurately as possible.

Techniques for Measuring Divisional Betas

In Chapter 2, we discussed the estimation of betas for stocks and indicated how difficult it is to measure beta precisely. Estimating divisional betas is much more difficult, primarily because divisions do not have their own publicly traded stock. Therefore, we must estimate the beta that the division would have if it were an independent, publicly traded company. Two approaches can be used to estimate divisional betas: the pure play method and the accounting beta method.

The Pure Play Method. In the **pure play method**, the company tries to find the betas of several publicly held specialized companies in the same line of business as the division being evaluated, and it then averages those betas to determine the cost of capital for its own division. For example, suppose Huron found three companies devoted exclusively to operating barges, and suppose that Huron's management believes its barge division would be subject to the same risks as those firms. Then Huron could use the average beta of those firms as an estimate of its barge division's beta.[17]

The Accounting Beta Method. As noted above, it may be impossible to find specialized publicly traded firms suitable for the pure play approach. If that is the case, we may be able to use the **accounting beta method**. Betas are normally found by regressing the returns of a particular company's *stock* against returns on a *stock market index*. However, we could run a regression of the division's *accounting return on assets* against the *average return on assets* for a large sample of companies, such as those included in the S&P 500. Betas determined in this way (that is, by using accounting data rather than stock market data) are called **accounting betas**.

---

17. If the pure play firms employ different capital structures than that of Huron, then this must be addressed by adjusting the beta coefficients. See Chapter 16 for a discussion of this aspect of the pure play method. For a technique that can be used when pure play firms are not available, see Yatin Bhagwat and Michael Ehrhardt, "A Full Information Approach for Estimating Divisional Betas," *Financial Management*, Summer 1991, pp. 60–69.

Estimating the Cost of Capital for Individual Projects

In Chapter 13, we examine ways to estimate the risk inherent in individual projects, but at this point it is useful to consider how project risk is reflected in measures of the firm's cost of capital. First, although it is intuitively clear that riskier projects have a higher cost of capital, it is difficult to measure projects' relative risks. Also, note that three separate and distinct types of risk can be identified.

1. **Stand-alone risk** is the variability of the project's returns.
2. **Corporate risk**, which is also called **within-firm risk**, is the variability the project contributes to the corporation's returns, giving consideration to the fact that the project represents only one asset of the firm's portfolio of assets and so some of its risk will be diversified away.
3. **Market risk**, which is also called **beta risk**, is the risk of the project as seen by a well-diversified stockholder who owns many different stocks. A project's market risk is measured by its effect on the firm's overall beta coefficient.

Taking on a project with a high degree of either stand-alone or corporate risk will not necessarily increase the corporate beta. However, if the project has highly uncertain returns and if those returns are highly correlated with returns on the firm's other assets and with most other assets in the economy, then the project will have a high degree of all types of risk.

Of the three measures, market risk is theoretically the most relevant because of its direct effect on stock prices. Unfortunately, the market risk for a project is also the most difficult to estimate. In practice, most decision makers consider all three risk measures in a subjective manner.

The first step is to determine the divisional cost of capital before grouping divisional projects into subjective risk categories. Then, using the divisional WACC as a starting point, **risk-adjusted costs of capital** are developed for each category. For example, a firm might establish three risk classes—high, average, and low—and then assign average-risk projects the divisional cost of capital, higher-risk projects an above-average cost, and lower-risk projects a below-average cost. Thus, if a division's WACC were 10%, its managers might use 10% to evaluate average-risk projects in the division, 12% for high-risk projects, and 8% for low-risk projects. Although this approach is better than ignoring project risk, these adjustments are necessarily subjective and somewhat arbitrary. Unfortunately, given the data, there is no completely satisfactory way to specify exactly how much higher or lower we should go in setting risk-adjusted costs of capital.

11-11c **Four Mistakes to Avoid**

We often see managers and students make the following mistakes when estimating the cost of capital. Although we have discussed these errors previously at separate places in the chapter, they are worth repeating here.

1. *Never base the cost of debt on the coupon rate on a firm's existing debt.* The cost of debt must be based on the interest rate the firm would pay if it issued new debt today.
2. *When estimating the market risk premium for the CAPM method, never use the historical average return on stocks in conjunction with the current return on T-bonds.* The historical average return on bonds should be subtracted from the past average return on stocks to calculate the *historical market risk premium.*

On the other hand, it is appropriate to subtract today's yield on T-bonds from an estimate of the expected future return on stocks to obtain the *forward-looking market risk premium*. A case can be made for using either the historical or the current risk premium, but it would be wrong to take the *historical* rate of return on stocks, subtract from it the *current* rate on T-bonds, and then use the difference as the market risk premium.

3. *Never use the current book value capital structure to obtain the weights when estimating the WACC.* Your first choice should be to use the firm's target capital structure for the weights. However, if you are an outside analyst and do not know the target weights, it would probably be best to estimate weights based on the current market values of the capital components. If the company's debt is not publicly traded, then it is reasonable to use the book value of debt to estimate the weights because book and market values of debt, especially short-term debt, are usually close to one another. However, stocks' market values in recent years have generally been at least 2–3 times their book values, so using book values for equity could lead to serious errors. The bottom line: If you don't know the target weights then use the market value, not the book value, of equity when calculating the WACC.

4. *Always remember that capital components are funds that come from investors.* If it's not from an investor, then it's not a capital component. Sometimes the argument is made that accounts payable and accruals should be included in the calculation of the WACC. However, these funds are not provided by investors, but instead, they arise from operating relationships with suppliers and employees. As such, the impact of accounts payable and accruals is incorporated into the calculations of free cash flows and project cash flows. Therefore, accounts payable and accruals should not be included as capital components when we calculate the WACC.

SELF TEST

Name some factors that are generally beyond the firm's control but still affect its cost of capital.

What three policies under the firm's control affect its cost of capital?

Explain how a change in interest rates in the economy would be expected to affect each component of the weighted average cost of capital.

Based on the CAPM, how would one adjust the corporation's overall cost of capital to establish the required return for most projects in a low-risk division and in a high-risk division?

Describe the pure play and the accounting beta methods for estimating divisional betas.

What are the three types of risk to which projects are exposed? Which type of risk is theoretically the most relevant? Why?

Describe a procedure firms can use to establish costs of capital for projects with differing degrees of risk.

What four mistakes are commonly made when estimating the WACC?

Summary

This chapter discussed how the cost of capital is developed for use in capital budgeting. The key points covered are listed below.

- The cost of capital used in capital budgeting is a **weighted average** of the types of capital the firm uses—typically long-term debt, short-term debt, preferred stock, and common equity.
- The **component cost of debt** is the **after-tax cost of new debt**. It is found by multiplying the interest rate paid on new debt by $1 - T$, where T is the firm's marginal tax rate: $r_d(1 - T)$.
- Most debt is raised directly from lenders without the use of investment bankers; hence no flotation costs are incurred. However, a **debt flotation cost adjustment** should be made if large flotation costs are incurred. We reduce the bond's issue price by the flotation expenses, reduce the bond's cash flows to reflect taxes, and then solve for the after-tax yield to maturity.
- The **component cost of preferred stock** is calculated as the preferred dividend divided by the net price the firm receives after deducting flotation costs: $r_{ps} = D_{ps}/[P_{ps}(1 - F)]$. Flotation costs on preferred stock are usually fairly high, so we typically include the impact of flotation costs when estimating r_{ps}.
- The **cost of common equity, r_s**, also called the **cost of common stock**, is the rate of return required by the firm's stockholders.
- To use the **CAPM approach,** we: (1) estimate the firm's beta, (2) multiply this beta by the market risk premium to obtain the firm's risk premium, and then (3) add the firm's risk premium to the risk-free rate to obtain its cost of common stock: $r_s = r_{RF} + (RP_M)b_i$.
- The best proxy for the **risk-free rate** is the yield on long-term T-bonds, with 10 years the maturity used most frequently.
- To use the **dividend-yield-plus-growth-rate approach**, which is also called the **discounted cash flow (DCF) approach**, add the firm's expected dividend growth rate to its expected dividend yield: $r_s = \hat{r}_s = D_1/P_0 + g$. *Web Extension 11A* shows how to estimate the DCF cost of equity (and the market risk premium) if dividends are not growing at a constant rate.
- The growth rate for use in the DCF model can be based on security analysts' **published forecasts**, on **historical growth rates** of earnings and dividends, or on the **retention growth model**, $g = (1 - Payout)(Return on equity)$.
- The **own-bond-yield-plus-judgmental-risk-premium approach** calls for adding a subjective risk premium of 3 to 5 percentage points to the interest rate on the firm's own long-term debt: $r_s = $ Bond yield + Judgmental risk premium.
- When calculating the **cost of new common stock, r_e**, the DCF approach can be used to estimate the flotation cost. For a constant growth stock, the flotation-adjusted cost can be expressed as $r_e = \hat{r}_e = D_1/[P_0(1 - F)] + g$. Note that flotation costs cause r_e to be greater than r_s. We can find the difference between r_e and r_s and then add this differential to the CAPM estimate of r_s to find the CAPM estimate of r_e.

- Each firm has a **target capital structure**, which is defined as the mix of debt, preferred stock, and common equity that minimizes its **weighted average cost of capital (WACC)**:

$$WACC = w_d r_d (1 - T) + w_{std} r_{std} (1 - T) + w_{ps} r_{ps} + w_s r_s$$

- Various factors affect a firm's cost of capital. Some are determined by the financial environment, but the firm can influence others through its financing, investment, and dividend policies.
- Many firms estimate **divisional costs of capital** that reflect each division's risk and capital structure.
- The **pure play** and **accounting beta methods** can be used to estimate betas for large projects or for divisions.
- A project's **stand-alone risk** is the risk the project would have if it were the firm's only asset and if stockholders held only that one stock. Stand-alone risk is measured by the variability of the asset's expected returns.
- **Corporate risk**, which is also called **within-firm risk**, reflects the effect of a project on the firm's risk, and it is measured by the project's effect on the firm's earnings variability.
- **Market risk**, which is also called **beta risk**, reflects the effects of a project on stockholders' risk, assuming they hold diversified portfolios. Market risk is measured by the project's effect on the firm's beta coefficient.
- Most decision makers consider all three risk measures in a subjective manner and then classify projects into risk categories. Using the firm's WACC as a starting point, risk-adjusted costs of capital are developed for each category. The **risk-adjusted cost of capital** is the cost of capital appropriate for a given project, given its risk. The greater a project's risk, the higher its cost of capital.

The cost of capital as developed in this chapter is used in the next two chapters to evaluate potential capital budgeting projects, and it is used later in the text to determine the value of a corporation.

Questions

11-1 Define each of the following terms:
   a. Weighted average cost of capital, WACC; after-tax cost of debt, $r_d(1 - T)$; after-tax cost of short-term debt, $r_{std}(1 - T)$
   b. Cost of preferred stock, r_{ps}; cost of common equity (or cost of common stock), r_s
   c. Target capital structure
   d. Flotation cost, F; cost of new external common equity, r_e

11-2 How can the WACC be both an average cost and a marginal cost?

11-3 How would each of the factors in the following table affect a firm's cost of debt, $r_d(1 - T)$; its cost of equity, r_s; and its weighted average cost of capital, WACC? Indicate by a plus (+), a minus (−), or a zero (0) if the factor would increase, reduce, or have an indeterminate effect on the item in question. Assume that all other factors are held constant. Be prepared to justify your answer, but recognize that several of the parts probably have no single correct answer; these questions are designed to stimulate thought and discussion.

	Effect on:		
	$r_d(1 - T)$	r_s	**WACC**
a. The corporate tax rate is lowered.	_____	_____	_____
b. The Federal Reserve tightens credit.	_____	_____	_____
c. The firm uses more debt.	_____	_____	_____
d. The firm doubles the amount of capital it raises during the year.	_____	_____	_____
e. The firm expands into a risky new area.	_____	_____	_____
f. Investors become more risk averse.	_____	_____	_____

11-4 Distinguish between beta (i.e., market) risk, within-firm (i.e., corporate) risk, and stand-alone risk for a potential project. Of the three measures, which is theoretically the most relevant, and why?

11-5 Suppose a firm estimates its overall cost of capital for the coming year to be 10%. What might be reasonable costs of capital for average-risk, high-risk, and low-risk projects?

Problems Answers Appear in Appendix B

Easy Problems 1–8

11-1 **After-Tax Cost of Debt**
Calculate the after-tax cost of debt under each of the following conditions:
a. r_d of 13%, tax rate of 0%
b. r_d of 13%, tax rate of 20%
c. r_d of 13%, tax rate of 35%

11-2 **After-Tax Cost of Debt**
LL Incorporated's currently outstanding 11% coupon bonds have a yield to maturity of 8%. LL believes it could issue new bonds at par that would provide a similar yield to maturity. If its marginal tax rate is 35%, what is LL's after-tax cost of debt?

11-3 Cost of Preferred Stock

Duggins Veterinary Supplies can issue perpetual preferred stock at a price of $50 a share with an annual dividend of $4.50 a share. Ignoring flotation costs, what is the company's cost of preferred stock, r_{ps}?

11-4 Cost of Preferred Stock with Flotation Costs

Burnwood Tech plans to issue some $60 par preferred stock with a 6% dividend. A similar stock is selling on the market for $70. Burnwood must pay flotation costs of 5% of the issue price. What is the cost of the preferred stock?

11-5 Cost of Equity: DCF

Summerdahl Resort's common stock is currently trading at $36 a share. The stock is expected to pay a dividend of $3.00 a share at the end of the year (D_1 = $3.00), and the dividend is expected to grow at a constant rate of 5% a year. What is its cost of common equity?

11-6 Cost of Equity: CAPM

Booher Book Stores has a beta of 0.8. The yield on a 3-month T-bill is 4%, and the yield on a 10-year T-bond is 6%. The market risk premium is 5.5%, and the return on an average stock in the market last year was 15%. What is the estimated cost of common equity using the CAPM?

11-7 WACC

Shi Importers' balance sheet shows $300 million in debt, $50 million in preferred stock, and $250 million in total common equity. Shi's tax rate is 40%, r_d = 6%, r_{ps} = 5.8%, and r_s = 12%. If Shi has a target capital structure of 30% debt, 5% preferred stock, and 65% common stock, what is its WACC?

11-8 WACC

David Ortiz Motors has a target capital structure of 40% debt and 60% equity. The yield to maturity on the company's outstanding bonds is 9%, and the company's tax rate is 40%. Ortiz's CFO has calculated the company's WACC as 9.96%. What is the company's cost of equity capital?

Intermediate Problems 9–14

11-9 Bond Yield and After-Tax Cost of Debt

A company's 6% coupon rate, semiannual payment, $1,000 par value bond that matures in 30 years sells at a price of $515.16. The company's federal-plus-state tax rate is 40%. What is the firm's after-tax component cost of debt for purposes of calculating the WACC? (*Hint:* Base your answer on the *nominal* rate.)

11-10 Cost of Equity

The earnings, dividends, and stock price of Shelby Inc. are expected to grow at 7% per year in the future. Shelby's common stock sells for $23 per share, its last dividend was $2.00, and the company will pay a dividend of $2.14 at the end of the current year.

a. Using the discounted cash flow approach, what is its cost of equity?

b. If the firm's beta is 1.6, the risk-free rate is 9%, and the expected return on the market is 13%, then what would be the firm's cost of equity based on the CAPM approach?

c. If the firm's bonds earn a return of 12%, then what would be your estimate of r_s using the own-bond-yield-plus-judgmental-risk-premium approach? (*Hint:* Use the midpoint of the risk premium range.)

d. On the basis of the results of parts a through c, what would be your estimate of Shelby's cost of equity?

11–11 Cost of Equity

Radon Homes' current EPS is $6.50. It was $4.42 5 years ago. The company pays out 40% of its earnings as dividends, and the stock sells for $36.

a. Calculate the historical growth rate in earnings. (*Hint:* This is a 5-year growth period.)

b. Calculate the *next* expected dividend per share, D_1. (*Hint:* $D_0 = 0.4(\$6.50) = \$2.60$.) Assume that the past growth rate will continue.

c. What is Radon's cost of equity, r_s?

11–12 Calculation of g and EPS

Spencer Supplies' stock is currently selling for $60 a share. The firm is expected to earn $5.40 per share this year and to pay a year-end dividend of $3.60.

a. If investors require a 9% return, what rate of growth must be expected for Spencer?

b. If Spencer reinvests earnings in projects with average returns equal to the stock's expected rate of return, then what will be next year's EPS? (*Hint:* $g = \text{ROE} \times \text{Retention ratio}$.)

11–13 The Cost of Equity and Flotation Costs

Messman Manufacturing will issue common stock to the public for $30. The expected dividend and the growth in dividends are $3.00 per share and 5%, respectively. If the flotation cost is 10% of the issue's gross proceeds, what is the cost of external equity, r_e?

11–14 The Cost of Debt and Flotation Costs

Suppose a company will issue new 20-year debt with a par value of $1,000 and a coupon rate of 9%, paid annually. The tax rate is 40%. If the flotation cost is 2% of the issue proceeds, then what is the after-tax cost of debt? Disregard the tax shield from the amortization of flotation costs.

Challenging Problems 15–17

11–15 WACC Estimation

On January 1, the total market value of the Tysseland Company was $60 million. During the year, the company plans to raise and invest $30 million in new projects. The firm's present market value capital structure, shown below, is considered to be optimal. There is no short-term debt.

Debt	$30,000,000
Common equity	30,000,000
Total capital	$60,000,000

New bonds will have an 8% coupon rate, and they will be sold at par. Common stock is currently selling at $30 a share. The stockholders' required rate of return is estimated to be 12%, consisting of a dividend yield of 4% and an expected constant growth rate of 8%. (The next expected dividend is $1.20, so the dividend yield is $1.20/$30 = 4%.) The marginal tax rate is 40%.

a. In order to maintain the present capital structure, how much of the new investment must be financed by common equity?

b. Assuming there is sufficient cash flow for Tysseland to maintain its target capital structure without issuing additional shares of equity, what is its WACC?

c. Suppose now that there is not enough internal cash flow and the firm must issue new shares of stock. Qualitatively speaking, what will happen to the WACC? No numbers are required to answer this question.

11-16 Market Value Capital Structure
Suppose the Schoof Company has this *book value* balance sheet:

Current assets	$ 30,000,000	Current liabilities	$ 20,000,000
		Notes payable	10,000,000
Fixed assets	70,000,000	Long-term debt	30,000,000
		Common stock (1 million shares)	1,000,000
		Retained earnings	39,000,000
Total assets	$100,000,000	Total liabilities and equity	$100,000,000

The notes payable are to banks, and the interest rate on this debt is 10%, the same as the rate on new bank loans. These bank loans are not used for seasonal financing but instead are part of the company's permanent capital structure. The long-term debt consists of 30,000 bonds, each with a par value of $1,000, an annual coupon interest rate of 6%, and a 20-year maturity. The going rate of interest on new long-term debt, r_d, is 10%, and this is the present yield to maturity on the bonds. The common stock sells at a price of $60 per share. Calculate the firm's *market value* capital structure.

11-17 WACC Estimation
The table below gives the balance sheet for Travelers' Inn Inc. (TII), a company that was formed by merging a number of regional motel chains.

Travelers' Inn: December 31, 2015 (Millions of Dollars)

Cash	$ 10	Accounts payable	$ 10
Accounts receivable	20	Accruals	10
Inventories	20	Short-term debt	5
Current assets	$ 50	Current liabilities	$ 25
Net fixed assets	50	Long-term debt	30
		Preferred stock	5
		Common equity	
		Common stock	$ 10
		Retained earnings	30
		Total common equity	$ 40
Total assets	$100	Total liabilities and equity	$100

The following facts also apply to TII.

(1) Short-term debt consists of bank loans that currently cost 10%, with interest payable quarterly. These loans are used to finance receivables and inventories on a seasonal basis, so bank loans are zero in the off-season.

(2) The long-term debt consists of 20-year, semiannual payment mortgage bonds with a coupon rate of 8%. Currently, these bonds provide a yield to investors of $r_d = 12\%$. If new bonds were sold, they would have a 12% yield to maturity.

(3) TII's perpetual preferred stock has a $100 par value, pays a quarterly dividend of $2, and has a yield to investors of 11%. New perpetual preferred stock would have to provide the same yield to investors, and the company would incur a 5% flotation cost to sell it.

(4) The company has 4 million shares of common stock outstanding. $P_0 = \$20$, but the stock has recently traded in the price range from $17 to $23. $D_0 = \$1$ and $EPS_0 = \$2$. ROE based on average equity was 24% in 2015, but management expects to increase this return on equity to 30%; however, security analysts and investors generally are not aware of management's optimism in this regard.

(5) Betas, as reported by security analysts, range from 1.3 to 1.7; the T-bond rate is 10%; and RP_M is estimated by various brokerage houses to range from 4.5% to 5.5%. Some brokerage house analysts report forecasted growth dividend growth rates in the range of 10% to 15% over the foreseeable future.

(6) TII's financial vice president recently polled some pension fund investment managers who hold TII's securities regarding what minimum rate of return on TII's common would make them willing to buy the common rather than TII bonds, given that the bonds yielded 12%. The responses suggested a risk premium over TII bonds of 4 to 6 percentage points.

(7) TII is in the 40% federal-plus-state tax bracket.

(8) TII's principal investment banker predicts a decline in interest rates, with r_d falling to 10% and the T-bond rate to 8%, although the bank acknowledges that an increase in the expected inflation rate could lead to an increase rather than a decrease in interest rates.

Assume that you were recently hired by TII as a financial analyst and that your boss, the treasurer, has asked you to estimate the company's WACC under the assumption that no new equity will be issued. Your cost of capital should be appropriate for use in evaluating projects that are in the same risk class as the assets TII now operates.

Spreadsheet Problem

11–18 Build a Model: WACC

Start with the partial model in the file *Ch11 P18 Build a Model.xls* on the textbook's Web site. The stock of Gao Computing sells for $50, and last year's dividend was $2.10. A flotation cost of 10% would be required to issue new common stock. Gao's preferred stock pays a dividend of $3.30 per share, and new preferred stock could be sold at a price to net the company $30 per share. Security analysts are projecting that the common dividend will grow at a rate of 7% a year. The firm can issue additional long-term debt at an interest rate (or a before-tax cost) of 10%, and its marginal tax rate is 35%. The market risk premium is 6%, the risk-free rate is 6.5%, and Gao's beta is 0.83. In its cost-of-capital calculations, Gao uses a target capital structure with 45% debt, 5% preferred stock, and 50% common equity.

a. Calculate the cost of each capital component—in other words, the after-tax cost of debt, the cost of preferred stock (including flotation costs), and the cost of equity (ignoring flotation costs). Use both the DCF method and the CAPM method to find the cost of equity.

b. Calculate the cost of new stock using the DCF model.

c. What is the cost of new common stock based on the CAPM? (*Hint:* Find the difference between r_e and r_s as determined by the DCF method and then add that difference to the CAPM value for r_s.)

d. Assuming that Gao will not issue new equity and will continue to use the same target capital structure, what is the company's WACC?

e. Suppose Gao is evaluating three projects with the following characteristics.

(1) Each project has a cost of $1 million. They will all be financed using the target mix of long-term debt, preferred stock, and common equity. The cost of the common equity for each project should be based on the beta estimated for the project. All equity will come from reinvested earnings.

(2) Equity invested in Project A would have a beta of 0.5 and an expected return of 9.0%.

(3) Equity invested in Project B would have a beta of 1.0 and an expected return of 10.0%.

(4) Equity invested in Project C would have a beta of 2.0 and an expected return of 11.0%.

f. Analyze the company's situation, and explain why each project should be accepted or rejected.

MINI CASE

During the last few years, Harry Davis Industries has been too constrained by the high cost of capital to make many capital investments. Recently, though, capital costs have been declining, and the company has decided to look seriously at a major expansion program proposed by the marketing department. Assume that you are an assistant to Leigh Jones, the financial vice president. Your first task is to estimate Harry Davis' cost of capital. Jones has provided you with the following data, which she believes may be relevant to your task:

(1) The firm's tax rate is 40%.
(2) The current price of Harry Davis' 12% coupon, semiannual payment, noncallable bonds with 15 years remaining to maturity is $1,153.72. Harry Davis does not use short-term interest-bearing debt on a permanent basis. New bonds would be privately placed with no flotation cost.
(3) The current price of the firm's 10%, $100 par value, quarterly dividend, perpetual preferred stock is $116.95. Harry Davis would incur flotation costs equal to 5% of the proceeds on a new issue.
(4) Harry Davis' common stock is currently selling at $50 per share. Its last dividend (D_0) was $3.12, and dividends are expected to grow at a constant rate of 5.8% in the foreseeable future. Harry Davis' beta is 1.2, the yield on T-bonds is 5.6%, and the market risk premium is estimated to be 6%. For the own-bond-yield-plus-judgmental-risk-premium approach, the firm uses a 3.2% risk premium.
(5) Harry Davis' target capital structure is 30% long-term debt, 10% preferred stock, and 60% common equity.

To help you structure the task, Leigh Jones has asked you to answer the following questions.

a. (1) What sources of capital should be included when you estimate Harry Davis' weighted average cost of capital?

(2) Should the component costs be figured on a before-tax or an after-tax basis?
(3) Should the costs be historical (embedded) costs or new (marginal) costs?

b. What is the market interest rate on Harry Davis' debt, and what is the component cost of this debt for WACC purposes?

c. (1) What is the firm's cost of preferred stock?
(2) Harry Davis' preferred stock is riskier to investors than its debt, yet the preferred stock's yield to investors is lower than the yield to maturity on the debt. Does this suggest that you have made a mistake? (*Hint:* Think about taxes.)

d. (1) What are the two primary ways companies raise common equity?
(2) Why is there a cost associated with reinvested earnings?
(3) Harry Davis doesn't plan to issue new shares of common stock. Using the CAPM approach, what is Harry Davis' estimated cost of equity?

e. (1) What is the estimated cost of equity using the discounted cash flow (DCF) approach?
(2) Suppose the firm has historically earned 15% on equity (ROE) and has paid out 62% of earnings, and suppose investors expect similar values to obtain in the future. How could you use this information to estimate the future dividend growth rate, and what growth rate would you get? Is this consistent with the 5.8% growth rate given earlier?
(3) Could the DCF method be applied if the growth rate were not constant? How?

f. What is the cost of equity based on the own-bond-yield-plus-judgmental-risk-premium method?

g. What is your final estimate for the cost of equity, r_s?

h. What is Harry Davis' weighted average cost of capital (WACC)?

i. What factors influence a company's WACC?

j. Should the company use its overall WACC as the hurdle rate for each of its divisions?

k. What procedures can be used to estimate the risk-adjusted cost of capital for a particular division? What approaches are used to measure a division's beta?

l. Harry Davis is interested in establishing a new division that will focus primarily on developing new Internet-based projects. In trying to determine the cost of capital for this new division, you discover that specialized firms involved in similar projects have, on average, the following characteristics: (1) their capital structure is 10% debt and 90% common equity, (2) their cost of debt is typically 12%, and (3) they have a beta of 1.7. Given this information, what would your estimate be for the new division's cost of capital?

m. What are three types of project risk? How can each type of risk be considered when thinking about the new division's cost of capital?

n. Explain in words why new common stock that is raised externally has a higher percentage cost than equity that is raised internally by retaining earnings.

o. (1) Harry Davis estimates that if it issues new common stock, the flotation cost will be 15%. Harry Davis incorporates the flotation costs into the DCF approach. What is the estimated cost of newly issued common stock, taking into account the flotation cost?

   (2) Suppose Harry Davis issues 30-year debt with a par value of $1,000 and a coupon rate of 10%, paid annually. If flotation costs are 2%, what is the after-tax cost of debt for the new bond issue?

p. What four common mistakes in estimating the WACC should Harry Davis avoid?

SELECTED ADDITIONAL CASES

The following cases from CengageCompose cover many of the concepts discussed in this chapter and are available at http://compose.cengage.com.

Klein-Brigham Series:

Case 42, "West Coast Semiconductor"; Case 54, "Ace Repair"; Case 55, "Premier Paint & Body"; Case 6, "Randolph Corporation"; Case 75, "The Western Company"; and Case 81, "Pressed Paper Products."

Brigham-Buzzard Series:

Case 5, "Powerline Network Corporation (Determining the Cost of Capital)."

Project Valuation

Capital Budgeting: Decision Criteria

In Chapters 12 and 13, we discuss *capital budgeting*. Here *capital* refers to long-term assets used in production, and a budget is a plan that outlines projected expenditures during a future period. Thus, the *capital budget* is a summary of planned investments of assets that will last for more than a year, and **capital budgeting** is the whole process of analyzing projects and deciding which ones to accept and thus include in the capital budget. Chapter 12 explains the measures companies use to evaluate projects, including the measures' strengths and weaknesses. Chapter 12 also describes several other issues that arise in the capital budgeting process. Chapter 13 explains how to estimate cash flows and evaluate project risk.

Beginning-of-Chapter Questions

As you read the chapter, consider how you would answer the following questions. You *should not* necessarily be able to answer the questions before you read the chapter. Rather, you should use them to get a sense of the issues covered in the chapter. After reading the chapter, you should be able to give at least partial answers to the questions, and you should be able to give better answers after the chapter has been discussed in class. Note, too, that it is often useful, when answering conceptual questions, to use hypothetical data to illustrate your answer. We illustrate the answers with an *Excel* model that is available on the textbook's Web site. Accessing the model and working through it is a useful exercise, and it provides insights that are useful when answering the questions.

1. Describe the **six primary capital budgeting decision criteria**. What are their pros and cons, and how are they related to maximizing shareholder wealth? Should managers use just one criterion, or are there good reasons for using two or more criteria in the decision process?

2. Why do conflicts sometimes arise between the **net present value (NPV)** and **internal rate of return (IRR)** methods; that is, what conditions can lead to conflicts? Can similar conflicts arise between **modified internal rate of return (MIRR)** and NPV rankings, or between rankings by the MIRR and IRR methods?

3. If management's goal is to maximize shareholder wealth, should it focus on the regular IRR or the MIRR? Explain your answer.

4. Under what conditions might you find more than one IRR for a project? How would you decide whether or not to accept the project? If you were comparing two mutually exclusive projects, one with a single IRR of 12% and the other with two different IRRs of 10% and 15%, how should you choose between the projects?

5. What is the **unequal life problem**, under what conditions is it relevant, and how should it be dealt with?

6. What is a **post-audit**, and what is the purpose of this audit?

7. What is **capital rationing**, what conditions lead to it, and how should it be dealt with?

CORPORATE VALUATION AND CAPITAL BUDGETING

You can calculate the cash flows (CF) for a project in much the same way as you do for a firm. When the project's cash flows are discounted at the appropriate risk-adjusted weighted average cost of capital ("r" for simplicity), the result is the project's value. When valuing an entire firm you discount its free cash flows at the overall weighted average cost of capital, but when valuing a project you discount its cash flows at the project's own risk-adjusted cost of capital. The firm's free cash flows are the total of all the net cash flows from its existing projects. Thus, if a project is accepted and put into operation, it will provide cash flows that add to the firm's free cash flows and thus to the firm's value.

Subtracting the initial cost of the project from the discounted future expected cash flows gives the project's net present value (NPV). A project that has a positive NPV adds value to the firm. In fact, the firm's Market Value Added (MVA) is the sum of all its projects' NPVs. The key point, though, is that the process of evaluating projects, or capital budgeting, is critical to a firm's success.

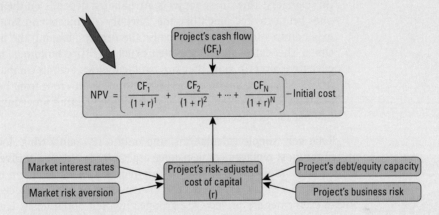

$$NPV = \left[\frac{CF_1}{(1+r)^1} + \frac{CF_2}{(1+r)^2} + \cdots + \frac{CF_N}{(1+r)^N} \right] - \text{Initial cost}$$

Source: From *Financial Management: Theory & Practice,* 2013, by Brigham and Ehrhardt. © Cengage Learning.

12-1 An Overview of Capital Budgeting

A firm's ability to remain competitive and to survive depends on a constant flow of ideas for new products, improvements in existing products, and ways to operate more efficiently. Therefore, it is vital for a company to evaluate proposed projects accurately. However, analyzing project proposals requires skill, effort, and time. For certain types of projects, an extremely detailed analysis may be warranted, whereas simpler procedures are adequate for other projects. Accordingly, firms generally categorize projects and analyze those in each category some what differently:

1. *Replacement needed to continue profitable operations.* An example would be replacing an essential pump on a profitable offshore oil platform. The platform manager could make this investment without an elaborate review process.
2. *Replacement to reduce costs.* An example would be the replacement of serviceable but obsolete equipment in order to lower costs. A fairly detailed analysis would be needed, with more detail required for larger expenditures.

3. *Expansion of existing products or markets.* These decisions require a forecast of growth in demand, so a more detailed analysis is required. Go/no-go decisions are generally made at a higher level in the organization than are replacement decisions.

4. *Expansion into new products or markets.* These investments involve strategic decisions that could change the fundamental nature of the business. A detailed analysis is required, and top officers make the final decision, possibly with board approval.

5. *Contraction decisions.* Especially during bad recessions, companies often find themselves with more capacity than they are likely to need. Rather than continue to operate plants at, say, 50% of capacity and incur losses as a result of excessive fixed costs, management decides to downsize. That generally requires payments to laid-off workers and additional costs for shutting down selected operations. These decisions are made at the board level.

6. *Safety and/or environmental projects.* Expenditures necessary to comply with environmental orders, labor agreements, or insurance policy terms fall into this category. How these projects are handled depends on their size, with small ones being treated much like the Category 1 projects and large ones requiring expenditures that might even cause the firm to abandon the line of business.

7. *Other.* This catch-all includes items such as office buildings, parking lots, and executive aircraft. How they are handled varies among companies.

8. *Mergers.* Buying a whole firm (or division) is different from buying a machine or building a new plant. Still, basic capital budgeting procedures are used when making merger decisions.

Relatively simple calculations, and only a few supporting documents, are required for most replacement decisions, especially maintenance investments in profitable plants. More detailed analyses are required as we move on to more complex expansion decisions, especially for investments in new products or areas. Also, within each category projects are grouped by their dollar costs: Larger investments require increasingly detailed analysis and approval at higher levels. Thus, a plant manager might be authorized to approve maintenance expenditures up to $10,000 using a simple payback analysis, but the full board of directors might have to approve decisions that involve either amounts greater than $1 million or expansions into new products or markets.

If a firm has capable and imaginative executives and employees, and if its incentive system is working properly, then many ideas for capital investment will be forthcoming. Some ideas will be good and should be funded, but others should be killed. Therefore, the following measures have been established for screening projects and deciding which to accept or reject:[1]

1. Net Present Value (NPV)
2. Internal Rate of Return (IRR)
3. Modified Internal Rate of Return (MIRR)
4. Profitability Index (PI)
5. Regular Payback
6. Discounted Payback

---

1. One other rarely used measure, the Accounting Rate of Return, is covered in the chapter's *Excel Tool Kit model* and *Web Extension 12A.*

As we shall see, the NPV is the best single measure, primarily because it directly relates to the firm's central goal of maximizing intrinsic value. However, all of the measures provide some useful information, and all are used in practice.

12-2 The First Step in Project Analysis

In the sections that follow, we will evaluate two projects that Guyton Products Company (GPC) is considering. GPC is a high-tech "lab-bench-to-market" development company that takes cutting-edge research advances and translates them into consumer products. GPC has recently licensed a nano-fabrication coating technology from a university that promises to significantly increase the efficiency with which solar energy can be harvested and stored as heat. GPC is considering using this technology in two different product lines. In the first, code-named "Project S" for "solid," the technology would be used to coat rock and concrete structures to be used as passive heat sinks and sources for energy-efficient residential and commercial buildings. In the second, code-named "Project L" for "liquid," it would be used to coat the collectors in a high-efficiency solar water heater. GPC must decide whether to undertake either of these two projects.

The first step in project analysis is to estimate the project's expected cash flows. We will explain cash flow estimation for Project L in Chapter 13, including the impact of depreciation, taxes, and salvage values. However, we want to focus now on the six evaluation measures, so we will specify the cash flows used in the following examples.[2]

Recall from Chapter 11 that a company's weighted average cost of capital (WACC) reflects the average risk of all the company's projects and that the appropriate cost of capital for a particular project may differ from the company's WACC. Chapter 13 explains how to estimate a project's risk-adjusted cost of capital, but for now assume that Projects L and S are equally risky and both have a 10% cost of capital.

Figure 12-1 shows the inputs for GPC's Projects S and L, including the projects' cost of capital and the time line of expected cash flows (with the initial cost shown at Year 0). Although Projects S and L are GPC's "solid" and "liquid" coating projects, you may also find it helpful to think of S and L as standing for *Short* and *Long*. Project S is a short-term project in the sense that its biggest cash inflows occur relatively soon; Project L has more total cash inflows, but its largest cash flows occur in the later years.

The second step in project analysis is to calculate the evaluation measures, which are shown in Panel B of Figure 12-1. The following sections explain how each measure is calculated.

---

2. We will see in Chapter 13 that project cash flows are, in fact, free cash flows as calculated in Chapter 6 and used in Chapter 8 to estimate corporate value.

FIGURE 12-1 Cash Flows and Selected Evaluation Measures for Projects S and L (Millions of Dollars)

	A	B	C	D	E	F
19	**Panel A: Inputs for Project Cash Flows and Cost of Capital, r**					
20						
21	**INPUTS:**					
22	r = 10%					
23		**Initial Cost and Expected Cash Flows**				
24	**Year**	**0**	**1**	**2**	**3**	**4**
25	**Project S**	−$10,000	$5,300	$4,300	$1,874	$1,500
26	**Project L**	−$10,000	$1,900	$2,700	$2,345	$7,800
27						
28	**Panel B: Summary of Selected Evaluation Measures**					
29			**Project S**	**Project L**		
30	Net present value, NPV		$804.38	$1,048.02		
31	Internal rate of return, IRR		14.69%	13.79%		
32	Modified IRR, MIRR		12.15%	10.19%		
33	Profitability index, PI		1.08	1.10		
34	Payback		2.21	3.39		
35	Discounted payback		3.21	3.80		

Microsoft Excel® is a registered trademark of Microsoft Corporation. © 2014 Microsoft.

SELF TEST   What is the first step in project analysis?

12-3 Net Present Value (NPV)

The **net present value (NPV)** is defined as the present value of a project's expected cash flows (including its initial cost) discounted at the appropriate risk-adjusted rate. The NPV measures how much wealth the project contributes to shareholders. When deciding which projects to accept, NPV is generally regarded as the best single criterion.

12-3a Calculating NPV

We can calculate NPV with the following steps.

1. Calculate the present value of each cash flow discounted at the project's risk-adjusted cost of capital, which is r = 10% in our example.
2. The sum of the discounted cash flows is defined as the project's NPV.

   The equation for the NPV is:

(12–1)

$$NPV = CF_0 + \frac{CF_1}{(1 + r)^1} + \frac{CF_2}{(1 + r)^2} + \cdots + \frac{CF_N}{(1 + r)^N}$$

$$= \sum_{t=0}^{N} \frac{CF_t}{(1 + r)^t}$$

Applying Equation 12-1 to Project S, we have:

$$NPV_S = -\$10,000 + \frac{\$5,300}{(1.10)^1} + \frac{\$4,300}{(1.10)^2} + \frac{\$1,874}{(1.10)^3} + \frac{\$1,500}{(1.10)^4}$$

$$= -\$10,000 + \$4,818.18 + \$3,553.72 + \$1,407.96 + \$1,024.52$$

$$= \$804.38 \text{ million}$$

Here CF_t is the expected net cash flow at Time t, r is the project's risk-adjusted cost of capital (or WACC), and N is its life. Projects generally require an initial investment—for example, developing the product, buying the equipment needed to make it, building a factory, and stocking inventory. The initial investment is a negative cash flow. For Projects S and L, only CF_0 is negative; large projects often have outflows for several years before cash inflows begin.

Figure 12-2 shows the cash flow time line for Project S as taken from Figure 12-1. The initial cash flow is $-\$10,000$, which is not discounted because it occurs at t = 0. The PV of each cash inflow and the sum of the PVs are shown in Column B. You could find the PVs of the cash flows with a calculator or with *Excel*, and the result would be the numbers in Column B. When we sum the PVs of the inflows and subtract the cost, the result is $804.38, which is NPV_S. The NPV for Project L, $1,048.02, can be found similarly, but there is a much easier way. The bottom section of Figure 12-2 shows how to use *Excel's* NPV function to calculate Project L's NPV. Notice that the NPV function uses the range of cash flows beginning with the Year 1 cash flow, not the Year 0 cash flow. Therefore, you must add the Year 0 cash flow to the result of the NPV function to calculate the net present value.

It is also possible to calculate the NPV with a financial calculator. As we discussed in Web Chapter 28, all calculators have a "cash flow register" that can be used to evaluate uneven cash flows such as those for Projects S and L. Equation 12-1 is programmed into these calculators, and all you need to do is enter the cash flows

See ***Ch12 Tool Kit.xls*** on the textbook's Web site.

FIGURE 12-2   **Finding the NPV for Projects S and L (Millions of Dollars)**

	A	B	C	D	E	F
46	INPUTS:					
47	r =	10%				
48			**Initial Cost and Expected Cash Flows**			
49	**Year**	**0**	**1**	**2**	**3**	**4**
50	**Project S**	**−$10,000**	**$5,300**	**$4,300**	**$1,874**	**$1,500**
51		4,818.18	← ← ↵	↓	↓	↓
52		3,553.72	← ← ← ← ← ← − ← ← ↵		↓	↓
53		1,407.96	← ← ← ← ← ← ← ← ← ← ← − ← ← ↵			↓
54		1,024.52	← ← ← ← ← ← ← ← ← ← ← ← ← ← ← ← ← − ← ← ↵			
55	**NPV_S =**	**$804.38**	Long way:			
56			**Sum the PVs of the CFs to find NPV**			
57			**Initial Cost and Expected Cash Flows**			
58	**Year**	**0**	**1**	**2**	**3**	**4**
59	**Project L**	**−$10,000**	**$1,900**	**$2,700**	**$2,345**	**$7,800**
60	**NPV_L =**	**$1,048.02**	**Short way: Use *Excel's* NPV function =NPV(B47,C59:F59)+B59**			
61						

(with the correct signs) along with r = I/YR = 10. Once you have entered the data, press the NPV key to get the answer, 804.38, on the screen.[3]

12-3b Applying NPV as an Evaluation Measure

Before using these NPVs in the decision process, we need to know whether Projects S and L are **independent** or **mutually exclusive**. The cash flows for independent projects are not affected by other projects. For example, if Walmart were considering a new store in Boise and another in Atlanta, those projects would be independent. If both had positive NPVs, Walmart should accept both.

Mutually exclusive projects, on the other hand, are two different ways of accomplishing the same result, so if one project is accepted then the other must be rejected. A conveyor-belt system to move goods in a warehouse and a fleet of forklifts for the same purpose would be mutually exclusive—accepting one implies rejecting the other.

What should the decision be if Projects S and L are independent? In this case, both should be accepted because both have positive NPVs and thus add value to the firm. However, if they are mutually exclusive, then Project L should be chosen because it has the higher NPV and thus adds more value than S. We can summarize these criteria with the following rules.

1. *Independent projects:* If NPV exceeds zero, accept the project. Because S and L both have positive NPVs, accept them both if they are independent.
2. *Mutually exclusive projects:* Accept the project with the highest positive NPV. If no project has a positive NPV, then reject them all. If S and L are mutually exclusive, the NPV criterion would select L.

Projects must be either independent or mutually exclusive, so one or the other of these rules applies to every project.

Why is NPV the primary capital budgeting decision criterion?

What is the difference between "independent" and "mutually exclusive" projects?

Projects SS and LL have the following cash flows:

	End-of-Year Cash Flows			
	0	**1**	**2**	**3**
SS	−700	500	300	100
LL	−700	100	300	600

If the cost of capital is 10%, then what are the projects' NPVs? (**NPV$_{SS}$ = $77.61; NPV$_{LL}$ = $89.63**)

What project or set of projects would be in your capital budget if SS and LL were: (a) independent or (b) mutually exclusive? (**Both; LL**)

3. The keystrokes for finding the NPV are shown for several calculators in the calculator tutorials we provide on the textbook's Web site.

12-4 **Internal Rate of Return (IRR)**

In Chapter 4, we discussed the yield to maturity on a bond, and we explained that if you hold a bond to maturity then you will earn the yield to maturity on your investment. The YTM is found as the discount rate that forces the present value of the cash inflows to equal the price of the bond and, as the name implies, is the rate of return you would actually earn if you held the bond to maturity. This same concept is used in capital budgeting when we calculate a project's **internal rate of return**, or **IRR**. A project's IRR is the discount rate that forces the PV of the expected future cash flows to equal the initial cash flow. This is equivalent to forcing the NPV to equal zero.

Why is the discount rate that causes a project's NPV to equal zero helpful as an evaluation measure? The reason is that the IRR is an estimate of the rate of return the company would actually earn if it invested in the project. If this return exceeds the opportunity cost of the funds used to finance the project, then the difference benefits the firm's stockholders. On the other hand, if the IRR is less than the cost of capital, stockholders suffer a loss in value.

12-4a **Calculating the IRR**

To calculate the IRR, begin with Equation 12-1 for the NPV, replace r in the denominator with the term "IRR," and choose a value of IRR so that the NPV is equal to zero. This transforms Equation 12-1 into Equation 12-2, the one used to find the IRR. The rate that forces NPV to equal zero is the IRR.[4]

For Project S, we have:

$$\text{NPV} = \text{CF}_0 + \frac{\text{CF}_1}{(1 + \text{IRR})^1} + \frac{\text{CF}_2}{(1 + \text{IRR})^2} + \cdots + \frac{\text{CF}_N}{(1 + \text{IRR})^N} = 0$$

$$= \sum_{t=0}^{N} \frac{\text{CF}_t}{(1 + \text{IRR})^t} = 0$$

(12–2)

$$\text{NPVs} = 0 = -\$10{,}000 + \frac{\$5{,}300}{(1 + \text{IRR})^1} + \frac{\$4{,}300}{(1 + \text{IRR})^2} + \frac{\$1{,}874}{(1 + \text{IRR})^3} + \frac{\$1{,}500}{(1 + \text{IRR})^4}$$

Figure 12-3 illustrates the process for finding the IRR of Project S.

Three procedures can be used to find the IRR:

1. *Trial-and-error.* We could use a trial-and-error procedure: Try a discount rate, see if the equation solves to zero, and if it doesn't, try a different rate. Continue until you find the rate that forces the NPV to zero, and that rate will be the IRR. This procedure is rarely used, however. IRR usually is calculated using either a financial calculator or *Excel* (or some other computer program), as described below.
2. *Calculator solution.* Enter the cash flows into the calculator's cash flow register just as you did to find the NPV, and then press the calculator key labeled "IRR."

---

4. For a large, complex project like a power plant, costs are incurred for several years before cash inflows begin. That simply means that we have a number of negative cash flows before the positive cash flows begin.

FIGURE 12-3   Finding the IRR for Projects S and L (Millions of Dollars)

	A	B	C	D	E	F
73	INPUTS:					
74		**Initial Cost and Expected Cash Flows**				
75	Year	0	1	2	3	4
76	Project S	−$10,000	$5,300	$4,300	$1,874	$1,500
77		4,621.33	← ← ← ↵	↓	↓	↓
78		3,269.26	← ← ← ← ← ← ←– ← ← ↵		↓	↓
79		1,242.34	← ← ← ← ← ← ← ← ← ← ← ← ← ← ↵			↓
80		867.07	← ↵			
81			Long way: Try a value for r, sum the PVs of the CFs to find NPV. If NPV is not zero, try another value for r. Or use Goal Seek to find the value of r that makes the NPV = 0.			
82	NPV$_S$ =	$0.00				
83						
84	IRR = r =	14.69%	Value of r that makes NPV = 0.			
85						
86		**Initial Cost and Expected Cash Flows**				
87	Year	0	1	2	3	4
88	Project L	−$10,000	$1,900	$2,700	$2,345	$7,800
89	IRR$_L$ =	13.79%	Short way: Use *Excel's* IRR function =IRR(B88:F88)			
90						

Microsoft Excel® is a registered trademark of Microsoft Corporation. © 2014 Microsoft.

See **Ch12 Tool Kit.xls** on the textbook's Web site.

Instantly, you get the internal rate of return. Here are the values for Projects S and L:

$$IRR_S = 14.686\%$$
$$IRR_L = 13.786\%$$

3. *Excel solution.* It is even easier to find IRRs using *Excel,* as Figure 12-3 shows for Project L. Notice that with *Excel's* IRR function, the range in the function includes the initial cash flow at Year 0. This is in contrast to the NPV function's range, which starts with the Year 1 cash flow. Be alert to this difference when you use these functions, because it is easy to mis-specify the range of inputs.

12-4b A Potential Problem with the IRR: Multiple Internal Rates of Return[5]

If a project has a *normal* cash flow pattern, which is one or more cash outflows followed only by cash inflows (or the reverse, one or more cash inflows followed only by outflows), then the project can have at most one positive IRR. Here are some examples of normal cash flow patterns:

Normal: − + + +   or   − − + + +   or   + + − −

Notice that the sign of the cash flows only changes once for any of these examples, either from negative to positive or positive to negative.

---

5. This section is relatively technical, and some instructors may choose to omit it without loss of continuity.

However, some projects have cash flows with signs that change more than once. For example, consider a strip coal mine where the company first spends money to buy the property and prepare the site for mining. The mining company has positive inflows for several years and then spends more money to return the land to its original condition. For this project, the cash flow sign goes from negative to positive and then changes again from positive to negative. This is a *nonnormal* cash flow pattern; here are some examples:

Nonnormal: $- + + + + -$ or $- + + + - + + +$

If a project's cash flows have a nonnormal pattern (i.e., the cash flows have more than one sign change), it is possible for the project to have more than one positive IRR—that is, **multiple IRRs**.[6]

To illustrate multiple IRRs, suppose a firm is considering a potential strip mine (Project M) that has a cost of $1.6 million and will produce a cash flow of $10 million at the end of Year 1; however, the firm must spend $10 million to restore the land to its original condition at the end of Year 2. Therefore, the project's expected net cash flows are as follows (in millions):

Year	0	1	2
Cash flows	−$1.6	+$10	−$10

We can substitute these values into Equation 12-2 and then solve for the IRR:

$$NPV = \frac{-\$1.6 \text{ million}}{(1 + IRR)^0} + \frac{\$10 \text{ million}}{(1 + IRR)^1} + \frac{-\$10 \text{ million}}{(1 + IRR)^2} = 0$$

See **Ch12 Tool Kit.xls** on the textbook's Web site.

For Project M's cash flows, the NPV equals zero when IRR = 25%, but it also equals zero when IRR = 400%.[7] Therefore, Project M has one IRR of 25% and another of 400%. Are either of these IRRs helpful in deciding whether to proceed with Project M? No! To see this, look at Figure 12-4, which shows Project M's NPV for different costs of capital. Notice that Project M has a negative NPV for costs of capital less than 25%. Therefore, Project M should be rejected for reasonable costs of capital.

When you evaluate a project, always look at the projected cash flows and count the number of times that the sign changes. If the sign changes more than once, don't even calculate the IRR, because it is at best useless and at worst misleading.

---

6. Equation 12-2 is a polynomial of degree n, so it has n different roots, or solutions. All except one of the roots are imaginary numbers when investments have normal cash flows (one or more cash outflows followed by cash inflows), so in the normal case only one value of IRR appears, and it may be positive, negative, or zero. However, the possibility of multiple real roots, and hence of multiple IRRs, arises when negative net cash flows occur after the project has been placed in operation.

7. If you attempt to find Project M's IRR with an HP calculator, you will get an error message, whereas TI calculators give only the IRR closest to zero. When you encounter either situation, you can find the approximate IRRs by first calculating NPVs using several different values for r = I/YR, constructing a graph with NPV on the vertical axis and cost of capital on the horizontal axis, and then visually determining approximately where NPV = 0. The intersection with the x-axis gives a rough idea of the IRRs' values. With some calculators and with *Excel*, you can find both IRRs by entering guesses, as we explain in our calculator and *Excel* tutorials.

| FIGURE 12-4 | Graph for Multiple IRRs: Project M (Millions of Dollars) |

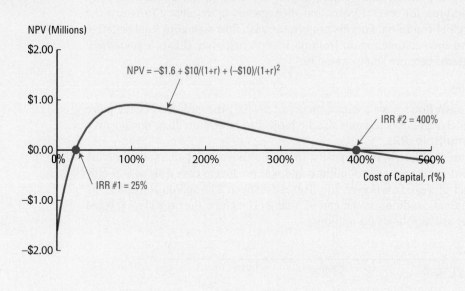

NPV (Millions)

$$NPV = -\$1.6 + \$10/(1+r) + (-\$10)/(1+r)^2$$

IRR #2 = 400%

IRR #1 = 25%

Cost of Capital, r(%)

12-4c Potential Problems When Using the IRR to Evaluate Mutually Exclusive Projects

Potential problems can arise when using the IRR to choose among mutually exclusive projects. Projects S and L are independent, but suppose for illustrative purposes that they are mutually exclusive. Their NPVs and IRRs are shown below:

	NPV	**IRR**
Project S	$804.38	14.69%
Project L	$1,048.02	13.79%

If using NPV as a decision criterion, Project L is preferred. But Project S is preferred if using IRR as a decision criterion. How do we resolve this conflict?

Resolving a Conflict between the IRR and NPV for Mutually Exclusive Projects: Pick the Project with the Highest NPV

Consider these two hypothetical games we offer our students in class. In Game 1, we offer to give a student $2 at the end of class if the student will give us $1 at the beginning. Assuming we can be trusted, Game 1 has a 100% rate of return. In Game 2, we offer to give a student $25 at the end of class in exchange for $20 at the beginning of class. The games are mutually exclusive and may not be repeated—a student can choose only one game and can play it only once. Which game would you choose? If you are like our students, you would choose Game 2 because your wealth goes up by $5, which is better than the $1 increase in wealth offered by Game 1. So even though Game 1 has a higher rate of return, people prefer more wealth to less wealth.

The same is true for the shareholders. If projects are mutually exclusive, managers should choose the project that provides the greatest increase in wealth (as measured by the NPV) even though it may not have the highest rate of return (as measured by the IRR). Therefore, if Projects S and L were mutually exclusive, managers would choose Project L because it has a higher NPV and generates more wealth for shareholders.

The Causes of Possible Conflicts between the IRR and NPV for Mutually Exclusive Projects: Timing and Scale Differences

Figure 12-5 illustrates the situation with a **net present value profile** for each project. This profile has a project's NPV plotted on the y-axis for different costs of capital. Notice the IRR for each project, which is the point at which the project has a zero NPV (it is also the place where the curve crosses the x-axis). As the figure shows, Project S has the largest IRR (the curve for Project S crosses the x-axis to the right of Project L's curve). Notice the NPV for each project when the cost of capital is 10%. Project L's NPV is above that of Project S.

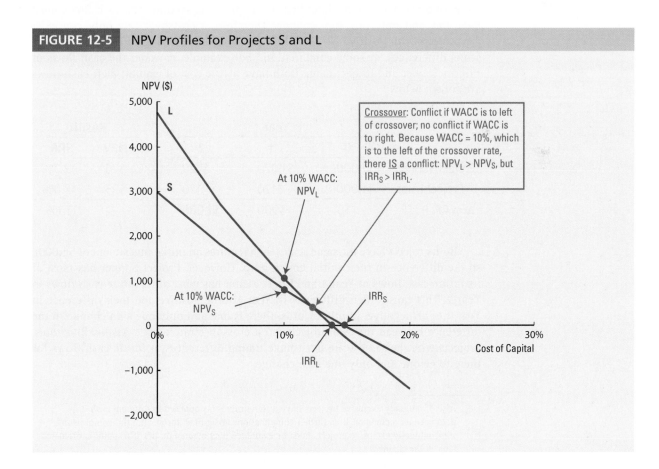

FIGURE 12-5   NPV Profiles for Projects S and L

The two NPV profile lines cross at a cost of capital of 12.274%, which is called the **crossover rate**. Find the crossover rate by calculating the IRR of the differences in the projects' cash flows, as demonstrated below:

	Year				
	0	**1**	**2**	**3**	**4**
Project S:	−$10,000	$5,300	$4,300	$1,874	$1,500
Project L:	−10,000	1,900	2,700	2,345	7,800
$\Delta = CF_S - CF_L$:	$0	$3,400	$1,600	−$471	−$6,300

$$\text{IRR } \Delta = 12.274\%$$

If the cost of capital is *less* than the crossover rate, Project L has the higher NPV. But if the cost of capital is *greater* than the crossover rate, Project S has the higher NPV.

Many projects don't have different rankings—if a project has a larger NPV, it usually has a higher IRR. But for projects whose rankings conflict, you must determine the source of the conflict. Note that in order for a conflict to exist, both projects must have positive NPVs and there must be a crossover rate. For a crossover rate to exist, the difference in cash flows between the two projects must have a normal pattern, as described in the previous section: The cash flows must have one and only one sign change. Therefore, a crossover rate only can exist for projects with positive NPVs if the cash flows have timing differences, size (or scale) differences, or some combination.[8] For example, consider the cash flows of Project Sooner and Project Later. Both have a 10% cost of capital; their cash flows are shown below:

	Year			Result	
	0	**1**	**2**	**NPV**	**IRR**
Project Sooner:	−$1,000	$1,020	$120	$26	12.7%
Project Later:	−$1,000	$120	$1,120	$35	12.0%
$\Delta = CF_S - CF_L$:	$0	$900	−$1,000		11.1%

Both projects have the same scale (each requires an initial investment of $1,000), so the difference in their initial cost is zero. However, Project Sooner has most of its future cash flows in Year 1 and Project Later has most of its future cash flows in Year 2. This causes their difference in Year 1 to be positive and their difference in Year 2 to be negative. In other words, there is one and only one sign change in the difference between the two projects, so a crossover rate exists. As this illustrates, projects with the same scale must have timing differences in future cash flows for there to be one and only one sign change.

---

8. Also, if mutually exclusive projects have different lives (as opposed to different cash flow patterns over a common life), further complications arise; thus, for meaningful comparisons, some mutually exclusive projects must be evaluated over a common life. This point is discussed later in the chapter.

What about a situation in which projects don't have timing differences but do have a scale difference? Projects Smaller and Larger each have a 10% cost of capital, and their cash flows are shown below:

	Year			Result	
	0	**1**	**2**	**NPV**	**IRR**
Smaller	−$90	$12	$112	$13	18.4%
Larger	−$1,000	$120	$1,120	$35	12.0%
$\Delta = CF_S - CF_L$	$910	−$108	−$1,008		11.3%

There are no timing differences in the future cash flows; in fact, Project Smaller's future cash flows are 10% of Project Larger's. However, there is a scale difference because Project Smaller's initial cost is much less than that of Project Larger. The scale difference causes the difference in the initial cash flow to be positive. However, the differences in the future cash flows are negative. This causes one and only one sign change, so a crossover rate exists.

12-4d Applying IRR as an Evaluation Measure

When using the IRR, it is important to distinguish between independent projects and mutually exclusive projects.

If you are evaluating an independent project with normal cash flows, then the NPV and IRR criteria always lead to the same accept/reject decision: If NPV says accept then IRR also says accept, and vice versa. To see why this is so, look at Figure 12-5 and notice: (1) that the IRR says accept Project S if the cost of capital is less than (or to the left of) the IRR and (2) that if the cost of capital is less than the IRR then the NPV must be positive. Thus, at any cost of capital less than 14.686%, Project S will be recommended by both the NPV and IRR criteria, but both methods reject the project if the cost of capital is greater than 14.686%. A similar statement can be made for Project L, or any other normal project, and we would always reach the same conclusion: For normal, independent projects, if the IRR says to accept it, then so will the NPV.

Now assume that Projects S and L are mutually exclusive rather than independent. Therefore, we can choose either S or L, or we can reject both, but we can't accept both. Now look at Figure 12-5 and note these points.

- $IRR_S > IRR_L$, so the IRR decision rule would say to accept Project S over Project L.
- As long as the cost of capital is *greater than* the crossover rate of 12.274%, both methods agree that Project S is better: NPV_S . NPV_L and IRR_S . IRR_L. Therefore, if r is *greater* than the crossover rate, no conflict occurs.
- However, if the cost of capital is *less than* the crossover rate, a conflict arises: NPV ranks L higher, but IRR ranks S higher. In this situation, select the project with the highest NPV even if it has a lower IRR.

In what sense is a project's IRR similar to the YTM on a bond?

The cash flows for Projects SS and LL are as follows:

SELF TEST

(Continued)

	End-of-Year Cash Flows			
	0	**1**	**2**	**3**
SS	−700	500	300	100
LL	−700	100	300	600

Assume that the firm's WACC = r = 10%. What are the two projects' IRRs?
(IRRSS = 18.0%; IRRLL = 15.6%)

Which project would the IRR method select if the firm has a 10% cost of capital and the projects are: (a) independent or (b) mutually exclusive?
(Both; SS)

What condition regarding cash flows would cause more than one IRR to exist?

Project MM has the following cash flows:

End-of-Year Cash Flows			
0	**1**	**2**	**3**
−$1,000	$2,000	$2,000	−$3,350

Calculate MM's NPV at discount rates of 0%, 10%, 12.2258%, 25%, 122.147%, and 150%. **(−$350; −$46; $0; $165; $0; −$94)** What are MM's IRRs?
(12.23% and 122.15%)

If the cost of capital were 10%, should the project be accepted or rejected?
(Rejected because NPV < 0)

Describe in words how an NPV profile is constructed. How do you determine the intercepts for the x-axis and the y-axis?

What is the crossover rate, and how does it interact with the cost of capital to determine whether or not a conflict exists between NPV and IRR?

What two characteristics can lead to conflicts between the NPV and the IRR when evaluating mutually exclusive projects?

12-5 **Modified Internal Rate of Return (MIRR)**

Recall from Chapter 4 that an investor who purchases a bond and holds it to maturity (assuming no default) will receive the bond's yield to maturity (YTM) even if interest rates change. This happens because the realized rate of return on an investment is by definition the rate that sets the present value of the realized cash flows equal to the purchase price. However, the realized rate of return on the investment in the bond and the subsequent reinvestment of the coupons will only equal the YTM if the coupons are reinvested at a rate equal to the YTM. Similar reasoning can be applied to a project—the project's expected return is equal to its IRR, but the expected return on the project plus any return on reinvested cash flows is equal to the IRR only if the cash flows are reinvested at a rate equal to the IRR.

If a manager wishes to evaluate a project based on the return expected from the project and its reinvested cash flows, then the IRR overstates this return because it is

FIGURE 12-6	Finding the MIRR for Projects S and L

	A	B	C	D	E	F	G
303	INPUTS:						
304	r = 10%						
305			**Initial Cost and Expected Cash Flows**				
306	Year	0	1	2	3	4	
307	Project S	–$10,000	$5,300	$4,300	$1,874	$1,500	
308		↓	↓	↓	↳ → →	$2,061	
309		↓	↓	↳ → → –	→ → → → →	$5,203	
310	Present Value of	↓	↳ → →·	→ → → → →	→ → → → →	$7,054	
311	Negative CF (PV) =	–$10,000	**Terminal Value of Positive CF (TV) =**			$15,819	
312							
313	Calculator: N = 4, PV = –10000, PMT = 0, FV = 15819. Press I/YR to get:					MIRR$_S$ =	12.15%
314	*Excel* Rate function–Easier:		=RATE(F306,0,B311,F311)			MIRR$_S$ =	12.15%
315	*Excel* MIRR function–Easiest:		=MIRR(B307:F307,B304,B304)			MIRR$_S$ =	12.15%
316							
317	Year	0	1	2	3	4	
318	Project L	–$10,000	$1,900	$2,700	$2,345	$7,800	
319							
320	For Project L, using the MIRR function:		=MIRR(B318:F318,B304,B304)			MIRR$_L$ =	12.78%

Notes:

1. The terminal value (TV) is the future value of all positive cash flows. The present value (PV) is the present value of all negative cash flows.
2. Find the discount rate that forces the TV positive cash flows to equal the PV of negative cash flows. That discount rate is defined as the MIRR.

   PV of negative cash flows = (TV of positive cash flows)/(1+MIRR)^N

   $$\$10,000 = \$15,819/(1+MIRR)^4$$
   We can find the MIRR with a calculator or *Excel*.

Microsoft Excel® is a registered trademark of Microsoft Corporation. © 2014 Microsoft.

more likely that the project's future cash flows can be reinvested at the cost of capital and not at the project's IRR. The **Modified IRR (MIRR)** is similar to the regular IRR, except it is based on the assumption that cash flows are reinvested at the WACC (or some other explicit rate if that is a more reasonable assumption). Refer to Figure 12-6 as you read the following steps that explain the MIRR's calculation.

See *Ch12 Tool Kit.xls* on the textbook's Web site.

1. Project S has just one outflow, a negative $10,000 at t = 0. Because it occurs at Time 0, it is not discounted, and its PV is −$10,000. If the project had additional outflows, we would find the PV at t = 0 for each one and then sum them for use in the MIRR calculation.
2. Next, we find the future value of each *inflow*, compounded at the WACC out to the "terminal year," which is the year the last inflow is received. We assume that cash flows are reinvested at the WACC. For Project S, the first cash flow, $5,300, is compounded at WACC = 10% for 3 years, and it grows to $7,054. The second inflow, $4,300, grows to $5,203, and the third inflow, $1,874, grows to $2,061. The last inflow, $1,500, is received at the end, so it is not compounded at all. The sum of the future values, $15,819, is called the "terminal value," or TV.
3. We now have the PV at t = 0 of all negative cash flows, −$10,000, and the TV at Year 4 of all positive cash flows, $15,819. There is some discount rate that will cause the PV of the terminal value to equal the cost. *That interest rate is defined as the Modified Internal Rate of Return (MIRR)*. In a calculator, enter N = 4, PV = −10000, PMT = 0, and FV = 15819. Then pressing the I/YR key yields the MIRR, 12.15%.

4. The MIRR can be found in a number of ways. Figure 12-6 illustrates how the MIRR is calculated: We compound each cash inflow, sum them to determine the TV, and then find the rate that causes the PV of the TV to equal the cost. That rate in this example is 12.15%. However, *Excel* and some of the better calculators have a built-in MIRR function that streamlines the process. We explain how to use the MIRR function in our calculator tutorials, and we explain how to find MIRR with *Excel* in this chapter's *Excel Tool Kit*.[9]

The MIRR has two significant advantages over the regular IRR. First, the MIRR assumes that cash flows are reinvested at the cost of capital (or some other explicit rate) rather than at the IRR. Because reinvestment at the IRR is generally not correct, the MIRR is usually a better indicator of the rate of return on the project and its reinvested cash flows. Second, the MIRR eliminates the multiple IRR problem—there can never be more than one MIRR, and it can be compared with the cost of capital when deciding to accept or reject projects.

Our conclusion is that the MIRR is better than the regular IRR; however, this question remains: Is MIRR as good as the NPV? Here is our take on the situation.

*   For *independent* projects, the NPV, IRR, and MIRR always reach the same accept–reject conclusion, so the three criteria are equally good when evaluating independent projects.
*   However, if projects are *mutually exclusive* and if they differ in size, conflicts can arise. In such cases the NPV is best because it selects the project that maximizes value.[10]
*   Our overall conclusions are that: (1) the MIRR is superior to the regular IRR as an indicator of a project's "true" rate of return, but (2) NPV is better than either IRR or MIRR when choosing among competing projects. If managers want to know the expected rates of return on projects, it would be better to give them MIRRs than IRRs because MIRRs are more likely to be the rates that are actually earned if the projects' cash flows are reinvested in future projects.

---

9. If we let COF_t and CIF_t denote cash outflows and inflows, respectively, then Equations 12-2a and 12-2b summarize the steps just described:

(12–2a)
$$\sum_{t=0}^{N} \frac{COF_t}{(1+r)^t} = \frac{\sum_{t=0}^{N} CIF_t (1+r)^{N-t}}{(1+MIRR)^N}$$

(12–2b)
$$PV \text{ costs} = \frac{TV}{(1+MIRR)^N}$$

Also, note that there are alternative definitions for the MIRR. One difference relates to whether negative cash flows after the positive cash flows begin should be compounded and treated as part of the TV or discounted and treated as a cost. A related issue is whether negative and positive flows in a given year should be netted or treated separately. For more discussion, see David M. Shull, "Interpreting Rates of Return: A Modified Rate of Return Approach," *Financial Practice and Education*, Fall 1993, pp. 67–71.

10. For projects of equal size but different lives, the MIRR will always lead to the same decision as the NPV if the MIRRs are both calculated using as the terminal year the life of the longer project. (Fill in zeros for the shorter project's missing cash flows.)

What's the primary difference between the MIRR and the regular IRR?

Projects A and B have the following cash flows:

	0	1	2
A	−$1,000	$1,150	$100
B	−$1,000	$100	$1,300

The cost of capital is 10%. What are the projects' IRRs, MIRRs, and NPVs?
(IRR$_A$ = 23.1%, IRR$_B$ = 19.1%; MIRR$_A$ = 16.8%, MIRR$_B$ =18.7%; NPV$_A$ = $128.10, NPV$_B$ = $165.29)

Which project would each method select? **(IRR: A; MIRR: B; NPV: B)**

12-6 Profitability Index (PI)

The **profitability index (PI)** measures how much value a project creates for each dollar of the project's cost. The PI is calculated as:

$$PI = \frac{\text{PV of future cash flows}}{\text{Initial cost}} = \frac{\sum\limits_{t=1}^{N} \dfrac{CF_t}{(1+r)^t}}{CF_0}$$

(12–3)

Here CF_t represents the expected future cash flows and CF_0 represents the initial cost. As we can see from Figure 12-7, the PI for Project S, based on a 10% cost of capital, is $10,804.38/$10,000 = 1.0804; the PI for Project L is 1.1048. Thus, Project S is expected to produce $1.0804 of present value for each $1 of investment, whereas L should produce $1.1048 for each dollar invested.

A project is acceptable if its PI is greater than 1.0. Projects with higher PIs should be ranked above projects with lower PIs. Projects S and L would be accepted by the PI criterion if they were independent, and L would be ranked ahead of S if they were mutually exclusive.

FIGURE 12-7 Profitability Index (PI)

		A	B	C	D	E
342	**Project S:**		PI$_S$ =	**PV of future cash flows** ÷		**Initial cost**
343			PI$_S$ =	$10,804	÷	$10,000
344			PI$_S$ =	1.0804		
345						
346	**Project L:**		PI$_L$ =	**PV of future cash flows** ÷		**Initial cost**
347			PI$_L$ =	$11,048	÷	$10,000
348			PI$_L$ =	1.1048		

Mathematically, the NPV, IRR, MIRR, and PI methods will always lead to the same accept/reject decisions for *normal, independent* projects: If a project's NPV is positive, its IRR and MIRR will always exceed r and its PI will always be greater than 1.0. However, these methods can give conflicting rankings for *mutually exclusive* projects if the projects differ in size or in the timing of cash flows. If the PI ranking conflicts with the NPV, then the NPV ranking should be used.

SELF TEST

Explain how the PI is calculated. What does it measure?

A project has the following expected cash flows: $CF_0 = -\$500$, $CF_1 = \$200$, $CF_2 = \$200$, and $CF_3 = \$400$. If the project's cost of capital is 9%, what is the PI? **(1.32)**

12-7 **Payback Period**

NPV and IRR are the most commonly used methods today, but historically the first selection criterion was the **payback period**, defined as the number of years required to recover the funds invested in a project from its operating cash flows. Equation 12-4 is used for the calculation, and the process is diagrammed in Figure 12-8. We start with the project's cost, a negative number, and then add the cash inflow for each year until the cumulative cash flow turns positive. The payback year is the year *prior to* full recovery, plus a fraction equal to the shortfall at the end of the prior year divided by the cash flow during the year when full recovery occurs:[11]

(12–4)

$$\text{Payback} = \begin{array}{c}\text{Number of}\\\text{years prior to}\\\text{full recovery}\end{array} + \frac{\begin{array}{c}\text{Unrecovered cost}\\\text{at start of year}\end{array}}{\begin{array}{c}\text{Cash flow during}\\\text{full recovery year}\end{array}}$$

The cash flows for Projects S and L, together with their paybacks, are shown in Figure 12-8.[12] The shorter the payback, the better the project. Therefore, if the firm requires a payback of 3 years or less, then S would be accepted but L would be rejected. If the projects were mutually exclusive, S would be ranked over L because of its shorter payback.

The regular payback has three flaws: (1) Dollars received in different years are all given the same weight—that is, the time value of money is ignored. (2) Cash flows beyond the payback year are given no consideration whatsoever, regardless of how large they might be. (3) Unlike the NPV or the IRR, which tell us how much wealth a project adds or how much a project's rate of return exceeds the cost of

---

11. Equation 12-4 assumes that cash flows come in uniformly during the full recovery year.
12. There is not an *Excel* function for payback. But if the cash flows are normal then the
    PERCENTRANK function can be used to find payback, as illustrated in Figures 12-8 and 12-9.

FIGURE 12-8	Payback Period

	A	B	C	D	E	F	G
374							
375	Project S	Year	0	1	2	3	4
376		Cash flow	–$10,000	$5,300	$4,300	$1,874	$1,500
377		Cumulative cash flow	–$10,000	–$4,700	–$400	$1,474	$2,974
378		Intermediate calculation for payback	—	—	—	2.21	3.98
379						↑	
380					Intermediate calculation:		
381	Manual calculation of Payback S = 2 + $400/$1,874 =			2.21	=IF(F377>0,E375+ABS(E377/F376),"—")		
382	Excel calculation of Payback S =			2.21	2.21		
383							
384	Project L	Year	0	1	2	3	4
385		Cash flow	–$10,000	$1,900	$2,700	$2,345	$7,800
386		Cumulative cash flow	–$10,000	–$8,100	–$5,400	–$3,055	$4,745
387							
388	Manual calculation of Payback L = 3 + $3,055/$7,800 =			3.39	Payback switches from negative to positive cash flow.		
389	Alternative Excel calculation of Payback L =						
390	=PERCENTRANK(C386:G386,0,6)*G384 =			3.39			

Microsoft Excel® is a registered trademark of Microsoft Corporation. © 2014 Microsoft.

capital, the payback merely tells us how long it takes to recover our investment. There is no necessary relationship between a given payback period and investor wealth, so we don't know how to specify an acceptable payback. The firm might use 2 years, 3 years, or any other number as the minimum acceptable payback, but the choice is arbitrary.

To counter the first criticism, financial analysts developed the **discounted payback**, where cash flows are discounted at the WACC and then those discounted cash flows are used to find the payback. In Figure 12-9, we calculate the discounted paybacks for S and L, assuming both have a 10% cost of capital. Each inflow is divided by $(1 + r)^t = (1.10)^t$, where t is the year in which the cash flow occurs and r is the project's cost of capital, and then those PVs are used to find the payback. Project S's discounted payback is 3.21 years and L's is 3.80 years.

Note that the payback is a "break-even" calculation in the sense that if cash flows come in at the expected rate, then the project will at least break even. However, because the regular payback doesn't consider the cost of capital, it doesn't specify the true break-even year. The discounted payback does consider capital costs, but it disregards cash flows beyond the payback year, which is a serious flaw. Further, if mutually exclusive projects vary in size, both payback methods can conflict with the NPV, and that might lead to poor decisions. Finally, there is no way to determine how short the payback periods must be to justify accepting a project.

Although the payback methods have faults as ranking criteria, they do provide information about *liquidity* and *risk*. The shorter the payback, other things held constant, the greater the project's liquidity. This factor is often important for smaller firms that don't have ready access to the capital markets. Also, cash flows expected in the distant future are generally riskier than near-term cash flows, so the payback period is also a risk indicator.

See *Ch12 Tool Kit.xls* on the textbook's Web site.

FIGURE 12-9   Discounted Payback

	A	B	C	D	E	F	G
403	Project r =	10%					
404	Project S	Year	0	1	2	3	4
405		Cash flow	−$10,000	$5,300	$4,300	$1,874	$1,500
406		Discounted cash flow	−$10,000	$4,818	$3,554	$1,408	$1,025
407		Cumulative discounted CF	−$10,000	−$5,182	−$1,628	−$220	$804
408							
409	Discounted Payback S = 3 + $220.14/$1,024.52 =		3.21			Switches from negative to	
410	*Excel* calculation of Discounted Payback S =					positive cash flow.	
411	=PERCENTRANK(C407:G407,0,6)*G404		3.21				
412							
413	Project L	Year	0	1	2	3	4
414		Cash flow	−$10,000	$1,900	$2,700	$2,345	$7,800
415		Discounted cash flow	−$10,000	$1,727	$2,231	$1,762	$5,328
416		Cumulative discounted CF	−$10,000	−$8,273	−$6,041	−$4,279	$1,048
417							
418	Discounted Payback L = 3 + $4,279.49/$5,327.50 =		3.80			Switches from negative to	
419	*Excel* calculation of Discounted Payback L =					positive cash flow.	
420	=PERCENTRANK(C416:G416,0,6)*G413		3.80				

Microsoft Excel® is a registered trademark of Microsoft Corporation. © 2014 Microsoft.

SELF TEST

What two pieces of information does the payback method provide that are absent from the other capital budgeting decision methods?

What three flaws does the regular payback method have? Does the discounted payback method correct all of those flaws? Explain.

Project P has a cost of $1,000 and cash flows of $300 per year for 3 years plus another $1,000 in Year 4. The project's cost of capital is 15%. What are P's regular and discounted paybacks? **(3.10, 3.55)** If the company requires a payback of 3 years or less, would the project be accepted? Would this be a good accept–reject decision, considering the NPV and/or the IRR? **(NPV = $256.72, IRR = 24.78%)**

12-8 How to Use the Different Capital Budgeting Methods

We have discussed six capital budgeting decision criteria: NPV, IRR, MIRR, PI, payback, and discounted payback. We compared these methods and highlighted their strengths and weaknesses. In the process, we may have created the impression that "sophisticated" firms should use only one method, the NPV. However, virtually all capital budgeting decisions are analyzed by computer, so it is easy to use all six methods. In making the accept–reject decision, most firms usually calculate and consider all six because each method provides a somewhat different piece of information about the decision.

12-8a **A Comparison of the Methods**

NPV is the single best criterion because it provides a direct measure of the value a project adds to shareholder wealth. IRR and MIRR measure profitability expressed as a percentage rate of return, which decision makers like to consider. The PI also measures profitability but in relation to the amount of the investment. Further, IRR, MIRR, and PI all contain information concerning a project's "safety margin." To illustrate, consider a firm, whose WACC is 10%, which must choose between these two mutually exclusive projects: SS (for small) has a cost of $10,000 and is expected to return $16,500 at the end of 1 year; LL (for large) has a cost of $100,000 and is expected to return $115,550 at the end of 1 year. SS has a huge IRR, 65%, while LL's IRR is a more modest 15.6%. The NPV paints a somewhat different picture: At the 10% cost of capital, SS's NPV is $5,000 while LL's is $5,045. By the NPV rule, we would choose LL. However, SS's IRR indicates that it has a much larger margin for error: Even if its cash flow were only 66.6% of the $16,500 forecast, the project would still have a barely positive NPV. On the other hand, if LL's inflow were to fall a much smaller percentage, to just 95.1% of its forecasted $115,550, it would have a negative NPV.

The modified IRR has all the virtues of the IRR, but it avoids the problem of multiple rates of return that can occur with the IRR. The MIRR also measures the expected return of the project and its reinvested cash flows, which provides additional insight into the project. So if decision makers want to know projects' rates of return, the MIRR is a better indicator than the regular IRR.

The PI tells a similar story to the IRR. Here PI_{LL} is only 1.05 while PI_{SS} is 1.50. As with the IRR, this indicates that Project SS is less risky: Its cash inflow could decline by 33.3% before the PI is unacceptable, whereas a decline of only 4.8% in LL's cash flows would result in an unacceptable PI.

Payback and discounted payback provide indications of a project's *liquidity* and *risk*. A long payback means that investment dollars will be locked up for a long time; hence, the project is relatively illiquid. In addition, a long payback means that cash flows must be forecast far into the future, and that probably makes the project riskier than one with a shorter payback. A good analogy for this is bond valuation. An investor should never compare the yields to maturity on two bonds without also considering their terms to maturity, because a bond's risk is influenced significantly by its maturity. The same holds true for capital projects.

In summary, the different measures provide different types of useful information. It is easy to calculate all of them: Simply put the cost of capital and the cash flows into an *Excel* model like the one provided in this chapter's *Tool Kit* and the model will instantly calculate all six criteria. Therefore, most sophisticated companies consider all six measures when making capital budgeting decisions. For most decisions, the greatest weight should be given to the NPV, but it would be foolish to ignore the information provided by the other criteria.

12-8b **The Decision Process: What Is the Source of a Project's NPV?**

Just as it would be foolish to ignore these capital budgeting methods, it would also be foolish to make decisions based *solely* on them. One cannot know at Time 0 the exact cost of future capital or the exact future cash flows. These inputs are simply estimates, and if they turn out to be incorrect then so will be the calculated NPVs and IRRs. Thus, *quantitative methods provide valuable information, but they should not be used as the sole criteria for accept–reject decisions* in the capital budgeting process. Rather, managers should use quantitative methods in the decision-making process but should also consider the likelihood that actual results will differ from the forecasts. Qualitative factors, such as the chances of a tax increase, or a war, or a major product liability suit, should also be considered. In summary, *quantitative methods such as NPV and IRR should be considered as an aid to informed decisions but not as a substitute for sound managerial judgment.*

In this same vein, managers should ask sharp questions about any project that has a large NPV, a high IRR, or a high PI. In a perfectly competitive economy, there would be no positive-NPV projects—all companies would have the same opportunities, and competition would quickly eliminate any positive NPV. The existence of positive-NPV projects must be predicated on some imperfection in the marketplace, and the longer the life of the project, the longer that imperfection must last. Therefore, managers should be able to identify the imperfection and explain why it will persist before accepting that a project will really have a positive NPV. Valid explanations might include patents or proprietary technology, which is how pharmaceutical and software firms create positive-NPV projects. Pfizer's Lipitor (a cholesterol-reducing medicine) and Microsoft's Windows 8 operating system are examples. Companies can also create positive NPV by being the first entrant into a new market or by creating new products that meet some previously unidentified consumer needs. Post-it notes invented by 3M are an example. Similarly, Dell developed procedures for direct sales of microcomputers and, in the process, created projects with enormous NPV. Also, companies such as Southwest Airlines have trained and motivated their workers better than their competitors, and this has led to positive-NPV projects. In all of these cases, the companies developed some source of competitive advantage, and that advantage resulted in positive-NPV projects.

This discussion suggests three things: (1) If you can't identify the reason a project has a positive projected NPV, then its actual NPV will probably not be positive. (2) Positive-NPV projects don't just happen—they result from hard work to develop some competitive advantage. At the risk of oversimplification, the primary job of a manager is to find and develop areas of competitive advantage. (3) Some competitive advantages last longer than others, with their durability depending on competitors' ability to replicate them. Patents, the control of scarce resources, or large size in an industry where strong economies of scale exist can keep competitors at bay. However, it is relatively easy to replicate product features that cannot be patented. The bottom line is that managers should strive to develop nonreplicable sources of competitive advantage. If such an advantage cannot be demonstrated, then you should question projects with high NPV—especially if they have long lives.

12-8c **Decision Criteria Used in Practice**

Table 12-1 reports survey evidence and shows that a large majority of companies use NPV and IRR. As we suggested in the previous section, other methods are also used.

TABLE 12-1	Capital Budgeting in Practice		
Quantitative Measures Used by Companies	**Percent Using**	**Factors Considered Important by CEOs when Allocating Capital within the Company**	**Percent Agreeing**
NPV	75%	Project's ranking based on NPV	78.6%
IRR	76	Proposing manager's track record	71.3
Payback	57	Proposing manager's confidence in project	68.8
Discounted payback	29	Timing of project's cash flows	65.3
		Project's ability to protect market share	51.9
		Proposing division's track record	51.2

Sources: The percentages of companies using particular quantitative measures are from John R. Graham and Campbell R. Harvey, "The Theory and Practice of Corporate Finance: Evidence from the Field," *Journal of Financial Economics*, 2001, pp. 187–244. The percentages of CEOs agreeing with the capital allocation factors are from John R. Graham, Campbell R. Harvey, and Manju Puri, "Capital Allocation and Delegation of Decision Making Authority within Firms," NBER Working Paper 1730, 2011, **www.nber.org/papers/w17370**.

The table also reports the factors CEOs consider important in allocating capital within the firm. The ranking of projects by NPV is the factor that most CEOs consider important. Interestingly, CEOs also consider the manager who is proposing the project, both in terms of the manager's past success and the manager's confidence in the project. Confidence is often expressed through the range of possible outcomes for the project, with smaller ranges conveying more confidence. Chapter 13 explains how to estimate such confidence intervals.

Describe the advantages and disadvantages of the six capital budgeting methods.

Should capital budgeting decisions be made solely on the basis of a project's NPV, with no regard to the other criteria? Explain your answer.

What are some possible reasons that a project might have a high NPV?

SELF TEST

12-9 Other Issues in Capital Budgeting

Three other issues in capital budgeting are discussed in this section: (1) how to deal with mutually exclusive projects whose lives differ; (2) the potential advantage of terminating a project before the end of its physical life; and (3) the optimal capital budget when the cost of capital rises as the size of the capital budget increases.

12-9a Mutually Exclusive Projects with Unequal Lives

When choosing between two mutually exclusive alternatives with significantly different lives, an adjustment is necessary. For example, suppose a company is planning to modernize its production facilities and is considering either a conveyor system (Project C) or a fleet of forklift trucks (Project F) for moving materials. The

FIGURE 12-10 Analysis of Projects C and F (r = 12%)

	A	B	C	D	E	F	G	H
448	WACC = r = 12.0%							
449								
450	Data on Project C, Conveyor System:							
451	Year	0	1	2	3	4	5	6
452	Cash flows for C	−$40,000	$8,000	$14,000	$13,000	$12,000	$11,000	$10,000
453		NPV$_C$ =	$6,491		IRR$_C$ =	17.5%		
454								
455	Data on Project F, Forklifts:							
456	Year	0	1	2	3			
457	Cash flows for F	−$20,000	$7,000	$13,000	$12,000			
458		NPV$_F$ =	$5,155		IRR$_F$ =	25.2%		
459								
460	Common Life Approach with F Repeated (Project FF):							
461	Year	0	1	2	3	4	5	6
462	CF$_t$ for 1st F	−$20,000	$7,000	$13,000	$12,000			
463	CF$_t$ for 2nd F				−$20,000	$7,000	$13,000	$12,000
464	All CFs for FF	−$20,000	$7,000	$13,000	−$8,000	$7,000	$13,000	$12,000
465		NPV$_{FF}$ =	$8,824		IRR$_{FF}$ =	25.2%		

See **Ch12 Tool Kit.xls** on the textbook's Web site.

first two sections of Figure 12-10 show the expected net cash flows, NPVs, and IRRs for these two mutually exclusive alternatives. We see that Project C, when discounted at the firm's 12% cost of capital, has the higher NPV and thus appears to be the better project.

Although the NPVs shown in Figure 12-10 suggest that Project C should be selected, this analysis is incomplete, and the decision to choose Project C is actually incorrect. Since the company will require a means of moving materials around in the plant for at least 6 years, if we choose Project F, we will have to make a similar investment in 3 years when Project F wears out. If cost and revenue conditions continue at the levels shown in Figure 12-10, then this second investment will also be profitable. However, if we choose Project C, we cannot make this second investment. Two approaches can be used to compare Projects C and F, as shown in Figure 12-10 and discussed next.

Replacement Chains

The key to the *replacement chain,* or *common life, approach* for projects that will have to be repeated in the future is to analyze both projects over an equal life. In our example, Project C has a 6-year life, so we assume that Project F will be repeated after 3 years and then analyze it over the same 6-year period. We can then calculate the NPV of C and compare it to the extended-life NPV of Project F. The NPV for Project C, as shown in Figure 12-10, is already based on the 6-year common life. For Project F, however, we must add in a second version of it to extend the overall life to 6 years. The time line for this extended project, denoted as "All CFs for FF," is shown in Figure 12-10. Here we assume: (1) that Project F's cost and annual cash inflows will not change if the project is repeated in 3 years and (2) that the cost of capital will remain at 12%.

The NPV of this extended Project F is $8,824, and its IRR is 25.2%. (The IRR of two Project Fs is the same as the IRR for one Project F.) However, the $8,824 extended NPV of Project F is greater than Project C's $6,491 NPV, so Project F should be selected.

Alternatively, we could recognize that Project F has an NPV of $5,155 at Time 0 and a second NPV of that same amount at Time 3, find the PV of the second NPV at Time 0, and then sum the two to find Project F's extended-life NPV of $8,824.

Equivalent Annual Annuities (EAA)

Electrical engineers designing power plants and distribution lines were the first to encounter the unequal life problem. They could install transformers and other equipment that had relatively low initial costs but short lives, or they could use equipment that had higher initial costs but longer lives. The services would be required into the indefinite future, so this was the issue: Which choice would result in a higher NPV in the long run? The engineers converted the annual cash flows under the alternative investments into a constant cash flow stream whose NPV was equal to, or equivalent to, the NPV of the initial stream. This was called the **equivalent annual annuity (EAA) method**. To apply the EAA method to Projects C and F, for each project find the constant payment streams that the projects' NPVs ($6,491 for C and $5,155 for F) would provide over their respective lives. Project C's 6-year life and NPV of $6,491 is equivalent to a 6-year annuity of $1,579 per year. To find this using a financial calculator, we enter N = 6, I/YR = 12, PV = −6491, and FV = 0. Then, when we press the PMT key, we find EAA_C = $1,579. For Project F, we enter N = 3, I/YR = 12, PV = −5155, and FV = 0; solving for PMT, we find EAA_F = $2,146. Thus, whether Project F is repeated once, twice, or more times, it is equivalent to cash flow of $2,146 per year for the total length of the project. Project F would thus produce a higher annual cash flow, so it is the better project.

Conclusions about Unequal Lives

When should we worry about analysis of unequal lives? The unequal life issue: (1) does not arise for independent projects but (2) can arise if mutually exclusive projects with significantly different lives are being compared. However, even for mutually exclusive projects, it is not always appropriate to extend the analysis to a common life. This should be done if and only if there is a high probability that the projects will actually be repeated at the end of their initial lives.

We should note several potentially serious weaknesses in this type of analysis. (1) If inflation occurs, then replacement equipment will have a higher price. Moreover, both sales prices and operating costs would probably change. Thus, the static conditions built into the analysis would be invalid. (2) Replacements that occur down the road would probably employ new technology, which in turn might change the cash flows. (3) It is difficult enough to estimate the lives of most projects, and even more so to estimate the lives of a series of projects. In view of these problems, no experienced financial analyst would be too concerned about comparing mutually exclusive projects with lives of, say, 8 years and 10 years. Given all the uncertainties in the estimation process, we would assume that such projects would, for all practical purposes, have the same life. Still, it is important to recognize that a problem exists if mutually exclusive projects have substantially different lives.

When we encounter situations with significant differences in project lives, we first use a computer spreadsheet to build expected inflation and/or possible efficiency gains directly into the cash flow estimates and then use the replacement chain approach. We prefer the replacement chain approach for two reasons. First, it is easier to explain to those who are responsible for approving capital budgets. Second, it is easier to build inflation and other modifications into a spreadsheet and then go on to make the replacement chain calculations.

12-9b Economic Life versus Physical Life

Projects are normally evaluated under the assumption that the firm will operate them over their full physical lives. However, this may not be the best plan—it may be better to terminate a project before the end of its potential life. For example, the cost of maintenance for trucks and machinery can become quite high if they are used for too many years, so it might be better to replace them before the end of their potential lives.

Figure 12-11 provides data for an asset with a physical life of 3 years. However, the project can be terminated at the end of any year and the asset sold at the indicated salvage values. All of the cash flows are after taxes, and the firm's cost of capital is 10%. The undiscounted cash flows are shown in Columns C and D in the upper part of the figure, and the present values of these flows are shown in Columns E and F. We find the project's NPV under different assumptions about how long it will be operated. If the project is operated for its full 3-year life, it will have a negative NPV. The NPV will be positive if it is operated for 2 years and then the asset is sold for a relatively high salvage value; the NPV will be negative if the asset is disposed after only 1 year of operation. Therefore, the project's optimal life is 2 years.

This type of analysis is used to determine a project's **economic life**, which is the life that maximizes the NPV and thus shareholder wealth. For our project, the economic life is 2 years versus the 3-year **physical life**, or **engineering life**. Note

WEB

See *Ch12 Tool Kit.xls* on the textbook's Web site.

FIGURE 12-11 Economic Life versus Physical Life

	A	B	C	D	E	F	G
505	r = 10%				PVs of the Cash Flows		
506			Operating		Operating		
507		Year	Cash Flow	Salvage Value	Cash Flow	Salvage Value	
508		0	−$4,800				
509		1	2,000	$3,000	$1,818.18	$2,727.27	
510		2	2,000	1,650	1,652.89	1,363.64	
511		3	1,750	0	1,314.80	0.00	
512					PV of		PV of Salvage
513	NPV at Different Operating Lives:		Initial Cost	+	Operating	+	Value
514					Cash Flows		
515	Operate for 3 Years:						
516	NPV₃: −$14.12		−$4,800	+	$4,785.88	+	$0.00
517	Operate for 2 Years:						
518	NPV₂: $34.71		−$4,800	+	$3,471.07	+	$1,363.64
519	Operate for 1 Year:						
520	NPV₁: −$254.55		−$4,800	+	$1,818.18	+	$2,727.27
521							

Note: The project is profitable if and only if it is operated for just 2 years.

that this analysis was based on the expected cash flows and the expected salvage values, and it should always be conducted as a part of the capital budgeting evaluation if salvage values are relatively high.

12-9c **The Optimal Capital Budget**

The **optimal capital budget** is defined as the set of projects that maximizes the value of the firm. Finance theory states that all independent projects with positive NPVs should be accepted, as should the mutually exclusive projects with the highest NPVs. Therefore, the optimal capital budget consists of that set of projects. However, two complications arise in practice: (1) The cost of capital might increase as the size of the capital budget increases, making it hard to know the proper discount rate to use when evaluating projects; and (2) sometimes firms set an upper limit on the size of their capital budgets, which is also known as *capital rationing*.

An Increasing Cost of Capital

The cost of capital may increase as the capital budget increases—this is called an *increasing marginal cost of capital*. As we discussed in Chapter 11, flotation costs associated with issuing new equity can be quite high. This means that the cost of capital will increase once a company has invested all of its internally generated cash and must sell new common stock. In addition, once a firm has used up its normal credit lines and must seek additional debt capital, it may encounter an increase in its cost of debt. This means that a project might have a positive NPV if it is part of a $10 million capital budget but the same project might have a negative NPV if it is part of a $20 million capital budget because the cost of capital might increase.

Fortunately, these problems rarely occur for most firms, especially those that are stable and well established. When a rising cost of capital is encountered, we would proceed as indicated below. You can look at Figure 12-12 as you read through our points.

- Find the IRR (or MIRR) on all potential projects, arrange them in rank order (along with their initial costs), and then plot them on a graph with the IRR on the vertical axis and the cumulative costs on the horizontal axis. The firm's data are shown in Figure 12-12, and the IRRs are plotted in the graph. The line is called the Investment Opportunity Schedule (IOS), and it shows the marginal return on capital.
- Next, determine how much capital can be raised before it is necessary to issue new common stock or go to higher-cost sources of debt, and identify the amounts of higher-cost capital to be used. Use this information to calculate the WACC that corresponds to the different amounts of capital raised. In this example, the firm can raise $300 before the WACC rises, and the WACC increases as additional capital is raised. The increasing WACC represents the marginal cost of capital, and its graph is called the Marginal Cost of Capital (MCC) schedule.
- The intersection of the IOS and MCC schedules indicates the amount of capital the firm should raise and invest, and it is analogous to the familiar marginal cost versus marginal revenue schedule discussed in introductory economics courses. In our example, the firm should have a capital budget of $400; if it uses a WACC of 10% then it will accept projects A, B, C, and D, which have a cumulative cost of $400. The 10% WACC should be used for average-risk projects, but it should be scaled up or down for more or less risky projects, as discussed in Chapter 11.

FIGURE 12-12   IOS and MCC Schedules

	A	B	C	D	E	F
527	**Investment Opportunity Schedule (IOS)**			**Marginal Cost of Capital (MCC)**		
528			**Highest to**	**Cumulative**	**Lowest to**	
529	**Projects**	**Cost**	**Lowest IRR**	**Cost**	**Highest WACC**	
530	A	$100	14.0%	$100	9.0%	
531	B	$100	13.0%	$200	9.0%	
532	C	$100	11.5%	$300	9.0%	
533	D	$100	10.0%	$400	10.0%	
534	E	$50	9.5%	$450	11.0%	
535	F	$50	9.0%	$500	12.0%	
536	G	$100	8.5%	$600	15.0%	

MCC and IOS Schedules

MCC and IOS

IOS

MCC

16%
14%
12%
10%
8%
6%
4%
2%
0%

$100 $200 $300 $400 $500 $600

Dollars Raised and Invested

Note: Use WACC = 10% as the base rate for finding base risk-adjusted project WACCs.

See *Ch12 Tool Kit.xls* on the textbook's Web site.

Our example illustrates the case of a firm that cannot raise all the money it needs at a constant WACC. Firms should not try to be too precise with this process—the data are not good enough for precision—but they should be aware of the concept and get at least a rough idea of how raising additional capital will affect the WACC.

Capital Rationing

Armbrister Pyrotechnics, a manufacturer of fireworks and lasers for light shows, has identified 40 potential independent projects, of which 15 have a positive NPV based on the firm's 12% cost of capital. The total investment required to implement these 15 projects would be $75 million and so, according to finance theory, the optimal capital budget is $75 million. Thus, Armbrister should accept the 15 projects with positive NPVs and invest $75 million. However, Armbrister's management has imposed a limit of $50 million for capital expenditures during the upcoming year. Because of this restriction, the company must forgo a number of value-adding projects. This is an example of **capital rationing**, defined as a situation in which a firm limits its capital expenditures to an amount less than would be required to fund the optimal capital budget. Despite being at odds with finance theory, this practice is quite common.

Why would any company forgo value-adding projects? Here are some potential explanations, along with some suggestions for better ways to handle these situations.

1. *Reluctance to issue new stock.* Many firms are extremely reluctant to issue new stock, so they must fund all of their capital expenditures with debt and internally generated cash. Also, most firms try to stay near their target capital structure, and, when combined with the limit on equity, this limits the amount of debt that can be added during any one year without raising the cost of that debt as well as the cost of equity. The result can be a serious constraint on the amount of funds available for investment in new projects.

   The reluctance to issue new stock could be based on some sound reasons: (a) flotation costs can be very expensive, (b) investors might perceive new stock offerings as a signal that the company's equity is overvalued, and (c) the company might have to reveal sensitive strategic information to investors, thereby reducing some of its competitive advantages. To avoid these costs, many companies simply limit their capital expenditures.

   However, rather than placing a somewhat artificial limit on capital expenditures, companies might be better off explicitly incorporating the costs of raising external capital into their costs of capital along the lines shown in Figure 12-12. If there still are positive-NPV projects even with the higher cost of capital, then the company should go ahead and raise external equity and accept the projects.

2. *Constraints on nonmonetary resources.* Sometimes a firm simply doesn't have the necessary managerial, marketing, or engineering talent to immediately accept all positive-NPV projects. In other words, the potential projects may be independent from a demand standpoint but not from an internal standpoint, because accepting them all would raise the firm's costs. To avoid potential problems due to spreading existing talent too thin, many firms simply limit the capital budget to a size that can be accommodated by their current personnel.

   A better solution might be to employ a technique called **linear programming**. Each potential project has an expected NPV, and each potential project requires a certain level of support by different types of employees. A linear program can identify the set of projects that maximizes NPV *subject to the constraint* that the total amount of support required for these projects does not exceed the available resources.

3. *Controlling estimation bias.* Many managers become overly optimistic when estimating the cash flows for a project. Some firms try to control this estimation bias by requiring managers to use an unrealistically high cost of capital. Others try to control the bias by limiting the size of the capital budget. Neither solution is generally effective, because managers quickly learn the rules of the game and then increase their own estimates of project cash flows, which might have been biased upward to begin with.

   A better solution is to implement a post-audit program and to link the accuracy of forecasts to the compensation of the managers who initiated the projects.

Briefly describe the replacement chain (common life) approach and differentiate it from the Equivalent Annual Annuity (EAA) approach.

Differentiate between a project's *physical* life and its *economic* life.

What factors can lead to an increasing marginal cost of capital? How might this affect capital budgeting?

What is capital rationing?

What are three explanations for capital rationing? How might firms otherwise handle these situations?

Summary

This chapter has described six techniques used in capital budgeting analysis: NPV, IRR, MIRR, PI, payback, and discounted payback. Each approach provides a different piece of information, so in this age of computers, managers often look at all of them when evaluating projects. However, NPV is the best single measure, and almost all firms now use NPV. The key concepts covered in this chapter are listed below.

- **Capital budgeting** is the process of analyzing potential projects. Capital budgeting decisions are probably the most important ones that managers must make.
- The **net present value (NPV) method** discounts all cash flows at the project's cost of capital and then sums those cash flows. The project should be accepted if the NPV is positive because such a project increases shareholders' value.
- The **internal rate of return (IRR)** is defined as the discount rate that forces a project's NPV to equal zero. The project should be accepted if the IRR is greater than the cost of capital.
- The NPV and IRR methods make the same accept–reject decisions for **independent projects**, but if projects are **mutually exclusive** then ranking conflicts can arise. In such cases, the NPV method should generally be relied upon.
- It is possible for a project to have more than one IRR if the project's cash flows change signs more than once.
- Unlike the IRR, a project never has more than one **modified IRR (MIRR)**. MIRR requires finding the **terminal value (TV)** of the cash inflows, compounding them at the firm's cost of capital, and then determining the discount rate that forces the present value of the TV to equal the present value of the outflows.
- The **profitability index (PI)** is calculated by dividing the present value of cash inflows by the initial cost, so it measures relative profitability—that is, the amount of the present value per dollar of investment.

- The regular **payback period** is defined as the number of years required to recover a project's cost. The regular payback method has three flaws: It ignores cash flows beyond the payback period, it does not consider the time value of money, and it doesn't give a precise acceptance rule. The payback method does, however, provide an indication of a project's risk and liquidity, because it shows how long the invested capital will be tied up.

- The **discounted payback** is similar to the regular payback except that it discounts cash flows at the project's cost of capital. It considers the time value of money, but it still ignores cash flows beyond the payback period.

- The chapter's *Tool Kit Excel* model and *Web Extension 12A* describe another, but seldom-used, evaluation method—the **accounting rate of return**.

- If mutually exclusive projects have **unequal lives**, it may be necessary to adjust the analysis to put the projects on an equal-life basis. This can be done using the **replacement chain (common life) approach** or the **equivalent annual annuity (EAA) approach**.

- A project's true value may be greater than the NPV based on its **physical life** if it can be **terminated** at the end of its **economic life**.

- Flotation costs and increased risk associated with unusually large expansion programs can cause the **marginal cost of capital** to increase as the size of the capital budget increases.

- **Capital rationing** occurs when management places a constraint on the size of the firm's capital budget during a particular period.

Questions

12-1 Define each of the following terms:
   a. Capital budgeting; regular payback period; discounted payback period
   b. Independent projects; mutually exclusive projects
   c. DCF techniques; net present value (NPV) method; internal rate of return (IRR) method; profitability index (PI)
   d. Modified internal rate of return (MIRR) method
   e. NPV profile; crossover rate
   f. Nonnormal cash flow projects; normal cash flow projects; multiple IRRs
   g. Reinvestment rate assumption
   h. Replacement chain; economic life; capital rationing; equivalent annual annuity (EAA)

12-2 What types of projects require the least detailed and the most detailed analysis in the capital budgeting process?

12-3 Explain why the NPV of a relatively long-term project, defined as one for which a high percentage of its cash flows are expected in the distant future, is more sensitive to changes in the cost of capital than is the NPV of a short-term project.

12-4 When two mutually exclusive projects are being compared, explain why the short-term project might be ranked higher under the NPV criterion if the cost of capital is high, whereas the long-term project might be deemed better if the cost of capital is low. Would changes in the cost of capital ever cause a change in the IRR ranking of two such projects? Why or why not?

12-5 Suppose a firm is considering two mutually exclusive projects. One has a life of 6 years and the other a life of 10 years. Would the failure to employ some type of replacement chain analysis bias an NPV analysis against one of the projects? Explain.

Problems   Answers Appear in Appendix B

Easy Problems 1–7

12-1 NPV
A project has an initial cost of $40,000, expected net cash inflows of $9,000 per year for 7 years, and a cost of capital of 11%. What is the project's NPV? (*Hint:* Begin by constructing a time line.)

12-2 IRR
Refer to Problem 12-1. What is the project's IRR?

12-3 MIRR
Refer to Problem 12-1. What is the project's MIRR?

12-4 Profitability Index
Refer to Problem 12-1. What is the project's PI?

12-5 Payback
Refer to Problem 12-1. What is the project's payback period?

12-6 Discounted Payback
Refer to Problem 12-1. What is the project's discounted payback period?

12-7 NPV
Your division is considering two investment projects, each of which requires an up-front expenditure of $15 million. You estimate that the investments will produce the following net cash flows:

Year	Project A	Project B
1	$ 5,000,000	$20,000,000
2	10,000,000	10,000,000
3	20,000,000	6,000,000

a. What are the two projects' net present values, assuming the cost of capital is 5%? 10%? 15%?
b. What are the two projects' IRRs at these same costs of capital?

Intermediate Problems 8–18

12-8 NPVs, IRRs, and MIRRs for Independent Projects
Edelman Engineering is considering including two pieces of equipment, a truck and an overhead pulley system, in this year's capital budget. The projects are independent. The cash outlay for the truck is $17,100 and that for the pulley system is $22,430. The firm's cost of capital is 14%. After-tax cash flows, including depreciation, are as follows:

Year	Truck	Pulley
1	$5,100	$7,500
2	5,100	7,500
3	5,100	7,500
4	5,100	7,500
5	5,100	7,500

Calculate the IRR, the NPV, and the MIRR for each project, and indicate the correct accept–reject decision for each.

12–9 NPVs and IRRs for Mutually Exclusive Projects

Davis Industries must choose between a gas-powered and an electric-powered forklift truck for moving materials in its factory. Because both forklifts perform the same function, the firm will choose only one. (They are mutually exclusive investments.) The electric-powered truck will cost more, but it will be less expensive to operate; it will cost $22,000, whereas the gas-powered truck will cost $17,500. The cost of capital that applies to both investments is 12%. The life for both types of truck is estimated to be 6 years, during which time the net cash flows for the electric-powered truck will be $6,290 per year and those for the gas-powered truck will be $5,000 per year. Annual net cash flows include depreciation expenses. Calculate the NPV and IRR for each type of truck, and decide which to recommend.

12–10 Capital Budgeting Methods

Project S has a cost of $10,000 and is expected to produce benefits (cash flows) of $3,000 per year for 5 years. Project L costs $25,000 and is expected to produce cash flows of $7,400 per year for 5 years. Calculate the two projects' NPVs, IRRs, MIRRs, and PIs, assuming a cost of capital of 12%. Which project would be selected, assuming they are mutually exclusive, using each ranking method? Which should actually be selected?

12–11 MIRR and NPV

Your company is considering two mutually exclusive projects, X and Y, whose costs and cash flows are shown below:

Year	X	Y
0	−$5,000	−$5,000
1	1,000	4,500
2	1,500	1,500
3	2,000	1,000
4	4,000	500

The projects are equally risky, and their cost of capital is 12%. You must make a recommendation, and you must base it on the modified IRR (MIRR). Which project has the higher MIRR?

12–12 NPV and IRR Analysis

After discovering a new gold vein in the Colorado mountains, CTC Mining Corporation must decide whether to go ahead and develop the deposit. The most cost-effective method of mining gold is sulfuric acid extraction, a process that could result in environmental damage. Before proceeding with the extraction, CTC must spend $900,000 for new mining equipment and pay $165,000 for its installation. The gold mined will net the firm an estimated $350,000 each year for the 5-year life of the vein. CTC's cost of capital is 14%. For the purposes of this problem, assume that the cash inflows occur at the end of the year.

a. What are the project's NPV and IRR?

b. Should this project be undertaken if environmental impacts were not a consideration?

c. How should environmental effects be considered when evaluating this, or any other, project? How might these concepts affect the decision in part b?

12–13 NPV and IRR Analysis

Cummings Products is considering two mutually exclusive investments whose expected net cash flows are as follows:

	EXPECTED NET CASH FLOWS	
Year	Project A	Project B
0	−$400	−$650
1	−528	210
2	−219	210
3	−150	210
4	1,100	210
5	820	210
6	990	210
7	−325	210

a. Construct NPV profiles for Projects A and B.

b. What is each project's IRR?

c. If each project's cost of capital were 10%, which project, if either, should be selected? If the cost of capital were 17%, what would be the proper choice?

d. What is each project's MIRR at the cost of capital of 10%? At 17%? (*Hint:* Consider Period 7 as the end of Project B's life.)

e. What is the crossover rate, and what is its significance?

12–14 Timing Differences

The Ewert Exploration Company is considering two mutually exclusive plans for extracting oil on property for which it has mineral rights. Both plans call for the expenditure of $10 million to drill development wells. Under Plan A, all the oil will be extracted in 1 year, producing a cash flow at t = 1 of $12 million; under Plan B, cash flows will be $1.75 million per year for 20 years.

a. What are the annual incremental cash flows that will be available to Ewert Exploration if it undertakes Plan B rather than Plan A? (*Hint:* Subtract Plan A's flows from B's.)

b. If the company accepts Plan A and then invests the extra cash generated at the end of Year 1, what rate of return (reinvestment rate) would cause the cash flows from reinvestment to equal the cash flows from Plan B?

c. Suppose a firm's cost of capital is 10%. Is it logical to assume that the firm would take on all available independent projects (of average risk) with returns greater than 10%? Further, if all available projects with returns greater than 10% have been taken, would this mean that cash flows from past investments would have an opportunity cost of only 10%, because all the firm could do with these cash flows would be to replace money that has a cost of 10%? Finally, does this imply that the cost of capital is the correct rate to assume for the reinvestment of a project's cash flows?

d. Construct NPV profiles for Plans A and B, identify each project's IRR, and indicate the crossover rate.

12–15 Scale Differences

The Pinkerton Publishing Company is considering two mutually exclusive expansion plans. Plan A calls for the expenditure of $50 million on a large-scale, integrated plant that will provide an expected cash flow stream of $8 million per year for 20 years. Plan B calls for the expenditure of $15 million to build a somewhat less efficient, more labor-intensive plant that has an expected cash flow stream of $3.4 million per year for 20 years. The firm's cost of capital is 10%.

a. Calculate each project's NPV and IRR.

b. Set up a Project Δ by showing the cash flows that will exist if the firm goes with the large plant rather than the smaller plant. What are the NPV and the IRR for this Project Δ?

c. Graph the NPV profiles for Plan A, Plan B, and Project Δ.

12–16 Unequal Lives

Shao Airlines is considering the purchase of two alternative planes. Plane A has an expected life of 5 years, will cost $100 million, and will produce net cash flows of $30 million per year. Plane B has a life of 10 years, will cost $132 million, and will produce net cash flows of $25 million per year. Shao plans to serve the route for only 10 years. Inflation in operating costs, airplane costs, and fares is expected to be zero, and the company's cost of capital is 12%. By how much would the value of the company increase if it accepted the better project (plane)? What is the equivalent annual annuity for each plane?

12–17 Unequal Lives

The Perez Company has the opportunity to invest in one of two mutually exclusive machines that will produce a product it will need for the foreseeable future. Machine A costs $10 million but realizes after-tax inflows of $4 million per year for 4 years. After 4 years, the machine must be replaced. Machine B costs $15 million and realizes after-tax inflows of $3.5 million per year for 8 years, after which it must be replaced. Assume that machine prices are not expected to rise because inflation will be offset by cheaper components used in the machines. The cost of capital is 10%. By how much would the value of the company increase if it accepted the better machine? What is the equivalent annual annuity for each machine?

12-18 Unequal Lives

Filkins Fabric Company is considering the replacement of its old, fully depreciated knitting machine. Two new models are available: Machine 190-3, which has a cost of $190,000, a 3-year expected life, and after-tax cash flows (labor savings and depreciation) of $87,000 per year; and Machine 360-6, which has a cost of $360,000, a 6-year life, and after-tax cash flows of $98,300 per year. Knitting machine prices are not expected to rise, because inflation will be offset by cheaper components (microprocessors) used in the machines. Assume that Filkins's cost of capital is 14%. Should the firm replace its old knitting machine? If so, which new machine should it use? By how much would the value of the company increase if it accepted the better machine? What is the equivalent annual annuity for each machine?

Challenging Problems 19–22

12-19 Multiple Rates of Return

The Ulmer Uranium Company is deciding whether or not to open a strip mine whose net cost is $4.4 million. Net cash inflows are expected to be $27.7 million, all coming at the end of Year 1. The land must be returned to its natural state at a cost of $25 million, payable at the end of Year 2.
a. Plot the project's NPV profile.
b. Should the project be accepted if $r = 8\%$? If $r = 14\%$? Explain your reasoning.
c. Can you think of some other capital budgeting situations in which negative cash flows during or at the end of the project's life might lead to multiple IRRs?
d. What is the project's MIRR at $r = 8\%$? At $r = 14\%$? Does the MIRR method lead to the same accept–reject decision as the NPV method?

12-20 Present Value of Costs

The Aubey Coffee Company is evaluating the within-plant distribution system for its new roasting, grinding, and packing plant. The two alternatives are: (1) a conveyor system with a high initial cost but low annual operating costs, and (2) several forklift trucks, which cost less but have considerably higher operating costs. The decision to construct the plant has already been made, and the choice here will have no effect on the overall revenues of the project. The cost of capital for the plant is 8%, and the projects' expected net costs are listed in the following table:

	Expected Net Cost	
Year	Conveyor	Forklift
0	−$500,000	−$200,000
1	−120,000	−160,000
2	−120,000	−160,000
3	−120,000	−160,000
4	−120,000	−160,000
5	−20,000	−160,000

a. What is the IRR of each alternative?

b. What is the present value of the costs of each alternative? Which method should be chosen?

12-21 Payback, NPV, and MIRR

Your division is considering two investment projects, each of which requires an up-front expenditure of $25 million. You estimate that the cost of capital is 10% and that the investments will produce the following after-tax cash flows (in millions of dollars):

Year	Project A	Project B
1	5	20
2	10	10
3	15	8
4	20	6

a. What is the regular payback period for each of the projects?

b. What is the discounted payback period for each of the projects?

c. If the two projects are independent and the cost of capital is 10%, which project or projects should the firm undertake?

d. If the two projects are mutually exclusive and the cost of capital is 5%, which project should the firm undertake?

e. If the two projects are mutually exclusive and the cost of capital is 15%, which project should the firm undertake?

f. What is the crossover rate?

g. If the cost of capital is 10%, what is the modified IRR (MIRR) of each project?

12-22 Economic Life

The Scampini Supplies Company recently purchased a new delivery truck. The new truck cost $22,500, and it is expected to generate net after-tax operating cash flows, including depreciation, of $6,250 per year. The truck has a 5-year expected life. The expected salvage values after tax adjustments for the truck are given below. The company's cost of capital is 10%.

Year	Annual Operating Cash Flow	Salvage Value
0	−$22,500	$22,500
1	6,250	17,500
2	6,250	14,000
3	6,250	11,000
4	6,250	5,000
5	6,250	0

a. Should the firm operate the truck until the end of its 5-year physical life? If not, then what is its optimal economic life?

b. Would the introduction of salvage values, in addition to operating cash flows, ever *reduce* the expected NPV and/or IRR of a project?

Spreadsheet Problem

12–23 Build a Model: Capital Budgeting Tools

Start with the partial model in the file *Ch12 P23 Build a Model.xls* on the textbook's Web site. Gardial Fisheries is considering two mutually exclusive investments. The projects' expected net cash flows are as follows:

	Expected Net Cash Flows	
Year	Project A	Project B
0	−$375	−$575
1	−300	190
2	−200	190
3	−100	190
4	600	190
5	600	190
6	926	190
7	−200	0

a. If each project's cost of capital is 12%, which project should be selected? If the cost of capital is 18%, what project is the proper choice?

b. Construct NPV profiles for Projects A and B.

c. What is each project's IRR?

d. What is the crossover rate, and what is its significance?

e. What is each project's MIRR at a cost of capital of 12%? At r = 18%? (*Hint:* Consider Period 7 as the end of Project B's life.)

f. What is the regular payback period for these two projects?

g. At a cost of capital of 12%, what is the discounted payback period for these two projects?

h. What is the profitability index for each project if the cost of capital is 12%?

MINI CASE

You have just graduated from the MBA program of a large university, and one of your favorite courses was "Today's Entrepreneurs." In fact, you enjoyed it so much you have decided you want to "be your own boss." While you were in the master's program, your grandfather died and left you $1 million to do with as you please. You are not an inventor, and you do not have a trade skill that you can market; however, you have decided that you would like to purchase at least one established franchise in the fast-foods area, maybe two (if profitable). The problem is that you have never been one to stay with any project for too long, so you figure that your time frame is 3 years. After 3 years you will go on to something else.

You have narrowed your selection down to two choices: (1) Franchise L, Lisa's Soups, Salads & Stuff, and (2) Franchise S, Sam's Fabulous Fried Chicken. The net cash flows shown below include the price you would receive for selling the franchise in Year 3 and the forecast of how each franchise will do over the 3-year period. Franchise L's cash flows will start off slowly but will increase rather quickly as people become more health-conscious, while Franchise S's cash flows will start off high but will trail off as other chicken competitors enter the marketplace and as people become more health-conscious and avoid fried foods. Franchise L serves breakfast and lunch whereas Franchise S serves only dinner, so it is possible for you to invest in both franchises. You see these franchises as perfect complements to one another: You could attract both the lunch and dinner crowds and the health-conscious and not-so-health-conscious crowds without the franchises directly competing against one another.

Here are the net cash flows (in thousands of dollars):

Expected Net Cash Flows

Year	Franchise L	Franchise S
0	−$100	−$100
1	10	70
2	60	50
3	80	20

Depreciation, salvage values, net working capital requirements, and tax effects are all included in these cash flows.

You also have made subjective risk assessments of each franchise and concluded that both franchises have risk characteristics that require a return of 10%. You must now determine whether one or both of the franchises should be accepted.

a. What is capital budgeting?
b. What is the difference between independent and mutually exclusive projects?
c. (1) Define the term *net present value (NPV)*. What is each franchise's NPV?
   (2) What is the rationale behind the NPV method? According to NPV, which franchise or franchises should be accepted if they are independent? Mutually exclusive?
   (3) Would the NPVs change if the cost of capital changed?

d. (1) Define the term *internal rate of return (IRR)*. What is each franchise's IRR?
   (2) How is the IRR on a project related to the YTM on a bond?
   (3) What is the logic behind the IRR method? According to IRR, which franchises should be accepted if they are independent? Mutually exclusive?
   (4) Would the franchises' IRRs change if the cost of capital changed?
e. (1) Draw NPV profiles for Franchises L and S. At what discount rate do the profiles cross?
f. (2) Look at your NPV profile graph without referring to the actual NPVs and IRRs. Which franchise or franchises should be accepted if they are independent? Mutually exclusive? Explain. Are your answers correct at any cost of capital less than 23.6%?
g. What is the underlying cause of ranking conflicts between NPV and IRR?
h. Define the term *modified IRR (MIRR)*. Find the MIRRs for Franchises L and S.
i. What does the profitability index (PI) measure? What are the PIs of Franchises S and L?
   (1) What is the payback period? Find the paybacks for Franchises L and S.
   (2) What is the rationale for the payback method? According to the payback criterion, which franchise or franchises should be accepted if the firm's maximum acceptable payback is 2 years and if Franchises L and S are independent? If they are mutually exclusive?
   (3) What is the difference between the regular and discounted payback periods?
   (4) What is the main disadvantage of discounted payback? Is the payback method of any real usefulness in capital budgeting decisions?
j. As a separate project (Project P), you are considering sponsorship of a pavilion at the upcoming World's Fair. The pavilion would cost $800,000, and it is expected to result in $5 million of incremental cash inflows during its single year of operation. However, it would then take another year, and $5 million of costs, to demolish the site and return it to its original condition. Thus, Project P's expected net cash flows look like this (in millions of dollars):

Year	Net Cash Flows
0	−$0.8
1	5.0
2	−5.0

The project is estimated to be of average risk, so its cost of capital is 10%.

(1) What are normal and nonnormal cash flows?

(2) What is Project P's NPV? What is its IRR? Its MIRR?

(3) Draw Project P's NPV profile. Does Project P have normal or nonnormal cash flows? Should this project be accepted?

k. In an unrelated analysis, you have the opportunity to choose between the following two mutually exclusive projects, Project T (which lasts for 2 years) and Project F (which lasts for 4 years):

	Expected Net Cash Flows	
Year	Project T	Project F
0	−$100,000	−$100,000
1	60,000	33,500
2	60,000	33,500
3	—	33,500
4	—	33,500

The projects provide a necessary service, so whichever one is selected is expected to be repeated into the foreseeable future. Both projects have a 10% cost of capital.

(1) What is each project's initial NPV without replication?

(2) What is each project's equivalent annual annuity?

(3) Apply the replacement chain approach to determine the projects' extended NPVs. Which project should be chosen?

(4) Assume that the cost to replicate Project T in 2 years will increase to $105,000 due to inflation. How should the analysis be handled now, and which project should be chosen?

l. You are also considering another project that has a physical life of 3 years; that is, the machinery will be totally worn out after 3 years. However, if the project were terminated prior to the end of 3 years, the machinery would have a positive salvage value. Here are the project's estimated cash flows:

Year	Initial Investment and Operating Cash Flows	End-of-Year Net Salvage Value
0	−$5,000	$5,000
1	2,100	3,100
2	2,000	2,000
3	1,750	0

Using the 10% cost of capital, what is the project's NPV if it is operated for the full 3 years? Would the NPV change if the company planned to terminate the project at the end of Year 2? At the end of Year 1? What is the project's optimal (economic) life?

SELECTED ADDITIONAL CASES

The following cases from CengageCompose cover many of the concepts discussed in this chapter and are available at http://compose.cengage.com.

Klein-Brigham Series:

Case 11, "Chicago Valve Company."

Brigham-Buzzard Series:

Case 6, "Powerline Network Corporation (Basics of Capital Budgeting)."

Capital Budgeting: Estimating Cash Flows and Analyzing Risk

Chapter 12 assumed that a project's cash flows had already been estimated. Now we cover cash flow estimation and identify the issues a manager faces in producing relevant and realistic cash flow estimates. In addition, cash flow estimates are just that: estimates! It is crucial for a manager to incorporate uncertainty into project analysis if a company is to make informed decisions regarding project selection. We begin with a discussion of procedures for estimating relevant and realistic cash flows.

WEB

The textbook's Web site contains an *Excel* file that will guide you through the chapter's calculations. The file for this chapter is ***Ch13 Tool Kit.xls***, and we encourage you to open the file and follow along as you read the chapter.

Beginning-of-Chapter Questions

As you read the chapter, consider how you would answer the following questions. You *should not* necessarily be able to answer the questions before you read the chapter. Rather, you should use them to get a sense of the issues covered in the chapter. After reading the chapter, you should be able to give at least partial answers to the questions, and you should be able to give better answers after the chapter has been discussed in class. Note, too, that it is often useful, when answering conceptual questions, to use hypothetical data to illustrate your answer. We illustrate the answers with an *Excel* model that is available on the textbook's Web site. Accessing the model and working through it is a useful exercise, and it provides insights that are useful when answering the questions.

1. How do **project cash flows** as calculated in this chapter affect a firm's **corporate free cash flows** as defined in Chapter 6 and then used in Chapter 9 to calculate a firm's value? How does a proposed project's **estimated NPV** affect the **value of the firm**?

2. Define (a) **externalities** and (b) **sunk costs,** and then give examples of each that might be involved in a proposal by an energy company to build a new coal-fired electric power generating unit. How would these factors be worked into the analysis?

3. If Congress shortened depreciation lives for tax purposes, how would this affect the energy project's NPV, assuming nothing else changes?

4. If the company's capital budgeting analyst decided to show all projected cash flows, both positive and negative, in current dollars rather than inflation-adjusted dollars, would this affect the calculated NPV?

5. Discuss some ways the company could estimate the project's risk, and then explain how risk might be incorporated into the decision analysis.

6. What are **real options**, and why are they important to capital budgeting?

PROJECT VALUATION, CASH FLOWS, AND RISK ANALYSIS

When we estimate a project's cash flows (CF) and then discount them at the project's risk-adjusted cost of capital, r, the result is the project's NPV, which tells us how much the project increases the firm's value. This chapter focuses on how to estimate the size and risk of a project's cash flows.

Note too that project cash flows, once a project has been accepted and placed in operation, are added to the firm's free cash flows from other sources. Therefore, projects' cash flows essentially determine the firm's free cash flows as discussed in Chapter 6 and thus form the basis for the firm's market value and stock price.

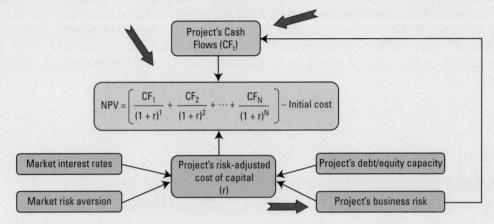

$$NPV = \left[\frac{CF_1}{(1 + r)^1} + \frac{CF_2}{(1 + r)^2} + \cdots + \frac{CF_N}{(1 + r)^N} \right] - \text{Initial cost}$$

Source: From *Financial Management: Theory & Practice*, 2013, by Brigham and Ehrhardt. © Cengage Learning.

13-1 Identifying Relevant Cash Flows

The most important—and difficult—step in capital budgeting is estimating a proposal's relevant **project cash flows**, which are the differences between the cash flows the firm will have if it implements the project versus the cash flows it will have if it rejects the project. These are called **incremental cash flows**:

$$\text{Incremental cash flows} = \frac{\text{Company's cash flows}}{\textit{with} \text{ the project}} - \frac{\text{Company's cash flows}}{\textit{without} \text{ the project}}$$

Estimating incremental cash flows might sound easy, but there are many potential pitfalls. In this section, we identify the key concepts that will help you avoid these pitfalls and then apply the concepts to an actual project to illustrate their application to cash flow estimation.

13-1a Cash Flow versus Accounting Income

We saw in Chapter 6 that free cash flow differs from accounting income: Free cash flow is cash flow that is available for distribution to all investors, making free cash flow the basis of a firm's value. It is common in finance to speak of a firm's free cash flow and a project's cash flow (or net cash flow), but these are based on the same concepts. In fact, a project's cash flow is identical to the project's free cash flow, and a firm's total net cash flow from all projects is equal to the firm's free cash flow. We will follow the typical convention and refer to a project's free cash flow simply as project cash flow, but keep in mind that the two concepts are identical.[1]

Because net income is not equal to the cash flow available for distribution to all investors, in the last chapter we discounted *net cash flows,* not accounting income, to find projects' NPVs. *For capital budgeting purposes it is the project's net cash flow, not its accounting income, which is relevant.* Therefore, when analyzing a proposed capital budgeting project, disregard the project's net income and focus exclusively on its net cash flow. Be especially alert to the following differences between cash flow and accounting income.

The Cash Flow Effect of Asset Purchases and Depreciation

Most projects require assets, and asset purchases represent *negative* cash flows. Even though the acquisition of assets results in a cash outflow, accountants do not show the purchase of fixed assets as a deduction from accounting income. Instead, they deduct a depreciation expense each year throughout the life of the asset. Depreciation shelters income from taxation, and this has an impact on cash flow, but depreciation itself is not a cash flow. Therefore, depreciation must be added back when estimating a project's operating cash flow.

Depreciation is the most common noncash charge, but there are many other noncash charges that might appear on a company's financial statements. Just as with depreciation, all other noncash charges should be added back when calculating a project's net cash flow.

Changes in Net Operating Working Capital

Normally, additional inventories are required to support a new operation, and expanded sales tie up additional funds in accounts receivable. However, payables and accruals increase as a result of the expansion, and this reduces the cash needed to finance inventories and receivables. The difference between the required increase in operating current assets and the increase in operating current liabilities is the change in net operating working capital. If this change is positive, as it generally is for expansion projects, then additional financing—beyond the cost of the fixed assets—will be needed.

Toward the end of a project's life, inventories will be used but not replaced, and receivables will be collected without corresponding replacements. As these changes occur the firm will receive cash inflows; as a result, the investment in net operating working capital will be returned by the end of the project's life.

---

1. There are several terms with "cash flow" in them. Some are the same, and some are different! When the financial press refers to a firm's "net cash flow," it is almost always equal to the definition of net cash flow we provide in Chapter 6 (which simply adds back depreciation and any other noncash charges to net income). However, as we explained in Chapter 6, the "net cash flow from operations" (from the statement of cash flows) and the firm's "free cash flow" are different from "net cash flow" and are much more useful measures. When financial analysts within a company use the term "a project's net cash flow," they almost always calculate it as we do in this chapter, which is in essence the project's free cash flow. Thus, free cash flow means the same thing whether you calculate it for a firm or for a project. On the other hand, a firm's net cash flow as discussed in the financial press and a project's net cash flow as calculated by an internal analyst are not the same.

Interest Charges Are Not Included in Project Cash Flows

Interest is a cash expense, so at first blush it would seem that interest on any debt used to finance a project should be deducted when we estimate the project's net cash flows. However, this is not correct. Recall from Chapter 12 that we discount a project's cash flows by its risk-adjusted cost of capital, which is a weighted average (WACC) of the costs of debt, preferred stock, and common equity, adjusted for the project's risk and debt capacity. This project cost of capital is the rate of return necessary to satisfy *all* of the firm's investors, including stockholders and debtholders. A common mistake made by many students and financial managers is to subtract interest payments when estimating a project's cash flows. This is a mistake because the cost of debt is already embedded in the cost of capital, so subtracting interest payments from the project's cash flows would amount to double-counting interest costs. Therefore, *you should not subtract interest expenses when finding a project's cash flows.*

13-1b **Timing of Cash Flows: Yearly versus Other Periods**

In theory, in capital budgeting analyses we should discount cash flows based on the exact moment when they occur. Therefore, one could argue that daily cash flows would be better than annual flows. However, it would be costly to estimate daily cash flows and laborious to analyze them. In general, the analysis would be no better than one using annual flows because we simply can't make accurate forecasts of daily cash flows more than a couple of months into the future. Therefore, it is generally appropriate to assume that all cash flows occur at the end of the various years. We would analyze projects with highly predictable cash flows, such as constructing a building and then leasing it on a long-term basis (with monthly payments) to a financially sound tenant, using monthly periods.

13-1c **Expansion Projects and Replacement Projects**

Two types of projects can be distinguished: (1) *expansion projects,* in which the firm makes an investment in, for example, a new Home Depot store in Seattle; and (2) *replacement projects,* in which the firm replaces existing assets, generally to reduce costs. In expansion projects, the cash expenditures on buildings, equipment, and required working capital are obviously incremental, as are the sales revenues and operating costs associated with the project. The incremental costs associated with replacement projects are not so obvious. For example, Home Depot might replace some of its delivery trucks to reduce fuel and maintenance expenses. Replacement analysis is complicated by the fact that most of the relevant cash flows are the cash flow differences between the existing project and the replacement project. For example, the fuel bill for a more efficient new truck might be $10,000 per year versus $15,000 for the old truck, and the $5,000 fuel savings would be an incremental cash flow associated with the replacement decision. We analyze an expansion and replacement decision later in the chapter.

13-1d **Sunk Costs**

A **sunk cost** is an outlay related to the project that was incurred in the past and that cannot be recovered in the future regardless of whether or not the project is accepted. Therefore, sunk costs are *not incremental costs* and thus are not relevant in a capital budgeting analysis.

To illustrate, suppose Home Depot spent $2 million to investigate sites for a potential new store in a given area. That $2 million is a sunk cost—the money is gone, and it won't come back regardless of whether or not a new store is built. Therefore, the $2 million should not be included in a capital budgeting decision.

Improper treatment of sunk costs can lead to bad decisions. For example, suppose Home Depot completed the analysis for a new store and found that it must spend an additional (or incremental) $17 million to build and supply the store, on top of the $2 million already spent on the site study. Suppose the present value of future cash flows is $18 million. Should the project be accepted? If the sunk costs are mistakenly included, the NPV is −$2 million + (−$17 million) + $18 million = −$1 million and the project would be rejected. However, *that would be a bad decision.* The real issue is whether the *incremental* $17 million would result in enough *incremental* cash flow to produce a positive NPV. If the $2 million sunk cost were disregarded, as it should be, then the NPV on an incremental basis would be a *positive* $1 million.

13-1e Opportunity Costs Associated with Assets the Firm Already Owns

Another conceptual issue relates to **opportunity costs** related to assets the firm already owns. Continuing our example, suppose Home Depot (HD) owns land with a current market value of $2 million that can be used for the new store if it decides to build the store. If HD goes forward with the project, only another $15 million will be required, not the full $17 million, because it will not need to buy the required land. Does this mean that HD should use the $15 million incremental cost as the cost of the new store? The answer is definitely "no." If the new store is *not* built, then HD could sell the land and receive a cash flow of $2 million. This $2 million is an *opportunity cost*—it is cash that HD would not receive if the land is used for the new store. Therefore, the $2 million must be charged to the new project, and failing to do so would cause the new project's calculated NPV to be too high.

13-1f Externalities

Another conceptual issue relates to **externalities**, which are the effects of a project on other parts of the firm or on the environment. As explained in what follows, there are three types of externalities: negative within-firm externalities, positive within-firm externalities, and environmental externalities.

Negative Within-Firm Externalities

If a retailer like Home Depot opens a new store that is close to its existing stores, then the new store might attract customers who would otherwise buy from the existing stores, reducing the old stores' cash flows. Therefore, the new store's incremental cash flow must be reduced by the amount of the cash flow lost by its other units. This type of externality is called **cannibalization**, because the new business eats into the company's existing business. Many businesses are subject to cannibalization. For example, each new iPod model cannibalizes existing models. Those lost cash flows should be considered, and that means charging them as a cost when analyzing new products.

Dealing properly with negative externalities requires careful thinking. If Apple decided not to come out with a new model of iPod because of cannibalization, another company might come out with a similar new model, causing Apple to lose sales on existing models. Apple must examine the total situation, and this is definitely more than a simple, mechanical analysis. Experience and knowledge of the industry is required to make good decisions in most cases.

One of the best examples of a company getting into trouble as a result of not dealing correctly with cannibalization was IBM's response to the development of the first personal computers in the 1970s. IBM's mainframes dominated the computer industry, and they generated huge profits. IBM used its technology to enter the PC market, and initially it was the leading PC company. However, its top managers decided to deemphasize the PC division because they were afraid it would hurt the more profitable mainframe business. That decision opened the door for Apple, Dell, Hewlett Packard, Sony, and Chinese competitors to take PC business away from IBM. As a result, IBM went from being the most profitable firm in the world to one whose very survival was threatened. IBM's experience highlights that it is just as important to understand the industry and the long-run consequences of a given decision as it is to understand the theory of finance. Good judgment is an essential element for good financial decisions.

Positive Within-Firm Externalities

As we noted earlier, cannibalization occurs when a new product competes with an old one. However, a new project can also be *complementary* to an old one, in which case cash flows in the old operation will be *increased* when the new one is introduced. For example, Apple's iPod was a profitable product, but when Apple considered an investment in its iTunes music store it realized that the store would boost sales of iPods. So, even if an analysis of the proposed music store indicated a negative NPV, the analysis would not be complete unless the incremental cash flows that would occur in the iPod division were credited to the music store. Consideration of positive externalities often changes a project's NPV from negative to positive.

Environmental Externalities

The most common type of negative externality is a project's impact on the environment. Government rules and regulations constrain the minimal amount of environmental protection companies are required to provide, but firms have some flexibility in dealing with environmental issues over and above this minimum amount. For example, suppose a manufacturer is studying a proposed new plant. The company could meet current environmental regulations at a cost of $1 million, but the plant would still emit fumes that would cause some bad will in its neighborhood. Those ill feelings would not show up in the cash flow analysis, but they should be considered. Perhaps a relatively small additional expenditure would reduce the emissions substantially, make the plant look good relative to other plants in the area, and provide goodwill that in the future would help the firm's sales and its negotiations with governmental agencies.

Of course, all firms' profits ultimately depend on the Earth remaining healthy, so companies have some incentive to do things that protect the environment even though those actions are not currently required. However, if one firm decides to take actions that are good for the environment but quite costly, then it must either raise its prices or suffer a decline in earnings. If its competitors decide to get by with less costly but environmentally unfriendly processes, they can price their products lower and make more money. Of course, the more environmentally friendly companies can advertise their environmental efforts, and this might—or might not—offset their higher costs. All this illustrates why government regulations are often necessary. Finance, politics, and the environment are all interconnected.

Why should companies use a project's net cash flows rather than accounting income when determining a project's NPV?

Explain the following terms: incremental cash flow, sunk cost, opportunity cost, externality, cannibalization, and complementary project.

Provide an example of a "good" externality—that is, one that increases a project's true NPV over what it would be if just its own cash flows were considered.

13-2 Analysis of an Expansion Project

In Chapter 12, we worked with the cash flows associated with one of Guyton Products Company's expansion projects. Recall that Project L is the application of a radically new liquid nano-coating technology to a new type of solar water heater module, which will be manufactured under a 4-year license from a university. In this section, we show how these cash flows are estimated. (We only show estimates for Project L in the chapter, but we also show estimates for GPC's other project from Chapter 12, Project S, in *Ch13 Tool Kit.xls*.) It's not clear how well the water heater will work, how strong demand for it will be, how long it will be before the product becomes obsolete, or whether the license can be renewed after the initial 4 years. Still, the water heater has the potential for being profitable, though it could also fail miserably. GPC is a relatively large company and this is one of many projects, so a failure would not bankrupt the firm but would hurt profits and the stock's price.

13-2a Base Case Inputs and Key Results

We used *Excel* to do the analysis. We could have used a calculator and paper, but *Excel is much* easier to use for capital budgeting problems. You don't need to know *Excel* to understand our discussion, but if you plan to work in finance—or, really, in any business field—you must know how to use *Excel*, so we recommend that you open the *Excel Tool Kit* for this chapter and scroll through it as the textbook explains the analysis.

WEB

See *Ch13 Tool Kit.xls* on the textbook's Web site.

Figure 13-1 shows Part 1 of the *Excel* model used in this analysis; see the first worksheet in *Ch13 Tool Kit.xls*, named *1-Base-Case*. The base-case inputs are in the blue section. For example, the cost of required equipment to manufacture the water heaters is $7,750 and is shown in the blue input section. (All dollar values in Figure 13-1 and in our discussion here are reported in thousands, so the equipment actually costs $7,750,000.) The actual number-crunching takes place in Part 2 of the model, shown in Figure 13-2. Part 2 takes the inputs from the blue section of Figure 13-1 and generates the project's cash flows. Part 2 of the model also performs calculations of the project performance measures discussed in Chapter 12 and then reports those results in the orange section of Figure 13-1. This structure allows you (or your manager) to change and input and instantly see the impact on the reported performance measures.

FIGURE 13-1   Analysis of an Expansion Project: Inputs and Key Results (Thousands of Dollars)

	A	B	C	D	E	F	G	H	I
54	Part 1. Inputs and Key Results								
55									
56	Inputs				Base-Case		Key Results		
57	Equipment cost				$7,750		NPV		$1,048
58	Salvage value, equipment, Year 4				$639		IRR		13.79%
59	Opportunity cost				$0		MIRR		12.78%
60	Externalities (cannibalization)				$0		PI		1.10
61	Units sold, Year 1				10,000		Payback		3.39
62	Annual change in units sold, after Year 1				15%		Discounted payback		3.80
63	Sales price per unit, Year 1				$1.50				
64	Annual change in sales price, after Year 1				4%				
65	Variable cost per unit (VC), Year 1				$1.07				
66	Annual change in VC, after Year 1				3%				
67	Nonvariable cost (Non-VC), Year 1				$2,120				
68	Annual change in Non-VC, after Year 1				3%				
69	Project cost of capital, r				10%				
70	Tax rate				40%				
71	Working capital as % of next year's sales				15%				

Microsoft Excel® is a registered trademark of Microsoft Corporation. © 2014 Microsoft.

See ***Ch13 Tool Kit.xls***
on the textbook's
Web site.

We have saved these base-case inputs in ***Ch13 Tool Kit.xls*** with *Excel's* Scenario Manager. If you change some inputs but want to return to the original base-case inputs, you can select Data, What-If Analysis, Scenario Manager, pick the scenario named "Base-Case for Project L," and click Show. This will replace any changes with the original inputs. Scenario Manager is a very useful tool and we will have more to say about it later in this chapter.

13-2b Cash Flow Projections: Intermediate Calculations

Figure 13-2 shows Part 2 of the model. When setting up *Excel* models, we prefer to have more rows but shorter formulas. So instead of having very complicated formulas in the section for cash flow forecasts, we put intermediate calculations in a separate section. The blue section of Figure 13-2 shows these intermediate calculations for the GPC project, as we explain in the following sections.

Annual Unit Sales, Unit Prices, Unit Costs, and Inflation

Rows 85–88 show annual unit sales, unit sale prices, unit variable costs, and nonvariable costs. These values are all projected to grow at the rates assumed in Part 1 of the model in Figure 13-1. If you ignore growth in prices and costs when estimating cash flows, you are likely to *underestimate* a project's value because the project's weighted average cost of capital (WACC) includes the impact of inflation. In other words, the estimated cash flows will be too low relative to the WACC, so the estimated net present value (NPV) also will be too low relative to the true NPV. To see that the WACC includes inflation, recall from Chapter 4 that the cost of debt

FIGURE 13-2	Analysis of an Expansion Project: Cash Flows and Performance Measures (Thousands of Dollars)

	A	B	C	D	E	F	G	H	I
83	**Part 2. Cash Flows and Performance Measures**								
84	**Intermediate Calculations**				**0**	**1**	**2**	**3**	**4**
85	Unit sales					10,000	11,500	13,225	15,209
86	Sales price per unit					$1.50	$1.56	$1.62	$1.69
87	Variable cost per unit (excl. depr.)					$1.07	$1.10	$1.14	$1.17
88	Nonvariable costs (excl. depr.)					$2,120	$2,184	$2,249	$2,317
89	Sales revenues = Units × Price/unit					$15,000	$17,940	$21,456	$25,662
90	NOWC$_t$ = 15%(Revenues$_{t+1}$)				$2,250	$2,691	$3,218	$3,849	$0
91	Basis for depreciation				$7,750				
92	Annual depreciation rate (MACRS)					33.33%	44.45%	14.81%	7.41%
93	Annual depreciation expense					$2,583	$3,445	$1,148	$574
94	Remaining undepreciated value (book value)					$5,167	$1,722	$574	$0
95	**Cash Flow Forecast**					**Cash Flows at End of Year**			
96						**0**	**1**	**2**	**3**	**4**
97	Sales revenues = Units × Price/unit					$15,000	$17,940	$21,456	$25,662
98	Variable costs = Units × Cost/unit					$10,700	$12,674	$15,013	$17,782
99	Nonvariable costs (excluding depr.)					$2,120	$2,184	$2,249	$2,317
100	Depreciation					$2,583	$3,445	$1,148	$574
101	Earnings before int. and taxes (EBIT)					−$403	−$363	$3,047	$4,988
102	Taxes on operating profit (40% rate)					−$161	−$145	$1,219	$1,995
103	Net operating profit after taxes					−$242	−$218	$1,828	$2,993
104	Add back depreciation					$2,583	$3,445	$1,148	$574
105	Equipment purchases				−$7,750				
106	Salvage value								$639
107	Cash flow due to tax on salv. val.								−$256
108	Cash flow due to change in WC				−$2,250	−$441	−$527	−$631	$3,849
109	Opportunity cost, after taxes				$0	$0	$0	$0	$0
110	After-tax externalities					$0	$0	$0	$0
111	**Project net cash flows: Time Line**				**−$10,000**	**$1,900**	**$2,700**	**$2,345**	**$7,800**
112	**Project Evaluation Measures**								
113	NPV		$1,048	=NPV(E69,F111:I111)+E111					
114	IRR		13.79%	=IRR(E111:I111)					
115	MIRR		12.78%	=MIRR(E111:I111,E69,E69)					
116	Profitability index		1.10	=NPV(E69,F111:I111)/(−E111)					
117	Payback		3.39	=PERCENTRANK(E120:I120,0,6)*I119					
118	Disc. payback		3.80	=PERCENTRANK(E122:I122,0,6)*I119					
119	**Calculations for Payback**			Year:	**0**	**1**	**2**	**3**	**4**
120	Cumulative cash flows for payback				−$10,000	−$8,100	−$5,400	−$3,055	$4,745
121	Disc. cash flows for disc. payback				−$10,000	$1,727	$2,231	$1,762	$5,328
122	Cumulative discounted cash flows				−$10,000	−$8,273	−$6,041	−$4,279	$1,048

includes an inflation premium. Also, the capital asset pricing model from Chapter 2 defines the cost of equity as the sum of the risk-free rate and a risk premium. Like the cost of debt, the risk-free rate also has an inflation premium. Therefore, if the WACC includes the impact of inflation, the estimated cash flows must also include inflation. It is theoretically possible to ignore inflation when estimating the cash flows but adjust the WACC so that it, too, doesn't incorporate inflation, but we have

See **Ch13 Tool Kit.xls** on the textbook's Web site.

never seen this accomplished correctly in practice. Therefore, you should always include growth rates in prices and costs when estimating cash flows.

Net Operating Working Capital (NOWC)

Virtually all projects require working capital, and this one is no exception. For example, raw materials must be purchased and replenished each year as they are used. In Part 1 (Figure 13-1), we assume that GPC must have an amount of net operating working capital on hand equal to 15% of the upcoming year's sales. For example, in Year 0, GPC must have 15%($15,000) = $2,250 in working capital on hand. As sales grow, so does the required working capital. Rows 89–90 show the annual sales revenues (the product of units sold and sales price) and the required working capital.

Depreciation Expense

Rows 91–94 report intermediate calculations related to depreciation, beginning with the depreciation basis, which is the cost of acquiring and installing a project. The basis for GPC's project is $7,750.[2] The depreciation expense for a year is the product of the basis and that year's depreciation rate. Depreciation rates depend on the type of property and its useful life. Even though GPC's project will operate for 4 years, it is classified as 3-year property for tax purposes. The depreciation rates in Row 92 are for 3-year property using the modified cost accelerated cost recovery system (MACRS); see Appendix 13A and the chapter's *Tool Kit* for more discussion of depreciation.[3] The remaining undepreciated value is equal to the original basis less the accumulated depreciation; this is called the book value of the asset and is used later in the model when calculating the tax on the salvage value.

See *Ch13 Tool Kit.xls* on the textbook's Web site.

13-2c **Cash Flow Projections: Estimating Net Operating Profit After Taxes (NOPAT)**

The yellow section in the middle of Figure 13-2 shows the steps in calculating the project's net operating profit after taxes (NOPAT). Projected sales revenues are on Row 97. Annual variable unit costs are multiplied by the number of units sold to determine total variable costs, as shown on Row 98. Nonvariable costs are shown on Row 99, and depreciation expense is shown on Row 100. Subtracting variable costs, nonvariable costs, and depreciation from sales revenues results in operating profit, as shown on Row 101.

When discussing a company's income statement, operating profit often is called earnings before interest and taxes (EBIT). Remember, though, that we do not subtract interest when estimating a project's cash flows, because the project's WACC is the overall rate of return required by all the company's investors and not just shareholders. Therefore, the cash flows must also be the cash flows available to all investors and not just shareholders, so we do not subtract interest expense.

---

2. Regardless of whether accelerated or straight-line depreciation is used, the basis is not adjusted by the expected salvage value when calculating the depreciation expense that is used to determine taxable income. This is different from the calculation of depreciation for purposes of financial reporting.

3. MACRS assumes that property is placed in service in the middle of a year, so only one-half a year's depreciation is allowed in the first year. A final one-half year's depreciation is allowed in the fourth year.

We calculate taxes in Row 102 and subtract them to get the project's net operating profit after taxes (NOPAT) on Row 103. The project has negative earnings before interest and taxes in Years 1 and 2. When multiplied by the 40% tax rate, Row 102 shows negative taxes for Years 1 and 2. This negative tax is subtracted from EBIT and actually makes the after-tax operating profit larger than the pre-tax profit! For example, the Year 1 pre-tax profit is −$403 and the reported tax is −$161, leading to an after-tax profit of −$403 − (−$161) = −$242. In other words, it is as though the IRS is sending GPC a check for $161. How can this be correct?

Recall the basic concept underlying the relevant cash flows for project analysis— what are the company's cash flows with the project versus the company's cash flows without the project? Applying this concept, if GPC expects to have taxable income from other projects in excess of $403 in Year 1, then the project will shelter that income from $161 in taxes. Therefore, the project will generate $161 in cash flow for GPC in Year 1 due to the tax savings.[4]

13-2d **Cash Flow Projections: Adjustments to NOPAT**

Row 103 reports the project's NOPAT, but we must adjust NOPAT to determine the project's actual cash flows. In particular, we must account for depreciation, asset purchases and dispositions, changes in working capital, opportunity costs, externalities, and sunk costs.

Adjustments to Determine Cash Flows: Depreciation

The first step is to add back depreciation, which is a noncash expense. You might be wondering why we subtract depreciation on Row 100 only to add it back on Row 104, and the answer is due to depreciation's impact on taxes. If we had ignored the Year 1 depreciation of $2,583 when calculating NOPAT, the pre-tax income (EBIT) for Year 1 would have been $15,000 − $10,700 − $2,120 = $2,180 instead of −$403. Taxes would have been 40%($2,180) = $872 instead of −$161. This is a difference of $872 − (−$161) = $1,033. Cash flows should reflect the actual taxes, but we must add back the noncash depreciation expense to reflect the actual cash flow.[5]

Adjustments to Determine Cash Flows: Asset Purchases and Dispositions

GPC purchased the asset at the beginning of the project for $7,750, which is a negative cash flow shown on Row 105. Had GPC purchased additional assets in other years, we would report those purchases, too.

GPC expects to salvage the investment at Year 4 for $639. In our example, GPC's project was fully depreciated by the end of the project, so the $639 salvage value is a taxable profit. At a 40% tax rate, GPC will owe 40%($639) = $256 in taxes, as shown on Row 107.

---

4. Even if GPC doesn't expect to have other taxable income in Year 1 but does have taxable income from the past 2 years, GPC can carry back the loss in Year 1 and receive a tax refund. If GPC doesn't have past taxable income, then we would report zero taxes for the project in Year 1 and carry forward the loss until GPC or the project does have taxable income.
5. Notice that the tax savings due to depreciation also may be calculated as the product of the tax rate and the depreciation expense: 40%($2,583) = $1,033.20. The numbers shown in the textbook are rounded, but the numbers used in the *Excel* model are not.

Suppose instead that GPC terminates operations before the equipment is fully depreciated. The after-tax salvage value depends on the price at which GPC can sell the equipment *and* on the book value of the equipment (i.e., the original basis less all previous depreciation charges). Suppose GPC terminates at Year 2, at which time the book value is $1,722, as shown on Row 94. We consider two cases, gains and losses. In the first case, the salvage value is $2,200 and so there is a reported gain of $2,200 − $1,722 = $478. This gain is taxed as ordinary income, so the tax is 40%($478) = $191. The after-tax cash flow is equal to the sales price less the tax: $2,200 − $191 = $2,009.

Now suppose the salvage value at Year 2 is only $500. In this case, there is a reported loss: $500 − $1,722 = −$1,222. This is treated as an ordinary expense, so its tax is 40%(−$1,222) = −$489. This "negative" tax acts as a credit if GPC has other taxable income, so the net after-tax cash flow is $500 − (−$489) = $989.

Adjustments to Determine Cash Flows: Working Capital

Row 90 shows the total amount of net operating working capital needed each year. Row 108 shows the incremental investment in working capital required each year. For example, at the start of the project, Cell E108 shows a cash flow of −$2,250 will be needed at the beginning of the project to support Year 1 sales. Row 90 shows working capital must increase from $2,250 to $2,691 to support Year 2 sales. Thus, GPC must invest $2,691 − $2,250 = $441 in working capital in Year 1, and this is shown as a negative number (because it is an investment) in Cell F108. Similar calculations are made for Years 2 and 3. At the end of Year 4, all of the investments in working capital will be recovered. Inventories will be sold and not replaced, and all receivables will be collected by the end of Year 4. Total net working capital recovered at t = 4 is the sum of the initial investment at t = 0, $2,250, plus the additional investments during Years 1 through 3; the total is $3,849.

Adjustments to Determine Cash Flows: Sunk Costs, Opportunity Costs, and Externalities

GPC's project doesn't have any sunk costs, opportunity costs, or externalities, but the following sections show how we would adjust the cash flows if GPC did have some of these issues.

Sunk Costs. Suppose that last year GPC spent $1,500 on a marketing and feasibility study for the project. Should $1,500 be included in the project's cost? The answer is no. That money already has been spent and accepting or rejecting the project will not change that fact.

Opportunity Costs. Now suppose GPC's new equipment will be installed in a building that GPC now owns but that the space could be leased to another company for $200 per year, after taxes, if the project is rejected. The $200 per year would be an *opportunity cost*, and it should be reflected as a reduction in the calculated annual cash flows.

Externalities. As noted earlier, the solar water heater project does not lead to any cannibalization effects. Suppose, however, that it would reduce the net after-tax cash flows of another GPC division by $50 per year and that no other firm could take on this project if GPC turns it down. In this case, we would use the cannibalization line at Row 110, deducting $50 each year. As a result, the project would have a lower NPV. On the other hand, if the project would cause additional inflows to some other GPC division because it was complementary to that other division's products (i.e., if a positive externality exists), then those after-tax inflows should be attributed to the water heater project and thus shown as a positive inflow on Row 110.

13-2e Evaluating Project Cash Flows

We sum Rows 103 to 110 to get the project's annual net cash flows, set up as a time line on Row 111. These cash flows are then used to calculate NPV, IRR, MIRR, PI, payback, and discounted payback, performance measures that are shown in the orange portion at the bottom of Figure 13-2.

Preliminary Evaluation of the Base-Case Scenario

Based on this analysis, the preliminary evaluation indicates that the project is acceptable. The NPV is $1,048, which is fairly large when compared to the initial investment of $10,000. Its IRR and MIRR are both greater than the 10% WACC, and the PI is larger than 1.0. The payback and discounted payback are almost as long as the project's life, which is somewhat concerning, and is something that needs to be explored by conducting a risk analysis of the project.

Scenario Manager

Excel's Scenario Manager is a very powerful and useful tool. We illustrate its use here as we examine two topics, the impact of forgetting to include inflation and the impact of accelerated depreciation versus straight-line depreciation. To use Scenario Manager in the worksheet named *1-Base-Case* in *Ch13 Tool Kit.xls,* Select Data, What-If Analysis, and Scenario Manager. There are five scenarios: (1) Base-Case for Project L but Forget Inflation, (2) Base-Case for Project L, (3) Project S, (4) MACRS Depreciation, and (5) Straight-Line Depreciation. The first three scenarios change the inputs in Rows 57–71. The last two scenarios change the depreciation rates in Row 92. This structure allows you to choose a set of inputs and then choose a depreciation method. Sometimes we include all the changing cells in each scenario, and sometimes we separate the scenarios into different groups as we did in this example.

The advantage of having all changing cells in each scenario is that you only have to select a single scenario to show all the desired inputs in the model. The disadvantage is that each scenario can get complicated by having many changing cells.

The advantage of having groups of scenarios is that you can focus on particular aspects of the analysis, such as the choice of depreciation methods. The disadvantage is that you must know which other scenarios are active in order to properly interpret your results.

For some models it makes sense to have only one group of scenarios in which each scenario has the same changing cells; for other models it makes sense to have different groups of scenarios. In any case, be sure to have at least one cell in your model that has a written description that changes with each scenario. In our case, Cell E56 gives a description that changes with each scenario, and Cell A92 says whether the depreciation is straight-line or MACRS.

The Impact of Inflation. It is easy to overlook inflation, but it is important to include it. For example, had we forgotten to include inflation in the GPC example,

MISTAKES IN CASH FLOW ESTIMATION CAN KILL INNOVATION

Estimating a project's relevant incremental cash flows takes work, but the idea is simple: Forecast a company's after-tax cash flows assuming the company takes the project and then forecast cash flows assuming the company doesn't take the project. The difference between the with-the-project cash flows and the without-the project cash flows defines the project's relevant incremental cash flows. But as Harvard Business School faculty Clayton Christensen, Stephen Kaufman, and Willy Shih show, ignoring or incorrectly applying this simple rule can kill innovation and harm companies.

First, managers sometimes implicitly assume the company will operate in the future as it has in the past. For example, consider a new product introduction. The analysis might include only the cash flows directly attributable to the new product. But suppose the company's cash flows would decline due to obsolescence or competition if the new product were not introduced. Ignoring this fact would cause the company to underestimate the *incremental* cash flows of the new product and perhaps incorrectly reject a value-adding project.

Second, some managers focus too much on the short term. For example, consider a manager faced with the choice of expanding production by using the company's existing technology or by using a newer and more efficient technology with a longer expected life. The initial cost of the old technology might be less, but a reduction in operating costs over the long run might make the new technology a better choice. If managers don't consider long-term cash flows, they will underestimate the value of long-lived assets.

Third, some managers' bonuses are based on reported earnings per share (EPS) rather than a market-based measure of performance. These managers may (and do) take actions to maximize EPS (and their bonus!) rather than shareholder value. For example, research and development expenses and start-up costs for new products reduce net income and EPS in the short term, leading some managers to cut these expenses and maximize their current bonuses. However, this kills the pipeline for new products, which reduces the company's expected long-term cash flows. Changing the link for executive compensation from EPS to market-based measures that take long-run expected cash flows into account can improve managers' incentives to invest for the long term.

The moral of the story is that ignoring or misapplying the capital budgeting principles developed in this chapter can cause a manager to destroy value rather than create it!

Note: See Christensen, Clayton M, Stephen P. Kaufman, and Willy C. Shih, "Innovation Killers: How Financial Tools Destroy your Capacity to Do New Things," *Harvard Business Review*, January 2008, pp. 98–105.

---

the estimated NPV would have dropped from $1,048 to $225. You can see this by changing all the price and cost growth rates to zero and then looking at the NPV. An easy way to do this is with the Scenario Manager—just choose the scenario named "Base-Case Project L but Forget Inflation." Forgetting to include inflation in a capital budgeting analysis typically causes the estimated NPV to be lower than the true NPV, which could cause a company to reject a project that it should have accepted. You can return to the original inputs by going back into Scenario Manager, selecting "Base-Case for Project L," and clicking on "Show."

Accelerated Depreciation versus Straight-Line Depreciation. Congress permits firms to depreciate assets using either the straight-line method or an accelerated method. The results we have discussed thus far were based on accelerated depreciation. To see the impact of using straight-line depreciation, go to the Scenario Manager and select "Straight-Line Depreciation." Be sure that you have also selected "Base-Case for Project L." After selecting and showing these two scenarios, you will have a set of inputs for the base-case and straight-line deprecation rates.

The results indicate that the project's NPV is $921 when using straight-line depreciation, which is lower than the $1,048 NPV when using accelerated depreciation. In general, *profitable firms are better off using accelerated depreciation* because more depreciation is taken in the early years under the accelerated method, so taxes are lower in those years and higher in later years. Total depreciation, total cash flows, and total taxes are the same under both depreciation methods, but receiving the cash earlier under the accelerated method results in a higher NPV, IRR, and MIRR.

Suppose Congress wants to encourage companies to increase their capital expenditures and thereby boost economic growth and employment. What changes in depreciation regulations would have the desired effect? The answer is, "Make accelerated depreciation even more accelerated." For example, if GPC could write off equipment at rates of 67%, 22%, 7%, and 4% rather than 33.33%, 44.45%, 14.81%, and 7.41%, then its early tax payments would be even lower, early cash flows would be even higher, and the project's NPV would exceed the value shown in Figure 13-2.[6]

Be sure to return the scenarios to "Base-Case for Project L" and "MACRS Depreciation."

Project S. Recall from Chapter 12 that GPC was also considering Project S, which used solid coatings. You can use the Scenario Manager to show this project by selecting the scenario "Project S," which will show the cash flows used in Chapter 12. Be sure to return the scenarios in the worksheet *1-Base-Case* to "Base-Case for Project L" and "MACRS Depreciation."

SELF TEST

In what way is the setup for finding a project's cash flows similar to the projected income statements for a new, single-product firm? In what way would the two statements be different?

Would a project's NPV for a typical firm be higher or lower if the firm used accelerated rather than straight-line depreciation? Explain.

How could the analysis in Figure 13-2 be modified to consider cannibalization, opportunity costs, and sunk costs?

Why does net working capital appear with both negative and positive values in Figure 13-2?

---

6. This is exactly what Congress did in 2008 and 2009, in response to the global economic crisis, by establishing a temporary "bonus" depreciation to stimulate investment. The depreciation in the first year is the regular accelerated depreciation plus a bonus of 50% of the original basis. This bonus was increased to 100% of the original basis for 2011, effectively allowing companies to fully expense certain capital expenditures in 2011. The bonus dropped back to 50% for 2012 and 2013 and expired at the end of 2013.

13-3 Risk Analysis in Capital Budgeting[7]

Projects differ in risk, and risk should be reflected in capital budgeting decisions. There are three separate and distinct types of risk.

1. **Stand-alone risk** is a project's risk assuming: (a) that it is the firm's only asset and (b) that each of the firm's stockholders holds only that one stock in his portfolio. Stand-alone risk is based on uncertainty about the project's expected cash flows. It is important to remember that *stand-alone risk ignores diversification by both the firm and its stockholders.*

2. **Within-firm risk** (also called **corporate risk**) is a project's risk to the corporation itself. Within-firm risk recognizes that the project is only one asset in the firm's portfolio of projects; hence, some of its risk is eliminated by diversification within the firm. However, *within-firm risk ignores diversification by the firm's stockholders.* Within-firm risk is measured by the project's impact on uncertainty about the firm's future total cash flows.

3. **Market risk** (also called **beta risk**) is the risk of the project as seen by a well-diversified stockholder who recognizes that: (a) the project is only one of the firm's projects and (b) the firm's stock is but one of her stocks. The project's market risk is measured by its effect on the firm's beta coefficient.

Taking on a project with a lot of stand-alone and/or corporate risk will not necessarily affect the firm's beta. However, if the project has high stand-alone risk and if its cash flows are highly correlated with cash flows on the firm's other assets and with cash flows of most other firms in the economy, then the project will have a high degree of all three types of risk. Market risk is, *theoretically*, the most relevant because it is the one that, according to the CAPM, is reflected in stock prices. Unfortunately, market risk is also the most difficult to measure, primarily because new projects don't have "market prices" that can be related to stock market returns.

Most decision makers conduct a *quantitative* analysis of stand-alone risk and then consider the other two types of risk in a *qualitative* manner. They classify projects into several categories; then, using the firm's overall WACC as a starting point, they assign a **risk-adjusted cost of capital** to each category. For example, a firm might establish three risk classes and then assign the corporate WACC to average-risk projects, add a 5% risk premium for higher-risk projects, and subtract 2% for low-risk projects. Under this setup, if the company's overall WACC were 10%, then 10% would be used to evaluate average-risk projects, 15% for high-risk projects, and 8% for low-risk projects. Although this approach is probably better than not making any risk adjustments, these adjustments are highly subjective and difficult to justify. Unfortunately, there's no perfect way to specify how high or low the risk adjustments should be.[8]

---

7. Some professors may choose to cover some of the risk sections and skip others. We offer a range of choices, and we tried to make the exposition clear enough that interested and self-motivated students can read these sections on their own if they are not assigned.

8. Note that the CAPM approach can be used for projects provided there are specialized publicly traded firms in the same business as that of the project under consideration. See the discussion in Chapter 11 regarding techniques for measuring divisional betas.

What are the three types of project risk?

Which type is theoretically the most relevant? Why?

Describe a type of classification scheme that firms often use to obtain risk-adjusted costs of capital.

13-4 Measuring Stand-Alone Risk

A project's stand-alone risk reflects uncertainty about its cash flows. The required dollars of investment, unit sales, sales prices, and operating costs as shown in Figure 13-1 for GPC's project are all subject to uncertainty. First-year sales are projected at 10,000 units to be sold at a price of $1.50 per unit (recall that all dollar values are reported in thousands). However, unit sales will almost certainly be somewhat higher or lower than 10,000, and the price will probably turn out to be different from the projected $1.50 per unit. Similarly, the other variables would probably differ from their indicated values. Indeed, *all the inputs are expected values, not known values, and actual values can and do vary from expected values.* That's what risk is all about!

Three techniques are used in practice to assess stand-alone risk: (1) sensitivity analysis, (2) scenario analysis, and (3) Monte Carlo simulation. We discuss them in the sections that follow.

What does a project's stand-alone risk reflect?

What three techniques are used to assess stand-alone risk?

13-5 Sensitivity Analysis

Intuitively, we know that a change in a key input variable such as units sold or the sales price will cause the NPV to change. **Sensitivity analysis** *measures the percentage change in NPV that results from a given percentage change in an input variable when other inputs are held at their expected values.* This is by far the most commonly used type of risk analysis. It begins with a base-case scenario in which the project's NPV is found using the base-case value for each input variable. GPC's base-case inputs were given in Figure 13-1, but it's easy to imagine changes in the inputs, and any changes would result in a different NPV. See the worksheet *2-Sens* in *Ch13 Tool Kit.xls* for all calculations in the following sections.

13-5a Sensitivity Graph

When GPC's senior managers review a capital budgeting analysis, they are interested in the base-case NPV, but they always go on to ask a series of "what if" questions: "What if unit sales fall to 9,000?" "What if market conditions force us to price the product at $1.40, not $1.50?" "What if variable costs are higher than we have forecasted?" Sensitivity analysis is designed to provide answers to such questions. Each variable is increased or decreased by a specified percentage from its expected value, holding other variables constant at their base-case levels. Then the NPV is calculated using the changed input. Finally, the resulting set of NPVs is plotted to show how sensitive NPV is to changes in the different variables.

Figure 13-3 shows GPC's project's sensitivity graph for six key variables. The data below the graph give the NPVs based on different values of the inputs, and those NPVs were then plotted to make the graph. Figure 13-3 shows that, as unit sales and the sales price are increased, the project's NPV increases; in contrast, increases in variable costs, nonvariable costs, equipment costs, and WACC lower the project's NPV. The slopes of the lines in the graph and the ranges in the table below the graph indicate how sensitive NPV is to each input: *The larger the range, the steeper the variable's slope, and the more sensitive the NPV is to this variable.* We see that NPV is extremely sensitive to changes in the sales price; fairly sensitive to changes in variable costs, units sold, and fixed costs; and not especially sensitive to changes in the equipment's cost and the WACC. Management should, of course, try especially hard to obtain accurate estimates of the variables that have the greatest impact on the NPV.

If we were comparing two projects, then the one with the steeper sensitivity lines would be riskier (other things held constant), because relatively small changes in the

WEB

See **Ch13 Tool Kit.xls** on the textbook's Web site.

FIGURE 13-3   Sensitivity Graph for Solar Water Heater Project (Thousands of Dollars)

Deviation from Base	NPV with Variables at Different Deviations from Base					
	Equip.	Price	Units	VC/Unit	Non-VC	r
−30%	$2,599	−$9,852	−$1,999	$8,901	$2,309	$1,999
0%	$1,048	$1,048	$1,048	$1,048	$1,048	$1,048
30%	−$503	$11,949	$4,096	−$6,805	−$213	$205
Range	$3,102	$21,801	$6,095	$15,706	$2,521	$1,794

input variables would produce large changes in the NPV. Thus, sensitivity analysis provides useful insights into a project's risk.[9] Note, however, that even though NPV may be highly sensitive to certain variables, if those variables are not likely to change much from their expected values, then the project may not be very risky in spite of its high sensitivity. Also, if several of the inputs change at the same time, the combined effect on NPV can be much greater than sensitivity analysis suggests.

13-5b **Tornado Diagrams**

Tornado diagrams are another way to present results from sensitivity analysis. The first steps are to calculate the range of possible NPVs for each of the input variables being changed and then rank these ranges. In our example, the range for sales price per unit is the largest and the range for WACC is the smallest. The ranges for each variable are then plotted, with the largest range on top and the smallest range on the bottom. It is also helpful to plot a vertical line showing the base-case NPV. We present a tornado diagram in Figure 13-4. Notice that the diagram is like a tornado in the sense that it is widest at the top and smallest at the bottom, hence its name. The tornado diagram makes it immediately obvious which inputs have the greatest impact on NPV: sales price and variable costs in this case.

See *Ch13 Tool Kit.xls* on the textbook's Web site.

| FIGURE 13-4 | Tornado Diagram for Solar Water Heater Project: Range of Outcomes for Input Deviations from Base Case (Thousands of Dollars) |

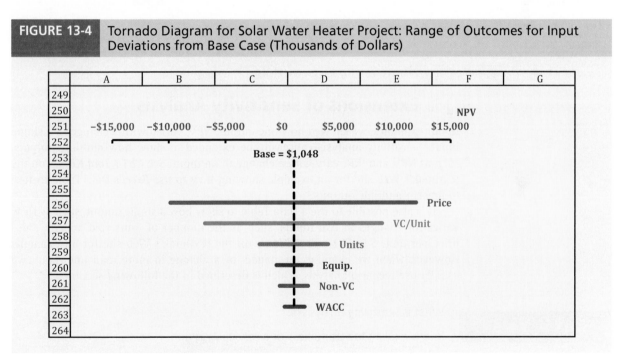

Microsoft Excel® is a registered trademark of Microsoft Corporation. © 2014 Microsoft.

---

9. Sensitivity analysis is tedious with a regular calculator but easy with a spreadsheet. We used the chapter's *Excel Tool Kit* to calculate the NPVs and then to draw the graph in Figure 13-3. To conduct such an analysis by hand would be quite time-consuming, and if the basic data were changed even slightly—say, the cost of the equipment was increased slightly—then all of the calculations would have to be redone. With a spreadsheet, we can simply type over the old input with the new one, and the analysis and the graph change instantaneously.

13-5c **NPV Break-Even Analysis**

A special application of sensitivity analysis is called **NPV break-even analysis**. In a break-even analysis, we find the level of an input that produces an NPV of exactly zero. We used *Excel*'s Goal Seek feature to do this. See *Ch13 Tool Kit.xls* on the textbook's Web site for an explanation of how to use this *Excel* feature.

See *Ch13 Tool Kit.xls* on the textbook's Web site.

Table 13-1 shows the values of the inputs discussed previously that produce a zero NPV. For example, the number of units sold in Year 1 can drop to 8,968 before the project's NPV falls to zero. Break-even analysis is helpful in determining how bad things can get before the project has a negative NPV.

TABLE 13-1	NPV Break-Even Analysis (Thousands of Dollars)
Input	**Input Value That Produces Zero NPV, Holding All Else Constant**
Sales price per unit, Year 1	$1.457
Variable cost per unit (VC), Year 1	$1.113
Annual change in units sold after Year 1	7.40%
Units sold, Year 1	8,968
Nonvariable cost (Non-VC), Year 1	$2,649
Project WACC	13.79%

Source: From *Financial Management: Theory & Practice*, 2013, by Brigham and Ehrhardt. © Cengage Learning.

13-5d **Extensions of Sensitivity Analysis**

In our examples, we showed how one output, NPV, varied with a change in a single input. Sensitivity analysis can easily be extended to show how multiple outputs, such as NPV and IRR, vary with a change in an input. See *Ch13 Tool Kit.xls* on the textbook's Web site for an example showing how to use *Excel*'s Data Table feature to present multiple outputs.

It is also possible to use a Data Table to show how a single output, such as NPV, varies for changes in two inputs, such as the number of units sold and the sales price per unit. See *Ch13 Tool Kit.xls* on the textbook's Web site for an example. However, when we examine the impact of a change in more than one input, we usually use scenario analysis, which is described in the following section.

SELF TEST

What is sensitivity analysis?

Briefly explain the usefulness of a sensitivity graph.

Discuss the following statement: "A project may not be very risky in spite of its high sensitivity to certain variables."

13-6 **Scenario Analysis**

In the sensitivity analysis just described, we changed one variable at a time. However, it is useful to know what would happen to the project's NPV if several of the inputs turn out to be better or worse than expected, and this is what we do in a

scenario analysis. Also, scenario analysis allows us to assign probabilities to the base (or most likely) case, the best case, and the worst case; then we can find the *expected value and standard deviation* of the project's NPV to get a better idea of the project's risk.

In a scenario analysis, we begin with the base-case scenario, which uses the most likely value for each input variable. We then ask marketing, engineering, and other operating managers to specify a worst-case scenario (low unit sales, low sales price, high variable costs, and so on) and a best-case scenario. Often, the best and worst cases are defined as having a 25% probability of occurring, with a 50% probability for the base-case conditions. Obviously, conditions could take on many more than three values, but such a scenario setup is useful to help get some idea of the project's riskiness.

After much discussion with the marketing staff, engineers, accountants, and other experts in the company, a set of worst-case and best-case values were determined for several key inputs. Figure 13-5, taken from worksheet *3a-Scen* of the chapter *Tool Kit* model, shows the probability and inputs assumed for the base-case, worst-case, and best-case scenarios, along with selected key results.

The project's cash flows and performance measures under each scenario are calculated; see the worksheet *3a-Scen* in the *Tool Kit* for the calculations. The net

WEB

See **Ch13 Tool Kit.xls** on the textbook's Web site.

FIGURE 13-5   Inputs and Key Results for Each Scenario (Thousands of Dollars)

	A	B	C	D	E	F	G
34						Scenarios:	
35	Scenario Name				Base	Worst	Best
36	Probability of Scenario				50%	25%	25%
37	Inputs:						
38	Equipment cost				$7,750	$8,250	$7,250
39	Salvage value of equip. in Year 4				$639	$639	$639
40	Opportunity cost				$0	$0	$0
41	Externalities (cannibalization)				$0	$0	$0
42	Units sold, Year 1				10,000	8,500	11,500
43	% Δ in units sold, after Year 1				15%	5%	25%
44	Sales price per unit, Year 1				$1.50	$1.25	$1.75
45	% Δ in sales price, after Year 1				4%	4%	4%
46	Var. cost per unit (VC), Year 1				$1.07	$1.17	$0.97
47	% Δ in VC, after Year 1				3%	3%	3%
48	Nonvar. cost (Non-VC), Year 1				$2,120	$2,330	$1,910
49	% Δ in Non-VC, after Year 1				3%	3%	3%
50	Project cost of capital (r)				10%	10%	10%
51	Tax rate				40%	50%	30%
52	NOWC as % of next year's sales				15%	15%	15%
53	Key Results:						
54				NPV	$1,048	–$7,543	$19,468
55				IRR	13.79%	–29.40%	62.41%
56				MIRR	12.78%	–22.23%	43.49%
57			Profitability index		1.10	0.23	2.90
58				Payback	3.39	Not found	1.83
59			Discounted payback		3.80	Not found	2.07

cash flows for each scenario are shown in Figure 13-6, along with a probability distribution of the possible outcomes for NPV. If the project is highly successful, then a low initial investment, high sales price, high unit sales, and low production costs would combine to result in a very high NPV, $19,468. However, if things turn out badly, then the NPV would be a *negative* $7,543. This wide range of possibilities, and especially the large potential negative value, suggests that this is a risky project. If bad conditions materialize, the project will not bankrupt the company—this is just one project for a large company. Still, losing $7,543 (actually $7,543,000, as the units are thousands of dollars) would certainly hurt the company's value and the reputation of the project's manager.

Note that it becomes cumbersome to manage more than a couple of scenarios for analysis such as this. In the worksheet tab 3a-Scen, we created three separate models, one for each scenario. The analysis can be simplified somewhat by using *Excel's* Scenario Manager to manage multiple scenarios, which we show in worksheet *3b-ScenMgr* in the *Tool Kit*. Adding many scenarios to Scenario Manager can also be tedious, and in those cases we use simulation, described in the next section.

If we multiply each scenario's probability by the NPV for that scenario and then sum the products, we will have the project's expected NPV of $3,505, as shown in Figure 13-6. Note that the *expected* NPV differs from the *base-case* NPV, which is the most likely outcome because it has a 50% probability. This is not an error—mathematically they are not equal.[10] We also calculate the standard deviation of the expected NPV; it is $9,861. Dividing the standard deviation by the expected NPV yields the **coefficient of variation**, 2.81, which is a measure of stand-alone risk. The coefficient of variation measures the amount of risk per dollar of NPV, so the coefficient of variation can be helpful when comparing the risk of projects with different NPVs. GPC's average project has a coefficient of variation of about 1.2, so the 2.81 indicates that this project is riskier than most of GPC's other typical projects.

GPC's corporate WACC is 9%, so that rate should be used to find the NPV of an average-risk project. However, the water heater project is riskier than average, so a higher discount rate should be used to find its NPV. There is no way to determine the precisely correct discount rate—this is a judgment call. Management decided to evaluate the project using a 10% rate.[11]

Note that the base-case results are the same in our sensitivity and scenario analyses, but in the scenario analysis the worst case is much worse than in the sensitivity analysis and the best case is much better. This is because in scenario analysis all of the variables are set at their best or worst levels, whereas in sensitivity analysis only one variable is adjusted and all the others are left at their base-case levels.

---

10. This result occurs for two reasons. First, although in this scenario analysis, the base-case input values happen to equal the average of the best- and worst-case values, this is by no means necessary. Best- and worst-case values need not be the same distance from the base case. Second, even though the base-case values are midway between the best- and worst-case values, in our model two uncertain variables, sales volume and sales price, are multiplied together to obtain dollar sales, and this process causes the NPV distribution to be skewed to the right. A large number multiplied by another large number produces a very big number, and this in turn causes the average value (or expected value) to increase.

11. One could argue that the best-case scenario should be evaluated with a relatively low WACC, the worst-case scenario with a relatively high WACC, and the base case with the average corporate WACC. However, one could also argue that, at the time of the initial decision, we don't know what case will occur and hence a single rate should be used. Observe that, in the worst-case scenario, all of the cash flows are negative. If we used a high WACC because of this branch's risk, this would lower the PV of these negative cash flows, making the worst case much better than if we used the average WACC. Determining the "right" WACC to use in the analysis is not an easy task!

FIGURE 13-6 Scenario Analysis: Expected NPV and Its Risk (Thousands of Dollars)

	A	B	C	D	E	F	G	H	I
94			Predicted Cash Flows for Alternative Scenarios						
95		Prob:	0	1	2	3	4	r	NPV
96	Best →	25%	−$10,269	$4,761	$6,673	$8,237	$20,065	10.00%	$19,468
97									
98	Base →	50%	−$10,000	$1,900	$2,700	$2,345	$7,800	10.00%	$1,048
99									
100	Worst →	25%	−$9,844	$403	$897	−$281	$2,055	10.00%	−$7,543
101							Expected NPV =		$3,505
102							Standard Deviation (SD) =		$9,861
103						Coefficient of Variation (CV) = Std. Dev./Expected NPV =			2.81

(Circled **1** with arrows pointing to Best, Base, and Worst)

Probability Distribution of Scenarios:
Outcomes and Probabilities

(Bar chart)
- Worst-Case: −$7,543 (25%)
- Base-Case: $1,048 (50%)
- Best-Case: $19,468 (25%)
- Exp. NPV $3,505
- NPV (horizontal axis)

Microsoft Excel® is a registered trademark of Microsoft Corporation. © 2014 Microsoft.

The project has a positive NPV, but its coefficient of variation (CV) is 2.81, which is more than double the 1.2 CV of an average project. With the higher risk, it is not clear if the project should be accepted or not. At this point, GPC's CEO will ask the CFO to investigate the risk further by performing a simulation analysis, as described in the next section.

WEB

See **Ch13 Tool Kit.xls** on the textbook's Web site.

What is scenario analysis?

Differentiate between sensitivity analysis and scenario analysis. What advantage does scenario analysis have over sensitivity analysis?

SELF TEST

13-7 Monte Carlo Simulation[12]

Monte Carlo simulation ties together sensitivities, probability distributions, and correlations among the input variables. It grew out of work in the Manhattan Project to build the first atomic bomb and was so named because it utilized the

---

12. This section is relatively technical, and some instructors may choose to skip it with no loss in continuity.

mathematics of casino gambling. Although Monte Carlo simulation is considerably more complex than scenario analysis, simulation software packages make the process manageable. Many of these packages can be used as add-ins to *Excel* and other spreadsheet programs.

In a simulation analysis, a probability distribution is assigned to each input variable—sales in units, the sales price, the variable cost per unit, and so on. The computer begins by picking a random value for each variable from its probability distribution. Those values are then entered into the model, the project's NPV is calculated, and the NPV is stored in the computer's memory. This is called a trial. After completing the first trial, a second set of input values is selected from the input variables' probability distributions, and a second NPV is calculated. This process is repeated many times. The NPVs from the trials can be charted on a histogram, which shows an estimate of the project's outcomes. The average of the trials' NPVs is interpreted as a measure of the project's expected NPV, with the standard deviation (or the coefficient of variation) of the trials' NPV as a measure of the project's risk.

Using this procedure, we conducted a simulation analysis of GPC's solar water heater project. To compare apples and apples, we focused on the same six variables that were allowed to change in the previously conducted scenario analysis. We assumed that each variable can be represented by its own continuous normal distribution with means and standard deviations that are consistent with the base-case scenario. For example, we assumed that the units sold in Year 1 come from a normal distribution with a mean equal to the base-case value of 10,000. We used the probabilities and outcomes of the three scenarios from Section 13-6 to estimate the standard deviation (all calculations are in the *Tool Kit*). The standard deviation of units sold is 1,061, as calculated using the scenario values. We made similar assumptions for all variables. In addition, we assumed that the annual change in unit sales will be positively correlated with unit sales in the first year: If demand is higher than expected in the first year, it will continue to be higher than expected. In particular, we assume a correlation of 0.65 between units sold in the first year and growth in units sold in later years. For all other variables, we assumed zero correlation. Figure 13-7 shows the inputs used in the simulation analysis.

Figure 13-7 also shows the current set of random variables that were drawn from the distributions at the time we created the figure for the textbook—you will see different values for the key results when you look at the *Excel* model because the values are updated every time the file is opened. We used a two-step procedure to create the random variables for the inputs. First, we used *Excel*'s functions to generate standard normal random variables with a mean of 0 and a standard deviation of 1; these are shown in Cells E38:E51.[13] To create the random values for the inputs used in the analysis, we multiplied a random standard normal variable by the standard deviation and added the expected value. For example, *Excel* drew the value for first-year unit sales (Cell E42) from a standard normal distribution. We calculated the value for first-year unit sales to use in the current trial as 10,000 + 1,061(−0.045) = 9,952, which is shown in Cell F42.[14]

---

13. See the *Tool Kit* for detailed explanations on using *Excel* to generate random variables.

14. There may be slight rounding differences because *Excel* doesn't round in intermediate steps. We used a slightly more complicated procedure to generate a random variable for the annual change in sales to ensure that it had 0.65 correlation with the first-year units sold. See the *Tool Kit* for details.

FIGURE 13-7	Inputs and Key Results for the Current Simulation Trial (Thousands of Dollars)

	A	B	C	D	E	F
33			Inputs for Simulation Probability Distributions		Random Variables Used in Current Simulation Trial	
34						
35			Expected Value of Input	Standard Deviation of Input	Standard Normal Random Variable	Value Used in Current Trial
36						
37						
38	Equipment cost		$7,750	$354	0.534	$7,939
39	Salvage value of equip. in Year 4		—	—		$639
40	Opportunity cost		—	—		$0
41	Externalities (cannibalization)		—	—		$0
42	Units sold, Year 1		10,000	1,061	−0.045	9,952
43	% Δ in units sold, after Year 1		15.00%	7.07%	0.198	16.40%
44	Sales price per unit, Year 1		$1.50	$0.18	0.837	$1.65
45	% Δ in sales price, after Year 1		—	—		4.00%
46	Var. cost per unit (VC), Year 1		$1.07	$0.07	−0.706	$1.02
47	% Δ in VC, after Year 1		—	—		3.00%
48	Nonvar. cost (Non-VC), Year 1		$2,120	$148	0.277	$2,161
49	% Δ in Non-VC, after Year 1		—	—		3.00%
50	Project WACC		—	—		10.00%
51	Tax rate		40.00%	7.07%	0.494	43.50%
52	NOWC as % of next year's sales		—	—		15.00%
53	Assumed correlation between units sold in Year 1 and annual change in units sold in later years:		ρ = 65.00%			
54						
55	Key Results Based on Current Trial					
56		NPV	$5,391			
57		IRR	27.75%			
58		MIRR	22.11%			
59		PI	1.52			
60		Payback	2.91			
61		Discounted payback	$3.23			

Microsoft Excel® is a registered trademark of Microsoft Corporation. © 2014 Microsoft.

We used the inputs in Cells F38:F52 to generate cash flows and to calculate performance measures for the project (the calculations are in the *Tool Kit*). For the trial reported in Figure 13-7, the NPV is $5,391. We used a Data Table in the *Tool Kit* to generate additional trials. For each trial, the Data Table saved the value of the input variables and the value of the trial's NPV. Figure 13-8 presents selected results from the simulation for 10,000 trials. (The worksheet *4a-Sim100* in the *Tool Kit* shows only 100 trials; the worksheet *4b-Sim10000* has the ability to perform 10,000 simulations, but we have turned off the Data Table in that worksheet because simulating 10,000 trials reduces *Excel*'s speed when performing other calculations in the file.)

After running a simulation, the first thing we do is verify that the results are consistent with our assumptions. The resulting sample mean and standard deviation of units sold in the first year are 9,993 and 1,060, which are virtually identical to our assumptions in Figure 13-7. The same is true for all the other

See **Ch13 Tool Kit.xls** on the textbook's Web site.

FIGURE 13-8   Summary of Simulation Results (Thousands of Dollars)

	A	B	C	D	E	F	G	H	I
156	Number of Trials 10,000		Input Variables						
157					Annual		Variable	Nonvariable	
158					change in	Sales price	cost per	cost	
159	Summary Statistics for		Equipment	Units sold,	units sold,	per unit,	unit (VC),	(Non-VC),	
160	Simulated Input Variables		cost	Year 1	after Year 1	Year 1	Year 1	Year 1	Tax rate
161	Average		$7,746	9,993	15%	$1.50	$1.07	$2,119	40.0%
162	Standard deviation		$355	1,060	7%	$0.18	$0.07	$148	7.1%
163	Maximum		$9,360	14,121	43%	$2.14	$1.34	$2,685	66.2%
164	Minimum		$6,489	5,893	−14%	$0.87	$0.81	$1,581	15.4%
165	Correlation with unit sales				64%				
166									
167	Summary Statistics for Simulated Results		NPV						
168	Average		$1,149						
169	Standard deviation		$5,189						
170	Maximum		$32,616						
171	Minimum		−$20,251						
172	Median		$790						
173	Probability of NPV > 0		56.6%						
174	Coefficient of variation		4.52						
175									
176									
177									
178									
179									
180									
181									
182									
183									
184				−32,616	−16,308	0	16,308	32,616	
185								NPV ($)	
186									

Probability

Microsoft Excel® is a registered trademark of Microsoft Corporation. © 2014 Microsoft.

See **Ch13 Tool Kit.xls** on the textbook's Web site.

inputs, so we can be reasonably confident that the simulation is doing what we are asking.

Figure 13-8 also reports summary statistics for the project's NPV. The mean is $1,149, which suggests that the project should be accepted. However, the range of outcomes is quite large, from a loss of $20,251 to a gain of $32,616, so the project is clearly risky. The standard deviation of $5,189 indicates that losses could easily occur, which is consistent with this wide range of possible outcomes.[15]

15. Note that the standard deviation of NPV in the simulation is much smaller than the standard deviation in the scenario analysis. In the scenario analysis, we assumed that all of the poor outcomes would occur together in the worst-case scenario and that all of the positive outcomes would occur together in the best-case scenario. In other words, we implicitly assumed that all of the risky variables were perfectly positively correlated. In the simulation, we assumed that the variables were independent (except for the correlation between unit sales and growth). The independence of variables in the simulation reduces the range of outcomes. For example, in the simulation, sometimes the sales price is high but the sales growth is low. In the scenario analysis, a high sales price is always coupled with high growth. Because the scenario analysis assumption of perfect correlation is unlikely, simulation may provide a better estimate of project risk. However, if the standard deviations and correlations used as inputs in the simulation are inaccurately estimated, then the simulation output will likewise be inaccurate.

Figure 13-8 also reports a median NPV of $790, which means that half the time the project will have an NPV of less than $790. In fact, there is only a 56.6% probability that the project will have a positive NPV.

A picture is worth a thousand words, and Figure 13-8 shows the probability distribution of the outcomes. Note that the distribution of outcomes is slightly skewed to the right. As the figure shows, the potential downside losses are not as large as the potential upside gains. Our conclusion is that this is a very risky project, as indicated by the coefficient of variation, but it does have a positive expected NPV and the potential to be a "home run."

If the company decides to go ahead with the project, senior management should also identify possible contingency plans for responding to changes in market conditions. Senior managers always should consider qualitative factors in addition to the quantitative project analysis.

What is Monte Carlo simulation?

SELF TEST

13-8 Project Risk Conclusions

We have discussed the three types of risk normally considered in capital budgeting: stand-alone risk, within-firm (or corporate) risk, and market risk. However, two important questions remain: (1) Should firms care about stand-alone and corporate risk, given that finance theory says that market (beta) risk is the only relevant risk? (2) What do we do when the stand-alone, within-firm, and market risk assessments lead to different conclusions?

There are no easy answers to these questions. Strict adherents of the CAPM would argue that well-diversified investors are concerned only with market risk, that managers should be concerned only with maximizing stock price, and thus that market (beta) risk ought to be given virtually all the weight in capital budgeting decisions. However, we know that not all investors are well diversified, that the CAPM does not operate exactly as the theory says it should, and that measurement problems keep managers from having complete confidence in the CAPM inputs. In addition, the CAPM ignores bankruptcy costs, even though such costs can be substantial, and the probability of bankruptcy depends on a firm's corporate risk, not on its beta risk. Therefore, even well-diversified investors should want a firm's management to give at least some consideration to a project's corporate risk, and that means giving some consideration to stand-alone project risk.

Although it would be nice to reconcile these problems and to measure risk on some absolute scale, the best we can do in practice is to estimate risk in a somewhat nebulous, relative sense. For example, we can generally say with a fair degree of confidence that a particular project has more, less, or about the same stand-alone risk as the firm's average project. Then, because stand-alone and corporate risks generally are correlated, the project's stand-alone risk generally is a reasonably good measure of its corporate risk. Finally, assuming that market risk and corporate risk are correlated, as is true for most companies, a project with a relatively high or low corporate risk will also have a relatively high or low market risk. We wish we could be more specific, but one simply must use a lot of judgment when assessing projects' risks.

SELF TEST

In theory, should a firm be equally concerned with stand-alone, corporate, and market risk? Would your answer be the same if we substituted "In practice" for "In theory"? Explain your answers.

If a project's stand-alone, corporate, and market risk are known to be highly correlated, would this make the task of evaluating the project's risk easier or harder? Explain.

13-9 Replacement Analysis

In the previous sections, we assumed that the solar water heater project was an entirely new project, so all of its cash flows were incremental—they would occur if and only if the project were accepted. However, for replacement projects we must find the cash flow *differentials* between the new and old projects, and these differentials are the *incremental cash flows* that we must analyze.

We evaluate a replacement decision in Figure 13-9, which is set up much like Figures 13-1 and 13-2 but with data on both a new, highly efficient machine and data on the old machine. In Part I we show the key inputs in the analysis, including depreciation on the new and old machines. In Part II we find the cash flows the firm will have if it continues to use the old machine, and in Part III we find the cash flows if the firm replaces the old machine. Then, in Part IV, we subtract the old flows from the new to arrive at the *incremental cash flows*, and we evaluate those flows in Part V to find the NPV, IRR, and MIRR. Replacing the old machine appears to be a good decision.[16]

In some instances, replacements add capacity as well as lower operating costs. In this case, sales revenues in Part III would be increased, and if that leads to a need for more working capital, then this would be shown as a Time 0 expenditure along with a recovery at the end of the project's life. These changes would, of course, be reflected in the incremental cash flows on Row 52.

SELF TEST

How are incremental cash flows found in a replacement analysis?

If you were analyzing a replacement project and suddenly learned that the old equipment could be sold for $1,000 rather than $400, would this new information make the replacement look better or worse? Explain.

In Figure 13-9 we assumed that output would remain stable if the old machine were replaced. Suppose output would double. How would this change be dealt with in the framework of Figure 13-9?

13-10 Real Options

According to traditional capital budgeting theory, a project's NPV is the present value of its expected future cash flows discounted at a rate that reflects the riskiness of those cash flows. Note, however, that this says nothing about actions taken *after* the

16. The same sort of risk analysis discussed in previous sections can be applied to replacement decisions.

FIGURE 13-9   Replacement Analysis

	A	B	C	D	E	F	G	H	I
16	**Part I. Inputs:**				**Both Machines**	**Old Machine**	**New Machine**		
17	**Cost of new machine**						$2,000		
18	**After-tax salvage value old machine**					$400			
19	**Sales revenues (fixed)**				$2,500				
20	**Annual operating costs except depr.**					$1,200	$280		
21	**Tax rate**				40%				
22	**WACC**				10%				
23	**Depreciation**			1	2	3	4	**Totals:**	
24	**Depr. rates (new machine)**			33.33%	44.45%	14.81%	7.41%	100%	
25	**Depreciation on new machine**			$667	$889	$296	$148	$2,000	
26	**Depreciation on old machine**			$334	$333	$0	$0	$667	
27									
28	**Part II. Net Cash Flows before Replacement: Old Machine**								
29					0	1	2	3	4
30	**Sales revenues**					$2,500	$2,500	$2,500	$2,500
31	**Operating costs except depreciation**					1,200	1,200	1,200	1,200
32	**Depreciation**					334	333	0	0
33	**Total operating costs**					$1,534	$1,533	$1,200	$1,200
34	**Operating income**					$966	$967	$1,300	$1,300
35	**Taxes 40%**					386	387	520	520
36	**After-tax operating income**					$580	$580	$780	$780
37	**Add back depreciation**					334	333	0	0
38	**Net cash flows <u>before</u> replacement**				$0	$914	$913	$780	$780
39	**Part III. Net Cash Flows after Replacement: New Machine**								
40					0	1	2	3	4
41	**New machine cost:**				−$2,000				
42	**After-tax salvage value, old machine**				$400				
43	**Sales revenues**					$2,500	$2,500	$2,500	$2,500
44	**Operating costs except depreciation**					$280	$280	$280	$280
45	**Depreciation**					$667	$889	$296	$148
46	**Total operating costs**					$947	$1,169	$576	$428
47	**Operating income**					$1,553	$1,331	$1,924	$2,072
48	**Taxes 40%**					$621	$532	$770	$829
49	**After-tax operating income**					$932	$799	$1,154	$1,243
50	**Add back depreciation**					$667	$889	$296	$148
51	**Net cash flows <u>after</u> replacement**				−$1,600	$1,599	$1,688	$1,450	$1,391
52	**Part IV. Incremental CF: Row 51 − Row 38**				−$1,600	$685	$774	$670	$611
53	**Part V. Evaluation**			**NPV =**	$584.02	**IRR =**	26.33%	**MIRR =**	18.90%

project has been accepted and placed in operation that might lead to an increase in the cash flows. In other words, traditional capital budgeting theory assumes that a project is like a roulette wheel. A gambler can choose whether to spin the wheel, but once the wheel has been spun, nothing can be done to influence the outcome. Once the game begins, the outcome depends purely on chance, and no skill is involved.

See **Ch13 Tool Kit.xls** on the textbook's Web site.

Contrast roulette with a game such as poker. Chance plays a role in poker, and it continues to play a role after the initial deal because players receive additional cards throughout the game. However, poker players are able to respond to their opponents' actions, so skilled players are more likely to win.

Capital budgeting decisions have more in common with poker than roulette because: (1) chance plays a continuing role throughout the life of the project, but (2) managers can respond to changing market conditions and to competitors' actions. Opportunities to respond to changing circumstances are called **managerial options** (because they give managers a chance to influence the outcome of a project), **strategic options** (because they are often associated with large, strategic projects rather than routine maintenance projects), and **embedded options** (because they are a part of the project). Finally, they are called **real options** to differentiate them from financial options because they involve real, rather than financial, assets. The following sections describe projects with several types of real options.

13-10a **Investment Timing Options**

Conventional NPV analysis implicitly assumes that projects either will be accepted or rejected, which implies they will be undertaken now or never. In practice, however, companies sometimes have a third choice—delay the decision until later, when more information is available. Such **investment timing options** can dramatically affect a project's estimated profitability and risk, as we saw in our example of GPC's solar water heater project.

Keep in mind, though, that the *option to delay* is valuable only if it more than offsets any harm that might result from delaying. For example, while one company delays, some other company might establish a loyal customer base that makes it difficult for the first company to enter the market later. The option to delay is usually most valuable to firms with proprietary technology, patents, licenses, or other barriers to entry, because these factors lessen the threat of competition. The option to delay is valuable when market demand is uncertain, but it is also valuable during periods of volatile interest rates, because the ability to wait can allow firms to delay raising capital for a project until interest rates are lower.

13-10b **Growth Options**

A **growth option** allows a company to increase its capacity if market conditions are better than expected. There are several types of growth options. One lets a company *increase the capacity of an existing product line*. A "peaking unit" power plant illustrates this type of growth option. Such units have high variable costs and are used to produce additional power only if demand is high (and thus prices are high).

The second type of growth option allows a company to *expand into new geographic markets*. Many companies are investing in China, Eastern Europe, and Russia even though standard NPV analysis produces negative NPVs. However, if these developing markets really take off, the option to open more facilities could be quite valuable.

The third type of growth option is the opportunity to *add new products,* including complementary products and successive "generations" of the original product. Auto companies are losing money on their first electric autos, but the manufacturing skills and consumer recognition those cars will provide should help turn subsequent generations of electric autos into moneymakers.

13-10c **Abandonment Options**

Consider the value of an **abandonment option**. Standard DCF analysis assumes that a project's assets will be used over a specified economic life. But even though some projects must be operated over their full economic life—in spite of deteriorating market conditions and hence lower than expected cash flows—other projects can be abandoned. Smart managers negotiate the right to abandon if a project turns out to be unsuccessful as a condition for undertaking the project.

Note, too, that some projects can be structured so that they provide the option to *reduce capacity* or *temporarily suspend operations*. Such options are common in the natural resources industry, including mining, oil, and timber, and they should be reflected in the analysis when NPVs are being estimated.

13-10d **Flexibility Options**

Many projects offer **flexibility options** that permit the firm to alter operations depending on how conditions change during the life of the project. Typically, either inputs or outputs (or both) can be changed. BMW's auto assembly plant in Spartanburg, South Carolina, provides a good example of output flexibility. BMW needed the plant to produce sports coupes. If it built the plant configured to produce only these vehicles, the construction cost would be minimized. However, the company thought that later on it might want to switch production to some other vehicle type, and that would be difficult if the plant were designed just for coupes. Therefore, BMW decided to spend additional funds to construct a more flexible plant: one that could produce different types of vehicles should demand patterns shift. Sure enough, things did change. Demand for coupes dropped a bit and demand for sport-utility vehicles soared. But BMW was ready, and the Spartanburg plant began to produce hot-selling SUVs. The plant's cash flows were much higher than they would have been without the flexibility option that BMW "bought" by paying more to build a more flexible plant.

Electric power plants provide an example of input flexibility. Utilities can build plants that generate electricity by burning coal, oil, or natural gas. The prices of those fuels change over time in response to events in the Middle East, changing environmental policies, and weather conditions. Some years ago, virtually all power plants were designed to burn just one type of fuel, because this resulted in the lowest construction costs. However, as fuel cost volatility increased, power companies began to build higher-cost but more flexible plants, especially ones that could switch from oil to gas and back again depending on relative fuel prices.

13-10e **Valuing Real Options**

A full treatment of real option valuation is beyond the scope of this chapter, but there are some things we can say. First, if a project has an embedded real option, then management should at least recognize and articulate its existence. Second, we know that a financial option is more valuable if it has a long time until maturity or if the underlying asset is very risky. If either of these characteristics applies to a project's real option, then management should know that its value is probably relatively high. Third, management might be able to model the real option along the lines of a decision tree, as we illustrate in the following section.

Explain the relevance of the following statement: "Capital budgeting decisions have more in common with poker than roulette."

What are managerial options? Strategic options?

Identify some different types of real options and differentiate among them.

13-11 Phased Decisions and Decision Trees

Up to this point we have focused primarily on techniques for estimating a project's risk. Although this is an integral part of capital budgeting, managers are just as interested in *reducing* risk as in *measuring* it. One way to reduce risk is to structure projects so that expenditures can be made in stages over time rather than all at once. This gives managers the opportunity to reevaluate decisions using new information and then to either invest additional funds or terminate the project. This type of analysis involves the use of *decision trees*.

13-11a The Basic Decision Tree

GPC's analysis of the solar water heater project thus far has assumed that the project cannot be abandoned once it goes into operation, even if the worst-case situation arises. However, GPC is considering the possibility of terminating (abandoning) the project at Year 2 if the demand is low. The net after-tax cash flow from salvage, legal fees, liquidation of working capital, and all other termination costs and revenues is $5,000. Using these assumptions, the GPC ran a new scenario analysis; the results are shown in Figure 13-10, which is a simple decision tree.

WEB

See *Ch13 Tool Kit.xls* on the textbook's Web site.

Here we assume that, if the worst case materializes, then this will be recognized after the low Year-1 cash flow and GPC will abandon the project. Rather than continue realizing low cash flows in Years 2, 3, and 4, the company will shut down the operation and liquidate the project for $5,000 at t = 2. Now the expected NPV rises

FIGURE 13-10 Simple Decision Tree: Abandoning Project in Worst-Case Scenario

	A	B	C	D	E	F	G	H	I
123			Predicted Cash Flows for Alternative Scenarios						
124		Prob:	0	1	2	3	4	WACC	NPV
125	Best→	25%	−$10,269	$4,761	$6,673	$8,237	$20,065	10%	$19,468
126									
127	→Base→	50%	−$10,000	$1,900	$2,700	$2,345	$7,800	10%	$1,048
128									
129			−$9,844	$403	$897	−$281	$2,055		
130	Worst→	25%							
131			−$9,844	$403	$5,000	$0	$0	10%	−$5,345
132	If abandon, can liquidate for $5,000 at t = 2.								
133							Expected NPV =		$4,055
134							Standard Deviation (SD) =		$9,273
135						Coefficient of Variation (CV) = Std. Dev./Expected NPV =			2.29

from \$3,505 to \$4,055 and the CV declines from 2.81 to 2.29. So, securing the right to abandon the project if things don't work out raised the project's expected return and lowered its risk. This will give you an approximate value, but keep in mind that you may not have a good estimate of the appropriate discount rate because the real option changes the risk, and hence the required return, of the project.[17]

13-11b **Staged Decision Tree**

After the management team thought about the decision-tree approach, other ideas for improving the project emerged. The marketing manager stated that he could undertake a study that would give the firm a better idea of demand for the product. If the marketing study found favorable responses to the product, the design engineer stated that she could build a prototype solar water heater to gauge consumer reactions to the actual product. After assessing consumer reactions, the company could either go ahead with the project or abandon it. This type of evaluation process is called a **staged decision tree** and is shown in Figure 13-11.

Decision trees such as the one in Figure 13-11 often are used to analyze multistage, or sequential, decisions. Each circle represents a decision point, also known as a **decision node.** The dollar value to the left of each decision node represents the net cash flow at that point, and the cash flows shown under t = 3, 4, 5, and 6 represent the cash inflows if the project is pushed on to completion. Each diagonal line leads to a **branch** of the decision tree, and each branch has an estimated probability. For example, if the firm decides to "go" with the project

FIGURE 13-11 Decision Tree with Multiple Decision Points

	A	B	C	D	E	F	G	H	I	J	K
144	Firm can abandon the project at t = 2									WACC =	10%
145			Time Periods, Cash Flows, Probabilities, and Decision Points							WACC =	10%
146	0		1		2	3	4	5	6	WACC =	10%
147	1st Invest	Prob.	2nd Invest	Prob.	3rd Invest	Inflow	Inflow	Inflow	Inflow	NPV	Joint Prob
148											
149				45%	–\$10,269 ③ \$4,761	\$6,673	\$8,237	\$20,065		\$15,534	36%
150											
151		80%	–\$500② →	40%	–\$10,000 ③ \$1,900	\$2,700	\$2,345	\$7,800		\$312	32%
152											
153	–\$100 ①			15%	Stop ③ \$0	\$0	\$0	\$0		–\$555	12%
154											
155		20%	Stop ②		\$0	\$0	\$0	\$0	\$0	–\$100	20%
156											100%
157									Expected NPV =	\$5,606	
158								Standard Deviation (SD) =		\$7,451	
159							Coefficient of Variation (CV) = Std. Dev./Expected NPV =			1.33	

17. For more on real option valuation, see M. Amram and N. Kulatilaka, *Real Options: Managing Strategic Investment in an Uncertain World* (Boston: Harvard Business School Press, 1999); and H. Smit and L. Trigeorgis, *Strategic Investments: Real Options and Games* (Princeton, NJ: Princeton University Press, 2004).

at Decision Point 1, then it will spend $100,000 on the marketing study. Management estimates that there is a 0.8 probability that the study will produce *positive* results, leading to the decision to make an additional investment and thus move on to Decision Point 2, and a 0.2 probability that the marketing study will produce *negative* results, indicating that the project should be canceled after Stage 1. If the project is canceled, the cost to the company will be the $100,000 spent on the initial marketing study.

If the marketing study yields positive results, then the firm will spend $500,000 on the prototype water heater module at Decision Point 2. Management estimates (even before making the initial $100,000 investment) that there is a 45% probability of the pilot project yielding good results, a 40% probability of average results, and a 15% probability of bad results. If the prototype works well, then the firm will spend several millions more at Decision Point 3 to build a production plant, buy the necessary inventory, and commence operations. The operating cash flows over the project's 4-year life will be good, average, or bad, and these cash flows are shown under Years 3 through 6.

The column of joint probabilities in Figure 13-11 gives the probability of occurrence of each branch—and hence of each NPV. Each joint probability is obtained by multiplying together all the probabilities on that particular branch. For example, the probability that the company will, if Stage 1 is undertaken, move through Stages 2 and 3, and that a strong demand will produce the indicated cash flows, is (0.8)(0.45) = 0.36 = 36.0%. There is a 32% probability of average results, a 12% probability of building the plant and then getting bad results, and a 20% probability of getting bad initial results and stopping after the marketing study.

The NPV of the top (most favorable) branch as shown in Column J is $15,534, calculated as follows:

$$NPV = -\$100 - \frac{\$500}{(1.10)^1} - \frac{\$10,269}{(1.10)^2} + \frac{\$4,761}{(1.10)^3} + \frac{\$6,673}{(1.10)^4} + \frac{\$8,237}{(1.10)^5} + \frac{\$20,065}{(1.10)^6}$$

$$= \$15,534$$

The NPVs for the other branches are calculated similarly.[18]

The expected NPV is calculated by multiplying each branch's NPV by the joint probability that the branch will occur and then summing this product for all the branches. Based on the expectations used to create Figure 13-11 and a cost of capital of 10%, the project's expected NPV is $5,606, or $5.606 million.[19] In addition, the CV declines from 2.81 to 1.33, and the maximum anticipated loss is a manageable −$555,000. At this point, the solar water heater project looked good, and GPC's management decided to accept it.

As this example shows, decision-tree analysis requires managers to articulate explicitly the types of risk a project faces and to develop responses to potential scenarios. Note also that our example could be extended to cover many other types of decisions and could even be incorporated into a simulation analysis. All in all, decision-tree analysis is a valuable tool for analyzing project risks.[20]

18. The calculations in *Excel* use nonrounded annual cash flows, so there may be small differences when calculating by hand with rounded annual cash flows.
19. As we mentioned concerning the abandonment option, the presence of the real options in Figure 13-11 might cause the discount rate to change.

What is a decision tree? A branch? A node?

If a firm can structure a project such that expenditures can be made in stages rather than all at the beginning, how would this affect the project's risk and expected NPV? Explain.

---

20. In this example we glossed over an important issue: the appropriate cost of capital for the project. Adding decision nodes to a project clearly changes its risk, so we would expect the cost of capital for a project with few decision nodes to have a different risk than one with many nodes. If this is so, then the projects should have different costs of capital. In fact, we might expect the cost of capital to change over time as the project moves to different stages, because the stages themselves differ in risk.

Summary

In this chapter, we developed a framework for analyzing a project's cash flows and its risk. The key concepts covered are listed below.

- The most important (and most difficult) step in analyzing a capital budgeting project is **estimating the incremental after-tax cash flows** the project will produce.
- A project's **net cash flow** is different from its accounting income. Project net cash flow reflects: (1) cash outlays for fixed assets, (2) sales revenues, (3) operating costs, (4) the tax shield provided by depreciation, and (5) cash flows due to changes in net working capital. A project's net cash flow does *not* include interest payments, because they are accounted for by the discounting process. If we deducted interest and then discounted cash flows at the WACC, this would double-count interest charges.
- In determining incremental cash flows, **opportunity costs** (the cash flows forgone by using an asset) must be included, but **sunk costs** (cash outlays that have been made and that cannot be recouped) are not included. Any **externalities** (effects of a project on other parts of the firm) should also be reflected in the analysis. Externalities can be *positive* or *negative* and may be *environmental*.
- **Cannibalization** is an important type of externality that occurs when a new project leads to a reduction in sales of an existing product.
- **Tax laws** affect cash flow analysis in two ways: (1) taxes reduce operating cash flows, and (2) tax laws determine the depreciation expense that can be taken in each year.
- **Price level changes (inflation** or **deflation)** must be considered in project analysis. The best procedure is to build expected price changes into the cash flow estimates. Recognize that output prices and costs for a product can decline over time even though the economy is experiencing inflation.

- The chapter illustrates both **expansion projects**, in which the investment generates new sales, and **replacement projects**, where the primary purpose of the investment is to operate more efficiently and thus reduce costs.
- We discuss three types of risk: **Stand-alone risk**, **corporate risk** (or **within-firm risk**), and **market risk** (or **beta risk**). Stand-alone risk does not consider diversification at all; corporate risk considers risk among the firm's own assets; and market risk considers risk at the stockholder level, where stockholders' own diversification is considered.
- **Risk** is important because it affects the discount rate used in capital budgeting; in other words, a project's WACC depends on its risk.
- Assuming the CAPM holds true, **market risk** is the most important risk because (according to the CAPM) it is the risk that affects stock prices. However, usually *it is difficult to measure a project's market risk*.
- **Corporate risk** is important because it influences the firm's ability to use low-cost debt, to maintain smooth operations over time, and to avoid crises that might consume management's energy and disrupt its employees, customers, suppliers, and community. Also, a project's corporate risk is generally easier to measure than its market risk. Because corporate and market risks usually are generally correlated, corporate risk can often serve as a proxy for market risk.
- **Stand-alone risk** is easier to measure than either market or corporate risk. Also, most of a firm's projects' cash flows are correlated with one another, and the firm's total cash flows are correlated with those of most other firms. These correlations mean that a project's stand-alone risk generally can be used as a proxy for hard-to-measure market and corporate risk. As a result, most risk analysis in capital budgeting focuses on stand-alone risk.
- **Sensitivity analysis** is a technique that shows how much a project's NPV will change in response to a given change in an input variable, such as sales, when all other factors are held constant.
- **Scenario analysis** is a risk analysis technique in which the best- and worst-case NPVs are compared with the project's base-case NPV.
- **Monte Carlo simulation** is a risk analysis technique that uses a computer to simulate future events and thereby estimate a project's profitability and riskiness.
- The **risk-adjusted discount rate**, or **project cost of capital**, is the rate used to evaluate a particular project. It is based on the corporate WACC, a value that is increased for projects that are riskier than the firm's average project and decreased for less risky projects.
- A **decision tree** shows how different decisions during a project's life can affect its value.
- A **staged decision tree** divides the analysis into different phases. At each phase a decision is made either to proceed or to stop the project. These decisions are represented on the decision trees by circles and are called **decision nodes**.
- Opportunities to respond to changing circumstances are called **real options** or **managerial options** because they give managers the option to influence the returns on a project. They are also called **strategic options** if they are associated with large, strategic projects rather than routine maintenance projects. Finally, they are also called "real" options because they involve "real" (or "physical") rather than "financial" assets. Many projects include a variety of these **embedded options** that can dramatically affect the true NPV.

- An **investment timing option** involves the possibility of delaying major expenditures until more information on likely outcomes is known. The opportunity to delay can dramatically change a project's estimated value.
- A **growth option** occurs if an investment creates the opportunity to make other potentially profitable investments that would not otherwise be possible. These include: (1) options to expand the original project's output, (2) options to enter a new geographical market, and (3) options to introduce complementary products or successive generations of products.
- An **abandonment option** is the ability to discontinue a project if the operating cash flow turns out to be lower than expected. It reduces the risk of a project and increases its value. Instead of total abandonment, some options allow a company to reduce capacity or temporarily suspend operations.
- A **flexibility option** is the option to modify operations depending on how conditions develop during a project's life, especially the type of output produced or the inputs used.

Questions

13-1 Define each of the following terms:
a. Project cash flow; accounting income
b. Incremental cash flow; sunk cost; opportunity cost; externality; cannibalization; expansion project; replacement project
c. Net operating working capital changes; salvage value
d. Stand-alone risk; corporate (within-firm) risk; market (beta) risk
e. Sensitivity analysis; scenario analysis; Monte Carlo simulation analysis
f. Risk-adjusted discount rate; project cost of capital
g. Decision tree; staged decision tree; decision node; branch
h. Real options; managerial options; strategic options; embedded options
i. Investment timing option; growth option; abandonment option; flexibility option

13-2 Operating cash flows, rather than accounting profits, are used in project analysis. What is the basis for this emphasis on cash flows as opposed to net income?

13-3 Why is it true, in general, that a failure to adjust expected cash flows for expected inflation biases the calculated NPV downward?

13-4 Explain why sunk costs should not be included in a capital budgeting analysis but opportunity costs and externalities should be included.

13-5 Explain how net operating working capital is recovered at the end of a project's life and why it is included in a capital budgeting analysis.

13-6 How do simulation analysis and scenario analysis differ in the way they treat very bad and very good outcomes? What does this imply about using each technique to evaluate project riskiness?

13-7 Why are interest charges not deducted when a project's cash flows are calculated for use in a capital budgeting analysis?

13-8 Most firms generate cash inflows every day, not just once at the end of the year. In capital budgeting, should we recognize this fact by estimating daily project cash flows and then using them in the analysis? If we do not, will this bias our results? If it does, would the NPV be biased up or down? Explain.

13-9 What are some differences in the analysis for a replacement project versus that for a new expansion project?

13-10 Distinguish among beta (or market) risk, within-firm (or corporate) risk, and stand-alone risk for a project being considered for inclusion in a firm's capital budget.

13-11 In theory, market risk should be the only "relevant" risk. However, companies focus as much on stand-alone risk as on market risk. What are the reasons for the focus on stand-alone risk?

Problems   Answers Appear in Appendix B

Easy Problems 1–4

13-1 Investment Outlay
Talbot Industries is considering launching a new product. The new manufacturing equipment will cost $17 million, and production and sales will require an initial $5 million investment in net operating working capital. The company's tax rate is 40%.
a. What is the initial investment outlay?
b. The company spent and expensed $150,000 on research related to the new product last year. Would this change your answer? Explain.
c. Rather than build a new manufacturing facility, the company plans to install the equipment in a building it owns but is not now using. The building could be sold for $1.5 million after taxes and real estate commissions. How would this affect your answer?

13-2 Operating Cash Flow
The financial staff of Cairn Communications has identified the following information for the first year of the roll-out of its new proposed service:

Projected sales	$18 million
Operating costs (not including depreciation)	$9 million
Depreciation	$4 million
Interest expense	$3 million

The company faces a 40% tax rate. What is the project's operating cash flow for the first year $(t = 1)$?

13-3 Net Salvage Value
Allen Air Lines must liquidate some equipment that is being replaced. The equipment originally cost $12 million, of which 75% has been depreciated.

The used equipment can be sold today for $4 million, and its tax rate is 40%. What is the equipment's after-tax net salvage value?

13-4 Replacement Analysis

Although the Chen Company's milling machine is old, it is still in relatively good working order and would last for another 10 years. It is inefficient compared to modern standards, though, and so the company is considering replacing it. The new milling machine, at a cost of $110,000 delivered and installed, would also last for 10 years and would produce after-tax cash flows (labor savings and depreciation tax savings) of $19,000 per year. It would have zero salvage value at the end of its life. The firm's WACC is 10%, and its marginal tax rate is 35%. Should Chen buy the new machine?

Intermediate Problems 5–11

13-5 Depreciation Methods

Wendy's boss wants to use straight-line depreciation for the new expansion project because he said it will give higher net income in earlier years and give him a larger bonus. The project will last 4 years and requires $1,700,000 of equipment. The company could use either straight line or the 3-year MACRS accelerated method. Under straight-line depreciation, the cost of the equipment would be depreciated evenly over its 4-year life (ignore the half-year convention for the straight-line method). The applicable MACRS depreciation rates are 33.33%, 44.45%, 14.81%, and 7.41%, as discussed in Appendix 13A. The company's WACC is 10%, and its tax rate is 40%.

a. What would the depreciation expense be each year under each method?

b. Which depreciation method would produce the higher NPV, and how much higher would it be?

c. Why might Wendy's boss prefer straight-line depreciation?

13-6 New-Project Analysis

The Campbell Company is considering adding a robotic paint sprayer to its production line. The sprayer's base price is $1,080,000, and it would cost another $22,500 to install it. The machine falls into the MACRS 3-year class, and it would be sold after 3 years for $605,000. The MACRS rates for the first three years are 0.3333, 0.4445, and 0.1481. The machine would require an increase in net working capital (inventory) of $15,500. The sprayer would not change revenues, but it is expected to save the firm $380,000 per year in before-tax operating costs, mainly labor. Campbell's marginal tax rate is 35%.

a. What is the Year 0 net cash flow?

b. What are the net operating cash flows in Years 1, 2, and 3?

c. What is the additional Year-3 cash flow (i.e., the after-tax salvage and the return of working capital)?

d. If the project's cost of capital is 12%, should the machine be purchased?

13-7 New-Project Analysis

The president of the company you work for has asked you to evaluate the proposed acquisition of a new chromatograph for the firm's R&D department. The equipment's basic price is $70,000, and it would cost another $15,000 to modify it for special use by your firm. The chromatograph, which falls into the MACRS 3-year class, would be sold after 3 years for $30,000. The MACRS rates for the first three years are 0.3333, 0.4445, and 0.1481. Use of the equipment would require an increase in net working capital (spare parts inventory) of $4,000. The machine would have no effect on revenues, but it is expected to save the firm $25,000 per year in before-tax operating costs, mainly labor. The firm's marginal federal-plus-state tax rate is 40%.

a. What is the Year-0 net cash flow?

b. What are the net operating cash flows in Years 1, 2, and 3?

c. What is the additional (nonoperating) cash flow in Year 3?

d. If the project's cost of capital is 10%, should the chromatograph be purchased?

13–8 Inflation Adjustments

The Rodriguez Company is considering an average-risk investment in a mineral water spring project that has a cost of $150,000. The project will produce 1,000 cases of mineral water per year indefinitely. The current sales price is $138 per case, and the current cost per case is $105. The firm is taxed at a rate of 34%. Both prices and costs are expected to rise at a rate of 6% per year. The firm uses only equity, and it has a cost of capital of 15%. Assume that cash flows consist only of after-tax profits, because the spring has an indefinite life and will not be depreciated.

a. Should the firm accept the project? (*Hint:* The project is a growing perpetuity, so you must use the constant growth formula to find its NPV.)

b. Suppose that total costs consisted of a fixed cost of $10,000 per year plus variable costs of $95 per unit and only the variable costs were expected to increase with inflation. Would this make the project better or worse? Continue to assume that the sales price will rise with inflation.

13–9 Replacement Analysis

The Gilbert Instrument Corporation is considering replacing the wood steamer it currently uses to shape guitar sides. The steamer has 6 years of remaining life. If kept, the steamer will have depreciation expenses of $650 for 5 years and $325 for the sixth year. Its current book value is $3,575, and it can be sold on an Internet auction site for $4,150 at this time. If the old steamer is not replaced, it can be sold for $800 at the end of its useful life.

Gilbert is considering purchasing the *Side Steamer 3000*, a higher-end steamer, which costs $12,000 and has an estimated useful life of 6 years with an estimated salvage value of $1,500. This steamer falls into the MACRS 5-year class, so the applicable depreciation rates are 20.00%, 32.00%, 19.20%, 11.52%, 11.52%, and 5.76%. The new steamer is faster and allows for an output expansion, so sales would rise by $2,000 per year; the new machine's much greater efficiency would reduce operating expenses by $1,900 per year. To support the greater sales, the new machine would require that inventories increase by $2,900, but accounts payable would simultaneously increase by $700. Gilbert's marginal federal-plus-state tax rate is 40%, and its WACC is 15%. Should it replace the old steamer?

13–10 Replacement Analysis

St. Johns River Shipyard's welding machine is 15 years old, fully depreciated, and has no salvage value. However, even though it is old, it is still functional as originally designed and can be used for quite a while longer. A new welder will cost $182,500 and have an estimated life of 8 years with no salvage value. The new welder will be much more efficient, however, and this enhanced efficiency will increase earnings before depreciation from $27,000 to $74,000 per year. The new machine will be depreciated over its 5-year MACRS recovery period, so the applicable depreciation rates are 20.00%, 32.00%, 19.20%, 11.52%, 11.52%, and 5.76%. The applicable corporate tax rate is 40%, and the firm's WACC is 12%. Should the old welder be replaced by the new one?

Challenging Problems 11–17

13–11 Scenario Analysis

Shao Industries is considering a proposed project for its capital budget. The company estimates the project's NPV is $12 million. This estimate assumes that the economy and market conditions will be average over the next few years. The company's CFO, however, forecasts there is only a 50% chance that the economy will be average. Recognizing this uncertainty, she has also performed the following scenario analysis:

Economic Scenario	Probability of Outcome	NPV
Recession	0.05	−$70 million
Below average	0.20	−25 million
Average	0.50	12 million
Above average	0.20	20 million
Boom	0.05	30 million

What is the project's expected NPV, its standard deviation, and its coefficient of variation?

13–12 New-Project Analysis

Madison Manufacturing is considering a new machine that costs $350,000 and would reduce pre-tax manufacturing costs by $110,000 annually. Madison would use the 3-year MACRS method to depreciate the machine, and management thinks the machine would have a value of $33,000 at the end of its 5-year operating life. The applicable depreciation rates are 33.33%, 44.45%, 14.81%, and 7.42%, as discussed in Appendix 13A. Working capital would increase by $35,000 initially, but it would be recovered at the end of the project's 5-year life. Madison's marginal tax rate is 40%, and a 10% WACC is appropriate for the project.

a. Calculate the project's NPV, IRR, MIRR, and payback.

b. Assume management is unsure about the $110,000 cost savings—this figure could deviate by as much as plus or minus 20%. What would the NPV be under each of these extremes?

c. Suppose the CFO wants you to do a scenario analysis with different values for the cost savings, the machine's salvage value, and the working capital (WC) requirement. She asks you to use the following probabilities and values in the scenario analysis:

Scenario	Probability	Cost Savings	Salvage Value	WC
Worst case	0.35	$ 88,000	$28,000	$40,000
Base case	0.35	110,000	33,000	35,000
Best case	0.30	132,000	38,000	30,000

Calculate the project's expected NPV, its standard deviation, and its coefficient of variation. Would you recommend that the project be accepted?

13–13 Replacement Analysis

The Everly Equipment Company's flange-lipping machine was purchased 5 years ago for $55,000. It had an expected life of 10 years when it was bought and its remaining depreciation is $5,500 per year for each year of its remaining life. As older flange-lippers are robust and useful machines, this one can be sold for $20,000 at the end of its useful life.

A new high-efficiency, digital-controlled flange-lipper can be purchased for $120,000, including installation costs. During its 5-year life, it will reduce cash operating expenses by $30,000 per year, although it will not affect sales. At the end of its useful life, the high-efficiency machine is estimated to be worthless. MACRS depreciation will be used, and the machine will be depreciated over its 3-year class life rather than its 5-year economic life, so the applicable depreciation rates are 33.33%, 44.45%, 14.81%, and 7.41%.

The old machine can be sold today for $35,000. The firm's tax rate is 35%, and the appropriate WACC is 16%.

a. If the new flange-lipper is purchased, what is the amount of the initial cash flow at Year 0?

b. What are the incremental net cash flows that will occur at the end of Years 1 through 5?

c. What is the NPV of this project? Should Everly replace the flange-lipper?

13–14 Replacement Analysis

DeYoung Entertainment Enterprises is considering replacing the latex molding machine it uses to fabricate rubber chickens with a newer, more efficient model. The old machine has a book value of $450,000 and a remaining useful life of 5 years. The current machine would be worn out and worthless in 5 years, but DeYoung can sell it now to a Halloween mask manufacturer for $135,000. The old machine is being depreciated by $90,000 per year for each year of its remaining life.

The new machine has a purchase price of $775,000, an estimated useful life and MACRS class life of 5 years, and an estimated salvage value of $105,000. The applicable depreciation rates are 20.00%, 32.00%, 19.20%, 11.52%, 11.52%, and 5.76%. Being highly efficient, it is expected to economize on electric power usage, labor, and repair costs, and, most importantly, to reduce the number of defective chickens. In total, an annual savings of $185,000 will be realized if the new machine is installed. The company's marginal tax rate is 35%, and it has a 12% WACC.

a. What is the initial net cash flow if the new machine is purchased and the old one is replaced?

b. Calculate the annual depreciation allowances for both machines, and compute the change in the annual depreciation expense if the replacement is made.

c. What are the incremental net cash flows in Years 1 through 5?

d. Should the firm purchase the new machine? Support your answer.

e. In general, how would each of the following factors affect the investment decision, and how should each be treated?

(1) The expected life of the existing machine decreases.

(2) The WACC is not constant but is increasing as DeYoung adds more projects into its capital budget for the year.

13–15 **Risky Cash Flows**

The Bartram-Pulley Company (BPC) must decide between two mutually exclusive investment projects. Each project costs $6,750 and has an expected life of 3 years. Annual net cash flows from each project begin 1 year after the initial investment is made and have the following probability distributions:

Project A		Project B	
Probability	Net Cash Flows	Probability	Net Cash Flows
0.2	$6,000	0.2	$ 0
0.6	6,750	0.6	6,750
0.2	7,500	0.2	18,000

BPC has decided to evaluate the riskier project at a 12% rate and the less risky project at a 10% rate.

a. What is the expected value of the annual net cash flows from each project? What is the coefficient of variation (CV)? (*Hint:* $\sigma_B = \$5,798$ and $CV_B = 0.76$.)

b. What is the risk-adjusted NPV of each project?

c. If it were known that Project B is negatively correlated with other cash flows of the firm whereas Project A is positively correlated, how would this affect the decision? If Project B's cash flows were negatively correlated with gross domestic product (GDP), would that influence your assessment of its risk?

13–16 **Simulation**

Singleton Supplies Corporation (SSC) manufactures medical products for hospitals, clinics, and nursing homes. SSC may introduce a new type of X-ray scanner designed to identify certain types of cancers in their early stages. There are a number of uncertainties about the proposed project, but the following data are believed to be reasonably accurate:

Probability	Developmental Costs	Random Numbers
0.3	$2,000,000	00–29
0.4	4,000,000	30–69
0.3	6,000,000	70–99

Probability	Project Life	Random Numbers
0.2	3 years	00–19
0.6	8 years	20–79
0.2	13 years	80–99

Probability	Sales in Units	Random Numbers
0.2	100	00–19
0.6	200	20–79
0.2	300	80–99

Probability	Sales Price	Random Numbers
0.1	$13,000	00–09
0.8	13,500	10–89
0.1	14,000	90–99

Probability	Cost per Unit (Excluding Developmental Costs)	Random Numbers
0.3	$5,000	00–29
0.4	6,000	30–69
0.3	7,000	70–99

SSC uses a cost of capital of 15% to analyze average-risk projects, 12% for low-risk projects, and 18% for high-risk projects. These risk adjustments primarily reflect the uncertainty about each project's NPV and IRR as measured by their coefficients of variation. The firm is in the 40% federal-plus-state income tax bracket.

a. What is the expected IRR for the X-ray scanner project? Base your answer on the expected values of the variables. Also, assume the after-tax "profits" figure that you develop is equal to annual cash flows. All facilities are leased, so depreciation may be disregarded. Can you determine the value of σ_{IRR} short of actual simulation or complex statistical analysis?

b. Assume that SSC uses a 15% cost of capital for this project. What is the project's NPV? Could you estimate σ_{NPV} without either simulation or a complex statistical analysis?

c. Show the process by which a computer would perform a simulation analysis for this project. Use the random numbers 44, 17, 16, 58, 1; 79, 83, 86; and 19, 62, 6 to illustrate the process with the first computer run. Calculate the first-run NPV and IRR. Assume the cash flows for each year are independent of cash flows for other years. Also, assume the computer operates as follows: (1) A developmental cost and a project life are estimated for the first run using the first two random numbers. (2) Next, sales volume, sales price, and cost per unit are estimated using the next three random numbers and used to derive a cash flow for the first year.

(3) Then, the next three random numbers are used to estimate sales volume, sales price, and cost per unit for the second year, hence the cash flow for the second year. (4) Cash flows for other years are developed similarly, on out to the first run's estimated life. (5) With the developmental cost and the cash flow stream established, NPV and IRR for the first run are derived and stored in the computer's memory. (6) The process is repeated to generate perhaps 500 other NPVs and IRRs. (7) Frequency distributions for NPV and IRR are plotted by the computer, and the distributions' means and standard deviations are calculated.

13–17 Decision Tree

The Yoran Yacht Company (YYC), a prominent sailboat builder in Newport, may design a new 30-foot sailboat based on the "winged" keels first introduced on the 12-meter yachts that raced for the America's Cup.

First, YYC would have to invest $10,000 at t = 0 for the design and model tank testing of the new boat. YYC's managers believe there is a 60% probability that this phase will be successful and the project will continue. If Stage 1 is not successful, the project will be abandoned with zero salvage value.

The next stage, if undertaken, would consist of making the molds and producing two prototype boats. This would cost $500,000 at t = 1. If the boats test well, YYC would go into production. If they do not, the molds and prototypes could be sold for $100,000. The managers estimate the probability is 80% that the boats will pass testing and that Stage 3 will be undertaken.

Stage 3 consists of converting an unused production line to produce the new design. This would cost $1 million at t = 2. If the economy is strong at this point, the net value of sales would be $3 million; if the economy is weak, the net value would be $1.5 million. Both net values occur at t = 3, and each state of the economy has a probability of 0.5. YYC's corporate cost of capital is 12%.

a. Assume this project has average risk. Construct a decision tree and determine the project's expected NPV.
b. Find the project's standard deviation of NPV and coefficient of variation of NPV. If YYC's average project had a CV of between 1.0 and 2.0, would this project be of high, low, or average stand-alone risk?

Spreadsheet Problem

13–18 Build a Model: Issues in Capital Budgeting

Start with the partial model in the file *Ch13 P18 Build a Model.xls* on the textbook's Web site. Webmaster.com has developed a powerful new server that would be used for corporations' Internet activities. It would cost $10 million at Year 0 to buy the equipment necessary to manufacture the server. The project would require net working capital at the beginning of a year in an amount equal to 10% of the year's projected sales: $NOWC_0 = 10\%(Sales_1)$. The servers would sell for $24,000 per unit, and Webmasters

WEB

believes that variable costs would amount to $17,500 per unit. After Year 1, the sales price and variable costs will increase at the inflation rate of 3%. The company's nonvariable costs would be $1 million at Year 1 and would increase with inflation.

The server project would have a life of 4 years. If the project is undertaken, it must be continued for the entire 4 years. Also, the project's returns are expected to be highly correlated with returns on the firm's other assets. The firm believes it could sell 1,000 units per year.

The equipment would be depreciated over a 5-year period, using MACRS rates. The estimated market value of the equipment at the end of the project's 4-year life is $500,000. Webmaster's federal-plus-state tax rate is 40%. Its cost of capital is 10% for average-risk projects, defined as projects with an NPV coefficient of variation between 0.8 and 1.2. Low-risk projects are evaluated with a WACC of 8% and high-risk projects at 13%.

a. Develop a spreadsheet model, and use it to find the project's NPV, IRR, MIRR, PI, payback, and discounted payback.

b. Conduct a sensitivity analysis to determine the sensitivity of NPV to changes in the sales price, variable costs per unit, and number of units sold. Set these variables' values at 10% and 20% above and below their base-case values.

c. Conduct a scenario analysis. Assume that there is a 25% probability that best-case conditions, with each of the variables discussed in part b being 20% better than its base-case value, will occur. There is a 25% probability of worst-case conditions, with the variables 20% worse than base, and a 50% probability of base-case conditions.

d. If the project appears to be more or less risky than an average project, find its risk-adjusted NPV, IRR, and payback.

e. On the basis of information in the problem, would you recommend the project should be accepted?

MINI CASE

Shrieves Casting Company is considering adding a new line to its product mix, and the capital budgeting analysis is being conducted by Sidney Johnson, a recently graduated MBA. The production line would be set up in unused space in Shrieves' main plant. The machinery's invoice price would be approximately $200,000, another $10,000 in shipping charges would be required, and it would cost an additional $30,000 to install the equipment. The machinery has an economic life of 4 years, and Shrieves has obtained a special tax ruling that places the equipment in the MACRS 3-year class. The machinery is expected to have a salvage value of $25,000 after 4 years of use.

The new line would generate incremental sales of 1,250 units per year for 4 years at an incremental cost of $100 per unit in the first year, excluding depreciation. Each unit can be sold for $200 in the first year. The sales price and cost are both expected to increase by 3% per year due to inflation. Further, to handle the new line, the firm's net working capital would have to increase by an amount equal to 12% of sales revenues. The firm's tax rate is 40%, and its overall weighted average cost of capital is 10%.

a. Define "incremental cash flow."
   (1) Should you subtract interest expense or dividends when calculating project cash flow?
   (2) Suppose the firm spent $100,000 last year to rehabilitate the production line site. Should this be included in the analysis? Explain.
   (3) Now assume the plant space could be leased out to another firm at $25,000 per year. Should this be included in the analysis? If so, how?
   (4) Finally, assume that the new product line is expected to decrease sales of the firm's other lines by $50,000 per year. Should this be considered in the analysis? If so, how?

b. Disregard the assumptions in part a. What is Shrieves' depreciable basis? What are the annual depreciation expenses?

c. Calculate the annual sales revenues and costs (other than depreciation). Why is it important to include inflation when estimating cash flows?

d. Construct annual incremental operating cash flow statements.

e. Estimate the required net working capital for each year and the cash flow due to investments in net working capital.

f. Calculate the after-tax salvage cash flow.

g. Calculate the net cash flows for each year. Based on these cash flows, what are the project's NPV, IRR, MIRR, PI, payback, and discounted payback? Do these indicators suggest that the project should be undertaken?

h. What does the term "risk" mean in the context of capital budgeting; to what extent can risk be quantified; and, when risk is quantified, is the quantification based primarily on statistical analysis of historical data or on subjective, judgmental estimates?

i. (1) What are the three types of risk that are relevant in capital budgeting?
   (2) How is each of these risk types measured, and how do they relate to one another?
   (3) How is each type of risk used in the capital budgeting process?

j. (1) What is sensitivity analysis?
   (2) Perform a sensitivity analysis on the unit sales, salvage value, and cost of capital for the project. Assume each of these variables can vary from its base-case, or expected, value by ±10%, ±20%, and ±30%. Include a sensitivity diagram, and discuss the results.
   (3) What is the primary weakness of sensitivity analysis? What is its primary usefulness?

k. Assume that Sidney Johnson is confident in her estimates of all the variables that affect the project's cash flows except unit sales and sales price. If product acceptance is poor, unit sales would be only 900 units a year and the unit price would only be $160; a strong consumer response would produce sales of 1,600 units and a unit price of $240. Johnson believes there is a 25% chance of poor acceptance, a 25% chance of excellent acceptance, and a 50% chance of average acceptance (the base case).
   (1) What is scenario analysis?
   (2) What is the worst-case NPV? The best-case NPV?
   (3) Use the worst-, base-, and best-case NPVs and probabilities of occurrence to find the project's expected NPV, as well as the NPV's standard deviation and coefficient of variation.

l. Are there problems with scenario analysis? Define simulation analysis, and discuss its principal advantages and disadvantages.

m. (1) Assume Shrieves' average project has a coefficient of variation in the range of 0.2 to 0.4. Would the new line be classified as high risk, average risk, or low risk? What type of risk is being measured here?
   (2) Shrieves typically adds or subtracts 3 percentage points to the overall cost of capital to adjust for risk. Should the new line be accepted?
   (3) Are there any subjective risk factors that should be considered before the final decision is made?

n. What is a real option? What are some types of real options?

SELECTED ADDITIONAL CASES

The following cases from CengageCompose cover many of the concepts discussed in this chapter and are available at http://compose.cengage.com.

Klein-Brigham Series:

Case 12, "Indian River Citrus Company (A)," Case 44, "Cranfield, Inc. (A)," and Case 14, "Robert Montoya, Inc.," focus on cash flow estimation. Case 13, "Indian River Citrus (B)," Case 45, "Cranfield, Inc. (B)," Case 58, "Tasty Foods (B)," Case 60, "Heavenly Foods," and Case 15, "Robert Montoya, Inc. (B)," illustrate project risk analysis. Cases 75, 76, and 77, "The Western Company (A and B)," are comprehensive cases.

Brigham-Buzzard Series:

Case 7, "Powerline Network Corporation (Risk and Real Options in Capital Budgeting)."

Tax Depreciation

Companies often calculate depreciation one way when figuring taxes and another way when reporting income to investors: Many use the **straight-line method** for stockholder reporting (or "book" purposes), but they use the fastest rate permitted by law for tax purposes. Under the straight-line method used for stockholder reporting, one normally takes the cost of the asset, subtracts its estimated salvage value, and divides the net amount by the asset's useful economic life. For example, consider an asset with a 5-year life that costs $100,000 and has a $12,500 salvage value; its annual straight-line depreciation charge is ($100,000 − $12,500)/5 = $17,500. Note, however, as we stated earlier, salvage value is a factor in financial reporting but it is *not* considered for tax depreciation purposes.

For tax purposes, Congress changes the permissible tax depreciation methods from time to time. Prior to 1954, the straight-line method was required for tax purposes, but in 1954 **accelerated methods** (double-declining balance and sum-of-years'-digits) were permitted. Then, in 1981, the old accelerated methods were replaced by a simpler procedure known as the Accelerated Cost Recovery System (ACRS). The ACRS system was changed again in 1986 as a part of the Tax Reform Act, and it is now known as the **Modified Accelerated Cost Recovery System (MACRS)**; a 1993 tax law made further changes in this area.

Note that U.S. tax laws are complicated, and in this text we can provide only an overview of MACRS that will give you a basic understanding of the impact of depreciation on capital budgeting decisions. Further, the tax laws change so often that the numbers we present may be outdated before the book is published. Thus, when dealing with tax depreciation in real-world situations, always consult current Internal Revenue Service (IRS) publications or individuals with expertise in tax matters.

For tax purposes, the entire cost of an asset is expensed over its depreciable life. Historically, an asset's depreciable life was set equal to its estimated useful economic life; it was intended that an asset would be fully depreciated at approximately the same time that it reached the end of its useful economic life. However, MACRS totally abandoned that practice and set simple guidelines that created several classes of assets, each with a more-or-less arbitrarily prescribed life called a *recovery period* or *class life*. The MACRS class lives bear only a rough relationship to assets' expected useful economic lives.

A major effect of the MACRS system has been to shorten the depreciable lives of assets, thus giving businesses larger tax deductions early in the assets' lives and thereby increasing the present value of the cash flows. Table 13A-1 describes the types of property that fit into the different class life groups, and Table 13A-2 sets forth the MACRS recovery allowance percentages (depreciation rates) for selected classes of investment property.

TABLE 13A-1	Major Classes and Asset Lives for MACRS
Class	**Type of Property**
3-year	Certain special manufacturing tools
5-year	Automobiles, light-duty trucks, computers, and certain special manufacturing equipment
7-year	Most industrial equipment, office furniture, and fixtures
10-year	Certain longer-lived types of equipment
27.5-year	Residential rental real property such as apartment buildings
39-year	All nonresidential real property, including commercial and industrial buildings

Consider Table 13A-1, which gives the MACRS class lives and the types of assets that fall into each category. Property in the 27.5- and 39-year categories (real estate) must be depreciated by the straight-line method, but 3-, 5-, 7-, and 10-year property (personal property) can be depreciated either by the accelerated method set forth in Table 13A-2 or by the straight-line method.[1]

As we saw earlier in the chapter, higher depreciation expenses result in lower taxes in the early years and hence lead to a higher present value of cash flows. Therefore, because firms have the choice of using straight-line rates or the accelerated rates shown in Table 13A-2, most elect to use the accelerated rates.

The yearly recovery allowance, or depreciation expense, is determined by multiplying each asset's *depreciable basis* by the applicable recovery percentage shown in Table 13A-2. You might be wondering why 4 years of deprecation rates are shown for property in the 3-year class. Under MACRS, the assumption is generally made that property is placed in service in the middle of the first year. Thus, for 3-year-class property, the recovery period begins in the middle of the year the asset is placed in service and ends 3 years later. The effect of the *half-year convention* is to extend the recovery period out one more year, so 3-year-class property is depreciated over 4 calendar years, 5-year property is depreciated over 6 calendar years, and so on. This convention is incorporated into Table 13A-2's recovery allowance percentages.[2]

---

1. The Tax Code currently (for 2014) permits companies to *expense*, which is equivalent to depreciating over 1 year, up to $25,000 of equipment; see IRS Publication 946 for details. This is a benefit primarily for small companies. Thus, if a small company bought one asset worth up to $25,000, it could write the asset off in the year it was acquired. This is called "Section 179 expensing." We shall disregard this provision throughout the book. Also, Congress enacted the Job Creation and Worker Assistance Act of 2002 following the terrorist attacks on the World Trade Center and Pentagon. This act, among other things, temporarily changed how depreciation is charged for property acquired after September 10, 2001, and before September 11, 2004, and put in service before January 1, 2005. We shall disregard this provision throughout the book as well.

2. The half-year convention also applies if the straight-line alternative is used, with half of one year's depreciation taken in the first year, a full year's depreciation taken in each of the remaining years of the asset's class life, and the remaining half-year's depreciation taken in the year following the end of the class life. You should recognize that virtually all companies have computerized depreciation systems. Each asset's depreciation pattern is programmed into the system at the time of its acquisition, and the computer aggregates the depreciation allowances for all assets when the accountants close the books and prepare financial statements and tax returns.

What do the acronyms ACRS and MACRS stand for?

Briefly describe the tax depreciation system under MACRS.

SELF TEST

See **Ch13 Tool Kit.xls** on the textbook's Web site for all calculations.

TABLE 13A-2	Recovery Allowance Percentage for Personal Property			
	Class of Investment			
Ownership Year	**3-Year**	**5-Year**	**7-Year**	**10-Year**
1	33.33%	20.00%	14.29%	10.00%
2	44.45	32.00	24.49	18.00
3	14.81	19.20	17.49	14.40
4	7.41	11.52	12.49	11.52
5		11.52	8.93	9.22
6		5.76	8.92	7.37
7			8.93	6.55
8			4.46	6.55
9				6.56
10				6.55
11				3.28
	100%	100%	100%	100%

Notes:

1. We developed these recovery allowance percentages based on the 200% declining balance method prescribed by MACRS, with a switch to straight-line depreciation at some point in the asset's life. For example, consider the 5-year recovery allowance percentages. The straight-line percentage would be 20% per year, so the 200% declining balance multiplier is 2.0(20%) = 40% = 0.4. However, because the half-year convention applies, the MACRS percentage for Year 1 is 20%. For Year 2, there is 80% of the depreciable basis remaining to be depreciated, so the recovery allowance percentage is 0.40(80%) = 32%. In Year 3, 20% + 32% = 52% of the depreciation has been taken, leaving 48%, so the percentage is 0.4(48%) = 19.2%. In Year 4, the percentage is 0.4(28.8%) = 11.52%. After 4 years, straight-line depreciation exceeds the declining balance depreciation, so a switch is made to straight-line (which is permitted under the law). However, the half-year convention must also be applied at the end of the class life, and the remaining 17.28% of depreciation must be taken (amortized) over 1.5 years. Thus, the percentage in Year 5 is 17.28%/1.5 = 11.52%, and in Year 6 it is 17.28% − 11.52% = 5.76%. Although the tax tables carry the allowance percentages out to two decimal places, we have rounded to the nearest whole number for ease of illustration. See the worksheet **7. App. A** in the file **Ch13 Tool Kit.xls** on the textbook's Web site for the exact recovery percentages specified by the IRS.

2. Residential rental property (apartments) is depreciated over a 27.5-year life, whereas commercial and industrial structures are depreciated over 39 years. In both cases, straight-line depreciation must be used. The depreciation allowance for the first year is based, pro rata, on the month the asset was placed in service, with the remainder of the first year's depreciation being taken in the 28th or 40th year. A half-month convention is assumed; that is, an asset placed in service in February would receive 10.5 months of depreciation in the first year.

WEB

The textbook's Web site contains an *Excel* file that will guide you through the chapter's calculations. The file for this chapter is ***Ch14 Tool Kit.xls***, and we encourage you to open the file and follow along as you read the chapter.

Traditional discounted cash flow (DCF) analysis—in which an asset's cash flows are estimated and then discounted to obtain the asset's NPV—has been the cornerstone for valuing all types of assets since the 1950s. Accordingly, most of our discussion of capital budgeting has focused on DCF valuation techniques. However, in recent years, academics and practitioners have demonstrated that DCF valuation techniques do not always tell the complete story about a project's value and that rote use of DCF can, at times, lead to incorrect capital budgeting decisions.[1]

DCF techniques were originally developed to value securities such as stocks and bonds. Securities are passive investments: Once they have been purchased, most investors have no influence over the cash flows the assets produce. However, real assets are not passive investments, because managerial actions after an investment has been made can influence its results. Furthermore, investing in a new project often brings with it the potential for increasing the firm's future investment opportunities. Such opportunities are, in effect, options—the right (but not the obligation) to take some action in the future. As we demonstrate in the next section, options are valuable, so projects that expand the firm's set of opportunities have positive **option values**. Similarly, any project that reduces the set of future opportunities destroys option value. A project's impact on the firm's opportunities, or its option value, may not be captured by conventional NPV analysis, so this option value should be considered separately, as we do in this chapter.

Beginning-of-Chapter Questions

As you read the chapter, consider how you would answer the following questions. You *should not* necessarily be able to answer the questions before you read the chapter. Rather, you should use them to get a sense of the issues covered in the chapter. After reading the chapter, you should be able to give at least partial answers to the questions, and you should be able to give better answers after the chapter has been discussed in class. Note, too, that it is often useful, when answering conceptual questions, to use hypothetical data to illustrate your answer. We illustrate the answers with an *Excel* model that is available on the textbook's Web site. Accessing the model and working through it is a useful exercise, and it provides insights that are useful when answering the questions.

---

1. For an excellent general discussion of the problems inherent in discounted cash flow valuation techniques as applied to capital budgeting, see Avinash K. Dixit and Robert S. Pindyck, "The Options Approach to Capital Investment," *Harvard Business Review*, May/June 1995, pp. 105–115.

1. What's the difference between a **financial option** and a **real option**? What are some specific types of real options? Do real options just occur, or can they be "created"?

2. Real options can be analyzed using a **scenario approach** with decision trees or using the **Black-Scholes Option Pricing Model**. What are the pros and cons of the two approaches? Is one procedure "better" than the other?

3. Option values are extinguished when they are exercised. How does this influence capital budgeting decisions? What considerations, or types of analysis, might lead management to "take the plunge" and proceed with a project rather than keep delaying it?

4. Suppose a company uses the NPV method, along with risk-adjusted WACCs, to calculate project NPVs. However, it has not been considering real options in its capital budgeting decisions. Now suppose the company changes its capital budgeting process to take account of four types of real options—**timing, flexibility, growth**, and **abandonment**. Would this decision be likely to affect some of the calculated NPVs? Explain your answer.

5. Good managers not only identify and evaluate real options in projects—they also structure projects so as to create real options. Suppose a company is considering a project to build an electric generating plant. Name some real options that might be built into the project, explain how they could be evaluated, and discuss their effects on the project's NPV.

14-1 **Valuing Real Options**

Recall from Chapter 13 that real options are opportunities for management to change the timing, scale, or other aspects of an investment in response to changes in market conditions. These opportunities are options in the sense that management can, if it is in the company's best interest, undertake some action; management is not *required* to undertake the action. These opportunities are real (as opposed to financial) because they involve decisions regarding real assets—such as plants, equipment, and land—rather than financial assets like stocks or bonds. Four examples of real options are investment timing options, growth options, abandonment options, and flexibility options. This chapter provides an example of how to value an investment timing option and a growth option. *Web Extension 14A* on the textbook's Web site shows how to value an abandonment option.

Valuing a real option requires judgment, both to formulate the model and to estimate the inputs. Does this mean the answer won't be useful? Definitely not. For example, the models used by NASA only approximate the centers of gravity for the moon, the Earth, and other heavenly bodies, yet even with these "errors" in their models, NASA has been able to put astronauts on the moon. As one professor said, "All models are wrong, but some are still quite useful." This is especially true for real options. We might not be able to find the exact value of a real option, but the value we find can be helpful in deciding whether or not to accept the project. Equally important, the process of looking for and then valuing real options often identifies critical issues that might otherwise go unnoticed.

Five possible procedures can be used to deal with real options. Starting with the simplest, they are as follows.

1. Use discounted cash flow (DCF) valuation and ignore any real options by assuming their values are zero.
2. Use DCF valuation and include a qualitative recognition of any real option's value.

3. Use decision-tree analysis.
4. Use a standard model for a financial option.
5. Develop a unique, project-specific model using financial engineering techniques.

The following sections illustrate these procedures.

SELF TEST   List the five possible procedures for dealing with real options.

WEB

All calculations for the analysis of the investment timing option are shown in **Ch14 Tool Kit.xls** on the textbook's Web site.

14-2 The Investment Timing Option: An Illustration

There is frequently an alternative to investing immediately—the decision to invest or not can be postponed until more information becomes available. By waiting, a better-informed decision can be made, and this investment timing option adds value to the project and reduces its risk.

Murphy Systems is considering a project for a new type of handheld device that provides wireless Internet connections. The cost of the project is $50 million, but the future cash flows depend on the demand for wireless Internet connections, which is uncertain. Murphy believes there is a 25% chance that demand for the new device will be high, in which case the project will generate cash flows of $33 million each year for 3 years. There is a 50% chance of average demand, with cash flows of $25 million per year, and a 25% chance that demand will be low and annual cash flows will be only $5 million. A preliminary analysis indicates that the project is somewhat riskier than average, so it has been assigned a cost of capital of 14% versus 12% for an average project at Murphy Systems. Here is a summary of the project's data:

Demand	Probability	Annual Cash Flow
High	0.25	$33 million
Average	0.50	25 million
Low	0.25	5 million
Expected annual cash flow		$22 million
Project's cost of capital	14%	
Life of project	3 years	
Required investment, or cost of project	$50 million	

Murphy could accept the project and implement it immediately; however, because the company has a patent on the device's core modules, it could also choose to delay the decision until next year, when more information about demand will be available. The cost will still be $50 million if Murphy waits, and the project will still be expected to generate the indicated cash flows, but each flow will be pushed back 1 year. However, if Murphy waits, then it will know which of the demand conditions—and hence which set of cash flows—will occur. If Murphy waits, then it will, of course, make the investment only if demand is sufficient to yield a positive NPV.

Observe that this real timing option resembles a call option on a stock. A call gives its owner the right to purchase a stock at a fixed strike price, but only if the stock's price is higher than the strike price will the owner exercise the option and buy the stock. Similarly, if Murphy defers implementation, then it will have the right to "purchase" the project by making the $50 million investment if the NPV as calculated next year, when new information is available, is positive.

14-2a **Approach 1: DCF Analysis Ignoring the Timing Option**

Based on probabilities for the different levels of demand, the expected annual cash flows are $22 million per year:

$$\text{Expected cash flow per year} = 0.25(\$33) + 0.50(\$25) + 0.25(\$5)$$
$$= \$22 \text{ million}$$

Ignoring the investment timing option, the traditional NPV is $1.08 million, found as follows:

$$\text{NPV} = -\$50 + \frac{\$22}{(1 + 0.14)^1} + \frac{\$22}{(1 + 0.14)^2} + \frac{\$22}{(1 + 0.14)^3} = \$1.08$$

The present value of the cash inflows is $51.08 million while the cost is $50 million, leaving an NPV of $1.08 million.

Based just on this DCF analysis, Murphy should accept the project. Note, however, that if the expected cash flows had been slightly lower—say, $21.5 million per year—then the NPV would have been negative and the project would have been rejected. Also, note that the project is risky: There is a 25% probability that demand will be weak, in which case the NPV will turn out to be a negative $38.4 million.

14-2b **Approach 2: DCF Analysis with a Qualitative Consideration of the Timing Option**

The discounted cash flow analysis suggests that the project should be accepted, but just barely, and it ignores the existence of a possibly valuable real option. If Murphy implements the project now, it gains an expected (but risky) NPV of $1.08 million. However, accepting now means that it is also giving up the option to wait and learn more about market demand before making the commitment. Thus, the decision is this: Is the option Murphy would be giving up worth more or less than $1.08 million? If the option is worth more than $1.08 million, then Murphy should not give up the option, which means deferring the decision—and vice versa if the option is worth less than $1.08 million.

Based on the discussion of financial options in Chapter 5, what qualitative assessment can we make regarding the option's value? Put another way: Without doing any additional calculations, does it appear that Murphy should go forward now or wait? In thinking about this decision, first note that the value of an option is higher if the current value of the underlying asset is high relative to its strike price, other things held constant. For example, a call option with a strike price of $50 on a stock with a current price of $50 (an at-the-money call) is worth more than if the current price were $20 (an out-of-the-money call). The strike price of the project is $50 million, and our first guess at the value of its cash flows is $51.08 million. We will calculate the exact value of Murphy's underlying asset later, but the DCF analysis does suggest that the underlying asset's value will be close to the strike price, so the option should be valuable. We also know that an option's value is higher the longer its time to expiration. Here the option has a 1-year life, which is fairly long for an option, and this also suggests that the option is probably valuable. Finally, we know that the value of an option increases with the risk of the underlying asset. The data used in the DCF analysis indicate that the project is quite risky, which again suggests that the option is valuable.

Thus, our qualitative assessment indicates that the option to delay might well be more valuable than the expected NPV of $1.08 if we undertake the project immediately. This conclusion is subjective, but the qualitative assessment suggests that Murphy's management should go on to make a quantitative assessment of the situation.

14-2c **Approach 3: Scenario Analysis and Decision Trees**

Part 1 of Figure 14-1 presents a scenario analysis and decision tree similar to the examples in Chapter 13. Each possible outcome is shown as a "branch" on the tree. Each branch shows the cash flows and probability of a scenario laid out as a time line. Thus, the top line, which gives the payoffs of the high-demand scenario, has positive cash flows of $33 million for the next 3 years, and its NPV is $26.61 million. The average-demand branch in the middle has an NPV of $8.04 million, while the NPV of the low-demand branch is a negative $38.39 million. Because Murphy will suffer a $38.39 million loss if demand is weak, and there is a 25% probability of weak demand, the project is clearly risky.

The expected NPV is the weighted average of the three possible outcomes, where the weight for each outcome is its probability. The weighted sum in the last column in Part 1 shows that the expected NPV is $1.08 million, the same as in the original DCF analysis. Part 1 also shows a standard deviation of $24.02 million for the NPV and a coefficient of variation (defined as the ratio of standard deviation to the expected NPV) of 22.32, which is extremely large. Clearly, the project is quite risky under the analysis thus far.

Part 2 is set up similarly to Part 1 except that it shows what happens if Murphy delays the decision and then implements the project only if demand turns out to be high or average. No cost is incurred now at Year 0—here the only action is to wait. Then, if demand is average or high, Murphy will spend $50 million at Year 1 and receive either $33 million or $25 million per year for the following 3 years. If demand is low, as shown on the bottom branch, Murphy will spend nothing at Year 1 and will receive no cash flows in subsequent years. The NPV of the high-demand branch is $23.35 million and that of the average-demand branch is $7.05 million. Because all cash flows under the low-demand scenario are zero, the NPV in this case will also be zero. The expected NPV if Murphy delays the decision is $9.36 million.

This analysis shows that the project's expected NPV will be much higher if Murphy delays than if it invests immediately. Also, because there is no possibility of losing money under the delay option, this decision also lowers the project's risk. This plainly indicates that the option to wait is valuable; hence, Murphy should wait until Year 1 before deciding whether to proceed with the investment.

Before we conclude the discussion of decision trees, note that we used the same cost of capital, 14%, to discount cash flows in the "proceed immediately" scenario

| FIGURE 14-1 | DCF and Decision-Tree Analysis for the Investment Timing Option (Millions of Dollars) |

	A	B	C	D	E	F	G	H
41	Part 1. Scenario Analysis: Proceed with Project Today							
42								
43					Future Cash Flows			NPV of This
44	Now: Year 0		Probability	Year 1	Year 2	Year 3		Scenario[a]
45								
46		→ High→	0.25	$33	$33	$33		$26.61
47		↗						
48	−$50	→Average→	0.50	$25	$25	$25		$8.04
49		↘						
50		→ Low→	0.25	$5	$5	$5		−$38.39
51			1.00					
52						Expected value of NPV[b] =		$1.08
53						Standard deviation[b] =		$24.02
54						Coefficient of variation[c] =		22.32
55								
56	Part 2. Decision-Tree Analysis: Implement in One Year Only if Optimal							
57								
58					Future Cash Flows			NPV of This
59	Now: Year 0		Probability	Year 1	Year 2	Year 3	Year 4	Scenario[d]
60								
61		→ High→	0.25	−$50	$33	$33	$33	$23.35
62		↗						
63	Wait	→Average→	0.50	−$50	$25	$25	$25	$7.05
64		↘						
65		→ Low→	0.25	$0	$0	$0	$0	$0.00
66			1.00					
67						Expected value of NPV[b] =		$9.36
68						Standard deviation[b] =		$8.57
69						Coefficient of variation[c] =		0.92

Notes:
[a] The WACC is 14%.
[b] The expected value and standard deviation are calculated as explained in Chapter 2.
[c] The coefficient of variation is the standard deviation divided by the expected value.
[d] The NPV in Part 2 is as of Year 0. Therefore, each of the project cash flows is discounted back 1 more year than in Part 1.

Microsoft Excel® is a registered trademark of Microsoft Corporation. © 2014 Microsoft.

analysis in Part 1 and under the "delay 1 year" scenario in Part 2. However, this is not appropriate for three reasons. First, because there is no possibility of losing money if Murphy delays, the investment under that plan is clearly less risky than if Murphy charges ahead today. Second, the 14% cost of capital might be appropriate for risky cash flows, yet the investment in the project at Year 1 in Part 2 is known with certainty. Perhaps, then, we should discount it at the risk-free rate.[2] Third, the

2. For a more detailed explanation of the rationale behind using the risk-free rate to discount the project cost, see Timothy A. Luehrman, "Investment Opportunities as Real Options: Getting Started on the Numbers," *Harvard Business Review*, July/August 1998, pp. 51–67. This paper also provides a discussion of real option valuation. Professor Luehrman also wrote a follow-up paper that provides an excellent discussion of the ways real options affect strategy: "Strategy as a Portfolio of Real Options," *Harvard Business Review*, September/October 1998, pp. 89–99.

project's cash inflows (excluding the initial investment) are different in Part 2 than in Part 1 because the low-demand cash flows are eliminated. This suggests that if 14% is the appropriate cost of capital in the "proceed immediately" case then some lower rate would be appropriate in the "delay decision" case.

In Figure 14-2, Part 1, we repeat the "delay decision" analysis but with one exception. We continue to discount the operating cash flows in Year 2 through Year 4 at the 14% WACC, but now we discount the project's cost at Year 1 using the risk-free rate of 6%. This increases the PV of the cost, which lowers the NPV from $9.36 million to $6.88 million. Yet we really don't know the precise WACC for this project—the 14% we used might be

FIGURE 14-2 Decision-Tree and Sensitivity Analysis for the Investment Timing Option (Millions of Dollars)

	A	B	C	D	E	F	G	H	I
80	Part 1. Decision-Tree Analysis: Implement in One Year Only if Optimal								
81	(Discount Cost at the Risk-Free Rate and Operating Cash Flows at the WACC)								
82									
83					Future Cash Flows			NPV of This	
84	Now: Year 0		Probability	Year 1	Year 2	Year 3	Year 4	Scenario[a]	
85									
86		→ High →	0.25	−$50	$33	$33	$33	$20.04	
87	↗								
88	Wait	→Average→	0.50	−$50	$25	$25	$25	$3.74	
89	↘								
90		→ Low →	0.25	$0	$0	$0	$0	$0.00	
91			1.00						
92						Expected value of NPV[b] =		$6.88	
93						Standard deviation[b] =		$7.75	
94						Coefficient of variation[c] =		1.13	
95									
96	Part 2. Sensitivity Analysis of NPV to Changes in the Cost of Capital Used to								
97	Discount Cost and Cash Flows								
98									
99				Cost of Capital Used to Discount the Year-1 Cost					
100				3%	4%	5%	6%	7%	8%	9%
101			8%	$13.1	$13.5	$13.8	$14.1	$14.5	$14.8	$15.1
102			9%	$11.8	$12.1	$12.5	$12.8	$13.1	$13.5	$13.8
103			10%	$10.5	$10.9	$11.2	$11.5	$11.9	$12.2	$12.5
104			11%	$9.3	$9.6	$10.0	$10.3	$10.6	$11.0	$11.3
105			12%	$8.1	$8.4	$8.8	$9.1	$9.5	$9.8	$10.1
106			13%	$6.9	$7.3	$7.6	$8.0	$8.3	$8.6	$9.0
107			14%	$5.9	$6.2	$6.5	$6.9	$7.2	$7.5	$7.9
108			15%	$4.8	$5.1	$5.5	$5.8	$6.2	$6.5	$6.8
109			16%	$3.8	$4.1	$4.5	$4.8	$5.1	$5.5	$5.8
110			17%	$2.8	$3.1	$3.5	$3.8	$4.1	$4.5	$4.8
111			18%	$1.8	$2.2	$2.5	$2.9	$3.2	$3.5	$3.8

(Rows 101–111, columns A–B: "Cost of Capital Used to Discount the Year-2 through Year-4 Operating Cash Flows")

Notes:
[a]The operating cash flows in Year 2 through Year 4 are discounted at the WACC of 14%. The cost in Year 1 is discounted at the risk-free rate of 6%.
[b]The expected value and standard deviation are calculated as explained in Chapter 2.
[c]The coefficient of variation is the standard deviation divided by the expected value.

too high or too low for the operating cash flows in Year 2 through Year 4.[3] Therefore, in Part 2 of Figure 14-2 we show a sensitivity analysis of the NPV in which the discount rates used for both the operating cash flows and for the project's cost vary. This sensitivity analysis shows that, under all reasonable WACCs, the NPV of delaying is greater than $1.08 million. This confirms that the option to wait is more valuable than the $1.08 million NPV resulting from immediate implementation. Therefore, Murphy should wait rather than implement the project immediately.

14-2d Approach 4: Valuing the Timing Option with the Black-Scholes Option Pricing Model

The decision-tree approach, coupled with a sensitivity analysis, may provide enough information for a good decision. However, it is often useful to obtain additional insights into the real option's value, which means using the fourth procedure, an option pricing model. To do this, the analyst must find a standard financial option that resembles the project's real option.[4] As noted earlier, Murphy's option to delay the project is similar to a call option on a stock. Hence, the Black-Scholes option pricing model can be used. This model requires five inputs: (1) the risk-free rate, (2) the time until the option expires, (3) the strike price, (4) the current price of the stock, and (5) the variance of the stock's rate of return. Therefore, we need to estimate values for those five inputs.

First, if we assume that the rate on a 52-week Treasury security is 6%, then this rate can be used as the risk-free rate. Second, Murphy must decide within a year whether or not to implement the project, so there is 1 year until the option expires. Third, it will cost $50 million to implement the project, so $50 million can be used for the strike price. Fourth, we need a proxy for the value of the underlying asset, which in Black-Scholes is the current price of the stock. Note that a stock's current price is the present value of its expected future cash flows. For Murphy's real option, the underlying asset is the project itself, and its current "price" is the present value of its expected future cash flows. Therefore, as a proxy for the stock price we can use the present value of the project's future cash flows. And fifth, the variance of the project's return can be used to represent the variance of the stock's return in the Black-Scholes model.

Figure 14-3 shows how to estimate the present value of the project's cash inflows. We need to find the current value of the underlying asset—that is, the project. For a stock, the current price is the present value of all expected future cash flows, including those that are expected even if we do not exercise the call option. Note also that the strike price for a call option has no effect on the stock's current price.[5] For our real option, the underlying asset is the delayed project, and its current "price" is the present value of all its future expected cash flows. Just as the price of a stock

3. Murphy might gain information by waiting, which could reduce risk, but if a delay would enable others to enter and perhaps preempt the market, this could increase risk. In our example, we assumed that Murphy has a patent on critical components of the device, precluding the entrance of a competitor that could preempt its position in the market.

4. In theory, financial option pricing models apply only to assets that are continuously traded in a market. Even though real options usually don't meet this criterion, financial option models often provide a reasonably accurate approximation of the real option's value.

5. The company itself is not involved with traded stock options. However, if the option were a warrant issued by the company, then the strike price would affect the company's cash flows and hence its stock price.

FIGURE 14-3 Estimating the Input for Stock Price in the Option Analysis of the Investment Timing Option (Millions of Dollars)

	A	B	C	D	E	F	G	H
140					**Future Cash Flows**			**PV of This**
141	Now: Year 0		Probability	Year 1	Year 2	Year 3	Year 4	Scenario[a]
142								
143		→ High →	0.25	$0	$33	$33	$33	$67.21
144	↗							
145	"P_0" →	→Average →	0.50	$0	$25	$25	$25	$50.91
146	↘							
147		→ Low →	0.25	$0	$5	$5	$5	$10.18
148			1.00					
149						Expected value of NPV[b] =		$44.80
150						Standard deviation[b] =		$21.07
151						Coefficient of variation[c] =		0.47

Notes:
[a]Here we find the PV, not the NPV, because the project's cost is ignored. The WACC is 14%. All cash flows in this scenario are discounted back to Year 0.
[b]The expected value and standard deviation are calculated as explained in Chapter 2.
[c]The coefficient of variation is the standard deviation divided by the expected value.

Microsoft Excel® is a registered trademark of Microsoft Corporation. © 2014 Microsoft.

includes all of its future cash flows, so should the present value of the project include all of its possible future cash flows. Moreover, because the price of a stock is not affected by the strike price of a call option, we ignore the project's "strike price," or cost, when we find its present value. Figure 14-3 shows the expected cash flows if the project is delayed. The PV of these cash flows as of now (Year 0) is $44.80 million, and this is the input we should use for the current price in the Black-Scholes model.

The last required input is the variance of the project's return. Three different approaches could be used to estimate this input. First, we could use judgment—an educated guess. Here we would begin by recalling that a company is a portfolio of projects (or assets), with each project having its own risk. Because returns on the company's stock reflect the diversification gained by combining many projects, we might expect the variance of the stock's returns to be lower than the variance of one of its average projects. The variance of an average company's stock return is about 12%, so we might expect the variance for a typical project to be somewhat higher, say, 15% to 25%. Companies in the Internet infrastructure industry are riskier than average, so we might subjectively estimate the variance of Murphy's project to be in the range of 18% to 30%.

The second approach, called the *direct* method, is to estimate the rate of return for each possible outcome and then calculate the variance of those returns. First, Part 1 in Figure 14-4 shows the PV for each possible outcome as of Year 1, the time when the option expires. Here we simply find the present value of all future operating cash flows discounted back to Year 1, using the WACC of 14%. The Year-1 present value is $76.61 million for high demand, $58.04 million for average demand, and $11.61 million for low demand. Then, in Part 2, we show the percentage return from the current time until the option expires for each scenario, based on the $44.80 million starting "price"

FIGURE 14-4   Estimating the Input for Variance in the Option Analysis of the Investment Timing Option (Millions of Dollars)

	A	B	C	D	E	F	G	H	I
160	Part 1. Find the Value and Risk of Future Cash Flows at the Time the Option Expires								
161									
162								PV in Year 1	
163					Future Cash Flows			for This	
164	Now: Year 0		Probability	Year 1	Year 2	Year 3	Year 4	Scenario[a]	
165									
166	→ High →		0.25		$33	$33	$33	$76.61	
167	↗				↗				
168	Scenario·Average →		0.50	"P_1" →	$25	$25	$25	$58.04	
169	↘				↘				
170	→ Low →		0.25		$5	$5	$5	$11.61	
171			1.00						
172						Expected value of NPV[b] =		$51.08	
173						Standard deviation[b] =		$24.02	
174						Coefficient of variation[c] =		0.47	
175									
176	Part 2. Direct Method: Use the Scenarios to Directly Estimate the Variance of the Project's Return								
177									
178	Price$_{Year\,0}$[d]		Probability	PV$_{Year\,1}$[e]	Return$_{Year\,1}$[f]				
179									
180	→ High →		0.25	$76.61	71.0%				
181	↗								
182	$44.80	Average →	0.50	$58.04	29.5%				
183	↘								
184	→ Low →		0.25	$11.61	−74.1%				
185			1.00						
186									
187			Expected return[b] =	14.0%					
188			Variance of return[b] =	28.7%					
189									
190	Part 3. Indirect Method: Use the Scenarios to Indirectly Estimate the Variance of the Project's Return								
191									
192		Expected "price" at the time the option expires[g] =			$51.08				
193		Std. dev. of expected "price" at the time the option expires[h] =			$24.02				
194		Coefficient of variation (CV) =			0.47				
195		Time (in years) until the option expires (t) =			1.00				
196		Variance of the project's expected return = ln(CV^2+1)/t =			20.0%				

Notes:
[a]The WACC is 14%. The Year-2 through Year-4 cash flows are discounted back to Year 1.
[b]The expected value, variance, and standard deviation are calculated as explained in Chapter 2.
[c]The coefficient of variation is the standard deviation divided by the expected value.
[d]The Year-0 price is the expected PV from Figure 14-3.
[e]The Year-1 PVs are from Part 1.
[f]The returns for each scenario are calculated as (PV$_{Year\,1}$ − Price$_{Year\,0}$)/Price$_{Year\,0}$.
[g]The expected "price" at the time the option expires is taken from Part 1.
[h]The standard deviation of expected "price" at the time the option expires is taken from Part 1.

Microsoft Excel® is a registered trademark of Microsoft Corporation. © 2014 Microsoft.

of the project at Year 0 as calculated in Figure 14-3. If demand is high, we will obtain a return of 71.0%: ($76.61 − $44.80)/$44.80 = 0.710 = 71.0%. Similar calculations show returns of 29.5% for average demand and −74.1% for low demand. The expected percentage return is 14%, the standard deviation is 53.6%, and the variance is 28.7%.[6]

The third approach for estimating the variance of the annual rate of return is also based on the scenario data, but the data are used in a different manner. First, we know that demand is not really limited to three scenarios, which means the direct approach in Figure 14-4 isn't necessarily reliable. We could overcome this problem by estimating thousands of scenarios, but that would require a lot of effort. Fortunately, there is a simple shortcut we can use. From Part 1 of Figure 14-4, we have estimates of the expected value of the project and its standard deviation at the time the option expires. Using this information (and a lot of complicated mathematics), we can estimate the variance of the project's annual rate of return, σ^2, with this formula:[7]

(14–1)

$$\sigma^2 = \frac{\ln(CV^2 + 1)}{t}$$

Here CV is the coefficient of variation of the underlying asset's price at the time the option expires, and t is the time until the option expires. Although the three outcomes in the scenarios represent a small sample of the many possible outcomes, we can still use the scenario data to estimate the variance that the project's rate of return would have if there were an infinite number of possible outcomes. For Murphy's project, this indirect method produces the following estimate of the variance of the project's return:

(14–1a)

$$\sigma^2 = \frac{\ln(0.47^2 + 1)}{1} = 0.20 = 20\%$$

Which of the three approaches is best? Obviously, they all involve judgment, so an analyst might want to consider all three. In our example, all three methods produce similar estimates, but for illustrative purposes we will simply use 20% as our initial estimate for the variance of the project's rate of return.

In Part 1 of Figure 14-5, we calculate the value of the option to defer investment in the project based on the Black-Scholes model, and the result is $7.04 million. Because this is significantly higher than the $1.08 million NPV under immediate implementation and because the option would be forfeited if Murphy goes ahead right now, we conclude as before that the company should defer the final decision until more information is available.

---

6. Two points should be made about the percentage return. First, for use in the Black-Scholes model, we need a percentage return calculated as shown, not an IRR return. The IRR is not used in the option pricing approach. Second, the expected return comes to 14%, the same as the WACC. This is because the Year-0 price and the Year-1 PVs were all calculated using the 14% WACC and because we measured return over only 1 year. If we measure the compound return over more than 1 year, then the average return generally will not equal 14%.

7. For a more detailed discussion of the relationship between the variance of a stock's price and the variance of its return, see David C. Shimko, *Finance in Continuous Time* (Miami, FL: Kolb Publishing, 1992).

FIGURE 14-5 Estimating the Value of the Investment Timing Option Using a Standard Financial Option (Millions of Dollars)

	A	B	C	D	E	F	G	H	I
210	Part 1. Find the Value of a Call Option Using the Black-Scholes Model								
211									
212		Inputs for Real "Call" Option:							
213		r_{RF} = Risk-free interest rate					=	6%	
214		t = Time until the option expires					=	1	
215		X = Cost to implement the project					=	$50.00	
216		P = Current value of the project					=	$44.80 [a]	
217		σ^2 = Variance of the project's rate of return					=	20.0% [b]	
218		Intermediate Calculations:							
219		$d_1 = \{ \ln (P/X) + [r_{RF} + (\sigma^2/2)]\, t \}/(\sigma\, t^{1/2})$					=	0.1124	
220		$d_2 = d_1 - \sigma\, (t^{1/2})$					=	−0.3348	
221		$N(d_1)$ = Area to left of d_1 in Normal PD function					=	0.5447	
222		$N(d_2)$ = Area to left of d_2 in Normal PD function					=	0.3689	
223									
224		V =	$P[\, N(d_1)\,] - Xe^{-(\text{risk-free rate})(t)}\, [\, N(d_2)\,]$				=	$7.04	
225									
226	Part 2. Sensitivity Analysis of Option Value to Changes in Variance								
227									
228			Variance	Option Value					
229			12.0%	$5.24					
230			14.0%	$5.74					
231			16.0%	$6.20					
232			18.0%	$6.63					
233			20.0%	$7.04					
234			22.0%	$7.42					
235			24.0%	$7.79					
236			26.0%	$8.15					
237			28.0%	$8.49					
238			30.0%	$8.81					
239			32.0%	$9.13					

Notes:
[a] The current value of the project is taken from Figure 14-3.
[b] The variance of the project's rate of return is taken from Part 3 of Figure 14-4..

Microsoft Excel® is a registered trademark of Microsoft Corporation. © 2014 Microsoft.

Many inputs were based on subjective estimates, so it is important to determine how sensitive the final outcome is to key inputs. Therefore, in Part 2 of Figure 14-5, we show the sensitivity of the option's value to different estimates of the variance. It is reassuring to see that, for all reasonable estimates of variance, the option to delay remains more valuable than immediate implementation.

14-2e **Approach 5: Financial Engineering**

Sometimes an analyst might not be satisfied with the results of a decision-tree analysis and cannot find a standard financial option that corresponds to the real option. In such a situation the only alternative is to develop a unique model for the specific real option being analyzed, a process called **financial engineering**. When financial engineering is applied on Wall Street, where it was developed, the result is a newly designed financial product.[8] When it is applied to real options, the result is the value of a project that contains embedded options.

Although financial engineering was originally developed on Wall Street, many financial engineering techniques have been applied to real options during the last 20 years. We expect this trend to continue, especially in light of the rapid improvements in computer processing speed and spreadsheet software capabilities. One financial engineering technique is called **risk-neutral valuation**. This technique uses simulation, and we discuss it in *Web Extension 14B*. Most other financial engineering techniques are too complicated for a course in financial management, so we leave a detailed discussion of them to a specialized course.

SELF TEST

What is a decision tree?

In a qualitative analysis, what factors affect the value of a real option?

14-3 The Growth Option: An Illustration

As we saw with the investment timing option, there is frequently an alternative to merely accepting or rejecting a static project. Many investment opportunities, if successful, lead to other investment opportunities. The production capacity of a successful product line can later be expanded to satisfy increased demand, or distribution can be extended to new geographic markets. A company with a successful name brand can capitalize on its success by adding complementary or new products under the same brand. These growth options add value to a project and explain, for example, why companies are flocking to make inroads into the very difficult business environment in China.

Kidco Corporation designs and manufactures products aimed at the preteen market. Most of its products have a very short life, given the rapidly changing tastes of preteens. Kidco is now considering a project that will cost $30 million. Management believes there is a 25% chance that the project will "take off" and generate operating cash flows of $34 million in each of the next 2 years, after which preteen tastes will change and the project will be terminated. There is a 50% chance of average demand, in which case cash flows will be $20 million annually for 2 years. Finally, there is a 25% chance that preteens won't like the product at all, and it will generate cash flows of only $2 million per year. The estimated cost of capital for the project is 14%.

Based on its experience with other projects, Kidco believes it will be able to launch a second-generation product if demand for the original product is average or above. This second-generation product will cost the same as the first-generation product, $30 million, and the cost will be incurred at Year 2. However, given the success of the first-generation product, Kidco believes that the second-generation product would be just as successful as the first-generation product.

---

8. Financial engineering techniques are widely used for the creation and valuation of derivative securities.

This growth option resembles a call option on a stock, because it gives Kidco the opportunity to "purchase" a successful follow-on project at a fixed cost if the value of the project is greater than the cost. Otherwise, Kidco will let the option expire by not implementing the second-generation product.

The following sections apply the first four valuation approaches: (1) DCF, (2) DCF and qualitative assessment, (3) decision-tree analysis, and (4) analysis with a standard financial option.

14-3a Approach 1: DCF Analysis Ignoring the Growth Option

Based on probabilities for the different levels of demand, the expected annual operating cash flows for the project are $19 million per year:

$$0.25(\$34) + 0.50(\$20) + 0.25(\$2) = \$19.00$$

Ignoring the investment timing option, the traditional NPV is $1.29 million:

$$\text{NPV} = -\$30 + \frac{\$19}{(1 + 0.14)^1} + \frac{\$19}{(1 + 0.14)^2} = \$1.29$$

Based on this DCF analysis, Kidco should accept the project.

14-3b Approach 2: DCF Analysis with a Qualitative Consideration of the Growth Option

Although the DCF analysis indicates that the project should be accepted, it ignores a potentially valuable real option. The option's time to maturity and the volatility of the underlying project provide qualitative insights into the option's value. Kidco's growth option has 2 years until maturity, which is a relatively long time, and the cash flows of the project are volatile. Taken together, this qualitative assessment indicates that the growth option should be quite valuable.

14-3c Approach 3: Decision-Tree Analysis of the Growth Option

Part 1 of Figure 14-6 shows a scenario analysis for Kidco's project. The top line, which describes the payoffs for the high-demand scenario, has operating cash flows of $34 million for the next 2 years. The NPV of this branch is $25.99 million. The NPV of the average-demand branch in the middle is $2.93 million, and it is −$26.71 million for the low-demand scenario. The sum in the last column of Part 1 shows the expected NPV of $1.29 million. The coefficient of variation is 14.54, indicating that the project is very risky.

Part 2 of Figure 14-6 shows a decision-tree analysis in which Kidco undertakes the second-generation product only if demand is average or high. In these scenarios, shown on the top two branches of the decision tree, Kidco will incur a cost of $30 million at Year 2 and receive operating cash flows of either $34 million or $20 million for the next 2 years, depending on the level of demand. If the demand is low, shown on the bottom branch, Kidco has no cost at Year 2

FIGURE 14-6　Scenario Analysis and Decision-Tree Analysis for the Kidco Project (Millions of Dollars)

	A	B	C	D	E	F	G	H
281	**Part 1. Scenario Analysis of Kidco's First-Generation Project**							
282								
283				**Future Cash Flows**			**NPV of This**	
284	**Now: Year 0**		**Probability**	**Year 1**	**Year 2**		**Scenario**[a]	
285								
286		→ **High** →	25%	$34	$34		$25.99	
287	↗							
288	−$30.00	→**Average**→	50%	$20	$20		$2.93	
289	↘							
290		→ **Low** →	25%	$2	$2		−$26.71	
291								
292					**Expected value of NPV**[b] =		$1.29	
293					**Standard deviation**[b] =		$18.70	
294					**Coefficient of variation**[c] =		14.54	
295								
296	**Part 2. Decision-Tree Analysis of the Growth Option**							
297								
298					**Future Cash Flows**			**NPV of This**
299	**Now: Year 0**		**Probability**	**Year 1**	**Year 2**[d]	**Year 3**	**Year 4**	**Scenario**[e]
300								
301			25%	$34	$34	$34	$34	$42.37
302		→ **High** →			−$30			
303	↗							
304	−$30.00	→**Average**→	50%	$20	$20	$20	$20	$1.57
305	↘				−$30			
306		↘						
307		→ **Low** →	25%	$2	$2	$0	$0	−$26.71
308			1.00					
309								
310					**Expected value of NPV**[b] =		$4.70	
311					**Standard deviation**[b] =		$24.62	
312					**Coefficient of variation**[c] =		5.24	

Notes:

[a] The operating cash flows are discounted by the WACC of 14%.

[b] The expected value, standard deviation, and variance are calculated as in Chapter 2.

[c] The coefficient of variation is the standard deviation divided by the expected value.

[d] The total cash flows at Year 2 are equal to the operating cash flows for the first-generation product minus the $30 million cost to implement the second-generation product, if the firm chooses to do so. For example, the Year-2 cash flow in the high-demand scenario is $34 − $30 = $4 million. Based on Part 1, it makes economic sense to implement the second-generation product only if demand is high or average.

[e] The operating cash flows in Year 1 through Year 2, which do not include the $30 million cost of implementing the second-generation project at Year 2 for the high-demand and average-demand scenarios, are discounted at the WACC of 14%. The $30 million implementation cost at Year 2 for the high-demand and average-demand scenarios is discounted at the risk-free rate of 6%.

Microsoft Excel® is a registered trademark of Microsoft Corporation. © 2014 Microsoft.

and receives no additional cash flows in subsequent years. All operating cash flows (which do not include the cost of implementing the second-generation project at Year 2) are discounted at the WACC of 14%. Because the $30 million implementation cost is known, it is discounted at the risk-free rate of 6%. As shown in

FIGURE 14-7 | Sensitivity Analysis of the Kidco Decision-Tree Analysis in Figure 14-6 (Millions of Dollars)

	B	C	D	E	F	G	H	I
329		Cost of Capital Used to Discount the $30 Million Implementation						
330		Cost in Year 2 of the Second-Generation Project						
331		3%	4%	5%	6%	7%	8%	9%
332	8%	$11.0	$11.4	$11.8	$12.1	$12.5	$12.9	$13.2
333	9%	$9.6	$10.0	$10.4	$10.8	$11.2	$11.5	$11.9
334	10%	$8.3	$8.7	$9.1	$9.5	$9.9	$10.2	$10.6
335	11%	$7.0	$7.4	$7.8	$8.2	$8.6	$9.0	$9.3
336	12%	$5.8	$6.2	$6.6	$7.0	$7.4	$7.7	$8.1
337	13%	$4.7	$5.1	$5.5	$5.8	$6.2	$6.6	$6.9
338	14%	$3.5	$3.9	$4.3	$4.7	$5.1	$5.4	$5.8
339	15%	$2.4	$2.8	$3.2	$3.6	$4.0	$4.3	$4.7
340	16%	$1.4	$1.8	$2.2	$2.5	$2.9	$3.3	$3.6
341	17%	$0.3	$0.7	$1.1	$1.5	$1.9	$2.3	$2.6
342	18%	−$0.7	−$0.3	$0.1	$0.5	$0.9	$1.3	$1.6

Note:
The operating cash flows do not include the $30 million implementation cost of the second-generation project in Year 2.

Microsoft Excel® is a registered trademark of Microsoft Corporation. © 2014 Microsoft.

Part 2 of Figure 14-6, the expected NPV is $4.70 million, indicating that the growth option is quite valuable.

The option itself alters the risk of the project, which means that 14% is probably not the appropriate cost of capital. Figure 14-7 presents the results of a sensitivity analysis in which the cost of capital for the operating cash flows varies from 8% to 18%. The sensitivity analysis also allows the rate used to discount the implementation cost at Year 2 to vary from 3% to 9%. The resulting NPV is positive for all reasonable combinations of discount rates.

14-3d Approach 4: Valuing the Growth Option with the Black-Scholes Option Pricing Model

The fourth approach is to use a standard model for a corresponding financial option. As we noted earlier, Kidco's growth option is similar to a call option on a stock, so we will use the Black-Scholes model to find the value of the growth option. The time until the growth option expires is 2 years. The rate on a 2-year Treasury security is 6%, and this provides a good estimate of the risk-free rate. Implementing the project will cost $30 million, which is the strike price.

The input for stock price in the Black-Scholes model is the current value of the underlying asset. For the growth option, the underlying asset is the second-generation project, and its current value is the present value of its cash flows. The calculations in Figure 14-8 show that this value is $24.07 million. Because the strike price of $30 million is greater than the current "price" of $24.07 million, the growth option is currently out-of-the-money.

FIGURE 14-8	Estimating the Input for Stock Price in the Growth Option Analysis of the Investment Timing Option (Millions of Dollars)

	A	B	C	D	E	F	G	H
350					**Future Cash Flows**			**PV of This**
351	**Now: Year 0**		**Probability**	**Year 1**	**Year 2**	**Year 3**	**Year 4**	**Scenario**[a]
352								
353		→ High →	25%	$0	$0	$34	$34	$43.08
354	↗							
355	"P_0" →→Average →		50%	$0	$0	$20	$20	$25.34
356	↘							
357		→ Low →	25%	$0	$0	$2	$2	$2.53
358			1.00					
359						Expected value of NPV[b] =		$24.07
360						Standard deviation[b] =		$14.39
361						Coefficient of variation[c] =		0.60

Notes:
[a] The WACC is 14%. All cash flows in this scenario are discounted back to Year 0.
[b] The expected value, standard deviation, and variance are calculated as in Chapter 2.
[c] The coefficient of variation is the standard deviation divided by the expected value.

Microsoft Excel® is a registered trademark of Microsoft Corporation. © 2014 Microsoft.

WEB

See **Ch14 Tool Kit.xls** on the textbook's Web site for all calculations.

Figure 14-9 shows the estimates for the variance of the project's rate of return using the two methods described earlier in the chapter for the analysis of the investment timing option. The direct method, shown in Part 2 of the figure, produces an estimate of 17.9% for the variance of return. The indirect method, in Part 3, estimates the variance as 15.3%. Both estimates are somewhat higher than the 12% variance of a typical company's stock return, which is consistent with the idea that a project's variance is higher than a stock's because of diversification effects. Thus, an estimated variance of 15% to 20% seems reasonable. We use an initial estimate of 15.3% in our initial application of the Black-Scholes model, shown in Part 1 of Figure 14-10.

Using the Black-Scholes model for a call option, Figure 14-10 shows a $4.34 million value for the growth option. The total NPV is the sum of the first-generation project's NPV and the value of the growth option: Total NPV = $1.29 + $4.34 = $5.63 million, which is much higher than the NPV of the first-generation project alone. As this analysis shows, the growth option adds considerable value to the original project. In addition, the sensitivity analysis in Part 2 of Figure 14-10 indicates that the growth option's value is large for all reasonable values of variance. Kidco should therefore accept the project.

For an illustrative valuation of an abandonment option, *see Web Extension 14A.*

SELF TEST   Explain how growth options are like call options.

FIGURE 14-9 Estimating the Input for Stock Return Variance in the Growth Option Analysis (Millions of Dollars)

	A	B	C	D	E	F	G	H	I
372	Part 1. Find the Value and Risk of Future Cash Flows at the Time the Option Expires								
373									
374								PV in Year 2	
375					Future Cash Flows			for This	
376	Now: Year 0		Probability	Year 1	Year 2	Year 3	Year 4	Scenario[a]	
377									
378		→ High →	25%			$34	$34	$55.99	
379	↗					↗			
380	Scenario	→Average→	50%		"P_2"→	$20	$20	$32.93	
381	↘					↘			
382		→ Low→	25%			$2	$2	$3.29	
383			1.00						
384						Expected value of $PV_{Year\,2}^{b}$ =		$31.29	
385						Standard deviation of $PV_{Year\,2}^{b}$ =		$18.70	
386						Coefficient of variation of $PV_{Year\,2}^{c}$ =		0.60	
387	Part 2. Direct Method: Use the Scenarios to Directly Estimate the Variance of the Project's Return								
388									
389	$Price_{Year\,0}^{d}$		Probability	$PV_{Year\,2}^{e}$	$Return_{Year\,2}^{f}$				
390									
391		→ High →	25%	$55.99	52.5%				
392	↗								
393	$24.07	→Average→	50%	$32.93	17.0%				
394	↘								
395		→ Low→	25%	$3.29	−63.0%				
396			1.00						
397									
398			Expected return[b,g] =		5.9%				
399			Variance of return[b] =		17.9%				
400									
401	Part 3. Indirect Method: Use the Scenarios to Indirectly Estimate the Variance of the Project's Return								
402									
403			Expected "price" at the time the option expires[h] =			$31.29			
404			Std. dev. of expected "price" at the time the option expires[i] =			$18.70			
405			Coefficient of variation (CV) =			0.60			
406			Time (in years) until the option expires (t) =			2			
407			Variance of the project's expected return = $\ln(CV^2+1)/t$ =			15.3%			

Notes:

[a]The WACC is 14%. The Year-3 through Year-4 cash flows are discounted back to Year 2.

[b]The standard deviation, variance, and expected value are calculated as in Chapter 2.

[c]The coefficient of variation is the standard deviation divided by the expected value.

[d]The Year-0 price is the expected PV from Figure 14-8.

[e]The Year-2 PVs are from Part 1.

[f]The annualized returns for each scenario are calculated as $(PV_{Year\,2}/Price_{Year\,0})^{0.5} - 1$.

[g]The expected annualized return is not equal to the cost of capital, 14%. However, if you do the calculations, then you'll see that the expected 2-year return is 29.26%, which is equal to the 2-year compounded cost of capital: $(1.14)^2 - 1 = 29.26\%$.

[h]The expected "price" at the time the option expires is taken from Part 1.

[i]The standard deviation of the expected "price" at the time the option expires is taken from Part 1.

FIGURE 14-10	Estimating the Value of the Growth Option Using a Standard Financial Option (Millions of Dollars)

	A	B	C	D	E	F	G	H	I
424	Part 1. Find the Value of a Call Option Using the Black-Scholes Model								
425									
426		Inputs for Real "Call" Option:							
427		r_{RF} = Risk-free interest rate					=	6%	
428		t = Time until the option expires					=	2	
429		X = Cost to implement the project					=	$30.00	
430		P = Current value of the project					=	$24.07 [a]	
431		σ^2 = Variance of the project's rate of return					=	15.3% [b]	
432		Intermediate Calculations:							
433		$d_1 = \{ \ln(P/X) + [r_{RF} + (\sigma^2/2)]\,t \}/(\sigma\, t^{1/2})$					=	0.095	
434		$d_2 = d_1 - \sigma\,(t^{1/2})$					=	−0.46	
435		$N(d_1)$ = Area to left of d_1 in Normal PD function					=	0.54	
436		$N(d_2)$ = Area to left of d_2 in Normal PD function					=	0.32	
437									
438		V =	$P[\,N(d_1)\,] - Xe^{-(\text{risk-free rate})(t)}\,[\,N(d_2)\,]$				=	$4.34	
439									
440	Part 2. Sensitivity Analysis of Option Value to Changes in Variance								
441									
442			Variance	Option Value					
443			11.3%	$3.60					
444			13.3%	$3.98					
445			15.3%	$4.34					
446			17.3%	$4.68					
447			19.3%	$4.99					
448			21.3%	$5.29					
449			23.3%	$5.57					
450			25.3%	$5.84					
451			27.3%	$6.10					
452			29.3%	$6.35					
453			31.3%	$6.59					

Notes:
[a] The current value of the project is taken from Figure 14-8.
[b] The variance of the project's rate of return is taken from Part 3 of Figure 14-9.

14-4 Concluding Thoughts on Real Options

We don't deny that real options can be complicated. Keep in mind, however, that 60 years ago very few companies used NPV because it seemed too complicated. Now NPV is a basic tool used by virtually all companies and taught in all business schools. A similar but more rapid pattern of adoption is occurring with real options. Twenty years ago very few companies used real options, but a survey of CFOs reported that more than 26% of companies now use real option techniques when evaluating projects.[9] Just as with NPV, it's only a matter of time before virtually all companies use real option techniques.

We have provided you with some basic tools for evaluating real options, starting with the ability to identify real options and make qualitative assessments regarding a real option's value. Decision trees are another important tool, because they facilitate an explicit identification of the embedded options, which is critical in the decision-making process. However, keep in mind that the decision tree should not use the original project's cost of capital. Although finance theory has not yet provided a way to estimate the appropriate cost of capital for a decision tree, sensitivity analysis can identify the effect that different costs of capital have on the project's value.

Many real options can be analyzed using a standard model for an existing financial option, such as the Black-Scholes model for calls and puts. There are also other financial models for a variety of options. These include the option to exchange one asset for another, the option to purchase the minimum or the maximum of two or more assets, the option on an average of several assets, and even an option on an option.[10] In fact, there are entire textbooks that describe even more options.[11] Given the large number of standard models for existing financial options, it is often possible to find a financial option that resembles the real option being analyzed.

Sometimes there are some real options that don't resemble any financial options. But the good news is that many of these options can be valued using techniques from financial engineering. This is frequently the case if there is a traded financial asset that matches the risk of the real option. For example, many oil companies use oil futures contracts to price the real options that are embedded in various exploration and leasing strategies. With the explosion in the markets for derivatives, there are now financial contracts that span an incredible variety of risks. This means that an ever-increasing number of real options can be valued using these financial instruments. Most financial engineering techniques are beyond the scope of this book, but *Web Extension 14B* on the textbook's Web site describes one particularly useful financial engineering technique called risk-neutral valuation.[12]

---

9. See John R. Graham and Campbell R. Harvey, "The Theory and Practice of Corporate Finance: Evidence from the Field," *Journal of Financial Economics*, May 2001, pp. 187–243.

10. See W. Margrabe, "The Value of an Option to Exchange One Asset for Another," *Journal of Finance*, March 1978, pp. 177–186; R. Stulz, "Options on the Minimum or Maximum of Two Risky Assets: Analysis and Applications," *Journal of Financial Economics*, Vol. 10, 1982, pp. 161–185; H. Johnson, "Options on the Maximum or Minimum of Several Assets," *Journal of Financial and Quantitative Analysis*, September 1987, pp. 277–283; P. Ritchken, L. Sankarasubramanian, and A. M. Vijh, "Averaging Options for Capping Total Costs," *Financial Management*, Autumn 1990, pp. 35–41; and R. Geske, "The Valuation of Compound Options," *Journal of Financial Economics*, March 1979, pp. 63–81.

11. See John C. Hull, *Options, Futures, and Other Derivatives*, 9th ed. (Boston: Pearson, 2015).

12. For more on real options, see Martha Amram, *Value Sweep: Mapping Corporate Growth Opportunities* (Boston: Harvard Business School Press, 2002); Martha Amram and Nalin Kulatilaka, *Real Options: Managing Strategic Investment in an Uncertain World* (Boston: Harvard Business School Press, 1999); Michael Brennan and Lenos Trigeorgis, *Project Flexibility, Agency, and Competition: New Developments in the Theory and Application of Real Options* (New York: Oxford University Press, 2000); Eduardo Schwartz and Lenos Trigeorgis, *Real Options and Investment Under Uncertainty* (Cambridge, MA: MIT Press, 2001); Han T. J. Smit and Lenos Trigeorgis, *Strategic Investment: Real Options and Games* (Princeton, NJ: Princeton University Press, 2004); Lenos Trigeorgis, *Real Options in Capital Investment: Models, Strategies, and Applications* (Westport, CT: Praeger, 1995); and Lenos Trigeorgis, *Real Options: Managerial Flexibility and Strategy in Resource Allocation* (Cambridge, MA: MIT Press, 1996).

SELF TEST

How widely used is real option analysis?

What techniques can be used to analyze real options?

Summary

In this chapter, we discussed some topics that go beyond the simple capital budgeting framework, including the following:

- Investing in a new project often brings with it a potential increase in the firm's future opportunities. Opportunities are, in effect, options—the right but not the obligation to take some future action.
- A project may have an **option value** that is not accounted for in a conventional NPV analysis. Any project that expands the firm's set of opportunities has positive option value.
- **Real options** are opportunities for management to respond to changes in market conditions and involve "real" rather than "financial" assets.
- There are five possible **procedures for valuing real options**: (1) DCF analysis only, and ignore the real option; (2) DCF analysis and a qualitative assessment of the real option's value; (3) decision-tree analysis; (4) analysis with a standard model for an existing financial option; and (5) financial engineering techniques.
- Many **investment timing options** and **growth options** can be valued using the Black-Scholes call option pricing model.
- See *Web Extension 14A* on the textbook's Web site for an illustration of valuing the **abandonment option**.
- See *Web Extension 14B* on the textbook's Web site for a discussion of **risk-neutral valuation**.

Questions

14–1 Define each of the following terms:
   a. Real option; managerial option; strategic option; embedded option
   b. Investment timing option; growth option; abandonment option; flexibility option
   c. Decision tree

14–2 What factors should a company consider when it decides whether to invest in a project today or to wait until more information becomes available?

14–3 In general, do timing options make it more or less likely that a project will be accepted today?

14–4 If a company has an option to abandon a project, would this tend to make the company more or less likely to accept the project today?

Problems

Answers Appear in Appendix B

Intermediate Problems 1–5

14–1 Investment Timing Option: Decision-Tree Analysis
Kim Hotels is interested in developing a new hotel in Seoul. The company estimates that the hotel would require an initial investment of $20 million. Kim expects the hotel will produce positive cash flows of $3 million a year at the end of each of the next 20 years. The project's cost of capital is 13%.
a. What is the project's net present value?
b. Kim expects the cash flows to be $3 million a year, but it recognizes that the cash flows could actually be much higher or lower, depending on whether the Korean government imposes a large hotel tax. One year from now, Kim will know whether the tax will be imposed. There is a 50% chance that the tax will be imposed, in which case the yearly cash flows will be only $2.2 million. At the same time, there is a 50% chance that the tax will not be imposed, in which case the yearly cash flows will be $3.8 million. Kim is deciding whether to proceed with the hotel today or to wait a year to find out whether the tax will be imposed. If Kim waits a year, the initial investment will remain at $20 million. Assume that all cash flows are discounted at 13%. Use decision-tree analysis to determine whether Kim should proceed with the project today or wait a year before deciding.

14–2 Investment Timing Option: Decision-Tree Analysis
The Karns Oil Company is deciding whether to drill for oil on a tract of land the company owns. The company estimates the project would cost $8 million today. Karns estimates that, once drilled, the oil will generate positive net cash flows of $4 million a year at the end of each of the next 4 years. Although the company is fairly confident about its cash flow forecast, in 2 years it will have more information about the local geology and about the price of oil. Karns estimates that if it waits 2 years then the project would cost $9 million. Moreover, if it waits 2 years, then there is a 90% chance that the net cash flows would be $4.2 million a year for 4 years and a 10% chance that they would be $2.2 million a year for 4 years. Assume all cash flows are discounted at 10%.
a. If the company chooses to drill today, what is the project's net present value?
b. Using decision-tree analysis, does it make sense to wait 2 years before deciding whether to drill?

14–3 Investment Timing Option: Decision-Tree Analysis
Hart Lumber is considering the purchase of a paper company, which would require an initial investment of $300 million. Hart estimates that the paper company would provide net cash flows of $40 million at the end of each of the next 20 years. The cost of capital for the paper company is 13%.
a. Should Hart purchase the paper company?
b. Hart's best guess is that cash flows will be $40 million a year, but it realizes that the cash flows are as likely to be $30 million a year as $50 million. One year from now, it will find out whether the cash flows will be $30 million or $50 million. In addition, Hart could sell the paper company

at Year 3 for $280 million. Given this additional information, does decision-tree analysis indicate that it makes sense to purchase the paper company? Again, assume that all cash flows are discounted at 13%.

14–4 Real Options: Decision-Tree Analysis
Utah Enterprises is considering buying a vacant lot that sells for $1.2 million. If the property is purchased, the company's plan is to spend another $5 million today (t = 0) to build a hotel on the property. The after-tax cash flows from the hotel will depend critically on whether the state imposes a tourism tax in this year's legislative session. If the tax is imposed, the hotel is expected to produce after-tax cash inflows of $600,000 at the end of each of the next 15 years, versus $1,200,000 if the tax is not imposed. The project has a 12% cost of capital. Assume at the outset that the company does not have the option to delay the project. Use decision-tree analysis to answer the following questions.

a. What is the project's expected NPV if the tax is imposed?
b. What is the project's expected NPV if the tax is not imposed?
c. Given that there is a 50% chance that the tax will be imposed, what is the project's expected NPV if the company proceeds with it today?
d. Although the company does not have an option to delay construction, it does have the option to abandon the project 1 year from now if the tax is imposed. If it abandons the project, it would sell the complete property 1 year from now at an expected price of $6 million. Once the project is abandoned, the company would no longer receive any cash inflows from it. If all cash flows are discounted at 12%, would the existence of this abandonment option affect the company's decision to proceed with the project today?
e. Assume there is no option to abandon or delay the project but that the company has an option to purchase an adjacent property in 1 year at a price of $1.5 million. If the tourism tax is imposed, then the net present value of developing this property (as of t = 1) is only $300,000 (so it wouldn't make sense to purchase the property for $1.5 million). However, if the tax is not imposed, then the net present value of the future opportunities from developing the property would be $4 million (as of t = 1). Thus, under this scenario it would make sense to purchase the property for $1.5 million. Given that cash flows are discounted at 12% and that there's a 50-50 chance the tax will be imposed, how much would the company pay today for the option to purchase this property 1 year from now for $1.5 million?

14–5 Growth Option: Decision-Tree Analysis
Fethe's Funny Hats is considering selling trademarked, orange-haired curly wigs for University of Tennessee football games. The purchase cost for a 2-year franchise to sell the wigs is $20,000. If demand is good (40% probability), then the net cash flows will be $25,000 per year for 2 years. If demand is bad (60% probability), then the net cash flows will be $5,000 per year for 2 years. Fethe's cost of capital is 10%.

a. What is the expected NPV of the project?
b. If Fethe makes the investment today, then it will have the option to renew the franchise fee for 2 more years at the end of Year 2 for an additional payment of $20,000. In this case, the cash flows that occurred in Years 1 and 2 will be repeated (so if demand was good in Years 1 and 2, it will continue to be good in Years 3 and 4). Write out the decision tree and use

decision-tree analysis to calculate the expected NPV of this project, including the option to continue for an additional 2 years. *Note:* The franchise fee payment at the end of Year 2 is known, so it should be discounted at the risk-free rate, which is 6%.

Challenging Problems 6–8

14–6 Investment Timing Option: Option Analysis
Rework Problem 14-1 using the Black-Scholes model to estimate the value of the option. Assume that the variance of the project's rate of return is 6.87% and that the risk-free rate is 8%.

14–7 Investment Timing Option: Option Analysis
Rework Problem 14-2 using the Black-Scholes model to estimate the value of the option. Assume that the variance of the project's rate of return is 1.11% and that the risk-free rate is 6%.

14–8 Growth Option: Option Analysis
Rework Problem 14-5 using the Black-Scholes model to estimate the value of the option. Assume that the variance of the project's rate of return is 20.25% and that the risk-free rate is 6%.

Spreadsheet Problem

14–9 Build a Model: Real Options
Start with the partial model in the file *Ch14 P09 Build a Model.xls* on the textbook's Web site. Bradford Services Inc. (BSI) is considering a project with a cost of $10 million and an expected life of 3 years. There is a 30% probability of good conditions, in which case the project will provide a cash flow of $9 million at the end of each of the next 3 years. There is a 40% probability of medium conditions, in which case the annual cash flows will be $4 million, and there is a 30% probability of bad conditions with a cash flow of −$1 million per year. BSI uses a 12% cost of capital to evaluate projects like this.

a. Find the project's expected present value, NPV, and the coefficient of variation of the present value.

b. Now suppose that BSI can abandon the project at the end of the first year by selling it for $6 million. BSI will still receive the Year-1 cash flows, but will receive no cash flows in subsequent years.

c. Now assume that the project cannot be shut down. However, expertise gained by taking it on would lead to an opportunity at the end of Year 3 to undertake a venture that would have the same cost as the original project, and the new project's cash flows would follow whichever branch resulted for the original project. In other words, there would be a second $10 million cost at the end of Year 3 followed by cash flows of either $9 million, $4 million, or −$1 million for the subsequent 3 years. Use decision-tree analysis to estimate the value of the project, including the opportunity to implement the new project at Year 3. Assume that the $10 million cost at Year 3 is known with certainty and should be discounted at the risk-free rate of 6%.

d. Now suppose the original project (no abandonment option or additional growth option) could be delayed a year. All the cash flows would remain unchanged, but information obtained during that year would tell the company exactly which set of demand conditions existed. Use decision-tree analysis to estimate the value of the project if it is delayed by 1 year. (*Hint:* Discount the $10 million cost at the risk-free rate of 6% because the cost is known with certainty.)

e. Go back to part c. Instead of using decision-tree analysis, use the Black-Scholes model to estimate the value of the growth option. The risk-free rate is 6%, and the variance of the project's rate of return is 22%.

MINI CASE

Assume you have just been hired as a financial analyst by Tropical Sweets Inc., a mid-sized California company that specializes in creating exotic candies from tropical fruits such as mangoes, papayas, and dates. The firm's CEO, George Yamaguchi, recently returned from an industry corporate executive conference in San Francisco, and one of the sessions he attended addressed real options. Because no one at Tropical Sweets is familiar with the basics of real options, Yamaguchi has asked you to prepare a brief report that the firm's executives can use to gain a cursory understanding of the topic.

To begin, you gathered some outside materials on the subject and used these materials to draft a list of questions that need to be answered. Now that the questions have been drafted, you must develop the answers.

a. What are some types of real options?

b. What are five possible procedures for analyzing a real option?

c. Tropical Sweets is considering a project that will cost $70 million and will generate expected cash flows of $30 million per year for 3 years. The cost of capital for this type of project is 10%, and the risk-free rate is 6%. After discussions with the marketing department, you learn that there is a 30% chance of high demand with associated future cash flows of $45 million per year. There is also a 40% chance of average demand with cash flows of $30 million per year as well as a 30% chance of low demand with cash flows of only $15 million per year. What is the expected NPV?

d. Now suppose this project has an investment timing option, because it can be delayed for a year. The cost will still be $70 million at the end of the year, and the cash flows for the scenarios will still last 3 years. However, Tropical Sweets will know the level of demand and will implement the project only if it adds value to the company. Perform a qualitative assessment of the investment timing option's value.

e. Use decision-tree analysis to calculate the NPV of the project with the investment timing option.

f. Use a financial option pricing model to estimate the value of the investment timing option.

g. Now suppose that the cost of the project is $75 million and the project cannot be delayed. However, if Tropical Sweets implements the project, then the firm will have a growth option: the opportunity to replicate the original project at the end of its life. What is the total expected NPV of the two projects if both are implemented?

h. Tropical Sweets will replicate the original project only if demand is high. Using decision-tree analysis, estimate the value of the project with the growth option.

i. Use a financial option model to estimate the value of the project with the growth option.

j. What happens to the value of the growth option if the variance of the project's return is 14.2%? What if it is 50%? How might this explain the high valuations of many start-up high-tech companies that have yet to show positive earnings?

Strategic Financing Decisions

15

Distributions to Shareholders: Dividends and Repurchases

Because a company's value depends on its ability to generate free cash flow (FCF), most of this book has focused on aspects of FCF generation, including measurement, forecasts, and risk analysis. In contrast, this chapter focuses on the use of FCF for cash distributions to shareholders. Here are the central issues addressed in this chapter: Can a company increase its value through its choice of **distribution policy**, defined as: (1) the *level* of distributions, (2) the *form* of distributions (cash dividends versus stock repurchases), and (3) the *stability* of distributions? Do different groups of shareholders prefer one form of distribution over the other? Do shareholders perceive distributions as signals regarding a firm's risk and expected future free cash flows?

Before addressing these questions, let's take a look at the big picture regarding cash distributions.

Beginning-of-Chapter Questions

As you read the chapter, consider how you would answer the following questions. You *should not* necessarily be able to answer the questions before you read the chapter. Rather, you should use them to get a sense of the issues covered in the chapter. After reading the chapter, you should be able to give at least partial answers to the questions, and you should be able to give better answers after the chapter has been discussed in class. Note, too, that it is often useful, when answering conceptual questions, to use hypothetical data to illustrate your answer. We illustrate the answers with an *Excel* model that is available on the textbook's Web site. Accessing the model and working through it is a useful exercise, and it provides insights that are useful when answering the questions.

1. In your judgment, what are some characteristics of the type of investor who would likely prefer a **high dividend payout**, and what are some characteristics of one who would prefer a **low payout**? Would you personally prefer to own a stock with a high or a low payout, other things held constant? If you had a low-payout stock that you wanted to keep but you wanted more cash income, what could you do to increase your cash flow? Would those actions cause you to incur costs? What could you do, and what costs would you incur, if you owned a high-payout stock but did not need cash income?

2. Describe the three theories that have been advanced regarding whether investors in the aggregate tend to favor high or low dividend payout ratios. What results were reached from empirical tests of these theories?

3. How should (a) **signaling** and (b) the **clientele effect** be taken into account by a firm as it considers its dividend decision? Do signaling and clientele effects make it easier or harder to determine if investors prefer high or low payout ratios? Do these factors influence the desirability of a **stable dividend policy** versus one that is **flexible** and thus varies with the company's cash flows and investment opportunities?

4. Describe the **residual dividend model**. Explain how it operates and how firms use it in practice. In your answer, discuss any influences signaling and the clientele effect might have on a firm's decision to use, not use, or modify this model.

5. If a company is thinking about distributing excess cash through a **stock repurchase program** in lieu of continuing to pay regular cash dividends, what are some factors it should consider before making the change?

6. What is a **stock split**? As an investor, would you like to see shares you own be split?

7. In 2003, President Bush proposed a change in the tax law that would have eliminated the tax on dividends received by stockholders. The same proposal also would have increased the basis of stocks by the amount of new retained earnings per share—in effect reducing the capital gains tax to almost zero. In total, the proposal would have, to a large extent, put debt and equity financing on equal footing from a tax standpoint. The proposal did not pass, and instead, the tax rate on dividends was reduced to the rate on capital gains. However, if a similar proposal at some point becomes law, how would it tend to affect: (a) corporate capital structures, (b) corporate share repurchases, (c) dividend payout ratios, and (d) any conclusions one might reach regarding the three dividend preference theories?

USES OF FREE CASH FLOW: DISTRIBUTIONS TO SHAREHOLDERS

Free cash flow is generated from operations and is available for distribution to all investors. This chapter focuses on the distributions of FCF to shareholders in the form of dividends and stock repurchases.

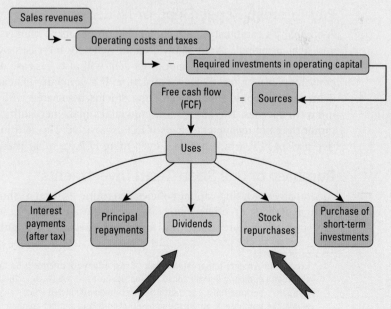

Source: From *Financial Management: Theory & Practice,* 2013, by Brigham and Ehrhardt. © Cengage Learning.

15-1 **An Overview of Cash Distributions**

At the risk of stating the obvious, a company must have cash before it can make a cash distribution to shareholders, so we begin by examining a company's sources of cash.

15-1a **Sources of Cash**

Occasionally the cash comes from a recapitalization or the sale of an asset, but in most cases it comes from the company's internally generated free cash flow. Recall that FCF is defined as the amount of cash flow available for distribution to investors after expenses, taxes, and the necessary investments in operating capital. Thus, the *source* of FCF depends on a company's investment opportunities and its effectiveness in turning those opportunities into realities. Notice that a company with many opportunities will have large investments in operating capital and might have negative FCF even if it is profitable. When growth begins to slow, a profitable company's FCF will be positive and very large. Home Depot and Microsoft are good examples of once-fast-growing companies that are now generating large amounts of free cash flows.

15-1b **Uses of Cash**

There are only five potentially "good" ways to use free cash flow: (1) pay interest expenses (after tax), (2) pay down the principal on debt, (3) pay dividends, (4) repurchase stock, or (5) buy short-term investments or other nonoperating assets.[1] If a company's FCF is negative, then its "uses" of FCF must also be negative. For example, a growing company often issues new debt rather than repaying debt and issues new shares of stock rather than repurchasing outstanding shares. Even after FCF becomes positive, some of its "uses" can be negative, as we explain next.

Pay Interest, Repay Debt, or Issue New Debt

A company's capital structure choice determines its payments for interest expenses and debt principal.[2] A company's value typically increases over time, even if the company is mature, which implies its debt will also increase over time if the company maintains a target capital structure. If a company instead were to pay off its debt, then it would lose valuable tax shields associated with the deductibility of interest expenses. Therefore, most companies make net additions to debt over time rather than net repayments, even if FCF is positive. The addition of debt is a "negative use" of FCF, which provides even more FCF for other uses.

Purchase or Sell Short-Term Investments

A company's working capital policies determine its level of short-term investments, such as T-bills or other marketable securities. Chapter 21 discusses short-term investments in more detail, but for now you should recognize that the decision

---

1. Recall from Chapter 6 that the company's cost of paying interest is on an after-tax basis. Recall also that a company doesn't *spend* FCF on operating assets (such as the acquisition of another company), because those expenditures were already deducted when calculating FCF. In other words, the purchase of an operating asset (even if it is another company) is not a *use* of FCF; instead, it is a *source* of FCF (albeit a "negative source").

2. We discuss capital structure choices in more detail in Chapter 16.

involves a trade-off between the benefits and costs of holding a large amount of short-term investments. In terms of benefits, a large holding reduces the risk of financial distress should there be an economic downturn. Also, if growth opportunities turn out to be better than expected, short-term investments provide a ready source of funding that does not incur the flotation or signaling costs due to raising external funds. However, there is a potential agency cost: If a company has a large investment in marketable securities, then managers might be tempted to squander the money on perks (such as corporate jets) or high-priced acquisitions.

However, many companies have much bigger short-term investments than the previous reasons can explain. For example, Apple has over $25 billion and Microsoft has about $70 billion. The most rational explanation is that such companies are using short-term investments temporarily until deciding how to use the cash.

Purchasing short-term investments is a positive use of FCF, and selling short-term investments is negative use. If a particular use of FCF is negative, then some other use must be larger than it otherwise would have been.

Pay Dividends, Repurchase Stock, or Issue New Shares of Stock

In summary, a company's investment opportunities and operating plans determine its level of FCF. The company's capital structure policy determines the amount of debt and interest payments. Working capital policy determines the investment in marketable securities. The remaining FCF should be distributed to shareholders, with the only question being how much to distribute in the form of dividends versus stock repurchases.

Obviously this is a simplification, because companies: (1) sometimes scale back their operating plans for sales and asset growth if such reductions are needed to maintain an existing dividend, (2) temporarily adjust their current financing mix in response to market conditions, and (3) often use marketable securities as shock absorbers for fluctuations in short-term cash flows. Still, there is an interdependence among operating plans (which have the biggest impact on free cash flow), financing plans (which have the biggest impact on the cost of capital), working capital policies (which determine the target level of marketable securities), and shareholder distributions.

What are the five uses of free cash flows?

How do a company's investment opportunities, capital structure, and working capital policies affect its distributions to shareholders?

SELF TEST

15-2 Procedures for Cash Distributions

Companies can distribute cash to shareholders via cash dividends or stock repurchases. In this section, we describe the actual procedures used to make cash distributions.

15-2a Dividend Payment Procedures

Companies normally pay dividends quarterly, and, if conditions permit, increase the dividend once each year. For example, Katz Corporation paid a $0.50

dividend per share in each quarter of 2015, for an annual dividend per share of $2.00. In common financial parlance, we say that in 2015 Katz's *regular quarterly dividend* was $0.50, and its *annual dividend* was $2.00. In late 2015, Katz's board of directors met, reviewed projections for 2016, and decided to keep the 2016 dividend at $2.00. The directors announced the $2 rate, so stockholders could count on receiving it unless the company experienced unanticipated operating problems.

The actual payment procedure is as follows.

1. *Declaration date.* On the **declaration date**—say, on Thursday, November 19—the directors meet and declare the regular dividend, issuing a statement similar to the following: "On November 19, 2015, the directors of Katz Corporation met and declared the regular quarterly dividend of 50 cents per share, payable to holders of record as of Friday, December 18, payment to be made on Friday, January 8, 2016." For accounting purposes, the declared dividend becomes an actual liability on the declaration date. If a balance sheet were constructed, an amount equal to $\$0.50 \times n_0$, where n_0 is the number of shares outstanding, would appear as a current liability, and retained earnings would be reduced by a like amount.

2. *Holder-of-record date.* At the close of business on the **holder-of-record date**, December 18, the company closes its stock transfer books and makes up a list of shareholders as of that date. If Katz Corporation is notified of the sale before 5 p.m. on December 18, then the new owner receives the dividend. However, if notification is received after 5 p.m. on December 18, the previous owner gets the dividend check.

3. *Ex-dividend date.* Suppose Jean Buyer buys 100 shares of stock from John Seller on December 15. Will the company be notified of the transfer in time to list Buyer as the new owner and thus pay the dividend to her? To avoid conflict, the securities industry has set up a convention under which the right to the dividend remains with the stock until two business days prior to the holder-of-record date; on the second day before that date, the right to the dividend no longer goes with the shares. The date when the right to the dividend leaves the stock is called the **ex-dividend date**. In this case, the ex-dividend date is two days prior to December 18, which is December 16:

Dividend goes with stock:	Tuesday, December 15
Ex-dividend date:	Wednesday, December 16
	Thursday, December 17
Holder-of-record date:	Friday, December 18

Therefore, if Buyer is to receive the dividend, she must buy the stock on or before December 15. If she buys it on December 16 or later, Seller will receive the dividend because he will be the official holder of record.

Katz's dividend amounts to $0.50, so the ex-dividend date is important. Barring fluctuations in the stock market, we would normally expect the price of a stock to drop by approximately the amount of the dividend on the ex-dividend date. Thus, if Katz closed at $30.50 on December 15, it would probably open at about $30 on December 16.

4. *Payment date.* The company actually pays the dividend on January 8, the **payment date**, to the holders of record.

15-2b **Stock Repurchase Procedures**

Stock repurchases occur when a company buys back some of its own outstanding stock.[3] Three situations can lead to stock repurchases. First, a company may decide to increase its leverage by issuing debt and using the proceeds to repurchase stock; we discuss recapitalizations in more detail in Chapter 16. Second, many firms have given their employees stock options, and companies often repurchase their own stock to sell to employees when employees exercise the options. In this case, the number of outstanding shares reverts to its pre-repurchase level after the options are exercised. Third, a company may have excess cash. This may be due to a one-time cash inflow, such as the sale of a division, or the company may simply be generating more free cash flow than it needs to service its debt.[4]

Stock repurchases are usually made in one of three ways. (1) A publicly owned firm can buy back its own stock through a broker on the open market.[5] (2) The firm can make a tender offer, under which it permits stockholders to send in (that is, "tender") shares in exchange for a specified price per share. In this case, the firm generally indicates it will buy up to a specified number of shares within a stated time period (usually about two weeks). If more shares are tendered than the company wants to buy, purchases are made on a pro rata basis. (3) The firm can purchase a block of shares from one large holder on a negotiated basis. This is a targeted stock repurchase, as discussed in Chapter 10.

15-2c **Patterns of Cash Distributions**

The occurrence of dividends versus stock repurchases has changed dramatically during the past 30 years. First, total cash distributions as a percentage of net income have remained fairly stable at around 26% to 28%, but the mix of dividends and repurchases has changed.[6] The average dividend payout ratio fell from 22.3% in 1974 to 13.8% in 1998, while the average repurchase payout as a percentage of net income rose from 3.7% to 13.6%. Since 1985, large companies have repurchased more shares than they have issued. Since 1998, more cash has been returned to shareholders in repurchases than as dividend payments.

---

3. The repurchased stock is called "treasury stock" and is shown as a negative value on the company's detailed balance sheet. On the consolidated balance sheet, treasury shares are deducted to find shares outstanding, and the price paid for the repurchased shares is deducted when determining common equity.

4. See Benton Gup and Doowoo Nam, "Stock Buybacks, Corporate Performance, and EVA," *Journal of Applied Corporate Finance*, Spring 2001, pp. 99–110. The authors show that the firms that repurchase stock have superior operating performance to those that do not buy back stock, which is consistent with the notion that firms buy back stock when they generate additional free cash flow. They also show that operating performance improves in the year after the buyback, indicating that the superior performance is sustainable.

5. Many firms announce their plans to repurchase stock on the open market. For example, a company might announce it plans to repurchase 4 million shares of stock. However, companies usually don't buy back all the shares they announce but instead repurchase only about 80% of the announced number. See Clifford Stephens and Michael Weisbach, "Actual Share Reacquisitions in Open-Market Repurchase Programs," *Journal of Finance*, February 1998, pp. 313–333.

6. See Gustavo Grullon and Roni Michaely, "Dividends, Share Repurchases, and the Substitution Hypothesis," *Journal of Finance*, August 2002, pp. 1649–1684; and Eugene Fama and Kenneth French, "Disappearing Dividends: Changing Firm Characteristics or Lower Propensity to Pay?" *Journal of Applied Corporate Finance*, Spring 2001, pp. 67–79.

Second, companies today are less likely to pay a dividend. In 1978, about 66.5% of NYSE, AMEX, and NASDAQ firms paid a dividend. In 1999, only 20.8% paid a dividend. Part of this reduction can be explained by the large number of IPOs in the 1990s, because young firms rarely pay a dividend. However, that doesn't explain the entire story, as many mature firms now do not pay dividends. For example, consider the way in which a maturing firm will make its first cash distribution. In 1973, 73% of firms making an initial distribution did so with a dividend. By 1998, only 19% initiated distributions with dividends.[7]

Third, the aggregate dividend payouts have become more concentrated in the sense that a relatively small number of older, more established, and more profitable firms accounts for most of the cash distributed as dividends.[8]

Fourth, Table 15-1 shows there is considerable variation in distribution policies, with some companies paying a high percentage of their income as dividends and others paying none. The next section discusses some theories about distribution policies.

> **SELF TEST**
>
> Explain the procedures used to actually pay the dividend.
>
> Why is the ex-dividend date important to investors?
>
> What are the three ways in which a company can repurchase stock?

TABLE 15-1	Dividend Payouts (April 2014)		
Company	**Industry**	**Dividend Payout**	**Dividend Yield**
Empire District Electric (EDE)	Electric utility	68%	4.2%
Rayonier Inc. (RYN.N)	Forest products	71	4.5
Regions Financial Corp. (RF)	Regional banks	17	1.2
Reynolds American Inc. (RAI)	Tobacco products	79	5.0
WD-40 Company (WDFC)	Household products	48	1.9
Harley-Davidson Inc. (HOG)	Recreational products	25	1.7
Ingles Markets Inc. (IMKTA)	Retail (grocery)	59	2.9
Microsoft Corp. (MSFT)	Software and programming	37	2.9
Tiffany and Company (TIF)	Specialty retail	94	1.6

Source: **www.reuters.com**, April 2014.

7. See Gustavo Grullon and David Ikenberry, "What Do We Know about Stock Repurchases?" *Journal of Applied Corporate Finance,* Spring 2000, pp. 31–51.
8. For example, see Harry DeAngelo, Linda DeAngelo, and Douglas J. Skinner, "Are Dividends Disappearing? Dividend Concentration and the Consolidation of Earnings," *Journal of Financial Economics,* June 2004, pp. 425–456.

15-3 Cash Distributions and Firm Value

A company can change its value of operations only if it changes the cost of capital or investors' perceptions regarding expected free cash flow. This is true for all corporate decisions, including the distribution policy. Is there an **optimal distribution policy** that maximizes a company's intrinsic value?

The answer depends in part on investors' preferences for returns in the form of dividend yields versus capital gains. The relative mix of dividend yields and capital gains is determined by the **target distribution ratio**, which is the percentage of net income distributed to shareholders through cash dividends or stock repurchases, and the **target payout ratio**, which is the percentage of net income paid as a cash dividend. Notice that the payout ratio must be less than the distribution ratio because the distribution ratio includes stock repurchases as well as cash dividends.

A high distribution ratio and a high payout ratio mean that a company pays large dividends and has small (or zero) stock repurchases. In this situation, the dividend yield is relatively high and the expected capital gain is low. If a company has a large distribution ratio but a small payout ratio, then it pays low dividends but regularly repurchases stock, resulting in a low dividend yield but a higher expected capital gain yield. If a company has a low distribution ratio, then it must also have a relatively low payout ratio, again resulting in a low dividend yield and, it is hoped, a relatively high capital gain yield.

In this section, we examine three theories of investor preferences for dividend yield versus capital gains: (1) the dividend irrelevance theory, (2) the dividend preference theory (also called the "bird-in-the-hand" theory), and (3) the tax effect theory.

15-3a Dividend Irrelevance Theory

The original proponents of the **dividend irrelevance theory** were Merton Miller and Franco Modigliani (MM).[9] They argued that the firm's value is determined only by its basic earning power and its business risk. In other words, MM argued that the value of the firm depends only on the income produced by its assets, not on how this income is split between dividends and retained earnings.

To understand MM's argument, recognize that any shareholder can in theory construct his own dividend policy. For example, if a firm does not pay dividends, a shareholder who wants a 5% dividend can "create" it by selling 5% of his stock. Conversely, if a company pays a higher dividend than an investor desires, the investor can use the unwanted dividends to buy additional shares of the company's stock. If investors could buy and sell shares and thus create their own dividend policy without incurring costs, then the firm's dividend policy would truly be irrelevant.

In developing their dividend theory, MM made a number of important assumptions, especially the absence of taxes and brokerage costs. If these assumptions are not true, then investors who want additional dividends must incur brokerage costs

---

9. See Merton H. Miller and Franco Modigliani, "Dividend Policy, Growth, and the Valuation of Shares," *Journal of Business*, October 1961, pp. 411–433. However, their conclusion is valid only if investors expect managers eventually to pay out the equivalent of the present value of all future free cash flows; see Harry DeAngelo and Linda DeAngelo, "The Irrelevance of the MM Dividend Irrelevance Theorem," *Journal of Financial Economics*, Vol. 79, 2006, pp. 293–315.

to sell shares and must pay taxes on any capital gains. Investors who do not want dividends must incur brokerage costs to purchase shares with their dividends. Because taxes and brokerage costs certainly exist, dividend policy may well be relevant. We will discuss empirical tests of MM's dividend irrelevance theory shortly.

15-3b **Dividend Preference (Bird-in-the-Hand) Theory**

The principal conclusion of MM's dividend irrelevance theory is that dividend policy does not affect a stock's value or risk. Therefore, it does not affect the required rate of return on equity, r_s. In contrast, Myron Gordon and John Lintner both argued that a stock's risk declines as dividends increase: A return in the form of dividends is a sure thing, but a return in the form of capital gains is risky. In other words, a **bird in the hand** is worth more than two in the bush. Therefore, shareholders prefer dividends and are willing to accept a lower required return on equity.[10]

The possibility of agency costs leads to a similar conclusion. First, high payouts reduce the risk that managers will squander cash because there is less cash on hand. Second, a high-payout company must raise external funds more often than a low-payout company, all else held equal. If a manager knows that the company will receive frequent scrutiny from external markets, then the manager will be less likely to engage in wasteful practices. Therefore, high payouts reduce the risk of agency costs. With less risk, shareholders are willing to accept a lower required return on equity.

15-3c **Tax Effect Theory: Capital Gains Are Preferred**

Before 2003, individual investors paid ordinary income taxes on dividends but lower rates on long-term capital gains. The Jobs and Growth Act of 2003 changed this, reducing the tax rate on dividend income to the same as on long-term capital gains.[11] However, there are two reasons why stock price appreciation still is taxed more favorably than dividend income. First, an increase in a stock's price isn't taxable until the investor sells the stock, whereas a dividend payment is taxable immediately; a dollar of taxes paid in the future has a lower effective cost than a dollar paid today because of the time value of money. So even when dividends and gains are taxed equally, capital gains are never taxed sooner than dividends. Second, if a stock is held until the shareholder dies, then no capital gains tax is due at all: The beneficiaries who receive the stock can use its value on the date of death as their cost basis and thus completely escape the capital gains tax.

---

10. Myron J. Gordon, "Optimal Investment and Financing Policy," *Journal of Finance*, May 1963, pp. 264–272; and John Lintner, "Dividends, Earnings, Leverage, Stock Prices, and the Supply of Capital to Corporations," *Review of Economics and Statistics*, August 1962, pp. 243–269.

11. Of course, nothing involving taxes is quite this simple. The dividend must be from a domestic company, and the investor must own the stock for more than 60 days during the 120-day period beginning 60 days before the ex-dividend date. There are restrictions for dividends other than regular cash dividends. The Tax Increase Prevention and Reconciliation Act of 2005 cut the long-term capital gains tax rate to zero for low-income investors (that is, those whose marginal tax rate is 15% or less) and kept it at 15% for those with more income. Starting in 2014, the capital gains rates are 0%, 15%, or 20%, depending on income. In addition, higher income filers will pay an additional 3.8% on net investment income, making their effective capital gains rate 23.8%. Also, the Alternative Minimum Tax (AMT) increases the effective tax rate on dividends and capital gains by 7% for some moderately high-income earners. See Leonard Burman, William Gale, Greg Leiserson, and Jeffrey Rohaly, "The AMT: What's Wrong and How to Fix It," *National Tax Journal*, September 2007, pp. 385–405.

Because dividends are in some cases taxed more highly than capital gains, investors might require a higher pre-tax rate of return to induce them to buy dividend-paying stocks. Therefore, investors may prefer that companies minimize dividends. If so, then investors should be willing to pay more for low-payout companies than for otherwise similar high-payout companies.[12]

15-3d **Empirical Evidence on Distribution Policies**

It is very difficult to construct a perfect empirical test of the relationship between payout policy and the required rate of return on stock. First, all factors other than distribution level should be held constant; that is, the sample companies should differ only in their distribution levels. Second, each firm's cost of equity should be measured with a high degree of accuracy. Unfortunately, we cannot find a set of publicly owned firms that differ only in their distribution levels, nor can we obtain precise estimates of the cost of equity. Therefore, no one has yet identified a completely unambiguous relationship between the distribution level and the cost of equity or firm value.

Although none of the empirical tests is perfect, recent evidence does suggest that firms with higher dividend payouts also have higher required returns.[13] This tends to support the tax effect hypothesis, although the size of the required return is too high to be fully explained by taxes.

Agency costs should be most severe in countries with poor investor protection. In such countries, companies with high dividend payouts should be more highly valued than those with low payouts because high payouts limit the extent to which managers can expropriate shareholder wealth. Recent research shows that this is the case, which supports the dividend preference hypothesis in the case of companies with severe agency problems.[14]

Although the evidence from these studies is mixed as to whether the *average* investor uniformly prefers either higher or lower distribution levels, other research does show that *individual* investors have strong preferences. Also, other research shows that investors prefer stable, predictable dividend payouts (regardless of the payout level) and that they interpret dividend changes as signals about firms' future prospects. We discuss these issues in the next several sections.

SELF TEST

What did Modigliani and Miller assume about taxes and brokerage costs when they developed their dividend irrelevance theory?

How did the bird-in-the-hand theory get its name?

What have been the results of empirical tests of the dividend theories?

---

12. For more on tax-related issues, see Eli Talmor and Sheridan Titman, "Taxes and Dividend Policy," *Financial Management,* Summer 1990, pp. 32–35; and Rosita P. Chang and S. Ghon Rhee, "The Impact of Personal Taxes on Corporate Dividend Policy and Capital Structure Decisions," *Financial Management,* Summer 1990, pp. 21–31.

13. See A. Naranjo, N. Nimalendran, and M. Ryngaert, "Stock Returns, Dividend Yields, and Taxes," *Journal of Finance,* December 1998, pp. 2029–2057.

14. See L. Pinkowitz, R. Stulz, and R. Williamson, "Does the Contribution of Corporate Cash Holdings and Dividends to Firm Value Depend on Governance? A Cross-Country Analysis," *Journal of Finance,* December 2006, pp. 2725–2751.

15-4 **Clientele Effect**

As we indicated earlier, different groups, or *clienteles*, of stockholders prefer different dividend payout policies. For example, retired individuals, pension funds, and university endowment funds generally prefer cash income, so they may want the firm to pay out a high percentage of its earnings. Such investors are often in low or even zero tax brackets, so taxes are of no concern. On the other hand, stockholders in their peak earning years might prefer reinvestment, because they have less need for current investment income and would simply reinvest dividends received—after first paying income taxes on those dividends.

For updates of industry payout ratios, go to **www.reuters.com /finance/stocks.** After picking a company, select Ratios.

If a firm retains and reinvests income rather than paying dividends, those stockholders who need current income would be disadvantaged. The value of their stock might increase, but they would be forced to go to the trouble and expense of selling some of their shares to obtain cash. Also, some institutional investors (or trustees for individuals) would be legally precluded from selling stock and then "spending capital." On the other hand, stockholders who are saving rather than spending dividends might favor the low-dividend policy: The less the firm pays out in dividends, the less these stockholders will have to pay in current taxes, and the less trouble and expense they will have to go through to reinvest their after-tax dividends. Therefore, investors who want current investment income should own shares in high–dividend payout firms, while investors with no need for current investment income should own shares in low–dividend payout firms. For example, investors seeking high cash income might invest in the household products industry, which averaged a 47% payout in April 2014, while those favoring growth could invest in the automotive industry, which paid out only 3% during the same time period.

To the extent that stockholders can switch firms, a firm can change from one dividend payout policy to another and then let stockholders who do not like the new policy sell to other investors who do. However, frequent switching would be inefficient because of: (1) brokerage costs, (2) the likelihood that stockholders who are selling will have to pay capital gains taxes, and (3) a possible shortage of investors who like the firm's newly adopted dividend policy. Thus, management should be hesitant to change its dividend policy, because a change might cause current shareholders to sell their stock, forcing the stock price down. Such a price decline might be temporary but might also be permanent—if few new investors are attracted by the new dividend policy, then the stock price would remain depressed. Of course, the new policy might attract an even larger clientele than the firm had before, in which case the stock price would rise.

Evidence from several studies suggests that there is, in fact, a **clientele effect**. For example, low-tax or tax-free institutions hold relatively more high-dividend stocks than taxable investors, and taxable institutions hold fewer high-dividend stocks than non-taxed investors.[15] MM and others have argued that one clientele is as good as another, so the existence of a clientele effect does not necessarily imply that one dividend policy is better than any other. However, MM may be wrong, and neither they nor anyone else can prove that the aggregate makeup of investors permits firms to disregard clientele effects. This issue, like most others in the dividend arena, is still up in the air.

---

15. For example, see R. Richardson Pettit, "Taxes, Transactions Costs and the Clientele Effect of Dividends," *Journal of Financial Economics,* December 1977, pp. 419–436; and William J. Moser and Andy Puckett, "Dividend Tax Clienteles: Evidence from Tax Law Changes," *Journal of the American Taxation Association,* Spring 2009, pp. 1–22.

15-5 Information Content, or Signaling, Hypothesis

When MM set forth their dividend irrelevance theory, they assumed that everyone—investors and managers alike—has identical information regarding a firm's future earnings and dividends. In reality, however, different investors have different views on both the level of future dividend payments and the uncertainty inherent in those payments, and managers have better information about future prospects than public stockholders.

It has been observed that an increase in the dividend is often accompanied by an increase in the price of a stock and that a dividend cut generally leads to a stock price decline. Some have argued this indicates that investors prefer dividends to capital gains. However, MM saw this differently. They noted the well-established fact that corporations are reluctant to cut dividends, which implies that corporations do not raise dividends unless they anticipate higher earnings in the future. Thus, MM argued that a higher than expected dividend increase is a signal to investors that the firm's management forecasts good future earnings. Conversely, a dividend reduction, or a smaller than expected increase, is a signal that management is forecasting poor earnings in the future. Thus, MM argued that investors' reactions to changes in dividend policy do not necessarily show that investors prefer dividends to retained earnings. Rather, they argue that price changes following dividend actions simply indicate that there is important **information content**, or **signaling content**, in dividend announcements.

The initiation of a dividend by a firm that formerly paid no dividend is certainly a significant change in distribution policy. It appears that initiating firms' future earnings and cash flows are less risky than before the initiation. However, the evidence is mixed regarding the future profitability of initiating firms: Some studies find slightly higher earnings after the initiation but others find no significant change in earnings.[16] What happens when firms with existing dividends unexpectedly increase or decrease the dividend? Early studies, using small data samples, concluded that unexpected dividend changes did not provide a signal about future earnings.[17] However, more recent data with larger samples provide mixed evidence.[18] On average, firms that cut dividends had poor earnings in the years directly

---

16. See Edward Dyl and Robert Weigand, "The Information Content of Dividend Initiations: Additional Evidence," *Financial Management,* Autumn 1998, pp. 27–35; P. Asquith and D. Mullins, "The Impact of Initiating Dividend Payments on Shareholders' Wealth," *Journal of Business,* January 1983, pp. 77–96; and P. Healy and K. Palepu, "Earnings Information Conveyed by Dividend Initiations and Omissions," *Journal of Financial Economics,* September 1988, pp. 149–175.

17. For example, see N. Gonedes, "Corporate Signaling, External Accounting, and Capital Market Equilibrium: Evidence of Dividends, Income, and Extraordinary Items," *Journal of Accounting Research,* Spring 1978, pp. 26–79; and R. Watts, "The Information Content of Dividends," *Journal of Business,* April 1973, pp. 191–211.

18. See Shlomo Benartzi, Roni Michaely, and Richard Thaler, "Do Changes in Dividends Signal the Future or the Past?" *Journal of Finance,* July 1997, pp. 1007–1034; and Yaron Brook, William Charlton Jr., and Robert J. Hendershott, "Do Firms Use Dividends to Signal Large Future Cash Flow Increases?" *Financial Management,* Autumn 1998, pp. 46–57.

preceding the cut but actually improved earnings in subsequent years. Firms that increased dividends had earnings increases in the years preceding the increase but did not appear to have subsequent earnings increases. However, neither did they have subsequent declines in earnings, so it appears that the increase in dividends is a signal that past earnings increases were not temporary. Also, a relatively large number of firms that expect a large permanent increase in cash flow (as opposed to earnings) do in fact increase their dividend payouts in the year prior to the cash flow increase.

All in all, there is clearly some information content in dividend announcements: Stock prices tend to fall when dividends are cut, even if they don't always rise when dividends are increased. However, this doesn't necessarily validate the signaling hypothesis, because it is difficult to tell whether any stock price change following a change in dividend policy reflects only signaling effects or reflects both signaling and dividend preferences.

SELF TEST Define signaling content, and explain how it affects dividend policy.

15-6 Implications for Dividend Stability

The clientele effect and the information content in dividend announcements definitely have implications regarding the desirability of stable versus volatile dividends. For example, many stockholders rely on dividends to meet expenses, and they would be seriously inconvenienced if the dividend stream were unstable. Further, reducing dividends to make funds available for capital investment could send incorrect signals to investors, who might push down the stock price because they interpret the dividend cut to mean that the company's future earnings prospects have been diminished. Thus, maximizing its stock price probably requires a firm to maintain a steady dividend policy. Because sales and earnings are expected to grow for most firms, a stable dividend policy means a company's regular cash dividends should also grow at a steady, predictable rate.[19] But, as we explain in the next section, most companies will probably move toward small, sustainable, regular cash dividends that are supplemented by stock repurchases.

SELF TEST Why do the clientele effect and the information content hypotheses imply that investors prefer stable dividends?

---

19. For more on announcements and stability, see Jeffrey A. Born, "Insider Ownership and Signals—Evidence from Dividend Initiation Announcement Effects," *Financial Management,* Spring 1988, pp. 38–45; Chinmoy Ghosh and J. Randall Woolridge, "An Analysis of Shareholder Reaction to Dividend Cuts and Omissions," *Journal of Financial Research,* Winter 1988, pp. 281–294; C. Michael Impson and Imre Karafiath, "A Note on the Stock Market Reaction to Dividend Announcements," *Financial Review,* May 1992, pp. 259–271; James W. Wansley, C. F. Sirmans, James D. Shilling, and Young-jin Lee, "Dividend Change Announcement Effects and Earnings Volatility and Timing," *Journal of Financial Research,* Spring 1991, pp. 37–49; and J. Randall Woolridge and Chinmoy Ghosh, "Dividend Cuts: Do They Always Signal Bad News?" *Midland Corporate Finance Journal,* Summer 1985, pp. 20–32.

WILL DIVIDENDS EVER BE THE SAME?

The global economic crisis has had dramatic effects on dividend policies. According to Standard & Poor's, companies announcing dividend increases have exceeded those announcing decreases by a factor of 15 to 1 since 1955—at least until the first 5 months of 2009. Out of 7,000 publicly traded companies, only 283 announced dividend increases in the first quarter of 2009, while 367 cut dividends, a stunning reversal in the normal ratio of increasers to decreasers. Even the S&P 500 companies weren't immune to the crisis, with only 74 increasing dividends as compared with 54 cutting dividends and 9 suspending dividend payments altogether. To put this in perspective, only *one* S&P 500 company cut its dividend during the first quarter of 2007. The dividend decreases in 2009 aren't minor cuts, either. Howard Silverblatt, a Senior Index Analyst at Standard & Poor's, estimates the cuts add up to $77 billion.

How did the market react to cuts by these companies? JPMorgan Chase's stock price went up on the announcement, presumably because investors thought a stronger balance sheet at JPM would increase its intrinsic value by more than the loss investors incurred because of the lower dividend. On the other hand, GE's stock fell by more than 6% on the news of its 68% dividend cut, perhaps because investors feared this was a signal that GE's plight was worse than they had expected.

One thing is for certain: The days of large "permanent" dividends are over!

Sources: "S&P: Q1 Worst Quarter for Dividends Since 1955; Companies Reduce Shareholder Payments by $77 Billion," press release, April 7, 2009; also see **www2.standardandpoors.com/spf/xls/index /INDICATED_RATE_CHANGE.xls**.

15-7 Setting the Target Distribution Level: The Residual Distribution Model

When deciding how much cash to distribute to stockholders, two points should be kept in mind: (1) The overriding objective is to maximize shareholder value, and (2) the firm's cash flows really belong to its shareholders, so a company should not retain income unless managers can reinvest that income to produce returns higher than shareholders could themselves earn by investing the cash in investments of equal risk. On the other hand, recall from Chapter 11 that internal equity (reinvested earnings) is cheaper than external equity (new common stock issues) because it avoids flotation costs and adverse signals. This encourages firms to retain earnings so as to avoid having to issue new stock.

When establishing a distribution policy, one size does not fit all. Some firms produce a lot of cash but have limited investment opportunities—this is true for firms in profitable but mature industries in which few opportunities for growth exist. Such firms typically distribute a large percentage of their cash to shareholders, thereby attracting investment clienteles that prefer high dividends. Other firms generate little or no excess cash because they have many good investment opportunities. Such firms generally don't distribute much cash but do enjoy rising earnings and stock prices, thereby attracting investors who prefer capital gains.

As Table 15-1 suggests, dividend payouts and dividend yields for large corporations vary considerably. Generally, firms in stable, cash-producing industries such as utilities, financial services, and tobacco pay relatively high dividends, whereas companies in rapidly growing industries such as computer software tend to pay lower dividends.

For a given firm, the optimal distribution ratio is a function of four factors: (1) investors' preferences for dividends versus capital gains, (2) the firm's investment opportunities, (3) its target capital structure, and (4) the availability and cost of external capital. The last three elements are combined in what we call the **residual distribution model**. Under this model a firm follows these four steps when establishing its target distribution ratio: (1) it determines the optimal capital budget; (2) it determines the amount of equity needed to finance that budget, given its target capital structure (we explain the choice of target capital structures in Chapter 16); (3) it uses reinvested earnings to meet equity requirements to the extent possible; and (4) it pays dividends or repurchases stock only if more earnings are available than are needed to support the optimal capital budget. The word *residual* implies "leftover," and the residual policy implies that distributions are paid out of "leftover" earnings.

If a firm rigidly follows the residual distribution policy, then distributions paid in any given year can be expressed as follows:

(15–1)

$$\text{Distributions} = \text{Net income} - \frac{\text{Retained earnings needed to}}{\text{finance new investments}}$$

$$= \text{Net income} - [(\text{Target equity ratio}) \times (\text{Total capital budget})]$$

As an illustration, consider the case of Texas and Western (T&W) Transport Company, which has $60 million in net income and a target capital structure of 60% equity and 40% debt.

If T&W forecasts poor investment opportunities, then its estimated capital budget will be only $40 million. To maintain the target capital structure, 40% ($16 million) of this capital must be raised as debt and 60% ($24 million) must be equity. If it followed a strict residual policy, T&W would retain $24 million of its $60 million earnings to help finance new investments and then distribute the remaining $36 million to shareholders:

$$\begin{aligned} \text{Distributions} &= \text{Net income} - [(\text{Target equity ratio})(\text{Total capital budget})] \\ &= \$60 - [(60\%)(\$40)] \\ &= \$60 - \$24 = \$36 \end{aligned}$$

Under this scenario, the company's distribution ratio would be $36 million ÷ $60 million = 0.6 = 60%. These results are shown in Table 15-2.

In contrast, if the company's investment opportunities are average, its optimal capital budget would rise to $70 million. Here it would require $42 million of retained earnings, so distributions would be $60 − $42 = $18 million, for a ratio of $18/$60 = 30%. Finally, if investment opportunities are good then the capital budget would be $150 million, which would require 0.6($150) = $90 million of equity. In this case, T&W would retain all of its net income ($60 million) and thus make no distributions. Moreover, because the required equity exceeds the retained earnings, the company would have to issue some new common stock to maintain the target capital structure.

Because investment opportunities and earnings will surely vary from year to year, a strict adherence to the residual distribution policy would result in unstable distributions. One year the firm might make no distributions because it needs the

TABLE 15-2	T&W's Distribution Ratio with $60 Million of Net Income and a 60% Target Equity Ratio When Faced with Different Investment Opportunities (Millions of Dollars)		
	Investment Opportunities		
	Poor	**Average**	**Good**
Capital budget	$40	$70	$150
Required equity (0.6 × Capital budget)	$24	$42	$ 90
Net income	$60	$60	$ 60
Required equity (from above)	24	42	90
Distributions paid (NI − Required equity)	$36	$18	−$ 30[a]
Distribution ratio (Dividend/NI)	60%	30%	0%

[a]With a $150 million capital budget, T&W would retain all of its earnings and also issue $30 million of new stock.

money to finance good investment opportunities, but the next year it might make a large distribution because investment opportunities are poor and so it does not need to retain much. Similarly, fluctuating earnings could also lead to variable distributions, even if investment opportunities were stable. Until now, we have not addressed whether distributions should be in the form of dividends, stock repurchases, or some combination. The next sections discuss specific issues associated with dividend payments and stock repurchases; this is followed by a comparison of their relative advantages and disadvantages.

SELF TEST

Explain the logic of the residual dividend model and the steps a firm would take to implement it.

Hamilton Corporation has a target equity ratio of 65%, and its capital budget is $2 million. If Hamilton has net income of $1.6 million and follows a residual distribution model, how much will its distribution be? **($300,000)**

15-8 The Residual Distribution Model in Practice

If distributions were solely in the form of dividends, then rigidly following the residual policy would lead to fluctuating, unstable dividends. Because investors dislike volatile regular dividends, r_s would be high and the stock price low. Therefore, firms should proceed as follows.

1. Estimate earnings and investment opportunities, on average, for the next 5 or so years.
2. Use this forecasted information and the target capital structure to find the average residual model distributions and dollars of dividends during the planning period.
3. Set a *target payout ratio* based on the average projected data.

Thus, *firms should use the residual policy to help set their long-run target distribution ratios, but not as a guide to the distribution in any one year.*

Companies often use financial forecasting models in conjunction with the residual distribution model discussed here to help understand the determinants of an optimal dividend policy. Most large corporations forecast their financial statements over the next 5 to 10 years. Information on projected capital expenditures and working capital requirements is entered into the model, along with sales forecasts, profit margins, depreciation, and the other elements required to forecast cash flows. The target capital structure is also specified, and the model shows the amount of debt and equity that will be required to meet the capital budgeting requirements while maintaining the target capital structure. Then, dividend payments are introduced. Naturally, the higher the payout ratio, the greater the required external equity. Most companies use the model to find a dividend pattern over the forecast period (generally 5 years) that will provide sufficient equity to support the capital budget without forcing them to sell new common stock or move the capital structure ratios outside their optimal range.

Some companies set a very low "regular" dividend and then supplement it with an "extra" dividend when times are good, such as Microsoft now does. This **low-regular-dividend-plus-extras policy** ensures that the regular dividend can be maintained "come hell or high water" and that stockholders can count on receiving that dividend under all conditions. Then, when times are good and profits and cash flows are high, the company can either pay a specially designated extra dividend or repurchase shares of stock. Investors recognize that the extras might not be maintained in the future, so they do not interpret them as a signal that the companies' earnings are going up permanently; nor do they take the elimination of the extra as a negative signal.

SELF TEST

Why is the residual model more often used to establish a long-run payout target than to set the actual year-by-year dividend payout ratio?

How do firms use planning models to help set dividend policy?

15-9 A Tale of Two Cash Distributions: Dividends versus Stock Repurchases

WEB

See *Ch15 Tool Kit.xls* on the textbook's Web site.

Benson Conglomerate, a prestigious publishing house with several Nobel laureates among its authors, recently began generating positive free cash flow and is analyzing the impact of different distribution policies. Benson anticipates extremely stable cash flows and will use the residual model to determine the level of distributions, but it has not yet chosen the form of the distribution. In particular, Benson is comparing distributions via dividends versus repurchases and wants to know the impact the different methods will have on financial statements, shareholder wealth, the number of outstanding shares, and the stock price.

15-9a The Impact on Financial Statements

Consider first the case in which distributions are in the form of dividends. Figure 15-1 shows the most recent financial statements and the inputs we will use to forecast

FIGURE 15-1	Projecting Benson Conglomerate's Financial Statements: Distributions as Dividends (Millions of Dollars)

	A	B	C	D	E	F
77	**1. Inputs**	Actual	Projected			
78		12/31/2015	2016		2017	
79	Sales growth rate		5%		5%	
80	Costs/Sales	70%	70%		70%	
81	Depreciation/Net PPE	10%	10%		10%	
82	Cash/Sales	1%	1%		1%	
83	Acct. rec./Sales	15%	15%		15%	
84	Inventories/Sales	12%	12%		12%	
85	Net PPE/Sales	85%	85%		85%	
86	Acct. pay./Sales	8%	8%		8%	
87	Accruals/Sales	2%	2%		2%	
88	Tax rate	40%	40%		40%	
89	**2. Income Statement**[a]	Actual	Projected			
90		12/31/2015	12/31/2016		12/31/2017	
91	Net Sales	$8,000.0	$8,400.0		$8,820.0	
92	Costs (except depr.)	5,600.0	5,880.0		6,174.0	
93	Depreciation	680.0	714.0		749.7	
94	EBIT	$1,720.0	$1,806.0		$1,896.3	
95	Interest expense[b]	0.0	0.0		0.0	
96	Pre-tax earnings	$1,720.0	$1,806.0		$1,896.3	
97	Taxes	688.0	722.4		758.5	
98	Net income	$1,032.0	$1,083.6		$1,137.8	
99	Regular dividends	$0.0	$0.0		$0.0	
100	Special dividends		$671.6		$705.2	
101	Addition to RE		$412.0		$432.6	
102	**3. Balance Sheets**	Actual	Projected			
103		12/31/2015	2016		2017	
104	*Assets*		12/30	12/31	12/30	12/31
105	Cash	$80.0	$84.0	$84.0	$88.2	$88.2
106	Short-term investments[c]	0.0	671.6	0.0	705.2	0.0
107	Accounts receivable	1,200.0	1,260.0	1,260.0	1,323.0	1,323.0
108	Inventories	960.0	1,008.0	1,008.0	1,058.4	1,058.4
109	Total current assets	$2,240.0	$3,023.6	$2,352.0	$3,174.8	$2,469.6
110	Net plant and equipment	6,800.0	7,140.0	7,140.0	7,497.0	7,497.0
111	Total assets	$9,040.0	$10,163.6	$9,492.0	$10,671.8	$9,966.6
112	*Liabilities & Equity*					
113	Accounts payable	$640.0	$672.0	$672.0	$705.6	$705.6
114	Accruals	160.0	168.0	168.0	176.4	176.4
115	Line of credit	0.0	0.0	0.0	0.0	0.0
116	Total current liabilities	$800.0	$840.0	$840.0	$882.0	$882.0
117	Long-term debt	0.0	0.0	0.0	0.0	0.0
118	Total liabilities	$800.0	$840.0	$840.0	$882.0	$882.0
119	Common stock	2,400.0	2,400.0	2,400.0	2,400.0	2,400.0
120	Retained earnings[d]	5,840.0	6,923.6	6,252.0	7,389.8	6,684.6
121	Total common equity	$8,240.0	$9,323.6	$8,652.0	$9,789.8	$9,084.6
122	Total liabilities & equity	$9,040.0	$10,163.6	$9,492.0	$10,671.8	$9,966.6
123	Check for balancing:		Yes	Yes	Yes	Yes
124	**4. Financial Deficit or Surplus**		12/30/16	12/31/16	12/30/17	12/31/17
125	Incr. spon. liab.		$40.0		$42.0	
126	+ Incr. LT debt and stock		$0.0		$0.0	
127	− Previous line of credit		$0.0		$0.0	
128	+ NI minus regular dividends		$1,083.6		$1,137.8	
129	Increase in financing		$1,123.6		$1,179.8	
130	− Increase in operating assets		$452.0		$474.6	
131	Amount of deficit or surplus financing:		$671.6		$705.2	
132	Line of credit		$0.0	$0.0	$0.0	$0.0
133	Short-term investment		$671.6	$0.0	$705.2	$0.0
134	Special dividend		$0.0	$671.6	$0.0	$705.2

(continued)

Notes:

[a]All significant digits are used in calculations, but numbers in the figure are rounded, so columns may not total exactly.
[b]To simplify the example, we assume any short-term investments are held for only part of the year and earn no interest.
[c]If there is a financial surplus, it is shown as a short-term investment on December 30. These funds are distributed to investors on December 31, so the balance of short-term investments goes to zero on December 31.
[d]Because no special dividends have been paid out as of December 30, the retained earnings balance for that date is equal to the previous year's retained earnings balance plus the current year's net income less the regular dividends. When short-term investments are sold and their proceeds are used to make the special cash dividend payments on December 31, the balance of retained earnings is reduced by the amount of the total dividend payments (which is equal to the regular dividend and the reduction in short-term investments that funded the special dividend).

its financial statements. The forecasted financial statements for the next 2 years are shown in the figure. (The file *Ch15 Tool Kit.xls* shows 4 years of projected statements.) Benson has no debt, so its interest expense is zero.

Section 4 of Figure 15-1 shows the identification and elimination of any financing deficit or surplus using the same methods we described in Chapter 9. The increase in financing is the sum of the increase in spontaneous financing (the sum of accounts payable and accruals), external financing (the increase in long-term debt and common stock), and internal financing (net income less any regular dividends); also, we subtract any beginning of year balance for the line of credit because Benson must pay off the line of credit each year even if it draws on it the next year. The increase in operating assets is the increase in all assets except the short-term investments. We subtract the increase in operating assets from the increase in financing. If the difference is negative, there is a financing deficit that must be met by drawing on the line of credit. If the difference is positive, there is a financing surplus that will be used by paying a special dividend.

We show balance sheets in Figure 15-1 for both December 30 and 31 of each year to better illustrate the impact of the distribution, which we assume occurs once each year on December 31.[20] We assume that the financing surplus is temporarily used to purchase short-term investments that are held until the distribution to shareholders. At the time of the distribution, all short-term investments will be converted to cash and paid out as special dividends. Thus, the 2016 short-term investments total $671.6 on December 30 and drop to zero on December 31, when they are distributed to investors.[21] Observe that the retained earnings account also drops by $671.6 on December 31 as funds that were previously retained are paid out as dividends.

Now let's consider the case of stock repurchases. The projected income statements and asset portion of the balance sheets are the same whether the distribution is in the form of dividends or repurchases, but this is not true for the liabilities-and-equity side of the balance sheet. Figure 15-2 reports the case in which distributions are in the form of stock repurchases. As in the case of dividend distributions, the December 30 balance of the retained earnings account is equal to the previous

---

20. As we noted earlier in the chapter, when dividends are declared, a new current liability called "dividends payable" would be added to current liabilities and then retained earnings would be reduced by that amount. To simplify the example, we ignore that provision and assume that there is no balance sheet effect on the declaration date.

21. As explained previously, there is a difference between the actual payment date and the ex-dividend date. To simplify the example, we assume that the dividends are paid on the ex-dividend date to the shareholder owning the stock the day before it goes ex-dividend.

FIGURE 15-2	Projecting Benson Conglomerate's Liabilities & Equity: Distributions as Stock Repurchases (Millions of Dollars)

	A	B	C	D	E	F
148				Projected		
149		12/31/2015	2016		2017	
150	Liabilities & Equity[a]		12/30	12/31	12/30	12/31
151	Accounts payable	$640.0	$672.0	$672.0	$705.6	$705.6
152	Accruals	160.0	168.0	168.0	176.4	176.4
153	Line of credit	0.0	0.0	0.0	0.0	0.0
154	Total current liabilities	$800.0	$840.0	$840.0	$882.0	$882.0
155	Long-term debt	0.0	0.0	0.0	0.0	0.0
156	Total liabilities	$800.0	$840.0	840.0	882.0	882.0
157	Common stock	2,400.0	2,400.0	2,400.0	2,400.0	2,400.0
158	Treasury stock[b]	0.0	0.0	(671.6)	(671.6)	(1,376.8)
159	Retained earnings[c]	5,840.0	6,923.6	6,923.6	8,061.4	8,061.4
160	Total common equity	$8,240.0	$9,323.6	8,652.0	9,789.8	9,084.6
161	Total liabilities & equity	$9,040.0	$10,163.6	9,492.0	10,671.8	9,966.6

Notes:

[a]All significant digits are used in calculations, but numbers in the figure are rounded and so columns may not total exactly. See Figure 15-1 for income statements and assets.

[b]When distributions are made as repurchases, a negative entry equal to the dollar amount of the repurchase is made in the treasury stock account at the time of the repurchase, which occurs when short-term investments are liquidated and used to repurchase stock.

[c]No funds are paid out in dividends, so the retained earnings balance is equal to the previous balance plus the year's net income (all net income is being retained).

Microsoft Excel® is a registered trademark of Microsoft Corporation. © 2014 Microsoft.

retained earnings balance plus the year's net income, because all income is retained. However, when funds in the short-term investments account are used to repurchase stock on December 31, the repurchase is shown as a negative entry in the treasury stock account.

To summarize, the projected income statements and assets are identical, whether the distribution is made in the form of dividends or stock repurchases. There also is no difference in liabilities. However, distributions as dividends reduce the retained earnings account, whereas stock repurchases reduce the treasury stock account.

See **Ch15 Tool Kit.xls** on the textbook's Web site.

15-9b The Residual Distribution Model

Figures 15-1 and 15-2 illustrate the residual distribution model in Equation 15-1 as applied to entire financial statements. The projected capital budget is equal to the net addition to total operating capital from the projected balance sheets in Figure 15-1. For example, for 2016 the capital budget is:

$$
\begin{aligned}
\text{Capital budget} &= (\Delta\text{Cash} + \Delta\text{Accounts receivable} + \Delta\text{Inventories} \\
&\quad + \Delta\text{Net plant \& equipment}) \\
&\quad - (\Delta\text{Accounts payable} + \Delta\text{Accruals}) \\
&= (\$84 - \$80) + (\$1,260 - \$1,200) + (\$1,008 - \$960) \\
&\quad + (\$7,140 - \$6,800) - (\$672 - \$640) - (\$168 - \$160) \\
&= \$452 - \$40 = \$412
\end{aligned}
$$

With a 100% target equity ratio and net income of $1,083.6, the residual distribution is:

$$\text{Distribution} = \text{Net income} - [(\text{Target equity ratio})(\text{Total capital budget})]$$
$$= \$1{,}083.6 - [(100\%)(\$412)]$$
$$= \$1{,}083.6 - \$412 = \$671.6$$

Notice that this is the same as the financial surplus we calculated in Figure 15-1.

15-9c The Impact of Distributions on Intrinsic Value

What is the impact of cash distributions on intrinsic value? We use Benson Conglomerate to illustrate the answer to that question next.

Free Cash Flow

We begin by calculating expected free cash flows and performance measures as shown in Figure 15-3. Notice that Benson's expected return on invested capital is

FIGURE 15-3	Benson Conglomerate's Value of Operations Under Different Distribution Methods (Millions of Dollars)

	A	B	C	D	E	F	G	H	I	J
199	WACC = 12.0%			Projected						
200		12/31/2015		12/31/2016		12/31/2017		12/31/2018		12/31/2019
201	1. Calculation of Free Cash Flow									
202	Operating current assets[a]	$2,240.00		$2,352.00		$2,469.60		$2,593.08		$2,722.73
203	Operating current liabilities[b]	800.00		840.00		882.00		926.10		972.41
204	NOWC[c]	$1,440.00		$1,512.00		$1,587.60		$1,666.98		$1,750.33
205	Net plant & equipment	6,800.00		7,140.00		7,497.00		7,871.85		8,265.44
206	Net operating capital[d]	$8,240.00		$8,652.00		$9,084.60		$9,538.83		$10,015.77
207	NOPAT[e]	$1,032.00		$1,083.60		$1,137.78		$1,194.67		$1,254.40
208	Inv. in operating capital[f]			412.00		432.60		454.23		476.94
209	Free cash flow (FCF)[g]			$671.60		$705.18		$740.44		$777.46
210	2. Performance Measures	12/31/2015		12/31/2016		12/31/2017		12/31/2018		12/31/2019
211	Expected ROIC[h]			13.15%		13.15%		13.15%		13.15%
212	Growth in FCF			na		5.00%		5.00%		5.00%
213	Growth in sales			5.00%		5.00%		5.00%		5.00%
214	3. Valuation	12/31/2015		12/31/2016		12/31/2017		12/31/2018		12/31/2019
215	Horizon value at 2019 (after FCF paid)[i]									$11,661.91
216	Value of operations[j]	$9,594.29		$10,074.00		$10,577.70		$11,106.58		$11,661.91

Notes:
[a] Sum of cash, accounts receivable, and inventories.
[b] Sum of accounts payable and accruals.
[c] Net operating working capital is equal to operating current assets minus operating current liabilities.
[d] Sum of NOWC and net plant & equipment.
[e] Net operating profit after taxes = (EBIT)(1 − T). In this example, NOPAT is equal to net income because there is no interest expense or interest income.
[f] Change in net operating capital from previous year.
[g] FCF = NOPAT − Investment in operating capital.
[h] Expected return on invested capital = NOPAT divided by beginning capital.
[i] Horizon value at 2019 is immediately after the FCF at 2019 has been paid, which makes the horizon value at 2019 the present value of all FCF from 2020 and beyond when discounted back to 12/31/2019: $HV_{2019} = [FCF_{2019}(1+g)]/(WACC-g)$.
[j] Value of operations before horizon = $V_{op(t)} = (V_{op(t+1)} + FCF_{t+1})/(1+WACC)$.

greater than the cost of capital, indicating that the managers are creating value for their shareholders. Also notice that the company is beyond its high-growth phase, so FCF is positive and growing at a constant rate of 5%. Therefore, Benson has cash flow available for distribution to investors.

The Value of Operations

Figure 15-3 also shows the horizon value at 2019, which is the value immediately after the payment of the FCF at 2019—it is the value of all FCF from 2020 and beyond discounted back to 12/31/2019. We can use the projected FCFs to determine the horizon value at the end of the projections and then estimate the value of operations for each year prior to the horizon. For Benson, the horizon value on December 31, 2019, is:

$$HV_{12/31/19} = \frac{FCF_{12/31/19}(1 + g)}{WACC - g}$$

$$= \frac{\$777.46(1 + 0.05)}{0.12 - 0.05} = \$11,661.9$$

The value of operations on 12/31/2019 is the present value of all FCF from 2020 and beyond discounted back to 12/31/2019, which is exactly the definition of the horizon value on 12/31/2019. Therefore, the value of operations on 12/31/2019 is $11,661.9.

To estimate the value of operations at dates prior to the horizon, consider the following logic. Suppose you own the operations on 12/31/2018 and have just received the 2018 FCF. You plan to sell the operations in a year, after receiving the 2019 FCF. Your expected cash flows in 1 year would be the 2019 FCF and the value at which you expect to sell the operations on 12/31/2019. What is the expected sales price of the operations on 12/31/19? It is the value of all cash flows in 2020 and beyond, discounted back to 12/31/2019, which is the definition of the previously calculated value of 12/31/2019 value of operations. Therefore, the value of operations on 12/31/2018 (after the 2018 FCF has been paid) is the sum of the 12/31/2019 FCF and value of operations, discounted back 1 year at the WACC:

$$V_{op(12/31/18)} = \frac{FCF_{12/31/19} + V_{op(12/31/19)}}{(1 + WACC)}$$

$$= \frac{\$777.46 + \$11,661.9}{1 + 0.12} = \$11,106.6$$

We can repeat this process to obtain the current value of operations (i.e., as of December 31, 2015): $9,549.29.

Notice that the choice of how to distribute the residual does not affect the value of operations because the distribution choice does not affect the projected free cash flows.

The Intrinsic Stock Price: Distributions as Dividends.

Figure 15-4 shows the intrinsic stock price each year using the corporate valuation approach described in Chapter 8. Section 1 provides calculations assuming cash is distributed via dividends. (See *Ch15 Tool Kit.xls* for projections for 4 years.) Notice

FIGURE 15-4   Benson Conglomerate's Intrinsic Stock Price for Each Method of Distribution (Millions of Dollars)

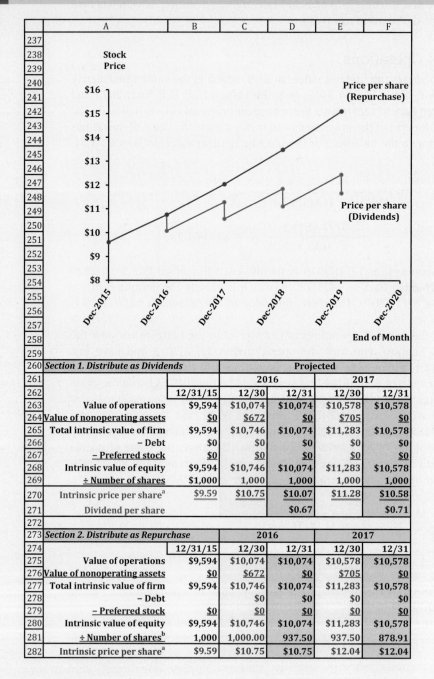

	12/31/15	2016		2017	
Section 1. Distribute as Dividends		**Projected**			
		2016		**2017**	
	12/31/15	**12/30**	**12/31**	**12/30**	**12/31**
Value of operations	$9,594	$10,074	$10,074	$10,578	$10,578
Value of nonoperating assets	$0	$672	$0	$705	$0
Total intrinsic value of firm	$9,594	$10,746	$10,074	$11,283	$10,578
– Debt	$0	$0	$0	$0	$0
– Preferred stock	$0	$0	$0	$0	$0
Intrinsic value of equity	$9,594	$10,746	$10,074	$11,283	$10,578
÷ Number of shares	$1,000	1,000	1,000	1,000	1,000
Intrinsic price per share[a]	$9.59	$10.75	$10.07	$11.28	$10.58
Dividend per share			$0.67		$0.71

	12/31/15	2016		2017	
Section 2. Distribute as Repurchase		**2016**		**2017**	
	12/31/15	**12/30**	**12/31**	**12/30**	**12/31**
Value of operations	$9,594	$10,074	$10,074	$10,578	$10,578
Value of nonoperating assets	$0	$672	$0	$705	$0
Total intrinsic value of firm	$9,594	$10,746	$10,074	$11,283	$10,578
– Debt		$0	$0	$0	$0
– Preferred stock	$0	$0	$0	$0	$0
Intrinsic value of equity	$9,594	$10,746	$10,074	$11,283	$10,578
÷ Number of shares[b]	1,000	1,000.00	937.50	937.50	878.91
Intrinsic price per share[a]	$9.59	$10.75	$10.75	$12.04	$12.04

Notes:

[a]The projected intrinsic stock prices for 4 years are shown in **Ch15 Tool Kit.xls**.
[b]The number of shares after the repurchase is $n_{Post} = n_{Prior} - (Cash_{Rep}/P_{Prior})$. In this example, the entire amount of ST investments (i.e., the balance of nonoperating assets) is used to repurchase stock.

that on December 31 the intrinsic value of equity drops because the firm no longer owns the short-term investments. This causes the intrinsic stock price also to drop. In fact, the drop in stock price is equal to the dividend per share. For example, the 2016 dividend per share (DPS) is $0.67 and the drop in stock price is $10.75 − $10.07 = $0.68 ≈ $0.67. (The penny difference here is due to rounding in intermediate steps.)

Notice that if the stock price did *not* fall by the amount of the DPS, then there would be an opportunity for arbitrage. If the price were to drop by less than the DPS—say, by $0.50 to $10.25—then you could buy the stock on December 30 for $10.75, receive a DPS of $0.67 on December 31, and then immediately sell the stock for $10.25, reaping a sure profit of −$10.75 + $0.67 + $10.25 = $0.17. Of course, you'd want to implement this strategy with a million shares, not just a single share. But if everyone tried to use this strategy, the increased demand would drive up the stock price on December 30 until there was no more sure profit to be made. The reverse would happen if investors expected the stock price to fall by more than the DPS.[22]

Here is an important observation: Even though the stock price falls, shareholder wealth does not fall. For example, on December 30, a shareholder owns stock worth $10.75. On December 31, the shareholder owns stock worth $10.07 but has cash of $0.67 from the dividend, for total wealth of $10.75 (subject to rounding differences). Thus, the shareholder's wealth is the same before and after the dividend payment, with the only difference being that part of the shareholder's wealth is in the form of cash from the dividend payment.

The Intrinsic Stock Price: Distributions as Repurchases

Section 2 of Figure 15-4 provides calculations of intrinsic value for the case in which stock is repurchased. Observe that the intrinsic value of equity is the same for both methods of distributions, but the analysis of a repurchase is a little more complicated because the number of shares changes. The key to solving this additional complexity is to recognize that the repurchase does not change the stock price. If the price did change due to the repurchase, then there would be an arbitrage opportunity. For example, suppose the stock price is expected to increase after the repurchase. If this were true, then it should be possible for an investor to buy the stock the day before the repurchase and then reap a reward the very next day. Current stockholders would realize this and would refuse to sell the stock unless they were paid the price that is expected immediately after the repurchase. Now suppose the stock price is expected to fall immediately after the repurchase. In this case, current shareholders should try to sell the stock prior to the repurchase, but their actions would drive the price down to the price that is expected after the repurchase. As you can see, the repurchase itself does not change the stock price.

In summary, the events leading up to a repurchase generate cash (the sale of a division, a recapitalization, or the generation of high free cash flows from operations). Generating cash can certainly change the stock price, but the repurchase itself doesn't change the stock price. We can use this fact to determine the number of shares repurchased. First, though, we must define some notation.

---

22. We ignore taxes in this description. Empirical evidence suggests that the actual drop in stock price is equal to about 90% of the DPS, with all pre-tax profit being eliminated by taxes.

n_{Prior} = The number of shares outstanding prior to the repurchase

n_{Post} = The number of shares outstanding after the repurchase

S_{Prior} = The intrinsic value of equity prior to the repurchase

S_{Post} = The intrinsic value of equity after the repurchase

P_{Prior} = The intrinsic stock price prior to the repurchase

P_{Post} = The intrinsic stock price after the repurchase

$P = P_{\text{Prior}} = P_{\text{Post}}$ = The intrinsic stock price during, before, and after the repurchase

Cash_{Rep} = The amount of cash used to repurchase shares

As we explained, the repurchase itself doesn't change the stock price. Therefore, the number of shares repurchased is equal to the amount of cash used to repurchase stocks divided by the stock price:

(15–2)

$$\text{Number of shares repurchased} = n_{\text{Prior}} - n_{\text{Post}} = \frac{\text{Cash}_{\text{Rep}}}{P_{\text{Prior}}}$$

We can rewrite Equation 15-2 to find an expression for the number of shares after the repurchase:

(15–3)

$$n_{\text{Post}} = n_{\text{Prior}} - \frac{\text{Cash}_{\text{Rep}}}{P_{\text{Prior}}}$$

$$= n_{\text{Prior}} - \frac{\text{Cash}_{\text{Rep}}}{S_{\text{Prior}}/n_{\text{Prior}}}$$

$$= n_{\text{Prior}}\left(1 - \frac{\text{Cash}_{\text{Rep}}}{S_{\text{Prior}}}\right)$$

For example, as shown in Section 2 of Figure 15-4, the intrinsic stock price on December 30, 2016, the day before the repurchase, is \$10.75, and there are 1,000 shares of stock. Using Equation 15-3, the number of shares after the repurchase is equal to:

$$n_{\text{Post}} = n_{\text{Prior}} - \frac{\text{Cash}_{\text{Rep}}}{P_{\text{Prior}}}$$

$$= 1,000 - \frac{\$671.6}{\$10.75}$$

$$= 1,000 - 62.47 = 937.5$$

Section 2 of Figure 15-4 also shows that on December 31, 2016, the intrinsic value of equity prior to the repurchase, S_{Prior}, drops from $10,745.6 to a value after the repurchase, S_{Post}, of $10,074.0. This decrease in the intrinsic value of equity is equal to the amount of the cash used in the repurchase, $671.6. However, the stock price remains at $10.75 after the repurchase because the number of shares also drops:

$$P_{Post} = \frac{S_{Post}}{n_{Post}} = \frac{\$10,074}{937.5} = \$10.75$$

How does the repurchase affect shareholder wealth? The aggregate value of outstanding stock drops after the repurchase, but the aggregate wealth of the shareholders remains unchanged. Before the repurchase, shareholders own a total of equity worth S_{Prior}, $10,745.6. After the repurchase, shareholders own a total of equity worth S_{Post}, $10,074, but they also own cash (received in the repurchase) in the amount of $671.6, for a total wealth of $10,745.6. Thus, the repurchase does not change shareholders' aggregate wealth; it only changes the form in which they hold wealth (all stock versus a combination of stock and cash).

Comparing Intrinsic Stock Prices: Dividends vs. Repurchases

The chart at the top of Figure 15-4 shows the projected intrinsic stock prices for the two different distribution methods. Notice that the prices begin at the same level (because Benson has not yet begun making any distributions). The price for the repurchase scenario climbs smoothly and grows to a higher level than does the price for the dividend scenario, which drops by the DPS each time it is paid. However, the number of shares falls in the repurchase scenario. As shown in Rows 268 and 280 of the figure, the intrinsic values of equity are identical for both distribution methods.

This example illustrates three key results: (1) Ignoring possible tax effects and signals, the total market value of equity will be the same whether a firm pays dividends or repurchases stock. (2) The repurchase itself does not change the stock price (compared with using the cash to buy marketable securities) at the time of the repurchase, although it does reduce the number of outstanding shares. (3) Because a company that repurchases stock will have fewer shares than an otherwise identical company that pays dividends, the stock price of a repurchasing company will climb faster than that of the dividend-paying company. However, the total return to the two companies' shareholders will be the same.[23]

---

23. For more on repurchases, see David J. Denis, "Defensive Changes in Corporate Payout Policy: Share Repurchases and Special Dividends," *Journal of Finance,* December 1990, pp. 1433–1456; Gerald D. Gay, Jayant R. Kale, and Thomas H. Noe, "Share Repurchase Mechanisms: A Comparative Analysis of Efficacy, Shareholder Wealth and Corporate Control Effects," *Financial Management,* Spring 1991, pp. 44–59; Jeffry M. Netter and Mark L. Mitchell, "Stock-Repurchase Announcements and Insider Transactions after the October 1987 Stock Market Crash," *Financial Management,* Autumn 1989, pp. 84–96; William Pugh and John S. Jahera, Jr., "Stock Repurchases and Excess Returns: An Empirical Examination," *The Financial Review,* February 1990, pp. 127–142; and James W. Wansley, William R. Lane, and Salil Sarkar, "Managements' View on Share Repurchase and Tender Offer Premiums," *Financial Management,* Autumn 1989, pp. 97–110.

SELF TEST

Explain how a repurchase changes the number of shares but not the stock price.

A firm's most recent FCF was $2.4 million, and its FCF is expected to grow at a constant rate of 5%. The firm's WACC is 14%, and it has 2 million shares outstanding. The firm has $12 million in short-term investments that it plans to liquidate and then distribute in a stock repurchase; the firm has no other financial investments or debt. Verify that the value of operations is $28 million. Immediately prior to the repurchase, what are the intrinsic value of equity and the intrinsic stock price? **($40 million; $20/share)** How many shares will be repurchased? **(0.6 million)** How many shares will remain after the repurchase? **(1.4 million)** Immediately after the repurchase, what are the intrinsic value of equity and the intrinsic stock price? **($28 million; $20/share)**

15-10 The Pros and Cons of Dividends and Repurchases

The advantages of repurchases can be listed as follows.

1. Repurchase announcements are viewed as positive signals by investors because the repurchase is often motivated by management's belief that the firm's shares are undervalued.
2. Stockholders have a choice when the firm distributes cash by repurchasing stock—they can sell or not sell. Those stockholders who need cash can sell back some of their shares while others can simply retain their stock. With a cash dividend, on the other hand, stockholders must accept a dividend payment.
3. Dividends are "sticky" in the short run because management is usually reluctant to raise the dividend if the increase cannot be maintained in the future, and cutting cash dividends is always avoided because of the negative signal it gives. Hence, if the excess cash flow is thought to be only temporary, management may prefer making the distribution in the form of a stock repurchase to declaring an increased cash dividend that cannot be maintained.
4. Companies can use the residual model to set a *target cash distribution* level and then divide the distribution into a *dividend component* and a *repurchase component*. The dividend payout ratio will be relatively low, but the dividend itself will be relatively secure, and it will grow as a result of the declining number of shares outstanding. The company has more flexibility in adjusting the total distribution than it would if the entire distribution were in the form of cash dividends, because repurchases can be varied from year to year without giving off adverse signals.
5. Repurchases can be used to produce large-scale changes in capital structures. For example, several years ago PepsiCo borrowed $4 billion to use in its stock repurchase plan. The repurchases totaled over 4% of the firm's market value, allowing PepsiCo to quickly change its capital structure.

6. Companies that use stock options as an important component of employee compensation usually repurchase shares in the secondary market and then use those shares when employees exercise their options. This technique allows companies to avoid issuing new shares and thus diluting earnings.

Repurchases have three principal disadvantages.

1. Stockholders may not be indifferent between dividends and capital gains, and the price of the stock might benefit more from cash dividends than from repurchases. Cash dividends are generally dependable, but repurchases are not.
2. The *selling* stockholders may not be fully aware of all the implications of a repurchase, or they may not have all the pertinent information about the corporation's present and future activities. However, in order to avoid potential stockholder suits, firms generally announce repurchase programs before embarking on them.
3. The corporation may pay too much for the repurchased stock—to the disadvantage of remaining stockholders. If the firm seeks to acquire a relatively large amount of its stock, then the price may be bid above its equilibrium level and then fall after the firm ceases its repurchase operations.

When all the pros and cons on stock repurchases versus dividends have been totaled, where do we stand? Our conclusions may be summarized as follows.

1. Because of the deferred tax on capital gains, repurchases have a tax advantage over dividends as a way to distribute income to stockholders. This advantage is reinforced by the fact that repurchases provide cash to stockholders who want cash while allowing those who do not need current cash to delay its receipt. On the other hand, dividends are more dependable and thus are better suited for those who need a steady source of income.
2. The danger of signaling effects requires that a company not have volatile dividend payments, which would lower investors' confidence in the company and adversely affect its cost of equity and its stock price. However, cash flows vary over time, as do investment opportunities, so the "proper" dividend in the residual model sense varies. To get around this problem, a company can set its dividend low enough to keep dividend payments from constraining operations and then use repurchases on a more or less regular basis to distribute excess cash. Such a procedure will provide regular, dependable dividends plus additional cash flow to those stockholders who want it.
3. Repurchases are also useful when a firm wants to make a large shift in its capital structure, wants to distribute cash from a one-time event such as the sale of a division, or wants to obtain shares for use in an employee stock option plan.

What are some advantages and disadvantages of stock repurchases?

How can stock repurchases help a company operate in accordance with the residual distribution model?

SELF TEST

DIVIDEND YIELDS AROUND THE WORLD

D ividend yields vary considerably in different stock markets throughout the world. In 1999, dividend yields in the United States averaged 1.6% for the large blue-chip stocks in the Dow Jones Industrials, 1.2% for a broader sample of stocks in the S&P 500, and 0.3% for stocks in the NASDAQ, where high-tech firms predominate. Outside the United States, average dividend yields ranged from 5.7% in New Zealand to 0.7% in Taiwan. The accompanying table summarizes the dividend picture in 1999.

World Stock Market (Index)	Dividend Yield	World Stock Market (Index)	Dividend Yield
New Zealand	5.7%	United States (Dow Jones Industrials)	1.6%
Australia	3.1	Canada (TSE 300)	1.5
Britain (FTSE 100)	2.4	United States (S&P 500)	1.2
Hong Kong	2.4	Mexico	1.1
France	2.1	Japan (Nikkei)	0.7
Germany	2.1	Taiwan	0.7
Belgium	2.0	United States (NASDAQ)	0.3
Singapore	1.7		

Source: From Alexandra Eadie, "On the Grid Looking for Dividend Yield around the World," *The Globe and Mail,* June 23, 1999, p. B16. Eadie's source was Bloomberg Financial Services. Reprinted with permission from *The Globe and Mail.*

15-11 Other Factors Influencing Distributions

In this section, we discuss several other factors that affect the dividend decision. These factors may be grouped into two broad categories: (1) constraints on dividend payments and (2) availability and cost of alternative sources of capital.

15-11a Constraints

Constraints on dividend payments can affect distributions, as the following examples illustrate.

1. *Bond indentures.* Debt contracts often limit dividend payments to earnings generated after the loan was granted. Also, debt contracts often stipulate that no dividends can be paid unless the current ratio, times-interest-earned ratio, and other safety ratios exceed stated minimums.
2. *Preferred stock restrictions.* Typically, common dividends cannot be paid if the company has omitted its preferred dividend. The preferred arrearages must be satisfied before common dividends can be resumed.
3. *Impairment of capital rule.* Dividend payments cannot exceed the balance sheet item "retained earnings." This legal restriction, known as the "impairment of capital rule," is designed to protect creditors. Without the rule, a company in trouble might distribute most of its assets to stockholders and leave its debt-holders out in the cold. (*Liquidating dividends* can be paid out of capital, but

they must be indicated as such and must not reduce capital below the limits stated in debt contracts.)

4. *Availability of cash.* Cash dividends can be paid only with cash, so a shortage of cash in the bank can restrict dividend payments. However, the ability to borrow can offset this factor.

5. *Penalty tax on improperly accumulated earnings.* To prevent wealthy individuals from using corporations to avoid personal taxes, the Tax Code provides for a special surtax on improperly accumulated income. Thus, if the IRS can demonstrate that a firm's dividend payout ratio is being deliberately held down to help its stockholders avoid personal taxes, the firm is subject to heavy penalties. This factor is generally relevant only to privately owned firms.

15-11b **Alternative Sources of Capital**

The second factor that influences the dividend decision is the cost and availability of alternative sources of capital.

1. *Cost of selling new stock.* If a firm needs to finance a given level of investment, it can obtain equity by retaining earnings or by issuing new common stock. If flotation costs (including any negative signaling effects of a stock offering) are high then the required return on new equity, r_e, will be well above the required return on internally generated equity, r_s, making it better to set a low payout ratio and to finance through retention rather than through the sale of new common stock. On the other hand, a high dividend payout ratio is more feasible for a firm whose flotation costs are low. Flotation costs differ among firms—for example, the flotation percentage is generally higher for small firms, so they tend to set low payout ratios.

2. *Ability to substitute debt for equity.* A firm can finance a given level of investment with either debt or equity. As just described, low stock flotation costs permit a more flexible dividend policy because equity can be raised either by retaining earnings or by selling new stock. A similar situation holds for debt policy: If the firm can adjust its debt ratio without raising costs sharply, then it can pay the expected dividend—even if earnings fluctuate—by increasing its debt ratio.

3. *Control.* If management is concerned about maintaining control, it may be reluctant to sell new stock; hence, the company may retain more earnings than it otherwise would. However, if stockholders want higher dividends and a proxy fight looms, then the dividend will be increased.

What constraints affect dividend policy?

How do the availability and cost of outside capital affect dividend policy?

SELF TEST

15-12 **Summarizing the Distribution Policy Decision**

In practice, the distribution decision is made jointly with capital structure and capital budgeting decisions. The underlying reason for joining these decisions is asymmetric information—managers know more than investors know about their company's prospects. Here is how asymmetric information influences managerial actions.

1. In general, managers do not want to issue new common stock. First, new common stock involves issuance costs—commissions, fees, and so on—and those costs can be avoided by reinvesting earnings to finance equity needs. Second, as we will explain in Chapter 16, asymmetric information causes investors to view new common stock issues as negative signals and thus lowers expectations regarding the firm's future prospects. The end result is that the announcement of a new stock issue usually leads to a decrease in the stock price. Considering the total costs due to issuance and asymmetric information, managers prefer to use retained earnings as the primary source of new equity.

2. Dividend changes provide signals about managers' beliefs concerning their firms' future prospects. Thus, dividend reductions generally have a significant negative effect on a firm's stock price. Because managers recognize this, they try to set dollar dividends low enough so there is only a remote chance the dividend will have to be reduced in the future.

The effects of asymmetric information suggest that, to the extent possible, managers should avoid both new common stock sales and dividend cuts, because both actions tend to lower the stock price. Thus, in setting distribution policy, managers should begin by considering the firm's future investment opportunities relative to its projected internal sources of funds. The target capital structure also plays a part, but because it is a *range*, firms can vary their actual capital structures somewhat from year to year. Because it is best to avoid issuing new common stock, the target long-term payout ratio should be designed to permit the firm to meet all of its equity capital requirements by retaining earnings. In effect, *managers should use the residual model to set dividends, but in a long-term framework*. Finally, the current dollar dividend should be set so that there is an extremely low probability that the dividend, once set, will ever have to be lowered or omitted.

Of course, the dividend decision is made during the planning process, so there is uncertainty about future investment opportunities and operating cash flows. The actual payout ratio in any year will therefore likely be above or below the firm's long-range target. However, the dollar dividend should be maintained, or increased as planned, unless the firm's financial condition deteriorates to the point at which the planned policy simply cannot be maintained. A steady or increasing stream of dividends over the long run signals that the firm's financial condition is under control. Moreover, investor uncertainty is decreased by stable dividends, so a steady dividend stream reduces the negative effect of a new stock issue—should one become absolutely necessary.

In general, firms with superior investment opportunities should set lower payouts, and hence retain more earnings, than firms with poor investment opportunities. The degree of uncertainty also influences the decision. If there is a great deal of uncertainty regarding the forecasts of free cash flows, which are defined here as the firm's operating cash flows minus mandatory equity investments, then it is best to be conservative and to set a lower current dollar dividend. Also, firms with postponable investment opportunities can afford to set a higher dollar dividend, because in times of stress investments can be postponed for a year or two, thus increasing the cash available for dividends. Finally, firms whose cost of capital is largely unaffected by changes in the debt ratio can also afford to set a higher payout ratio, because in times of stress they can more easily issue additional debt to maintain the capital budgeting program without having to cut dividends or issue stock.

The net result of these factors is that many firms' dividend policies are consistent with the life-cycle theory in which younger firms with many investment opportunities but relatively low cash flows reinvest their earnings so that they can avoid the large flotation costs associated with raising external capital.[24] As firms mature and begin to generate more cash flow, they tend to pay more dividends and issue more debt as a way to "bond" their cash flows (as described in Chapter 16) and thereby reduce the agency costs of free cash flow.

What do executives think? A recent survey indicates financial executives believe that it is extremely important to *maintain* dividends but much less important to initiate or increase dividend payments. In general, they view the cash distribution decision as being much less important than capital budgeting decisions. Managers like the flexibility provided by repurchases instead of regular dividends. They tend to repurchase shares when they believe their stock price is undervalued, and they believe that shareholders view repurchases as positive signals. In general, the different taxation of dividends and repurchases is not a major factor when a company chooses how to distribute cash to investors.[25]

> Describe the decision process for distribution policy and dividend payout. Be sure to discuss all the factors that influence this decision.
>
> **SELF TEST**

15-13 Stock Splits and Stock Dividends

The rationale for stock splits and dividends can best be explained through an example. We will use Porter Electronic Controls Inc., a $700 million electronic components manufacturer, for this purpose. Since its inception, Porter's markets have been expanding, and the company has enjoyed growth in sales and earnings. Some of its earnings have been paid out in dividends, but some are also retained each year, causing its earnings per share and stock price to grow. The company began its life with only a few thousand shares outstanding, and after some years of growth the stock price was high. Porter's CFO thought this high price limited the number of investors who could buy the stock, which reduced demand for the stock and thus kept the firm's total market value below what it could be if there were more shares, at a lower price, outstanding. To correct this situation, Porter "split its stock," as we describe next.

15-13a Stock Splits

Although there is little empirical evidence to support the contention, there is nevertheless a widespread belief in financial circles that an *optimal price range* exists for stocks. "Optimal" means that if the price is within this range, the firm's value will be

---

24. For a test of the life-cycle theory, see Harry DeAngelo, Linda DeAngelo, and René Stulz, "Dividend Policy and the Earned/Contributed Capital Mix: A Test of the Life-Cycle Theory," *Journal of Financial Economics*, August 2006, pp. 227–254.

25. See Alon Brav, John R. Graham, Campbell R. Harvey, and Roni Michaely, "Payout Policy in the 21st Century," *Journal of Financial Economics*, September 2005, pp. 483–527.

THE GLOBAL ECONOMIC CRISIS

Talk about a Split Personality!

Sun Microsystems once was among the highest of the high-flying companies in the tech boom of the 1990s. Sun went public in 1986 and its stock price grew rapidly, with Sun declaring seven different 2-1 stock splits between 1988 and 2000. Without these splits, Sun's stock price would have grown from about $30 in late 1988 to over $1,700 in mid-2000, a staggering return of over 40% per year! However, Sun's fortunes fell when the tech bubble burst, and the company never recovered. With its stock price languishing around $5, Sun declared a 1-4 reverse stock split in late 2007, which boosted the stock price to over $20, but subsequently it

sank into the $3–$4 range by the spring of 2009. In April 2009, Sun announced that it had agreed to be acquired by Oracle for about $9.50 per share. This would have been only $2.375 = $9.50/4 if not for the reverse split in 2007, quite a fall from its former highs.

Reverse splits were rare when Sun Microsystems declared its split in 2007, but now Sun might have plenty of company caused by the economic crisis. Such well-known companies as Citigroup and Duke Energy effected reverse splits in 2011 and 2012, and many more are potential candidates. In fact, 36 companies trading on the NASDAQ had stock prices of less than a dollar per share in April 2014.

maximized. Many observers, including Porter's management, believe the best range for most stocks is from $20 to $80 per share. Accordingly, if the price of Porter's stock rose to $80, management would probably declare a 2-for-1 **stock split**, thus doubling the number of shares outstanding, halving the earnings and dividends per share, and thereby lowering the stock price. Each stockholder would have more shares, but each share would be worth less. If the post-split price were $40, then Porter's stockholders would be exactly as well off as before the split. However, if the stock price were to stabilize above $40, stockholders would be better off. Stock splits can be of any size—for example, the stock could be split 2-for-1, 3-for-1, 1.5-for-1, or in any other way.

Sometimes a company will have a **reverse split**. For example, the financial services company Citigroup (C) was trading in the $55 per share range in 2007 prior to the global financial meltdown. After the meltdown, the stock traded as low as $1 in 2009 and had recovered only to $4.52 per share by May 6, 2011. On May 9, 2011 Citigroup had a 1-10 reverse stock split before trading began, with its shareholders exchanging 10 shares of stock for a single new share. In theory, the stock price should have increased by a factor of 10, to around $45.20, and Citigroup indeed closed that day at a price of $44.16. Even though Citigroup was again trading in the same per-share price range as it did before the global financial meltdown, with only 1/10 the number of shares outstanding, its market value of equity was still less than 10% of what it had been in 2007.

15-13b **Stock Dividends**

Stock dividends are similar to stock splits in that they "divide the pie into smaller slices" without affecting the fundamental position of the current stockholders. On a 5% stock dividend, the holder of 100 shares would receive an additional 5 shares (without cost); on a 20% stock dividend, the same holder would receive 20 new shares, and so on. Again, the total number of shares is increased, so earnings, dividends, and price per share all decline.

If a firm wants to reduce the price of its stock, should it use a stock split or a stock dividend? Stock splits are generally used after a sharp price run-up to produce a large price reduction. Stock dividends used on a regular annual basis will keep the stock price more or less constrained. For example, if a firm's earnings and dividends were growing at about 10% per year, its stock price would tend to go up at about the same rate, and it would soon be outside the desired trading range. A 10% annual stock dividend would maintain the stock price within the optimal trading range. Note, however, that small stock dividends create bookkeeping problems and unnecessary expenses, so firms today use stock splits far more often than stock dividends.[26]

15-13c **Effect on Stock Prices**

If a company splits its stock or declares a stock dividend, will this increase the market value of its stock? Many empirical studies have sought to answer this question. Here is a summary of their findings.

1. On average, the price of a company's stock rises shortly after it announces a stock split or a stock dividend.
2. However, these price increases are probably due to signaling rather than a desire for stock splits or dividends per se. Only managers who think future earnings will be higher tend to split stocks, so investors often view the announcement of a stock split as a positive signal. Thus, it is the signal of favorable prospects for earnings and dividends that causes the price to increase.
3. If a company announces a stock split or stock dividend, its price will tend to rise. However, if during the next few months it does not announce an increase in earnings and dividends, then its stock price will drop back to the earlier level.
4. As we noted earlier, brokerage commissions are generally higher in percentage terms on lower-priced stocks. This means that it is more expensive to trade low-priced than high-priced stocks—which, in turn, means that stock splits may reduce the liquidity of a company's shares. This particular piece of evidence suggests that stock splits/dividends might actually be harmful, although a lower price does mean that more investors can afford to trade in round lots (100 shares), which carry lower commissions than do odd lots (fewer than 100 shares).

What can we conclude from all this? From a purely economic standpoint, stock dividends and splits are just additional pieces of paper. However, they provide management with a relatively low-cost way of signaling that the firm's prospects look good.[27] Further, we should note that since few large, publicly owned stocks sell at

---

26. Accountants treat stock splits and stock dividends somewhat differently. For example, in a 2-for-1 stock split, the number of shares outstanding is doubled and the par value is halved. With a stock dividend, a bookkeeping entry is made transferring "retained earnings" to "common stock."

27. For more on stock splits and stock dividends, see H. Kent Baker, Aaron L. Phillips, and Gary E. Powell, "The Stock Distribution Puzzle: A Synthesis of the Literature on Stock Splits and Stock Dividends," *Financial Practice and Education,* Spring/Summer 1995, pp. 24–37; Maureen McNichols and Ajay Dravid, "Stock Dividends, Stock Splits, and Signaling," *Journal of Finance,* July 1990, pp. 857–879; and David R. Peterson and Pamela P. Peterson, "A Further Understanding of Stock Distributions: The Case of Reverse Stock Splits," *Journal of Financial Research,* Fall 1992, pp. 189–205.

prices above several hundred dollars, we simply do not know what the effect would be if Microsoft, Walmart, Hewlett-Packard, and other highly successful firms had never split their stocks and consequently sold at prices in the thousands or even tens of thousands of dollars. All in all, it probably makes sense to employ stock splits (or stock dividends) when a firm's prospects are favorable, especially if the price of its stock has gone beyond the normal trading range.[28]

SELF TEST

What are stock splits and stock dividends?

How do stock splits and dividends affect stock prices?

In what situations should managers consider the use of stock splits?

In what situations should managers consider the use of stock dividends?

Suppose you have 1,000 common shares of Burnside Bakeries. The EPS is $6.00, the DPS is $3.00, and the stock sells for $90 per share. Burnside announces a 3-for-1 split. Immediately after the split, how many shares will you have? **(3,000)** What will the adjusted EPS and DPS be? **($2 and $1)** What would you expect the stock price to be? **($30)**

15-14 Dividend Reinvestment Plans

During the 1970s, most large companies instituted **dividend reinvestment plans (DRIPs)**, under which stockholders can choose to automatically reinvest their dividends in the stock of the paying corporation. Today most large companies offer DRIPs; participation rates vary considerably, but about 25% of the average firm's shareholders are enrolled. There are two types of DRIPs: (1) plans that involve only "old stock" that is already outstanding and (2) plans that involve newly issued stock. In either case, the stockholder must pay taxes on the amount of the dividends, even though stock rather than cash is received.

Under both types of DRIPs, stockholders choose between continuing to receive dividend checks or having the company use the dividends to buy more stock in the corporation. Under the "old stock" type of plan, if a stockholder elects reinvestment then a bank, acting as trustee, takes the total funds available for reinvestment, purchases the corporation's stock on the open market, and allocates the shares purchased to the participating stockholders' accounts on a pro rata basis. The transaction costs of buying shares (brokerage costs) are low because of volume purchases, so these plans benefit small stockholders who do not need cash dividends for current consumption.

The "new stock" type of DRIP uses the reinvested funds to buy newly issued stock; hence these plans raise new capital for the firm. AT&T, Union Carbide, and

---

28. It is interesting to note that Berkshire Hathaway (controlled by billionaire Warren Buffett) has never had a stock split, and its stock (BRKa) sold on the NYSE for $190,720 per share in April 2014. Yet in response to investment trusts that were being formed in 1996 to sell fractional units of the stock and thus—in effect—split it, Buffett himself created a new class of Berkshire Hathaway stock (Class B) now worth about 1/1,500 of a Class A (regular) share.

many other companies have used new stock plans to raise substantial amounts of new equity capital. No fees are charged to stockholders, and many companies offer stock at a discount of 3% to 5% below the actual market price. The companies offer discounts as a trade-off against flotation costs that would have been incurred if new stock had been issued through investment bankers instead of through the dividend reinvestment plans.

One interesting aspect of DRIPs is that they cause corporations to re-examine their basic dividend policies. A high participation rate in a DRIP suggests that stockholders might be better off if the firm simply reduced cash dividends, which would save stockholders some personal income taxes. Quite a few firms are surveying their stockholders to learn more about their preferences and to find out how they would react to a change in dividend policy. A more rational approach to basic dividend policy decisions may emerge from this research.

Note that companies start or stop using new stock DRIPs depending on their need for equity capital. For example, Union Carbide and AT&T recently stopped offering new stock DRIPs with a 5% discount because their needs for equity capital declined.

Some companies have expanded their DRIPs by moving to "open enrollment," whereby anyone can purchase the firm's stock directly and thus bypass brokers' commissions. ExxonMobil not only allows investors to buy their initial shares at no fee but also lets them pick up additional shares through automatic bank account withdrawals. Several plans, including ExxonMobil's, offer dividend reinvestment for individual retirement accounts, and some, such as U.S. West's, allow participants to invest weekly or monthly rather than on the quarterly dividend schedule. In all of these plans, and many others, stockholders can invest more than the dividends they are forgoing—they simply send a check to the company and buy shares without a brokerage commission. According to First Chicago Trust, which handles the paperwork for 13 million shareholder DRIP accounts, at least half of all DRIPs will offer open enrollment, extra purchases, and other expanded services within the next few years.

> What are dividend reinvestment plans?
>
> What are their advantages and disadvantages from both the stockholders' and the firm's perspectives?

SELF TEST

Summary

- **Distribution policy** involves three issues: (1) What fraction of earnings should be distributed? (2) Should the distribution be in the form of cash dividends or stock repurchases? (3) Should the firm maintain a steady, stable dividend growth rate?

- The **optimal distribution policy** strikes a balance between current dividends and future growth so as to maximize the firm's stock price.
- Miller and Modigliani (MM) developed the **dividend irrelevance theory**, which holds that a firm's dividend policy has no effect on either the value of its stock or its cost of capital.
- The **dividend preference theory**, also called the **bird-in-the-hand theory**, holds that the firm's value will be maximized by a high dividend payout ratio, because investors regard cash dividends as being less risky than potential capital gains.
- The **tax effect theory** states that because long-term capital gains are subject to lower taxes than dividends, investors prefer to have companies retain earnings rather than pay them out as dividends.
- Dividend policy should take account of the **information content of dividends (signaling)** and the **clientele effect**. The information content, or signaling, effect stems from investors regarding an unexpected dividend change as a signal of management's forecast of future earnings. The clientele effect suggests that a firm will attract investors who like the firm's dividend payout policy. Both factors should be taken into account by firms that are considering a change in dividend policy.
- In practice, dividend-paying firms follow a policy of paying a **steadily increasing dividend**. This policy provides investors with stable, dependable income, and departures from it give investors signals about management's expectations for future earnings.
- Most firms use the **residual distribution model** to set the long-run target distribution ratio at a level that will permit the firm to meet its equity requirements with retained earnings.
- Under a **stock repurchase plan**, a firm buys back some of its outstanding stock, thereby decreasing the number of shares but leaving the stock price unchanged.
- Legal constraints, investment opportunities, availability and cost of funds from other sources, and taxes are also considered when firms establish dividend policies.
- A **stock split** increases the number of shares outstanding. Normally, splits reduce the price per share in proportion to the increase in shares because splits merely "divide the pie into smaller slices." However, firms generally split their stocks only if: (1) the price is quite high and (2) management thinks the future is bright. Therefore, stock splits are often taken as positive signals and thus boost stock prices.
- A **stock dividend** is a dividend paid in additional shares rather than in cash. Both stock dividends and splits are used to keep stock prices within an "optimal" trading range.
- A **dividend reinvestment plan (DRIP)** allows stockholders to have the company automatically use dividends to purchase additional shares. DRIPs are popular because they allow stockholders to acquire additional shares without brokerage fees.

Questions

15–1 Define each of the following terms:
   a. Optimal distribution policy

b. Dividend irrelevance theory; bird-in-the-hand theory; tax effect theory

c. Information content, or signaling, hypothesis; clientele effect

d. Residual distribution model; extra dividend

e. Declaration date; holder-of-record date; ex-dividend date; payment date

f. Dividend reinvestment plan (DRIP)

g. Stock split; stock dividend; stock repurchase

15-2 How would each of the following changes tend to affect aggregate payout ratios (that is, the average for all corporations), other things held constant? Explain your answers.

a. An increase in the personal income tax rate

b. A liberalization of depreciation for federal income tax purposes—that is, faster tax write-offs

c. A rise in interest rates

d. An increase in corporate profits

e. A decline in investment opportunities

f. Permission for corporations to deduct dividends for tax purposes as they now do interest charges

g. A change in the Tax Code so that both realized and unrealized capital gains in any year were taxed at the same rate as dividends

15-3 What is the difference between a stock dividend and a stock split? As a stockholder, would you prefer to see your company declare a 100% stock dividend or a 2-for-1 split? Assume that either action is feasible.

15-4 One position expressed in the financial literature is that firms set their dividends as a residual after using income to support new investments. Explain what a residual policy implies (assuming that all distributions are in the form of dividends), illustrating your answer with a table showing how different investment opportunities could lead to different dividend payout ratios.

15-5 Indicate whether the following statements are true or false. If the statement is false, explain why.

a. If a firm repurchases its stock in the open market, the shareholders who tender the stock are subject to capital gains taxes.

b. If you own 100 shares in a company's stock and the company's stock splits 2-for-1, then you will own 200 shares in the company following the split.

c. Some dividend reinvestment plans increase the amount of equity capital available to the firm.

d. The Tax Code encourages companies to pay a large percentage of their net income in the form of dividends.

e. A company that has established a clientele of investors who prefer large dividends is unlikely to adopt a residual dividend policy.

f. If a firm follows a residual dividend policy then, holding all else constant, its dividend payout will tend to rise whenever the firm's investment opportunities improve.

Problems

Answers Appear in Appendix B

Easy Problems 1–5

15-1 **Residual Distribution Model**

Puckett Products is planning for $5 million in capital expenditures next year. Puckett's target capital structure consists of 60% debt and 40% equity. If net income next year is $3 million and Puckett follows a residual distribution policy with all distributions as dividends, what will be its dividend payout ratio?

15-2 **Residual Distribution Policy**

Petersen Company has a capital budget of $1.2 million. The company wants to maintain a target capital structure which is 60% debt and 40% equity. The company forecasts that its net income this year will be $600,000. If the company follows a residual distribution model and pays all distributions as dividends, what will be its payout ratio?

15-3 **Dividend Payout**

The Wei Corporation expects next year's net income to be $15 million. The firm's debt ratio is currently 40%. Wei has $12 million of profitable investment opportunities, and it wishes to maintain its existing debt ratio. According to the residual distribution model (assuming all payments are in the form of dividends), how large should Wei's dividend payout ratio be next year?

15-4 **Stock Repurchase**

A firm has 10 million shares outstanding with a market price of $20 per share. The firm has $25 million in extra cash (short-term investments) that it plans to use in a stock repurchase; the firm has no other financial investments or any debt. What is the firm's value of operations, and how many shares will remain after the repurchase?

15-5 **Stock Split**

JPix management is considering a stock split. JPix currently sells for $120 per share and a 3-for-2 stock split is contemplated. What will be the company's stock price following the stock split, assuming that the split has no effect on the total market value of JPix's equity?

Intermediate Problems 6–9

15-6 **External Equity Financing**

Gardial GreenLights, a manufacturer of energy-efficient lighting solutions, has had such success with its new products that it is planning to substantially expand its manufacturing capacity with a $15 million investment in new machinery. Gardial plans to maintain its current 30% debt-to-total-assets ratio for its capital structure and to maintain its dividend policy in which at the end of each year it distributes 55% of the year's net income. This year's net income was $8 million. How much external equity must Gardial seek now to expand as planned?

15–7 Stock Split

Suppose you own 2,000 common shares of Laurence Incorporated. The EPS is $10.00, the DPS is $3.00, and the stock sells for $80 per share. Laurence announces a 2-for-1 split. Immediately after the split, how many shares will you have, what will the adjusted EPS and DPS be, and what would you expect the stock price to be?

15–8 Stock Split

Fauver Enterprises declared a 3-for-1 stock split last year, and this year its dividend is $1.50 per share. This total dividend payout represents a 6% increase over last year's pre-split total dividend payout. What was last year's dividend per share?

15–9 Residual Distribution Policy

Harris Company must set its investment and dividend policies for the coming year. It has three independent projects from which to choose, each of which requires a $3 million investment. These projects have different levels of risk, and therefore different costs of capital. Their projected IRRs and costs of capital are as follows:

> Project A: Cost of capital = 17%; IRR = 20%
>
> Project B: Cost of capital = 13%; IRR = 10%
>
> Project C: Cost of capital = 7%; IRR = 9%

Harris intends to maintain its 35% debt and 65% common equity capital structure, and its net income is expected to be $4,750,000. If Harris maintains its residual dividend policy (with all distributions in the form of dividends), what will its payout ratio be?

Challenging Problems 10–12

15–10 Alternative Dividend Policies

Boehm Corporation has had stable earnings growth of 8% a year for the past 10 years and in 2015 Boehm paid dividends of $2.6 million on net income of $9.8 million. However, in 2016 earnings are expected to jump to $12.6 million, and Boehm plans to invest $7.3 million in a plant expansion. This one-time unusual earnings growth won't be maintained, though, and after 2016 Boehm will return to its previous 8% earnings growth rate. Its target debt ratio is 35%.

a. Calculate Boehm's total dividends for 2016 under each of the following policies:

   (1) Its 2016 dividend payment is set to force dividends to grow at the long-run growth rate in earnings.

   (2) It continues the 2015 dividend payout ratio.

   (3) It uses a pure residual policy with all distributions in the form of dividends (35% of the $7.3 million investment is financed with debt).

   (4) It employs a regular-dividend-plus-extras policy, with the regular dividend being based on the long-run growth rate and the extra dividend being set according to the residual policy.

b. Which of the preceding policies would you recommend? Restrict your choices to the ones listed, but justify your answer.

c. Does a 2016 dividend of $9 million seem reasonable in view of your answers to parts a and b? If not, should the dividend be higher or lower?

15–11 Residual Distribution Model

Kendra Brown is analyzing the capital requirements for Reynolds Corporation for next year. Kendra forecasts that Reynolds will need $15 million to fund all of its positive-NPV projects and her job is to determine how to raise the money. Reynolds's net income is $11 million, and it has paid a $2 dividend per share (DPS) for the past several years (1 million shares of common stock are outstanding); its shareholders expect the dividend to remain constant for the next several years. The company's target capital structure is 30% debt and 70% equity.

a. Suppose Reynolds follows the residual model and makes all distributions as dividends. How much retained earnings will it need to fund its capital budget?

b. If Reynolds follows the residual model with all distributions in the form of dividends, what will be its dividend per share and payout ratio for the upcoming year?

c. If Reynolds maintains its current $2 DPS for next year, how much retained earnings will be available for the firm's capital budget?

d. Can Reynolds maintain its current capital structure, maintain its current dividend per share, and maintain a $15 million capital budget *without* having to raise new common stock? Why or why not?

e. Suppose Reynolds' management is firmly opposed to cutting the dividend; that is, it wishes to maintain the $2 dividend for the next year. Suppose also that the company is committed to funding all profitable projects and is willing to issue more debt (along with the available retained earnings) to help finance the company's capital budget. Assume the resulting change in capital structure has a minimal impact on the company's composite cost of capital, so that the capital budget remains at $15 million. What portion of this year's capital budget would have to be financed with debt?

f. Suppose once again that Reynolds' management wants to maintain the $2 DPS. In addition, the company wants to maintain its target capital structure (30% debt, 70% equity) and its $15 million capital budget. What is the minimum dollar amount of new common stock the company would have to issue in order to meet all of its objectives?

g. Now consider the case in which Reynolds' management wants to maintain the $2 DPS and its target capital structure but also wants to avoid issuing new common stock. The company is willing to cut its capital budget in order to meet its other objectives. Assuming the company's projects are divisible, what will be the company's capital budget for the next year?

h. If a firm follows the residual distribution policy, what actions can it take when its forecasted retained earnings are less than the retained earnings required to fund its capital budget?

15–12 Stock Repurchase

Bayani Bakery's most recent FCF was $48 million; the FCF is expected to grow at a constant rate of 6%. The firm's WACC is 12%, and it has 15 million shares of common stock outstanding. The firm has $30 million in short-term investments, which it plans to liquidate and distribute to common shareholders via a stock repurchase; the firm has no other nonoperating assets. It has $368 million in debt and $60 million in preferred stock.

a. What is the value of operations?

b. Immediately prior to the repurchase, what is the intrinsic value of equity?

c. Immediately prior to the repurchase, what is the intrinsic stock price?

d. How many shares will be repurchased? How many shares will remain after the repurchase?

e. Immediately after the repurchase, what is the intrinsic value of equity? The intrinsic stock price?

Spreadsheet Problem

15-13 Build a Model: Distributions as Dividends or Repurchases

Start with the partial model in the file *Ch15 P13 Build a Model.xls* on the textbook's Web site. J. Clark Inc. (JCI), a manufacturer and distributor of sports equipment, has grown until it has become a stable, mature company. Now JCI is planning its first distribution to shareholders. (See the file for the most recent year's financial statements and projections for the next year, 2016; JCI's fiscal year ends on June 30.) JCI plans to liquidate and distribute $500 million of its short-term securities on July 1, 2016, the first day of the next fiscal year, but it has not yet decided whether to distribute with dividends or with stock repurchases.

a. Assume first that JCI distributes the $500 million as dividends. Fill in the missing values in the file's balance sheet column for July 1, 2016, which is labeled "Distribute as Dividends." (*Hint:* Be sure that the balance sheets balance after you fill in the missing items.) Assume that JCI did not have to establish an account for dividends payable prior to the distribution.

b. Now assume that JCI distributes the $500 million through stock repurchases. Fill in the missing values in the file's balance sheet column for July 1, 2016, which is labeled "Distribute as Repurchase." (*Hint:* Be sure that the balance sheets balance after you fill in the missing items.)

c. Calculate JCI's projected free cash flow; the tax rate is 40%.

d. What is JCI's current intrinsic stock price (the price on 6/30/2015)? What is the projected intrinsic stock price for 6/30/2016?

e. What is the projected intrinsic stock price on 7/1/2016 if JCI distributes the cash as dividends?

f. What is the projected intrinsic stock price on 7/1/2016 if JCI distributes the cash through stock repurchases? How many shares will remain outstanding after the repurchase?

MINI CASE

Integrated Waveguide Technologies Inc. (IWT) is a 6-year-old company founded by Hunt Jackson and David Smithfield to exploit metamaterial plasmonic technology to develop and manufacture miniature microwave frequency directional transmitters and receivers for use in mobile Internet and communications applications. IWT's technology, although highly advanced, is relatively inexpensive to implement, and its patented manufacturing techniques require little capital as compared to many electronics fabrication ventures. Because of the low capital requirement, Jackson and Smithfield have been able to avoid issuing new stock and thus own all of the shares. Because of the explosion in demand for its mobile Internet applications, IWT must now access outside equity capital to fund its growth, and Jackson and Smithfield have decided to take the company public. Until now, Jackson and Smithfield have paid themselves reasonable salaries but routinely reinvested all after-tax earnings in the firm, so dividend policy has not been an issue. However, before talking with potential outside investors, they must decide on a dividend policy.

Your new boss at the consulting firm Flick and Associates, which has been retained to help IWT prepare for its public offering, has asked you to make a presentation to Jackson and Smithfield in which you review the theory of dividend policy and discuss the following issues.

a. (1) What is meant by the term "distribution policy"? How has the mix of dividend payouts and stock repurchases changed over time?

   (2) The terms "irrelevance," "dividend preference" (or "bird-in-the-hand"), and "tax effect" have been used to describe three major theories regarding the way dividend payouts affect a firm's value. Explain these terms, and briefly describe each theory.

   (3) What do the three theories indicate regarding the actions management should take with respect to dividend payouts?

   (4) What results have empirical studies of the dividend theories produced? How does all this affect what we can tell managers about dividend payouts?

b. Discuss: (1) the information content, or signaling, hypothesis, (2) the clientele effect, and (3) their effects on distribution policy.

c. (1) Assume that IWT has completed its IPO and has a $112.5 million capital budget planned for the coming year. You have determined that its present capital structure (80% equity and 20% debt) is optimal, and its net income is forecasted at $140 million. Use the residual distribution approach to determine IWT's total dollar distribution. Assume for now that the distribution

is in the form of a dividend. Suppose IWT has 100 million shares of stock outstanding. What is the forecasted dividend payout ratio? What is the forecasted dividend per share? What would happen to the payout ratio and DPS if net income were forecasted to decrease to $90 million? To increase to $160 million?

   (2) In general terms, how would a change in investment opportunities affect the payout ratio under the residual distribution policy?

   (3) What are the advantages and disadvantages of the residual policy? (*Hint:* Don't neglect signaling and clientele effects.)

d. (1) Describe the procedures a company follows when it makes a distribution through dividend payments.

   (2) What is a stock repurchase? Describe the procedures a company follows when it makes a distribution through a stock repurchase.

e. Discuss the advantages and disadvantages of a firm repurchasing its own shares.

f. Suppose IWT has decided to distribute $50 million, which it presently is holding in liquid short-term investments. IWT's value of operations is estimated to be about $1,937.5 million, and it has $387.5 million in debt (it has no preferred stock). As mentioned previously, IWT has 100 million shares of stock outstanding.

   (1) Assume that IWT has not yet made the distribution. What is IWT's intrinsic value of equity? What is its intrinsic stock price per share?

   (2) Now suppose that IWT has just made the $50 million distribution in the form of dividends. What is IWT's intrinsic value of equity? What is its intrinsic stock price per share?

   (3) Suppose instead that IWT has just made the $50 million distribution in the form of a stock repurchase. Now what is IWT's intrinsic value of equity? How many shares did IWT repurchase? How many shares remained outstanding after the repurchase? What is its intrinsic stock price per share after the repurchase?

g. Describe the series of steps that most firms take when setting dividend policy.

h. What are stock splits and stock dividends? What are the advantages and disadvantages of each?

i. What is a dividend reinvestment plan (DRIP), and how does it work?

SELECTED ADDITIONAL CASES

The following cases from CengageCompose cover many of the concepts discussed in this chapter and are available at http://compose.cengage.com.

Klein-Brigham Series:

Case 19, "Georgia Atlantic Company," Case 20, "Bessemer Steel Products, Inc.," Case 47, "Floral Fragrance, Inc.," and Case 80, "The Western Company."

Brigham-Buzzard Series:

Case 9, "Powerline Network Corporation (Dividend Policy)."

Capital Structure Decisions

As explained in Chapters 9 and 10, growth in sales requires growth in operating capital, and this often requires that external funds be raised through a combination of equity and debt. The firm's mixture of debt and equity is called its **capital structure**. Although actual levels of debt and equity may vary somewhat over time, most firms try to keep their financing mix close to a **target capital structure**. A firm's **capital structure decision** includes its choice of a target capital structure, the average maturity of its debt, and the specific types of financing it decides to use at any particular time. As with operating decisions, managers should make capital structure decisions that are designed to maximize the firm's intrinsic value.

Beginning-of-Chapter Questions

A s you read this chapter, consider how you would answer the following questions. You *should not* necessarily be able to answer the questions before you read the chapter. Rather, you should use them to get a sense of the issues covered in the chapter. After reading the chapter, you should be able to give at least partial answers to the questions, and you should be able to give better answers after the chapter has been discussed in class. Note, too, that it is often useful, when answering conceptual questions, to use hypothetical data to illustrate your answer. We illustrate the answers with an *Excel* model that is available on the textbook's Web site. Accessing the model and working through it is a useful exercise, and it provides insights that are useful when answering the questions.

1. What is **business risk**? List and then discuss some factors that affect business risk.
2. What is **financial risk**? How is it related to business risk?

3. Who are **Modigliani and Miller (MM)**, and what were their conclusions regarding the effect of capital structure on a firm's value and cost of capital under the assumption of no corporate taxes? How do their conclusions change when they introduce corporate taxes? If a firm's managers thought that MM were exactly right, and they wanted to maximize the firm's value what capital structure would they choose?
4. Does the MM theory appear to be correct according to either empirical research or observations of firms' actual behavior? How do assumptions affect your conclusion about whether the MM theory appears to be correct?
5. What is the **trade-off theory** of capital structure? How does it differ from MM's theory?
6. In general, does the market view the **announcement of a new stock issue** to be a good **signal**? Does the signaling theory lead to the

same conclusions regarding the optimal capital structure as the trade-off theory and/or the MM theory?

7. What does it mean to be at the **optimal capital structure**? What is optimized? What is maximized and what is minimized?

8. Should firms focus on **book value** or **market value** capital structures? How would the calculated

WACC be affected by the use of book weights rather than market weights?

9. What would you expect to happen to an all-equity firm's stock price if its management announced a **recapitalization** under which debt would be issued and used to repurchase common stock?

CORPORATE VALUATION AND CAPITAL STRUCTURE

A firm's financing choices obviously have a direct effect on the weighted average cost of capital (WACC). Financing choices also have an indirect effect on the costs of debt and equity because they change the risk and required returns of debt and equity. Financing choices can also affect free cash flows if the probability of bankruptcy becomes high. This chapter focuses on the debt–equity choice and its effect on value.

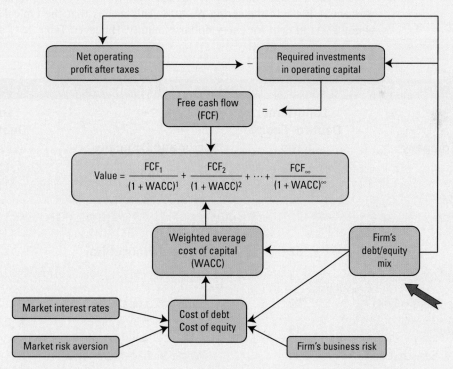

Source: From *Financial Management: Theory & Practice*, 2013, by Brigham and Ehrhardt. © Cengage Learning.

16-1 **An Overview of Capital Structure**

The value of a firm's operations is the present value of its expected future free cash flows (FCF) discounted at its weighted average cost of capital (WACC):

(16–1)

$$V_{op} = \sum_{t=1}^{\infty} \frac{FCF_t}{(1 + WACC)^t}$$

The WACC of a firm financed only by debt and common stock depends on the percentages of debt and common stock (w_d and w_s), the cost of debt (r_d), the cost of stock (r_s), and the corporate tax rate (T):

(16–2)

$$WACC = w_d(1 - T)r_d + w_s r_s$$

As these equations show, the only way any decision can change the value of operations is by changing either expected free cash flows or the cost of capital. As you read the chapter, think about the ways the capital structure choices can affect FCF or the WACC.

For the average company in the S&P 500, the ratio of long-term debt to equity was about 104% in the spring of 2014. This means that the typical company had about $1.04 in debt for every dollar of equity. However, Table 16-1 shows that the

TABLE 16-1	Long-Term Debt-to-Equity Ratios for Selected Firms and Industries		
Sector and Company	**Long-Term Debt-to- Equity Ratio**	**Sector and Company**	**Long-Term Debt-to- Equity Ratio**
Technology	**9%**	**Capital Goods**	**44%**
Microsoft (MSFT)	24	Winnebago Industries (WGO)	0
Ricoh (RICOF.PK)	52	Caterpillar Inc. (CAT)	144
Energy	**37**	**Consumer/Noncyclical**	**44**
ExxonMobil (XOM)	4	Starbucks (SBUX)	42
Chesapeake Energy (CHK)	79	Kellogg Company (K)	224
Transportation	**49**	**Services**	**49**
United Parcel Service (UPS)	299	Waste Management (WM)	141
United Continental Holdings (UAL)	—	Republic Services (RSG)	91

Basic Materials	18	Utilities	132
Anglo American PLC (AAL.L)	—	NRG Energy (NRG)	153
Century Aluminum (CENX)	27	CMS Energy (CMS)	213

Source: For updates on a company's ratio, go to **www.reuters.com** and enter the ticker symbol for a stock quote. Click on Financials tab for updates on the sector ratio.

average ratios diverge widely for different business sectors and for different companies within a sector. For example, the technology sector has a very low average ratio (9%) while the utilities sector has a much higher ratio (132%). Even so, within each sector there are some companies with low levels of debt and others with high levels. For example, the average debt ratio for the consumer/noncyclical sector is 44%, but in this sector Starbucks has a ratio of 42% while Kellogg has a ratio of 224%. Why do we see such variation across companies and business sectors? Can a company make itself more valuable through its choice of debt ratio? We address these questions in the rest of this chapter, beginning with a description of business risk and financial risk.

What are some ways in which the capital structure decisions can affect the value of operations?

SELF TEST

16-2 Business Risk and Financial Risk

Business risk and financial risk combine to determine the total risk of a firm's future return on equity, as we explain in the next sections.

16-2a Business Risk and Operating Leverage

Business risk is the risk a firm's common stockholders would face if the firm had no debt. In other words, it is the risk inherent in the firm's operations, which arises from uncertainty about future operating profits and capital requirements.

Business risk depends on a number of factors, beginning with variability in product demand and production costs. If a high percentage of a firm's costs are fixed and hence do not decline when demand falls, then the firm has high *operating leverage,* which increases its business risk.

A high degree of **operating leverage** implies that a relatively small change in sales results in a relatively large change in EBIT, net operating profits after taxes (NOPAT), return on invested capital (ROIC), return on assets (ROA), and return on equity (ROE). Other things held constant, the higher a firm's fixed costs, the greater its operating leverage. Higher fixed costs are generally associated with: (1) highly automated, capital-intensive firms; (2) businesses that employ highly skilled workers who must be retained and paid even when sales are low; and (3) firms with high product development costs that must be maintained to complete ongoing R&D projects.

To illustrate the relative impact of fixed versus variable costs, consider Strasburg Electronics Company, a manufacturer of components used in cell phones.

Strasburg is considering several different operating technologies and several different financing alternatives. We will analyze its financing choices in the next section, but for now we will focus on its operating plans.

Strasburg is comparing two plans, each requiring a capital investment of $200 million; assume for now that Strasburg will finance its choice entirely with equity. Each plan is expected to produce 110 million units (Q) per year at a sales price (P) of $2 per unit. As shown in Figure 16-1, Plan A's technology requires a smaller annual fixed cost (F) than Plan U's, but Plan A has higher variable costs (V). (We denote the second plan with U because it has no financial leverage, and we denote the third plan with L because it does have financial leverage; Plan L is discussed in the next section.) Figure 16-1 also shows the projected income statements and selected performance measures for the first year. Notice that Plan U's performance measures are superior to Plan A's if the expected sales occur.

Notice that the projections in Figure 16-1 are based on the 110 million units expected to be sold. But what if demand is lower than expected? It often is useful

FIGURE 16-1 Illustration of Operating and Financial Leverage (Millions of Dollars and Millions of Units, Except Per Unit Data)

	A	B	C	D	E
17	1. Input Data		Plan A	Plan U	Plan L
18	Required operating current assets		$3	$3	$3
19	Required long-term assets		$199	$199	$199
20	Resulting operating current liabilities		$2	$2	$2
21	Total assets		$202	$202	$202
22	Required capital (TA – Op. CL)		$200	$200	$200
23	Book equity		$200	$200	$150
24	Debt		$0	$0	$50
25	Interest rate		8%	8%	8%
26	Sales price (P)		$2.00	$2.00	$2.00
27	Tax rate (T)		40%	40%	40%
28	Expected units sold (Q)		110	110	110
29	Fixed costs (F)		$20	$60	$60
30	Variable costs (V)		$1.50	$1.00	$1.00
31	2. Income Statements		Plan A	Plan U	Plan L
32	Sales revenue (P x Q)		$220.0	$220.0	$220.0
33	Fixed costs		20.0	60.0	60.0
34	Variable costs (V x Q)		165.0	110.0	110.0
35	EBIT		$35.0	$50.0	$50.0
36	Interest		0.0	0.0	4.0
37	EBT		$35.0	$50.0	$46.0
38	Tax		14.0	20.0	18.4
39	Net income		$21.0	$30.0	$27.6
40	3. Key Performance Measures		Plan A	Plan U	Plan L
41	NOPAT = EBIT(1 – T)		$21.0	$30.0	$30.0
42	ROIC = NOPAT/Capital		10.5%	15.0%	15.0%
43	ROA = NI/Total assets		10.4%	14.9%	13.7%
44	ROE = NI/Equity		10.5%	15.0%	18.4%

Note: ROA is not exactly equal to ROE for the Plan L or Plan U, because total assets are not quite equal to equity for these plans. This is because the operating current liabilities, such as accounts payable and accruals, reduce the required equity capital investment.

to know how far sales can fall before operating profits become negative. The **operating break-even point** occurs when earnings before interest and taxes (EBIT) equal zero:[1]

$$EBIT = PQ - VQ - F = 0 \qquad \textbf{(16–3)}$$

If we solve for the break-even quantity, Q_{BE}, we get this expression:

$$Q_{BE} = \frac{F}{P - V} \qquad \textbf{(16–4)}$$

The break-even quantities for Plans A and U are:

$$\text{Plan A: } Q_{BE} = \frac{\$20 \text{ million}}{\$2.00 - \$1.50} = 40 \text{ million units}$$

$$\text{Plan U: } Q_{BE} = \frac{\$60 \text{ million}}{\$2.00 - \$1.00} = 60 \text{ million units}$$

Plan A will be profitable if unit sales are above 40 million, whereas Plan U requires sales of 60 million units before it is profitable. This difference occurs because Plan U has higher fixed costs, so more units must be sold to cover these fixed costs. Panel A of Figure 16-2 illustrates the operating profitability of these two plans for different levels of unit sales. Because these companies have no debt, the return on assets measures operating profitability; we report ROA instead of EBIT to facilitate comparisons when we discuss financial risk in the next section.

Suppose sales are at 80 million units. In this case, the ROA is identical for each plan. As unit sales begin to climb above 80 million, both plans increase in profitability, but ROA increases more for Plan U than for Plan A. If sales fall below 80 million, then both plans become less profitable, but ROA decreases more for Plan U than for Plan A. This illustrates that the combination of higher fixed costs and lower variable costs of Plan U magnifies its gain or loss relative to Plan A. In other words, because Plan U has higher operating leverage, it also has greater business risk.

16-2b **Financial Risk and Financial Leverage**

Financial risk is the additional risk placed on the common stockholders as a result of the decision to finance with debt.[2] Conceptually, stockholders face a certain amount of risk that is inherent in a firm's operations—this is its business risk, which is defined as the uncertainty in projections of future EBIT, NOPAT, and ROIC. If a

---

1. This definition of the break-even point does not include any fixed financial costs because it focuses on operating profits. We could also examine net income, in which case a firm with debt would have negative net income even at the operating break-even point. We introduce financial costs shortly.
2. Preferred stock also adds to financial risk. To simplify matters, we examine only debt and common equity in this chapter.

FIGURE 16-2   Operating Leverage and Financial Leverage

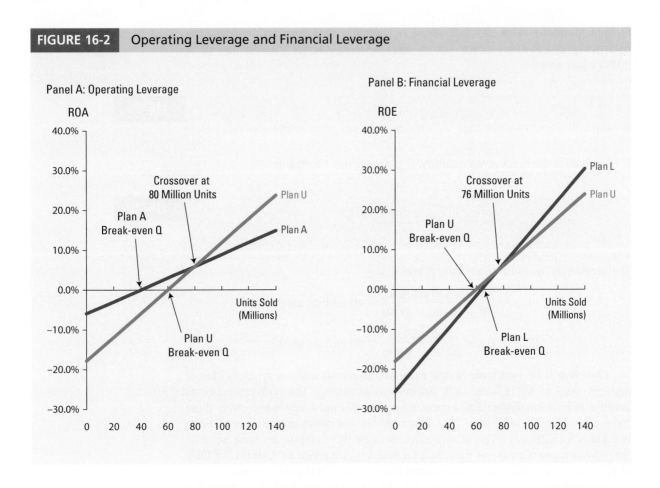

firm uses debt (financial leverage), then the business risk is concentrated on the common stockholders. To illustrate, suppose 10 people decide to form a corporation to manufacture flash memory drives. There is a certain amount of business risk in the operation. If the firm is capitalized only with common equity and if each person buys 10% of the stock, then each investor shares equally in the business risk. However, suppose the firm is capitalized with 50% debt and 50% equity, with five of the investors putting up their money by purchasing debt and the other five putting up their money by purchasing equity. In this case, the five debtholders are paid before the five stockholders, so *virtually all* of the business risk is borne by the stockholders. Thus, the use of debt, or **financial leverage**, concentrates business risk on stockholders.[3]

To illustrate the impact of financial risk, we can extend the Strasburg Electronics example. Strasburg initially decided to use the technology of Plan U, which is unlevered (financed with all equity), but now it's considering financing the technology with $150 million of equity and $50 million of debt at an 8% interest rate, as shown for Plan L in Figure 16-1 (recall that L denotes leverage). Compare Plans U

---

3. Holders of corporate debt generally do bear some business risk, because they may lose some of their investment if the firm goes bankrupt. We discuss this in more depth later in the chapter.

and L. Notice that the ROIC of 15% is the same for the two plans. Since the financing choice doesn't affect operations, the ROICs of the two plans will be equal for any level of sales. Plan L has lower net income ($27.6 million versus $30 million) because it must pay interest, but it has a higher ROE (18.4%) because the net income is shared over a smaller equity base.[4]

But there is more to the story than just a higher ROE with financial leverage. Just as operating leverage adds risk, so does financial leverage. We used the Data Table feature in the file *Ch16 Tool Kit.xls* to generate performance measures for plans U and L at different levels of unit sales. Panel B of Figure 16-2 shows the ROE of Plan L versus quantity sold.

At the crossover, when the quantity sold is 76 million, both plans have an ROE and ROIC of 4.8%. (See the *Tool Kit* for the calculations.) The after-tax cost of debt also is 8%(1 − 0.40) = 4.8%, which is no coincidence. As sales increase above 76 million units and ROIC increases above 4.8%, the ROE increases for each plan, but more for Plan L than for Plan U. However, if sales fall below 76 million units and ROIC falls below 4.8%, then the ROE falls further for Plan L than for Plan U. Thus, financial leverage magnifies the ROE for good or ill, depending on the ROIC, and so increases the risk of a levered firm relative to an unlevered firm.

We see, then, that using leverage has both good and bad effects: If expected ROIC is greater than the after-tax cost of debt, then higher leverage increases expected ROE but also increases risk.

SELF TEST

What is business risk, and how can it be measured?

What are some determinants of business risk?

How does operating leverage affect business risk?

What is financial risk, and how does it arise?

Explain this statement: "Using leverage has both good and bad effects."

A firm has fixed operating costs of $100,000 and variable costs of $4 per unit. If it sells the product for $6 per unit, what is the break-even quantity? **(50,000)**

16-3 Capital Structure Theory

In the previous section, we showed how capital structure choices affect a firm's ROE and its risk. For a number of reasons, we would expect capital structures to vary considerably across industries. For example, pharmaceutical companies generally have very different capital structures than airline companies. Moreover, capital structures vary among firms within a given industry. What factors explain these differences? In an attempt to answer this question, academics and practitioners have developed a number of theories, and the theories have been

---

4. Recall that Strasburg has $202 million in total assets, all of which are operating assets. With $2 million in operating current liabilities, Strasburg has $202 − $2 = $200 million in operating capital, which must be financed with a combination of debt and equity.

subjected to many empirical tests. The following sections examine several of these theories.[5]

16-3a **Modigliani and Miller: No Taxes**

Modern capital structure theory began in 1958, when Professors Franco Modigliani and Merton Miller (hereafter MM) published what has been called the most influential finance article ever written.[6] MM's study was based on some strong assumptions, which included the following:

1. There are no brokerage costs.
2. There are no taxes.
3. There are no bankruptcy costs.
4. Investors can borrow at the same rate as corporations.
5. All investors have the same information as management about the firm's future investment opportunities.
6. EBIT is not affected by the use of debt.

Modigliani and Miller imagined two hypothetical portfolios. The first contains all the equity of an unlevered firm, so the portfolio's value is V_U, the value of an unlevered firm. Because the firm has no growth (which means it does not need to invest in any new net assets) and because it pays no taxes, the firm can pay out all of its EBIT in the form of dividends. Therefore, the cash flow from owning this first portfolio is equal to EBIT.

Now consider a second firm that is identical to the unlevered firm *except* that it is partially financed with debt. The second portfolio contains all of the levered firm's stock (S_L) and debt (D), so the portfolio's value is V_L, the total value of the levered firm. If the interest rate is r_d, then the levered firm pays out interest in the amount r_dD. Because the firm is not growing and pays no taxes, it can pay out dividends in the amount EBIT $- r_dD$. If you owned all of the firm's debt and equity, your cash flow would be equal to the sum of the interest and dividends: $r_dD + (EBIT - r_dD) = EBIT$. Therefore, the cash flow from owning this second portfolio is equal to EBIT.

Notice that the cash flow of each portfolio is equal to EBIT. Thus, MM concluded that two portfolios producing the same cash flows must have the same value:[7]

---

5. For additional discussion of capital structure theories, see John C. Easterwood and Palani-Rajan Kadapakkam, "The Role of Private and Public Debt in Corporate Capital Structures," *Financial Management,* Autumn 1991, pp. 49–57; Gerald T. Garvey, "Leveraging the Underinvestment Problem: How High Debt and Management Shareholdings Solve the Agency Costs of Free Cash Flow," *Journal of Financial Research,* Summer 1992, pp. 149–166; Milton Harris and Artur Raviv, "Capital Structure and the Informational Role of Debt," *Journal of Finance,* June 1990, pp. 321–349; and Ronen Israel, "Capital Structure and the Market for Corporate Control: The Defensive Role of Debt Financing," *Journal of Finance,* September 1991, pp. 1391–1409.
6. Franco Modigliani and Merton H. Miller, "The Cost of Capital, Corporation Finance, and the Theory of Investment," *American Economic Review,* June 1958, pp. 261–297. Modigliani and Miller each won a Nobel Prize for their work.
7. They actually showed that if the values of the two portfolios differed, then an investor could engage in riskless arbitrage: The investor could create a trading strategy (buying one portfolio and selling the other short) that had no risk, required none of the investor's own cash, and resulted in a positive cash flow for the investor. This would be such a desirable strategy that everyone would try to implement it. But if everyone tries to buy the same portfolio, its price will be driven up by market demand, and if everyone tries to short sell a portfolio, its price will be driven down. The net result of the trading activity would be to change the portfolio's values until they were equal and no more arbitrage was possible.

$$V_L = V_U = S_L + D \qquad (16\text{–}5)$$

Given their assumptions, MM proved that a firm's value is unaffected by its capital structure.

Recall that the WACC is a combination of the cost of debt and the relatively higher cost of equity, r_s. As leverage increases, more weight is given to low-cost debt but equity becomes riskier, which drives up r_s. Under MM's assumptions, r_s increases by exactly enough to keep the WACC constant. Put another way: If MM's assumptions are correct, then it doesn't matter how a firm finances its operations, so capital structure decisions are irrelevant.

Even though some of their assumptions are obviously unrealistic, MM's irrelevance result is extremely important. By indicating the conditions under which capital structure is irrelevant, MM also provided us with clues about what is required for capital structure to be relevant and hence to affect a firm's value. The work of MM marked the beginning of modern capital structure research, and subsequent research has focused on relaxing the MM assumptions in order to develop a more realistic theory of capital structure.

Modigliani and Miller's thought process was just as important as their conclusion. It seems simple now, but their idea that two portfolios with identical cash flows must also have identical values changed the entire financial world because it led to the development of options and derivatives. It is no surprise that Modigliani and Miller received Nobel awards for their work.

16-3b Modigliani and Miller II: The Effect of Corporate Taxes

In 1963, MM published a follow-up paper in which they relaxed the assumption that there are no corporate taxes.[8] The Tax Code allows corporations to deduct interest payments as an expense, but dividend payments to stockholders are not deductible. The differential treatment encourages corporations to use debt in their capital structures. This means that interest payments reduce the taxes a corporation pays, and if a corporation pays less to the government, then more of its cash flow is available for investors. In other words, the tax deductibility of the interest payments shields the firm's pre-tax income.

To illustrate, look at Figure 16-1 and see that Plan U (with no debt) pays taxes of $20, but Plan L (with leverage) pays taxes of only $18.40. What happens to the difference of $1.60 = $20 − $18.40? This extra amount is paid out to investors! Notice that Plan U has $30 of net income for shareholders, but Plan L has $4 of interest for debtholders and $27.60 of net income for shareholders for a combined total of $31.60, which is exactly $1.60 more than Plan U. With more cash flows available for investors, a levered firm's total value should be greater than that of an unlevered firm, and this is what MM showed.

8. Franco Modigliani and Merton H. Miller, "Corporate Income Taxes and the Cost of Capital: A Correction," *American Economic Review*, June 1963, pp. 433–443.

YOGI BERRA ON THE MM PROPOSITION

When a waitress asked Yogi Berra, Baseball Hall of Fame catcher for the New York Yankees, whether he wanted his pizza cut into four pieces or eight, Yogi replied: "Better make it four. I don't think I can eat eight."[a]

Yogi's quip helps convey the basic insight of Modigliani and Miller. The firm's choice of leverage "slices" the distribution of future cash flows in a way that is like slicing a pizza. MM recognized that holding a company's investment activities fixed is like fixing the size of the pizza; no information costs means that everyone sees the same pizza; no taxes means the IRS gets none of the pie; and no "contracting costs" means nothing sticks to the knife.

So, just as the substance of Yogi's meal is unaffected by whether the pizza is sliced into four pieces or eight, the economic substance of the firm is unaffected by whether the liability side of the balance sheet is sliced to include more or less debt—at least under the MM assumptions.

[a]Lee Green, *Sportswit* (New York: Fawcett Crest, 1984), p. 228.

Source: "Yogi Berra on the MM Proposition," *Journal of Applied Corporate Finance,* Winter 1995, p. 6. Reprinted by permission of Stern Stewart Management.

As in their earlier paper, MM introduced a second important way of looking at the effect of capital structure: The value of a levered firm is the value of an otherwise identical unlevered firm plus the value of any "side effects." While others have expanded on this idea by considering other side effects, MM focused on the tax shield:

(16–6)
$$V_L = V_U + \text{Value of side effects} = V_U + \text{Present value of tax shield}$$

Under their assumptions, they showed that the present value of the tax shield is equal to the corporate tax rate, T, multiplied by the amount of debt, D:

(16–7)
$$V_L = V_U + TD$$

With a tax rate of about 40%, this implies that every dollar of debt adds about 40 cents of value to the firm, and this leads to the conclusion that the optimal capital structure is virtually 100% debt. MM also showed that the cost of equity, r_s, increases as leverage increases but that it doesn't increase quite as fast as it would if there were no taxes. As a result, under MM with corporate taxes the WACC falls as debt is added.

16-3c **Miller: The Effect of Corporate and Personal Taxes**

Merton Miller (this time without Modigliani) later brought in the effects of personal taxes.[9] The income from bonds is generally interest, which is taxed as personal

---

9. See Merton H. Miller, "Debt and Taxes," *Journal of Finance,* May 1977, pp. 261–275.

income at rates (T_d) going up to 39.6%, while income from stocks generally comes partly from dividends and partly from capital gains. Long-term capital gains are taxed at a rate of 20%, and this tax is deferred until the stock is sold and the gain realized. If stock is held until the owner dies, no capital gains tax whatsoever must be paid. So, on average, returns on stocks are taxed at lower effective rates (T_s) than returns on debt.[10]

Because of the tax situation, Miller argued that investors are willing to accept relatively low before-tax returns on stock relative to the before-tax returns on bonds. (The situation here is similar to that with tax-exempt municipal bonds as discussed in Chapter 4 and preferred stocks held by corporate investors, as discussed in Chapter 8.) For example, an investor might require a return of 10% on Strasburg's bonds, and if stock income were taxed at the same rate as bond income, the required rate of return on Strasburg's stock might be 16% because of the stock's greater risk. However, in view of the favorable treatment of income on the stock, investors might be willing to accept a before-tax return of only 14% on the stock.

Thus, as Miller pointed out: (1) the *deductibility of interest* favors the use of debt financing, but (2) the *more favorable tax treatment of income from stock* lowers the required rate of return on stock and thus favors the use of equity financing.

Miller showed that the net impact of corporate and personal taxes is given by this equation:

$$V_L = V_U + \left[1 - \frac{(1 - T_c)(1 - T_s)}{(1 - T_d)}\right] D \tag{16-8}$$

Here T_c is the corporate tax rate, T_s is the personal tax rate on income from stocks, and T_d is the tax rate on income from debt. Miller argued that the marginal tax rates on stock and debt balance out in such a way that the bracketed term in Equation 16-8 is zero and so $V_L = V_U$, but most observers believe there is still a tax advantage to debt if reasonable values of tax rates are assumed. For example, if the marginal corporate tax rate is 40%, the marginal rate on debt is 30%, and the marginal rate on stock is 12%, then the advantage of debt financing is:

$$V_L = V_U + \left[1 - \frac{(1 - 0.40)(1 - 0.12)}{(1 - 0.30)}\right] D \tag{16-8a}$$

$$= V_U + 0.25D$$

Thus it appears that the presence of personal taxes reduces but does not completely eliminate the advantage of debt financing.

---

10. The Tax Code isn't quite as simple as this. An increasing number of investors face the Alternative Minimum Tax (AMT); see **Web Extension 6A** for a discussion. The AMT imposes a 28% tax rate on most income and an effective rate of 22% on long-term capital gains and dividends. Under the AMT there is still a spread between the tax rates on interest income and stock income, but the spread is narrower. See Leonard Burman, William Gale, Greg Leiserson, and Jeffrey Rohaly, "The AMT: What's Wrong and How to Fix It," *National Tax Journal*, September 2007, pp. 385–405.

16-3d **Trade-Off Theory**

The results of Modigliani and Miller also depend on the assumption that there are no **bankruptcy costs**. However, bankruptcy can be quite costly. Firms in bankruptcy have very high legal and accounting expenses, and they also have a hard time retaining customers, suppliers, and employees. Moreover, bankruptcy often forces a firm to liquidate or sell assets for less than they would be worth if the firm were to continue operating. For example, if a steel manufacturer goes out of business it might be hard to find buyers for the company's blast furnaces. Such assets are often illiquid because they are configured to a company's individual needs and also because they are difficult to disassemble and move.

Note, too, that the *threat of bankruptcy*, not just bankruptcy per se, causes many of these same problems. Key employees jump ship, suppliers refuse to grant credit, customers seek more stable suppliers, and lenders demand higher interest rates and impose more restrictive loan covenants if potential bankruptcy looms. Therefore, even the threat of bankruptcy can cause free cash flows to fall, causing further declines in a company's value.

Bankruptcy-related problems are most likely to arise when a firm includes a great deal of debt in its capital structure. Therefore, bankruptcy costs discourage firms from pushing their use of debt to excessive levels.

Bankruptcy-related costs have two components: (1) the probability of financial distress and (2) the costs that would be incurred if financial distress does occur. Firms whose earnings are more volatile, all else equal, face a greater chance of bankruptcy and should therefore use less debt than more stable firms. This is consistent with our earlier point that firms with high operating leverage, and thus greater business risk, should limit their use of financial leverage. Likewise, firms that would face high costs in the event of financial distress should rely less heavily on debt. For example, firms whose assets are illiquid and thus would have to be sold at "fire sale" prices should limit their use of debt financing.

The preceding arguments led to the development of what is called the trade-off theory of leverage, in which firms trade off the benefits of debt financing (favorable corporate tax treatment) against higher interest rates and bankruptcy costs. In essence, the **trade-off theory** says that the value of a levered firm is equal to the value of an unlevered firm plus the value of any side effects, which include the tax shield and the expected costs due to financial distress. A summary of the trade-off theory is expressed graphically in Figure 16-3, and a list of observations about the figure follows here.

1. Under the assumptions of the MM model with corporate taxes, a firm's value increases linearly for every dollar of debt. The line labeled "MM Result Incorporating the Effects of Corporate Taxation" in Figure 16-3 expresses the relationship between value and debt under those assumptions.

2. There is some threshold level of debt, labeled D_1 in Figure 16-3, below which the probability of bankruptcy is so low as to be immaterial. Beyond D_1, however, expected bankruptcy-related costs become increasingly important, and they reduce the tax benefits of debt at an increasing rate. In the range from D_1 to D_2, expected bankruptcy-related costs reduce but do not completely offset the tax benefits of debt, so the stock price rises (but at a decreasing rate) as the debt ratio increases. However, beyond D_2, expected bankruptcy-related costs exceed the tax benefits, so from this point on increasing the debt ratio lowers the value

FIGURE 16-3	Effect of Financial Leverage on Value

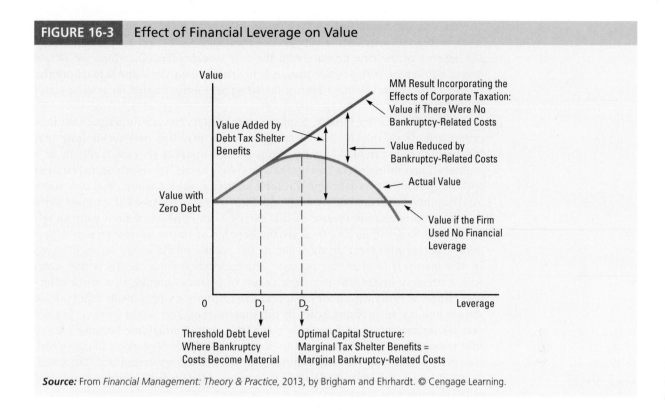

Source: From *Financial Management: Theory & Practice*, 2013, by Brigham and Ehrhardt. © Cengage Learning.

of the stock. Therefore, D_2 is the optimal capital structure. Of course, D_1 and D_2 vary from firm to firm, depending on their business risks and bankruptcy costs.

3. Although theoretical and empirical work confirms the general shape of the curve in Figure 16-3, this graph must be taken as an approximation and not as a precisely defined function.

16-3e **Signaling Theory**

MM assumed that investors have the same information about a firm's prospects as its managers—this is called **symmetric information**. However, managers in fact often have better information than outside investors. This is called **asymmetric information**, and it has an important effect on the optimal capital structure. To see why, consider two situations, one in which the company's managers know that its prospects are extremely positive (Firm P) and one in which the managers know that the future looks negative (Firm N).

Suppose, for example, that Firm P's R&D labs have just discovered a cure for the common cold. Firm P can't provide investors with any details about the product because that might give competitors an advantage. But if they don't provide details, then investors will underestimate the value of the discovery. Given the inability to provide accurate, verifiable information to the market, how should Firm P's management raise the needed capital?

Suppose Firm P issues stock. When profits from the new product start flowing in, the price of the stock would rise sharply and the purchasers of the new stock would make a bonanza. The current stockholders (including the managers) would also do well, but not as well as they would have done if the company had not sold stock before the price increased, because then they would not have had to share the benefits of the new product with the new stockholders. Therefore, *we should expect a firm with very positive prospects to avoid selling stock and instead to raise required new capital by other means, including debt usage beyond the normal target capital structure.*[11]

Now let's consider Firm N. Suppose its managers have information that new orders are off sharply because a competitor has installed new technology that has improved its products' quality. Firm N must upgrade its own facilities, at a high cost, just to maintain its current sales. As a result, its return on investment will fall (but not by as much as if it took no action, which would lead to a 100% loss through bankruptcy). How should Firm N raise the needed capital? Here the situation is just the reverse of that facing Firm P, which did not want to sell stock so as to avoid having to share the benefits of future developments. *A firm with negative prospects would want to sell stock, which would mean bringing in new investors to share the losses!*[12] The conclusion from all this is that firms with extremely bright prospects prefer not to finance through new stock offerings, whereas firms with poor prospects like to finance with outside equity. How should you, as an investor, react to this conclusion? You ought to say: "If I see that a company plans to issue new stock, this should worry me because I know that management would not want to issue stock if future prospects looked good. However, management *would* want to issue stock if things looked bad. Therefore, I should lower my estimate of the firm's value, other things held constant, if it plans to issue new stock."

If you gave this answer, then your views are consistent with those of sophisticated portfolio managers. In a nutshell: *The announcement of a stock offering is generally taken as a* **signal** *that the firm's prospects as seen by its own management are not good; conversely, a debt offering is taken as a positive signal.* Notice that Firm N's managers cannot make a false signal to investors by mimicking Firm P and issuing debt. With its unfavorable future prospects, issuing debt could soon force Firm N into bankruptcy. Given the resulting damage to the personal wealth and reputations of N's managers, they cannot afford to mimic Firm P. All of this suggests that when a firm announces a new stock offering, more often than not the price of its stock will decline. Empirical studies have shown that this is indeed true.

16-3f **Reserve Borrowing Capacity**

Because issuing stock sends a negative signal and tends to depress the stock price even if the company's true prospects are bright, a company should try to maintain a **reserve borrowing capacity** so that debt can be used if an especially good investment opportunity comes along. This means that *firms should, in normal times, use more equity and less debt than is suggested by the tax benefit–bankruptcy cost trade-off model depicted in Figure 16-3.*

---

11. It would be illegal for Firm P's managers to personally purchase more shares on the basis of their inside knowledge of the new product.
12. Of course, Firm N would have to make certain disclosures when it offered new shares to the public, but it might be able to meet the legal requirements without fully disclosing management's worst fears.

16-3g **The Pecking Order Hypothesis**

The presence of flotation costs and asymmetric information may cause a firm to raise capital according to a **pecking order**. In this situation, a firm first raises capital internally by reinvesting its net income and selling its short-term marketable securities. When that supply of funds has been exhausted, the firm will issue debt and perhaps preferred stock. Only as a last resort will the firm issue common stock.[13]

16-3h **Using Debt Financing to Constrain Managers**

Agency problems may arise if managers and shareholders have different objectives. Such conflicts are particularly likely when the firm's managers have too much cash at their disposal. Managers often use excess cash to finance pet projects or for perquisites such as nicer offices, corporate jets, and skyboxes at sports arenas—none of which have much to do with maximizing stock prices. Even worse, managers might be tempted to pay too much for an acquisition, something that could cost shareholders hundreds of millions of dollars. By contrast, managers with limited "excess cash flow" are less able to make wasteful expenditures.

Firms can reduce excess cash flow in a variety of ways. One way is to funnel some of it back to shareholders through higher dividends or stock repurchases. Another alternative is to shift the capital structure toward more debt in the hope that higher debt service requirements will force managers to be more disciplined. If debt is not serviced as required then the firm will be forced into bankruptcy, in which case its managers would likely lose their jobs. Therefore, a manager is less likely to buy an expensive new corporate jet if the firm has large debt service requirements that could cost the manager his or her job. In short, high levels of debt **bond the cash flow**, because much of it is precommitted to servicing the debt.

A **leveraged buyout (LBO)** is one way to bond cash flow. In an LBO, a large amount of debt and a small amount of cash are used to finance the purchase of a company's shares, after which the firm "goes private." The first wave of LBOs was in the mid-1980s; private equity funds led the buyouts of the late 1990s and early 2000s. Many of these LBOs were specifically designed to reduce corporate waste. As noted, high debt payments force managers to conserve cash by eliminating unnecessary expenditures.

Of course, increasing debt and reducing the available cash flow has its downside: It increases the risk of bankruptcy. Ben Bernanke, former chairman of the Fed, has argued that adding debt to a firm's capital structure is like putting a dagger into the steering wheel of a car.[14] The dagger—which points toward your stomach—motivates you to drive more carefully, but you may get stabbed if someone runs into you—even if you are being careful. The analogy applies to corporations in the following sense: Higher debt forces managers to be more careful with shareholders' money, but even well-run firms could face bankruptcy (get stabbed) if some event beyond their control occurs: a war, an earthquake, a strike, or a recession. To complete the analogy, the capital structure decision comes down to deciding how long a dagger stockholders should use to keep managers in line.

---

13. For more information, see Jonathon Baskin, "An Empirical Investigation of the Pecking Order Hypothesis," *Financial Management,* Spring 1989, pp. 26–35.

14. See Ben Bernanke, "Is There Too Much Corporate Debt?" *Federal Reserve Bank of Philadelphia Business Review,* September/October 1989, pp. 3–13.

Finally, too much debt may overly constrain managers. A large portion of a manager's personal wealth and reputation is tied to a single company, so managers are not well diversified. When faced with a positive-NPV project that is risky, a manager may decide that it's not worth taking on the risk even though well-diversified stockholders would find the risk acceptable. As previously mentioned, this is an underinvestment problem. The more debt the firm has, the greater the likelihood of financial distress and thus the greater the likelihood that managers will forgo risky projects even if they have positive NPVs.

16-3i The Investment Opportunity Set and Reserve Borrowing Capacity

Bankruptcy and financial distress are costly, and, as just reiterated, this can discourage highly levered firms from undertaking risky new investments. If potential new investments, although risky, have positive net present values, then high levels of debt can be doubly costly—the expected financial distress and bankruptcy costs are high, and the firm loses potential value by not making some potentially profitable investments. On the other hand, if a firm has very few profitable investment opportunities then high levels of debt can keep managers from wasting money by investing in poor projects. For such companies, increases in the debt ratio can actually increase the value of the firm.

Thus, in addition to the tax, signaling, bankruptcy, and managerial constraint effects discussed previously, the firm's optimal capital structure is related to its set of investment opportunities. Firms with many profitable opportunities should maintain their ability to invest by using low levels of debt, which is also consistent with maintaining reserve borrowing capacity. Firms with few profitable investment opportunities should use high levels of debt (which have high interest payments) to impose managerial constraint.[15]

16-3j The Market Timing Theory

If markets are efficient, then security prices should reflect all available information; hence they are neither underpriced nor overpriced (except during the time it takes prices to move to a new equilibrium caused by the release of new information). The *market timing theory* states that managers don't believe this and supposes instead that stock prices and interest rates are sometimes either too low or too high relative to their true fundamental values. In particular, the theory suggests that managers issue equity when they believe stock market prices are abnormally high and issue debt when they believe interest rates are abnormally low. In other words, they try to time the market.[16] Notice that this differs from signaling theory because no asymmetric information is involved. These managers aren't basing their beliefs on insider information, just on a different opinion than the market consensus.

---

15. See Michael J. Barclay and Clifford W. Smith, Jr., "The Capital Structure Puzzle: Another Look at the Evidence," *Journal of Applied Corporate Finance,* Spring 1999, pp. 8–20.

16. See Malcolm Baker and Jeffrey Wurgler, "Market Timing and Capital Structure," *Journal of Finance,* February 2002, pp. 1–32.

SELF TEST

Why does the MM theory with corporate taxes lead to 100% debt?

Explain how *asymmetric information* and *signals* affect capital structure decisions.

What is meant by *reserve borrowing capacity,* and why is it important to firms?

How can the use of debt serve to discipline managers?

16-4 Capital Structure Evidence and Implications

There have been hundreds, perhaps even thousands, of papers testing the capital structure theories described in the previous section. We can cover only the high-lights here, beginning with the empirical evidence.[17]

16-4a Empirical Evidence

Here is a brief summary of findings from the many papers that test the theories of capital structure discussed in the previous section.

The Trade-Off Between Tax Benefits and Bankruptcy Costs

Recent studies by Professors Van Binsbergen, Graham, and Yang and by Professor Korteweg suggest that the average net benefits of leverage (i.e., the value of the tax shield less the expected cost of financial distress) make up about 3% to 6% of a levered firm's value.[18] To put this into perspective, let's look at the impact of debt on an average company's value. The average company is financed with about 25% to 35% debt, so let's suppose that the company has $25 debt and $75 of equity, just to keep the arithmetic simple. The total net benefit of debt is about $5, based on the recent research. This implies that each dollar of debt adds (on average) about $0.20 of value ($5/$25 = 0.2) to the company. The first dollar of debt adds a bigger net benefit because bankruptcy risk is low when debt is low. By the time the 25th dollar of debt is added, its incremental net benefit is close to zero—the incremental expected costs of financial distress are about equal to the incremental expected tax shield.

These studies also showed that the net benefits of debt increase slowly until reaching the optimal level but decline rapidly thereafter. In other words, it isn't very costly to be somewhat below the optimal level of debt, but it is costly to exceed it.

A particularly interesting study by Professors Mehotra, Mikkelson, and Partch examined the capital structure of firms that were spun off from their parent

---

17. This section also draws heavily from Barclay and Smith, "The Capital Structure Puzzle," cited in footnote 19; Jay Ritter, ed., *Recent Developments in Corporate Finance* (Northampton, MA: Edward Elgar Publishing Inc., 2005); and a presentation by Jay Ritter at the 2003 FMA meeting, "The Windows of Opportunity Theory of Capital Structure."

18. See Jules H. Van Binsbergen, John H. Graham, and Jie Yang, "The Cost of Debt," *Journal of Finance*, Vol. 65, No. 6, December, 2010, pp. 2089–2135; also see Arthur Korteweg, "The Net Benefits to Leverage," *Journal of Finance*, Vol. 65, No. 6, December, 2010, pp. 2137–2169.

companies.[19] The financing choices of existing firms might be influenced by their past financing choices and by the costs of moving from one capital structure to another, but because spin-offs are newly created companies, managers can choose a capital structure without regard to these issues. The study found that more profitable firms (which have a lower expected probability of bankruptcy) and more asset-intensive firms (which have better collateral and thus a lower cost of bankruptcy should one occur) have higher levels of debt. These findings support the trade-off theory.

A Dynamic Trade-Off Theory

However, there is also evidence that is inconsistent with the static optimal target capital structure implied by the trade-off theory. For example, stock prices are volatile, which frequently causes a firm's actual market-based debt ratio to deviate from its target. However, such deviations don't cause firms to immediately return to their target by issuing or repurchasing securities. Instead, Professors Flannery and Rangan show that firms tend to make a partial adjustment each year, moving about 30% of the way toward their target capital structure. In a more recent study, Professors Faulkender, Flannery, Hankins, and Smith show that the speed of adjustment depends on a company's cash flows—companies with high cash flows adjust by about 50%. This effect is even more pronounced if the company's leverage exceeds its target—high cash flow companies in this situation have a 70% speed of adjustment. This is consistent with the idea that it is more costly to exceed the target debt ratio than to be lower than the target. [20]

Market Timing

If a stock price has a big run-up, which reduces the debt ratio, then the trade-off theory suggests that the firm should issue debt to return to its target. However, firms tend to do the opposite, issuing stock after big run-ups. This is much more consistent with the market timing theory, with managers trying to time the market by issuing stock when they perceive the market to be overvalued. Furthermore, firms tend to issue debt when stock prices and interest rates are low. The maturity of the issued debt seems to reflect an attempt to time interest rates: Firms tend to issue short-term debt if the term structure is upward sloping but long-term debt if the term structure is flat. Again, these facts suggest that managers try to time the market.

Signaling and the Pecking Order

Firms issue equity much less frequently than debt. On the surface, this seems to support both the pecking order hypothesis and the signaling hypothesis. The pecking order hypothesis predicts that firms with a high level of informational asymmetry, which causes equity issuances to be costly, should issue debt before issuing equity. Yet we often see the opposite, with high-growth firms (which usually have greater

---

19. See V. Mehotra, W. Mikkelson, and M. Partch, "The Design of Financial Policies in Corporate Spin-offs," *Review of Financial Studies*, Winter 2003, pp. 1359–1388.

20. See Mark Flannery and Kasturi Rangan, "Partial Adjustment toward Target Capital Structures," *Journal of Financial Economics*, Vol. 79, 2006, pp. 469–506. Also see Michael Faulkender, Mark Flannery, Kristine Hankins, and Jason Smith, "Cash Flows and Leverage," *Journal of Financial Economics*, Vol. 103, 2012, pp. 632–646.

informational asymmetry) issuing more equity than debt. Also, many highly profitable firms could afford to issue debt (which comes before equity in the pecking order) but instead choose to issue equity. With respect to the signaling hypothesis, consider the case of firms that have large increases in earnings that were unanticipated by the market. If managers have superior information, then they will anticipate these upcoming performance improvements and issue debt before the increase. Such firms do, in fact, tend to issue debt slightly more frequently than other firms, but the difference isn't economically meaningful.

Reserve Borrowing Capacity

Many firms have less debt than might be expected, and many have large amounts of short-term investments. This is especially true for firms with high market/book ratios (which indicate many growth options as well as informational asymmetry). This behavior is consistent with the hypothesis that investment opportunities influence attempts to maintain reserve borrowing capacity. It is also consistent with tax considerations, because low-growth firms (which have more debt) are more likely to benefit from the tax shield. This behavior is not consistent with the pecking order hypothesis, where low-growth firms (which often have high free cash flow) would be able to avoid issuing debt by raising funds internally.

Summary of Empirical Tests

To summarize these results, it appears that firms try to capture debt's tax benefits while avoiding financial distress costs. However, they also allow their debt ratios to deviate from the static optimal target ratio implied by the trade-off theory. In fact, Professors DeAngelo, DeAngelo, and Whited extend the dynamic trade-off model by showing that firms often deliberately issue debt to take advantage of unexpected investment opportunities, even if this causes them to exceed their target debt ratio.[21] Firms often maintain reserve borrowing capacity, especially firms with many growth opportunities or problems with informational asymmetry.[22] There is a little evidence indicating that firms follow a pecking order and use security issuances as signals, but there is some evidence in support of the market timing theory.

16-4b **Implications for Managers**

Managers should explicitly consider tax benefits when making capital structure decisions. Tax benefits obviously are more valuable for firms with high tax rates. Firms can utilize tax loss carryforwards and carrybacks, but the time value of money means that tax benefits are more valuable for firms with stable, positive pre-tax

---

21. See Harry DeAngelo, Linda DeAngelo, and Toni Whited, "Capital Structure Dynamics and Transitory Debt," *Journal of Financial Economics*, Vol. 99, 2011, pp. 235–261.

22. For more on empirical tests of capital structure theory, see Gregor Andrade and Steven Kaplan, "How Costly Is Financial (Not Economic) Distress? Evidence from Highly Leveraged Transactions That Became Distressed," *Journal of Finance*, Vol. 53, 1998, pp. 1443–1493; Malcolm Baker, Robin Greenwood, and Jeffrey Wurgler, "The Maturity of Debt Issues and Predictable Variation in Bond Returns," *Journal of Financial Economics*, November 2003, pp. 261–291; Murray Z. Frank and Vidhan K. Goyal, "Testing the Pecking Order Theory of Capital Structure," *Journal of Financial Economics*, February 2003, pp. 217–248; and Michael Long and Ileen Malitz, "The Investment-Financing Nexus: Some Empirical Evidence," *Midland Corporate Finance Journal*, Fall 1985, pp. 53–59.

income. Therefore, a firm whose sales are relatively stable can safely take on more debt and incur higher fixed charges than a company with volatile sales. Other things being equal, a firm with less operating leverage is better able to employ financial leverage because it will have less business risk and less volatile earnings.

Managers should also consider the expected cost of financial distress, which depends on the probability and cost of distress. Notice that stable sales and lower operating leverage provide tax benefits but also reduce the *probability* of financial distress. One *cost* of financial distress comes from lost investment opportunities. Firms with profitable investment opportunities need to be able to fund them, either by holding higher levels of marketable securities or by maintaining excess borrowing capacity.

Another cost of financial distress is the possibility of being forced to sell assets to meet liquidity needs. General-purpose assets that can be used by many businesses are relatively liquid and make good collateral, in contrast to special-purpose assets. Thus, real estate companies are usually highly leveraged, whereas companies involved in technological research are not.

Asymmetric information also has a bearing on capital structure decisions. For example, suppose a firm has just successfully completed an R&D program, and it forecasts higher earnings in the immediate future. However, the new earnings are not yet anticipated by investors and hence are not reflected in the stock price. This company should not issue stock—it should finance with debt until the higher earnings materialize and are reflected in the stock price. Then it could issue common stock, retire the debt, and return to its target capital structure.

Managers should consider conditions in the stock and bond markets. For example, during a recent credit crunch, the junk bond market dried up and there was simply no market at a "reasonable" interest rate for any new long-term bonds rated below BBB. Therefore, low-rated companies in need of capital were forced to go to the stock market or to the short-term debt market, regardless of their target capital structures. When conditions eased, however, these companies sold bonds to get their capital structures back on target.

Finally, managers should always consider lenders' and rating agencies' attitudes. For example, Moody's and Standard & Poor's told a large utility that its bonds would be downgraded if it issued more debt. This influenced the utility's decision to finance its expansion with common equity. This doesn't mean that managers should never increase debt if it will cause their bond rating to fall, but managers should always factor this into their decision making.[23]

> **SELF TEST**
>
> Which capital structure theories does the empirical evidence seem to support?
>
> What issues should managers consider when making capital structure decisions?

---

23. For some insights into how practicing financial managers view the capital structure decision, see John Graham and Campbell Harvey, "The Theory and Practice of Corporate Finance: Evidence from the Field," *Journal of Financial Economics,* Vol. 60, 2001, pp. 187–243; Ravindra R. Kamath, "Long-Term Financing Decisions: Views and Practices of Financial Managers of NYSE Firms," *Financial Review,* May 1997, pp. 331–356; and Edgar Norton, "Factors Affecting Capital Structure Decisions," *Financial Review,* August 1991, pp. 431–446.

16-5 **Estimating the Optimal Capital Structure**

Managers should choose the capital structure that maximizes shareholders' wealth. The basic approach is to consider a trial capital structure, based on the market values of the debt and equity, and then estimate the wealth of the shareholders under this capital structure. This approach should be repeated until an optimal capital structure is identified. There are several steps in the analysis of each potential capital structure: (1) Estimate the interest rate the firm will pay. (2) Estimate the cost of equity. (3) Estimate the weighted average cost of capital. (4) Estimate the value of operations, which is the present value of free cash flows discounted by the new WACC. The objective is to find the amount of debt financing that maximizes the value of operations. As we will show, this capital structure maximizes both shareholder wealth and the intrinsic stock price. The following sections explain each of these steps, using the company we considered earlier, Strasburg Electronics.

16-5a **Strasburg's Current Value and Capital Structure**

In Section 16-2, Strasburg was examining several different capital structure plans. Strasburg implemented Plan L, the one with high operating leverage and $50 million in debt financing. The plan has been in place for a year, and Strasburg's stock price is now $20 per share. With 10 million shares, Strasburg's market value of equity is $20(10) = $200 million. Strasburg has no short-term investments, so Strasburg's total enterprise value is the sum of its debt and equity: V = $50 + $200 = $250 million. In terms of market values, Strasburg's capital structure has 20% debt (w_d = $50/$250 = 0.20) and 80% equity (w_s = $200/$250 = 0.80). These calculations are reported in Figure 16-4 along with other input data.

Is this the optimal capital structure? We will address the question in more detail later, but for now let's focus on understanding Strasburg's current valuation, beginning with its cost of capital. Strasburg has a beta of 1.25. We can use the Capital Asset Pricing Model (CAPM) to estimate the cost of equity. The risk-free rate, r_{RF}, is 6.3% and the market risk premium, RP_M, is 6%, so the cost of equity is:

$$r_s = r_{RF} + b(RP_M) = 6.3\% + 1.25(6\%) = 13.8\%$$

The weighted average cost of capital is:

$$\begin{aligned} WACC &= w_d(1 - T)r_d + w_s r_s \\ &= 20\%(1 - 0.40)(8\%) + 80\%(13.8\%) \\ &= 12\% \end{aligned}$$

As shown previously in Figure 16-1, Plan L has a NOPAT of $30 million. Strasburg expects zero growth, which means there are no required investments in capital. Therefore, FCF is equal to NOPAT. Using the constant growth formula, the value of operations is:

$$V_{op} = \frac{FCF(1 + g)}{WACC - g} = \frac{\$30(1 + 0)}{0.12 - 0} = \$250$$

Figure 16-4 illustrates the calculation of the intrinsic stock price. For Strasburg, the intrinsic stock price and the market price are each equal to $20. Can Strasburg increase its value by changing its capital structure? The next sections answer that question.

FIGURE 16-4 Strasburg's Current Value and Capital Structure (Millions of Dollars, Except for Per Share Data)

	A	B	C	D	E
109	Input Data:		Capital Structure:		
110	Tax rate	40.00%	Market value of equity (S = P x n)		$200
111	Debt (D)	$50.00	Total value (V = D + S)		$250
112	# of shares (n)	10.00	% financed with debt (w_d = D/V)		20%
113	Stock price (P)	$20.00	% financed with stock (w_s = S/V)		80%
114	NOPAT	$30.00			
115	Free Cash Flow (FCF)[a]	$30.00			
116	Growth rate in FCF[a]	0.00%			
117	Cost of Capital:		Estimated Intrinsic Value:		
118	Cost of debt (r_d)	8.00%	Value of operations:		
119	Beta (b)	1.25	V_{op} = [FCF(1+g)]/(WACC−g)		$250.00
120	Risk-free rate (r_{RF})	6.30%	+ Value of ST investments		$0.00
121	Mkt. risk prem. (RP_M)	6.00%	Estimated total intrinsic value		$250.00
122	Cost of equity:		− Debt		$50.00
123	r_s = r_{RF} + b(RP_M)	13.80%	Estimated intrinsic value of equity		$200.00
124	WACC	12.00%	÷ Number of shares		10.00
125			Estimated intrinsic price per share		$20.00

Note:
[a]Strasburg's sales, earnings, and assets are not growing, so it does not need investments in operating capital. Therefore, FCF = NOPAT (1 − T). The growth in FCF also is zero.

Microsoft Excel® is a registered trademark of Microsoft Corporation. © 2014 Microsoft.

16-5b Estimating the Weighted Average Cost of Capital (WACC) for Different Levels of Debt

Following is a description of the steps to estimate the weighted average cost of capital for different levels of debt.

Estimating the Cost of Debt (r_d)

The CFO asked Strasburg's investment bankers to estimate the cost of debt at different capital structures. The investment bankers began by analyzing industry conditions and prospects. They appraised Strasburg's business risk based on its past financial statements and its current technology and customer base. The bankers also forecasted financial statements with different capital structures and analyzed such key ratios as the current ratio and the times-interest-earned ratio. Finally, they factored in current conditions in the financial markets, including interest rates paid by firms in Strasburg's industry. Based on their analysis and judgment, they estimated interest rates at various capital structures as shown in Row 2 of Figure 16-5, starting with a 7.7% cost of debt for the first dollar of debt.[24] This rate increases to 16% if

---

24. For a description of a technique for estimating the cost of debt, see Jules H. Van Binsbergen, John H. Graham, and Jie Yang, "An Empirical Model of Optimal Capital Structure," *Journal of Applied Corporate Finance*, Vol. 23, No. 4, Fall, 2011, pp. 34–59. They also provide an approach for estimating the optimal capital structure that explicitly incorporates the tax benefits of debt net of the financial distress costs and other costs.

FIGURE 16-5	Estimating Strasburg's Optimal Capital Structure (Millions of Dollars)

	A	B	C	D	E	F	G	H
140		**Percent of Firm Financed with Debt (w$_d$)**						
141		0%	10%	20%	30%	40%	50%	60%
142	1. w_s	100.00%	90.00%	80.00%	70.00%	60.00%	50.00%	40.00%
143	2. r_d	7.70%	7.80%	8.00%	8.50%	9.90%	12.00%	16.00%
144	3. b	1.09	1.16	1.25	1.37	1.52	1.74	2.07
145	4. r_s	12.82%	13.26%	13.80%	14.50%	15.43%	16.73%	18.69%
146	5. r_d (1−T)	4.62%	4.68%	4.80%	5.10%	5.94%	7.20%	9.60%
147	6. WACC	12.82%	12.40%	12.00%	11.68%	11.63%	11.97%	13.24%
148	7. V_{op}	$233.98	$241.96	$250.00	$256.87	$257.86	$250.68	$226.65
149	8. Debt	$0.00	$24.20	$50.00	$77.06	$103.14	$125.34	$135.99
150	9. Equity	$233.98	$217.76	$200.00	$179.81	$154.72	$125.34	$90.66
151	10. # Shares	12.72	11.34	10.00	8.69	7.44	6.25	5.13
152	11. Stock price	$18.40	$19.20	$20.00	$20.69	$20.79	$20.07	$17.66
153	12. Net income	$30.00	$28.87	$27.60	$26.07	$23.87	$20.98	$16.95
154	13. EPS	$2.36	$2.54	$2.76	$3.00	$3.21	$3.36	$3.30

Notes:

1. The percent financed with equity is $w_s = 1 − w_d$.
2. The interest rate on debt, r_d, is obtained from investment bankers.
3. Beta is estimated using Hamada's formula, the unlevered beta of 1.09, and a tax rate of 40%: $b = b_U [1 + (1 − T)(w_d/w_s)]$.
4. The cost of equity is estimated using the CAPM formula with a risk-free rate of 6.3% and a market risk premium of 6%: $r_s = r_{RF} + b(RP_M)$.
5. The after-tax cost of debt is $r_d(1 − T)$, where T = 40%.
6. The weighted average cost of capital is calculated as WACC $= w_d r_d(1 − T) + w_s r_s$.
7. The value of the firm's operations is calculated as $V_{op} = [FCF(1 + g)] / (WACC − g)$, where FCF = $30 million and g = 0.
8. Debt $= w_d × V_{op}$.
9. The intrinsic value of equity after the recapitalization and repurchase is $S_{Post} = V_{op} − Debt = w_s × V_{op}$.
10. The number of shares after the recap has been completed is found using this equation: $n_{Post} = n_{Prior} × [(V_{opNew} − D_{New}) / (V_{opNew} − D_{Old})]$. The subscript "Old" indicates values from the original capital structure, where w_d = 20%; the subscript "New" indicates values at the current capital structure after the recap and repurchase; and the subscript "Post" indicates values after the recap and repurchase.
11. The price after the recap and repurchase is $P_{Post} = S_{Post}/n_{Post}$, but we can also find the price as $P_{Post} = (V_{opNew} − D_{Old})/n_{Prior}$.
12. EBIT is $50 million; see Figure 16-1. Net income is NI $= (EBIT − r_d D)(1 − T)$.
13. Earnings per share is EPS $= NI/n_{Post}$.

Microsoft Excel® is a registered trademark of Microsoft Corporation. © 2014 Microsoft.

the firm finances 60% of its capital structure with debt. Strasburg's current situation is in Column D and is shown in blue. (We will explain all the rows in Figure 16-5 in the following discussion.)

Estimating the Cost of Equity (r$_s$) Using the Hamada Equation

An increase in the debt ratio also increases the risk faced by shareholders, and this has an effect on the cost of equity, r_s. Recall from Chapter 2 that a stock's beta is the relevant measure of risk for diversified investors. Moreover, it has been demonstrated, both theoretically and empirically, that beta increases with financial leverage. The **Hamada equation** specifies the effect of financial leverage on beta:[25]

(16–9)	$$b = b_U[1 + (1 - T)(D/S)]$$

Here D is the market value of the debt and S is the market value of the equity. The Hamada equation shows how increases in the market value debt/equity ratio increase beta. Here **b_U** is the firm's **unlevered beta** coefficient—that is, the beta it would have if it had no debt. In that case, beta would depend entirely on business risk and thus be a measure of the firm's "basic business risk."

Sometimes it is more convenient to work with the percentages of debt and equity at which the firm is financed (w_d and w_s) rather than the dollar values of D and S. Notice that w_d and w_s are defined as D/(D + S) and S/(D + S), respectively. This means that the ratio w_d/w_s is equal to the ratio D/S. Substituting these values gives us another form of Hamada's formula:

(16–9a)	$$b = b_U[1 + (1 - T)(w_d/w_s)]$$

Often we know the current capital structure and beta but wish to know the unlevered beta. We find this by rearranging Equation 16-9a as follows:

(16–10)	$$b_U = b/[1 + (1 - T)(w_d/w_s)]$$

For Strasburg, the unlevered beta is:

$$b_U = 1.25/[1 + (1 - 0.40)(0.20/0.80)]$$
$$= 1.087$$

Using this unlevered beta, we can then apply Hamada's formula in Equation 16-9a to determine estimates of Strasburg's beta for different capital structures. These results are reported in Line 3 of Figure 16-5.

Recall from Section 16.2 that the risk-free rate is 6.3% and the market risk premium is 6%. We can use the CAPM and the previously estimated betas to estimate Strasburg's cost of equity for different capital structures (which cause Strasburg's beta to change). These results are shown in Line 4 of Figure 16-5. As expected, Strasburg's cost of equity increases as its debt increases. Figure 16-6 graphs Strasburg's required return on equity at different debt ratios. Observe that the cost of equity consists of the 6.3% risk-free rate, a constant premium for business risk in the amount of $RP_M(b_U) = 6.522\%$, and a premium for financial risk in the amount of

---

25. See Robert S. Hamada, "Portfolio Analysis, Market Equilibrium, and Corporation Finance," *Journal of Finance*, March 1969, pp. 13–31. For a comprehensive framework, see Robert A. Taggart, Jr., "Consistent Valuation and Cost of Capital Expressions with Corporate and Personal Taxes," *Financial Management*, Autumn 1991, pp. 8–20.

| FIGURE 16-6 | Strasburg's Required Rate of Return on Equity at Different Debt Levels |

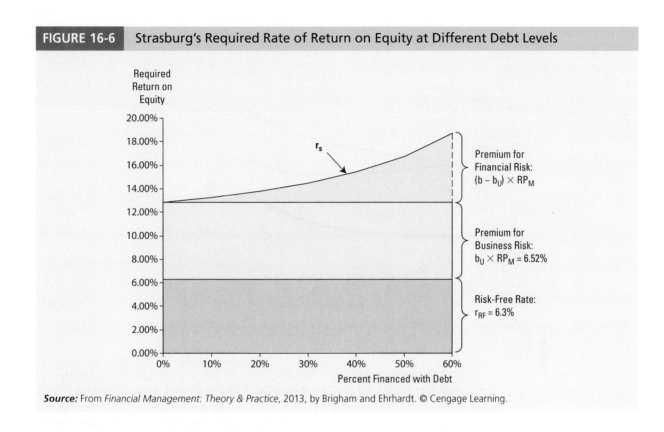

Source: From *Financial Management: Theory & Practice*, 2013, by Brigham and Ehrhardt. © Cengage Learning.

$RP_M(b - b_U)$ that starts at zero (because $b = b_U$ for zero debt) but rises at an increasing rate as the debt ratio increases.

The Weighted Average Cost of Capital at Different Levels of Debt

Line 6 of Figure 16-5 shows Strasburg's weighted average cost of capital, WACC, at different capital structures. As the debt ratio increases, the costs of both debt and equity rise, at first slowly but then at an accelerating rate. Eventually, the increasing costs of these two components offset the fact that more debt (which is still less costly than equity) is being used. At 40% debt, Strasburg's WACC hits a minimum of 11.63%; Column F is shown in silver to indicate that it is the capital structure with the minimum WACC. Notice that the WACC begins to increase for capital structures with more than 40% debt. Figure 16-7 shows how the WACC changes as debt increases.

Also note that, even though the component cost of equity is always higher than that of debt, only using debt would not maximize value. If Strasburg were to issue more than 40% debt, then the costs of both debt and equity would increase in such a way that the overall WACC would increase, because the cost of debt would increase by more than the cost of equity.

16-5c **Estimating the Firm's Value**

As we showed previously, Strasburg currently has a $250 million intrinsic value of operations: $w_d = 20\%$, WACC = 12%, FCF = $30 million, and zero growth in FCF.

| FIGURE 16-7 | Effects of Capital Structure on the Cost of Capital |

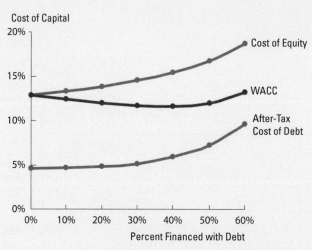

Source: From *Financial Management: Theory & Practice,* 2013, by Brigham and Ehrhardt. © Cengage Learning.

Using the same approach as in Section 16-2, we can use the data in Figure 16-5 to estimate Strasburg's value of operations at different capital structures; these results are reported in Line 7 of Figure 16-5 and are graphed in Figure 16-8.[26] The maximum value of $257.86 million occurs at a capital structure with 40% debt, which also is the capital structure that minimizes the WACC.

Notice that the value of the firm initially increases but then begins to fall. As discussed earlier, the value initially rises because the WACC initially falls. But the rising costs of equity and debt eventually cause the WACC to increase, causing the value of the firm to fall. Notice how flat the curve is around the optimal level of debt. Thus, it doesn't make a great deal of difference whether Strasburg's capital structure has 30% debt or 40% debt. Also, notice that the maximum value is about 10% greater than the value with no debt. Although this example is for a single company, the results are not unrealistic: The optimal capital structure for most firms can add 2% to 15% more value relative to zero debt, and there is a fairly wide range of w_d (from about 20% to 50%) over which value changes very little.

Figures 16-5 and 16-8 also show the values of debt and equity for each capital structure. The value of debt is found by multiplying the value of operations by the percentage of the firm that is financed by debt: Debt = $w_d \times V_{op}$. The intrinsic value of equity is found in a similar manner: S = V_{op} − Debt = $w_s \times V_{op}$. Even though the intrinsic value of equity falls as debt increases, the wealth of shareholders is maximized at the maximum value of operations, as we explain in the next section.

---

26. In this analysis, we assume that Strasburg's expected EBIT and FCF are constant for the various capital structures. In a more refined analysis, we might try to estimate any possible declines in FCF at high levels of debt as the threat of bankruptcy becomes imminent.

FIGURE 16-8	Effects of Capital Structure on the Value of Operations

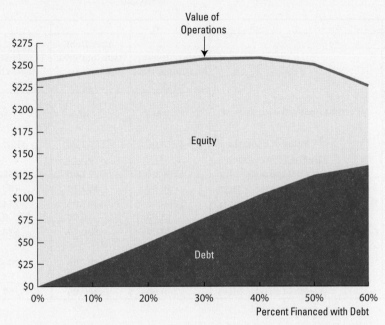

Source: From *Financial Management: Theory & Practice*, 2013, by Brigham and Ehrhardt. © Cengage Learning.

What happens to the costs of debt and equity when the leverage increases? Explain.

Use the Hamada equation to calculate the unlevered beta for JAB Industries, assuming the following data: Levered beta = b = 1.4; T = 40%; w_d = 45%. **(0.939)**

Suppose r_{RF} = 6% and RP_M = 5%. What would be the cost of equity for JAB Industries if it had no debt? **(10.7%)** If w_d were 45%? **(13.0%)**

16-6 **Anatomy of a Recapitalization**

Strasburg should **recapitalize**, meaning that it should issue enough additional debt to optimize its capital structure and then use the debt proceeds to repurchase stock. As shown in Figure 16-5, a capital structure with 40% debt is optimal. But before tackling the **recap**, as it is commonly called, let's consider the sequence of events, starting with the situation before Strasburg issues any additional debt. Figure 16-4 shows the valuation analysis of Strasburg at a capital structure consisting of 20% debt and 80% equity. These results are repeated in Column 1 of Figure 16-9, along with the shareholder wealth, which consists entirely of $200 million in stock before the repurchase. The next step is to examine the impact of Strasburg's debt issuance.

FIGURE 16-9	Anatomy of a Recapitalization (Millions, Except for Per Share Data)

	A	B	C	D	E
324				After Debt	
325			Before Issuing	Issue, but Prior	Post
326			Additional Debt	to Repurchase	Repurchase
327			(1)	(2)	(3)
328					
329	**Percent financed with debt: w_d**		20%	40%	40%
330					
331	Value of operations		$250.00	$257.86	$257.86
332	+ Value of ST investments		0.00	53.14	0.00
333	Estimated total intrinsic value		$250.00	$311.00	$257.86
334	− Debt		50.00	103.14	103.14
335	Estimated intrinsic value of equity		$200.00	$207.86	$154.72
336	÷ Number of shares		10.00	10.00	7.44
337	Estimated intrinsic price per share		$20.00	$20.79	$20.79
338					
339	Value of stock		$200.00	$207.86	$154.72
340	+ Cash distributed in repurchase		0.00	0.00	53.14
341	Wealth of shareholders		$200.00	$207.86	$207.86

Notes:
1. The value of ST investments in Column 2 is equal to the amount of cash raised by issuing additional debt. This cash has not yet been used to repurchase shares, so it is held in the form of short-term investments: ST investments = $D_{New} - D_{Old}$.
2. The value of ST investments in Column 3 is zero because the funds have been used to repurchase shares of stock.
3. The number of shares in Column 3 reflects the shares repurchased: $n_{Post} = n_{Prior} - (Cash_{Rep}/P_{Prior}) = n_{Prior} - [(D_{New} - D_{Old})/P_{Prior}]$.

Microsoft Excel® is a registered trademark of Microsoft Corporation. © 2014 Microsoft.

16-6a Strasburg Issues New Debt but Has Not Yet Repurchased Stock

The next step in the recap is to issue debt and announce the firm's intent to repurchase stock with the newly issued debt. At the optimal capital structure of 40% debt, the value of the firm's operations is $257.86 million, as calculated in Figure 16-5 and repeated in Column 2 of Figure 16-9. This value of operations is greater than the $250 million value of operations for $w_d = 20\%$ because the WACC is lower. Notice that Strasburg raised its debt from $50 million to $103.14 million, an increase of $53.14 million. Because Column 2 reports data prior to the repurchase, Strasburg has short-term investments in the amount of $53.14 million, the amount that was raised in the debt issuance but that has not yet been used to repurchase stock.[27] As Figure 16-9 shows, Strasburg's intrinsic value of equity is $207.86 million.

Because Strasburg has not yet repurchased any stock, it still has 10 million shares outstanding. Therefore, the price per share after the debt issue but prior to the repurchase is:

$$P_{Prior} = S_{Prior}/n_{Prior}$$
$$= \$207.86/10 = \$20.79$$

---

27. These calculations are shown in the *Excel* file **Ch16 Tool Kit.xls** on the textbook's Web site. The values reported in the text are rounded, but the values used in calculations in the spreadsheet are not rounded.

Column 2 of Figure 16-9 summarizes these calculations and also shows the wealth of the shareholders. The shareholders own Strasburg's equity, which is worth $207.86 million. Strasburg has not yet made any cash distributions to shareholders, so the total wealth of shareholders is $207.86 million. The new wealth of $207.86 million is greater than the initial wealth of $200 million, so the recapitalization has added value to Strasburg's shareholders. This increase in value comes from reducing the amount of taxes Strasburg pays and represents a transfer of value from the government to Strasburg's shareholders. By increasing the level of debt, interest expense increases and taxes go down. Notice also that the recapitalization caused the intrinsic stock price to increase from $20.00 to $20.79.[28]

Summarizing these results, we see that the issuance of debt and the resulting change in the optimal capital structure caused: (1) the WACC to decrease, (2) the value of operations to increase, (3) shareholder wealth to increase, and (4) the stock price to increase.

16-6b **Strasburg Repurchases Stock**

What happens to the stock price during the repurchase? In Chapter 15, we discussed repurchases and noted that a repurchase does not change the stock price. It is true that the additional debt will change the WACC and the stock price prior to the repurchase (P_{Prior}), but the subsequent repurchase itself will not affect the post-repurchase stock price (P_{Post}).[29] Therefore, $P_{Post} = P_{Prior}$. (Keep in mind that P_{Prior} is the price immediately prior to the repurchase, not the price prior to announcing the recapitalization and issuing the debt in this example.)

Strasburg uses the entire amount of cash raised by the debt issue to repurchase stock. The total cash raised is equal to $D_{New} - D_{Old}$. The number of shares repurchased is equal to the cash raised by issuing debt divided by the repurchase price:

$$\text{Number of shares repurchased} = \frac{D_{new} - D_{Old}}{P_{Prior}}$$

(16–11)

Strasburg repurchases ($103.14 − $50)/$20.79 = 2.56 million shares of stock.

The number of remaining shares after the repurchase, n_{Post}, is equal to the initial number of shares minus the number that is repurchased:

$$
\begin{aligned}
n_{Post} &= \text{Number of outstanding shares remaining after the repurchase} \\
&= n_{Prior} - \text{Number of shares repurchased} \\
&= n_{Prior} - \frac{D_{new} - D_{Old}}{P_{Prior}}
\end{aligned}
$$

(16–12)

---

28. The increase in value is, in principle, the present value of the new interest tax shields as in Equation 16-6. Hamada's formula for levering beta, Equation 16-9, was developed for the special case in which debt is risk free. Since $r_d > r_f$ in this example, the additional value doesn't exactly equal the present value of the tax shields. Chapter 17 develops an equation similar to Equation 16-9 that deals with risky debt, and when it is used to lever and unlever beta, the additional value from a recapitalization is precisely equal to the present value of the new interest tax shields.

29. As we discuss in Chapter 15, a stock repurchase may be a signal of a company's future prospects or it may be the way a company "announces" a change in capital structure, and either of these situations could have an impact on estimated free cash flows or WACC. However, neither situation applies to Strasburg.

For Strasburg, the number of remaining shares after the repurchase is:

$$n_{Post} = n_{Prior} - (D_{New} - D_{Old})/P_{Prior}$$
$$= 10 - (\$103.14 - \$50)/\$20.79$$
$$= 7.44 \text{ million}$$

Column 3 of Figure 16-9 summarizes these post-repurchase results. The repurchase doesn't change the value of operations, which remains at $257.86 million. However, the short-term investments are sold and the cash is used to repurchase stock. Strasburg is left with no short-term investments, so the intrinsic value of equity is:

$$S_{Post} = \$257.86 - \$103.14 = \$154.72 \text{ million}$$

After the repurchase, Strasburg has 7.44 million shares of stock. We can verify that the intrinsic stock price has not changed:[30]

$$P_{Post} = S_{Post}/n_{Post} = \$154.72/7.44 = \$20.79$$

Shareholders now own an equity position in the company worth only $154.72 million, but they have received a cash distribution in the amount of $53.14 million, so their total wealth is equal to the value of their equity plus the amount of cash they received: $154.72 + $53.14 = $207.86.

Here are some points worth noting. As shown in Column 3 of Figure 16-9, the change in capital structure clearly added wealth to the shareholders, increased the price per share, and increased the cash (in the form of short-term investments) temporarily held by the company. However, the repurchase itself did not affect shareholder wealth or the price per share. The repurchase did reduce the cash held by the company and the number of shares outstanding, but shareholder wealth stayed constant. After the repurchase, shareholders directly own the funds used in the repurchase; before the repurchase, shareholders indirectly own the funds. In either case, shareholders own the funds. The repurchase simply takes them out of the company's account and puts them into the shareholders' personal accounts.

The approach we've described here is based on the corporate valuation model, and it will always provide the correct value for S_{Post}, n_{Post}, and P_{Post}. However, there is a quicker way to calculate these values if the firm has no short-term investments either before or after the recap (other than the temporary short-term investments held between the time debt was issued and shares repurchased). After the recap is completed, the percentage of equity in the capital structure, based on market values, is equal to $1 - w_d$ if the firm holds no other short-term investments. Therefore, the value of equity after the repurchase is:

(16–13)

$$S_{Post} = V_{opNew}(1 - w_d)$$

where we use the subscript "New" to indicate the value of operations at the new capital structure and the subscript "Post" to indicate the post-repurchase intrinsic value of equity.

---

30. There may be a small rounding difference due to using rounded numbers in intermediate steps. See the *Excel* file *Ch16 Tool Kit.xls* for the exact calculations.

The post-repurchase number of shares can be found using this equation:

$$n_{Post} = n_{Prior} \left[\frac{V_{opNew} - D_{New}}{V_{opNew} - D_{Old}} \right]$$

(16–14)

Given the value of equity and the number of shares, it is straightforward to calculate the intrinsic price per share as $P_{Post} = S_{Post}/n_{Post}$. But we can also calculate the post-repurchase price using:

$$P_{Post} = \frac{V_{opNew} - D_{Old}}{n_{Prior}}$$

(16–15)

Figure 16-5 reports the number of shares and the intrinsic price per share in Lines 10–11. Notice that the number of shares goes down as debt goes up because the debt proceeds are used to buy back stock. Notice also that the capital structure that maximizes stock price, $w_d = 40\%$, is the same capital structure that optimizes the WACC and the value of operations.

Figure 16-5 also reports the earnings per share for the different levels of debt. Figure 16-10 graphs the intrinsic price per share and the earnings per share. Notice that the maximum earnings per share is at 50% debt even though the optimal capital structure is at 40% debt. This means that maximizing EPS will not maximize shareholder wealth.

FIGURE 16-10   **Effects of Capital Structure on Stock Price and Earnings Per Share**

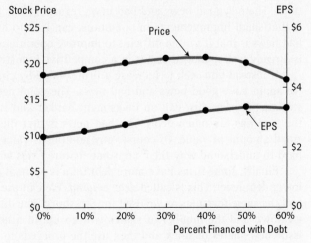

Source: From *Financial Management: Theory & Practice*, 2013, by Brigham and Ehrhardt. © Cengage Learning.

THE GLOBAL ECONOMIC CRISIS

Deleveraging

Many households, nonfinancial businesses, and financial institutions loaded up on easy credit during the run-up to the global economic crisis and found themselves with too much debt during the recession that began in 2007. The process of reducing debt is called *deleveraging,* and it is painful for individuals and the economy.

The debt-to-income ratio for households increased from around 80%–90% during the 1990s to a peak of 133% in 2007. To deleverage, many households cut spending on consumer goods and paid off some of their debt. This belt-tightening is difficult for the individual households, but it also is difficult for the economy because decreased spending leads to economic contraction and job losses. Other households deleveraged by declaring bankruptcy, with over 1.5 million people filing in 2010.

Like individuals, businesses can deleverage by paying off debt or by declaring bankruptcy, and many did so during this global economic crisis. But businesses can also deleverage by issuing equity. For example, Dunkin' Brands Group, owner of the Dunkin' Donuts and Baskin-Robbins brands, issued $427 million in stock in July 2011, part of which was used to pay down debt. And Wells Fargo and Morgan Stanley issued over $12 billion in stock in May of 2009. A problem with deleveraging via stock issuances is that the stock price usually has been beaten down so much by the time of deleveraging that the new investors get a larger stake in the company, which dilutes the existing stockholders. But the bottom line is that dilution is better than bankruptcy!

Sources: Reuven Glick and Kevin J. Lansing, "U.S. Household Deleveraging and Future Consumption Growth," FRBSF Economic Letter, May 15, 2009, **www.frbsf.org/publications/economics/letter/2009/el2009-16.pdf**; and BankruptcyAction.com, **www.bankruptcyaction.com/USbankstats.htm**, May 2009.

16-6c **Recapitalization: A Post-Mortem**

In Chapter 9, we saw how a company can increase its value by improving its operations. There is good news and bad news regarding this connection. The good news is that small improvements in operations can lead to huge increases in value. The bad news is that it's often difficult to improve operations, especially if the company is already well managed and is in a competitive industry.

If instead you seek to increase a firm's value by changing its capital structure, we again have good news and bad news. The good news is that changing capital structure is easy—just call an investment banker and issue debt (or issue equity if the firm has too much debt). The bad news is that this will add only a relatively small amount of value. Of course, any additional value is better than none, so it's hard to understand why there are some mature firms with zero debt.

Finally, some firms have more debt than is optimal and should recapitalize to a lower debt level. This is called *deleveraging.* We can use exactly the same approach and the same formulas as we used for Strasburg. The difference is that the debt will go down and the number of shares will go up. In other words, the company will issue new shares of stock and then use the proceeds to pay off debt, resulting in a capital structure with less debt and lower interest payments.

A firm's value of operations is equal to $800 million after a recapitalization. (The firm had no debt before the recap.) The firm raised $200 million in new debt and used this to buy back stock. The firm had no short-term investments before or after the recap. After the recap, w_d = 25%. The firm had 10 million shares before the recap. What is S (the value of equity after the recap)? **($600 million)** What is P (the stock price after the recap)? **($80/share)** What is n (the number of remaining shares after the recap)? **(7.5 million)**

Summary

This chapter examined the effects of financial leverage on stock prices, earnings per share, and the cost of capital. The key concepts covered are listed below.

- A firm's **optimal capital structure** is the mix of debt and equity that maximizes the stock price. At any point in time, management has a specific **target capital structure** in mind, presumably the optimal one, but this target may change over time.
- Several factors influence a firm's capital structure. These include its: (1) **business risk**, (2) **tax position**, (3) need for **financial flexibility**, (4) **managerial conservatism or aggressiveness**, and (5) **growth opportunities**.
- **Business risk** is the risk inherent in the firm's operations if it uses no debt. A firm will have little business risk if the demand for its products is stable, if the prices of its inputs and products remain relatively constant, if it can adjust its prices freely if costs increase, and if a high percentage of its costs are variable and hence will decrease if sales decrease. Other things the same, the lower a firm's business risk, the higher its optimal debt ratio.
- **Financial leverage** is the extent to which fixed-income securities (debt and preferred stock) are used in a firm's capital structure. **Financial risk** is the added risk borne by stockholders as a result of financial leverage.
- **Operating leverage** is the extent to which fixed costs are used in a firm's operations. In business terminology, a high degree of operating leverage, other factors held constant, implies that a relatively small change in sales results in a large change in ROIC. *Web Extension 16A* describes additional measures of operating and financial leverage.
- If there are no corporate or personal taxes, Modigliani and Miller showed that the value of a levered firm is equal to the value of an otherwise identical but unlevered firm:

$$V_L = V_U$$

- If there are only corporate taxes, Modigliani and Miller showed that a firm's value increases as it adds debt due to the interest rate deductibility of debt:

$$V_L = V_U + TD$$

- If there are personal and corporate taxes, Miller showed that:

$$V_L = V_U + \left[1 - \frac{(1 - T_c)(1 - T_s)}{(1 - T_d)} \right] D$$

- The **Hamada equation** shows the effect of financial leverage on beta as follows:

$$b = b_U[1 + (1 - T)(D/S)]$$

Firms can use their current beta, tax rate, and debt/equity ratio to derive their **unlevered beta, b_U**, as follows:

$$b_U = b/[1 + (1 - T)(D/S)] = b/[1 + (1 - T)(w_d/w_s)]$$

- The **trade-off theory** of capital structure states that debt initially adds value because interest is tax deductible but that debt also brings costs associated with actual or potential bankruptcy. The optimal capital structure strikes a balance between the tax benefits of debt and the costs associated with bankruptcy.
- A firm's decision to use debt versus stock to raise new capital sends a **signal** to investors. A stock issue is viewed as a negative signal, whereas a debt issuance is a positive (or at least a neutral) signal. As a result, companies try to avoid having to issue stock by maintaining a **reserve borrowing capacity**, and this means using less debt in "normal" times than the trade-off theory would suggest.
- A firm's owners may decide to use a relatively large amount of debt to constrain the managers. A *high debt ratio raises the threat of bankruptcy,* which not only carries a cost but also forces managers to be more careful and less wasteful with shareholders' money. Many of the corporate takeovers and leveraged buyouts in recent years were designed to improve efficiency by reducing the cash flow available to managers.

Questions

16–1 Define each of the following terms:
  a. Capital structure; business risk; financial risk
  b. Operating leverage; financial leverage; break-even point
  c. Reserve borrowing capacity

16–2 What term refers to the uncertainty inherent in projections of future ROIC?

16–3 Firms with relatively high nonfinancial fixed costs are said to have a high degree of what?

16–4 "One type of leverage affects both EBIT and EPS. The other type affects only EPS." Explain this statement.

16-5 Why is the following statement true? "Other things being the same, firms with relatively stable sales are able to carry relatively high debt ratios."

16-6 Why do public utility companies usually have capital structures that are different from those of retail firms?

16-7 Why is EBIT generally considered to be independent of financial leverage? Why might EBIT be influenced by financial leverage at high debt levels?

16-8 If a firm went from zero debt to successively higher levels of debt, why would you expect its stock price to first rise, then hit a peak, and then begin to decline?

Problems

Answers Appear in Appendix B

Easy Problems 1–6

16-1 Break-even Quantity
Shapland Inc. has fixed operating costs of $500,000 and variable costs of $50 per unit. If it sells the product for $75 per unit, what is the break-even quantity?

16-2 Unlevered Beta
Counts Accounting has a beta of 1.15. The tax rate is 40%, and Counts is financed with 20% debt. What is Counts' unlevered beta?

16-3 Premium for Financial Risk
Ethier Enterprise has an unlevered beta of 1.0. Ethier is financed with 50% debt and has a levered beta of 1.6. If the risk-free rate is 5.5% and the market risk premium is 6%, how much is the additional premium that Ethier's shareholders require to be compensated for financial risk?

16-4 Value of Equity after Recapitalization
Nichols Corporation's value of operations is equal to $500 million after a recapitalization (the firm had no debt before the recap). It raised $200 million in new debt and used this to buy back stock. Nichols had no short-term investments before or after the recap. After the recap, w_d = 40%. What is S (the value of equity after the recap)?

16-5 Stock Price after Recapitalization
Lee Manufacturing's value of operations is equal to $900 million after a recapitalization. (The firm had no debt before the recap.) Lee raised $300 million in new debt and used this to buy back stock. Lee had no short-term investments before or after the recap. After the recap, w_d = 1/3. The firm had 30 million shares before the recap. What is P (the stock price after the recap)?

16-6 Shares Remaining after Recapitalization
Dye Trucking raised $150 million in new debt and used this to buy back stock. After the recap, Dye's stock price is $7.50. If Dye had 60 million shares of stock before the recap, how many shares does it have after the recap?

Intermediate Problems 7-8

16-7 Break-Even Point

Schweser Satellites Inc. produces satellite earth stations that sell for $100,000 each. The firm's fixed costs, F, are $2 million, 50 earth stations are produced and sold each year, profits total $500,000, and the firm's assets (all equity financed) are $5 million. The firm estimates that it can change its production process, adding $4 million to investment and $500,000 to fixed operating costs. This change will: (1) reduce variable costs per unit by $10,000 and (2) increase output by 20 units, but (3) the sales price on all units will have to be lowered to $95,000 to permit sales of the additional output. The firm has tax loss carryforwards that render its tax rate zero, its cost of equity is 16%, and it uses no debt.

a. What is the incremental profit? To get a rough idea of the project's profitability, what is the project's expected rate of return for the next year (defined as the incremental profit divided by the investment)? Should the firm make the investment? Why or why not?

b. Would the firm's break-even point increase or decrease if it made the change?

c. Would the new situation expose the firm to more or less business risk than the old one?

16-8 Capital Structure Analysis

The Rivoli Company has no debt outstanding, and its financial position is given by the following data:

Assets (Market value = Book value)	$3,000,000
EBIT	$ 500,000
Cost of equity, r_s	10%
Stock price, P_0	$ 15
Shares outstanding, n_0	200,000
Tax rate, T (federal-plus-state)	40%

The firm is considering selling bonds and simultaneously repurchasing some of its stock. If it moves to a capital structure with 30% debt based on market values, its cost of equity, r_s, will increase to 11% to reflect the increased risk. Bonds can be sold at a cost, r_d, of 7%. Rivoli is a no-growth firm. Hence, all its earnings are paid out as dividends. Earnings are expected to be constant over time.

a. What effect would this use of leverage have on the value of the firm?

b. What would be the price of Rivoli's stock?

c. What happens to the firm's earnings per share after the recapitalization?

d. The $500,000 EBIT given previously is actually the expected value from the following probability distribution:

Probability	EBIT
0.10	($ 100,000)
0.20	200,000
0.40	500,000
0.20	800,000
0.10	1,100,000

Determine the times-interest-earned ratio for each probability. What is the probability of not covering the interest payment at the 30% debt level?

Challenging Problems 9–11

16–9 Capital Structure Analysis

Pettit Printing Company has a total market value of $100 million, consisting of 1 million shares selling for $50 per share and $50 million of 10% perpetual bonds now selling at par. The company's EBIT is $13.24 million, and its tax rate is 15%. Pettit can change its capital structure by either increasing its debt to 70% (based on market values) or decreasing it to 30%. If it decides to *increase* its use of leverage, it must call its old bonds and issue new ones with a 12% coupon. If it decides to *decrease* its leverage, it will call its old bonds and replace them with new 8% coupon bonds. The company will sell or repurchase stock at the new equilibrium price to complete the capital structure change.

The firm pays out all earnings as dividends; hence, its stock is a zero-growth stock. Its current cost of equity, r_s, is 14%. If it increases leverage, r_s will be 16%. If it decreases leverage, r_s will be 13%. What is the firm's WACC and total corporate value under each capital structure?

16–10 Optimal Capital Structure with Hamada

Beckman Engineering and Associates (BEA) is considering a change in its capital structure. BEA currently has $20 million in debt carrying a rate of 8%, and its stock price is $40 per share with 2 million shares outstanding. BEA is a zero-growth firm and pays out all of its earnings as dividends. The firm's EBIT is $14.933 million, and it faces a 40% federal-plus-state tax rate. The market risk premium is 4%, and the risk-free rate is 6%. BEA is considering increasing its debt level to a capital structure with 40% debt, based on market values, and repurchasing shares with the extra money that it borrows. BEA will have to retire the old debt in order to issue new debt, and the rate on the new debt will be 9%. BEA has a beta of 1.0.

a. What is BEA's unlevered beta? Use market value D/S (which is the same as w_d/w_s) when unlevering.

b. What are BEA's new beta and cost of equity if it has 40% debt?

c. What are BEA's WACC and total value of the firm with 40% debt?

16–11 WACC and Optimal Capital Structure

F. Pierce Products Inc. is considering changing its capital structure. F. Pierce currently has no debt and no preferred stock, but it would like to add some debt to take advantage of low interest rates and the tax shield. Its investment banker has indicated that the pre-tax cost of debt under various possible capital structures would be as follows:

Market Debt-to-Value Ratio (w_d)	Market Equity-to-Value Ratio (w_s)	Market Debt-to-Equity Ratio (D/S)	Before-Tax Cost of Debt (r_d)
0.0	1.0	0.00	6.0%
0.2	0.8	0.25	7.0
0.4	0.6	0.67	8.0
0.6	0.4	1.50	9.0
0.8	0.2	4.00	10.0

F. Pierce uses the CAPM to estimate its cost of common equity, r_s and at the time of the analysis the risk-free rate is 5%, the market risk premium is 6%, and the company's tax rate is 40%. F. Pierce estimates that its beta now (which is "unlevered" because it currently has no debt) is 0.8. Based on this information, what is the firm's optimal capital structure, and what would be the weighted average cost of capital at the optimal capital structure?

Spreadsheet Problem

16–12 **Build a Model: WACC and Optimal Capital Structure**

Start with the partial model in the file *Ch16 P12 Build a Model.xls* on the textbook's Web site. Reacher Technology has consulted with investment bankers and determined the interest rate it would pay for different capital structures, as shown in the following table. Data for the risk-free rate, the market risk premium, an estimate of Reacher's unlevered beta, and the tax rate are also shown. Based on this information, what is the firm's optimal capital structure, and what is the weighted average cost of capital at the optimal structure?

Percent Financed with Debt (w_d)	Before-Tax Cost Debt (r_d)	Input Data	
0%	6.0%	Risk-free rate	4.5%
10	6.1	Market risk premium	5.5%
20	7.0	Unlevered beta	0.8
30	8.0	Tax rate	40.0%
40	10.0		
50	12.5		
60	15.5		
70	18.0		

MINI CASE

Assume you have just been hired as a business manager of PizzaPalace, a regional pizza restaurant chain. The company's EBIT was $50 million last year and is not expected to grow. The firm is currently financed with all equity, and it has 10 million shares outstanding. When you took your corporate finance course, your instructor stated that most firms' owners would be financially better off if the firms used some debt. When you suggested this to your new boss, he encouraged you to pursue the idea. As a first step, assume that you obtained from the firm's investment banker the following estimated costs of debt for the firm at different capital structures:

Percent Financed with Debt, w_d	r_d
0%	—
20	8.0%
30	8.5
40	10.0
50	12.0

If the company were to recapitalize, then debt would be issued and the funds received would be used to repurchase stock. PizzaPalace is in the 40% state-plus-federal corporate tax bracket, its beta is 1.0, the risk-free rate is 6%, and the market risk premium is 6%.

a. Using the free cash flow valuation model, show the only avenues by which capital structure can affect value.

b. (1) What is business risk? What factors influence a firm's business risk?

(2) What is operating leverage, and how does it affect a firm's business risk? Show the operating break-even point if a company has fixed costs of $200, a sales price of $15, and variable costs of $10.

c. Now, to develop an example that can be presented to PizzaPalace's management to illustrate the effects of financial leverage, consider two hypothetical firms: Firm U, which uses no debt financing, and Firm L, which uses $10,000 of 12% debt. Both firms have $20,000 in assets, a 40% tax rate, and an expected EBIT of $3,000.

(1) Construct partial income statements, which start with EBIT, for the two firms.

(2) Now calculate ROE for both firms.

(3) What does this example illustrate about the impact of financial leverage on ROE?

d. Explain the difference between financial risk and business risk.

e. What happens to ROE for Firm U and Firm L if EBIT falls to $2,000? What does this imply about the impact of leverage on risk and return?

f. What does capital structure theory attempt to do? What lessons can be learned from capital structure theory? Be sure to address the MM models.

g. What does the empirical evidence say about capital structure theory? What are the implications for managers?

h. With the preceding points in mind, now consider the optimal capital structure for PizzaPalace.

(1) For each capital structure under consideration, calculate the levered beta, the cost of equity, and the WACC.

(2) Now calculate the corporate value for each capital structure.

i. Describe the recapitalization process and apply it to PizzaPalace. Calculate the resulting value of the debt that will be issued, the resulting market value of equity, the price per share, the number of shares repurchased, and the remaining shares. Considering only the capital structures under analysis, what is PizzaPalace's optimal capital structure?

SELECTED ADDITIONAL CASES

The following cases from CengageCompose cover many of the concepts discussed in this chapter and are available at http://compose.cengage.com.

Klein-Brigham Series:

Case 9, "Kleen Kar, Inc.," Case 43, "Mountain Springs, Inc.," and Case 57, "Greta Cosmetics, Inc.," each present a situation similar to the Strasburg example in the text. Case 74, "The Western Company," and Case 99, "Moore Plumbing Supply," explore capital structure policies.

Brigham-Buzzard Series:

Case 8, "Powerline Network Corporation (Operating Leverage, Financial Leverage, and the Optimal Capital Structure)."

Dynamic Capital Structures and Corporate Valuation

Chapter 16 described capital structure decisions, including the selection of an optimal capital structure. The analysis assumed a static capital structure in the sense that managers have a target and try to keep the actual capital structure equal to the target. However, capital structures often are dynamic. Some variation occurs without managerial actions, such as changes in the stock price due to overall market conditions. Some changes occur due to economies of scale with respect to raising capital—because of transaction costs, companies raise large amounts of capital less frequently instead of small amounts often. Other changes occur as companies deliberately deviate from their target to take advantage of unexpected opportunities. The first part of the chapter provides a general framework for analyzing capital structure effects on value, including applications for familiar cases, such as the Modigliani and Miller models. The second part shows how to evaluate companies with dynamic capital structures.

Beginning-of-Chapter Questions

As you read the chapter, consider how you would answer the following questions. You *should not* necessarily be able to answer the questions before you read the chapter. Rather, you should use them to get a sense of the issues covered in the chapter. After reading the chapter, you should be able to give at least partial answers to the questions, and you should be able to give better answers after the chapter has been discussed in class. Note, too, that it is often useful, when answering conceptual questions, to use hypothetical data to illustrate your answer. We illustrate the answers with an *Excel* model that is available on the textbook's Web site. Accessing the model and working through it is a useful exercise, and it provides insights that are useful when answering the questions.

1. What is and how did Modigliani and Miller use the **arbitrage** concept in developing their theory that (with no corporate taxes) capital structure has no effect on value or the cost of capital? What real-world impediments exist to creating one's own "homemade" leverage?

2. What is the essence of Miller's contribution to the theory of capital structure, and how does it relate to the earlier MM with-taxes position?

3. MM and Miller assumed that firms do not grow. If they grow, how would this affect the value of the debt tax shield? What does growth do to the required rate of return on equity and the WACC as a firm increases its use of debt?

4. What is the compressed adjusted present value (APV) model and how does this differ from the Modigliani and Miller models? (*Hint:* think of the discount rate on the tax shield. What is "compressed" about this model?)

5. In what circumstances is the compressed adjusted present value (APV) model useful and how would it be applied?

6. MM and Miller also assumed that debt is riskless. How does the possibility of default on debt cause equity to take on the characteristics of an option? What types of incentives for shareholders does this lead to?

CORPORATE VALUATION AND CAPITAL STRUCTURE DECISIONS

A firm's financing choices obviously have a direct effect on its weighted average cost of capital (WACC). Financing choices also have an indirect effect because they change the risk and required return of debt and equity. This chapter focuses on the debt–equity choice and its effect on value in a dynamic environment.

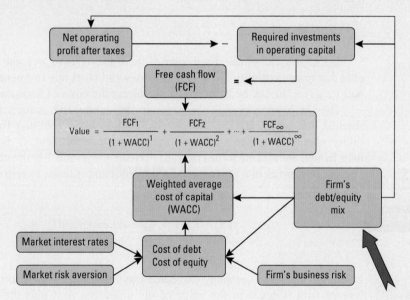

17-1 **The Impact of Growth and Tax Shields on Value**

Before addressing issues arising from dynamic capital structures, we need a framework for analyzing the impact of capital structure on a levered firm's value, V_L. The most general conceptual framework is to start with the value of an unlevered but otherwise identical firm, V_U, and adjust the unlevered value for any side effects due to leverage:

$$V_L = V_U + \text{Value of side effects} \tag{17-1}$$

WEB

The textbook's Web site contains an *Excel* file that will guide you through the chapter's calculations. The file for this chapter is ***Ch17 Tool Kit.xls***, and we encourage you to open the file and follow along as you read the chapter.

The value of an unlevered firm is the present value of its free cash flows (FCF) discounted at the weighted average cost of capital (WACC). For an unlevered firm, the WACC is the unlevered cost of equity: WACC $= r_{sU}$. As we saw in the free cash flow corporate valuation model from Chapter 8, this present value is:

(17–2)

$$V_U = \sum_{t=1}^{\infty} \frac{FCF_t}{(1 + r_{sU})^t}$$

As we saw in Chapter 8, Equation (17-2) can be simplified to be:

(17–3)

$$V_U = \sum_{t=1}^{\infty} \frac{FCF_0(1 + g)^t}{(1 + r_{sU})^t} = \frac{FCF_1}{r_{sU} - g}$$

In Chapter 16, we discussed some of the side effects of leverage, including benefits due to deductibility of interest expenses and costs due to financial distress. We will focus on the tax benefits now and address the costs of financial distress later.

The tax benefits due to leverage are the annual tax savings (also called tax shields), TS_t, which are the annual reductions in taxes resulting from the deductibility of interest expenses. If r_d is the interest rate on debt, D_t is the amount of debt (which we assume to be constant over the year), and T is the tax rate, then the reduction in taxes in a given year due to deducting interest expense is:

(17–4)

$$TS_t = r_d D_t T = (\text{Interest expense})(T)$$

Each year a levered company can deduct its interest expenses, so the value of the levered firm is equal to the value of the unlevered firm plus the gain from leverage, which is the present value of the interest tax savings, also known as the **interest tax shield**:

(17–1a)

$$V_L = V_U + V_{\text{Tax shield}}$$

The value of the tax shield is the present value of all of the interest tax savings (TS), discounted at the appropriate rate, r_{TS}:

(17–5)

$$V_{\text{Tax shield}} = \sum_{t=1}^{\infty} \frac{TS_t}{(1 + r_{TS})^t} = \sum_{t=1}^{\infty} \frac{r_d T D_t}{(1 + r_{TS})^t}$$

If free cash flows grow at a constant rate and the proportions of debt and equity in the capital structure remain constant, then the annual tax savings grow at a constant rate. Using the constant growth model, the present value of these growing tax savings is:

$$V_{\text{Tax shield}} = \frac{r_d TD_1}{r_{TS} - g}$$

(17–6)

Substituting Equations 17-3 and 17-6 into Equation 17-1a yields a valuation expression that separately identifies the impact of leverage and growth on value:

$$V_L = V_U + \left(\frac{r_d}{r_{TS} - g}\right)TD_1$$

(17–7)

With considerable algebra, the levered cost of equity (r_{sL}) can be expressed in terms of: (1) the unlevered cost of equity, (2) the capital structure weights (w_d is the percentage of the firm financed with debt and w_s is the percentage financed with common stock), (3) the cost of debt (r_d), and (4) the discount rate for the tax shield:

$$r_{sL} = r_{sU} + (r_{sU} - r_d)\frac{w_d}{w_s} - (r_{sU} - r_{TS})\left[\frac{r_d T}{r_{TS} - g}\right]\frac{w_d}{w_s}$$

(17–8)

The ratio of w_d/w_s is also equal to the ratio D/S, where S is the value of the stock. For some problems it is easier to use the ratio of D/S if you have already calculated D and S; in other problems, you might have a target capital structure, so it is easier to use the ratio w_d/w_s. We usually use the ratio that saves calculations and time, so be aware of this as you read the chapter and work problems.

Surprisingly, Equation 17-8 shows that growth actually can cause the levered cost of equity to be *less* than the unlevered cost of equity when a very low discount rate for the tax shield is used, $r_{TS} < r_{sU}$, and the last term is very large.[1] This could happen when growth is rapid and a low discount rate for the tax shield is used, which causes the value of the tax shield to be very large. If this were the case, then you would expect to see high-growth firms that wanted to minimize their cost of capital using large amounts of debt, and lower-growth firms using lower amounts of debt. But this is not consistent either with intuition

---

1. See Michael C. Ehrhardt and Phillip R. Daves, "Corporate Valuation: The Combined Impact of Growth and the Tax Shield of Debt on the Cost of Capital and Systematic Risk," *Journal of Applied Finance*, Fall/Winter 2002, pp. 31–38.

or observations in the market: High-growth firms actually tend to have lower levels of debt. And regardless of the growth rate, firms with more debt should have a higher cost of equity than firms with no debt. This means that a low discount rate for the tax shield isn't consistent with either intuition or observations in the market. It is worth mentioning now that these counterintuitive results in which growth causes the levered cost of equity to be lower than the unlevered cost of equity cannot happen if $r_{TS} = r_{sU}$. We will use this finding later in the chapter when we discuss dynamic capital structures.

With a little more algebra, we can express a company's beta as a function of the unlevered beta of stock, b_U, the beta of the debt, b_D, and the beta of the tax shield, b_{TS}; the betas of the debt and the tax shield reflect the systematic risk of debt and the tax shield. The levered beta of a company is:

(17–9)

$$b = b_U + (b_U - b_D)\frac{w_d}{w_s} - (b_U - b_{TS})\left[\frac{r_d T}{r_{TS} - g}\right]\frac{w_d}{w_s}$$

Observe that Equation 17-9 includes the term b_D. If corporate debt is not riskless, then its beta, b_D, may not be zero. If we assume that bonds lie on the Security Market Line, then a bond's required return, r_d, can be expressed as $r_d = r_{RF} + b_D RP_M$. Solving for b_D then gives $b_D = (r_d - r_{RF})/RP_M$.

Armed with this general framework, let's examine some special cases, including the Modigliani and Miller models from Chapter 16 and a new model, the compressed adjusted present value (APV) model.

SELF TEST

What is the value of an unlevered firm?

What is the tax shield due to debt in the capital structure?

How does the value of a levered firm compare to the value of an unlevered firm that is otherwise identical?

17-2 The Modigliani and Miller Models and the Compressed Adjusted Present Value (APV) Model

Recall from Chapter 16 that Modigliani and Miller (MM) developed a model of capital structure based on the assumption of zero growth and no risk of bankruptcy. In addition, they assumed that the appropriate discount rate for the tax shield is $r_{TS} = r_d$. They made this assumption because the annual tax savings are proportional to the annual debt, which implies that the tax savings have the same risk as debt. MM examined two situations, one with no taxes and one with corporate taxes.

17-2a **Modigliani and Miller: No Taxes**

In addition to the previous assumptions, MM's first model assumed no taxes. We show a proof of their model in Section 17-6, but here are three of their results:

$$V_L = V_U = FCF/r_{sU} \tag{17-10}$$

and

$$r_{sL} = r_{sU} + (r_{sU} - r_d)(w_d/w_s) \tag{17-11}$$

The Hamada adjustment that we discussed in Chapter 16 becomes:

$$b = b_U[1 + (w_d/w_s)] \tag{17-12}$$

Notice that these three equations are exactly equal to the corresponding equations for the general framework (Equations 17-7, 17-8, and 17-9) if $g = 0$, $r_{TS} = r_d$, and $T = 0$.

17-2b **Modigliani and Miller: Corporate Taxes**

When MM include corporate taxes (but keep all their previous assumptions), their models become:

$$V_L = V_U + TD = FCF/r_{sU} + TD \tag{17-13}$$

and

$$r_{sL} = r_{sU} + (r_{sU} - r_d)(1 - T)(w_d/w_s) \tag{17-14}$$

The Hamada model is shown below:

$$b = b_U[1 + (1 - T)(w_d/w_s)] \tag{17-15}$$

Again, these three equations are exactly equal to the corresponding equations for the general framework (Equations 17-7, 17-8, and 17-9) if $g = 0$ and $r_{TS} = r_d$.

17-2c **The Compressed Adjusted Present Value Model (APV)**

The compressed **adjusted present value (APV) model** allows nonzero growth and risky debt with a nonzero beta.[2] It also differs from the MM models in its assumption regarding the appropriate discount rate for the tax shield. In particular, it assumes that $r_{TS} = r_{sU}$. Here is the logic behind that choice.

A fundamental concept in finance is that the appropriate discount rate is the rate of return that investors require to compensate them for risk. So what is the risk of the tax shield? If the company will always get to deduct interest expenses, then the tax shield has no risk and should be discounted at the risk-free rate. However, corporate debt is not riskless—firms do occasionally default on their loans if cash flows from operations are so low that the firm's value is less than the debt's value. Even if a company doesn't default on its debt, a company might not be able to use tax savings from interest deductions in the current year if it has a pre-tax operating loss. Therefore, the future tax savings are not risk-free and hence should be discounted using a higher rate than the risk-free rate.

How much higher should the discount rate be? The risk that the company will not be able to use future interest rate deductions stems from the risk of its pre-tax operating profit. This suggests that the unlevered cost of equity, which reflects the risk of operations, should be an upper limit for the required return on the tax shield.

Based on the previous logic, r_{TS} should be between the risk-free rate and the unlevered cost of equity. As we previously showed, the cost of levered equity can be less than the cost of unlevered equity unless $r_{TS} = r_{sU}$. Therefore, the compressed APV assumes that $r_{TS} = r_{sU}$.[3] Substituting this into the general valuation model in Equation 17-7, we get:

(17–16)

$$V_L = V_U + \left(\frac{r_d T D_1}{r_{sU} - g} \right)$$

Notice that the gain from leverage (the second term in Equation 17-16) can be larger or smaller than the gain from leverage in the MM model with taxes, depending on the fraction $r_d/(r_{sU} - g)$. If the cost of debt is low relative to the spread between the unlevered cost of equity and the growth rate, then a growing tax shield is very valuable. On the other hand, if growth is very low (or zero), then fraction $r_d/(r_{sU} - g)$ is less than 1, which means that the gain from leverage is bigger in the MM

---

2. For a discussion of the *compressed APV* valuation method, which assumes that $r_{TS} = r_{sU}$, see Steven N. Kaplan and Richard S. Ruback, "The Valuation of Cash Flow Forecasts: An Empirical Analysis," *Journal of Finance*, September 1995, pp. 1059–1093. For evidence showing the effectiveness of the adjusted present value approach, see S. N. Kaplan and R. S. Ruback, "The Market Pricing of Cash Flow Forecasts: Discounted Cash Flow vs. the Method of 'Comparables,'" *Journal of Applied Corporate Finance*, Winter 1996, pp. 45–60.

3. It is called the *compressed* APV because it is not necessary to separate the NOPAT and the interest expenses since all cash flows are discounted at the unlevered cost of equity. This means you can define the cash flow as net income minus required investments in operating capital. However, we usually keep interest expenses separate from free cash flow so that we can more easily identify the impact on value due to operations versus leverage.

model than in the APV model. This makes sense, because the MM model discounts the tax savings at the relatively low cost of debt, r_d, while the APV model discounts the tax savings at the relatively high unlevered cost of equity, r_{sU}.

Substituting $r_{TS} = r_{sU}$ into Equation 17-8 shows that the levered cost of equity is:

$$r_{sL} = r_{sU} + (r_{sU} - r_d)(w_d/w_s)$$

(17–17)

Although the derivation of Equation 17-17 reflects corporate taxes and growth, neither of these expressions includes the corporate tax rate or the growth rate. Perhaps unintuitively, this means that the expression for the levered required rate of return, Equation 17-17, is exactly the same as MM's expression for the levered required rate of return *without taxes*, Equation 17-11. The reason the tax rate and the growth rate drop out of these two expressions is that the growing tax shield is discounted at the unlevered cost of equity, r_{sU}, not at the cost of debt as in the MM model. The tax rate drops out because no matter how high the level of T, the total risk of the firm will not be changed—the unlevered cash flows and the tax shield are discounted at the same rate. The growth rate drops out for the same reason—an increasing debt level will not change the risk of the entire firm no matter what rate of growth prevails.

Substituting $b_{TS} = b_U$ into Equation 17-9 shows the levered beta:

$$b = b_U + (b_U - b_D)(w_d/w_s)$$

(17–18)

If the systematic risk of debt is small enough to neglect, then the relationship between the levered beta and the unlevered beta is:

$$b = b_U[1 + (w_d/w_s)]$$

(17–18a)

This expression for the levered beta is exactly the same as Hamada's formula in Equation 17-12 (and 17-15 but *without taxes*).

17-2d Illustration of the Models

To illustrate the models, we will examine the impact of leverage on Fredrickson Water Company, an established firm that supplies water to residential customers in several no-growth upstate New York communities. Following is some information about the company.

The Example Company

Following are the required data for the analysis.

1. Fredrickson currently has no debt.
2. Expected EBIT = $2.4 million.
3. Fredrickson is in a no-growth situation, so g = 0.

WEB

See *Ch17 Tool Kit.xls* on the textbook's Web site for all calculations.

4. If Frederickson begins to use debt, it can borrow at a rate $r_d = 8\%$. This borrowing rate is constant—it does not increase regardless of the amount of debt used. Any money raised by selling debt would be used to repurchase common stock, so *Frederickson's assets would remain constant.*

5. The business risk inherent in Frederickson's assets, and thus in its EBIT, is such that its beta is 0.80; this is called the unlevered beta, b_U, because Frederickson has no debt. The risk-free rate is 8%, and the market risk premium (RP_M) is 5%. Using the Capital Asset Pricing Model (CAPM), Frederickson's required rate of return on stock, r_{sU}, is 12% if no debt is used:

$$r_{sU} = r_{RF} + b_U(RP_M) = 8\% + 0.80(5\%) = 12\%$$

MM with Zero Taxes

To begin, assume that there are no taxes and so $T = 0\%$. Free cash flow is defined as NOPAT less required investments in capital. With zero growth, Frederickson doesn't require any investments in capital. NOPAT is defined as EBIT(1 – T), but no taxes mean that FCF is equal to EBIT.

Using Equation 17-10, Frederickson's value is $20 million (no matter how much debt it has):

$$V_L = V_U = \frac{FCF}{r_{sU}} = \frac{EBIT}{r_{sU}} = \frac{\$2.4 \text{ million}}{0.12} = \$20.0 \text{ million}$$

If Frederickson uses $10 million of debt, then the value of its stock, S, must be $10 million:

$$V_L = S + D$$
$$S = V - D = \$20 \text{ million} - \$10 \text{ million} = \$10 \text{ million}$$

With $10 million in debt and $10 million in stock, Frederickson would be financed with capital structure weights of $w_d = 50\%$ and $w_s = 50\%$.

We can also find Frederickson's cost of equity, r_{sL}, and its WACC at a debt level of $10 million. First, we use Equation 17-11 to find r_{sL}, Frederickson's levered cost of equity:

$$r_{sL} = r_{sU} + (r_{sU} - r_d)(w_d/w_s)$$
$$= 12\% + (12\% - 8\%) (0.5/0.5)$$
$$= 12\% + 4.0\% = 16.0\%$$

Now we can find the company's weighted average cost of capital:

$$WACC = w_d(r_d)(1 - T) + w_s\,r_{sL}$$
$$= 0.5(8\%)(1.0) + 0.5(16.0\%) = 12.0\%$$

Frederickson's value based on the MM model without taxes at various debt levels is shown in Panel A in Figure 17-1. Panel B reports the cost of equity and WACC. Here we see that, in an MM world without taxes, financial leverage simply does not matter: *The value of the firm and its overall cost of capital are both independent of the amount of debt.*

MM with Corporate Taxes

To illustrate the MM model with corporate taxes, assume that all of the previous conditions hold except for the following changes:

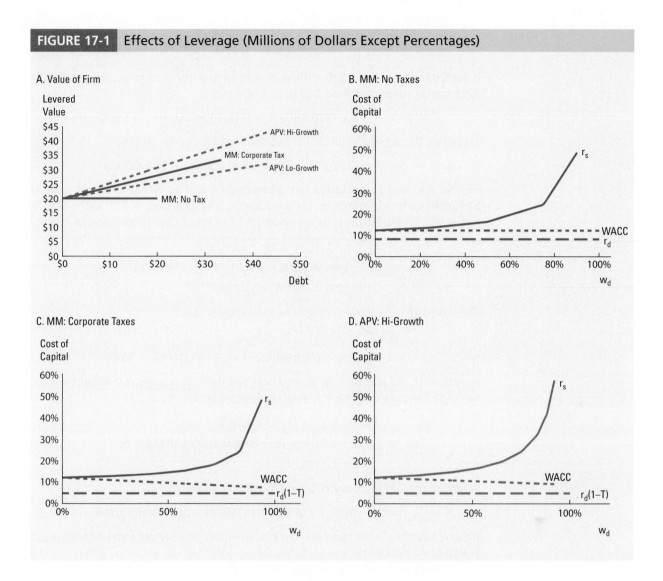

| FIGURE 17-1 | Effects of Leverage (Millions of Dollars Except Percentages) |

1. Expected EBIT = $4 million.[4]
2. Fredrickson has a 40% federal-plus-state tax rate, so T = 40%.

Other things held constant, the introduction of corporate taxes would lower Fredrickson's net income and hence its value, so we increased EBIT from $2.4 million to $4 million to facilitate comparisons between the two models.

When Fredrickson has zero debt but pays taxes, Equation 17-13 can be used to find its current zero debt value:

---

4. If we had left Fredrickson's EBIT at $2.4 million, then introducing corporate taxes would have reduced the firm's value from $20 million to $12 million:

$$V_U = \frac{EBIT(1-T)}{r_{sU}} = \frac{\$2.4 \text{ million}(0.6)}{0.12} = \$12.0 \text{ million}$$

Corporate taxes reduce the amount of operating income available to investors in an unlevered firm by the factor $(1-T)$, so the value of the firm would be reduced by the same amount, holding r_{sU} constant.

$$V_U = \frac{EBIT(1 - T)}{r_{sU}} + TD = \frac{\$4\ million(0.6)}{0.12} + \$0 = \$20\ million$$

If Fredrickson now uses $10 million of debt in a world with taxes, we see that its total market value rises from $20 to $24 million:

$$V_L = V_U + TD = \$20\ million + 0.4(\$10\ million) = \$24\ million$$

Therefore, the implied value of Fredrickson's equity is $14 million:

$$S = V - D = \$24\ million - \$10\ million = \$14\ million$$

We can also find Fredrickson's cost of equity, r_{sL}, and its WACC at a debt level of $10 million, which is equivalent to capital structure weights of $w_d = \$10/\$24 = 41.67\%$ and $w_s = 58.33\%$. First, we use Equation 17-14 to find r_{sL}, the levered cost of equity:

$$\begin{aligned}
r_{sL} &= r_{sU} + (r_{sU} - r_d)(1 - T)(w_d/w_s) \\
&= 12\% + (12\% - 8\%)(0.6)(0.4167/0.5833) \\
&= 12\% + 1.71\% = 13.71\%
\end{aligned}$$

The company's weighted average cost of capital is then:

$$\begin{aligned}
WACC &= w_d(r_d)(1 - T) + w_s r_{sL} \\
&= (0.4167)(8\%)(0.6) + 0.5833(13.71\%) = 10.0\%
\end{aligned}$$

Note that we can also find the levered beta and then the levered cost of equity. First, we apply Hamada's equation to find the levered beta:

$$\begin{aligned}
b &= b_U[1 + (1 - T)(w_d/w_s)] \\
&= 0.80[1 + (1 - 0.4)(0.4167/0.5833)] \\
&= 1.1429
\end{aligned}$$

Applying the CAPM then yields the levered cost of equity as:

$$r_{sL} = r_{RF} + b(RP_M) = 8\% + 1.1429(5\%) = 0.1371 = 13.71\%$$

Observe that this is the same levered cost of equity that we obtained directly using Equation 17-14.

Fredrickson's value at various debt levels with corporate taxes is shown in Panel A of Figure 17-1; Panel C shows the cost of equity and the WACC. In an MM world with corporate taxes, financial leverage does matter: The value of the firm is maximized—and its overall cost of capital is minimized—if it uses almost 100% debt financing. The increase in value is due solely to the tax deductibility of interest payments, which lowers both the cost of debt and the equity risk premium by $(1 - T)$.[5]

---

5. In the limit case where the firm used 100% debt financing, the bondholders would own the entire company and so would bear all the business risk. (Up until this point, MM assume that stockholders bear all the risk.) If the bondholders bear all the risk, then the capitalization rate on the debt should be equal to the equity capitalization rate at zero debt, $r_d = r_{sU} = 12\%$.

The income stream to the stockholders in the all-equity case was $4,000,000(1 - T) = \$2,400,000$, and the value of the firm was:

$$V_U = \frac{\$2,400,000}{0.12} = \$20,000,000$$

With all debt, the entire $4,000,000 of EBIT would be used to pay interest charges: r_d would be 12%, so $I = 0.12(Debt) = \$4,000,000$. Taxes would be zero, so the investors (bondholders)

APV: Hi-Growth and Lo-Growth

This section illustrates the compressed adjusted present value model in a Hi-Growth scenario and a Lo-Growth scenario. Assume that all of the previous conditions hold except for the following changes:

1. Required investment in operating capital = $0.60 million.
2. Hi-Growth scenario: Expected EBIT = $3 million and constant growth rate = 6%.[6]
3. Lo-Growth scenario: Expected EBIT = $4.83 million and constant growth rate = 0.5%.

Fredrickson's expected free cash flow in the Hi-Growth scenario is:

$$FCF = \$3(1 - 0.4) - \$0.60 = \$1.2 \text{ million}$$

Frederickson's unlevered value is $20 million:

$$V_U = \frac{FCF}{r_{sU} - g} = \frac{\$1.2 \text{ million}}{0.12 - 0.6} = \$20.0 \text{ million}$$

With $10 million in debt financing, we use Equation 17-16 to estimate the levered value:

$$V_L = \$20 + \left(\frac{0.08(0.4)(\$10)}{0.12 - 0.06}\right) = \$20 + \$5.33 = \$25.33$$

The capital structure weights are $w_d = \$10/(\$25.33) = 39.48\%$ and $w_s = 60.52\%$. Using Equation 17-17, the levered cost of equity is:

$$r_{sL} = 12\% + (12\% - 8\%)(0.3948/0.6052) = 14.61\%$$

The WACC is:

$$WACC = (0.3948)(8\%)(1 - 0.4) + 0.6052(14.61\%) = 10.74\%$$

We repeated all calculations for the Lo-Growth scenario; see *Ch17 Tool Kit.xls* for the calculations. Look at Panel A in Figure 17-1, which shows the value of the firm at different levels of debt for the MM model with no taxes, the MM model with taxes, and the two APV scenarios. With zero taxes, there is no tax shield and the value of a levered firm is the same as the value of an unlevered firm. For the MM model with corporate taxes, the value increases as debt increases, but it tops out at around $33 million. At this level of debt, virtually all operating earnings are being used to pay interest. For the APV scenarios, the value steadily increases as debt is added. For the Lo-Growth scenario, its value is less than the MM model with taxes because the APV model discounts the tax savings at the relatively high unlevered cost of equity whereas the MM model discounts tax savings at the much lower cost of debt.

---

would get the entire $4,000,000 of operating income (they would not have to share it with the government). Thus, the value of the firm at 100% debt would be:

$$V_L = \frac{\$4,000,000}{0.12} = \$33,333,333 = D$$

There is, of course, a transition problem in all this. Modigliani and Miller assume that $r_d = 8\%$ regardless of how much debt the firm has until debt reaches 100%, at which point r_d jumps to 12%, the cost of equity. As we shall see later in the chapter, r_d actually rises as the risk of financial distress increases.

6. We made these changes so that the unlevered value would remain at $20 million.

Panels B, C, and D show the levered cost of equity, the WACC and the cost of debt for the two MM models and for the Hi-Growth APV scenario. With zero taxes (Panel B), the cost of equity goes up just fast enough to keep the WACC constant. However, when taxes are considered (Panels C and D), the combination of the after-tax cost of debt and the levered cost of equity results in a decrease in the WACC as more debt is added. The WACC falls faster for the MM model in Panel C than in the APV model in Panel D because the MM model discounts the tax savings at the relatively low cost of debt.

SELF TEST

Is there an optimal capital structure under the MM zero-tax model?

What is the optimal capital structure under the MM model with corporate taxes?

Why do taxes result in a "gain from leverage" in the MM model with corporate taxes?

How does growth affect the value of the tax shield?

How will your estimates of the levered cost of equity be biased if you use the MM or Hamada models when growth is present?

An unlevered firm has a value of $100 million. An otherwise identical but levered firm has $30 million in debt. Under the MM zero-tax model, what is the value of the levered firm? **($100 million)** Under the MM corporate tax model, what is the value of a levered firm if the corporate tax rate is 40%? **($112 million)**

An unlevered firm has a value of $100 million. An otherwise identical but levered firm has $30 million in debt. Both firms are growing at a constant rate of 5%, the corporate tax rate is 40%, the cost of debt is 6%, and the unlevered cost of equity is 8% (assume r_{sU} is the appropriate discount rate for the tax shield). What is the value of the levered firm? **($124 million)** What is the value of the stock? **($94 million)** What is the levered cost of equity? **(8.64%)**

17-3 Dynamic Capital Structures and the Adjusted Present Value (APV) Model

A dynamic capital structure implies that a company's capital structure weights are changing over time. What impact does that have on a company's value? We can't use the dividend growth model or the free cash flow valuation model to answer that question—both models assume that the rates used to discount future cash flows (the required return on stock in the dividend growth model and the weighted average cost of capital in the free cash flow valuation model) are constant over time, but these rates definitely change if the capital structure changes. Therefore, a different approach must be used. Fortunately, the adjusted present value model is ideally suited for such situations.

17-3a An Overview of the APV Model for Dynamic Capital Structures

Even for dynamic capital structures, the value of operations can be decomposed into the portions due to unlevered operations and the tax shield:

$$V_{\text{Operations}} = V_{\text{Unlevered}} + V_{\text{Tax shield}} \qquad \textbf{(17–1b)}$$

To estimate the unlevered value of operations, $V_{\text{Unlevered}}$, we need the projected free cash flows and the unlevered cost of equity, r_{sU}. It is straightforward to estimate the projected free cash flows, as shown in Chapter 9. It can be a bit more complicated to estimate the unlevered cost of equity. If the company being analyzed currently has no debt, then its current cost of equity *is* the unlevered cost of equity. If the company already has some debt, then we need to unlever its current cost of equity. As mentioned previously, the Hamada equation is based on the MM model with corporate taxes, which discounts the tax savings at the cost of debt and which assumes zero growth, which makes the Hamada equation inappropriate for applications of the APV model. Instead, we use Equation 17-18 (or 17-18a if we neglect the systematic risk of debt). Given the estimated FCF and unlevered cost of equity, the unlevered value of operations is the present value of the firm's free cash flows discounted at the unlevered cost of equity:

$$V_{\text{Unlevered}} = \sum_{t=1}^{\infty} \frac{\text{FCF}_t}{(1 + r_{sU})^t} \qquad \textbf{(17–19)}$$

As described earlier, the compressed APV discounts the tax savings at the unlevered cost of equity, so the value of the tax shield is:

$$V_{\text{Tax shield}} = \sum_{t=1}^{\infty} \frac{\text{TS}_t}{(1 + r_{sU})^t} \qquad \textbf{(17–20)}$$

Application of the APV model to a dynamic capital structure still requires that the capital structure must eventually stabilize. It also requires that the FCF and TS eventually must grow at a constant rate, which allows us to find the horizon values using an approach similar to the ones we used in Chapter 8 for the nonconstant dividend model and the free cash flow corporate valuation model. Recall that those approaches explicitly projected the values for years with nonconstant growth rates, estimated the horizon value at the end of the nonconstant growth period, and then calculated the present value of the horizon value and the cash flows during the forecast period.

17-3b **Application of the APV Model in a Dynamic Capital Structure**

We illustrate the APV model with the following example. Mencer's Extreme Gear (MEG) borrowed heavily and is reducing its debt over the next 3 years to a sustainable level. MEG has forecast free cash flows, interest expenses, and the tax savings due to the deductibility of interest expense for the next 3 years, as shown below:

	1	2	3
Free cash flow	$1,000	$1,200	$1,350
Interest expense	$ 800	$ 600	$ 400
Tax savings (T = 40%)	$ 320	$ 240	$ 160

The FCF and interest expenses are expected to grow at a constant rate of 4% after Year 3. MEG's unlevered cost of equity 10% and its tax rate is 40%.

The Unlevered Value of Operations

The horizon value of an unlevered firm at Year N ($HV_{U,N}$) is the value of all free cash flows beyond the horizon discounted back to the horizon at the unlevered cost of equity. Because FCF grows at a constant rate of g_L in the post-horizon period, we can use the constant growth formula:

(17–21)

$$\text{Horizon value of unlevered firm} = HV_{U,N} = \frac{FCF_{N+1}}{r_{sU} - g_L} = \frac{FCF_N(1 + g_L)}{r_{sU} - g_L}$$

For MEG, the horizon value of operations is:

$$HV_{U,3} = \frac{\$1,350(1 + 0.04)}{0.10 - 0.04} = \$23,400$$

This is the value of all free cash flows from Year 4 and beyond discounted back to Year 3.

The next step is to calculate the present value of the horizon value and the present values of all the free cash flows during the forecast period. Their sum is the current unlevered value of operations:

(17–22)

$$V_{Unlevered} = \sum_{t=1}^{N} \frac{FCF_t}{(1 + r_{sU})^t} + \frac{HV_{U,N}}{(1 + r_{sU})^N}$$

$$= \left[\frac{FCF_1}{(1 + r_{sU})^1} + \frac{FCF_2}{(1 + r_{sU})^2} + \cdots + \frac{FCF_N}{(1 + r_{sU})^N} \right] + \frac{[(TS_{N+1})/(r_{sU} - g_L)]}{(1 + r_{sU})^N}$$

For MEG, the unlevered value of operations is:

$$V_{Unlevered} = \left[\frac{\$1,000}{(1.10)^1} + \frac{\$1,200}{(1.10)^2} + \frac{\$1,350}{(1.10)^3} \right] + \frac{\$23,400}{(1.10)^3}$$

$$= \$2,915.10 + \$17,580.77 = \$20,495.87$$

MEG's unlevered value of operations is $20,495.87. This would be the value of the company if it had no debt or nonoperating assets.

The Value of the Tax Shield

The horizon value of the tax shield, $HV_{TS,N}$, is the value of all tax savings beyond the horizon, discounted back to the horizon:

$$
\begin{array}{cc}
\text{Horizon value of} & \\
\text{tax shield} & = HV_{TS,N} = \dfrac{TS_{N+1}}{r_{sU} - g_L} = \dfrac{TS_N(1 + g_L)}{r_{sU} - g_L}
\end{array}
\qquad \text{(17–23)}
$$

For Mencer's, the horizon value of the tax shield is:

$$
HV_{TS,3} = \frac{160(1 + 0.04)}{0.10 - 0.04} = \$2{,}773.33
$$

This is the value of all tax savings from Year 4 and beyond discounted back to Year 3.

The next step is to calculate the present value of the horizon value and the present values of all the tax savings during the forecast period. Their sum is the current value of the tax shield:

$$
\begin{aligned}
V_{\text{Tax shield}} &= \sum_{t=1}^{N} \frac{TS_t}{(1 + r_{sU})^t} + \frac{HV_{TS,N}}{(1 + r_{sU})^N} \\[2mm]
&= \left[\frac{TS_1}{(1 + r_{sU})^1} + \frac{TS_2}{(1 + r_{sU})^2} + \cdots + \frac{TS_N}{(1 + r_{sU})^N} \right] + \frac{[(FCF_{N+1})/(r_{sU} - g_L)]}{(1 + r_{sU})^N}
\end{aligned}
\qquad \text{(17–24)}
$$

For MEG, the value of the tax shield is:

$$
\begin{aligned}
V_{\text{Tax shield}} &= \left[\frac{\$320}{(1.10)^1} + \frac{\$240}{(1.10)^2} + \frac{\$160}{(1.10)^3} \right] + \frac{\$2{,}773.33}{(1.10)^3} \\[2mm]
&= \$609.47 + \$2{,}083.64 = \$2{,}693.11
\end{aligned}
$$

The Levered Value of Operations

The horizon value of the tax shield, $HV_{TS,N}$, is the value of all tax savings beyond the horizon, discounted back to the horizon:

$$
\begin{aligned}
V_{\text{Operations}} &= V_{\text{Unlevered}} + V_{\text{Tax shield}} \\
&= \$20{,}495.87 + \$2{,}693.11 \\
&= \$23{,}189
\end{aligned}
$$

The APV approach gives the same answer as the dividend growth model and the free cash flow valuation model if the capital structure is constant. In a dynamic situation with a nonconstant capital structure, however, only the APV approach gives the correct value.

Why is the adjusted present value approach appropriate for situations with a changing capital structure?

Describe the steps required to apply the APV approach.

A company forecasts free cash flow of $400 at Year 1, $600 at Year 2; after Year 2, the FCF grow at a constant rate of 5%. The company forecasts the tax savings from interest deductions as $200 in Year 1, $100 in Year 2; after Year 2, the tax savings grow at a constant rate of 5%. The unlevered cost of equity is 9%. What is the horizon value of operations at Year 2? **($15,750.0)** What is the current unlevered value of operations? **($14,128.4)** What is the horizon value of the tax shield at Year 2? **($2,625.0)** What is the current value of the tax shield? **($2,477.1)** What is the levered value of operations at Year 0? **($16,605.5)**

17-4 Risky Debt and Equity as an Option

In the previous sections, we evaluated equity and debt using the standard discounted cash flow techniques. However, we learned in Chapter 13 that if there is an opportunity for management to make a change as a result of new information after a project or investment has been started, then there might be an option component to the project or investment being evaluated. This is the case with equity. To see why, consider Kunkel Inc., a small manufacturer of electronic wiring harnesses and instrumentation located in Minot, North Dakota. Kunkel's current value (debt plus equity) is $20 million, and its debt consists of $10 million face value of 5-year zero coupon bonds. What decision does management make when the debt comes due? In most cases, it would pay the $10 million that is due. But what if the company has done poorly and the firm is worth only $9 million? In that case, the firm is technically bankrupt, because its value is less than the amount of debt due. Management will choose to default on the loan; in this case, the firm will be liquidated or sold for $9 million, the debtholders will get all $9 million, and the stockholders will get nothing. Of course, if the firm is worth $10 million or more then management will choose to repay the loan. The ability to make this decision—to pay or not to pay—looks very much like an option, and the techniques we developed in Chapter 5 can be used to value it.

17-4a Using the Black-Scholes Option Pricing Model to Value Equity

To put this decision into an option context, suppose P is Kunkel's total value when the debt matures. Then, if the debt is paid off, Kunkel's stockholders will receive the equivalent of P − $10 million if P > $10 million.[7] They will receive nothing if P ≤ $10 million because management will default on the bond and the bondholders will take over the company. These facts can be summarized as follows:

$$\text{Payoff to stockholders} = \text{MAX}(P - \$10 \text{ million}, 0)$$

---

7. Actually, rather than receive cash of P − $10 million, the stockholders will keep the company (which is worth P − $10 million after the debt is repaid) rather than turn it over to the bondholders.

This is exactly the same payoff as a European call option on the total value (P) of the firm with a strike price equal to the face value of the debt, $10 million. We can use the Black-Scholes option pricing model from Chapter 5 to determine the value of this asset.

Recall from Chapter 5 that the value of a call option depends on five factors: the price of the underlying asset, the strike price, the risk-free rate, the time to expiration, and the volatility of the market value of the underlying asset. Here the underlying asset is the total value of the firm. If we assume that volatility is 40% and that the risk-free rate is 6%, then the inputs for the Black-Scholes model are as follows:

$$
\begin{aligned}
P &= \$20 \text{ million} \\
X &= \$10 \text{ million} \\
t &= 5 \text{ years} \\
r_{RF} &= 6\% \\
\sigma &= 40\%
\end{aligned}
$$

The value of a European call option, as shown in Chapter 5, is:

$$V = P[N(d_1)] - Xe^{-r_{RF}t}[N(d_2)] \tag{17-25}$$

where

$$d_1 = \frac{\ln(P/X) + (r_{RF} + \sigma^2/2)t}{\sigma\sqrt{t}} \tag{17-26}$$

and

$$d_2 = d_1 - \sigma\sqrt{t} \tag{17-27}$$

For Kunkel Inc.:

$$d_1 = \frac{\ln(20/10) + (0.06 + 0.40^2/2)5}{0.40\sqrt{5}} = 1.5576$$

$$d_2 = 1.5576 - 0.40\sqrt{5} = 0.6632$$

Using the *Excel* NORMSDIST function gives $N(d_1) = N(1.5576) = 0.9403$, $N(d_2) = N(0.6632) = 0.7464$, and $V = \$20(0.9403) - \$10e^{-0.06(5)}(0.7464) = \$13.28$ million. So Kunkel's equity is worth $13.28 million, and its debt must be worth what is left over: $20 - $13.28 = $6.72 million. Because this is 5-year, zero coupon debt, its yield must be:

$$\text{Yield on debt} = \left(\frac{10}{6.72}\right)^{1/5} - 1 = 0.0827 = 8.27\%$$

Thus, when Kunkel issued the debt, it received $6.72 million and the yield on the debt was 8.27%. Notice that the yield on the debt, 8.27%, is greater than the 6% risk-free rate. This is because the firm might default if its value falls enough, so the bonds are risky. Note also that the yield on the debt depends on the value of the option and hence on the riskiness of the firm. The debt will have a lower value—and a higher yield—the more the option is worth.

17-4b **Managerial Incentives**

The only decision an investor in a stock option can make, once the option is purchased, is whether and when to exercise it. However, this restriction does not apply to equity when it is viewed as an option on the total value of the firm. Management has some leeway to affect the riskiness of the firm through its capital budgeting and investment decisions, and it can affect the amount of capital invested in the firm through its dividend policy.

17-4c **Capital Budgeting Decisions**

See **Ch17 Tool Kit.xls** on the textbook's Web site for all calculations.

When Kunkel issued the $10 million face value debt discussed previously, the yield was determined in part by Kunkel's riskiness, which in turn was determined in part by what management intended to do with the $6.72 million it raised. We know from our analysis in Chapter 5 that options are worth more when volatility is higher. This means that if Kunkel's management can find a way to increase its riskiness without decreasing the total value of the firm, then doing so will increase the equity's value while decreasing the debt's value. Management can accomplish this by selecting risky rather than safe investment projects. Table 17-1 shows the value of equity, the value of debt, and the yield on debt for a range of possible volatilities. See *Ch17 Tool Kit.xls* for the calculations.

Kunkel's current volatility is 40%, so its equity is worth $13.28 million, and its debt is worth $6.72 million. But if, after incurring the debt, management

TABLE 17-1	The Value of Kunkel's Debt and Equity for Various Levels of Volatility (Millions of Dollars)		
Standard Deviation	**Equity**	**Proceeds from Debt**	**Debt Yield**
20%	$12.62	$7.38	6.25%
30	12.83	7.17	6.89
40	**13.28**	**6.72**	**8.27**
50	13.86	6.14	10.25
60	14.51	5.49	12.74
70	15.17	4.83	15.66
80	15.81	4.19	18.99
90	16.41	3.59	22.74
100	16.96	3.04	26.92
110	17.46	2.54	31.56
120	17.90	2.10	36.68

undertakes projects that increase its riskiness from a volatility of 40% to a volatility of 80%, then the value of Kunkel's equity will increase by $2.53 million to $15.81 million, and the value of its debt will decrease by the same amount. This 19% increase in the value of the equity represents a transfer of wealth from bondholders to stockholders. A corresponding transfer of wealth from stockholders to bondholders would occur if Kunkel undertook projects that were safer than originally planned. Table 17-1 shows that if management undertakes safe projects and drives the volatility down to 30%, then stockholders will lose (and bondholders will gain) $0.45 million.

Such a strategy of investing borrowed funds in risky assets is called **bait and switch** because the firm obtains the money by promising one investment policy and then switching to another policy. The bait-and-switch problem is more severe when a firm's value is low relative to its level of debt. If Kunkel's total value is $20 million, then doubling its volatility from 40% to 80% increases its equity value by 19%. But if Kunkel had done poorly in recent years and its total value were only $10 million, then the impact of increasing volatility would be much greater. Table 17-2 shows that if Kunkel's total value were only $10 million and it issued $10 million face value of 5-year, zero coupon debt, then its equity would be worth $4.46 million at a volatility of 40%. Doubling the volatility to 80% would increase the value of the equity to $6.83 million, or by 53%. The incentive for management to "roll the dice" with borrowed funds can be enormous—if management owns many stock options, then their payoff from rolling the dice is even greater than the payoff to stockholders!

Bondholders are aware of these incentives and write covenants into debt issues that restrict management's ability to invest in riskier projects than originally promised. However, their attempts to protect themselves are not always successful, as the failures of Enron, Lehman Brothers, and AIG demonstrate. The combination of a risky industry, high levels of debt, and option-based compensation has proven to be very dangerous.

Notice that for extremely high volatilities, the yield on the debt is much higher than any reasonable required return on stock. When debt is supposedly safer than

TABLE 17-2	Debt and Equity Values for Various Levels of Volatility When the Firm's Total Value is $10 Million (Millions of Dollars)		
Standard Deviation	**Equity**	**Value of Debt**	**Debt Yield**
20%	$3.16	$6.84	7.90%
30	3.80	6.20	10.02
40	**4.46**	**5.54**	**12.52**
50	5.10	4.90	15.35
60	5.72	4.28	18.49
70	6.30	3.70	21.98
80	6.83	3.17	25.81
90	7.31	2.69	30.04
100	7.74	2.26	34.68
110	8.13	1.87	39.77
120	8.46	1.54	45.36

equity, why would its yield be so high? The answer is that although debtholders are indeed paid before stockholders, they don't get to participate in the very high payouts stockholders receive when the company does extremely well—debtholders only get the face value of the debt in those cases. But when the company does poorly, the debtholders only get to take over a poorly performing company. As the volatility increases, the probability of getting a poorly performing company instead of the face value of debt increases, driving down the value of the debt. In the limit, as the volatility continues to increase, the value of the debt is driven to zero. Thus the debt is actually much riskier than the stock when volatility is high!

17-4d **Equity with Risky Coupon Debt**

We have analyzed the simple case when a firm has zero coupon debt outstanding. The analysis becomes much more complicated when a firm has debt that requires periodic interest payments, because then management can decide whether to default on each interest payment date. For example, suppose Kunkel's $10 million of debt is a 1-year, 8% loan with semiannual payments. The scheduled payments are $400,000 in 6 months, and then $10.4 million at the end of the year. If management makes the scheduled $400,000 interest payment, then the stockholders will acquire the right to make the next payment of $10.4 million. If it does not make the $400,000 payment, then by defaulting the stockholders lose the right to make that next payment and hence lose the firm.[8] In other words, at the beginning of the year the stockholders have an option to purchase an option. The option they own has an exercise price of $400,000 and it expires in 6 months, and if they exercise it, they will acquire an option to purchase the entire firm for $10.4 million in another 6 months.

If the debt were 2-year debt, then there would be four decision points for management and the stockholders' position would be like an option on an option on an option on an option! These types of options are called **compound options**, and techniques for valuing them are beyond the scope of this book. However, the incentives discussed previously for the case when a firm has risky zero coupon debt still apply when the firm has periodic interest payments to make.[9]

SELF TEST

Discuss how equity can be viewed as an option. Who has the option and what decision can they make?

Why would management want to increase the riskiness of the firm? Why would this make bondholders unhappy?

What can bondholders do to limit management's ability to bait and switch?

---

8. Bankruptcy is far more complicated than our example suggests. As a firm approaches default it can take a number of actions, and even after filing for bankruptcy the stockholders can substantially delay a takeover by bondholders, during which time the value of the firm can deteriorate further. As a result, stockholders can often extract concessions from bondholders in situations in which it would seem that the bondholders should get all of the firm's value. Bankruptcy is discussed in more detail in Chapter 25.

9. For more on viewing equity as an option, see D. Galai and R. Masulis, "The Option Pricing Model and the Risk Factor of Stock," *Journal of Financial Economics*, Vol. 3, 1976, pp. 53–81. For a discussion on compound options, see Robert Geske, "The Valuation of Corporate Liabilities as Compound Options," *Journal of Financial and Quantitative Analysis*, June 1984, pp. 541–552.

17-5 **Introducing Personal Taxes: The Miller Model**

Although MM included *corporate taxes* in the second version of their model, they did not extend the model to include *personal taxes*. However, in his presidential address to the American Finance Association, Merton Miller presented a model to show how leverage affects firms' values when both personal and corporate taxes are taken into account.[10]

17-5a **The Miller Model**

To explain Miller's model, we begin by defining T_c as the corporate tax rate, T_s as the personal tax rate on income from stocks, and T_d as the personal tax rate on income from debt. Note that stock returns are expected to come partly as dividends and partly as capital gains, so T_s is a weighted average of the effective tax rates on dividends and capital gains. However, essentially all debt income comes from interest, which is effectively taxed at investors' top rates; thus T_d is higher than T_s.

With personal taxes included and under the same set of assumptions used in the earlier MM models, the value of an unlevered firm is found as follows:

$$
\begin{aligned}
V_U &= \frac{\text{EBIT}(1 - T_c)}{r_{sU}} \\
&= \frac{\text{EBIT}(1 - T_c)(1 - T_s)}{r_{sU}(1 - T_s)}
\end{aligned}
\tag{17–28}
$$

The $(1 - T_s)$ term takes account of personal taxes. Note that, in order to find the value of the unlevered firm, we can either discount pre-personal-tax cash flows at the pre-personal-tax rate of r_{sU} or discount after-personal-tax cash flows at the after-personal-tax rate of $r_{sU}(1 - T_s)$. Therefore, the numerator in the second line of Equation 17-28 shows how much of the firm's operating income is left after the unlevered firm pays corporate income taxes and its stockholders subsequently pay personal taxes on their equity income. Note also that the discount rate, r_{sU}, in Equation 17-28 is not necessarily equal to the discount rate in Equation 17-13. The r_{sU} from Equation 17-13 is the required discount rate in a world with corporate taxes but no personal taxes; the r_{sU} in Equation 17-28 is the required discount rate in a world with both corporate and personal taxes.

17-5b **Derivation of the Miller Model**

To begin, we partition the levered firm's annual cash flows, CF_L, into those going to stockholders and those going to bondholders *after* corporate and personal taxes:

$$
\begin{aligned}
CF_L &= \text{Net CF to stockholders} + \text{Net CF to bondholders} \\
&= (\text{EBIT} - I)(1 - T_c)(1 - T_s) + I(1 - T_d)
\end{aligned}
\tag{17–29}
$$

---

10. See Merton H. Miller, "Debt and Taxes," *Journal of Finance*, May 1977, pp. 261–275.

where I is the annual interest payment. Equation 17-29 can be rearranged as follows:

(17–29a)

$$CF_L = [EBIT(1 - T_c)(1 - T_s)] - [I(1 - T_c)(1 - T_s)] + [I(1 - T_d)]$$

The first term in Equation 17-29a is identical to the after-personal-tax cash flow of an unlevered firm as shown in the numerator of Equation 17-28, and its present value is found by discounting the perpetual cash flow by $r_{sU}(1 - T_s)$.

The second and third terms reflect leverage and result from the cash flows associated with debt financing, which under the MM assumptions are riskless (because the firm's debt is riskless under those assumptions). We can either discount pre-personal-tax interest payments at the pre-personal-tax rate of r_d or discount after-personal-tax interest payments at the after-personal-tax rate of $r_d(1 - T_d)$. Because they are after-personal-tax cash flows to debtholders, the present value of the last two right-hand terms in Equation 17-29a can be obtained by discounting at the after-personal-tax cost of debt, $r_d(1 - T_d)$. Combining the present values of the three terms, we obtain this value for the levered firm:

(17–30)

$$V_L = \frac{EBIT(1 - T_c)(1 - T_s)}{r_{sU}(1 - T_s)} - \frac{I(1 - T_c)(1 - T_s)}{r_d(1 - T_d)} + \frac{I(1 - T_d)}{r_d(1 - T_d)}$$

The first right-hand term in Equation 17-30 is identical to V_U in Equation 17-28. Recognizing this and consolidating the second two terms, we obtain:

(17–30a)

$$V_L = V_U + \left[1 - \frac{(1 - T_c)(1 - T_s)}{(1 - T_d)} \right]\left[\frac{I(1 - T_d)}{r_d(1 - T_d)} \right]$$

Now recognize that the after-tax perpetual interest payment divided by the after-tax required rate of return on debt, $I(1 - T_d)/r_d(1 - T_d)$, is equal to the market value of the perpetual debt, D:

(17–31)

$$D = \frac{I}{r_d} = \frac{I(1 - T_d)}{r_d(1 - T_d)}$$

Substituting D into Equation 17-30a and rearranging, we obtain the following expression, which is called the **Miller model**:

$$\text{Miller model: } V_L = V_U + \left[1 - \frac{(1 - T_c)(1 - T_s)}{(1 - T_d)}\right]D$$

The Miller model provides an estimate of the value of a levered firm in a world with both corporate and personal taxes.

The Miller model has several important implications, as follows.

1. The term in brackets,

$$\left[1 - \frac{(1 - T_c)(1 - T_s)}{(1 - T_d)}\right]$$

when multiplied by D, represents the gain from leverage. The bracketed term thus replaces the corporate tax rate, T, in the earlier MM model with corporate taxes ($V_L = V_U + TD$).

2. If we ignore all taxes (i.e., if $T_c = T_s = T_d = 0$), then the bracketed term is zero, so in this case Equation 17-32 is the same as the original MM model without taxes.

3. If we ignore personal taxes (i.e., if $T_s = T_d = 0$), then the bracketed term reduces to $[1 - (1 - T_c)] = T_c$, so in this case Equation 17-32 is the same as the MM model with corporate taxes.

4. If the effective personal tax rates on stock and bond incomes were equal (i.e., if $T_s = T_d$), then $(1 - T_s)$ and $(1 - T_d)$ would cancel, and so the bracketed term would again reduce to T_c.

5. If $(1 - T_c)(1 - T_s) = (1 - T_d)$, then the bracketed term would be zero, and so the value of using leverage would also be zero. This implies that the tax advantage of debt to the firm would be exactly offset by the personal tax advantage of equity. Under this condition, capital structure would have no effect on a firm's value or its cost of capital, so we would be back to MM's original zero-tax proposition.

17-5c **Application of the Miller Model**

Because taxes on capital gains are lower than on ordinary income and can be deferred, the effective tax rate on stock income is normally less than that on bond income. This being the case, what would the Miller model predict as the gain from leverage? To answer this question, assume the tax rate on corporate income is $T_c = 34\%$, the effective rate on bond income is $T_d = 28\%$, and the effective rate on stock income is $T_s = 15\%$. Using these values in the Miller model, we find that a levered firm's value exceeds that of an unlevered firm by 22% of the market value of corporate debt:

$$\begin{aligned}
\text{Gain from leverage} &= \left[1 - \frac{(1 - T_c)(1 - T_s)}{(1 - T_d)}\right]D \\
&= \left[1 - \frac{(1 - 0.34)(1 - 0.15)}{(1 - 0.28)}\right]D \\
&= (1 - 0.78)D \\
&= 0.22D
\end{aligned}$$

Note that the MM model with corporate taxes would indicate a gain from leverage of $T_c(D) = 0.34D$, or 34% of the amount of corporate debt. Thus, with these assumed tax rates, adding personal taxes to the model reduces, but does not eliminate, the benefit from corporate debt. In general, whenever the effective tax rate on income from stock is less than the effective rate on income from bonds, the Miller model produces a lower gain from leverage than is produced by the MM model with taxes.

In his paper, Miller argued that firms in the aggregate would issue a mix of debt and equity securities such that the before-tax yields on corporate securities and the personal tax rates of the investors who bought these securities would adjust until equilibrium was reached. At equilibrium, $(1 - T_d)$ would equal $(1 - T_c)(1 - T_s)$ and so, as we noted in item 5 above, the tax advantage of debt to the firm would be exactly offset by personal taxation and thus capital structure would have no effect on a firm's value or its cost of capital. Hence, according to Miller, the conclusions derived from the original MM zero-tax model are correct!

Others have extended and tested Miller's analysis. Generally, these extensions question Miller's conclusion that there is no advantage to the use of corporate debt. In fact, Equation 17-31 shows that both T_c and T_s must be less than T_d if there is to be zero gain from leverage. For most U.S. corporations and investors, the effective tax rate on income from stock is less than the rate on income from bonds; that is, $T_s < T_d$. However, many corporate bonds are held by tax-exempt institutions, and in those cases T_c is generally greater than T_d. Also, for those high-tax-bracket individuals with $T_d > T_c$, T_s may be large enough that $(1 - T_c)(1 - T_s)$ is less than $(1 - T_d)$; in this case there would be an advantage to using corporate debt. Still, Miller's work does show that personal taxes offset some of the benefits of corporate debt. This means that the tax advantages of corporate debt are less than were implied by the earlier MM model, which considered only corporate taxes.

As we discuss in the next section, both the MM and the Miller models are based on strong but unrealistic assumptions, so we should regard our examples as indicating the general effects of leverage on a firm's value and not a precise relationship.

SELF TEST

How does the Miller model differ from the MM model with corporate taxes?

What are the implications of the Miller model if $T_c = T_s = T_d = 0$? If $T_s = T_d = 0$?

Considering the current tax structure in the United States, what is the primary implication of the Miller model?

An unlevered firm has a value of $100 million. An otherwise identical but levered firm has $30 million in debt. Use the Miller model to calculate the value of a levered firm if the corporate tax rate is 40%, the personal tax rate on equity is 15%, and the personal tax rate on debt is 35%. **($106.46 million)**

17-6 **Capital Structure Theory: Arbitrage Proofs of the Modigliani-Miller Theorems**

Until 1958, capital structure theory consisted of loose assertions about investor behavior rather than carefully constructed models that could be tested by formal statistical analysis. In what has been called the most influential set of financial papers ever published, Franco Modigliani and Merton Miller (MM) addressed capital structure in a rigorous, scientific fashion, and they set off a chain of research that continues to this day.[11]

17-6a **Assumptions**

As we explain in this chapter, MM employed the concept of **arbitrage** to develop their theory. Arbitrage occurs if two similar assets—in this case, levered and unlevered stocks—sell at different prices. Arbitrageurs will buy the undervalued stock and simultaneously sell the overvalued stock, earning a profit in the process, and will continue doing so until market forces of supply and demand cause the prices of the two assets to be equal. For arbitrage to work, the assets must be equivalent, or nearly so. MM show that, under their assumptions, levered and unlevered stocks are sufficiently similar for the arbitrage process to operate.

No one, not even MM, believes their assumptions are sufficiently correct that their models will hold exactly in the real world. However, their models do show how money can be made through arbitrage if one can find ways around problems with the assumptions. Though some of them were later relaxed, here are the initial MM assumptions.

1. There are *no taxes*, either personal or corporate.
2. Business risk can be measured by σ_{EBIT}, and firms with the same degree of business risk are said to be in a *homogeneous risk class*.
3. All present and prospective investors have identical estimates of each firm's future EBIT; that is, investors have *homogeneous expectations* about expected future corporate earnings and the riskiness of those earnings.
4. Stocks and bonds are traded in *perfect capital markets*. This assumption implies, among other things: (a) that there are no brokerage costs and (b) that investors (both individuals and institutions) can borrow at the same rate as corporations.
5. *Debt is riskless.* This applies to both firms and investors, so the interest rate on all debt is the risk-free rate. Further, this situation holds regardless of how much debt a firm (or individual) uses.

---

11. See Franco Modigliani and Merton H. Miller, "The Cost of Capital, Corporation Finance and the Theory of Investment," *American Economic Review*, June 1958, pp. 261–297; "The Cost of Capital, Corporation Finance and the Theory of Investment: Reply," *American Economic Review*, September 1958, pp. 655–669; "Taxes and the Cost of Capital: A Correction," *American Economic Review*, June 1963, pp. 433–443; and "Reply," *American Economic Review*, June 1965, pp. 524–527. In a survey of Financial Management Association members, the original MM article was judged to have had the greatest impact on the field of finance of any work ever published. See Philip L. Cooley and J. Louis Heck, "Significant Contributions to Finance Literature," *Financial Management*, Tenth Anniversary Issue, 1981, pp. 23–33. Note that both Modigliani and Miller won Nobel Prizes—Modigliani in 1985 and Miller in 1990.

6. All cash flows are *perpetuities*. This means that growth is zero, expected EBIT is constant, and all bonds are perpetuities with no maturity dates.

17-6b **MM without Taxes**

MM first analyzed leverage under the assumption that there are no corporate or personal income taxes. On the basis of their assumptions, they stated and algebraically proved two propositions.[12]

Proposition I

The value of any firm is established by capitalizing its expected net operating income (EBIT) at a constant rate (r_{sU}) that is based on the firm's risk class:

(17–33)
$$V_L = V_U = \frac{\text{EBIT}}{\text{WACC}} = \frac{\text{EBIT}}{r_{sU}}$$

Here the subscript L designates a levered firm and U designates an unlevered firm. Both firms are assumed to be in the same business risk class, and r_{sU} is the required rate of return for an unlevered (i.e., all-equity) firm of this risk class when there are no taxes. For our purposes, it is easiest to think in terms of a single firm that has the option of financing either with all equity or with some combination of debt and equity. Hence, L designates a firm that uses some amount of debt and U designates a firm that uses no debt.

As established by Equation 17-33, V is a constant; therefore, *under the MM model, if there are no taxes then the value of the firm is independent of its leverage.* As we shall see, this also implies the following statements.

1. The weighted average cost of capital, WACC, is completely independent of a firm's capital structure.
2. Regardless of the amount of debt a firm uses, its WACC is equal to the cost of equity that it would have if it used no debt.

Proposition II

When there are no taxes, the cost of equity to a levered firm, r_{sL}, is equal to (1) the cost of equity to an unlevered firm in the same risk class, r_{sU}, plus (2) a risk premium whose size depends on (a) the difference between an unlevered firm's costs of debt and equity and (b) the amount of debt used:

(17–34)
$$r_{sL} = r_{sU} + \text{Risk premium} = r_{sU} + (r_{sU} - r_d)(D/S)$$

Here D is the market value of the firm's debt, S is the market value of its equity, and r_d is the constant cost of debt. Equation 17-34 states that, *as debt increases, the cost*

---

12. Modigliani and Miller actually stated and proved three propositions, but the third one is not material to our discussion here.

of equity rises in a mathematically precise manner (even though the cost of debt does not rise).

Taken together, the two MM propositions imply that using more debt in the capital structure will not increase the value of the firm, because the benefits of cheaper debt will be exactly offset by an increase in the riskiness of the equity and hence in its cost. Thus, MM argue that, *in a world without taxes, both the value of a firm and its WACC would be unaffected by its capital structure.*

17-6c **MM's Arbitrage Proof**

Propositions I and II are important because they showed for the first time that any valuation effects due to the use of debt must arise from taxes or other market frictions. The technique that MM used to prove these propositions is equally important, however, so we discuss it in detail here. They used an *arbitrage proof* to support their propositions, and this proof technique was later used in the development of option pricing models that revolutionized the securities industry.[13] Modigliani and Miller showed that, under their assumptions, if two companies differed only: (1) in the way they were financed and (2) in their total market values, then investors would sell shares of the higher-valued firm, buy those of the lower-valued firm, and continue this process until the companies had exactly the same market value. To illustrate, assume that two firms, L and U, are identical in all important respects except that Firm L has $4,000,000 of 7.5% debt while Firm U uses only equity. Both firms have EBIT = $900,000, and σ_{EBIT} is the same for both firms, so they are in the same business risk class.

Modigliani and Miller assumed that all firms are in a zero-growth, zero-tax situation. In other words, EBIT is expected to remain constant; this will occur if ROE is constant and all earnings are paid out as dividends. Under the constant EBIT assumption, the total market value of the common stock, S, is the present value of a perpetuity, which is found as follows:

$$S = \frac{\text{Dividends}}{r_{sL}} = \frac{\text{Net income}}{r_{sL}} = \frac{\text{EBIT} - r_d D}{r_{sL}}$$

(17–35)

Equation 17-35 is merely the value of a perpetuity, where the numerator is the net income available to common stockholders (all of which is paid out as dividends) and the denominator is the cost of common equity. Since there are no taxes, the numerator is not multiplied by $(1 - T)$, as it was when we calculated NOPAT in Chapters 6 and 9.

Assume that initially, *before any arbitrage occurs*, both firms have the same equity capitalization rate (that is, required rate of return on equity): $r_{sU} = r_{sL} = 10\%$. Under this condition, according to Equation 17-35, the following situation would exist.

---

13. By *arbitrage* we mean the simultaneous buying and selling of essentially identical assets that sell at different prices. The buying increases the price of the undervalued asset, and the selling decreases the price of the overvalued asset. Arbitrage operations will continue until prices have adjusted to the point where the arbitrageur can no longer earn a profit, at which point the market is in equilibrium. In the absence of transaction costs, equilibrium requires that the prices of the two assets be equal.

Firm U

$$\text{Value of Firm U's stock} = S_U = \frac{\text{EBIT} - r_d D}{r_{sU}}$$

$$= \frac{\$900,000 - \$0}{0.10} = \$9,000,000$$

$$\text{Total market value of Firm U} = V_U = D_U + S_U = \$0 + \$9,000,000$$
$$= \$9,000,000$$

Firm L

$$\text{Value of Firm L's stock} = S_L = \frac{\text{EBIT} - r_d D}{r_{sL}}$$

$$= \frac{\$900,000 - 0.075(\$4,000,000)}{0.10} = \frac{\$600,000}{0.10}$$

$$= \$6,000,000$$

$$\text{Total market value of Firm L} = V_L = D_L + S_L = \$4,000,000 + \$6,000,000$$
$$= \$10,000,000$$

Thus, before arbitrage (and assuming that $r_{sU} = r_{sL}$, which implies that capital structure has no effect on the cost of equity), the value of the levered Firm L exceeds that of the unlevered Firm U.

Modigliani and Miller argued that this result is a disequilibrium that cannot persist. To see why, suppose you owned 10% of L's stock and so the market value of your investment was $0.10(\$6,000,000) = \$600,000$. According to MM, you could increase your income without increasing your exposure to risk. For example, you could: (1) sell your stock in L for $600,000, (2) borrow an amount equal to 10% of L's debt ($400,000), and then (3) buy 10% of U's stock for $900,000. Note that you would receive $1,000,000 from the sale of your 10% of L's stock plus your borrowing, and you would be spending only $900,000 on U's stock. Hence, you would have an extra $100,000, which you could invest in riskless debt to yield 7.5%, or $7,500 annually.

Now consider your income positions:

Old Portfolio		New Portfolio	
10% of L's $600,000 equity income	$60,000	10% of U's $900,000 equity income	$90,000
		Less 7.5% interest on $400,000 loan	(30,000)
		Plus 7.5% interest on extra $100,000	7,500
Total income	$60,000	Total income	$67,500

Thus, your net income from common stock would be exactly the same as before, $60,000, but you would have $100,000 left over for investment in riskless debt and this would increase your income by $7,500. Therefore, the total return on your $600,000 net worth would rise to $67,500. And your risk, according to MM, would be the same as before, because you would have simply substituted $400,000 of "homemade" leverage for your 10% share of Firm L's $4 million of corporate leverage. Thus, neither your "effective" debt nor your risk would have changed. Therefore, you would have increased your income without raising your risk, which is obviously desirable.

Modigliani and Miller argued that this arbitrage process would actually occur, with sales of L's stock driving its price down and purchases of U's stock driving its price up, until the market values of the two firms were equal. Until this equality was established, gains could be obtained by switching from one stock to the other; hence, the profit motive would force equality to be reached. When equilibrium is established, the values of Firms L and U must be equal, which is what Proposition I states. If their values are equal, then Equation 17-33 implies that WACC $= r_{sU}$. Because there are no taxes, we have:

$$\text{WACC} = [D/(D+S)]r_d + [S/(D+S)]r_{sL}$$

A little algebra then yields:

$$r_{sL} = r_{sU} + (r_{sU} - r_d)(D/S)$$

which is what Proposition II states. Thus, according to MM, both a firm's value and its WACC must be independent of capital structure.

Note that each of the assumptions listed at the beginning of this section is necessary for the arbitrage proof to work exactly. For example, if the companies did not have identical business risk or if transaction costs were significant, then the arbitrage process could not be invoked. We discuss other implications of the assumptions later in the chapter.

17-6d **Arbitrage with Short Sales**

Even if you did not own any stock in L, you still could reap benefits if U and L did not have the same total market value. Your first step would be to sell short $600,000 of stock in L. To do this, your broker would let you borrow stock in L from another client. Your broker would then sell the stock for you and give you the proceeds, or $600,000 in cash. You would supplement this $600,000 by borrowing $400,000. With the $1 million total, you would buy 10% of the stock in U for $900,000 and have $100,000 remaining.

Your position would then consist of $100,000 in cash and two portfolios. The first portfolio would contain $900,000 of stock in U, which would generate $90,000 of income. Because you would own the stock, we'll call it the "long" portfolio. The other portfolio would consist of $600,000 of stock in L and $400,000 of debt. The value of this portfolio is $1 million, and it would generate $60,000 of dividends and $30,000 of interest. However, you would not own this second portfolio—you would "owe" it. Because you borrowed the $400,000, you would owe the $30,000 in interest. And because you borrowed the stock in L, you would "owe the stock" to the client from whom it was borrowed. Therefore, you would have to pay your broker the $60,000 of dividends paid by L, which the broker would then pass on to the client from whom the stock was borrowed. Thus your net cash flow from the second portfolio would be a negative $90,000. Because you would "owe" this portfolio, we'll call it the "short" portfolio.

Where would you get the $90,000 that you must pay on the short portfolio? The good news is that this is exactly the amount of cash flow generated by your long portfolio. Because the cash flows generated by each portfolio are the same, the short portfolio "replicates" the long portfolio.

Here is the bottom line. You started out with no money of your own. By selling L short, borrowing $400,000, and purchasing stock in U, you ended up with $100,000 in cash plus the two portfolios. The portfolios mirror one another, so their net cash flow is zero. This is perfect arbitrage: You invest none of your own money, you have no risk, you have no future negative cash flows, but you end up with cash in your pocket.

Not surprisingly, many traders would want to do this. The selling pressure on L would cause its price to fall, and the buying pressure on U would cause its price to rise, until the two companies' values were equal. To put it another way, *if the long and short replicating portfolios have the same cash flows, then arbitrage will force them to have the same value.*

This is one of the most important ideas in modern finance. Not only does it give us insights into capital structure, but it is the fundamental building block underlying the valuation of real and financial options and derivatives as discussed in Chapters 5 and 14. Without the concept of arbitrage, the options and derivatives markets we have today simply would not exist.

17-6e **MM with Corporate Taxes**

Modigliani and Miller's original work, published in 1958, assumed zero taxes. In 1963, they published a second article that incorporated corporate taxes. With corporate income taxes, they concluded that leverage will increase a firm's value. This occurs because interest is a tax-deductible expense; hence more of a levered firm's operating income flows through to investors.

Previously in this chapter we presented a proof of the MM propositions when personal taxes as well as corporate taxes are allowed. The situation in which there are corporate taxes but no personal taxes is a special instance of the situation with both personal and corporate taxes, so we only present results in this case.

Proposition I

The value of a levered firm is equal to the value of an unlevered firm in the same risk class (V_U) *plus* the value of the tax shield ($V_{Tax\ shield}$) due to the tax deductibility of interest expenses. The value of the tax shield, which is often called *the gain from leverage*, is the present value of the annual tax savings. The annual tax saving is equal to the interest payment multiplied by the tax rate, T:

$$\text{Annual tax saving} = r_dD(T)$$

Modigliani and Miller assume a no-growth firm, so the present value of the annual tax saving is the present value of a perpetuity. They assume that the appropriate discount rate for the tax shield is the interest rate on debt, so the value of the tax shield is:

$$V_{Tax\ shield} = \frac{r_dD(T)}{r_d} = TD$$

Therefore, the value of a levered firm is:

$$V_L = V_U + V_{\text{Tax shield}}$$
$$= V_U + TD$$

(17–36)

The important point here is that, when corporate taxes are introduced, the value of the levered firm exceeds that of the unlevered firm by the amount TD. Because the gain from leverage increases as debt increases, this implies that a firm's value is maximized at 100% debt financing.

Because all cash flows are assumed to be perpetuities, the value of the unlevered firm can be found by using Equation 17-35 and incorporating taxes. With zero debt (D = $0), the value of the firm is its equity value:

$$V_U = S = \frac{\text{EBIT}(1 - T)}{r_{sU}}$$

(17–37)

Note that the discount rate, r_{sU}, is not necessarily equal to the discount rate in Equation 17-33. The r_{sU} from Equation 17-33 is the required discount rate in a world with no taxes, whereas the r_{sU} in Equation 17-37 is the required discount rate in a world with taxes.

Proposition II

The cost of equity to a levered firm is equal to (1) the cost of equity to an unlevered firm in the same risk class plus (2) a risk premium whose size depends on (a) the difference between the costs of equity and debt to an unlevered firm, (b) the amount of financial leverage used, and (c) the corporate tax rate:

$$r_{sL} = r_{sU} + (r_{sU} - r_d)(1 - T)(D/S)$$

(17–38)

Observe that Equation 17-38 is identical to the corresponding without-tax Equation 17-34 except for the term $(1 - T)$, which appears only in Equation 17-38. Because $(1 - T)$ is less than 1, corporate taxes cause the cost of equity to rise less rapidly with leverage than it would in the absence of taxes. Proposition II, coupled with the reduction (due to taxes) in the effective cost of debt, is what produces the Proposition I result—namely, that the firm's value increases as its leverage increases.

As shown in Chapter 16, Professor Robert Hamada extended the MM analysis to define the relationship between a firm's beta, b, and the amount of leverage it has. The beta of an unlevered firm is denoted by b_U, and Hamada's equation is:

$$b = b_U[1 + (1 - T)(D/S)]$$

(17–39)

Note that beta, like the cost of stock shown in Equation 17-38, increases with leverage.

Is there an optimal capital structure under the MM zero-tax model?

What is the optimal capital structure under the MM model with corporate taxes?

How does the Proposition I equation differ between the two models?

How does the Proposition II equation differ between the two models?

Why do taxes result in a "gain from leverage" in the MM model with corporate taxes?

Summary

In this chapter, we discussed a variety of topics related to capital structure decisions. The key concepts covered are listed below.

- The most general approach to analyzing capital structure effects expresses the levered value of a company as the combination of its unlevered value and the value of side effects due to leverage:

$$V_L = V_U + \text{Value of side effects}$$

- MM stated that the primary benefit of debt stems from the **tax deductibility of interest payments**. The present value of the tax savings due to interest expense deductibility is called the **tax shield**. If we ignore other side effects, the value of an unlevered firm is:

$$V_L = V_U + V_{\text{Tax shield}}$$

- In 1958, **Franco Modigliani and Merton Miller (MM)** proved, under a restrictive set of assumptions including zero taxes, that capital structure is irrelevant; thus, according to the original MM article, a firm's value is not affected by its financing mix.

- Modigliani and Miller later added **corporate taxes** to their model and reached the conclusion that capital structure does matter. Indeed, their model led to the conclusion that firms should use 100% debt financing.

- Later, Miller extended the theory to include **personal taxes**. The introduction of personal taxes reduces, but does not eliminate, the benefits of debt financing. Thus, the **Miller model** also leads to 100% debt financing.

- The compressed **adjusted present value (APV)** model incorporates nonconstant growth and assumes that the tax savings should be discounted at the unlevered cost of equity.

- The levered cost of equity and the levered beta are different in the APV model than in the MM and Hamada models. In the APV model, the relationships are:

$$r_{sL} = r_{sU} + (r_{sU} - r_d)\left(\frac{w_d}{w_s}\right)$$

and

$$b = b_U + (b_U - b_D)\left(\frac{w_d}{w_s}\right)$$

- When debt is risky, management may choose to default. If the debt is zero coupon debt, then this makes equity like an option on the value of the firm with a strike price equal to the face value of the debt. If the debt has periodic interest payments, then the equity is like an option on an option, or a **compound option**.
- When a firm has risky debt and equity is like an option, management has an incentive to increase the firm's risk in order to increase the equity value at the expense of the debt value. This is called **bait and switch**.

Questions

17-1 Define each of the following terms:
  a. MM Proposition I without taxes and with corporate taxes
  b. MM Proposition II without taxes and with corporate taxes
  c. Miller model
  d. Adjusted present value (APV) model
  e. Value of debt tax shield
  f. Equity as an option

17-2 Explain, in your own words, how MM uses the arbitrage process to prove the validity of Proposition I. Also, list the major MM assumptions and explain why each of these assumptions is necessary in the arbitrage proof.

17-3 A utility company is allowed to charge prices high enough to cover all costs, including its cost of capital. Public service commissions are supposed to take actions that stimulate companies to operate as efficiently as possible in order to keep costs, and hence prices, as low as possible. Some time ago, AT&T's debt ratio was about 33%. Some individuals (Myron J. Gordon, in particular) argued that a higher debt ratio would lower AT&T's cost of capital and permit it to charge lower rates for telephone service. Gordon thought an optimal debt ratio for AT&T was about 50%. Do the theories presented in the chapter support or refute Gordon's position?

17-4 Modigliani and Miller assumed that firms do not grow. How does positive growth change their conclusions about the value of the levered firm and its cost of capital?

17-5 Your firm's CEO has just learned about options and how your firm's equity can be viewed as an option. Why might he want to increase the riskiness of the firm, and why might the bondholders be unhappy about this?

Problems   Answers Appear in Appendix B

Easy Problems 1–4

17-1 MM Model with Zero Taxes
An unlevered firm has a value of $500 million. An otherwise identical but levered firm has $50 million in debt. Under the MM zero-tax model, what is the value of the levered firm?

17-2 MM Model with Corporate Taxes
An unlevered firm has a value of $800 million. An otherwise identical but levered firm has $60 million in debt at a 5% interest rate. Its cost of debt is 5% and its unlevered cost of equity is 11%. No growth is expected. Assuming the corporate tax rate is 35%, use the MM model with corporate taxes to determine the value of the levered firm.

17-3 Miller Model with Corporate and Personal Taxes
An unlevered firm has a value of $600 million. An otherwise identical but levered firm has $240 million in debt. Under the Miller model, what is the value of the levered firm if the corporate tax rate is 34%, the personal tax rate on equity is 10%, and the personal tax rate on debt is 35%?

17-4 APV Model with Constant Growth
An unlevered firm has a value of $800 million. An otherwise identical but levered firm has $60 million in debt at a 5% interest rate. Its cost of debt is 5% and its unlevered cost of equity is 11%. After Year 1, free cash flows and tax savings are expected to grow at a constant rate of 3%. Assuming the corporate tax rate is 35%, use the compressed adjusted present value model to determine the value of the levered firm. (*Hint:* The interest expense at Year 1 is based on the current level of debt.)

Intermediate Problems 5–8

17-5 Business and Financial Risk—MM Model
Air Tampa has just been incorporated, and its board of directors is grappling with the question of optimal capital structure. The company plans to offer commuter air services between Tampa and smaller surrounding cities. Jaxair has been around for a few years, and it has about the same basic business risk as Air Tampa would have. Jaxair's market-determined beta is 1.8, and it has a current market value debt ratio (total debt to total assets) of 50% and a federal-plus-state tax rate of 40%. Air Tampa expects to be only marginally profitable at start-up; hence, its tax rate would only be 25%. Air Tampa's owners expect that the total book and market value of the firm's stock, if it uses zero debt, would be $10 million. Air Tampa's CFO believes that the MM and Hamada formulas for the value of a levered firm and the levered firm's cost of capital should be used. (These are given in Equations 17-13, 17-14, and 17-15.)

a. Estimate the beta of an unlevered firm in the commuter airline business based on Jaxair's market-determined beta. (*Hint:* This is a levered beta; use Equation 17-15 and solve for b_U.)

b. Now assume that $r_d = r_{RF} = 10\%$ and that the market risk premium $RP_M = 5\%$. Find the required rate of return on equity for an unlevered commuter airline.

c. Air Tampa is considering three capital structures: (1) \$2 million debt, (2) \$4 million debt, and (3) \$6 million debt. Estimate Air Tampa's r_s for these debt levels.

d. Calculate Air Tampa's r_s at \$6 million debt while assuming its federal-plus-state tax rate is now 40%. Compare this with your corresponding answer to part c. (*Hint*: The increase in the tax rate causes V_U to drop to \$8 million.)

17-6 MM without Taxes

Companies U and L are identical in every respect except that U is unlevered while L has \$10 million of 5% bonds outstanding. Assume that: (1) there are no corporate or personal taxes, (2) all of the other MM assumptions are met, (3) EBIT is \$2 million, and (4) the cost of equity to Company U is 10%.

a. What value would MM estimate for each firm?

b. What is r_s for Firm U? For Firm L?

c. Find S_L, and then show that $S_L + D = V_L = \$20$ million.

d. What is the WACC for Firm U? For Firm L?

e. Suppose $V_U = \$20$ million and $V_L = \$22$ million. According to MM, are these values consistent with equilibrium? If not, explain the process by which equilibrium would be restored.

17-7 MM with Corporate Taxes

Companies U and L are identical in every respect except that U is unlevered while L has \$10 million of 5% bonds outstanding. Assume that: (1) all of the MM assumptions are met, (2) both firms are subject to a 40% federal-plus-state corporate tax rate, (3) EBIT is \$2 million, and (4) the unlevered cost of equity is 10%.

a. What value would MM now estimate for each firm? (*Hint*: Use Proposition I.)

b. What is r_s for Firm U? For Firm L?

c. Find S_L, and then show that $S_L + D = V_L$ results in the same value as obtained in part a.

d. What is the WACC for Firm U? For Firm L?

17-8 Miller Model

Companies U and L are identical in every respect except that U is unlevered while L has \$10 million of 5% bonds outstanding. Both firms have an EBIT of \$2 million. Assume that all of the MM assumptions are met.

a. Suppose that both firms are subject to a 40% federal-plus-state corporate tax rate, investors in both firms face a tax rate of $T_d = 28\%$ on debt income and $T_s = 20\%$ (on average) on stock income, and the appropriate required pre-personal-tax rate r_{sU} is 10%. What is the value of the unlevered firm, V_U? What is the value of the levered firm, V_L? What is the gain from leverage?

b. Now keep the other assumptions ($D = \$10$ million, $r_d = 5\%$, EBIT $= \$2$ million, and $r_{sU} = 10\%$) but set $T_c = T_s = T_d = 0$. What is the value of the unlevered firm, V_U? What is the value of the levered firm, V_L? What is the gain from leverage?

c. Keep the other assumptions ($D = \$10$ million, $r_d = 5\%$, EBIT $= \$2$ million, and $r_{sU} = 10\%$), but now suppose $T_s = T_d = 0$ and $T_c = 40\%$. What is the value of the unlevered firm, V_U? What is the value of the levered firm, V_L? What is the gain from leverage?

d. Keep the other assumptions (D = $10 million, r_d = 5%, EBIT = $2 million, and r_{sU} = 10%), but now suppose that T_d = 28%, T_s = 28%, and T_c = 40%. Now what is the value of the levered firm? What is the gain from leverage?

Challenging Problems 9–12

17-9 Adjusted Present Value

Schwarzentraub Industries' expected free cash flow for the year is $500,000; in the future, free cash flow is expected to grow at a rate of 9%. The company currently has no debt, and its cost of equity is 13%. Its tax rate is 40%. (*Hint:* Use Equations 17-16 and 17-17.)

a. Find V_U.

b. Find V_L and r_{sL} if Schwarzentraub uses $5 million in debt with a cost of 7%. Use the APV model that allows for growth.

c. Based on V_U from part a, find V_L and r_{sL} using the MM model (with taxes) if Schwarzentraub uses $5 million in 7% debt.

d. Explain the difference between your answers to parts b and c.

17-10 MM with and without Taxes

International Associates (IA) is about to commence operations as an international trading company. The firm will have book assets of $10 million, and it expects to earn a 16% return on these assets before taxes. However, because of certain tax arrangements with foreign governments, IA will not pay any taxes; that is, its tax rate will be zero. Management is trying to decide how to raise the required $10 million. It is known that the capitalization rate r_U for an all-equity firm in this business is 11%, and IA can borrow at a rate r_d = 6%. Assume that the MM assumptions apply.

a. According to MM, what will be the value of IA if it uses no debt? If it uses $6 million of 6% debt?

b. What are the values of the WACC and r_s at debt levels of D = $0, D = $6 million, and D = $10 million? What effect does leverage have on firm value? Why?

c. Assume the initial facts of the problem (r_d = 6%, EBIT = $1.6 million, r_{sU} = 11%), but now assume that a 40% federal-plus-state corporate tax rate exists. Use the MM formulas to find the new market values for IA with zero debt and with $6 million of debt.

d. What are the values of the WACC and r_s at debt levels of D = $0, D = $6 million, and D = $10 million if we assume a 40% corporate tax rate? Plot the relationship between the value of the firm and the debt ratio as well as that between capital costs and the debt ratio.

e. What is the maximum dollar amount of debt financing that can be used? What is the value of the firm at this debt level? What is the cost of this debt?

f. How would each of the following factors tend to change the values you plotted in your graph?

(1) The interest rate on debt increases as the debt ratio rises.

(2) At higher levels of debt, the probability of financial distress rises.

17–11 Equity Viewed as an Option

A. Fethe Inc. is a custom manufacturer of guitars, mandolins, and other stringed instruments and is located near Knoxville, Tennessee. Fethe's current value of operations, which is also its value of debt plus equity, is estimated to be $5 million. Fethe has $2 million face value, zero coupon debt that is due in 2 years. The risk-free rate is 6%, and the standard deviation of returns for companies similar to Fethe is 50%. Fethe's owners view their equity investment as an option and they would like to know the value of their investment.

a. Using the Black-Scholes option pricing model, how much is Fethe's equity worth?

b. How much is the debt worth today? What is its yield?

c. How would the equity value and the yield on the debt change if Fethe's managers could use risk management techniques to reduce its volatility to 30%? Can you explain this?

17–12 Compressed APV with Nonconstant Growth

Sheldon Corporation projects the following free cash flows (FCFs) and interest expenses for the next 3 years, after which FCF and interest expenses are expected to grow at a constant 7% rate. Sheldon's unlevered cost of equity is 13% its tax rate is 40%.

	Year		
	1	2	3
Free cash flow ($ millions)	$20	$30	$40
Interest expense ($ millions)	$ 8	$ 9	$10

a. What is Sheldon's unlevered horizon value of operations at Year 3?

b. What is the current unlevered value of operations?

c. What is horizon value of the tax shield at Year 3?

d. What is the current value of the tax shield?

e. What is the current total value of the company?

Spreadsheet Problems

17–13 Build a Model: Equity Viewed as an Option

Higgs Bassoon Corporation is a custom manufacturer of bassoons and other wind instruments. Its current value of operations, which is also its value of debt plus equity, is estimated to be $200 million. Higgs has zero coupon debt outstanding that matures in 3 years with $110 million face value. The risk-free rate is 5%, and the standard deviation of returns for similar companies is 60%. The owners of Higgs Bassoon view their equity investment as an option and would like to know its value. Start with the partial model in the file *Ch17 P13 Build a Model.xls* on the textbook's Web site and answer the following questions:

a. Using the Black-Scholes option pricing model, how much is the equity worth?

b. How much is the debt worth today? What is its yield?

c. How would the equity value change if Fethe's managers could use risk management techniques to reduce its volatility to 45%? Can you explain this?

d. Graph the cost of debt versus the face value of debt for values of the face value from $10 to $160 million.

e. Graph the values of debt and equity for volatilities from 0.10 to 0.90 when the face value of the debt is $100 million.

17–14 **Build a Model: Compressed Adjusted Value Model**

Start with the partial model in the file *Ch17 P14 Build a Model.xls* on the textbook's Web site. Kasperov Corporation has an unlevered cost of equity of 12% and is taxed at a 40% rate. The 4-year forecasts of free cash flow and interest expenses are shown below. Free cash flow and interest expenses are expected to grow at a 5% rate starting after Year 4. Answer the following questions.

INPUTS (In Millions)		Projected		
Year:	1	2	3	4
Free cash flow	$200	$280	$320	$340
Interest expense	$100	$120	$120	$140

a. Calculate the estimated horizon value of unlevered operations at Year 4 (i.e., immediately after the Year-4 free cash flow).

b. Calculate the current value of unlevered operations.

c. Calculate the estimated horizon value of the tax shield at Year 4 (i.e., immediately after the Year-4 free cash flow).

d. Calculate the current value of the tax shield.

e. Calculate the current total value.

MINI CASE

David Lyons, CEO of Lyons Solar Technologies, is concerned about his firm's level of debt financing. The company uses short-term debt to finance its temporary working capital needs, but it does not use any permanent (long-term) debt. Other solar technology companies average about 30% debt, and Mr. Lyons wonders why they use so much more debt and how it affects stock prices. To gain some insights into the matter, he poses the following questions to you, his recently hired assistant.

a. Who were Modigliani and Miller (MM), and what assumptions are embedded in the MM and Miller models?

b. Assume that Firms U and L are in the same risk class and that both have EBIT = $500,000. Firm U uses no debt financing, and its cost of equity is r_{sU} = 14%. Firm L has $1 million of debt outstanding at a cost of r_d = 8%. There are no taxes. Assume that the MM assumptions hold.

(1) Find V, S, r_s, and WACC for Firms U and L.

(2) Graph (a) the relationships between capital costs and leverage as measured by D/V and (b) the relationship between V and D.

c. Now assume that Firms L and U are both subject to a 40% corporate tax rate. Using the data given in part b, repeat the analysis called for in b(1) and b(2) under the MM model with taxes.

d. Suppose investors are subject to the following tax rates: $T_d = 30\%$ and $T_s = 12\%$.
   (1) According to the Miller model, what is the gain from leverage?
   (2) How does this gain compare with the gain in the MM model with corporate taxes?
   (3) What does the Miller model imply about the effect of corporate debt on the value of the firm; that is, how do personal taxes affect the situation?

e. What capital structure policy recommendations do the three theories (MM without taxes, MM with corporate taxes, and Miller) suggest to financial managers? Empirically, do firms appear to follow any one of these guidelines?

f. Suppose that Firms U and L are growing at a constant rate of 7% and that the investment in net operating assets required to support this growth is 10% of EBIT. Use the compressed adjusted present value (APV) model to estimate the value of U and L. Also estimate the levered cost of equity and the weighted average cost of capital.

g. Suppose the expected free cash flow for Year 1 is $250,000 but it is expected to grow unevenly over the next 3 years: FCF2 = $290,000 and FCF3 = $320,000, after which it will grow at a constant rate of 7%. The expected interest expense at Year 1 is $80,000, but it is expected to grow over the next couple of years before the capital structure becomes constant: Interest expense at Year 2 will be $95,000, at Year 3 it will be $120,000 and it will grow at 7% thereafter. What is the estimated horizon unlevered value of operations (i.e., the value at Year 3 immediately after the FCF at Year 3)? What is the current unlevered value of operations? What is the horizon value of the tax shield at Year 3? What is the current value of the tax shield? What is the current total value? The tax rate and unlevered cost of equity remain at 40% and 14%, respectively.

h. Suppose there is a large probability that L will default on its debt. For the purpose of this example, assume that the value of L's operations is $4 million (the value of its debt plus equity). Assume also that its debt consists of 1-year, zero coupon bonds with a face value of $2 million. Finally, assume that L's volatility, σ, is 0.60 and that the risk-free rate r_{RF} is 6%.

i. What is the value of L's stock for volatilities between 0.20 and 0.95? What incentives might the manager of L have if she understands this relationship? What might debtholders do in response?

SELECTED ADDITIONAL CASES

The following cases from CengageCompose cover many of the concepts discussed in this chapter and are available at http://compose.cengage.com.

Klein-Brigham Series:

Case 7, "Seattle Steel Products," Case 9, "Kleen Kar, Inc.," Case 10, "Aspeon Sparkling Water," Case 43, "Mountain Springs," Case 57, "Greta Cosmetics," Case 74, "The Western Company," Case 83, "Armstrong Production Company," and Case 99, "Moore Plumbing Supply Company," focus on capital structure theory. Case 8, "Johnson Window Company," and Case 56, "Isle Marine Boat Company," cover operating and financial leverage.

Brigham-Buzzard Series:

Case 8, "Powerline Network Corporation," covers operating leverage, financial leverage, and the optimal capital structure.

CHAPTER 18

Initial Public Offerings, Investment Banking, and Financial Restructuring

WEB

The textbook's Web site contains an *Excel* file that will guide you through the chapter's calculations. The file for this chapter is **Ch18 Tool Kit.xls**, and we encourage you to open the file and follow along as you read the chapter.

Previous chapters described how a company selects projects, chooses its capital structure, and implements its dividend policy. These activities determine the amount of new capital a company must raise and the debt/equity mix of that new capital. In this chapter, we describe the actual process of raising capital from the public markets (such as selling stock in an initial public offering) and private markets (such as selling stock to a private investor like a pension fund). We also describe the roles investment banks and regulatory agencies play in raising capital.

Beginning-of-Chapter Questions

As you read the chapter, consider how you would answer the following questions. You *should not* necessarily be able to answer the questions before you read the chapter. Rather, you should use them to get a sense of the issues covered in the chapter. After reading the chapter, you should be able to give at least partial answers to the questions, and you should be able to give better answers after the chapter has been discussed in class. Note, too, that it is often useful, when answering conceptual questions, to use hypothetical data to illustrate your answer. We illustrate the answers with an *Excel* model that is available on the textbook's Web site. Accessing the model and working through it is a useful exercise, and it provides insights that are useful when answering the questions.

1. What are some reasons why companies decide to **go public**? If going public is a good idea, why don't all companies do so?

2. On the day an IPO comes out, the market price can rise above the offering price or fall below that price. Is it more common for the market price to close above or below the offering price on the day of an IPO? If a company's market price rises above the IPO price, does that suggest that the company **left money on the table** and thus received less for its shares than it should have received? If most companies do leave money on the table, does that indicate the IPO market is inefficient? How might systematic underpricing be explained? Has the amount of underpricing been constant over time? Explain.

3. What's the difference between an IPO and an SEO? Would you view purchasing a stock in an SEO to be more or less risky than purchasing a stock in an IPO? Would you expect the same first-day returns for an SEO purchase as for an IPO purchase? Why?

4. How do companies decide whether or not to **refund their outstanding bonds**? If the NPV as calculated in a bond refunding analysis is positive, does that mean that the company should call and refund the bond? What is the effect of calling a bond on its bondholders?

18-1 The Financial Life Cycle of a Start-up Company

Most businesses begin life as proprietorships or partnerships, and if they become successful and grow, at some point they find it desirable to become corporations. Initially, most corporate stock is owned by the firms' founding managers and key employees. Even start-up firms that are ultimately successful usually begin with negative free cash flows because of their high growth rates and product development costs; hence, they must raise capital during these high-growth years. If the founding owner-managers have invested all of their own financial resources in the company, then they must turn to outside sources of capital. Start-up firms generally have high growth opportunities, and they suffer from especially large problems due to asymmetric information. Therefore, as we discussed in Chapter 16, they must raise external capital primarily as equity rather than debt.

To protect investors from fraudulent stock issues, in 1933 Congress enacted the Securities Act, which created the **Securities and Exchange Commission (SEC)** to regulate the financial markets.[1] The Securities Act regulates interstate public offerings, which we explain later in this section, but it also provides several exemptions that allow companies to issue securities through **private placements** that are not registered with the SEC. The rules governing these exemptions are quite complex, but in general they restrict the number and type of investors who may participate in an issue. **Accredited investors** include the officers and directors of the company, high-wealth individuals, and institutional investors. In a nonregistered private placement, the company may issue securities to an unlimited number of accredited investors but to only 35 nonaccredited investors. In addition, none of the investors can sell their securities in the secondary market to the general public.

For most start-ups, the first round of external financing comes through a private placement of equity to one or two individual investors, called **angel investors**. In return for a typical investment in the range of $50,000 to $400,000, the angels receive stock and perhaps also a seat on the board of directors. Because angels can influence the strategic direction of the company, it is best when they bring experience and industry contacts to the table in addition to cash.

As the company grows, its financing requirements may exceed the resources of individual investors, in which case it is likely to turn to a **venture capital fund**. A venture capital fund is a private limited partnership, which typically raises $30 million to $80 million from a relatively small group of primarily institutional investors, including pension funds, college endowments, and corporations.[2] The managers of a venture capital fund, called **venture capitalists**, or **VCs**, are usually very knowledgeable and experienced in a particular industry, such as health care or

---

1. In addition to federal statutes, which affect transactions that cross state borders, states have "blue sky" laws that regulate securities sold just within the state. These laws were designed to prevent unscrupulous dealers from selling something of little worth, such as the blue sky, to naïve investors.

2. The typical venture capital fund is a private limited partnership, with limited partners and a general partner. The limited partners contribute cash but are prohibited from being involved in the partnership's decision making. Because of their limited participation, they are not held liable for any of the partnership's liabilities, except to the extent of their original investment. The general partner usually contributes a relatively modest amount of cash but acts as the partnership's manager. In return, the general partner normally receives annual compensation equal to 1% to 2% of the fund's assets plus a 20% share of the fund's eventual profits.

biotechnology. They screen hundreds of companies and ultimately fund around a dozen, called **portfolio companies**. The venture fund buys shares of the portfolio companies, and the VCs sit on the companies' boards of directors. The venture capital fund usually has a prespecified life of 7 to 10 years, after which it is dissolved, either by selling the portfolio companies' stock and distributing the proceeds to the funds' investors or by directly distributing the stock to the investors.

SELF TEST

What is a private placement?

What is an angel investor?

What is a venture capital fund? A VC?

18-2 **The Decision to Go Public**

Going public means selling some of a company's stock to outside investors in an initial public offering (IPO) and then letting the stock trade in public markets. For example, the babysitting, nanny and eldercare company Care.com, the performance boat manufacturer Malibu Boats Inc., the financial services company Ally Financial, and the online takeout food ordering portal Grubhub.com all went public in 2014. There are advantages and disadvantages for going public, as explained next.

18-2a **Advantages of Going Public**

The advantages to going public include the following.

1. *Increases liquidity and allows founders to harvest their wealth.* The stock of a private, or closely held, corporation is illiquid. It may be hard for one of the owners who wants to sell some shares to find a ready buyer, and even if a buyer is located, there is no established price on which to base the transaction.
2. *Permits founders to diversify.* As a company grows and becomes more valuable, its founders often have most of their wealth tied up in the company. By selling some of their stock in a public offering, they can diversify their holdings, thereby reducing the riskiness of their personal portfolios.
3. *Facilitates raising new corporate cash.* If a privately held company wants to raise cash by selling new stock, it must either go to its existing owners, who may not have any money or may not want to put more eggs in this particular basket, or else shop around for wealthy investors. However, it is usually quite difficult to get outsiders to put money into a closely held company: If the outsiders do not have voting control (more than 50% of the stock), then the inside stockholders/managers can take advantage of them. Going public, which brings with it both public disclosure of information and regulation by the SEC, greatly reduces this problem and thus makes people more willing to invest in the company, which makes it easier for the firm to raise capital.
4. *Establishes a value for the firm.* If a company wants to give incentive stock options to key employees, it is useful to know the exact value of those options. Employees much prefer to own stock, or options on stock, that is publicly traded and therefore liquid. Also, when the owner of a privately owned business dies, state and federal tax appraisers must set a value on the company for

estate tax purposes. Often these appraisers set a higher value than that of a similar publicly traded company.

5. *Facilitates merger negotiations.* Having an established market price helps when a company either is being acquired or is seeking to acquire another company in which the payment will be with stock.

6. *Increases potential markets.* Many companies report that it is easier to sell their products and services to potential customers after they become publicly traded.

18-2b Disadvantages of Going Public

The disadvantages associated with going public include the following.

1. *Increases reporting costs.* A publicly owned company must file quarterly and annual reports with the SEC and/or various state agencies. These reports can be a costly burden, especially for small firms. In addition, compliance with the Sarbanes-Oxley Act often requires considerable expense and manpower.

2. *Increases disclosure requirements.* Management may not like the idea of reporting operating data, because these data will then be available to competitors. Similarly, the owners of the company may not want people to know their net worth. But because a publicly owned company must disclose the number of shares its officers, directors, and major stockholders own, it is easy enough for anyone to multiply shares held by price per share to estimate the net worth of the insiders.

3. *Increases risk of having an inactive market and/or low price.* If the firm is very small and if its shares are not traded frequently, then its stock will not really be liquid and so the market price may not represent the stock's true value. Security analysts and stockbrokers simply will not follow the stock, because there will not be sufficient trading activity to generate enough brokerage commissions to cover the costs of following it.

4. *Reduces owner/manager control.* Because of possible tender offers and proxy fights, the managers of publicly owned firms who do not have voting control must be concerned about maintaining control. Further, there is pressure on such managers to produce annual earnings gains, even when it might be in the shareholders' best long-term interests to adopt a strategy that reduces short-term earnings but raises them in future years. These factors have led a number of public companies to "go private" in leveraged buyout deals, where the managers borrow the money to buy out the nonmanagement stockholders. We discuss the decision to go private in a later section.

5. *Increases time spent on investor relations.* Public companies must keep investors abreast of current developments. Many CFOs of newly public firms report that they spend 2 full days a week talking with investors and analysts.

What are the major advantages of going public?

What are the major disadvantages?

SELF TEST

18-3 The Process of Going Public: An Initial Public Offering

An initial public offering is complicated, expensive, and time-consuming, as the following explains.

18-3a **Selecting an Investment Bank**

After a company decides to go public, it faces the problem of how to sell its stock to a large number of investors. Although most companies know how to sell their products, few have experience in selling securities. To help in this process, the company will interview a number of different **investment banks**, also called **underwriters**, and then select one to be the lead underwriter. To understand the factors that affect this choice, it helps to understand exactly what investment banks do in an IPO.

First, the investment bank helps the firm determine the preliminary offering price, or price range, for the stock and the number of shares to be sold. The investment bank's reputation and experience in the company's industry are critical in convincing potential investors to purchase the stock at the offering price. In effect, the investment bank implicitly certifies that the stock is not overpriced, which obviously comforts investors. Second, the investment bank actually sells the shares to its existing clients, which include a mix of institutional investors and retail (that is, individual) customers. Third, the investment bank, through its associated brokerage house, will have an analyst "cover" the stock after it is issued. This analyst will regularly distribute reports to investors describing the stock's prospects, which will help to maintain an interest in the stock. Well-respected analysts increase the likelihood that there will be a liquid secondary market for the stock and that its price will reflect the company's true value.

Some activities in finance involve as much marketing skill as finance expertise. For example, the selection of an underwriter often is described as a bake-off in which the competing investment banks woo the company with their best sales pitch, much like a cake-baking contest in which bakers vie for first prize.

Facebook chose Morgan Stanley to be its lead underwriter, but other investment banks were also involved, as we explain next.

18-3b **The Underwriting Syndicate**

The firm and its investment bank must next decide whether the bank will work on a **best efforts basis** or will **underwrite** the issue. In a best efforts sale, the bank does not guarantee that the securities will be sold or that the company will get the cash it needs, only that it will put forth its "best efforts" to sell the issue. On an underwritten issue, in contrast, the company does get a guarantee: The bank agrees to buy the entire issue and then resell the stock to its customers. Therefore, the bank bears significant risks in underwritten offerings.

Except for extremely small issues, virtually all IPOs are underwritten. Investors are required to pay for securities within 10 days, and the investment bank must pay the issuing firm within 4 days of the official commencement of the offering. Typically, the bank sells the stock within a day or two after the offering begins, but on occasion the bank miscalculates, sets the offering price too high, and thus is unable to move the issue. At other times, the market declines during the offering period, forcing the bank to reduce the price of the stock or bonds. In either instance, on an underwritten offering the firm receives the price that was agreed upon, so the bank must absorb any losses that are incurred.

Because they are exposed to large potential losses, investment banks typically do not handle the purchase and distribution of issues single-handedly unless the issue is very small. If the sum of money involved is large, then investment banks form **underwriting syndicates** in an effort to minimize the risk each individual bank faces. The banking house that sets up the deal is called the **lead underwriter** or the **managing underwriter**. Syndicated offerings are usually covered by more analysts, which contribute to greater liquidity in the post-IPO secondary market. Thus, syndication provides benefits to both underwriters and issuers.

In addition to the underwriting syndicate, on larger offerings still more investment banks are included in a **selling group**, which handles the distribution of securities to individual investors. The selling group includes all members of the underwriting syndicate plus additional dealers who take relatively small percentages of the total issue from the members of the underwriting syndicate. Thus, the underwriters act as wholesalers while members of the selling group act as retailers. The number of brokerage houses in a selling group depends partly on the size of the issue, but it is normally in the range of 10 to 15.

In addition to Morgan Stanley, Facebook's underwriting and sales syndicate included over 30 firms, including Goldman Sachs, Merrill Lynch, Barclays, Citigroup, Credit Suisse Securities, Deutsche Bank Securities, and Wells Fargo.

A new selling procedure has recently emerged that takes advantage of the trend toward institutional ownership of stock. In this type of sale, called an **unsyndicated stock offering**, the managing underwriter—acting alone—sells the issue entirely to a group of institutional investors, thus bypassing both retail stockbrokers and individual investors. In recent years, about 50% of all stock sold has been by unsyndicated offerings. Behind this phenomenon is a simple motivating force: money. The fees that issuers pay on a syndicated offering, which include commissions paid to retail brokers, can run a full percentage point higher than those on unsyndicated offerings. Moreover, although total fees are lower in unsyndicated offerings, managing underwriters usually come out ahead because they do not have to share the fees with an underwriting syndicate. However, some types of stock do not appeal to institutional investors, so not all firms can use unsyndicated offers.

18-3c **Regulation of Securities Sales**

Sales of new securities, and also sales in the secondary markets, are regulated by the Securities and Exchange Commission and, to a lesser extent, by each of the 50 states. There are four primary elements of SEC regulation.

1. *Jurisdiction.* The SEC has jurisdiction over all **interstate public offerings** in amounts of $1.5 million or more.
2. *Registration.* Newly issued securities (stocks and bonds) must be registered with the SEC at least 20 days before they are publicly offered. The **registration statement**, called Form S-1, provides financial, legal, and technical information about the company to the SEC. A **prospectus**, which is embedded in the S-1, summarizes this information for investors. The SEC's lawyers and accountants analyze both the registration statement and the prospectus; if the information is inadequate or misleading, the SEC will delay or stop the public offering.[3]

w w w

The SEC Web site allows users to search for any filings by a company, including Form S-1. See **www.sec.gov/edgar .shtml.**

---

3. It is easy to obtain the S-1 form, which typically has 50 to 200 pages of financial statements in addition to a detailed discussion of the firm's business, the risks and opportunities the firm faces, its principal stockholders and managers, what will be done with the funds raised, and the like. The company seeking to go public files the statement with the SEC, which makes it immediately available to investors via the Internet. The SEC staff reviews the filed S-1, and amendments may be issued (labeled S-1A, S-1B, etc.). The likely range for the offering price will be reported—for example, $13 to $15 per share. If the market strengthens or weakens during the SEC review, the price may be increased or decreased right up until the last day. The SEC Web site for these and other filings is www.sec.gov.

Among its disclosures, the S-1 document and subsequent amendments (S-1/A) show the proposed number of shares to be sold (including a breakdown between shares sold by the company and shares sold by current stockholders, including the founders and investors) and a range of possible offering prices (the prices at which the first investors may purchase the stock). For example, Facebook's S-1 filing on February 1, 2012, did not specify either the number of shares or price range, but its amended statement on May 3, 2012, stated that Facebook would offer 337 million shares (180 million from the company and 157 million shares from its current stockholders) at a price between $28 and $35 per shares.

3. *Prospectus.* After the SEC declares the registration to be effective, new securities may be advertised, but all sales solicitations must be accompanied by the prospectus. **Preliminary prospectuses**, which are also called **"red herring" prospectuses,** may be distributed to potential buyers during the 20-day waiting period after the registration is effective, but no sales may be finalized during this time. The "red herring" prospectus (so called because it has a standard legal disclaimer printed in red across its cover) contains all the key information that will appear in the final prospectus except the final price, which is generally set after the market closes the day before the new securities are offered to the public.

4. *Truth in reporting.* If the registration statement or prospectus contains **misrepresentations** or **omissions** of material facts, then any purchaser who suffers a loss may sue for damages. Severe penalties may be imposed on the issuer or its officers, directors, accountants, engineers, appraisers, underwriters, and all others who participated in the preparation of the registration statement or prospectus.

18-3d **The Roadshow and Book-Building**

After the registration statement has been filed, the senior management team, the investment banker, and the company's lawyers go on a **roadshow**. The management team will make three to seven presentations each day to potential institutional investors, who typically are existing clients of the underwriters. The institutional investors ask questions during the presentation, but the management team may not give any information that is not in the registration statement. Nor may the management team make any forecasts or express any opinions about the value of their company. These provisions are due to the SEC-mandated **quiet period**. This quiet period begins when the registration statement is made effective and lasts for 40 days after the stock begins trading. Its purpose is to create a level playing field for all investors by ensuring that they all have access to the same information. It is not uncommon for the SEC to delay an IPO if managers violate the quiet period rules. The typical roadshow may last 10 to 14 days, with stops in 10 to 20 different cities. In many ways the process resembles a coming-out party for the company, but it is more grueling and has much higher stakes.

After each presentation, the investment banker asks the investor for an indication of interest based on the offering price range shown in the registration statement. The investment banker records the number of shares each investor is willing to buy, which is called **book-building**. As the roadshow progresses, an investment bank's "book" shows how demand for the offering is building. Many

IPOs are **oversubscribed**, with investors wishing to purchase more shares than are available. In such a case, the investment bank will allocate shares to the investors on a pro rata basis.[4] If demand is high enough, the banks may increase the offering price; if demand is low, they will either reduce the offering price or withdraw the IPO. Sometimes low demand is specifically due to concern over the company's future prospects, but sometimes low demand is caused by a fall in the general stock market. Thus, the timing of the roadshow and offering date are important. As the old saying goes, sometimes it is better to be lucky than good.

18-3e **Setting the Offer Price**

Before trading can begin, a company must file a final amended registration statement showing the actual number of shares to be sold and the final price range. A company usually announces the actual offering price the day before the IPO. This is the price at which the investment banking syndicate sells stocks to the buyers it lined up during the roadshow. The investment bank then pays these proceeds to the issuing company, less a percentage that is called the underwriting spread (we discuss all the costs of an IPO in following sections).

How do the company and its investment bankers set the offering price? It is simple in theory but complicated in practice, so we will start with theory. There are two situations: (1) a company knows how many shares it plans to sell or (2) it knows how much cash it needs to raise.

Setting the Offer Price If the Number of New Shares Is Known

A company must decide how much ownership it wishes to sell to new investors, and this depends on the number of shares owned by the founder and previous investors, $n_{Existing}$, and the number of new shares purchased by new investors, n_{New}:

$$\text{Percentage shares owned by new investors} = \frac{n_{New}}{n_{New} + n_{Existing}} \qquad \textbf{(18-1)}$$

Given the target percentage to be sold, Equation 18-1 can be solved for the required number of new shares to sell:

$$n_{New} = \frac{(\% \text{ owned by new investors})n_{Existing}}{1 - (\% \text{ owned by new investors})} \qquad \textbf{(18-1a)}$$

The company and investment banker must estimate the value of the company and the value of its equity prior to the IPO, $V_{Pre\text{-}IPO}$. The total value of equity after the IPO is the sum of the pre-IPO value and the proceeds from the IPO, net of the

---

4. Most underwriting agreements contain an "overallotment option" that permits the underwriter to purchase additional shares from the company, up to 15% of the issue size, to cover promises made to potential buyers. This is called a "green shoe" agreement because it was first used in the 1963 underwriting of a company named Green Shoe.

underwriter's spread. Letting P_{Offer} denote the offer price, and F denote the percentage spread, the post-IPO value of equity, $V_{Post-IPO}$, is:

(18–2)

$$V_{Post-IPO} = V_{Pre-IPO} + P_{Offer}(1 - F)n_{New}$$

The new investors will buy stock only if their stake after the IPO is at least as big as the amount they pay for the shares. Their stake is equal to the post-IPO value of the company multiplied by the percentage of the company that they own, and the amount they pay is equal to the offer price multiplied by the number of new shares. Using this observation, Equations 18-1 and 18-2, and considerable algebra we get:

(18–3)

$$P_{Offer} = \left[\frac{V_{Pre-IPO}}{F(n_{New}) + n_{Existing}}\right]$$

For example, Facebook's founders and early investors owned 1.96 billion shares before the IPO and Facebook sold 0.18 billion in the IPO. If the pre-IPO value of Facebook was $75 billion and the investment bank's spread was 7%, the offer price should have been:

$$P_{Offer} = \left[\frac{\$75}{(0.07)(0.18) + 1.96}\right] = \$38.02$$

After a company announces the offer price, analysts can use Equation 18-3 to solve for the pre-IPO value implied by the pricing, which is what we did for the example using Facebook. After the investment banker's spread, Facebook's proceeds were about $38.02(1 − 0.07)(0.18 billion) = $6.4 billion. The new investors owned about 8.4% of Facebook: 0.18/(0.18 + 1.96) = 8.4%.

Setting the Offer Price If the Target Proceeds Are Known

How does a company set the offer price if it needs a certain amount of proceeds? The basic idea is to determine the ratio of the value of the investment by new investors to the post-IPO value. From the new investors' perspectives, this is the percentage of ownership they must have to justify their investment. The post-IPO value is equal to the pre-IPO value plus the net proceeds, so the percentage ownership required by new investors is:

(18–4)

$$\% \text{ of shares required by new investors} = \frac{Investment}{(1 - F)Investment + V_{Pre-IPO}}$$

For example, suppose a company has a pre-IPO value of $50 million, has 2 million existing shares, needs $9.3 million in net proceeds, and the investment bank charges a 7% spread. The company must sell $10 million of stock to investors in order to net the desired $9.3 million: ($10 million)(1 − 0.07) = $9.3 million. Using Equation 18-4, the new investors will require a 16.86% stake in the company:

$$\% \text{ of shares required by new investors} = \frac{\$10}{(1 - 0.07)\$10 + \$50} = 16.86\%$$

Equation 18-1a can be used to solve for the number of new shares:

$$n_{New} = \frac{(0.1686)(2,000,000)}{(1 - 0.1686)} = 405,581$$

The price per share is found by dividing the investment by the number of new shares: $10,000,000/405,581 = $24.656 ≈ $24.65.

A quicker way to make this calculation is to recognize that the existing shareholders bear the underwriting cost because the new investors must receive stock exactly equal to their cost. For this example, the underwriting cost is 0.07($10 million) = $0.7 million. Subtracting this from the pre-IPO value and dividing by the existing number of shares gives the same price of $24.65 = ($10 − $0.07)/2. After calculating the IPO price of $24.65, it is a simple matter to find the number of new shares by dividing the investment of $10 million by the price per share: $10,000,000/$24.65 = 405,680 shares, the same as we found previously, except for rounding differences.

Conflicts Between the Company and the Investment Bank

Although the pricing is simple in theory, there are big conflicts of interest in practice. The issuing company wants the offer price to be high because that will generate more cash in the IPO or reduce the number of shares that must be sold. However, the investment banker in an underwritten IPO is afraid of being stuck with over-valued stock if the offer price is too high. Although rare, some IPOs have been cancelled at the last moment because the company and the underwriters could not reach an agreement.

18-3f **The First Day of Trading**

The first day of trading for many IPOs can be wild and exciting. Table 18-1 shows the largest first-day returns for IPOs during 2013. Some stocks end the day with large gains, such as the 123% price increase of Sprouts Farmers Market, Inc., as shown in Line 1 of the table. Others have a sharp run-up and then fall back by the end of the day. A few IPOs actually end their first day with a loss. Professor Jay Ritter of the University of Florida reported that the average first-day return in 2013 was about 21.2%, a bit higher than the 1980–2013 return of 18.0%.[5]

In one of the most famous IPOs of the decade, Facebook broke even on the first day, May 18, 2012, and would have fallen if the underwriters had not created artificial demand by purchasing the falling shares. On the second day, Facebook fell by 11%. Facebook's amended filings in the week before its IPO may have contributed to its weak first-day performance. On May 15, 2012, Facebook filed an amended S-1/A increasing the range of prices from $28–$35 to $34–$38. On May 16, Facebook

---

5. See Jay R. Ritter, http://bear.warrington.ufl.edu/ritter/IPOStatistics.pdf

TABLE 18-1	Highest First-Day IPO Returns in 2013[a]			
Rank	Company	Offering Price	First-Day Closing Price	Gain
1	Sprouts Farmers Market Inc.	$18.00	$40.11	123%
2	Noodles & Company	$18.00	$36.75	104%
3	Benefitfocus Inc.	$26.50	$53.55	102%
4	The Container Store Group Inc.	$18.00	$36.20	101%
5	Foundation Medicine Inc.	$18.00	$35.35	96%
6	Rocket Fuel Inc.	$29.00	$56.10	93%
7	China Commercial Credit Inc.	$ 6.50	$12.45	92%
8	Qunar Cayman Islands Limited	$15.00	$28.40	89%
9	FireEye Inc.	$20.00	$36.00	80%
10	Marketo Inc.	$13.00	$23.10	78%

[a]These are the highest first-day IPO returns in 2013.

Source: Compiled from **www.hoovers.com/100007201-1.html.**

filed another amendment increasing by 84 million shares the amount to be sold by insiders. On May 17, Facebook announced that the offer price would be $38 per share, at the very top of the already higher range. Facebook's stock began trading the next day.

Many analysts were surprised by these increases in the offer price and the number of shares to be sold, especially the proportion of shares from insiders, which rose to 57% of the total sold in the IPO. To put this in perspective, Google's insiders represented about 28% of its IPO, and some insiders don't sell any of their shares, like the insiders at Amazon in 1994. It is possible that this increase in supply and cost drove down demand for the stock.

According to a study of IPOs during 1990–1998 by Professors Tim Loughran and Jay Ritter, about 27.3% of the IPOs had an offer price that was lower than the low range in their initial registration filing, and these stocks had an average first-day return of 4.0%.[6] Even though the average return was positive, 47% of these stocks actually ended the day with a loss or no gain. About 48.4% of IPOs had an offering price that was within the range of their initial filing. For such companies, the average first-day return was 10.8%. As a result of high demand during the roadshow, 24.3% of IPOs had a final offer price that exceeded their original range. These stocks had an average first-day return of 31.9%. Overall, the average first-day return was 14.1% during 1990–1998, with 75% of all IPOs having a positive return. During 1999, the average first-day return was an astronomical 70%!

---

6. See Tim Loughran and Jay R. Ritter, "Why Don't Issuers Get Upset about Leaving Money on the Table in IPOs?" *Review of Financial Studies*, 2002, pp. 413–444.

You're probably asking yourself two questions: (1) How can I get in on these deals? (2) Why is the offering price so low? First, you probably can't get the chance to buy an IPO at its offering price, especially not a "hot" one. Virtually all sales go to institutional investors and preferred retail customers. A few Web-based investment banks are trying to change this, such as the OpenIPO of W. R. Hambrecht & Co., but right now it is difficult for small investors to get in on the first day for hot IPOs.

Various theories have been put forth to explain IPO underpricing. As long as issuing companies don't complain, investment banks have strong incentives to underprice the issue. First, underpricing increases the likelihood of oversubscription, which reduces the risk to the underwriter. Second, most investors who get to purchase the IPO at its offering price are preferred customers of the investment bank, and they became preferred customers by generating lots of commissions in the investment bank's sister brokerage company. Therefore, the IPO is an easy way for the underwriter to reward customers for past and future commissions. Third, the underwriter needs an honest indication of interest when building the book prior to the offering, and underpricing is a possible way to secure this information from the institutional investors.

But why don't issuing companies object to underpricing? Some do, and they are seeking alternative ways to issue securities, such as OpenIPO. However, most seem content to leave some money on the table. The best explanations seem to be that: (1) the company wants to create excitement, and a price run-up on the first day does that; (2) only a small percentage of the company's stock generally is offered to the public, so current stockholders lose less to underpricing than appears at first glance; and (3) IPO companies generally plan to have additional offerings in the future, and the best way to ensure future success is to have a successful IPO, which underpricing guarantees.

Although IPOs on average provide large first-day returns, their long-term returns over the following 3 years are below average. For example, if you could not get in at the IPO price but purchased a portfolio of IPO stocks on their second day of trading, your 3-year return would have been lower than the return on a portfolio of similar but seasoned stocks. In summary, the offering price appears to be too low, but the first-day run-up is generally too high.

18-3g **The Costs of Going Public**

During recent years, virtually all investment banks have charged a 7% **spread** between the price they pay the issuing company and the price at which they sell shares to the public. Thus, they keep 7% of the offering price as their compensation. For example, Malibu Boats (MBUU), a manufacturer of watersport boats, went public in 2014. MBUU sold 7.642 million shares at an offering price of $14.00 to the public, while the founders and other shareholders sold an additional 571,289 of their own shares. In this IPO, the underwriters' direct compensation was $0.98 per share, which means that the stock was sold at a price of $14 to the public but MBUU received only $14.00 − $0.98 = $13.02 per share. For the 7.642 million shares issued by MBUU, these direct underwriting costs totaled about $0.98(7.642) = $7.5 million, and some $559 thousand for the shares sold by the founders and other existing shareholders.

There are other direct costs as well, such as lawyers' fees, accountants' costs, printing, engraving, and so on. MBUU estimated that these fees totaled about $800 thousand.

Last but not least are the indirect costs. The money left on the table, which is equal to the number of shares multiplied by the difference in the closing price and the offering price, can be quite large. MBUU experienced a first-day run-up to $17.00 from an offering price of $14.00, so its indirect costs totaled 7.642 ($17.00 − $14.00) = $22.9 million. In addition, senior managers spend an enormous amount of time working on the IPO rather than managing the business, which certainly carries a high cost even if it cannot be easily measured.

Thus, MBUU received proceeds of 7.642 ($14 − $0.98) = $99.50 million, the underwriters and their sales forces received $7.5 million, other expenses totaled about $0.8 million, and $22.9 million was left on the table. There were undoubtedly other indirect costs due to the time management spent on the IPO instead of running the company. As you can see, an IPO is quite expensive.[7]

18-3h **The Importance of the Secondary Market**

An active secondary market after the IPO provides the pre-IPO shareholders with a chance to convert some of their wealth into cash, makes it easier for the company to raise additional capital later, makes employee stock options more attractive, and makes it easier for the company to use its stock to acquire other companies. Without an active secondary market, there would be little reason to have an IPO. Thus, companies should try to ensure that their stock will trade in an active secondary market before they incur the high costs of an IPO.

There are several types of secondary markets: physical stock exchanges, dealer markets, and bulletin boards. We discuss each of these below.

The physical exchanges, such as the NYSE and AMEX (called the NYSE MKT since its acquisition by NYSE Euronext in 2008), conduct their trading in an actual location. In general, the NYSE and AMEX provide excellent liquidity. In order to have its stock listed, a company must apply to an exchange, pay a relatively small fee, and meet the exchange's minimum requirements. These requirements relate to the size of the company's net income, its market value, and its "float," which is the number of shares outstanding and in the hands of outsiders (as opposed to the number held by insiders, who generally do not actively trade their stock). Also, the company must agree to disclose certain information to the exchange and to help the exchange track trading patterns and thus ensure that no one is attempting to manipulate the stock's price. The size qualifications increase as a company moves from the AMEX to the NYSE.

Assuming a company qualifies, many believe that listing is beneficial to the company and to its stockholders. Listed companies receive a certain amount of free advertising and publicity, and their status as listed companies may enhance their prestige and reputation, which often leads to higher sales. Investors respond favorably to increased information, increased liquidity, and the confidence that the quoted price is not being manipulated. Listing provides investors with these

---

7. For more on IPOs, see Roger G. Ibbotson, Jody L. Sindelar, and Jay R. Ritter, "The Market's Problems with the Pricing of Initial Public Offerings," *Journal of Applied Corporate Finance,* Spring 1994, pp. 66–74; Chris J. Muscarella and Michael R. Vetsuypens, "The Underpricing of 'Second' Initial Public Offerings," *Journal of Financial Research,* Fall 1989, pp. 183–192; Jay R. Ritter, "The Long-Run Performance of Initial Public Offerings," *Journal of Finance,* March 1991, pp. 3–27; and Jay R. Ritter, "Initial Public Offerings," *Contemporary Finance Digest,* Spring 1998, pp. 5–30.

benefits, which may help managers reduce their firms' cost of equity and increase the value of their stock.[8]

The advantages of physical exchanges have been eroded—some would say eliminated—by computers and the Internet, which have benefited the dealer markets. The primary equity dealer markets are administered by NASDAQ, and they include the NASDAQ National Market and the NASDAQ SmallCap Market. Almost 85% of new IPO stocks trade in these markets. Unlike the physical exchanges, these consist of a network of dealers, with each dealer making a market in one or more stocks. A dealer makes a market in a company's stock by holding an inventory of the shares and then making offers to buy or sell the stock. Many stocks have excellent liquidity in these markets and remain there even though they easily meet the requirements for listing on the NYSE. Examples include Microsoft, Intel, Apple, and Cisco Systems.

Investment banks generally agree to make a market in a company's stock as part of their IPO duties. The diligence with which they carry out this task can have a huge effect on the stock's liquidity in the secondary market and thus on the success of the IPO.

Although the requirements for listing on the NASDAQ National Market or SmallCap Market are not as stringent as for the NYSE, some companies fail to maintain them and hence are "delisted." For these companies, offers to buy or sell the stock may be posted on the OTC Bulletin Board, an electronic bulletin board administered by NASDAQ. However, there is very little liquidity in these stocks, and an IPO would be considered a failure if the company's stock ended up on the OTC Bulletin Board.

18-3i **Regulating the Secondary Market**

As we stated earlier, a liquid and crime-free secondary market is critical to the success of an IPO or any other publicly traded security. So, in addition to regulating the process for issuing securities, the Securities Exchange Commission also has responsibilities in the secondary markets. The primary elements of SEC regulation are set forth below.

1. *Stock exchanges.* The SEC *regulates all national stock exchanges*, and companies whose securities are listed on an exchange must file annual reports similar to the registration statement with both the SEC and the exchange.
2. *Insider trading.* The SEC has control over trading by corporate *insiders.* Officers, directors, and major stockholders must file monthly reports of changes in their holdings of the stock of the corporation. Any short-term profits from such transactions must be turned over to the corporation.
3. *Market manipulation.* The SEC has the power to *prohibit manipulation* by such devices as pools (large amounts of money used to buy or sell stocks to artificially affect prices) or wash sales (sales between members of the same group to record artificial transaction prices).

---

8. For additional discussion on the benefits of listing, see H. Kent Baker and Richard B. Edelman, "AMEX-to-NYSE Transfers, Market Microstructure, and Shareholder Wealth," *Financial Management,* Winter 1992, pp. 60–72; and Richard B. Edelman and H. Kent Baker, "Liquidity and Stock Exchange Listing," *The Financial Review,* May 1990, pp. 231–249.

4. *Proxy statements.* The SEC has *control over the proxy statement* and the way the company uses it to solicit votes.

Control over credit used to buy securities is exercised by the Federal Reserve Board through **margin requirements**, which specify the maximum percentage of the purchase price someone can borrow. If a great deal of margin borrowing has persisted, then a decline in stock prices can result in inadequate coverages. This could force stockbrokers to issue **margin calls**, which require investors either to put up more money or have their margined stock sold to pay off their loans. Such forced sales further depress the stock market and thus can set off a downward spiral. The required "initial margin" at the time a stock is purchased has been 50% since 1974; required "maintenance margin" after the initial purchase is lower than the initial margin and is set by individual lender.

The securities industry itself realizes the importance of stable markets, sound brokerage firms, and the absence of stock manipulation.[9] Therefore, the various exchanges work closely with the SEC to police transactions and to maintain the integrity and credibility of the system. Similarly, the **National Association of Securities Dealers (NASD)** cooperates with the SEC to police trading in its dealer and OTC markets. These industry groups also cooperate with regulatory authorities to set net worth and other standards for securities firms, to develop insurance programs to protect the customers of failed brokerage houses, and the like.

In general, government regulation of securities trading, as well as industry self-regulation, is designed to ensure that: (1) investors receive information that is as accurate as possible, (2) no one artificially manipulates the market price of a given stock, and (3) corporate insiders do not take advantage of their position to profit in their companies' stocks at the expense of other stockholders. Neither the SEC, the state regulators, nor the industry itself can prevent investors from making foolish decisions or from having "bad luck," but they can and do help investors obtain the best data possible for making sound investment decisions.

18-3j **Questionable IPO Practices**

Among the many revelations to come out during 2002 regarding investment banking was the practice by some investment banking houses of letting CEOs and other high-ranking corporate executives in on "hot" IPOs. In these deals, the demand for the new stock was far greater than supply at the offering price, so the investment banks were virtually certain that the stock would soar far above the offering price.

Some investment banks systematically allocated shares of hot IPOs to executives of companies that were issuing stocks and bonds—and thus generating fees to the banks who underwrote the deals. Bernie Ebbers, the chairman and CEO of WorldCom—one of the biggest sources of underwriting fees for investment banks—was given huge allocations in hot IPOs, and he made millions on these deals. Ebbers

---

9. It is illegal for anyone to attempt to manipulate the price of a stock. During the 1920s and earlier, syndicates would buy and sell stocks back and forth at rigged prices so the public would believe that a particular stock was worth more or less than its true value. The stock exchanges, with the encouragement and support of the SEC, utilize sophisticated computer programs to help spot any irregularities that suggest manipulation, and they require disclosures to help identify manipulators. This system also helps to identify illegal insider trading. It is now illegal to manipulate a stock's price by spreading false news on the Internet.

is just one example; a lot of this was going on in the late 1990s, at the height of the tech/dot-com bubble.

Government regulators investigated this practice, called "spinning," and corporate executives and investment bankers were charged with something that amounts to a kickback scheme under which those executives who favored particular investment banks were rewarded with allocations in hot IPOs. Indeed, in 2003 ten Wall Street securities firms agreed to pay $1.4 billion in fines to settle charges of investor abuse, including spinning. The corporate executives were paid to work for their stockholders, so they should have turned over any IPO profits to their companies—not kept those profits for themselves. This practice was found to be a form of bribery by the New York Supreme Court and was ruled to be illegal in 2006.

This kind of unethical and illegal behavior may help to explain past IPO underpricing and "money left on the table" if executives allowed their IPOs to be underpriced in exchange for allocations of similarly underpriced shares in other IPOs. Whether or not similar activities take place now remains to be seen.

In summary, we have a hard time justifying IPO underpricing during the late 1990s on rational economic grounds. Researchers and analysts have come up with explanations for why companies let their investment banks price their stocks too low in IPOs, but those reasons seem rather weak. However, when coupled with what may have been a kickback scheme, the underpricing is less puzzling (but still ethically troubling). Before closing, we should make it clear that relatively few corporate executives were corrupt. However, just as one rotten apple can spoil an entire barrel, a few bad executives—when combined with lax regulation—can help a bad practice become "the industry standard," and thus become widespread.

SELF TEST

What is the difference between *best efforts* and *underwriting*?

What are some SEC regulations regarding sales of new securities?

What is a roadshow? What is book-building?

What is underpricing? What is leaving money on the table?

What are some of the costs of going public?

A privately held company has an estimated value of equity equal to $100 million. The founders own 10 million shares. If the company goes public and sells 1 million shares with no underwriting costs, how much should the per share offer price be? **($10.00)** If instead the underwriting spread is 7%, what should the offer price be? **($9.93)**

A company is planning an IPO. Its underwriters have said the stock will sell at $50 per share. The underwriters will charge a 7% spread. How many shares must the company sell to net $93 million, ignoring any other expenses? **(2 million)**

18-4 Equity Carve-Outs: A Special Type of IPO

In 2014, General Electric sold to the public about 15% of the equity in its wholly owned subsidiary, Synchrony Financial. In this transaction, the subsidiary, like the parent, became publicly owned, but the parent retained full control of the subsidiary by keeping about 85% of the subsidiary's common stock. (Parent companies typically retain at least 80% of the subsidiary's common stock to preserve their ability to file a consolidated tax return.) This type of transaction is called an **equity carve-out** (or **partial public offering**, or **spin-out**).[10] The market's response to Synchrony's carve-out was neutral—the stock price remained flat the first week of trading. The announcement (as opposed to the completion) of a carve-out, however, is typically associated with a stock price increase. This leads to an interesting question: Why do carve-out announcements typically result in stock price increases while the announcements of new stock issues by parent corporations generally decrease stock prices?

One possible answer is that carve-outs facilitate the evaluation of corporate growth opportunities on a line-of-business basis. Thus, analysts might have an easier time evaluating Synchrony as a separate company than when it was a part of General Electric. This also applies to providers of capital—Synchrony might be able to raise capital more effectively as a stand-alone company because investors are better able to evaluate its prospects. A third advantage to carve-outs is that they improve the ability of the parent to offer incentives to a subsidiary's managers. Thus, Synchrony can now offer equity incentives to its managers based on its own stock price rather than that of General Electric.

Equity carve-outs do have some associated costs. First, the underwriting commission involved in a carve-out is larger than for an equity offering by the parent. Second, because an equity carve-out is a type of initial public offering, there is a potential for underpricing the new offering. Third, key managers of the subsidiary must spend a significant amount of time marketing the new stock. Fourth, there are costs associated with the minority interest that is created in the carve-out. For example, the subsidiary's new board of directors must monitor all transactions between the subsidiary and the parent to ensure that the minority investors are not being exploited. Finally, there are additional costs such as annual reports, SEC filings, analyst presentations, and so on, which now must be borne both by parent and subsidiary.

SELF TEST

Explain what is meant by an equity carve-out.

On average, equity carve-outs have increased shareholder wealth. What are some potential explanations for this phenomenon?

18-5 Other Ways to Raise Funds in the Capital Markets

IPOs are exciting and play a vital role in stimulating the entrepreneurship and innovation that are vital for economic growth. However, the funds raised through IPOs are only a small fraction of the total funding that companies raise from commercial

---

10. For more information on equity carve-outs, see Roni Michaely and Wayne H. Shaw, "The Choice of Going Public: Spin-offs vs. Carve-outs," *Financial Management*, Autumn 1995, pp. 5–21; and Anand Vijh, "Long-Term Returns from Equity Carve-outs," *Journal of Financial Economics*, Vol. 51, 1999, pp. 273–308.

banks and capital markets. Of the roughly $2.3 trillion of debt and equity raised in 2010 in the United States, only about 1.6% ($36 billion) was through IPOs. Although 2013 was a bigger year for IPOs than 2010, only $55 billion was raised.[11] We discuss other ways that firms raise cash from capital markets in the following sections.[12]

18-5a **Preliminary Decisions**

Before raising capital, a firm must make some initial, preliminary decisions, which include the following:

1. *Dollars to be raised.* How much new capital is needed?
2. *Type of securities used.* Should common stock, preferred stock, bonds, hybrid securities, or a combination be used? Should the capital be public securities (which are registered and may be traded freely in the secondary markets), or should it be a private placement that might have restrictions on its subsequent trading? If common stock is to be issued, should it be done as a preemptive rights offering to current shareholders or by a direct sale to the general public?
3. *Competitive bid versus a negotiated deal.* Should the company simply offer a block of its securities for sale to the highest bidder, or should it negotiate a deal with an investment bank? These two procedures are called **competitive bids** and **negotiated deals**, respectively. Only about 100 of the largest firms listed on the NYSE, whose securities are already well known to the investment banking community, are in a position to use the competitive bidding process. The investment banks must do a great deal of investigative work ("due diligence") to bid on an issue unless they are already quite familiar with the firm, and such costs would be too high to make it worthwhile unless the bank was sure of getting the deal. Therefore, except for the largest firms, offerings of stock and bonds are generally on a negotiated basis. The exceptions are utilities, which are able to issue debt through competitive bids because the offerings are relatively easy for the investment banks to value and sell to clients.
4. *Selection of an investment bank.* Most deals are negotiated, so the firm must select an investment bank. This can be an important decision for a firm that is going public. On the other hand, an older firm that has already "been to market" will have an established relationship with an investment bank. However, it is easy to change banks if the firm is dissatisfied. Different investment banking houses are better suited for different companies. For example, Goldman Sachs and Morgan Stanley are the leading tech-IPO underwriters. Investment banking houses sell new issues largely to their own regular brokerage customers,

---

11. For IPO data, see the Global IPO Report from Renaissance Capital, **www.renaissancecapital.com /IPOHome/Press/MediaRoom.aspx?market=global**. For other data, see a special SEC report by Vlad Ivanov and Scott Bauguess, "Capital Raising in the U.S.: The Significance of Unregistered Offerings Using the Regulation D Exemption," February, 2012, **www.sec.gov/info/smallbus /acsec/acsec103111_analysis-reg-d-offering.pdf**.

12. For an excellent discussion of the various procedures used to raise capital, see Jay R. Ritter, "Investment Banking and Securities Issuance," in *North-Holland Handbook of the Economics of Finance*, George Constantinides, Milton Harris, and René Stulz, eds. (Amsterdam: North-Holland, 2002). Also see Claudio Loderer, John W. Cooney, and Leonard D. Van Drunen, "The Price Elasticity of Demand for Common Stock," *Journal of Finance*, June 1991, pp. 621–651.

so the nature of these customers has a major effect on the ability of the house to do a good job for corporate issuers. Finally, a major factor in choosing an underwriter is the reputation of the analyst who will cover the stock in the secondary market, because a strong buy recommendation from a well-respected analyst can trigger a sharp price run-up.

18-5b Seasoned Equity Offerings

When a company with publicly traded stock issues additional shares, this is called a **seasoned equity offering**, also known as a *secondary* or *follow-on offering*. Because the stock is already publicly traded, the offering price will be based upon the existing market price of the stock. Typically, the investment bank buys the securities at a prescribed number of points below the closing price on the last day of registration. For example, suppose that in August 2015 the stock of Microwave Telecommunications Inc. (MTI) had a price of $28.60 per share and that the stock had traded between $25 and $30 per share during the previous 3 months. Suppose further that MTI and its underwriter agreed that the investment bank would buy 10 million new shares at $1 per share below the closing price on the last day of registration. If the stock closed at $25 on the day the SEC released the issue, then MTI would receive $24 per share. Typically, such agreements have an escape clause that provides for the contract to be voided if the price of the securities drops below some predetermined figure. In the illustrative case, this "upset" price might be set at $24 per share. Thus, if the closing price of the shares on the last day of registration had been $23.50, MTI would have had the option of withdrawing from the agreement.

The investment bank will have an easier job if the issue is priced relatively low. However, the issuer naturally wants as high a price as possible. A conflict of interest on price therefore arises between the investment bank and the issuer. If the issuer is financially sophisticated and makes comparisons with similar security issues, the investment bank will be forced to price close to the market.

As we discussed in Chapter 16, the announcement of a new stock offering by a mature firm is often taken as a negative signal—if the firm's prospects were good, management would not want to issue new stock and thus share the rosy future with new stockholders. Therefore, the announcement of a new offering is taken as bad news. Consequently, the price will probably fall when the announcement is made, so the offering price will probably have to be set at a price below the pre-announcement market price.

One final point is that *if negative signaling effects drive down the price of the stock, then all shares outstanding, not just the new shares, are affected.* Thus, if MTI's stock should fall from $28.60 to $25 per share as a result of the financing and remains at the new level, then the company would incur a loss of $3.60 on each of the 50 million shares previously outstanding, or a total market value loss of $180 million. This loss, like underwriting expenses, is a flotation cost, and it should be considered as a cost associated with the stock issue. Of course, if the company's prospects really were poorer than investors thought, then the price decline would have occurred sooner or later anyway. On the other hand, if the company's prospects are really not all that bad (the signal was incorrect), then over time MTI's price should move back to its previous level. Yet even if the price does revert to its former level, there will have been a transfer of wealth from the original shareholders to the new shareholders.

To prevent dilution due to a regular seasoned equity offering, companies occasionally sell additional shares of stock through a rights offering (also called a preemptive rights offering). The issuing company gives the owner of each share of outstanding stock a "right," which is similar to a stock option: each right's holder has the option to purchase a specified number of new shares of the company's stock at a specified purchase price on a certain date. The purchase price usually is very low relative to the current stock price, so the rights are valuable and will be exercised. The rights usually are transferable, so a shareholder can sell the right if she so chooses. This allows each shareholder the opportunity to maintain a proportional ownership stake in the company, but it also gives each shareholder a chance to receive cash from selling the right if the shareholder doesn't want to maintain a proportional ownership. See *Web Extension 18A* for more details and numerical examples.

See **Web Extension 18A** on the textbook's Web site for a discussion of rights offerings.

18-5c Shelf Registrations

The selling procedures described so far, including the 20-day waiting period after registration with the SEC, apply to most security sales. However, under the SEC's Rule 415, large, well-known public companies that issue securities frequently may file a master registration statement with the SEC and then update it with a short-form statement just prior to each individual offering. Under this procedure, a company can decide at 10 a.m. to sell securities and have the sale completed before noon. This procedure is known as **shelf registration** because, in effect, the company puts its new securities "on the shelf" and then sells them to investors when it feels the market is "right." Firms with less than $150 million in stock held by outside investors cannot use shelf registrations. The rationale for this distinction is to protect investors who may not be able to obtain adequate financial data about a little-known company in the short time between announcement of a shelf issue and its sale. Shelf registrations have two advantages over standard registrations: (1) lower flotation costs and (2) more control over the timing of the issue.[13]

18-5d Private Placements

The 1933 Securities Act regulates the issuance and subsequent trading of securities. Public offerings must be registered with the SEC, but several exemptions allow companies meeting certain conditions to issue unregistered securities in a process called a private placement.[14] The regulations are complex, but the basic idea is to

---

13. In 2005, the SEC began allowing very large firms, known as "well known seasoned issuers" or WKSIs, even greater flexibility in selling shelf-registered shares. WKSIs may now bypass SEC review and automatically shelf-register an unspecified number of securities to sell at times of their choosing. This speeds up even more the process for these large issuers. For more on shelf registrations, see David J. Denis, "The Costs of Equity Issues Since Rule 415: A Closer Look," *Journal of Financial Research,* Spring 1993, pp. 77–88.

14. Following is a brief and simplified explanation of the major exemptions. Regulation D permits the sale of securities to accredited investors but places restrictions on the subsequent trading of those securities. Rule 144A allows qualified institutional buyers to trade restricted securities among themselves, including securities issued by non-U.S. companies. Regulation S allows U.S. companies to sell unregistered securities abroad. Section 4(2) allows the sale of unregistered securities if the purchaser is knowledgeable and agrees not to resell them to the public.

speed up the process by allowing companies to offer securities to accredited investors, such as financial institutions, security dealers, and high-wealth individuals. The primary advantages of private placements are: (1) lower flotation costs and (2) greater speed, because the securities do not have to go through the SEC registration process at the time they are offered.

Private placements are a very important source of financing. In 2010, U.S. companies raised about $1.16 trillion from private placements of debt and equity versus about $1.07 trillion from public offerings.[15]

Private Placements of Equity

Sometimes a privately held firm makes a private placement of equity. For example, Facebook placed $1 billion of common stock with non-U.S. investors in 2011. At other times, it is a public company making a private placement. For example, General Growth Properties, which develops real estate properties such as shopping malls, raised $6.8 billion by selling stock directly to a consortium of investment funds, including Pershing Square Capital Management and Blackstone Group. Because GGP is a publicly held company, this is called a **private placement of public equity**, or a **PIPE**. The most common type of private placement occurs when a company places securities directly with a financial institution, often an insurance company or a pension fund.

Many large companies make equity investments in suppliers or in start-up companies that are developing a related technology. For example, Microsoft's 2014 3rd quarter report showed $11.6 billion of investments in the common and preferred stock of other companies.

Private Placements of Debt

Before 1990, debt could be issued privately (without SEC registration), but the purchasers faced restrictions on their abilities to resell the debt. This changed in 1990 with SEC Rule 144A, which allows qualified institutional buyers to trade unregistered securities among themselves. This opened the door for non-U.S. companies to raise capital in the states. In addition, subsequent amendments permit Rule 144A securities to be registered shortly after they have been issued, providing companies a quicker way to issue debt that ultimately will trade in public markets. The increased liquidity has made private placement of debt the preferred choice, with the majority of debt being placed privately rather than being issued publicly.

Companies issued over $1.1 trillion in public debt in 2013.[16] Exact numbers are difficult to find, but it is likely that companies sold twice this amount in private placements.

18-5e **Securitization**

In Chapter 1, we discussed securitization in the context of mortgage markets, and now we discuss it in the context of capital formation. As the term is generally used, a **security** refers to a publicly traded financial instrument as opposed to a privately placed instrument. Thus, securities have greater liquidity than otherwise similar

---

15. See the SEC report by Vlad Ivanov and Scott Bauguess cited in footnote 11.
16. See the SEC report by Vlad Ivanov and Scott Bauguess cited in footnote 11. For 2013 totals, see
    http://online.wsj.com/mdc/public/page/2_3106-IGUS-Q42013.html.

instruments that are not traded in an open market. In recent years, procedures have been developed to **securitize** various types of debt instruments, thus increasing their liquidity, lowering the cost of capital to borrowers, and generally increasing the efficiency of the financial markets.

Securitization occurs in two ways. First, a debt instrument that formerly was rarely traded becomes actively traded, usually because the size of the market increases and the terms of the debt instrument become more standardized. For example, this has occurred with commercial paper and junk bonds, both of which are now considered to be securities.

Second, a security can be created by the pledging of specific assets. This is called **asset securitization**, resulting in the creation of **asset-backed securities**. The oldest type of asset securitization was in the mortgage industry, as we described in Chapter 1. Today, many different types of assets are used as collateral, including auto loans, and credit card balances.

WHERE THERE'S SMOKE THERE'S FIRE

For an unusual example of securitization, consider the 1998 settlement of several lawsuits in which the major tobacco firms agreed to pay a percentage of their cigarette revenues each year to state governments. The payments, which totaled over $7.3 billion in 2012, were intended to compensate states for costs due to smoking-related illness and for expenses related to anti-smoking campaigns. It sounds like a reasonable settlement, but many states have used the money for other purposes.

For example, in 2001 Virginia's governor proposed using the funds to pay for a tax cut, and for many years thereafter Virginia allocated 40% of its annual share of the settlement to its general fund, 50% to a fund for economic assistance to tobacco farmers, and 10% to smoking cessation programs. Prior to 2008, Tennessee committed no funds at all to smoking prevention. In 2012, Tennessee received $139 million from the settlement and devoted only $200,000 to prevention programs. The rest went to fund general government operations.

Some states didn't want to wait on the annual payments, so they securitized the future stream of settlement cash flows by issuing tobacco bonds—investors gave the state cash on the issue date, and the states will pay the investors annually with future tobacco settlement revenues. In 2012, California, Iowa, Louisiana,

Minnesota, New Jersey, New York, Rhode Island, South Carolina, Virginia, Washington, and West Virginia all had tobacco bonds outstanding.

As with the annual payments, not all bond proceeds were used for the intended purpose. For example, Wisconsin sold over $1 billion of tobacco bonds in 2002, much of which was used to balance the budget that year. In March 2012, Alabama issued $92.8 million of tobacco bonds, using the proceeds to retire tobacco bonds they had issued 12 years earlier which were used to make grants to companies for economic development and to pay for flood levee improvements.

Virginia issued $448 million worth of tobacco bonds in 2005. Instead of spending it in the annual budget as Wisconsin did, Virginia contributed $390 million to the Tobacco Indemnification and Community Revitalization Endowment, a program whose earnings subsidize tobacco farmers based on the amount of tobacco they produced in 1998.

Some observers might say that the tobacco settlement is going up in smoke.

Sources: See Mike Cherney, "New Flavor of Tobacco Bonds," *The Wall Street Journal,* March 17, 2012, B6; also see www.tobaccofreekids.org /what_we_do/state_local/tobacco_settlement/ and **http://kff.org/other /state-indicator/tobacco-settlement-payments/#**.

The asset securitization process involves the pooling and repackaging of loans secured by relatively homogeneous, small-dollar assets (such as an automobile) into liquid securities. Usually several different financial institutions are involved, with each playing a different functional role. For example, an auto dealer might sell a car, the auto manufacturer's lending operation might originate the loan, an investment bank might pool similar car loans and structure the security, a federal agency might insure against credit risk, a second investment bank might sell the securities, and a pension fund might supply the final capital.

A similar process can occur with equipment or cell-tower leases, student loans, or more exotic assets like Miramax's 2011 sale of $550 million of bonds backed by revenues from its library of films, including *Pulp Fiction* and *Good Will Hunting*.[17]

The process of securitization lowers costs and increases the availability of funds to borrowers, with the risk being transferred to the investor. But as we described in Chapter 1, if loans are originated to borrowers with high credit risk, then the cash flows received by the ultimate investor are likely to be low.

SELF TEST

What is the difference between a competitive bid and a negotiated deal?

What is a private placement?

What is shelf registration?

What is securitization? What are its advantages to borrowers? What are its advantages to lenders?

18-6 Investment Banking Activities and Their Role in the Global Economic Crisis

Investment banks underwrite IPOs, underwrite seasoned equity offerings, and manage debt offerings. In other words, investment banks help firms raise capital, and lots of it: Table 18-2 shows that investment banks helped firms raise almost *$7 trillion* during 2013. Investment banks also engage in other activities. Because of increasingly relaxed regulations that culminated with the repeal of the Glass-Steagall Act in 1999, there is no longer a clear delineation between investment banks, brokerage firms, and commercial banks. In the following sections, we discuss activities that are primarily associated with the investment banking arm of the financial conglomerates.

18-6a Mergers and Acquisitions

Many investment banks are actively involved in mergers and acquisitions (M&As) through three activities.

1. *Matchmaking.* Investment banks often find potential targets for acquirers, sometimes earning a finder's fee if the deal is successful.

---

17. See Liz Moyer and Al Yoon, "Jury Out on Uma-Backed Securities," online.wsj.com, November 19, 2011.

TABLE 18-2	Top Five Underwriters of Global Debt and Equity in 2013
Manager	**Proceeds (Billions)**
JP Morgan	$ 504
Deutsche Bank AG	436
Citi	414
Barclays	412
Bank of America Merrill Lynch	388
Industry total	$6,923

Source: *The Wall Street Journal Online*, January 7, 2014.

2. *Advising.* Both the target and acquirer must document that the deal is "fair" for their stockholders by performing a due diligence valuation analysis. Investment banks often provide consulting advice during this stage of the M&A.

3. *Underwriting.* Most M&As require that new capital be raised. Investment banks underwrite these new issues.

Underwriting is the most lucrative of these activities, but if the deal falls through then no new securities will be underwritten. This makes one wonder how unbiased investment bankers are when finding targets and providing advice during negotiations.

18-6b **Securitization**

Investment banks often provide advice to financial institutions regarding the securitization of the institutions' loans or leases. In fact, investment banks frequently provide turnkey service by purchasing an institution's loans, securitizing the loans, and selling the newly created securities. Thus, the investment bank becomes the securitizer, not just the advisor. During the build-up to the global economic crisis, many investment banks were unable to sell all the mortgage-backed securities they created and were left holding some of them in their own portfolios. When the original borrowers began defaulting, the values of these securities owned by the investment banks plummeted, contributing to the downfall of Bear Stearns, Lehman Brothers, and Merrill Lynch.

18-6c **Asset Management**

Many investment banking companies create investment funds, such as a limited partnership (LP) that might invest in real estate in developing nations or an LP that might seek to exploit mispricing in various asset classes. In other words, they run their own hedge funds, which can be quite lucrative. Like any other hedge fund, they raise capital for these funds from a variety of sources. But unlike other hedge funds, investment banks often have access to a special source—their own clients!

Here is how that works. Many investment banks have "wealth management" divisions or subsidiaries that provide investment advice to wealthy individuals or institutions such as pension funds. As advisors, they recommend investment strategies, including specific investments, to their clients. Some of these investments might be individual securities or mutual funds managed by other organizations. However, some of the recommended investments might be funds managed by the advisor's own investment bank. These might be great investments, but there is at least the appearance of a conflict of interest when advisors recommend funds managed by their own company.

In addition to managing clients' money, investment banks also invest their own money (actually, the money of their own stockholders and creditors) in financial securities. Sometimes the choice of investment is intentional, but sometimes it is not—as we mentioned previously, some investment banks were unable to sell all the mortgage-backed securities they created and were left holding some in their own portfolios.

18-6d **Trading Operations**

Many investment banking companies have trading operations through which they actively trade on the behalf of clients. For example, a client might need help in selling a large block of debt. Also, investment banking companies usually make a market in the stock of companies that they took public. Thus, these activities can be viewed as services provided to clients.

However, many investment banks also view their trading operations as profit centers. In other words, the traders try to buy low and sell high, and in the process they sometimes accumulate large positions that become difficult to unload.

WHAT WAS THE ROLE OF INVESTMENT BANKS?

There is plenty of blame to spread around for the cause of the global economic crisis, but investment banks certainly played a special role.

Among their many strategic errors, investment banks morphed from organizations that earned money primarily through fee-generating activities into organizations that earned money as highly leveraged investors. Investing is an inherently risky business, especially when the investments include extremely complicated mortgage-backed securities and credit default swaps. Investing becomes even riskier when you borrow $33 for every $1 of equity, as many investment banks did. This strategy is great if you earn more than you owe on your debt because leverage magnifies returns, and these magnified returns generated gigantic bonuses for senior managers at the investment banks. But it doesn't take too much of a decline in asset values and investment income to cause failure. In essence, the investment bankers were willing to risk it all for the chance of mind-boggling bonuses.

In addition to selling toxic investments (such as complex mortgage-backed securities) to pension funds and other financial institutions, the interconnectedness of failing investment banks threatened the entire world economy. Lehman Brothers had been borrowing short-term in the commercial paper market and investing long-term in risky assets. When those assets failed, Lehman defaulted on its commercial paper obligations, many of which were owned by money market funds. This caused some funds, like the large Primary Reserve Fund, to "break the buck," which means that their reported net asset value dropped below $1, something that investors never expected. This led to a run on many money market funds and a huge disruption in the financial commercial paper markets.

Investment banks also were major players in the market for credit default swaps (CDS). If investment banks defaulted on their CDS, then it would cause potentially bankrupting financial distress at many other financial institutions.

Because many investment banks are subsidiaries of bank holding companies, the failure of the investment banks threatened the viability of the holding company and its other subsidiaries, such as commercial banks, which began limiting the credit they provided to their borrowers. In short, the financial crisis spread to the nonfinancial sector as financial institutions began cutting back on the credit they provided to the nonfinancial sector.

The investment banking landscape has certainly changed during the global economic crisis. Bear Stearns was acquired by JP Morgan, Lehman Brothers went bankrupt and was sold piecemeal, Merrill Lynch was acquired by Bank of America, and several investment banks, including Goldman Sachs, rechartered themselves as banks to qualify for TARP funds.

What are some investment banking activities?

SELF TEST

18-7 The Decision to Go Private

In a **going private** transaction, the entire equity of a publicly held firm is purchased by a small group of investors, with the firm's current senior management usually maintaining or increasing their ownership stakes. The outside investors typically place directors on the now-private firm's board and arrange for the financing needed to purchase the publicly held stock. When the financing involves substantial borrowing, as it usually does, it is known as a **leveraged buyout (LBO)**. In some cases, the current management group raises the financing and acquires all of the equity of the company; these are called management buyouts (MBOs).

The outside equity in a buyout often comes from a **private equity (PE) fund**, which is a limited liability partnership created to own and manage investments in nontraded equity. Private equity funds raise money from wealthy investors and institutions such as university endowments, pension funds, and insurance companies. The PE funds then take public firms private or invest in firms that already are privately held. Most PE funds plan on improving the companies' performance and then harvesting their investments by selling the company, perhaps in an IPO.[18]

Regardless of the deal's structure, going private initially affects the right-hand side of the balance sheet, the liabilities and capital, and not the assets: Going private simply rearranges the ownership structure. Thus, going private involves no obvious operating economies, yet the new owners are generally willing to pay a large premium over the stock's current price in order to take the firm private. For

---

18. For more information on private equity, see Steve Kaplan, "Private Equity: Past, Present, and Future," *Journal of Applied Corporate Finance*, Summer 2007, pp. 8–16; "Morgan Stanley Roundtable on Private Equity and Its Import for Public Companies," *Journal of Applied Corporate Finance*, Summer 2006, pp. 8–37; and Stephen D. Prowse, "The Economics of the Private Equity Market," *Economic Review*, third quarter 1998, pp. 21–33.

example, in 2006 HCA Inc., a large health care corporation, was taken private by the original family owners, the Frists, and a group of private equity firms and investment banks, including Bain Capital and Kohlberg Kravis Roberts & Co. (KKR), for $51 per share. The stock had been selling in the low $40s the month prior to the announcement. The investors put up about $4.9 billion in equity and borrowed about $28 billion to fund the purchase of equity and refinance some of the company's debt. It is hard to believe that these sophisticated investors and managers would knowingly pay too much for the firm. Thus, the investors and managers must have regarded the firm as being grossly undervalued, even at $51 per share, or else thought that they could significantly boost the firm's value under private ownership. In fact, after 4 years as a private company HCA went public again in 2011. The owners received $4.3 billion in dividends during 2010 and an additional $1.1 billion in cash from shares they sold in the IPO, almost completely recovering their initial investment. After the IPO the stock was worth about $16 billion, with about 25% of the company in public hands, and 75%, or about $12 billion, remaining with the private equity fund. Although the total return the investors ultimately earn depends on how much they receive for the shares they still hold in the company, the $4.9 billion investment has currently reaped cash and stock worth some $16 billion. Not a bad return for a 4-year investment!

This suggests that going private can increase the value of some firms sufficiently to enrich both managers and public stockholders. Other large companies going private recently include Dell (2013), Frederick's of Hollywood (2013), the piano maker Steinway Musical Instruments (2013), and H.J. Heinz Co. (2013).

The primary advantages to going private are: (1) administrative cost savings, (2) increased managerial incentives, (3) increased managerial flexibility, (4) increased shareholder oversight and participation, and (5) increased use of financial leverage, which of course reduces taxes. We discuss each of these advantages in more detail in the following paragraphs.

1. *Administrative cost savings.* Because going private takes the stock of a firm out of public hands, it saves on the time and costs associated with securities registration, annual reports, SEC and exchange reporting, responding to stockholder inquiries, and so on.

2. *Increased managerial incentives.* Managers' increased ownership and equity incentive plans mean that managers benefit more directly from their own efforts; hence, managerial efficiency tends to increase after going private. If the firm is highly successful, then its managers can easily see their personal net worth increase twentyfold, but if the firm fails, then its managers end up with nothing.

3. *Increased managerial flexibility.* Managers at private companies do not have to worry about what a drop in the next quarter's earnings will do to the firm's stock price, so they can focus on long-term, strategic actions that ultimately will have the greatest positive impact on the firm's value. Managerial flexibility concerning asset sales is also greater in a private firm, because such sales need not be justified to a large number of shareholders with potentially diverse interests.

4. *Increased shareholder oversight and participation.* Going private typically results in replacing a dispersed, largely passive group of public shareholders with a small group of investors who take a much more active role in managing the firm. These new equity investors have a substantial position in the private firm; hence, they have a greater motivation to monitor management and to

provide incentives to management than do the typical stockholders of a public corporation. Further, the new nonmanagement equity investors—frequently private equity firms, such as KKR, Carlyle Group, or Blackstone Group—are typically represented on the board, and they bring sophisticated industry and financial expertise and hard-nosed attitudes to the new firm.

5. *Increased financial leverage.* Going private usually entails a drastic increase in the firm's use of debt financing, which has two effects. First, the firm's taxes are reduced because of the increase in deductible interest payments, so more of the operating income flows through to investors. Second, the increased debt service requirements force managers to hold costs down to ensure that the firm has sufficient cash flow to meet its obligations—a highly leveraged firm simply cannot afford any fat.

One might ask why all firms are not privately held. The answer is that, although there are real benefits to private ownership, there are also benefits to being publicly owned. Most notably, public corporations have access to large amounts of equity capital on favorable terms, and for most companies, the advantage of access to public capital markets dominates the advantages of going private. Also, note that most companies that go private end up going public again after several years of operation as private firms. In addition to HCA, for example, Celanese AG, a global chemical company, went public in 1999. It was taken private in 2004 by Blackstone Capital Partners, a PE firm, and then taken public again in 2005.

What is meant by the term "going private"?

What is a private equity fund?

What are the main benefits of going private?

Why don't all firms go private to capture these benefits?

SELF TEST

18-8 Managing the Maturity Structure of Debt

Chapters 16 and 17 describe the capital structure decision. But after a firm chooses the total amount of debt in its capital structure, it must still choose the maturities of the various securities that make up its debt. The following sections explain the factors associated with the choice of maturity structure.

18-8a Maturity Matching

Assume that Consolidated Tools, a Cincinnati machine tool manufacturer, made the decision to float a $25 million nonconvertible bond issue to help finance its 2015 capital budget. It must choose a maturity for the issue, taking into consideration the shape of the yield curve, management's own expectations about future interest rates, and the maturity of the assets being financed. To illustrate how asset maturities affect the choice of debt maturities, suppose Consolidated's capital projects consist primarily of new milling machinery. This machinery has an expected economic life of 10 years (even though it falls into the MACRS 5-year class life).

Should Consolidated use debt with a 5-year, 10-year, 20-year, 30-year, or some other maturity?

Note that some of the new capital will come from common equity, which is permanent capital. On the other hand, debt maturities can be specified at the time of issue. If Consolidated financed its capital budget with 10-year sinking fund bonds, it would be matching asset and liability maturities. The cash flows resulting from the new machinery could be used to make the interest and sinking fund payments on the issue, so the bonds would be retired as the machinery wore out. If Consolidated used 1-year debt, then it would have to pay off this debt with cash flows derived from assets other than the machinery in question.

Of course, the 1-year debt could probably be rolled over year after year, out to the 10-year asset maturity. However, if interest rates rose, then Consolidated would have to pay a higher rate when it rolled over its debt, and if the company experienced difficulties, then it might not be able to refund the debt at a reasonable rate. Conversely, if it used 20-year or 30-year debt, it would have to service the debt long after the assets that were purchased with the funds had been scrapped and had ceased providing cash flows. This would worry lenders.

For all these reasons, *the safest all-around financing strategy is to match debt maturities with asset maturities.* In recognition of this fact, firms generally place great emphasis on maturity matching, and this factor often dominates the debt maturity decision.

Some firms use zero coupon bonds as a tool in matching maturities. We explain these bonds in *Web Extension 4A.*

WEB

See **Web Extension 4A** on the textbook's Web site for more on zero coupon bonds.

18-8b **Effects of Interest Rate Levels and Forecasts**

Financial managers also consider interest rate levels and forecasts, both absolute and relative, when making financing decisions. For example, if long-term interest rates are high by historical standards and are expected to fall, managers will be reluctant to issue long-term debt, which would lock in those costs for long periods. We already know that one solution to this problem is to use a call provision, because callability permits refunding should interest rates drop. This flexibility comes at a cost, however, because of the call premium and also because the firm must set a higher coupon on callable debt. Floating-rate debt could be used, but another alternative would be to finance with short-term debt whenever long-term rates are historically high, and then, assuming that interest rates subsequently fall, sell a long-term issue to replace the short-term debt. Of course, this strategy has its risks: If interest rates move even higher, the firm will be forced to renew its short-term debt at higher and higher rates or to replace the short-term debt with a long-term bond that costs even more than it would have when the original decision was made.

We could argue that capital markets are efficient and hence that it's not possible to predict future interest rates, because these rates will be determined by information that is not now known. Thus, under the efficient markets hypothesis, it would be unproductive for firms to try to "beat the market" by forecasting future capital costs and then acting on these forecasts. According to this view, financial managers ought to arrange their capital structures in such a manner that they can ride out almost any economic storm, and this generally calls for: (1) using some "reasonable" mix of debt and equity and (2) using debt with maturities that more or less match the maturities of the assets being financed.

18-8c **Information Asymmetries**

In Chapter 4, we discussed bond ratings and the effects of changes in ratings on the cost and availability of capital. If a firm's current financial condition is poor, then its managers may be reluctant to issue new long-term debt because: (1) a new debt issue would probably trigger a review by the rating agencies, and (2) debt issued when a firm is in poor financial shape would probably cost more and be subject to more severe restrictive covenants than debt issued from strength. Furthermore, in Chapters 16 and 17 we pointed out that firms are reluctant to use new common stock financing, especially when this might be taken as a negative signal. Thus, a firm that is in a weakened condition but whose internal forecasts indicate greater financial strength in the future would be inclined to delay long-term financing of any type until things improved. Such a firm would be motivated to use short-term debt even to finance long-term assets, with the expectation of replacing the short-term debt in the future with cheaper, higher-rated long-term debt.

Conversely, a firm that is strong now but that forecasts a potentially bad time in the period just ahead would be motivated to finance long term now rather than to wait. Each of these scenarios implies either that the capital markets are inefficient or that investors do not have the same information regarding the firm's future as does its financial manager. The second situation undoubtedly is true at times, and the first one possibly is true at times.

The firm's earnings outlook and the extent to which forecasted higher earnings per share are reflected in stock prices also have an effect on the choice of securities. If a successful R&D program has just been concluded and causes management to forecast higher earnings than do most investors, then the firm would not want to issue common stock. It would use debt and then, once earnings rise and push up the stock price, sell common stock to restore the capital structure to its target level.

18-8d **Amount of Financing Required**

Obviously, the amount of financing required will influence the financing decision. This is mainly because of flotation costs. A $5 million debt financing, which is small in Wall Street terms, would most likely be done with a term loan or a privately placed bond issue, whereas a firm seeking $2 billion of new debt would most likely use a public offering of long-term bonds.

18-8e **Availability of Collateral**

Generally, secured debt is less costly than unsecured debt. Thus, firms with large amounts of marketable fixed assets are likely to use a relatively large amount of long-term debt, especially mortgage bonds. Additionally, each year's financing decision would be influenced by the amount of qualified assets available as security for new bonds.

What are some factors that financial managers consider when choosing the maturity structure of their debt?

How do information asymmetries affect financing decisions?

SELF TEST

18-9 **Refunding Operations**

A great deal of corporate debt was sold during the late 1990s. Because the call protection on much of this debt has ended and because interest rates have fallen since the debt was issued, many companies are analyzing the pros and cons of bond refundings. The basic approach is to estimate the incremental after-tax cash flows associated with the refunding. The cash flows in a refunding decision are due to the presence of debt, so the cash flows should be discounted at the after-tax cost of debt.

The best way to examine the refunding decision is through an example. Microchip Computer Company has a $60 million bond issue outstanding that has a 12% annual coupon interest rate and 20 years remaining to maturity. This issue, which was sold 5 years ago, had flotation costs of $3 million that the firm has been amortizing on a straight-line basis over the 25-year original life of the issue. The bond has a call provision that makes it possible for the company to retire the issue at this time by calling the bonds in at a 10% call premium. Investment banks have assured the company that it could sell an additional $60 million to $70 million worth of new 20-year bonds at an interest rate of 9%. To ensure that the funds required to pay off the old debt will be available, the new bonds will be sold 1 month before the old issue is called; thus, for 1 month the company will have to pay interest on two issues. Current short-term interest rates are 6%. Predictions are that long-term interest rates are unlikely to fall below 9%.[19] Flotation costs on a new refunding issue will amount to $2,650,000, and the firm's marginal federal-plus-state tax rate is 40%. Should the company refund the $60 million of 12% bonds?

The following steps outline the decision process; they are summarized in the spreadsheet in Figure 18-1. This spreadsheet is part of the spreadsheet model, *Ch18 Tool Kit.xls*, developed for this chapter. The range of cells from A51 through H58 shows input data needed for the analysis, which were just discussed.

See *Ch18 Tool Kit.xls* on the textbook's Web site for details.

18-9a **Step 1: Determine the Investment Outlay Required to Refund the Issue**

Row 60

Call premium on old issue:

$$\text{Before tax: } 0.10(\$60,000,000) = \$6,000,000$$

$$\text{After tax: } \$6,000,000(1 - T) = \$6,000,000(0.6)$$
$$= \$3,600,000$$

Although Microchip must spend $6 million on the call premium, this is a deductible expense in the year the call is made. Because the company is in the 40% tax bracket, it saves $2.4 million in taxes; therefore, the after-tax cost of the call is only $3.6 million.

---

19. The firm's management has estimated that interest rates will probably remain at their present level of 9% or else rise; there is only a 25% probability that they will fall further.

FIGURE 18-1	Spreadsheet for the Bond Refunding Decision (Thousands of Dollars)

	A	B	C	D	E	F	G	H
51	**Input Data**							
52			Existing bond issue =	$60,000		New bond issue =		$60,000
53			Original flotation cost =	$3,000		New flotation cost =		$2,650
54			Maturity of original debt =	25		New bond maturity =		20
55			Years since old debt issue =	5		New cost of debt =		9.0%
56			Call premium (%) =	10.0%				
57			Original coupon rate =	12.0%		Tax rate =		40.0%
58			After-tax cost of new debt =	5.4%		Short-term interest rate =		6.0%
59	*Investment Outlay*					Before-tax	After-tax	
60			Call premium on the old bond			−$6,000	−$3,600	
61			Flotation costs on new issue			−$2,650	−$2,650	
62			Immediate tax savings on old flotation cost expense			$2,400	$960	
63			Extra interest paid on old issue			−$600	−$360	
64			Interest earned on short-term investment			$300	$180	
65			Total after-tax investment				−$5,470	
66								
67	*Annual Flotation Cost Tax Effects: t = 1 to 20*					Before-tax	After-tax	
68			Annual tax savings from new-issue flotation costs			$132.5	$53.0	
69			Annual lost tax savings from old-issue flotation costs			−$120.0	−$48.0	
70			Net flotation cost tax savings			$12.5	$5.0	
71								
72	*Annual Interest Savings Due to Refunding: t = 1 to 20*					Before-tax	After-tax	
73			Interest on old bond			$7,200	$4,320	
74			Interest on new bond			−$5,400	−$3,240	
75			Net interest savings			$1,800	$1,080	
76								
77	*Annual Flotation Cost Tax Effects*				*Annual Interest Savings*			
78	Annual flotation cost tax savings (Pmt)			$5	Annual interest savings (Pmt)			$1,080
79	Maturity of the new bond (Nper)			20	Maturity of the new bond (Nper)			20
80	After-tax cost of new debt (Rate)			5.4%	After-tax cost of new debt (Rate)			5.4%
81	NPV of annual flotation cost savings			$60	NPV of annual interest savings			$13,014
82								
83	*Total Net Present Value of the Refunding*							
84	Bond Refunding NPV =	Initial outlay		+	PV of flotation costs +		PV of interest savings	
85	Bond Refunding NPV =	−$5,470		+	$60	+	$13,014	
86								
87	Bond Refund NPV =		$7,604					

Row 61

Flotation costs on new issue: Flotation costs on the new issue will be $2,650,000. This amount cannot be expensed for tax purposes, so it provides no immediate tax benefit.

Row 62

Flotation costs on old issue: The old issue has an unamortized flotation cost of $(20/25)(\$3,000,000) = \$2,400,000$ at this time. If the issue is retired then the unamortized flotation cost may be recognized immediately as an expense, thus creating an after-tax savings of $2,400,000(T) = $960,000. Because this is a cash inflow, it is shown as a positive number.

Rows 63 and 64

Additional interest: One month's "extra" interest on the old issue, after taxes, costs $360,000:

$$\text{Interest cost} = (\text{Dollar amount})(1/12 \text{ of } 12\%)(1 - T)$$
$$= (\$60,000,000)(0.01)(0.6) = \$360,000$$

However, the proceeds from the new issue can be invested in short-term securities for 1 month. Thus, $60 million invested at a rate of 6% will return $180,000 in after-tax interest:

$$\text{Interest earned} = (\$60,000,000)(1/12 \text{ of } 6\%)(1 - T)$$
$$= (\$60,000,000)(0.005)(0.6) = \$180,000$$

Row 65

Total after-tax investment: The total investment outlay required to refund the bond issue, which will be financed by debt, is thus $5,470,000:[20]

Call premium	($3,600,000)
Flotation costs, new	(2,650,000)
Flotation costs, old, tax savings	960,000
Net additional interest	(180,000)
Total investment	($5,470,000)

18-9b Step 2: Calculate the Annual Flotation Cost Tax Effects

Row 68

Tax savings on flotation costs on the new issue: For tax purposes, flotation costs must be amortized over the life of the new bond, which is 20 years. Therefore, the annual tax deduction is:

$$\frac{\$2,650,000}{20} = \$132,500$$

Our spreadsheet shows dollars in thousands, so this number appears as $132.5 on the spreadsheet. Because the firm is in the 40% tax bracket, it has a tax savings of $132,500(0.4) = $53,000 a year for 20 years. This is an annuity of $53,000 for 20 years.

20. The investment outlay (in this case, $5,470,000) is usually obtained by increasing the amount of the new bond issue. In the example given, the new issue would be $65,470,000. However, the interest on the additional debt *should not* be deducted at Step 3 because the $5,470,000 itself will be deducted at Step 4. If additional interest on the $5,470,000 were deducted at Step 3 then interest would, in effect, be deducted twice. The situation here is exactly like that in regular capital budgeting decisions. Even though some debt may be used to finance a project, interest on that debt is not subtracted when developing the annual cash flows. Instead, the annual cash flows are *discounted* at the project's cost of capital.

Row 69

Tax benefits lost on flotation costs on the old issue: The firm, however, will no longer receive a tax deduction of $120,000 a year for 20 years, so it loses an after-tax
benefit of $48,000 a year.

Row 70

Net flotation amortization tax effect: The after-tax difference between the amortization tax effects of flotation on the new and old issues is $5,000 a year for
20 years.

18-9c **Step 3: Calculate the Annual Interest Savings**

Row 73

Interest on old bond, after tax: The annual after-tax interest on the old issue is
$4.32 million:

$$(\$60,000,000)(0.12)(0.6) = \$4,320,000$$

Row 74

Interest on new bond, after tax: The new issue has an annual after-tax cost of
$3,240,000:

$$(\$60,000,000)(0.09)(0.6) = \$3,240,000$$

Row 75

Net annual interest savings: Thus, the net annual interest savings is $1,080,000:

Interest on old bonds, after tax	$ 4,320,000
Interest on new bonds, after tax	(3,240,000)
Annual interest savings, after tax	$ 1,080,000

18-9d **Step 4: Determine the NPV of the Refunding**

Row 81

PV of the benefits: The PV of the annual after-tax flotation cost benefit can be found
using a financial calculator, with N = 20, I/YR = 5.4, PMT = 5000, and FV = 0.
Solving for PV shows that the flotation cost savings have a present value equal to
$60,251. The PV of the $1,080,000 annual after-tax interest savings is found with
N = 20, I/YR = 5.4, PMT = 1080000 and FV = 0; solving for PV shows that the
present value of after-tax interest cost savings is $13,014,174.

These values are used in Row 85 when finding the NPV of the refunding operation:

Amortization tax effects	$ 60,251
Interest savings	13,014,174
Net investment outlay	(5,470,000)
NPV from refunding	$ 7,604,425

TVA RATCHETS DOWN ITS INTEREST EXPENSES

In 1998, TVA raised $575 million in 30-year debt. If it had issued fixed-rate debt, it would be stuck with high coupon payments if interest rates in the market fall. If it had issued floating-rate debt, it would be stuck with high coupon payments if interest rates rise. If it had issued callable debt, then it could refinance if interest rates fall. But the costs of refunding are high, and TVA would have to agonize over the decision of whether to refund or wait in the hopes that rates will fall. None of these three choices seemed desirable, so TVA issued a new type of security that finesses these problems.

The new bonds are officially called Putable Automatic Rate Reset Securities (PARRS), but they are commonly known as ratchet bonds. These bonds have a feature that resets the coupon rate each year, starting in 2003, to 94 basis points over the rate on the prevailing 30-year Treasury bond—provided the new coupon would be lower than the ratchet bond's current coupon. In other words, the coupon on the bond will fall if interest rates fall, but it will never increase from year to year, allowing TVA to lock in the lowest interest rates that prevail during the

bond's life. In essence, TVA gets to refund its debt in any year when rates fall, hence the term "ratchet."

The 94-basis-point spread is higher than the spread over Treasuries that normally exists on TVA's noncallable bonds, given its bond rating. However, if the bond rating deteriorates, then investors can "put" the bond by selling it back to TVA. The net effect is that investors are exposed to interest rate risk but not to credit risk, and they are compensated for interest rate risk by the relatively high spread.

These bonds were originally issued with a 6.750% coupon, and on the first reset date (June 1, 2003) the rate ratcheted down to 5.952%, reflecting the decline in long-term interest rates since 1998. By April, 2014, long-term interest rates had fallen so that the coupon rate on the PARRS had ratcheted down to 3.830%.

Sources: Andrew Kalotay and Leslie Abreo, "Ratchet Bonds: Maximum Refunding Efficiency at Minimum Transaction Cost," *Journal of Applied Corporate Finance*, Vol. 41, No. 1, Spring 1999, pp. 40–47; and TVA's 10-K on its Web site, **www.tva.gov**.

Because the net present value of the refunding is positive, it would be profitable to refund the old bond issue.

We can summarize the data shown in Figure 18-1 using a time line (amounts in thousands) as shown below:

	0	5.4%	1	2	20
After-tax investment	−5,470				
Flotation cost tax effects			5	5	5
Interest savings			1,080	1,080	1,080
Net cash flows	−5,470		1,085	1,085	1,085

$\text{NPV}_{5.4\%} = \$7,604$

Several other points should be made. First, because the cash flows are based on differences between contractual obligations, their risk is the same as that of the underlying obligations. Therefore, the present values of the cash flows should be found by discounting at the firm's least risky rate—its after-tax cost of marginal debt. Second, because the refunding operation is advantageous to the firm, it must be disadvantageous to bondholders; they must give up their 12% bonds and reinvest in new ones yielding 9%. This points out the danger of the call provision to bondholders, and it also explains why noncallable bonds command higher prices than callable bonds with the same coupon rate. Third, although it is not emphasized in the example, we assumed that the firm raises the investment required to undertake the refunding operation (the $5,470,000 shown in Row 65 of Figure 18-1) as debt. This should be feasible because the refunding operation will improve the interest coverage ratio, even though a larger amount of debt is outstanding. Fourth, we set up our example in such a way that the new issue had the same maturity as the remaining life of the old one. Often, the old bonds have a relatively short time to maturity (say, 5 to 10 years), whereas the new bonds have a much longer maturity (say, 25 to 30 years). In such a situation, the analysis should be set up similarly to a replacement chain analysis in capital budgeting, which was discussed in Chapter 12. Fifth, refunding decisions are well suited for analysis with a computer spreadsheet program. Spreadsheets such as the one shown in Figure 18-1 are easy to set up, and once the model has been constructed, it is easy to vary the assumptions (especially the assumption about the interest rate on the refunding issue) and to see how such changes affect the NPV.

18-9e **Refund Now or Later?**

One final point should be addressed: Although our analysis shows that the refunding would increase the firm's value, would refunding *at this time* truly maximize the firm's expected value? If interest rates continue to fall, then the company might be better off waiting, for this would increase the NPV of the refunding operation even more. The mechanics of calculating the NPV in a refunding are easy, but the decision of *when* to refund is not at all simple because it requires a forecast of future interest rates. Thus, the final decision on refunding now versus waiting for a possibly more favorable time is a judgment call.

To illustrate the timing decision, assume Microchip's managers forecast that long-term interest rates have a 50% probability of remaining at their present level of 9% over the next year. However, there is a 25% probability that rates could fall to 7% and a 25% probability they could rise to 11%. Further, assume that short-term rates are expected to remain 3 percentage points below long-term rates and that the call premium would be reduced by 5% if the call were delayed for 1 year.

The refunding analysis could then be repeated, as previously, but as if it were a year later. Thus, the old bonds would have only 19 years remaining to maturity. We performed the analysis and found the NPV distribution of refunding 1 year from now:

Probability	Long-Term Interest Rate	NPV of Refunding 1 Year from Now
25%	7%	$17,947,071
50	9	7,390,083
25	11	(1,359,939)

At first blush, it would seem reasonable to calculate the expected NPV of refunding next year in terms of the probability distribution. However, that would not be correct. If interest rates did rise to 11%, Microchip would not refund the issue; therefore, the actual NPV if rates rose to 11% would be zero. The expected NPV from refunding 1 year hence is 0.25($17,947,071) + 0.50($7,390,083) + 0.25($0) = $8,181,809, versus $7,604,425 if refunding occurred today.

Even though the expected NPV of refunding in 1 year is higher, Microchip's managers would probably decide to refund today. The $7,604,425 represents a sure increase in firm value, whereas the $8,181,809 is risky. Also, proper comparison requires that the $8,181,809 be discounted back 1 year to today. Microchip's managers should opt to delay refunding only if the expected NPV from later refunding is sufficiently above today's sure NPV to compensate for the risk and time value involved.

Clearly, the decision to refund now versus refund later is complicated by the fact that there would be numerous opportunities to refund in the future rather than just a single opportunity 1 year from now. Furthermore, the decision must be based on a large set of interest rate forecasts, a daunting task in itself. Fortunately, financial managers making bond refunding decisions can now use the values of derivative securities to estimate the value of the bond issue's embedded call option. If the call option is worth more than the NPV of refunding today, the issue should not be immediately refunded. Rather, the issuer should either delay the refunding to take advantage of the information obtained from the derivative market or actually create a derivative transaction to lock in the value of the call option.[21]

SELF TEST   How is bond refunding like a capital budgeting project?

18-10 Managing the Risk Structure of Debt with Project Financing

Historically, many large projects such as the Alaska pipeline have been financed by what is called **project financing**.[22] We can only present an overview of the concept, for in practice it involves complicated provisions and can take on many forms.

Project financing has been used to finance energy explorations, oil tankers, refineries, and electric generating plants. Generally, one or more firms will sponsor

---

21. For a discussion of the time to call and refund, see Andrew J. Kalotay, Deane Yang, and Frank J. Fabozzi, "Refunding Efficiency: A Generalized Approach," *Applied Financial Economics Letters,* 2007, No. 3, pp. 141–146. For more information on the use of derivatives to help make call decisions, see Andrew J. Kalotay and George O. Williams, "How to Succeed in Derivatives without Really Buying," *Journal of Applied Corporate Finance,* Fall 1993, pp. 100–103. For more on bond refunding, see Raymond C. Chiang and M. P. Narayanan, "Bond Refunding in Efficient Markets: A Dynamic Analysis with Tax Effects," *Journal of Financial Research,* Winter 1991, pp. 287–302; David C. Mauer, "Optimal Bond Call Policies under Transactions Costs," *Journal of Financial Research,* Spring 1993, pp. 23–37; and Janet S. Thatcher and John G. Thatcher, "An Empirical Test of the Timing of Bond-Refunding Decisions," *Journal of Financial Research,* Fall 1992, pp. 219–230.

22. For an excellent discussion of project financing, see Benjamin C. Esty, "Petrozuata: A Case Study on the Effective Use of Project Finance," *Journal of Applied Corporate Finance,* Fall 1999, pp. 26–42.

the project, putting up the required equity capital, while the remainder of the financing is furnished by lenders or lessors. Most often, a separate legal entity is formed to operate the project. Normally, the project's creditors do not have full recourse against the sponsors. In other words, the lenders and lessors must be paid from the project's cash flows and from the sponsors' equity in the project, because the creditors have no claims against the sponsors' other assets or cash flows. Often the sponsors write "comfort" letters, giving general assurances that they will strive diligently to make the project successful. However, these letters are not legally binding, so in project financing the lenders and lessors must focus their analysis on the inherent merits of the project and on the equity cushion provided by the sponsors.[23]

Project financing is not a new development. Indeed, back in 1299 the English Crown negotiated a loan with Florentine merchant banks that was to be repaid with 1 year's output from the Devon silver mines. Essentially, the Italians were allowed to operate the mines for 1 year, paying all the operating costs and mining as much ore as they could. The Crown made no guarantees as to how much ore could be mined or the value of the refined silver. A more current example involved GE Capital, the credit arm of General Electric, which recently financed a $72 million project to build an aluminum can plant. The plant is owned by several beverage makers but it is operated independently, and GE Capital must depend on the cash flows from the plant to repay the loan. About half of all project financings in recent years have been for electric generating plants, including plants owned by electric utilities and cogeneration plants operated by industrial companies. Project financings are generally characterized by large size and a high degree of complexity. However, because project financing is tied to a specific project, it can be tailored to meet the specific needs of both the creditors and the sponsors. In particular, the financing can be structured so that both the funds provided during the construction phase and the subsequent repayments match the timing of the project's projected cash outflows and inflows.

Project financing offers several potential benefits over conventional debt financing. For one, project financing usually restricts the use of the project's cash flows, which means that the lenders—rather than the managers—can decide whether excess cash flows should be reinvested or instead used to reduce the loan balance by more than the minimum required. Conferring this power on the lenders reduces their risks. Project financings also have advantages for borrowers. First, because risks to the lenders are reduced, the interest rate built into a project financing deal may be relatively low. Second, because suppliers of project financing capital have no recourse against the sponsoring firms' other assets and cash flows, project financings insulate the firms' other assets from risks associated with the project being financed. Managers may be more willing to take on a large, risky project if they know that the company's existence would not be threatened if it fails.

---

23. In another type of project financing, each sponsor guarantees its share of the project's debt obligations. Here the creditors also consider the creditworthiness of the sponsors in addition to the project's own prospects. It should be noted that project financing with multiple sponsors in the electric utility industry has led to problems when one or more of the sponsors has landed in financial trouble. For example, Long Island Lighting, one of the sponsors in the Nine Mile Point nuclear project, became unable to meet its commitments to the project, which forced other sponsors to shoulder an additional burden or else see the project cancelled and lose all their investment up to that point. The risk of such default makes many companies reluctant to enter into such projects.

Project financings increase the number and type of investment opportunities; hence they make capital markets "more complete." At the same time, project financings reduce the costs to investors of obtaining information and monitoring the borrower's operations. To illustrate, consider an oil and gas exploration project that is funded using project financing. If the project were financed as an integral part of the firm's normal operations, investors in all the firm's outstanding securities would need information on the project. By isolating the project, the need for information is confined to the investors in the project financing, who need to monitor only the project's operations and not those of the entire firm.

Project financings also permit firms whose earnings are below the minimum requirements specified in their existing bond indentures to obtain additional debt financing. In such situations, lenders look only at the merits of the new project, and its cash flows may support additional debt even though the firm's overall situation does not. Project financings also permit managers to reveal proprietary information to a smaller group of investors, so project financings increase the ability of a firm to maintain confidentiality. Finally, project financings can improve incentives for key managers by enabling them to take direct ownership stakes in the operations under their control. By establishing separate projects, companies can provide incentives that are much more directly based on individual performance than is typically possible within a large corporation.

> **SELF TEST**   What is project financing? What are its advantages and disadvantages?

Summary

- The **Securities and Exchange Commission (SEC)** regulates securities markets.
- **Private placements** are securities offerings to a limited number of investors and are exempt from registration with the SEC.
- **Accredited investors** include the officers and directors of a company, high-wealth individuals, and institutional investors. These investors are eligible to buy securities in private placements.
- An **angel investor** is a wealthy individual who makes an equity investment in a start-up company.
- The managers of a **venture capital fund** are called **venture capitalists**, or **VCs.** They raise money from investors and make equity investments in start-up companies, called **portfolio companies**.
- **Going public** in an **initial public offering (IPO)** facilitates stockholder diversification, increases liquidity of the firm's stock, makes it easier for the firm to raise capital, establishes a value for the firm, and makes it easier for a firm to sell its products. However, reporting costs are high, operating data must be

disclosed, management self-dealings are harder to arrange, the price may sink to a low level if the stock is not traded actively, and public ownership may make it harder for management to maintain control.

- **Investment banks** assist in issuing securities by helping the firm determine the size of the issue and the type of securities to be used, by establishing the selling price, by selling the issue, and, in some cases, by maintaining an after-market for the stock.
- An investment bank may sell a security issue on a **best efforts basis,** or it may guarantee the sale by **underwriting** the issue.
- Before an IPO, the investment bank and management team go on a **roadshow** and make presentations to potential institutional investors.
- An IPO is **oversubscribed** if investors are willing to purchase more shares than are being offered at the IPO price.
- The **spread** is the difference between the price at which an underwriter sells a security and the proceeds that the underwriter gives to the issuing company. In recent years the spread for almost all IPOs has been 7%.
- An **equity carve-out** (also called a **partial public offering** or **spin-out**) is a special IPO in which a publicly traded company converts a subsidiary into a separately traded public company by selling shares of stock in the subsidiary. The parent typically retains a controlling interest.
- SEC Rule 415, also known as **shelf registration**, allows a company to register an issue and then sell that issue in pieces over time rather than all at once.
- A **seasoned equity offering** occurs when a public company issues additional shares of stock.
- A **private equity fund** is a limited liability partnership created to own and manage investments in the nontraded equity of firms.
- A company **goes private** when a small group of investors, including the firm's senior management, purchases all of the equity in the company. Such deals usually involve high levels of debt and are commonly called **leveraged buyouts (LBOs)**.
- If a bond has a call provision, then the issuer may **refund (call)** the bond prior to maturity and pay for it with a new debt issue at a lower interest rate.
- In **project financing**, the payments on debt are secured by the cash flows of a particular project.
- **Asset securitization** occurs when assets such as mortgages or credit card receivables are bundled together into a pool. Then bonds are created that use the payments in the pool to make interest and principal payments on the bonds.
- *Web Extension 18A* describes a *rights offering*.

Questions

18-1 Define each of the following terms:
   a. Going public; new issue market; initial public offering (IPO)
   b. Public offering; private placement
   c. Venture capitalists; roadshow; spread
   d. Securities and Exchange Commission (SEC); registration statement; shelf registration; margin requirement; insiders

e. Prospectus; "red herring" prospectus
f. National Association of Securities Dealers (NASD)
g. Best efforts arrangement; underwritten arrangement
h. Refunding; project financing; securitization; maturity matching

18-2 Is it true that the "flatter" (more nearly horizontal) the demand curve for a particular firm's stock and the less important investors regard the signaling effect of the offering, the more important the role of investment banks when the company sells a new issue of stock? Explain your answer.

18-3 The SEC attempts to protect investors who are purchasing newly issued securities by making sure that the information put out by a company and its investment banks is correct and is not misleading. However, the SEC does not provide an opinion about the real value of the securities; hence, an investor might pay too much for some new stock and consequently lose heavily. Do you think the SEC should, as a part of every new stock or bond offering, render an opinion to investors on the proper value of the securities being offered? Explain.

18-4 How do you think each of the following items would affect a company's ability to attract new capital and the flotation costs involved in doing so?
a. A decision of a privately held company to go public
b. The increasing institutionalization of the "buy side" of the stock and bond markets
c. The trend toward financial conglomerates as opposed to stand-alone investment banking houses
d. Elimination of the preemptive right
e. The introduction in 1981 of shelf registration of securities

18-5 Before entering a formal agreement, investment banks carefully investigate the companies whose securities they underwrite; this is especially true of the issues of firms going public for the first time. Because the banks do not themselves plan to hold the securities but intend to sell them to others as soon as possible, why are they so concerned about making careful investigations?

Problems   Answers Appear in Appendix B

Easy Problems 1–2

18-1 Profit or Loss on New Stock Issue
Security Brokers Inc. specializes in underwriting new issues by small firms. On a recent offering of Beedles Inc., the terms were as follows:

Price to public:	$5 per share
Number of shares:	3 million
Proceeds to Beedles:	$14,000,000

The out-of-pocket expenses incurred by Security Brokers in the design and distribution of the issue were $300,000. What profit or loss would Security Brokers incur if the issue were sold to the public at the following average price?

a. $5 per share

b. $6 per share

c. $4 per share

18-2 Underwriting and Flotation Expenses

The Beranek Company, whose stock price is now $25, needs to raise $20 million in common stock. Underwriters have informed the firm's management that they must price the new issue to the public at $22 per share because of signaling effects. The underwriters' compensation will be 5% of the issue price, so Beranek will net $20.90 per share. The firm will also incur expenses in the amount of $150,000. How many shares must the firm sell to net $20 million after underwriting and flotation expenses?

Intermediate Problems 3-4

18-3 Pricing Stock Issues

Benjamin Garcia's start-up business is succeeding, but he needs $200,000 in additional funding to fund continued growth. Benjamin and an angel investor agree the business is worth $800,000 and the angel has agreed to invest the $200,000 that is needed. Benjamin presently owns all 40,000 shares in his business. What is a fair price per share and how many additional shares must Benjamin sell to the angel? Because the stock will be sold directly to an investor, there is no spread; the other flotation costs are insignificant.

18-4 New Stock Issue

Bynum and Crumpton Inc. (B&C), a small jewelry manufacturer, has been successful and has enjoyed a positive growth trend. Now B&C is planning to go public with an issue of common stock, and it faces the problem of setting an appropriate price for the stock. The company and its investment banks believe that the proper procedure is to conduct a valuation and select several similar firms with publicly traded common stock and to make relevant comparisons.

Several jewelry manufacturers are reasonably similar to B&C with respect to product mix, asset composition, and debt/equity proportions. Of these companies, Abercrombe Jewelers and Gunter Fashions are most similar.

Company Data	Abercrombe	Gunter	B&C
Shares outstanding	5 million	10 million	500,000
Price per share	$35.00	$47.00	NA
Earnings per share	$2.20	$3.13	$2.60
Free cash flow per share	$1.63	$2.54	$2.00
Book value per share	$16.00	$20.00	$18.00
Total assets	$115 million	$250 million	$11 million
Total debt	$35 million	$50 million	$2 million

When analyzing the following data, assume that the most recent year has been reasonably "normal" in the sense that it was neither especially good nor especially bad in terms of sales, earnings, and free cash flows. Abercrombie is listed on the AMEX and Gunter on the NYSE, while B&C will be traded in the NASDAQ market.

a. B&C is a closely held corporation with 500,000 shares outstanding. Free cash flows have been low and in some years negative due to B&C's recent high sales growth rates, but as its expansion phase comes to an end B&C's free cash flows should increase. B&C anticipates the following free cash flows over the next 5 years:

Year	1	2	3	4	5
FCF	$1,000,000	$1,050,000	$1,208,000	$1,329,000	$1,462,000

After Year 5, free cash flow growth will be stable at 7% per year. Currently, B&C has no nonoperating assets, and its WACC is 12%. Using the free cash flow valuation model (see Chapters 8 and 9), estimate B&C's intrinsic value of equity and intrinsic per share price.

b. Calculate debt to total assets, P/E, market to book, P/FCF, and ROE for Abercrombie, Gunter, and B&C. For calculations that require a price for B&C, use the per share price you obtained with the corporate valuation model in part a.

c. Using Abercrombie's and Gunter's P/E, Market/Book, and Price/FCF ratios, calculate the range of prices for B&C's stock that would be consistent with these ratios. For example, if you multiply B&C's earnings per share by Abercrombie's P/E ratio you get a price. What range of prices do you get? How does this compare with the price you get using the corporate valuation model?

18-5 Pricing Stock Issues in an IPO

Zang Industries has hired the investment banking firm of Eric, Schwartz, & Mann (ESM) to help it go public. Zang and ESM agree that Zang's current value of equity is $60 million. Zang currently has 4 million shares outstanding and will issue 1 million new shares. ESM charges a 7% spread. What is the correctly valued offer price? How much cash will Zang raise net of the spread?

Challenging Problems 6–7

18-6 Refunding Analysis

Jan Volk, financial manager of Green Sea Transport (GST), has been asked by her boss to review GST's outstanding debt issues for possible bond refunding. Five years ago, GST issued $40,000,000 of 11%, 25-year debt. The issue, with semiannual coupons, is currently callable at a premium of 11%, or $110 for each $1,000 par value bond. Flotation costs on this issue were 6%, or $2,400,000.

Volk believes that GST could issue 20-year debt today with a coupon rate of 8%. The firm has placed many issues in the capital markets during the last 10 years, and its debt flotation costs are currently estimated to be 4% of the issue's value. GST's federal-plus-state tax rate is 40%.

Help Volk conduct the refunding analysis by answering the following questions.

a. What is the total dollar call premium required to call the old issue? Is it tax deductible? What is the net after-tax cost of the call?

b. What is the dollar flotation cost on the new issue? Is it immediately tax deductible? What is the after-tax flotation cost?

c. What amounts of old-issue flotation costs have not been expensed? Can these deferred costs be expensed immediately if the old issue is refunded? What is the value of the tax savings?

d. What is the net after-tax cash outlay required to refund the old issue?

e. What is the semiannual tax savings that arises from amortizing the flotation costs on the new issue? What is the forgone semiannual tax savings on the old-issue flotation costs?

f. What is the semiannual after-tax interest savings that would result from the refunding?

g. Thus far, Volk has identified two future cash flows: (1) the net of new-issue flotation cost tax savings and old-issue flotation cost tax savings that are lost if refunding occurs and (2) after-tax interest savings. What is the sum of these two semiannual cash flows? What is the appropriate discount rate to apply to these future cash flows? What is their present value?

h. What is the NPV of refunding? Should GST refund now or wait until later?

18–7 Refunding Analysis
Mullet Technologies is considering whether or not to refund a $75 million, 12% coupon, 30-year bond issue that was sold 5 years ago. It is amortizing $5 million of flotation costs on the 12% bonds over the issue's 30-year life. Mullet's investment banks have indicated that the company could sell a new 25-year issue at an interest rate of 10% in today's market. Neither they nor Mullet's management anticipate that interest rates will fall below 10% any time soon, but there is a chance that rates will increase.

A call premium of 12% would be required to retire the old bonds, and flotation costs on the new issue would amount to $5 million. Mullet's marginal federal-plus-state tax rate is 40%. The new bonds would be issued 1 month before the old bonds are called, with the proceeds being invested in short-term government securities returning 6% annually during the interim period.

a. Conduct a complete bond refunding analysis. What is the bond refunding's NPV?

b. What factors would influence Mullet's decision to refund now rather than later?

Spreadsheet Problem

18–8 Build a Model: Bond Refunding
Start with the partial model in the file *Ch18 P08 Build a Model.xls* on the textbook's Web site. Schumann Shoe Manufacturer is considering whether or not to refund a $70 million, 10% coupon, 30-year bond issue that was sold 8 years ago. It is amortizing $4.5 million of flotation costs on the 10%

bonds over the issue's 30-year life. Schumann's investment bankers have indicated that the company could sell a new 22-year issue at an interest rate of 8% in today's market. Neither they nor Schumann's management anticipate that interest rates will fall below 6% anytime soon, but there is a chance that interest rates will increase.

a. Conduct a complete bond refunding analysis. What is the bond refunding's NPV?

b. At what interest rate on the new debt is the NPV of the refunding no longer positive?

MINI CASE

Randy's, a family-owned restaurant chain operating in Alabama, has grown to the point that expansion throughout the entire Southeast is feasible. The proposed expansion would require the firm to raise about $18.3 million in new capital. Because Randy's currently has a debt ratio of 50% and because family members already have all their personal wealth invested in the company, the family would like to sell common stock to the public to raise the $18.3 million. However, the family wants to retain voting control. You have been asked to brief family members on the issues involved by answering the following questions.

a. What agencies regulate securities markets?

b. How are start-up firms usually financed?

c. Differentiate between a private placement and a public offering.

d. Why would a company consider going public? What are some advantages and disadvantages?

e. What are the steps of an initial public offering?

f. What criteria are important in choosing an investment bank?

g. Would companies going public use a negotiated deal or a competitive bid?

h. Would the sale be on an underwritten or best efforts basis?

i. The estimated pre-IPO value of equity in the company is about $63 million and there are 4 million shares of existing shares of stock held by family members. The investment bank will charge a 7% spread, which is the difference between the price the new investor pays and the proceeds to the company. To net $18.3 million, what is the value of stock that must be sold? What is the total post-IPO value of equity? What percentage of this equity will the new investors require? How many shares will the new investors require? What is the estimated offer price per share?

j. What is a roadshow? What is book-building?

k. Describe the typical first-day return of an IPO and the long-term returns to IPO investors.

l. What are the direct and indirect costs of an IPO?

m. What are equity carve-outs?

n. Describe some ways other than an IPO that companies can use to raise funds from the capital markets.

o. What are some other investment banking activities? How did these increase investment banks' risk?

p. What is meant by "going private"? What are some advantages and disadvantages? What role do private equity funds play?

q. How do companies manage the maturity structure of their debt?

r. Under what conditions would a firm exercise a bond call provision?

s. Explain how firms manage the risk structure of their debt with project financing.

SELECTED ADDITIONAL CASES

The following cases from CengageCompose cover many of the concepts discussed in this chapter and are available at **http://compose.cengage.com.** Klein-Brigham Series:

Case 21, "Sun Coast Savings Bank," illustrates the decision to go public; Case 22, "Precision Tool Company," emphasizes the investment banking process; Case 23, "Art Deco Reproductions, Inc.," focuses on the analysis of a rights offering; and Case 24, "Bay Area Telephone Company," Case 24A, "Shenandoah Power Company," and Case 24B, "Tucson Entertainment, Inc.," illustrate the bond refunding decision.

Lease Financing

Firms generally own fixed assets and report them on their balance sheets, but it is the use of assets that is important, not their ownership per se. One way to obtain the *use* of facilities and equipment is to buy them, but an alternative is to lease them. Prior to the 1950s, leasing was generally associated with real estate—land and buildings. Today, however, it is possible to lease virtually any kind of fixed asset, and currently over 50% of all new capital equipment and software is financed through lease arrangements.[1] In fact, the Equipment Leasing and Finance Foundation estimates that over $700 billion in equipment and software is acquired through leases each year.[2] Because leases are so frequently used by virtually all businesses, it is important for every manager to understand them.

Beginning-of-Chapter Questions

As you read the chapter, consider how you would answer the following questions. You *should not* necessarily be able to answer the questions before you read the chapter. Rather, you should use them to get a sense of the issues covered in the chapter. After reading the chapter, you should be able to give at least partial answers to the questions, and you should be able to give better answers after the chapter has been discussed in class. Note, too, that it is often useful, when answering conceptual questions, to use hypothetical data to illustrate your answer. We illustrate the answers with an *Excel* model that is available on the textbook's Web site. Accessing the model and working through it is a useful exercise, and it provides insights that are useful when answering the questions.

1. Differentiate between an **operating lease**, a **capital lease** (also known as a **financial lease**), and a **sale and leaseback arrangement**. How might investors be misled by firms that use lease financing extensively, and what rules have accounts put in place in an effort to mitigate this problem?
2. What is a **synthetic lease**? How are such leases structured, and what is their primary purpose? Is it likely that the use of synthetic leases will increase or decrease?
3. How do **IRS regulations** affect leasing decisions?
4. Assuming that **FASB Statement 13** is working as it is supposed to work, should traditional leasing arrangements enable a firm to use more financial leverage than it otherwise could? How do synthetic

---

1. For a detailed treatment of leasing, see James S. Schallheim, *Lease or Buy? Principles for Sound Decision Making* (Boston: Harvard Business School Press, 1994).
2. See Tammy Whitehouse, "FASB to Revisit Lease Accounting," Compliance Week, May 9, 2006, **www.complianceweek.com/article/2488/fasb-to-revisit-lease-accounting**. For current leasing statistics, see the annual U.S. Equipment Market Finance study by the Equipment Leasing and Finance Foundation at www.leasefoundation.org/IndRsrcs/MO/USMkts/.

leases alter the situation? How do FASB Statement 13 and synthetic leases affect the rate at which cash flows are discounted in a lease analysis?

5. Define the term **NAL** as it is used in lease analysis, and then explain how the NAL is calculated.

6. Is leasing a **zero sum game** in the sense that any gain to the lessee is a cost to the lessor? If not, how might both parties gain from a lease transaction? In your answer, explain how the lessee and the lessor analyze the situation, why they might use different inputs in their analyses, and how those input differences could affect the outcome. To help you with this analysis, the BOC model for this chapter has a "negotiation graph" that should help tie things together.

19-1 **Types of Leases**

Lease transactions involve two parties: the lessor, who owns the property, and the lessee, who obtains use of the property in exchange for one or more lease, or rental, payments. (Note that the term *lessee* is pronounced "less-ee," not "lease-ee," and *lessor* is pronounced "less-or.") Because both parties must agree before a lease transaction can be completed, this chapter discusses leasing from the perspectives of both the lessor and the lessee.

Leasing takes several different forms, of which the five most important are: (1) operating leases; (2) financial, or capital, leases; (3) sale-and-leaseback arrangements; (4) combination leases; and (5) synthetic leases.

19-1a **Operating Leases**

Operating leases generally provide for both *financing* and *maintenance*. IBM was one of the pioneers of the operating lease contract, and computers and office copying machines—together with automobiles, trucks, and aircraft—are the primary types of equipment involved in operating leases. Ordinarily, operating leases require the lessor to maintain and service the leased equipment, and the cost of the maintenance is built into the lease payments.

Another important characteristic of operating leases is the fact that they are *not fully amortized*. In other words, the rental payments required under the lease contract are not sufficient for the lessor to recover the full cost of the asset. However, the lease contract is written for a period considerably shorter than the expected economic life of the asset, so the lessor can expect to recover all costs either by subsequent renewal payments, by re-leasing the asset to another lessee, or by selling the asset.

A final feature of operating leases is that they often contain a *cancellation clause* that gives the lessee the right to cancel the lease and return the asset before the expiration of the basic lease agreement. This is an important consideration to the lessee, for it means that the asset can be returned if it is rendered obsolete by technological developments or is no longer needed because of a change in the lessee's business.

19-1b **Financial, or Capital, Leases**

Financial leases, sometimes called **capital leases**, differ from operating leases in that they: (1) *do not* provide for maintenance service, (2) *are not* cancellable, and (3) *are* fully amortized (that is, the lessor receives rental payments equal to the full price of the leased equipment plus a return on invested capital). In a typical arrangement, the firm that will use the equipment (the lessee) selects the specific items it requires and negotiates the price with the manufacturer. The user firm then arranges to have a leasing company (the lessor) buy the equipment from the manufacturer and simultaneously executes a lease contract. The terms of the lease generally call for full amortization of the lessor's investment, plus a rate of return on the unamortized balance that is close to the percentage rate the lessee would have paid on a secured loan. For example, if the lessee had to pay 10% for a loan, then a rate of about 10% would be built into the lease contract.

The lessee is generally given an option to renew the lease at a reduced rate upon expiration of the basic lease. However, the basic lease usually cannot be cancelled unless the lessor is paid in full. Also, the lessee generally pays the property taxes and insurance on the leased property. Because the lessor receives a return *after*, or *net of*, these payments, this type of lease is often called a "net, net" lease.

19-1c Sale-and-Leaseback Arrangements

Under a sale-and-leaseback arrangement, a firm that owns land, buildings, or equipment sells the property to another firm and simultaneously executes an agreement to lease the property back for a stated period under specific terms. The capital supplier could be an insurance company, a commercial bank, a specialized leasing company, the finance arm of an industrial firm, a limited partnership, or an individual investor. The sale-and-leaseback plan is an alternative to a mortgage.

Note that the seller immediately receives the purchase price put up by the buyer. At the same time, the seller-lessee retains the use of the property. The parallel to borrowing is carried over to the lease payment schedule. Under a mortgage loan arrangement, the lender would normally receive a series of equal payments just sufficient to amortize the loan and to provide a specified rate of return on the outstanding loan balance. Under a sale-and-leaseback arrangement, the lease payments are set up exactly the same way—the payments are just sufficient to return the full purchase price to the investor plus a stated return on the lessor's investment.

Sale-and-leaseback arrangements are almost the same as financial leases; the major difference is that the leased equipment is used, not new, and the lessor buys it from the user-lessee instead of a manufacturer or a distributor. A sale-and-leaseback is thus a special type of financial lease.

19-1d Combination Leases

Many lessors offer a wide variety of terms. Therefore, in practice leases often do not fit exactly into the operating lease or financial lease category but combine some features of each. Such leases are called **combination leases**. To illustrate, cancellation clauses are normally associated with operating leases, but many of today's financial leases also contain cancellation clauses. However, in financial leases these clauses generally include prepayment provisions whereby the lessee must make penalty payments sufficient to enable the lessor to recover the unamortized cost of the leased property.

19-1e Synthetic Leases

A fifth type of lease, the *synthetic lease*, also should be mentioned. These leases were first used in the early 1990s, and they became very popular in the mid- to late-1990s when companies such as Enron and Tyco, as well as companies that did not engage in fraud, discovered that synthetic leases could be used to keep debt off their balance sheets. In a typical **synthetic lease**, a corporation that wanted to acquire an asset—generally real estate, with a very long life—with debt would first establish a **special purpose entity**, or **SPE**. The SPE would then obtain financing, typically 97% debt provided by a financial institution and 3% equity provided by a party other than the corporation itself.[3] The SPE would then use the funds to acquire the property, and the corporation would lease the asset from the SPE, generally for a term of 3 to 5 years but with an option to extend the lease, which the firm generally expected to exercise. Because of the relatively short term of the lease, it was deemed to be an operating lease and hence did not have to be capitalized and shown on the balance sheet.

A corporation that set up an SPE was required to do one of three things when the lease expired: (1) pay off the SPE's 97% loan; (2) refinance the loan at the current interest rate, if the lender was willing to refinance at all; or (3) sell the asset and make up any shortfall between the sale price and the amount of the loan. Thus, the corporate user was guaranteeing the loan, yet it did not have to show an obligation on its balance sheet.

Synthetic leases stayed under the radar until 2001. As we discuss in the next section, long-term leases must be capitalized and shown on the balance sheet. Synthetic leases were designed to get around this requirement, and neither the corporations that used them (such as Enron and Tyco) nor the accounting firms that approved them (such as Arthur Andersen) wanted anyone to look closely at them. However, the scandals of the early 2000s led security analysts, the SEC, banking regulators, the FASB, and even corporate boards of directors to begin seriously discussing SPEs and synthetic leases. Investors and bankers subjectively downgraded companies that made heavy use of them, and boards of directors began to tell their CFOs to stop using them and to close down the ones that existed. In 2003, the FASB put in place rules that require companies to report on their balance sheets most special purpose entities and synthetic leases of the type Enron abused, limiting management's opportunity to hide these transactions from shareholders.

Who are the two parties to a lease transaction?

What is the difference between an operating lease and a financial, or capital, lease?

What is a sale-and-leaseback transaction?

What is a combination lease?

What is a synthetic lease?

SELF TEST

---

3. Enron's CFO, Andy Fastow, and other insiders provided the equity for many of Enron's SPEs. Also, a number of Merrill Lynch's executives provided SPE equity, allegedly to enable Merrill Lynch to obtain profitable investment banking deals. The very fact that SPEs are so well suited to conceal what is going on helped those who used them engage in shady deals that would have at least raised eyebrows had they been disclosed. In fact, Fastow pled guilty to two counts of conspiracy in connection to Enron's accounting fraud and ultimate bankruptcy. For more on this subject, see W. R. Pollert and E. J. Glickman, "Synthetic Leases Under Fire," at **www.strategicfinancemag.com**, October 2002.

19-2 **Tax Effects**

The full amount of the lease payments is a tax-deductible expense for the lessee *provided the Internal Revenue Service agrees that a particular contract is a genuine lease and not simply a loan called a lease.* This makes it important that a lease contract be written in a form acceptable to the IRS. A lease that complies with all IRS requirements is called a **guideline**, or **tax-oriented, lease**, and the tax benefits of ownership (depreciation and any investment tax credits) belong to the lessor. The main provisions of the tax guidelines are as follows:

1. The lease term (including any extensions or renewals at a fixed rental rate) must not exceed 80% of the estimated useful life of the equipment at the commencement of the lease transaction. Thus, an asset with a 10-year life can be leased for no more than 8 years. Further, the remaining useful life must not be less than 1 year. Note that an asset's expected useful life is normally much longer than its MACRS depreciation class life.
2. The equipment's estimated residual value (in constant dollars without adjustment for inflation) at the expiration of the lease must be at least 20% of its value at the start of the lease. This requirement can have the effect of limiting the maximum lease term.
3. Neither the lessee nor any related party can have the right to purchase the property at a predetermined fixed price. However, the lessee can be given an option to buy the asset at its fair market value.
4. Neither the lessee nor any related party can pay or guarantee payment of any part of the price of the leased equipment. Simply put, the lessee cannot make any investment in the equipment other than through the lease payments.
5. The leased equipment must not be "limited use" property, defined as equipment that can be used only by the lessee or a related party at the end of the lease.

The reason for the IRS's concern about lease terms is that, without restrictions, a company could set up a "lease" transaction calling for very rapid payments, which would be tax deductible. The effect would be to depreciate the equipment over a much shorter period than its MACRS class life. For example, suppose a firm planned to acquire a $2 million computer that had a 3-year MACRS class life. The annual depreciation allowances would be $666,600 in Year 1, $889,000 in Year 2, $296,200 in Year 3, and $148,200 in Year 4. If the firm were in the 40% federal-plus-state tax bracket, the depreciation would provide a tax savings of $266,640 in Year 1, $355,600 in Year 2, $118,480 in Year 3, and $59,280 in Year 4, for a total savings of $800,000. At a 6% discount rate, the present value of these tax savings would be $714,463.

Now suppose the firm could acquire the computer through a 1-year lease arrangement with a leasing company for a payment of $2 million, with a $1 purchase option. If the $2 million payment were treated as a lease payment, it would be fully deductible, so it would provide a tax savings of 0.4($2,000,000) = $800,000 versus a present value of only $714,463 for the depreciation shelters. Thus, the lease payment and the depreciation would both provide the same total amount of tax savings (40% of $2,000,000, or $800,000), but the savings would come in faster with the 1-year lease, giving it a higher present value. Therefore, if just any type of contract could be called a lease and given tax treatment as a lease, then the timing of the tax shelters could be speeded up as compared with ownership depreciation tax shelters. This speedup would benefit companies, but it would be costly to the government. For this reason, the IRS has established the rules just described for defining a lease for tax purposes.

Even though leasing can be used only within limits to speed up the effective depreciation schedule, there are still times when very substantial tax benefits can be derived from a leasing arrangement. For example, if a firm has incurred losses and hence has no current tax liabilities, then its depreciation shelters are not very useful. In this case, a leasing company set up by profitable companies such as GE or Philip Morris can buy the equipment, receive the depreciation shelters, and then share these benefits with the lessee by charging lower lease payments. This will be discussed in detail later in the chapter, but the point now is that if firms are to obtain tax benefits from leasing, the lease contract must be written in a manner that will qualify it as a true lease under IRS guidelines. If there is any question about the legal status of the contract, the financial manager must be sure to have the firm's lawyers and accountants check the latest IRS regulations.

Note that a lease that does not meet the tax guidelines is called a **non-tax-oriented lease**. For this type of lease, the lessee: (1) is the effective owner of the leased property, (2) can depreciate it for tax purposes, and (3) can deduct only the interest portion of each lease payment.

> What is the difference between a tax-oriented lease and a non-tax-oriented lease?
>
> What are some lease provisions that would cause a lease to be classified as a non-tax-oriented lease?
>
> Why does the IRS place limits on lease provisions?

SELF TEST

19-3 Financial Statement Effects

Under certain conditions, neither the leased assets nor the liabilities under the lease contract appear directly on the firm's balance sheet. For this reason, leasing is often called **off–balance sheet financing**. This point is illustrated in Table 19-1 by the balance sheets of two hypothetical firms, B (for "borrow") and L (for "lease"). Initially, the balance sheets of both firms are identical, and they both have debt ratios of 50%. Next, each firm decides to acquire a fixed asset costing $100. Firm B borrows $100 and buys the asset, so both an asset and a liability go on its balance sheet, and its debt ratio rises from 50% to 75%. Firm L leases the equipment. The lease may call for fixed charges as high as or even higher than the loan, and the obligations assumed under the lease may be equally or more dangerous from the standpoint of potential bankruptcy, but the firm's debt ratio remains at only 50%.

TABLE 19-1	Balance Sheet Effects of Leasing

Panel A: Before Asset Increase

Firms B and L

Current assets	$ 50	Debt	$ 50
Fixed assets	50	Equity	50
	$100		$100
Debt/assets ratio:		50%	

Panel B: After Asset Increase

Firm B, Which Borrows and Buys				**Firm L, Which Leases**			
Current assets	$ 50	Debt	$150	Current assets	$ 50	Debt	$ 50
Fixed assets	150	Equity	50	Fixed assets	50	Equity	50
	$200		$200		$100		$100
Debt/assets ratio:		75%				50%	

To correct this problem, the Financial Accounting Standards Board (FASB) issued FASB Statement 13, which requires that, for an unqualified audit report, firms entering into financial (or capital) leases must restate their balance sheets and report the leased asset as a fixed asset and the present value of the future lease payments as a liability. This process is called **capitalizing the lease**, and its net effect is to cause Firms B and L to have similar balance sheets—both of which will, in essence, resemble the one shown for Firm B.[4]

The logic behind Statement 13 is as follows: If a firm signs a financial lease contract, its obligation to make lease payments is just as binding as if it had signed a loan agreement—the failure to make lease payments can bankrupt a firm just as fast as the failure to make principal and interest payments on a loan. Therefore, for all intents and purposes, a financial lease is identical to a loan.[5] This being the

---

4. FASB Statement 13, "Accounting for Leases," spells out in detail both the conditions under which the lease must be capitalized and the procedures for capitalizing it. See also Chapter 4 of Schallheim's *Lease or Buy?* (cited in footnote 1) for more on the accounting treatment of leases.

5. There are, however, certain legal differences between loans and leases. In the event of liquidation in bankruptcy, a lessor is entitled to take possession of the leased asset, and if the value of the asset is less than the required payments under the lease, the lessor can enter a claim (as a general creditor) for 1 year's lease payments. Also, after bankruptcy has been declared but before the case has been resolved, lease payments may be continued, whereas all payments on debts are generally stopped. In a reorganization, the lessor receives the asset plus 3 years' lease payments if needed to cover the value of the lease. The lender under a secured loan arrangement has a security interest in the asset; this means that, if the asset is sold, then the lender will be given the proceeds and the full unsatisfied portion of the lender's claim will be treated as a general creditor obligation. It is not possible to state, as a general rule, whether a supplier of capital is in a stronger position as a secured creditor or as a lessor. However, in certain situations, lessors may bear less risk than secured lenders if financial distress occurs.

case, if a firm signs a financial lease agreement, then the effect is to raise its true debt ratio, and hence its true capital structure is changed. Therefore, if the firm had previously established a target capital structure and if there is no reason to think the optimal capital structure has changed, then lease financing requires additional equity support, just as debt financing does.

If disclosure of the lease in our Table 19-1 example were not made, then Firm L's investors could be deceived into thinking its financial position is stronger than it really is. Thus, even before FASB Statement 13 was issued, firms were required to disclose the existence of long-term leases in footnotes to their financial statements. At that time, it was debated as to whether or not investors recognized fully the impact of leases and, in effect, would see that Firms B and L were in essentially the same financial position. Some people argued that leases were not fully recognized, even by sophisticated investors. If this were the case, then leasing could alter the capital structure decision in a significant manner—a firm could increase its true leverage through a lease arrangement, and this procedure would have a smaller effect on its cost of conventional debt, r_d, and on its cost of equity, r_s, than if it had borrowed directly and reflected this fact on its balance sheet. These benefits of leasing would accrue to existing investors at the expense of new investors, who would be deceived because the firm's balance sheet did not reflect its true financial leverage.

The question of whether investors were truly deceived was debated but never resolved. Those who believed strongly in efficient markets thought investors were not deceived and that footnotes were sufficient, while those who questioned market efficiency thought all leases should be capitalized. Statement 13 represents a compromise between these two positions, though one that is tilted heavily toward those who favor capitalization.

A lease is classified as a capital lease—and hence must be capitalized and shown directly on the balance sheet—if one or more of the following conditions exist:

1. Under the terms of the lease, ownership of the property is effectively transferred from the lessor to the lessee.
2. The lessee can purchase the property at less than its true market value when the lease expires.
3. The lease runs for a period equal to or greater than 75% of the asset's life. Thus, if an asset has a 10-year life and the lease is written for 8 years, the lease must be capitalized.
4. The present value of the lease payments is equal to or greater than 90% of the initial value of the asset.[6]

These rules, together with strong footnote disclosure rules for operating leases, were supposed to be sufficient to ensure that no one would be fooled by lease financing. Thus, leases should be regarded as debt for capital structure purposes, and they should have the same effects as debt on r_d and r_s. Therefore, leasing is not likely to permit a firm to use more financial leverage than could be obtained with conventional debt.

---

6. The discount rate used to calculate the present value of the lease payments must be the lower of: (1) the rate used by the lessor to establish the lease payments (this rate is discussed later in the chapter) or (2) the rate of interest that the lessee would have to pay for new debt with a maturity equal to that of the lease. Also, note that any maintenance payments embedded in the lease payment must be stripped out prior to checking this condition.

OFF–BALANCE SHEET FINANCING: IS IT GOING TO DISAPPEAR?

There is currently (early 2014) a movement to standardize global accounting regulations, with the IASB (International Accounting Standards Board) and the FASB working toward this goal. One element of any agreement will be the treatment of leases. It appears likely that the FASB and IASB will require all leases to be capitalized, even those that are now classified as operating leases. In fact, they have agreed that the leases should be shown on the balance sheets, but they are still debating how to recognize the lease-associated expenses on the income statements.

This could have a huge impact on many companies' financial statements. For example, Credit Suisse estimated that the S&P 500 firms use about $369 billion in assets that are in the form of operating leases. As such, these are not shown as either assets or liabilities and instead are off the balance sheets. Putting these leases on the balance sheets by capitalizing them would boost the average liabilities by about 2%, but the impact would be much higher for some companies. This might be painful for businesses, but it certainly would help investors identify a company's obligations and liabilities.

SELF TEST

Why is lease financing sometimes referred to as off–balance sheet financing?

What is the intent of FASB Statement 13?

What is the difference in the balance sheet treatment of a lease that is capitalized versus one that is not?

WEB

See **Ch19 Tool Kit.xls** on the textbook's Web site for all calculations.

WEB

See **Web Extension 19A** on the textbook's Web site for more information on such feedback effects.

19-4 Evaluation by the Lessee

Leases are evaluated by both the lessee and the lessor. The lessee must determine whether leasing an asset is less costly than buying it, and the lessor must decide whether the lease payments provide a satisfactory return on the capital invested in the leased asset. This section focuses on the lessee's analysis.

In the typical case, the events leading to a lease arrangement follow the sequence described below. Note that a degree of uncertainty exists regarding the theoretically correct way to evaluate lease-versus-purchase decisions, and some very complex decision models have been developed to aid in the analysis. However, the simple analysis given here leads to the correct decision in all the cases we have ever encountered.

1. When the firm decides to acquire a particular building or piece of equipment, the decision is based on regular capital budgeting procedures. Whether or not to acquire the asset is *not* part of the typical lease analysis—in a lease analysis, we are concerned simply with whether to obtain the use of the machine by lease or by purchase. Thus, for the lessee, the lease decision is typically just a financing decision. However, if the effective cost of capital obtained by leasing

is substantially lower than the cost of debt, then the cost of capital used in the capital budgeting decision would have to be recalculated, and perhaps projects formerly deemed unacceptable might become acceptable. Such feedback effects usually are very small and can safely be ignored.

2. Once the firm has decided to acquire the asset, the next question is how to finance it. Well-run businesses do not have excess cash lying around, so capital to finance new assets must be obtained from some source.

3. Funds to purchase the asset could be obtained from internally generated cash flows, by borrowing, or by selling new equity. Alternatively, the asset could be leased. Because of the capitalization/disclosure provision for leases, leasing normally has the same capital structure effect as borrowing.

4. As indicated earlier, a lease is comparable to a loan in the sense that the firm is required to make a specified series of payments, and a failure to meet these payments could result in bankruptcy. If a company has a target capital structure, then $1 of lease financing displaces $1 of debt financing. Thus, the most appropriate comparison is lease financing versus debt financing. Note that the analysis should compare the cost of leasing with the cost of debt financing *regardless* of how the asset purchase is actually financed. The asset may be purchased with available cash or with cash raised by issuing stock, but because leasing is a substitute for debt financing and has the same capital structure effect, the appropriate comparison would still be with debt financing.

To illustrate the basic elements of lease analysis, consider this simplified example. (See *Ch19 Tool Kit.xls* on the textbook's Web site for this analysis.) The Thompson-Grammatikos Company (TGC) needs a 2-year asset that costs $100 million, and the company must choose between leasing and buying the asset. TGC's tax rate is 40%. If the asset is purchased, the bank would lend TGC the $100 million at a rate of 10% on a 2-year, simple interest loan. Thus, the firm would have to pay the bank $10 million in interest at the end of each year *and* return the $100 million of principal at the end of Year 2. However, the interest expense is deductible, so the tax shelter is T(Interest expense) = 0.4($10 million) = $4 million. For simplicity, assume that: (1) TGC could depreciate the asset over 2 years for tax purposes by the straight-line method if it is purchased, resulting in tax depreciation of $50 million and tax savings of T(Depreciation) = 0.4($50) = $20 million in each year; and (2) the asset's value at the end of 2 years will be $0.

See *Ch19 Tool Kit.xls* on the textbook's Web site for this analysis.

Alternatively, TGC could lease the asset under a guideline lease (by a special IRS ruling) for 2 years for a payment of $55 million at the end of each year. These payments are deductible, so the tax shelter is T(Lease payment) = 0.4($55 million) = $22 million.

The analysis for the lease-versus-borrow decision consists of: (1) estimating the cash flows associated with borrowing and buying the asset—that is, the flows associated with debt financing; (2) estimating the cash flows associated with leasing the asset; and (3) comparing the two financing methods to determine is preferable. Figure 19-1 reports the borrow-and-buy flows, set up to produce a cash flow time line for owning option.

The net cash flow for owning is zero in Year 0, positive in Year 1, and negative in Year 2. The operating cash flows are not shown, but they must, of course, have a PV greater than the PV of the financing costs or else TGC would not want to acquire the asset. Because the operating cash flows will be the same regardless of whether the asset is leased or purchased, they can be ignored.

FIGURE 19-1	Analysis of the TGC Lease-versus-Buy Decision (Millions of Dollars)

	A	B	C	D	E
83	**Cost of Owning**			**Year**	
84			**0**	**1**	**2**
85	Equipment cost		−$100		
86	Loan amount		$100		
87	Interest expense			−$10	−$10
88	Tax savings from interest = (−Interest exp.)(Tax rate)			$4	$4
89	Principal repayment				−$100
90	Tax savings from depr.			$20	$20
91	Net cash flow (NCF)		$0	$14	−$86
92					
93	PV ownership NCF @ 6%		−$63.33		
94	**Cost of Leasing**			**Year**	
95			**0**	**1**	**2**
96	Lease payment			−$55	−$55
97	Tax savings from lease = (−Lease pmt)(Tax rate)			$22	$22
98	Net cash flow (NCF)		$0	−$33	−$33
99					
100	PV of leasing NCF @ 6%		−$60.50		
101	**Net advantage to leasing (NAL)**				
102	NAL =PV of leasing − PV of owning				$2.83

Figure 19-1 also shows the cash flows associated with leasing. Note that the two sets of cash flows reflect the tax deductibility of interest and depreciation if the asset is purchased or the deductibility of lease payments if it is leased. Thus, the net cash flows include the tax savings from these items.[7]

To compare the cost streams of buying versus leasing, we must put them on a present value basis. As we explain later, the correct discount rate is the after-tax cost of debt, which for TGC is $10\%(1 − 0.4) = 6.0\%$. Applying this rate, we find the present value of the ownership cash flows is −$63.33 million versus a present value of leasing cash flows of −$60.50 million.

We define the **net advantage to leasing (NAL)** as follows:

(19–1)

$$NAL = PV \text{ of leasing} − PV \text{ of owning}$$

For TGC, the NAL is $−\$60.50 − (−\$63.33) = \$2.83$ million. The PV of owning is more negative than the PV of leasing, so leasing is preferable.

WEB

See **Ch19 Tool Kit.xls** on the textbook's Web site for all calculations.

---

7. If the lease had not met IRS guidelines, then ownership would effectively reside with the lessee, and TGC would depreciate the asset for tax purposes whether it was leased or purchased. However, only the implied interest portion of the lease payment would be tax deductible. Thus, the analysis for a nonguideline lease would consist of simply comparing the after-tax financing flows on the loan with the after-tax lease payment stream.

Now we examine a more realistic example, one from the Anderson Company, which is conducting a lease analysis on some assembly line equipment it will procure during the coming year. (See *Ch19 Tool Kit.xls* on the textbook's Web site for this analysis.) The following data have been collected:

1. Anderson plans to acquire automated assembly line equipment with a 10-year life at a cost of $10 million, delivered and installed. However, Anderson plans to use the equipment for only 5 years and then discontinue the product line.
2. Anderson can borrow the required $10 million at a pre-tax cost of 10%.
3. The equipment's estimated scrap value is $50,000 after 10 years of use, but its estimated salvage value after only 5 years of use is $2,000,000. Thus, if Anderson buys the equipment, it would expect to receive $2,000,000 before taxes when the equipment is sold in 5 years. In leasing, the asset's value at the end of the lease is called its **residual value**.
4. Anderson can lease the equipment for 5 years for an annual rental charge of $2,600,000, payable at the beginning of each year, but the lessor will own the equipment upon the expiration of the lease. (The lease payment schedule is established by the potential lessor, as described in the next section, and Anderson can accept it, reject it, or negotiate modifications.)
5. The lease contract stipulates that the lessor will maintain the equipment at no additional charge to Anderson. However, if Anderson borrows and buys, it will have to bear the cost of maintenance, which will be done by the equipment manufacturer at a fixed contract rate of $500,000 per year, payable at the beginning of each year.
6. The equipment falls in the MACRS 5-year class, Anderson's marginal tax rate is 35%, and the lease qualifies as a guideline lease.

Figure 19-2 shows the steps involved in the analysis. Part A of the table is devoted to the costs of borrowing and buying. The company borrows $10 million and uses it to pay for the equipment, so these two items net out to zero and thus are not shown in the figure. Then, the company makes the *after-tax* payments shown in Line 1. In Year 1, the after-tax interest charge is $0.10(\$10 \text{ million})(1 - 0.35) = \$650,000$, and other payments are calculated similarly. The $10 million loan is repaid at the end of Year 5. Line 2 shows the maintenance cost. Line 3 gives the maintenance tax savings. Line 4 contains the annual depreciation tax savings, which are the depreciation expenses multiplied by the tax rate. The notes to Figure 19-2 explain the depreciation calculation. Lines 5 and 6 contain the residual (or salvage) value cash flows. The tax is on the excess of the residual value over the asset's book value, not on the full residual value. Line 7 contains the net cash flows, and Line 8 shows the net present value of these flows discounted at 6.5%, which is negative.

Part B of Figure 19-2 analyzes the lease. The lease payments, shown in Line 9, are $2,600,000 per year; this rate, which includes maintenance, was established by the prospective lessor and offered to Anderson Equipment. If Anderson accepts the lease then the full amount will be a deductible expense, so the annual tax savings, shown in Line 10, are $0.35(\text{Lease payment}) = 0.35(\$2,600,000) = \$910,000$. Thus, the after-tax cost of the lease payment is Lease payment − Tax savings = $2,600,000 − $910,000 = $1,690,000. This amount is shown in Line 11 for Years 0 through 4.

The next step is to compare leasing versus owning. However, we must first put the annual cash flows of leasing and borrowing on a common basis. This requires converting them to present values, which brings up the question of the proper rate at which to discount the costs. Because leasing is a substitute for debt, most analysts recommend that the company's cost of debt be used, and this rate seems reasonable

FIGURE 19-2 Anderson Company: Lease Analysis (Thousands of Dollars)

	A	B	C	D	E	F	G	H
141	**Part A: Cost of Owning**					Year		
142			**0**	**1**	**2**	**3**	**4**	**5**
143								
144	**1. After-tax loan payments**			−$650	−$650	−$650	−$650	−$10,650
145	**2. Maintenance cost**		−$500	−$500	−$500	−$500	−$500	
146	**3. Maintenance tax savings**		$175	$175	$175	$175	$175	
147	**4. Depreciation tax savings**			$700	$1,120	$672	$403	$403
148	**5. Residual value**							$2,000
149	**6. Tax on residual value**							−$498
150	**7. Net cash flow**		−$325	−$275	$145	−$303	−$572	−$8,745
151								
152	**8. PV ownership CF @ 6.5%**		−$7,534					
153	**Part B: Cost of Leasing**					Year		
154			**0**	**1**	**2**	**3**	**4**	**5**
155	**9. Lease payment**		−$2,600	−$2,600	−$2,600	−$2,600	−$2,600	
156	**10. Tax savings from lease**		$910	$910	$910	$910	$910	
157	**11. Net cash flow**		−$1,690	−$1,690	−$1,690	−$1,690	−$1,690	$0
158								
159	**12. PV of leasing CF @ 6.5%**		−$7,480					
160	**Part C: Net advantage to leasing (NAL)**							
161	**13. NAL = PV of leasing − PV of owning =**				$54			

Notes:
(1) The after-tax loan payments consist of after-tax interest for Years 1–4 and after-tax interest plus the principal amount in Year 5.
(2) The net cash flows shown in Lines 7 and 11 are discounted at the lessee's after-tax cost of debt, 6.5%.
(3) The MACRS depreciation allowances are 0.20, 0.32, 0.192, 0.1152, and 0.1152 in Years 1 through 5, respectively. Thus, the depreciation expense is 0.20($10,000) = $2,000 in Year 1, and so on. The depreciation tax savings in each year is 0.35(Depreciation).
(4) The residual value is $2,000, while the book value is $576. Thus, Anderson would have to pay 0.35($2,000 − $576) = $498.4 in taxes, producing a net after-tax residual value of $2,000 − $498.4 = $1,501.6. These amounts are shown in Lines 5 and 6 in the cost-of-owning analysis.

See **Ch19 Tool Kits.xls** on the textbook's Web site for all calculations.

in our example. Moreover, because the cash flows are after taxes, *we should use the after-tax cost of debt*, which is 10%(1 − T) = 10%(0.65) = 6.5%. Accordingly, we discount the net cash flows in Lines 7 and 11 using a rate of 6.5%. The resulting present values are −$7,480,000 for the present value of leasing and −$7,534,000 for the present value of owning. The net advantage to leasing is about $54 thousand (ignoring rounding differences):

$$NAL = PV \text{ of leasing} - PV \text{ of owning}$$
$$= -\$7,480,000 - (-\$7,534,000)$$
$$= \$54,000$$

Owning is more costly than leasing, so the NAL is positive. Therefore, Anderson should lease the equipment.[8]

---

8. The more complicated methods that exist for analyzing leasing generally focus on the issue of what discount rate should be used to discount the cash flows—especially the residual value, because its risk might be different from the risk of the other cash flows. For more on residual value risk, see Chapter 8 of Schallheim's *Lease or Buy?* (cited in footnote 1).

In this example, Anderson did not plan on using the equipment beyond Year 5. But if Anderson instead had planned on using the equipment after Year 5, the analysis would be modified. For example, suppose Anderson planned on using the equipment for 10 years and the lease allowed Anderson to purchase the equipment at the residual value. First, how do we modify the cash flows due to owning? Lines 5 and 6 (for residual value and tax on residual value) in Figure 19-2 will be zero at Year 5, because Anderson will not sell the equipment then.[9] However, there will be the additional remaining year of depreciation tax savings in Line 4 for Year 6. There will be no entries for Years 6–10 for Line 1, the after-tax loan payments, because the loan is completely repaid at Year 5. Also, there will be no incremental maintenance costs and tax savings in Lines 2 and 3 for Years 6–10, because Anderson will have to perform its own maintenance on the equipment in those years whether it initially purchases the equipment or whether it leases the equipment for 5 years and then purchases it. Either way, Anderson will own the equipment in Years 6–10 and must pay for its own maintenance.

Second, how do we modify the cash flows if Anderson leases the equipment and then purchases it at Year 5? There will be a negative cash flow at Year 5 reflecting the purchase. Because the equipment was originally classified with a MACRS 5-year life, Anderson will be allowed to depreciate the purchased equipment (even though it is not new) with a MACRS 5-year life. Therefore, in Years 6–10, there will be after-tax savings due to depreciation.[10] Given the modified cash flows, we can calculate the NAL just as we did in Figure 19-2.

In this section, we focused on the dollar cost of leasing versus borrowing and buying, which is analogous to the NPV method used in capital budgeting. A second method that lessees can use to evaluate leases focuses on the percentage cost of leasing and is analogous to the IRR method used in capital budgeting.

The percentage approach is discussed in **Web Extension 19B** on the textbook's Web site.

Explain how the cash flows are structured in order to estimate the net advantage to leasing.

What discount rate should be used to evaluate a lease? Why?

Define the term *net advantage to leasing* (NAL).

19-5 Evaluation by the Lessor

Thus far, we have considered leasing only from the lessee's viewpoint. It is also useful to analyze the transaction as the lessor sees it: Is the lease a good investment for the party who must put up the money? The lessor will generally be a specialized leasing company, a bank or bank affiliate, an individual or group of individuals organized as a limited partnership or limited liability corporation, or

---

9. There might be a salvage value in Line 5 at Year 10 (and a corresponding tax adjustment in Line 6) if the equipment is not completely worn out or obsolete.

10. There will also be an after-tax cash flow at Year 10 that depends on the salvage value of the equipment at that date.

a manufacturer such as IBM or GM that uses leasing as a sales tool. The specialized leasing companies are often owned by profitable companies such as General Electric, which owns General Electric Capital, the largest leasing company in the world. Investment banking houses such as Goldman Sachs also set up and/or work with specialized leasing companies, where brokerage clients' money is made available to leasing customers in deals that permit the investors to share in tax shelters provided by leases.

Any potential lessor needs to know the rate of return on the capital invested in the lease, and this information is also useful to the prospective lessee: Lease terms on large leases are generally negotiated, so the lessee should know what return the lessor is earning. The lessor's analysis involves: (1) determining the net cash outlay, which is usually the invoice price of the leased equipment less any lease payments made in advance; (2) determining the periodic cash inflows, which consist of the lease payments minus both income taxes and any maintenance expense the lessor must bear; (3) estimating the after-tax residual value of the property when the lease expires; and (4) determining whether the rate of return on the lease exceeds the lessor's opportunity cost of capital or, equivalently, whether the NPV of the lease exceeds zero.

19-5a **Analysis by the Lessor**

See **Ch19 Tool Kits.xls** on the textbook's Web site for all calculations.

To illustrate the lessor's analysis, we assume the same facts as for the Anderson Company lease, plus the following: (1) The potential lessor is a wealthy individual whose current income is in the form of interest and whose marginal federal-plus-state income tax rate, T, is 40%. (2) The investor can buy 5-year bonds that have a 9% yield to maturity, providing an after-tax yield of $(9\%)(1 - T) = (9\%)(0.6) = 5.4\%$. This is the after-tax return the investor can obtain on alternative investments of similar risk. (3) The before-tax residual value is $2,000,000. Because the asset will be depreciated to a book value of $600,000 at the end of the 5-year lease, $1,400,000 of this $2 million will be taxable at the 40% rate by the depreciation recapture rule, so the lessor can expect to receive $2,000,000 − 0.4($1,400,000) = $1,440,000 after taxes from the sale of the equipment after the lease expires.

The lessor's cash flows are developed in Figure 19-3. Here we see that the lease as an investment has a net present value of $81,091. On a present value basis, the investor who invests in the lease rather than in the 9% bonds (5.4% after taxes) is better off by $81,091, indicating that he or she should be willing to write the lease. As we saw earlier, the lease is also advantageous to Anderson Company, so the transaction should be completed.

The investor can also calculate the lease investment's internal rate of return based on the net cash flows shown in Line 9 of Figure 19-3. The IRR of the lease, which is that discount rate that forces the NPV of the lease to zero, is 5.8%. Thus, the lease provides a 5.8% after-tax return to this 40% tax rate investor, which exceeds the 5.4% after-tax return on 9% bonds. So, using either the IRR or the NPV method, the lease would appear to be a satisfactory investment.[11]

---

11. Note that the lease investment is actually slightly more risky than the alternative bond investment because the residual value cash flow is less certain than a principal repayment. Thus, the lessor might require an expected return somewhat above the 5.4% promised on a bond investment.

FIGURE 19-3	Lease Analysis from the Lessor's Viewpoint (Thousands of Dollars)

	A	B	C	D	E	F	G	H
218						Year		
219			0	1	2	3	4	5
220								
221	1. Net purchase price		–$10,000					
222	2. Maintenance cost		–$500	–$500	–$500	–$500	–$500	
223	3. Maintenance tax savings		$200	$200	$200	$200	$200	
224	4. Depreciation tax savings[a]			$800	$1,280	$768	$461	$461
225	5. Lease payment		$2,600	$2,600	$2,600	$2,600	$2,600	
226	6. Tax on lease payment		–$1,040	–$1,040	–$1,040	–$1,040	–$1,040	
227	7. Residual value							$2,000
228	8. Tax on residual value[b]							–$570
229	9. Net cash flow		–$8,740	$2,060	$2,540	$2,028	$1,721	$1,891
230	10. NPV @ 5.4% =		$81.091					
231	11. IRR =		5.8%					
232	12. MIRR=		5.6%					

[a]Depreciation tax savings = Depreciation × (Tax rate).
[b](Residual value − Book value) × (Tax rate).

19-5b Setting the Lease Payment

So far we have evaluated leases assuming that the lease payments have already been specified. However, in large leases the parties generally sit down and work out an agreement on the size of the lease payments, with these payments being set so as to provide the lessor with some specific rate of return. In situations in which the lease terms are not negotiated, which is often the case for small leases, the lessor must still go through the same type of analysis, setting terms that provide a target rate of return and then offering these terms to the potential lessee on a take-it-or-leave-it basis.

To illustrate all this, suppose the potential lessor described earlier, after examining other alternative investment opportunities, decides that the 5.4% after-tax bond return is too low to use for evaluating the lease and that the required after-tax return on the lease should be 6.0%. What lease payment schedule would provide this return?

To answer this question, note again that Figure 19-3 contains the lessor's cash flow analysis. We used the *Excel* Goal Seek function to set the lessor's IRR equal to 6% by changing the lease payment; see the analysis in *Ch19 Tool Kit.xls*. We found that the lessor must set the lease payment at $2,621,278 to obtain an after-tax rate of return of 6.0%. If this lease payment is not acceptable to the lessee, Anderson Company, then it may not be possible to strike a deal. Naturally, competition among leasing companies forces lessors to build market-related returns into their lease payment schedules.[12]

---

12. For a discussion of realized returns on lease contracts, see Ronald C. Lease, John J. McConnell, and James S. Schallheim, "Realized Returns and the Default and Prepayment Experience of Financial Leasing Contracts," *Financial Management*, Summer 1990, pp. 11–20.

If the inputs to the lessee and the lessor are identical, then a positive NAL to the lessee implies an equal but negative NPV to the lessor. However, *conditions are often such that leasing can provide net benefits to both parties. This situation arises because of differentials in taxes, in borrowing rates, in estimated residual values, or in the ability to bear the residual value risk.* We will explore these issues in detail in the next section.

Note that the lessor can, under certain conditions, increase the return on the lease by borrowing some of the funds used to purchase the leased asset. Such a lease is called a **leveraged lease**. Whether or not a lease is leveraged has no effect on the lessee's analysis, but it can have a significant effect on the cash flows to the lessor and hence on the lessor's expected rate of return.

WEB

We discuss leveraged leases in more detail in **Web Extension 19C** on the textbook's Web site.

SELF TEST

What discount rate is used in a lessor's NPV analysis?

Under what conditions will the lessor's NPV be the negative of the lessee's NAL?

19-6 Other Issues in Lease Analysis

The basic methods of analysis used by lessees and lessors were presented in the previous sections. However, some other issues warrant discussion.[13]

19-6a Estimated Residual Value

It is important to note that the lessor owns the property upon expiration of a lease, so the lessor has claim to the asset's residual value. Superficially, it would appear that if residual values are expected to be large, then owning would have an advantage over leasing. However, this apparent advantage does not hold up. If expected residual values are large—as they may be under inflation for certain types of equipment and also if real estate is involved—then competition between leasing companies and other financing sources, as well as competition among leasing companies themselves, will force leasing rates down to the point where potential residual values are fully recognized in the lease contract. Thus, the existence of large residual values is not likely to result in materially higher costs for leasing.

19-6b Increased Credit Availability

As noted earlier, leasing is sometimes said to be advantageous for firms that are seeking to increase their financial leverage. First, it is sometimes argued that firms can obtain more money, and for longer terms, under a lease arrangement than under a loan secured by a specific piece of equipment. Second, because some leases do not appear on the balance sheet, lease financing has been said to give the firm

---

13. For a description of lease analysis in practice as well as a comprehensive bibliography of the leasing literature, see Tarun K. Mukherjee, "A Survey of Corporate Leasing Analysis," *Financial Management*, Autumn 1991, pp. 96–107.

WHAT YOU DON'T KNOW CAN HURT YOU!

A leasing decision seems to be pretty straightforward, at least from a financial perspective: Calculate the NAL for the lease and undertake it if the NAL is positive. Right? But tracking down all the financial implications from lease contract provisions can be difficult, requiring the lessee to make assumptions about future costs that are not explicitly spelled out in the lease contract. For example, consider the purchase option embedded in the lease that Rojacks Food Stores undertook with GE Capital for restaurant equipment. Upon expiration, the lease allowed Rojacks either to return the equipment or purchase it at the current market value. When the lease expired, GE set a purchase price that was much higher than Rojacks expected. Rojacks needed the equipment for its day-to-day operations, so it couldn't just return the equipment without disrupting its business. Ultimately, Rojacks hired an independent appraiser for the equipment and negotiated a lower purchase price—but without the appraiser, Rojacks would have been stuck with the price GE decided to set for the equipment. The Rojacks–GE situation isn't that unusual.

Lessors often use high expected residual values or high expected penalties to offset low lease payments. In addition, some contracts may require that: (1) all of the equipment covered under a lease must either be purchased or returned in its entirety, (2) equipment that is moved must be purchased, (3) large fees must be paid even for minor damage or missing parts, and/or (4) equipment must be returned in its original packaging. These conditions impose costs on the lessee when the lease is terminated and should be considered explicitly when making the leasing decision.

The moral of the story for lessees is to read the fine print and request changes to objectionable terms before signing the lease. Here are some ways to reduce the likelihood of unanticipated costs: (1) specify residual value as a percentage of the initial cost of the equipment; (2) allow for portions of the equipment to be returned and portions to be purchased at the end of the lease; and (3) specify that disagreements will be settled by arbitration.

Source: Linda Corman, "(Don't) Look Deep into My Lease," *CFO*, July 2006, pp. 71–75.

a stronger appearance in a *superficial* credit analysis and thus to permit the firm to use more leverage than would be possible if it did not lease.

There may be some truth to these claims for smaller firms. However, because firms are required to capitalize financial leases and to report them on their balance sheets, this point is of questionable validity for any firm large enough to have audited financial statements. However, leasing can be a way to circumvent existing loan covenants. If restrictive covenants prohibit a firm from issuing more debt but fail to restrict lease payments, then the firm could effectively increase its leverage by leasing additional assets. Also, firms that are in poor financial condition and face possible bankruptcy may be able to obtain lease financing at a lower cost than comparable debt financing because: (1) lessors often have a more favorable position than lenders should the lessee actually go bankrupt, and (2) lessors that specialize in certain types of equipment may be in a better position to dispose of repossessed equipment than banks or other lenders.

19-6c **Real Estate Leases**

Most of our examples have focused on equipment leasing. However, leasing originated with real estate, and such leases still constitute a huge segment of total lease financing. (We distinguish between housing rentals and long-term business leases; our concern is with business leases.) Retailers lease many of their stores. In some situations, retailers have no choice but to lease—this is true of locations in malls and certain office buildings. In other situations, they have a choice of building and owning versus leasing. Law firms and accounting firms, for example, can choose to buy their own facilities or to lease them on a long-term basis (up to 20 or more years).

The type of lease-versus-purchase analysis we discussed in this chapter is just as applicable for real estate as for equipment—conceptually, there is no difference. Of course, such things as maintenance, who the other tenants will be, what alterations can be made, who will pay for alterations, and the like become especially important with real property, but the analytical procedures upon which the lease-versus-buy decision is based are no different from any other lease analysis.

19-6d **Vehicle Leases**

Vehicle leasing is very popular today both for large corporations and for individuals, especially professionals such as MBAs, doctors, lawyers, and accountants. For corporations, the key factor involved with transportation is often maintenance and disposal of used vehicles—the leasing companies are specialists here, and many businesses prefer to "outsource" services related to autos and trucks. For individuals, leasing is often more convenient, and it may be easier to justify tax deductions on leased than on owned vehicles. Also, most auto leasing to individuals is through dealers. These dealers (and manufacturers) use leasing as a sales tool, and they often make the terms quite attractive—especially when it comes to the down payment, which may be nonexistent in the case of a lease.

Vehicle leasing also permits many individuals to drive more expensive cars than they could otherwise afford. For example, the monthly payment on a new BMW might be $1,500 when financed with a 3-year loan, but the same car, if leased for 3 years, might cost only $749 a month. At first glance, it appears that leasing is less expensive than owning because the monthly payment is so much lower. However, such a simplistic analysis ignores the fact that payments end after the loan is paid off but continue indefinitely under leasing. By using the techniques described in this chapter, individuals can assess the true costs associated with auto leases and then rationally judge the merits of each type of auto financing.

19-6e **Leasing and Tax Laws**[14]

The ability to structure leases that are advantageous to both lessor and lessee depends in large part on tax laws. The four major tax factors that influence leasing are: (1) investment tax credits, (2) depreciation rules, (3) tax rates, and (4) the alternative minimum tax. In this section, we briefly discuss each of these factors and how they influence leasing decisions.

The investment tax credit (ITC), when it is allowed, is a direct reduction of taxes that occurs when a firm purchases new capital equipment. Prior to 1987, firms could immediately deduct up to 10% of the cost of new capital investments from their corporate tax bills. Thus, a company that bought a $1,000,000 mainframe

---

14. See Chapters 3 and 6 of Schallheim's *Lease or Buy?* (cited in footnote 1) for an in-depth discussion of tax effects on leasing.

computer system would get a $100,000 reduction in current-year taxes. Because the ITC goes to the owner of the capital asset, low-tax-bracket companies that could not otherwise use the ITC could use leasing as a vehicle to pass immediate tax savings to high-tax-bracket lessors. The ITC is not currently in effect, but it could be reinstated in the future. If the ITC is put back into law, leasing will become especially attractive to low-tax-bracket firms.

To stimulate the economy in the wake of the global financial crisis of 2007, Congress authorized bonus depreciation rates. For example, in 2011, companies could claim a depreciation expense equal to 100% of the property's basis. Because of the time value of money, the faster an asset can be depreciated, the greater the tax advantages of ownership. However, many companies have lost money in recent years, so they are unable to fully utilize the bonus depreciation, which would reduce the stimulating impact of bonus deprecation. This is where leasing comes into play. Lessors in higher tax brackets can take advantage of the bonus depreciation and pass some of the savings on to low-tax-bracket lessees in the form of lower lease payments. The bonus depreciation provision expired at the beginning of 2014, but in July 2014 the House voted to reinstate it and make it permanent. As of fall 2014, the Senate has not acted on the legislation and so for now bonus depreciation is not in effect.

LEASE SECURITIZATION

Compared with many markets, the leasing market is fragmented and inefficient. There are millions of potential lessees, including all equipment users. Some are in high tax brackets, some are in low brackets. Some are financially sophisticated, some are not. Some have excellent credit ratings, some have poor credit. On the other side of the market are millions of potential lessors—including equipment manufacturers, banks, and individual investors—with different tax brackets and risk tolerances. If each lessee had to negotiate a separate deal for each lease, then information and search costs would be so high that few leases would be written.

Tax laws complicate the picture. For example, the alternative minimum tax (AMT) often has the effect of limiting the amount of depreciation a firm can utilize. In addition, a firm can't take a full half-year's depreciation on purchases in the fourth quarter if those purchases amount to more than 40% of total annual purchases. In this case the firm can take only a half-quarter's depreciation, which is the equivalent of one-eighth of a year's depreciation.

Lease brokers often served as facilitators in this complicated and inefficient market. Working with many different equipment manufacturers and lenders, brokers are in a position to match lessees with appropriate lessors in such a way that the full benefit of tax laws can be utilized.

Lease securitization, a new procedure, is the ultimate method of matching lessees with appropriate lessors. The first step is to create a portfolio consisting of numerous leases. The second step is to divide the leasing cash flows into different streams of income, called *tranches*. For example, one tranche might contain only lease payments, which would appeal to an investor in a low tax bracket. A second tranche might consist of depreciation, which a high-tax-bracket investor could use to shelter income from other sources. A third might contain the residual cash flows, which will occur in the future when the leases end. This tranche would appeal to a high-tax-bracket investor who can take some risk. Tranches can also be allocated according to the credit rating of the lessees, allowing investors with different risk tolerances to take on their desired level of risk.

In addition, a company might obtain a lease in its fourth quarter, but if this is the third quarter of the *lessor's* fiscal year, the lessor can take a full half-year's depreciation.

Sound complicated? It is, but it's an efficient answer to an inefficient market.

Source: SMG Fairfax, Knoxville, Tennessee.

Finally, the alternative minimum tax (AMT) also affects leasing activity. Corporations are permitted to use accelerated depreciation and other tax shelters on their tax books but then use straight-line depreciation for reporting results to shareholders. Thus, some firms report to the IRS that they are doing poorly, and hence pay little or no taxes, but report high earnings to shareholders. The corporate AMT, which is roughly computed by applying a 20% tax rate to the profits reported to shareholders, is designed to force highly profitable companies to pay at least some taxes even if they have tax shelters that push their taxable income to zero. In effect, all firms (and individuals) must compute the "regular" tax and the AMT tax, and then pay the higher of the two.

Companies with large AMT liabilities look for ways to reduce their tax bills by lowering reported income. Leasing can be beneficial here—a relatively short-term lease with high annual payments will increase reported expenses and thus lower reported profits. Note that the lease does not have to qualify as a guideline lease and be deducted for regular tax purposes—all that is needed is to lower reported income as shown on the income statement.

We see that tax laws and differential tax rates between lessors and lessees can be a motivating force for leasing. However, as we discuss in the next section, there are some sound nontax economic reasons why firms lease plants and equipment.

> **SELF TEST**
>
> Does leasing lead to increased credit availability?
>
> How do tax laws affect leasing?

19-7 **Other Reasons for Leasing**

Up to this point, we have noted that the tax rate or other differentials are generally necessary to make leasing attractive to both the lessee and the lessor. If the lessee and the lessor are facing different tax situations, including the alternative minimum tax, then it is often possible to structure a lease that is beneficial to both parties. However, there are other reasons that firms might want to lease an asset rather than buy it.

More than half of all commercial aircraft are leased, and smaller airlines, especially in developing nations, lease an especially high percentage of their planes. One of the reasons for this is that airlines can reduce their risks by leasing. If an airline purchased all its aircraft, it would be hampered in its ability to respond to changing market conditions. Because they have become specialists at matching airlines with available aircraft, the aircraft lessors (which are multibillion-dollar concerns) are quite good at managing the changing demand for different types of aircraft. This permits them to offer attractive lease terms. In this situation, *leasing provides operating flexibility*. Leasing is not necessarily less expensive than buying, but the operating flexibility is quite valuable.

Leasing is also an attractive alternative for many high-technology items that are subject to rapid and unpredictable technological obsolescence. Suppose a small rural hospital wants to buy a magnetic resonance imaging (MRI) device. If it buys the MRI equipment, then it is exposed to the risk of technological obsolescence. In a short time, some new technology might lower the value of the current system and thus render the project unprofitable. Because it does not use much equipment of this nature, the hospital would bear a great deal of risk if it bought the MRI device. However, a lessor that specializes in state-of-the-art medical equipment would be exposed to significantly less risk. By purchasing and then leasing many different items, the lessor benefits from diversification. Of course, over time some items will probably lose more value than the lessor expected, but this will be offset by other items that retain more value than expected. Also, because such a leasing company will be especially familiar with the market for used medical equipment, it can refurbish the equipment and then get a better price in the resale market than could a remote rural hospital. For these reasons, *leasing can reduce the risk of technological obsolescence.*

Leasing can also be attractive when a firm is uncertain about the demand for its products or services and thus about how long the equipment will be needed. Again, consider the hospital industry. Hospitals often offer services that are dependent on a single staff member—for example, a physician who performs liver transplants. To support the physician's practice, the hospital might have to invest millions in equipment that can be used only for this particular procedure. The hospital will charge for the use of the equipment, and if things go as expected, the investment will be profitable. However, if the physician leaves the hospital and if no replacement can be recruited, then the project is dead and the equipment becomes useless to the hospital. In this case, a lease with a cancellation clause would permit the hospital to simply return the equipment. The lessor would charge something for the cancellation clause, and this would lower the expected profitability of the project, but it would provide the hospital with an option to abandon the equipment, and the value of the option could easily exceed the incremental cost of the cancellation clause. The leasing company would be willing to write this option because it is in a better position to remarket the equipment, either by writing another lease or by selling it outright.

The leasing industry recently introduced a type of lease that even transfers some of a project's operating risk from the lessee to the lessor and also motivates the lessor to maintain the leased equipment in good working order. Instead of making a fixed rental payment, the lessee pays a fee each time the leased equipment is used. This type of lease originated with copy machines, where the lessee pays so much per month plus an additional amount per copy made. If the machine breaks down, no copies are made and the lessor's rental income declines. This motivates the lessor to repair the machine quickly.

This type of lease is also used in the health care industry, where it is called a "per-procedure lease." For example, a hospital might lease an X-ray machine for a fixed fee per X-ray, say, $5. If demand for the machine's X-rays is less than expected by the hospital, then revenues will be lower than expected—but so will the machine's capital costs. Conversely, high demand would lead to higher than expected lease costs—but these would be offset by higher than expected revenues. By using a per-procedure lease, the hospital is converting a fixed cost for the equipment into a variable cost and thereby reducing the machine's operating leverage and break-even point. The net effect is to reduce the project's risk. Of course, the expected cost of a per-procedure lease might be more than the cost of a conventional lease, but the risk reduction benefit could be worth the cost. Note too that if the lessor writes a large number of per-procedure leases then much of the riskiness inherent in such leases can be eliminated by diversification, so the risk premiums that lessors build into per-procedure lease payments could be low enough to attract potential lessees.

Some companies also find leasing attractive because the lessor is able to provide servicing on favorable terms. For example, Virco Manufacturing, a company that makes school desks and other furniture, recently leased 25 truck tractors and 140 trailers that it uses to ship furniture from its plant. The lease agreement, with a large leasing company that specializes in purchasing, maintaining, and then reselling trucks, permitted the replacement of an aging fleet that Virco had built up over the years. "We are pretty good at manufacturing furniture, but we aren't very good at maintaining a truck fleet," said Virco's CFO.

There are other reasons that might cause a firm to lease an asset rather than buy it. Often these reasons are difficult to quantify and so cannot be easily incorporated into an NPV or IRR analysis. Nevertheless, a sound lease decision must begin with a quantitative analysis, and then qualitative factors can be considered before making the final lease-or-buy decision.[15]

> **SELF TEST**   Describe some economic factors that might provide an advantage to leasing.

---

15. For more on leasing, see Thomas J. Finucane, "Some Empirical Evidence on the Use of Financial Leases," *The Journal of Financial Research*, Fall 1988, pp. 321–333; and Lawrence D. Schall, "The Evaluation of Lease Financing Opportunities," *Midland Corporate Finance Journal*, Spring 1985, pp. 48–65.

Summary

In the United States, more than 30% of all equipment is leased, as is a great deal of real estate. Consequently, leasing is an important financing vehicle. In this chapter, we discussed the leasing decision from the standpoints of both the lessee and the lessor. The key concepts covered are listed below.

- The five most important types of lease agreement are: (1) the **operating lease;** (2) the **financial lease**, which is also called a **capital lease;** (3) the **sale-and-leaseback;** (4) the **combination lease;** and (5) the **synthetic lease.**
- The IRS has specific guidelines that apply to lease arrangements. A lease that meets these guidelines is called a **guideline lease**, or a **tax-oriented lease**, because the IRS permits the lessor to deduct the asset's depreciation and allows the lessee to deduct the lease payments. A lease that does not meet the IRS guidelines is called a **non-tax-oriented lease**, in which case ownership for tax purposes resides with the lessee rather than the lessor.
- **FASB Statement 13** spells out the conditions under which a lease must be **capitalized** (shown directly on the balance sheet) as opposed to shown only in the notes to the financial statements. Generally, leases that run for a period equal to or greater than 75% of the asset's life must be capitalized.

- The lessee's analysis consists basically of a comparison of the PV of leasing versus the PV of owning. The difference in these PV's is called the **net advantage to leasing (NAL)**.

- One of the key issues in the lessee's analysis is the appropriate discount rate. A lease is a substitute for debt, cash flows in a lease analysis are stated on an after-tax basis, and cash flows are known with relative certainty, so the appropriate discount rate is the lessee's after-tax cost of debt. A higher discount rate may be used on the **residual value** if it is substantially riskier than the other flows.

- The lessor evaluates the lease as an **investment**. If the lease's NPV is greater than zero or if its IRR is greater than the lessor's opportunity cost, then the lease should be written.

- Leasing is motivated by various differences between lessees and lessors. Three of the most important reasons for leasing are: (1) **tax rate differentials**, (2) leases in which the lessor is better able than the lessee to bear the **residual value risk**, and (3) situations in which the lessor can maintain the leased equipment more efficiently than the lessee can.

- *Web Extension 19A* explains leasing feedback effects, *Web Extension 19B* explains the percentage cost of leasing, and *Web Extension 19C* explains leveraged leases.

Questions

19-1 Define each of the following terms:
   a. Lessee; lessor
   b. Operating lease; financial lease; sale-and-leaseback; combination lease; synthetic lease; SPE
   c. Off-balance sheet financing; capitalizing
   d. FASB Statement 13
   e. Guideline lease
   f. Residual value
   g. Lessee's analysis; lessor's analysis
   h. Net advantage to leasing (NAL)
   i. Alternative minimum tax (AMT)

19-2 Distinguish between operating leases and financial leases. Would you be more likely to find an operating lease employed for a fleet of trucks or for a manufacturing plant?

19-3 Are lessees more likely to be in higher or lower income tax brackets than lessors?

19-4 Commercial banks moved heavily into equipment leasing during the early 1970s, acting as lessors. One major reason for this invasion of the leasing industry was to gain the benefits of accelerated depreciation and the investment tax credit on leased equipment. During this same period, commercial banks were investing heavily in municipal securities, and they were also making loans to real estate investment trusts (REITs). In the mid-1970s, these REITs got into such serious difficulty that many banks suffered large losses on their REIT loans. Explain how its investments in municipal bonds and REITs could reduce a bank's willingness to act as a lessor.

19-5 One advantage of leasing voiced in the past is that it kept liabilities off the balance sheet, thus making it possible for a firm to obtain more leverage than it otherwise could have. This raised the question of whether or not both the lease obligation and the asset involved should be capitalized and shown on the balance sheet. Discuss the pros and cons of capitalizing leases and related assets.

19-6 Suppose there were no IRS restrictions on what constituted a valid lease. Explain, in a manner a legislator might understand, why some restrictions should be imposed. Illustrate your answer with numbers.

19-7 Suppose Congress enacted new tax law changes that would: (1) permit equipment to be depreciated over a shorter period, (2) lower corporate tax rates, and (3) reinstate the investment tax credit. Discuss how each of these potential changes would affect the relative volume of leasing versus conventional debt in the U.S. economy.

19-8 In our Anderson Company example, we assumed that the lease could not be canceled. What effect would a cancellation clause have on the lessee's analysis? On the lessor's analysis?

Problems   Answers Appear in Appendix B

Easy Problems 1–2

19-1 Balance Sheet Effects
Reynolds Construction needs a piece of equipment that costs $200. Reynolds can either lease the equipment or borrow $200 from a local bank and buy the equipment. If the equipment is leased, the lease would *not* have to be capitalized. Reynolds' balance sheet prior to the acquisition of the equipment is as follows:

Current assets	$300	Debt	$400
Net fixed assets	500	Equity	400
Total assets	$800	Total claims	$800

a. (1) What is Reynolds' current debt ratio?
   (2) What would be the company's debt ratio if it purchased the equipment?
   (3) What would be the debt ratio if the equipment were leased?
b. Would the company's financial risk be different under the leasing and purchasing alternatives?

19-2 Lease versus Buy
Consider the data in Problem 19-1. Assume that Reynolds' tax rate is 40% and that the equipment's depreciation would be $100 per year. If the company leased the asset on a 2-year lease, the payment would be $110 at the beginning of each year. If Reynolds borrowed and bought, the bank would charge 10% interest on the loan. In either case, the equipment is

worth nothing after 2 years and will be discarded. Should Reynolds lease or buy the equipment?

Intermediate Problems 3–4

19–3 Balance Sheet Effects

Two companies, Energen and Hastings Corporation, began operations with identical balance sheets. A year later, both required additional fixed assets at a cost of $50,000. Energen obtained a 5-year, $50,000 loan at an 8% interest rate from its bank. Hastings, on the other hand, decided to lease the required $50,000 capacity for 5 years, and an 8% return was built into the lease. The balance sheet for each company, before the asset increases, follows:

Current assets	$ 25,000	Debt	$ 50,000
Fixed assets	125,000	Equity	100,000
Total assets	$150,000	Total claims	$150,000

a. Show the balance sheets for both firms after the asset increases, and calculate each firm's new debt ratio. (Assume that the lease is not capitalized.)

b. Show how Hastings' balance sheet would look immediately after the financing if it capitalized the lease.

19–4 Lease versus Buy

Big Sky Mining Company must install $1.5 million of new machinery in its Nevada mine. It can obtain a bank loan for 100% of the purchase price, or it can lease the machinery. Assume that the following facts apply.

1. The machinery falls into the MACRS 3-year class.
2. Under either the lease or the purchase, Big Sky must pay for insurance, property taxes, and maintenance.
3. The firm's tax rate is 40%.
4. The loan would have an interest rate of 15%. It would be nonamortizing, with only interest paid at the end of each year for four years and the principal repaid at Year 4.
5. The lease terms call for $400,000 payments at the end of each of the next 4 years.
6. Big Sky Mining has no use for the machine beyond the expiration of the lease, and the machine has an estimated residual value of $250,000 at the end of the 4th year.

What is the NAL of the lease?

Challenging Problem 5

19–5 Lease versus Buy

Sadik Industries must install $1 million of new machinery in its Texas plant. It can obtain a bank loan for 100% of the required amount. Alternatively, a Texas investment banking firm that represents a group of investors believes it can arrange for a lease financing plan. Assume that the following facts apply.

1. The equipment falls in the MACRS 3-year class.
2. Estimated maintenance expenses are $50,000 per year.
3. The firm's tax rate is 34%.

4. If the money is borrowed, the bank loan will be at a rate of 14%, amortized in six equal installments at the end of each year.
5. The tentative lease terms call for payments of $280,000 at the end of each year for 3 years. The lease is a guideline lease.
6. Under the proposed lease terms, the lessee must pay for insurance, property taxes, and maintenance.
7. Sadik must use the equipment if it is to continue in business, so it will almost certainly want to acquire the property at the end of the lease. If it does, then under the lease terms it can purchase the machinery at its fair market value at Year 3. The best estimate of this market value is $200,000, but it could be much higher or lower under certain circumstances. If purchased at Year 3, the used equipment would fall into the MACRS 3-year class. Sadik would actually be able to make the purchase on the last day of the year (i.e., slightly before Year 3), so Sadik would get to take the first depreciation expense at Year 3 (the remaining depreciation expenses would be at Year 4 through Year 6). On the time line, Sadik would show the cost of the used equipment at Year 3 and its depreciation expenses starting at Year 3.

To assist management in making the proper lease-versus-buy decision, you are asked to answer the following questions:

a. What is the net advantage of leasing? Should Sadik take the lease?
b. Consider the $200,000 estimated residual value. How high could the residual value get before the net advantage of leasing falls to zero?
c. The decision almost can be considered a bet on the future residual value. Do you think the residual cash flows are equal in risk to the other cash flows? If not, how might you address this issue? (*Hint:* if you discount a negative cash flow at a higher rate, you get a better NPV—the NPV of a negative cash flow stream is less negative at high discount rates.)

Spreadsheet Problem

19–6 Build a Model: Lessee's Analysis

Start with the partial model in the file *Ch19 P06 Build a Model.xls* on the textbook's Web site. As part of its overall plant modernization and cost reduction program, Western Fabrics' management has decided to install a new automated weaving loom. In the capital budgeting analysis of this equipment, the IRR of the project was found to be 20% versus the project's required return of 12%.

The loom has an invoice price of $250,000, including delivery and installation charges. The funds needed could be borrowed from the bank through a 4-year amortized loan at a 10% interest rate, with payments to be made at the end of each year. In the event the loom is purchased, the manufacturer will contract to maintain and service it for a fee of $20,000 per year paid at the end of each year. The loom falls in the MACRS 5-year class, and Western's marginal federal-plus-state tax rate is 40%.

Aubey Automation Inc., maker of the loom, has offered to lease the loom to Western for $70,000 upon delivery and installation (at t = 0) plus four additional annual lease payments of $70,000 to be made at the end of Years 1 to 4. (Note that there are five lease payments in total.) The lease agreement includes maintenance and servicing. The loom has an expected life of 8 years, at which time its expected salvage value is zero; however, after 4 years its market value is expected to equal its book value of $42,500. Western plans to build an entirely new plant in 4 years, so it has no interest in either leasing or owning the proposed loom for more than that period.

a. Should the loom be leased or purchased?

b. The salvage value is clearly the most uncertain cash flow in the analysis. What effect would a salvage value risk adjustment have on the analysis? (Assume that the appropriate salvage value pre-tax discount rate is 15%.)

c. Assuming that the after-tax cost of debt should be used to discount all anticipated cash flows, at what lease payment would the firm be indifferent to either leasing or buying?

MINI CASE

Lewis Securities Inc. has decided to acquire a new market data and quotation system for its Richmond home office. The system receives current market prices and other information from several online data services and then either displays the information on a screen or stores it for later retrieval by the firm's brokers. The system also permits customers to call up current quotes on terminals in the lobby.

The equipment costs $1,000,000 and, if it were purchased, Lewis could obtain a term loan for the full purchase price at a 10% interest rate. Although the equipment has a 6-year useful life, it is classified as a special-purpose computer and therefore falls into the MACRS 3-year class. If the system were purchased, a 4-year maintenance contract could be obtained at a cost of $20,000 per year, payable at the beginning of each year. The equipment would be sold after 4 years, and the best estimate of its residual value is $200,000. However, because real-time display system technology is changing rapidly, the actual residual value is uncertain.

As an alternative to the borrow-and-buy plan, the equipment manufacturer informed Lewis that Consolidated Leasing would be willing to write a 4-year guideline lease on the equipment, including maintenance, for payments of $260,000 at the beginning of

each year. Lewis' marginal federal-plus-state tax rate is 40%. You have been asked to analyze the lease-versus-purchase decision and, in the process, to answer the following questions:

a. (1) Who are the two parties to a lease transaction?
   (2) What are the five primary types of leases, and what are their characteristics?
   (3) How are leases classified for tax purposes?
   (4) What effect does leasing have on a firm's balance sheet?
   (5) What effect does leasing have on a firm's capital structure?

b. (1) What is the present value cost of owning the equipment? (*Hint:* Set up a time line that shows the net cash flows over the period t = 0 to t = 4, and then find the PV of these net cash flows, or the PV cost of owning.)
   (2) Explain the rationale for the discount rate you used to find the PV.

c. What is Lewis' present value cost of leasing the equipment? (*Hint:* Again, construct a time line.)

d. What is the net advantage to leasing (NAL)? Does your analysis indicate that Lewis should buy or lease the equipment? Explain.

e. Now assume that the equipment's residual value could be as low as $0 or as high as $400,000, but $200,000 is the expected value. Because the residual value is riskier than the other relevant cash flows, this differential risk should be incorporated into the analysis. Describe how this could be accomplished. (No calculations are necessary, but explain how you would modify the analysis if calculations were required.) What effect would the residual value's increased uncertainty have on Lewis' lease-versus-purchase decision?

f. The lessee compares the cost of owning the equipment with the cost of leasing it. Now put yourself in the lessor's shoes. In a few sentences, how should you analyze the decision to write or not to write the lease?

g. (1) Assume that the lease payments were actually $280,000 per year, that Consolidated Leasing is also in the 40% tax bracket, and that it also forecasts a $200,000 residual value. Also, to furnish the maintenance support, Consolidated would have to purchase a maintenance contract from the manufacturer at the same $20,000 annual cost, again paid in advance. Consolidated Leasing can obtain an expected 10% pre-tax return on investments of similar risk. What would be Consolidated's NPV and IRR of leasing under these conditions?

(2) What do you think the lessor's NPV would be if the lease payment were set at $260,000 per year? (*Hint:* The lessor's cash flows would be a "mirror image" of the lessee's cash flows.)

h. Lewis' management has been considering moving to a new downtown location, and they are concerned that these plans may come to fruition prior to the equipment lease's expiration. If the move occurs, then Lewis would buy or lease an entirely new set of equipment, so management would like to include a cancellation clause in the lease contract. What effect would such a clause have on the riskiness of the lease from Lewis' standpoint? From the lessor's standpoint? If you were the lessor, would you insist on changing any of the other lease terms if a cancellation clause were added? Should the cancellation clause contain provisions similar to call premiums or any restrictive covenants and/or penalties of the type contained in bond indentures? Explain your answer.

SELECTED ADDITIONAL CASES

The following cases from CengageCompose cover many of the concepts discussed in this chapter and are available at **http://compose.cengage.com.**

Klein-Brigham Series:

Case 25, "Environmental Sciences, Inc.," Case 49, "Agro Chemical Corporation," Case 69, "Friendly Food Stores, Inc.," and Case 26, "Prudent Solutions, Inc.," all examine the lease decision from the perspectives of both the lessee and the lessor.

Brigham-Buzzard Series:

Case 12, "Powerline Network Corporation (Leasing)."

Hybrid Financing: Preferred Stock, Warrants, and Convertibles

In previous chapters, we examined common stocks and various types of long-term debt. In this chapter, we examine three other securities used to raise long-term capital: (1) *preferred stock*, which is a hybrid security that represents a cross between debt and common equity, (2) *warrants*, which are derivative securities issued by firms to facilitate the issuance of some other type of security, and (3) *convertibles*, which combine the features of debt (or preferred stock) and warrants.

Beginning-of-Chapter Questions

As you read this chapter, consider how you would answer the following questions. You *should not* necessarily be able to answer the questions before you read the chapter. Rather, you should use them to get a sense of the issues covered in the chapter. After reading the chapter, you should be able to give at least partial answers to the questions, and you should be able to give better answers after the chapter has been discussed in class. Note, too, that it is often useful, when answering conceptual questions, to use hypothetical data to illustrate your answer. We illustrate the answers with an *Excel* model that is available on the textbook's Web site. Accessing the model and working through it is a useful exercise, and it provides insights that are useful when answering the questions.

1. Why do companies use so many different types of instruments to raise capital? Why not just use debt and common stock?

2. If a company is thinking about issuing **preferred stock** to raise capital, what are some factors that it

should consider? What factors should an investor consider before buying preferred stock?

3. What is a **warrant**? If a company decides to raise capital by issuing bonds with warrants, how would the terms on both the bond and the warrant be set? Consider in particular how the coupon rate and maturity of the bond would be related to the exercise price and life of the warrant, together with any other factors that might affect the decision.

4. What is a **convertible**? If a company decides to raise capital by issuing convertible bonds, how would the terms on the bond be set? Consider specifically the maturity, coupon rate, and call features of the bond, as well as the conversion price (or conversion ratio), together with any other parameters required for the analysis.

5. Suppose you just bought a convertible bond at its par value. Your broker gives you information on the bond's conversion ratio, coupon rate, maturity,

years of call protection, and the yield on noncon-vertible bonds of similar risk and maturity. The company has a well-established payout ratio, and you also know the stock's price, beta, and expected ROE. You also know the risk-free rate and the market risk premium.

a. How could you use this information to determine how much you are paying for the option to convert?

b. How would you determine the expected rate of return on the convertible, along with the expected return on the common stock and the straight bonds?

c. Now suppose the company unexpectedly announced: (1) an increase in its target dividend payout ratio from, say, 25% to 75% and (2) an increase in the dividend from $1 to $3 to conform to the new policy. Would the new dividend policy help or hurt you and other holders of the convertible bond? Explain.

20-1 **Preferred Stock**

Preferred stock is a hybrid—it is similar to bonds in some respects and to common stock in other ways. Accountants classify preferred stock as equity; hence they show it on the balance sheet as an equity account. However, from a financial perspective preferred stock lies somewhere between debt and common equity: It imposes a fixed charge and thus increases the firm's financial leverage, yet omitting the preferred dividend does not force a company into bankruptcy. Also, unlike interest on debt, preferred dividends are not deductible by the issuing corporation, so preferred stock has a higher cost of capital than debt. We first describe the basic features of preferred stock, after which we discuss the types of preferred stock and the advantages and disadvantages of preferred stock.

20-1a **Basic Features**

Preferred stock has a par (or liquidating) value, often either $25 or $100. The dividend is stated as either a percentage of par, as so many dollars per share, or both ways. For example, several years ago Klondike Paper Company sold 150,000 shares of $100 par value perpetual preferred stock for a total of $15 million. This preferred stock had a stated annual dividend of $12 per share, so the preferred dividend yield was $12/$100 = 0.12, or 12%, at the time of issue. The dividend was set when the stock was issued; it will not be changed in the future. Therefore, if the required rate of return on preferred, r_{ps}, changes from 12% after the issue date—as it did—then the market price of the preferred stock will go up or down. Currently, r_{ps} for Klondike Paper's preferred is 9%, and the price of the preferred has risen from $100 to $12/0.09 = $133.33.

If the preferred dividend is not earned, the company does not have to pay it. However, most preferred issues are **cumulative**, meaning that the cumulative total of unpaid preferred dividends must be paid before dividends can be paid on the common stock. Unpaid preferred dividends are called **arrearages**. Dividends in arrears do not earn interest; thus, arrearages do not grow in a compound interest sense, they only grow from additional nonpayments of the preferred dividend. Also, many preferred stocks accrue arrearages for only a limited number of years—so that, for example, the cumulative feature may cease after 3 years. However, the dividends in arrears continue in force until they are paid.

Preferred stock normally has no voting rights. However, most preferred issues stipulate that the preferred stockholders can elect a minority of the directors—say, three out of ten—if the preferred dividend is passed (omitted). Some preferreds even entitle their holders to elect a majority of the board.

Although nonpayment of preferred dividends will not trigger bankruptcy, corporations issue preferred stock with every intention of paying the dividend. Even if passing the dividend does not give the preferred stockholders control of the company, failure to pay a preferred dividend precludes payment of common dividends. In addition, passing the dividend makes it difficult to raise capital by selling bonds and virtually impossible to sell more preferred or common stock except at rock-bottom prices. However, having preferred stock outstanding does give a firm the chance to overcome its difficulties: If bonds had been used instead of preferred stock, a company could be forced into bankruptcy before it could straighten out its problems. Thus, *from the viewpoint of the issuing corporation, preferred stock is less risky than bonds.*

For an investor, however, preferred stock is riskier than bonds: (1) preferred stockholders' claims are subordinated to those of bondholders in the event of liquidation, and (2) bondholders are more likely to continue receiving income during hard times than are preferred stockholders. Accordingly, investors require a higher after-tax rate of return on a given firm's preferred stock than on its bonds. However, because 70% of preferred dividends is exempt from corporate taxes, preferred stock is attractive to corporate investors. Indeed, high-grade preferred stock, on average, sells on a lower pre-tax yield basis than high-grade bonds. As an example, Alcoa has preferred stock with an annual dividend of $3.75 (a 3.75% rate applied to

For updates, go to
http://finance.yahoo .com and get quotes for AA-P, Alcoa's 3.75% preferred stock. For an updated bond yield, go to FINRA's site at
http://finra-markets .morningstar.com /BondCenter/Default .jsp and search for Alcoa bonds.

THE ROMANCE HAD NO CHEMISTRY, BUT IT HAD A LOT OF PREFERRED STOCK!

On April 1, 2009, Dow Chemical Company merged with Rohm & Haas after a bitter dispute over the interpretation of their previous merger agreement. So even though the two companies make chemicals, there apparently wasn't much chemistry by the time the merger was completed.

To raise cash for the $78.97 per share purchase of Rohm & Haas' outstanding shares, Dow borrowed over $9 billion from Citibank and also issued $4 billion in convertible preferred stock to Berkshire Hathaway and The Kuwait Investment Authority.

The Haas Family Trusts and Paulson & Company were large shareholders in Rohm & Haas. As part of the deal,

they sold their shares to Dow with one hand and bought $3 billion in preferred stock from Dow with the other. This preferred stock pays a cash dividend of 7%. It also pays an 8% "dividend" that either can be cash or additional shares of the preferred stock, with the choice left to Dow; this is called a payment-in-kind (PIK) dividend.

These terms mean that Dow can conserve cash if it runs into difficult times: Dow can pay the 8% in additional stock and Dow can even defer payment of the 7% cash dividend without risk of bankruptcy. But if this happens, a troubled marriage is likely to cause even more grief.

Source: 8-K reports from the SEC filed on March 12, 2009 and April 1, 2009.

$100 par value). In May 2014, Alcoa's preferred stock had a price of $86.50, for a market yield of about $3.75/$84.50 = 4.44%. Alcoa's long-term bonds that mature in 2037 provided a yield of 6.0%, which is 1.56 percentage points *more* than its preferred, even though preferred stock is riskier than debt. The tax treatment accounted for this differential; the *after-tax yield* to corporate investors was greater on the preferred stock than on the bonds because 70% of the dividend may be excluded from taxation by a corporate investor.[1]

About half of all preferred stock issued in recent years has been convertible into common stock. We discuss convertibles in Section 20-3.

Some preferred stocks are similar to perpetual bonds in that they have no maturity date, but most new issues now have specified maturities. For example, many preferred shares have a sinking fund provision that calls for the retirement of 2% of the issue each year, meaning the issue will "mature" in a maximum of 50 years. Also, many preferred issues are callable by the issuing corporation, which can also limit the life of the preferred.[2]

Nonconvertible preferred stock is virtually all owned by corporations, which can take advantage of the 70% dividend exclusion to obtain a higher after-tax yield on preferred stock than on bonds. Individuals should not own preferred stocks (except convertible preferreds)—they can get higher yields on safer bonds, so it is not logical for them to hold preferreds.[3] As a result of this ownership pattern, the volume of preferred stock financing is geared to the supply of money in the hands of corporate investors. When the supply of such money is plentiful, the prices of preferred stocks are bid up, their yields fall, and investment bankers suggest that companies in need of financing consider issuing preferred stock.

---

1. For example, the after-tax yield on an 8.1% bond to a corporate investor in the 34% marginal tax rate bracket is 8.1%(1 − T) = 5.3%. The after-tax yield on a 7.0% preferred stock is 7.0%(1 − Effective T) = 7.0%[1 − (0.30)(0.34)] = 6.3%. Also, note that tax law prevents arbitrage. If a firm issues debt and uses the proceeds to purchase another firm's preferred stock, then the 70% dividend exclusion is voided.

2. Prior to the late 1970s, virtually all preferred stock was perpetual and almost no issues had sinking funds or call provisions. Then insurance company regulators, worried about the unrealized losses the companies had been incurring on preferred holdings as a result of rising interest rates, made changes essentially mandating that insurance companies buy only limited life preferreds. From that time on, virtually no new preferred has been perpetual. This example illustrates the way securities change as a result of changes in the economic environment.

3. Since 2003, qualified dividends received by individuals are taxed at a capital gains rate rather than as ordinary income. This makes preferred stock more attractive relative to bonds, putting individual investors in much the same boat as corporations. For example, a corporation in the 35% tax bracket with a 70% dividend exclusion faces a (0.35)(1 − 0.70) = 10.5% tax rate on dividend income as compared to a 35% rate on interest income. Most individuals face a dividend tax rate of 15%, and high income earners would face a 35% tax on ordinary income. Thus there is a tax advantage for dividend income for both individuals and corporations, although the advantage is larger for corporations.

    Also, some financially engineered preferred stock has "dividends" that the paying company can deduct for tax purposes in the same way that interest payments are deductible. Therefore, the company is able to pay a higher rate on such preferred stock, making it potentially attractive to individual investors. These securities trade under a variety of colorful names, including MIPS (Modified Income Preferred Securities), QUIPS (Quarterly Income Preferred Securities), TOPrS (Trust Originated Preferred Stock), and QUIDS (Quarterly Income Debt Securities). However, dividends from these hybrid securities are not subject to the 70% corporate exclusion and are taxed as ordinary income for individual investors.

For issuers, preferred stock has a tax *disadvantage* relative to debt: Interest expense is deductible, but preferred dividends are not. Still, firms with low tax rates may have an incentive to issue preferred stock that can be bought by high-tax-rate corporate investors, who can take advantage of the 70% dividend exclusion. If a firm has a lower tax rate than potential corporate buyers, then the firm might be better off issuing preferred stock than debt. The key here is that the tax advantage to a high-tax-rate corporation is greater than the tax disadvantage to a low-tax-rate issuer. As an illustration, assume that risk differentials between debt and preferred would require an issuer to set the interest rate on new debt at 10% and the dividend yield on new preferred stock 2% higher, or at 12% in a no-tax world. However, when taxes are considered, a corporate buyer with a high tax rate—say, 40%—might be willing to buy the preferred stock if it has an 8% before-tax yield. This would produce an $8\%(1 - \text{Effective T}) = 8\%[1 - 0.30(0.40)] = 7.04\%$ after-tax return on the preferred versus $10\%(1 - 0.40) = 6.0\%$ on the debt. If the issuer has a low tax rate—say, 10%—then its after-tax costs would be $10\%(1 - T) = 10\%(0.90) = 9\%$ on the bonds and 8% on the preferred. Thus, the security with lower risk to the issuer, preferred stock, also has a lower cost. Such situations can make preferred stock a logical financing choice.[4]

HYBRIDS AREN'T ONLY FOR CORPORATIONS

The Cooperative Regions of Organic Producer Pools (CROPP) markets organic produce under such brand names as Organic Valley and Organic Prairie and is a supplier to Stonyfield, maker of organic yogurt. CROPP is not a corporation or a partnership. It is a cooperative, which is an organization that provides services for its owner/members. In this case, CROPP purchases produce from its members, processes the produce, and then resells it. Profits are redistributed to the owner/members as dividends.

With the beginnings of the financial recovery and an overall increase in the demand for organic products, CROPP's sales grew 18% in 2009 to over $600 million. High growth requires investments in operating assets, causing CROPP to need $14 million in additional external financing. CROPP decided to raise the funds by issuing preferred stock to members and non-members. CROPP had successfully issued preferred stock in the past and this issue was a $50 par, 6% cumulative dividend, non-voting preferred stock, and was sold for $50 per share. CROPP chose not to use an investment banker for this issue; the co-op's investor relations manager was in charge of marketing and selling the preferred stock and CROPP saved quite a bit of money in fees with issuance costs totaling about 4.5% rather than the 7% or more charged by an investment bank.

Unlike preferred stock issued by corporations, dividends on preferred stock issued by a Section 521 cooperative such as CROPP can be deducted from its pre-tax income, and the dividend recipient treats it as ordinary income for tax purposes. Therefore this preferred stock is treated like perpetual debt for tax purposes. Why then would CROPP issue preferred stock rather than debt? The simple reason is that preferred stock is non-recourse. If CROPP misses a dividend payment, the dividend accrues, but the preferred stockholder cannot force CROPP into bankruptcy. This flexibility is valuable, especially in an industry as volatile as farming.

---

4. For more on preferred stock, see Arthur L. Houston Jr. and Carol Olson Houston, "Financing with Preferred Stock," *Financial Management*, Autumn 1990, pp. 42–54; and Michael J. Alderson and Donald R. Fraser, "Financial Innovations and Excesses Revisited: The Case of Auction Rate Preferred Stock," *Financial Management*, Summer 1993, pp. 61–75.

20-1b **Other Types of Preferred Stock**

In addition to "plain vanilla" preferred stock, there are two other variations: adjustable rate and market auction preferred stock.

Adjustable Rate Preferred Stock

Instead of paying fixed dividends, **adjustable rate preferred stock (ARP)** has dividends tied to the rate on Treasury securities. ARPs are issued mainly by utilities and large commercial banks. When ARPs were first developed, they were touted as nearly perfect short-term corporate investments because: (1) only 30% of the dividends are taxable to corporations, and (2) the floating-rate feature was supposed to keep the issue trading at near par. The new security proved to be popular as a short-term investment for firms with idle cash, so mutual funds that held ARPs sprouted like weeds (and shares of these funds, in turn, were purchased by corporations). However, the ARPs still had some price volatility due to: (1) changes in the riskiness of the issuers (some big banks that had issued ARPs, such as Continental Illinois, ran into serious loan default problems) and (2) fluctuations in Treasury yields between dividend rate adjustment dates. Therefore, the ARPs had too much price instability to be held in the liquid asset portfolios of many corporate investors.

Market Auction Preferred Stock

In 1984, investment bankers introduced **money market preferred stock**, which is also called **market auction preferred stock**.[5] Here the underwriter conducts an auction on the issue every 7 weeks. (To get the 70% exclusion from taxable income, buyers must hold the stock for at least 46 days.) Holders who want to sell their shares can put them up for auction at par value. Buyers then submit bids in the form of the yields they are willing to accept over the next 7-week period. The yield set on the issue for the coming period is the lowest yield sufficient to sell all the shares being offered at that auction. The buyers pay the sellers the par value; hence holders are virtually assured that their shares can be sold at par. The issuer then must pay a dividend rate over the next 7-week period as determined by the auction. From the holder's standpoint, market auction preferred is a low-risk, largely tax-exempt, 7-week maturity security that can be sold between auction dates at close to par.

  In practice, things may not go quite so smoothly. If there are few potential buyers, then an excessively high yield might be required to clear the market. To protect the issuing firms or mutual funds from high dividend payments, the securities have a cap on the allowable dividend yield. If the market-clearing yield is higher than this cap, then the next dividend yield will be set equal to this cap rate, but the auction will fail and the owners of the securities who wish to sell will not be able to do so. This happened in February 2008, and many market auction preferred stockholders were left holding securities they wanted to liquidate.

---

5. Confusingly, market auction preferred stock is frequently referred to as *auction-rate preferred* stock and with the acronym ARP as well.

20-1c **Advantages and Disadvantages of Preferred Stock**

There are both advantages and disadvantages to financing with preferred stock. Here are the major advantages from the issuer's standpoint.

1. In contrast to bonds, the obligation to pay preferred dividends is not firm, and passing (not paying) a preferred dividend cannot force a firm into bankruptcy.
2. By issuing preferred stock, the firm avoids the dilution of common equity that occurs when common stock is sold.
3. Because preferred stock sometimes has no maturity and because preferred sinking fund payments (if present) are typically spread over a long period, preferred issues reduce the cash flow drain from repayment of principal that occurs with debt issues.

There are two major disadvantages as follows.

1. Preferred stock dividends are not normally deductible to the issuer, so the after-tax cost of preferred is typically higher than the after-tax cost of debt. However, the tax advantage of preferreds to corporate purchasers lowers its pre-tax cost and thus its effective cost.
2. Although preferred dividends can be passed, investors expect them to be paid and firms intend to pay them if conditions permit. Thus, preferred dividends are considered to be a fixed cost. As a result, their use—like that of debt—increases financial risk and hence the cost of common equity.

SELF TEST

Should preferred stock be classified as equity or debt? Explain.

Who are the major purchasers of nonconvertible preferred stock? Why?

Briefly explain the mechanics of adjustable rate and market auction preferred stock.

What are the advantages and disadvantages of preferred stock to the issuer?

A company's preferred stock has a pre-tax dividend yield of 7%, and its debt has a pre-tax yield of 8%. If an investor is in the 34% marginal tax bracket, what are the after-tax yields of the preferred stock and debt? **(6.29% and 5.28%)**

20-2 **Warrants**

A **warrant** is a certificate issued by a company that gives the holder the right to buy a stated number of shares of the company's stock at a specified price for some specified length of time. Generally, warrants are issued along with debt, and they are used to induce investors to buy long-term debt with a lower coupon rate than would otherwise be required. For example, when Infomatics Corporation, a rapidly growing high-tech company, wanted to sell $50 million of 20-year bonds in 2015, the company's investment bankers informed the financial vice president that the bonds would be difficult to sell and that a coupon rate of 10% would be required. However, as an alternative the bankers suggested that investors might be willing to buy the bonds with a coupon rate of only 8% if the company would offer 20 warrants with each $1,000 bond, each warrant entitling the holder to buy one share of common stock at a strike price (also called an *exercise price*) of $22 per share. The stock was selling for $20 per share at the time, and the warrants would expire in the year 2025 if they had not been exercised previously.

Why would investors be willing to buy Infomatics' bonds at a yield of only 8% in a 10% market just because warrants were also offered as part of the package? It's because the warrants are long-term *call options* that allow holders to buy the firm's common stock at the strike price regardless of how high the market price climbs. The value of this option offsets the low interest rate on the bonds and makes the package of low-yield bonds plus warrants attractive to investors. (See Chapter 5 for a discussion of options.)

20-2a **Initial Market Price of a Bond with Warrants**

If the Infomatics bonds had been issued as straight debt, they would have carried a 10% interest rate. However, with warrants attached, the bonds were sold to yield 8%. Someone buying the bonds at their $1,000 initial offering price would thus be receiving a package consisting of an 8%, 20-year bond plus 20 warrants. Because the going interest rate on bonds as risky as those of Infomatics was 10%, we can find the straight-debt value of the bonds, assuming an annual coupon for ease of illustration, as follows:

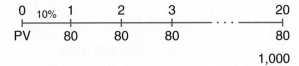

Using a financial calculator, input N = 20, I/YR = 10, PMT = 80, and FV = 1000. Then press the PV key to obtain the bond's value of $829.73, or approximately $830. Thus, a person buying the bonds in the initial underwriting would pay $1,000 and receive in exchange a straight bond worth about $830 plus 20 warrants that are presumably worth about $1,000 − $830 = $170:

(20–1)

$$\frac{\text{Price paid for}}{\text{bond with warrants}} = \frac{\text{Straight-debt}}{\text{value of bond}} + \frac{\text{Value of}}{\text{warrants}}$$

$$\$1,000 = \$830 + \$170$$

Because investors receive 20 warrants with each bond, each warrant has an implied value of $170/20 = $8.50.

The key issue in setting the terms of a bond-with-warrants deal is valuing the warrants. The straight-debt value can be estimated quite accurately, as we have shown. However, it is more difficult to estimate the value of the warrants. The Black-Scholes option pricing model (OPM), discussed in Chapter 5, can be used to find the value of a call option. There is a temptation to use this model to find the value of a warrant, because call options are similar to warrants in many respects: Both give the investor the right to buy a share of stock at a fixed strike price on or before the expiration date. However, there are major differences between call options and warrants. When call options are exercised, the stock provided to the option holder comes from the secondary market, but when warrants are exercised, the stock provided to the warrant holder is either newly issued shares or treasury stock the company has previously purchased. This means that the exercise of warrants dilutes the value of the original equity, which could cause the value of the original warrant to differ from the value of a similar call option. Also, call options typically have a life of just a few months, whereas warrants often have lives of 10 years or more. Finally, the Black-Scholes model assumes that the underlying stock pays no dividend, which is not unreasonable over a short period but is unreasonable for 5 or 10 years. Therefore, investment bankers cannot use the original Black-Scholes model to determine the value of warrants.

Even though the original Black-Scholes model cannot be used to determine a precise value for a warrant, there are more sophisticated models that work reasonably well.[6] In addition, investment bankers can simply contact portfolio managers of mutual funds, pension funds, and other organizations that would be interested in buying the securities to get an indication of how many they would buy at different prices. In effect, the bankers hold a presale auction and determine the set of terms that will just clear the market. If they do this job properly then they will, in effect, be letting the market determine the value of the warrants.

20-2b **Use of Warrants in Financing**

Warrants generally are used by small, rapidly growing firms as **sweeteners** when they sell debt or preferred stock. Such firms frequently are regarded by investors as being highly risky, so their bonds can be sold only at extremely high coupon rates and with very restrictive indenture provisions. To avoid such restrictions, firms like Infomatics often offer warrants along with the bonds.

Getting warrants along with bonds enables investors to share in the company's growth, assuming it does in fact grow and prosper. Therefore, investors are willing to accept a lower interest rate and less restrictive indenture provisions. A bond with warrants has some characteristics of debt and some characteristics of equity. It is a hybrid security that provides the financial manager with an opportunity to expand the firm's mix of securities and thereby appeal to a broader group of investors.

---

6. For example, see John C. Hull, *Options, Futures, and Other Derivatives*, 9th ed. (Boston: Prentice-Hall, 2015). Hull shows that if there are m warrants outstanding, each of which can be converted into γ shares of common stock at an exercise price of X, as well as n shares of common stock outstanding, then the price ω of a warrant is given by this modification of the Black-Scholes option pricing formula from Chapter 5:

$$\omega = \left(\frac{n\gamma}{n + m\gamma}\right)\left[S^*N(d_1^*) - Xe^{-r_{RF}(T-t)}N(d_2^*)\right] \text{ where } d_1^* = \frac{\ln(S^*/X) + (r_{RF} + \sigma_0^2/2)(T-t)}{\sigma_0 \sqrt{T-t}}$$

Here $d_2^* = d_1^* - \sigma_0(T-t)^{1/2}$ and $S^* = S + m\omega/n$, where S is the underlying stock price, T is the maturity date, r_{RF} is the risk free rate, σ_0 is the volatility of the stock and the warrants together, and $N(\cdot)$ is the cumulative normal distribution function. See Chapter 5 for more on the Black-Scholes option pricing formula. If $\gamma = 1$ and n is very much larger than m, so that the number of warrants issued is very small compared to the number of shares of stock outstanding, then this simplifies to the standard Black-Scholes option pricing formula.

Virtually all warrants issued today are **detachable**. In other words, after a bond with attached warrants is sold, the warrants can be detached and traded separately from the bond. Further, even after the warrants have been exercised, the bond (with its low coupon rate) remains outstanding.

The strike price on warrants is generally set some 20% to 30% above the market price of the stock on the date the bond is issued. If the firm grows and prospers, causing its stock price to rise above the strike price at which shares may be purchased, warrant holders could exercise their warrants and buy stock at the stated price. However, without some incentive, warrants would never be exercised prior to maturity—their value in the open market would be greater than their value if exercised, so holders would sell warrants rather than exercise them. There are three conditions that cause holders to exercise their warrants: (1) Warrant holders will surely exercise and buy stock if the warrants are about to expire and the market price of the stock is above the exercise price. (2) Warrant holders will exercise voluntarily if the company raises the dividend on the common stock by a sufficient amount. No dividend is earned on the warrant, so it provides no current income. However, if the common stock pays a high dividend, then it provides an attractive dividend yield but limits stock price growth. This induces warrant holders to exercise their option to buy the stock. (3) Warrants sometimes have stepped-up strike prices (also called stepped-up exercise prices), which prod owners into exercising them. For example, Williamson Scientific Company has warrants outstanding with a strike price of $25 until December 31, 2018, at which time the strike price rises to $30. If the price of the common stock is over $25 just before December 31, 2018, many warrant holders will exercise their options before the stepped-up price takes effect and the value of the warrants falls.

Another desirable feature of warrants is that they generally bring in funds only if funds are needed. If the company grows, it will probably need new equity capital. At the same time, growth will cause the price of the stock to rise and the warrants to be exercised; hence the firm will obtain the cash it needs. If the company is not successful and it cannot profitably employ additional money, then the price of its stock will probably not rise enough to induce exercise of the warrants.

20-2c **The Component Cost of Bonds with Warrants**

When Infomatics issued its bonds with warrants, the firm received $1,000 for each bond. The pre-tax cost of debt would have been 10% if no warrants had been attached, and this is the component cost of debt that would have been used for calculating the company's weighed average cost of capital as we did in Chapter 11. However, each Infomatics bond has 20 warrants, each of which entitles its holder to buy one share of stock for $22. The presence of warrants also allows Infomatics to pay only 8% interest on the bonds, obligating it to pay $80 interest for 20 years plus $1,000 at the end of 20 years. So given these complicating factors, what is the component cost of capital for bonds with warrants? As we shall see, the cost is well above the 8% coupon rate on the bonds and is also above the 10% cost if the company had issued straight debt.

The best way to approach this analysis is to break the $1,000 bond with warrants attached into two components, one consisting of an $830 bond and the other consisting of $170 of warrants, and calculate the cost of capital for each of these components. Thus, the $1,000 bond-with-warrants package consists of $830/$1,000 = 0.83 = 83% straight debt and $170/$1,000 = 0.17 = 17% warrant.

We will find the cost of capital for the straight bonds and the cost of capital for the warrant, and then weight them to derive the cost of capital for the bond-with-warrants package.

Finding the cost of capital for the straight bond component is easy. The pre-tax component cost of debt is 10% because this is the pre-tax cost of debt for a straight bond. Estimating the cost of capital for the warrant component, however, is fairly complicated in theory, but we can use the following simplified procedure to obtain a reasonable approximation.[7] The basic idea is to estimate the firm's expected dollar cost of satisfying the warrant holders at the time the warrants expire and use this to calculate the warrant holders' expected return from owning the warrants. This expected return will be our component cost of capital for the warrants.

To calculate the firm's expected cost of satisfying the warrants, we need an estimate of the value of the firm's stock price on the warrants' expiration date, T. From the Corporate Valuation Model in Chapter 8, this price will be the expected intrinsic value of the total firm less the value of the debt, all divided by the number of shares. Each of these three pieces is estimated for the date the warrants expire, T:

$$\frac{\text{Estimated}}{\text{price of stock}_T} = \frac{\text{Intrinsic value of equity}_T}{\text{Shares outstinding}_T}$$

$$= \frac{\substack{\text{Estimated total} \\ \text{value of firm}_T} - \substack{\text{Estimated value} \\ \text{of debt}_T}}{\text{Shares outstanding}_T}$$

Assume that the total value of Infomatics' operations and investments, which is $250 million immediately after issuing the bonds with warrants, is expected to grow at 9% per year. When the warrants are due to expire in 10 years, the total value of Infomatics is expected to be $250(1.09)^{10}$ = $591.841 million.

Infomatics will receive $22 per warrant when exercised; with 1 million warrants, this creates a $22 million cash flow to Infomatics. The total value of Infomatics will be equal to the value of operations plus the value of this cash. This will make the total value of Infomatics equal to $591.84 + $22 = $613.841 million.

When the warrants expire, the bonds will have 10 more years remaining until maturity with a fixed coupon payment of $80. If the expected market interest rate is still 10%, then the time line of cash flows will be:

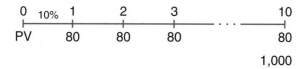

Using a financial calculator, input N = 10, I/YR = 10, PMT = 80, and FV = 1000; then press the PV key to obtain the bond's value, $877.11. The total value of all of the bonds is therefore expected to be 50,000($877.11) = $43.856 million.

The intrinsic value of equity is equal to the total value of the firm minus the value of debt: $613.841 − $43.856 = $569.985 million.

---

7. For an exact solution, see P. Daves and M. Ehrhardt, "Convertible Securities, Employee Stock Options, and the Cost of Equity," *The Financial Review,* Vol. 42, 2007, pp. 267–288.

TABLE 20-1	Valuation Analysis after Exercise of Warrants in 10 Years (Millions of Dollars, Except for Per Share
	Warrants Are Exercised
Expected value of operations and investments[a]	$591.841
Plus new cash from exercise of warrants[b]	22.000
Total value of firm	$613.841
Minus value of bonds	43.856
Value remaining for shareholders	$569.985
Divided by shares outstanding[c]	11
Price per share	$ 51.82

[a]The value of operations and investments is expected to grow from its current $250 million at a rate of 9%: $250(1.09)^{10} = $591.841 million.
[b]The warrants will be exercised only if the stock price at expiration is above $22. If the stock price is less than $22, then the warrants will expire worthless and there will be no new capital. Our calculations show that the expected stock price is much greater than $22, so the warrants are expected to be exercised.
[c]Before the warrants are exercised, there are 10 million shares of stock. After the warrants are exercised, there will be 10 + 1 = 11 million shares outstanding.

Infomatics had 10 million shares outstanding prior to the warrants' exercise, so it will have 11 million after the 1 million options are exercised. The predicted intrinsic stock price is equal to the intrinsic value of equity divided by the number of shares: $569.985/11 = $51.82 per share.[8] These calculations are summarized in Table 20-1.

To find the component cost of the warrants, consider that Infomatics will have to issue one share of stock worth $51.82 for each warrant exercised and, in return, Infomatics will receive the strike price from the warrant holder, $22. Thus, a purchaser of the bonds with warrants, if she holds the complete package, would expect to realize a profit in Year 10 of $51.82 − $22 = $29.82 for each warrant exercised.[9] Because each bond has 20 warrants attached and because each warrant entitles the holder to buy one share of common stock, it follows that warrant holders will have an expected cash flow of 20($29.82) = $596.40 per bond at the end of Year 10. Here is a time line of the expected cash flow stream to a warrant holder:

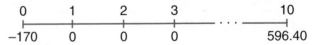

0	1	2	3	10
−170	0	0	0	596.40

8. If the stock price had been less than the strike price of $22 at expiration, then the warrants would not have been exercised. Based on the expected growth in the firm's value, there is little chance that the stock price will not be greater than $22.

9. It is not strictly accurate to say that the expected profit from the warrant position is the expected stock price less the strike price: $29.82 = $51.82 − $22. This is because if the stock price drops below the strike price, in this case $22, then the warrant profit is $0, regardless of how low the stock price goes. Thus, the expected payoff will be somewhat more than $29.82. Although this expectation can be calculated using options techniques similar to those in Chapter 5, it is beyond the scope of this chapter. However, if there is a very small probability that the stock price will drop below the exercise price, then $29.82 is very close to the true expected payoff.

The IRR of this stream is 13.35%, which is an approximation of the warrant holder's expected return on the warrants (r_w) in the bond with warrants. The overall pre-tax cost of capital for the bonds with warrants is the weighted average of the cost of straight debt and the cost of warrants:

$$\text{Pre-tax cost of bonds with warrants} = r_d(\$830/\$1,000) + r_w(\$170/\$1,000)$$
$$= 10\%(0.83) + 13.35\%(0.17) = 10.57\%$$

The cost of the warrants is higher than the cost of debt because warrants are riskier than debt; in fact, the cost of warrants is greater than the cost of equity because warrants also are riskier than equity. Thus, the cost of capital for a bond with warrants is somewhere between the cost of debt and the much higher cost of equity. This means the overall cost of capital for the bonds with warrants will be greater than the cost of straight debt and will be much higher than the 8% coupon rate on the bonds-with-warrants package.[10]

Bonds with warrants and preferred stock with warrants have become an important source of funding for companies during the global economic crisis. But as our example shows, this form of financing has a much higher cost of capital than its low coupon and preferred dividend might lead you to think.[11]

SELF TEST

What is a warrant?

Describe how a new bond issue with warrants is valued.

How are warrants used in corporate financing?

The use of warrants lowers the coupon rate on the corresponding debt issue. Does this mean that the component cost of a debt-plus-warrants package is less than the cost of straight debt? Explain.

Shanton Corporation could issue 15-year straight debt at a rate of 8%. Instead, Shanton issues 15-year debt with a coupon rate of 6%, but each bond has 25 warrants attached. The bonds can be issued at par ($1,000 per bond). Assuming annual interest payments, what is the implied value of each warrant? **($6.85)**

---

10. In order to estimate the after-tax cost of capital, the after-tax cost of each component must be estimated. The after-tax cost of the warrant is the same as the pre-tax cost because warrants do not affect the issuer's tax liability. This is not true for the bond component. *Web Extension 4A* on the textbook's Web site shows that the after-tax cost of debt when the bond is issued at a price less than par is equal to the yield on that debt multiplied by 1–T, just like when the bond is issued at par. Thus the after-tax cost of Infomatics' bond component is 10%(1 − 0.40) = 6%, assuming a 40% tax rate. We also show this calculation as well as the complete after-tax cost of capital calculation for the bonds with warrants attached in the *Ch20 Tool Kit.xlsx*.

11. For more on warrant pricing, see Michael C. Ehrhardt and Ronald E. Shrieves, "The Impact of Warrants and Convertible Securities on the Systematic Risk of Common Equity," *Financial Review*, November 1995, pp. 843–856; Beni Lauterbach and Paul Schultz, "Pricing Warrants: An Empirical Study of the Black-Scholes Model and Its Alternatives," *Journal of Finance,* September 1990, pp. 1181–1209; David C. Leonard and Michael E. Solt, "On Using the Black-Scholes Model to Value Warrants," *Journal of Financial Research*, Summer 1990, pp. 81–92; and Katherine L. Phelps, William T. Moore, and Rodney L. Roenfeldt, "Equity Valuation Effects of Warrant-Debt Financing," *Journal of Financial Research*, Summer 1991, pp. 93–103.

20-3 **Convertible Securities**

Convertible securities are bonds or preferred stocks that, under specified terms and conditions, can be exchanged for (that is, converted into) common stock at the option of the holder. Unlike the exercise of warrants, which brings in additional funds to the firm, conversion does not provide new capital; debt (or preferred stock) is simply replaced on the balance sheet by common stock. Of course, reducing the debt or preferred stock will improve the firm's financial strength and make it easier to raise additional capital, but that requires a separate action.

20-3a **Conversion Ratio and Conversion Price**

See **Ch20 Tool Kit.xls** on the textbook's Web site for details.

The **conversion ratio (CR)** is defined as the number of shares of stock a bond-holder will receive upon conversion. The **conversion price (P_c)** is defined as the effective price investors pay for the common stock when conversion occurs. The relationship between the conversion ratio and the conversion price can be illustrated by Silicon Valley Software Company's convertible debentures issued at their $1,000 par value in July of 2015. At any time prior to maturity on July 15, 2035, a debenture holder can exchange a bond for 18 shares of common stock. Therefore, the conversion ratio, CR, is 18. The bond cost a purchaser $1,000, the par value, when it was issued. Dividing the $1,000 par value by the 18 shares received gives a conversion price of $55.56 a share:

(20–2)

$$\text{Conversion price } = P_c = \frac{\text{Par value of bond given up}}{\text{Shares received}}$$

$$= \frac{\$1,000}{\text{CR}} = \frac{\$1,000}{18} = \$55.56$$

Conversely, by solving for CR, we obtain the conversion ratio:

(20–3)

$$\text{Conversion ratio } = \text{CR} = \frac{\$1,000}{P_c}$$

$$= \frac{\$1,000}{\$55.56} = 18 \text{ Shares}$$

Once CR is set, the value of P_c is established, and vice versa.

Like a warrant's exercise price, the conversion price is typically set some 20% to 30% above the prevailing market price of the common stock on the issue date. Generally, the conversion price and conversion ratio are fixed for the life of the bond, with the exception of protection against dilutive actions the company might take, including stock splits, stock dividends, and the sale of common stock at prices below the conversion price.[12]

---

12. Some convertible bonds have a stepped-up conversion price. For example, a convertible bond might be convertible into 12 shares for the first 10 years, into 11 shares for the next 10, and 10 shares for the remainder of its life. This has the effect of increasing the conversion price over time, so that the holder of a convertible bond won't get rewarded if the stock price grows slowly.

The typical protective provision states that if the stock is split or if a stock dividend is declared, the conversion price must be lowered by the percentage amount of the stock dividend or split. For example, if Silicon Valley Software (SVS) were to have a 2-for-1 stock split, then the conversion ratio would automatically be adjusted from 18 to 36 and the conversion price lowered from $55.56 to $27.73. Also, if SVS sells common stock at a price below the conversion price, then the conversion price must be lowered (and the conversion ratio raised) to the price at which the new stock is issued. If protection were not contained in the contract, then a company could always prevent conversion by the use of stock splits and stock dividends. Warrants have similar protection against dilution.

However, this standard protection against dilution from selling new stock at prices below the conversion price can get a company into trouble. For example, SVS's stock was selling for $35 per share at the time the convertible was issued. Now suppose that the market went sour and the stock price dropped to $15 per share. If SVS needs new equity to support operations, a new common stock sale would require the company to lower the conversion price on the convertible debentures from $55.56 to $15. What impact would this have on the existing shareholders?

First, think about the value of a convertible bond as consisting of a straight bond and an option to convert. Reducing the conversion price is like reducing the strike price on an option, which would make the option to convert much more valuable. Second, recall the approach taken by the free cash flow valuation model to determine the value of equity—start with the value of operations, add the value of any nonoperating assets (like T-bills), and subtract the value of any debt, including convertible bonds. We can estimate the value of equity at the original conversion price and compare it to the value of equity at the new conversion price. At the new conversion price, the value of the convertible bond goes up, so the value of equity goes down, causing a transfer of wealth from the existing shareholders to the convertible bondholders. Therefore, the protective reset feature on the conversion price makes it very costly for existing shareholders to raise additional equity in the times when new equity is needed.

20-3b **The Component Cost of Convertibles**

See **Ch20 Tool Kit.xls** on the textbook's Web site for details.

In the spring of 2015, Silicon Valley Software was evaluating the use of the convertible bond issue described earlier. The issue would consist of 20-year convertible bonds that would sell at a price of $1,000 per bond; this $1,000 would also be the bond's par (and maturity) value. The bonds would pay an 8% annual coupon interest rate, which is $80 per year. Each bond would be convertible into 18 shares of stock, so the conversion price would be $1,000/18 = $55.56. Its stock price was $35. If the bonds were not made convertible then they would have to provide a yield of 10%, given their risk and the general level of interest rates. The convertible bonds would not be callable for 10 years, after which they could be called at a price of $1,050, with this price declining by $5 per year thereafter. If, after 10 years, the conversion value exceeded the call price by at least 20%, management would probably call the bonds.

For a more detailed discussion of call strategies, see **Web Extension 20A** on the textbook's Web site.

SVS's cost of equity is 13%, with a 4% dividend yield and expected capital gain of 9% per year (Silicon Valley Software is a high-risk company with low dividends and occasional stock repurchases, so its stock price has a high expected growth rate).

Figure 20-1 shows the expectations of both an average investor and the company. Refer to the figure as you consider the following points:

1. The horizontal dashed line at $1,000 represents the par (and maturity) value. Also, $1,000 is the price at which the bond is initially offered to the public.
2. The bond is protected against a call for 10 years. It is initially callable at a price of $1,050; the call price declines thereafter by $5 per year, as shown by the pink line in Figure 20-1.
3. Because the convertible has an 8% coupon rate and because the yield on a non-convertible bond of similar risk is 10%, it follows that the expected "straight-bond" value of the convertible, B_t, must be less than par. At the time of issue and assuming an annual coupon, B_0 is $830:

FIGURE 20-1   Silicon Valley Software: Convertible Bond Model

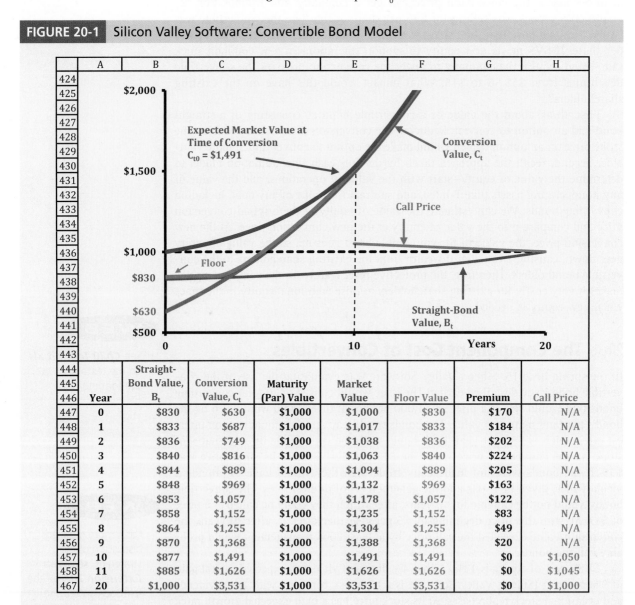

Year	Straight-Bond Value, B_t	Conversion Value, C_t	Maturity (Par) Value	Market Value	Floor Value	Premium	Call Price
0	$830	$630	$1,000	$1,000	$830	$170	N/A
1	$833	$687	$1,000	$1,017	$833	$184	N/A
2	$836	$749	$1,000	$1,038	$836	$202	N/A
3	$840	$816	$1,000	$1,063	$840	$224	N/A
4	$844	$889	$1,000	$1,094	$889	$205	N/A
5	$848	$969	$1,000	$1,132	$969	$163	N/A
6	$853	$1,057	$1,000	$1,178	$1,057	$122	N/A
7	$858	$1,152	$1,000	$1,235	$1,152	$83	N/A
8	$864	$1,255	$1,000	$1,304	$1,255	$49	N/A
9	$870	$1,368	$1,000	$1,388	$1,368	$20	N/A
10	$877	$1,491	$1,000	$1,491	$1,491	$0	$1,050
11	$885	$1,626	$1,000	$1,626	$1,626	$0	$1,045
20	$1,000	$3,531	$1,000	$3,531	$3,531	$0	$1,000

$$\text{Straight-debt value} = B_0 = \sum_{t=1}^{N} \frac{\text{Coupon interest}}{(1 + r_d)^t} + \frac{\text{Maturity value}}{(1 + r_d)^N} \qquad \textbf{(20–4)}$$

$$= \sum_{t=1}^{20} \frac{\$80}{(1.10)^t} + \frac{\$1,000}{(1.10)^{20}} = \$830$$

Note, however, that the bond's straight-debt value must be $1,000 at maturity, so the straight-debt value rises over time; this is plotted by the brown line in Figure 20-1.

4. The bond's initial **conversion value, C,** or the value of the stock an investor would receive if the bonds were converted at t = 0, is $P_0(CR) = \$35(18\text{ shares}) = \$630$. Because the stock price is expected to grow at a 9% rate, the conversion value should rise over time. For example, in Year 5 it should be $P_5(CR) = \$35(1.09)^5(18) = \$969$. The expected conversion value is shown by the green line in Figure 20-1.

5. If the market price dropped below the straight-bond value, then those who wanted bonds would recognize the bargain and buy the convertible as a bond. Similarly, if the market price dropped below the conversion value, people would buy the convertibles, exercise them to get stock, and then sell the stock at a profit. Therefore, the higher of the bond value and conversion value curves in the graph represents a *floor price* for the bond. In Figure 20-1, the floor price is represented by the red line.

6. The convertible bond's market price will exceed the straight-bond value because the option to convert is worth something—an 8% bond with conversion possibilities is worth more than an 8% bond without this option. The convertible's price will also exceed its conversion value because holding the convertible is equivalent to holding a call option and, prior to expiration, the option's true value is higher than its exercise (or conversion) value. Without using financial engineering models, we cannot say exactly where the market value line will lie, but as a rule it will be above the floor, as shown by the blue line in Figure 20-1.

7. If the stock price continues to increase, then it becomes more and more likely that the bond will be converted. As this likelihood increases, the market value line will begin to converge with the conversion value line.

After the bond becomes callable, its market value cannot exceed the higher of the conversion value and the call price without exposing investors to the danger of a call. For example, suppose that 10 years after issue (when the bonds become callable) the market value of the bond is $1,600, the conversion value is $1,500, and the call price is $1,050. If the company called the bonds the day after you bought one for $1,600, you would choose to convert them to stock worth only $1,500 (rather than let the company buy the bond from you at the $1,050 call price), so you would suffer a loss of $100. Recognizing this danger, you and other investors would refuse to pay a premium over the higher of the call price or the conversion value after the bond becomes callable. Therefore, in Figure 20-1, we assume that the market value line hits the conversion value line in Year 10, when the bond becomes callable.

8. In our example, the call-protection period ends in 10 years. At this time, the expected stock price is so high that the conversion value is almost certainly going to be greater than the call price; hence, we assume that the bond will be converted immediately prior to the company calling the bond, which would happen in 10 years.

9. The expected market value at Year 10 is $35(1.09)^{10}(18) = \$1,491$. An investor can find the expected rate of return on the convertible bond, r_c, by finding the IRR of the following cash flow stream:

With a financial calculator, we set N = 10, PV = −1000, PMT = 80, and FV = 1491; we then solve for I/YR = r_c = IRR = 10.94%.[13]

10. A convertible bond is riskier than straight debt but less risky than stock, so its cost of capital should be somewhere between the cost of straight debt and the cost of equity. This is true in our example: r_d = 10%, r_c = 10.94%, and r_s = 13%.[14]

20-3c **Use of Convertibles in Financing**

Convertibles have two important advantages from the issuer's standpoint: (1) Convertibles, like bonds with warrants, offer a company the chance to sell debt with a low coupon rate in exchange for giving bondholders a chance to participate in the company's success if it does well. (2) In a sense, convertibles provide a way to sell common stock at prices higher than those currently prevailing. Some companies actually want to sell common stock, not debt, but feel that the price of their stock is temporarily depressed. Management may know, for example, that earnings are depressed because of start-up costs associated with a new project, but they expect

---

13. As in the case with warrants, the expected conversion value is not precisely equal to the expected stock price multiplied by the conversion ratio. Here is the reason: If after 10 years the stock price happens to be low, so that the conversion value is less than the call price, then the bondholders would not choose to convert—instead, they would surrender their bonds if the company called them. In this example, conversion does not occur if the stock price is less than $1,050/18 = \$58.33$ after 10 years. Because the company makes a call in order to force conversion, it won't call the bonds if the stock price is less than $58.33. So when the stock price is low, the bondholders will keep the bonds, whose value will depend primarily on interest rates at that time. Finding the expected value in this situation is a difficult problem (and is beyond the scope of this text). However, if the expected stock price is much greater than the conversion price when the bonds are called (in this case, $35[1.09]^{10} = \$82.86$ is much more than $58.33), then the difference between the true expected conversion value and the conversion value that we calculated using the expected stock price will be very small. Therefore, we can approximate the component cost reasonably accurately with the approach used in the example.

14. To find the after-tax cost of the convertible, you can replace the pre-tax coupons with the after-tax coupons paid by the company. If the corporate tax rate is 40%, then we have N = 10, PV = −1000, PMT = 80(1 − 0.40) = 48, and FV = 1491; we solve for I/YR = $r_{c,AT}$ = 8.16%. Notice that this after-tax cost is not equal to $r_c(1 − T)$. Note also that this tax treatment is different from that of bonds with warrants as discussed earlier in this chapter. The company receives no tax benefits from the conversion feature in convertible bonds.

earnings to rise sharply during the next year or so, pulling the price of the stock up with them. Thus, if the company sold stock now, it would be giving up more shares than necessary to raise a given amount of capital. However, if it set the conversion price 20% to 30% above the present market price of the stock, then 20% to 30% fewer shares would be given up when the bonds were converted than if stock were sold directly at the current time. Note, however, that management is counting on the stock's price to rise above the conversion price, thus making the bonds attractive in conversion. If earnings do not rise and pull the stock price up, so that conversion does *not* occur, then the company will be saddled with debt in the face of low earnings, which could be disastrous. How can the company be sure that conversion will occur if the price of the stock rises above the conversion price? Typically, convertibles contain a call provision that enables the issuing firm to force holders to convert. Suppose the conversion price is $50, the conversion ratio is 20, the market price of the common stock has risen to $60, and the call price on a convertible bond is $1,050. If the company calls the bond, bondholders can either convert into common stock with a market value of 20($60) = $1,200 or allow the company to redeem the bond for $1,050. Naturally, bondholders prefer $1,200 to $1,050, so conversion would occur. The call provision thus gives the company a way to force conversion, provided the market price of the stock is greater than the conversion price. Note, however, that most convertibles have a fairly long period of call protection—10 years is typical. Therefore, if the company wants to be able to force conversion early, it will have to set a short call-protection period. This will, in turn, require that it set a higher coupon rate or a lower conversion price.

From the standpoint of the issuer, convertibles have three important disadvantages: (1) Even though the use of a convertible bond may give the company the opportunity to sell stock at a price higher than the current price, if the stock greatly increases in price then, the firm would be better off if it had used straight debt (in spite of its higher cost) and then later sold common stock and refunded the debt. (2) Convertibles typically have a low coupon interest rate, and the advantage of this low-cost debt will be lost when conversion occurs. (3) If the company truly wants to raise equity capital and if the price of the stock does not rise sufficiently after the bond is issued, then the company will be stuck with debt.

20-3d **Convertibles and Agency Costs**

A potential agency conflict between bondholders and stockholders is asset substitution, also known as "bait and switch." Suppose a company has been investing in low-risk projects, and because risk is low, bondholders charge a low interest rate. What happens if the company is considering a very risky but highly profitable venture that potential lenders don't know about? The company might decide to raise low-interest-rate debt without revealing that the funds will be invested in a risky project. After the funds have been raised and the investment is made, the value of the debt should fall because its interest rate will be too low to compensate debtholders for the high risk they bear. This is a "heads I win, tails you lose" situation, and it results in a wealth transfer from bondholders to stockholders.

Let's use some numbers to illustrate this scenario. The value of a company, based on the present value of its future free cash flows, is $800 million. It has $300 million of debt, based on market values. Therefore, its equity is worth $800 − $300 = $500 million. The company now undertakes some projects with high but risky expected returns, and its expected NPV remains unchanged. In other words, the actual NPV will probably end up much higher or much lower than under the old situation, but the firm still has the same expected value. Even though its total value is still $800 million, the value of the debt falls because its risk has increased. Note that the debtholders don't benefit if the venture's value is higher than expected, because the most they can receive is the contracted coupon and the principal repayment. However, they will suffer if the value of the projects turns out to be lower than expected, because they might not receive the full value of their contracted payments. In other words, risk doesn't give them any upside potential but does expose them to downside losses, so the bondholders' expected value must decline.

With a constant total firm value, if the value of the debt falls from $300 to $200 million, then the value of equity must increase from $500 to $800 − $200 = $600 million. Thus, the bait-and-switch tactic causes a wealth transfer of $100 million from debtholders to stockholders.

If debtholders think a company might employ the bait-and-switch tactic, they will charge a higher interest rate, and this higher interest rate is an agency cost. Debtholders will charge this higher rate even if the company has no intention of engaging in bait-and-switch behavior, because they can't know the company's true intentions. Therefore, they assume the worst and charge a higher interest rate.

Convertible securities are one way to mitigate this type of agency cost. Suppose the debt is convertible and the company does take on the high-risk project. If the value of the company turns out to be higher than expected, then bondholders can convert their debt to equity and benefit from the successful investment. Therefore, bondholders are willing to charge a lower interest rate on convertibles, and this serves to minimize the agency costs.

Note that if a company does not engage in bait-and-switch behavior by swapping low-risk projects for high-risk projects, then the chance of "hitting a home run" is reduced. Because there is less chance of a home run, the convertible bond is less likely to be converted. In this situation, the convertible bonds are actually similar to nonconvertible debt, except that they carry a lower interest rate.

Now consider a different agency cost, one due to asymmetric information between the managers and potential new stockholders. Suppose a firm's managers know that its future prospects are not as good as the market believes, which means the current stock price is too high. Acting in the interests of existing stockholders, managers can issue stock at the current high price. When the poor future prospects are eventually revealed, the stock price will fall, causing a transfer of wealth from the new shareholders to old shareholders.

To illustrate this, suppose the market estimates an $800 million present value of future free cash flows. For simplicity, assume the firm has no nonoperating assets and no debt, so the total value of both the firm and the equity is $800 million. However, its managers know the market has overestimated the future free cash flows and that the true value is only $700 million. When investors eventually discover this, the value of the company will drop to $700 million. But before this happens, suppose the company raises $200 million of new equity. The company uses this new cash to invest in projects with a present value of $200 million, which shouldn't be too hard, because these projects have a zero NPV. Right after the new stock is sold, the company will have a market value of $800 + $200 = $1,000 million, based on the market's overly optimistic estimate of the company's future prospects. Observe that the new shareholders own 20% of the company ($200/$1,000 = 0.20) and the original shareholders own 80%.

As time passes, the market will realize that the previously estimated value of $800 million for the company's original set of projects was too high and that these projects are worth only $700 million. The new projects are still worth $200 million, so the total value of the company will fall to $700 + $200 = $900 million. The original shareholders' value is now 80% of $900 million, which is $720 million. Note that this is $20 million *more* than it would have been if the company had issued no new stock. The new shareholders' value is now 0.20($900) = $180 million, which is $20 million *less* than their original investment. The net effect is a $20 million wealth transfer from the new shareholders to the original shareholders.

Because potential shareholders know this might occur, they interpret an issue of new stock as a signal of poor future prospects, which causes the stock price to fall. Note also that this will occur even for companies whose future prospects are actually quite good, because the market has no way of distinguishing between companies with good versus poor prospects.

A company with good future prospects might want to issue equity, but it knows the market will interpret this as a negative signal. One way to obtain equity and yet avoid this signaling effect is to issue convertible bonds. Because the company knows its true future prospects are better than the market anticipates, it knows the bonds will likely end up being converted to equity. Thus, a company in this situation is issuing equity "through the back door" when it issues convertible debt.

In summary, convertibles are logical securities to use in at least two situations. First, if a company would like to finance with straight debt but lenders are afraid the funds will be invested in a manner that increases the firm's risk profile, then convertibles are a good choice. Second, if a company wants to issue stock but thinks such a move would cause investors to interpret a stock offering as a signal of tough times ahead, then again convertibles would be a good choice.[15]

SELF TEST

What is a conversion ratio? A conversion price? A straight-bond value?

What is meant by a convertible's *floor value*?

What are the advantages and disadvantages of convertibles to issuers? To investors?

How do convertibles reduce agency costs?

A convertible bond has a par value of $1,000 and a conversion price of $25. The stock currently trades for $22 a share. What are the bond's conversion ratio and conversion value at t = 0? **(40, $880)**

---

15. See Craig M. Lewis, Richard J. Rogalski, and James K. Seward, "Understanding the Design of Convertible Debt," *Journal of Applied Corporate Finance*, Vol. 11, No. 1, Spring 1998, pp. 45–53. For more insights into convertible pricing and use, see Paul Asquith and David W. Mullins Jr., "Convertible Debt: Corporate Call Policy and Voluntary Conversion," *Journal of Finance*, September 1991, pp. 1273–1289; Randall S. Billingsley and David M. Smith, "Why Do Firms Issue Convertible Debt?" *Financial Management*, Summer 1996, pp. 93–99; Douglas R. Emery, Mai E. Iskandor-Datta, and Jong-Chul Rhim, "Capital Structure Management as a Motivation for Calling Convertible Debt," *Journal of Financial Research*, Spring 1994, pp. 91–104; T. Harikumar, P. Kadapakkam, and Ronald F. Singer, "Convertible Debt and Investment Incentives," *Journal of Financial Research*, Spring 1994, pp. 15–29; and V. Sivarama Krishnan and Ramesh P. Rao, "Financial Distress Costs and Delayed Calls of Convertible Bonds," *Financial Review*, November 1996, pp. 913–925.

20-4 **A Final Comparison of Warrants and Convertibles**

Convertible debt can be thought of as straight debt with nondetachable warrants. Thus, at first blush, it might appear that debt with warrants and convertible debt are more or less interchangeable. However, a closer look reveals one major and several minor differences between these two securities.[16] First, as we discussed previously, the exercise of warrants brings in new equity capital, whereas the conversion of convertibles results only in an accounting transfer.

A second difference involves flexibility. Most convertibles contain a call provision that allows the issuer either to refund the debt or to force conversion, depending on the relationship between the conversion value and call price. However, most warrants are not callable, so firms must wait until maturity for the warrants to generate new equity capital. Generally, maturities also differ between warrants and convertibles. Warrants typically have much shorter maturities than convertibles, and warrants typically expire before their accompanying debt matures. Warrants also provide for fewer future common shares than do convertibles, because with convertibles all of the debt is converted to stock, whereas debt remains outstanding when warrants are exercised. Together, these facts suggest that debt-plus-warrant issuers are actually more interested in selling debt than in selling equity.

In general, firms that issue debt with warrants are smaller and riskier than those that issue convertibles. One possible rationale for the use of option securities, especially the use of debt with warrants by small firms, is the difficulty investors have in assessing the risk of small companies. If a start-up with a new, untested product seeks debt financing, then it's difficult for potential lenders to judge the riskiness of the venture and so it's difficult to set a fair interest rate. Under these circumstances, many potential investors will be reluctant to invest, making it necessary to set a very high interest rate to attract debt capital. By issuing debt with warrants, investors obtain a package that offers upside potential to offset the risks of loss.

Finally, there is a significant difference in issuance costs between debt with warrants and convertible debt. Bonds with warrants typically require issuance costs that are about 1.2 percentage points more than the flotation costs for convertibles. In general, bond-with-warrant financings have underwriting fees that approximate the weighted average of the fees associated with debt and equity issues, whereas underwriting costs for convertibles are more like those associated with straight debt.

SELF TEST

What are some differences between debt-with-warrant financing and convertible debt?

Explain how bonds with warrants might help small, risky firms sell debt securities.

16. For a more detailed comparison of warrants and convertibles, see Michael S. Long and Stephen F. Sefcik, "Participation Financing: A Comparison of the Characteristics of Convertible Debt and Straight Bonds Issued in Conjunction with Warrants," *Financial Management*, Autumn 1990, pp. 23–34.

20-5 Reporting Earnings When Warrants or Convertibles Are Outstanding

If warrants or convertibles are outstanding, the Financial Accounting Standard Board requires that a firm report basic earnings per share and diluted earnings per share.[17]

1. *Basic* EPS is calculated as earnings available to common stockholders divided by the average number of shares actually outstanding during the period.
2. *Diluted* EPS is calculated as the earnings that would have been available to common shareholders divided by the average number of shares that would have been outstanding if "dilutive" securities had been converted. The rules governing the calculation of diluted EPS are quite complex; here we present a simple illustration using convertible bonds. If the bonds had been converted at the beginning of the accounting period, then the firm's interest payments would have been lower because it would not have had to pay interest on the bonds, and this would have caused earnings to be higher. But the number of outstanding shares of stock also would have increased because of the conversion. If the higher earnings and higher number of shares caused EPS to fall, then the convertible bonds would be defined as dilutive securities because their conversion would decrease (or dilute) EPS. All convertible securities with a net dilutive effect are included when calculating diluted EPS. Therefore, this definition means that diluted EPS always will be lower than basic EPS. In essence, the diluted EPS measure is an attempt to show how the presence of convertible securities reduces common shareholders' claims on the firm.

Under SEC rules, firms are required to report both basic and diluted EPS. For firms with large amounts of option securities outstanding, there can be a substantial difference between the basic and diluted EPS figures. This makes it easier for investors to compare the performance of U.S. firms with their foreign counterparts, which tend to use basic EPS.

> What are the three possible methods for reporting EPS when warrants and convertibles are outstanding?
>
> Which methods are most used in practice?
>
> Why should investors be concerned about a firm's outstanding warrants and convertibles?

SELF TEST

---

17. FAS 128 was issued in February of 1997. It simplified the calculations required by firms, made U.S. standards more consistent with international standards, and required the presentation of both basic EPS and diluted EPS for those firms with significant amounts of convertible securities. In addition, it replaced a measure called *primary EPS* with basic EPS. In general, the calculation of primary EPS required the company to estimate whether or not a security was "likely to be converted in the near future" and to base the calculation of EPS on the assumption that those securities would in fact have been converted. In June 2008 the FASB issued FSP APB 14-1, which (although not changing how EPS is reported under FAS 128) requires that convertibles be split into their implied equity and debt components for accounting purposes, in much the same way as we analyze them in this chapter.

Summary

Although common stock and long-term debt provide most of the capital used by corporations, companies also use several forms of "hybrid securities." The hybrids include preferred stock, convertibles, and warrants, and they generally have some characteristics of debt and some of equity. The key concepts covered are listed below.

- **Preferred stock** is a hybrid—it is similar to bonds in some respects and to common stock in other ways.
- **Adjustable rate preferred stocks (ARPs)** pay dividends tied to the rate on Treasury securities. **Market auction (money market) preferred stocks** are low-risk, largely tax-exempt securities of 7-week maturity that can be sold between auction dates at close to par.
- A **warrant** is a long-term call option issued along with a bond. Warrants are generally detachable from the bond, and they trade separately in the market. When warrants are exercised, the firm receives additional equity capital, and the original bonds remain outstanding.
- A **convertible** security is a bond or preferred stock that can be exchanged for common stock at the option of the holder. When a security is converted, debt or preferred stock is replaced with common stock, and no money changes hands.
- Warrant and convertible issues generally are structured so that the **strike price** (also called the **exercise price**) or **conversion price** is 20% to 30% above the stock's price at time of issue.
- Although both warrants and convertibles are option securities, there are several differences between the two, including separability, impact when exercised, callability, maturity, and flotation costs.
- Warrants and convertibles are **sweeteners** used to make the underlying debt or preferred stock issue more attractive to investors. Although the coupon rate or dividend yield is lower when options are part of the issue, the overall cost of the issue is higher than the cost of straight debt or preferred, because option-related securities are riskier.
- For a more detailed discussion of call strategies, see *Web Extension 20A* on the textbook's Web site.

Questions

20-1 Define each of the following terms:
   a. Preferred stock
   b. Cumulative dividends; arrearages
   c. Warrant; detachable warrant
   d. Stepped-up price
   e. Convertible security
   f. Conversion ratio; conversion price; conversion value
   g. Sweetener

20–2 Is preferred stock more like bonds or common stock? Explain.

20–3 What effect does the trend in stock prices (subsequent to issue) have on a firm's ability to raise funds through: (a) convertibles and (b) warrants?

20–4 If a firm expects to have additional financial requirements in the future, would you recommend that it use convertibles or bonds with warrants? What factors would influence your decision?

20–5 How does a firm's dividend policy affect each of the following?
a. The value of its long-term warrants
b. The likelihood that its convertible bonds will be converted
c. The likelihood that its warrants will be exercised

20–6 Evaluate the following statement: "Issuing convertible securities is a means by which a firm can sell common stock for more than the existing market price."

20–7 Suppose a company simultaneously issues $50 million of convertible bonds with a coupon rate of 10% and $50 million of straight bonds with a coupon rate of 14%. Both bonds have the same maturity. Does the convertible issue's lower coupon rate suggest that it is less risky than the straight bond? Is the cost of capital lower on the convertible than on the straight bond? Explain.

Problems   Answers Appear in Appendix B

Easy Problems 1–2

20–1 Warrants
Neubert Enterprises recently issued $1,000 par value 15-year bonds with a 5% coupon paid annually and warrants attached. These bonds are currently trading for $1,000. Neubert also has outstanding $1,000 par value 15-year straight debt with a 7% coupon paid annually, also trading for $1,000. What is the implied value of the warrants attached to each bond?

20–2 Convertibles
Breuer Investment's convertible bonds have a $1,000 par value and a conversion price of $50 a share. What is the convertible issue's conversion ratio?

Intermediate Problems 3–4

20–3 Warrants
Maese Industries Inc. has warrants outstanding that permit the holders to purchase 1 share of stock per warrant at a price of $25.
a. Calculate the exercise value of the firm's warrants if the common sells at each of the following prices: (1) $20, (2) $25, (3) $30, (4) $100. (*Hint*: A warrant's exercise value is the difference between the stock price and the purchase price specified by the warrant if the warrant were to be exercised.)

b. Assume the firm's stock now sells for $20 per share. The company wants to sell some 20-year, $1,000 par value bonds with interest paid annually. Each bond will have attached 50 warrants, each exercisable into 1 share of stock at an exercise price of $25. The firm's straight bonds yield 12%. Assume that each warrant will have a market value of $3 when the stock sells at $20. What coupon interest rate, and dollar coupon, must the company set on the bonds with warrants if they are to clear the market? (*Hint*: The convertible bond should have an initial price of $1,000.)

20-4 Convertible Premiums

The Tsetsekos Company was planning to finance an expansion. The principal executives of the company all agreed that an industrial company such as theirs should finance growth by means of common stock rather than by debt. However, they felt that the current $42 per share price of the company's common stock did not reflect its true worth, so they decided to sell a convertible security. They considered a convertible debenture but feared the burden of fixed interest charges if the common stock did not rise enough in price to make conversion attractive. They decided on an issue of convertible preferred stock, which would pay a dividend of $2.10 per share.

a. The conversion ratio will be 1.0; that is, each share of convertible preferred can be converted into a single share of common. Therefore, the convertible's par value (and also the issue price) will be equal to the conversion price, which in turn will be determined as a premium (i.e., the percentage by which the conversion price exceeds the stock price) over the current market price of the common stock. What will the conversion price be if it is set at a 10% premium? At a 30% premium?

b. Should the preferred stock include a call provision? Why or why not?

Challenging Problems 5–7

20-5 Convertible Bond Analysis

Fifteen years ago, Roop Industries sold $400 million of convertible bonds. The bonds had a 40-year maturity, a 5.75% coupon rate, and paid interest annually. They were sold at their $1,000 par value. The conversion price was set at $62.75, and the common stock price was $55 per share. The bonds were subordinated debentures and were given an A rating; straight non-convertible debentures of the same quality yielded about 8.75% at the time Roop's bonds were issued.

a. Calculate the premium on the bonds—that is, the percentage excess of the conversion price over the stock price at the time of issue.

b. What is Roop's annual before-tax interest savings on the convertible issue versus a straight-debt issue?

c. At the time the bonds were issued, what was the value per bond of the conversion feature?

d. Suppose the price of Roop's common stock fell from $55 on the day the bonds were issued to $32.75 now, 15 years after the issue date (also assume the stock price never exceeded $62.75). Assume interest rates remained constant. What is the current price of the straight-bond portion of the convertible bond? What is the current value if a bondholder converts a bond? Do you think it is likely that the bonds will be converted? Why or why not?

e. The bonds originally sold for $1,000. If interest rates on A-rated bonds had remained constant at 8.75% and if the stock price had fallen to $32.75, then what do you think would have happened to the price of the convertible bonds? (Assume no change in the standard deviation of stock returns.)

f. Now suppose that the price of Roop's common stock had fallen from $55 on the day the bonds were issued to $32.75 at present, 15 years after the issue. Suppose also that the interest rate on similar straight debt had fallen from 8.75% to 5.75%. Under these conditions, what is the current price of the straight-bond portion of the convertible bond? What is the current value if a bondholder converts a bond? What do you think would have happened to the price of the bonds?

20–6 Warrant/Convertible Decisions

The Howland Carpet Company has grown rapidly during the past 5 years. Recently, its commercial bank urged the company to consider increasing its permanent financing. Its bank loan under a line of credit has risen to $250,000, carrying an 8% interest rate. Howland has been 30 to 60 days late in paying trade creditors.

Discussions with an investment banker have resulted in the decision to raise $500,000 at this time. Investment bankers have assured the firm that the following alternatives are feasible (flotation costs will be ignored).

- *Alternative 1:* Sell common stock at $8.
- *Alternative 2:* Sell convertible bonds at an 8% coupon, convertible into 100 shares of common stock for each $1,000 bond (i.e., the conversion price is $10 per share).
- *Alternative 3:* Sell debentures at an 8% coupon, each $1,000 bond carrying 100 warrants to buy common stock at $10.

John L. Howland, the president, owns 80% of the common stock and wishes to maintain control of the company. There are 100,000 shares outstanding. The following are extracts of Howland's latest financial statements:

Balance Sheet

	Current liabilities	$400,000
	Common stock, par $1	100,000
	Retained earnings	50,000
Total assets	$550,000	Total claims	$ 550,000

Income Statement	
Sales	$1,100,000
All costs except interest	990,000
EBIT	$ 110,000
Interest	20,000
Pre-tax earnings	$ 90,000
Taxes (40%)	36,000
Net income	$ 54,000
Shares outstanding	100,000
Earnings per share	$0.54
Price/earnings ratio	15.83
Market price of stock	$8.55

a. Show the new balance sheet under each alternative. For Alternatives 2 and 3, show the balance sheet after conversion of the bonds or exercise of the warrants. Assume that half of the funds raised will be used to pay off the bank loan and half to increase total assets.
b. Show Mr. Howland's control position under each alternative, assuming that he does not purchase additional shares.
c. What is the effect on earnings per share of each alternative, assuming that profits before interest and taxes will be 20% of total assets?
d. What will be the debt ratio (TL/TA) under each alternative?
e. Which of the three alternatives would you recommend to Howland, and why?

20-7 Convertible Bond Analysis

Niendorf Incorporated needs to raise $25 million to construct production facilities for a new type of USB memory device. The firm's straight non-convertible debentures currently yield 9%. Its stock sells for $23 per share, has an expected constant growth rate of 6%, and has an expected dividend yield of 7%, for a total expected return on equity of 13%. Investment bankers have tentatively proposed that the firm raise the $25 million by issuing convertible debentures. These convertibles would have a $1,000 par value, carry a coupon rate of 8%, have a 20-year maturity, and be convertible into 35 shares of stock. Coupon payments would be made annually. The bonds would be noncallable for 5 years, after which they would be callable at a price of $1,075; this call price would decline by $5 per year in Year 6 and each year thereafter. For simplicity, assume that the bonds may be called or converted only at the end of a year, immediately after the coupon and dividend payments. Also assume that management would call eligible bonds if the conversion value exceeded 20% of par value (not 20% of call price).

a. At what year do you expect the bonds will be forced into conversion with a call? What is the bond's value in conversion when it is converted at this time? What is the cash flow to the bondholder when it is converted at this time? (*Hint:* The cash flow includes the conversion value and the coupon payment, because the conversion occurs immediately after the coupon is paid.)

b. What is the expected rate of return (i.e., the before-tax component cost) on the proposed convertible issue?

Spreadsheet Problem

20–8 Build a Model: Convertible Bond Analysis

Start with the partial model in the file *Ch20 P08 Build a Model.xls* on the textbook's Web site. Maggie's Magazines (MM) has straight nonconvertible bonds that currently yield 9%. MM's stock sells for $22 per share, has an expected constant growth rate of 6%, and has a dividend yield of 4%. MM plans on issuing convertible bonds that will have a $1,000 par value, a coupon rate of 8%, a 20-year maturity, and a conversion ratio of 32 (i.e., each bond could be convertible into 32 shares of stock). Coupon payments will be made annually. The bonds will be noncallable for 5 years, after which they will be callable at a price of $1,090; this call price would decline by $6 per year in Year 6 and each year thereafter. For simplicity, assume that the bonds may be called or converted only at the end of a year, immediately after the coupon and dividend payments. Management will call the bonds when their conversion value exceeds 25% of their par value (not their call price).

a. For each year, calculate: (1) the anticipated stock price, (2) the anticipated conversion value, (3) the anticipated straight-bond price, and (4) the cash flow to the investor assuming conversion occurs. At what year do you expect the bonds will be forced into conversion with a call? What is the bond's value in conversion when it is converted at this time? What is the cash flow to the bondholder when it is converted at this time? (*Hint:* The cash flow includes the conversion value and the coupon payment, because the conversion occurs immediately after the coupon is paid.)

b. What is the expected rate of return (i.e., the before-tax component cost) on the proposed convertible issue?

c. Assume that the convertible bondholders require a 9% rate of return. If the coupon rate remains unchanged, then what conversion ratio will give a bond price of $1,000?

MINI CASE

Paul Duncan, financial manager of EduSoft Inc., is facing a dilemma. The firm was founded 5 years ago to provide educational software for the rapidly expanding primary and secondary school markets. Although EduSoft has done well, the firm's founder believes an industry shakeout is imminent. To survive, EduSoft must grab market share now, and this will require a large infusion of new capital.

Because he expects earnings to continue rising sharply and looks for the stock price to follow suit, Mr. Duncan does not think it would be wise to issue new common stock at this time. On the other hand, interest rates are currently high by historical standards, and the firm's B rating means that interest payments on a new debt issue would be prohibitive. Thus, he has narrowed his choice of financing alternatives to: (1) preferred stock, (2) bonds with warrants, or (3) convertible bonds.

As Duncan's assistant, you have been asked to help in the decision process by answering the following questions.

a. How does preferred stock differ from both common equity and debt? Is preferred stock more risky than common stock? What is floating rate preferred stock?

b. How can knowledge of call options help a financial manager to better understand warrants and convertibles?

c. Mr. Duncan has decided to eliminate preferred stock as one of the alternatives and focus on the others. EduSoft's investment banker estimates that EduSoft could issue a bond-with-warrants package consisting of a 20-year bond and 27 warrants. Each warrant would have a strike price of $25 and 10 years until expiration. It is estimated that each warrant, when detached and traded separately, would have a value of $5. The coupon on a similar bond but without warrants would be 10%.

   (1) What coupon rate should be set on the bond with warrants if the total package is to sell at par ($1,000)?

   (2) When would you expect the warrants to be exercised? What is a stepped-up exercise price?

   (3) Will the warrants bring in additional capital when exercised? If EduSoft issues 100,000 bond-with-warrant packages, how much cash will EduSoft receive when the warrants are exercised? How many shares of stock will be outstanding after the warrants are exercised? (EduSoft currently has 20 million shares outstanding.)

   (4) Because the presence of warrants results in a lower coupon rate on the accompanying debt issue, shouldn't all debt be issued with warrants? To answer this, estimate the anticipated stock price in 10 years when the warrants are expected to be exercised, and then estimate the return to the holders of the bond-with-warrants packages. Use the corporate valuation model to estimate the expected stock price in 10 years. Assume that EduSoft's current value of operations is $500 million and it is expected to grow at 8% per year.

   (5) How would you expect the cost of the bond with warrants to compare with the cost of straight debt? With the cost of common stock (which is 13.4%)?

   (6) If the corporate tax rate is 40%, what is the after-tax cost of the bond with warrants?

d. As an alternative to the bond with warrants, Mr. Duncan is considering convertible bonds. The firm's investment bankers estimate that EduSoft could sell a 20-year, 8.5% coupon (paid annually), callable convertible bond for its $1,000 par value, whereas a straight-debt issue would require a 10% coupon (paid annually). The convertibles would be call protected for 5 years, the call price would be $1,100, and the company would probably call the bonds as soon as possible after their conversion value exceeds $1,200. Note, though, that the call must occur on an issue-date anniversary. EduSoft's current stock price is $20, its last dividend was $1, and the dividend is expected to grow at a constant 8% rate. The convertible could be converted into 40 shares of EduSoft stock at the owner's option.

   (1) What conversion price is built into the bond?

(2) What is the convertible's straight-debt value? What is the implied value of the convertibility feature?

(3) What is the formula for the bond's expected conversion value in any year? What is its conversion value at Year 0? At Year 10?

(4) What is meant by the "floor value" of a convertible? What is the convertible's expected floor value at Year 0? At Year 10?

(5) Assume that EduSoft intends to force conversion by calling the bond as soon as possible after its conversion value exceeds 20% above its par value, or 1.2($1,000) = $1,200. When is the issue expected to be called? (*Hint:* Recall that the call must be made on an anniversary date of the issue.)

(6) What is the expected cost of capital for the convertible to EduSoft? Does this cost appear to be consistent with the riskiness of the issue?

(7) What is the after-tax cost of the convertible bond?

e. Mr. Duncan believes that the costs of both the bond with warrants and the convertible bond are close enough to call them even and that the costs are consistent with the risks involved. Thus, he will make his decision based on other factors. What are some of the factors that he should consider?

f. How do convertible bonds help reduce agency costs?

SELECTED ADDITIONAL CASES

The following cases from CengageCompose cover many of the concepts discussed in this chapter and are available at http://compose.cengage.com.

Klein-Brigham Series:

Case 27, "Virginia May Chocolate Company," which illustrates convertible bond valuation, and Case 98, "Levinger Organic Snack," which illustrates the use of convertibles and warrants.

Working capital management involves two basic questions: (1) What is the appropriate amount of working capital, both in total and for each specific account, and (2) how should working capital be financed? Note that sound working capital management goes beyond finance. Indeed, improving the firm's working capital position generally comes from improvements in the operating divisions. For example, experts in logistics, operations management, and information technology often work with engineers and production specialists to develop ways to speed up the manufacturing process and thus reduce the goods-in-process inventory. Similarly, marketing managers and logistics experts cooperate to develop better ways to deliver the firm's products to customers. Finance comes into play in evaluating how effective the firm's operating departments are relative to other firms in its industry and also in evaluating the profitability of alternative proposals for improving working capital management. In addition, financial managers decide how much cash their companies should keep on hand and how much short-term financing should be used to finance their working capital.

Beginning-of-Chapter Questions

As you read this chapter, consider how you would answer the following questions. You *should not* necessarily be able to answer the questions before you read the chapter. Rather, you should use them to get a sense of the issues covered in the chapter. After reading the chapter, you should be able to give at least partial answers to the questions, and you should be able to give better answers after the chapter has been discussed in class. Note, too, that it is often useful, when answering conceptual questions, to use hypothetical data to illustrate your answer. We illustrate the answers with an *Excel* model that is available on the textbook's Web site. Accessing the model and working through it is a useful exercise, and it provides insights that are useful when answering the questions.

1. What is the **cash conversion cycle (CCC)**? Why is it better, other things held constant, to have a shorter rather than a longer CCC? Suppose you know a company's annual sales, average inventories, average accounts receivable, average accounts payable, and annual cost of goods sold. How could you use that information to determine the company's CCC? If you also knew its cost of capital, how could you determine its annual cost of carrying working capital? How could you determine how much the company would save if it could reduce the CCC by, say, 5 days? What are some actions it might take to reduce the CCC?

2. What is a **cash budget**, and how is this statement used by a business? How is the cash budget affected by the CCC? By credit policy?

3. Differentiate between **free** and **costly trade credit**. What is the formula for determining the **nominal annual cost rate** associated with a credit policy? What is the formula for the **effective annual cost rate**? How would these cost rates be affected if a firm buying on credit could "stretch" either the discount days or the net payment days— that is, take discounts on payments made after the discount period or else pay later than the stated payment date?

4. What are some advantages of **matching the maturities** of claims against assets with the lives of the assets financed by those claims? Is it feasible for a firm to match perfectly the maturities of all assets and claims against assets? Why might a firm deliberately mismatch some asset and claim maturities?

5. Define the terms **aggressive** and **conservative** when applied to financing, give examples of each, and then discuss the pros and cons of each approach. Would you expect to find entrenched firms in monopolistic (or oligopolistic) industries leaning more toward the aggressive or the conservative approach?

CORPORATE VALUATION AND WORKING CAPITAL MANAGEMENT

S uperior working capital management can dramatically reduce required investments in operating capital, which can lead, in turn, to larger free cash flows and greater firm value.

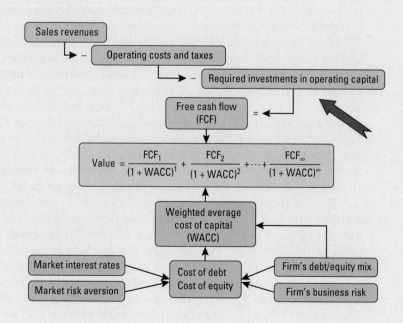

21-1 **Overview of Working Capital Management**

Consider some of the activities involved in a company's supply chain. The company places an order with a supplier. The supplier ships the order and bills the company. The company either pays immediately or waits, in which case the unpaid amount is called an account payable. The newly arrived shipment goes into inventory until it is needed. If the supplier shipped finished products, the company will distribute the goods to its warehouses or retail facilities. If instead the supplier shipped components or raw materials, the company will use the shipment in a manufacturing or assembly process, putting the final product into its finished goods inventory. Items from the finished goods inventory will be shipped either directly to customers or to warehouses for later shipments. When a customer purchases the product, the company bills the customer and often offers the customer credit. If the customer doesn't pay immediately, the unpaid balance is called an account receivable. During this process, the company has been accruing unpaid wages (because the company doesn't pay its employees daily) and unpaid taxes (because the company doesn't pay the IRS daily).

Several current assets and current liabilities are involved in this process—cash is spent (when paying suppliers, employees, taxes, etc.) and collected (when customers pay), accounts receivable are created and collected, inventory ebbs and flows, accounts payable are generated and paid, and accruals accumulate until paid. Notice that these are the same operating current assets (cash, accounts receivable, and inventories) and operating current liabilities (accounts payable and accruals) that are used in calculating **net operating working capital (NOWC)**, which is defined as operating current assets minus operating current liabilities.

In addition to operating current assets and operating current liabilities, there are two other current accounts related to working capital management: short-term investments and short-term debt. We discuss each current asset and liability later in the chapter, but it will be helpful if we first distinguish between cash and short-term investments because this can be a source of confusion.

Many dictionaries define cash as currency (coins and bills) and demand deposit accounts (such as a checking account at a bank). Most companies have very little currency on hand, and most have relatively small checking accounts. However, most companies own a wide variety of short-term financial assets. For example, Apple and Microsoft own: (1) checking accounts, (2) U.S. Treasury and agency securities, (3) certificates of deposits and time deposits, (4) commercial paper, (5) money market funds and other mutual funds (with low price volatility), (6) short-term or floating-rate corporate and municipal notes and bonds, and (7) and floating-rate preferred stock. Most of these holdings can be converted into cash very quickly at prices identical or very close to their book values, so sometimes they are called cash equivalents.

Some of these financial assets are held to support current ongoing operations and some are held for future purposes, and this is the distinction we make when defining cash and short-term investments. In particular, we define cash as the total value of the short-term financial assets that are held to support ongoing operations because this is the definition of cash that is required to be consistent with the definition of cash used to calculate NOWC (which is used, in turn, to calculated free cash flow and the intrinsic value of the company). We define short-term investments as the total value of short-term financial assets held for future purposes. Keep these distinctions in mind when we discuss cash management and short-term investments later in the chapter.

We normally use the term NOWC, but the term *working capital* is also used for slightly different purposes, so be aware of this when you see it in the financial press. For example, the financial press defines **working capital**, sometimes called *gross working capital*, as current assets used in operations.[1] The press also defines **net working capital** as all current assets minus all current liabilities. Of course, neither of these is equal to net operating working capital.

21-2 Using and Financing Operating Current Assets

Operating current assets (CA) are used to support sales. Having too much invested in operating CA is inefficient, but having too little might constrain sales. Many companies have seasonal, growing sales, so they have seasonal growing operating CA, which has an implication for the pattern of financing that companies choose. The next sections address these issues.

21-2a Efficient Use of Operating Current Assets

Most companies can influence their ratios of operating current assets to sales. Some companies choose a relaxed policy and hold a lot of cash, receivables, and inventories relative to sales. This is a **relaxed policy**. On the other hand, if a firm has a **restricted policy**, holdings of current assets are minimized and we say that the firm's policy is *tight* or *"lean-and-mean."* A **moderate policy** lies between the two extremes.

We can use the DuPont equation to demonstrate how working capital management affects the return on equity:

$$\text{ROE} = \text{Profit margin} \times \text{Total assets turnover} \times \text{Equity multiplier}$$
$$= \frac{\text{Net income}}{\text{Sales}} \times \frac{\text{Sales}}{\text{Assets}} \times \frac{\text{Assets}}{\text{Equity}}$$

A relaxed policy means a high level of assets and hence a low total assets turnover ratio; this results in a low ROE, other things held constant. Conversely, a restricted policy results in low current assets, a high turnover, and hence a relatively high ROE. However, the restricted policy exposes the firm to risk, because shortages can lead to work stoppages, unhappy customers, and serious long-run problems. The moderate policy falls between the two extremes. The optimal strategy is the one that management believes will maximize the firm's long-run free cash flow and thus the stock's intrinsic value.

Note that changing technologies can lead to changes in the optimal policy. For example, if a new technology makes it possible for a manufacturer to produce a given product in 5 rather than 10 days, then work-in-progress inventories can be cut in half. Similarly, most retailers have inventory management systems that use bar codes on all merchandise. These codes are read at the cash register; this information

---

1. The term "working capital" originated with the old Yankee peddler, who would load his wagon with pots and pans and then take off to peddle his wares. His horse and wagon were his fixed assets, while his merchandise was sold, or turned over at a profit, and thus was called his *working capital*.

is transmitted electronically to a computer that adjusts the remaining stock of the item; and the computer automatically places an order with the supplier's computer when the stock falls to a specified level. This process lowers the "safety stocks" that would otherwise be necessary to avoid running out of stock. Such systems have dramatically lowered inventories and thus boosted profits.

21-2b **Financing Operating Current Assets**

Investments in operating current assets must be financed, and the primary sources of funds include bank loans, credit from suppliers (accounts payable), accrued liabilities, long-term debt, and common equity. Each of those sources has advantages and disadvantages, so a firm must decide which sources are best for it.

To begin, note that most businesses experience seasonal and/or cyclical fluctuations. For example, construction firms tend to peak in the summer, retailers peak around Christmas, and the manufacturers who supply both construction companies and retailers follow related patterns. Similarly, the sales of virtually all businesses increase when the economy is strong, so they increase operating current assets during booms but let inventories and receivables fall during recessions. However, current assets rarely drop to zero—companies maintain some **permanent operating current assets**, which are the operating current assets needed even at the low point of the business cycle. For a growing firm in a growing economy, permanent current assets tend to increase over time. Also, as sales increase during a cyclical upswing, current assets are increased; these extra current assets are defined as **temporary operating current assets** as opposed to permanent current assets. The way permanent and temporary current assets are financed is called the firm's **operating current assets financing policy**. Three alternative policies are discussed next.

Maturity Matching Approach

The **maturity matching approach**, which is also called the **"self-liquidating approach"**, calls for matching asset and liability maturities as shown in Panel A of Figure 21-1. All of the fixed assets plus the permanent current assets are financed with long-term capital, but temporary current assets are financed with short-term debt. Inventory expected to be sold in 30 days would be financed with a 30-day bank loan; a machine expected to last for 5 years would be financed with a 5-year loan; a 20-year building would be financed with a 20-year mortgage bond; and so on. Actually, two factors prevent exact maturity matching, uncertain asset lives and equity financing. For example, a firm might finance inventories with a 30-day bank loan, expecting to sell the inventories and use the cash to retire the loan. But if sales are slow, then the "life" of the inventories would exceed the original 30-day estimate and the cash from sales would not be forthcoming, perhaps causing the firm problems in paying off the loan when it comes due. In addition, some common equity financing must be used, and common equity has no maturity. Still, if a firm attempts to match or come close to matching asset and liability maturities, this is defined as a *moderate current asset financing policy*.

Aggressive Approach

Panel B of Figure 21-1 illustrates the situation for a more aggressive firm that finances some of its permanent assets with short-term debt. Note that we used the term "relatively" in the title for Panel B because there can be different *degrees*

FIGURE 21-1	Alternative Operating Current Assets Financing Policies

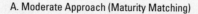

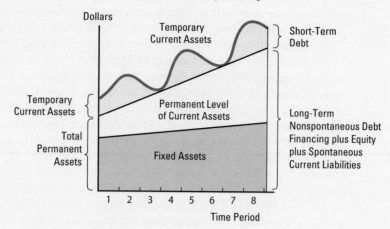

A. Moderate Approach (Maturity Matching)

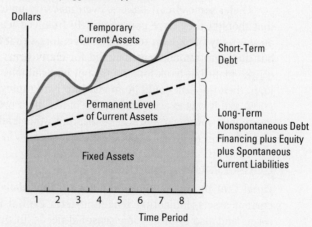

B. Relatively Aggressive Approach

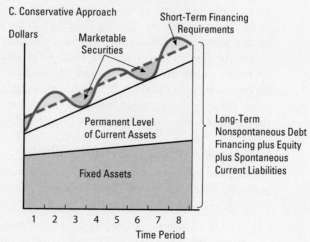

C. Conservative Approach

of aggressiveness. For example, the dashed line in Panel B could have been drawn *below* the line designating fixed assets, indicating that all of the current assets—both permanent and temporary—and part of the fixed assets were financed with short-term credit. This policy would be highly aggressive, and the firm would be subject to dangers from loan renewal as well as rising interest rates. However, short-term interest rates are generally lower than long-term rates, and some firms are willing to gamble by using a large amount of low-cost, short-term debt in hopes of earning higher profits.

A possible reason for adopting the aggressive policy is to take advantage of an upward sloping yield curve, for which short-term rates are lower than long-term rates. However, as many firms learned during the financial crisis of 2009, a strategy of financing long-term assets with short-term debt is really quite risky. As an illustration, suppose a company borrowed $1 million on a 1-year basis and used the funds to buy machinery that would lower labor costs by $200,000 per year for 10 years.[2] Cash flows from the equipment would not be sufficient to pay off the loan at the end of only 1 year, so the loan would have to be renewed. If the economy were in a recession like that of 2009, the lender might refuse to renew the loan, and that could lead to bankruptcy. Had the firm matched maturities and financed the equipment with a 10-year loan, then the annual loan payments would have been lower and better matched with the cash flows, and the loan renewal problem would not have arisen.

Under some circumstances, even maturity matching can be risky, as many firms that thought they were conservatively financed learned in 2009. If a firm borrowed on a 30-day bank loan to finance inventories that it expected to sell within 30 days but then sales dropped, as they did for many firms in 2009, the funds needed to pay off the maturing bank loan might not be available. If the bank would not extend the loan, then the firm could be forced into bankruptcy. This happened to many firms in 2009, and it was exacerbated by the banks' own problems. The banks lost billions on mortgages, mortgage-backed bonds, and other bad investments, which led them to restrict credit to their normal business customers in order to conserve their own cash.

Conservative Approach

Panel C of the figure shows the dashed line *above* the line designating permanent current assets, indicating that long-term capital is used to finance all permanent assets and also to meet some seasonal needs. In this situation, the firm uses a small amount of short-term credit to meet its peak requirements, but it also meets a part of its seasonal needs by "storing liquidity" in the form of marketable securities. The humps above the dashed line represent short-term financings, while the troughs below the dashed line represent short-term security holdings. This conservative financing policy is fairly safe, and the wisdom of using it was demonstrated in 2009—when credit dried up, firms with adequate cash holdings were able to operate more effectively than those that were forced to cut back their operations because they couldn't order new inventories or pay their normal workforce.

Choosing among the Approaches

Because the yield curve is normally upward sloping, *the cost of short-term debt is generally lower than that of long-term debt.* However, *short-term debt is riskier for*

---

2. We are oversimplifying here. Few lenders would explicitly lend money for 1 year to finance a 10-year asset. What would actually happen is that the firm would borrow on a 1-year basis for "general corporate purposes" and then actually use the money to purchase the 10-year machinery.

the borrowing firm for two reasons: (1) If a firm borrows on a long-term basis then its interest costs will be relatively stable over time, but if it uses short-term credit then its interest expense can fluctuate widely—perhaps reaching such high levels that profits are extinguished.[3] (2) If a firm borrows heavily on a short-term basis, then a temporary recession may adversely affect its financial ratios and render it unable to repay its debt. Recognizing this fact, the lender may not renew the loan if the borrower's financial position is weak, which could force the borrower into bankruptcy.

Note also that *short-term loans can generally be negotiated much faster* than long-term loans. Lenders need to make a thorough financial examination before extending long-term credit, and the loan agreement must be spelled out in great detail because a lot can happen during the life of a 10- to 20-year loan.

Finally, *short-term debt generally offers greater flexibility*. If the firm thinks that interest rates are abnormally high and due for a decline, it may prefer short-term credit because prepayment penalties are often attached to long-term debt. Also, if its needs for funds are seasonal or cyclical, then the firm may not want to commit itself to long-term debt because of its underwriting costs and possible prepayment penalties. Finally, long-term loan agreements generally contain provisions, or *covenants*, that constrain the firm's future actions in order to protect the lender, whereas short-term credit agreements generally have fewer restrictions.

All things considered, it is not possible to state that either long-term or short-term financing is generally better. The firm's specific conditions will affect its decision, as will the risk preferences of managers. Optimistic and/or aggressive managers will lean more toward short-term credit to gain an interest cost advantage, whereas more conservative managers will lean toward long-term financing to avoid potential renewal problems. The factors discussed here should be considered, but the final decision will reflect managers' personal preferences and subjective judgments.

SELF TEST

Identify and explain three alternative current asset investment policies.

Use the DuPont equation to show how working capital policy can affect a firm's expected ROE.

What are the reasons for not wanting to hold too little working capital? For not wanting to hold too much?

Differentiate between permanent operating current assets and temporary operating current assets.

What does maturity matching mean, and what is the logic behind this policy?

What are some advantages and disadvantages of short-term versus long-term debt?

---

3. The prime interest rate—the rate banks charge very good customers—hit 21% in the early 1980s. This produced a level of business bankruptcies that was not seen again until 2009. The primary reason for the very high interest rate was that the inflation rate was up to 13%, and high inflation must be compensated by high interest rates. Also, the Federal Reserve was tightening credit in order to hold down inflation, and it was encouraging banks to restrict their lending.

21-3 **The Cash Conversion Cycle**

All firms follow a "working capital cycle" in which they purchase or produce inventory, hold it for a time, and then sell it and receive cash. This process is known as the **cash conversion cycle (CCC)**.

21-3a **Calculating the Target CCC**

Assume that Great Basin Medical Equipment (GBM), a start-up business, buys orthopedic devices from a manufacturer in China and sells them through distributors in the United States, Canada, and Mexico. Its business plan calls for it to purchase $10,000,000 of merchandise at the start of each month and sell it within 50 days. The company will have 40 days to pay its suppliers, and it will give its customers 60 days to pay for their purchases. GBM expects to just break even during its first few years and so its monthly sales will be $10,000,000, the same as its purchases (or cost of goods sold). For simplicity, assume that there are no administrative costs. Also, any funds required to support operations will be obtained from the bank, and those loans must be repaid as soon as cash becomes available.

This information can be used to calculate GBM's target, or theoretical, cash conversion cycle, which "nets out" the three time periods described below.

1. **Inventory conversion period**. For GBM, this is the 50 days it expects to take to sell the equipment, converting it from equipment to accounts receivable.[4]
2. **Average collection period (ACP)**. This is the length of time customers are given to pay for goods following a sale. The ACP is also called the *days sales outstanding* (DSO). GBM's business plan calls for an ACP of 60 days based on its 60-day credit terms. This is also called the *receivables conversion period*, as it is supposed to take 60 days to collect and thus convert receivables to cash.
3. **Payables deferral period**. This is the length of time GBM's suppliers give it to pay for its purchases, which in our example is 40 days.

On Day 1, GBM expects to buy merchandise, and it expects to sell the goods and thus convert them to accounts receivable within 50 days. It should then take 60 days to collect the receivables, making a total of 110 days between receiving merchandise and collecting cash. However, GBM is able to defer its own payments for only 40 days.

We can combine these three periods to find the theoretical, or target, cash conversion cycle, shown below as an equation and diagrammed in Figure 21-2:

(21–1)

$$\begin{array}{ccccc} \text{Inventory} & \text{Average} & \text{Payables} & & \text{Cash} \\ \text{conversion} + \text{collection} - \text{deferral} & = & \text{conversion} \\ \text{period} & \text{period} & \text{period} & & \text{cycle} \end{array}$$

$$50 \quad + \quad 60 \quad - \quad 40 \quad = \quad 70 \text{ days}$$

Although GBM is supposed to pay its suppliers $10,000,000 after 40 days, it does not expect to receive any cash until $50 + 60 = 110$ days into the cycle. Therefore, it

---

4. If GBM were a manufacturer, the inventory conversion period would be the time required to convert raw materials into finished goods and then to sell those goods.

FIGURE 21-2	The Cash Conversion Cycle

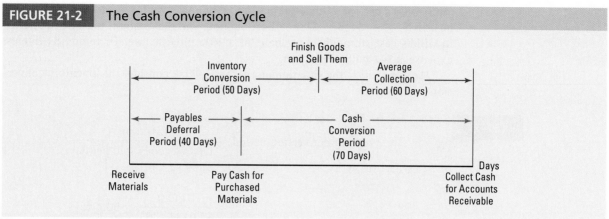

Microsoft Excel® is a registered trademark of Microsoft Corporation. © 2014 Microsoft.

will have to borrow the $10,000,000 cost of the merchandise from its bank on Day 40, and it does not expect to be able to repay the loan until it collects on Day 110. Thus, for 110 − 40 = 70 days–which is the theoretical cash conversion cycle (CCC)–it will owe the bank $10,000,000 and it will be paying interest on this debt. The shorter the cash conversion cycle the better, because a shorter CCC means lower interest charges.

Observe that if GBM could sell goods faster, collect receivables faster, or defer its payables longer without hurting sales or increasing operating costs, then its CCC would decline, its expected interest charges would be reduced, and its expected profits and stock price would increase.

21-3b Calculating the Actual CCC from Financial Statements

So far we have illustrated the CCC from a theoretical standpoint. However, in practice we would generally calculate the CCC based on the firm's financial statements, and the actual CCC would almost certainly differ from the theoretical value because of real-world complexities such as shipping delays, sales slowdowns, and slow-paying customers. Moreover, a firm such as GBM would be continually starting new cycles before the earlier ones ended, and this too would muddy the waters.

To see how the CCC is calculated in practice, assume that GBM has been in business for several years and is in a stable position, placing orders, making sales, receiving payments, and making its own payments on a recurring basis. The following data were taken from its latest financial statements:

Selected Items from GBM's Financial Statements (Millions of Dollars)	
Annual sales	$1,216.7
Cost of goods sold	1,013.9
Inventories	140.0
Accounts receivable	445.0
Accounts payable	115.0

Thus, GBM's net operating working capital due to inventory, receivables, and payables is $140 + $445 − $115 = $470 million, and that amount must be financed—in GBM's case, through bank loans at a 10% interest rate. Therefore, its interest expense is $47 million per year.

We can analyze the situation more closely. First, consider the inventory conversion period:

(21–2)

$$\text{Inventory conversion period} = \frac{\text{Inventory}}{\text{Cost of goods sold per day}}$$

$$= \frac{\$140.0}{\$1,013.9/365} = 50.4 \text{ days}$$

Thus, it takes GBM an average of 50.4 days to sell its merchandise, which is very close to the 50 days called for in the business plan. Note also that inventory is carried at cost, which explains why the denominator in Equation 21-2 is the cost of goods sold per day, not daily sales.

The average collection period (or days sales outstanding) is calculated next:

(21–3)

$$\text{Average collection period} = \text{ACP (or DSO)} = \frac{\text{Receivables}}{\text{Sales}/365}$$

$$= \frac{\$445.0}{\$1,216.7/365} = 133.5 \text{ days}$$

Thus, it takes GBM 133.5 days after a sale to receive cash, not the 60 days called for in its business plan. Because receivables are recorded at the sales price, we use daily sales (rather than the cost of goods sold per day) in the denominator for the ACP.

The payables deferral period is found as follows, again using daily cost of goods sold in the denominator because payables are recorded at cost:

(21–4)

$$\frac{\text{Payables}}{\text{deferral period}} = \frac{\text{Payables}}{\text{Purchases per day}} = \frac{\text{Payables}}{\text{Cost of goods sold}/365}$$

$$= \frac{\$115.0}{\$1,013.9/365} = 41.4 \text{ days}$$

GBM is supposed to pay its suppliers after 40 days, but it actually pays on average just after Day 41. This slight delay is normal, because mail delays and time for checks to be cashed generally slow payments down a bit.

We can now combine the three periods to calculate GBM's actual cash conversion cycle:

Cash conversion cycle (CCC) = 50.4 days + 133.5 days − 41.4 days = 142.5 days

Figure 21-3 summarizes all of these calculations and then analyzes why the actual CCC exceeds the theoretical CCC by such a large amount. It is clear from the

See **Ch21 Tool Kit.xls** on the textbook's Web site for details.

FIGURE 21-3	Summary of the Cash Conversion Cycle (Millions of Dollars)

	A	B	C	D	E	F	G
9	**Panel A. Target CCC: Based on Planned Conditions**						
10	**Cash Conversion Cycle (CCC)**	**=**	**Planned Inventory Conversion Period (ICP)**	**+**	**Credit Terms Offered to Our Customers**	**−**	**Credit Terms Our Supplier Offers Us**
11		**=**	50.0	**+**	60.0	**−**	40.0
12	**Target CCC**	**=**	**70.0**				
13	**Panel B. Actual CCC: Based on Financial Statements**						
14							
15	Sales	$1,216.7					
16	COGS	$1,013.9					
17	Inventories	$140.0					
18	Receivables	$445.0					
19	Payables	$115.0					
20	Days/year	365					
21	**Actual CCC**	**=**	**Inventory ÷ (COGS/365)**	**+**	**Receivables ÷ (Sales/365)**		**Payables ÷ (COGS/365)**
22		**=**	$140 ÷ ($1,013.9/365)	**+**	$445 ÷ ($1,216.7/365)		$115 ÷ ($1,013.9/365)
23		**=**	50.4	**+**	133.5		41.4
24	**Actual CCC**	**=**	**142.5**				
25	**Panel C. Actual versus Target Components**						
26			**ICP**		**ACP**		**PDP**
27	**Actual − Target**	**=**	50.4 - 50.0		133.5 - 60.0		41.4 - 40.0
28		**=**	0.4	**+**	73.5	**−**	1.4
29	**% Difference**	**=**	**0.8%**		**122.5%**		**3.5%**
30	**Evaluation**	**=**	**OK**		**VERY BAD**		**OK**

Notes: GBM's inventories are in line with its plans, and it is paying its suppliers nearly on time. However, some of its customers are paying quite late, so its average collection period (or DSO) is 133.5 days even though all customers are supposed to pay by Day 60.

Microsoft Excel® is a registered trademark of Microsoft Corporation. © 2014 Microsoft.

figure that the firm's inventory control is working as expected in that sales match the inflow of new inventory items quite well. Also, its own payments match reasonably well the terms under which it buys. However, its accounts receivable are much higher than they should be, indicating that customers are not paying on time. In fact, they are paying 73.5 days late, which is increasing GBM's working capital. Because working capital must be financed, the collections delay is lowering the firm's profits and presumably hurting its stock price.

When the CFO reviewed the situation, she discovered that GBM's customers—doctors, hospitals, and clinics—were themselves reimbursed by insurance companies and government units, and those organizations were paying late. The credit manager was doing everything he could to collect faster, but the customers said that they just could not make their own payments until they themselves were paid. If GBM wanted to keep making sales, it seemed that it would have to accept late-paying customers. However, the CFO wondered if collections might come in faster if GBM offered substantial discounts for early payments. We will take up this issue later in the chapter.

21-3c Benefits of Reducing the CCC

As we have seen, GBM currently has a CCC of 142.5 days, which results in $470 million being tied up in net operating working capital. Assuming that its cost of debt to carry working capital is 10%, this means that the firm is incurring interest charges of $47 million per year to carry its working capital. Now suppose the company can speed up its sales enough to reduce the inventory conversion period from 50.4 to 35.0 days. In addition, it begins to offer discounts for early payment and thereby reduces its average collection period to 40 days. Finally, assume that it could negotiate a change in its own payment terms from 40 to 50 days. The "New" column of Figure 21-4 shows the net effects of these improvements: a 117.5-day reduction in the cash conversion cycle and a reduction in net operating working capital from $470.0 to $91.7 million, which saves $37.8 million of interest.

Recall also that free cash flow (FCF) is equal to NOPAT minus the net new investment in operating capital. Therefore, if working capital *decreases* by a given amount while other things remain constant, then FCF *increases* by that same amount—$378.3 million in the GBM example. If sales remained constant in the following years, then this reduction in working capital would simply be a one-time cash inflow. However, suppose sales grow in future years. When a company improves its working capital management, the components (inventory conversion period, collection period, and payments period) usually remain at their improved levels, which means the NOWC-to-Sales ratio remains at its new level. With an improved NOWC-to-Sales ratio, less working capital will be required to support future sales, leading to higher annual FCFs than would have otherwise existed.

Thus, an improvement in working capital management creates a large one-time increase in FCF at the time of the improvement as well as higher FCF in future years. Therefore, an improvement in working capital management is a gift that keeps on giving.

FIGURE 21-4   Benefits from Reducing the Cash Conversion Cycle (Millions of Dollars)

	A	B	C	D	E	F	G
39					Old (Actual)		New (Target)
40	Inventory conversion period (ICP, days)				50.4		35.0
41	Average collection period (ACP, days)				133.5		40.0
42	Payable deferral period (PDP, days)				–41.4		–50.0
43	Cash Collection Cycle (CCC, days)				142.5		25.0
44							
45	Reduction in CCC				117.5		
46							
47	**Effects of the CCC Reduction**						
48	Annual sales				$1,216.7		$1,216.7
49	Costs of goods sold (COGS)				$1,013.9		$1,013.9
50	Inventory = Actual Old, New = new ICP(COGS/365)				$140.0		$97.2
51	Receivables = Actual Old, New = new ACP(Sales/365)				$445.0		$133.3
52	Payables = Actual Old, New = new PDP(COGS/365)				–$115.0		–$138.9
53	Net operating WC = Inv + Receivables – Payables				$470.0		$91.7
54							
55	Reduction in NOWC				$378.3		
56	Reduction in interest expense @ 10%				$37.8		

These benefits can add substantial value to the company. Professors Hyun-Han Shin and Luc Soenen studied more than 2,900 companies over a 20-year period, finding a strong relationship between a company's cash conversion cycle and its stock performance.[5] For an average company, a 10-day improvement in its CCC was associated with an increase in pre-tax operating profit margin from 12.76% to 13.02%. Moreover, companies with cash conversion cycles 10 days shorter than the average for their industry had annual stock returns that were 1.7 percentage points higher than the average company. Given results like these, it's no wonder firms place so much emphasis on working capital management![6]

SELF TEST

Define the following terms: inventory conversion period, average collection period, and payables deferral period. Give the equation for each term.

What is the cash conversion cycle? What is its equation?

What should a firm's goal be regarding the cash conversion cycle, holding other things constant? Explain your answer.

What are some actions a firm can take to shorten its cash conversion cycle?

A company has $20 million of inventory, $5 million of receivables, and $4 million of payables. Its annual sales revenue is $80 million, and its cost of goods sold is $60 million. What is its CCC? **(120.15)**

SOME FIRMS OPERATE WITH NEGATIVE WORKING CAPITAL!

Some firms are able to operate with zero or even negative net working capital. Dell Computer and Amazon are examples. When customers order computers from Dell's Web site or books from Amazon, they must provide a credit card number. Dell and Amazon then receive next-day cash, even before the product is shipped and even before they have paid their own suppliers. This results in a negative CCC, which means that working capital *provides* cash rather than *uses* it.

In order to grow, companies normally need cash for working capital. However, if the CCC is negative then growth in sales *provides* cash rather than *uses* it. This cash can be invested in plant and equipment, research and development, or for any other corporate purpose. Analysts recognize this point when they value Dell and Amazon, and it certainly helps their stock prices.

---

5. Hyun-Han Shin and Luc Soenen, "Efficiency of Working Capital Management and Corporate Profitability," *Financial Practice and Education*, Fall/Winter 1998, pp. 37–45.

6. For more on the CCC, see James A. Gentry, R. Vaidyanathan, and Hei Wai Lee, "A Weighted Cash Conversion Cycle," *Financial Management*, Spring 1990, pp. 90–99.

21-4 The Cash Budget

Firms must forecast their cash flows. If they are likely to need additional cash, then they should line up funds well in advance. Yet if they are likely to generate surplus cash, then they should plan for its productive use. The primary forecasting tool is the cash budget, illustrated in Figure 21-5, which is taken from the chapter's *Excel Tool Kit* model. The illustrative company is Educational Products Corporation (EPC), which supplies educational materials to schools and retailers in the Midwest. Sales are cyclical, peaking in September and then declining for the balance of the year.

21-4a Monthly Cash Budgets

Cash budgets can be of any length, but EPC and most companies use a monthly cash budget such as the one in Figure 21-5, but set up for 12 months. We used only 6 months for the purpose of illustration. The monthly budget is used for

FIGURE 21-5   EPC's Cash Budget, July–December 2016 (Millions of Dollars)

	A	B	C	D	E	F	G	H	I	J	K	L	M	N
144	**Base Case**					**May**	**June**	**July**	**August**	**Sept**	**Oct**	**Nov**	**Dec**	**Jan**
145	*Forecasted gross sales (manual inputs):*					$200	$250	$300	$400	$500	$350	$250	$200	$200
146	Adjustment: % deviation from forecast					0%	0%	0%	0%	0%	0%	0%	0%	0%
147	Adjusted gross sales forecast					$200	$250	$300	$400	$500	$350	$250	$200	$200
148	*Collections on sales:*													
149	During sales' month: 0.2 (Sales)(1 – discount %)							$58.8	$78.4	$98.0	$68.6	$49.0	$39.2	
150	During 2nd month: 0.7 (prior month's sales)							$175.0	$210.0	$280.0	$350.0	$245.0	$175.0	
151	Due in 3rd month: 0.1 (sales 2 months ago)							$20.0	$25.0	$30.0	$40.0	$50.0	$35.0	
152	Less bad debts (BD% × Sales 2 months ago)							$0.0	$0.0	$0.0	$0.0	$0.0	$0.0	
153	Total collections							$253.8	$313.4	$408.0	$458.6	$344.0	$249.2	
154	*Purchases: 60% of next month's sales*						$180.0	$240.0	$300.0	$210.0	$150.0	$120.0	$120.0	
155	*Payments*													
156	Pmt for last month's purchases (30 days of credit)							$180.0	$240.0	$300.0	$210.0	$150.0	$120.0	
157	Wages and salaries							$30.0	$40.0	$50.0	$40.0	$30.0	$30.0	
158	Lease payments							$30.0	$30.0	$30.0	$30.0	$30.0	$30.0	
159	Other payments (interest on LT bonds, dividends, etc.)							$30.0	$30.0	$30.0	$30.0	$30.0	$30.0	
160	Taxes									$30.0			$30.0	
161	Payment for plant construction									$150.0				
162	Total payments							$270.0	$340.0	$590.0	$310.0	$240.0	$240.0	
163	*Net cash flows:*													
164	Assumed *excess* cash on hand at start of forecast period							$0.0						
165	Net cash flow (NCF): Total collections – Total payments							–$16.2	–$26.6	–$182.0	$148.6	$104.0	$9.2	
166	Cumulative NCF: Prior month cum plus this month's NCF							–$16.2	–$42.8	–$224.8	–$76.2	$27.8	$37.0	
167	*Cash surplus (or loan requirement)*													
168	Target cash balance							$10.0	$10.0	$10.0	$10.0	$10.0	$10.0	
169	Surplus cash or loan needed: Cum NCF – Target cash							–$26.2	–$52.8	–$234.8	–$86.2	$17.8	$27.0	
170	Max required loan (most <u>negative</u> on Row 169)			$234.8										
171	Max investable funds (most <u>positive</u> on Row 169			$27.0										

Notes:

1. Although the budget period is July through December, sales and purchases data for May and June are needed to determine collections and payments during July and August.

2. Firms can both borrow and pay off commercial loans on a daily basis, so the $26.2 million loan needed for July would likely be gradually borrowed as needed on a daily basis, and during October the $234.8 million loan that presumably existed at the beginning of the month would be reduced daily to the $86.2 million ending balance—which, in turn, would be completely paid off sometime during November.

3. The data in the figure are for EPC's base-case forecast. Data for alternative scenarios are shown in the chapter's *Excel Tool Kit* model.

longer-range planning, but a daily cash budget is also prepared at the start of each month to provide a more precise picture of the daily cash flows for use in scheduling actual payments on a day-by-day basis.

The cash budget focuses on cash flows, but it also includes information on forecasted sales, credit policy, and inventory management. Because the statement is a forecast and not a report on historical results, actual results could vary from the figures given. Therefore, the cash budget is generally set up as an expected, or base-case, forecast, but it is created with a model that makes it easy to generate alternative forecasts to see what would happen under different conditions.

Figure 21-5 begins with a forecast of sales for each month on Row 145. Then, on Row 146, it shows possible percentage deviations from the forecasted sales. Because we are showing the base-case forecast, no adjustments are made, but the model is set up to show the effects if sales increase or decrease and so result in "adjusted sales" that are above or below the forecasted levels.

The company sells on terms of "2/10, net 60." This means that a 2% discount is given if payment is made within 10 days; otherwise, the full amount is due in 60 days. However, like most companies, EPC finds that some customers pay late. Experience shows that 20% of customers pay during the month of the sale and take the discount. Another 70% pay during the month immediately following the sale, and 10% are late, paying in the second month after the sale.[7]

The statement (Line 154) next shows forecasted materials purchases, which equal 60% of the following month's sales. EPC buys on terms of net 30, meaning that it receives no discounts and is required to pay for its purchases within 30 days of the purchase date. The purchases information is followed by forecasted payments for materials, labor, leases, other payments such as dividends and interest on long-term bonds, taxes (due in September and December), and a payment of $150 million in September for a new plant that is being constructed.

When the total forecasted payments are subtracted from the forecasted collections, the result is the expected net cash gain or loss for each month. This gain or loss is added to or subtracted from the excess cash on hand at the start of the forecast (which we assume was zero), and the result—the *cumulative net cash flow*—is the amount of cash the firm would have on hand at the end of the month if it neither borrowed nor invested.

EPC's target cash balance is $10 million, and it plans either to borrow to meet this target or to invest surplus funds if it generates more cash than it needs. How the target cash balance is determined is discussed later in the chapter, but EPC believes that it needs $10 million.

By subtracting the target cash balance from the cumulative cash flow, we calculate the *loan needed or surplus cash*, as shown on Row 169. A negative number indicates that we need a loan, whereas a positive number indicates that we forecast surplus cash that is available for investment or other uses.

---

7. Because we are using a monthly forecast instead of a daily forecast, we assume that all purchases are made on the first day of the month. Thus, discounted payments are received in the month of the sale, regular payments are received in the month after the sale, and late payments are received two months after the sale. Obviously, a daily budget would be more accurate. Also, a negligible percentage of sales results in bad debts. The low bad-debt losses evident here result from EPC's careful screening of customers and its generally tight credit policies. However, the cash budget model is able to show the effects of bad debts, so EPC's CFO could show top management how cash flows would be affected if the firm relaxed its credit policy in order to stimulate sales or if the recession worsened and more customers were forced to delay payments.

We total the net cash flows on Row 165 and show the cumulative total on Row 166. Cell M166 shows that the cumulative for the forecast period is $37 million. Because this number is positive, it indicates that EPC's cumulative cash flow is positive. Also, note that EPC borrows on a basis that allows it to borrow or repay loans on a daily basis. Thus, it would borrow a total of $26.2 million in July, increasing the loan daily, and would continue to build up the loan through September. Then, when its cash flows turn positive in October, it would start repaying the loan on a daily basis and completely pay it off sometime in November, assuming that everything works out as forecasted.

Note that our cash budget is incomplete in that it shows neither interest paid on the working capital loans nor interest earned on the positive cash balances. These amounts could be added to the budget simply by adding rows and including them. Similarly, if the firm makes quarterly dividend payments, principal payments on its long-term bonds, or any other payments, or if it has investment income, then those cash flows also could be added to the statement. In our simplified statement, we just lumped all such payments into "other payments."

Under the base-case forecast, the CFO will need to arrange a line of credit so that the firm can borrow up to $234.8 million, increasing the loan over time as funds are needed and repaying it later when cash flows become positive. The treasurer would show the cash budget to the bankers when negotiating for the line of credit. Lenders would want to know how much the firm expects to need, when the funds will be needed, and when the loan will be repaid. The lenders—and EPC's top executives—would question the treasurer about the budget, and they would want to know how the forecasts would be affected if sales were higher or lower than those projected, how changes in customers' payment times would affect the forecasts, and the like. The focus would be on these two questions: *How accurate is the forecast likely to be? What would be the effects of significant errors?* The first question could best be answered by examining historical forecasts, and the second by running different scenarios as we do in the *Excel Tool Kit* model.

No matter how hard we try, no forecast will ever be exactly correct, and this includes cash budgets. You can imagine the bank's reaction if the company negotiated a loan of $235 million and then came back a few months later saying that it had underestimated its requirements and needed to boost the loan to say $260 million. The banker might refuse, thinking the company was not managed very well. Therefore, EPC's treasurer would undoubtedly want to build a cushion into the line of credit—say, a maximum commitment of $260 million rather than the forecasted requirement of $234.8 million. However, as we discuss later in the chapter, banks charge commitment fees for guaranteed lines of credit; thus, the higher the cushion built into the line of credit, the more costly the credit will be. This is another reason why it is important to develop accurate forecasts.

See **Ch21 Tool Kit.xls** on the textbook's Web site for details.

21-4b **Cash Budgets versus Income Statements and Free Cash Flows**

If you look at the cash budget, it looks similar to an income statement. However, the two statements are quite different. Here are some key differences: (1) In an income statement, the focus would be on sales, not collections. (2) An income statement would show accrued taxes, wages, and so forth, not the actual payments. (3) An income statement would show depreciation as an expense, but it would not show expenditures on new fixed assets. (4) An income statement would show a cost for goods purchased when those goods were sold, not for when they were ordered or paid.

These are obviously large differences, so it would be a big mistake to confuse a cash budget with an income statement. Also, the cash flows shown on the cash budget are different from the firm's free cash flows, because FCF reflects after-tax operating income and the investments required to maintain future operations whereas the cash budget reflects only the actual cash inflows and outflows during a particular period.

The bottom line is that cash budgets, income statements, and free cash flows are all important and are related to one another, but they are also quite different. Each is designed for a specific purpose, and the main purpose of the cash budget is to forecast the firm's liquidity position, not its profitability.

21-4c Daily Cash Budgets

Note that if cash inflows and outflows do not occur uniformly during each month, then the actual funds needed might be quite different from the indicated amounts. The data in Figure 21-5 show the situation on the last day of each month, and we see that the maximum projected loan during the forecast period is $234.8 million. Yet if all payments had to be made on the 1st of the month but most collections came on the 30th, then EPC would have to make $270 million of payments in July before it received the $253.8 million from collections. In that case, the firm would need to borrow about $270 million in July, not the $26.2 million shown in Figure 21-5. This would make the bank unhappy—perhaps so unhappy that it would not extend the requested credit. A daily cash budget would have revealed this situation.

Figure 21-5 was prepared using *Excel*, which makes it easy to change the assumptions. In the *Tool Kit* model, we examine the cash flow effects of changes in sales, in customers' payment patterns, and so forth. Also, the effects of changes in credit policy and inventory management could be examined through the cash budget.

See *Ch21 Tool Kit.xls* on the textbook's Web site for details.

> **SELF TEST**
>
> How could the cash budget be used when negotiating the terms of a bank loan?
>
> How would a shift from a tight credit policy to a relaxed policy be likely to affect a firm's cash budget?
>
> How would the cash budget be affected if our firm's suppliers offered us terms of "2/10, net 30," rather than "net 30," and we decided to take the discount?
>
> Suppose a firm's cash flows do not occur uniformly throughout the month. What effect would this have on the accuracy of the forecasted borrowing requirements based on a monthly cash budget? How could the firm deal with this problem?

21-5 Cash Management and the Target Cash Balance

Companies need cash to pay for expenses related to daily ongoing operations, including labor, raw materials, utility bills, and taxes. Companies also need cash for several other predictable purposes, including major purchases and payments to investors (interest payments, principal payments, and dividend payments). Following are the issues that companies consider when deciding how much cash to hold in support of ongoing operations. We discuss major purchases and payments to investors in Section 21-10.

21-5a **Routine (but Uncertain) Operating Transactions**

Cash balances are necessary in business operations. Payments must be made in cash, and receipts are deposited in the cash account. Cash balances associated with routine payments and collections are known as **transactions balances**. Cash inflows and outflows are unpredictable, and the degree of predictability varies among firms and industries. Therefore, firms need to hold some cash to meet random, unforeseen fluctuations in inflows and outflows. These "safety stocks" are called **precautionary balances**, and the less predictable the firm's cash flows, the larger such balances should be. Research confirms this and shows that companies with volatile cash flows do in fact hold higher cash balances. [8]

In addition to holding cash for transactions and precautionary reasons, it is essential that the firm have sufficient cash to take **trade discounts**. Suppliers frequently offer customers discounts for early payment of bills. As we will see later in this chapter, the cost of not taking discounts is sometimes very high, so firms should have enough cash to permit payment of bills in time to take advantage of discounts.

Many companies have a line of credit to cover unexpected cash needs; we discuss lines of credit in Section 21-12.

21-5b **Compensating Balances**

A bank makes money by lending out funds that have been deposited with it, so the larger its deposits, the better the bank's profit position. If a bank is providing services to a customer, then it may require that customer to leave a minimum balance on deposit to help offset the costs of providing those services. Also, banks may require borrowers to hold their transactions deposits at the bank. Both types of deposits are called **compensating balances**. In a 1979 survey, 84.7% of responding companies reported they were required to maintain compensating balances to help pay for bank services; only 13.3% reported paying direct fees for banking services. [9] By 1996, those findings were reversed: Only 28% paid for bank services with compensating balances, while 83% paid direct fees. [10] Although the use of compensating balances to pay for services has declined, these balances improve a firm's relationship with its bank and are still a reason why some companies hold additional cash.

SELF TEST

Why is cash management important?

What are the primary motives for holding cash?

---

8. See Tim Opler, Lee Pinkowitz, René Stulz, and Rohan Williamson, "The Determinants and Implications of Corporate Cash Holdings," *Journal of Financial Economics*, 1999, pp. 3–46.

9. See Lawrence J. Gitman, E. A. Moses, and I. T. White, "An Assessment of Corporate Cash Management Practices," *Financial Management*, Spring 1979, pp. 32–41.

10. See Charles E. Maxwell, Lawrence J. Gitman, and Stephanie A. M. Smith, "Working Capital Management and Financial-Service Consumption Preferences of US and Foreign Firms: A Comparison of 1979 and 1996 Preferences," *Financial Practice and Education*, Fall/Winter 1998, pp. 46–52.

21-6 **Cash Management Techniques**

In terms of dollar volume, most business is conducted by large firms, many of which operate nationally or globally. They collect cash from many sources and make payments from a number of different cities or even countries. For example, companies such as IBM, General Electric, and Hewlett-Packard have manufacturing plants all around the world, even more sales offices, and bank accounts in virtually every city in which they do business. Their collection centers follow sales patterns. However, while some disbursements are made from local offices, most are made in the cities where manufacturing occurs or from the home office. Thus, a major corporation might have hundreds or even thousands of bank accounts located in cities all over the globe, but there is no reason to think that inflows and outflows will balance in each account. Therefore, a system must be in place to transfer funds from where they come in to where they are needed, to arrange loans to cover net corporate shortfalls, and to invest net corporate surpluses without delay. Some commonly used techniques for accomplishing these tasks are discussed next.[11]

21-6a **Synchronizing Cash Flow**

If you as an individual were to receive income once a year, then you would probably put it in the bank, draw down your account periodically, and have an average balance for the year equal to about half of your annual income. If instead you received income weekly and paid rent, tuition, and other charges on a daily basis, then your average bank balance would still be about half of your periodic receipts and thus only 1/52 as large as if you received income only once annually.

Exactly the same situation holds for businesses: By timing their cash receipts to coincide with their cash outlays, firms can hold their transactions balances to a minimum. Recognizing this fact, firms such as utilities, oil companies, and credit card companies arrange to bill customers—and to pay their own bills—on regular "billing cycles" throughout the month. This **synchronization of cash flows** provides cash when it is needed and thus enables firms to reduce their average cash balances.

21-6b **Speeding Up the Check-Clearing Process**

When a customer writes and mails a check, the funds are not available to the receiving firm until the **check-clearing process** has been completed. First, the check must be delivered through the mail. Checks received from customers in distant cities are especially subject to mail delays.

When a customer's check is written on one bank and a company deposits the check in another bank, the company's bank must verify that the check is valid before the payee can use those funds. Checks are generally cleared through the

11. For more information on cash management, see Bruce J. Summers, "Clearing and Payment Systems: The Role of the Central Bank," *Federal Reserve Bulletin*, February 1991, pp. 81–91.

Federal Reserve System or through a clearinghouse set up by the banks in a particular city.[12] Before 2004, this process sometimes took 2 to 5 days. But with the passage of a federal law in 2004 known as "Check 21," banks can exchange digital images of checks. This means that most checks now clear in a single day.

21-6c **Using Float**

Float is defined as the difference between the balance shown in a firm's (or individual's) checkbook and the balance on the bank's records. Suppose a firm writes, on average, checks in the amount of $5,000 each day, and suppose it takes 6 days for these checks to clear and be deducted from the firm's bank account. This will cause the firm's own checkbook to show a balance that is $30,000 smaller than the balance on the bank's records; this difference is called **disbursement float**. Now suppose the firm also receives checks in the amount of $5,000 daily but that it loses 4 days while those checks are being deposited and cleared. This will result in $20,000 of **collections float**. In total, the firm's **net float**—the difference between the $30,000 positive disbursement float and the $20,000 negative collections float—will be $10,000. In sum, collections float is bad, disbursement float is good, and positive net float is even better.

Delays that cause float will occur because it takes time for checks to: (1) travel through the mail (mail float), (2) be processed by the receiving firm (processing float), and (3) clear through the banking system (clearing, or availability, float). Basically, the size of a firm's net float is a function of its ability to speed up collections on checks it receives and to slow down collections on checks it writes. Efficient firms go to great lengths to speed up the processing of incoming checks, thus putting the funds to work faster, and they try to stretch their own payments out as long as possible, sometimes by disbursing checks from banks in remote locations.

21-6d **Speeding Up Collections**

Two major techniques are used to speed collections and to get funds where they are needed: lockboxes and electronic transfers.

Lockboxes

A **lockbox system** is one of the oldest cash management tools. In a lockbox system, incoming checks are sent to post office boxes rather than to the firm's corporate headquarters. For example, a firm headquartered in New York City might have its West Coast customers send their payments to a post office box in San Francisco, its customers in the Southwest send their checks to Dallas, and so on, rather than having all checks sent to New York City. Several times a day, a local bank will empty the lockbox and deposit the checks into the company's local account. The

---

12. For example, suppose a check for $100 is written on Bank A and deposited at Bank B. Bank B will usually contact either the Federal Reserve System or a clearinghouse to which both banks belong. The Fed or the clearinghouse will then verify with Bank A that the check is valid and that the account has sufficient funds to cover the check. Bank A's account with the Fed or the clearinghouse is then reduced by $100, and Bank B's account is increased by $100. Of course, if the check is deposited in the same bank on which it was drawn, that bank merely transfers funds by bookkeeping entries from one depositor to another.

YOUR CHECK ISN'T IN THE MAIL

Issuing payroll checks to thousands of employees is expensive—in both the time and resources it takes the company to print, process, and deliver the checks, and in the time it takes the employee to deposit or cash the check. Paper checks cost a company between $1 and $2 each, and multiply that by thousands of employees, some of whom are paid weekly or biweekly, it adds up to a lot of money every year. Direct deposit of payroll checks into the employee's checking account reduces these costs, but there are still many employees, especially seasonal, temporary, part-time, or young employees, who don't have a checking account.

A growing solution to high check costs and the needs of these "unbanked" employees is the payroll debit card. Companies, in partnership with a bank, issue the employee a debit card that is automatically filled each payday. The employee either uses the debit card to make purchases or withdraws cash at an ATM. The cost to load a debit card is around $0.20, and so saves the companies 80% to 90% of the cost to print a check, and saves the unbanked employee from paying the frequently usurious check-cashing fees that can be 10% or more. In fact, because debit card transactions that are processed as a credit card result in fees to the merchant, there is a small amount of money available to provide a rebate to the employer. For example, Premier Pay Cards offers a 0.1% rebate to the employer on certain purchases the employee makes with the debit card.

Although payroll debit cards may be good for companies, they aren't always as good for employees as advertised. *The New York Times* reported that high ATM transaction fees, balance inquiry fees, inactivity fees, and overdraft protection fees can eat up $40 per month in fees—even more than the frequently usurious fees charged by check cashing services. These high fees help banks offer those attractive rebates to the employers, with the employees essentially paying their employers for the privilege of being paid.

Sources: "The End of the Paycheck," *Fortune Small Business Magazine*, December 5, 2006, "Paid via Card, Workers Feel Sting of Fees," *The New York Times*, June 30, 2013, and **www.premierpaycards.com**.

bank then provides the firm with a daily record of the receipts collected, usually via an electronic data transmission system in a format that permits online updating of the firm's accounts receivable records.

A lockbox system reduces the time required to receive incoming checks, to deposit them, and to get them cleared through the banking system and available for use. Lockbox services can make funds available as many as 2 to 5 days faster than via the "regular" system.

Payment by Wire or Automatic Debit

Firms are increasingly demanding payments of larger bills by wire or by automatic electronic debits. Under an electronic debit system, funds are automatically deducted from one account and added to another. This is, of course, the ultimate in speeding up a collection process, and computer technology is making such a process increasingly feasible and efficient, even for retail transactions.

What is float? How do firms use float to increase cash management efficiency?

What are some methods firms can use to accelerate receipts?

SELF TEST

21-7 **Inventory Management**

Inventory management techniques are covered in depth in production management courses. Still, financial managers have a responsibility for raising the capital needed to carry inventory and for overseeing the firm's overall profitability, so it is appropriate that we cover the financial aspects of inventory management here.

The twin goals of inventory management are: (1) ensuring that the inventories needed to sustain operations are available, while (2) holding the costs of ordering and carrying inventories to the lowest possible level. In analyzing improvements in the cash conversion cycle, we identified some of the cash flows associated with a reduction in inventory. In addition to the points made earlier, lower inventory levels reduce costs due to storage and handling, insurance, property taxes, spoilage, and obsolescence.

Before the computer age, companies used simple inventory control techniques such as the "red line" system, where a red line was drawn around the inside of a bin holding inventory items; when the actual stock declined to the level where the red line showed, inventory would be reordered. Now computers have taken over, and supply chains have been established that provide inventory items just before they are needed—the *just-in-time* system. For example, consider Trane Corporation, which makes air conditioners and currently uses just-in-time procedures. In the past, Trane produced parts on a steady basis, stored them as inventory, and had them ready whenever the company received an order for a batch of air conditioners. However, the company's inventory eventually covered an area equal to three football fields, and it still could take as long as 15 days to fill an order. To make matters worse, occasionally some of the necessary components simply could not be located; in other instances, the components were located but found to have been damaged from long storage.

Then Trane adopted a new inventory policy—it began producing components only after receiving an order and then sending the parts directly from the machines that make them to the final assembly line. The net effect: Inventories fell nearly 40% even as sales were increasing by 30%.

SUPPLY CHAIN MANAGEMENT

Herman Miller Inc. manufactures a wide variety of office furniture, and a typical order from a single customer might require work at five different plants. Each plant uses components from different suppliers, and each plant works on orders for many customers. Imagine all the coordination this requires. The sales force generates the order, the purchasing department orders components from suppliers, and the suppliers must order materials from their own suppliers. The suppliers make and then ship the components to Herman Miller, the factory builds the products, the different products are gathered together to complete the order, and then the order is shipped to the customer. If one part of that process malfunctions, then the order will be delayed, inventory will pile up, extra costs to expedite the order will be incurred, and the customer's goodwill will be damaged, hurting future growth.

To prevent such consequences, many companies employ supply chain management (SCM). The key element in SCM is sharing information all the way back from the retailer where the product is sold, to the company's own plant, then back to the firm's suppliers, and even back to the suppliers' suppliers. SCM requires special computer software, but even more importantly, it requires cooperation among the different companies and departments in the supply chain. This culture of open communication is often difficult for companies, because they are reluctant to divulge operating information. For example, EMC Corp., a manufacturer of data storage systems, has become deeply involved in the design processes and financial controls of its key suppliers. Many of EMC's suppliers were initially wary of these new relationships. However, SCM has been a win–win proposition, resulting in higher profits for both EMC and its suppliers.

The same is true at many other companies. After implementing SCM, Herman Miller was able to reduce its days of inventory on hand by a week and to cut 2 weeks off delivery times to customers. It was also able to operate its plants at a 20% higher volume without additional capital expenditures, because downtime due to inventory shortages was virtually eliminated. As another example, Heineken USA can now get beer from its Dutch breweries to its customers' shelves in less than 6 weeks, compared with 10 to 12 weeks before implementing SCM. As these and other companies have found, SCM increases free cash flows, and that leads to more profits and higher stock prices.

Sources: Elaine L. Appleton, "Supply Chain Brain," *CFO*, July 1997, pp. 51–54; and Kris Frieswick, "Up Close and Virtual," *CFO*, April 1998, pp. 87–91.

Such improvements in inventory management can free up considerable amounts of cash. For example, suppose a company has sales of $120 million and an inventory turnover ratio of 3. This means the company has an inventory level of:

$$\text{Inventory} = \text{Sales} / (\text{Inventory turnover ratio})$$
$$= \$120/3 = \$40 \text{ million}$$

If the company can improve its inventory turnover ratio to 4, then its inventory will fall to:

$$\text{Inventory} = \$120/4 = \$30 \text{ million}$$

This $10 million reduction in inventory boosts free cash flow by $10 million.

However, there are costs associated with holding too little inventory, and these costs can be severe. If a business lowers its inventories, then it must reorder frequently, which increases ordering costs. Even worse, if stocks become depleted then firms can miss out on profitable sales and also suffer lost goodwill, which may lead to lower future sales. Therefore, it is important to have enough inventory on hand to meet customer demands but not so much as to incur the costs we discussed previously. Inventory optimization models have been developed, but the best approach—and the one most firms today are following—is to use supply chain management and monitor the system closely.[13]

SELF TEST

What are some costs associated with high inventories? With low inventories?

What is a "supply chain," and how are supply chains related to just-in-time inventory procedures?

A company has $20 million in sales and an inventory turnover ratio of 2.0. If it can reduce its inventory and improve its inventory turnover ratio to 2.5 with no loss in sales, by how much will FCF increase? **($2 million)**

13. For additional insights into the problems of inventory management, see Richard A. Followill, Michael Schellenger, and Patrick H. Marchard, "Economic Order Quantities, Volume Discounts, and Wealth Maximization," *The Financial Review*, February 1990, pp. 143–152.

21-8 Receivables Management

Firms would, in general, rather sell for cash than on credit, but competitive pressures force most firms to offer credit for substantial purchases, especially to other businesses. Thus, goods are shipped, inventories are reduced, and an **account receivable** is created.[14] Eventually, the customer will pay the account, at which time: (1) the firm will receive cash and (2) its receivables will decline. Carrying receivables has both direct and indirect costs, but selling on credit also has an important benefit: increased sales.

Receivables management begins with the firm's credit policy, but a monitoring system is also important to keep tabs on whether the terms of credit are being observed. Corrective action is often needed, and the only way to know whether the situation is getting out of hand is with a good receivables control system.[15]

21-8a Credit Policy

The success or failure of a business depends primarily on the demand for its products—as a rule, high sales lead to larger profits and a higher stock price. Sales, in turn, depend on a number of factors: Some, like the state of the economy, are exogenous, but others are under the firm's control. The major controllable factors are sales prices, product quality, advertising, and the firm's **credit policy**. Credit policy, in turn, consists of the following four variables:

1. *Credit period.* A firm might sell on terms of "net 30," which means that the customer must pay within 30 days.
2. *Discounts.* If the credit terms are stated as "2/10, net 30," then buyers may deduct 2% of the purchase price if payment is made within 10 days; otherwise, the full amount must be paid within 30 days. Thus, these terms allow a discount to be taken.
3. *Credit standards.* How much financial strength must a customer show to qualify for credit? Lower credit standards boost sales, but they also increase bad debts.
4. *Collection policy.* How tough or lax is a company in attempting to collect slow-paying accounts? A tough policy may speed up collections, but it might also anger customers and cause them to take their business elsewhere.

The credit manager is responsible for administering the firm's credit policy. However, because of the pervasive importance of credit, the credit policy itself is normally established by the executive committee, which usually consists of the president plus the vice presidents of finance, marketing, and production.

---

14. Whenever goods are sold on credit, two accounts are created—an asset item entitled *accounts receivable* appears on the books of the selling firm, and a liability item called *accounts payable* appears on the books of the purchaser. At this point, we are analyzing the transaction from the viewpoint of the seller, so we are concentrating on the variables under its control (i.e., the receivables). We examine the transaction from the viewpoint of the purchaser later in this chapter, where we discuss accounts payable as a source of funds and consider their cost.

15. For more on credit policy and receivables management, see Shehzad L. Mian and Clifford W. Smith, "Extending Trade Credit and Financing Receivables," *Journal of Applied Corporate Finance,* Spring 1994, pp. 75–84; and Paul D. Adams, Steve B. Wyatt, and Yong H. Kim, "A Contingent Claims Analysis of Trade Credit," *Financial Management,* Autumn 1992, pp. 104–112.

21-8b **The Accumulation of Receivables**

The total amount of accounts receivable outstanding at any given time is determined by two factors: (1) the credit sales per day and (2) the average length of time it takes to collect cash on accounts receivable:

$$\text{Accounts receivable} = \text{Credit sales per day} \times \text{Length of collection period} \qquad (21\text{--}5)$$

For example, suppose Boston Lumber Company (BLC), a wholesale distributor of lumber products, opens a warehouse on January 1 and, starting the first day, makes sales of $1,000 each day. For simplicity, we assume that all sales are on credit and that customers are given 10 days to pay. At the end of the first day, accounts receivable will be $1,000; they will rise to $2,000 by the end of the second day; and by January 10, they will have risen to 10($1,000) = $10,000. On January 11, another $1,000 will be added to receivables, but payments for sales made on January 1 will be collected and thus will reduce receivables by $1,000, so total accounts receivable will remain constant at $10,000. Once the firm's operations have stabilized, the following situation will exist:

$$\text{Accounts receivable} = \text{Credit sales per day} \times \text{Length of collection period}$$
$$= \$1,000 \quad \times \quad 10 \text{ days} \quad = \$10,000$$

If either credit sales or the collection period changes, these changes will be reflected in the accounts receivable balance.

21-8c **Monitoring the Receivables Position**

Both investors and bank loan officers should pay close attention to accounts receivable, because what you see on a financial statement is not necessarily what you end up getting. To see why, consider how the accounting system operates. When a credit sale is made, these events occur: (1) inventories are reduced by the cost of goods sold; (2) accounts receivable are increased by the sales price; and (3) the difference is reported as a profit, which is adjusted for taxes and then added to the previous retained earnings balance. If the sale is for cash, then the cash from the sale has actually been received by the firm and the scenario just described is completely valid. If the sale is on credit, however, then the firm will not receive the cash from the sale unless and until the account is collected. Firms have been known to encourage "sales" to weak customers in order to report high current profits. This could boost the firm's stock price—but only for a short time. Eventually, credit losses will lower earnings, at which time the stock price will fall. This is another example of how differences between a firm's stock price and its intrinsic value can arise, and it is something that security analysts must keep in mind.

An analysis along the lines suggested in the following sections will detect any such questionable practice, and it will also help a firm's management learn of problems that might be arising. Such early detection helps both investors and bankers avoid losses, and it also helps a firm's management maximize intrinsic values.

SUPPLY CHAIN FINANCE

In our global economy, companies purchase parts and materials from suppliers located all over the world. For small and mid-sized suppliers, especially those in less developed economies, selling to international customers can lead to cash flow problems. First, many suppliers have no way of knowing when their invoices have been approved by their customers. Second, they have no way of knowing when they will actually receive payment from their customers. With a 4–5-month lag between the time an order is received and the time the payment occurs, many suppliers resort to expensive local financing that can add as much as 4% to their costs. Even worse, some suppliers go out of business, which reduces competition and ultimately leads to higher prices.

Although most companies work very hard with their suppliers to improve their supply chain operations—which is at the heart of supply management—a recent poll shows that only 13% actively use supply chain finance (SCF)

techniques. However, that figure is likely to rise in the near future. For example, Big Lots joined a Web-based service operated by PrimeRevenue that works like this: First, invoices received by Big Lots are posted to the system as soon as they are approved. The supplier doesn't need specialized software but can check its invoices using a Web browser. Second, the supplier has the option of selling the approved invoices at a discount to financial institutions and banks that have access to the PrimeRevenue network. A further advantage to the supplier is that it receives cash within a day of the invoices' approval. In addition, the effective interest rate built into the discounted price is based on the credit rating of Big Lots, not that of the supplier.

As Big Lots treasurer Jared Poff puts it, this allows vendors to "compete on their ability to make the product and not on their ability to access financing."

Source: Kate O'Sullivan, "Financing the Chain," *CFO*, February 2007, pp. 46–53.

Days Sales Outstanding (DSO)

Suppose Super Sets Inc., a television manufacturer, sells 200,000 television sets a year at a price of $198 each. Assume that all sales are on credit under the terms 2/10, net 30. Finally, assume that 70% of the customers take the discount and pay on Day 10 and that the other 30% pay on Day 30.[16]

Super Sets' **days sales outstanding (DSO)**, sometimes called the *average collection period (ACP),* is 16 days:

$$\text{DSO} = \text{ACP} = 0.7(10 \text{ days}) + 0.3(30 \text{ days}) = 16 \text{ days}$$

Super Sets' *average daily sales (ADS)* is $108,493:

(21–6)

$$\text{ADS} = \frac{\text{Annual sales}}{365} = \frac{(\text{Units sold})(\text{Sales price})}{365}$$

$$= \frac{200,000(\$198)}{365} = \frac{\$39,600,000}{365} = \$108,493$$

---

16. Unless otherwise noted, we assume throughout that payments are made either on the *last day* for taking discounts or on the *last day* of the credit period. It would be foolish to pay on (say) the 5th day or on the 20th day if the credit terms were 2/10, net 30.

Super Sets' accounts receivable—assuming a constant, uniform rate of sales through-out the year—will at any point in time be $1,735,888:

$$\text{Receivables} = (\text{DSO}) (\text{ADS})$$
(21-7)

$$= (16) (\$108,493) = \$1,735,888$$

Note that DSO, or average collection period, is a measure of the average length of time it takes the firm's customers to pay off their credit purchases. Super Sets' DSO is 16 days versus an industry average of 25 days, so either Super Sets has a higher percentage of discount customers or else its credit department is exceptionally good at ensuring prompt payment.

Finally, note that you can derive both the annual sales and the receivables balance from the firm's financial statements, so you can calculate DSO as follows:

$$\text{DSO} = \frac{\text{Receivables}}{\text{Sales per day}} = \frac{\$1,735,888}{\$108,493} = 16 \text{ days}$$

The DSO can also be compared with the firm's own credit terms. For example, suppose Super Sets' DSO had been averaging 35 days. With a 35-day DSO, some customers obviously are taking more than 30 days to pay their bills. In fact, if many customers are paying by Day 10 to take advantage of the discount, then the others must be taking, on average, *much* longer than 35 days. A way to check this possibility is to use an aging schedule, as described next.

Aging Schedules

An **aging schedule** breaks down a firm's receivables by age of account. Table 21-1 shows the December 31, 2015, aging schedules of two television manufacturers, Super Sets and Wonder Vision. Both firms offer the same credit terms, and they have the same total receivables. Super Sets' aging schedule indicates that all of its customers pay on time: 70% pay by Day 10 and 30% pay by Day 30. In contrast, Wonder Vision's schedule, which is more typical, shows that many of its customers

TABLE 21-1	Aging Schedules			
	Super Sets		**Wonder Vision**	
Age of Account (Days)	**Value of Account**	**Percentage of Total Value**	**Value of Account**	**Percentage of Total Value**
0–10	$1,215,122	70%	$ 815,867	47%
11–30	520,766	30	451,331	26
31–45	0	0	260,383	15
46–60	0	0	173,589	10
Over 60	0	0	34,718	2
Total receivables	$1,735,888	100%	$1,735,888	100%

are not paying on time: 27% of its receivables are more than 30 days old, even though Wonder Vision's credit terms call for full payment by Day 30.

Aging schedules cannot be constructed from the type of summary data reported in financial statements; rather, they must be developed from the firm's accounts receivable ledger. However, well-run firms have computerized accounts receivable records, so it is easy to determine the age of each invoice, to sort electronically by age categories, and thus to generate an aging schedule.

Management should constantly monitor both the DSO and the aging schedule to detect any trends, to see how the firm's collections experience compares with its credit terms, and to see how effectively the credit department is operating in comparison with other firms in the industry. If the DSO starts to lengthen or the aging schedule begins to show an increasing percentage of past-due accounts, then the credit manager should examine why these changes are occurring.

Although increases in the DSO and the aging schedule are warning signs, this does not necessarily indicate the firm's credit policy has weakened. If a firm experiences sharp seasonal variations or if it is growing rapidly, then both the aging schedule and the DSO may be distorted. To see this point, note that the DSO is calculated as follows:

$$DSO = \frac{\text{Accounts receivable}}{\text{Annual sales}/365}$$

Receivables at any point in time reflect sales in the past 1 or 2 months, but sales as shown in the denominator are for the past 12 months. Therefore, a seasonal increase in sales will increase the numerator more than the denominator and hence will raise the DSO, even if customers continue to pay just as quickly as before. Similar problems arise with the aging schedule, because if sales are rising then the percentage in the 0–10-day category will be high, and the reverse will occur if sales are falling. Therefore, a change in either the DSO or the aging schedule should be taken as a signal to investigate further; it is not necessarily a sign that the firm's credit policy has weakened.

SELF TEST

Explain how a new firm's receivables balance is built up over time.

Define days sales outstanding (DSO). What can be learned from it? How is it affected by sales fluctuations?

What is an aging schedule? What can be learned from it? How is it affected by sales fluctuations?

A company has annual sales of $730 million. If its DSO is 35, what is its average accounts receivables balance? **($70 million)**

21-9 Accruals and Accounts Payable (Trade Credit)

Recall that net operating working capital is equal to operating current assets minus operating current liabilities. The previous sections discussed the management of operating current assets (cash, inventory, and accounts receivable), and the following sections discuss the two major types of operating current liabilities: accruals and accounts payable.[17]

21-9a Accruals

Firms generally pay employees on a weekly, biweekly, or monthly basis, so the balance sheet will typically show some accrued wages. Similarly, the firm's own estimated income taxes, employment and income taxes with held from employees, and sales taxes collected are generally paid on a weekly, monthly, or quarterly basis. Therefore, the balance sheet will typically show some accrued taxes along with accrued wages.

These **accruals** can be thought of as short-term, interest-free loans from employees and taxing authorities, and they increase automatically (that is, *spontaneously*) as a firm's operations expand. However, a firm cannot ordinarily control its accruals: The timing of wage payments is set by economic forces and industry norms, and tax payment dates are established by law. Thus, firms generally use all the accruals they can, but they have little control over the levels of these accounts.

21-9b Accounts Payable (Trade Credit)

Firms generally make purchases from other firms on credit, recording the debt as an *account payable*. Accounts payable, or **trade credit**, is the largest single operating current liability, representing about 40% of the current liabilities for an average nonfinancial corporation. The percentage is somewhat larger for smaller firms: Because small companies often have difficulty obtaining financing from other sources, they rely especially heavily on trade credit.

Trade credit is a spontaneous source of financing in the sense that it arises from ordinary business transactions. For example, suppose a firm makes average purchases of $2,000 a day on terms of net 30, meaning that it must pay for goods 30 days after the invoice date. On average, it will owe 30 times $2,000, or $60,000, to its suppliers. If its sales, and consequently its purchases, were to double, then its accounts payable would also double, to $120,000. So simply by growing, the firm would spontaneously generate an additional $60,000 of financing. Similarly, if the terms under which the firm buys were extended from 30 to 40 days, then its accounts payable would expand from $60,000 to $80,000 even with no growth in sales. Thus, both expanding sales and lengthening the credit period generate additional amounts of financing via trade credit.

21-9c The Cost of Trade Credit

Firms that sell on credit have a *credit policy* that includes their *terms of credit*. For example, Microchip Electronics sells on terms of 2/10, net 30: It gives customers a 2% discount if they pay within 10 days of the invoice date, but the full invoice amount is due and payable within 30 days if the discount is not taken.

The "true price" of Microchip's products is the net price, or 0.98 times the list price, because any customer can purchase an item at that price as long as payment is made within 10 days. Now consider Personal Computer Company (PCC), which

---

17. For more on accounts payable management, see James A. Gentry and Jesus M. De La Garza, "Monitoring Accounts Payables," *Financial Review*, November 1990, pp. 559–576.

A WAG OF THE FINGER OR TIP OF THE HAT? *THE COLBERT REPORT* AND SMALL BUSINESS PAYMENT TERMS

On February 17, 2011, *The Colbert Report* featured an interview with Jeffrey Leonard. During a spirited exchange with Stephen Colbert, Leonard accused many large businesses of imposing onerous payment terms on their small suppliers. According to Leonard, when Cisco Systems sells to the U.S. government, Cisco receives its payment in 30 days, the standard credit terms used by the federal government. Yet Cisco changed its own credit policy in 2010 to "net 60," meaning that Cisco's suppliers don't get paid for 60 days. In other words, many small companies essentially are helping Cisco finance its working capital, even though Cisco has over $39 billion in cash. Cisco isn't alone in delaying its payments: Dell, Walmart, and AB InBev (the owner of Anheuser-Busch) also pay slower than 30 days.

Colbert and Leonard agreed on the facts but interpreted them differently. Leonard suggested that the government should help small businesses by requiring its own supplier companies to offer their vendors the same terms as the government does. Colbert, however, suggested (perhaps with tongue-in-cheek) that this was just the natural result of free markets and that no government interference was warranted.

You be the judge. When big companies legally take what they can from smaller companies, should they receive a wag of the finger or a tip of the hat?

Sources: **www.washingtonmonthly.com/features/2011/1101.leonard .html; www.colbertnation.com/the-colbert-report-videos/374633 /february-17-2011/jeffrey-leonard**; and **www.allbusiness.com /company-activities-management/management-benchmarking /15472247-1.html.**

buys its memory chips from Microchip. One chip is listed at $100, so its "true" price to PCC is $98. Now if PCC wants an additional 20 days of credit beyond the 10-day discount period, it must incur a finance charge of $2 per chip for that credit. Thus, the $100 list price consists of two components:

$$\text{List price} = \$98 \text{ true price} + \$2 \text{ finance charge}$$

The question PCC must ask before it turns down the discount to obtain the additional 20 days of credit is this: Could credit be obtained at a lower cost from a bank or some other lender?

Now assume that PCC buys $11,923,333 of memory chips from Microchip each year at the net, or true, price. This amounts to $11,923,333/365 = $32,666.67 per day. For simplicity, assume that Microchip is PCC's only supplier. If PCC decides not to take the additional 20 days of trade credit—that is, if it pays on the 10th day and takes the discount—then its payables will average 10($32,666.67) = $326,667. Thus, PCC will be receiving $326,667 of credit from Microchip.

Now suppose PCC decides to take the additional 20 days credit and so must pay the full list price. Because PCC will now pay on the 30th day, its accounts payable will increase to 30($32,666.67) = $980,000.[18] Microchip will now be supplying PCC

---

18. A question arises here: Should accounts payable reflect gross purchases or purchases net of discounts? Generally accepted accounting principles permit either treatment if the difference is not material, but if the discount is material then the transaction must be recorded net of discounts, or at "true" prices. Then, the higher payment that results from not taking discounts is reported as an expense called "discounts lost." Therefore, *we show accounts payable net of discounts even if the company does not expect to take discounts.*

with an additional $980,000 − $326,667 = $653,333 of credit, which PCC could use to build up its cash account, to pay off debt, to expand inventories, or even to extend credit to its own customers, hence increasing its own accounts receivable.

Thus the additional trade credit offered by Microchip has a cost: PCC must pay a finance charge equal to the 2% discount it is forgoing. PCC buys $11,923,333 of chips at the true price, so the added finance charge would increase the total cost to $11,923,333/0.98 = $12,166,666. Therefore, the annual financing cost is $12,166,666 − $11,923,333 = $243,333. Dividing the $243,333 financing cost by the $653,333 of additional credit, we calculate the nominal annual cost rate of the additional trade credit to be 37.2%:

$$\text{Nominal annual costs} = \frac{\$243,333}{\$653,333} = 37.2\%$$

If PCC can borrow from its bank (or some other source) at an interest rate less than 37.2%, then it should take the 2% discount and forgo the additional trade credit.

The following equation can be used to calculate the nominal cost (on an annual basis) of not taking discounts, illustrated with terms of 2/10, net 30:

$$\frac{\text{Nominal cost}}{\text{of trade credit}} = \text{Cost per period} \times \text{Number of periods per year}$$

$$\frac{\text{Nominal cost}}{\text{of trade credit}} = \frac{\text{Discount percentage}}{100 - \dfrac{\text{Discount}}{\text{percentage}}} \times \frac{365}{\dfrac{\text{Days credit is}}{\text{outstanding}} - \dfrac{\text{Discount}}{\text{period}}} \qquad \textbf{(21–8)}$$

$$= \frac{2}{98} \times \frac{365}{20} = 2.04\%, \times 18.25 = 37.2\%$$

The numerator of the first term, Discount percentage, is the cost per dollar of credit, while the denominator, 100 − Discount percentage, represents the funds made available by not taking the discount. Thus, the first term, 2.04%, is the cost per period for the trade credit. The denominator of the second term is the number of days of extra credit obtained by not taking the discount, so the entire second term shows how many times each year the cost is incurred—18.25 times in this example.

This nominal annual cost formula does not consider the compounding of interest. In terms of effective annual interest, the cost of trade credit is even higher:

$$\text{Effective annual rate} = (1.0204)^{18.25} - 1.0 = 1.4459 - 1.0 = 44.6\%$$

Thus, the 37.2% nominal cost calculated with Equation 21-8 actually understates the true cost.

Note, however, that the calculated cost of trade credit can be reduced by paying late. Thus, if PCC could get away with paying in 60 days rather than the specified 30 days, then the effective credit period would become 60 − 10 = 50 days, the number of times the discount would be lost would fall to 365/50 = 7.3, and the nominal cost would drop from 37.2% to 2.04% × 7.3 = 14.9%. Then the effective annual rate would drop from 44.6% to 15.9%:

$$\text{Effective annual rate} = (1.0204)^{7.3} - 1.0 = 1.1589 - 1.0 = 15.9\%$$

FIGURE 21-6	Varying Credit Terms and Their Associated Costs

	A	B	C	D	E	F
277	Days in year: 365				Cost of additional credit	
278						
279	Credit terms	Discount	Discount period	Net period	Nominal	Effective
280	1/10, net 20	1%	10	20	36.87%	44.32%
281	1/10, net 30	1%	10	30	18.43%	20.13%
282	1/10, net 90	1%	10	90	4.61%	4.69%
283	2/10, net 20	2%	10	20	74.49%	109.05%
284	2/10, net 30	2%	10	30	37.24%	44.59%
285	3/15, net 45	3%	15	45	37.63%	44.86%

Microsoft Excel® is a registered trademark of Microsoft Corporation. © 2014 Microsoft.

See **Ch21 Tool Kit.xls** on the textbook's Web site for details.

In periods of excess capacity, firms may be able to get away with deliberately paying late, or **stretching accounts payable**. However, they will also suffer a variety of problems associated with being a "slow payer." These problems are discussed later in the chapter.

The costs of the additional trade credit from forgoing discounts under some other purchase terms are taken from the chapter's *Excel Tool Kit* model and shown here as Figure 21-6. As these numbers indicate, the cost of not taking discounts can be substantial.

On the basis of the preceding discussion, trade credit can be divided into two components: (1) **free trade credit**, which involves credit received during the discount period, and (2) **costly trade credit**, which involves credit in excess of the free trade credit and whose cost is an implicit one based on the forgone discounts. *Firms should always use the free component, but they should use the costly component only after analyzing the cost of this capital to make sure it is less than the cost of funds that could be obtained from other sources.* Under the terms of trade found in most industries, the costly component is relatively expensive, so stronger firms generally avoid using it.

Note, though, that firms sometimes offer favorable credit terms in order to stimulate sales. For example, suppose a firm has been selling on terms of 2/10, net 30, with a nominal cost of 37.24%, but a recession has reduced sales and the firm now has excess capacity. It wants to boost the sales of its product without cutting the list price, so it might offer terms of 1/10, net 90, which implies a nominal cost of additional credit of only 4.61%. In this situation, its customers would probably be wise to take the additional credit and reduce their reliance on banks and other lenders. So, turning down discounts is not always a bad decision.

SELF TEST

What are accruals? How much control do managers have over accruals?

What is trade credit?

What's the difference between free trade credit and costly trade credit?

How does the cost of costly trade credit generally compare with the cost of short-term bank loans?

A company buys on terms of 2/12, net 28. What is its nominal cost of trade credit? (**46.6%**) The effective cost? (**58.5%**)

21-10 **Managing Short-Term Investments**

Short-term investments include short-term financial assets such as U.S. Treasury securities, U.S. agency securities, certificates of deposits, time deposits, and commercial paper. There are three reasons companies hold short-term investments: (1) for liquidation just prior to scheduled transactions, (2) for unexpected opportunities, and (3) to reduce the company's risk.

Some future transaction dates and amounts are known with a high degree of certainty. For example, a company knows the dates on which it will need cash to make interest, principal, and dividend payments; if a company has decided to make a major purchase, such as a new machine or even a new factory, the company knows the dates on which it will pay for the purchase. A company's payment isn't complete until the funds have been deducted from the company's bank account and credited to the depositor's bank account. Because a company doesn't actually need a balance in the bank account until the payment is deducted, most companies try to keep their bank account balances (which pay zero or very low interest rates) as low as possible until the day the payment is deducted. For example, if a company has a scheduled dividend payment, the company is likely to hold the amount needed for the payment in the form short-term investments such as T-bills or other interest-paying short-term securities. The company will liquidate these short-term investments and deposit the proceeds into its bank accounts just prior to the required payment date.

Short-term investments that are designated for making scheduled payments, such as those just described, are temporary in the sense that a company acquires these short-term investments and plans to hold them for a specific period and for a particular use. The following sections describe short-term investments that are less transitory.

Some companies hold short-term investments even though they haven't planned a specific use for them and even though the rate of return on short-term investments is very low. For example, some companies compete in businesses that have growth opportunities that arise unexpectedly. If such a company doesn't have stable cash flows or ready access to credit markets (perhaps because the company is small or doesn't have a high credit rating), it might not be able to take advantage of an unexpected opportunity. Therefore, the company might hold short-term investments, which are **speculative balances** in the sense that the company speculates that it will have an opportunity to use them and subsequently earn much more than the rate on short-term investments. Studies show that such firms do hold relatively high levels of marketable securities. In contrast, cash holdings are less important to large firms with high credit ratings, because they have quick and inexpensive access to capital markets. As expected, such firms hold relatively low levels of cash.[19]

---

19. See the study by Opler, Pinkowitz, Stulz, and Williamson cited in footnote 9.

Holding short-term investments reduces a company's risk of facing a liquidity crisis, such as the ones that occurred during the economic downturn and credit crunch of the 2007 recession. A stockpile of short-term investments also reduces transaction costs due to issuing securities because the investments can be liquidated instead.

Although there are good reasons many companies hold short-term investments, there are too many companies holding too much cash. As we write this in mid-2014, U.S. nonfinancial companies hold about $1.02 trillion in cash, making up about 5% of their total assets. Some companies, such as Apple and Microsoft, have much larger cash-to-assets ratios. Even with the uncertain economic environment, it is hard to believe that investors would not benefit by cash distributions instead of cash stockpiles.

> **SELF TEST**   Why might a company hold low-yielding marketable securities when it could earn a much higher return on operating assets?

21-11 Short-Term Financing

The three possible short-term financing policies described earlier in the chapter were distinguished by the relative amounts of short-term debt used under each policy. The aggressive policy called for the greatest use of short-term debt, and the conservative policy called for using the least; maturity matching fell in between. Although short-term credit is generally riskier than long-term credit, using short-term funds does have some significant advantages. The pros and cons of short-term financing are considered in this section.

21-11a Advantages of Short-Term Financing

First, a short-term loan can be obtained much faster than long-term credit. Lenders will insist on a more thorough financial examination before extending long-term credit, and the loan agreement will have to be spelled out in considerable detail because a lot can happen during the life of a 10- to 20-year loan. Therefore, if funds are needed in a hurry, the firm should look to the short-term markets.

Second, if its needs for funds are seasonal or cyclical, then a firm may not want to commit itself to long-term debt. There are three reasons for this: (1) Flotation costs are higher for long-term debt than for short-term credit. (2) Although long-term debt can be repaid early (provided the loan agreement includes a prepayment provision), prepayment penalties can be expensive. Accordingly, if a firm thinks its need for funds will diminish in the near future, it should choose short-term debt. (3) Long-term loan agreements always contain provisions, or covenants, that constrain the firm's future actions. Short-term credit agreements are generally less restrictive.

The third advantage is that, because the yield curve is normally upward sloping, interest rates are generally lower on short-term debt. Thus, under normal conditions, interest costs at the time the funds are obtained will be lower if the firm borrows on a short-term rather than a long-term basis.

21-11b **Disadvantages of Short-Term Debt**

Even though short-term rates are often lower than long-term rates, using short-term credit is riskier for two reasons: (1) If a firm borrows on a long-term basis, then its interest costs will be relatively stable over time, but if it uses short-term credit, then its interest expense will fluctuate widely, at times going quite high. For example, the rate banks charged large corporations for short-term debt more than tripled over a 2-year period in the 1980s, rising from 6.25% to 21%. Many firms that had borrowed heavily on a short-term basis simply could not meet their rising interest costs; as a result, bankruptcies hit record levels during that period. (2) If a firm borrows heavily on a short-term basis, a temporary recession may render it unable to repay this debt. If the borrower is in a weak financial position, then the lender may not extend the loan, which could force the firm into bankruptcy.

> What are the advantages and disadvantages of short-term debt compared with long-term debt?

SELF TEST

21-12 **Short-Term Bank Loans**

Loans from commercial banks generally appear on balance sheets as notes payable. A bank's importance is actually greater than it appears from the dollar amounts shown on balance sheets because banks provide *nonspontaneous* funds. As a firm's financing needs increase, it requests additional funds from its bank. If the request is denied, the firm may be forced to abandon attractive growth opportunities. The key features of bank loans are discussed in the following paragraphs.

21-12a **Maturity**

Although banks do make longer-term loans, *the bulk of their lending is on a short-term basis*—about two-thirds of all bank loans mature in a year or less. Bank loans to businesses are frequently written as 90-day notes, so the loan must be repaid or renewed at the end of 90 days. Of course, if a borrower's financial position has deteriorated, then the bank may refuse to renew the loan. This can mean serious trouble for the borrower.

21-12b **Promissory Notes**

When a bank loan is approved, the agreement is executed by signing a **promissory note**. The note specifies: (1) the amount borrowed, (2) the interest rate, (3) the repayment schedule, which can call for either a lump sum or a series of installments, (4) any collateral that might have to be put up as security for the loan, and (5) any other terms and conditions to which the bank and the borrower have agreed. When the note is signed, the bank credits the borrower's checking account with the funds; hence both cash and notes payable increase on the borrower's balance sheet.

21-12c **Compensating Balances**

Banks sometimes require borrowers to maintain an average demand deposit (checking account) balance of 10% to 20% of the loan's face amount. This is called a compensating balance, and such balances raise the effective interest rate on the loans. For example, if a firm needs $80,000 to pay off outstanding obligations but it must maintain a 20% compensating balance, then it must borrow $100,000 to obtain a usable $80,000. If the stated annual interest rate is 8%, the effective cost is actually 10%: $8,000 interest divided by $80,000 of usable funds equals 10%.[20]

As we noted earlier in the chapter, recent surveys indicate that compensating balances are much less common now than earlier. In fact, compensating balances are now illegal in many states. Despite this trend, some small banks in states where compensating balances are legal still require their customers to maintain them.

21-12d **Informal Line of Credit**

A **line of credit** is an informal agreement between a bank and a borrower indicating the maximum credit the bank will extend to the borrower. For example, on December 31, a bank loan officer might indicate to a financial manager that the bank regards the firm as being "good" for up to $80,000 during the forthcoming year, provided the borrower's financial condition does not deteriorate. If on January 10 the financial manager signs a 90-day promissory note for $15,000, this would be called "taking down" $15,000 of the total line of credit. This amount would be credited to the firm's checking account at the bank, and the firm could borrow additional amounts up to a total of $80,000 outstanding at any one time.

21-12e **Revolving Credit Agreement**

A **revolving credit agreement** is a formal line of credit often used by large firms. To illustrate, suppose in 2015 Texas Petroleum Company negotiated a revolving credit agreement for $100 million with a group of banks. The banks were formally committed for 4 years to lend the firm up to $100 million if the funds were needed. Texas Petroleum, in turn, paid an annual commitment fee of 0.25% on the unused balance of the commitment to compensate the banks for making the commitment. Thus, if Texas Petroleum did not take down any of the $100 million commitment during a year, it would still be required to pay a $250,000 annual fee, normally in monthly installments of $20,833.33. If it borrowed $50 million on the first day of the agreement, then the unused portion of the line of credit would fall to $50 million and the annual fee would fall to $125,000. Of course, interest would also have to be paid on the money Texas Petroleum actually borrowed. As a general rule, the interest rate on "revolvers" is pegged to the London Interbank Offered Rate (LIBOR), the T-bill rate, or some other market rate, so the cost of the loan varies over time as interest rates change. The interest that Texas Petroleum must pay was set at the prime lending rate plus 1.0%.

---

20. Note, however, that the compensating balance may be set as a minimum monthly *average*, and if the firm would maintain this average anyway then the compensating balance requirement would not raise the effective interest rate. Also, note that these loan compensating balances are *added to* any compensating balances that the firm's bank may require for services performed, such as clearing checks.

Observe that a revolving credit agreement is similar to an informal line of credit but has an important difference: The bank has a *legal obligation* to honor a revolving credit agreement, and it receives a commitment fee. Neither the legal obligation nor the fee exists under the informal line of credit.

Often a line of credit will have a **cleanup clause** that requires the borrower to reduce the loan balance to zero at least once a year. Keep in mind that a line of credit typically is designed to help finance seasonal or cyclical peaks in operations, not as a source of permanent capital. For example, our cash budget for Educational Products Corporation showed negative flows from July through September but positive flows from October through December. Also, the cumulative net cash flow goes positive in November, indicating that the firm could pay off its loan at that time. If the cumulative flows were always negative, this would indicate that the firm was using its credit lines as a permanent source of financing.

21-12f **Costs of Bank Loans**

The costs of bank loans vary for different types of borrowers at any given point in time and for all borrowers over time. Interest rates are higher for riskier borrowers, and rates are also higher on smaller loans because of the fixed costs involved in making and servicing loans. If a firm can qualify for "prime credit" because of its size and financial strength, it can borrow at the **prime rate**, which at one time was the lowest rate banks charged. Rates on other loans are generally scaled up from the prime rate. Loans to large, strong customers are made at rates tied to LIBOR and the costs of such loans are generally well below prime:

Rates on March 19, 2014	
Prime	3.25%
1-Year LIBOR	0.55%

The rate to smaller, riskier borrowers is generally stated something like "prime plus 1.0%"; but for a larger borrower it is generally stated as something like "LIBOR plus 1.5%."

Bank rates vary widely over time depending on economic conditions and Federal Reserve policy. When the economy is weak, loan demand is usually slack, inflation is low, and the Fed makes plenty of money available to the system. As a result, rates on all types of loans are relatively low. Conversely, when the economy is booming, loan demand is typically strong, the Fed restricts the money supply to fight inflation, and the result is high interest rates. As an indication of the kinds of fluctuations that can occur, the prime rate during 1980 rose from 11% to 21% in just 4 months; during 1994, it rose from 6% to 9%.

Calculating Banks' Interest Charges: Regular (or "Simple") Interest

Banks calculate interest in several different ways. In this section, we explain the procedure used for most business loans. For illustration purposes, we assume a loan of $10,000 at the prime rate, currently 3.25%, with a 360-day year. Interest must be paid monthly, and the principal is payable "on demand" if and when the bank wants to end the loan. Such a loan is called a **regular interest** loan or a **simple interest** loan.

We begin by dividing the nominal interest rate (3.25% in this case) by 360 to obtain the rate per day. This rate is expressed as a *decimal fraction,* not as a percentage:

$$\text{Simple interest rate per day} = \frac{\text{Nominal rate}}{\text{Days in year}}$$
$$= 0.0325/360 = 0.000090278$$

To find the monthly interest payment, the daily rate is multiplied by the amount of the loan, and then by the number of days during the payment period. For our illustrative loan, the daily interest charge would be $0.902777778, and the total for a 30-day month would be $27.08:

$$\text{Interest charge for month} = (\text{Rate per day})(\text{Amount of loan})(\text{Days in month})$$
$$= (0.000090278)(\$10{,}000)(30 \text{ days}) = \$27.08$$

The *effective interest rate* on a loan depends on how frequently interest must be paid—the more frequently interest is paid, the higher the effective rate. If interest is paid once per year, then the nominal rate is also the effective rate. However, if interest must be paid monthly, then the effective rate is $(1 + 0.0325/12)^{12} - 1 = 3.2989\%$.

Calculating Banks' Interest Charges: Add-on Interest

Banks and other lenders typically use **add-on interest** for automobiles and other types of installment loans. The term *add-on* means that the interest is calculated and then added to the amount borrowed to determine the loan's face value. To illustrate, suppose you borrow $10,000 on an add-on basis at a nominal rate of 7.25% to buy a car, with the loan to be repaid in 12 monthly installments. At a 7.25% add-on rate, you would make total interest payments of $10,000(0.0725) = $725. Because the loan is paid off in monthly installments, you would have the use of the full $10,000 for only the first month. The outstanding balance would decline in subsequent months until, during the last month, only 1/12 of the original loan was still outstanding.

To find the annual percentage rate (APR), we first find the payment per month, $10,725/12 = $893.75. With a financial calculator, enter N = 12, PV = 10000, PMT = −893.75, and FV = 0; then press I/YR to obtain 1.093585%. This is a monthly rate, so multiply by 12 to get 13.12%, which is the APR the bank would report to the borrower. This is quite a bit above the 7.25% rate, and the effective rate on an add-on loan is even higher. The effective annual rate is $(1.010936)^{12} - 1 = 13.94\%$. All in all, add-on interest loans can be very costly.

What is a promissory note, and what are some terms that are normally included in promissory notes?

What is a line of credit? A revolving credit agreement?

What's the difference between simple interest and add-on interest?

Explain how a firm that expects to need funds during the coming year might make sure that the needed funds will be available.

How does the cost of costly trade credit generally compare with the cost of short-term bank loans?

If a firm borrowed $500,000 at a rate of 10% simple interest with monthly interest payments and a 365-day year, what would be the required interest payment for a 30-day month? **($4,109.59)** If interest must be paid monthly, what would be the effective annual rate? **(10.47%)**

If this loan had been made on a 10% add-on basis, payable in 12 end-of-month installments, what would be the monthly payment amount? **($45,833.33)** What is the annual percentage rate? **(17.97%)** The effective annual rate? **(19.53%)**

21-13 **Commercial Paper**

Commercial paper is a type of unsecured promissory note issued by large, strong firms and sold primarily to other business firms, to insurance companies, to pension funds, to money market mutual funds, and to banks. In March 2014, there was approximately $1.0 trillion of commercial paper outstanding, versus nearly $1.6 trillion of commercial and industrial bank loans. Most, but not all, commercial paper outstanding is issued by financial institutions.

21-13a **Maturity and Cost**

Maturities of commercial paper generally vary from 1 day to 9 months, with an average of about 5 months.[21] The interest rate on commercial paper fluctuates with supply and demand conditions—it is determined in the marketplace, varying daily as conditions change. Recently, commercial paper rates have ranged from 1.5 to 3.5 percentage points below the stated prime rate and up to half of a percentage point above the T-bill rate. For example, in March 2014, the average rate on 3-month commercial paper was 0.10%, the prime rate was 3.25%, and the 3-month T-bill rate was 0.06%.

21-13b **Use of Commercial Paper**

The use of commercial paper is restricted to a comparatively small number of very large companies that are exceptionally good credit risks. Dealers prefer to handle the paper of firms whose net worth is $100 million or more and whose annual borrowing exceeds $10 million. One potential problem with commercial paper is that a debtor who has a temporary financial difficulty may receive little help because commercial paper dealings are generally less personal than are bank relationships. Thus, banks are generally more able and willing to help a good customer weather a temporary storm than is a commercial paper dealer. On the other hand, using commercial paper permits a corporation to tap a wide range of credit sources, including financial institutions outside its own area and industrial corporations across the country, and this can reduce interest costs.

W W W

For updates on the outstanding balances of commercial paper, go to **www.federalreserve .gov/econresdata /releases/ statisticsdata.htm** and check out the volume statistics for Commercial Paper and the weekly releases for Assets and Liabilities of Commercial Banks in the United States.

W W W

For current rates, see **www .federalreserve.gov /econresdata /releases /statisticsdata.htm** and look at the Daily Releases for Selected Interest Rates.

---

21. The maximum maturity without SEC registration is 270 days. Also, commercial paper can be sold only to "sophisticated" investors; otherwise, SEC registration would be required even for maturities of 270 days or less.

SELF TEST

What is commercial paper?

What types of companies can use commercial paper to meet their short-term financing needs?

How does the cost of commercial paper compare with the cost of short-term bank loans? With the cost of Treasury bills?

WEB

For a more detailed discussion of secured financing, see **Web Extension 21A** on the textbook's Web site.

21-14 Use of Security in Short-Term Financing

Thus far, we have not addressed the question of whether or not short-term loans should be secured. Commercial paper is never secured, but other types of loans can be secured if this is deemed necessary or desirable. Other things held constant, it is better to borrow on an unsecured basis because the bookkeeping costs of **secured loans** are often high. However, firms often find that they can borrow only if they put up some type of collateral to protect the lender or that, by using security, they can borrow at a much lower rate.

Companies can employ several different kinds of collateral, including marketable stocks or bonds, land or buildings, equipment, inventory, and accounts receivable. Marketable securities make excellent collateral, but few firms that need loans also hold portfolios of stocks and bonds. Similarly, real property (land and buildings) and equipment are good forms of collateral, but they are generally used as security for long-term loans rather than for working capital loans. Therefore, most secured short-term business borrowing involves the use of accounts receivable and inventories as collateral.

Consider the case of a Chicago hardware dealer who requested a $200,000 bank loan to modernize and expand his store. After examining the business' financial statements, his bank indicated that it would lend him a maximum of $100,000 and that the effective interest rate would be 9%. The owner had a substantial personal portfolio of stocks, and he offered to put up $300,000 of high-quality stocks to support the $200,000 loan. The bank then granted the full $200,000 loan at the prime rate of 3.25%. The store owner might also have used his inventories or receivables as security for the loan, but processing costs would have been high.[22]

SELF TEST

What is a secured loan?

What are some types of current assets that are pledged as security for short-term loans?

---

22. The term "asset-based financing" is often used as a synonym for "secured financing." In recent years, accounts receivable have been used as security for long-term bonds, permitting corporations to borrow from lenders such as pension funds rather than just from banks and other traditional short-term lenders.

Summary

This chapter discussed working capital management and short-term financing. The key concepts covered are listed below.

- **Working capital** refers to current assets used in operations, and **net working capital** is defined as current assets minus all current liabilities. **Net operating working capital** is defined as operating current assets minus operating current liabilities.
- Under a **relaxed working capital policy**, a firm would hold relatively large amounts of each type of current asset. Under a **restricted working capital policy**, the firm would hold minimal amounts of these items.
- **Permanent operating current assets** are the operating current assets the firm holds even during slack times, whereas **temporary operating current assets** are the additional operating current assets needed during seasonal or cyclical peaks. The methods used to finance permanent and temporary operating current assets define the firm's **short-term financing policy**.
- A **moderate** approach to short-term financing involves matching, to the extent possible, the maturities of assets and liabilities, so that temporary operating current assets are financed with short-term debt and permanent operating current assets and fixed assets are financed with long-term debt or equity. Under an **aggressive** approach, some permanent operating current assets, and perhaps even some fixed assets, are financed with short-term debt. A **conservative** approach would be to use long-term sources to finance all permanent operating capital and some of the temporary operating current assets.
- The **inventory conversion period** is the average time required to convert materials into finished goods and then to sell those goods:

    Inventory conversion period = Inventory ÷ Cost of goods sold per day

- The **average collection period** is the average length of time required to convert the firm's receivables into cash—that is, to collect cash following a sale:

    Average collection period = DSO = Receivables ÷ (Sales/365)

- The **payables deferral period** is the average length of time between the purchase of materials and labor and the payment of cash for them:

    Payables deferral period = Payables ÷ Cost of goods sold per day

- The **cash conversion cycle (CCC)** is the length of time between the firm's actual cash expenditures to pay for productive resources (materials and labor) and its own cash receipts from the sale of products (that is, the length of time between paying for labor and materials and collecting on receivables):

$$
\begin{array}{ccccc}
\text{Cash} & & \text{Inventory} & \text{Average} & \text{Payables} \\
\text{conversion} & = & \text{conversion} + & \text{collection} - & \text{deferral} \\
\text{cycle} & & \text{period} & \text{period} & \text{period}
\end{array}
$$

- A **cash budget** is a schedule showing projected cash inflows and outflows over some period. The cash budget is used to predict cash surpluses and deficits, and it is the primary cash management planning tool.
- The **primary goal of cash management** is to minimize the amount of cash the firm must hold for conducting its normal business activities while at the same time maintaining a sufficient cash reserve to take discounts, pay bills promptly, and meet any unexpected cash needs.
- The **transactions balance** is the cash necessary to conduct routine day-to-day business; **precautionary balances** are cash reserves held to meet random, unforeseen needs. A **compensating balance** is a minimum checking account balance that a bank requires as compensation either for services provided or as part of a loan agreement.
- The twin goals of **inventory management** are: (1) to ensure that the inventories needed to sustain operations are available, but (2) to hold the costs of ordering and carrying inventories to the lowest possible level.
- When a firm sells goods to a customer on credit, an **account receivable** is created.
- A firm can use an **aging schedule** and the **days sales outstanding (DSO)** to monitor its receivables balance and to help avoid an increase in bad debts.
- A firm's **credit policy** consists of four elements: (1) credit period, (2) discounts given for early payment, (3) credit standards, and (4) collection policy.
- **Accounts payable**, or **trade credit**, arises spontaneously as a result of credit purchases. Firms should use all the **free trade credit** they can obtain, but they should use **costly trade credit** only if it is less expensive than other forms of short-term debt. Suppliers often offer discounts to customers who pay within a stated period. The following equation may be used to calculate the nominal cost, on an annual basis, of not taking such discounts:

$$\begin{array}{c} \text{Nominal annual cost} \\ \text{of trade credit} \end{array} = \frac{\text{Discount percentage}}{100 - \begin{array}{c}\text{Discount}\\\text{percentage}\end{array}} \times \frac{365}{\begin{array}{c}\text{Days credit is}\\\text{outstanding}\end{array} - \begin{array}{c}\text{Discount}\\\text{period}\end{array}}$$

- The advantages of short-term credit are: (1) the *speed* with which short-term loans can be arranged, (2) increased *flexibility,* and (3) generally *lower interest rates* than with long-term credit. The principal disadvantage of short-term credit is the *extra risk* the borrower must bear because: (1) the lender can demand payment on short notice, and (2) the cost of the loan will increase if interest rates rise.
- **Bank loans** are an important source of short-term credit. When a bank loan is approved, a **promissory note** is signed. It specifies: (1) the amount borrowed, (2) the percentage interest rate, (3) the repayment schedule, (4) the collateral, and (5) any other conditions to which the parties have agreed.
- Banks sometimes require borrowers to maintain **compensating balances**, which are deposit requirements set at between 10% and 20% of the loan amount. Compensating balances raise the effective interest rate on bank loans.
- A **line of credit** is an informal agreement between the bank and the borrower indicating the maximum amount of credit the bank will extend to the borrower.
- A **revolving credit agreement** is a formal line of credit often used by large firms; it involves a **commitment fee**.

- A **simple interest** loan is one in which interest must be paid monthly and the principal is payable "on demand" if and when the bank wants to end the loan.
- An **add-on interest loan** is one in which interest is calculated and added to the funds received to determine the face amount of the installment loan.
- **Commercial paper** is unsecured short-term debt issued by large, financially strong corporations. Although the cost of commercial paper is lower than the cost of bank loans, it can be used only by large firms with exceptionally strong credit ratings.
- Sometimes a borrower will find it is necessary to borrow on a **secured basis**, in which case the borrower pledges assets such as real estate, securities, equipment, inventories, or accounts receivable as collateral for the loan. For a more detailed discussion of secured financing, see *Web Extension 21A*.

Questions

21-1 Define each of the following terms:
   a. Working capital; net working capital; net operating working capital
   b. Relaxed policy; restricted policy; moderate policy
   c. Permanent operating current assets; temporary operating current assets
   d. Moderate (maturity matching) financing policy; aggressive financing policy; conservative financing policy
   e. Inventory conversion period; average collection period; payables deferral period; cash conversion cycle
   f. Cash budget; target cash balance
   g. Transactions balances; compensating balances; precautionary balances
   h. Trade discounts
   i. Credit policy; credit period; credit standards; collection policy; cash discounts
   j. Account receivable; days sales outstanding; aging schedule
   k. Accruals; trade credit
   l. Stretching accounts payable; free trade credit; costly trade credit
   m. Promissory note; line of credit; revolving credit agreement
   n. Commercial paper; secured loan

21-2 What are the two principal reasons for holding cash? Can a firm estimate its target cash balance by summing the cash held to satisfy each of the two reasons?

21-3 Is it true that, when one firm sells to another on credit, the seller records the transaction as an account receivable while the buyer records it as an account payable and that, disregarding discounts, the receivable typically exceeds the payable by the amount of profit on the sale?

21-4 What are the four elements of a firm's credit policy? To what extent can firms set their own credit policies as opposed to accepting policies that are dictated by its competitors?

21-5 What are the advantages of matching the maturities of assets and liabilities? What are the disadvantages?

21-6 From the standpoint of the borrower, is long-term or short-term credit riskier? Explain. Would it ever make sense to borrow on a short-term basis if short-term rates were above long-term rates?

21-7 Discuss this statement: "Firms can control their accruals within fairly wide limits."

21-8 Is it true that most firms are able to obtain some free trade credit and that additional trade credit is often available, but at a cost? Explain.

21-9 What kinds of firms use commercial paper?

Problems   Answers Appear in Appendix B

Easy Problems 1–5

21-1 Cash Management
Williams & Sons last year reported sales of $10 million and an inventory turnover ratio of 2. The company is now adopting a new inventory system. If the new system is able to reduce the firm's inventory level and increase the firm's inventory turnover ratio to 5 while maintaining the same level of sales, how much cash will be freed up?

21-2 Receivables Investment
Medwig Corporation has a DSO of 17 days. The company averages $3,500 in credit sales each day. What is the company's average accounts receivable?

21-3 Cost of Trade Credit
What is the nominal and effective cost of trade credit under the credit terms of 3/15, net 30?

21-4 Cost of Trade Credit
A large retailer obtains merchandise under the credit terms of 1/15, net 45, but routinely takes 60 days to pay its bills. (Because the retailer is an important customer, suppliers allow the firm to stretch its credit terms.) What is the retailer's effective cost of trade credit?

21-5 Accounts Payable
A chain of appliance stores, APP Corporation, purchases inventory with a net price of $500,000 each day. The company purchases the inventory under the credit terms of 2/15, net 40. APP always takes the discount but takes the full 15 days to pay its bills. What is the average accounts payable for APP?

Intermediate Problems 6–12

21-6 Receivables Investment
Snider Industries sells on terms of 2/10, net 45. Total sales for the year are $1,500,000. Thirty percent of customers pay on the 10th day and take discounts; the other 70% pay, on average, 50 days after their purchases.
a. What is the days sales outstanding?
b. What is the average amount of receivables?
c. What would happen to average receivables if Snider toughened its collection policy with the result that all nondiscount customers paid on the 45th day?

21-7 Cost of Trade Credit

Calculate the nominal annual cost of nonfree trade credit under each of the following terms. Assume that payment is made either on the discount date or on the due date.

a. 1/15, net 20

b. 2/10, net 60

c. 3/10, net 45

d. 2/10, net 45

e. 2/15, net 40

21-8 Cost of Trade Credit

a. If a firm buys under terms of 3/15, net 45, but actually pays on the 20th day and *still takes the discount,* what is the nominal cost of its nonfree trade credit?

b. Does it receive more or less credit than it would if it paid within 15 days?

21-9 Cost of Trade Credit

Grunewald Industries sells on terms of 2/10, net 40. Gross sales last year were $4,562,500 and accounts receivable averaged $437,500. Half of Grunewald's customers paid on the 10th day and took discounts. What are the nominal and effective costs of trade credit to Grunewald's nondiscount customers? (*Hint:* Calculate daily sales based on a 365-day year, then calculate average receivables of discount customers, and then find the DSO for the nondiscount customers.)

21-10 Effective Cost of Trade Credit

The D.J. Masson Corporation needs to raise $500,000 for 1 year to supply working capital to a new store. Masson buys from its suppliers on terms of 3/10, net 90, and it currently pays on the 10th day and takes discounts. However, it could forgo the discounts, pay on the 90th day, and thereby obtain the needed $500,000 in the form of costly trade credit. What is the effective annual interest rate of this trade credit?

21-11 Cash Conversion Cycle

Negus Enterprises has an inventory conversion period of 50 days, an average collection period of 35 days, and a payables deferral period of 25 days. Assume that cost of goods sold is 80% of sales.

a. What is the length of the firm's cash conversion cycle?

b. If Negus' annual sales are $4,380,000 and all sales are on credit, what is the firm's investment in accounts receivable?

c. How many times per year does Negus Enterprises turn over its inventory?

21-12 Working Capital Cash Flow Cycle

Strickler Technology is considering changes in its working capital policies to improve its cash flow cycle. Strickler's sales last year were $3,250,000 (all on credit), and its net profit margin was 7%. Its inventory turnover was 6.0 times during the year, and its DSO was 41 days. Its annual cost of goods sold was $1,800,000. The firm had fixed assets totaling $535,000. Strickler's payables deferral period is 45 days.

a. Calculate Strickler's cash conversion cycle.

b. Assuming Strickler holds negligible amounts of cash and marketable securities, calculate its total assets turnover and ROA.

c. Suppose Strickler's managers believe the annual inventory turnover can be raised to 9 times without affecting sales. What would Strickler's cash conversion cycle, total assets turnover, and ROA have been if the inventory turnover had been 9 for the year?

Challenging Problems 13–17

21-13 Working Capital Policy

Payne Products had $1.6 million in sales revenues in the most recent year and expects sales growth to be 25% this year. Payne would like to determine the effect of various current assets policies on its financial performance. Payne has $1 million of fixed assets and intends to keep its debt ratio at its historical level of 60%. Payne's debt interest rate is currently 8%. You are to evaluate three different current asset policies: (1) a tight policy in which current assets are 45% of projected sales, (2) a moderate policy with 50% of sales tied up in current assets, and (3) a relaxed policy requiring current assets of 60% of sales. Earnings before interest and taxes is expected to be 12% of sales. Payne's tax rate is 40%.

a. What is the expected return on equity under each current asset level?
b. In this problem, we have assumed that the level of expected sales is independent of current asset policy. Is this a valid assumption? Why or why not?
c. How would the overall riskiness of the firm vary under each policy?

21-14 Cash Budgeting

Dorothy Koehl recently leased space in the Southside Mall and opened a new business, Koehl's Doll Shop. Business has been good, but Koehl frequently runs out of cash. This has necessitated late payment on certain orders, which is beginning to cause a problem with suppliers. Koehl plans to borrow from the bank to have cash ready as needed, but first she needs a forecast of how much she should borrow. Accordingly, she has asked you to prepare a cash budget for the critical period around Christmas, when needs will be especially high.

Sales are made on a cash basis only. Koehl's purchases must be paid for during the following month. Koehl pays herself a salary of $4,800 per month, and the rent is $2,000 per month. In addition, she must make a tax payment of $12,000 in December. The current cash on hand (on December 1) is $400, but Koehl has agreed to maintain an average bank balance of $6,000—this is her target cash balance. (Disregard the amount in the cash register, which is insignificant because Koehl keeps only a small amount on hand in order to lessen the chances of robbery.)

The estimated sales and purchases for December, January, and February are shown below. Purchases during November amounted to $140,000.

	Sales	Purchases
December	$160,000	$40,000
January	40,000	40,000
February	60,000	40,000

a. Prepare a cash budget for December, January, and February.

b. Suppose that Koehl starts selling on a credit basis on December 1, giving customers 30 days to pay. All customers accept these terms, and all other facts in the problem are unchanged. What would the company's loan requirements be at the end of December in this case? (*Hint:* The calculations required to answer this part are minimal.)

21-15 Cash Discounts

Suppose a firm makes purchases of $3.65 million per year under terms of 2/10, net 30, and takes discounts.

a. What is the average amount of accounts payable net of discounts? (Assume the $3.65 million of purchases is net of discounts—that is, gross purchases are $3,724,489.80, discounts are $74,489.80, and net purchases are $3.65 million.)

b. Is there a cost of the trade credit the firm uses?

c. If the firm did not take discounts but did pay on the due date, what would be its average payables and the cost of this nonfree trade credit?

d. What would be the firm's cost of not taking discounts if it could stretch its payments to 40 days?

21-16 Trade Credit

The Thompson Corporation projects an increase in sales from $1.5 million to $2 million, but it needs an additional $300,000 of current assets to support this expansion. Thompson can finance the expansion by no longer taking discounts, thus increasing accounts payable. Thompson purchases under terms of 2/10, net 30, but it can delay payment for an additional 35 days—paying in 65 days and thus becoming 35 days past due—without a penalty because its suppliers currently have excess capacity. What is the effective, or equivalent, annual cost of the trade credit?

21-17 Bank Financing

The Raattama Corporation had sales of $3.5 million last year, and it earned a 5% return (after taxes) on sales. Recently, the company has fallen behind in its accounts payable. Although its terms of purchase are net 30 days, its accounts payable represents 60 days' purchases. The company's treasurer is seeking to increase bank borrowing in order to become current in meeting its trade obligations (that is, to have 30 days' payables outstanding). The company's balance sheet is as follows (in thousands of dollars):

Cash	$ 100	Accounts payable	$ 600
Accounts receivable	300	Bank loans	700
Inventory	1,400	Accruals	200
Current assets	$1,800	Current liabilities	$1,500
Land and buildings	600	Mortgage on real estate	700
Equipment	600	Common stock, $0.10 par	300
		Retained earnings	500
Total assets	$3,000	Total liabilities and equity	$3,000

a. How much bank financing is needed to eliminate the past-due accounts payable?

b. Assume that the bank will lend the firm the amount calculated in part a. The terms of the loan offered are 8%, simple interest, and the bank uses a 360-day year for the interest calculation. What is the interest charge for 1 month? (Assume there are 30 days in a month.)

c. Now ignore part b and assume that the bank will lend the firm the amount calculated in part a. The terms of the loan are 7.5%, add-on interest, to be repaid in 12 monthly installments.

(1) What is the total loan amount?

(2) What are the monthly installments?

(3) What is the APR of the loan?

(4) What is the effective rate of the loan?

d. Would you, as a bank loan officer, make this loan? Why or why not?

Spreadsheet Problem

21–18 Build a Model: Cash Budgeting

Start with the partial model in the file *Ch21 P18 Build a Model.xls* on the textbook's Web site. Rusty Spears, CEO of Rusty's Renovations, a custom building and repair company, is preparing documentation for a line of credit request from his commercial banker. Among the required documents is a detailed sales forecast for parts of 2016 and 2017:

	Sales	Labor and Raw Materials
May 2016	$ 60,000	$75,000
June	100,000	90,000
July	130,000	95,000
August	120,000	70,000
September	100,000	60,000
October	80,000	50,000
November	60,000	20,000
December	40,000	20,000
January 2017	30,000	NA

Estimates obtained from the credit and collection department are as follows: collections within the month of sale, 15%; collections during the month following the sale, 65%; collections the second month following the sale, 20%. Payments for labor and raw materials are typically made during the month following the one in which these costs were incurred. Total costs for labor and raw materials are estimated for each month as shown in the table.

General and administrative salaries will amount to approximately $15,000 a month; lease payments under long-term lease contracts will be $5,000 a month; depreciation charges will be $7,500 a month; miscellaneous expenses will be $2,000 a month; income tax payments of $25,000 will be due in both September and December; and a progress payment of $80,000 on a new office suite must be paid in October. Cash on hand on July 1 will amount to $60,000, and a minimum cash balance of $40,000 will be maintained throughout the cash budget period.

a. Prepare a monthly cash budget for the last 6 months of 2016.

b. Prepare an estimate of the required financing (or excess funds)—that is, the amount of money Rusty's Renovations will need to borrow (or will have available to invest)—for each month during that period.

c. Assume that receipts from sales come in uniformly during the month (i.e., cash receipts come in at the rate of 1/30 each day) but that all outflows are paid on the 5th of the month. Will this have an effect on the cash budget—in other words, would the cash budget you have prepared be valid under these assumptions? If not, what can be done to make a valid estimate of peak financing requirements? No calculations are required, although calculations can be used to illustrate the effects.

d. Rusty's Renovations produces on a seasonal basis, just ahead of sales. Without making any calculations, discuss how the company's current ratio and debt ratio would vary during the year assuming all financial requirements were met by short-term bank loans. Could changes in these ratios affect the firm's ability to obtain bank credit? Why or why not?

e. If its customers began to pay late, this would slow down collections and thus increase the required loan amount. Also, if sales dropped off, this would have an effect on the required loan amount. Perform a sensitivity analysis that shows the effects of these two factors on the maximum loan requirement.

MINI CASE

Karen Johnson, CFO for Raucous Roasters (RR), a specialty coffee manufacturer, is rethinking her company's working capital policy in light of a recent scare she faced when RR's corporate banker, citing a nationwide credit crunch, balked at renewing RR's line of credit. Had the line of credit not been renewed, RR would not have been able to make payroll, potentially forcing the company out of business. Although the line of credit was ultimately renewed, the scare has forced Johnson to examine carefully each component of RR's working capital to make sure it is needed, with the goal of determining whether the line of credit can be eliminated entirely. In addition to (possibly) freeing RR from the need for a line of credit, Johnson is well aware that reducing working capital can also add value to a company by improving its EVA (Economic

Value Added). In her corporate finance course Johnson learned that EVA is calculated by taking net operating profit after taxes (NOPAT) and then subtracting the dollar cost of all the capital the firm uses:

EVA = NOPAT − Capital costs
    = EBIT(1 − T) − WACC (Total capital employed)

If EVA is positive, then the firm's management is creating value. On the other hand, if EVA is negative, then the firm is not covering its cost of capital and stockholders' value is being eroded. If RR could generate its current level of sales with fewer assets, it would need less capital. This would, other things held constant, lower capital costs and increase its EVA.

Historically, RR has done little to examine working capital, mainly because of poor communication among business functions. In the past, the production manager resisted Johnson's efforts to question his holdings of raw materials, the marketing manager resisted questions about finished goods, the sales staff resisted questions about credit policy (which affects accounts receivable), and the treasurer did not want to talk about the cash and securities balances. However, with the recent credit scare, this resistance became unacceptable and Johnson has undertaken a company-wide examination of cash, marketable securities, inventory, and accounts receivable levels.

Johnson also knows that decisions about working capital cannot be made in a vacuum. For example, if inventories could be lowered without adversely affecting operations, then less capital would be required, the dollar cost of capital would decline, and EVA would increase. However, lower raw materials inventories might lead to production slowdowns and higher costs, and lower finished goods inventories might lead to stock-outs and loss of sales. So, before inventories are changed, it will be necessary to study operating as well as financial effects. The situation is the same with regard to cash and receivables. Johnson has begun her investigation by collecting the ratios shown below.

	RR	Industry
Current	1.75	2.25
Quick	0.92	1.16
Total liabilities/assets	58.76%	50.00%
Turnover of cash and securities	16.67	22.22
Days sales outstanding (365-day basis)	45.63	32.00
Inventory turnover	10.80	20.00
Fixed assets turnover	7.75	13.22
Total assets turnover	2.60	3.00
Profit margin on sales	2.07%	3.50%
Return on equity (ROE)	10.45%	21.00%
Payables deferral period	30.00	33.00

a. Johnson plans to use the preceding ratios as the starting point for discussions with RR's operating team. She wants everyone to think about the pros and cons of changing each type of current asset and how changes would interact to affect profits and EVA. Based on the data, does RR seem to be following a relaxed, moderate, or restricted working capital policy?

b. How can one distinguish between a relaxed but rational working capital policy and a situation in which a firm simply has excessive current assets because it is inefficient? Does RR's working capital policy seem appropriate?

c. Calculate the firm's cash conversion cycle given that annual sales are $660,000 and cost of goods sold represents 90% of sales. Assume a 365-day year.

d. What might RR do to reduce its cash without harming operations?

e. In an attempt to better understand RR's cash position, Johnson developed a cash budget for the first 2 months of the year. This budget appears on the next page. She has the figures for the other months, but they are not shown. Should depreciation expense be explicitly included in the cash budget? Why or why not?

f. In her preliminary cash budget, Johnson has assumed that all sales are collected and thus that RR has no bad debts. Is this realistic? If not, how would bad debts be dealt with in a cash budgeting sense? (*Hint:* Bad debts will affect collections but not purchases.)

g. Johnson's cash budget for the entire year, although not given here, is based heavily on her forecast for monthly sales. Sales are expected to be extremely low between May and September but then to increase dramatically in the fall and winter. November is typically the firm's best month, when RR ships its holiday blend of coffee. Johnson's forecasted cash budget indicates that the company's cash holdings will exceed the targeted cash balance every month except for October and November, when shipments will be high but collections will not be coming in until later. Based on the ratios shown earlier, does it appear that RR's target cash balance is appropriate? In addition to possibly lowering the target cash balance, what actions might RR take to better improve its cash management policies, and how might that affect its EVA?

Cash Budget (Thousands of Dollars)	Nov	Dec	Jan	Feb	Mar	Apr
Sales Forecast						
(1) Sales (gross)	$71,218.00	$68,212.00	$65,213.00	$52,475.00	$42,909.00	$30,524.00
Collections						
(2) During month of sale: (0.2)(0.98)(month's sales)			12,781.75	10,285.10		
(3) During first month after sale: (0.7)(previous month's sales)			47,748.40	45,649.10		
(4) During second month after sale: (0.1)(sales 2 months ago)			7,121.80	6,821.20		
(5) Total collections (Lines 2 + 3 + 4)			$67,651.95	$62,755.40		
Purchases						
(6) (0.85)(forecasted sales 2 months from now)		$44,603.75	$36,472.65	$25,945.40		
Payments						
(7) Payments (1-month lag)			44,603.75	36,472.65		
(8) Wages and salaries			6,690.56	5,470.90		
(9) Rent			2,500.00	2,500.00		
(10) Taxes						
(11) Total payments			$53,794.31	$44,443.55		
NCFs						
(12) Cash on hand at start of forecast			$ 3,000.00			
(13) NCF: Collections – Payments. = Line 5 – Line 11			$13,857.64	$ 18,311.85		
(14) Cum NCF: Prior + this mos. NCF			$16,857.64	$ 35,169.49		
Cash Surplus (or Loan Requirement)						
(15) Target cash balance			1,500.00	1,500.00		
(16) Surplus cash or loan needed			$15,357.64	$33,669.49		

h. What reasons might RR have for maintaining a relatively high amount of cash?

i. Is there any reason to think that RR may be holding too much inventory? If so, how would that affect EVA and ROE?

j. If the company reduces its inventory without adversely affecting sales, what effect should this have on the company's cash position: (1) in the short run and (2) in the long run? Explain in terms of the cash budget and the balance sheet.

k. Johnson knows that RR sells on the same credit terms as other firms in its industry. Use the ratios presented earlier to explain whether RR's customers pay more or less promptly than those of its competitors. If there are differences, does that suggest RR should tighten or loosen its credit policy? What four variables make up a firm's credit policy, and in what direction should each be changed by RR?

l. Does RR face any risks if it tightens its credit policy?

m. If the company reduces its DSO without seriously affecting sales, what effect would this have on its cash position: (1) in the short run and (2) in the long run? Answer in terms of the cash budget and the balance sheet. What effect should this have on EVA in the long run?

n. In addition to improving the management of its current assets, RR is also reviewing the ways in which it finances its current assets. Is it likely that RR could make significantly greater use of accruals?

o. Assume that RR purchases $200,000 (net of discounts) of materials on terms of 1/10, net 30, but that it can get away with paying on the 40th day if it chooses not to take discounts. How much free trade credit can the company get from its equipment supplier, how much costly trade credit can it get, and what is the nominal annual interest rate of the costly credit? Should RR take discounts?

p. RR tries to match the maturity of its assets and liabilities. Describe how RR could adopt either a more aggressive or a more conservative financing policy.

q. What are the advantages and disadvantages of using short-term debt as a source of financing?

r. Would it be feasible for RR to finance with commercial paper?

SELECTED ADDITIONAL CASES

The following cases from CengageCompose cover many of the concepts discussed in this chapter and are available at http://compose.cengage.com.

Klein-Brigham Series:

Case 29, "Office Mates, Inc.," which illustrates how changes in current asset policy affect expected profitability and risk; Case 32, "Alpine Wear, Inc.," which illustrates the mechanics of the cash budget and the rationale behind its use; Case 50, "Toy World, Inc.," and Case 66, "Sorenson Stove Company," which deal with cash budgeting; Case 33, "Upscale Toddlers, Inc.," which deals with credit policy changes; and Case 34, "Texas Rose Company," which focuses on receivables management.

Brigham-Buzzard Series:

Case 11, "Powerline Network Corporation (Working Capital Management)."

Providing and Obtaining Credit

WEB

The textbook's Web site contains an *Excel* file that will guide you through the chapter's calculations. The file for this chapter is **Ch22 Tool Kit.xls**, and we encourage you to open the file and follow along as you read the chapter.

Chapter 21 covered the basics of working capital management, including a brief discussion of trade credit from the standpoint of firms that grant credit and report it as accounts receivable and also from the standpoint of firms that use credit and report it as accounts payable. In this chapter, we expand the discussion of this important topic and also discuss the cost of the other major source of short-term financing, bank loans.

Beginning-of-Chapter Questions

As you read the chapter, consider how you would answer the following questions. You *should not* necessarily be able to answer the questions before you read the chapter. Rather, you should use them to get a sense of the issues covered in the chapter. After reading the chapter, you should be able to give at least partial answers to the questions, and you should be able to give better answers after the chapter has been discussed in class. Note, too, that it is often useful, when answering conceptual questions, to use hypothetical data to illustrate your answer. We illustrate the answers with an *Excel* model that is available on the textbook's Web site. Accessing the model and working through it is a useful exercise, and it provides insights that are useful when answering the questions.

1. How do each of the items in a firm's **credit policy**—defined to include the credit period, the discount and discount period, the credit standards used, and the collection policy—affect its sales, the level of its accounts receivable, and its profitability?

2. Does its management typically have complete control over a firm's credit policy? As a general rule, is it more likely that a company would increase its profitability if it tightened or loosened its credit policy?

3. How does credit policy affect the cash conversion cycle as discussed in the last chapter?

4. Suppose a company's current credit terms are 1/10, net 30, but management is considering changing its terms to 2/10, net 40, relaxing its credit standards, and putting less pressure on slow-paying customers. How would you expect these changes to affect: (a) sales, (b) the percentage of customers who take discounts, (c) the percentage of customers who pay late, and (d) the percentage of customers who end up as bad debts?

5. How would you decide whether or not to make the change described in question 4? Assume you also have information on the company's cost of capital, tax rate, and variable costs. How would the company's capacity utilization affect the decision?

6. What are some ways banks can state their charges, and how should the cost of bank debt be analyzed? In the early 1970s, Congress debated the need for new legislation, and it ended up passing a "Truth in Lending" law. One part of the law was the requirement that banks disclose their **APR**. How is the APR calculated? Do you think the Truth in Lending law was really necessary?

22-1 **Credit Policy**

As we stated in Chapter 21, the success or failure of a business depends primarily on the demand for its products: As a rule, the higher its sales, the larger its profits and the higher its stock price. Sales, in turn, depend on a number of factors, some exogenous but others under the firm's control. The major controllable determinants of demand are sales price, product quality, advertising, and the firm's **credit policy**. Credit policy, in turn, consists of these four variables:

1. *Credit period,* which is the length of time buyers are given to pay for their purchases.
2. *Discounts* given for early payment, including the discount percentage and how rapidly payment must be made to qualify for the discount.
3. *Credit standards,* which refer to the required financial strength of acceptable credit customers.
4. *Collection policy,* which is measured by the firm's toughness or laxity in attempting to collect on slow-paying accounts.

The credit manager is responsible for administering the firm's credit policy. However, because of the pervasive importance of credit, the credit policy normally is established by the executive committee, which usually consists of the president plus the vice presidents of finance, marketing, and production.

> **SELF TEST**   What are the four credit policy variables?

22-2 **Setting the Credit Period and Standards**

A firm's regular **credit terms**, which include the **credit period** and **discount**, might call for sales terms of 2/10, net 30 to all "acceptable" customers. Here customers are required to pay within 30 days, but they are given a 2% discount if they pay by the 10th day. The firm's *credit standards* would be applied to determine which customers qualify for the regular credit terms and the amount of credit available to each customer.

22-2a **Credit Standards**

Credit standards refer to the financial strength and creditworthiness a customer must exhibit in order to qualify for credit. A customer that does not qualify for the regular credit terms can still purchase from the firm but only under more restrictive terms. For example, a firm's "regular" credit terms might call for payment within 30 days, and these terms might be offered to all qualified customers; the firm's credit standards are applied when determining which customers qualify. The major factors to consider when setting credit standards concern the likelihood that a given customer will pay slowly or perhaps end up as a bad-debt loss.

Setting credit standards requires a measurement of *credit quality*, which is defined in terms of the probability of a customer's default. The probability estimate for a given customer is, for the most part, a subjective judgment. Nevertheless, credit evaluation is a well-established practice, and a good credit manager can make reasonably accurate judgments of the probability of default by different classes of customers.

Managing a credit department requires fast, accurate, and up-to-date information. To help get such information, the National Association of Credit Management (a group with 16,000 member firms) persuaded TRW, a large credit-reporting agency, to develop a computer-based telecommunications network for the collection, storage, retrieval, and distribution of credit information. A typical business credit report would include the following pieces of information:

1. A summary balance sheet and income statement
2. A number of key ratios, including trend information
3. Information obtained from the firm's suppliers telling whether it pays promptly or slowly and whether it has recently failed to make any payments
4. A verbal description of the physical condition of the firm's operations
5. A verbal description of the backgrounds of the firm's owners, including any previous bankruptcies, lawsuits, divorce settlement problems, and the like
6. A summary rating, ranging from A for the best credit risks down to F for those deemed likely to default

Consumer credit is appraised similarly, using income, years of employment, ownership of home, and past credit history (pays on time or has defaulted) as criteria.

Although a great deal of credit information is available, it must still be processed using judgment. Computerized information systems can assist in making better credit decisions, but, in the final analysis, most credit decisions are really exercises in informed judgment.[1]

> What are credit terms?
>
> What is credit quality, and how is it assessed?

SELF TEST

22-3 Setting the Collection Policy

Collection policy refers to the procedures the firm follows to collect past-due accounts. For example, a company might send a letter to customers when a bill is 10 days past due; it would send a more severe letter, followed by a telephone call, if payment is not received within 30 days; and it would turn the account over to a collection agency after 90 days.

---

1. Credit analysts use procedures ranging from highly sophisticated, computerized "creditscoring" systems, which actually calculate the statistical probability that a given customer will default, to informal procedures, which involve going through a checklist of factors that should be considered when processing a credit application. The credit-scoring systems use various financial ratios such as the current ratio and the debt ratio (for businesses) and income, years with the same employer, and the like (for individuals) to determine the statistical probability of default. Credit is then granted to those with low default probabilities. The informal procedures often involve examining the "5 C's of Credit": character, capacity, capital, collateral, and conditions. Character is obvious; capacity is a subjective estimate of ability to repay; capital means how much net worth the borrower has; collateral means assets pledged to secure the loan; and conditions refers to business conditions that affect ability to repay.

The collection process can be expensive in terms of both out-of-pocket expenditures and lost goodwill—customers dislike being turned over to a collection agency. However, at least some firmness is needed to prevent an undue lengthening of the collection period and to minimize outright losses. A balance must be struck between the costs and benefits of different collection policies.

Changes in collection policy influence sales, the collection period, and the bad-debt loss percentage. All of this should be taken into account when setting the credit policy.

> **SELF TEST**   How does collection policy influence sales, the collection period, and the bad-debt loss percentage?

22-4 Cash Discounts

The last element in the credit policy decision, the use of **cash discounts** for early payment, is analyzed by balancing the costs and benefits of different cash discounts. For example, a firm might decide to change its credit terms from "net 30," which means that customers must pay within 30 days, to "2/10, net 30," in which a 2% discount is given if payment is made within 10 days. This change should produce two benefits: (1) it should attract new customers who consider the discount to be a price reduction and (2) it should lead to a reduction in the days sales outstanding (DSO), because some existing customers will pay more promptly in order to get the discount. Offsetting these benefits is the dollar cost of the discounts. The optimal discount percentage is established at the point at which the marginal costs and benefits are exactly offsetting.

If sales are seasonal, a firm may use **seasonal dating** on discounts. For example, Slimware Inc., a swimsuit manufacturer, sells on terms of 2/10, net 30, May 1 dating. This means that the effective invoice date is May 1, even if the sale was made back in January. The discount may be taken up to May 10; otherwise, the full amount must be paid by May 30. Slimware produces swimsuits throughout the year, but retail sales are concentrated in the spring and early summer. By offering seasonal dating, the company induces some of its customers to stock up early, saving Slimware some storage costs and also "nailing down sales."

> **SELF TEST**   How can cash discounts be used to influence sales volume and the DSO?
>
> What is seasonal dating?

22-5 Other Factors Influencing Credit Policy

In addition to the factors discussed in previous sections, two other points should be made regarding credit policy: the potential for profit and the legal considerations.

22-5a Profit Potential

We have emphasized the costs of granting credit. However, *if it is possible to sell on credit and also to impose a carrying charge on receivables that are outstanding, then credit sales can actually be more profitable than cash sales.* This is especially true for consumer durables (autos, appliances, and so on), but it is also true for certain types of industrial equipment.[2]

The carrying charges on outstanding credit are generally about 18% on a nominal basis: 1.5% per month, so $1.5\% \times 12 = 18\%$. This is equivalent to an effective annual rate of $(1.015)^{12} - 1.0 = 19.6\%$. Having receivables outstanding that earn more than 18% is highly profitable unless there are too many bad-debt losses.

22-5b Legal Considerations

It is illegal, under the Robinson-Patman Act, for a firm to charge prices that discriminate between customers unless these differential prices are cost-justified. The same holds true for credit—it is illegal to offer more favorable credit terms to one customer or class of customers than to another unless the differences are cost-justified.

How do profit potential and legal considerations affect a firm's credit policy?

SELF TEST

22-6 The Payments Pattern Approach to Monitoring Receivables

In Chapter 21, we discussed two methods for monitoring a firm's receivables position: days sales outstanding and aging schedules. These procedures are useful, particularly for monitoring an individual customer's account, but neither is totally suitable for changes in aggregate payment behavior, especially for a firm that experiences fluctuating credit sales. Fortunately, the **payments pattern approach** is ideally suited for identifying payment trends.

The primary point in analyzing the aggregate accounts receivable situation is to see if customers, on average, are paying more slowly. If so, then accounts receivable will build up, as will the cost of carrying receivables. Furthermore, the payment slowdown may signal a decrease in the quality of the receivables and hence an increase in bad-debt losses down the road. The DSO and aging schedules are useful in monitoring credit operations, but both are affected by increases and decreases in the level of sales. Thus, changes in sales levels, including seasonal or cyclical changes, can change a firm's DSO and aging schedule even though its customers' payment behavior has not changed at all. For this reason, a procedure called the *payments pattern approach* has been developed to measure any changes that might be occurring in customers' payment behavior. To illustrate the payments pattern approach, consider the Hanover Company, a small manufacturer of hand tools that commenced operations in January 2015. Table 22-1 contains Hanover's credit sales and receivables data for 2015. Column 2 shows that Hanover's credit sales are seasonal, with the lowest sales in the fall and winter months and the highest during the summer.

---

2. Companies that do a large volume of sales financing typically set up subsidiary companies called *captive finance companies* to do the actual financing.

TABLE 22-1	Hanover Company: Receivables Data for 2015 (Thousands of Dollars)						
			Based on Quarterly Sales Data		Based on Year-to-Date Sales Data		
Month (1)	Credit Sales for Month (2)	Receivables at End of Month (3)	ADS[a] (4)	DSO[b] (5)	ADS[c] (6)	DSO[c] (7)
January	$ 60	$ 54				
February	60	90				
March	60	102	$1.98	52 days	$1.98	52 days
April	60	102				
May	90	129				
June	120	174	2.97	59	2.47	70
July	120	198				
August	90	177				
September	60	132	2.97	44	2.64	50
October	60	108				
November	60	102				
December	60	102	1.98	52	2.47	41

[a]ADS = Average daily sales.
[b]DSO = Days sales outstanding.
[c]We assume that each quarter is 91 days long.

Now assume that 10% of Hanover's customers pay in the month the sale is made, 30% pay in the first month following the sale, 40% pay in the second month, and the remaining 20% pay in the third month. Further, assume that Hanover's customers have the same payment behavior throughout the year; that is, they always take the same length of time to pay. Column 3 of Table 22-1 contains Hanover's receivables balance at the end of each month. For example, during January Hanover had $60,000 in sales. Because 10% of the customers paid during the month of sale, the receivables balance at the end of January was $60,000 − 0.1($60,000) = (1.0 − 0.1)($60,000) = 0.9($60,000) = $54,000. By the end of February, 10% + 30% = 40% of the customers had paid for January's sales and 10% had paid for February's sales. Thus, the receivables balance at the end of February was 0.6($60,000) + 0.9($60,000) = $90,000. By the end of March, 80% of January's sales had been collected, 40% of February's sales had been collected, and 10% of March's sales had been collected, so the receivables balance was 0.2($60,000) + 0.6($60,000) + 0.9($60,000) = $102,000, and so on.

Columns 4 and 5 give Hanover's average daily sales (ADS) and days sales outstanding (DSO), respectively, as these measures would be calculated from quarterly financial statements. For example, in the April–June quarter, ADS = ($60,000 + $90,000 + $120,000)/91 = $2,967, and the end-of-quarter (June 30) DSO = $174,000/$2,967 = 58.6 days. Columns 6 and 7 also show ADS and DSO, but here they are calculated on the basis of accumulated sales throughout the year. For example, at the end of June ADS = $450,000/182 = $2,473 and DSO = $174,000/$2,473 = 70 days. (For the entire year, sales are $900,000; ADS = $2,466 and DSO at year-end = 41 days. These last two figures are shown at the bottom of the last two columns.)

The data in Table 22-1 illustrate two major points. First, fluctuating sales lead to changes in the DSO, which suggests that customers are paying faster or slower even though we know that customers' payment patterns are not changing at all. The rising monthly sales trend causes the calculated DSO to rise, whereas declining sales (as in the third quarter) cause the calculated DSO to fall, even though nothing is changing with regard to when customers actually pay. Second, we see that the DSO depends on an averaging procedure; however, regardless of whether quarterly, semiannual, or annual data are used, the DSO is unstable even when payment patterns are *not* changing. Therefore, it is inadvisable to use the DSO as a monitoring device if the firm's sales exhibit seasonal or cyclical patterns.

Seasonal or cyclical variations also make it difficult to interpret aging schedules. Table 22-2 contains Hanover's aging schedules at the end of each quarter. At the end of June, Table 22-2 shows that Hanover's receivables balance was $174,000: 0.2($60,000) + 0.6($90,000) + 0.9($120,000) = $174,000. Note again that Hanover's customers had not changed their payment patterns. However, rising sales during the second quarter created the impression of faster payments when judged by the percentage aging schedule, and declining sales after July created the opposite appearance. Thus, neither the DSO nor the aging schedule provides an accurate picture of customers' payment patterns if sales fluctuate during the year or are trending up or down.

The days sales outstanding and quarterly aging schedules are unable to identify changes in payments patterns due to changes in payment behavior, so we need a better tool. This tool is the **uncollected balances schedule**, which each quarter shows the month's remaining receivables as a percentage of the month's sales; see Table 22-3. At the end of each quarter, the dollar amount of receivables remaining from each of the 3 month's sales is divided by that month's sales to obtain three receivables-to-sales ratios. For example, at the end of the first quarter, $12,000 of the $60,000 January sales, or 20%, are still outstanding, 60% of February sales

TABLE 22-2	Hanover Company: Quarterly Aging Schedules for 2015 (Thousands of Dollars)							
Ages of Accounts (Days)	**Value and Percentage of Total Accounts Receivable at the End of Each Quarter**							
	March 31		**June 30**		**September 30**		**December 31**	
0–30	$ 54	53%	$108	62%	$ 54	41%	$ 54	53%
31–60	36	35	54	31	54	41	36	35
61–90	12	12	12	7	24	18	12	12
	$102	100%	$174	100%	$132	100%	$102	100%

TABLE 22-3	Hanover Company: Quarterly Uncollected Balances Schedules for 2015 (Thousands of Dollars)		
Quarter	Monthly Sales	Remaining Receivables at End of Quarter	Month's Remaining Receivables at End of Quarter as a Percentage of Month's Sales
Quarter 1:			
January	$ 60	$ 12	20%
February	60	36	60
March	60	54	90
		$102	170%
Quarter 2:			
April	$ 60	$ 12	20%
May	90	54	60
June	120	108	90
		$174	170%
Quarter 3:			
July	$120	$ 24	20%
August	90	54	60
September	60	54	90
		$132	170%
Quarter 4:			
October	$ 60	$ 12	20%
November	60	36	60
December	60	54	90
		$102	170%

are still out, and 90% of March sales are uncollected. Exactly the same pattern is revealed at the end of each of the next three quarters. Therefore, to implement the payments pattern approach, you must construct the uncollected balances schedule and compare the month's remaining receivables at the end of quarter (as a percentage of the month's sales). As shown in the last column in Table 22-3, Hanover's customers' payment patterns have remained constant.

Recall that, at the beginning of the example, we assumed the existence of a constant payments pattern. In a normal situation, the firm's customers' payments pattern would probably vary somewhat over time. Such variations would be shown in the last column of the uncollected balances schedule. For example, suppose customers began to pay their accounts more slowly in the second quarter. That might cause the second-quarter uncollected balances schedule to look like this (in thousands of dollars):

Quarter 2, 2015	Sales	New Remaining Receivables	New Receivables/Sales
April	$ 60	$ 16	27%
May	90	70	78
June	120	110	92
		$196	197%

We see that the receivables-to-sales ratios are now higher than in the corresponding months of the first quarter—customers have changed their payments patterns. This causes the total uncollected balances percentage to rise from 170% to 197%, which should alert Hanover's managers that customers are paying more slowly than they did earlier in the year.

The uncollected balances schedule permits a firm to monitor its receivables better, and it can also be used to forecast future receivables balances. When Hanover's projected 2016 quarterly balance sheets are constructed, management can use the historical receivables-to-sales ratios, coupled with 2016 sales estimates, to project each quarter's receivables balance. For example, with projected sales as given below and using the same payments pattern as in 2015, Hanover's projected end-of-June 2016 receivables balance would be as follows:

Quarter 2, 2016	Projected Sales	Receivables/Sales	Projected Receivables
April	$ 70	20%	$ 14
May	100	60	60
June	140	90	126
		Total projected receivables =	$200

The payments pattern approach permits us to remove the effects of seasonal and/or cyclical sales variation and to construct a more accurate measure of customers' payments patterns. Thus, it provides financial managers with better aggregate information than the days sales outstanding or the aging schedule. Managers should use the payments pattern approach to monitor collection performance as well as to project future receivables requirements.

Nowhere in the typical firm have computers had more of an effect than in accounts receivable management, with the possible exception of the inventory and cash management areas. A well-run business will use a computer system to record sales, to send out bills, to keep track of when payments are made, to alert the credit manager when an account becomes past due, and to take action automatically to collect past-due accounts (for example, to prepare form letters requesting payment). Additionally, the payment history of each customer can be summarized and used to help establish credit limits for customers and classes of customers, and the data on each account can be aggregated and used for the firm's accounts receivable monitoring system. Finally, historical data can be stored in the firm's database and used to develop inputs for studies related to credit policy changes, as we discuss in the next section.

> **SELF TEST**

Define days sales outstanding. What can be learned from it? Does it have any deficiencies when used to monitor collections over time?

What is an aging schedule? What can be learned from it? Does it have any deficiencies when used to monitor collections over time?

What is the uncollected balances schedule? What advantages does it have over the DSO and the aging schedule for monitoring receivables? How can it be used to forecast a firm's receivables balance?

22-7 Analyzing Proposed Changes in Credit Policy

In Chapter 21, our discussion of credit policy included setting the credit period, credit standards, collection policy, and discount percentage as well as the factors that influence credit policy. A firm's credit policy is reviewed periodically, and policy changes may be proposed. However, before a new policy is adopted, it should be analyzed to determine whether it is indeed preferable to the existing policy. In this section, we discuss procedures for analyzing proposed changes in credit policy.

If a firm's credit policy is *eased* by such actions as lengthening the credit period, relaxing credit standards, following a less tough collection policy, or offering cash discounts, then sales should increase: *Easing the credit policy stimulates sales.* Of course, if credit policy is eased and sales rise, then costs will also rise because more labor, materials, and other inputs will be required to produce the additional goods. Additionally, receivables outstanding will also increase, which will increase carrying costs. Moreover, bad debts and/or discount expenses may also rise. Thus, the key question when deciding on a proposed credit policy change is this: Will sales revenues increase more than costs, including credit-related costs, or will the increase in sales revenues be more than offset by higher costs?

Table 22-4 illustrates the general idea behind the analysis of credit policy changes. Column 1 shows the projected income statement for Monroe Manufacturing under the assumption that the firm's current credit policy is maintained throughout the upcoming year. Column 2 shows the expected effects of easing the credit policy by extending the credit period, offering larger discounts, relaxing credit standards, and easing collection efforts. Specifically, Monroe is analyzing the effects of changing its credit terms from 1/10, net 30, to 2/10, net 40; relaxing its credit standards; and putting less pressure on slow-paying customers. Column 3 shows the projected 2016 income statement incorporating the expected effects of easing the credit policy. The looser policy is expected to increase sales and lower collection costs, but discounts and several other types of costs would rise. The overall, bottom-line effect is a $7 million increase in projected net income. In the following paragraphs, we explain how the numbers in the table were calculated.

Monroe's annual sales are $400 million. Under its current credit policy, 50% of those customers who pay do so on Day 10 and take the discount, 40% pay on Day 30,

TABLE 22-4	Monroe Manufacturing Company: Analysis of Changing Credit Policy (Millions of Dollars)		
	Projected 2016 Net Income under Current Credit Policy (1)	**Effect of Credit Policy Change (2)**	**Projected 2016 Net Income under New Credit Policy (3)**
Gross sales	$400	+ $130	$530
Less discounts	2	+ 4	6
Net sales	$398	+ $126	$524
Production costs, including overhead	280	+ 91	371
Profit before credit costs and taxes	$ 118	+ $ 35	$ 153
Credit-related costs			
Cost of carrying receivables	3	+ 2	5
Credit analysis and collection expenses	5	− 3	2
Bad-debt losses	10	+ 22	32
Profit before taxes	$ 100	+ 14	$ 114
State-plus-federal taxes (50%)	50	+ 7	57
Net income	$ 50	+ $ 7	$ 57

Note: The table reports only those cash flows that are related to the credit policy decision.

and 10% pay late, on Day 40. Thus, Monroe's days sales outstanding is $(0.5)(10) + (0.4)(30) + (0.1)(40) = 21$ days, and discounts total $(0.01)($400,000,000)(0.5) = $2,000,000$.

The cost of carrying receivables is equal to the average receivables balance multiplied by the variable cost ratio times the cost of money used to carry receivables. The firm's variable cost ratio is 70%, and its pre-tax cost of capital invested in receivables is 20%. Thus, its annual cost of carrying receivables is $3 million:

$$(DSO)\left(\begin{array}{c}\text{Sales}\\\text{per day}\end{array}\right)\left(\begin{array}{c}\text{Variable}\\\text{cost ratio}\end{array}\right)\left(\begin{array}{c}\text{Cost of}\\\text{funds}\end{array}\right) = \text{Cost of carrying receivables}$$

$$(21)($400,000,000/365)(0.70)(0.20) = $3,221,918 \approx $3 \text{ million}$$

Only variable costs enter this calculation, because this is the only cost element in receivables that must be financed. We are seeking the cost of carrying receivables, and variable costs represent the firm's investment in the cost of goods sold.

Even though Monroe spends $5 million annually to analyze accounts and to collect bad debts, 2.5% of sales will never be collected. Bad-debt losses therefore amount to $(0.025)($400,000,000) = $10,000,000$.

Monroe's new credit policy would be 2/10, net 40 versus the old policy of 1/10, net 30, so it would call for a larger discount and a longer payment period in addition to a relaxed collection effort and lower credit standards. The company believes these changes will lead to a $130 million increase in sales to $530 million per year. Under the new terms, management believes that 60% of the customers who pay will take the 2% discount, so discounts will increase to $(0.02)(\$530,000,000)(0.60) = \$6,360,000 \approx \$6$ million. Half of the nondiscount customers will pay on Day 40 and the remainder on Day 50. The new DSO is thus estimated to be 24 days:

$$(0.6)(10) + (0.2)(40) + (0.2)(50) = 24 \text{ days}$$

Also, the cost of carrying receivables will increase to $5 million:[3]

$$(24)(\$530,000,000/365)(0.70)(0.20) = \$4,878,904 \approx \$5 \text{ million}$$

The company plans to reduce its annual credit analysis and collection expenditures to $2 million. The reduced credit standards and the relaxed collection effort are expected to raise bad-debt losses to about 6% of sales, or to $(0.06)(\$530,000,000) = \$31,800,000 \approx \$32,000,000$, which is an increase of $22 million from the previous level.

The combined effect of all the changes in credit policy is a projected $7 million annual increase in net income. There would, of course, be corresponding changes on the projected balance sheet—the higher sales would necessitate somewhat larger cash balances, inventories, and (depending on the capacity situation) perhaps more fixed assets. Accounts receivable would, of course, also increase. Because these asset increases would have to be financed, certain liabilities and/or equity would have to be increased.

The $7 million expected increase in net income is, of course, an estimate, and the actual effects of the change could be quite different. In the first place, there is uncertainty—perhaps quite a lot—about the projected $130 million increase in sales. Indeed, if the firm's competitors matched its changes, then sales might not rise at all. Similar uncertainties must be attached to the number of customers who would take discounts, to production costs at higher or lower sales levels, to the costs of carrying additional receivables, and to bad-debt losses. In the final analysis, the decision will be based on judgment, especially concerning the risks involved, but the type of quantitative analysis set forth in this section is essential to the process.

SELF TEST

Describe the procedure for evaluating a change in credit policy using the income statement approach.

Do you think that credit policy decisions are made more on the basis of numerical analyses or on subjective judgment?

---

3. Because the credit policy change will result in a longer DSO, the firm will have to wait longer to receive its profit on the goods it sells. Therefore, the firm will incur an opportunity cost due to not having the cash from these profits available for investment. The dollar amount of this opportunity cost is equal to the old sales per day multiplied by the change in DSO times the contribution margin (1 − Variable cost ratio) times the firm's cost of carrying receivables, or:

$$\text{Opportunity cost} = (\text{Old sales}/365)(\Delta DSO)(1 - V)(r)$$
$$= (\$400 \text{ million}/365)(3)(0.3)(0.20)$$
$$= \$0.197 \text{ million} = \$197,000$$

For simplicity, we have ignored this opportunity cost in our analysis. However, we consider opportunity costs in the next section, where we discuss incremental analysis.

22-8 **Analyzing Proposed Changes in Credit Policy: Incremental Analysis**

To evaluate a proposed change in credit policy, one could compare alternative projected income statements, as we did in Table 22-4. Alternatively, one could develop the data in Column 2, which shows the incremental effect of the proposed change, without first developing the projected financial statements. This second approach is often preferable: Given that firms usually change their credit policies in specific divisions or on specific products, and not across the board, it may not be feasible to develop complete corporate income statements. Of course, the two approaches are based on exactly the same data, so they should produce identical results.

In an incremental analysis, we attempt to determine the increase or decrease in both sales and costs associated with a given easing or tightening of credit policy. The difference between incremental sales and incremental costs is defined as **incremental profit**. If the expected incremental profit is positive and if it is sufficiently large to compensate for the risks involved, then the proposed credit policy change should be accepted.

22-8a **The Basic Equations**

In order to ensure that all relevant factors are considered, it is useful to set up some equations for analyzing changes in credit policy. We begin by defining the following terms and symbols:

S_0 = Current gross sales.

S_N = New gross sales after the change in credit policy; note that S_N can be greater or less than S_0.

$S_N - S_0$ = Incremental (change in) gross sales.

V = Variable costs as a percentage of gross sales; V includes production costs, inventory carrying costs, the cost of administering the credit department, and all other variable costs *except* bad-debt losses, financing costs associated with carrying the investment in receivables, and costs of giving discounts.

$1 - V$ = Contribution margin, or the percentage of each gross sales dollar that goes toward covering overhead and increasing profits; the contribution margin is sometimes called the *gross profit* margin.

r = Cost of financing the investment in receivables.

DSO_0 = Days sales outstanding prior to the change in credit policy.

DSO_N = New days sales outstanding after the credit policy change.

B_0 = Average bad-debt loss at the current sales level as a percentage of current gross sales.

B_N = Average bad-debt loss at the new sales level as a percentage of new gross sales.

(*Continued*)

P_0 = Percentage of total customers (by dollar amount) who take discounts under the current credit policy; in other words, the percentage of gross sales that is discount sales.

P_N = Percentage of total customers (by dollar amount) that will take discounts under the new credit policy.

D_0 = Discount percentage offered at the present time.

D_N = Discount percentage offered under the new credit policy.

With these definitions in mind, we can calculate values for the incremental change in the level of the firm's investment in receivables, ΔI, and the incremental change in pre-tax profits, ΔP. The formula for calculating ΔI differs depending on whether the change in credit policy results in an increase or decrease in sales. We first present the equations that show the incremental changes in the investment in receivables and pre-tax profits. We then will discuss and explain them, through use of examples, after all the equations have been set forth.

If the change is expected to *increase* sales—either additional sales to old customers or sales to newly attracted customers, or both—then we have the following situation.

Formula for ΔI if Sales Increase:

(22–1)

$$\Delta I = \left(\begin{array}{c}\text{Increased investment in}\\ \text{receivables associated}\\ \text{with original sales}\end{array}\right) + \left(\begin{array}{c}\text{Increased investment in}\\ \text{receivables associated}\\ \text{with incremental sales}\end{array}\right)$$

$$= \left(\begin{array}{c}\text{Change in}\\ \text{days sales}\\ \text{outstanding}\end{array}\right)\left(\begin{array}{c}\text{Old}\\ \text{sales}\\ \text{per day}\end{array}\right) + V\left(\text{DSO}_N\left(\begin{array}{c}\text{Incremental}\\ \text{sales}\\ \text{per day}\end{array}\right)\right)$$

$$= [(\text{DSO}_N - \text{DSO}_0)(S_0/365)] + V[(\text{DSO}_N)(S_N - S_0)/365]$$

However, if the change in credit policy is expected to *decrease* sales, then the change in the level of investment in receivables is calculated as follows.

Formula for ΔI if Sales Decrease:

(22–2)

$$\Delta I = \left(\begin{array}{c}\text{Decreased investment in}\\ \text{receivables associated with}\\ \text{remaining original customers}\end{array}\right) + \left(\begin{array}{c}\text{Decreased investment in}\\ \text{receivables associated}\\ \text{with customers who left}\end{array}\right)$$

$$= \left(\begin{array}{c}\text{Change in}\\ \text{days sales}\\ \text{outstanding}\end{array}\right)\left(\begin{array}{c}\text{Remaining}\\ \text{sales}\\ \text{per day}\end{array}\right) + V\left(\text{DSO}_0\left(\begin{array}{c}\text{Incremental}\\ \text{sales}\\ \text{per day}\end{array}\right)\right)$$

$$= [(\text{DSO}_N - \text{DSO}_0)(S_N/365)] + V[(\text{DSO}_0)(S_N - S_0)/365]$$

Having calculated the change in receivables investment, we can now analyze the pre-tax profitability of the proposed change.

Formula for ΔP:

$$\Delta P = \begin{pmatrix} \text{Change in} \\ \text{gross} \\ \text{profit} \end{pmatrix} - \begin{pmatrix} \text{Change in cost} \\ \text{of carrying} \\ \text{receivables} \end{pmatrix} - \begin{pmatrix} \text{Change in} \\ \text{bad-debt} \\ \text{losses} \end{pmatrix} - \begin{pmatrix} \text{Change in} \\ \text{cost of} \\ \text{discounts} \end{pmatrix}$$

$$= (S_N - S_0)(1 - V) - r(\Delta I) - (B_N S_N - B_0 S_0) - (D_N S_N P_N - D_0 S_0 P_0)$$

(22–3)

Thus, changes in credit policy are analyzed by using either Equation 22-1 or 22-2, depending on whether the proposed change is expected to increase or decrease sales, together with Equation 22-3. The rationale behind these equations will become clear as we work through several illustrations. Note that all the terms in Equation 22-3 need not be used in a particular analysis. For example, a change in credit policy might not affect discount sales or bad-debt losses, in which case the last two terms of the equation would both be zero. Note also that the form of the equations depends on the way in which the variables are first defined.[4]

22-8b Changing the Credit Period

In this section, we examine the effects of changing the credit period, and in the subsequent sections we consider changes in credit standards, collection policy, and cash discounts. Throughout, we illustrate the situation with data on Stylish Fashions Inc.

Lengthening the Credit Period

Stylish Fashions currently sells on a cash-only basis. Because it extends no credit, the company has no funds tied up in receivables, no bad-debt losses, and no credit expenses of any kind. On the other hand, its sales volume is lower than it would be if credit terms were offered. Stylish is now considering offering credit on 30-day terms. Current sales are $100,000 per year, variable costs are 60% of sales, excess production capacity exists (so no new fixed costs would be incurred as a result of expanded sales), and the cost of capital invested in receivables is 10%. Stylish estimates sales would increase to $150,000 per year if credit were extended and that bad-debt losses would be 2% of total sales. Thus, we have the following:

$S_0 = \$100,000$

$S_N = \$150,000$

$V = 60\% = 0.6$

---

4. For example, P_0 and P_N are defined as the percentage of *total* customers who take discounts. If P_0 and P_N were defined as the percentage of *paying* customers (excluding bad debts) who take discounts, then Equation 22-3 would become:

$$\Delta P = (S_N - S_0)(1 - V) - r(\Delta I) - (B_N S_N - B_0 S_0) - [D_N S_N P_N (1 - B_N) - D_0 S_0 P_0 (1 - B_0)]$$

Similarly, changing the definitions of B_0 and B_N would affect the third term of Equation 22-3, as we discuss later.

$1 - V = 1 - 0.6 = 0.4$

$r = 10\% = 0.10$

$DSO_0 = 0$ days

$DSO_N = 30$ days Here we assume that all customers will pay on time, so DSO = specified credit period. Generally, some customers pay late, so in most cases DSO is greater than the specified credit period.

$B_0 = 0\% = 0.00$ There are currently no bad-debt losses.

$B_N = 2\% = 0.02$ These losses apply to the entire $150,000 new level of sales.

$D_0 = D_N = 0\%$ No discounts are given under either the current or the proposed credit policies.

Because sales are expected to increase, Equation 22-1 is used to determine the change in the investment in receivables:

$$\Delta I = [(DSO_N - DSO_0)(S_0/365)] + V[(DSO_N)(S_N - S_0)/365]$$
$$= [(30 - 0)(\$100,000/365)] + 0.6[30(\$150,000 - \$100,000)/365]$$
$$= \$8,219 + \$2,466 = \$10,685$$

Note that the first term, the increased investment in accounts receivable associated with *old sales*, is based on the full amount of the receivables, whereas the second term, the investment associated with *incremental sales*, consists of incremental receivables multiplied by V, the variable cost percentage. This difference reflects that: (1) the firm invests only its variable cost in incremental receivables, but (2) it would have collected the full sales price on the old sales earlier had it not made the credit policy change. There is an *opportunity cost* on the profit and a *direct financing cost* associated with the $8,219 additional investment in receivables from old sales, but only a direct financing cost associated with the $2,466 investment in receivables from incremental sales.

Looking at this another way, incremental sales will generate an actual increase in receivables of $(DSO_N)(S_N - S_0)/365 = 30(\$50,000/365) = \$4,110$. However, the only part of that increase that must be financed (by bank borrowing or from other sources) and reported as a liability on the right-hand side of the balance sheet is the cash outflow required to support the incremental sales—that is, the variable costs $V(\$4,110) = 0.6(\$4,110) = \$2,466$. The remainder of the receivables increase, $1,644 of accrued before-tax profit, is reflected on the balance sheet not as some type of credit used to finance receivables but rather as an increase in retained earnings generated by the sales. On the other hand, the old receivables level was zero, meaning that the original sales produced cash of $\$100,000/365 = \$273.97$ per day, which was immediately available for investing in assets or for reducing capital from other sources. The change in credit policy will cause a delay in the collection of these funds and hence will require the firm: (1) to borrow to cover the variable costs of the sales and (2) to forgo a return on the retained earnings portion, which would have been available immediately had the credit policy change not been made.

Given ΔI, we may now use Equation 22-3 to determine the incremental profit, ΔP, associated with the proposed credit period change:

$$\Delta P = (S_N - S_0)(1 - V) - r(\Delta I) - (B_N S_N - B_0 S_0) - (D_N S_N P_N - D_0 S_0 P_0)$$
$$= (\$50,000)(0.4) - 0.10(\$10,685) - [0.02(\$150,000) - 0.00(\$100,000)] - \$0$$
$$= \$20,000 - \$1,069 - \$3,000 = \$15,931$$

Because pre-tax profits are expected to increase by \$15,931, the credit policy change appears to be desirable.

Two simplifying assumptions that were made in our analysis should be noted. We assumed: (1) that all customers paid on time (DSO = credit period) and (2) that there were no current bad-debt losses. The assumption of prompt payment can be relaxed quite easily—we can simply use the actual days sales outstanding (say, 40 days), rather than the 30-day credit period, to calculate the investment in receivables and then use this new (higher) value of ΔI in Equation 22-3 to calculate ΔP. Thus, if DSO_N were 40 days then the increased investment in receivables would be:

$$\Delta I = [(40 - 0)(\$100{,}000/365)] + 0.6[40(\$50{,}000/365)]$$
$$= \$10{,}959 + \$3{,}288 = \$14{,}247$$

And the change in pre-tax profits would be:

$$\Delta P = \$50{,}000(0.4) - 0.10(\$14{,}247) - 0.02(\$150{,}000)$$
$$= \$20{,}000 - \$1{,}425 - \$3{,}000 = \$15{,}575$$

The longer collection period causes incremental profits to fall slightly, but they are still positive and so the credit policy should probably be relaxed.

If the company had been selling on credit initially and therefore incurring some bad-debt losses, then this information would need to be included in Equation 22-3. In our example, B_0S_0 was equal to zero because Stylish Fashions did not previously sell on credit; therefore, the change in bad-debt losses was equal to B_NS_N.

Note that B_N is defined as the average credit loss as a percentage of total sales, not of incremental sales. Bad debts might be higher for new customers attracted by the credit terms than for old customers who take advantage of them, but B_N is an average of these two groups. However, if one wanted to keep the two groups separate, it would be easy enough to define B_N as the bad-debt percentage of the incremental sales only.

Other factors could also be introduced into the analysis. For example, the company could consider a further easing of credit by extending the credit period to 60 days, or it could analyze the effects of a sales expansion so great that fixed assets, and hence fixed costs, had to be added. Or the variable cost ratio might change as sales increased, falling if economies of scale were present or rising if diseconomies were present. Adding such factors complicates the analysis, but the basic principles are the same; just bear in mind that we are seeking to determine the *incremental sales revenues*, the *incremental costs*, and consequently the *incremental before-tax profit* associated with a given change in credit policy.

Shortening the Credit Period

Suppose that a year after Stylish Fashions began offering 30-day credit terms its management decided to consider the possibility of shortening the credit period from 30 to 20 days. It was believed that sales would decline by \$20,000 per year from the current level of \$150,000, so S_N = \$130,000. It was also believed that the bad-debt percentage on these lost sales would be 2%, the same as on other sales, and that all other values would remain as given in the previous section.

We first calculate the incremental investment in receivables. Because the change in credit policy is expected to decrease sales, Equation 22-2 is used:

$$\Delta I = [(DSO_N - DSO_0)(S_N/365)] + V[(DSO_0)(S_N - S_0)/365]$$
$$= [(20 - 30)(\$130{,}000/365)] + 0.6[30(\$130{,}000 - \$150{,}000)/365]$$
$$= (-10)(\$356.16) + 0.6[(30)(-\$54.79)]$$
$$= -\$3{,}562 - \$986 = -\$4{,}548$$

With a shorter credit period, there is a shorter collection period, so sales are collected sooner. There is also a smaller volume of business, and hence a smaller investment in receivables. The first term captures the speedup in collections, while the second reflects the reduced sales and hence the lower receivables investment (at variable cost).

Note that V is included in the second term but not in the first. The logic here is similar to the logic underlying Equation 22-1: V is included in the second term because, by shortening the credit period, Stylish Fashions will drive off some customers and forgo sales of $20,000 per year, or $54.79 per day. The firm's investment in those sales was only 60% of the average receivables outstanding, or $0.6(30)(\$54.79) = \$986$. However, the situation is different for the remaining customers. They would have paid their full purchase price—variable cost plus profit—after 30 days. Now, however, they will have to pay this amount 10 days sooner, so those funds will be available to meet operating costs or for investment. Therefore, the first term should not be reduced by the variable cost factor. In total, then, reducing the credit period would result in a $4,548 reduction in the investment in receivables, consisting of a $3,562 decline in receivables associated with continuing customers and a further $986 decline in investment as a result of the reduced sales volume.

Having calculated the change in investment, we can now use Equation 22-3 to analyze the profitability of the proposed change:

$$
\begin{aligned}
\Delta P &= (S_N - S_0)(1 - V) - r(\Delta I) - (B_N S_N - B_0 S_0) - (D_N S_N P_N - D_0 S_0 P_0) \\
&= (\$130{,}000 - \$150{,}000)(0.4) - 0.10(-\$4{,}548) \\
&\quad - [(0.02)(\$130{,}000) - (0.02)(\$150{,}000)] - \$0 \\
&= -\$8{,}000 + \$455 + \$400 = -\$7{,}145
\end{aligned}
$$

Because the expected incremental pre-tax profits are negative, the firm should not reduce its credit period from 30 to 20 days.

22-8c Changes in Other Credit Policy Variables

In the preceding section, we examined the effects of changes in the credit period. Changes in other credit policy variables may be analyzed similarly. In general, we would follow these steps.

Step 1 Estimate the effect of the policy change on sales, on DSO, on bad-debt losses, and so on.

Step 2 Determine the change in the firm's investment in receivables. If the change will increase sales, use Equation 22-1 to calculate ΔI. Conversely, if the change will decrease sales, then use Equation 22-2.

Step 3 Use Equation 22-3, or one of its variations, to calculate the effect of the change on pre-tax profits. If profits are expected to increase, the policy change should be made—unless it is judged to increase the firm's risk by a disproportionate amount.

22-8d Simultaneous Changes in Policy Variables

In the preceding discussion, we considered the effects of changes in only one credit policy variable. The firm could, of course, change several or even all policy variables simultaneously. An almost endless variety of equations could be developed, depending on which policy variables are manipulated and on the assumed effects on sales, discounts taken, the collection period, bad-debt losses, the existence of excess capacity, changes in credit department costs, changes in the variable cost percentage, and so on. The analysis would get "messy" and the incremental profit equation would be complex, but the principles we have developed could be used to handle any type of policy change.

Describe the incremental analysis approach for evaluating a proposed credit policy change.

How can risk be incorporated into the analysis?

SELF TEST

22-9 **The Cost of Bank Loans**

The terms on a short-term bank loan to a business are spelled out in the promissory note. Here are the key elements contained in most promissory notes.

1. *Interest-only versus amortized.* Loans are either *interest-only*, meaning that only interest is paid during the life of the loan and the principal is repaid when the loan matures, or *amortized*, meaning that some of the principal is repaid on each payment date. Amortized loans are called *installment loans*. Note, too, that loans can be fully or partially amortized. For example, a loan may mature after 10 years, but payments may be based on 20 years, so an unpaid balance will still exist at the end of the 10th year. Such a loan is called a "balloon" loan.

2. *Collateral.* If a short-term loan is secured by some specific collateral, generally accounts receivable or inventories, then this fact is indicated in the note. If the collateral is to be kept on the premises of the borrower, then a form called a *UCC-1* (Uniform Commercial Code-1) is filed with the Secretary of State for the state in which the collateral resides, along with a *Security Agreement* (also part of the Uniform Commercial Code) that describes the nature of the agreement. These filings prevent the borrower from using the same collateral to secure loans from different lenders, and they spell out conditions under which the lender can seize the collateral.

3. *Loan guarantees.* If the borrower is a small corporation, its bank will probably insist that the larger stockholders *personally guarantee* the loan. Banks have often seen a troubled company's owner divert assets from the company to some other entity he or she owned, so banks protect themselves by insisting on personal guarantees. However, stockholder guarantees are virtually impossible to secure in the case of larger corporations that have many stockholders. Also, guarantees are unnecessary for proprietorships or partnerships because in those cases the owners are already personally liable for the businesses' debts.

4. *Nominal, or stated, interest rate.* The interest rate can be either *fixed* or *floating.* If it floats, then it is generally indexed to LIBOR. Most loans of any size ($25,000 and up) have floating rates if their maturities are greater than 90 days. The note will also indicate whether the bank uses a *360- or 365-day year* for purposes of calculating interest.

5. *Frequency of interest payments.* If the note is on an interest-only basis, it will indicate *how frequently interest must be paid.* Interest is typically calculated on a daily basis but paid monthly.

6. *Maturity.* Long-term loans always have specific maturity dates. A short-term loan may or may not have a specified maturity. For example, a loan may mature in 30 days, 90 days, 6 months, or 1 year; or it may call for "payment on demand," in which case the loan can remain outstanding as long as the borrower wants to continue using the funds and the bank agrees. Banks virtually never call demand notes unless the borrower's creditworthiness deteriorates, so some "short-term loans" remain outstanding for years, with the interest rate floating with rates in the economy.

7. *Calculation and payment of interest.* For most loans, interest is paid after it is earned. But not all loans follow this convention, and the method by which interest is calculated and paid affects the overall cost of credit. One alternate method is *discount interest.* A *discount loan* requires that interest be paid in advance. If the loan is on a discount basis, the borrower actually receives less than the face amount of the loan, and this increases the loan's effective cost. We discuss discount loans in a later section. Another method is used in an *add-on basis installment loan.* Auto loans and other types of consumer installment loans are generally set up on an "add-on basis," which means that interest over the life of the loan is calculated and then added to the face amount of the loan. Thus, the borrower signs a note for the funds received plus the interest. The add-on feature also raises the effective cost of a loan, as we demonstrate in a later section.

8. *Other cost elements.* Some commercial loans require the borrower to keep a percentage of the borrowed funds in an account at the lending bank. These held funds are called *compensating balances.* In addition, revolving credit agreements often require *commitment fees* in which the borrower pays interest on the amount actually drawn plus a separate fee based either on the total size of the line of credit or on the unused credit. Both of these conditions will be spelled out in the loan agreement, and both raise the effective cost of a loan above its stated nominal rate.

9. *The annual percentage rate (APR).* The various fees and methods of calculating interest mean that the nominal, or stated, interest rate may not reflect the true cost of the loan. The annual percentage rate calculation incorporates all of the costs of borrowing and reports a single nominal rate that reflects all of these costs. However, this rate is required to be reported only for consumer loans.

10. *Key-person insurance.* Often the success of a small company is linked to its owner or to a few important managers. It's a sad fact, but many small companies fail when one of these key individuals dies. Therefore, banks often require small companies to take out *key-person insurance* on their most important managers as part of the loan agreement. Usually the loan becomes due and payable should there be an untimely demise, with the insurance benefits being used to repay the loan. This makes the best of a bad situation—the bank gets its money, and the company reduces its debt burden without having to use any of its operating cash.

In the following sections, we explain how to calculate the effective cost of different bank loans. For illustrative purposes, we assume a loan of $10,000 at a nominal interest rate of 12% and with a 365-day year.

22-9a **Regular, or Simple, Interest**

In Chapter 21, we explained **simple interest,** which is also called **regular interest.** We review that discussion here. Most short-term business lending is with interest-only loans. The first step is to divide the nominal interest rate, 12% in this case, by 365 (or 360 in some cases) to obtain the rate per day:

$$\text{Interest rate per day} = \frac{\text{Nominal rate}}{\text{Days in year}}$$

$$= 0.12/365 = 0.00032876712$$

(22–4)

This rate is then multiplied by the number of days during the specific payment period and then by the amount of the loan. For example, if the loan is interest-only with monthly payments, then the interest payment for January would be $101.92:

$$\frac{\text{Interest charge}}{\text{for period}} = (\text{Days in period})(\text{Rate per day})(\text{Amount of loan})$$

$$= (31 \text{ days})(0.00032876712)(\$10{,}000) = \$101.92$$

(22–5)

If interest were payable quarterly and if there were 91 days in the quarter, then the interest payment would be $299.18. The annual interest would be 365 × 0.00032876712 × $10,000 = $1,200.00. Note that if the bank had based the interest calculation on a 360-day year, as most banks do, then the interest charges would have been slightly higher and the annual charge would have been $1,216.67. Obviously, banks use a 360-day year to boost their earnings.

The effective interest rate on a loan depends on how frequently interest must be paid—the more frequent, the higher the effective rate. We demonstrate this point with two time lines, one for interest paid once a year and one for quarterly payments:

Interest Paid Annually:

```
        0          0.25        0.5         0.75        1.0
        |           |           |           |           |
     10,000         0           0           0       -1,200.00
                                                   -10,000.00
                                                   -11,200.00
```

The borrower gets $10,000 at t = 0 and pays $11,200 at t = 1. On a financial calculator, enter N = 1, PV = 10000, PMT = 0, and FV = −11200; then press I/YR to get the effective cost of the loan, 12%.

Interest Paid Quarterly:

```
        0          0.25        0.5         0.75        1.0
        |           |           |           |           |
     10,000      -299.18     -299.18     -302.47     -299.18
                                                   -10,000.00
                                                   -10,299.18
```

Note that the third quarter has 92 days. After entering the data in the cash flow register of a financial calculator (being sure to use the $+/-$ key to enter -299.18), we find the periodic rate to be 2.9999%. The effective annual rate is 12.55%:

$$\text{Effective annual rate, quarterly} = (1 + 0.029999)^4 - 1 = 12.55\%$$

Had the loan called for interest to be paid monthly then the effective rate would have been 12.68%, and if interest had been paid daily then the rate would have been 12.75%. These rates would be higher if the bank used a 360-day year.

In these examples, we assumed that the loan matured in 1 year but that interest was paid at various times during the year. The rates we calculated would have been exactly the same even if the loan had matured on each interest payment date. In other words, the effective rate on a monthly payment loan would be 12.68% regardless of whether it matured after 1 month, 6 months, 1 year, or 10 years, providing the stated rate remained at 12%.

22-9b **Discount Interest**

In a **discount interest loan**, the bank deducts the interest in advance (*discounts the loan*). Thus, the borrower receives less than the face value of the loan. On a 1-year, $10,000 loan with a 12% (nominal) rate and discount basis, the interest is $10,000(0.12) = $1,200$. Therefore, the borrower obtains the use of only $10,000 − $1,200 = $8,800$. If the loan were for less than a year then the interest charge (the discount) would be lower; in our example, it would be $600 if the loan were for 6 months and so the amount received would be $9,400.

The effective rate on a discount loan is always higher than the rate on an otherwise similar simple interest loan. To illustrate, consider the situation for a discounted 12% loan for 1 year, as follows.

Discount Interest, Paid Annually:

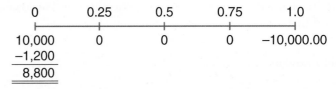

On a financial calculator, enter N = 1, PV = 8800, PMT = 0, and FV = -10000; then press I/YR to get the effective cost of the loan, 13.64%.[5]

If a discount loan matures in less than a year—say, after 1 quarter—then we have the following situation.

---

5.   Note that the firm actually receives less than the face amount of the loan:

$$\text{Funds received} = (\text{Face amount of loan})(1.0 - \text{Nominal interest rate})$$

We can solve for the face amount as follows:

$$\text{Face amount of loan} = \frac{\text{Funds received}}{1.0 - \text{Nominal interest rate}}$$

Therefore, if the borrowing firm actually requires $10,000 of cash, it must borrow $11,363.64:

$$\text{Face value} = \frac{\$10,000}{1.0 - 0.12} = \frac{\$10,000}{0.88} = \$11,363.64$$

Now the borrower will receive $11,363.64 − 0.12($11,363.64) = $10,000. Increasing the face value of the loan does not change the effective rate of 13.64% on the $10,000 of usable funds.

Discount Interest, One Quarter:

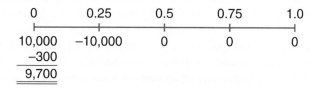

Enter N = 1, PV = 9700, PMT = 0, and FV = −10000, and then press I/YR to find the periodic rate, 3.092784% per quarter, that corresponds to an effective annual rate of 12.96%. Thus, shortening the period of a discount loan lowers the effective rate of interest.

22-9c Effects of Compensating Balances

If the bank requires a compensating balance and if the amount of the required balance exceeds the amount the firm would normally hold on deposit, then the excess must be deducted at t = 0 and then added back when the loan matures. This has the effect of raising the effective rate on the loan. To illustrate, here is the setup for a 1-year discount loan requiring a 20% compensating balance that the firm would not otherwise hold on deposit.

Discount Interest, Paid Annually, with 20% Compensating Balance:

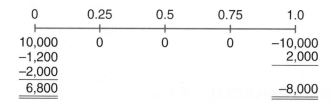

Note that the bank initially gives, and the borrower gets, $10,000 at time 0. However, the bank takes out the $1,200 of interest in advance, and the company must leave $2,000 in the bank as a compensating balance; hence, the borrower's effective net cash flow at t = 0 is $6,800. At t = 1, the borrower must repay the $10,000, but $2,000 is already in the bank (the compensating balance), so the company must repay a net amount of $8,000.

On a financial calculator, enter N = 1, PV = 6800, PMT = 0, and FV = −8000; then press I/YR to get the effective cost of the discount loan with a compensating balance, 17.65%.

Note that banks recently have moved away from requiring compensating balances for fear of violating antitrust regulations. Tying deposit services to lending services can be viewed as anticompetitive.

22-9d Installment Loans: Add-on Interest

Lenders typically charge **add-on interest** on automobile and other types of installment loans. The term "add-on" means the interest is calculated and then added to the amount received to determine the loan's face value. To illustrate, suppose you borrow $10,000 on an add-on basis at a nominal rate of 12% to buy a car, with the loan to be repaid in 12 monthly installments. At a 12% add-on rate, you will pay a total interest charge of $10,000(0.12) = $1,200. However, because the loan is paid off in monthly installments, you have the use of the full $10,000 for only the first month; then the outstanding balance declines until, during the last month, only one-twelfth of the original loan is still outstanding. Thus, you are paying $1,200 for the use of only about half the loan's face amount, as the average usable funds are only about $5,000.

To determine the effective rate of an add-on loan, we proceed as follows.

1. The total amount to be repaid is $10,000 of principal, plus $1,200 of interest, or $11,200.
2. The monthly payment is $11,200/12 = $933.33.
3. You are, in effect, paying off a 12-period annuity of $933.33 in order to receive $10,000 today, so $10,000 is the present value of the annuity. Here is the time line:

$$
\begin{array}{ccccccc}
0 & i = ? & 1 & 2 & & 11 & 12 \text{ Months} \\
\vdash & & \vdash & \vdash & \cdots & \vdash & \dashv \\
10{,}000 & & -933.33 & -933.33 & & -933.33 & -933.33
\end{array}
$$

4. On a financial calculator, enter N = 12, PV = 10000, PMT = −933.33, and FV = 0; then press I/YR to obtain 1.7880%. However, this is a monthly rate.
5. The effective annual rate is found as follows:[6]

(22–6)

$$
\text{Effective annual rate}_{\text{Add-on}} = (1 + r_d)^n - 1.0
$$

$$
= (1.01788)^{12} - 1.0
$$
$$
= 1.2370 - 1.0 = 23.7\%
$$

22-9e **Annual Percentage Rate**

The various ways of calculating interest (simple, discount, add-on), together with the various costs that are also frequently associated with smaller loans (e.g., credit report, loan processing, and origination fees), cause the effective annual rate to differ even for loans that have identical stated interest rates. For example, although the add-on interest rate in our example above is 12%, its effective rate is 23.7%. If the loan used discount interest paid quarterly then the effective rate would be 12.96%, and if the loan used monthly simple interest the effective rate would be $(1.01)^{12} - 1.0 = 12.68\%$. In order to attempt to bring some consistency to reporting the cost of credit across various loan types, Congress passed the Truth in Lending Act in 1968. This legislation required that the annual percentage rate (APR) for all "consumer loans" be stated in bold print on the loan agreement.

The APR is the annual nominal effective cost of the credit, taking into account fees and the timing of payments:

APR = (Periods per year)(Rate per period)

6. Note that if an installment loan is paid off ahead of schedule, additional complications arise. For the classic discussion of this point, see Dick Bonker, "The Rule of 78," *Journal of Finance*, June 1976, pp. 877–888.

So for a loan with 1% monthly simple interest, the APR would be 12(1%) = 12%. For the 12% add-on loan with monthly payments, the APR would be 12(1.788%) = 21.46%. For the 12% discount loan with quarterly payments, the APR would be 4(3.093%) = 12.37%. In most cases, this means that the effective annual rate can easily be calculated from the APR by compounding:

$$\text{Effective annual rate} = (1 + \text{APR}/n)^n - 1$$

where n is the number of periods per year.

The truth-in-lending laws apply primarily to consumer (not business) loans, so the APR does not necessarily appear on a business loan. In these cases, the all-in borrowing cost must be calculated by the borrower.

Name four ways that banks can calculate interest on loans.

What is a compensating balance? What effect does a compensating balance requirement have on the effective interest rate on a loan?

SELF TEST

22-10 Choosing a Bank

Individuals whose only contact with their bank is through the use of its checking services generally choose a bank for the convenience of its location and the competitive cost of its services. However, a business that borrows from banks must look at other criteria and recognize that important differences exist among banks. Some of these differences are considered next.

22-10a Willingness to Assume Risks

Banks have different basic policies toward risk. Some follow relatively conservative lending practices, while others engage in what are properly termed "creative banking practices." These policies reflect partly the personalities of bank officers and partly the characteristics of the bank's deposit liabilities. Thus, a bank with fluctuating deposit liabilities in a static community will tend to be a conservative lender, whereas a bank whose deposits are growing with little interruption may follow more liberal credit policies. Similarly, a large bank with broad diversification over geographic regions and across industries can obtain the benefit of combining and averaging risks. Thus, marginal credit risks that might be unacceptable to a small or specialized bank can be pooled by a branch banking system to reduce the overall risk of a group of marginal accounts.[7]

---

7. Bank deposits are insured by a federal agency, and banks are required to pay premiums toward the cost of this insurance. Riskier banks pay higher premiums and are required to hold more equity capital per dollar of deposits than less risky banks. Until the 1980s, the savings and loan industry had federal insurance, no risk-based insurance premiums, no differential capital requirements, and lax regulations. As a result, some S&L operators wrote risky loans at high interest rates using low-cost, insured deposits. If the loans paid off, the S&L owners would get rich. If they went into default, the taxpayers would have to pay off the deposits. Those government policies ended up costing taxpayers more than $100 billion.

22-10b **Advice and Counsel**

Some bank loan officers are active in providing counsel and in granting loans to firms in their early and formative years. Certain banks have specialized departments that make loans to firms that are expected to grow and thus to become more important customers. The personnel of these departments can provide valuable counseling to customers: The bankers' experience with other firms in growth situations may enable them to spot, and then to warn their customers about, developing problems.

22-10c **Loyalty to Customers**

Banks differ in their support of borrowers in bad times. This characteristic is referred to as the degree of *loyalty* of the bank. Some banks may put great pressure on a business to liquidate its loans when the firm's outlook becomes clouded, whereas others will stand by the firm and work diligently to help it get back on its feet. An especially dramatic illustration of this point was Bank of America's bailout of Memorex Corporation. The bank could have forced Memorex into bankruptcy, but instead it loaned the company additional capital and helped it survive a bad period. Memorex's stock price subsequently rose from $1.50 to $68, so Bank of America's help was indeed beneficial.

22-10d **Specialization**

Banks differ greatly in their degrees of loan specialization. Larger banks have separate departments that specialize in different kinds of loans—for example, real estate loans, farm loans, and commercial loans. Within these broad categories, there may be a specialization by line of business, such as steel, machinery, cattle, or textiles. The strengths of banks are also likely to reflect the nature of the businesses and the economic environment in the areas in which they operate. For example, some California banks have become specialists in lending to electronics companies, while many Midwestern banks are agricultural specialists. A sound firm can obtain more creative cooperation and more active support by going to a bank that has experience and familiarity with its particular type of business. Therefore, a bank that is excellent for one firm may be unsatisfactory for another.

22-10e **Maximum Loan Size**

The size of a bank can be an important factor. Because the maximum loan a bank can make to any one customer is limited to 15% of the bank's capital accounts (capital stock plus retained earnings), it is generally not appropriate for large firms to develop borrowing relationships with small banks.

22-10f **Other Services**

Banks also provide cash management services, assist with electronic funds transfers, help firms obtain foreign exchange, and the like; and the availability of such services should be taken into account when selecting a bank. Also, if the firm is a small business whose manager owns most of its stock, the bank's willingness and ability to provide trust and estate services should be considered.

> **SELF TEST**   What are some factors to consider when choosing a bank?

Summary

This chapter discussed granting credit and the conventions for interest rates on bank loans. It is important to monitor the results of credit policy by monitoring accounts receivable. A firm can affect its level of accounts receivable by changing its credit and collections policy, but doing so also affects sales. Therefore, a complete analysis of the effects of changes in credit policy is necessary. The key concepts covered in this chapter are listed below.

- A firm's credit policy consists of four elements: (1) **credit period**, (2) **discounts** given for early payment, (3) **credit standards**, and (4) **collection policy**. The first two, when combined, are called the **credit terms**.
- Additional factors that influence a firm's overall credit policy are *profit potential* and *legal considerations*.
- The basic objective of the credit manager is to increase profitable sales by extending credit to worthy customers and therefore adding value to the firm.
- Firms can use **days sales outstanding (DSO)** and **aging schedules** to help monitor their receivables position, but the best way to monitor aggregate receivables is the **payments pattern approach**. Using the *uncollected balances schedule,* the payments pattern approach examines each month's remaining uncollected balance (as a percentage of the month's sales) and compares it over time to identify any changes in customers' payment behaviors.
- If a firm *eases its credit policy* by lengthening the credit period, relaxing its credit standards and collection policy, and offering (or raising) its cash discount, then its sales should increase; however, its costs will also increase. A firm should ease its credit policy only if the costs of doing so will be offset by higher expected revenues. In general, credit policy changes should be evaluated on the basis of incremental profits.
- Changes in credit policy can be analyzed in two ways. First, *projected income statements* can be constructed for both the current and the proposed policies. Second, equations can be used to estimate the *incremental change* in profits resulting from a proposed new credit policy.
- With a **regular**, or **simple, interest loan**, interest is not compounded; that is, interest is not earned on interest.
- In a **discount interest loan**, the bank deducts the interest in advance. Interest is calculated on the face amount of the loan but it is paid in advance.
- Installment loans are typically **add-on interest loans**. Interest is calculated and added to the funds received to determine the face amount of the loan.
- The *annual percentage rate (APR)* is a rate reported by banks and other lenders on consumer loans that reflects all of the various loan fees and the timing of interest and principal payments.

Questions

22–1 Define each of the following terms:
   a. Cash discounts
   b. Seasonal dating

   c. Aging schedule; days sales outstanding (DSO)

   d. Payments pattern approach; uncollected balances schedule

   e. Simple interest; discount interest; add-on interest

22-2 Suppose a firm makes a purchase and receives the shipment on February 1. The terms of trade as stated on the invoice read "2/10, net 40, May 1 dating." What is the latest date on which payment can be made and the discount still be taken? What is the date on which payment must be made if the discount is not taken?

22-3 Is it true that if a firm calculates its days sales outstanding, it has no need for an aging schedule? Explain your answer.

22-4 Firm A had no credit losses last year, but 1% of Firm B's accounts receivable proved to be uncollectible and resulted in losses. Can you determine which firms credit manager is performing better? Why or why not?

22-5 Indicate by a (+), (−), or (0) whether each of the following events would most likely cause accounts receivable (AR), sales, and profits to increase, decrease, or be affected in an indeterminate manner:

	AR	Sales	Profits
The firm tightens its credit standards.	_____	_____	_____
The terms of trade are changed from 2/10, net 30, to 3/10, net 30.	_____	_____	_____
The terms are changed from 2/10, net 30, to 3/10, net 40.	_____	_____	_____
The credit manager gets tough with past-due accounts.	_____	_____	_____

Problems

Easy Problems 1–4

22-1   Cost of Bank Loan

On March 1, Minnerly Motors obtains a business loan from a local bank. The loan is a $25,000 interest-only loan with a nominal rate of 11%. Interest is calculated on a simple interest basis with a 365-day year. What is Minnerly's interest charge for the first month (assuming 31 days in the month)?

22-2   Cost of Bank Loan

Mary Jones recently obtained an equipment loan from a local bank. The loan is for $15,000 with a nominal interest rate of 11%. However, this is an installment loan, so the bank also charges add-on interest. Mary must make monthly payments on the loan, and the loan is to be repaid in 1 year. What is the effective annual rate on the loan (assuming a 365-day year)?

22–3 **Cost of Bank Loans**

Del Hawley, owner of Hawley's Hardware, is negotiating with First City Bank for a 1-year loan of $50,000. First City has offered Hawley the alternatives listed below. Calculate the effective annual interest rate for each alternative. Which alternative has the lowest effective annual interest rate?

a. A 12% annual rate on a simple interest loan, with no compensating balance required and interest due at the end of the year.

b. A 9% annual rate on a simple interest loan, with a 20% compensating balance required and interest due at the end of the year.

c. An 8.75% annual rate on a discounted loan, with a 15% compensating balance.

d. Interest figured as 8% of the $50,000 amount, *payable at the end of the year,* but with the loan amount repayable in monthly installments during the year.

22–4 **Cost of Bank Loans**

Gifts Galore Inc. borrowed $1.5 million from National City Bank. The loan was made at a simple annual interest rate of 9% a year for 3 months. A 20% compensating balance requirement raised the effective interest rate.

a. The nominal annual rate on the loan was 11.25%. What is the true effective rate?

b. What would be the effective cost of the loan if the note required discount interest?

c. What would be the nominal annual interest rate on the loan if the bank did not require a compensating balance but required repayment in three equal monthly installments?

Intermediate Problems 5–7

22–5 **Relaxing Collection Efforts**

The Boyd Corporation has annual credit sales of $1.6 million. Current expenses for the collection department are $35,000, bad-debt losses are 1.5%, and the days sales outstanding is 30 days. The firm is considering easing its collection efforts such that collection expenses will be reduced to $22,000 per year. The change is expected to increase bad-debt losses to 2.5% and to increase the days sales outstanding to 45 days. In addition, sales are expected to increase to $1,625,000 per year.

Should the firm relax collection efforts if the opportunity cost of funds is 16%, the variable cost ratio is 75%, and taxes are 40%?

22–6 **Tightening Credit Terms**

Kim Mitchell, the new credit manager of the Vinson Corporation, was alarmed to find that Vinson sells on credit terms of net 90 days while industry-wide credit terms have recently been lowered to net 30 days. On annual credit sales of $2.5 million, Vinson currently averages 95 days of sales in accounts receivable. Mitchell estimates that tightening the credit terms to 30 days would reduce annual sales to $2,375,000, but accounts receivable would drop to 35 days of sales and the savings on investment in them should more than overcome any loss in profit.

Vinson's variable cost ratio is 85%, and taxes are 40%. If the interest rate on funds invested in receivables is 18%, should the change in credit terms be made?

22–7 Effective Cost of Short-Term Credit

Yonge Corporation must arrange financing for its working capital requirements for the coming year. Yonge can: (a) borrow from its bank on a simple interest basis (interest payable at the end of the loan) for 1 year at a 12% nominal rate; (b) borrow on a 3-month, but renewable, loan basis at an 11.5% nominal rate; (c) borrow on an installment loan basis at a 6% add-on rate with 12 end-of-month payments; or (d) obtain the needed funds by no longer taking discounts and thus increasing its accounts payable. Yonge buys on terms of 1/15, net 60. What is the effective annual cost (*not* the nominal cost) of the *least expensive* type of credit, assuming 360 days per year?

Challenging Problems 8–10

22–8 Monitoring of Receivables

The Russ Fogler Company, a small manufacturer of cordless telephones, began operations on January 1. Its credit sales for the first 6 months of operations were as follows:

Month	Credit Sales
January	$ 50,000
February	100,000
March	120,000
April	105,000
May	140,000
June	160,000

Throughout this entire period, the firm's credit customers maintained a constant payments pattern: 20% paid in the month of sale, 30% paid in the first month following the sale, and 50% paid in the second month following the sale.

a. What was Fogler's receivables balance at the end of March and at the end of June?

b. Assume 90 days per calendar quarter. What were the average daily sales (ADS) and days sales outstanding (DSO) for the first quarter and for the second quarter? What were the cumulative ADS and DSO for the first half-year?

c. Construct an aging schedule as of June 30. Use account ages of 0–30, 31–60, and 61–90 days.

d. Construct the uncollected balances schedule for the second quarter as of June 30.

22–9 Short-Term Financing Analysis

Malone Feed and Supply Company buys on terms of 1/10, net 30, but it has not been taking discounts and has actually been paying in 60 rather than

30 days. Assume that the accounts payable are recorded at full cost, not net of discounts. Malone's balance sheet follows (thousands of dollars):

Cash	$ 50	Accounts payable	$ 500
Accounts receivable	450	Notes payable	50
Inventory	750	Accruals	50
Current assets	$ 1,250	Current liabilities	$ 600
		Long-term debt	150
Fixed assets	750	Common equity	1,250
Total assets	$2,000	Total liabilities and equity	$2,000

Malone's suppliers are threatening to stop shipments unless the company begins making prompt payments (that is, paying within 30). The firm can borrow on a 1-year note (call this a current liability) from its bank at a rate of 15% discount interest with a 20% compensating balance required. (Malone's $50,000 in cash is needed for transactions; it cannot be used as part of the compensating balance.)

a. How large would the accounts payable balance be if Malone takes discounts? If it does not take discounts and pays in 30 days?

b. How large must the bank loan be if Malone takes discounts? If Malone doesn't take discounts?

c. What are the nominal and effective costs of costly trade credit? What is the effective cost of the bank loan? Based on these costs, what should Malone do?

d. Assume Malone forgoes the discount and borrows the amount needed to become current on its payables. Construct a projected balance sheet based on this decision. (*Hint:* You will need to include an account called "prepaid interest" under current assets.)

e. Now assume that the $500,000 shown on the balance sheet is recorded net of discounts. How much would Malone have to pay its suppliers in order to reduce its accounts payable to $250,000? If Malone's tax rate is 40%, then what is the effect on its net income due to the lost discount when it reduces its accounts payable to $250,000? How much would Malone have to borrow? (*Hint:* Malone will receive a tax deduction due to the lost discount, which will affect the amount it must borrow.) Construct a projected balance sheet based on this scenario. (*Hint:* You will need to include an account called "prepaid interest" under current assets and then adjust retained earnings by the after-tax amount of the lost discount.)

22–10 **Alternative Financing Arrangements**
Suncoast Boats Inc. estimates that, because of the seasonal nature of its business, it will require an additional $2 million of cash for the month of July. Suncoast Boats has the following four options available for raising the needed funds.

1. Establish a 1-year line of credit for $2 million with a commercial bank. The commitment fee will be 0.5% per year on the unused portion, and the interest charge on the used funds will be 11% per annum. Assume

the funds are needed only in July and that there are 30 days in July and 360 days in the year.

2. Forgo the trade discount of 2/10, net 40, on $2 million of purchases during July.

3. Issue $2 million of 30-day commercial paper at a 9.5% annual interest rate. The total transaction fee (including the cost of a backup credit line) for using commercial paper is 0.5% of the amount of the issue.

4. Issue $2 million of 60-day commercial paper at a 9% annual interest rate plus a transaction fee of 0.5%. Because the funds are required for only 30 days, the excess funds ($2 million) can be invested in 9.4% per annum marketable securities for the month of August. The total transaction costs of purchasing and selling the marketable securities is 0.4% of the amount of the issue.

   a. What is the dollar cost of each financing arrangement?

   b. Is the source with the lowest expected cost necessarily the one to select? Why or why not?

Spreadsheet Problem

22–11 Build a Model: Short-Term Financing Analysis

Start with the partial model in the file *Ch22 P11 Build a Model.xls* on the textbook's Web site. Rework parts a through d of Problem 22-9 using a spreadsheet model. Answer the following questions:

   a. How large would the accounts payable balance be if Malone takes discounts? If it does not take discounts and pays in 30 days?

   b. How large must the bank loan be if Malone takes discounts? If Malone doesn't take discounts?

   c. What are the nominal and effective costs of costly trade credit? What is the effective cost of the bank loan? Based on these costs, what should Malone do?

   d. Assume Malone forgoes the discount and borrows the amount needed to become current on its payables. Construct a projected balance sheet based on this decision. (*Hint:* You will need to include an account called "prepaid interest" under current assets.)

   e. Using interest rates in the range of 5% to 25% and compensating balances in the range of 0% to 30%, perform a sensitivity analysis that shows how the size of the bank loan would vary with changes in the interest rate and the compensating balance percentage.

MINI CASE

Rich Jackson, a recent finance graduate, is planning to go into the wholesale building supply business with his brother, Jim, who majored in building construction. The firm would sell primarily to general contractors, and it would start operating next January. Sales would be slow during the cold months, rise during the spring, and then fall off again in the summer, when new construction in the area slows. Sales estimates for the first 6 months are as follows (in thousands of dollars):

January	February	March
$100	$200	$300

April	May	June
$300	$200	$100

The terms of sale are net 30 but, because of special incentives, the brothers expect 30% of the customers (by dollar value) to pay on the 10th day following the sale, 50% to pay on the 40th day, and the remaining 20% to pay on the 70th day. No bad-debt losses are expected because Jim, the building construction expert, knows which contractors are having financial problems.

a. Discuss, in general, what it means for the brothers to set a credit and collections policy.

b. Assume that, on average, the brothers expect annual sales of 18,000 items at an average price of $100 per item. (Use a 365-day year.)

   (1) What is the firm's expected days sales outstanding (DSO)?

   (2) What is its expected average daily sales (ADS)?

   (3) What is its expected average accounts receivable (AR) level?

   (4) Assume the firm's profit margin is 25%. How much of the receivables balance must be financed? What would the firm's balance sheet figures be for accounts receivable, notes payable, and retained earnings at the end of 1 year if notes payable are used to finance the investment in receivables? Assume that the cost of carrying receivables had been deducted when the 25% profit margin was calculated.

   (5) If bank loans have a cost of 12%, what is the annual dollar cost of carrying the receivables?

c. What are some factors that influence: (1) a firm's receivables level and (2) the dollar cost of carrying receivables?

d. Assuming the monthly sales forecasts given previously are accurate and that customers pay exactly as predicted, what would the receivables level be at the end of each month? To reduce calculations, assume that 30% of the firm's customers pay in the month of sale, 50% pay in the month following the sale, and the remaining 20% pay in the second month following the sale. (*Note:* This is a different assumption than was made earlier.) Also assume there are 91 days in each quarter. Use the following format to answer parts d and e:

Month	Sales	End-of-Month Receivables	Quarterly Sales	ADS	DSO = (AR)÷(ADS)
January	$100	$ 70			
February	200	160			
March	300	250	$600	$6.59	37.9
April	300				
May	200				
June	100				

e. What is the firm's forecasted average daily sales for the first 3 months? For the entire half-year? The days sales outstanding is commonly used to measure receivables performance. What DSO is expected at the end of March? At the end of June? What does the DSO indicate about customers'

payments? Is DSO a good management tool in this situation? If not, why not?

f. Construct aging schedules for the end of March and the end of June (use the format given below). Do these schedules properly measure customers' payment patterns? If not, why not?

	March		June	
Age of Account (Days)	**AR**	**%**	**AR**	**%**
0–30	$210	84%		
31–60	40	16		
61–90	0	0	___	___
	$250	100%		

g. Construct the uncollected balances schedules for the end of March and the end of June. Use the

format given below. Do these schedules properly measure customers' payment patterns?

	March			June		
Month	**Sales**	**Contribution to AR**	**AR-to-Sales Ratio**	**Month**	**Sales**	**Contribution to AR**	**AR-to-Sales Ratio**
January	$100	$ 0	0%	April			
February	200	40	20	May			
March	300	210	70	June		___	___

h. Assume that it is now July of Year 1 and that the brothers are developing projected financial statements for the following year. Further, assume that sales and collections in the first half-year matched the predicted levels. Use the Year-2 sales forecasts shown below to estimate next year's receivables levels for the end of March and for the end of June.

Month	Predicted Sales	Predicted AR-to-Sales Ratio	Predicted Contribution to Receivables
January	$150	0%	$ 0
February	300	20	60
March	500	70	350

Projected March 31 AR balance = $410

Month	Predicted Sales		
April	$400		
May	300		
June	200		

Projected June 30 AR balance = _____

i. Now assume that it is several years later. The brothers are concerned about the firm's current credit terms of net 30, which means that contractors buying building products from the firm are not offered a discount and are supposed to pay the full amount in 30 days. Gross sales are now running $1,000,000 a year, and 80% (by dollar volume) of the firm's *paying* customers generally pay the full amount on Day 30; the other 20% pay, on average, on Day 40. Of the firm's gross sales, 2% ends up as bad-debt losses.

The brothers are now considering a change in the firm's credit policy. The change would entail: (1) changing the credit terms to 2/10, net 20, (2) employing stricter credit standards before granting credit, and (3) enforcing collections with greater vigor than in the past. Thus, cash customers and those paying within 10 days would receive a 2% discount, but all others would have to pay the full amount after only 20 days. The brothers believe the discount would both attract additional customers and encourage some existing customers to purchase more from the firm—after all, the discount amounts to a price reduction. Of course, these customers would take the discount and hence would pay in only 10 days. The net expected result is for sales to increase to $1,100,000; for 60% of the paying customers to take the discount and pay on the 10th day; for 30% to pay the full amount on Day 20; for 10% to pay late on Day 30; and for bad-debt losses to fall from 2% to 1% of gross sales. The firm's operating cost ratio will remain unchanged at 75%, and its cost of carrying receivables will remain unchanged at 12%.

To begin the analysis, describe the four variables that make up a firm's credit policy, and explain how each of them affects sales and collections. Then use the information given in part h to answer parts j through p.

j. Under the current credit policy, what is the firm's days sales outstanding? What would the expected DSO be if the credit policy change were made?

k. What is the dollar amount of the firm's current bad-debt losses? What losses would be expected under the new policy?

l. What would be the firm's expected dollar cost of granting discounts under the new policy?

m. What is the firm's current dollar cost of carrying receivables? What would it be after the proposed change?

n. What is the incremental after-tax profit associated with the change in credit terms? Should the company make the change? (Assume a tax rate of 40%.)

o. Suppose the firm makes the change but its competitors react by making similar changes to their own credit terms, with the net result being that gross sales remain at the current $1,000,000 level. What would be the impact on the firm's after-tax profitability?

	New	Old	Difference
Gross sales		$1,000,000	
Less discounts	_____	0	_____
Net sales		$1,000,000	
Production costs	_____	750,000	_____
Profit before credit costs and taxes		$ 250,000	
Credit-related costs:			
Carrying costs		8,000	
Bad-debt losses	_____	20,000	_____
Profit before taxes		$ 222,000	
Taxes (40%)	_____	88,800	_____
Net income		$ 133,200	

p. The brothers need $100,000 and are considering a 1-year bank loan with a quoted annual rate of 8%. The bank is offering the following alternatives: (1) simple interest, (2) discount interest, (3) discount interest with a 10% compensating balance, and (4) add-on interest on a 12-month installment loan. What is the effective annual cost rate for each alternative? For the first three of these assumptions, what is the effective rate if the loan is for 90 days but renewable? How large must the face value of the loan amount actually be in each of the four alternatives to provide $100,000 in usable funds at the time the loan is originated?

SELECTED ADDITIONAL CASES

The following cases from CengageCompose cover many of the concepts discussed in this chapter and are available at http://compose.cengage.com.

Klein-Brigham Series:

Case 33, "Upscale Toddlers, Inc.," which deals with credit policy changes; Case 34, "Texas Rose Company," and Case 67, "Bridgewater Pool Company," which focus on receivables management; Case 79, "Mitchell Lumber Company," which deals with credit policy; Case 88, "Chef's Selection," which deals with short-term financing; and Case 96, "Lifeline Health Products," which deals with credit policy.

CHAPTER 23

Other Topics in Working Capital Management

This chapter provides detailed coverage of several working capital topics, including: (1) the target cash balance, (2) inventory control systems, (3) accounting treatments for inventory, and (4) the EOQ model.

WEB

The textbook's Web site contains an *Excel* file that will guide you through the chapter's calculations. The file for this chapter is *Ch23 Tool Kit.xls,* and we encourage you to open the file and follow along as you read the chapter.

Beginning-of-Chapter Questions

As you read the chapter, consider how you would answer the following questions. You *should not* necessarily be able to answer the questions before you read the chapter. Rather, you should use them to get a sense of the issues covered in the chapter. After reading the chapter, you should be able to give at least partial answers to the questions, and you should be able to give better answers after the chapter has been discussed in class. Note, too, that it is often useful, when answering conceptual questions, to use hypothetical data to illustrate your answer. We illustrate the answers with an *Excel* model that is available on the textbook's Web site. Accessing the model and working through it is a useful exercise, and it provides insights that are useful when answering the questions.

1. Explain briefly what the **EOQ model** is and how it can be used to help establish an optimal inventory policy. Is the EOQ concept consistent with **just-in-time** procedures for managing inventories?

2. Explain how the EOQ inventory model can be modified and used to help determine the optimal size of a firm's cash balances. Do you think the EOQ approach to cash management is more or less relevant today than it was in precomputer, preelectronic communications days?

3. What four methods are used to account for inventory? What are the financial implications of one method over another? How does the choice of inventory accounting method affect the order in which actual items in inventory are sold? Is it possible for the choice of accounting method for inventory to affect the free cash flow value of a firm as discussed in Chapter 9? How?

23-1 **The Concept of Zero Working Capital**

At first glance, it might seem that working capital management is not as important as capital budgeting, dividend policy, and other decisions that determine a firm's long-term direction. However, in today's world of intense global competition, working capital management is receiving increasing attention from managers striving for peak efficiency. In fact, the goal of many leading companies today is *zero working capital*. Proponents of the zero working capital concept claim that a movement toward this goal not only generates cash but also speeds up production and helps businesses make more timely deliveries and operate more efficiently. The concept has its own definition of working capital: Inventories + Receivables – Payables. The rationale here is: (1) that inventories and receivables are the keys to making sales, but (2) that inventories can be financed by suppliers through accounts payable.

Companies generally use about 20 cents of working capital for each dollar of sales. So, on average, working capital is turned over five times per year. Reducing working capital and thus increasing turnover has two major financial benefits. First, every dollar freed up by reducing inventories or receivables, or by increasing payables, results in a one-time contribution to cash flow. Second, a movement toward zero working capital permanently raises a company's earnings. Like all capital, funds invested in working capital cost money, so reducing those funds yields permanent savings in capital costs. In addition to the financial benefits, reducing working capital forces a company to produce and deliver faster than its competitors, which helps it gain new business and charge premium prices for providing good service. As inventories disappear, warehouses can be sold off, both labor and handling equipment needs are reduced, and obsolete and/or out-of-style goods are minimized.

The most important factor in moving toward zero working capital is increased speed. If the production process is fast enough, companies can produce items as they are ordered rather than having to forecast demand and build up large inventories that are managed by bureaucracies. The best companies are able to start production after an order is received yet still meet customer delivery requirements. This system is known as *demand flow*, or *demand-based management*, and it builds on the just-in-time method of inventory control discussed later in this chapter. However, demand flow management is broader than just-in-time, because it requires that all elements of a production system operate quickly and efficiently.

Achieving zero working capital requires that every order and part move at maximum speed, which generally means replacing paper with electronic data. Then, orders streak from the processing department to the plant, where flexible production lines produce each product every day and finished goods flow directly from the production line onto waiting trucks or rail cars. Instead of cluttering plants or warehouses with inventories, products move directly into the pipeline. As efficiency rises, working capital dwindles.

Clearly, it is not possible for most firms to achieve zero working capital and perfectly efficient production. Still, a focus on minimizing cash, receivables, and inventories while maximizing payables will help a firm lower its investment in working capital and achieve financial and production economies.

SELF TEST   What is the basic idea of zero working capital, and how is working capital defined for this purpose?

23-2 **Setting the Target Cash Balance**

Recall from Chapter 21 that firms hold cash balances primarily for two reasons: to pay for *transactions* they must make in their day-to-day operations and to maintain *compensating balances* that banks may require in return for loans. In addition, firms maintain additional cash balances as a *precaution* against unforeseen fluctuations in cash flows and in order to take advantage of *trade discounts*. Given that cash is necessary for these purposes but is also a nonearning asset, the primary goal of cash management is to minimize the amount of cash a firm holds while maintaining a sufficient *target cash balance* to conduct business.

In Chapter 21, when we discussed Educational Products Corporation's cash budget, we took as a given the $10 million target cash balance. We also discussed how lockboxes, synchronizing inflows and outflows, and float can reduce the required cash balance. Now we consider how target cash balances are set in practice.

Note that: (1) cash per se earns no return, (2) cash is an asset that appears on the left side of the balance sheet, (3) cash holdings must be financed by raising either debt or equity, and (4) both debt and equity capital have a cost. If cash holdings could be reduced without hurting sales or other aspects of a firm's operations, then this reduction would permit a reduction in either debt or equity or both, which would increase the return on capital and thus boost the value of the firm's stock. Therefore, *the general operating goal of the cash manager is to minimize the amount of cash held subject to the constraint that enough cash be held to enable the firm to operate efficiently.*

For most firms, cash as a percentage of assets and/or sales has declined sharply over the last couple of decades as a direct result of technological developments in computers and telecommunications. Years ago, it was difficult to move money from one location to another, and it was also difficult to forecast exactly how much cash would be needed in different locations at different points in time. As a result, firms had to hold relatively large "safety stocks" of cash to be sure they had enough when and where it was needed. Also, they held relatively large amounts of short-term securities as a backup, and they also had backup lines of credit that permitted them to borrow on short notice to build up the cash account if it became depleted.

Think about how computers and telecommunications now affect the situation. With a good computer system tied together with good telecommunications links, a company can get real-time information on its cash balances regardless of whether it operates in a single location or all over the world. Furthermore, it can use statistical procedures to forecast cash inflows and outflows, and good forecasts reduce the need for safety stocks. Finally, improvements in telecommunications systems make it possible for a treasurer to replenish the firm's cash accounts within minutes simply by calling a lender and stating that the firm wants to borrow a given amount under its line of credit. The lender then wires the funds to the desired location. Similarly, marketable securities can be sold with close to the same speed and with the same minimal transactions cost. This trend toward lower cash levels, however, was reversed in the wake of the financial crisis in 2008 and 2009, when firms found it difficult to obtain or renew lines of credit. As they became profitable moving out of the accompanying recession, many firms squirreled away relatively larger amounts of cash as a safeguard against turmoil in the banking industry.

Super Cell, a provider of cell phone services, can be used to illustrate the impact of computers and high-speed telecommunications on cash management. Super Cell knows exactly how much it must pay and when, and it can forecast quite accurately when it will receive checks. For example, the treasurer of Super Cell's Florida operation knows when the major employers in Tampa pay their workers and how long after that people generally pay their phone bills. Armed with this information, Super Cell's Florida treasurer can forecast with great accuracy any cash surpluses or deficits on a daily basis. Of course, no forecast will be exact, so slight overages or underages will occur. But this presents no problem. The treasurer knows by 11 a.m. the checks that must be covered by 4 p.m. that day, how much cash has come in, and consequently how much of a cash surplus or deficit will exist. Then, with a single phone call, the company borrows to cover any deficit or buys securities (or pays off outstanding loans) with any surplus. Thus, Super Cell can maintain cash balances that are very close to zero.

Today, cash management in reasonably sophisticated firms is largely a job for systems people. Except for the very largest firms, it is generally most efficient to have a bank handle the actual operations of the cash management system. When it comes to operating a cash management system, banks have extensive experience and are able to capture economies of scale that are unobtainable by individual nonfinancial firms. Also, many banks are willing and able to offer such services, so competition has driven the cost of cash management down to a reasonable level. Still, it is essential that corporate treasurers know enough about cash management procedures to be able to negotiate and then work with the banks to ensure that they get the best price (interest rate) on credit lines, the best yield on short-term investments, and a reasonable cost for other banking services. To provide perspective on these issues, we next discuss a theoretical model for cash balances as well as a practical approach to setting the target cash balance.

23-2a **The Baumol Model**

William Baumol first noted that cash balances are, in many respects, similar to inventories and that the EOQ inventory model, which will be developed in a later section, can be used to establish a target cash balance.[1] Baumol's model assumes that the firm uses cash at a steady, predictable rate—say, $1,000,000 per week—and that the firm's cash inflows from operations also occur at a steady, predictable rate—say, $900,000 per week. Therefore, the firm's net cash outflows, or net need for cash, also occur at a steady rate—in this case, $100,000 per week.[2] Under these steady-state assumptions, the firm's cash position will resemble the situation shown in Figure 23-1.

If our illustrative firm started at Time 0 with a cash balance of C = $300,000 and if its outflows exceeded its inflows by $100,000 per week, then its cash balance would drop to zero at the end of Week 3, and its average cash balance would be C/2 = $300,000/2 = $150,000. Therefore, at the end of Week 3, the firm would

---

1. William J. Baumol, "The Transactions Demand for Cash: An Inventory Theoretic Approach," *Quarterly Journal of Economics*, November 1952, pp. 545–556.

2. Our hypothetical firm is experiencing a $100,000 weekly cash shortfall, but this does not necessarily imply it is headed for bankruptcy. The firm could, for example, be highly profitable and be enjoying high earnings yet be expanding so rapidly that it experiences chronic cash shortages that must be made up by borrowing or by selling common stock. Or the firm could be in the construction business and therefore receive major cash inflows at widely spaced intervals but still have net cash outflows of $100,000 per week between these inflows.

FIGURE 23-1	Cash Balances under the Baumol Model's Assumptions

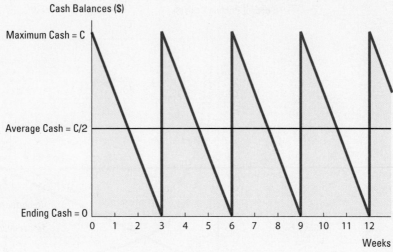

have to replenish its cash balance by selling marketable securities (if it had any) or by borrowing.

If C were set at a higher level—say, $600,000—then the cash supply would last longer (6 weeks), and the firm would have to sell securities (or borrow) less frequently. However, its average cash balance would rise from $150,000 to $300,000. A brokerage or some other type of transaction cost must be incurred to sell securities (or to borrow), so holding larger cash balances will lower the transaction cost associated with obtaining cash. On the other hand, cash provides no income, so larger average cash balances entail a higher opportunity cost, which is the return that could have been earned on securities or other assets held in lieu of cash. Thus, we have the situation graphed in Figure 23-2. The optimal cash balance is found by using the following variables and equations:

C = Amount of cash raised by selling marketable securities or by borrowing

$C/2$ = Average cash balance

C^* = Optimal amount of cash to be raised by selling marketable securities or by borrowing

$C^*/2$ = Optimal average cash balance

F = Fixed cost of selling securities or of obtaining a loan

T = Total amount of net new cash needed for transactions during the entire period (usually a year)

r = Opportunity cost of holding cash, set equal to either the rate of return forgone on marketable securities or the cost of borrowing to hold cash

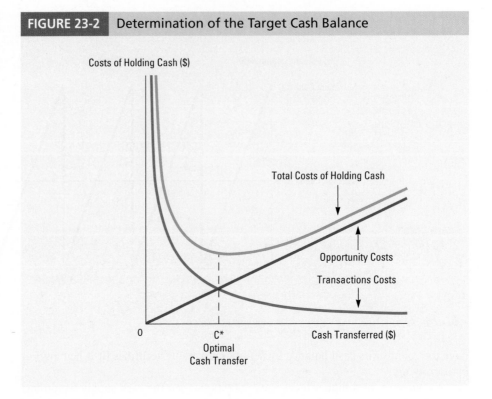

FIGURE 23-2   Determination of the Target Cash Balance

The total costs of cash balances consist of holding (or opportunity) cost plus transactions cost:[3]

(23–1)

$$\frac{\text{Total}}{\text{costs}} = \text{Holding cost} + \text{Transaction cost}$$

$$= \left(\begin{array}{c}\text{Average cash}\\\text{balance}\end{array}\right)\left(\begin{array}{c}\text{Opportunity}\\\text{cost rate}\end{array}\right) + \left(\begin{array}{c}\text{Number of}\\\text{transactions}\end{array}\right)\left(\begin{array}{c}\text{Cost per}\\\text{transaction}\end{array}\right)$$

$$= \qquad \frac{c}{2}\,(r) \qquad + \qquad \frac{T}{c}\,(F)$$

The minimum total cost is achieved when C is set equal to C*, the optimal cash transfer. The value of C* is found as follows:[4]

(23–2)

$$C^* = \sqrt{\frac{2(F)(T)}{r}}$$

---

3. Total cost can be expressed on either a before-tax or an after-tax basis. Both methods lead to the same conclusions regarding target cash balances and comparative costs. For simplicity, we present the model here on a before-tax basis.

4. Equation 23-1 is differentiated with respect to C. The derivative is set equal to zero, and we then solve for C = C* to derive Equation 23-2. This model, applied to inventories and called the EOQ model, is discussed further in a later section.

Equation 23-2 is the **Baumol model** for determining the optimal cash balance. To illustrate its use, suppose F = \$150, T = 52 weeks × \$100,000/week = \$5,200,000, and r = 15% = 0.15. Then:

$$C^* = \sqrt{\frac{2(\$150)(\$5,200,000)}{0.15}} = \$101,980$$

Therefore, the firm should sell securities (or borrow if it does not hold securities) in the amount of \$101,980 when its cash balance approaches zero, thus building its cash balance back up to \$101,980. Dividing T by C* yields the number of transactions per year: \$5,200,000/\$101,980 = 50.99 ≈ 51, or about once a week. The firm's average cash balance is \$101,980/2 = \$50,990 ≈ \$51,000.

Note that the optimal cash balance increases less than proportionately with increases in the amount of cash needed for transactions. For example, if the firm's size, and consequently its net new cash needs, doubled from \$5,200,000 to \$10,400,000 per year, then the average cash balance would increase by only 41%, from \$51,000 to \$72,000. This suggests that there are economies of scale in holding cash balances, and this, in turn, gives larger firms an edge over smaller ones.[5]

Of course, the firm would probably want to hold a safety stock of cash designed to reduce the probability of a cash shortage. However, if the firm is able to sell securities or to borrow on short notice—and most larger firms can do so in a matter of minutes simply by making a telephone call—then the safety stock can be quite low.

The Baumol model is obviously simplistic. Most important, it assumes relatively stable, predictable cash inflows and outflows, and it does not take into account seasonal or cyclical trends. Other models have been developed to deal both with uncertainty and with trends, but all of them have limitations and are more useful as conceptual models than for actually setting target cash balances.

23-2b **Monte Carlo Simulation**

Although the Baumol model and other theoretical models provide insights into the optimal cash balance, they are generally not practical for actual use. Rather, firms generally set their target cash balances based on some "safety stock" of cash that holds the risk of running out of money to some acceptably low level. One commonly used procedure is **Monte Carlo simulation**. To illustrate, consider the cash budget for Educational Products Corporation (EPC) presented in Figure 21-5 in Chapter 21. Sales and collections are the driving forces in the cash budget and, of course, are subject to uncertainty. In the cash budget, we used expected values for sales and collections as well as for all other cash flows. However, it would be relatively easy to use Monte Carlo simulation, first discussed in Chapter 13, to introduce uncertainty. If the cash budget were constructed using a spreadsheet program with Monte Carlo add-in software, then the key uncertain variables could be specified as continuous probability distributions rather than point values.

---

5. This edge may, of course, be more than offset by other factors—after all, cash management is only one aspect of running a business.

The end result of the simulation would be a distribution for each month's net cash flow instead of the single values shown on Row 165 of Figure 21-5. Suppose September's net cash flow distribution looked like this (in millions):

September Net Cash Flow	Probability of This Cash Flow or Less
−$208	10%
−200	20
−193	30
−187	40
−182 Expected CF	50
−177	60
−171	70
−164	80
−156	90

Now suppose EPC's managers want to be 90% confident that the firm will not run out of cash during September, because they don't want to borrow to cover any shortfall. They would set the beginning-of-month target balance at $200 million, well above the current target balance of $10 million, because there is only a 10% probability that September's cash flow will be worse than a $200 million outflow. With a balance of $200 million at the beginning of the month, there would be only a 10% chance that EPC would run out of cash during September. Of course, Monte Carlo simulation could be applied to the remaining months in the Figure 21-5 cash budget, and the amounts so obtained to match a given confidence level could be used to set each month's target cash balance instead of using a fixed target across all months.

The same type of analysis could be used to determine the amount of short-term securities to hold or the size of a requested line of credit. Of course, as in all simulations, the hard part is estimating the probability distributions for sales, collections, and the other highly uncertain variables. If these inputs are not good representations of the actual uncertainty facing the firm, then the resulting target balances will not offer the protection against cash shortages implied by the simulation. There is no substitute for experience, and cash managers will adjust the target balances obtained by Monte Carlo simulation based on their own judgment.

SELF TEST

How has technology changed the way target cash balances are set?

What is the Baumol model, and how is it used?

Explain how Monte Carlo simulation can be used to help set a firm's target cash balance.

23-3 **Inventory Control Systems**

Inventory management requires the establishment of an *inventory control system.* Inventory control systems run the gamut from very simple to extremely complex, depending on the size of the firm and the nature of its inventory. For example, one simple control procedure is the **red-line method**—inventory items are stocked in a bin, a red line is drawn around the inside of the bin at the level of the reorder point, and the inventory clerk places an order when the red line shows. The **two-bin method** has inventory items stocked in two bins. When the working bin is empty, an order is placed and inventory is drawn from the second bin. These procedures work well for parts such as bolts in a manufacturing process or for many items in retail businesses.

23-3a **Computerized Systems**

Most companies today employ **computerized inventory control systems**. The computer starts with an inventory count in memory. As withdrawals are made, they are recorded by the computer, and the inventory balance is revised. When the reorder point is reached, the computer automatically places an order, and when the order is received, the recorded balance is increased. As we noted earlier, retailers such as Walmart have carried this system quite far: Each item has a bar code and, as an item is checked out, the code is read, a signal is sent to the computer, and the inventory balance is adjusted at the same time the price is fed into the cash register tape. When the balance drops to the reorder point, an order is placed. In Walmart's case, the order goes directly from its computers to those of its suppliers.

A good inventory control system is dynamic, not static. A company such as Walmart or General Motors stocks hundreds of thousands of different items. The sales (or use) of individual items can rise or fall quite separately from rising or falling overall corporate sales. As the usage rate for an individual item begins to rise or fall, the inventory manager must adjust its balance to avoid running short or ending up with obsolete items. If the change in the usage rate appears to be permanent, then the safety stock level should be reconsidered and the computer model used in the control process should be reprogrammed.

23-3b **Just-in-Time Systems**

An approach to inventory control called the **just-in-time (JIT) system** was developed by Japanese firms but is now used throughout the world. Toyota provides a good example of the just-in-time system. Many of Toyota's suppliers are located near its factories. Delivery of components is tied to the speed of the assembly line, and parts are generally delivered no more than a few hours before they are used. The just-in-time system reduces the need for Toyota and other manufacturers to carry large inventories, but it requires a great deal of coordination between the manufacturer and its suppliers—both in the timing of deliveries and the quality of the parts. The component parts must be perfect, because a few bad parts could stop the entire production line. Therefore, JIT inventory management has been developed in conjunction with total quality management (TQM).

The close coordination required between the parties using JIT procedures has led to an overall reduction of inventory throughout the production–distribution system and to a general improvement in economic efficiency. This point is borne out by economic statistics, which show that inventory as a percentage of sales has been declining since the use of just-in-time procedures began. Also, with smaller inventories in the system, economic recessions have become shorter and less severe.

23-3c Outsourcing

Another important development related to inventory is **outsourcing,** which is the practice of purchasing components rather than making them in-house. Thus, GM has been moving toward buying radiators, axles, and other parts from suppliers rather than making them itself, so it has been increasing its use of outsourcing. Outsourcing is often combined with just-in-time systems to reduce inventory levels. However, perhaps the major reason for outsourcing has nothing to do with inventory policy: A bureaucratic, unionized company like GM can often buy parts from a smaller, nonunionized supplier at a lower cost than it can make them itself.

23-3d The Relationship between Production Scheduling and Inventory Levels

A final point relating to inventory levels is the relationship between production scheduling and inventory levels. For example, a greeting card manufacturer has highly seasonal sales. Such a firm could produce on a steady, year-round basis, or it could let production rise and fall with sales. If it established a level production schedule, its inventory would rise sharply during periods when sales were low and then decline during peak sales periods, but its average inventory would be substantially higher than if production rose and fell with sales.

Our discussions of just-in-time systems, outsourcing, and production scheduling all point out the necessity of coordinating inventory policy with manufacturing/procurement policies. Companies try to minimize *total production and distribution costs,* and inventory cost is just one part of total cost. Still, it is an important cost, and financial managers should be aware of its determinants and how it can be minimized.

> **SELF TEST**
>
> Describe some inventory control systems that are used in practice.
>
> What are just-in-time systems? What are their advantages? Why is quality especially important if a JIT system is used?
>
> What is outsourcing?
>
> Describe the relationship between production scheduling and inventory levels.

23-4 Accounting for Inventory

When finished goods are sold, the firm must assign a cost of goods sold. The cost of goods sold appears on the income statement as an expense for the period, and the balance sheet inventory account is reduced by a like amount. Four methods can be used to value the cost of goods sold and hence to value the remaining inventory:

(1) specific identification, (2) first-in, first-out (FIFO), (3) last-in, first-out (LIFO), and (4) weighted average.

23-4a Specific Identification

Under **specific identification**, a unique cost is attached to each item in inventory. Then, when an item is sold, the inventory value is reduced by that specific amount. This method is used only when the items are high cost and move relatively slowly, such as cars for an automobile dealer.

23-4b First-In, First-Out (FIFO)

In the **FIFO** method, the units sold during a given period are assumed to be the first units that were placed in inventory. As a result, the cost of goods sold is based on the cost of the oldest inventory items, and the remaining inventory consists of the newest goods.

23-4c Last-In, First-Out (LIFO)

LIFO is the opposite of FIFO. The cost of goods sold is based on the last units placed in inventory, while the remaining inventory consists of the first goods placed in inventory. Note that this is purely an accounting convention—the actual physical units sold could be either the earlier or the later units placed in inventory, or some combination. For example, Del Monte has in its LIFO inventory accounts catsup bottled in the 1920s, but all the catsup in its warehouses was bottled in 2014 or 2015. If Del Monte were to switch from LIFO to FIFO for tax reporting, then its reported cost of goods sold would plummet as it "used up" all of the cheap catsup that was booked years ago when the price level was lower. This would increase substantially its tax liability. If international financial reporting standards (IFRS) are ever adopted for U.S. companies, LIFO accounting for inventory will no longer be allowed. This is one reason adoption of IFRS by U.S. companies has been delayed over and over, and may never take place.[6]

23-4d Weighted Average

The **weighted average** method involves calculating the weighted average unit cost of goods available for sale from inventory; the average is then used to determine the cost of goods sold. This method results in a cost of goods sold and an ending inventory that fall somewhere between the FIFO and LIFO methods.

23-4e Comparison of Inventory Accounting Methods

To illustrate these methods and their effects on financial statements, assume that Custom Furniture Inc. manufactured five identical faux antique dining tables during

---

6. As we shall see, when there is inflation, LIFO gives a higher reported cost of goods sold. U.S. Companies choose LIFO instead of FIFO in order to maximize the reported cost of goods sold for tax purposes and essentially defer the taxes that should have been due had the company reported the actual inventory it sold. As long as companies never have to switch back to FIFO, those additional taxes can be deferred indefinitely. However, if they have to switch to LIFO, those taxes it owes will come due!

a 1-year accounting period. During the year, a new labor contract and dramatically increasing mahogany prices caused manufacturing costs to almost double, resulting in the following inventory costs:

Table Number:	1	2	3	4	5	Total
Cost:	$10,000	$12,000	$14,000	$16,000	$18,000	$70,000

There were no tables in stock at the beginning of the year, and Tables 1, 3, and 5 were sold during the year.

If Custom used the specific identification method, then the cost of goods sold would be reported as $10,000 + $14,000 + $18,000 = $42,000 and the end-of-period inventory value would be $70,000 − $42,000 = $28,000. If Custom used the FIFO method, then its cost of goods sold would be $10,000 + $12,000 + $14,000 = $36,000 and ending inventory would be $70,000 − $36,000 = $34,000. If Custom used the LIFO method, then its cost of goods sold would be $48,000 and its ending inventory would be $22,000. Finally, if Custom used the weighted average method, then its average cost per unit of inventory would be $70,000/5 = $14,000, its cost of goods sold would be 3($14,000) = $42,000, and its ending inventory would be $70,000 − $42,000 = $28,000.

If Custom's actual sales revenues from the tables were $80,000, or an average of $26,667 per unit sold, and if its other costs were minimal, then the following table summarizes the effects of the four methods:

Method	Sales	Cost of Goods Sold	Reported Profit	Ending Inventory Value
Specific identification	$80,000	$42,000	$38,000	$28,000
FIFO	80,000	36,000	44,000	34,000
LIFO	80,000	48,000	32,000	22,000
Weighted average	80,000	42,000	38,000	28,000

If we ignore taxes, then Custom's cash flows would not be affected by its choice of inventory methods, yet its balance sheet and reported profits would vary with each method. In an inflationary period such as in our example, FIFO gives the lowest cost of goods sold and thus the highest net income. FIFO also shows the highest inventory value, so it produces the strongest apparent liquidity position as measured by net working capital or the current ratio. On the other hand, LIFO produces the highest cost of goods sold, the lowest reported profits, and the weakest apparent liquidity position. However, when taxes are considered, LIFO provides the greatest tax deductibility and therefore results in the lowest tax burden. Consequently, after-tax cash flows are highest when LIFO is used.

Of course, these results apply only to periods when costs are increasing. If costs were constant, then all four methods would produce the same cost of goods sold, ending inventory, taxes, and cash flows. However, inflation has been a fact of life in recent years, so most firms use LIFO to take advantage of its greater tax and cash flow benefits.

23-5 **The Economic Ordering Quantity (EOQ) Model**

As discussed in Chapter 21, inventories are obviously necessary, but it is equally obvious that a firm's profitability will suffer if it has too much or too little inventory. Most firms take a pragmatic approach to setting inventory levels in which past experience plays a major role. However, as a starting point in the process, it is useful for managers to consider the insights provided by the **Economic Ordering Quantity (EOQ) model**. The EOQ model first specifies the costs of ordering and carrying inventories and then combines these costs to obtain the total cost associated with inventory holdings. Finally, optimization techniques are used to find the order quantity, and hence inventory level, that minimizes total cost. Note that a third category of inventory cost, the cost of running short (stock-out cost), is not considered in our initial discussion. This cost is dealt with by adding safety stocks, as we discuss later. Similarly, we shall discuss quantity discounts in a later section. The costs that remain for consideration at this stage are carrying, ordering, shipping, and receiving costs.

23-5a **Carrying Cost**

Carrying cost generally rises in direct proportion to the average amount of inventory carried. Inventories carried, in turn, depend on the frequency with which orders are placed. To illustrate, suppose a firm sells S units per year and places equal-sized orders N times per year; then S/N units will be purchased with each order. If the inventory is used evenly over the year and if no safety stocks are carried, then the average inventory, A, will be:

$$A = \frac{\text{Units per order}}{2} = \frac{S/N}{2} \qquad (23\text{–}3)$$

For example, if S = 120,000 units in a year and N = 4, then the firm will order 30,000 units at a time and its average inventory will be 15,000 units:

$$A = \frac{S/N}{2} = \frac{120,000/4}{2} = \frac{30,000}{2} = 15,000 \text{ units}$$

Just after a shipment arrives, the inventory will be 30,000 units; just before the next shipment arrives, it will be zero; and on average, 15,000 units will be carried.

Now assume the firm purchases its inventory at a price P = $2 per unit. The average inventory value is thus (P)(A) = $2(15,000) = $30,000. If the firm has a cost of capital of 10%, it will incur $3,000 in financing charges to carry the inventory for 1 year. Further, assume that each year the firm incurs $2,000 of storage costs (space, utilities, security, taxes, and so forth), that its inventory insurance cost is $500, and that it must mark down inventories by $1,000 because of depreciation and obsolescence. The firm's total cost of carrying the $30,000 average inventory is thus $3,000 + $2,000 + $500 + $1,000 = $6,500, and the annual percentage cost of carrying the inventory is $6,500/$30,000 = 0.217 = 21.7%.

Defining the annual percentage carrying cost as C, we can, in general, find the annual total carrying cost, TCC, as the percentage carrying cost (C) multiplied by the price per unit (P) times the average number of units (A):

(23–4)
$$\text{Total carrying cost} = \text{TCC} = (C)(P)(A)$$

In our example:

$$\text{TCC} = (0.217)(\$2)(15,000) \approx \$6,500$$

23-5b Ordering Cost

Although we assume that carrying cost is entirely variable and rises in direct proportion to the average size of inventories, *ordering cost* is often fixed. For example, the cost of placing and receiving an order—interoffice memos, long-distance telephone calls, setting up a production run, and taking delivery—is essentially fixed regardless of the size of an order, so this part of inventory cost is simply the fixed cost of placing and receiving orders multiplied by the number of orders placed per year.[7] We define the fixed cost associated with ordering inventories as F, and if we place N orders per year then the total ordering cost is given by Equation 23-5:

(23–5)
$$\text{Total ordering cost} = \text{TOC} = (F)(N)$$

---

7. Note that, in reality, both carrying and ordering costs can have variable and fixed-cost elements—at least over certain ranges of average inventory. For example, security and utilities charges are probably fixed in the short run over a wide range of inventory levels. Similarly, labor cost in receiving inventory could be tied to the quantity received and hence could be variable. To simplify matters, we treat all carrying cost as variable and all ordering cost as fixed. However, if these assumptions do not fit the situation at hand, the cost definitions can be changed. For example, one could add another term for shipping cost if there are economies of scale in shipping such that the cost of shipping a unit is smaller if shipments are larger. However, in most situations shipping cost is not sensitive to order size, so total shipping cost is simply the shipping cost per unit times the units ordered (and sold) during the year. Under this condition, shipping cost is not influenced by inventory policy; hence it may be disregarded for purposes of determining the optimal inventory level and the optimal order size.

Here TOC = total ordering cost, F = fixed cost per order, and N = number of orders placed per year.

Equation 23-3 may be rewritten as N = S/2A and then substituted into Equation 23-5:

$$\text{Total ordering cost} = \text{TOC} = F\left(\frac{S}{2A}\right)$$

(23–6)

To illustrate the use of Equation 23-6, let F = $100, S = 120,000 units, and A = 15,000 units. Then TOC, the total annual ordering cost, is $400:

$$\text{TOC} = \$100\left(\frac{120,000}{30,000}\right) = \$100(4) = \$400$$

23-5c Total Inventory Costs

Total carrying cost, TCC, as defined in Equation 23-4, and total ordering cost, TOC, as defined in Equation 23-6, may be combined to find *total inventory costs*, TIC, as follows:

$$\text{Total inventory costs} = \text{TIC} = \quad \text{TCC} \quad + \quad \text{TOC}$$
$$= (C)(P)(A) + F\left(\frac{S}{2A}\right)$$

(23–7)

Recognizing that the average inventory carried is A = Q/2, or one-half the size of each order quantity, Q, we may rewrite Equation 23-7 as:

$$\text{TIC} = \quad \text{TCC} \quad + \quad \text{TOC}$$
$$= (C)(P)\left(\frac{Q}{2}\right) + (F)\left(\frac{S}{Q}\right)$$

(23–8)

Here we see that total carrying cost equals average inventory in units, Q/2, multiplied by unit price, P, times the percentage annual carrying cost, C. Total ordering cost equals the number of orders placed per year, S/Q, multiplied by the fixed cost of placing and receiving an order, F. Finally, total inventory costs equal the sum of total carrying cost plus total ordering cost. We will use this equation in the next section to develop the optimal inventory ordering quantity.

23-5d Derivation of the EOQ Model

Figure 23-3 illustrates the basic premise on which the EOQ model is built—namely, that some costs rise with larger inventories while other costs decline, and there is an optimal order size (and associated average inventory) that minimizes the total costs of inventories. First, as noted earlier, the average investment in

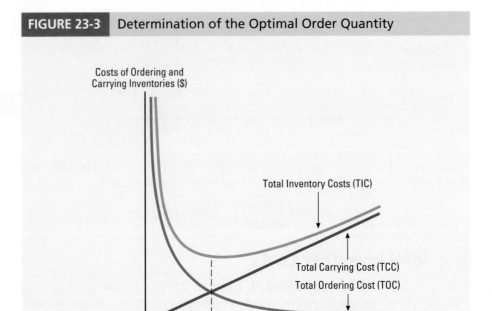

FIGURE 23-3 Determination of the Optimal Order Quantity

inventories depends on how frequently orders are placed and the size of each order—if we fill orders every day, then average inventories will be much smaller than if we fill orders once a year. Further, as Figure 23-3 shows, the firm's carrying costs rise with larger orders; larger orders mean larger average inventories and so warehousing costs, interest on funds tied up in inventory, insurance, and obsolescence costs will all increase. However, ordering costs decline with larger orders and inventories; the cost of placing orders, suppliers' production setup costs, and order-handling costs will all decline if we order infrequently and consequently hold larger quantities.

If the carrying and ordering cost curves in Figure 23-3 are added, the sum represents total inventory costs, TIC. The point at which the TIC is minimized represents the Economic Ordering Quantity, and this, in turn, determines the optimal average inventory level.

The EOQ is found by differentiating Equation 23-8 with respect to ordering quantity, Q, and setting the derivative equal to zero:

$$\frac{d(TIC)}{dQ} = \frac{(C)(P)}{2} - \frac{(F)(S)}{Q^2} = 0$$

Now, solving for Q, we obtain:

$$\frac{(C)(P)}{2} = \frac{(F)(S)}{Q^2}$$

$$Q^2 = \frac{2(F)(S)}{(C)(P)}$$

$$Q = EOQ = \sqrt{\frac{2(F)(S)}{(C)(P)}}$$

(23–9)

Here:

EOQ = Economic Ordering Quantity—the optimal quantity to be ordered each time an order is placed

F = Fixed cost of placing and receiving an order

S = Annual sales in units

C = Annual carrying cost expressed as a percentage of average inventory value

P = Purchase price the firm must pay per unit of inventory

Equation 23-9 is the EOQ model.[8] The assumptions of the model, which will be relaxed shortly, include the following: (1) sales can be forecasted perfectly, (2) sales are evenly distributed throughout the year, and (3) orders are received when expected.

23-5e EOQ Model Illustration

As an illustration of the EOQ model, consider the following data supplied by Cotton Tops Inc., a distributor of budget-priced, custom-designed T-shirts that it sells to concessionaires at various theme parks in the United States:

S = Annual sales = 26,000 shirts per year

C = Percentage carrying cost = 25% of inventory value

P = Purchase price per shirt = $4.92 per shirt

F = Fixed cost per order = $1,000. Cotton Tops designs and distributes the shirts, but the actual production is done by another company. The bulk of this $1,000 cost is the labor cost for setting up the equipment for the production run, which the manufacturer bills separately from the $4.92 cost per shirt.

Substituting these data into Equation 23-9, we obtain an EOQ of 6,500 units:

$$EOQ = \sqrt{\frac{2(F)(S)}{(C)(P)}} = \sqrt{\frac{(2)(\$1,000)(26,000)}{(0.25)(\$4.92)}}$$
$$= \sqrt{42,276,423} \approx 6,500 \text{ units}$$

---

8. The EOQ model can also be written as:

$$EOQ = \sqrt{\frac{2(F)(S)}{C^*}}$$

where C* is the annual carrying cost per unit expressed in dollars.

FIGURE 23-4   Inventory Position without Safety Stock

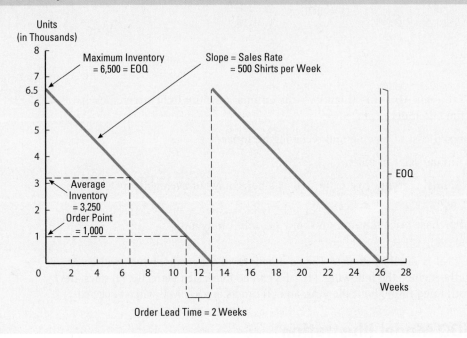

With an EOQ of 6,500 shirts and annual usage of 26,000 shirts, Cotton Tops will place 26,000/6,500 = 4 orders per year. Note that average inventory holdings depend directly on the EOQ. This relationship is illustrated graphically in Figure 23-4, where we see that average inventory = EOQ/2. Immediately after an order is received, 6,500 shirts are in stock. The usage rate, or sales rate, is 500 shirts per week (26,000/52 weeks), so inventories are drawn down by this amount each week. Thus, the actual number of units held in inventory will vary from 6,500 shirts just after an order is received to zero just before a new order arrives. With a 6,500 beginning balance, a zero ending balance, and a uniform sales rate, inventories will average one-half the EOQ, or 3,250 shirts, during the year. At a cost of $4.92 per shirt, the average investment in inventories will be (3,250)($4.92) ≈ $16,000. If inventories are financed by bank loans then the loan will vary from a high of $32,000 to a low of $0, but the average amount outstanding over the course of a year will be $16,000.

Note that the EOQ, and hence the average inventory holdings, rises with the square root of sales. Therefore, a given increase in sales will result in a less-than-proportionate increase in inventories, so the inventory/sales ratio will tend to decline as a firm grows. For example, Cotton Tops' EOQ is 6,500 shirts at an annual sales level of 26,000, and the average inventory is 3,250 shirts, or $16,000. However, if sales were to increase by 100% to 52,000 shirts per year, then the EOQ would rise only to 9,195 units or by 41%, and the average inventory would rise by this same percentage. This suggests there are economies of scale in holding inventories.[9]

---

9. Note, however, that these scale economies relate to each particular item, not to the entire firm. Thus, a large distributor with $500 million of sales might have a higher inventory/sales ratio than a much smaller distributor if the small firm has only a few items with high sales volume and the large firm distributes a great many low-volume items.

Finally, look at Cotton Tops' total inventory costs for the year, assuming that the EOQ is ordered each time. Using Equation 23-8, we find that total inventory cost is $8,000:

$$
\begin{aligned}
\text{TIC} &= & \text{TCC} & + & \text{TOC} \\
&= & (C)(P)\left(\dfrac{Q}{2}\right) & + & (F)\left(\dfrac{S}{Q}\right) \\
&= & 0.25(\$4.92)\left(\dfrac{6{,}500}{2}\right) & + & (\$1{,}000)\left(\dfrac{26{,}000}{6{,}500}\right) \\
&\approx & \$4{,}000 & + & \$4{,}000 & = \$8{,}000
\end{aligned}
$$

Note these two points: (1) The $8,000 total inventory cost represents the total of carrying costs and ordering costs, but this amount does *not* include the 26,000 ($4.92) = $127,920 annual purchasing cost of the inventory itself. (2) As we see both in Figure 23-3 and in the calculation above, at the EOQ, total carrying cost (TCC) equals total ordering cost (TOC). This property is not unique to our Cotton Tops illustration; it always holds.

23-5f **Setting the Order Point**

If a 2-week lead time is required for production and shipping, what is Cotton Tops' order point level? Cotton Tops sells 26,000/52 = 500 shirts per week. Thus, if a 2-week lag occurs between placing an order and receiving goods, Cotton Tops must place the order when there are 2(500) = 1,000 shirts on hand. During the 2-week production and shipping period, the inventory balance will continue to decline at the rate of 500 shirts per week, and the inventory balance will hit zero just as the order of new shirts arrives.

If Cotton Tops knew for certain that both the sales rate and the order lead time would never vary, then it could operate exactly as shown in Figure 23-4. However, sales do change, and production and/or shipping delays are sometimes encountered. To guard against these events, the firm must carry additional inventories, or safety stocks, as discussed in the next section.

SELF TEST

What are some specific inventory carrying costs? As defined here, are these costs fixed or variable?

What are some inventory ordering costs? As defined here, are these costs fixed or variable?

What are the components of total inventory costs?

What is the concept behind the EOQ model?

What is the relationship between total carrying cost and total ordering cost at the EOQ?

What assumptions are inherent in the EOQ model as presented here?

23-6 **EOQ Model Extensions**

The basic EOQ model was derived under several restrictive assumptions. In this section, we relax some of these assumptions and, in the process, extend the model to make it more useful.

23-6a **The Concept of Safety Stocks**

The concept of a **safety stock** is illustrated in Figure 23-5. First, note that the slope of the sales line measures the expected rate of sales. The company *expects* to sell 500 shirts per week, but let us assume that the maximum likely sales rate is twice this amount, or 1,000 units each week. Further, assume that Cotton Tops sets the safety stock at 1,000 shirts, so it initially orders 7,500 shirts, the EOQ of 6,500 plus the 1,000-unit safety stock. Subsequently, it reorders the EOQ whenever the inventory level falls to 2,000 shirts, the safety stock of 1,000 shirts plus the 1,000 shirts expected to be used while awaiting delivery of the order.

Note that the company could, over the 2-week delivery period, sell 1,000 units a week, or double its normal expected sales. This maximum rate of sales is shown by the steeper dashed line in Figure 23-5. The condition that makes this higher sales rate possible is the safety stock of 1,000 shirts.

The safety stock is also useful to guard against delays in receiving orders. The expected delivery time is 2 weeks, but with a 1,000-unit safety stock, the company

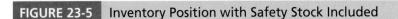

FIGURE 23-5   Inventory Position with Safety Stock Included

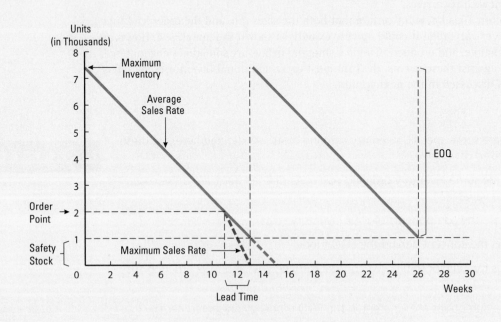

could maintain sales at the expected rate of 500 units per week for an additional 2 weeks if something should delay an order.

However, carrying a safety stock has a cost. The average inventory is now EOQ/2 plus the safety stock, or 6,500/2 + 1,000 = 3,250 + 1,000 = 4,250 shirts, and the average inventory value is now (4,250)($4.92) = $20,910. This increase in average inventory causes an increase in annual inventory carrying cost equal to (Safety stock)(P)(C) = 1,000($4.92)(0.25) = $1,230.

The optimal safety stock varies from situation to situation, but in general it *increases:* (1) with the uncertainty of demand forecasts, (2) with the cost (in terms of lost sales and lost goodwill) that results from inventory shortages, and (3) with the probability that delays will occur in receiving shipments. The optimal safety stock *decreases* as the cost of carrying this additional inventory increases.

23-6b Setting the Safety Stock Level

The critical question with regard to safety stocks is this: How large should the safety stock be? To answer this question, first examine Table 23-1, which contains the probability distribution of Cotton Tops' unit sales for an average 2-week period, the time it takes to receive an order of 6,500 T-shirts. Note that the expected sales over an average 2-week period are 1,000 units. Why do we focus on a 2-week period? Because shortages can occur only during the 2 weeks it takes for an order to arrive.

Cotton Tops' managers have estimated that the annual carrying cost is 25% of inventory value. Because each shirt has an inventory value of $4.92, the annual carrying cost per unit is 0.25($4.92) = $1.23, and the carrying cost for each 13-week inventory period is $1.23(13/52) = $0.308 per unit. Even though shortages can occur only during the 2-week order period, safety stocks must be carried over the full 13-week inventory cycle. Next, Cotton Tops' managers must estimate the cost of shortages. Assume that when shortages occur, 50% of Cotton Tops' buyers are willing to accept back orders, but 50% of its potential customers simply cancel their orders. Remember that each shirt sells for $9.00, so each one-unit shortage produces expected lost profits of 0.5($9.00 − $4.92) = $2.04. With this information, the firm can calculate the expected costs of different safety stock levels. This is done in Table 23-2.

TABLE 23-1	Two-Week Sales Probability Distribution
Probability	**Unit Sales**
0.1	0
0.2	500
0.4	1,000
0.2	1,500
0.1	2,000
1.0	Expected sales = 1,000

TABLE 23-2   Safety Stock Analysis

Safety Stock (1)	Sales During 2-Week Delivery Period (2)	Probability (3)	Shortage[a] (4)	Shortage Cost (Lost Profits): $2.04 × (4) = (5)	Expected Shortage Cost: (3) × (5) = (6)	Safety Stock Carrying Cost: $0.308 × (1) = (7)	Expected Total Cost: (6) + (7) = (8)
0	0	0.1	0	$ 0	$ 0		
	500	0.2	0	0	0		
	1,000	0.4	0	0	0		
	1,500	0.2	500	1,020	204		
	2,000	0.1	1,000	$2,040	204		
		1.0		Expected shortage cost = $408		$ 0	$408
500	0	0.1	0	$ 0	$ 0		
	500	0.2	0	0	0		
	1,000	0.4	0	0	0		
	1,500	0.2	0	0	0		
	2,000	0.1	500	1,020	102		
		1.0		Expected shortage cost = $102		$154	$256
1,000	0	0.1	0	$ 0	$ 0		
	500	0.2	0	0	0		
	1,000	0.4	0	0	0		
	1,500	0.2	0	0	0		
	2,000	0.1	0	0	0		
		1.0		Expected shortage cost = $ 0		$308	$308

[a]Shortage = Actual sales − (1,000 Stock at order point − Safety stock); positive values only.

For each safety stock level, we determine the expected cost of a shortage based on the sales probability distribution in Table 23-1. There is an expected shortage cost of $408 if no safety stock is carried; $102 if the safety stock is set at 500 units; and no expected shortage, hence no shortage cost, with a safety stock of 1,000 units. The cost of carrying each safety level is merely the cost of carrying a unit of inventory over the 13-week inventory period, $0.308, multiplied by the safety stock; for example, the cost of carrying a safety stock of 500 units is $0.308(500) = $154. Finally, we sum the expected shortage cost in Column 6 and the safety stock carrying cost in Column 7 to obtain the total cost figures given in Column 8. Because the 500-unit safety stock has the lowest expected total cost, Cotton Tops should carry this safety level.

Of course, the optimal safety level is highly sensitive to the estimates of the sales probability distribution and shortage costs. Errors here could result in incorrect safety stock levels. Note also that, in calculating the shortage cost of $2.04 per unit, we implicitly assumed that a lost sale in one period would not result in lost sales in future periods. If shortages cause customer ill will, the result could be permanent sales reductions. Then the situation would be much more serious, stock-out costs would be far higher, and the firm should consequently carry a larger safety stock.

The stock-out example is just one example of the many judgments required in inventory management—the mechanics are relatively simple, but the inputs are based on judgment and difficult to obtain.

23-6c **Quantity Discounts**

Now suppose the T-shirt manufacturer offered Cotton Tops a **quantity discount** of 2% on large orders. If the quantity discount applied to orders of 5,000 or more, then Cotton Tops would continue to place the EOQ order of 6,500 shirts and take the quantity discount. However, if the quantity discount required orders of 10,000 or more, then Cotton Tops would have to compare the savings in purchase price that would result if its ordering quantity were increased to 10,000 units with the increase in total inventory cost caused by deviating from the 6,500-unit EOQ.

First, consider the total cost associated with Cotton Tops' EOQ of 6,500 units. We found earlier that total inventory cost is $8,000:

$$
\begin{aligned}
\text{TIC} &= \quad\quad \text{TCC} &+& \quad\quad \text{TOC} \\
&= \quad\quad (C)(P)\!\left(\frac{Q}{2}\right) &+& \quad\quad (F)\!\left(\frac{S}{Q}\right) \\
&= 0.25(\$4.92)\!\left(\frac{6{,}500}{2}\right) &+& \ (\$1{,}000)\!\left(\frac{26{,}000}{6{,}500}\right) \\
&\approx \quad\quad \$4{,}000 &+& \quad\quad \$4{,}000 \quad = \$8{,}000
\end{aligned}
$$

Now, what would total inventory cost be if Cotton Tops ordered 10,000 units instead of 6,500? The answer is $8,625:

$$
\begin{aligned}
\text{TIC} &= 0.25(\$4.82)\!\left(\frac{10{,}000}{2}\right) + \ (\$1{,}000)\!\left(\frac{26{,}000}{10{,}000}\right) \\
&\approx \quad\quad \$6{,}025 \quad\quad + \quad\quad \$2{,}600 \quad\quad = \$8{,}625
\end{aligned}
$$

Note that when the discount is taken, the price, P, is reduced by the amount of the discount; the new price per unit would be 0.98($4.92) = $4.82. Also note that, when the ordering quantity is increased, carrying cost *increases* (because the firm is carrying a larger average inventory) but ordering cost *decreases* (because the number of orders per year decreases). If we were to calculate total inventory cost at an ordering quantity less than the EOQ—say, 5,000—then we would find carrying cost to be less than $4,000 and ordering cost to be more than $4,000; however, the total inventory cost would be more than $8,000 because it is at a minimum when only 6,500 units are ordered.[10]

Thus, inventory cost would increase by $8,625 − $8,000 = $625 if Cotton Tops were to increase its order size to 10,000 shirts. However, *this cost increase must be compared with Cotton Tops' savings if it takes the discount.* Taking the discount would save 0.02($4.92) = $0.0984 per unit. Over the year, Cotton Tops orders 26,000 shirts, so the annual savings is $0.0984(26,000) ≈ $2,558. Here is a summary:

Reduction in purchase price = 0.02($4.92)(26,000) =	$2,558
Increase in total inventory cost =	625
Net savings from taking discounts	$1,933

Obviously, the company should order 10,000 units at a time and take advantage of the quantity discount.

23-6d **Inflation**

Moderate inflation—say, 3% per year—can largely be ignored for purposes of inventory management, but higher rates of inflation must be considered. If the rate of inflation in the types of goods the firm stocks tends to be relatively constant, then it can be dealt with quite easily: Simply deduct the expected annual rate of inflation from the carrying cost percentage, C, in Equation 23-9; then use this modified version of the EOQ model to establish the ordering quantity. The reason for making this deduction is that inflation causes the value of the inventory to rise, thus offsetting somewhat the effects of depreciation and other carrying costs. Now C will be smaller, assuming other factors are held constant, so the calculated EOQ and the average inventory will increase. However, higher rates of inflation usually mean higher interest rates, and this will cause C to increase, thus lowering the EOQ and average inventory.

On balance, there is no evidence that inflation either raises or lowers the optimal inventories of firms in the aggregate. Inflation should still be explicitly considered, however, for it will raise the individual firm's optimal holdings if the rate of inflation for its own inventories is above average (and is greater than the effects of inflation on interest rates), and vice versa.

23-6e **Seasonal Demand**

For most firms, it is unrealistic to assume that the demand for an inventory item is uniform throughout the year. What happens when there is seasonal demand, as would hold true for an ice cream company? Here the standard annual EOQ model is obviously not appropriate. However, it does provide a point of departure for setting inventory parameters, which are then modified to fit the particular seasonal pattern. We divide the year into the seasons in which annualized sales are relatively constant; for example, sales might be relatively constant in the spring and fall,

---

10. At an ordering quantity of 5,000 units, total inventory cost is $8,275:

$$\text{TIC} = (0.25)(\$4.92)\left(\frac{5,000}{2}\right) + (\$1,000)\left(\frac{26,000}{5,000}\right)$$

$$= \$3,075 + \$5,200 = \$8,275$$

TABLE 23-3	EOQ Sensitivity Analysis	
Ordering Quantity	Total Inventory Cost	Percentage Deviation from Optimal
3,000	$10,512	+31.4%
4,000	8,960	+12.0
5,000	8,275	+3.4
6,000	8,023	+0.3
6,500	8,000	0.0
7,000	8,019	+0.2
8,000	8,170	+2.1
9,000	8,423	+5.3
10,000	8,750	+9.1

but different in the summer and winter. The EOQ model then is applied separately to each constant-sales period. During the transitions between seasons, inventories would be either run down or else built up with special seasonal orders.

23-6f **EOQ Range**

Thus far, we have interpreted the EOQ and the resulting inventory values as single-point estimates. It can be easily demonstrated that small deviations from the EOQ do not appreciably affect total inventory cost and consequently that the optimal ordering quantity should be viewed more as a range than as a single value.[11]

To illustrate this point, we examine the sensitivity of total inventory cost to ordering quantity for Cotton Tops. Table 23-3 contains the results. We conclude that the ordering quantity could range from 5,000 to 8,000 units without affecting total inventory cost by more than 3.4%. Thus, managers can adjust the ordering quantity within a fairly wide range without significantly increasing total inventory cost.

Why are safety stocks required?

Conceptually, how would you evaluate a quantity discount offer from a supplier?

What effect does inflation typically have on the EOQ?

Can the EOQ model be used when a company faces seasonal demand fluctuations?

What effect do minor deviations from the EOQ have on total inventory cost?

SELF TEST

---

11. This is somewhat analogous to the optimal capital structure in that small changes in capital structure around the optimum do not have much effect on the firm's weighted average cost of capital.

Summary

This chapter discussed the goals of cash management and how a company might determine its optimal cash balance using the Baumol model. It also discussed how an optimal inventory policy might be identified using the Economic Ordering Quantity (EOQ) model. The key concepts covered are listed below.

- A policy that strives for **zero working capital** not only generates cash but also speeds up production and helps businesses operate more efficiently. This concept has its own definition of working capital: Inventories + Receivables − Payables. The rationale is that inventories and receivables are the keys to making sales and that inventories can be financed by suppliers through accounts payable.
- The primary goal of cash management is to minimize the amount of cash a firm holds while maintaining a sufficient **target cash balance** to conduct business.
- The **Baumol model** provides insights into the optimal cash balance. The model balances the opportunity cost of holding cash against the transaction cost associated with obtaining cash either by selling marketable securities or by borrowing:

$$\text{Optimal cash infusion} = \sqrt{\frac{2(F)(T)}{r}}$$

- Firms generally set their target cash balances at the level that holds the risk of running out of cash to some acceptable level. **Monte Carlo simulation** can be helpful in setting the target cash balance.
- Firms use inventory control systems such as the **red-line method**, the **two-bin method**, and **computerized inventory control systems** to help them keep track of actual inventory levels and to ensure that inventory levels are adjusted as sales change. **Just-in-time (JIT) systems** are used to hold down inventory costs and, simultaneously, to improve the production process. **Outsourcing** is the practice of purchasing components rather than making them in-house.
- Inventory can be accounted for in four different ways: (1) **specific identification**, (2) **first-in, first-out (FIFO)**, (3) **last-in, first-out (LIFO)**, and (4) **weighted average**.
- **Inventory costs** can be divided into three parts: **carrying cost**, **ordering cost**, and **stock-out cost**. In general, carrying cost increases as the level of inventory rises, but ordering cost and stock-out cost decline with larger inventory holdings.
- **Total carrying cost (TCC)** is equal to the percentage cost of carrying inventory (C) multiplied by the purchase price per unit of inventory (P) times the average number of units held (A): TCC = (C)(P)(A).
- **Total ordering cost (TOC)** is equal to the fixed cost of placing an order (F) multiplied by the number of orders placed per year (N): TOC = (F)(N).
- **Total inventory costs (TIC)** equal total carrying cost (TCC) plus total ordering cost (TOC): TIC = TCC + TOC.

- The **Economic Ordering Quantity (EOQ) model** is a formula for determining the order quantity that will minimize total inventory cost:

$$EOQ = \sqrt{\frac{2(F)(S)}{(C)(P)}}$$

Here F is the fixed cost per order, S is annual sales in units, C is the percentage cost of carrying inventory, and P is the purchase price per unit.

- The **order point** is the inventory level at which new items must be ordered.
- **Safety stocks** are held to avoid shortages, which can occur if (1) sales increase by more than expected or (2) shipping delays are encountered on inventory ordered. The cost of carrying a safety stock, which is separate from that based on the EOQ model, is equal to the percentage cost of carrying inventory multiplied by the purchase price per unit times the number of units held as the safety stock.

Questions

23–1 Define each of the following terms:
   a. Baumol model
   b. Total carrying cost; total ordering cost; total inventory costs
   c. Economic Ordering Quantity (EOQ); EOQ model; EOQ range
   d. Reorder point; safety stock
   e. Red-line method; two-bin method; computerized inventory control system
   f. Just-in-time system; outsourcing

23–2 Indicate by a (+), (−), or (0) whether each of the following events would probably cause average annual inventory holdings to rise, fall, or be affected in an indeterminate manner:
   a. Our suppliers change from delivering by trainto air freight.   _____
   b. We change from producing just-in-time to meet seasonal demand to steady, year-round production.   _____
   c. Competition in the markets in which we sell increases.   _____
   d. The general rate of inflation rises.   _____
   e. Interest rates rise; other things are constant.   _____

23–3 Assuming the firm's sales volume remained constant, would you expect it to have a higher cash balance during a tight-money period or during an easy-money period? Why?

23–4 Explain how each of the following factors would probably affect a firm's target cash balance if all other factors were held constant.
   a. The firm institutes a new billing procedure that better synchronizes its cash inflows and outflows.
   b. The firm develops a new sales forecasting technique that improves its forecasts.

c. The firm reduces its portfolio of U.S. Treasury bills.

d. The firm arranges to use an overdraft system for its checking account.

e. The firm borrows a large amount of money from its bank and also begins to write far more checks than it did in the past.

f. Interest rates on Treasury bills rise from 5% to 10%.

Problems

Intermediate Problems 1–2

23–1 Economic Ordering Quantity

The Gentry Garden Center sells 90,000 bags of lawn fertilizer annually. The optimal safety stock (which is on hand initially) is 1,000 bags. Each bag costs the firm $1.50, inventory carrying cost is 20%, and the cost of placing an order with its supplier is $15.

a. What is the Economic Ordering Quantity?

b. What is the maximum inventory of fertilizer?

c. What will be the firm's average inventory?

d. How often must the company order?

23–2 Optimal Cash Transfer

Barenbaum Industries projects that cash outlays of $4.5 million will occur uniformly throughout the year. Barenbaum plans to meet its cash requirements by periodically selling marketable securities from its portfolio. The firm's marketable securities are invested to earn 12%, and the cost per transaction of converting securities to cash is $27.

a. Use the Baumol model to determine the optimal transaction size for transfers from marketable securities to cash.

b. What will be Barenbaum's average cash balance?

c. How many transfers per year will be required?

d. What will be Barenbaum's total annual cost of maintaining cash balances? What would the total cost be if the company maintained an average cash balance of $50,000 or of $0 (it deposits funds daily to meet cash requirements)?

Spreadsheet Problem

23–3 Build a Model: Inventory Management

Start with the partial model in the file *Ch23 P03 Build a Model.xls* on the textbook's Web site. The following inventory data have been established for the Adler Corporation.

(1) Orders must be placed in multiples of 100 units.

(2) Annual sales are 338,000 units.

(3) The purchase price per unit is $3.

(4) Carrying cost is 20% of the purchase price of goods.

(5) Cost per order placed is $24.

(6) Desired safety stock is 14,000 units; this amount is on hand initially.

(7) Two weeks are required for delivery.

   a. What is the EOQ?

   b. How many orders should the firm place each year?

   c. At what inventory level should a reorder be made? (*Hint:* Reorder point = (Safety stock + Weeks to deliver × Weekly usage) − Goods in transit.)

   d. Calculate the total cost of ordering and carrying inventories if the order quantity is: (1) 4,000 units, (2) 4,800 units, or (3) 6,000 units. What is the total cost of ordering if the order quantity is the EOQ?

   e. What are the EOQ and total inventory cost if the following were to occur?

     (1) Sales increase to 500,000 units.

     (2) Fixed order cost increases to $30; sales remain at 338,000 units.

     (3) Purchase price increases to $4; sales and fixed costs remain at original values.

MINI CASE

Andria Mullins, financial manager of Webster Electronics, has been asked by the firm's CEO, Fred Weygandt, to evaluate the company's inventory control techniques and to lead a discussion of the subject with the senior executives. Andria plans to use as an example one of Webster's "big ticket" items, a customized computer microchip that the firm uses in its laptop computers. Each chip costs Webster $200, and it must also pay its supplier a $1,000 setup fee on each order; the minimum order size is 250 units. Webster's annual usage forecast is 5,000 units, and the annual carrying cost of this item is estimated to be 20% of the average inventory value.

Andria plans to begin her session with the senior executives by reviewing some basic inventory concepts, after which she will apply the EOQ model to Webster's microchip inventory. As her assistant, you have been asked to help her by answering the following questions:

a. Why is inventory management vital to the financial health of most firms?

b. What assumptions underlie the EOQ model?

c. Write out the formula for the total costs of carrying and ordering inventory, and then use the formula to derive the EOQ model.

d. What is the EOQ for custom microchips? What are total inventory costs if the EOQ is ordered?

e. What is Webster's added cost if it orders 400 units at a time rather than the EOQ quantity? What if it orders 600 units?

f. Suppose it takes 2 weeks for Webster's supplier to set up production, make and test the chips, and deliver them to Webster's plant. Assuming certainty in delivery times and usage, at what inventory level should Webster reorder? (Assume a 52-week year, and assume Webster orders the EOQ amount.)

g. Of course, there is uncertainty in Webster's usage rate as well as in delivery times, so the company must carry a safety stock to avoid running out of chips and having to halt production. If a 200-unit safety stock is carried, what effect would this have on total inventory costs? What is the new reorder point? What protection does the safety stock provide if usage increases or if delivery is delayed?

h. Now suppose Webster's supplier offers a discount of 1% on orders of 1,000 or more. Should Webster take the discount? Why or why not?

i. For many firms, inventory usage is not uniform throughout the year but instead follows some seasonal pattern. Can the EOQ model be used in this situation? If so, how?

j. How would these factors affect an EOQ analysis?
  (1) The use of just-in-time procedures.
  (2) The use of air freight for deliveries.
  (3) The use of a computerized inventory control system, in which an electronic system automatically reduced the inventory account as units were removed from stock and, when the order point was hit, automatically sent an electronic message to the supplier placing an order. The electronic system would ensure that inventory records are accurate and that orders are placed promptly.
  (4) The manufacturing plant is redesigned and automated. Computerized process equipment and state-of-the-art robotics are installed, making the plant highly flexible in the sense that the company can quickly switch from the production of one item to another at a minimum cost. This makes short production runs more feasible than under the old plant setup.

k. Webster runs a $100,000 per month cash deficit, requiring periodic transfers from its portfolio of marketable securities. Broker fees are $32 per transaction, and Webster earns 7% on its investment portfolio. How can Andria use the EOQ model to determine how Webster should liquidate part of its portfolio to provide cash?

SELECTED ADDITIONAL CASES

The following cases from CengageCompose cover many of the concepts discussed in this chapter and are available at http://compose.cengage.com. Klein-Brigham Series:

Case 33, "Upscale Toddlers, Inc.," Case 79, "Mitchell Lumber Co.," Case 34, "Texas Rose Company," and Case 67, "Bridgewater Pool Company," all of which focus on receivables management.

Special Topics

Enterprise Risk Management

Defining risk management is simple: Identify events that could have adverse consequences and then take actions to prevent or minimize the damage caused by these events. Applying risk management is more difficult, but it is vital for a company's success, and perhaps even its survival. In this chapter, we explain how risk management adds value to a corporation, describe an enterprise risk management framework, identify different categories of risks, explain how to measure selected risks, and show how to manage those risks.[1] We also illustrate how companies can use **derivatives**, which are securities whose values are determined by the market price of some other asset, to manage certain types of risk.

Beginning-of-Chapter Questions

As you read this chapter, consider how you would answer the following questions. You *should not* necessarily be able to answer the questions before you read the chapter. Rather, you should use them to get a sense of the issues covered in the chapter. After reading the chapter, you should be able to give at least partial answers to the questions, and you should be able to give better answers after the chapter has been discussed in class. Note, too, that it is often useful, when answering conceptual questions, to use hypothetical data to illustrate your answer. We illustrate the answers with an *Excel* model that is available on the textbook's Web site. Accessing the model and working through it is a useful exercise, and it provides insights that are useful when answering the questions.

1. What does it mean to "manage" **risk**? Should its stockholders want a firm to "manage" all of the risks it faces?

2. What types of risks are **interest-rate and exchange-rate swaps** designed to mitigate? Why might one company prefer fixed-rate payments while another company prefers floating-rate payments, or payments in one currency versus another?

3. SafeCo can issue floating-rate debt at **LIBOR + 1%** or fixed-rate debt at 8%, but it would prefer to use fixed-rate debt. RiskyCo can issue floating-rate debt at LIBOR + 2% or fixed-rate debt at 8.8%, but it would prefer to use floating-rate debt. Explain why both companies might be better off if SafeCo issues floating-rate debt,

---

1. For excellent overviews of risk management, see Kenneth A. Froot, David S. Scharfstein, and Jeremy Stein, "A Framework for Risk Management," *Journal of Applied Corporate Finance*, Fall 1994, pp. 22–32; Brian Nocco and Rene Stultz, "Enterprise Risk Management, Theory and Practice," *Journal of Applied Corporate Finance*, Fall 2006, pp. 8–20; Walter Dolde, "The Trajectory of Corporate Financial Risk Management," *Journal of Applied Corporate Finance*, Fall 1993, pp. 33–41; and Marshall Blake and Nelda Mahady, "How Mid-Sized Companies Manage Risk," *Journal of Applied Corporate Finance*, Spring 1991, pp. 59–65.

RiskyCo issues fixed-rate debt, and they then swap payment streams. Assume that if they do arrange a swap, SafeCo will make a fixed payment of 6.9 percent to RiskyCo, and RiskyCo will make a payment of LIBOR (which is currently 6%) to SafeCo.

4. What is a **futures contract**, and how are futures used to manage risk? What are you protecting against if you buy Treasury futures contracts? What if you sell Treasury futures short?

5. Stohs Semiconductor Corporation plans to issue $50 million of 20-year bonds in 6 months. The interest rate would be 9% if the bonds were issued today. How can Stohs set up a hedge against an increase in interest rates over the next 6 months? Assume that 6-month futures sell for 100'22.

CORPORATE VALUATION AND RISK MANAGEMENT

All companies are exposed to risk from volatility in product prices, demand, input costs, and other sources of business risk, such as the risk stemming from the choice of production technology. Many companies also are exposed to risk from volatility in exchange rates and interest rates. Risk management can reduce firm risk, preventing catastrophes and leading to a lower cost of capital. In some instances, derivatives such as swaps can reduce the effective interest rate paid by a corporation, again reducing its cost of capital.

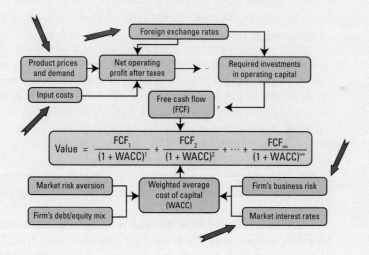

24-1 **Reasons to Manage Risk**

Will reducing risk make a company more valuable? Consider Plastic Inc., which manufactures dashboards, interior door panels, and other plastic components used by auto companies. Petroleum is the key feedstock for plastic and thus makes up a large percentage of its costs. Plastic has a 3-year contract with an auto company to deliver 500,000 door panels each year at a price of $20 each. When the company recently signed this contract, oil sold for $100 per barrel and was expected to stay at that level for the next 3 years. If oil prices fell during this time, Plastic would have higher than expected profits and free cash flows, but if oil prices rose, profits would fall. Because Plastic's value depends on its profits and free cash flows, a change in the price of oil would cause stockholders to earn either more or less than they anticipated.

Now suppose that, shortly after signing the contract with its door panel supplier, Plastic announces that it plans to lock in a 3-year supply of oil at a guaranteed price of $100 per barrel *and* that the cost of this guarantee is zero. Would that cause its stock price to rise? At first glance, it seems the answer should be "yes," but that might not be correct. Recall that the value of a stock depends on the present value of its expected future free cash flows, discounted at the weighted average cost of capital (WACC). Locking in the cost of oil will cause an increase in Plastic's stock price if and only if: (1) it causes the expected future free cash flows to increase or (2) it causes the WACC to decline.

Consider first the free cash flows. Before the announcement of guaranteed oil costs, investors had formed an estimate of the expected future free cash flows based on an expected oil price of $100 per barrel. Locking in the cost of oil at $100 per barrel will lower the *risk* of the expected future free cash flows, but it might not change the expected *size* of these cash flows because investors already expected a price of $100 per barrel. Of course, smaller than expected cash flows can disrupt a firm's operation and that disruption can, in turn, adversely affect cash flows.

Now what about the WACC? It will change only if locking in the cost of oil causes a change either in the cost of debt or equity or in the target capital structure. If the foreseeable increases in the price of oil are not enough to increase the threat of bankruptcy, then Plastic's cost of debt should not change and neither should its target capital structure. Regarding the cost of equity, recall from Chapter 2 that most investors hold well-diversified portfolios, which means that the cost of equity should depend only on systematic risk. Moreover, even though an increase in oil prices would have a negative effect on Plastic's stock price, it would not have a negative effect on all stocks. Indeed, oil producers should have higher than expected returns and stock prices. Assuming that Plastic's investors hold well-diversified portfolios that include stocks of oil-producing companies, we should have little reason to expect its cost of equity to decrease. The bottom line is this: If Plastic's expected future cash flows and WACC will not change significantly as a consequence of eliminating the risk of oil price increases, then neither should the value of its stock.

We discuss futures contracts and hedging in detail in the next section, but for now let's assume that Plastic has *not* locked in oil prices. Therefore, if oil prices increase, its stock price will fall. However, if its stockholders know this, they can build portfolios that contain oil futures whose values will rise or fall with oil prices and thus offset changes in the price of Plastic's stock. By choosing the correct amount of futures contracts, investors can thus "hedge" their portfolios and completely eliminate the risk due to changes in oil prices. There will be a cost to hedging, but that cost to large investors should be about the same as the cost to Plastic. Because stockholders can hedge away oil price risk themselves, why should they pay a higher price for Plastic's stock just because the company itself hedged away that risk?

The previous points not with standing, companies clearly believe that active risk management is important. A 1998 survey reported that 83% of firms with market values greater than $1.2 billion engage in risk management.[2] A more recent 2005 survey of CFOs reported that 90% of the international and domestic firms responding considered risk in the planning process. The average of the estimates of the contribution that risk management made to the market value of the firm was 3.8%.[3] There are many reasons why companies manage their risks.

1. *Debt capacity.* Risk management can reduce the volatility of cash flows, which decreases the probability of bankruptcy. As we discussed in Chapter 16, firms with lower operating risks can use more debt, and this can lead to higher stock prices due to the interest tax savings.

2. *Maintaining the optimal capital budget over time.* Recall from Chapter 16 that firms are reluctant to raise external equity because of high flotation costs and market pressure. This means that the capital budget must generally be financed with a combination of debt and internally generated funds. In bad years, internal cash flows may be too low to support the optimal capital budget, causing firms to either slow investment below the optimal rate or else incur the high costs associated with external equity. By smoothing out the cash flows, risk management can alleviate this problem. This issue is most relevant for firms with large growth opportunities. A study by Professors Gerald Gay and Jouahn Nam found that such firms do in fact use derivatives more than low-growth firms.[4] Thus, maintaining an optimal capital budget is an important determinant of firms' risk management practices.

3. *Financial distress.* The stages of financial distress can range from stockholder concern and higher interest rates on debt to customer defections and bankruptcy. Any serious level of financial distress causes a firm to have lower cash flows than expected. Risk management can reduce the likelihood of low cash flows and hence of financial distress.

4. *Comparative advantages in hedging.* Most investors cannot hedge as efficiently as a company. First, firms generally incur lower transaction costs because of their larger volume of hedging activities. Second, there is the problem of asymmetric information: Managers know more about the firm's risk exposure than do outside investors, so managers can create more effective hedges. And third, effective risk management requires specialized skills and knowledge that firms are more likely to have.

5. *Borrowing costs.* As discussed later in the chapter, firms can sometimes reduce input costs—especially the interest rate on debt—through the use of derivative instruments called *swaps.* Any such cost reduction adds value to the firm.

6. *Tax effects.* The present value of taxes paid by companies with volatile earnings is higher than the present value of taxes paid by stable companies; this is because of the treatment of tax credits and the rules governing corporate loss carryforwards and carrybacks. Moreover, if volatile earnings cause a company to declare bankruptcy, then the company often will lose the value of its tax

---

2. See Gordon M. Bodnar, Gregory S. Hayt, and Richard C. Marston, "1998 Wharton Survey of Financial Risk Management by U.S. Non-Financial Firms," *Financial Management*, Winter, 1998, pp. 70–91.

3. See Henri Servaes, Ane Tamayo, and Peter Tufano, "The Theory and Practice of Corporate Risk Management," *Journal of Applied Corporate Finance*, Fall, 2009, pp. 60–78.

4. See Gerald D. Gay and Jouahn Nam, "The Underinvestment Problem and Corporate Derivatives Use," *Financial Management*, Winter, 1998, pp. 53–69.

loss carryforwards. Therefore, using risk management to stabilize earnings can reduce the present value of a company's tax burden.

7. *Compensation systems.* Many compensation systems establish "floors" and "ceilings" on bonuses and also reward managers for meeting targets. To illustrate, suppose a firm's compensation system calls for a manager to receive no bonus if net income is below $1 million, a bonus of $10,000 if income is between $1 million and $2 million, or a bonus of $20,000 if income is $2 million or more. The manager will also receive an additional $10,000 if actual income is at least 90% of the forecasted level, which is $1 million. Now consider the following two situations. First, if income is stable at $2 million each year then the manager receives a $30,000 bonus each year, for a 2-year total of $60,000. However, if income is zero the first year and $4 million the second, the manager gets no bonus the first year and $30,000 the second, for a 2-year total of $30,000. So, even though the company has the same total income ($4 million) over the 2 years, the manager's bonus is higher if earnings are stable. Therefore, even if hedging does not add much value for stockholders, it may still benefit managers.

There are regulatory and economically driven reasons to manage risk. The following section describes a typical enterprise risk management framework.

SELF TEST Explain why finance theory, combined with well-diversified investors and "homemade hedging," might suggest that risk management should not add much value to a company.

List and explain some reasons companies might employ risk management techniques.

24-2 An Overview of Enterprise Risk Management

The practice of enterprise risk management has evolved considerably over the last 20 years, due to advances in technology and regulatory changes. To better explain the framework for risk enterprise risk management, we begin with a brief history of risk management.

One of the earliest used tools in risk management is a futures contract, which is an agreement in which a buyer pledges to purchase a specific quantity of an item at a specific price on a specific future date from a seller who has pledged to provide the item at the agreed-upon terms. Written records show that commodity futures contracts were used and traded over 4,000 years ago in India, so risk management has been around a very long time. In the United States, grain traders used futures contracts as far back as the early 1800s.[5]

---

5. For a thorough treatment of the history of enterprise risk management, see Betty Simkins and Steven A. Ramirez, "Enterprise-Wide Risk Management and Corporate Governance," *Loyola University Chicago Law Journal*, Vol. 39, 2008, pp. 571–594.

The history of insurance also dates back hundreds of years, with maritime insurance offered in Genoa in the 1300s and fire insurance offered in London in 1680, not long after the Great Fire of London. In fact, Benjamin Franklin and the Union Fire Company began a fire insurance company in 1752.

As the previous examples illustrate, commodity futures contracts and insurance have been used worldwide for centuries. At the risk of oversimplification, not much new happened until the 1970s, probably because several sources of risk (interest rates, currency exchange rates, and oil prices) had been relatively stable, and perhaps because models for options and other derivatives had not yet been developed. However, the 1970s saw the end of the monetary gold standard (which dramatically increased foreign exchange rate volatility), runaway inflation in the United States, and a reversal in bargaining power between OPEC and oil companies during the Yom Kippur War between Egypt and Israel in 1973. These events, combined with the acceleration of international competition, exposed companies to much more risk than in the previous decades. In turn, these sources of risk made stocks, bonds, and other investments much more volatile.

With the development of pricing models for derivatives, most companies began to actively manage their exposures to interest rates, exchange rates, and a wide variety of commodities. However, few companies employed a systematic approach to risk management. Instead, most companies had a risk management group in charge of insurance-related issues, but different groups in charge of managing each of the other specific risks. For example, one group might manage foreign exchange risk and another might manage commodity risk.

The impetus for a more comprehensive and systematic approach to risk management came from several sources, including corporate bribery scandals in the 1970s, the S&L crisis in the early 1980s, the accounting scandals in the early 2000s (including Enron and WorldCom), and the banking crisis in the late 2000s. All of these events had several common factors, including accounting systems that lacked sufficient controls to identify improper activities.

Regulators responded to each of these crises in an effort to assign blame and prevent the next crisis. In 1977, Congress passed the Foreign Corrupt Practices Act (FCPA) to prevent corporate bribery, and one of its provisions requires companies to have an accounting system that can identify funds used for bribery. In the mid-1980s, a Congressional committee examined the S&L failures and found that some of the failed financial institutions had fraudulent financial statements. In addition to criticizing accounting standards, this committee hinted that Congress and the SEC would impose additional regulatory controls if the accounting profession did not take actions to prevent similar frauds. In 2002, Congress passed the Sarbanes-Oxley (SOX) Act to prevent accounting scandals like those that occurred at Enron, Arthur Andersen, and Tyco. Section 404 of SOX requires senior management to include a section in the annual report that addresses the internal control system, including the system's framework and an assessment of its ability to detect fraud.

In response to stinging criticism from Congress, five major accounting organizations formed the Committee of Sponsoring Organizations (COSO) and released several reports, including one in 1992 that provided a framework for an internal control system designed to prevent fraudulent accounting. The framework for the COSO accounting internal control system satisfied the reporting requirements made by the Foreign Corrupt Practices Act (FCPA) and SOX, so many companies adopted the framework. In 2004, COSO also issued a framework for enterprise risk management, which broadened the scope of the original internal control framework. Because many companies were already using the framework for internal controls, some adopted versions of the broader framework for enterprise risk management. Today, the COSO framework and similar frameworks are widely used.

COSO defines **enterprise risk management (ERM)** as follows:

> Enterprise risk management is a *process*, effected by an entity's *board of directors*, management and other personnel, applied in a *strategy setting* and across the *enterprise*, designed to identify *potential events* that may affect the entity, and manage risk to be within its *risk appetite*, to provide reasonable *assurance* regarding the achievement of entity objectives.[6]

Notice how this definition differs from the traditional compartmentalization of risk management. The COSO framework is inclusive, starting with the board of directors in addition to managers and other employees; COSO is broad in defining risk, ranging from strategic choices to specific events; COSO is unambiguous, with the company explicitly choosing an acceptable level of risk; and COSO is transparent, requiring monitoring and reporting.

Before we describe ERM frameworks in more detail, you should know about the Basel accords, another big regulatory wave that has had an impact on risk management. The Basel Committee, headquartered in Switzerland, is composed of the heads of the central banks from well-developed economies. In the past 25 years, the Committee has introduced three major accords designed to control risk in the global financial system, Basel I (1988), Basel II (2004), and Basel III (introduced in 2010 and revised in 2011). There are similarities in all three accords, but we focus on Basel III because it is the most recent.

The essence of banking is raising funds (from sales of stock, issuances of debt, borrowing through short-term loans, and taking deposits) and then investing the funds in assets (such as business loans and derivatives). A bank experiences financial distress when its assets' cash flows and values aren't sufficient to cover its obligations to its creditors. To prevent a bank from experiencing financial distress (and then passing its problems on to taxpayers and the global financial system), Basel III seeks to ensure that a bank is not financed with too much debt relative to the risk of its assets. In addition to regulations regarding the types and proportions of capital a bank must maintain relative to its assets' risks, Basel III also requires adequate internal control systems to supervise a bank's risk and goes on to suggest particular techniques for measuring risk. We will describe several of these measures later in the chapter, including *value at risk* and *expected shortfall*.

SELF TEST

Describe some regulatory actions that have influenced the evolution of risk management.

Define enterprise risk management.

---

6. We added the italics for emphasis. See page 2 of COSO, "Summary of Enterprise Risk Management—Integrated Framework," 2004, www.coso.org/documents/coso_erm _executivesummary.pdf.

24-3 A Framework for Enterprise Risk Management

No single framework is applicable to all companies, but the COSO framework (including modified versions) is widely used, so it provides an excellent example of an ERM framework.[7]

24-3a The Committee of Sponsoring Organizations' (COSO) Framework for Enterprise Risk Management (ERM)

COSO designed its enterprise risk management framework with three dimensions. The first dimension is the organizational level. The COSO framework applies ERM at all levels of an organization, including the corporate level, division levels, business units, and subsidiaries.

The second dimension is the category of objectives. Each organizational level should define its objectives in each of four categories: (1) *strategic objectives*, which are based on the company's mission and overall goals; (2) *operating objectives*, which focus on the selection, implementation, and ongoing execution of projects and other applications of corporate resources; (3) *reporting objectives*, which seek to disseminate accurate and up-to-date information to decision-makers inside the company and stakeholders outside the company (such as investors and regulators); and (4) *compliance objectives*, which seek to ensure the company complies with laws and regulatory requirements.

The third dimension is the process of risk management for an objective at a particular level within the organization. The risk management process for each objective has eight components, which we discuss in the following section.

24-3b The Components of the COSO Enterprise Risk Management Framework

The eight components of the COSO ERM process define the way in which an organization approaches and applies risk management.

Components 1 and 2: Internal Environment and Objective Setting

The first two components are related to a company's culture and mission, including the company's workplace environment, attitude toward risk, and goal-setting process. An important part of these processes is the identification of the amount of risk that a company is willing to take, which often is called the *risk appetite*.

---

7. For more on the COSO framework, see The Committee of Sponsoring Organizations of the Treadway Commission, *Enterprise Risk Management—Integrated Framework*, 2004, available at www.coso.org/guidance.htm. A summary of the framework is available for free at the same Web site. Another widely used framework is ISO 3100:2009, published by the International Organization for Standardization (ISO), headquartered in Switzerland. For an ERM framework that is consistent with COSO and ISO, see **www.theirm.org/documents/SARM_FINAL.pdf**, a report that is authored jointly by three major UK risk management associations.

Component 3: Event Identification

You can't manage a source of risk if you don't recognize it. A **risky event** is defined as any uncertain outcome that affects a company's previously defined objectives.[8] For example, risky events include increases in the prices of raw materials, an explosion at a factory, or a loss of customers to a competitor. To prevent overlooking risky events, ERM systems typically define categories and then identify the potential events within those categories. We will take a much closer look at risk categories later.

Component 4: Risk Assessment

After identifying a risk, a company should assess the risk. We will describe risk assessment in more detail later, but it always includes estimating both the probability that the event will occur and the resulting impact on the company's objectives. For example, an event might be an increase in interest rates, which would affect a company's cost when it issues debt. To assess this risk, the company would begin by forecasting the probabilities of different interest rates at the time it plans to issue the debt, and then estimate the cost of issuing debt at the different interest rates. As another example, an event might be a fire at a warehouse. In this case, a company would estimate the probability of a fire and the resulting cost. The insurance industry often uses the terms *loss frequency* and *loss severity* (the dollar value of each loss) for these concepts.

Component 5: Risk Response

After identifying and assessing a risky event, the next steps are to choose a response to the risk and implement that choice. There are several different types of responses, including these:

Totally avoid the activity that gives rise to the risk. For example, a company might discontinue a product or service line because the risks outweigh the rewards. This often is the case with pharmaceutical products that have potentially harmful side effects or global expansion into countries with civil unrest.

Reduce the probability of occurrence of an adverse event. The expected loss arising from any risk is a function of both the probability of occurrence and the dollar loss if the adverse event occurs. In some instances, it is possible to reduce the probability that an adverse event will occur. For example, the probability that a fire will occur can be reduced by instituting a fire prevention program, by replacing old electrical wiring, and by using fire-resistant materials in areas with the greatest fire potential.

Reduce the magnitude of the loss associated with an adverse event. In some instances, companies can take actions to reduce losses even if the event occurs. Continuing with the previous example, the dollar cost associated with a fire can be reduced by such actions as installing sprinkler systems, designing facilities with self-contained fire zones, and locating facilities close to a fire station.

Transfer the risk to an insurance company. Often, it is advantageous to insure against risk by transferring it to an insurance company. Even though an insured

---

8. COSO defines risk as an event that negatively affects an objective, and an opportunity as an event that can positively affect an objective. We don't make that distinction—we define risk as uncertainty, which can result in positive or negative outcomes.

item's expected loss is the same for its owner and for the insurance company, the insurance company benefits from diversification. For example, an insurance company might provide coverage for tractors, harvesters, and other types of agricultural equipment, which often cost several hundred thousand dollars or more. If the insurance company has a large number of customers, it can predict quite accurately the amounts it will pay in claims and then can set premiums high enough to pay the claims and provide the return required by its investors. In addition, insurance companies can themselves insure parts of their risk by purchasing reinsurance from another insurance company. Therefore, the potential loss of a harvester might be quite risky to a farmer, but it may not be risky to a large insurance company.

However, just because something can be insured does not mean that a company should insure it. In many instances, it might be better for the company to *self-insure*, which means bearing the risk directly rather than paying another party to bear it. In fact, many large companies choose to self-insure, or to insure only the part of an asset's loss that exceeds a certain amount, which is equivalent to an individual who has a large deductible on car or home insurance.

Insurance typically excludes acts of war or terrorism, but this became a major issue after the September 11, 2001, attacks on the World Trade Center and the Pentagon. Unless possible terrorist targets—including large malls, office buildings, oil refineries, airlines, and ships—can be insured against attacks, lenders may refuse to provide mortgage financing, and that would crimp the economy. Private insurance companies are reluctant to insure these projects, at least without charging prohibitive premiums, so the federal government has been asked to step in and provide terrorist insurance. However, losses due to terrorist attacks are potentially so large that they could bankrupt even strong insurance companies. Therefore, Congress passed the Terrorism Risk Insurance Act (TRIA) in 2002 and extended it in 2007 through 2014. Under the TRIA, the federal government and private insurers share the cost of benefits paid on insured losses caused by terrorists. As of late 2014, the act has not been extended. There is vigorous debate on both sides of the issue, with insurance companies pushing for its renewal and think tanks, such as the Heritage Foundation, pushing to let the insurance industry stand on its own.

Transfer the function that produces the risk to a third party. For example, suppose a furniture manufacturer is concerned about potential liabilities arising from its ownership of a fleet of trucks used to transfer products from its manufacturing plant to various points across the country. One way to eliminate this risk would be to contract with a trucking company to do the shipping, thus passing the risks to a third party.

Share or eliminate the risk by using derivative contracts. Many companies use derivative contracts to reduce or eliminate an event's risk. For example, a cereal company may use corn or wheat futures to hedge against increases in grain prices. Similarly, financial derivatives can be used to reduce risks that arise from changes in interest rates and exchange rates. As we will describe later, the risk doesn't disappear—it is just taken on by the other party in the derivative contract.

Accept the risk. In some instances, a company will decide to accept a risk because the expected benefits are greater than the expected costs and because the risk doesn't exceed the company's risk appetite. Indeed, accepting risk is the nature of most businesses—if they were riskless, then investors would expect to receive a return only equal to the risk-free rate. Also, some stand-alone risks may be quite large, but they may not contribute much to the total corporate risk if they are not highly correlated with the company's other risks.

Components 6, 7, and 8: Control Activities, Information and Communication, and Monitoring

The last three components focus on ensuring that risky events are in fact being treated according to the responses that were previously chosen—it doesn't do much good to develop strategies and tactics if employees don't follow them! For example, a single rogue trader lost €4.9 billion in 2008 at the French bank Societe Generale, and another lost £1.5 billion in 2011 at the London branch of UBS (headquartered in Switzerland).

> **SELF TEST**
>
> Define a risk event.
>
> What are the two stages in risk assessment?
>
> Describe some possible risk responses.
>
> Should a firm insure itself against all of the insurable risks it faces? Explain.

24-4 Categories of Risk Events

Before addressing alternative risk responses to specific risk events, it will be helpful to describe ways to categorize risk.

24-4a Major Categories

Following is a typical list of major categories that are representative of those at several organizations.[9]

1. *Strategy and reputation.* A company's strategic choices simultaneously influence and respond to its competitors' actions, corporate social responsibilities, the public's perception of its activities, and its reputation among suppliers, peers, and customers. ERM addresses the risk inherent in these strategic choices.
2. *Control and compliance.* This category includes risk events related to regulatory requirements, litigation risks, intellectual property rights, reporting accuracy, and internal control systems.
3. *Hazards.* These include fires, floods, riots, acts of terrorism, and other natural or man-made disasters. Notice that hazards only have negative outcomes—an earthquake might destroy a factory, but it isn't going to build one.

---

9. To see the way that several organizations have categorized risk and the ways that surveyors categorize risk, see the following: Mark L. Frigo and Hans Læssøe, "Strategic Risk Management at the LEGO Group," *Strategic Finance*, February, 2012, pp. 27–35; Henri Servaes, Ane Tamayo, and Peter Tufano, "The Theory and Practice of Corporate Risk Management," *Journal of Applied Corporate Finance*, Fall, 2009, pp. 60–78; Celina Rogers, The Risk Management Imperative, (Boston: CFO Publishing LLC), 2010, http://secure.cfo.com/whitepapers/index.cfm /download/14521624; Casualty Actuarial Society, *Overview of Risk Management*, 2003, www.casact.org/research/erm/overview.pdf; and the sources cited in footnote 12.

4. *Human resources.* Success often depends upon a company's employees. ERM addresses risk events related to employees, including recruiting, succession planning, employee health, and employee safety.
5. *Operations.* A company's operations include supply chains, manufacturing facilities, existing product lines, and business processes. Risk events include supply chain disruptions, equipment failures, product recalls, and changes in customer demand.
6. *Technology.* Technology changes rapidly and is a major source of risk, including risk events related to innovations, technological failures, and IT reliability and security.
7. *Financial management.* This category includes risk events related to: (1) foreign exchange risk, (2) commodity price risk, (3) interest rate risk, (4) project selection risk (including major capital expenditures, mergers, and acquisitions), (5) liquidity risk, (6) customer credit risk, and (7) portfolio risk (the risk that a portfolio of financial assets will decrease in value). For the remainder of the chapter, we will focus on the risk events related to financial management, but first we need to describe several other ways to think about risk.

24-4b **Dimensions of Risk**

Sometimes it is helpful to think about risk events based on different dimensions. For example, several risk management systems classify risk by whether it is driven by external forces or by internal decisions and activities. This is especially helpful in risk identification because it forces managers to look at a broader range of risk events.

Sometimes it is useful to classify risk by whether it is a pure risk that only has a downside (e.g., a hazard, such as a fire) or a speculative risk that has potential positive as well as negative outcomes (e.g., the exchange rate between dollars and euros can go up or down, which would have a big impact on the cash flows of U.S. importers). Most pure risks can be reduced or eliminated with insurance products.

When choosing among different risk responses, it is helpful to determine whether the source of risk is linear or nonlinear. For example, consider an agricultural company with access to a low-cost source of water for irrigation. The company grows corn and can predict its costs and the size of its harvest, but it is exposed to volatility in the price of corn. Notice that this is a linear risk—the company loses money when prices are low and makes money when they are high. We discuss the details later, but the company can enter into derivative contracts that provide positive cash flows when prices are low but create negative cash flows when prices are high. The derivative also has a linear payout, but its payouts are opposite those of the company. The combination of the company's internally generated cash flows from the harvest and its externally generated cash flows from the derivative can reduce or eliminate the company's risk.

In contrast, consider a company in the oil exploration and extraction industry.[10] The company will incur fixed costs and negative cash flows associated with

---

10. See Kenneth A. Froot, David S. Scharfstein, and Jeremy Stein, "A Framework for Risk Management," *Journal of Applied Corporate Finance*, Fall 1994, pp. 22–32; also see the paper by Servais et al, cited in footnote 14.

continuing operations when oil prices are too low to justify additional exploration. When oil prices are high, the company incurs fixed costs and also variable costs associated with expanded exploration and extraction. However, when oil prices are high, the company will generate enough positive cash flow to cover its fixed costs and also the new variable costs associated with the additional exploration and extraction. Therefore, the company is exposed to nonlinear risk—it needs additional cash flow to support its ongoing operations only when oil prices are low but not when prices are high. In this situation, the company might be willing to buy a derivative that pays out only when oil prices are low. In other words, the company reduces its nonlinear risk with a nonlinear hedging strategy.

SELF TEST

List and define the different major categories of risk events.

Should a firm insure itself against all of the insurable risks it faces? Explain.

Explain the difference between a linear risk and a nonlinear risk.

24-5 **Foreign Exchange (FX) Risk**

Foreign exchange (FX) risk occurs when a company's cash flows are affected by changes in currency exchange rates. This can occur if a company imports materials from other countries or sells its products in other countries. Some smaller companies manage FX risk for each transaction, but most large companies aggregate their transactions and manage their exposures centrally. For example, if one division is selling goods denominated in Canadian dollars and another division is purchasing goods denominated in Canadian dollars, the company would net out the two transactions and just manage any remaining exposure.

The primary tool used to manage FX risk is a **forward contract**, which is an agreement in which one party agrees to buy an item at a specific price on a specific future date and another party agrees to sell the item at the agreed upon terms. *Goods are actually delivered under forward contracts.* In the case of foreign exchange, the goods are the amount of foreign currency specified in the contract, paid for with the other currency specified in the contract.

Historically, FX trading has been directly between two parties using customized contracts with unique amounts and dates and no central market. This requires that both parties be morally and financially strong to minimize the danger that one party will default on the contract—this is called **counterparty risk**. In such contracts, major banks often act as counterparties for their customers. For example, a bank might agree to buy euros in 30 days at a price of 1.24 dollars per euro from one customer and agree to sell euros in 30 days at a rate of 1.25 dollars per euro to another customer. Depending on the change in the euro exchange rate, the bank will make money on one of the contracts and lose money on the other, netting only the spread on the difference in prices. This matching of contracts allows banks to reduce their net exposure to exchange rate volatility, but the bank is still exposed to counterparty risk from the customers.

The failure to manage counterparty risk was one of the causes of the 2007 global financial crisis. For example, Lehman Brothers was a counterparty to many other financial institutions in a variety of derivative contracts, so Lehman's failure caused distress at financial institutions throughout the world. In response to this and other causes of the financial crisis, the Dodd-Frank Consumer Protection Act was passed in 2010. One of its provisions required the Commodities and Futures Trading Commission (CFTC) to establish, among other things, a mechanism for centralized clearing of foreign exchange derivatives contracts, such as forward contracts. The CME Group is one company that provides this clearing function in the United States and acts as the counterparty to all trades that it clears. As of mid-2014, the CME Group is able to clear 38 cash-settled forward contracts involving 33 different currencies.[11]

Foreign exchange transactions are a big business. Contracts are based on the total amount of currency to be delivered at expiration, which is called the notional amount. In the middle of 2013, there was a total of over $39 *trillion* in notional value of forward and related contracts outstanding globally. Adding in other foreign exchange derivatives like options and currency swaps brings the total to over $81 trillion!

To illustrate how foreign exchange contracts are used, suppose GE arranges to buy electric motors from a European manufacturer on terms that call for GE to pay 10 million euros in 180 days. GE would not want to give up the free trade credit, but if the euro appreciated against the dollar during the next 6 months, then the dollar cost of the 10 million euros would rise. GE could hedge the transaction by buying a forward contract under which it agreed to buy the 10 million euros in 180 days at a fixed dollar price, which would lock in the dollar cost of the motors. This transaction would probably be conducted through a money center bank, which would try to find a European company that needed dollars in 6 months.

www

See the Quarterly Review from the Bank of International Settlements, **www.bis .org/publ/qtrpdf/r _qt1206.htm**.

> What is a forward contract?
>
> Explain how a company can use forward contracts to eliminate FX risk.
>
> What is counterparty risk?

SELF TEST

24-6 **Commodity Price Risk**

Many companies use or produce commodities, including agricultural products, energy, metals, and lumber. Because commodity prices can be quite volatile, many companies manage their exposure to commodity price risk. Before describing specific ways to manage commodity price risk, we begin with a brief overview of futures markets in the United States to illustrate some key concepts.

www

See the CME Group's Web site, **www .cmegroup.com**, for a wealth of information on the operation and history of the exchange.

---

11. When a traditional forward for delivery contract expires the two currencies are exchanged. In a cash-settled forward contract, however, the currencies are never exchanged. Rather, the difference between the contract price and the spot price at expiration is converted to U.S. dollars at the prevailing spot price and then these dollars are paid or received. The clearinghouse would require some form of collateral to reduce the risk that one of the parties didn't pay. In addition, cash-settled forward contracts can be "marked to market" every day like a futures contract, and this further reduces the clearinghouse's risk. See the CME Group's Web site, www.CMEGroup.com, for more information on their clearing mechanism and the products it clears.

24-6a **An Overview of Futures Markets**

As we noted earlier, Midwest farmers in the early 1800s were concerned about the price they would receive for their wheat when they sold it in the fall, and millers were concerned about the price they would have to pay. Each party soon realized that the risks they faced could be reduced if they established a price earlier in the year. Accordingly, mill agents began going out to the Wheat Belt with contracts that called for the farmers to deliver grain at a predetermined price, and both parties benefited from the transaction in the sense that their risks were reduced. The farmers could concentrate on growing their crop without worrying about the price of grain, and the millers could concentrate on their milling operations.

These early agreements were between two parties who arranged the transactions themselves. Soon, though, intermediaries came into the picture. The Chicago Board of Trade, founded in 1848, was an early marketplace where *futures dealers* helped make a market in futures contracts.

A **futures contract** is similar to a forward contract in that two parties are involved, with one party taking a long position (which obligates the party to buy the underlying asset) and the other party taking a short position (which obligates the party to sell the asset). However, there are three key differences. First, futures contracts are marked-to-market on a daily basis, meaning that gains and losses are recognized daily and money must be put up to cover losses. This greatly reduces the risk of default that exists with forward contracts because daily price changes are usually smaller than the cumulative change over the contract's life. For example, if a corn futures contract has a price of $7.00 per bushel and the price goes up to $7.10 the next day, a party with a short position must pay the $0.10 difference, and a party with a long position would receive the difference. This marking-to-market occurs daily until the delivery date. To see that this procedure does in fact lock in the price, suppose that the price doesn't change again. On the delivery date, the party with the short position would sell corn at the current price of $7.10. Because the short seller had already paid $0.10 from daily marking-to-market, the short seller's net cash flow is $7.00. The party with the long position would have to buy corn at the current price of $7.10, but because the purchaser had already received $0.10 from cumulative daily marking-to-market, the net purchase price would be $7.00.

The second major difference between a forward contract and a futures contract is that physical delivery of the underlying asset in a futures contract is virtually never taken—the two parties simply settle up with cash for the difference between the contracted price and the actual price on the expiration date. The third difference is that futures contracts are generally standardized instruments that are traded on exchanges, whereas forward contracts are usually tailor-made, negotiated between two parties, and not traded after they have been signed.

The needs of farmers and millers allowed a **natural hedge**, defined as a situation in which aggregate risk can be reduced by derivatives transactions between two parties. Natural hedges occur when futures are traded between cotton farmers and cotton mills, copper mines and copper fabricators, importers and foreign manufacturers for currency exchange rates, electric utilities and coal mines, and oil producers and oil users. In such situations, hedging reduces aggregate risk and thus benefits the economy.

There are two basic types of hedges: (1) **long hedges**, in which futures contracts are *bought* (obligating the hedger to purchase the underlying asset), providing protection against price increases, and (2) **short hedges**, where a firm or individual *sells* futures contracts (obligating the hedger to sell the underlying asset), providing protection against falling prices.

Not all participants in the futures markets are hedgers. **Speculation** involves betting on future price movements, and futures are used instead of the commodities because of the leverage inherent in the contract. For example, a speculator might buy corn for $7 a bushel. If corn goes up to $7.70, the speculator has a 10% return (assuming rats don't eat the corn before it can be sold). Now consider a futures contract for 5,000 bushels at $7 per bushel. The exchange requires an investor to put up a **margin requirement** to ensure that the investor will not renege on the daily marking to market. However, the margin is quite small relative to the size of a contract—the margin is only $1,500, but the total amount of corn is valued at $35,000 = $7(5,000).[12] If the price goes up to $7.70, the profit is $3,500 = ($7.70 − $7.00)(5,000). The rate of return on the invested margin is 233% = $3,500/$1,500. Of course, any losses on the contract also would be magnified.

At first blush, one might think that the appearance of speculators would increase risk, but this is not necessarily true. Speculators add capital and players to the market. Thus, to the extent that speculators broaden the market and make hedging possible, they help decrease risk for those who seek to avoid it. Unlike the natural hedge, however, risk is not eliminated. Instead, it is transferred from the hedgers to the speculators.

Today, futures contracts are available on hundreds of real and financial assets traded on dozens of U.S. and international exchanges, the largest of which are the Chicago Board of Trade (CBOT) and the Chicago Mercantile Exchange (CME), both of which are now part of the CME Group. Futures contracts are divided into two classes, **commodity futures** and **financial futures**. Commodity futures include oil, various grains, oilseeds, livestock, meats, fibers, metals, and wood. Financial futures, which were first traded in 1975, include Treasury bills, notes, bonds, certificates of deposit, Eurodollar deposits, foreign currencies, and stock indexes. We describe how financial futures can reduce interest rate risk in a later section.

24-6b Using Futures Contracts to Reduce Commodity Price Exposure

We will illustrate inventory hedging at Porter Electronics, which uses large quantities of copper and several precious metals in its manufacturing operations. Suppose that in May 2015, Porter foresaw a need for 100,000 pounds of copper in March 2016 for use in fulfilling a fixed-price contract to supply solar power cells to the U.S. government. Porter's managers are concerned that a strike by Chilean copper miners might occur, which would raise the price of copper in world markets and possibly turn Porter's expected profit into a loss.

Porter could go ahead and buy the copper it will need to fulfill the contract, but it would have to borrow money to pay for the copper and then pay for storage. As an alternative, the company could hedge against increasing copper prices in the futures market. COMEX, a division of The New York Commodity Exchange, trades standard copper futures contracts of 25,000 pounds each. Thus, Porter could buy four contracts (go long) for delivery in March 2016. Assume these contracts were trading in May 2015 for about $4.10 per pound and that the spot price at that date was about $4.08 per pound. If copper prices rose appreciably over the next 10 months, then the value of Porter's long position in copper futures would increase,

WWW

For current margin requirements, go to **www.cmegroup .com**, and select View Products under the Products and Trading tab. Under the Products heading select Agriculture, and scroll down to Corn Futures and click on it.

---

12. This is the margin requirement for hedgers. Speculators have a higher margin requirement.

thus offsetting some of the price increase in the commodity itself. Of course, if copper prices fell, then Porter would lose money on its futures contracts, but the company would be buying the copper on the spot market at a cheaper price, so it would make a higher than anticipated profit on its sale of solar cells. Thus, hedging in the copper futures market locks in the cost of raw materials and removes some risk to which the firm would otherwise be exposed.

Many other companies, such as Alcoa with aluminum and Archer Daniels Midland with grains, routinely use the futures markets to reduce the risks associated with price volatility.

24-6c **Options on Futures**

Futures contracts and options are similar to one another—so similar that people often confuse the two. Therefore, it is useful to compare the two instruments. A *futures contract* is a definite agreement on the part of one party to buy something on a specific date and at a specific price, and the other party agrees to sell on the same terms. No matter how low or how high the price goes, the two parties must settle the contract at the agreed-upon price and the losses of one party must exactly equal to the gains of the other. In addition, a dollar increase in the futures price has exactly the opposite effect of a dollar decrease in the futures price. A hedge constructed using futures contracts is called a **symmetric hedge** because of this feature—the payoff from an increase in the futures price is exactly opposite the payoff from a decrease in the futures price. For this reason, symmetric hedges are typically used to provide a fixed transaction price at some date in the future and are ideal for managing a risk that is linear.

For example, suppose an agricultural company has access to a source of low-cost water for irrigation. The company can predict its costs and the size of its harvest but is exposed to price risk. The company could sell futures contracts (take a long position, which obligates it to sell corn) for delivery when the corn is harvested in 6 months. If the corn price (and hence the corn futures price) decreases over the 6 months, then the company will receive less when selling the corn but will make up the difference when closing out the futures contract. If instead the corn price increases, then the company will make more money when selling the corn in 6 months but will lose money when closing out the futures contract. In this way the ending value of the position doesn't depend on the corn price in 6 months, and so the amount received for selling the corn in 6 months is locked in.

An *option*, on the other hand, gives someone the right to buy (call) or sell (put) an asset, but the holder of the option does not have to complete the transaction. The payoff from a hedge constructed using options will be different from a futures hedge because of this option feature. As discussed in Chapter 5, the payoff from a call option increases as the price of the underlying asset increases, but if the underlying asset price decreases, then the most the option holder can lose is the amount invested in the option. That is, upside gains are unlimited but downside losses are capped at the amount invested in the option. For this reason, an option is said to create an **asymmetric hedge**—it hedges price changes in one direction more than price changes in the other. As such, options are ideal for managing nonlinear risks.

For example, suppose the agricultural company did not have access to irrigation but operated many farms in different states. A widespread drought would reduce the size of the harvest but probably would cause the price of corn to increase due to the lower supply. If this happened, the company's revenues would fall but would not be eliminated—the higher corn price would partially compensate for the smaller harvest. This means the company faces nonlinear risk with respect to corn prices. Instead of going long in a futures contract, the company might buy a put option on a corn futures contract, giving the company the right to sell a futures contract at a fixed price. If the price of corn decreased, the value of the put option would increase, and the profits on the option would offset the loss from selling the corn at the lower price. However, if corn prices increased, then the investor would let the put option expire and simply sell its smaller harvest at the higher price.

How does a futures contract differ from a forward contract?

What is a "natural hedge"? Give some examples of natural hedges.

Suppose a company knows the quantity of a commodity that it will produce. Describe how it might hedge using a futures contract.

SELF TEST

24-7 **Interest Rate Risk**

Interest rates can be quite volatile, exposing a company to interest rate risk, especially if the company is planning to issue debt or if the company has floating rate debt. The following sections describe these two situations.

24-7a **Using Futures Contracts to Manage the Risk of Debt Issuances**

To illustrate, assume that Carson Foods is considering in May a plan to issue $10,000,000 of 20-year bonds in September to finance a capital expenditure program. The interest rate would be 9% paid semiannually if the bonds were issued today, and at that rate the project would have a positive NPV. However, interest rates may rise, and when the issue is actually sold, this would increase Carson's financing costs. Carson can protect itself against a rise in rates by hedging in the futures market using an interest rate futures contract.

Interest Rates Futures

To illustrate how interest rate futures work, consider the CBOT's contract on Treasury bonds. The basic contract is for $100,000 of a hypothetical 6% coupon, semiannual payment Treasury bond with 20 years to maturity.[13] Table 24-1 shows Treasury bond futures data from the Chicago Board of Trade.

---

13. The coupon rate on the hypothetical bond was changed to 6% from 8% in March 2000. The CBOT contract doesn't specify a 20-year bond but instead allows delivery of any noncallable bond with a remaining maturity greater than 15 years (or callable bond that is not callable for at least 15 years) and less than 25 years. Rather than simply deliver a bond, which might have an interest rate other than 6%, the actual bond price is adjusted by a conversion factor to make it equivalent to a 6% bond that is trading at par. Because the average maturity of bonds that are eligible for delivery is about 20 years, we use a 20-year maturity for the hypothetical bond in the futures contract. For even longer maturity hedging, the CBOT also has the Ultra T-Bond contract, which allows for delivery of a Treasury bond of at least 25 years to maturity.

TABLE 24-1	Futures Prices (Treasury Bonds: $100,000; Pts. 32nds of 100%)						
Delivery Month (1)	Settle (2)	Change (3)	Open (4)	High (5)	Low (6)	Estimated Volume (7)	Open Interest (8)
Jun 2014	137'12	0'14	136'31	137'15	136'21	495531	687917
Sep 2014	136'20	0'15	136'07	136'23	135'28	288550	92311
Dec 2014	135'13	0'15	135'13	135'13	135'13	0	51

Source: The Wall Street Journal Online, **www.wsj.com**, settlement prices for May 27, 2014.

See **Ch24 Tool Kit.xls** on the textbook's Web site for all calculations.

The first column of Table 24-1 shows the delivery month and year. Column 2 shows the last price of the day, also called the *settlement* price, and the next column shows the change in price from the previous day. For example, the settlement price for the September contract, 136'20, means 136 plus $^{20}/_{32}$, or 136.6250%, of par. The change was 0'15, which means the September 2014 contract's last price of the day was $^{15}/_{32}$ higher than the previous day's last trade, which must have been at 136'05. The next three columns show the opening, high, and low prices for the day. Column 7 shows the day's estimated trading volume. Notice that most of the trading occurs in the contract with the nearest delivery date. Finally, Column 8 shows the "open interest," which is the number of contracts outstanding.

To illustrate, we focus on the Treasury bonds for September delivery. The settlement price was 136.6250% of the $100,000 contract value. Thus, the price at which one could buy $100,000 face value of 6%, 20-year Treasury bonds to be delivered in December was 136.6250% ($100,000) = $136,625.0.

The contract price increased by $^{15}/_{32}$ of 1% of $100,000 from the previous day's price, so if you had bought the contract yesterday, you would have made $468.75 = $($^{15}/_{32})(0.01)($100,000)$. There were 92,311 contracts outstanding, representing a total value of about 92,311($136,625.0) = $12,611,990,375.

Note that the contract increased by $^{15}/_{32}$ of a percent on this particular day. Why would the value of the bond futures contract increase? Bond prices increase when interest rates fall, so interest rates must have fallen on that day. Moreover, we can calculate the implied rate inherent in the futures price. Recall that the contract relates to a hypothetical 20-year, semiannual payment, 6% coupon bond. The settlement price was 136.6250% of par, so a $1,000 par bond would have a price of 136.6250% ($1,000) = $1,366.25. We can solve for r_d by using the following equation:

$$\sum_{t=1}^{40} \frac{\$30}{(1 + r_d/2)^t} + \frac{\$1,000}{(1 + r_d/2)^{40}} = \$1,366.25$$

Using a financial calculator, input N = 40, PV = −1366.25, PMT = 30, and FV = 1000; then solve for I/YR = 1.7249%. This is the semiannual rate, which is equivalent to a nominal annual rate of 3.4498%, or approximately 3.45%.

The previous day's last (settlement) price was 136'05, or 136.15625%, for a bond price of $1,361.5625 = 136.15625($1,000). Setting N = 40, PV = −1361.5625, PMT = 30, and FV = 1000 and then solving for I/YR = 1.7382 implies an annual yield of 3.4764%, or approximately 3.48%. Therefore, interest rates fell from 3.48%

to 3.45%. This was only 3 basis points, but that was enough to increase the value of the contract by $468.75.

In May 2014, when the data in Table 24-1 were gathered, the yield on a 20-year T-bond was about 3.14%. But as we just calculated, the implied yield on the September futures contract was about 3.45%. The September yield reflects investors' beliefs as to what the interest rate level will be in September: The marginal trader in the futures market was predicting a 31-basis-point increase in yields between May and September. That prediction could, of course, turn out to be incorrect.

For example, suppose that 3 months later, in August, implied yields in the futures market had fallen by 50 basis points from the earlier levels—say, from 3.45% to 2.95%. Inputting N = 40, I/YR = 2.95/2 = 1.475, PMT = 30, and FV = 1000 and then solving for PV = −1458.3054 shows that the September contract would be worth about $145,830.54 in August if implied yields fell by 50 basis points. Thus, the contract's value would have increased by $145,830.54 − $136,625.00 ≈ $9,206.

Hedging with Treasury Bond Futures Contracts

Recall that Carson Foods plans to issue $10,000,000 of 9% semiannual 20-year bonds in September and would like to protect itself from a possible increase in interest rates by using T-bond futures contracts. Rising interest rates cause bond prices to fall, and thus decrease the value of bond futures contracts. Therefore, Carson can guard against an *increase* in interest rates by taking a short position on a T-bond futures contract—if rates go up, Carson will receive a cash flow from the futures contract equal to the original futures price less the now-lower futures price.

Carson would choose a futures contract on the security most similar to the one it plans to issue, long-term bonds, and so would probably hedge with September Treasury bond futures. In the previous section, we calculated the price of a contract, which was $136,625.00. Because Carson plans to issue $10,000,000 of bonds and because each contract is worth $136,625.00, Carson will sell $10,000,000/$136,625.00 = 73.193 ≈ 73 contracts for delivery in September.[14] The total value of the contracts is 73($136,625.00) = $9,973,625.00, which is very close to the value of the bonds Carson wants to issue.

Now suppose that in September, when Carson issues its bonds, renewed fears of inflation push interest rates up by 100 basis points. What would the bond proceeds be if Carson still tried to issue 9% coupon bonds when the market requires a 10% rate of return? We can find the total value of the offering with a financial calculator, inputting N = 40, I/YR = 5, PMT = −450000, and FV = −10000000 and then solving for PV = 9142046. Therefore, bonds with a 9% coupon, based upon its original plans, would bring proceeds of only $9,142,046, because investors now require a 10% return. Because Carson would have to issue $10 million worth of bonds at a 10% rate, Carson's cost would go up by $857,954 = $10,000,000 − $9,142,046 as a result of delaying the financing.

Alternatively, we can estimate Carson's cost of delaying by calculating the present value of the incremental payments Carson must make. The increase in interest rates from 9% to 10% would cause the semiannual coupon payments to go up from $45 to $50 on a per-bond basis. For 10,000 bonds, the total incremental semiannual coupon payments are $50,000 = ($50 − $45)(10,000). We can find the

WEB

See *Ch24 Tool Kit.xls* on the textbook's Web site for all calculations.

---

14. Carson will have to put up a margin of 67($2,700) = $180,900 and also pay brokerage commissions.

present value of these incremental payments by, inputting N = 40, I/YR = 5, PMT = −50000, and FV = 0 and then solving for PV = −857954 = −$857,954, which is the same cost found by the first method. Mathematically, this is true because a little bit of algebra will show that the two methods use the same formula. Intuitively, this is because the first method identifies the difference between an asset's par value and its market value given a change in interest rates. This difference can be thought of as the extra amount of value that would need to be added to bring the market value up to par. One way to add value would be to increase the payments, which is what the second approach does.

Either way we calculate it, Carson incurs a cost of $857,954 due to the increase in rates. However, the increase in interest rates would also bring about a change in the value of Carson's short position in the futures contract. When interest rates increase, the value of the futures contract will fall. If the interest rate on the futures contract also increased by the same full percentage point, from 3.4764% to 4.4764%, then the new contract value can be found by inputting N = 40, I/YR = 4.4764/2 = 2.2382, PMT = −3000, and FV = −100000 and then solving for PV = 119,994.750 per contract. With 73 contracts, the total value of the position is thus $8,759,617.00 = 73($119,994.75). Carson would then close its position in the futures market by repurchasing for $8,759,617 the contracts that it earlier sold for $9,973,625, giving it a profit of $1,214,008.

Thus, Carson would offset the loss on the bond issue if we ignore commissions and the opportunity cost of the margin money. In fact, in our example Carson more than offsets the loss, pocketing an additional $356,054.0 = $1,214,008 − $857,954.[15] Of course, if interest rates had fallen, then Carson would have lost on its futures position, but this loss would have been offset because Carson could now sell its bonds with a lower coupon.

If futures contracts existed on Carson's own debt and if interest rates moved identically in the spot and futures markets, then the firm could construct a **perfect hedge** in which gains on the futures contract would exactly offset losses on the bonds. In reality, it is virtually impossible to construct perfect hedges, because in most cases the underlying asset is not identical to the futures asset; and even when the assets are identical, prices (and interest rates) may not move exactly together in the spot and futures markets.[16]

---

15. Carson would have to pay taxes on the profit from the futures contract, so the after-tax value of the future's transaction can be found by multiplying the pretax profit by (1 − T). However, Carson would get to deduct the larger additional coupon payments from its income. To find the present value of the after-tax additional coupon payments, we multiply the additional pretax coupons by (1 − T) and calculate the present value. This gives the same result as first finding the present value of the additional pretax coupons and then multiplying the present value by (1 − T). In other words, the pretax cost of delaying and the pretax profit from the futures contract should be multiplied by (1 − T) to estimate the after-tax effectiveness of the hedge.

16. In this example, Carson hedged a 20-year bond with a T-bond futures contract. Rather than simply matching on maturity, it would be more accurate to match on duration (see *Web Extension 4C*, available on the textbook's Web site, for a discussion of duration). A matching duration in the futures contracts could be accomplished by taking positions in the T-bond futures contract and in another financial futures contract, such as the 10-Year Treasury note contract. Because Carson's bond had a 20-year maturity, matching on maturity instead of duration provided a good hedge. If Carson's bond had a different maturity, then it would be essential to match on duration.

Observe also that if Carson had been planning an equity offering and if its stock tended to move fairly closely with one of the stock indexes, then the company could have hedged against falling stock prices by selling the index future. Even better, if options on Carson's stock were traded in the options market, then it could use options rather than futures to hedge against falling stock prices.

The futures and options markets permit flexibility in the timing of financial transactions: The firm can be protected, at least partially, against changes that occur between the time a decision is reached and the time the transaction is completed. However, this protection has a cost—the firm must pay commissions. Whether or not the protection is worth the cost is a matter of judgment. The decision to hedge also depends on management's risk aversion and on the company's strength and ability to assume the risk in question.[17]

24-7b **Using Interest Rate Swaps: Managing Floating versus Fixed Rates**

Suppose that Company S has a 20-year, $100 million floating-rate bond outstanding and that Company F has a $100 million, 20-year, fixed-rate issue outstanding. Thus, each company has an obligation to make a stream of interest payments, but one payment stream is fixed while the other will vary as interest rates change in the future. This situation is shown in the top part of Figure 24-1.

Now suppose that Company S has stable cash flows and wants to lock in its cost of debt. Company F has cash flows that fluctuate with the economy, rising when the economy is strong and falling when it is weak. Recognizing that interest rates also move up and down with the economy, Company F has concluded it would be better off with variable-rate debt. Suppose the companies agreed to swap their payment obligations. The bottom half of Figure 24-1 shows that the net cash flows for Company S are at a fixed rate and those for Company F are based on a floating rate. Company S would now have to make fixed payments, which are consistent with its stable cash inflows, and Company F would have a floating obligation, which for it is less risky.

A **swap** is just what the name implies—two parties agree to swap something, generally obligations to make specified payment streams.

The previous example illustrates how swaps can reduce risks by allowing each company to match the variability of its interest payments with that of its cash flows. However, there are also situations in which swaps can reduce both the risk and the effective cost of debt. For example, Antron Corporation, which has a high credit rating, can issue either floating-rate debt at LIBOR + 1% or fixed-rate debt at 10%.[18] Bosworth Industries is less creditworthy, so its cost for floating-rate debt is LIBOR + 1.5% and its fixed-rate cost is 10.4%. Owing to the nature of Antron's operations, its CFO has decided that the firm would be better off with fixed-rate debt; meanwhile, Bosworth's CFO prefers floating-rate debt. Paradoxically, both firms can benefit by issuing the type of debt they do not want and then swapping their payment obligations.

---

17. For additional insights into the use of financial futures for hedging, see Mark G. Castelino, Jack C. Francis, and Avner Wolf, "Cross-Hedging: Basis Risk and Choice of the Optimal Hedging Vehicle," *The Financial Review,* May 1991, pp. 179–210.

18. LIBOR stands for the London Interbank Offered Rate, the rate charged on interbank dollar loans in the Eurodollar market.

FIGURE 24-1   Cash Flows under a Swap

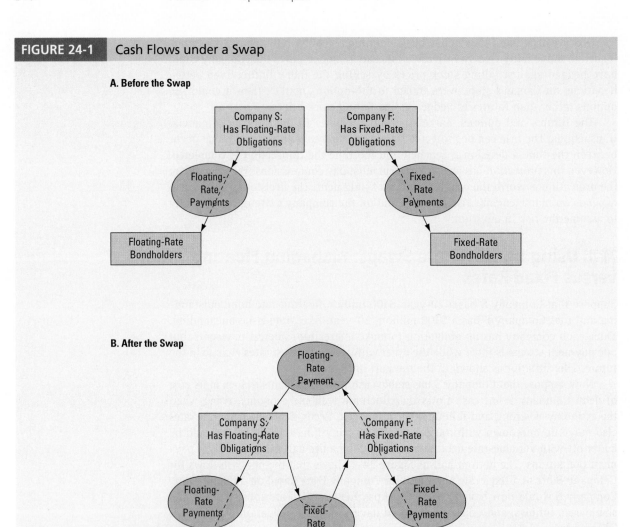

A. Before the Swap

B. After the Swap

Note: In Panel A, Company S must make floating-rate payments out of its own internal cash flows; but in Panel B, it uses the floating payments from Company F to pay its bondholders. Company F has a reversed position. After the swap, S has de facto fixed payments, which are consistent with its stable internal flows, and F has floating payments, which are consistent with its fluctuating flows.

First, each company will issue an identical amount of debt, which is called the **notional principal**. Even though Antron wants fixed-rate debt, it issues floating-rate debt at LIBOR + 1%, and Bosworth issues fixed-rate debt at 10.4%. Next, the two companies enter into an interest rate swap.[19] Assume the debt maturities are 5 years, which means the length of this swap will also be 5 years. By convention,

---

19. Such transactions are generally arranged by large money center banks, and payments are made to the bank, which in turn pays the interest on the original loans. The bank assumes the credit risk and guarantees the payments should one of the parties default. For its services, the bank receives a percentage of the payments as its fee. In addition, the CME clears swaps similar to these.

THE GAME OF TRUTH OR LIBOR

LIBOR stands for the London Interbank Offered Rate, the rate banks charge one another for loans in the Eurodollar market. LIBOR might possibly be the most important number reported in financial markets because many derivative contracts base payments on LIBOR. Some analysts estimate that there are over $300 trillion dollars of derivatives linked to LIBOR. Because LIBOR is such a widely used rate, you might think that it is reported with the utmost care and accuracy. Wrong!

The largest banks in London report to Thomson Reuters the rates they charge one another on loans. Each day Thomson Reuters collects these rates, throws out the highest and lowest percentiles, and uses the middle 50% to calculate the average rate, which it reports to the rest of the world. That part of the process is clear, but how do the banks define the rates that they report? It turns out that some of them just pick a number. On June 27, 2012, Barclays admitted that it had been fined £290 million by U.S. and U.K. regulators for knowingly reporting untrue rates. Barclays reported low rates at times to disguise how risky other banks viewed Barclays, according to its own emails. In addition, some emails suggest that Barclays manipulated LIBOR to profit on trades. In the wake of this news, Barclays's CEO and other senior executives were forced to resign.

The Barclays case was just the beginning of a much bigger scandal. In 2013 Deutsche Bank, Société Générale, and Royal Bank of Scotland admitted fixing reported interest rates on the euro version of LIBOR, the EURIBOR, and Citigroup, HSBC, JPMorgan, and Crédit Agricole are being investigated. As of mid-2014, $5.8 billion in fines have been assessed in the combined LIBOR and EURIBOR scandals, with more likely to come.

Note: For more information on the LIBOR and EURIBOR scandal, see **http://topics.nytimes.com/top/reference/timestopics/subjects/l/london_interbank_offered_rate_libor/index.html** and **http://www.ft.com/intl/indepth/libor-scandal**.

the floating-rate payments of most swaps are based on LIBOR, with the fixed rate adjusted upward or downward to reflect credit risk and the term structure. The riskier the company that will receive the floating-rate payments, the higher the fixed-rate payment it must make. In our example, Antron will be receiving floating-rate payments from Bosworth, and those payments will be set at LIBOR multiplied by the notional principal. Then, payments will be adjusted every 6 months to reflect changes in the LIBOR rate.

The fixed payment that Antron must make to Bosworth is set (that is, "fixed") for the duration of the swap at the time the contract is signed, and it depends primarily on two factors: (1) the level of fixed interest rates at the time of the agreement and (2) the relative creditworthiness of the two companies.

In our example, assume interest rates and creditworthiness are such that 8.95% is the appropriate fixed swap rate for Antron, so it will make 8.95% fixed-rate payments to Bosworth. In turn, Bosworth will pay the LIBOR rate to Antron. Table 24-2 shows the net rates paid by each participant, and Figure 24-2 graphs the flows. Note that Antron ends up making fixed payments, which it desires, but because of the swap the rate paid is 9.95% versus the 10% rate it would have paid had it issued fixed-rate debt directly. At the same time, the swap leaves Bosworth with floating-rate debt, which it wants, but at a rate of LIBOR + 1.45% versus the LIBOR + 1.50% it would have paid on directly issued floating-rate debt. As this example illustrates, swaps can sometimes lower the interest rate paid by each party.

TABLE 24-2	Anatomy of an Interest Rate Swap		
Antron's Payments: Borrows Floating, Swaps for Fixed		**Bosworth's Payments: Borrows Fixed, Swaps for Floating**	
Payment to lender	−(LIBOR + 1%)	Payment to lender	−10.40% fixed
Payment from Bosworth	+LIBOR	Payment from Antron	+8.95% fixed
Payment to Bosworth	−8.95% fixed	Payment to Antron	−LIBOR
Net payment by Antron	−9.95% fixed	Net payment by Bosworth	−(LIBOR + 1.45%)

Currency swaps are special types of interest rate swaps. To illustrate, suppose Company A, an American firm, had issued $100 million of dollar-denominated bonds in the United States to fund an investment in Germany. Meanwhile, Company G, a German firm, had issued $100 million of euro-denominated bonds in Germany to make an investment in the United States. Company A would earn euros but be required to make payments in dollars, and Company G would be in the opposite situation. Thus, both companies would be exposed to exchange rate risk. However, both companies' risks would be eliminated if they swapped payment obligations.

Originally, swaps were arranged between companies by money center banks, which would match up counterparties. Such matching still occurs, but today most swaps are between companies and banks, with the banks then taking steps to ensure that their own risks are hedged. For example, Citibank might arrange a swap with Company A. Company A would agree to make specified payments in euros to Citibank, while Citibank made dollar payments to Company A. Citibank would charge a fee for setting up the swap, and those charges would reflect the creditworthiness of Company A. To protect itself against exchange rate movements, the bank would

FIGURE 24-2	The Antron/Bosworth Swap

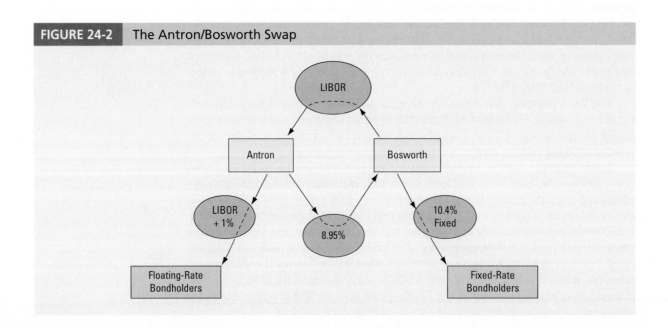

hedge its position, either by lining up a European company that needed to make dollar payments or else by using currency futures.[20]

Major changes have occurred over time in the swaps market. First, standardized contracts have been developed for the most common types of swaps, which has had two effects: (1) Standardized contracts lower the time and effort involved in arranging swaps, and this lowers transactions costs. (2) The development of standardized contracts has led to a secondary market for swaps, which has increased the liquidity and efficiency of the swaps market. A number of international banks now make markets in swaps and offer quotes on several standard types. Second, a provision in the Dodd-Frank Act mandated that certain standardized interest rate swaps be centrally cleared rather than managed by banks. The Chicago Mercantile Group (CME) is one of these clearing houses and as of October, 2014 the notional principal of the swaps outstanding with CME totaled $23 trillion.

Most swaps today involve either interest payments or currencies, but just about anything can be swapped, including equity swaps, credit spread swaps, and commodity swaps.[21]

24-7c **Inverse Floaters**

A floating-rate note has an interest rate that rises and falls with some interest rate index. For example, if the prime rate were currently 8.5%, then the interest rate on a $100,000 note at prime plus 1% would be 9.5% and the note's rate would move up and down with the prime rate. Because both the cash flows associated with the note and the discount rate used to value it would rise and fall together, the market value of the note would be relatively stable.

With an **inverse floater**, the rate paid on the note moves *counter* to market rates. Thus, if interest rates in the economy rise, the interest rate paid on an inverse floater will fall, reducing its cash interest payments. At the same time, the discount rate used to value the inverse floater's cash flows will rise along with other rates. The combined effect of lower cash flows and a higher discount rate would lead to a large decline in the value of the inverse floater. Thus, inverse floaters are exceptionally vulnerable to increases in interest rates. Of course, if interest rates fall then the value of an inverse floater will soar.

Could an inverse floater be used for hedging purposes? The answer is "yes, perhaps quite effectively." These securities have a magnified effect, so not many are required to hedge a given position. However, because they are so volatile, they could make what is supposed to be a hedged position quite risky.

---

20. For more information on swaps, see Keith C. Brown and Donald J. Smith, "Default Risk and Innovations in the Design of Interest Rate Swaps," *Financial Management*, Summer 1993, pp. 94–105; Robert Einzig and Bruce Lange, "Swaps at Transamerica: Applications and Analysis," *Journal of Applied Corporate Finance*, Winter 1990, pp. 48–58; John F. Marshall, Vipul K. Bansal, Anthony F. Herbst, and Alan L. Tucker, "Hedging Business Cycle Risk with Macro Swaps and Options,"*Journal of Applied Corporate Finance*, Winter 1992, pp. 103–108; and Laurie S. Goodman, "The Uses of Interest Rate Swaps in Managing Corporate Liabilities," *Journal of Applied Corporate Finance*, Winter 1990, pp. 35–47.

21. In an equity swap, the cash flow based on an equity index is swapped for some other cash flow. In a commodity swap, the swapped cash flow is based on commodity prices. In a credit swap, the cash flow usually is based on the spread between a risky bond and a U.S. Treasury bond.

SELF TEST

Explain how a company can use Treasury bond futures to hedge against rising interest rates.

What is an interest rate swap? Describe the mechanics of a fixed-rate to floating-rate swap.

A Treasury bond futures contract is selling for 94'16. What is the implied annual yield? **(6.5%)**

Messman Corporation issues fixed-rate debt at a rate of 9.00%. Messman agrees to an interest rate swap in which it pays LIBOR to Moore Inc. and Moore pays 8.75% to Messman. What is Messman's resulting net payment? **(LIBOR + 0.25%)**

24-8 Project Selection Risks

A project is any corporate undertaking that uses corporate assets such as cash, factories, buildings, equipment, IT infrastructure, intellectual property, and people.

A successful project creates value by generating a return that is commensurate with the size and risk of the assets invested in the project. Perhaps the most important factor for a company's success is its ability to select value-adding projects and avoid value-destroying projects.

24-8a Using Monte Carlo Simulation to Evaluate Project Risk

When evaluating a potential project, a company should assess the project qualitatively and quantitatively using the three-step approach we described in Chapters 12 and 13: (1) forecast the project's future cash flows, (2) estimate the value of the cash flows, and (3) analyze the risk of the cash flows.[22] Small projects, such as the replacement of a single machine, require less analysis than large projects, which include major capital expenditures, product line extensions, new products, geographic expansion, acquisitions, and mergers.

For larger projects, it is absolutely vital to conduct a thorough risk analysis, including sensitivity analysis and scenario analysis, as described in Chapter 13. Very large projects require even more risk analysis, including Monte Carlo simulation, which is widely used in enterprise risk management—you can't manage a risk very well if you can't measure it!

We repeat here some of the results from the simulation analysis in Chapter 13, and we include some new results. Recall that the analysis in Chapter 13 was for the application of a radically new liquid nano-coating technology to a new type of solar water heater module. We projected cash flows for the project, calculated NPV and other evaluation measures, performed a sensitivity analysis, and did a scenario analysis; see Section 13-2 for the basic analysis and Sections 13-5 and 13-6 for the sensitivity and scenario analyses.

---

22. Recall from Chapter 12 that cash flow evaluation methods include the net present value (NPV), the internal rate of return (IRR), the modified internal rate of return (MIRR), the profitability index (PI), the payback period, and the discounted payback period.

We conducted a Monte Carlo simulation analysis in Section 13-7. Recall that in a simulation analysis, a probability distribution is assigned to each input variable—sales in units, the sales price, the variable cost per unit, and so on. The computer begins by picking a random value for each variable from its probability distribution. Those values are then entered into the model, the project's NPV (and any other measures) is calculated, and the NPV is stored in the computer's memory. This is called a trial. After completing the first trial, a second set of input values is selected from the input variables' probability distributions, and a second NPV is calculated. This process is repeated until there are enough observations that the estimated NPV and any other outcome measures are stable.

We replicated the simulation analysis from Chapter 13 with 10,000 iterations; see *Ch24 Tool Kit.xls* and look in the worksheet *Simulation.* Figure 24-3 reports the

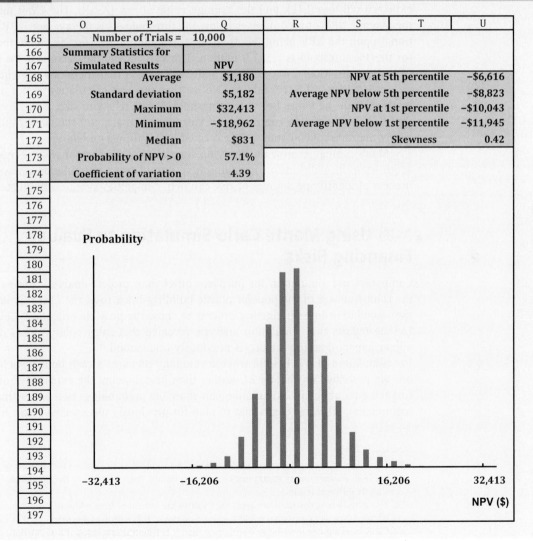

FIGURE 24-3   An Example of Monte Carlo Simulation Applied to Project Analysis (Thousands of Dollars)

	O	P	Q	R	S	T	U
165		Number of Trials =	10,000				
166		Summary Statistics for					
167		Simulated Results	NPV				
168		Average	$1,180		NPV at 5th percentile		−$6,616
169		Standard deviation	$5,182		Average NPV below 5th percentile		−$8,823
170		Maximum	$32,413		NPV at 1st percentile		−$10,043
171		Minimum	−$18,962		Average NPV below 1st percentile		−$11,945
172		Median	$831		Skewness		0.42
173		Probability of NPV > 0	57.1%				
174		Coefficient of variation	4.39				

estimated evaluation measures from Chapter 13 and some additional measures.[23] The measures from Chapter 13 for include NPV include its average, standard deviation, maximum, minimum, median, and the probability that the NPV will be positive. Based on these measures, the project has a positive expected NPV and will break even about 57% of the time.

In addition to the evaluation measures from Chapter 13, enterprise risk management systems often use another measure called **value at risk (VaR)**. Using the trials from the simulation analysis, the company specifies a threshold, such as the bottom 1% or 5% of outcomes. The basic idea is to measure the value of the project if things go badly. For example, Figure 24-3 shows that there is a 5% chance that the project will lose $6.6 million or more (the values are reported in thousands) and a 1% chance that the project will lose $10.0 million or more.

The VaR measures are helpful, but they don't measure the extent of possible losses if things go badly. A measure that many companies now apply is the **conditional value at risk (CVaR)**; it is also called the **expected shortfall**, the expected tail loss (ETL), and the average value at risk (AVaR). The CVaR measures the average NPV of all outcomes below the threshold—it is the average NPV conditional upon the NPV being less than the threshold value.[24] For example, the CVaR for the 1% threshold is −$11.9 million. The VaR shows that there is a 1% chance of losing more than $10.0 million, and CVaR shows that there is a 1% chance of an expected loss of $11.9 million. Notice that the VaR calculation is not affected by the size of the losses below the threshold—it just tells you size of the loss at the threshold percentile. In contrast, the CVaR takes into account the size of the losses below the threshold—it shows the expected loss if things go badly.

Many companies now are applying simulation when they analyze mergers and acquisition. In addition to the quantitative output from a simulation analysis, the process of identifying sources of risk can help companies avoid costly mistakes.

24-8b Using Monte Carlo Simulation to Evaluate Financing Risks

Companies use simulation for purposes other than project analysis. For example, the Danish maker of the popular plastic building-brick toys, the LEGO Group, also uses simulation in its budgeting process to show the possible outcomes. CFO Hans Læssøe reports that simulation analysis revealed that sales volatility has a much bigger impact than top managers previously understood.[25]

Simulation also is helpful when a company prepares a cash budget such as the one we described in Chapter 21. Rather than just showing the expected short-term financing requirements, simulation can show the probabilities of a larger financing requirement, allowing companies to plan for previously unexpected credit needs.

---

23. The values of the measures will be different in this figure than in Figure 13-7 since these results are from another run of 10,000 trials for the simulation. Each new run of the simulation will give slightly different results.

24. This definition is correct when applying CVaR to the outcomes from a Monte Carlo simulation because there is an equal probability of each outcome. It is a little more complicated to calculate CVaR from a given probability distribution than it is from the outcomes of a simulation.

25. See the paper by Mark Frigo and Hans Læssøe cited in footnote 14.

24-8c **Using Monte Carlo Simulation to Evaluate Portfolio Risks**

Many companies are exposed to portfolio risk, which is the risk that a portfolio of financial assets will decrease in value. For example, many companies offer pension plans to their employees. Defined benefit plans have a portfolio of stocks, bonds, and other financial assets that is used to support promised pension benefits to its employees. Such companies are exposed to significant portfolio risk—if the value of the pension assets portfolio drops too much relative to the value of the promised pension benefits, then the company will have to use its other resources to make additional contributions to the plan.

Most financial institutions are also exposed to portfolio risk because they own financial assets and have financial liabilities. Simulation is a widely used tool for measuring a bank's portfolio risk. In fact, the Basel II and III accords require banks to report their VaR and the Basel Committee is presently (2014) considering requiring banks to also report the expected shortfall (the CVar).

When the trading and risk management groups at financial institutions use VaR (or CVaR), they usually measure it over a very short time horizon because they want to know how much they might lose overnight or within a couple of days.

What is Monte Carlo simulation?

What is value at risk, VaR? What is conditional value at risk, CVaR?

SELF TEST

24-9 **Managing Credit Risks**

Nonfinancial companies are exposed to risk if they extend credit to their customers, and financial institutions are exposed to credit risk when they lend to their customers. Following are some key concepts in the management of credit risk.

24-9a **Managing Credit Risk at Nonfinancial Companies**

As we described in Chapter 21, when a company sells a product to a customer but does not require immediate payment, an account receivable is created. There are three primary tools that companies use to manage this credit risk.

First, a company evaluates its customers before extending credit. The company can do its own evaluation or purchase an evaluation from a third party. If the customer is an individual, credit evaluations are available from several companies, including as Equifax, Experian, and TransUnion. Each of these companies provides a numerical score, with the FICO score being the most widely used. The score ranges from 300 to 850, with lower scores indicating that the customer is more likely to default.

When the customer is another company, the evaluation is conducted using many of the same ratios and analyses we described in Chapter 7. In addition, some companies create their own credit scoring models based on past experience or statistical models (such as discriminant analysis).

A company can mitigate its credit risk by selling its accounts receivable to a third party in a process called factoring. Of course, the price a company receives from selling its receivables depends on the receivables' risk, with riskier receivables purchased for much less than their nominal value. A company can also buy insurance for some or all of its receivables. Many companies, including the LEGO Group, use simulation to estimate the risk of their receivables so that they can better negotiate with insurers.

24-9b Managing Credit Risk at Financial Institutions

W W W

See the Markit Group Limited's Web site for updates on CDS data. Free registration allows access to a variety of current data, including indexes: **www.markit.com/en/**.

In addition to the same techniques used at nonfinancial corporations (credit scoring models and simulation), many financial institutions use credit default swaps (CDS). Even though CDS are called swaps, they are like insurance. For example, an investor (which might be a financial institution) might purchase a CDS by making an annual payment to a counterparty to insure a particular bond or other security against default; if the bond defaults, the counterparty pays the purchaser the amount of the defaulted bond that was insured.

The CDS "price" is quoted in basis points and is called the CDS spread. For example, the spread on Unitymedia KabelBW GmbH, a German cable operator, was about 271 basis points in May 2014. An easy way to interpret the reported basis point spread is that it would be the annual fee in dollars (or euros) to protect $10,000 (or euros) of the bond. Therefore, it would cost €271 per year to insure €10,000 of Unitymedia's bonds.

To protect €10 million of Unitymedia's debt, a buyer would pay €271,000 = 0.0271(€10 million) per year. In contrast, the spread on the automobile manufacturer BMW's bonds was only 42 basis points, so insuring €10 million of BMW's debt would cost only €42,000 per year. If the investors owned the bonds, then the purchase of the CDS would reduce the investor's risk.

There is an active secondary market for CDS, and it is not necessary to own the underlying security. In fact, most participants in the CDS market don't own the underlying securities. For example, a speculator might purchase a CDS on Unitymedia for 271 basis points but only purchase coverage for 1 month, which would be a payment of €22,583 = €271,000/12. Now suppose the Eurozone's problems immediately worsened and drove Unitymedia's CDS spread up to 300 basis points. The investor could liquidate the position by selling 1-month credit protection for €25,000 = €300,000/12 and use the previously purchased CDS to offset the newly sold CDS. The investor's profit would be €2,417.

In addition to CDS for individual securities, there are CDS for indices. For example, the CDX.NA.IG is an index of 125 CDS for North American investment-grade debt. The index's movements are positively correlated with the overall level of default for many commercial loans—the index goes up when defaults increase. Therefore, a U.S. bank can protect itself from increasing default rates in its loan portfolio by taking a short position in the CDX.NA.IG. If defaults increase, then the index goes up, which means a short investor can profit by selling the now higher priced index at the lower price specified in the original short position. This is a situation in which the CDS help reduce a financial institution's risk—when defaults increase, the institution loses money on it loans but makes money on the index. Of course, if the index falls, then the bank loses on the short position but wins on its own loan portfolio because there are fewer defaults.

When banks and other major financial institutions take positions in swaps and CDS, they are themselves exposed to various risks, especially if their counterparties cannot meet their obligations. Furthermore, swaps are off–balance sheet transactions, making it impossible to tell just how large the swap market is or who has what obligation. The Bank of International Settlements estimates that as of the end of 2013 the notional value of all CDS was over $21 trillion. As we write this in the summer of 2014, the SEC and the Commodity Futures Trading Commission (CFTC) continue implementation of provisions in Title VII of the 2010 Dodd-Frank Act to improve transparency in the swaps markets. Standardized interest-rate and credit-default swaps must now be centrally cleared and the market is working to develop new products that provide the same benefits as these swaps, but with lower counterparty risk.[26]

Credit default swaps are traded on government debt as well as corporate debt. Before 2008, a CDS on a 5-year U.S. Treasury bond was trading at less than 7 basis points, which would be a $7 annual fee to protect $10,000 of the bond. The CDS price increased to almost 100 basis points in 2009 and is currently (mid 2014) trading around 17 basis points. Figure 24-4 shows the prices for the U.S. and selected European countries, some which have adopted the euro (Germany, France, Italy, Spain, and Portugal) and some which have not. The extremely high prices for Euro-zone debt indicate the problems facing these countries.

FIGURE 24-4	Credit Default Swap Spreads for Sovereign Debt (May 27, 2014)

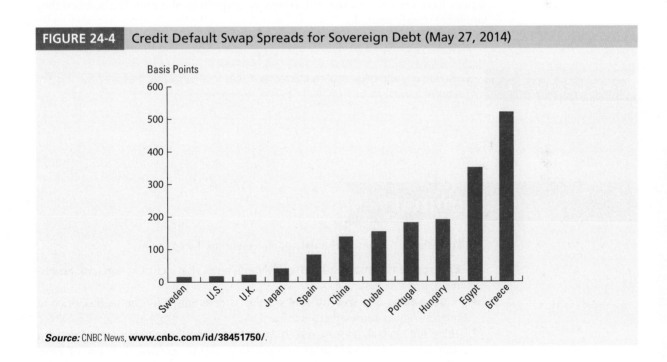

Source: CNBC News, **www.cnbc.com/id/38451750/**.

---

26. See the presentation "Swaps Regulation under Dodd-Frank's Title VII: Recent Developments" given March 6, 2014, by David Kaufman, Anna Pinedo, James Schwartz and Michael Sefton at http://www.mofo.com/files/Uploads/Images/140306-Swaps-Regulation-under-Dodd-Franks-Title-VII.pdf.

SELF TEST

Describe some ways to manage credit risk at a nonfinancial company.

What are credit default swaps?

24-10 Risk and Human Safety

Risk management decisions, like all corporate decisions, should begin with a cost–benefit analysis for each feasible alternative. For example, suppose it would cost $50,000 per year to conduct a comprehensive fire safety training program for all personnel in a high-risk plant. Presumably, this program would reduce the expected value of future fire losses. An alternative to the training program would be to place $50,000 annually in a reserve fund set aside to cover future fire losses. Both alternatives involve expected cash flows, and from an economic standpoint the choice should be made on the basis of the lowest present value of future costs.

However, suppose a fire occurs and a life is lost. In situations involving safety and health, the trade-off between expected profits and expected losses is not sufficient for making sound decisions. Companies must always consider the impact their decisions have on the safety of their employees and customers. Ignoring safety and health is an ethical mistake, but it also is a business mistake because many companies have been forced out of business or suffered debilitating losses when they produced unsafe products.

SELF TEST

Describe a situation in risk management that involves ethical as well as financial issues.

Summary

The key concepts in enterprise risk management are listed below.

- **Enterprise risk management (ERM)** includes risk identification, risk assessment, and risk responses.
- A **derivative** is a security whose value is determined by the market price or interest rate of some other security.
- There are several reasons **risk management** might increase the value of a firm. Risk management allows corporations: (1) to increase their **use of debt**, (2) to maintain their **capital budget** over time, (3) to avoid costs associated with **financial distress**, (4) to utilize their **comparative advantages in hedging** relative to the hedging ability of individual investors, (5) to reduce both the risks and costs of borrowing by using **swaps**, and (6) to reduce the **higher taxes** that result from fluctuating earnings. Managers may also want to stabilize earnings in order to boost their own compensation.

- Risk responses include: (1) avoiding the activity, (2) reducing the probability of occurrence of an adverse event, (3) reducing the magnitude of the loss associated with an adverse event, (4) transferring the risk to an insurance company, (5) transferring the function that produces the risk to a third party, and (6) sharing the risk by purchasing a derivative contract.
- Major categories of risk include: (1) strategy and reputation, (2) control and compliance, (3) hazards, (4) human resources, (5) operation, (6) technology, and (7) financial management.
- Types of financial risk include: (1) foreign exchange risk, (2) commodity price risk, (3) interest rate risk, (4) project selection risk, (5) liquidity risk, (6) customer credit risk, and (7) portfolio risk.
- A **hedge** is a transaction that lowers risk. A **natural hedge** is a transaction between two **counterparties** whose risks are mirror images of each other.
- A **futures contract** is a standardized contract that is traded on an exchange and is marked-to-market daily, although physical delivery of the underlying asset usually does not occur.
- Under a **forward contract**, one party agrees to buy a commodity at a specific price and a specific future date and the other party agrees to make the sale; delivery does occur.
- A **swap** is an exchange of cash payment obligations. Swaps occur because the parties involved prefer the other's payment stream.
- **Financial futures** permit firms to create hedge positions to protect themselves against fluctuating interest rates, stock prices, and exchange rates.
- **Commodity futures** can be used to hedge against input price increases.
- **Long hedges** involve buying futures contracts to guard against price increases.
- **Short hedges** involve selling futures contracts to guard against price declines.
- **Symmetric hedges** protect against price increases and price decreases. Futures contracts are frequently used for symmetric hedges.
- **Asymmetric hedges** protect against price movements in one direction more than movements in another. Options are frequently used for asymmetric hedges.
- A **perfect hedge** occurs when the gain or loss on the hedged transaction exactly offsets the loss or gain on the unhedged position.

Questions

24-1 Define each of the following terms:
  a. Derivatives
  b. Enterprise risk management
  c. Financial futures; forward contract
  d. Hedging; natural hedge; long hedge; short hedge; perfect hedge; symmetric hedge; asymmetric hedge
  e. Swap; structured note
  f. Commodity futures

24-2 Give two reasons stockholders might be indifferent between owning the stock of a firm with volatile cash flows and that of a firm with stable cash flows.

24-3 List six reasons why risk management might increase the value of a firm.

24-4 Discuss some of the techniques available to reduce risk exposures.

24-5 Explain how the futures markets can be used to reduce interest rate risk and input price risk.

24-6 How can swaps be used to reduce the risks associated with debt contracts?

Problems   Answers Appear in Appendix B

Easy Problems 1–2

24-1 Swaps
Zhao Automotive issues fixed-rate debt at a rate of 7.00%. Zhao agrees to an interest rate swap in which it pays LIBOR to Lee Financial and Lee pays 6.8% to Zhao. What is Zhao's resulting net payment?

24-2 Futures
A Treasury bond futures contract has a settlement price of 89'08. What is the implied annual yield?

Intermediate Problems 3-4

24-3 Futures
What is the implied interest rate on a Treasury bond ($100,000) futures contract that settled at 100'16? If interest rates increased by 1%, what would be the contract's new value?

24-4 Swaps
Carter Enterprises can issue floating-rate debt at LIBOR + 2% or fixed-rate debt at 10%. Brence Manufacturing can issue floating-rate debt at LIBOR + 3.1% or fixed-rate debt at 11%. Suppose Carter issues floating-rate debt and Brence issues fixed-rate debt. They are considering a swap in which Carter makes a fixed-rate payment of 7.95% to Brence and Brence makes a payment of LIBOR to Carter. What are the net payments of Carter and Brence if they engage in the swap? Would Carter be better off if it issued fixed-rate debt or if it issued floating-rate debt and engaged in the swap? Would Brence be better off if it issued floating-rate debt or if it issued fixed-rate debt and engaged in the swap? Explain your answers.

Challenging Problem 5

24-5 Hedging
The Zinn Company plans to issue $10,000,000 of 20-year bonds in June to help finance a new research and development laboratory. The bonds will pay interest semiannually. It is now November, and the current cost of debt to the high-risk biotech company is 11%. However, the firm's financial manager is concerned that interest rates will climb even higher in coming months. The following data are available:

Futures Prices: Treasury Bonds—$100,000; Pts. 32nds of 100%

Delivery Month (1)	Open (2)	High (3)	Low (4)	Settle (5)	Change (6)	Open Interest (7)
Dec	94'28	95'13	94'22	95'05	+0'07	591,944
Mar	96'03	96'03	95'13	95'25	+0'08	120,353
June	95'03	95'17	95'03	95'17	+0'08	13,597

a. Use the given data to create a hedge against rising interest rates.
b. Assume that interest rates in general increase by 200 basis points. How well did your hedge perform?
c. What is a perfect hedge? Are any real-world hedges perfect? Explain.

Spreadsheet Problem

24-6 Build a Model: Hedging

Start with the partial model in the file *Ch24 P06 Build a Model.xls* on the textbook's Web site. Use the information and data below.

F. Pierce Products Inc. is financing a new manufacturing facility with the issue in March of $20,000,000 of 20-year bonds with semiannual interest payments. It is now October, and if Pierce were to issue the bonds now, the yield would be 10% because of Pierce's high risk. Pierce's CFO is concerned that interest rates will climb even higher in coming months and is considering hedging the bond issue. The following data are available:

Futures Prices: Treasury Bonds—$100,000; Pts. 32nds of 100%

Delivery Month (1)	Open (2)	High (3)	Low (4)	Settle (5)	Change (6)	Open Interest (7)
Dec	93'28	94'13	93'22	94'05	+0'06	723,946
Mar	95'03	95'03	94'13	94'25	+0'07	97,254

a. Create a hedge with the futures contract for Pierce's planned March debt offering of $20 million using the March Treasury Bond futures contract. What is the implied yield on the bond underlying the futures contract?
b. Suppose that interest rates fall by 300 basis points. What are the dollar savings from issuing the debt at the new interest rate? What is the dollar change in value of the futures position? What is the total dollar value change of the hedged position?
c. Create a graph showing the effectiveness of the hedge if the change in interest rates, in basis points, is −300, −200, −100, 0, 100, 200, or 300. Show the dollar cost (or savings) from issuing the debt at the new interest rates, the dollar change in value of the futures position, and the total dollar value change.

MINI CASE

Assume you have just been hired as a financial analyst by Tennessee Sunshine Inc., a mid-sized Tennessee company that specializes in creating exotic sauces from imported fruits and vegetables. The firm's CEO, Bill Stooksbury, recently returned from an industry corporate executive conference in San Francisco, and one of the sessions he attended was on the pressing need for companies to institute enterprise risk management programs. Because no one at Tennessee Sunshine is familiar with the basics of enterprise risk management, Stooksbury has asked you to prepare a brief report that the firm's executives could use to gain at least a cursory understanding of the topics.

To begin, you gathered some outside materials on derivatives and risk management and used these materials to draft a list of pertinent questions that need to be answered. In fact, one possible approach to the paper is to use a question-and-answer format. Now that the questions have been drafted, you have to develop the answers.

a. Why might stockholders be indifferent to whether or not a firm reduces the volatility of its cash flows?

b. What are six reasons risk management might increase the value of a corporation?

c. What is COSO? How does COSO define enterprise risk management?

d. Describe the eight components of the COSO ERM framework.

e. Describe some of the risks events within the following major categories of risk: (1) strategy and reputation, (2) control and compliance, (3) hazards, (4) human resources, (5) operations, (6) technology, and (7) financial management.

f. What are some actions that companies can take to minimize or reduce risk exposures?

g. What are forward contracts? How can they be used to manage foreign exchange risk?

h. Describe how commodity futures markets can be used to reduce input price risk.

i. It is January, and Tennessee Sunshine is considering issuing $5 million in bonds in June to raise capital for an expansion. Currently, the firm can issue 20-year bonds with a 7% coupon (with interest paid semiannually), but interest rates are on the rise and Stooksbury is concerned that long-term interest rates might rise by as much as 1% before June. You looked online and found that June T-bond futures are trading at 111'25. What are the risks of not hedging, and how might TS hedge this exposure? In your analysis, consider what would happen if interest rates all increased by 1%.

j. What is a swap? Suppose two firms have different credit ratings. Firm Hi can borrow fixed at 11% and floating at LIBOR + 1%. Firm Lo can borrow fixed at 11.4% and floating at LIBOR + 1.5%. Describe a floating versus fixed interest rate swap between firms Hi and Lo in which Lo also makes a "side payment" of 45 basis points to Firm L.

CHAPTER 25

Bankruptcy, Reorganization, and Liquidation

WEB

The textbook's Web site contains an *Excel* file that will guide you through the chapter's calculations. The file for this chapter is ***Ch25 Tool Kit.xls***, and we encourage you to open the file and follow along as you read the chapter.

Thus far, we have dealt with issues faced by growing, successful enterprises. However, many firms encounter financial difficulties, and some—including such big names as General Motors, Chrysler, Delta Air Lines, and Lehman Brothers—are forced into bankruptcy. When a firm encounters financial distress, its managers must try to ward off a total collapse and thereby minimize losses. The ability to hang on during rough times often means the difference between forced liquidation versus rehabilitation and eventual success. An understanding of bankruptcy is also critical to the executives of healthy firms, because they must know the best actions to take when their customers or suppliers face the threat of bankruptcy.

Beginning-of-Chapter Questions

As you read the chapter, consider how you would answer the following questions. You *should not* necessarily be able to answer the questions before you read the chapter. Rather, you should use them to get a sense of the issues covered in the chapter. After reading the chapter, you should be able to give at least partial answers to the questions, and you should be able to give better answers after the chapter has been discussed in class. Note, too, that it is often useful, when answering conceptual questions, to use hypothetical data to illustrate your answer. (There is no model on the textbook's Web site for these Beginning-of-Chapter Questions.)

1. Is **bankruptcy** a fairly common occurrence among large companies, or is it restricted primarily to small firms?

2. How can a company use a bankruptcy to abrogate labor contracts? Has this occurred in certain industries in recent years?

3. In your answers to the following set of questions, assume that Ross Corporation has $200 million of assets at book value, $150 million of liabilities owed to 500 different creditors, and $50 million of common equity book value. Also, assume that Ross has failed to make timely payments on its debt. The assets are worth less than the $200 million shown on the balance sheet, although their actual market value is uncertain. The company issued mortgage bonds that are held by public bondholders and are secured by real estate, and 15 different banks hold loans secured by all of the company's accounts receivable, inventories, and equipment. There are also some 250 general (unsecured) creditors, including accounts payable, accrued wages and taxes, and pension plan obligations. Answer the following questions:

   a. Should Ross attempt to resolve its problems using **informal procedures**, or should it file for bankruptcy? Why?

b. What are the two key **chapters** in the bankruptcy code, and what is the primary effect of each one?

c. Who is more likely to initiate **formal bankruptcy proceedings**—the company or its creditors? What exactly would be filed to start the bankruptcy process?

d. If the company initiated the proceedings, would it be more likely to seek relief under **Chapter 7** or **Chapter 11**? Would the same be true if a creditor initiated the proceedings? Explain.

e. What is the **common pool problem**, and would it be likely to arise in Ross' case in the absence of a bankruptcy filing?

f. What is the **automatic stay**, and is it likely that it would be applied in this case?

g. What is a **pre-pack**, and is it likely that one would be used in this case?

h. What is a **cramdown**, and is it likely that one would be used in this case?

i. Define the terms **absolute priority doctrine** and **relative priority doctrine**.

j. If the assets were sold at auction and the company **liquidated**, how would the proceeds be divided up?

k. If the company were **reorganized**, who would get what in the reorganization?

25-1 Financial Distress and Its Consequences

We begin with some background on financial distress and its consequences.[1]

25-1a Causes of Business Failure

A company's intrinsic value is the present value of its expected future free cash flows. Many factors can cause this value to decline. These include general economic conditions, industry trends, and company-specific problems such as shifting consumer tastes, obsolete technology, and changing demographics in existing retail locations. Financial factors, such as too much debt and unexpected increases in interest rates, can also cause business failures. The importance of the different factors varies over time, and most business failures occur because a number of factors combine to make the business unsustainable. Further, case studies show that financial difficulties are usually the result of a series of errors, misjudgments, and interrelated weaknesses that can be attributed directly or indirectly to management. In a few cases, such as Enron and MF Global Holdings, fraud leads to bankruptcy.

As you might guess, signs of potential financial distress are generally evident in a ratio analysis long before the firm actually fails, and researchers use ratio analysis to estimate the probability that a given firm will go bankrupt. Financial analysts constantly are seeking ways to assess a firm's likelihood of going bankrupt. We discuss one method, multiple discriminant analysis (MDA), in *Web Extension 25A.*

---

1. Much of the current academic work in the area of financial distress and bankruptcy is based on writings by Edward I. Altman. See Edward I. Altman and Edith Hotchkiss, *Corporate Financial Distress and Bankruptcy: Predict and Avoid Bankruptcy, Analyze and Invest in Distressed Debt* (Hoboken, NJ: Wiley, 2006).

25-1b **The Business Failure Record**

Although bankruptcy is more frequent among smaller firms, it is clear from Table 25-1 that large firms are not immune. This was especially true during the global economic crisis: Six of the largest bankruptcies occurred in 2008 and 2009.

Bankruptcy obviously is painful for a company's shareholders, but it also can be harmful to the economy if the company is very large or is in a critical sector. For example, the failure of Lehman Brothers in September 2008 sparked a global run on financial institutions that froze credit markets and contributed to the ensuing global recession. It is not clear whether the damage to the world economy could have been mitigated if the government had intervened to prevent Lehman's failure, but the government subsequently decided not to take chances with many other troubled financial institutions. For example, the government helped arrange the 2008 acquisition of Wachovia by Wells Fargo, the 2008 acquisition of Bear Stearns by JPMorgan Chase, and the 2009 acquisition of Merrill Lynch by Bank of America (despite Bank of America's misgivings). In addition, the government provided billions of dollars of capital to many major financial institutions in 2008, including AIG. In each of these cases, the government decided that a complete failure of these institutions might cause the entire financial system to collapse.

In other cases, the government has decided that a company was too important to the nonfinancial side of the economy to be allowed to go through liquidation. For example, in 2008 and 2009 the government provided billions of dollars of financing to General Motors and Chrysler. Even though these companies subsequently went through bankruptcy proceedings in 2009, they avoided liquidation, still have a significant number of employees, and remain major players in the automobile industry. In past years, the government also has intervened to support troubled firms in other critical sectors, such as Lockheed and Douglas Aircraft in the defense industry.

TABLE 25-1	The Ten Largest Bankruptcies since 1980 (Billions of Dollars)		
Company	**Business**	**Assets**	**Date**
Lehman Brothers Holdings Inc.	Investment banking	$691.1	September 15, 2008
Washington Mutual Inc.	Financial services	327.9	September 26, 2008
WorldCom Inc.	Telecommunications	103.9	July 21, 2002
General Motors Corporation	Auto manufacturing	91.0	June 1, 2009
CIT Group Inc.	Financial services	80.4	November 1, 2009
Enron Corp.	Energy trading	63.4	December 2, 2001
Conseco Inc.	Financial services	61.4	December 17, 2002
Energy Future Holdings Corp.	Electric Utility	50.0	April 29, 2014
MF Global Holdings Ltd.	Commodities	40.5	October 31, 2011
Chrysler LLC	Auto manufacturing	39.3	April 30, 2009

Source: BankruptcyData.com, a division of New Generation Research, May, 2014.

What are the major causes of business failure?

Do business failures occur evenly over time?

Which size of firm, large or small, is most prone to business failure? Why?

25-2 Issues Facing a Firm in Financial Distress

Financial distress begins when a firm is unable to meet scheduled payments or when cash flow projections indicate that it will soon be unable to do so. As the situation develops, five central issues arise.

1. Is the firm's inability to meet scheduled debt payments a temporary cash flow problem, or is it a permanent problem caused by asset values having fallen below debt obligations?
2. If the problem is temporary, then an agreement with creditors that gives the firm time to recover and to satisfy everyone may be worked out. However, if basic long-run asset values have truly declined, then economic losses have occurred. In this event, who should bear the losses, and who should get whatever value remains?
3. Is the company "worth more dead than alive"? That is, would the business be more valuable if it were liquidated and sold off in pieces or if it were maintained and continued in operation?
4. Should the firm file for protection under Chapter 11 of the Bankruptcy Act, or should it try to use informal procedures? (Both reorganization and liquidation can be accomplished either informally or under the direction of a bankruptcy court.)
5. Who should control the firm while it is being liquidated or rehabilitated? Should the existing management be left in charge, or should a trustee be placed in charge of operations?

In the remainder of the chapter, we discuss these issues in turn.

What five major issues must be addressed when a firm faces financial distress?

25-3 Settlements without Going through Formal Bankruptcy

When a firm experiences financial distress, its managers and creditors must decide whether the problem is temporary and the firm is financially viable or whether a permanent problem exists that endangers the firm's life. Then the parties must decide whether to try to solve the problem informally or under the direction of a bankruptcy court. Because of costs associated with formal bankruptcy—including the disruptions that occur when a firm's customers, suppliers, and employees learn that it has filed under the Bankruptcy Act—it is preferable to reorganize (or liquidate) outside of formal bankruptcy. We first discuss informal settlement procedures and then the procedures under a formal bankruptcy.

25-3a **Informal Reorganization**

In the case of an economically sound company whose financial difficulties appear to be temporary, creditors are generally willing to work with the company to help it recover and reestablish itself on a sound financial basis. Such voluntary plans, commonly called **workouts**, usually require a **restructuring** of the firm's debt, because current cash flows are insufficient to service the existing debt. Restructuring typically involves extension and/or composition. In an **extension**, creditors postpone the dates of required interest or principal payments, or both. In a **composition**, creditors voluntarily reduce their fixed claims on the debtor by accepting a lower principal amount, by reducing the interest rate on the debt, by taking equity in exchange for debt, or by some combination of these changes.

A debt restructuring begins with a meeting between the failing firm's managers and creditors. The creditors appoint a committee consisting of four or five of the largest creditors plus one or two of the smaller ones. This meeting is often arranged and conducted by an **adjustment bureau** associated with and run by a local credit managers' association.[2] The first step is for management to draw up a list of creditors that shows the amounts of debt owed. There are typically different classes of debt, ranging from first-mortgage holders to unsecured creditors. Next, the company develops information showing the value of the firm under different scenarios. Typically, one scenario is going out of business, selling off the assets, and then distributing the proceeds to the various creditors in accordance with the priority of their claims, with any surplus going to the common stockholders. The company may hire an appraiser to get an appraisal of the value of the firm's property to use as a basis for this scenario. Other scenarios include continued operations, frequently with some improvements in capital equipment, marketing, and perhaps some management changes.

This information is then shared with the firm's bankers and other creditors. Frequently, the firm's debts exceed its liquidating value, and the legal fees and other costs associated with a formal liquidation under federal bankruptcy procedures will materially lower the net proceeds available to creditors. Furthermore, it generally takes at least a year (and often several years) to resolve matters in a formal proceeding, so the present value of the eventual proceeds will be lower still. This information, when presented in a credible manner, often convinces creditors they would be better off accepting something less than the full amount of their claims rather than holding out for the full face amount. If management and the major creditors agree that the problems can probably be resolved, then a more formal plan is drafted and presented to all the creditors, along with the reasons creditors should be willing to compromise on their claims.

In developing the reorganization plan, creditors prefer an extension because it promises eventual payment in full. In some cases, creditors may agree not only to postpone the date of payment but also to subordinate existing claims to vendors

---

2. There is a nationwide group called the National Association of Credit Management, which consists of bankers and industrial companies' credit managers. This group sponsors research on credit policy and problems, conducts seminars on credit management, and operates local chapters in cities throughout the nation. These local chapters frequently operate adjustment bureaus.

who are willing to extend new credit during the workout period. Similarly, creditors may agree to accept a lower interest rate on loans during the extension, perhaps in exchange for a pledge of collateral. Because of the sacrifices involved, the creditors must have faith that the debtor firm will be able to solve its problems.

In a composition, creditors agree to reduce their claims. Typically, creditors receive cash and/or new securities that have a combined market value that is less than the amounts owed them. The cash and securities, which might have a value of only 10% of the original claim, are taken as full settlement of the original debt. Bargaining will take place between the debtor and the creditors over the savings that result from avoiding the costs of legal bankruptcy: administrative costs, legal fees, investigative costs, and so on. In addition to escaping such costs, the debtor gains because the stigma of bankruptcy may be avoided. As a result, the debtor may be induced to part with most of the savings from avoiding formal bankruptcy.

Often, the bargaining process will result in a restructuring that involves both extension and composition. For example, the settlement may provide for a cash payment of 25% of the debt immediately plus a new note promising six future installments of 10% each, for a total payment of 85%.

Voluntary settlements are both informal and simple; they are also relatively inexpensive, because legal and administrative expenses are held to a minimum. Thus, voluntary procedures generally result in the largest return to creditors. Although creditors do not obtain immediate payment and may even have to accept less than is owed them, they generally recover more money, and sooner, than if the firm were to file for bankruptcy.

In recent years, the fact that restructurings can sometimes help creditors avoid showing a loss has motivated some creditors, especially banks and insurance companies, to agree to voluntary restructurings. Thus, a bank "in trouble" with its regulators over weak capital ratios may agree to extend loans that are used to pay the interest on earlier loans—in order to keep the bank from having to write down the value of those earlier loans. This particular type of restructuring depends on: (1) the willingness of the regulators to go along with the process, and (2) whether the bank is likely to recover more by restructuring the debt than by forcing the borrower into bankruptcy immediately.

We should point out that informal voluntary settlements are not reserved for small firms. International Harvester (now Navistar International) avoided formal bankruptcy proceedings by getting its creditors to agree to restructure more than $3.5 billion of debt. Likewise, Chrysler's creditors accepted both an extension and a composition to help it through its bad years in the late 1970s before it merged with Daimler-Benz. The biggest problem with informal reorganizations is getting all the parties to agree to the voluntary plan. This problem, called the *holdout* problem, is discussed in a later section.

25-3b **Informal Liquidation**

When it is obvious that a firm is more valuable dead than alive, informal procedures can also be used to **liquidate** the firm. **Assignment** is an informal procedure for liquidating a firm, and it usually yields creditors a larger amount than they would get in a formal bankruptcy liquidation. However, assignments are feasible only if the firm is small and its affairs are not too complex. An assignment calls for title to the debtor's assets to be transferred to a third party, known as an **assignee** or trustee. The assignee is instructed to liquidate the assets through a private sale or public auction and then to distribute the proceeds among the creditors on a pro rata basis. The assignment does not automatically discharge the debtor's obligations. However, the debtor may have the assignee write the requisite legal language on the check to each creditor so that endorsement of the check constitutes acknowledgment of full settlement of the claim.

Assignment has some advantages over liquidation in federal bankruptcy courts in terms of time, legal formality, and expense. The assignee has more flexibility in disposing of property than does a federal bankruptcy trustee, so action can be taken sooner, before inventory becomes obsolete or machinery rusts. Also, because the assignee is often familiar with the debtor's business, better results may be achieved. However, an assignment does not automatically result in a full and legal discharge of all the debtor's liabilities, nor does it protect the creditors against fraud. Both of these problems can be reduced by formal liquidation in bankruptcy, which we discuss in a later section.

Define the following terms: (1) restructuring, (2) extension, (3) composition, (4) assignment, and (5) assignee (trustee).

What are the advantages of liquidation by assignment versus a formal bankruptcy liquidation?

SELF TEST

25-4 **Federal Bankruptcy Law**

U.S. bankruptcy laws were first enacted in 1898. They were modified substantially in 1938 and again in 1978, and some fine-tuning was done in 1986. In 2005, Congress further modified the bankruptcy code, speeding up bankruptcy proceedings for companies and making it more difficult for consumers to take advantage of provisions that can wipe out certain debts. The primary purpose of the bankruptcy law is to prevent individual creditors from forcing the liquidation of firms that are worth more as ongoing concerns, and thus causing harm to other stakeholders.

Currently, our bankruptcy law consists of eight odd-numbered chapters, plus one even-numbered chapter. (The old even-numbered chapters were deleted when the act was revised in 1978.) Chapters 1, 3, and 5 contain general provisions applicable to the other chapters. **Chapter 11**, which deals with business reorganization, is the most important section from a financial management viewpoint. **Chapter 7** details the procedures to be followed when liquidating a firm; generally, Chapter 7 does not come into play unless it has been determined that reorganization under Chapter 11 is not feasible. Chapter 9 deals with financially distressed municipalities; Chapter 12 covers special procedures for family-owned farms; Chapter 13 covers the adjustment of debts for "individuals with regular income"; and Chapter 15 sets up a system of trustees who help administer proceedings under the act.

A firm is officially bankrupt when it files for bankruptcy with a federal court. When you read that a company such as General Motors has "filed for court protection under Chapter 11," this means the company is attempting to reorganize under the supervision of a bankruptcy court. Formal bankruptcy proceedings are designed to protect both the firm and its creditors. On the one hand, if the problem is temporary insolvency, then the firm may use bankruptcy proceedings to gain time to solve its cash flow problems without asset seizure by its creditors. On the other hand, if the firm is truly bankrupt in the sense that liabilities exceed assets, then creditors can use bankruptcy procedures to stop the firm's managers from continuing to operate, lose more money, and thus deplete assets that should go to creditors.

Bankruptcy law is flexible in that it provides scope for negotiations between a company, its creditors, its labor force, and its stockholders. A case is opened by filing a petition with one of the 291 bankruptcy courts serving 90 judicial districts. The petition may be either **voluntary** or **involuntary**; that is, it may be filed either by the firm's management or by its creditors. After a filing, a committee of unsecured creditors is then appointed by the Office of the U.S. Trustee to negotiate with management for a reorganization, which may include the restructuring of debt. Under Chapter 11, a **trustee** will be appointed to take over the company if the court deems current management incompetent or if fraud is suspected. Normally, though, the existing management retains control. If no fair and feasible reorganization can be worked out, the bankruptcy judge will order that the firm be liquidated under procedures spelled out in Chapter 7 of the Bankruptcy Act, in which case a trustee will always be appointed.[3]

> **SELF TEST**
>
> Define the following terms: bankruptcy law, Chapter 11, Chapter 7, trustee, voluntary bankruptcy, and involuntary bankruptcy.
>
> How does a firm formally declare bankruptcy?

25-5 Reorganization in Bankruptcy

It might appear that most reorganizations should be handled informally because informal reorganizations are faster and less costly than formal bankruptcy. However, two problems often arise to stymie informal reorganizations and thus force debtors into Chapter 11 bankruptcy: the common pool problem and the holdout problem.[4]

To illustrate these problems, consider a firm that is having financial difficulties. It is worth $9 million as a going concern (this is the present value of its expected future operating cash flows) but only $7 million if it is liquidated. The firm's debt totals $10 million at face value—ten creditors with equal priority each have a $1 million claim. Now suppose the firm's liquidity deteriorates to the point that it defaults on one of its loans. The holder of that loan has the contractual right to *accelerate* the claim, which means the creditor can *foreclose* on the loan and demand payment of the entire balance. Further, because most debt agreements have *cross-default provisions*, defaulting on one loan effectively places all loans in default.

---

3. For a discussion of European bankruptcy laws, see Kevin M. J. Kaiser, "European Bankruptcy Laws: Implications for Corporations Facing Financial Distress," *Financial Management,* Autumn 1996, pp. 67–85.

4. The issues discussed in this section are covered in more detail in Thomas H. Jackson, *The Logic and Limits of Bankruptcy Law* (Frederick, MD: Beard Group, 2001). Also see Stuart C. Gilson, "Managing Default: Some Evidence on How Firms Choose between Workouts and Chapter 11," *Journal of Applied Corporate Finance,* Summer 1991, pp. 62–70; and Yehning Chen, J. Fred Weston, and Edward I. Altman, "Financial Distress and Restructuring Models," *Financial Management,* Summer 1995, pp. 57–75.

The firm's market value is less than the $10 million face value of debt, regardless of whether it remains in business or liquidates. Therefore, it would be impossible to pay off all of the creditors in full. However, the creditors in total would be better off if the firm is not shut down, because they could ultimately recover $9 million if the firm remains in business but only $7 million if it is liquidated. The problem here, which is called the **common pool problem**, is that in the absence of protection under the Bankruptcy Act, individual creditors would have an incentive to foreclose on the firm even though it is worth more as an ongoing concern.

An individual creditor would have the incentive to foreclose because it could then force the firm to liquidate a portion of its assets to pay off that particular creditor's $1 million claim in full. The payment to that creditor would probably require the liquidation of vital assets, which might cause a shutdown of the firm and thus lead to a total liquidation. Therefore, the value of the remaining creditors' claims would decline. Of course, all the creditors would recognize the gains they could attain from this strategy, so they would storm the debtor with foreclosure notices. Even those creditors who understand the merits of keeping the firm alive would be forced to foreclose, because the foreclosures of the other creditors would reduce the payoff to those who do not. In our hypothetical example, if seven creditors foreclosed and forced liquidation, they would be paid in full, and the remaining three creditors would receive nothing.

With many creditors, as soon as a firm defaults on one loan, there is the potential for a disruptive flood of foreclosures that would make the creditors collectively worse off. In our example, the creditors would lose $9 − $7 = $2 million in value if a flood of foreclosures were to force the firm to liquidate. If the firm had only one creditor—say, a single bank loan—then the common pool problem would not exist. If a bank had loaned the company $10 million, it would not force liquidation to get $7 million when it could keep the firm alive and eventually realize $9 million.

Chapter 11 of the Bankruptcy Act provides a solution to the common pool problem through its **automatic stay** provision. *An automatic stay, which is forced on all creditors in a bankruptcy, limits the ability of creditors to foreclose to collect their individual claims.* However, the creditors can collectively foreclose on the debtor and force liquidation.

Although bankruptcy gives the firm a chance to work out its problems without the threat of creditor foreclosure, management does not have a completely free rein over the firm's assets. First, bankruptcy law requires the debtor firm to request permission from the court to take many actions, and the law also gives creditors the right to petition the bankruptcy court to block almost any action the firm might take while in bankruptcy. Second, **fraudulent conveyance** statutes, which are part of debtor–creditor law, protect creditors from unjustified transfers of property by a firm in financial distress.

To illustrate fraudulent conveyance, suppose a holding company is contemplating bankruptcy protection for one of its subsidiaries. The holding company might be tempted to sell some or all of the subsidiary's assets to itself (the parent company) for less than the true market value. This transaction would reduce the value of the subsidiary by the difference between the true market value of its assets and the amount paid, and the loss would be borne primarily by the subsidiary's creditors. Such a transaction would be voided by the courts as a fraudulent conveyance. Note also that transactions favoring one creditor at the expense of another can be voided under the same law. For example, a transaction in which an asset is sold and the proceeds are used to pay one creditor in full at the expense of other creditors could be voided. Thus, fraudulent conveyance laws also protect creditors from each other.[5]

The second problem that is mitigated by bankruptcy law is the **holdout problem**. To illustrate this, consider again our example firm with ten creditors owed $1 million each but with assets worth only $9 million. The goal of the firm is to avoid liquidation by remedying the default. In an informal workout, this would require a reorganization plan that is agreed to by each of the ten creditors. Suppose the firm offers each creditor new debt with a face value of $850,000 in exchange for the old $1,000,000 face value debt. If each of the creditors accepted the offer, the firm could be successfully reorganized. The reorganization would leave the equity holders with some value—the market value of the equity would be $9,000,000 − 10($850,000) = $500,000. Further, the creditors would have claims worth $8.5 million, much more than the $7 million value of their claims in liquidation.

Although such an exchange offer seems to benefit all parties, it might not be accepted by the creditors. Here's why: Suppose seven of the ten creditors tender their bonds; thus, seven creditors each now have claims with a face value of $850,000 each, or $5,950,000 in total, while the three creditors that did not tender their bonds each still have a claim with a face value of $1 million. The total face value of the debt at this point is $8,950,000, which is less than the $9 million value of the firm. In this situation, the three holdout creditors would receive the full face value of their debt. However, this probably would not happen, because: (1) all of the creditors would be sophisticated enough to realize this could happen, and (2) each creditor would want to be one of the three holdouts that gets paid in full. Thus, it is likely that none of the creditors would accept the offer. The holdout problem makes it difficult to restructure the firm's debts. Again, if the firm had a single creditor, there would be no holdout problem.

The holdout problem is mitigated in bankruptcy proceedings by the bankruptcy court's ability to lump creditors into classes. Each class is considered to have accepted a reorganization plan if two-thirds of the amount of debt and one-half the number of claimants vote for the plan, and the plan will be approved by the court if it is deemed to be "fair and equitable" to the dissenting parties. This procedure, in which the court mandates a reorganization plan in spite of dissent, is called a **cramdown**, because the court crams the plan down the throats of the dissenters. The ability of the court to force acceptance of a reorganization plan greatly reduces the incentive for creditors to hold out. Thus, in our example, if the reorganization plan offered each creditor a new claim worth $850,000 in face value along with information that each creditor would probably receive only $700,000 under the liquidation alternative, then reorganization would have a good chance of success.

It is easier for a firm with few creditors to reorganize informally than it is for a firm with many creditors. A 1990 study examined 169 publicly traded firms that experienced severe financial distress from 1978 to 1987.[6] About half of the

---

5. The bankruptcy code requires that all transactions undertaken by the firm in the 6 months prior to a bankruptcy filing be reviewed by the court for fraudulent conveyance, and the review can go back as far as 3 years.

6. See Stuart Gilson, Kose John, and Larry Lang, "Troubled Debt Restructurings: An Empirical Study of Private Reorganization of Firms in Default," *Journal of Financial Economics,* October 1990, pp. 315–354.

firms reorganized without filing for bankruptcy, while the other half were forced to reorganize in bankruptcy. The firms that reorganized without filing for bankruptcy owed most of their debt to a few banks and had fewer creditors. Generally, bank debt can be reorganized outside of bankruptcy, but a publicly traded bond issue held by thousands of individual bondholders makes reorganization difficult.

Filing for bankruptcy under Chapter 11 has several other features that help the bankrupt firm.

1. Interest and principal payments, including interest on delayed payments, may be delayed without penalty until a reorganization plan is approved, and the plan itself may call for even further delays. This permits cash generated from operations to be used to sustain operations rather than be paid to creditors.
2. The firm is permitted to issue **debtor-in-possession (DIP) financing**. DIP financing enhances the ability of the firm to borrow funds for short-term liquidity purposes, because such loans are, under the law, senior to all previous unsecured debt.
3. The debtor firm's managers are given the exclusive right for 120 days after filing for bankruptcy protection to submit a reorganization plan, plus another 60 days to obtain agreement on the plan from the affected parties. The court may also extend these dates up to 18 months. After management's first right to submit a plan has expired, any party to the proceedings may propose its own reorganization plan.

Under the early bankruptcy laws, most formal reorganization plans were guided by the **absolute priority doctrine**.[7] This doctrine holds that creditors should be compensated for their claims in a rigid hierarchical order and that senior claims must be paid in full before junior claims can receive even a dime. If there were any chance that a delay would lead to losses by senior creditors, then the firm would be shut down and liquidated. However, an alternative position, the **relative priority doctrine**, holds that more flexibility should be allowed in a reorganization and that a balanced consideration should be given to all claimants. The current law represents a movement away from absolute priority toward relative priority.

The primary role of the bankruptcy court in a reorganization is to determine the **fairness** and the **feasibility** of the proposed plan of reorganization. The basic doctrine of fairness states that claims must be recognized in the order of their legal and contractual priority. Feasibility means that there is a reasonable chance that the reorganized company will be viable. Carrying out the concepts of fairness and feasibility in a reorganization involves the following steps:

1. Future sales must be estimated.
2. Operating conditions must be analyzed so that future earnings and cash flows can be predicted.
3. The appropriate capitalization rate must be determined.

---

7. For more on absolute priority, see Lawrence A. Weiss, "The Bankruptcy Code and Violations of Absolute Priority," *Journal of Applied Corporate Finance,* Summer 1991, pp. 71–78; William Beranek, Robert Boehmer, and Brooke Smith, "Much Ado about Nothing: Absolute Priority Deviations in Chapter 11," *Financial Management,* Autumn 1996, pp. 102–109; and Allan C. Eberhart, William T. Moore, and Rodney Roenfeldt, "Security Pricing and Deviations from the Absolute Priority Rule in Bankruptcy Proceedings," *Journal of Finance,* December 1990, pp. 1457–1469.

4. This capitalization rate must then be applied to the estimated cash flows to obtain an estimate of the company's value.[8]
5. An appropriate capital structure for the company after it emerges from Chapter 11 must be determined.
6. The reorganized firm's securities must be allocated to the various claimants in a fair and equitable manner.

The primary test of feasibility in a reorganization is whether the fixed charges after reorganization will be adequately covered by earnings. Adequate coverage generally requires an improvement in earnings, a reduction of fixed charges, or both. Among the actions that must generally be taken are the following:

1. Debt maturities are usually lengthened, interest rates may be lowered, and some debt is usually converted into equity.
2. When the quality of management has been substandard, a new team must be given control of the company.
3. If inventories have become obsolete or depleted, they must be replaced.
4. Sometimes the plant and equipment must be modernized before the firm can operate and compete successfully.
5. Reorganization may also require an improvement in production, marketing, advertising, and/or other functions.
6. It is sometimes necessary to develop new products or markets to enable the firm to move from areas where economic trends are poor into areas with more potential for growth.
7. Labor unions must agree to accept lower wages and less restrictive work rules. This was a major issue for United Airlines in 2003 as it attempted to emerge from Chapter 11 bankruptcy protection. By threatening liquidation, UAL was able to squeeze a $6.6 billion reduction in payroll costs from its pilots over 6 years and another $2.6 billion from its ground-crew workers. This wasn't enough, though, and UAL didn't emerge from bankruptcy for another 3 years.

These actions usually require at least some new money, so most reorganization plans include new investors who are willing to put up capital.

It might appear that stockholders have very little to say in a bankruptcy situation in which the firm's assets are worth less than the face value of its debt. Under the absolute priority rule, stockholders in such a situation should get nothing of value under a reorganization plan. In fact, however, stockholders may be able to extract some of the firm's value. This occurs because: (1) stockholders generally continue to control the firm during the bankruptcy proceedings, (2) stockholders have the first right (after management's 120-day window) to file a reorganization plan, and (3) for the creditors, developing a plan and taking it through the courts would be expensive and time-consuming. Given this situation, creditors may support a plan under which they are not paid off in full and where the old stockholders

---

8. Several different approaches can be used to estimate a company's value. Market-determined multiples such as the price/earnings ratio, which are obtained from an analysis of comparable firms, can be applied to some measure of the company's earnings or cash flow. Alternatively, discounted cash flow techniques may be used. The key point here is that fairness requires the value of a company facing reorganization to be estimated so that potential offers can be evaluated rationally by the bankruptcy court.

will control the reorganized company, because the creditors want to get the problem behind them and to get some money in the near future.

25-5a Illustration of a Reorganization

Reorganization procedures may be illustrated with an example involving the Columbia Software Company, a regional firm that specializes in selling, installing, and servicing accounting software for small businesses.[9] Table 25-2 gives Columbia's balance sheet as of March 31, 2015. The company had been suffering losses running to $2.5 million a year, and (as the following discussion will make clear) the asset values in the balance sheet were overstated relative to their market values. The firm was *insolvent*, which means that the book values of its liabilities were greater than the market values of its assets, so it filed a petition with a federal court for reorganization

TABLE 25-2	Columbia Software Company: Balance Sheet as of March 31, 2015 (Millions of Dollars)
Assets	
Current assets	$ 3.50
Net fixed assets	12.50
Other assets	0.70
Total assets	$ 16.70
Liabilities and Equity	
Accounts payable	$ 1.00
Accrued taxes	0.25
Notes payable	0.25
Other current liabilities	1.75
7.5% first-mortgage bonds, due 2023	6.00
9% subordinated debentures, due 2018[a]	7.00
Total liabilities	$ 16.25
Common stock ($1 par)	1.00
Paid-in capital	3.45
Retained earnings	(4.00)
Total liabilities and equity	$ 16.70

[a]The debentures are subordinated to the notes payable.

9. This example is based on an actual reorganization, although the company name has been changed and the numbers have been changed slightly to simplify the analysis.

under Chapter 11. Management filed a plan of reorganization with the court on June 13, 2015. The plan was subsequently submitted for review by the SEC.[10]

The plan concluded that the company could not be internally reorganized and that the only feasible solution would be to combine Columbia with a larger, nationwide software company. Accordingly, management solicited the interest of a number of software companies. Late in July 2015, Moreland Software showed an interest in Columbia. On August 3, 2015, Moreland made a formal proposal to take over Columbia's $6 million of 7.5% first-mortgage bonds, to pay the $250,000 in taxes owed by Columbia, and to provide 40,000 shares of Moreland common stock to satisfy the remaining creditor claims. The Moreland stock had a market price of $75 per share, so the value of the stock was $3 million. Thus, Moreland was offering $3 million of stock plus assuming $6 million of loans and $250,000 of taxes—a total of $9.25 million for assets that had a book value of $16.7 million.

Moreland's plan is shown in Table 25-3. As in most Chapter 11 plans, the secured creditors' claims are paid in full (in this case, the mortgage bonds are taken over by Moreland Software). However, the total remaining unsecured claims equal $10 million against only $3 million of Moreland stock. Thus, each unsecured creditor would be entitled to receive 30% before the adjustment for subordination. Before this adjustment, holders of the notes payable would receive 30% of their

TABLE 25-3	Columbia Software Company: Reorganization Plan	
Senior Claims		
Taxes	$ 250,000	Paid off by Moreland
Mortgage bonds	$6,000,000	Assumed by Moreland

The reorganization plan for the remaining $10 million of liabilities, based on 40,000 shares at a price of $75 for a total market value of $3 million, or 30% of the remaining liabilities, is as follows:

Junior Claims (1)	Original Amount (2)	30% of Claim Amount (3)	Claim after Subordination (4)	Number of Shares of Common Stock (5)	Percentage of Original Claim Received (6)
Notes payable	$ 250,000	$ 75,000	$ 250,000[a]	3,333	100%
Unsecured creditors	2,750,000	825,000	825,000	11,000	30
Subordinated debentures	7,000,000	2,100,000	1,925,000[a]	25,667	28
	$10,000,000	$3,000,000	$3,000,000	40,000	30

[a]Because the debentures are subordinated to the notes payable, $250,000 − $75,000 = $175,000 must be redistributed from the debentures to the notes payable; this leaves a claim of $2,100,000 − $175,000 = $1,925,000 for the debentures.

---

10. Reorganization plans must be submitted to the Securities and Exchange Commission (SEC) if: (1) the securities of the debtor are publicly held and (2) total indebtedness exceeds $3 million. However, in recent years the only bankruptcy cases that the SEC has become involved in are those that set precedent or involve issues of national interest.

$250,000 claim, or $75,000 in stock. However, the debentures are subordinated to the notes payable, so an additional $175,000 must be allocated to notes payable (see footnote a in Table 25-3). In Column 5, the dollar claims of each class of debt are restated in terms of the number of shares of Moreland common stock received by each class of unsecured creditors. Finally, Column 6 shows the percentage of the original claim that each group received. Of course, both the taxes and the secured creditors were paid off in full, while the stockholders received nothing.[11]

The bankruptcy court first evaluated the proposal from the standpoint of fairness. The court began by considering the value of Columbia Software as estimated by the unsecured creditors' committee and by a subgroup of debenture holders. After discussions with various experts, one group had arrived at estimated post-reorganization sales of $25 million per year. It further estimated that the profit margin on sales would equal 6%, thus producing estimated future annual earnings of $1.5 million.

This subgroup analyzed price/earnings ratios for comparable companies and arrived at 8 times future earnings for a capitalization factor. Multiplying 8 by $1.5 million gave an indicated equity value of the company of $12 million. This value was 4 times that of the 40,000 shares of Moreland stock offered for the remainder of the company. Thus, the subgroup concluded that the plan for reorganization did not meet the test of fairness. Note that, under both Moreland's plan and the subgroup's plan, the holders of common stock were to receive nothing, which is one of the risks of ownership, while the holders of the first-mortgage bonds were to be assumed by Moreland, which amounts to being paid in full.

The bankruptcy judge examined management's plan for feasibility, observing that in the reorganization Moreland Software would take over Columbia's properties. The court judged that the direction and aid that Moreland could offer would remedy the deficiencies that had troubled Columbia. Whereas the debt/assets ratio of Columbia Software had become unbalanced, Moreland had only a moderate amount of debt. After consolidation, Moreland would still have a relatively low 27% debt ratio.

Moreland's net income before interest and taxes had been running at a level of approximately $15 million. The interest on its long-term debt after the merger would be $1.5 million and, taking short-term borrowings into account, would total a maximum of $2 million per year. The $15 million in earnings before interest and taxes would therefore provide an interest charge coverage of 7.5 times, exceeding the norm of 5 times for the industry.

Note that the question of feasibility would have been irrelevant if Moreland had offered $3 million in cash (rather than in stock) and payment of the bonds (rather than assuming them). It is the court's responsibility to protect the interests of Columbia's creditors. Because the creditors are being forced to take common stock or bonds guaranteed by another firm, the law requires the court to look into the feasibility of the transaction. However, if Moreland had made a cash offer, then the feasibility of its own operation after the transaction would not have been a concern.

Moreland Software was told of the subgroup's analysis and concern over the fairness of the plan. Further, Moreland was asked to increase the number of

---

11. We do not show it, but $365,000 of fees for Columbia's attorneys and $123,000 of fees for the creditors' committee lawyers were also deducted. The current assets shown in Table 25-2 were net of these fees. Creditors joke (often bitterly) about the "lawyers first" rule in payouts in bankruptcy cases. It is often said, with much truth, that the only winners in bankruptcy cases are the attorneys.

shares it offered. Moreland refused, and no other company offered to acquire Columbia. Because no better offer could be obtained and the only alternative to the plan was liquidation (with an even lower realized value), Moreland's proposal was ultimately accepted by the creditors despite some disagreement with the valuation.

One interesting aspect of this case concerned an agency conflict between Columbia's old stockholders and its management. Columbia's management knew when it filed for bankruptcy that the company was probably worth less than the amount of its debt and hence that stockholders would probably receive nothing. Indeed, that situation did materialize. If management has a primary responsibility to the stockholders, then why would it file for bankruptcy knowing that the stockholders would receive nothing? In the first place, management did not know for certain that stockholders would receive nothing. But they were certain that, if they did not file for bankruptcy protection, then creditors would foreclose on the company's property and shut the company down, which would surely lead to liquidation and a total loss to stockholders. Second, if the company were liquidated, then managers and workers would lose their jobs and the managers would have a black mark on their records. Finally, Columbia's managers thought (correctly) that there was nothing they could do to protect the stockholders, so they might as well do what was best for the workforce, the creditors, and themselves—and that meant realizing the most value possible for the company's assets.

Some of the stockholders felt betrayed by management—they thought management should have taken more heroic steps to protect them, regardless of the cost to other parties. One stockholder suggested management should have sold off assets, taken the cash to Las Vegas, and rolled the dice. Then, if they won, they should have paid off the debt and had something left for stockholders, leaving debtholders holding the bag if they lost. Actually, management had done something a bit like this in the year preceding the bankruptcy. Management realized the company was floundering, was likely to sink under its current operating plan, and that only a "big winner" project would save the company. Hence they took on several risky, "bet the company" projects with negative expected NPVs but at least some chance for high profits. Unfortunately, those projects did not work out.

25-5b **Prepackaged Bankruptcies**

One type of reorganization combines the advantages of both the informal workout and formal Chapter 11 reorganization. This hybrid is called a **prepackaged bankruptcy**, or **pre-pack**.[12]

In an informal workout, a debtor negotiates a restructuring with its creditors. Even though complex workouts typically involve corporate officers, lenders, lawyers, and investment bankers, workouts are still less expensive and less

---

12. For more information on prepackaged bankruptcies, see John J. McConnell and Henri Servaes, "The Economics of Pre-Packaged Bankruptcy," *Journal of Applied Corporate Finance,* Summer 1991, pp. 93–97; Brian L. Betker, "An Empirical Examination of Prepackaged Bankruptcy," *Financial Management,* Spring 1995, pp. 3–18; Sris Chatterjee, Upinder S. Dhillon, and Gabriel G. Ramirez, "Resolution of Financial Distress: Debt Restructurings via Chapter 11, Prepackaged Bankruptcies, and Workouts," *Financial Management,* Spring 1996, pp. 5–18; and John J. McConnell, Ronald C. Lease, and Elizabeth Tashjian, "Prepacks as a Mechanism for Resolving Financial Distress," *Journal of Applied Corporate Finance,* Winter 1996, pp. 99–106.

damaging to reputations than are Chapter 11 reorganizations. In a prepackaged bankruptcy, the debtor firm gets all, or most, of the creditors to agree to the reorganization plan *prior* to filing for bankruptcy. Then, a reorganization plan is filed along with, or shortly after, the bankruptcy petition. If enough creditors have signed on before the filing, a cramdown can be used to bring reluctant creditors along.

A logical question arises: Why would a firm that can arrange an informal reorganization want to file for bankruptcy? The three primary advantages of a prepackaged bankruptcy are: (1) reduction of the holdout problem, (2) preserving creditors' claims, and (3) taxes. Perhaps the biggest benefit of a prepackaged bankruptcy is the reduction of the holdout problem, because a bankruptcy filing permits a cramdown that would otherwise be impossible. By eliminating holdouts, bankruptcy forces all creditors in each class to participate on a pro rata basis, which preserves the relative value of all claimants. Also, filing for formal bankruptcy can at times have positive tax implications. First, in an informal reorganization in which the debtholders trade debt for equity, if the original equity holders end up with less than 50% ownership then the company loses its accumulated tax losses. In formal bankruptcy, in contrast, the firm may get to keep its loss carryforwards. Second, in a workout, when (say) debt worth $1,000 is exchanged for debt worth $500, the reduction in debt of $500 is considered to be taxable income to the corporation. However, if this same situation occurs in a Chapter 11 reorganization, the difference is not treated as taxable income.[13]

All in all, prepackaged bankruptcies make sense in many situations. If sufficient agreement can be reached among creditors through informal negotiations, a subsequent filing can solve the holdout problem and result in favorable tax treatment. For these reasons, the number of prepackaged bankruptcies has grown dramatically in recent years.

25-5c **Reorganization Time and Expense**

The time, expense, and headaches involved in a reorganization are almost beyond comprehension. Even in a small bankruptcy, such as one with assets valued between $2 million and $5 million, many people and groups are involved: lawyers representing the company, the U.S. Bankruptcy Trustee, each class of secured creditor, the general creditors as a group, tax authorities, and the stockholders if they are upset with management. There are time limits within which things are supposed to be done, but the process generally takes at least a year and usually much longer. The company must be given time to file its plan, and creditor groups must be given time to study and seek clarifications to it and then file counterplans, to which the company must respond. Also, different creditor classes often disagree among themselves as to how much each class should receive, and hearings must be held to resolve such conflicts.

Management will want to remain in business, whereas some well-secured creditors may want the company liquidated as quickly as possible. Often, some party's plan will involve selling the business to another concern, as was the case with

---

13. Note that in both tax situations—loss carryforwards and debt value reductions—favorable tax treatment can be available in workouts if the firm is deemed to be legally insolvent—that is, if the market value of its assets is demonstrated to be less than the face value of its liabilities.

Columbia Software in our earlier example. Obviously, it can take months to seek out and negotiate with potential merger candidates.

The typical bankruptcy case takes about 2 years from the time the company files for protection under Chapter 11 until the final reorganization plan is approved or rejected. While all of this is going on, the company's business suffers. Sales certainly won't be helped, key employees may leave, and the remaining employees will be worrying about their jobs rather than concentrating on their work. Further, management will be spending much of its time on the bankruptcy rather than running the business, and it won't be able to take any significant action without court approval, which requires filing a formal petition with the court and giving all parties involved a chance to respond.

Even if its operations do not suffer, the company's assets surely will be reduced by its own legal fees and the required court and trustee costs. Good bankruptcy lawyers charge from $200 to $400 or more per hour, depending on the location, so those costs are not trivial. The creditors also will be incurring legal costs. Indeed, the sound of all of those meters ticking at $400 or so an hour in a slow-moving hearing can be deafening.

Note that creditors also lose the time value of their money. A creditor with a $100,000 claim and a 10% opportunity cost who ends up getting $50,000 after 2 years would have been better off settling for $41,500 initially. When the creditor's legal fees, executive time, and general aggravation are taken into account, it might make sense to settle for $25,000 or even $20,000.

Both the troubled company and its creditors know the drawbacks of formal bankruptcy, or their lawyers will inform them. Armed with knowledge of how bankruptcy works, management may be in a strong position to persuade creditors to accept a workout that may seem to be unfair and unreasonable. Or, if a Chapter 11 case has already begun, creditors may at some point agree to settle just to stop the bleeding.

One final point should be made before closing this section. In most reorganization plans, creditors with claims of less than $1,000 are paid off in full. Paying off these "nuisance claims" does not cost much money, and it saves time and gets votes to support the plan.[14]

SELF TEST

Define the following terms: common pool problem, holdout problem, automatic stay, cramdown, fraudulent conveyance, absolute priority doctrine, relative priority doctrine, fairness, feasibility, debtor-in-possession financing, and prepackaged bankruptcy.

What are the advantages of a formal reorganization under Chapter 11?

What are some recent trends regarding absolute versus relative priority doctrines?

How do courts assess the fairness and feasibility of reorganization plans?

Why have prepackaged bankruptcies become so popular in recent years?

---

14. For more information on bankruptcy costs, see Daryl M. Guffey and William T. Moore, "Direct Bankruptcy Costs: Evidence from the Trucking Industry," *The Financial Review*, May 1991, pp. 223–235.

25-6 **Liquidation in Bankruptcy**

If a company is "too far gone" to be reorganized, then it must be liquidated. Liquidation should occur when the business is worth more dead than alive, or when the possibility of restoring it to financial health is remote and the creditors are exposed to a high risk of greater loss if operations are continued. Earlier we discussed assignment, which is an informal liquidation procedure. Now we consider **liquidation in bankruptcy**, which is carried out under the jurisdiction of a federal bankruptcy court.

Chapter 7 of the Federal Bankruptcy Reform Act of 1978 deals with liquidation. It: (1) provides safeguards against fraud by the debtor, (2) provides for an equitable distribution of the debtor's assets among the creditors, and (3) allows insolvent debtors to discharge all their obligations and thus be able to start new businesses unhampered by the burdens of prior debt. However, formal liquidation is time-consuming and costly, and it extinguishes the business.

The distribution of assets in a liquidation under Chapter 7 is governed by the following priority of claims[15]:

1. *Past-due property tax liens.*[16]
2. *Secured creditors, who are entitled to the proceeds of the sale of specific property pledged for a lien or a mortgage.* If the proceeds from the sale of the pledged property do not fully satisfy a secured creditor's claim, the remaining balance is treated as a general creditor claim (see Item 10 below).[17]
3. *Legal fees and other expenses to administer and operate the bankrupt firm.* These costs include legal fees incurred in trying to reorganize.
4. *Expenses incurred after an involuntary case has begun but before a trustee is appointed.*
5. *Wages due workers if earned within 6 months prior to the filing of the petition for bankruptcy.* The amount of wages is limited to $10,000 per employee.
6. *Claims for unpaid contributions to employee pension plans that should have been paid within 6 months prior to filing.* These claims, plus wages in Item 5, may not exceed the limit of $10,000 per wage earner.
7. *Unsecured claims for customer deposits.* These claims are limited to a maximum of $1,800 per individual.
8. *Taxes due to federal, state, county, and other government agencies.*
9. *Unfunded pension plan liabilities.* These liabilities have a claim above that of the general creditors for an amount up to 30% of the common and preferred

---

15. See www.law.cornell.edu/uscode/text/11/507 for a complete listing of the priority of claims.
16. See www.law.cornell.edu/uscode/text/11/724 for the priority rules regarding liens.
17. When a firm or individual who goes bankrupt has a bank loan, the bank will attach any deposit balances. The loan agreement may stipulate that the bank has a first-priority claim on any deposits. If so, then the deposits are used to offset all or part of the bank loan—in legal terms, "the right of offset." In this case, the bank will not have to share the deposits with other creditors. Loan contracts often designate compensating balances as security against a loan. Even if the bank has no explicit claim against deposits, the bank will attach the deposits and hold them for the general body of creditors, including the bank itself. Without an explicit statement in the loan agreement, the bank does not receive preferential treatment with regard to attached deposits.

equity, and any remaining unfunded pension claims rank with the general creditors.[18]

10. *General, or unsecured, creditors.* Holders of trade credit, unsecured loans, the unsatisfied portion of secured loans, and debenture bonds are classified as general creditors. Holders of subordinated debt also fall into this category, but they must turn over required amounts to the senior debt.

11. *Preferred stockholders.* These stockholders can receive an amount up to the par value of their stock.

12. *Common stockholders.* These stockholders receive any remaining funds.[19]

To illustrate how this priority system works, consider the balance sheet of Whitman Inc., shown in Table 25-4. Assets have a book value of $90 million. The claims are shown on the right-hand side of the balance sheet. Note that the debentures are subordinated to the notes payable to banks. Whitman filed for bankruptcy under Chapter 11, but because no fair and feasible reorganization could be arranged, the trustee is liquidating the firm under Chapter 7.

The assets as reported in the balance sheet are greatly overstated; they are, in fact, worth less than half the $90 million that is shown. The following amounts are realized on liquidation:

From sale of current assets	$28,000,000
From sale of fixed assets	5,000,000
Total receipts	$33,000,000

The distribution of proceeds from the liquidation is shown in Table 25-5. The first-mortgage holders receive the $5 million in net proceeds from the sale of fixed property, leaving $28 million available to the remaining creditors, including a $1 million unsatisfied claim of the first-mortgage holders. Next are the fees and expenses of administering the bankruptcy, which are typically about 20% of gross proceeds (including the bankrupt firm's own legal fees); in this example, they are assumed to be $6 million. Next in priority are wages due workers, which total $700,000, and taxes due, which amount to $1.3 million. Thus far, the total amount

---

18. Pension plan liabilities have a significant bearing on bankruptcy settlements. As we discuss in *Web Chapter 30*, pension plans may be funded or unfunded. With a *funded* plan, the firm makes cash payments to an insurance company or to a trustee (generally a bank), which then uses these funds (and the interest earned on them) to pay retirees' pensions. With an *unfunded* plan, the firm is obligated to make payments to retirees, but it does not provide cash in advance. Many plans are actually partially funded—some money has been paid in advance but not enough to provide full pension benefits to all employees.

   If a firm goes bankrupt, the funded part of the pension plan remains intact and is available for retirees. Prior to 1974, employees had no explicit claims for unfunded pension liabilities, but under the Employees' Retirement Income Security Act of 1974 (ERISA), an amount up to 30% of the equity (common and preferred) is earmarked for employees' pension plans and has a priority over the general creditors, with any remaining pension claims having status equal to that of the general creditors. This means, in effect, that the funded portion of a bankrupt firm's pension plan is completely secured, whereas the unfunded portion ranks just above the general creditors. Obviously, unfunded pension liabilities should be of great concern to a firm's unsecured creditors.

19. Note that if different classes of common stock have been issued, then differential priorities may exist in stockholder claims.

TABLE 25-4	Whitman Inc.: Balance Sheet at Liquidation (Millions of Dollars)		
Current assets	$80.0	Accounts payable	$20.0
Net fixed assets	10.0	Notes payable (to banks)	10.0
		Accrued wages (1,400 @ $500)	0.7
		Federal taxes	1.0
		State and local taxes	0.3
		Current liabilities	$32.0
		First mortgage	6.0
		Second mortgage	1.0
		Subordinated debentures[a]	8.0
		Total long-term debt	$15.0
		Preferred stock	2.0
		Common stock	26.0
		Paid-in capital	4.0
		Retained earnings	11.0
		Total equity	$43.0
Total assets	$90.0	Total liabilities and equity	$90.0

[a]The debentures are subordinated to the notes payable.

of claims paid from the $33 million received from the asset sale is $13 million, leaving $20 million for the general creditors. In this example, we assume there are no claims for unpaid benefit plans or unfunded pension liabilities.

The claims of the general creditors total $40 million. Because $20 million is available, claimants will be allocated 50% of their claims initially, as shown in Column 3. However, the subordination adjustment requires that the subordinated debentures turn over to the notes payable all amounts received until the notes are satisfied. In this situation, the claim of the notes payable is $10 million but only $5 million is available; the deficiency is therefore $5 million. After transfer of $4 million from the subordinated debentures, there remains a deficiency of $1 million on the notes; this amount will remain unsatisfied.

Note that 90% of the bank claim is satisfied, whereas a maximum of 50% of other unsecured claims will be satisfied. These figures illustrate the usefulness of the subordination provision to the security to which the subordination is made.

Because no other funds remain, the claims of the holders of preferred and common stocks, as well as the subordinated debentures, are completely wiped out.

TABLE 25-5   Whitman Inc.: Distribution of Liquidation Proceeds (Millions of Dollars)

Distribution to Priority Claimants

Proceeds from the sale of assets	$33.0
Less:	
1. First mortgage (paid from the sale of fixed assets)	5.0
2. Fees and expenses of bankruptcy	6.0
3. Wages due to workers within 3 months of bankruptcy	0.7
4. Taxes due to federal, state, and local governments	1.3
Funds available for distribution to general creditors	$20.0

Distribution to General Creditors

General Creditors' Claims (1)	Amount of Claim[a] (2)	Pro Rata Distribution[b] (3)	Distribution after Subordination Adjustment[c] (4)	Percentage of Original Claim Received[d] (5)
Unsatisfied portion of first mortgage	$ 1.0	$ 0.5	$ 0.5	92%
Second mortgage	1.0	0.5	0.5	50
Notes payable (to banks)	10.0	5.0	9.0	90
Accounts payable	20.0	10.0	10.0	50
Subordinated debentures	8.0	4.0	0.0	0
Total	$40.0	$20.0	$20.0	

[a]Column 2 is the claim of each class of general creditor. Total claims equal $40.0 million.
[b]From the top section of the table, we see that $20 million is available for distribution to general creditors. Because there is $40 million worth of general creditor claims, the pro rata distribution will be $20/$40 = 0.50, or 50 cents on the dollar.
[c]The debentures are subordinate to the notes payable, so up to $5 million could be reallocated from debentures to notes payable. However, only $4 million is available to the debentures, so this entire amount is reallocated.
[d]Column 5 shows the results of dividing the Column 4 final allocation by the original claim shown in Column 2—except for the first mortgage, where the $5 million received from the sale of fixed assets is included in the calculation.

Studies of the proceeds in bankruptcy liquidations reveal that unsecured creditors receive, on the average, about 15 cents on the dollar, while common stockholders generally receive nothing.

SELF TEST

Describe briefly the priority of claims in a formal liquidation.

What is the impact of subordination on the final allocation of proceeds from liquidation?

In general, how much do unsecured creditors receive from a liquidation? How much do stockholders receive?

A NATION OF DEFAULTERS?

Big corporate bankruptcies like those of Lehman Brothers and General Motors get the headlines, but they represent a small portion of the many bankruptcies each year, as shown in the accompanying table. Most business bankruptcies are liquidations (Chapter 7) of small businesses, and they rose steadily from 2006 through 2009 and then have declined steadily since then. Although there are fewer business reorganizations than liquidations, reorganizations also increased steadily from 2006 through 2009 and have declined steadily since then, with the overall level of business bankruptcy filings now about equal to their pre-financial crisis levels.

Personal bankruptcies can be liquidations (Chapter 7) or reorganizations (Chapter 13). In a Chapter 7 bankruptcy,

an individual can keep a small amount of exempt personal property, and the nonexempt property is sold to satisfy creditors. In a Chapter 13 bankruptcy, an individual is allowed to keep nonexempt personal property but typically must repay the debt within 3 to 5 years. A change in bankruptcy laws in 2005 made it more difficult for individuals to declare bankruptcy. Personal bankruptcies increased dramatically during the lead up to and following the financial crisis, with liquidations leading the way—they have yet to recover to pre-crisis levels.

Napoleon Bonaparte reputedly scorned England as "a nation of shopkeepers." If he had been able to see current U.S. bankruptcy statistics, would he have called modern America "a nation of defaulters"?

Year	Business					Personal			
	Ch. 7	Ch. 11	Ch. 12	Ch. 13	Total	Ch. 7	Ch. 11	Ch. 13	Total
2013	22,334	7,660	395	2,727	33,212	706,499	1,320	330,899	1,038,720
2012	27,274	8,900	512	3,252	40,075	816,271	1,461	363,280	1,181,016
2011	33,698	9,772	637	3,630	47,806	958,634	1,757	402,454	1,362,847
2010	39,485	11,774	723	4,174	56,282	1,100,116	1,939	434,739	1,536,799
2009	41,962	13,683	544	4,500	60,837	1,008,870	1,506	402,462	1,412,838
2008	30,035	9,272	345	3,815	43,546	714,389	888	358,947	1,074,225
2007	18,751	5,736	376	3,412	28,322	500,613	617	321,359	822,590
2006	11,878	4,643	348	2,749	19,695	349,012	520	248,430	597,965
2005	28,006	5,923	380	4,808	39,201	1,631,011	877	407,322	2,039,214
2004	20,192	9,186	108	4,701	34,317	1,117,766	946	444,428	1,563,145

Source: **www.uscourts.gov/Statistics/BankruptcyStatistics.aspx**.

25-7 Anatomy of a Bankruptcy: Transforming the GM *Corporation* into the GM *Company*

The General Motors *Corporation* was started in 1908 and became the world's largest automobile manufacturer, a distinction it held from 1931 until 2008. Despite its size and market power, GM lost a cumulative $82 billion from 2005 until 2008 and declared bankruptcy in 2009. Several factors contributed to GM's problems, including increased international competition, high costs associated with labor contracts (especially retirement benefits), the economic slowdown that began in 2007, and senior executives that the press labeled as out of touch.

A look at GM's financial statements reveals some of the major restructuring efforts prior to the bankruptcy. During the 1980s, GM became a major player in the financial services industries, and by 2005 its financing and insurance operations had assets of $312 billion, while its automotive business had assets of $162 billion. By this measure, GM was a "bank" with an auto manufacturer and not an auto company with a "bank." To refocus on its auto businesses and raise some cash in 2006, GM cut its dividend in half and sold a 51% stake of its financing company, GMAC, reducing its non-auto assets by about $290 billion to $22 billion. GM also sold its stakes in several other auto manufacturers in 2006 and 2007, to generate cash and to focus on its primary product line. With declining sales and profits, GM also closed factories and reduced its workforce.

When GM and the United Auto Workers were unable to reach a contract agreement in 2007, the UAW called a strike. After two days, GM and the UAW reached an agreement. In exchange for a lower wage structure, GM agreed to create a trust fund (a voluntary employees' beneficiary association, called a VEBA) that would be managed by the UAW and that would fund retiree health care coverage. The liabilities associated with the retiree health care were estimated to be over $50 billion. GM agreed to put about $35 billion of assets into the VEBA (GM and the UAW assumed that the trust's $35 billion in assets would grow faster than the $50 billion in liabilities) and make the majority of its future contributions in the form of GM stock rather than cash.

GM continued to lose money. In late 2008, the CEOs of GM, Chrysler, and Ford flew to Washington in private jets to ask for government assistance. Congress was unable to agree on a plan, so the Bush administration broadened the Trouble Asset Relief Program (TARP) to include the auto industry. GM received a loan of $13.4 billion in December 2008. GMAC also received a TARP loan ($6 billion), as did Chrysler and its financial subsidiary. These loans required GM and Chrysler to submit turnaround plans to the government by February 17, 2009.[20]

A task force from the Obama administration reviewed the plans, rejected them, and gave GM and Chrysler an opportunity to revise the plans. The task force also asked for and received the resignation of Rick Wagoner, GM's CEO. In addition, the government provided loans to GM and Chrysler, loans to their suppliers (who were reluctant to keep selling to the auto companies on credit), and created a program to ensure that customer warranty claims would be honored.

GM was unable to provide a turnaround plan that was acceptable to its debtholders, suppliers, dealers, and workforce, so it filed for Chapter 11 bankruptcy protection on June 1, 2009. GM's bankruptcy petition listed its assets and liabilities as of its most recent 10-Q filing for the quarter ending March 31, 2009. It was not a pretty picture. GM listed $82 billion in assets, but more than twice that amount ($173 billion) in liabilities, including short-term debt of $26 billion, long-term debt of $29 billion, and retiree obligations of $47 billion.

---

20. For a detailed treatment of the government's involvement in GM's bankruptcy, see a paper by Thomas H. Klier and James Rubenstein, "Detroit Back from the Brink? Auto Industry Crisis and Restructuring, 2008–11," *Economic Perspectives*, 2Q/2012, pp. 35–54.

Two days after filing for bankruptcy, TARP provided an additional $30 billion; because GM had filed for bankruptcy, this loan was debtor-in-possession financing (DIP). In total, TARP provided about $50 billion in financing to GM.

On July 10, 2009, GM emerged from bankruptcy as a new company—literally! GM and its creditors agreed to sell almost all of GM's assets to a new company, to be named the General Motors Company (instead of Corporation). In return, GM's creditors and stakeholders exchanged their old claims for new claims in the new GM Company. GM now had about less than $16 billion in debt (compared to $55 before the bankruptcy) and $36 billion in retiree obligations (down from $47 billion). In addition to a much lower debt load, the bankruptcy plan called for GM to close over 10 factories, reduce the number of brands it sells, and reduce the number of its dealers.

GM emerged from bankruptcy with about $75 billion less in liabilities. What happened to all those claims? Senior secured loans and suppliers were paid in full. Subordinated bondholders received about 1/8 the face value of their bonds. The common stockholders received nothing. As for other claimants, they received common stock in the new GM. The U.S. government received about 61% of the stock, the Canadian government received 11.7%, the VEBA trust received 17.5% (instead of the cash it was originally owed), and unsecured bondholders received 10%.

GM's shares were not publicly traded until November 18, 2010, when GM sold $20.1 billion in its IPO. GM's underwriters sold an additional $3 billion of stock, for a total of $23.1 billion, which made GM's IPO the biggest ever. GM didn't raise any cash in the IPO—all the shares were sold by existing stockholders, including the U.S. government, which reduced its ownership to about 33% of GM.

GM has been profitable since the IPO, but its stock price has been volatile, at one point falling to $19 from the IPO price of $33. GM stock has since recovered and is trading at about its IPO price in May 2014. It is probably safe to say that GM and the U.S. auto industry are in better shape than in 2008, but it will probably be another decade before we know for sure whether the government intervention, bankruptcy, and IPO ultimately were successful.

What events preceded GM's bankruptcy?

What happened to the pre-bankruptcy stockholders and the claims of creditors?

SELF TEST

25-8 Other Motivations for Bankruptcy

Normally, bankruptcy proceedings do not commence until a company has become so financially weak that it cannot meet its current obligations. However, bankruptcy law also permits a company to file for bankruptcy if its financial forecasts indicate that a continuation of current conditions would lead to insolvency.

Bankruptcy law has also been used to hasten settlements in major product liability suits. The Manville asbestos case is an example. Manville was being bombarded by thousands of lawsuits, and the very existence of such huge contingent liabilities made normal operations impossible. Further, it was relatively easy to prove that: (1) if the plaintiffs won, the company would be unable to pay the full amount of the claims, (2) a larger amount of funds would be available to the claimants if the company continued to operate rather than liquidate, (3) continued operations were possible only if the suits were brought to a conclusion, and (4) a timely resolution of all the suits was impossible because of their vast number and variety. Manville filed for bankruptcy in 1982, at that time the largest U.S. bankruptcy ever. The bankruptcy statutes were used to consolidate all the suits and to reach settlements under which the plaintiffs obtained more money than they otherwise would have received, and Manville was able to stay in business. (It was acquired in 2001 by Berkshire Hathaway.) The stockholders did poorly under these plans because most of the companies' future cash flows were assigned to the plaintiffs, but even so, the stockholders probably fared better than they would have if the suits had been concluded through the jury system.

> **SELF TEST**   What are some situations other than immediate financial distress that lead firms to file for bankruptcy?

25-9 **Some Criticisms of Bankruptcy Laws**

Although bankruptcy laws exist, for the most part, to protect creditors, many critics claim that current laws are not doing what they were intended to do. Before 1978, most bankruptcies ended quickly in liquidation. Then Congress rewrote the laws, giving companies more opportunity to stay alive on the grounds that this was best for managers, employees, creditors, and stockholders. Before the reform, 90% of Chapter 11 filers were liquidated, but now that percentage is less than 80%, and the average time between filing and liquidation has almost doubled. Indeed, large public corporations with the ability to hire high-priced legal help can avoid (or at least delay) liquidation, often at the expense of creditors and shareholders.

Critics believe that bankruptcy is great for businesses these days—especially for consultants, lawyers, and investment bankers, who reap hefty fees during bankruptcy proceedings, and for managers, who continue to collect their salaries and bonuses as long as the business is kept alive. The problem, according to critics, is that bankruptcy courts allow cases to drag on too long, depleting assets that could be sold to pay off creditors and shareholders. Too often, quick resolution is impossible because bankruptcy judges are required to deal with issues such as labor disputes, pension plan funding, and environmental liability—social questions that could be solved by legislative action rather than by bankruptcy courts.

Critics contend that bankruptcy judges ought to realize that some sick companies should be allowed to die—and die quickly. Maintaining companies on life support does not serve the interests of the parties that the bankruptcy laws were designed to protect. The 2005 changes to the bankruptcy code addressed this issue by limiting to 18 months the time that management has to file a reorganization plan. Prior to the change, judges could extend this time almost indefinitely. Now, creditors may propose a plan if an acceptable plan hasn't been filed by management within 18 months.

Other critics think the entire bankruptcy system of judicial protection and supervision needs to be scrapped. Some even have proposed an auction-like procedure, where shareholders and creditors would have the opportunity to gain control of a bankrupt company by raising the cash needed to pay the bills. The rationale here is that the market is a better judge than a bankruptcy court as to whether a company is worth more dead or alive.

According to critics, what are some problems with the bankruptcy system?

SELF TEST

Summary

This chapter discussed the main issues involved in bankruptcy and financial distress in general. The key concepts are listed below.

- The fundamental issue that must be addressed when a company encounters financial distress is whether it is "worth more dead than alive"; that is, would the business be more valuable if it continued in operation or if it were liquidated and sold off in pieces?
- In the case of a fundamentally sound company whose financial difficulties appear to be temporary, creditors will frequently work directly with the company, helping it recover and reestablish itself on a sound financial basis. Such voluntary reorganization plans are called **workouts**.
- Reorganization plans usually require some type of **restructuring** of the firm's debts; this may involve an **extension**, which postpones the date of required payment of past-due obligations, and/or a **composition**, by which the creditors voluntarily reduce their claims on the debtor or the interest rate on their claims.
- When it is obvious that a firm is worth more dead than alive, informal procedures can sometimes be used to **liquidate** the firm. **Assignment** is an informal procedure for liquidating a firm, and it usually yields creditors a larger amount than they would receive in a formal bankruptcy liquidation. However, assignments are feasible only if the firm is small and its affairs are not too complex.
- Current **bankruptcy law** consists of nine chapters, designated by Arabic numbers. For businesses, the most important chapters are **Chapter 7**, which details the procedures to be followed when liquidating a firm, and **Chapter 11**, which contains procedures for formal reorganizations.
- Since the first bankruptcy laws, the **absolute priority doctrine** has guided most formal reorganization plans. This doctrine holds that creditors should be compensated for their claims in a rigid hierarchical order and that senior claims must be paid in full before junior claims can receive even a dime.
- Another position, the **relative priority doctrine**, holds that more flexibility should be allowed in a reorganization and that a balanced consideration should be given to all claimants. In recent years, there has been a shift away from absolute priority toward relative priority. The primary effect of this shift has been to delay liquidations, giving managements more time to rehabilitate companies in an effort to provide value to junior claimants.
- The primary role of the bankruptcy court in a reorganization is to determine the **fairness** and the **feasibility** of proposed plans of reorganization.
- Even if some creditors or stockholders dissent and do not accept a reorganization plan, the plan may still be approved by the court if the plan is deemed to

be "fair and equitable" to all parties. This procedure, in which the court mandates a reorganization plan in spite of dissent, is called a **cramdown**.

- A **prepackaged bankruptcy** (also called a **pre-pack**) is a hybrid type of reorganization that combines the advantages of both an informal workout and a formal Chapter 11 reorganization.
- The distribution of assets in a **liquidation** under Chapter 7 of the Bankruptcy Act is governed by a specific priority of claims.
- **Multiple discriminant analysis (MDA)** is a method to identify firms with high bankruptcy risk. We discuss MDA in *Web Extension 25A*.

Questions

25-1 Define each of the following terms:
   a. Informal restructuring; reorganization in bankruptcy
   b. Assignment; liquidation in bankruptcy; fairness; feasibility
   c. Absolute priority doctrine; relative priority doctrine
   d. Bankruptcy Reform Act of 1978; Chapter 11; Chapter 7
   e. Priority of claims in liquidation
   f. Extension; composition; workout; cramdown; prepackaged bankruptcy; holdout

25-2 Why do creditors usually accept a plan for financial rehabilitation rather than demand liquidation of the business?

25-3 Would it be a sound rule to liquidate whenever the liquidation value is above the value of the corporation as a going concern? Discuss.

25-4 Why do liquidations usually result in losses for the creditors or the owners, or both? Would partial liquidation or liquidation over a period limit their losses? Explain.

25-5 Are liquidations likely to be more common for public utility, railroad, or industrial corporations? Why or why not?

Problems   Answers Appear in Appendix B

Easy Problem 1

25-1 Liquidation
Southwestern Wear Inc. has the following balance sheet:

Current assets	$1,875,000	Accounts payable	$ 375,000
Fixed assets	1,875,000	Notes payable	750,000
		Subordinated debentures	750,000
		Total debt	$1,875,000
		Common equity	1,875,000
Total assets	$3,750,000	Total liabilities and equity	$3,750,000

The trustee's costs total $281,250, and the firm has no accrued taxes or wages. The debentures are subordinated only to the notes payable. If the firm goes bankrupt and liquidates, how much will each class of investors receive if a total of $2.5 million is received from sale of the assets?

Intermediate Problem 2

25-2 Reorganization

The Verbrugge Publishing Company's 2015 balance sheet and income statement are as follows (in millions of dollars):

Balance Sheet

Current assets	$168	Current liabilities	$ 42
Net fixed assets	153	Advance payments	78
Goodwill	15	Reserves	6
		$6 preferred stock, $112.50 par value (1,200,000 shares)	135
		$10.50 preferred stock, no par, callable at $150 (60,000 shares)	9
		Common stock, $1.50 par value (6,000,000 shares)	9
		Retained earnings	57
Total assets	$336	Total claims	$336

Income Statement

Net sales	$540.0
Operating expense	516.0
Net operating income	$ 24.0
Other income	3.0
EBT	$ 27.0
Taxes (50%)	13.5
Net income	$ 13.5
Dividends on $6 preferred	7.2
Dividends on $10.50 preferred	0.6
Income available to common stockholders	$ 5.7

Verbrugge and its creditors have agreed upon a voluntary reorganization plan. In this plan, each share of the $6 preferred will be exchanged for one share of $2.40 preferred with a par value of $37.50 plus one 8% subordinated income debenture with a par value of $75. The $10.50 preferred issue will be retired with cash.

a. Construct the projected balance sheet while assuming that reorganization takes place. Show the new preferred stock at its par value.

b. Construct the projected income statement. What is the income available to common shareholders in the proposed recapitalization?

c. *Required earnings* is defined as the amount that is just enough to meet fixed charges (debenture interest and/or preferred dividends). What are the required pre-tax earnings before and after the recapitalization?

d. How is the debt ratio affected by the reorganization? If you were a holder of Verbrugge's common stock, would you vote in favor of the reorganization? Why or why not?

Challenging Problems 3–4

25–3 **Liquidation**

At the time it defaulted on its interest payments and filed for bankruptcy, the McDaniel Mining Company had the balance sheet shown below (in thousands of dollars). The court, after trying unsuccessfully to reorganize the firm, decided that the only recourse was liquidation under Chapter 7. Sale of the fixed assets, which were pledged as collateral to the mortgage bondholders, brought in $400,000, while the current assets were sold for another $200,000. Thus, the total proceeds from the liquidation sale were $600,000. The trustee's costs amounted to $50,000; no single worker was due more than $10,000 in wages; and there were no unfunded pension plan liabilities.

Current assets	$ 400	Accounts payable	$ 50
Net fixed assets	600	Accrued taxes	40
		Accrued wages	30
		Notes payable	180
		Total current liabilities	$ 300
		First-mortgage bonds[a]	300
		Second-mortgage bonds[a]	200
		Debentures	200
		Subordinated debentures[b]	100
		Common stock	50
		Retained earnings	(150)
Total assets	$1,000	Total claims	$1,000

[a]All fixed assets are pledged as collateral to the mortgage bonds.
[b]Subordinated to notes payable only.

a. How much will McDaniel's shareholders receive from the liquidation?

b. How much will the mortgage bondholders receive?

c. Who are the other priority claimants (in addition to the mortgage bond-holders)? How much will they receive from the liquidation?

d. Who are the remaining general creditors? How much will each receive from the distribution before subordination adjustment? What is the effect of adjusting for subordination?

25–4 Liquidation

The following balance sheet represents Boles Electronics Corporation's position at the time it filed for bankruptcy (in thousands of dollars):

Cash	$ 10	Accounts payable	$ 1,600
Receivables	100	Notes payable	500
Inventories	890	Wages payable	150
		Taxes payable	50
Total current assets	$ 1,000	Total current liabilities	$ 2,300
Net plant	4,000	Mortgage bonds	2,000
Net equipment	5,000	Subordinated debentures	2,500
		Preferred stock	1,500
		Common stock	1,700
Total assets	$10,000	Total claims	$10,000

The mortgage bonds are secured by the plant but not by the equipment. The subordinated debentures are subordinated to notes payable. The firm was unable to reorganize under Chapter 11; therefore, it was liquidated under Chapter 7. The trustee, whose legal and administrative fees amounted to $200,000, sold off the assets and received the following proceeds (in thousands of dollars):

Asset	Proceeds
Plant	$1,600
Equipment	1,300
Receivables	50
Inventories	240
Total	$3,190

In addition, the firm had $10,000 in cash available for distribution. No single wage earner had more than $10,000 in claims, and there were no unfunded pension plan liabilities.

a. What is the total amount available for distribution to all claimants? What is the total of creditor and trustee claims? Will the preferred and common stockholders receive any distributions?

b. Determine the dollar distribution to each creditor and to the trustee. What percentage of each claim is satisfied?

Spreadsheet Problem

25–5 Liquidation

Start with the partial model in the file *Ch25 P05 Build a Model.xls* on the textbook's Web site. Duchon Industries had the following balance sheet at the time it defaulted on its interest payments and filed for liquidation under Chapter 7. Sale of the fixed assets, which were pledged as collateral to the mortgage bondholders, brought in $900 million, while the current assets were sold for another $401 million. Thus, the total proceeds from the liquidation sales were $1,300 million. The trustee's costs amounted to $1 million; no single worker was due more than $10,000 in wages; and there were no unfunded pension plan liabilities. Determine the amount available for distribution to shareholders and all claimants.

Duchon Industries' Balance Sheets (Millions of Dollars)

Current assets	$ 400	Accounts payable	$ 50
Net fixed assets	600	Accrued taxes	40
		Accrued wages	30
		Notes payable	180
		Total current liabilities	$ 300
		First-mortgage bonds[a]	300
		Second-mortgage bonds[a]	200
		Debentures	200
		Subordinated debentures[b]	100
		Common stock	50
		Retained earnings	(150)
Total assets	$1,000	Total claims	$1,000

[a]All fixed assets are pledged as collateral to the mortgage bonds.
[b]Subordinated to notes payable only.

MINI CASE

Kimberly MacKenzie—president of Kim's Clothes Inc., a medium-sized manufacturer of women's casual clothing—is worried. Her firm has been selling clothes to Russ Brothers Department Store for more than 10 years, and she has never experienced any problems in collecting payment for the merchandise sold. Currently, Russ Brothers owes Kim's Clothes $65,000 for spring sportswear that was delivered to the store just 2 weeks ago. Kim's concern arose from reading an article in yesterday's *Wall Street Journal* that indicated Russ Brothers was having serious financial problems. Moreover, the article stated that Russ Brothers' management was considering filing for reorganization, or even liquidation, with a federal bankruptcy court.

Kim's immediate concern is whether her firm will collect its receivables if Russ Brothers goes bankrupt. In pondering the situation, Kim has also realized that she knows nothing about the process that firms go through when they encounter severe financial distress. To learn more about bankruptcy, reorganization, and liquidation, Kim has asked Ron Mitchell, her firm's chief financial officer, to prepare a briefing on the subject for the entire board of directors. In turn, Ron has asked you, a newly hired financial analyst, to do the groundwork for the briefing by answering the following questions:

a. (1) What are the major causes of business failure?
   (2) Do business failures occur evenly over time?
   (3) Which size of firm, large or small, is more prone to business failure? Why?

b. What key issues must managers face in the financial distress process?

c. What informal remedies are available to firms in financial distress? In answering this question, define the following terms:
   (1) Workout
   (2) Restructuring
   (3) Extension
   (4) Composition
   (5) Assignment
   (6) Assignee (trustee)

d. Briefly describe U.S. bankruptcy law, including the following terms:
   (1) Chapter 11
   (2) Chapter 7
   (3) Trustee
   (4) Voluntary bankruptcy
   (5) Involuntary bankruptcy

e. What are the major differences between an informal reorganization and reorganization in bankruptcy? In answering this question, be sure to discuss the following items:
   (1) Common pool problem
   (2) Holdout problem
   (3) Automatic stay
   (4) Cramdown
   (5) Fraudulent conveyance

f. What is a prepackaged bankruptcy? Why have prepackaged bankruptcies become more popular in recent years?

g. Briefly describe the priority of claims in a Chapter 7 liquidation.

h. Assume that Russ Brothers did indeed fail, and that it had the following balance sheet when it was liquidated (in millions of dollars):

Current assets	$40.0	Accounts payable	$10.0
Net fixed assets	5.0	Notes payable (to banks)	5.0
		Accrued wages	0.3
		Federal taxes	0.5
		State and local taxes	0.2
		Current liabilities	$16.0
		First-mortgage bonds	3.0
		Second-mortgage bonds	0.5
		Subordinated debentures[a]	4.0
		Total long-term debt	$ 7.5
		Preferred stock	1.0
		Common stock	13.0
		Paid-in capital	2.0
		Retained earnings	5.5
		Total equity	$21.5
Total assets	$45.0	Total claims	$45.0

[a]The debentures are subordinated to the notes payable.

The liquidation sale resulted in the following proceeds:

From sale of current assets	$14,000,000
From sale of fixed assets	2,500,000
Total receipts	$16,500,000

For simplicity, assume there were no trustee's fees or any other claims against the liquidation proceeds. Also, assume that the mortgage bonds are secured by the entire amount of fixed assets. What would each claimant receive from the liquidation distribution?

SELECTED ADDITIONAL CASE

The following case from CengageCompose covers many of the concepts discussed in this chapter and is available at **http://compose.cengage.com.**

Klein-Brigham Series:

Case 39, "Mark X Company (B)," which examines the allocation of proceeds under bankruptcy.

Mergers and Corporate Control

Most corporate growth occurs by *internal expansion*, which takes place when a firm's existing divisions grow through normal capital budgeting activities. However, the most dramatic examples of growth result from mergers, the first topic covered in this chapter. Other actions that alter corporate control are divestitures—conditions change over time, causing firms to sell off, or divest, major divisions to other firms that can better utilize the divested assets. A *holding company* is another form of corporate control in which one corporation controls other companies by owning some, or all, of their stocks.

WEB

The textbook's Web site contains an *Excel* file that will guide you through the chapter's calculations. The file for this chapter is *Ch26 Tool Kit.xls*, and we encourage you to open the file and follow along as you read the chapter.

Beginning-of-Chapter Questions

As you read this chapter, consider how you would answer the following questions. You *should not* necessarily be able to answer the questions before you read the chapter. Rather, you should use them to get a sense of the issues covered in the chapter. After reading the chapter, you should be able to give at least partial answers to the questions, and you should be able to give better answers after the chapter has been discussed in class. Note, too, that it is often useful, when answering conceptual questions, to use hypothetical data to illustrate your answer. We illustrate the answers with an *Excel* model that is available on the textbook's Web site. Accessing the model and working through it is a useful exercise, and it provides insights that are useful when answering the questions.

1. What are **horizontal**, **vertical**, **congeneric**, and **conglomerate mergers**? Are the different types of mergers equally likely to pass muster with the Justice Department?
2. What is **synergy**? What are some factors that might lead to synergy? How is the amount of synergy in a proposed merger measured, and how is it allocated between the two firms' stockholders? Would the four types of mergers as discussed in Question 1 be equally likely to produce synergy?
3. Many companies have serious discussions about merging. Sometimes these discussions lead to mergers, sometimes not. What are some factors that should be considered and that affect the likelihood of a merger actually being completed?
4. Explain how the **market multiples method** is used to determine the value of a target firm to a potential acquirer. Give several examples of this procedure.
5. Explain how the **corporate valuation model** and the **adjusted present value (APV) method** are used to estimate the value of a target company. If someone did a complete and careful analysis of a given target using both of these methods, would they produce the same results? Explain why, under certain growth and capital structure conditions, it is better to use the APV method.

6. If you were conducting a merger analysis, would you give the multiples method or one of the DCF methods (that is, the APV or corporate valuation model) more weight in your decision? Explain.

7. Explain how **purchase accounting** is implemented in a merger. Does the accounting profession now require this method? How is any premium that the acquiring firm paid over the acquired firm's book value treated subsequent to a merger?

8. Acquisitions can have important tax consequences depending on: (a) whether the acquiring firm purchases the target's stock or just its assets, (b) whether cash or stock is used for the payment, and (c) how the acquirer records the target's assets on its books after the merger. Suppose a target's assets have a value of $50 million, but the appraised value of those assets is $80 million. The target firm is in the 20% tax bracket. Here are four possible situations:

   (1) Acquirer pays $100 million in cash for the target's stock in a tender offer and records assets at their book value.

   (2) Same as in part (1) but acquirer records assets at their appraised value.

   (3) Acquirer pays $100 million worth of stock in exchange for the target's stock.

   (4) Acquirer pays $100 million in cash to the target for its assets.

   In each situation, answer the following questions. (*Hint:* The tax situation is complicated, but Figure 26-1 would be helpful in answering these questions.)

   a. How much would the target's shareholders receive from the acquirer, and how much of that total would be taxable?

   b. How much would the target's shareholders receive from the target firm, and how much of that total would be taxable?

   c. How much in taxes would the target firm have to pay on any gains it realizes?

   d. What would the total depreciable value of the target be once it has been acquired?

26-1 Rationale for Mergers

Many reasons have been proposed by financial managers and theorists to account for the high level of U.S. merger activity. The primary motives behind corporate **mergers** are presented in this section.[1]

26-1a Synergy

The primary motivation for most mergers is to increase the value of the combined enterprise. If Companies A and B merge to form Company C and if C's value exceeds that of A and B taken together, then **synergy** is said to exist, and such a merger should be beneficial to both A's and B's stockholders.[2] Synergistic effects can arise from five sources: (1) *operating economies*, which result from economies of scale in management, marketing, production, or distribution; (2) *financial economies*, including lower transaction costs and better coverage by security analysts; (3) *tax effects*, in which case the combined enterprise pays less in taxes than the separate firms would

---

1. As we use the term, *merger* means any combination that forms one economic unit from two or more previous ones. For legal purposes, there are distinctions among the various ways these combinations can occur, but our focus is on the fundamental economic and financial aspects of mergers.

2. If synergy exists, then the whole is greater than the sum of the parts. Synergy is also called the "2 plus 2 equals 5 effect." The distribution of the synergistic gain between A's and B's stockholders is determined by negotiation. This point is discussed later in the chapter.

pay; (4) *differential efficiency*, which implies that the management of one firm is more efficient and that the weaker firm's assets will be more productive after the merger; and (5) *increased market power* due to reduced competition. Operating and financial economies are socially desirable, as are mergers that increase managerial efficiency, but mergers that reduce competition are socially undesirable and illegal.[3]

Expected synergies are not always realized. For example, when AOL acquired Time Warner, it believed that Time Warner's extensive content library could be sold to AOL's Internet subscribers and that AOL subscribers could be shifted over to Time Warner's cable system. When the merger was announced, the new management estimated that such synergies would increase operating income by $1 billion per year. However, things didn't work out as expected, and in 2002 Time Warner had to write off about $100 billion in lost value associated with the merger.

Merrill Lynch (ML) was facing bankruptcy in late 2008, so federal officials encouraged Bank of America (BoA) to save ML from bankruptcy by acquiring it, creating one of the world's largest (if not the largest) financial conglomerate. But BoA tried to back out of the deal as it learned more about ML's situation. Under pressure from the government, BoA went through with the merger and almost immediately reported over $21 billion in associated losses.

As these examples illustrate, often it is blemishes, not synergies, that materialize after a merger.

26-1b **Tax Considerations**

Tax considerations have stimulated a number of mergers. For example, a profitable firm in the highest tax bracket could acquire a firm with large accumulated tax losses. These losses could then be turned into immediate tax savings rather than carried forward and used in the future.[4]

Also, mergers can serve as a way of minimizing taxes when disposing of excess cash. For example, if a firm has a shortage of internal investment opportunities compared with its free cash flow, it could: (1) pay an extra dividend, (2) invest in marketable securities, (3) repurchase its own stock, or (4) purchase another firm. If it pays an extra dividend, its stockholders would have to pay immediate taxes on the distribution. Marketable securities often provide a good temporary parking place for money, but they generally earn a rate of return less than that required by stockholders. A stock repurchase might result in a capital gain for the selling stockholders. However, using surplus cash to acquire another firm would avoid all these problems, and this has motivated a number of mergers. Still, as we discuss later, the tax savings are often less than the premium paid in the acquisition. Thus, mergers motivated only by tax considerations often reduce the acquiring shareholders' wealth.

---

3. In the 1880s and 1890s, many mergers occurred in the United States, and some of them were directed toward gaining market power rather than increasing efficiency. As a result, Congress passed a series of acts designed to ensure that mergers are not used to reduce competition. The principal acts include the Sherman Act (1890), the Clayton Act (1914), and the Celler Act (1950). These acts make it illegal for firms to combine if the combination tends to lessen competition. The acts are enforced by the Antitrust Division of the Justice Department and by the Federal Trade Commission.

4. Mergers undertaken only to use accumulated tax losses would probably be challenged by the IRS. In recent years, Congress has made it increasingly difficult for firms to pass along tax savings after mergers. Internal Revenue Code Section 382 spells out the limitations on the use of loss carryforwards in a merger.

26-1c **Purchase of Assets below Their Replacement Cost**

Sometimes a firm will be touted as an acquisition candidate because the cost of replacing its assets is considerably higher than its market value. This is especially true in the natural resources industry; for example, an oil company's reserves might be worth more on paper than the company's stock. (Of course, converting paper value to monetary value isn't always as easy as it sounds.)

26-1d **Diversification**

Managers often cite diversification as a reason for mergers. They contend that diversification helps stabilize a firm's earnings and thus benefits its owners. Stabilization of earnings is certainly beneficial to employees, suppliers, and customers, but its value to stockholders is less certain. Why should Firm A acquire Firm B to stabilize earnings when stockholders can simply buy the stocks of both firms? Indeed, research suggests that in most cases diversification does not increase the firm's value. In fact, many studies find that diversified firms are worth significantly *less* than the sum of their individual parts.[5]

Of course, if you were the owner-manager of a closely held firm, it might be nearly impossible to sell part of your stock to diversify. Also, selling your stock would probably lead to a large capital gains tax. So, a diversification merger might be the best way to achieve personal diversification for a privately held firm.

26-1e **Managers' Personal Incentives**

Financial economists like to think that business decisions are based only on economic considerations, especially maximization of firms' values. However, many business decisions are based more on managers' personal motivations than on economic analyses. Business leaders like power, and more power is attached to running a larger corporation than a smaller one. Most likely, no executive would admit that his or her ego was the primary reason behind a merger, but egos do play a prominent role in many mergers.[6]

It has also been observed that executive salaries are highly correlated with company size—the bigger the company, the higher the salaries of its top officers. This, too, could obviously cause unnecessary acquisitions, as managers seek to increase the size of their companies as a way of increasing their own compensation.

Personal considerations deter as well as motivate mergers. After most takeovers, some managers of the acquired companies lose their jobs, or at least their autonomy. Therefore, managers who own less than 51% of their firms' stock look to devices that will lessen the chances of a takeover, and a merger can serve as such a device. In 2005, for example, MCI's board of directors, over the objection of large shareholders, turned down repeated acquisition offers from Qwest, at the time the

---

5. See, for example, Philip Berger and Eli Ofek, "Diversification's Effect on Firm Value," *Journal of Financial Economics,* 1995, pp. 37–65; and Larry Lang and René Stulz, "Tobin's Q, Corporate Diversification, and Firm Performance," *Journal of Political Economy,* December 1994, pp. 1248–1280.

6. See Randall Morck, Andrei Shleifer, and Robert W. Vishny, "Do Managerial Objectives Drive Bad Acquisitions?" *Journal of Finance,* March 1990, pp. 31–48.

nation's fourth-largest local phone company, in favor of substantially smaller offers from Verizon, the nation's largest phone company. MCI's management viewed Verizon as a stronger, more stable partner than Qwest even though Qwest's bid was at times 20% higher than Verizon's. In response to management's refusal to accept the higher bid, the holders of some 28% of MCI's stock withheld their votes to re-elect the board of directors as a protest. Nonetheless, management proceeded with the Verizon merger negotiations, and the two companies merged in June of 2006. In such cases, management always argues that synergy, not a desire to protect their own jobs, is the motivation for the choice. However, it is difficult to rationalize rejecting a 20% larger bid for undocumented synergies, and some observers suspect that this merger—like many others—was ultimately designed to benefit managers rather than shareholders.

26-1f Breakup Value

Some takeover specialists estimate a company's **breakup value**, which is the value of the individual parts of the firm if they were sold off separately. If this value is higher than the firm's current market value, then a takeover specialist could acquire the firm at or even above its current market value, sell it off in pieces, and earn a profit.

26-2 Types of Mergers

Economists classify mergers into four types: (1) horizontal, (2) vertical, (3) congeneric, and (4) conglomerate. A **horizontal merger** occurs when one firm combines with another in its same line of business—the 2014 proposed Comcast-Time Warner merger and the 2013 Amgen-Onyx Pharmaceuticals merger are examples. An example of a **vertical merger** would be a steel producer's acquisition of one of its own suppliers, such as an iron or coal mining firm, or an oil producer's acquisition of a petrochemical firm that uses oil as a raw material. *Congeneric* means "allied in nature or action"; hence a **congeneric merger** involves related enterprises but not producers of the same product (horizontal) or firms in a producer–supplier relationship (vertical). Facebook's 2014 acquisition of WhatsApp is an example. A **conglomerate merger** occurs when unrelated enterprises combine.

Operating economies (and also anticompetitive effects) are at least partially dependent on the type of merger involved. Vertical and horizontal mergers generally provide the greatest synergistic operating benefits, but they are also the ones most likely to be attacked by the Department of Justice as being anticompetitive.[7] In any event, it is useful to think of these economic classifications when analyzing prospective mergers.

SELF TEST   What are the four types of mergers?

26-3 Level of Merger Activity

Five principal "merger waves" have occurred in the United States. The first was in the late 1800s, when consolidations occurred in the oil, steel, tobacco, and other basic industries. The second was in the 1920s, when the stock market boom helped financial promoters consolidate firms in a number of industries, including utilities, communications, and autos. The third was in the 1960s, when conglomerate mergers were the rage. The fourth occurred in the 1980s, when LBO firms and others began using junk bonds to finance all manner of acquisitions. The fifth, which involves strategic alliances designed to enable firms to compete better in the global economy, lasted throughout the 1990s. Some speculate that the 2000s were a sixth wave, driven by private equity.

As shown in Table 26-1, some huge mergers have occurred. Most recent mergers have been strategic in nature—companies are merging to gain economies of scale or scope and thus be better able to compete in the world economy. Indeed, many recent

TABLE 26-1	The Ten Largest Completed Mergers Worldwide through February, 2014		
Buyer	**Target**	**Completion Date**	**Value (Billions of U.S. Dollars)**
Vodafone AirTouch	Mannesmann	April 12, 2000	$161
Verizon Commuications	Verizon Wireless	February 21, 2014	130
Pfizer	Warner-Lambert	June 19, 2000	116
America Online	Time Warner	January 11, 2001	106
RFS Holdings	ABN-AMRO Holding	October 5, 2007	99
Exxon	Mobil	November 30, 1999	81
Glaxo Wellcome	SmithKline Beecham	December 27, 2000	74
Royal Dutch Petroleum	Shell Transport and Trading	July 20, 2005	74
ATT	BellSouth	December 29, 2006	73
SBC Communications	Ameritech	October 8, 1999	72

Sources: "A Look at the Top 10 Global Mergers," *Associated Press Newswires*, January 11, 2001; *The Wall Street Journal*, "Year-End Review of Markets and Finance World-Wide Deals," various issues.

---

7. For interesting insights into antitrust regulations and mergers, see B. Espen Eckbo, "Mergers and the Value of Antitrust Deterrence," *Journal of Finance*, July 1992, pp. 1005–1029.

mergers have involved companies in the financial, defense, media, computer, tele-communications, and health care industries, all of which are experiencing structural changes and intense competition.

In the 1980s, cash was the preferred method of payment, because large cash payments could convince even the most reluctant shareholder to approve the deal. However, the cash was generally obtained by borrowing, leaving the consolidated company with a heavy debt burden, which often led to difficulties. Through the mid-2010s, stock replaced borrowed cash as the merger currency for two reasons: (1) Many of the 1980s mergers were financed with junk bonds that later went into default. These defaults, along with the demise of Drexel Burnham, the leading junk bond dealer, have made it difficult to arrange debt-financed mergers. (2) Many of the mergers during that time were for strategic reasons, such as Eli Lilly's $6.5 billion acquisition of ImClone Systems in 2008 or for industry consolidation purposes, such as Sprint's acquisition of Clearwire in 2013. Most of these mergers have been friendly, and stock swaps are easier to arrange in friendly mergers than in hostile ones. Global merger activity declined significantly in the 4 years after the 2007–2008 financial crisis and subsequent recession but has since picked up.

There has also been an increase in cross-border mergers. For example, in 2011 the Swiss automation technology company ABB acquired Baldor Electric Company, a U.S.-based industrial motors manufacturer. Also in early 2011, Pepsico acquired a 66% interest in the Russian food company, Wimm-Bill-Dann Foods, and purchased the remaining shares in late 2011.

What major "merger waves" have occurred in the United States?   **SELF TEST**

26-4 Hostile versus Friendly Takeovers

In the vast majority of merger situations, one firm (generally the larger of the two) simply decides to buy another company, negotiates a price with the management of the target firm, and then acquires the target company. Occasionally, the acquired firm will initiate the action, but it is much more common for a firm to seek companies to acquire than to seek to be acquired. Following convention, we call a company that seeks to acquire another firm the **acquiring company** and the one that it seeks to acquire the **target company**.

Once an acquiring company has identified a possible target, it must: (1) establish a suitable price, or range of prices, and (2) decide on the terms of payment—will it offer cash, its own common stock, bonds, or some combination? Next, the acquiring firm's managers must decide how to approach the target company's managers. If the acquiring firm has reason to believe that the target's management will approve the merger, then one CEO will contact the other, propose a merger, and then try to work out suitable terms. If an agreement is reached, then the two management groups will issue statements to their stockholders indicating that they approve the merger, and the target firm's management will recommend to its stockholders that they agree to the merger. Generally, the stockholders are asked to *tender* (or send in) their shares to a designated financial institution, along with a signed power of attorney that transfers ownership of the shares to the acquiring firm. The target firm's stockholders then receive the specified payment, either common stock of the acquiring company (in which case the target company's stockholders become stockholders of the acquiring company), cash, bonds, or some mix of cash and securities. This is a **friendly merger**. Sprint's acquisition of Clearwire in 2013 is an example of a friendly merger, even though Clearwire entertained an offer from Dish Network after an initial offer from Sprint was too low.

Often, however, the target company's management resists the merger. Perhaps they feel that the price offered is too low, or perhaps they simply want to keep their jobs. Regardless of the reasons, in this case the acquiring firm's offer is said to be **hostile** rather than friendly, and the acquiring firm must make a direct appeal to the target firm's stockholders. In a hostile merger, the acquiring company will again make a **tender offer**, and again it will ask the stockholders of the target firm to tender their shares in exchange for the offered price. This time, though, the target firm's managers will urge stockholders not to tender their shares, generally stating that the price offered (cash, bonds, or stocks in the acquiring firm) is too low. For example, in late 2010 the board of directors for the biotech company Genzyme refused to consider a $69 per share offer from French pharmaceutical giant Sanofi. To encourage the board to actively consider the offer, Sanofi appealed directly to Genzyme's shareholders with a tender offer at $69 per share. The tender offer got the attention of Genzyme's board and in early 2011, Sanofi increased the cash component of the offer to $74 and added a security called a contingent value right (CVR) to the mix. The CVR would pay up to $14 per share more to the selling shareholders, depending on performance of one of Genzyme's drugs, and the merger was finally approved by management.[8]

Although most mergers are friendly, there are cases in which high-profile firms have attempted hostile takeovers. For example, Wachovia, before its acquisition by Wells Fargo during the financial crisis in 2008, defeated a hostile bid by SunTrust and was acquired, instead, by First Union. Looking overseas, Olivetti successfully conducted a hostile takeover of Telecom Italia, and, in another hostile telecommunications merger, Britain's Vodafone AirTouch acquired its German rival, Mannesmann AG.

Perhaps not surprisingly, hostile bids often fail. However, an all-cash offer that is high enough will generally overcome any resistance by the target firm's management. A hostile merger often begins with a "preemptive" or "blowout" bid. The idea is to offer such a high premium over the pre-announcement price that: (a) no other bidders will be willing to jump into the fray and (b) the target company's board cannot simply reject the bid. If a hostile bid is eventually accepted by the target's board, then the deal ends up as "friendly," despite any acrimony during the hostile phase.

SELF TEST   What is the difference between a hostile and a friendly merger?

8. See www.bloomberg.com/news/2011-02-16/sanofi-aventis-agrees-to-buy-genzyme-for-74-a-share-in-19-2-billion-deal.html for more information on the Sanofi-Genzyme acquisition.

26-5 Merger Regulation

Prior to the mid-1960s, friendly acquisitions generally took place as simple exchange-of-stock mergers, and a proxy fight was the primary weapon used in hostile control battles. In the mid-1960s, however, corporate raiders began to operate differently. First, it took a long time to mount a proxy fight—raiders had to first request a list of the target company's stockholders, be refused, and then get a court order forcing management to turn over the list. During that time, the target's management could think through and then implement a strategy to fend off the raider. As a result, management won most proxy fights.

Then raiders thought, "If we could bring the decision to a head quickly, before management can take countermeasures, it would greatly increase our probability of success." That led the raiders to turn from proxy fights to tender offers, which had a much shorter response time. For example, the stockholders of a company whose stock was selling for $20 might be offered $27 per share and be given 2 weeks to accept. The raider, meanwhile, would have accumulated a substantial block of the shares in open market purchases, and additional shares might have been purchased by institutional friends of the raider who promised to tender their shares in exchange for the tip that a raid was to occur.

Faced with a well-planned raid, managements were generally overwhelmed. The stock might actually be worth more than the offered price, but management simply did not have time to get this message across to stockholders or to find a competing bidder. This situation seemed unfair, so Congress passed the Williams Act in 1968. This law had two main objectives: (1) to regulate the way acquiring firms can structure takeover offers and (2) to force acquiring firms to disclose more information about their offers. In essence, Congress wanted to put target managements in a better position to defend against hostile offers. Additionally, Congress believed that shareholders needed easier access to information about tender offers—including information on any securities that might be offered in lieu of cash—in order to make rational tender-versus-don't-tender decisions.

The Williams Act placed the following four restrictions on acquiring firms: (1) Acquirers must disclose their current holdings and future intentions within 10 days of amassing at least 5% of a company's stock. (2) Acquirers must disclose the source of the funds to be used in the acquisition. (3) The target firm's shareholders must be allowed at least 20 days to tender their shares; that is, the offer must be "open" for at least 20 days. (4) If the acquiring firm increases the offer price during the 20-day open period, then all shareholders who tendered prior to the new offer must receive the higher price. In total, these restrictions were intended to reduce the acquiring firm's ability to surprise management and to stampede target shareholders into accepting an inadequate offer. Prior to the Williams Act, offers were generally made on a first-come, first-served basis, and they were often accompanied by an implicit threat to lower the bid price after 50% of the shares were in hand. The legislation also gave the target more time to mount a defense, and it gave rival bidders and white knights a chance to enter the fray and thus help a target's stockholders obtain a better price.

Many states have also passed laws designed to protect firms in their states from hostile takeovers. In 1987, the U.S. Supreme Court upheld an Indiana law that radically changed the rules of the takeover game. Specifically, the Indiana law first defined "control shares" as enough shares to give an investor 20% of the vote. It went on to state that when an investor buys control shares, those shares can be voted only after approval by a majority of "disinterested shareholders," defined as those who are neither officers nor inside directors of the company nor associates of the raider. The law also gives the buyer of control shares the right to insist that a shareholders' meeting be called within 50 days to decide whether the shares may be voted. The Indiana law dealt a major blow to raiders, mainly because it slows down the action and thus gives the target firm time to mount a defense. Delaware (the state in which most large companies are incorporated) later passed a similar bill, as did New York and a number of other important states.

State laws also have some features that protect target stockholders from their own managers. Included are limits on the use of golden parachutes, onerous debt financing plans, and some types of takeover defenses. Because these laws do not regulate tender offers per se but rather govern the practices of firms in the state, they have withstood all legal challenges to date. But when companies such as IBM offer 100% premiums for companies such as Lotus, it is hard for any defense to hold them off.

SELF TEST

Is there a need to regulate mergers? Explain.

Do the states play a role in merger regulation, or is it all done at the national level? Explain.

26-6 Overview of Merger Analysis

An acquiring firm must answer two questions. First, how much would the target be worth after being incorporated into the acquirer? Notice that this may be quite different from the target's current value, which does not reflect any post-merger synergies or tax benefits. Second, how much should the acquirer offer for the target? A low price is obviously better for the acquirer, but the target won't take the offer if it is too low. However, a higher offer price could scare off potential rival bidders. Later sections discuss setting the offer's price and structure (cash versus stock), but for now we focus on estimating the post-merger value of the target.

There are two basic approaches used in merger valuation: discounted cash flow (DCF) techniques and market multiple analysis.[9] Survey evidence shows that 49.3% of firms use only discounted cash flow techniques, 33.3% use both DCF and market multiples, and 12.0% use only market multiples. The market multiple approach assumes that a target is directly comparable to the average firm in its industry. Therefore, this procedure provides at best a ballpark estimate. Because the market multiple approach is less accurate and less frequently used than DCF approaches, we will focus on DCF methods.[10]

---

9. See Chapter 8 for an explanation of market multiple analysis.
10. For recent survey evidence on merger valuation methods, see Tarun K. Mukherjee, Halil Kiymaz, and H. Kent Baker, "Merger Motives and Target Valuation: A Survey of Evidence from CFOs," *Journal of Applied Finance*, Fall/Winter 2004, pp. 7–23. For evidence on the effectiveness of market multiples and DCF approaches, see S. N. Kaplan and R. S. Ruback, "The Market Pricing of Cash Flow Forecasts: Discounted Cash Flow vs. the Method of 'Comparables,'" *Journal of Applied Corporate Finance*, Winter 1996, pp. 45–60. Also see Samuel C. Weaver, Robert S. Harris, Daniel W. Bielinski, and Kenneth F. MacKenzie, "Merger and Acquisition Valuation," *Financial Management*, Summer 1991, pp. 85–96; and Nancy Mohan, M. Fall Ainina, Daniel Kaufman, and Bernard J. Winger, "Acquisition/Divestiture Valuation Practices in Major U.S. Firms," *Financial Practice and Education*, Spring 1991, pp. 73–81.

There are three widely used DCF methods: (1) the corporate free cash flow valuation method, (2) the adjusted present value method, and (3) the equity residual method, which is also called the "free cash flow to equity" method. Chapter 8 explained the corporate valuation model, Chapter 17 explained the adjusted present value model, and Section 26-7 explains the equity residual model. Section 26-8 provides a numerical illustration for a company with a constant capital structure and shows that all three models, when properly applied, produce identical valuations if the capital structure is held constant. However, in many situations, there will be a nonconstant capital structure in years immediately following the merger. For example, this often occurs if an acquisition is financed with a temporarily high level of debt that will be reduced to a sustainable level as the merger is digested. In such situations, it is extremely difficult to apply the corporate valuation model or the equity residual model correctly because the cost of equity and the cost of capital are changing as the capital structure changes. Fortunately, the adjusted present value model is ideally suited for such situations, as we illustrate in Section 26-10.

SELF TEST

What are the two questions that an acquirer must answer?

What are four methods for estimating a target's value?

26-7 The Free Cash Flow to Equity (FCFE) Approach

Free cash flow is the cash flow available for distribution to *all* investors. In contrast, **free cash flow to equity (FCFE)** is the cash flow available for distribution to *common shareholders*. Because FCFE is available for distribution only to shareholders, it should be discounted at the levered cost of equity, r_{sL}. Therefore, the **free cash flow to equity approach**, also called the **equity residual model**, discounts the projected FCFEs at the cost of equity to determine the value of the equity from operations.

Because FCFE is the cash flow available for distribution to shareholders, it may be used to pay common dividends, repurchase stock, purchase financial assets, or some combination of these uses. In other words, the uses of FCFE include all those of FCF except for distributions to debtholders. Therefore, one way to calculate FCFE is to start with FCF and reduce it by the net after-tax distributions to debtholders:

$$\text{FCFE} = \frac{\text{Free}}{\text{cash flow}} - \frac{\text{After-tax}}{\text{interest expense}} - \frac{\text{Principal}}{\text{payments}} + \frac{\text{Newly issued}}{\text{debt}}$$

$$= \frac{\text{Free}}{\text{cash flow}} - \frac{\text{Interest}}{\text{expense}} + \frac{\text{Interest}}{\text{tax shield}} + \frac{\text{Net change}}{\text{in debt}}$$

(26–1)

Alternatively, the FCFE can be calculated as:

(26–1a)

$$\text{FCFE} = \text{Net income} - \frac{\text{Net investment in}}{\text{operating capital}} + \frac{\text{Net change}}{\text{in debt}}$$

Both calculations provide the same value for FCFE, but Equation 26-1 is used more often because analysts don't always estimate the net income for a target after it has been acquired.

Given projections of FCFE, the value of a firm's equity due to operations, V_{FCFE}, is:

(26–2)

$$V_{\text{FCFE}} = \sum_{t=1}^{\infty} \frac{\text{FCFE}_t}{(1 + r_{sL})^t}$$

If we assume constant growth beyond the horizon, then the horizon value of the value of equity due to operations, $HV_{\text{FCFE,N}}$, is:

(26–3)

$$HV_{\text{FCFE,N}} = \frac{\text{FCFE}_{N+1}}{r_{sL} - g} = \frac{\text{FCFE}_N(1 + g)}{r_{sL} - g}$$

The value of equity due to operations is the present value of the horizon value and the FCFE during the forecast period:

(26–4)

$$V_{\text{FCFE}} = \sum_{t=1}^{N} \frac{\text{FCFE}_t}{(1 + r_{sL})^t} + \frac{HV_{\text{FCFE,N}}}{(1 + r_{sL})^N}$$

The total value of a company's equity, S, is the value of the equity from operations plus the value of any nonoperating assets:

(26–5)

$$S = V_{\text{FCFE}} + \text{Nonoperating assets}$$

To get a per share price, simply divide the total value of equity by the shares outstanding.[11] Like the corporate valuation model, the FCFE model can be applied only when the capital structure is constant.

---

11. The FCFE model is similar to the dividend growth model in that cash flows are discounted at the cost of equity. The cash flows in the FCFE model are those that are generated from operations, while the cash flows in the dividend growth model (i.e., the dividends) also contain cash flows due to interest earned on nonoperating assets.

Table 26-2 summarizes the three cash flow valuation methods and their assumptions.

TABLE 26-2	Summary of Cash Flow Approaches		
	Approach		
	Corporate FCF Valuation Model	**Free Cash Flow to Equity Model**	**APV Model**
Cash flow definition	FCF = NOPAT − Net investment in operating capital	FCFE = FCF − Interest expense + Interest tax shield + Net change in debt	(1) FCF and (2) Interest tax savings
Discount rate	WACC	r_{sL} = Cost of equity	r_{sU} = Unlevered cost of equity
Result of present value calculation	Value of operations	Value of equity due to operations	(1) Value of unlevered operations and (2) Value of the tax shield; together, these are the value of operations
How to get equity value	Value of operations + Value of nonoperating assets − Value of debt	Value of equity due to operations + Value of nonoperating assets	Value of operations + Value of nonoperating assets − Value of debt
Assumption about capital structure during forecast period	Capital structure is constant	Capital structure is constant	None
Requirement for analyst to project interest expense	No interest expense projections needed	Projected interest expense must be based on the assumed capital structure	Interest expense projections are unconstrained
Assumption at horizon	FCF grows at constant rate g	FCFE grows at constant rate g	FCF and interest tax savings grow at constant rate g

What cash flows are discounted in the FCFE model, and what is the discount rate?

How do the FCFE, corporate FCF valuation, and APV models differ? How are they similar?

SELF TEST

26-8 Illustration of the Three Valuation Approaches for a Constant Capital Structure

To illustrate the three valuation approaches, consider Caldwell Inc., a large technology company, as it evaluates the potential acquisition of Tutwiler Controls. If the acquisition takes place, it will occur on January 1, 2016, and so each valuation will be as of that date and will be based on the capital structure and synergies expected after the acquisition. Tutwiler currently has a $62.5 million market value of equity and $27 million in debt, for a total market value of $89.5 million. Thus, Tutwiler's capital structure consists of $27/($62.5 + $27) = 30.17% debt. Caldwell intends to finance the acquisition with this same proportion of debt and plans to maintain this constant capital structure throughout the projection period and thereafter. Tutwiler is a publicly traded company, and its market-determined pre-merger beta was 1.2. Given a risk-free rate of 7% and a 5% market risk premium, the Capital Asset Pricing Model produces a pre-merger required rate of return on equity, r_{sL}, of:

$$r_{sL} = r_{RF} + b(RP_M)$$
$$= 7\% + 1.2(5\%) = 13\%$$

Tutwiler's cost of debt is 9%. Its WACC is:

$$WACC = w_d(1 - T)r_d + w_s r_{sL}$$
$$= 0.3017(0.60)(9\%) + 0.6983(13\%)$$
$$= 10.707\%$$

How much would Tutwiler be worth to Caldwell after the merger? The following sections illustrate the application of the corporate valuation model, the APV model, and the FCFE model. All three models produce an identical value of equity, but keep in mind this is only because the capital structure is constant. If the capital structure were to change during the projection period before becoming stable, then only the APV model could be used. Section 26-10 illustrates the APV in the case of a nonconstant capital structure.

26-8a Projecting Post-Merger Cash Flows

See *Ch26 Tool Kit.xls* for details.

The first order of business is to estimate the post-merger cash flows that Tutwiler will produce. This is by far the most important task in any merger analysis. In a **pure financial merger**, defined as one in which no operating synergies are expected, the incremental post-merger cash flows are simply the target firm's expected cash flows. In an **operating merger**, in which the two firms' operations are to be integrated, forecasting future cash flows is obviously more difficult, because potential synergies must be estimated. People from marketing, production, human resources, and accounting play leading roles here, with financial managers focusing on financing the acquisition and performing an analysis designed to determine whether the projected cash flows are worth the cost. In this chapter, we take the projections as given and concentrate on how they are analyzed. See *Web Extension 26A*, available on the textbook's Web site, for a discussion that focuses on projecting financial statements in a merger analysis.

Table 26-3 shows the post-merger projections for Tutwiler, taking into account all expected synergies and maintaining a constant capital structure. Both Caldwell

TABLE 26-3	Post-Merger Projections for the Tutwiler Subsidiary (Millions of Dollars)					
	1/1/16	**12/31/16**	**12/31/17**	**12/31/18**	**12/31/19**	**12/31/20**
Panel A: Selected Items from Projected Financial Statements[a]						
1. Net sales		$105.0	$126.0	$151.0	$174.0	$191.0
2. Cost of goods sold		80.0	94.0	113.0	129.3	142.0
3. Selling and administrative expenses		10.0	12.0	13.0	15.0	16.0
4. Depreciation		8.0	8.0	9.0	9.0	10.0
5. EBIT		$ 7.0	$ 12.0	$ 16.0	$ 20.7	$ 23.0
6. Interest expense[b]		3.0	3.2	3.5	3.7	3.9
7. Debt[c]	$ 33.2	35.8	38.7	41.1	43.6	46.2
8. Total net operating capital	116.0	117.0	121.0	125.0	131.0	138.0
Panel B: Corporate Valuation Model Cash Flows						
9. NOPAT = EBIT(1 − T)		$ 4.2	$ 7.2	$ 9.6	$ 12.4	$ 13.8
10. Less net investment in operating capital		1.0	4.0	4.0	6.0	7.0
11. Free cash flow		$ 3.2	$ 3.2	$ 5.6	$ 6.4	$ 6.8
Panel C: APV Model Cash Flows						
12. Free cash flow		$ 3.2	$ 3.2	$ 5.6	$ 6.4	$ 6.8
13. Interest tax saving = Interest(T)		$ 1.2	$ 1.3	$ 1.4	$ 1.5	$ 1.6
Panel D: FCFE Model Cash Flows						
14. Free cash flow		$ 3.2	$ 3.2	$ 5.6	$ 6.4	$ 6.8
15. Less A-T interest = Interest(1 − T)		1.8	1.9	2.1	2.2	2.4
16. Plus change in debt[d]	6.2	2.6	2.9	2.5	2.5	2.6
17. FCFE	$ 6.2	$ 4.0	$ 4.1	$ 6.0	$ 6.7	$ 7.1

Notes:
[a]Rounded figures are presented here, but the full nonrounded values are used in all calculations. The tax rate is 40%.
[b]Interest payments are based on Tutwiler's existing debt, new debt to be issued to finance the acquisition, and additional debt required to finance annual growth.
[c]Debt is existing debt plus additional debt required to maintain a constant capital structure. Caldwell will increase Tutwiler's debt by $6.2 million, from $27 million to $33.2 million, at the time of the acquisition in order to keep the capital structure constant. This increase occurs because the post-merger synergies make Tutwiler more valuable to Caldwell than it was on a stand-alone basis. Therefore, it can support more dollars of debt and still maintain the constant debt ratio.
[d]The increase in debt at the time of acquisition is a source of free cash flow to equity.

and Tutwiler are in the 40% marginal federal-plus-state tax bracket. The cost of debt after the acquisition will remain at 9%. The projections assume that growth in the post-horizon period will be 6%.

Panel A of Table 26-3 shows selected items from the projected financial statements. Panel B shows the calculations for free cash flow, which is used in the corporate FCF valuation model. Row 9 shows net operating profit after taxes (NOPAT), which is equal to EBIT(1 – T). Row 10 shows the net investment in operating capital, which is the annual change in the total net operating capital in Row 8. Free cash flow, shown in Row 11, is equal to NOPAT less the net investment in operating capital. Panel C shows the cash flows that will be used in the APV model. In particular, Row 13 shows the annual tax shield, which is equal to the interest expense multiplied by the tax rate. Panel D provides the calculations for FCFE, based upon Equation 26-1.

Of course, the post-merger cash flows are extremely difficult to estimate, and in merger valuations—just as in capital budgeting analysis—sensitivity, scenario, and simulation analyses should be conducted.[12] Indeed, in a friendly merger the acquiring firm would send a team consisting of literally dozens of financial analysts, accountants, engineers, and so forth to the target firm's headquarters. They would go over its books, estimate required maintenance expenditures, set values on assets such as real estate and petroleum reserves, and the like. Such an investigation, which is one example of **due diligence**, is an essential part of any merger analysis.

Following are valuations of Tutwiler using all three methods, beginning with the corporate valuation model.

26-8b Valuation Using the Corporate FCF Valuation Model

Because Caldwell does not plan on changing Tutwiler's capital structure, the post-merger WACC will be equal to the pre-merger WACC of 10.707% that we calculated previously. Tutwiler's free cash flows are shown in Row 11 of Table 26-3. The horizon value of Tutwiler's operations as of 2020 can be calculated with the constant growth formula that we used in Chapter 8:

$$HV_{Operations,2020} = \frac{FCF_{2021}}{WACC - g_L} = \frac{FCF_{2020}(1 + g_L)}{WACC - g_L}$$

$$= \frac{\$6.800(1.06)}{0.10707 - 0.06} = \$153.1 \text{ million}$$

The value of operations as of January 1, 2016, is the present value of the cash flows in the forecast period and the horizon value:

$$V_{Operations} = \frac{\$3.2}{(1 + 0.10707)^1} + \frac{\$3.2}{(1 + 0.10707)^2} + \frac{\$5.6}{(1 + 0.10707)^3}$$
$$+ \frac{\$6.4}{(1 + 0.10707)^4} + \frac{\$6.8 + \$153.1}{(1 + 0.10707)^5}$$
$$= \$110.1$$

WEB

See *Ch26 Tool Kit.xls* on the textbook's Web site for all calculations. Note that rounded intermediate values are shown in the text, but all calculations are performed in *Excel* using nonrounded values.

---

12. We purposely kept the cash flows simple in order to focus on key analytical issues. In actual merger valuations, the cash flows would be much more complex, normally including such items as tax loss carryforwards, tax effects of plant and equipment valuation adjustments, and cash flows from the sale of some of the subsidiary's assets.

There are no nonoperating assets, so the value of equity to Caldwell if Tutwiler is acquired is equal to the value of operations less the value of Tutwiler's debt:[13]

$$\$110.1 - \$27 = \$83.1 \text{ million}$$

26-8c **Valuation Using the APV Approach**

The APV approach requires an estimate of Tutwiler's unlevered cost of equity. As shown in Chapter 17, the levered cost of equity is:

$$r_{sL} = r_{sU} + (r_{sU} - r_d)(w_d/w_s)$$

(26–6)

Inputting Tutwiler's capital structure, cost of equity, and cost of debt, Equation 26-6 can be rearranged to estimate the unlevered cost of equity:

$$r_{sU} = w_s r_{sL} + w_d r_d$$

(26–6a)

$$= 0.6983(13\%) + 0.3017(9\%)$$
$$= 11.793\%$$

In other words, if Tutwiler had no debt, its cost of equity would be 11.793%.[14]

Instead of directly estimating the unlevered cost of equity, we can estimate the unlevered beta, b_U, and then calculate the unlevered cost of equity. Chapter 17 shows an expression for the unlevered beta:

$$b = b_U + (b_U - b_D)(w_d/w_s)$$

(26–7)

where b_D is the beta of the debt.

Notice that this is different from the Hamada formula in Chapter 16. First, the Hamada formula assumes zero growth, but 26-7 incorporates growth. Second, the Hamada formula assumes away risky debt. But if the CAPM is used to estimate the risk of equity, then the CAPM must be used to estimate the risk of debt, otherwise we would be comparing apples to oranges.

---

13. Notice that we subtract the $27 million value of Tutwiler's debt, not the $33.2 million of debt supported *after* the merger, because $27 million is the amount that must be paid off or assumed by Caldwell.

14. Notice that we do not use the Hamada equation to lever or unlever beta or the required return on equity because the Hamada equation assumes zero growth. Instead, we use Equation 17-17, which assumes that the growing debt tax shield is discounted at the unlevered cost of equity.

To estimate the beta on debt due to systematic risk, we can start with the observed cost of debt and solve the CAPM for the implied beta on debt:

$$b_D = (r_d - r_{RF}) / RP_M$$
$$= (0.09 - 0.07)/0.05$$
$$= 0.4$$

Rearranging Equation 26-7, Tutwiler's unlevered beta is:

$$b_U = [b + b_D(w_d/w_s)]/[1 + (w_d/w_s)]$$
$$= [1.2 + 0.4(0.3017/0.6983)]/[1 + (0.3017/0.6983)]$$
$$= 0.9586$$

Using the CAPM, the unlevered cost of equity is:

$$r_{sU} = r_{RF} + b_U(RP_M)$$
$$= 7\% + 0.9586(5\%) = 11.79\%$$

This is exactly the same value previously estimated. Because this alternative approach requires that we assume the CAPM is the correct model, and because it takes extra steps, we usually use the first method shown in Equations 26-6 and 26-6a.

The horizon value of Tutwiler's unlevered cash flows ($HV_{U,2020}$) and tax shield ($HV_{TS,2020}$) can be calculated using the constant growth formula with the unlevered cost of equity as the discount rate, as shown in Chapter 17:[15]

$$HV_{U,2020} = \frac{FCF_{2021}}{r_{sU} - g_L} = \frac{FCF_{2020}(1 + g_L)}{r_{sU} - g_L} = \frac{\$6.800(1.06)}{0.11793 - 0.06} = \$124.4 \text{ million}$$

$$HV_{TS,2020} = \frac{TS_{2021}}{r_{sU} - g_L} = \frac{TS_{2020}(1 + g_L)}{r_{sU} - g_L} = \frac{\$1.57(1.06)}{0.11793 - 0.06} = \$28.7 \text{ million}$$

The sum of the two horizon values is $124.4 + $28.7 = $153.1 million. This is the horizon value of operations, which is the same as the horizon value calculation we reached with the corporate FCF valuation model.

Row 11 in Table 26-3 shows the projected free cash flows. The unlevered value of operations is calculated as the present value of the free cash flows during the forecast period and the horizon value of the free cash flows:

$$V_{Unlevered} = \frac{\$3.2}{(1 + 0.11793)^1} + \frac{\$3.2}{(1 + 0.11793)^2} + \frac{\$5.6}{(1 + 0.11793)^3}$$

$$+ \frac{\$6.4}{(1 + 0.11793)^4} + \frac{\$6.8 + \$124.4}{(1 + 0.11793)^5}$$

$$= \$88.7 \text{ million}$$

This shows that Tutwiler's operations would be worth $88.7 million if it had no debt.

---

15. Note that we report two decimal places for the 2021 tax shield even though Table 26-3 reports only one decimal place. All calculations are performed in *Excel*, which uses the full nonrounded values.

Row 13 shows the yearly interest tax savings. The value of the tax shield is calculated as the present value of the yearly tax savings and the horizon value of the tax shield:

$$V_{\text{Tax shield}} = \frac{\$1.2}{(1 + 0.11793)^1} + \frac{\$1.3}{(1 + 0.11793)^2} + \frac{\$1.4}{(1 + 0.11793)^3}$$
$$+ \frac{\$1.5}{(1 + 0.11793)^4} + \frac{\$1.57 + \$28.7}{(1 + 0.11793)^5}$$
$$= \$21.4 \text{ million}$$

Thus, Tutwiler's operations would be worth only $88.7 million if it had no debt, but its capital structure contributes $21.4 million in value due to the tax deductibility of its interest payments. Because Tutwiler has no nonoperating assets, the total value of the firm is the sum of the unlevered value of operations, $88.7 million, and the value of the tax shield, $21.4 million, for a total of $110.1 million. The value of the equity is this total value less Tutwiler's outstanding debt of $27 million: $110.1 − $27 = $83.1 million. Note that this is the same value we obtained using the corporate valuation model.

WEB

See *Ch26 Tool Kit.xls* on the textbook's Web site for all calculations. Note that rounded intermediate values are shown in the text, but all calculations are performed in *Excel* using nonrounded values.

26-8d Valuation Using the FCFE Model

The horizon value of Tutwiler's free cash flows to equity can be calculated using the constant growth formula of Equation 26-3:[16]

$$HV_{\text{FCFE,2020}} = \frac{FCF_{2020}(1 + g_L)}{r_{sL} - g_L} = \frac{\$7.06(1.06)}{0.13 - 0.06} = \$106.9 \text{ million}$$

Notice that this horizon value is different from the APV and corporate FCF valuation horizon values. That is because the FCFE horizon value is only for equity, whereas the other two horizon values are for the total value of operations. If the 2020 debt of $46.2 million shown in Row 7 of Table 26-3 is added to the $HV_{\text{FCFE,2020}}$, the result is the same $153.1 million horizon value of operations obtained with the corporate valuation model and APV model.

Row 17 in Table 26-3 shows the yearly projections of FCFE. When discounted at the 13% cost of equity, the present value of these yearly FCFEs and the horizon value is the value of equity due to operations, which is $83.1 million:[17]

$$V_{\text{FCFE}} = \$6.2 + \frac{\$4.0}{(1 + 0.13)^1} + \frac{\$4.1}{(1 + 0.13)^2} + \frac{\$6.0}{(1 + 0.13)^3}$$
$$+ \frac{\$6.7}{(1 + 0.13)^4} + \frac{\$7.1 + \$106.9}{(1 + 0.13)^5}$$
$$= \$83.1 \text{ million}$$

16. Note that we report two decimal places for the 2020 FCFE even though Table 26-3 reports only one decimal place. All calculations are performed in *Excel*, which uses the full nonrounded values.

17. Row 16 in Table 26-3 shows that debt is forecast to increase from its pre-merger $27 million to $33.2 million at the acquisition date. This is because Tutwiler is more valuable after the merger, so it can support more dollars of debt while still maintaining 30% debt in its capital structure. The increase in debt of $33.2 − $27 = $6.2 million is an FCFE that is immediately available to Caldwell and so is not discounted.

See **Ch26 Tool Kit .xls** on the textbook's Web site for complete calculations and **Web Extension 26A** for a more detailed explanation.

If Tutwiler had any nonoperating assets, we would add them to V_{FCFE} to determine the total value of equity. Because Tutwiler has no nonoperating assets, its total equity value is equal to the V_{FCFE} of $83.1 million. Notice that this is the same value given by the corporate valuation model and the APV approach.

All three models agree that the estimated equity value is $83.1 million, which is more than the $62.5 million current market value of Tutwiler's equity. This means that Tutwiler is more valuable as a part of Caldwell than as a stand-alone corporation being run by its current managers.

SELF TEST

Why is the adjusted present value approach appropriate for situations with a changing capital structure?

Describe the steps required to apply the APV approach.

How do the FCFE, APV, and corporate valuation approaches differ from one another?

26-9 Setting the Bid Price

Under the acquisition plan, Caldwell would assume Tutwiler's debt and would also take on additional short-term debt as necessary to complete the purchase. The valuation models show that $83.1 million is the most it should pay for Tutwiler's stock. If it paid more, then Caldwell's own value would be diluted. On the other hand, if it could get Tutwiler for less than $83.1 million, Caldwell's stockholders would gain value. Therefore, Caldwell should bid something less than $83.1 million when it makes an offer for Tutwiler.

Now consider the target company. As stated earlier, Tutwiler's value of equity as an independent operating company is $62.5 million. If Tutwiler were acquired at a price greater than $62.5 million, then its stockholders would gain value, whereas they would lose value at any lower price.

The difference between $62.5 million and $83.1 million, or $20.6 million, represents **synergistic benefits** expected from the merger. If there were no synergistic benefits, the maximum bid would be the current value of the target company. The greater the synergistic gains, the greater the gap between the target's current price and the maximum the acquiring company could pay.

The issue of how to divide the synergistic benefits is critically important. Obviously, both parties would want to get the best deal possible. In our example, if it knew the maximum price Caldwell could pay, Tutwiler's management would argue for a price close to $83.1 million. Caldwell, on the other hand, would try to get Tutwiler at a price as close to $62.5 million as possible.

Where, within the range of $62.5 to $83.1 million, will the actual price be set? The answer depends on a number of factors, including whether Caldwell offers to pay with cash or securities, the negotiating skills of the two management teams, and, most importantly, the bargaining positions of the two parties as determined by fundamental economic conditions. Let's first consider bargaining power and then examine the mechanics of a cash offer versus a stock offer.

26-9a **Relative Bargaining Power**

To illustrate the relative bargaining power of the target and the acquirer, assume there are many companies similar to Tutwiler that Caldwell could acquire, but suppose that no company other than Caldwell could gain synergies by acquiring Tutwiler. In this case, Caldwell would probably make a relatively low, take-it-or-leave-it offer, and Tutwiler would probably take it because some gain is better than none. On the other hand, if Tutwiler has some unique technology or other asset that many companies want, then once Caldwell announces its offer, others would probably make competing bids and the final price would probably be close to (or even above) $83.1 million. A price above $83.1 million presumably would be paid by some other company with a better synergistic fit or with a management that is more optimistic about Tutwiler's cash flow potential.

Caldwell would, of course, want to keep its maximum bid secret, and it would plan its bidding strategy carefully. If Caldwell thought other bidders would emerge or that Tutwiler's management might resist in order to preserve their jobs, Caldwell might make a high preemptive bid in hopes of scaring off competing bids or management resistance. On the other hand, it might make a lowball bid in hopes of "stealing" the company.[18]

26-9b **Cash Offers versus Stock Offers**

Most target stockholders prefer to sell their shares for cash rather than to exchange them for stock in the post-merger company. Following is a brief description of each payment method.

Cash Offers

Tutwiler's pre-merger equity is worth $62.5 million. With 10 million shares outstanding, Tutwiler's stock price is $62.5/10 = $6.25. If the synergies are realized, then Tutwiler's equity will be worth $83.1 million to Caldwell, so $83.1/10 = $8.31 is the maximum price per share that Caldwell should be willing to pay to Tutwiler's stockholders. For example, Caldwell might offer $7.75 cash for each share of Tutwiler stock.

Stock Offers

In a stock offer, Tutwiler's stockholders exchange their Tutwiler shares for new shares in the post-merger company, which will be named Caldwell-Tutwiler. Targets typically prefer cash offers to stock offers, all else equal, but taxation of the offer prevents all else from being equal. We discuss taxation in more detail in Section 26-11, but for now you should know that stock offerings are taxed more favorably than cash offerings. In this case, perhaps Caldwell should offer a package worth $7.50 per share. With 10 million outstanding Tutwiler shares, the Tutwiler shareholders must end up owning $7.50 × 10 million = $75 million worth of stock in the post-merger company.

Suppose Caldwell has 20 million shares of stock outstanding (n_{Old}) prior to the merger and the stock price per share is $15. Then the total pre-merger value of Caldwell's equity is $15 × 20 million = $300 million. As calculated previously, the

---

18. For an interesting discussion of the after effects of losing a bidding contest, see Mark L. Mitchell and Kenneth Lehn, "Do Bad Bidders Become Good Targets?" *Journal of Applied Corporate Finance*, Summer 1990, pp. 60–69.

post-merger value of Tutwiler to Caldwell is $83.1 million. Therefore, the total post-merger value of Caldwell-Tutwiler will be $300 + $83.1 = $383.1 million.

After the merger, Tutwiler's former stockholders should own $75/$383.1 = 0.196 = 19.58% of the post-merger Caldwell-Tutwiler. With 20 million Caldwell shares outstanding, Caldwell must issue enough new shares, n_{New}, to the Tutwiler stockholders (in exchange for the Tutwiler shares) so that Tutwiler's former stockholders will own 19.6% of the shares of Caldwell-Tutwiler:

$$\frac{\text{Percent required by}}{\text{target stockholders}} = \frac{n_{New}}{n_{New} + n_{Old}}$$

$$19.58\% = \frac{n_{New}}{n_{New} + 20}$$

$$n_{New} = \frac{20 \times 0.1958}{1 - 0.1958} = 4.87 \text{ million}$$

Tutwiler's former stockholders will exchange 10 million shares of stock in Tutwiler for 4.87 million shares of stock in the combined Caldwell-Tutwiler. Thus, the exchange ratio is $4.87/10 = 0.487$.

After the merger, there will be 4.87 million new shares for a total of 24.87 million shares. With a combined intrinsic equity value of $383.1 million, the resulting price per share will be $383.1/24.87 = $15.40. The total value owned by Tutwiler's shareholders is this price multiplied by their shares: 15.40×4.87 million = $75 million. Also notice that the price will increase from $15.00 per share before the merger to $15.40 after the merger, so the merger will benefit Caldwell's shareholders if the synergies are realized.

SELF TEST   Explain the issues involved in setting the bid price.

26-10 Analysis When There Is a Permanent Change in Capital Structure

Tutwiler currently has equity worth $62.5 million and debt of $27 million, giving it a capital structure financed with about 30% debt: $27.0/($62.5 + $27.0) = 0.302 = 30.2%. Suppose Caldwell has decided to increase Tutwiler's debt from 30% to 50% over the next 5 years and to maintain the capital structure at that level from 2020 on. How would this affect Tutwiler's valuation? The free cash flows will not change, but the interest tax shield, the WACC, and the bid price will all change.[19] At a 30% debt level, the interest rate on Tutwiler's debt was 9%. However, at a 50% debt level, Tutwiler is more risky, and its interest rate would rise to 9.5% to reflect this additional risk. Because the capital structure is changing, we will use only the APV for this analysis.

---

19. We are assuming for simplicity that Tutwiler has no more expected bankruptcy costs at 50% debt than at 30% debt. If Tutwiler's risk of bankruptcy and hence its expected bankruptcy costs are larger at this higher level of debt, then its projected free cash flows should be reduced by these expected costs. In practice it is extremely difficult to estimate expected bankruptcy costs. However, these costs can be significant and should be considered when a high degree of leverage is being used.

26-10a **The Effect on the Tax Shield**

It is reasonable to assume that Caldwell will use more debt during the first 5 years of the acquisition if its long-run target capital structure is 50% debt. With more debt and a higher interest rate, the interest payments will be higher than those shown in Table 26-3, thus increasing the tax savings shown in Line 13. The interest payments and tax savings with more debt and a higher interest rate are projected as follows:

	2016	2017	2018	2019	2020
Interest	$5.00	$6.00	$7.00	$7.50	$8.30
Interest tax savings	2.00	2.40	2.80	3.00	3.32

In these projections, Tutwiler will reach its target capital structure of 50% debt and 50% equity by the start of 2020.[20]

26-10b **The Effect on the Bid Price**

The new capital structure would affect the maximum bid price by changing the value of Tutwiler to Caldwell. Based on the new tax shields, the unlevered and tax shield horizon values in 2020 are calculated as:

$$HV_{U,2020} = \frac{FCF_{2021}}{r_{sU} - g} = \frac{FCF_{2020}(1 + g)}{r_{sU} - g} = \frac{\$6.800(1.06)}{0.11793 - 0.06} = \$124.4$$

$$HV_{TS,2020} = \frac{TS_{2021}}{r_{sU} - g} = \frac{TS_{2020}(1 + g)}{r_{sU} - g} = \frac{\$3.32(1.06)}{0.11793 - 0.06} = \$60.7$$

Based on the new interest payments and horizon values, the cash flows to be discounted at the unlevered cost of equity are as follows:

	2016	2017	2018	2019	2020
Free cash flow	$3.2	$3.2	$5.6	$6.4	$ 6.8
Unlevered horizon value					124.4
FCF plus horizon value	$3.2	$3.2	$5.6	$6.4	$131.2
Interest tax saving	2.0	2.4	2.8	3.0	3.3
Tax shield horizon value					$ 60.7
TS_t plus horizon value	$2.0	$2.4	$2.8	$3.0	$ 64.0

WEB

For more information on projecting financial statements, see **Web Extension 26A** and **Ch26 Tool Kit.xls** on the textbook's Web site.

---

20. The last year's projected interest expense must be consistent with the assumed capital structure in order to use the relation $TS_{N+1} = TS_N(1 + g)$ in calculating the tax shield horizon value.

The present value of the free cash flows and their horizon value is $88.7 million, just as it was under the 30% debt policy; the unlevered value of operations is not impacted by the change in capital structure:

$$
\begin{aligned}
V_{\text{Unlevered}} &= \frac{\$3.2}{(1 + 10.11793)^1} + \frac{\$3.2}{(1 + 0.11793)^2} + \frac{\$5.6}{(1 + 0.11793)^3} \\
&+ \frac{\$6.4}{(1 + 0.11793)^4} + \frac{\$6.8 + \$124.4}{(1 + 0.11793)^5} \\
&= \$88.7 \text{ million}
\end{aligned}
$$

The present value of the tax shields and their horizon value is $44.3 million, which is $22.9 million more than the value of the tax shield under the 30% debt policy:

$$
\begin{aligned}
V_{\text{Tax shield}} &= \frac{\$2.0}{(1 + 0.11793)^1} + \frac{\$2.4}{(1 + 0.11793)^2} + \frac{\$2.8}{(1 + 0.11793)^3} \\
&+ \frac{\$3.0}{(1 + 0.11793)^4} + \frac{\$3.3 + \$60.7}{(1 + 0.11793)^5} \\
&= \$44.3 \text{ million}
\end{aligned}
$$

Thus, Tutwiler is worth almost $23 million more to Caldwell if it is financed with 50% rather than 30% debt because of the added value of the tax shields.

The value of operations under the new 50% debt policy is the sum of the unlevered value of operations and the value of the tax shields, or $133.0 million. There are no nonoperating assets to add, and subtracting the debt of $27 million leaves the value of Tutwiler's equity at $106.0 million. Because Tutwiler has 10 million shares outstanding, the maximum amount Caldwell should be willing to pay per share, given a post-merger target capital structure of 50% debt, is $10.60. This is more than the $8.31 maximum price if the capital structure had 30% debt. The difference, $2.29 per share, reflects the added value of the interest tax shields under the higher-debt plan.

> **SELF TEST**   How does a change in capital structure affect the valuation analysis?

26-11 Taxes and the Structure of the Takeover Bid

In a merger, the acquiring firm can either buy the target's assets or buy shares of stock directly from the target's shareholders. If the offer is for the target's assets then the target's board of directors will make a recommendation to the shareholders, who will vote either to accept or reject the offer. If they accept the offer, the payment goes directly to the target corporation, which pays off any debt not assumed by the acquiring firm, pays any corporate taxes that are due, and then distributes the remainder of the payment to the shareholders, often in the form of a liquidating dividend. In this situation, the target firm is usually dissolved and no longer continues to exist as a separate legal entity, although its assets and work force may continue to function as a division or as a wholly owned subsidiary of the acquiring firm. The acquisition of assets is a common form of takeover for small and medium-sized firms, especially those that are not publicly traded. A major advantage of this method compared with the acquisition of the target's stock is that the acquiring firm simply acquires assets and is not saddled with any hidden liabilities. In contrast, if the acquiring firm buys the target's stock, then it is responsible for any legal contingencies against the target, even for those that might have occurred prior to the takeover.

An offer for a target's stock rather than its assets can be made either directly to the shareholders, as is typical in a hostile takeover, or indirectly through the board of directors, which in a friendly deal makes a recommendation to the shareholders to accept the offer. In a successful offer, the acquiring firm will end up owning a controlling interest or perhaps even all of the target's stock. Sometimes the target retains its identity as a separate legal entity and is operated as a subsidiary of the acquiring firm, and sometimes its corporate status is dissolved and it is operated as one of the acquiring firm's divisions.

The payment offered by the acquiring firm can be in the form of cash, stock of the acquiring firm, debt of the acquiring firm, or some combination. The structure of the bid affects: (1) the capital structure of the post-merger firm, (2) the tax treatment of both the acquiring firm and the target's stockholders, (3) the ability of the target firm's stockholders to benefit from future merger-related gains, and (4) the types of federal and state regulations to which the acquiring firm will be subjected.

The tax consequences of the merger depend on whether it is classified as a *taxable offer* or a *nontaxable offer*.[21] In general, a nontaxable offer is one in which the form of payment is predominately stock, although the application of this simple principle is much more complicated in practice. The Internal Revenue Code views a mostly stock merger as an exchange rather than a sale, making it a nontaxable event. However, if the offer includes a significant amount of cash or bonds, then the IRS views it as a sale, and it is a taxable transaction just like any other sale.

TEMPEST IN A TEAPOT?

In 2001, amid a flurry of warnings and lobbying, the Financial Accounting Standards Board (FASB) in its Statement 141 eliminated the use of pooling for merger accounting, requiring that purchase accounting be used instead. Because the change would otherwise have required that all purchased goodwill be amortized and reported earnings be reduced, the FASB also issued Statement 142, which eliminated the regular amortization of purchased goodwill, replacing it with an "impairment test." The impairment test requires that companies evaluate annually their purchased goodwill and write it down if its value has declined. This impairment test resulted in Time Warner's unprecedented 2002 write-down of $54 billion of goodwill associated with the AOL merger.

---

21. For more details, see J. Fred Weston, Mark L. Mitchell, and Harold Mulherin, *Takeovers, Restructuring, and Corporate Governance*, 4th ed. (Upper Saddle River, NJ: Prentice-Hall, 2004), especially Chapter 4. Also see Kenneth E. Anderson, Thomas R. Pope, and John L. Kramer, eds., *Prentice Hall's Federal Taxation 2015: Corporations, Partnerships, Estates, and Trusts*, 28th ed. (Upper Saddle River, NJ: Prentice-Hall, 2013), especially Chapter 7.

So what exactly is the effect of the change? First and foremost, the change does *nothing* to the firm's actual cash flows. Purchased goodwill may still be amortized for federal income tax purposes, so the change does not affect the actual taxes a company pays, nor does it affect the company's operating cash flows. However, it does affect the earnings that companies report to their shareholders. Firms that used to have large goodwill charges from past acquisitions have seen their reported earnings increase because they no longer have to amortize the remaining goodwill. Firms whose acquisitions have fared badly, such as Time Warner, must make large write-downs. Executives facing boosted earnings hope—and executives facing a write-down fear—that investors will not see through these accounting changes. However, evidence suggests that investors realize that a company's assets have deteriorated long before the write-down actually occurs, and they build this information into the price of the stock. For example, Time Warner's announcement of its $54 billion charge in January 2002 resulted in only a blip in its stock price at that time, even though the write-down totaled more than a third of its market value. The market had recognized the decline in value months earlier, and by the time of the announcement Time Warner had already lost more than $100 billion in market value.

In a nontaxable deal, target shareholders who receive shares of the acquiring company's stock do not have to pay any taxes at the time of the merger. When they eventually sell their stock in the acquiring company, they must pay a tax on the gain. The amount of the gain is the sales price of their stock in the acquiring company minus the price at which they purchased their original stock in the target company.[22] In a taxable offer, the gain between the offer price and the original purchase price of the target stock is taxed in the year of the merger.[23]

All other things equal, stockholders prefer nontaxable offers, because they may then postpone taxes on their gains. Furthermore, if the target firm's stockholders receive stock, they will benefit from any synergistic gains produced by the merger. Most target shareholders are thus willing to give up their stock for a lower price in a nontaxable offer than in a taxable one. As a result, one might expect nontaxable bids to dominate. However, this is not the case: Roughly half of all mergers have been taxable. The reason for this is explained in the following paragraphs.

The form of the payment also has tax consequences for the acquiring and target firms. To illustrate, consider the following situation. The target firm has assets with a book value of $100 million, but these assets have an appraised value of $150 million. The offer by the acquiring firm is worth $225 million. If it is a nontaxable offer, then after the merger the acquiring firm simply adds the $100 million book value of the target's assets to its own assets and continues to depreciate them according to their previous depreciation schedules. To keep the example simple, we assume the target has no debt.

The situation is more complicated for a taxable offer, and the treatment is different depending on whether the offer is for the target's assets or for its stock. If the

---

22. This is a capital gain if it has been at least 1 year since they purchased their original stock in the target.

23. Even in nontaxable deals, taxes must be paid in the year of the merger by any stockholders who receive cash.

acquiring firm offers $225 million for the target's assets, then the target firm must pay a tax on the gain of $225 − $100 = $125 million. Assuming a corporate tax rate of 40%, this tax is 0.40($125) = $50 million. This leaves the target with $225 − $50 = $175 million to distribute to its shareholders upon liquidation. Adding insult to injury, the target's shareholders must also pay individual taxes on any of their own gains.[24] This is truly a taxable transaction, with taxes assessed at both the corporate and individual levels!

In contrast to the tax disadvantages for the target and its shareholders, the acquiring firm receives two major tax advantages. First, it records the acquired assets at their appraised value and depreciates them accordingly. Thus, it will depreciate $150 million of assets in this taxable transaction versus only $100 million in a nontaxable transaction. Second, it will create $75 million in a new asset account called **goodwill**, which is the difference between the purchase price of $225 million and the appraised value of $150 million. Tax laws that took effect in 1993 permit companies to amortize this goodwill over 15 years using the straight-line method and also to deduct the amortization from taxable income. The net effect is that the full purchase price of $225 million can be written off in a taxable merger versus only the original book value of $100 million in a nontaxable transaction.

Now suppose the acquiring firm offers $225 million for the target's stock, rather than just its assets as in the preceding example, in a taxable offer. After completing the merger, the acquiring firm must choose between two tax treatments. Under the first alternative, it will record the assets at their book value of $100 million and continue depreciating them using their current schedules. This treatment does not create any goodwill. Under the second alternative, it will record the assets at their appraised value of $150 million and create $75 million of goodwill. As described earlier for the asset purchase, this allows the acquiring firm to effectively depreciate the entire purchase price of $225 million for tax purposes. However, there will also be an immediate tax liability on the $125 million gain, just as when the firm purchased assets.[25] Therefore, many companies choose not to mark up the assets. Figure 26-1 illustrates the tax implications for the various types of transactions.

If you think this is complicated, you are right! At this point, you should know enough to talk with specialized accountants and lawyers or be ready to delve into tax accounting texts, but merger taxation is too complex a subject to be covered thoroughly in a general finance textbook.

Securities laws also have an effect on the offer's construction. The SEC has oversight over the issuance of new securities, including stock or debt issued in connection with a merger. Therefore, whenever a corporation bids for control of another firm through the exchange of equity or debt, the entire process must take

---

24. Our example assumes that the target is a publicly owned firm, which means that it must be a "C corporation" for tax purposes. However, if it is privately held then it might be an "S corporation," in which case only the stockholders would be taxed. This helps smaller firms use mergers as an exit strategy.

25. Technically speaking, it is the target firm that is responsible for this tax on the write-up. Keep in mind, however, that the acquiring firm previously purchased the stock in the target and so, in reality, must bear the brunt of the tax.

FIGURE 26-1	Merger Tax Effects

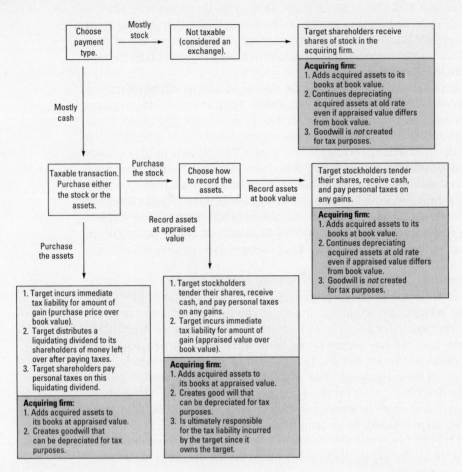

Note: These are actual cash tax effects. However, the tax effects reported to shareholders will be different because shareholder statements must conform to GAAP conventions, not to federal Tax Code conventions. For example, purchased goodwill can no longer be deducted for shareholder reporting under GAAP, even though it is still deductible for federal tax purposes. See the box entitled "Tempest in a Teapot?" which deals with changes in the accounting treatment of mergers and goodwill.

place under the scrutiny of the Securities and Exchange Commission. The time required for such reviews allows target managements to implement defensive tactics and other firms to make competing offers; as a result, nearly all hostile tender offers are for cash rather than securities.

> **SELF TEST**
>
> What are some alternative ways of structuring takeover bids?
>
> How do taxes influence the payment structure?
>
> How do securities laws affect the payment structure?

26-12 Financial Reporting for Mergers

Although a detailed discussion of financial reporting is best left to accounting courses, the accounting implications of mergers cannot be ignored. Currently, mergers are handled using **purchase accounting**.[26] Keep in mind, however, that all large companies are required to keep two sets of books. The first is for the IRS, and it reflects the tax treatment of mergers as described in the previous section. The second is for financial reporting, and it reflects the treatment described here. As you will see, the rules for financial reporting differ from those for the IRS.

26-12a Purchase Accounting

Table 26-4 illustrates purchase accounting. Here, Firm A is assumed to have "bought" Firm B using the stock of the acquiring company. If the price paid is exactly equal to the acquired firm's *net asset value,* which is defined as its total assets minus its liabilities, then the consolidated balance sheet will be as if the two statements were merged. Normally, though, there is an important difference. If the price paid *exceeds* the net asset value, then asset values will be increased to reflect the price actually paid, whereas if the price paid is *less* than the net asset value, then assets must be written down when preparing the consolidated balance sheet.

TABLE 26-4	Accounting for Mergers: Firm A Acquires Firm B with Stock				
			Post-Merger: Firm A		
	Firm A **(1)**	**Firm B** **(2)**	**$20 Paid[a]** **(3)**	**$30 Paid[a]** **(4)**	**$50 Paid[a]** **(5)**
Current assets	$ 50	$25	$ 75	$ 75	$ 80[b]
Fixed assets	50	25	65[c]	75	80[b]
Goodwill[d]	0	0	0	0	10[d]
Total assets	$100	$50	$140	$150	$ 170
Liabilities	$ 40	$20	$ 60	$ 60	$ 60
Equity	60	30	80[e]	90	110[f]
Total claims	$100	$50	$140	$150	$ 170

[a]The price paid is the *net asset value*—that is, total assets minus liabilities.
[b]Here we assume that Firm B's current and fixed assets are both increased to $30.
[c]Here we assume that Firm B's fixed assets are written down from $25 to $15 before constructing the consolidated balance sheet.
[d]*Goodwill* refers to the excess paid for a firm above the appraised value of the physical assets purchased. Goodwill represents payment both for intangibles such as patents and for "organization value," such as that associated with having an effective sales force. Beginning in 2001, purchased goodwill such as this may not be amortized for financial statement reporting purposes.
[e]Firm B's common equity is reduced by $10 prior to consolidation to reflect the fixed asset write-off.
[f]Firm B's equity is increased to $50 to reflect the above-book purchase price.

---

26. Recall that in 2001, the Financial Accounting Standards Board (FASB) issued Statement 141, which eliminated the use of *pooling* accounting.

Note that Firm B's net asset value is $30, which is also its reported common equity value. This $30 book value could be equal to the market value (which is determined by investors based on the firm's earning power), but book value could also be more or less than the market value. Three situations are considered in Table 26-4. First, in Column 3 we assume that Firm A gives stock worth $20 for Firm B. Thus, B's assets as reported on its balance sheet were overvalued, and A pays less than B's net asset value. The overvaluation could be in either fixed or current assets; an appraisal would be made, but we assume it is fixed assets that are overvalued. Accordingly, we reduce B's fixed assets and also its common equity by $10 before constructing the consolidated balance sheet shown in Column 3. Next, in Column 4, we assume that A pays exactly the net asset value for B. In this case, the financial statements are simply combined.

Finally, in Column 5 we assume that A pays more than the net asset value for B: $50 is paid for $30 of net assets. This excess is assumed to be partly attributable to undervalued assets (land, buildings, machinery, and inventories) and so, to reflect this undervaluation, current and fixed assets are each increased by $5. In addition, we assume that $10 of the $20 excess of market value over book value is due to a superior sales organization or to some other intangible factor, and we post this excess as goodwill. Firm B's common equity is increased by $20, the sum of the increases in current and fixed assets plus goodwill, and this markup is also reflected in Firm A's post-merger equity account.[27]

26-12b **Income Statement Effects**

A merger can have a significant effect on reported profits. If asset values are increased, as they often are under a purchase, then this must be reflected in higher depreciation charges (and also in a higher cost of goods sold if inventories are written up). This, in turn, will further reduce reported profits. Prior to 2001, goodwill was also amortized over its expected life. Now, however, goodwill is subject to an "annual impairment test." If the fair market value of the goodwill has declined over the year, then the amount of the decline must be charged to earnings. If not, then there is no charge, but gains in goodwill cannot be added to earnings.

Table 26-5 illustrates the income statement effects of the write-up of current and fixed assets. We assume A purchased B for $50, creating $10 of goodwill and $10 of higher physical asset value. As Column 3 indicates, the asset markups cause reported profits to be lower than the sum of the individual companies' reported profits.

The asset markup is also reflected in earnings per share. In our hypothetical merger, we assume that nine shares exist in the consolidated firm. (Six of these shares went to A's stockholders, and three went to B's.) The merged company's EPS is $2.33, whereas each of the individual companies' EPS was $2.40.

---

27. This example assumes that additional debt was not issued to help finance the acquisition. If the acquisition were totally debt financed, then the post-merger balance sheet would show an increase in debt rather than an increase in the equity account. If it were financed by a mix of debt and equity, both accounts would increase. If the acquisition were paid for with cash on hand, then current assets would decrease by the amount paid and the equity account would not increase.

TABLE 26-5	Income Statement Effects		
	Pre-Merger		**Post-Merger: Firm A**
	Firm A **(1)**	**Firm B** **(2)**	**Merged** **(3)**
Sales	$100.0	$50.0	$150.0
Operating costs	72.0	36.0	109.0[a]
Operating income	$ 28.0	$14.0	$ 41.0[a]
Interest (10%)	4.0	2.0	6.0
Taxable income	$ 24.0	$12.0	$ 35.0
Taxes (40%)	9.6	4.8	14.0
Net income	$ 14.4	$7.2	$ 21.0
EPS[b]	$ 2.40	$2.40	$ 2.33

[a]Operating costs are $1 higher than they otherwise would be; this reflects the higher reported costs (depreciation and cost of goods sold) caused by the physical asset markup at the time of purchase.
[b]Before the merger, Firm A had six shares and Firm B had three shares. Firm A gives one of its shares for each of Firm B's, so A has nine shares outstanding after the merger.

What is purchase accounting for mergers?

What is goodwill? What impact does goodwill have on the firm's balance sheet? On its income statement?

SELF TEST

26-13 Analysis for a "True Consolidation"

Most of our analysis in the preceding sections assumed that one firm plans to acquire another. However, in many situations it is hard to identify an "acquirer" and a "target"—the merger appears to be a true "merger of equals," as was the case with the Exxon–Mobil and First Union–Wachovia mergers. In such cases, how is the analysis handled?

The first step is to estimate the value of the combined enterprise, incorporating any synergies, tax effects, or capital structure changes. The second step is to decide how to allocate the new company's stock between the two sets of old stockholders. Because of synergy, one would normally expect the consolidated value to exceed the sum of the pre-announcement values of the two companies. For example, Company A might have had a pre-merger equity value of $10 billion, found as (Number of shares) (Price per share), and Company B might have had a pre-merger value of $15 billion. If the post-merger value of new Company AB is estimated to be $30 billion, then that value must be allocated. Company A's stockholders must receive enough shares to give them a projected value of at least $10 billion, and Company B's stockholders must receive at least $15 billion. But how will the remaining $5 billion of synergistically induced value be divided?

This is a key issue, requiring intense negotiation between the two management groups. There is no rule or formula to apply, but one basis for the allocation is the relative pre-announcement values of the two companies. For example, in our hypothetical merger of A and B to form AB, the companies might agree to give $10/$25 = 40% of the new stock to A's stockholders and 60% to B's stockholders. Unless a case could be made for giving a higher percentage of the shares to one of the companies because it was responsible for more of the synergistic value, then the pre-merger value proportions would seem to be a "fair" solution. In any event, the pre-merger proportions will probably be given the greatest weight in reaching the final decision.

It should also be noted that control of the consolidated company is always an issue. Generally, the companies hold a press conference and announce that the CEO of one firm will be chairman of the new company, that the other CEO will be president, that the new board will consist of directors from both old boards, and that power will be shared. With huge mergers such as those we have been seeing lately, there is plenty of power to be shared.

SELF TEST

How does merger analysis differ in the case of a large company acquiring a smaller one versus a "true merger of equals"?

Do you think the same guidelines for allocating synergistic gains would be used in both types of mergers?

26-14 The Role of Investment Bankers

Investment bankers are involved with mergers in a number of ways: (1) they help arrange mergers, (2) they help target companies develop and implement defensive tactics, (3) they help value target companies, (4) they help finance mergers, and (5) they invest in the stocks of potential merger candidates.

26-14a Arranging Mergers

The major investment banking firms have merger and acquisition groups that operate within their corporate finance departments. (Corporate finance departments offer advice, as opposed to underwriting or brokerage services, to business firms.) Members of these groups identify firms with excess cash that might want to buy other firms, companies that might be willing to be bought, and firms that might, for a number of reasons, be attractive to others. Sometimes dissident stockholders of firms with poor track records work with investment bankers to oust management by helping to arrange a merger.

26-14b Developing Defensive Tactics

Target firms that do not want to be acquired generally enlist the help of an investment banking firm along with a law firm that specializes in mergers. Defenses include such tactics as: (1) changing the bylaws so that only one-third of the directors are elected each year and/or so that a 75% approval (a *super majority*) rather than a simple majority is required to approve a merger, (2) trying to convince the target firm's stockholders that the price being offered is too low, (3) raising antitrust issues in the hope that the Justice Department will intervene, (4) repurchasing stock in the open market in an effort to push the price above that being offered by the potential acquirer, (5) finding a **white knight** who is acceptable to the target firm's management to compete with the potential acquirer, and (6) finding a **white squire** who is friendly to current management and can buy enough of the target firm's shares to block the merger.

26-14c **Establishing a Fair Value**

If a friendly merger is being worked out between two firms' managements, then it is important to document that the agreed-upon price is a fair one; otherwise, the stockholders of either company may sue to block the merger. Therefore, in most large mergers, each side will hire an investment banking firm to evaluate the target company and to help establish the fair price. Even if the merger is not friendly, investment bankers may still be asked to help establish a price. If a surprise tender offer is to be made, then the acquiring firm will want to know the lowest price at which it might be able to acquire the stock while the target firm may seek help in "proving" that the price being offered is too low.

26-14d **Financing Mergers**

To be successful in the mergers and acquisitions (M&A) business, an investment banker must be able to offer a financing package to clients—whether they are acquirers who need capital to take over companies or target companies trying to finance stock repurchase plans or other defenses against takeovers. In fact, the fees that investment banks generate through issuing merger-related debt often dwarf their other merger-related fees.

26-14e **Arbitrage Operations**

Arbitrage generally means simultaneously buying and selling the same commodity or security in two different markets at different prices and pocketing a risk-free return. However, the major brokerage houses, as well as some wealthy private investors, are engaged in a different type of arbitrage called *risk arbitrage.* The *arbitrageurs,* or "arbs," speculate in the stocks of companies that are likely takeover targets. Vast amounts of capital are required to speculate in a large number of securities and thus reduce risk, and also to make money on narrow spreads. Yet the large investment bankers have the wherewithal to play this game. To be successful, arbs must be able to sniff out likely targets, assess the probability of offers reaching fruition, and move in and out of the market quickly and with low transaction costs.

What are some defensive tactics that firms can use to resist hostile takeovers?

What is the difference between pure arbitrage and risk arbitrage?

SELF TEST

26-15 **Who Wins: The Empirical Evidence**

The magnitude of the merger market raises two questions: (1) Do corporate acquisitions create value? (2) If so, how is the value shared between the parties?

Most researchers agree that takeovers increase the wealth of the shareholders of target firms, otherwise they would not agree to the offer. However, there is a debate as to whether mergers benefit the acquiring firm's shareholders. In particular, managements of acquiring firms may be motivated by factors other than maximizing shareholder wealth. For example, they may want to merge merely to increase the size of the corporations they manage, because increased size usually brings larger salaries plus job security, perquisites, power, and prestige.

The question of who gains from corporate acquisitions can be tested by examining the stock price changes that occur around the time of a merger or takeover announcement. Changes in the stock prices of the acquiring and target firms represent market participants' beliefs about the value created by the merger and about how that value will be divided between the target and acquiring firms' shareholders. Therefore, examining a large sample of stock price movements can shed light on the issue of who gains from mergers.

MERGER MISTAKES

Academics have long known that acquiring firms' shareholders rarely reap the benefits of mergers. However, this important information never seemed to make it up to the offices of corporate America's decision makers; the 1990s saw bad deal after bad deal and with no apparent learning on the part of acquisitive executives. *BusinessWeek* published an analysis of 302 large mergers from 1995 to 2001, and it found that 61% of them led to losses by the acquiring firms' shareholders. Indeed, those losing shareholders' returns during the first post-merger year averaged 25 percentage points less than the returns on other companies in their industry. The average returns for all the merging companies, both winners and losers, were 4.3% below industry averages and 9.2% below the S&P 500.

The article cited four common mistakes:

1. The acquiring firms often overpaid. Generally, the acquirers gave away all of the synergies from the mergers to the acquired firms' shareholders, and then some.

2. Management overestimated the synergies (cost savings and revenue gains) that would result from the merger.

3. Management took too long to integrate operations between the merged companies. This irritated customers and employees alike, and it postponed any gains from the integration.

4. Some companies cut costs too deeply at the expense of maintaining sales and production infrastructures.

The worst performance came from companies that paid for their acquisitions with stock. The best performance, albeit a paltry 0.3% better than industry averages, came from companies that used cash for their acquisitions. On the bright side, the shareholders of the companies that were acquired fared quite well, earning on average 19.3% more than their industry peers, and all of those gains came in the two weeks surrounding the merger announcement.

Source: David Henry, "Mergers: Why Most Big Deals Don't Pay Off," *BusinessWeek*, October 14, 2002, pp. 60–70.

One cannot simply examine stock prices around merger announcement dates, because other factors influence stock prices. For example, if a merger was announced on a day when the entire market advanced, then a rise in the target firm's price would not necessarily signify that the merger was expected to create value. In other words, did the event (in this case, a merger announcement) cause a change in value? Hence, studies examine *abnormal returns* associated with merger announcements, where abnormal returns are defined as that part of a stock price change caused by factors other than changes in the general stock market. Some research defines abnormal returns as the return not explained by an asset pricing model, such as the CAPM or the Fama-French 3-Factor model, as we described in Chapter 2.

Event studies have examined both acquiring and target firms' stock price responses to mergers and tender offers. Jointly, they have covered nearly every acquisition involving publicly traded firms from the early 1960s to the present, and they are remarkably consistent in their results: On average, the stock prices of target firms increase by about 30% in hostile tender offers, whereas in friendly mergers the average increase is about 20%. However, for both hostile and friendly deals, the stock prices of acquiring firms, on average, remain constant. Thus, the event study evidence strongly indicates: (1) that acquisitions do create value but (2) that shareholders of target firms reap virtually all the benefits.

The event study evidence suggests that mergers benefit targets but not acquirers—and hence that an acquiring firm's stockholders should be skeptical of its managers' plans for acquisitions. This evidence cannot be dismissed out of hand, but neither is it entirely convincing. There are undoubtedly many good mergers, just as there are many poorly conceived ones. Like most of finance, merger decisions should be studied carefully, and it is best not to judge the outcome of a specific merger until the actual results start to come in.

> **SELF TEST**
>
> Explain how researchers can study the effects of mergers on shareholder wealth.
>
> Do mergers create value? If so, who profits from this value?
>
> Do the research results discussed in this section seem logical? Explain.

26-16 Corporate Alliances

Mergers are one way for two companies to join forces, but many companies are striking cooperative deals, called **corporate**, or **strategic, alliances**, which stop far short of merging. Whereas mergers combine all of the assets of the firms involved, as well as their ownership and managerial expertise, alliances allow firms to create combinations that focus on specific business lines that offer the most potential synergies. These alliances take many forms, from simple marketing agreements to joint ownership of worldwide operations.

One form of corporate alliance is the **joint venture**, in which parts of companies are joined to achieve specific, limited objectives. A joint venture is controlled by a management team consisting of representatives of the two (or more) parent companies. A study of 345 corporate alliances found that the stock prices of both partners in an alliance tended to increase when the alliance was announced, with an average abnormal return of about 0.64% on the day of the announcement.[28] About 43% of the alliances were marketing agreements, 14% were R&D agreements, 11% were for licensing technology, 7% for technology transfers, and 25% were for some combination of these four reasons. Although most alliances were for marketing agreements, the market reacted most favorably when the alliance was for technology sharing between two firms in the same industry. The study also found that the typical alliance lasted at least 5 years and that the allied firms had better operating performance than their industry peers during this period.

> **SELF TEST**
>
> What is the difference between a merger and a corporate alliance?
>
> What is a joint venture? Give some reasons why joint ventures may be advantageous to the parties involved.

26-17 **Divestitures**

There are four types of **divestitures**. A **sale to another firm** generally involves the sale of an entire division or unit, usually for cash but sometimes for stock in the acquiring firm. In a **spin-off**; the firm's existing stockholders are given new stock representing separate ownership rights in the division that was divested. The division establishes its own board of directors and officers, and it becomes a separate company. The stockholders end up owning shares of two firms instead of one, but no cash has been transferred. In a **carve-out**; a minority interest in a corporate subsidiary is sold to new shareholders, so the parent gains new equity financing yet retains control. In a **liquidation**, the assets of a division are sold off piecemeal to many purchasers rather than as an single operating entity to one purchaser. To illustrate the different types of divestitures, we now present some examples.

In mid-2014 Liberty Media made plans to divest itself of its cable business in an equity carve-out. Shares in the new, publicly traded company, Liberty Broadband, would be distributed to Liberty Media stockholders. This plan followed initial, but later scrapped, plans to create a tracking stock out of this same business line. In 2012, Ralcorp Holdings split the company into a Post Foods piece and a private-label business. The reason for the spin-off was to allow the two divisions to focus on their different product markets and also to allow ConAgra, which had been pursuing Ralcorp for its private-label business, to make a more limited acquisition. In 2009, Time Warner announced that it planned to spin off AOL, the dissolution of a merger that had never worked. And in 2008, Cadbury Schweppes decided to focus on its chocolate and candy businesses, so it spun off soft-drink brands into a separately traded company, the Dr Pepper Snapple Group.

As these examples illustrate, the reasons for divestitures vary widely. Sometimes the market feels more comfortable when firms "stick to their knitting," as the Cadbury Schweppes divestiture illustrates. Sometimes companies need cash either

---

28. See Su Han Chan, John W. Kensinger, Arthur J. Keown, and John D. Martin, "When Do Strategic Alliances Create Shareholder Value?" *Journal of Applied Corporate Finance*, Winter 1999, pp. 82–87.

to finance expansion in their primary business lines or to reduce a large debt burden, and divestitures can be used to raise this cash; for example, AMD spun off its manufacturing operations in 2009. The divestitures also show that running a business is a dynamic process—conditions change, corporate strategies change in response, and consequently firms alter their asset portfolios by acquisitions and/or divestitures. Some divestitures are designed to unload losing assets that would otherwise drag the company down, such as Time Warner's planned spin-off of AOL.

In general, the empirical evidence shows that the market reacts favorably to divestitures, with the divesting company typically having a small increase in stock price on the day of the announcement. The announcement-day returns are largest for companies that "undo" previous conglomerate mergers by divesting businesses in unrelated areas.[29] Studies also show that divestitures generally lead to superior operating performance for both the parent and the divested company.[30]

What are some types of divestitures?

What are some motives for divestitures?

SELF TEST

26-18 Holding Companies

Holding companies date from 1889, when New Jersey became the first state to pass a law permitting corporations to be formed for the sole purpose of owning the stocks of other companies. Many of the advantages and disadvantages of holding companies are identical to those of any large-scale organization. Whether a company is organized on a divisional basis or with subsidiaries kept as separate companies does not affect the basic reasons for conducting a large-scale, multiproduct, multiplant operation.

26-18a Advantages and Disadvantages of Holding Companies

There are two principal advantages of a holding company.

1. *Control with fractional ownership.* Through a holding company operation, a firm may buy 5%, 10%, or 50% of the stock of another corporation. Such fractional ownership may be sufficient to give the holding company effective working control over the operations of the company in which it has acquired stock ownership. Working control is often considered to entail more than 25% of the common stock, but it can be as low as 10% if the stock is widely distributed. One financier says that the attitude of management is more important than the number of shares owned: "If management thinks you can

---

29. For details, see Jeffrey W. Allen, Scott L. Lummer, John J. McConnell, and Debra K. Reed, "Can Takeover Losses Explain Spin-off Gains?" *Journal of Financial and Quantitative Analysis*, December 1995, pp. 465–485.

30. See Shane A. Johnson, Daniel P. Klein, and Verne L. Thibodeaux, "The Effects of Spin-offs on Corporate Investment and Performance," *Journal of Financial Research*, Summer 1996, pp. 293–307. Also see Steven Kaplan and Michael S. Weisbach, "The Success of Acquisitions: Evidence from Divestitures," *Journal of Finance*, March 1992, pp. 107–138.

control the company, then you do." In addition, control on a very slim margin can be held through relationships with large stockholders outside the holding company group.

2. *Isolation of risks*. Because the various **operating companies** in a holding company system are separate legal entities, the obligations of any one unit are separate from those of the other units. Therefore, catastrophic losses incurred by one unit of the holding company system may not be translatable into claims on the assets of the other units. However, we should note that while this is a customary generalization, it is not always valid. First, the **parent company** may feel obligated to make good on the subsidiary's debts, even though it is not legally bound to do so, in order to keep its good name and to retain customers. Second, a parent company may feel obligated to supply capital to an affiliate in order to protect its initial investment. And third, when lending to one of the units of a holding company system, an astute loan officer may require a guarantee by the parent holding company. To some degree, then, the assets in the various elements of a holding company are not really separate.

The main disadvantage of a holding company involves *partial multiple taxation*. Provided the holding company owns at least 80% of a subsidiary's voting stock, the IRS permits the filing of consolidated returns, in which case dividends received by the parent are not taxed. However, if less than 80% of the stock is owned, then tax returns cannot be consolidated. Firms that own more than 20% but less than 80% of another corporation can deduct 80% of the dividends received, whereas firms that own less than 20% may deduct only 70% of the dividends received. This partial double taxation somewhat offsets the benefits of holding company control with limited ownership, but whether the tax penalty is sufficient to offset other possible advantages varies from case to case.

26-18b **Holding Companies as a Leveraging Device**

The holding company vehicle has been used to obtain huge degrees of financial leverage. In the 1920s, several tiers of holding companies were established in the electric utility, railroad, and other industries. In those days, an operating company at the bottom of the pyramid might have $100 million of assets, financed by $50 million of debt and $50 million of equity. Then, a first-tier holding company might own the stock of the operating firm as its only asset and be financed with $25 million of debt and $25 million of equity. A second-tier holding company, which owned the stock of the first-tier company, might be financed with $12.5 million of debt and $12.5 million of equity. Such systems were extended to five or six levels. With six holding companies, $100 million of operating assets could be controlled at the top by only $0.78 million of equity, and the operating assets would have to provide enough cash income to support $99.22 million of debt. *Such a holding company system is highly leveraged—its consolidated debt ratio is 99.22%, even though each of the individual components shows only a 50% debt/assets ratio.* Because of this consolidated leverage, even a small decline in profits at the operating company level could bring the whole system down like a house of cards. This situation existed in the electric utility industry in the 1920s, and the Depression of the 1930s wreaked such havoc with the holding companies that federal legislation was enacted that constrained holding companies in that industry.

SELF TEST

What is a holding company?

What are some of the advantages of holding companies? Identify a disadvantage.

Summary

- A **merger** occurs when two firms combine to form a single company. The primary motives for mergers are: (1) synergy, (2) tax considerations, (3) purchase of assets below their replacement costs, (4) diversification, (5) gaining control over a larger enterprise, and (6) breakup value.
- Mergers can provide economic benefits through **economies of scale** and through putting assets in the hands of more efficient managers. However, mergers also have the potential for reducing competition, and for this reason they are carefully regulated by government agencies.
- In most mergers, one company (the **acquiring company**) initiates action to take over another (the **target company**).
- A **horizontal merger** occurs when two firms in the same line of business combine.
- A **vertical merger** combines a firm with one of its customers or suppliers.
- A **congeneric merger** involves firms in related industries but where no customer–supplier relationship exists.
- A **conglomerate merger** occurs when firms in totally different industries combine.
- In a **friendly merger**, the managements of both firms approve the merger, whereas in a **hostile merger**, the target firm's management opposes it.
- An **operating merger** is one in which the operations of the two firms are combined. A **financial merger** is one in which the firms continue to operate separately; hence no operating economies are expected.
- In a typical **merger analysis**, the key issues to be resolved are: (1) the price to be paid for the target firm and (2) the employment/control situation. If the merger is a consolidation of two relatively equal firms, at issue is the percentage of ownership that each merger partner's shareholders will receive.
- Four methods are commonly used to determine the **value of the target firm**: (1) **market multiple analysis**, (2) the **corporate valuation model**, (3) the **free cash flow to equity (FCFE) model**, and (4) the **adjusted present value (APV) model**. The three cash flow models give the same value if implemented correctly, but the APV model is the easiest to implement correctly and should be used when the capital structure is changing.
- **Purchase accounting** treats mergers as a purchase and is used for financial reporting.

- A **joint venture** is a **corporate alliance** in which two or more companies combine some of their resources to achieve a specific, limited objective.
- A **divestiture** is the sale of some of a company's operating assets. A divestiture may involve: (1) selling an operating unit to another firm, (2) **spinning off** a unit as a separate company, (3) **carving out** a unit by selling a minority interest, or (4) the outright **liquidation** of a unit's assets.
- The **reasons for divestiture** include: (1) settling antitrust suits, (2) improving the transparency of the resulting companies so that investors can more easily evaluate them, (3) enabling management to concentrate on a particular type of activity, and (4) raising the capital needed to strengthen the corporation's core business.
- A **holding company** is a corporation that owns sufficient stock in another firm to control it. The holding company is also known as the **parent company**, and the companies that it controls are called **subsidiaries**; or **operating companies**.
- Holding company operations are advantageous because: (1) control can often be obtained for a smaller cash outlay, (2) risks may be segregated, and (3) regulated companies can operate separate subsidiaries for their regulated and unregulated businesses.
- A major disadvantage to holding companies is the possibility of income being taxed at the subsidiary and at the parent.

Questions

26–1 Define each of the following terms:
    a. Synergy; merger
    b. Horizontal merger; vertical merger; congeneric merger; conglomerate merger
    c. Friendly merger; hostile merger; defensive merger; tender offer; target company; breakup value; acquiring company
    d. Operating merger; financial merger
    e. Free cash flow to equity
    f. Purchase accounting
    g. White knight; proxy fight
    h. Joint venture; corporate alliance
    i. Divestiture; spin-off
    j. Holding company; operating company; parent company
    k. Arbitrage; risk arbitrage

26–2 Four economic classifications of mergers are: (1) horizontal, (2) vertical, (3) conglomerate, and (4) congeneric. Explain the significance of these terms in merger analysis with regard to (a) the likelihood of governmental intervention and (b) possibilities for operating synergy.

26–3 Firm A wants to acquire Firm B. Firm B's management agrees that the merger is a good idea. Might a tender offer be used? Why or why not?

26–4 Distinguish between operating mergers and financial mergers.

26–5 Distinguish between the APV, FCFE, and corporate valuation models.

Problems

The following information is required to work Problems 26-1 through 26-4.

Hastings Corporation is interested in acquiring Vandell Corporation. Vandell has 1 million shares outstanding and a target capital structure consisting of 30% debt. Vandell's debt interest rate is 8%. Assume that the risk-free rate of interest is 5% and the market risk premium is 6%. Both Vandell and Hastings face a 40% tax rate.

Easy Problem 1

26-1 Valuation

Vandell's free cash flow (FCF_0) is $2 million per year and is expected to grow at a constant rate of 5% a year; its beta is 1.4. What is the value of Vandell's operations? If Vandell has $10.82 million in debt, what is the current value of Vandell's stock? (*Hint:* Use the corporate valuation model from Chapter 8.)

Intermediate Problems 2–3

26-2 Merger Valuation

Hastings estimates that if it acquires Vandell, interest payments will be $1.5 million per year for 3 years, after which the current target capital structure of 30% debt will be maintained. Interest in the fourth year will be $1.472 million, after which interest and the tax shield will grow at 5%. Synergies will cause the free cash flows to be $2.5 million, $2.9 million, $3.4 million, and $3.57 million in Years 1 through 4, respectively, after which the free cash flows will grow at a 5% rate. What is the unlevered value of Vandell, and what is the value of its tax shields? What is the per share value of Vandell to Hastings Corporation? Assume that Vandell now has $10.82 million in debt.

26-3 Merger Bid

On the basis of your answers to Problems 26-1 and 26-2, indicate the range of possible prices that Hastings could bid for each share of Vandell common stock in an acquisition.

Challenging Problems 4–6

26-4 Merger Valuation with Change in Capital Structure

Assuming the same information as for Problem 26-2, suppose Hastings will increase Vandell's level of debt at the end of Year 3 to $30.6 million so that the target capital structure is now 45% debt. Assume that with this higher level of debt the interest rate would be 8.5%, and assume that interest payments in Year 4 are based on the new debt level from the end of Year 3 and a new interest rate. Again, free cash flows and tax shields are projected to grow at 5% after Year 4. What are the values of the unlevered firm and the tax shield, and what is the maximum price that Hastings would bid for Vandell now?

26-5 Merger Analysis

Marston Marble Corporation is considering a merger with the Conroy Concrete Company. Conroy is a publicly traded company, and its beta is 1.30. Conroy has been barely profitable, so it has paid an average of only 20% in taxes during the last several years. In addition, it uses little debt; its target ratio is just 25%, with the cost of debt 9%.

If the acquisition were made, Marston would operate Conroy as a separate, wholly owned subsidiary. Marston would pay taxes on a consolidated basis, and the tax rate would therefore increase to 35%. Marston also would increase the debt capitalization in the Conroy subsidiary to $w_d = 40\%$, for a total of $22.27 million in debt by the end of Year 4, and pay 9.5% on the debt. Marston's acquisition department estimates that Conroy, if acquired, would generate the following free cash flows and interest expenses (in millions of dollars) in Years 1–5:

Year	Free Cash Flows	Interest Expense
1	$1.30	$1.2
2	1.50	1.7
3	1.75	2.8
4	2.00	2.1
5	2.12	?

In Year 5, Conroy's interest expense would be based on its beginning-of-year (that is, the end-of-Year-4) debt, and in subsequent years both interest expense and free cash flows are projected to grow at a rate of 6%.

These cash flows include all acquisition effects. Marston's cost of equity is 10.5%, its beta is 1.0, and its cost of debt is 9.5%. The risk-free rate is 6%, and the market risk premium is 4.5%.

a. What is the value of Conroy's unlevered operations, and what is the value of Conroy's tax shields under the proposed merger and financing arrangements?

b. What is the dollar value of Conroy's operations? If Conroy has $10 million in debt outstanding, how much would Marston be willing to pay for Conroy?

26–6 Merger Valuation with Change in Capital Structure

VolWorld Communications Inc., a large telecommunications company, is evaluating the possible acquisition of Bulldog Cable Company (BCC), a regional cable company. VolWorld's analysts project the following post-merger data for BCC (in thousands of dollars, with a year end of December 31):

	2015	2016	2017	2018	2019	2020
Net sales		$450	$518	$ 555	$ 600	$ 643
Selling and administrative expense		45	53	60	68	73
Interest		40	45	47	52	54
Total net operating capital	$800	850	930	1,005	1,075	1,150

Tax rate after merger: 35%

Cost of goods sold as a percent of sales: 65%

BCC's pre-merger beta: 1.40

Risk-free rate: 6%

Market risk premium: 4%

Terminal growth rate of free cash flows: 7%

If the acquisition is made, it will occur on January 1, 2016. All cash flows shown in the income statements are assumed to occur at the end of the year. BCC currently has a capital structure of 40% debt, which costs 10%, but over the next 4 years VolWorld would increase that to 50%, and the target capital structure would be reached by the start of 2020. BCC, if independent, would pay taxes at 20%, but its income would be taxed at 35% if it were consolidated. BCC's current market-determined beta is 1.4. The cost of goods sold is expected to be 65% of sales.

a. What is the unlevered cost of equity for BCC?

b. What are the free cash flows and interest tax shields for the first 5 years?

c. What is BCC's horizon value of interest tax shields and unlevered horizon value?

d. What is the value of BCC's equity to VolWorld's shareholders if BCC has $300,000 in debt outstanding now?

Spreadsheet Problem

26–7 Build a Model: Merger Analysis

Start with the partial model in the file *Ch26 P07 Build a Model.xls* on the textbook's Web site. Wansley Portal Inc., a large Internet service provider, is evaluating the possible acquisition of Alabama Connections Company (ACC), a regional Internet service provider. Wansley's analysts project the following post-merger data for ACC (in thousands of dollars):

	2016	2017	2018	2019	2020
Net sales	$500	$600	$700	$760	$806
Selling and administrative expense	60	70	80	90	96
Interest	30	40	45	60	74

If the acquisition is made, it will occur on January 1, 2016. All cash flows shown in the income statements are assumed to occur at the end of the year. ACC currently has a capital structure of 30% debt, which costs 9%, but Wansley would increase that over time to 40%, costing 10%, if the acquisition were made. ACC, if independent, would pay taxes at 30%, but its income would be taxed at 35% if it were consolidated. ACC's current market-determined beta is 1.4. The cost of goods sold, which includes depreciation, is expected to be 65% of sales, but it could vary somewhat. Required gross investment in operating capital is approximately equal to the depreciation charged, so there will be no investment in net operating capital. The risk-free rate is 7%, and the market risk premium is 6.5%. Wansley currently has $400,000 in debt outstanding.

a. What is the unlevered cost of equity?

b. What are the horizon value of the tax shields and the horizon value of the unlevered operations? What are the value of ACC's operations and the value of ACC's equity to Wansley's shareholders?

MINI CASE

Hager's Home Repair Company, a regional hardware chain that specializes in "do it yourself" materials and equipment rentals, is cash rich because of several consecutive good years. One of the alternative uses for the excess funds is an acquisition. Doug Zona, Hager's treasurer and your boss, has been asked to place a value on a potential target, Lyons Lighting (LL), a chain that operates in several adjacent states, and he has enlisted your help.

The table below indicates Zona's estimates of LL's earnings potential if it came under Hager's management (in millions of dollars). The interest expense listed here includes the interest: (1) on LL's existing debt, which is $55 million at a rate of 9%, and (2) on new debt expected to be issued over time to help finance expansion within the new "L division," the code name given to the target firm. If acquired, LL will face a 40% tax rate.

Security analysts estimate LL's beta to be 1.3. The acquisition would not change Lyons' capital structure, which is 20% debt. Zona realizes that Lyons Lighting's business plan also requires certain levels of operating capital and that the annual investment could be significant. The required levels of total net operating capital are listed in the table.

Zona estimates the risk-free rate to be 7% and the market risk premium to be 4%. He also estimates that free cash flows after 2020 will grow at a constant rate of 6%. Following are projections for sales and other items.

	2015	2016	2017	2018	2019	2020
Net sales		$ 60.00	$ 90.00	$112.50	$127.50	$139.70
Cost of goods sold (60%)		36.00	54.00	67.50	76.50	83.80
Selling/administrative expense		4.50	6.00	7.50	9.00	11.00
Interest expense		5.00	6.50	6.50	7.00	8.16
Total net operating capital	$150.00	150.00	157.50	163.50	168.00	173.00

Hager's management is new to the merger game, so Zona has been asked to answer some basic questions about mergers as well as to perform the merger analysis. To structure the task, Zona has developed the following questions, which you must answer and then defend to Hager's board.

a. Several reasons have been proposed to justify mergers. Among the more prominent are: (1) tax considerations, (2) risk reduction, (3) control, (4) purchase of assets at below replacement cost, (5) synergy, and (6) globalization. In general, which of the reasons are economically justifiable? Which are not? Which fit the situation at hand? Explain.

b. Briefly describe the differences between a hostile merger and a friendly merger.

c. What are the steps in valuing a merger?

d. Use the data developed in the table to construct the L division's free cash flows for 2016 through 2020. Why are we identifying interest expense separately when it is not normally included in calculating free cash flows or in a capital budgeting cash flow analysis? Why is investment in net operating capital included when calculating the free cash flow?

e. Conceptually, what is the appropriate discount rate to apply to the cash flows developed in part c? What is your actual estimate of this discount rate?

f. What is the estimated horizon, or continuing, value of the acquisition; that is, what is the estimated value of the L division's cash flows beyond 2020? What is LL's value to Hager's shareholders? Suppose another firm were evaluating LL as an acquisition candidate. Would it obtain the same value? Explain.

g. Assume that LL has 20 million shares outstanding. These shares are traded relatively infrequently, but the last trade (made several weeks ago) was at a

price of $11 per share. Should Hager's make an of-
fer for Lyons Lighting? If so, how much should it
offer per share?

h. How would the analysis be different if Hager's
intended to recapitalize LL with 40% debt costing 10% at the end of 4 years? This amounts to
$221.6 million in debt as of the end of 2019.

i. There has been considerable research undertaken
to determine whether mergers really create value
and, if so, how this value is shared between the

parties involved. What are the results of this
research?

j. What method is used to account for mergers?

k. What merger-related activities are undertaken
by investment bankers?

l. What are the major types of divestitures? What
motivates firms to divest assets?

m. What are holding companies? What are their advantages and disadvantages?

SELECTED ADDITIONAL CASES

*The following cases from CengageCompose cover many of the concepts discussed in this chapter and are available
at* **http://compose.cengage.com.**

Klein-Brigham Series:

Case 40, "Nina's Fashions, Inc."; Case 53, "Nero's Pasta, Inc."; and Case 70, "Computer Concepts/CompuTech."

Multinational Financial Management*

Managers of multinational companies must deal with a wide range of issues that are not present when a company operates in a single country. In this chapter, we highlight the key differences between multinational and domestic corporations, and we discuss the effects these differences have on the financial management of multinational businesses.

Beginning-of-Chapter Questions

As you read this chapter, consider how you would answer the following questions. You *should not* necessarily be able to answer the questions before you read the chapter. Rather, you should use them to get a sense of the issues covered in the chapter. After reading the chapter, you should be able to give at least partial answers to the questions, and you should be able to give better answers after the chapter has been discussed in class. Note, too, that it is often useful, when answering conceptual questions, to use hypothetical data to illustrate your answer. We illustrate the answers with an *Excel* model that is available on the textbook's Web site. Accessing the model and working through it is a useful exercise, and it provides insights that are useful when answering the questions.

1. How is **multinational financial management** different from financial management as practiced by a firm that has no direct contacts with foreign firms or customers? What special problems and challenges do multinational firms face? What factors cause companies to "go multinational"?

2. What is an **exchange rate**? What is the difference between **direct** and **indirect rates**? What is a **cross rate**?

3. What is the difference between a **spot rate** and a **forward rate**? How can forward rates be used for **hedging** purposes? Why would hedging occur?

4. What is **interest rate parity**? How might the treasurer of a multinational firm use the interest rate parity concept: (a) when deciding how to invest the firm's surplus cash and (b) when deciding where to borrow funds on a short-term basis?

5. What is **purchasing power parity**? How might a firm use this concept in its operations?

6. Suppose IBM signed a contract to buy a supply of computer chips from a German firm. The price is 10 million euros, and the chips will be delivered immediately, but IBM can delay payment for

---

*Earlier editions of this chapter benefited from the help of Professor Roy Crum of the University of Florida and Subu Venkataraman of Morgan Stanley.

6 months if it wants to. What risk would IBM be exposed to if it delays payment? Can it hedge this risk? Should it pay now or delay payment?

7. Much has been made about the sweeping changes that are occurring in Europe as a result of the **euro**.

Will the euro help European firms become more efficient? Will it change the way multinational corporations manage cash? Manage exchange risk? Borrow funds in local markets? What effects will the euro have on non-European firms?

CORPORATE VALUATION IN A GLOBAL CONTEXT

The intrinsic value of a firm is determined by the size, timing, and risk of its expected future free cash flows (FCF). This is true for foreign as well as domestic operations, but the FCF of a foreign operation is affected by exchange rates, cultural differences, and the host country's regulatory environment. In addition, global financial markets and political risk can affect the cost of capital.

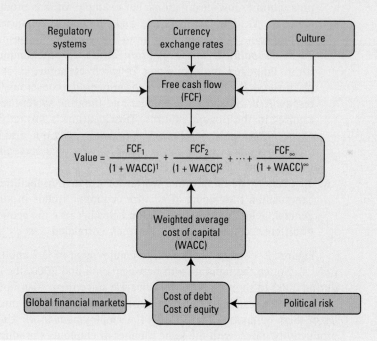

27-1 **Multinational, or Global, Corporations**

The terms **multinational corporations, transnational corporations,** and **global corporations** are used to describe firms that operate in an integrated fashion in a number of countries. Rather than merely buying resources from and selling goods to foreign nations, multinational firms often make direct investments in fully integrated operations, from extraction of raw materials, through the manufacturing process, and to distribution to consumers throughout the world. Today, multinational corporate networks control a large and growing share of the world's technological, marketing, and productive resources.

Companies "go global" for many reasons, including the following:

1. *To broaden their markets.* After a company has saturated its home market, growth opportunities are often better in foreign markets. Thus, such U.S. firms as Coca-Cola and McDonald's are aggressively expanding into overseas markets, and foreign firms such as Sony and Toshiba now dominate the U.S. consumer electronics market.

2. *To seek raw materials.* Many U.S. oil companies, such as ExxonMobil, have major subsidiaries around the world to ensure access to the basic resources needed to sustain the companies' primary business lines.

3. *To seek new technology.* No single nation holds a commanding advantage in all technologies, so companies scour the globe for leading scientific and design ideas. For example, Xerox has introduced more than 80 different office copiers in the United States that were engineered and built by its Japanese joint venture, Fuji Xerox.

4. *To seek production efficiency.* Companies in high-cost countries are shifting production to low-cost regions. For example, GE has production and assembly plants in Mexico, South Korea, and Singapore; Japanese manufacturers are shifting some of their production to lower-cost countries in the Pacific Rim.

5. *To avoid political and regulatory hurdles.* For example, when Germany's BASF launched biotechnology research at home, it confronted legal and political challenges from the environmentally conscious Green movement. In response, BASF shifted its cancer and immune system research to two laboratories in the Boston suburbs. This location is attractive not only because of its large number of engineers and scientists but also because the Boston area has resolved many controversies involving safety, animal rights, and the environment.

6. *To diversify.* By establishing worldwide production facilities and markets, firms can cushion the impact of adverse economic trends in any single country. In general, geographic diversification helps because the economic ups and downs of different countries are not perfectly correlated.

Figure 27-1 shows the growth in employment of U.S. multinational companies (MNCs). Notice the rapid growth between 1988 and 2000, the drop in employment during 2000 to through 2003, and the rise since then. Also notice that virtually all of the net new employees added after 2003 came from the international subsidiaries of these companies. Part of this flat employment in the United States is due to productivity gains, with the same number of employees producing more goods and services. But part is due to the growth in developing markets, which is likely to continue in the foreseeable future.

WWW

Interesting reports about the effect of trade on the U.S. economy can be found on the United States Trade Representative's home page at **www .ustr.gov**.

SELF TEST

What is a multinational corporation?

Why do companies "go global"?

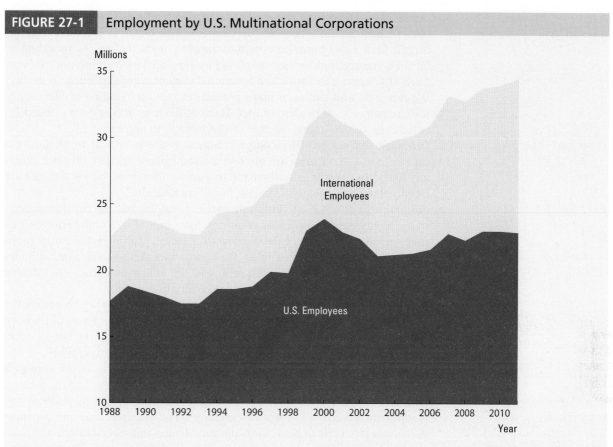

FIGURE 27-1 Employment by U.S. Multinational Corporations

Source: Data obtained from the Bureau of Economic Analysis, various issues of "Summary Estimates for Multinational Companies: Employment, Sales, and Capital Expenditures," including the most recent: **www.bea.gov/newsreleases/international/mnc/2013 /mnc2011.htm**.

27-2 Multinational versus Domestic Financial Management

In theory, the concepts and procedures discussed in earlier chapters are valid for both domestic and multinational operations. However, six major factors distinguish financial management in firms operating entirely within a single country from that of firms operating globally.

1. *Different currency denominations.* Cash flows in various parts of a multinational corporate system will be denominated in different currencies. Hence, the effects of exchange rates must be addressed in all financial analyses.

2. *Economic and legal ramifications.* Each country has its own unique economic and legal system, and the differences among the systems can cause significant problems when a corporation tries to coordinate and control its worldwide operations. For example, differences in tax laws among countries can cause a given economic transaction to have strikingly different after-tax consequences,

depending on where the transaction occurs. Similarly, differences in legal systems of host nations, such as the Common Law of Great Britain versus the French Civil Law, complicate matters ranging from the simple recording of business transactions to the role played by the judiciary in resolving conflicts. Such differences can restrict multinational corporations' flexibility in deploying resources and can even make procedures that are required in one part of the company illegal in another part. These differences also make it difficult for executives trained in one country to move easily to another.

3. *Language differences.* The ability to communicate is critical in all business transactions. U.S. citizens are often at a disadvantage because they are generally fluent only in English, whereas European and Japanese business people are usually fluent in several languages, including English.

4. *Cultural differences.* Even within geographic regions that are considered relatively homogeneous, different countries have unique cultural heritages that shape values and influence the conduct of business. Multinational corporations find that matters such as defining the appropriate goals of the firm, attitudes toward risk, dealings with employees, and the ability to curtail unprofitable operations vary dramatically from one country to the next.

5. *Role of governments.* In a foreign country, the terms under which companies compete, the actions that must be taken or avoided, and the terms of trade on various transactions often are determined not in the marketplace but by direct negotiation between host governments and multinational corporations.

6. *Political risk.* A nation might place constraints on the transfer of corporate resources or even expropriate assets within its boundaries. This is political risk, and it varies from country to country. Another aspect of political risk is terrorism against U.S. firms or executives. For example, U.S. and Japanese executives are at risk of being kidnapped in Mexico and several South American countries.

These factors complicate financial management, and they increase the risks faced by multinational firms. However, the prospects for high returns and better diversification make it worthwhile for firms to accept these risks and learn how to manage them.

> **SELF TEST**   Identify and briefly discuss six major factors that complicate financial management in multinational firms.

WWW

The Bloomberg World Currency Values site provides up-to-the-minute foreign currency values versus the U.S. dollar. The site can be accessed at **www.bloomberg.com/markets/currencies**

27-3 **Exchange Rates**

International transactions often require the purchaser to convert currency into the seller's currency. For example, a U.S. importer of wine from France might have to convert dollars into euros. Sometimes the reverse occurs. For example, OPEC member Saudi Arabia receives dollars for the oil it sells but must convert the dollars to riyals before spending it in Saudi Arabia. Similarly, Iran requires European and Asian countries to pay for oil in euros even though Iran's currency is the rial. Unless you regularly trade in foreign currencies, the notation can be confusing, so that is where we will begin.

27-3a **Foreign Exchange Notation**

An **exchange rate** specifies the number of units of a given currency that can be purchased with one unit of another currency. That sounds simple enough, but what does it mean if you see an exchange rate for dollars and euros posted at 1.25? Does it mean 1 dollar buys 1.25 euros or that 1 euro buys 1.25 dollars? Or if you see an exchange rate quote for dollars and the Japan yen of 80, what does that mean?

You are not the only one to ask such questions, so the International Organization for Standardization (ISO) defined specific labels for currencies. For example, the U.S. dollar is USD, the Japanese yen is JPY, and the euro is EUR. Most sources of exchange rate quotes, such as *The Wall Street Journal*, Reuters, Google Finance, and Yahoo! Finance would report the quote as USD/JPY = 80.[1] Here is how to interpret that quote. First, it is *not* the number of dollars per yen, as you might be led to think by the slash mark between USD and JPY—in fact, it is the opposite! It is the value of a dollar when expressed in yen, or 80 yen per dollar.

Here is the logic. Suppose you are doing business in Argentina and decide at dinner to buy a nice bottle of Malbec. One of your competitors from Japan also decides to buy the same bottle of wine. The quote of USD/JPY = 80 means that your competitor would need to spend 80 yen for each dollar that you spend. In other words, 1 dollar is 80 times more valuable than 1 yen. Therefore, the quote of USD/JPY shows the relative value of a dollar to a yen. If this quote were an equation, you could do some algebra and get:

$$USD/JPY = 80$$
$$USD = 80 \ JPY$$
$$\$1.00 = ¥80$$

This means that 1 dollar is worth 80 yen per dollar. Just remember that the "slash" in the notation shows the relative values of the two currencies and you will be able to keep exchange rates straight. For example, the quote of EUR/USD = 1.25 means that the euro is 25% more valuable than the dollar, so 1 euro can buy 1.25 dollars.

There are two other important concepts related to notation, home versus foreign and direct versus indirect. For example, sometimes the financial press will talk about a foreign currency and the home currency (also called the domestic currency). That is pretty straight forward—if you are in the United States and taking a U.S. perspective, then the U.S. dollar is the home currency and all other currencies are foreign currencies. Alternatively, if you are in India and taking a local perspective, the home currency is the rupee.

A **direct quote** reports the number of units of the home currency per unit of foreign currency. If we take a U.S. perspective, the quote EUR/USD = 1.25 is a direct quote because it shows the number of dollars per euro. When not shown in tables, the U.S. financial press often reports a direct quote with a dollar sign. For example, the press would report "the euro was at $1.25."

---

1. Some sources report quotes slightly differently. For example, **www.boomberg.com** would report it as USD-JPN. Some sources use currency notation, like the CFA Institute, which would report it as $:¥ = 80. But in all cases the notation shows the value of the first currency relative to the second currency.

TABLE 27-1	Selected Exchange Rates	
	Direct Quotation: U.S. Dollars Required to Buy One Unit of Foreign Currency (1)	**Indirect Quotation: Number of Units of Foreign Currency per U.S. Dollar (2)**
Canadian dollar	*0.9073*	1.1022
Japanese yen	*0.0098*	102.3130
Mexican peso	*0.0763*	13.1000
Swiss franc	*1.1343*	0.8816
U.K. (British) pound	1.6802	*0.5952*
Euro	1.3832	*0.7230*

Note: The financial press usually quotes British pounds and euros as direct quotations, so Column 2 equals 1.0 divided by Column 1 for these currencies. The financial press usually quotes all other currencies as indirect quotations, so Column 1 equals 1.0 divided by Column 2 for these currencies. We use italic to denote a quote that is an inverse of the actual reported quote.

Source: *The Wall Street Journal,* **http://online.wsj.com**; quotes for April 24, 2014.

An **indirect quote** is the inverse of a direct quote and shows the number of foreign currency per unit of home currency. For example, the quote USD/JPY = 80 is an indirect quote from a U.S. perspective. When not shown in tables, the U.S. financial press often reports an indirect quote with the foreign currency symbol. For example, the press would report "the dollar was at ¥80."

For consistency throughout this chapter, we will always take the U.S. perspective. A simple mnemonic device to help you remember is that a _D_irect quote is _D_ollars per unit of foreign currency.

27-3b **Converting Currencies**

Table 27-1 reports recent exchange rates for several currencies. The values shown in Column 1 are direct quotes and show the number of U.S. dollars required to purchase one unit of a foreign currency. The exchange rates in Column 2 are indirect quotes.

Normal practice in currency trading centers is to use indirect quotations (Column 2) for all currencies other than British pounds and euros, for which the direct quotations are given. Thus, we speak of the pound as "selling at 1.6802 dollars, or at $1.6802," and the euro as "selling at $1.3832." For all other currencies, the normal convention is to use indirect quotations. For example, for the Japanese yen, we would quote the dollar as "being at ¥102.3130," where the "¥" stands for *yen.* This convention eliminates confusion when comparing quotations from one trading center—say, New York—with those from another—say, London or Zurich.

We can use the data in Table 27-1 to show how to work with exchange rates. Suppose a tourist flies from New York to London, then to Paris, and then on to Geneva. She then flies to Montreal, and finally back to New York. Her tour package includes lodging, food, and transportation, but she must pay for any other expenses. When she arrives at London's Heathrow Airport, she goes to the bank to check the foreign exchange listings. The rate she observes for U.S. dollars is $1.6802, which is the number of dollars per pound. Summarizing her situation, she starts with dollars,

WEB

See *Ch27 Tool Kit.xls* on the textbook's Web site for all calculations.

sees the exchange rate posted as dollars/pound, and she wants to end with pounds. If she exchanges \$3,000, how many pounds will she get?[2]

$$\frac{3,000 \text{ dollars}}{1.6802 \text{ dollars/pound}} = 1,785.50 \text{ pounds}$$

She then enjoys a short vacation in London, ending with £1,000.

After taking a train under the English Channel to France, she realizes that she needs to exchange her 1,000 remaining pounds for euros. However, what she sees on the board is the direct quotation for dollars per pound and the direct quotation for dollars per euro. The exchange rate between any two currencies other than dollars is called a **cross rate**. Cross rates are actually calculated on the basis of various currencies relative to the U.S. dollar. For example, the cross rate between British pounds and euros is computed as follows:

$$\frac{1.6802 \left(\dfrac{\text{dollars}}{\text{pound}} \right)}{1.3832 \left(\dfrac{\text{dollars}}{\text{euro}} \right)} = \left(\frac{1.6802}{1.3832} \right) \left(\frac{\text{dollars}}{\text{pound}} \right) \left(\frac{\text{euros}}{\text{dollar}} \right) = 1.2147 \text{ euros per pound}$$

She would receive 1.2147 euros for every British pound, so she would receive:

$$(1,000 \text{ pounds}) \left(\frac{1.2147 \text{ euros}}{\text{pound}} \right) = 1,214.70 \text{ euros}$$

She has 800 euros remaining when she finishes touring in France and arrives in Geneva. She again needs to determine a cross rate, this time between euros and Swiss francs. The quotes she sees, as shown in Table 27-1, are a direct quote for euros (1.3832 dollars per euro) and an indirect quote for Swiss francs (0.8816 Swiss francs per dollar). To find the cross rate for Swiss francs per euro, she makes the following calculation:

$$\left(\frac{0.8816 \text{ Swiss francs}}{\text{dollar}} \right) \left(\frac{1.3832 \text{ dollars}}{\text{euro}} \right) = 1.2194 \text{ Swiss francs per euro}$$

Therefore, for every euro she would receive 1.2194 Swiss francs, so she would receive:

$$(800 \text{ euros}) \left(\frac{1.2194 \text{ Swiss francs}}{\text{euro}} \right) = 975.52 \text{ Swiss francs}$$

She has 500 Swiss francs remaining when she leaves Geneva and arrives in Montreal. She again needs to determine a cross rate, this time between Swiss francs and Canadian dollars. The quotes she sees, as shown in Table 27-1, are an indirect quote for Swiss francs (0.8816 Swiss francs per dollar) and an indirect quote for

WWW

For a nice currency calculator to determine the exchange rate between any two currencies, see **finance .yahoo.com/currency**.

---

2. For a quick refresher in algebra, recall that:

$$\frac{aX}{b \left(\dfrac{X}{Y} \right)} = \left(\frac{a}{b} \right) \left(\frac{X}{\left(\dfrac{X}{Y} \right)} \right) = \left(\frac{a}{b} \right) \left(\frac{XY}{X} \right) = \left(\frac{a}{b} \right) Y.$$

So if a = 3,000, X = dollars, b = 1.6802, and Y = pounds, then $\dfrac{aX}{b \left(\dfrac{X}{Y} \right)} = 1,785.50$ pounds.

Canadian dollars (1.1022 Canadian dollars per U.S. dollar). To find the cross rate for Canadian dollars per Swiss franc, she makes the following calculation:

$$\frac{1.1022\left(\dfrac{\text{Canadian dollars}}{\text{U.S. dollar}}\right)}{0.8816\left(\dfrac{\text{Swiss francs}}{\text{U.S. dollar}}\right)} = \left(\frac{1.1022}{0.8816}\right)\left(\frac{\text{Canadian dollars}}{\text{U.S. dollar}}\right)\left(\frac{\text{U.S. dollar}}{\text{Canadian dollars}}\right)$$

$$= 1.2502 \text{ Canadian dollars per Swiss franc}$$

Therefore, she would receive:

$$(500 \text{ Swiss francs})\left(\frac{1.2502 \text{ Canadian dollars}}{\text{Swiss franc}}\right) = 625.10 \text{ Canadian dollars}$$

After leaving Montreal and arriving at New York, she has 100 Canadian dollars remaining. She sees the indirect quote for Canadian dollars of 1.1022 Canadian dollars per U.S. dollar and converts the 100 Canadian dollars to U.S. dollars as follows:

$$\frac{100 \text{ canadian dollars}}{\left(1.1022\left(\dfrac{\text{Canadian dollars}}{\text{U.S. dollar}}\right)\right)} = \left(\frac{100}{1.1022}\right)(\text{Canadian dollars})\left(\frac{\text{U.S. dollars}}{\text{Canadian dollars}}\right)$$

$$= 90.73 \text{ U.S. dollars}$$

In this example, we made three assumptions. First, we assumed that our traveler had to calculate the cross rates. For retail transactions, it is customary to display the cross rates directly instead of a series of dollar rates. Second, we assumed that exchange rates remain constant over time. Actually, exchange rates vary every day, often dramatically. We will have more to say about exchange rate fluctuations in the next section. Finally, we assumed that there were no transaction costs involved in exchanging currencies. In reality, small retail exchange transactions such as those in our example usually involve fixed and/or sliding-scale fees that can easily consume 5% or more of the transaction amount. However, credit card purchases minimize these fees.

Major business publications, such as *The Wall Street Journal*, and Web sites, such as **www.bloomberg.com**, regularly report cross rates among key currencies. A set of cross rates is given in Table 27-2. When examining the table, note the following points:

1. Column 1 gives indirect quotes for dollars—that is, units of a foreign currency that can be bought with one U.S. dollar. Examples: $1 will buy 0.7230 euro or 0.8816 Swiss francs. This is consistent with Table 27-1, Column 2.
2. Other columns show number of units of other currencies that can be bought with one pound, one Swiss franc, etc. For example, the euro column shows that 1 euro will buy 1.5246 Canadian dollars, 141.5193 Japanese yen, or 1.3832 U.S. dollars.
3. The rows show direct quotes—that is, the number of units of the currency of the country listed in the left column required to buy one unit of the currency listed in the top row. The bottom row is particularly important for U.S. companies, as it shows the direct quotes for the U.S. dollar. This row is consistent with Column 1 of Table 27-1.
4. Observe that the values on the bottom row of Table 27-2 are reciprocals of the corresponding values in the first column. For example, the U.K. row in the first

TABLE 27-2	Key Currency Cross Rates						
	Dollar (1)	Euro (2)	Pound (3)	SFranc (4)	Peso (5)	Yen (6)	CdnDlr (7)
Canada	1.1022	1.5246	1.8519	1.2502	0.0841	0.0108	....
Japan	102.3130	141.5193	171.9063	116.0538	7.8102	....	92.8262
Mexico	13.1000	18.1199	22.0106	14.8593	....	0.1280	11.8853
Switzerland	0.8816	1.2194	1.4813	....	0.0673	0.0086	0.7999
United Kingdom	0.5952	0.8232	....	0.6751	0.0454	0.0058	0.5400
Euro	0.7230	....	1.2147	0.8201	0.0552	0.0071	0.6559
United States	....	1.3832	1.6802	1.1343	0.0763	0.0098	0.9073

Source: Derived from Table 27-1; quotes for April 24, 2014.

   column shows 0.5952 pound per dollar, and the pound column in the bottom row shows $1/0.5952 = 1.6802$ dollars per pound.
5. By reading down the euro column, you can see that 1 euro is worth 1.2194 Swiss francs. This is the same cross rate that we calculated for the U.S. tourist in our example.

The tie-in with the dollar ensures that all currencies are related to one another in a consistent manner—if this consistency did not exist, then currency traders could profit by buying undervalued and selling overvalued currencies. This process, known as *arbitrage*, works to bring about an equilibrium wherein the same relationship described earlier exists. Currency traders are constantly operating in the market, seeking small inconsistencies from which they can profit. The traders' existence enables the rest of us to assume that currency markets are in equilibrium and that, at any moment in time, cross rates are all internally consistent.[3]

SELF TEST

What is an exchange rate?

Explain the difference between direct and indirect quotations.

What is a cross rate?

Assume that the indirect quote is for 10.0 Mexican pesos per U.S. dollar. What is the direct quote for dollars per peso? **(0.10 dollars/peso)**

Assume that the indirect quote is for 115 Japanese yen per U.S. dollar and that the direct quote is for 1.25 U.S. dollars per euro. What is the yen per euro exchange rate? **(143.75 yen per euro)**

---

3. For more discussion of exchange rates, see Jongmoo Jay Choi and Anita Mehra Prasad, "Exchange Risk Sensitivity and Its Determinants: A Firm and Industry Analysis of U.S. Multinationals," *Financial Management*, Autumn 1995, pp. 77–88; Jerry A. Hammer, "Hedging Performance and Hedging Objectives: Tests of New Performance Measures in the Foreign Currency Market," *Journal of Financial Research*, Winter 1990, pp. 307–323; and William C. Hunter and Stephen G. Timme, "A Stochastic Dominance Approach to Evaluating Foreign Exchange Hedging Strategies," *Financial Management*, Autumn 1992, pp. 104–112.

27-4 **Exchange Rates and International Trade**

Just as the demand for consumer goods such as Tommy Hilfiger clothing and Nike shoes changes over time, so does the demand for currency. One factor affecting currency demand is the balance of trade between two countries. For example, U.S. importers must buy yen to pay for Japanese goods, whereas Japanese importers must buy U.S. dollars to pay for U.S. goods. If U.S. imports from Japan were to exceed U.S. exports to Japan, then the United States would have a **trade deficit** with Japan, and there would be a greater demand for yen than for dollars. Capital movements also affect currency demand. For example, suppose interest rates in the United States were higher than those in Japan. To take advantage of high U.S. interest rates, Japanese banks, corporations, and sophisticated individuals would buy dollars with yen and then use those dollars to purchase high-yielding U.S. securities. This would create greater demand for dollars than for yen.

Without any government intervention, the relative prices of yen and dollars would fluctuate in response to changes in supply and demand in much the same way that prices of consumer goods fluctuate. For example, if U.S. consumers were to increase their demand for Japanese electronic products, then the accompanying increase in demand for the yen would cause its value to increase relative to the dollar. In this situation, the yen would be strong due to fundamental economic forces.

However, governments can and do intervene. A country's central bank can artificially prop up its currency by using its reserves of gold or foreign currencies to purchase its own currency in the open market. This creates artificial demand for its own currency, thus causing its value to be artificially high. A central bank can also keep its currency at an artificially low value by selling its own currency in the open markets. This increases the currency's supply, which reduces its price.

Why might an artificially low currency be a problem? After all, a cheap currency makes it less expensive for other nations to purchase the country's goods, which creates jobs in the exporting country. However, an artificially low currency value raises the cost of imports, which increases inflation. In addition, high import prices allow competing domestic manufacturers to raise their prices as well, further boosting inflation. The government intervention that causes the artificially low value also contributes to inflation: When a government creates currency to sell in the open markets, this increases the money supply, and, all else held constant, an increasing money supply leads to still more inflation. Thus, artificially holding down the value of a currency stimulates exports but at the expense of potentially overheating and inflating the economy. Also, other countries—whose economies are being weakened because their manufacturers cannot compete against the artificially low prices—may retaliate and impose tariffs or other restrictions on the country that is holding its currency value down.

For example, China had for many years artificially held down the value of the yuan (also called the renminbi). This helped make China the world's largest exporter and greatly stimulated its economy. However, by 2004 the Chinese economy was growing at an unsustainably high rate, and inflation was rising rapidly. The United States and other nations began urging the Chinese government to allow the yuan to rise, which would help their economies by slowing Chinese exports and stimulating their own exports to China. On July 21, 2005, the Chinese government suddenly announced that it was changing the exchange rate to allow the yuan's value to rise by 2.1%. The Chinese government has continued to allow the yuan to appreciate

w w w

The International Monetary Fund reports a full listing of exchange rate arrangements. See **www.imf.org /external/data.htm**. The IMF also publishes a more detailed listing in its *Annual Report on Exchange Arrangements and Exchange Restrictions.* For another listing of world currencies, see **http://fx.sauder.ubc .ca/currency_table .html**.

slowly, and it now (May 2014) stands at about 0.1601 dollars per yuan versus 0.1217 dollars per yuan in June 2005. Notice that this change has made it somewhat cheaper for Chinese to buy from America (a yuan now buys more dollars) and more expensive for Americans to buy from China.

A currency that is artificially high has the opposite effects: Inflation will be held down and citizens can purchase imported goods at low domestic prices, but exporting industries are hurt, as are domestic industries that compete with the cheap imports. Because there is relatively little external demand for the currency, the government will have to create demand by purchasing its own currency, paying with either gold or foreign currencies held by its central bank. Over time, supporting an inflated currency can deplete the gold and foreign currency reserves, making it impossible to continue propping up the currency.

The following sections describe ways that governments handle changes in currency demands.

> What is the effect on a country's economy of an artificially low exchange rate? Of an artificially high exchange rate?

SELF TEST

27-5 The International Monetary System and Exchange Rate Policies

Every nation has a monetary system and a monetary authority. In the United States, the Federal Reserve is our monetary authority, and its task is to hold down inflation while promoting economic growth and raising our national standard of living. Moreover, if countries are to trade with one another, there must be some sort of system in place to facilitate payments between nations. The international monetary system is the framework within which exchange rates are determined. As we describe in this section, there are several different policies used by various countries to determine exchange rates.[4]

27-5a A Short History Lesson: The Bretton Woods Fixed Exchange Rate System

From the end of World War II until August 1971, most of the industrialized world operated under the Bretton Woods **fixed exchange rate system** administered by the International Monetary Fund (IMF). Under this system, the U.S. dollar was linked to gold (at $35 per ounce), and other currencies were then tied to the dollar. The United States took actions to keep the price of gold at $35 per ounce,

---

4. For a comprehensive history of the international monetary system and details of how it has evolved, consult one of the many economics books on the subject, which include Robert Carbaugh, *International Economics*, 14th ed. (Mason, OH: South-Western Cengage Learning, 2012); Mordechai Kreinin, *International Economics: A Policy Approach*, 10th ed. (Mason, OH: Thomson/South-Western, 2006); Jeff Madura, *International Financial Management*, 11th ed. (Mason, OH: Thomson/South-Western, 2012); and Joseph P. Daniels and David D. Van Hoose, *International Monetary and Financial Economics*, 3rd ed. (Mason, OH: South-Western, 2005).

and central banks acted to keep exchange rates between other currencies and the dollar within narrow limits. For example, when the demand for pounds was falling, the Bank of England would step in and buy pounds to push up their price, offering gold or foreign currencies in exchange for pounds. Conversely, when the demand for pounds was too high, the Bank of England would sell pounds for dollars or gold. The Federal Reserve in the United States performed the same functions, and central banks of other countries operated similarly. These actions artificially matched supply and demand, keeping exchange rates stable, but they didn't address the underlying imbalance. For example, if the high demand for pounds occurred because British productivity was rising and British goods were improving in quality, then the underlying demand for pounds would continue in spite of central bank intervention. In such a situation, the Bank of England would find it necessary to continually sell pounds. If the central bank stopped selling pounds then their value would rise; that is, the pound would strengthen and exceed the agreed-upon limits.

Many countries found it difficult and economically painful to maintain the fixed exchange rates required by Bretton Woods. This system began to crumble in August 1971, and it was abandoned completely by the end of 1973. The following sections describe several modern exchange rate systems.

27-5b **Freely, or Independently, Floating Rates**

In the early 1970s, the U.S. dollar was cut loose from the gold standard and, in effect, allowed to "float" in response to supply and demand caused by international trade and international investing activities. Figure 27-2 shows the value of the U.S. dollar

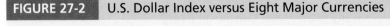

FIGURE 27-2   U.S. Dollar Index versus Eight Major Currencies

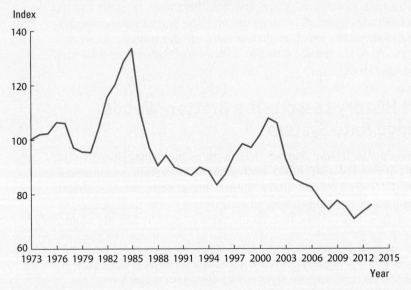

Source: Data obtained from the St. Louis Federal Reserve. The Federal Reserve defines the index as "Averages of daily figures. A weighted average of the foreign exchange value of the U.S. dollar against a subset of the broad index currencies that circulate widely outside the country of issue. Major currency index includes the Euro Area, Canada, Japan, United Kingdom, Switzerland, Australia, and Sweden." See **http://research.stlouisfed.org/fred2/series/TWEXMANL?cid = 105**.

relative to eight major currencies since it was allowed to float. There have been some peaks when demand for the dollar was high (such as in the mid-1980s and early 2000s), but the overall trend has been down. When we wrote this in mid-2014, the dollar was at an all-time low. This bodes well for exports, but it hurts U.S. consumers.

According to the International Monetary Fund, about 42 countries currently operate under a system of **floating exchange rates**, whereby currency prices are allowed to seek their own levels, with only modest central bank intervention to smooth out extreme exchange rate fluctuations. The IMF reports that about 31 currencies have freely, or independently, floating exchange rates; these currencies include the dollar, euro, pound, and yen.

Currency Appreciation and Depreciation

Currency appreciation occurs when one currency gains value relative to another currency—in other words, the appreciating currency can buy more of the other currency than it could before appreciating. For example, suppose the current exchange rate is EUR/USD = 1.25, which means that 1 euro can buy 1.25 dollars. Suppose the euro appreciates 20% against the dollar. In this case, the euro would be able to purchase 20% more dollars, so the new exchange rate would be EUR/USD = 1.25(1 + 0.20) = 1.50, which means the euro can purchase 1.50 dollars.

It is easy to get mixed up when calculating rates of appreciation, so here are some suggestions. Notice that two currencies are involved (euros and dollar) and the euro is the one appreciating. This means we need to express the original exchange rate as the number of dollars per euro in order to find the number of dollars per euro after the appreciation.

To apply these suggestions, consider a situation in which the dollar appreciates 10% versus the euro. This means the dollar now can purchase 10% more euros, so we need to express the exchange rate as the number of euros that can be purchased by 1 dollar. We can't use the direct quote of $1.25 (which is EUR/USD = 1.25) because it is the number of dollars that can be purchased by 1 euro. Instead, we need to find the indirect quote, which is 1/(1.25): USD/EUR = 1/1.25 = 0.80, the number of euros that 1 dollar can purchase. Now we apply the 10% appreciation rate and get the new exchange rate of USD/EUR = 0.80(1 + 0.10) = 0.88, which means that 0.88 euros can be purchased by $1.

Currency depreciation occurs when one currency loses value relative to another currency—the depreciating currency now buys less of the other currency than it could before depreciating. For example, suppose the dollar depreciates 10% with respect to the Mexican peso. We want to start with the number of pesos that 1 dollar could purchase before depreciating, so this is the indirect quote. Suppose the exchange rate is USD/MXN = 10, which is the number of pesos that can be purchased by 1 dollar. The exchange rate after the dollar depreciates is USD/MXN = 10(1 − 0.10) = 9. Therefore, the dollar is only able to purchase 10% less (9 pesos) than it could prior to depreciating.

Perhaps contrary to intuition, the percentage that one currency appreciates with respect to a second currency usually is not the same as the percentage that the second currency depreciates with respect to the first currency. To see this, consider the first example in which the euro appreciated by 20% against the dollar, with the exchange rate changing from EUR/USD = 1.25 to 1.50. Let's calculate by how much the dollar depreciated against the euro. Start by finding the indirect rates: 1/1.25 = 0.80 and 1/1.5 = 0.6667. This means that the dollar could purchase 0.80 euros before the dollar depreciated, and 0.6667 euros after it depreciated, for a change of 16.67%: $(0.80 - 0.6667)/0.80 = 0.1667 = 16.67\%$. This shows that the euro appreciated by 20% and the dollar depreciated by 16.67%. As this example shows, you need to be very careful when analyzing currency appreciation or deprecation.

Exchange Rate Risk

Exchange rate fluctuations can have a profound effect on profits and trade. For example, in 2002 the euro exchange rate was about $0.87 (i.e., 0.87 dollars per euro). In 2014, the exchange rate was about $1.38. Consider the impact this has on profits and trade. For example, a hand-blown glass from the Italian island of Murano cost about €50 in 2002. Ignoring shipping costs and taxes, a consumer in the United States could have purchased this glass for €50($0.87/€) = $43.50. Assuming the price in 2014 still was €50, it would cost €50($1.38/€) = $69.00. Thus, the change in exchange rates obviously hurt Italian exports to the United States.

On the other hand, U.S. vintners were able to export wines to Italy much more profitably in 2014 than in 2002. For example, suppose a bottle of Pinot Noir cost a California vineyard $10 to produce in 2002 but could be sold for €17 in Europe. In 2002, the profit would have been €17($0.87/€) − $10 = $14.79 − $10 = $4.79. Assuming no change in production costs, the bottle's profit in 2014 is €17($1.38/€) − $10 = $23.46 − $10 = $13.46. Thus, U.S. exporters to Europe have benefited by the change in exchange rates.

The volatility of exchange rates under a floating system increases the uncertainty of the cash flows for a multinational corporation. Because its cash flows are generated in many parts of the world, they are denominated in many different currencies. When exchange rates change, the dollar-equivalent value of the company's consolidated cash flows also fluctuates. This is known as **exchange rate risk**, and it is a major factor differentiating a global company from a purely domestic one.

27-5c **Managed Floating Rates**

In a **managed floating rate** system, there is significant government intervention to manage the exchange rate by manipulating the currency's supply and demand. The government rarely reveals its target exchange rate levels if it uses a managed float regime because this would make it too easy for currency speculators to profit. According to the IMF, about 48 countries have a managed floating rate system, including Colombia, India, Singapore, and Burundi.

27-5d **Pegged Exchange Rates**

In a **pegged exchange rate** system, a country locks, or "pegs," its currency's exchange rate to another currency or basket of currencies. It is common for a country with a pegged exchange rate to allow its currency to vary within specified limits or bands (often set at ±1% of the target rate) before the country intervenes to force the currency back within the limits. Examples in which a currency is pegged to another country's currency include Bhutan's ngultrum, which is pegged to the Indian rupee; the Falkland Islands' pound, which is pegged to the British pound; and Barbados' dollar, which is pegged to the U.S. dollar. An example of a currency being pegged to a basket is China, where the yuan is no longer just pegged to the U.S. dollar but rather to a basket of currencies. The Chinese government will not reveal exactly which currencies make up the basket, but the U.S. dollar, the euro, the yen, and the South Korean won are certainly components.

Currency Devaluation and Revaluation

As indicated previously, countries with pegged exchange rates establish a fixed exchange rate with some other major currency or basket of currencies. When a government reduces its target fixed exchange rate, the result is a currency **devaluation**; increasing the rate results in a currency **revaluation**. For example, from 1991 through early 2002, Argentina had a fixed exchange rate of 1 peso per U.S. dollar. Imports were high, exports were low, and the Argentinean government had to purchase huge amounts of pesos to maintain that artificially high exchange rate. The government borrowed heavily to finance these purchases, and eventually it was unable to continue supporting the peso. (Indeed, the government defaulted on some of its obligations.) As a result, the government had to devalue the peso to 1.4 pesos per dollar in early 2002. Notice that this made the peso weaker: Before the devaluation, 1 peso would buy 1 dollar, but afterward 1 peso would buy only 71 cents (1.4 pesos per dollar $= 1/1.4 = 0.71$ dollar per peso). The devaluation lowered the prices of Argentine goods on the world market, which helped its exporters, but prices rose for imported goods, including oil. The initial shock to the Argentine economy was severe, as employment fell in those industries that were not exporters. The problem was exacerbated because many Argentine companies and individuals had incurred debt that was denominated in dollars, which instantly cost much more to service. However, the economy gradually improved, aided by increased exports, tourism, and employment rates. Still, the initial pain caused by devaluation helps explain why many countries with fixed exchange rates tend to postpone needed measures until economic pressures build to explosive levels.

Given the expense of maintaining an artificially high exchange rate and the pain of large devaluations, many countries that once had pegged exchange rates now allow their currencies to float. For example, Mexico had a pegged exchange rate prior to 1994, but it depleted its foreign reserves trying to support the peso and was forced to devalue it. Mexico's currency now floats, as does that of Argentina.

Convertible versus Nonconvertible Securities

A pegged exchange rate isn't necessarily a deterrent to direct investment in the country by foreign corporations—as long as the local government's central bank supports the currency and devaluations are unlikely. This was generally the case in the Bretton Woods era, so those currencies were considered to be **convertible** because the nation that issued them allowed them to be traded in the currency markets and was willing to redeem them at market rates. This is true today for all floating-rate currencies, which are also called **hard currencies** because of their convertibility. Some pegged currencies are also at least partially convertible, because their central banks will redeem them at market rates under specified conditions.

However, some countries set the exchange rate but do not allow their currencies to be traded on world markets. For example, the Chinese yuan is allowed to float in a very narrow band against a basket of securities. However, the yuan can be legally used and exchanged only within China. Furthermore, the Chinese government imposes restrictions on both residents and nonresidents from freely converting their holdings of yuans into another currency. Thus, the yuan is a **nonconvertible currency**, also called a **soft currency**. When official exchange rates differ from "market rates" or when there are restrictions on convertibility, a black market will often arise. For example, in early 2014 Venezuela's official exchange rate was about 6.3 bolivars per dollar, but black market prices were estimated to be as high as 90. In response to shortages of dollars used to import food and medicine, Venezuela opened a currency market in April 2014 to supply a small fraction of the dollars needed for international trade. On it, the bolivar immediately traded at about 52 bolivars per dollar. Although the official exchange rate remains at 6.3 in June 2014, the bolivar is still trading in the 52 range on the new exchange.

A nonconvertible currency creates problems for foreign companies looking to make direct investments. Consider the situation faced by Pizza Hut when it wanted to open a chain of restaurants in the former Soviet Union. The Russian ruble was not convertible, so Pizza Hut could not take the profits from its restaurants out of the Soviet Union in the form of dollars. Because there was no mechanism to exchange the rubles it earned in Russia for dollars, it seemed that investing in the Soviet Union was essentially worthless to a U.S. company. However, Pizza Hut arranged to use the ruble profit from the restaurants to buy Russian vodka, which it then shipped to the United States and sold for dollars. Pizza Hut managed to find a solution, but lack of convertibility significantly inhibits the ability of a country to attract foreign investment.

27-5e **No Local Currency**

A few countries don't have their own separate legal tender but instead use the currency of another nation. For example, Ecuador has used the U.S. dollar since September 2000. Other countries belong to a monetary union, such as the 18 European Monetary Union nations in 2014 whose currency is the euro, which is allowed to float. In contrast, member nations of the Eastern Caribbean Currency Union, the West African Economic and Monetary Union (WAEMU), and the Central African Economic and Monetary Community (CAEMC) use their respective unions' currency, which is itself pegged to some other currency. For example, the Eastern Caribbean dollar is pegged to the U.S. dollar, and the CFA franc (used by both the WAEMU and CAEMC) is pegged to the euro.[5]

SELF TEST

What is the difference between a fixed exchange rate system and a floating rate system?

What are pegged exchange rates?

What does it mean to say that the dollar is depreciating with respect to the euro?

What is a convertible currency?

---

5. A few countries, such as Bosnia and Herzegovina, have currency board arrangements. Under this system, a country technically has its own currency but commits to exchange it for a specified foreign money unit at a fixed exchange rate. This requires it to impose domestic currency restrictions unless it has the foreign currency reserves to cover requested exchanges.

27-6 Trading in Foreign Exchange

Importers, exporters, tourists, and governments buy and sell currencies in the foreign exchange market. For example, when a U.S. trader imports automobiles from Japan, payment will probably be made in Japanese yen. The importer buys yen (through its bank) in the foreign exchange market, much as one buys common stocks on the New York Stock Exchange or pork bellies on the Chicago Mercantile Exchange. However, whereas stock and commodity exchanges have organized trading floors, the foreign exchange market consists of a network of brokers and banks based in New York, London, Tokyo, and other financial centers. Most buy and sell orders are conducted by computer and telephone.

27-6a Spot Rates and Forward Rates

The exchange rates shown in Tables 27-1 and 27-2 are known as **spot rates**, which mean the rate paid for delivery of the currency "on the spot" or, in reality, no more than 2 days after the day of the trade. For most of the world's major currencies, it is also possible to buy (or sell) currencies for delivery at some agreed-upon future date, usually 30, 90, or 180 days from the day the transaction is negotiated. This rate is known as the **forward exchange rate**.

For example, suppose that a U.S. firm must pay 500 million yen to a Japanese firm in 30 days and that the current spot rate is 102.31 yen per dollar. If spot rates remain constant, then the U.S. firm will pay the Japanese firm the equivalent of $4.887 million (500 million yen divided by 102.31 yen per dollar) in 30 days. But if the spot rate falls to, say, 93 yen per dollar, then the U.S. firm will have to pay the equivalent of 500¥/(93 ¥/$) = $5.376 million. If the spot rate increases to 113, the firm will pay only 500¥/(113 ¥/$) = $4.425 million. The treasurer of the U.S. firm can avoid this variability by entering into a 30-day forward exchange contract. Suppose this contract promises delivery of yen to the U.S. firm in 30 days at a guaranteed price of 102.30 yen per dollar. No cash changes hands at the time the treasurer signs the forward contract, although the U.S. firm might have to put some collateral down as a guarantee against default. Yet because the firm can use an interest-bearing instrument for the collateral, this requirement is not costly. The counterparty to the forward contract must deliver the yen to the U.S. firm in 30 days, and the U.S. firm is obligated to purchase the 500 million yen at the previously agreed-upon rate of 102.30 yen per dollar. Therefore, the treasurer of the U.S. firm is able to lock in a payment equivalent to $4.888 million = (¥500 million)/(102.30 ¥/$), no matter what happens to spot rates. This technique is called *hedging*.

Forward rates for 30-, 90-, and 180-day delivery, along with the current spot rates for some commonly traded currencies, are given in Table 27-3. If you can obtain *more* of the foreign currency for a dollar in the forward than in the spot market, then the forward currency is less valuable than the spot currency and the forward currency is said to be selling at a **discount**. In other words, if the foreign currency is expected to depreciate (based on the forward rates) with respect to the home currency, then the forward currency is at a discount. Conversely, because a dollar would buy *fewer* yen and francs in the forward than in the spot market, the forward yen and francs are selling at a **premium**.

WWW

Currency futures prices are available from the Chicago Mercantile Exchange (CME) on its Web site at **www.cme.com**. Currency spot and forward rates are available from the Bank of Montreal Financial Group at **www.bmo.com**.

TABLE 27-3	Selected Spot and Forward Exchange Rates, Indirect Quotation: Number of Units of Foreign Currency per U.S. Dollar				
		Forward Rates[a]			
	Spot Rate	**30 days**	**90 days**	**180 days**	**Forward Rate at a Premium or Discount**[b]
Britain (Pound)	0.5952	0.5953	0.5956	0.5960	Discount
Canada (Dollar)	1.0795	1.0817	1.0862	1.0931	Discount
Japan (Yen)	102.31	102.30	102.26	102.20	Premium
Switzerland (Franc)	0.8816	0.8814	0.8810	0.8802	Premium

[a] These are representative quotes as provided by a sample of New York banks. Forward rates for other currencies and for other lengths of time can often be negotiated.
[b] When it takes more units of a foreign currency to buy a dollar in the future, then the value of the foreign currency is less in the forward market than in the spot market; hence the forward rate is at a *discount* to the spot rate. When it takes fewer units of a foreign currency to buy a dollar in the future, the forward rate is at a *premium*.

Source: *The Wall Street Journal,* **http://online.wsj.com**; quotes for April 24, 2014.

SELF TEST

Differentiate between spot and forward exchange rates.

Explain what it means for a forward currency to sell at a discount and at a premium.

27-7 Interest Rate Parity

Market forces determine whether a currency sells at a forward premium or a discount, and the general relationship between spot and forward exchange rates is specified by a concept called "interest rate parity."

Interest rate parity means that investors should expect to earn the same return on security investments in all countries after adjusting for risk. It recognizes that when you invest in a country other than your home country, you are affected by two factors—returns on the investment itself and changes in the exchange rate. It follows that your overall return will be higher than the investment's stated return if the currency in which your investment is denominated appreciates relative to your home currency. Likewise, your overall return will be lower if the foreign currency that you receive declines in value.

To illustrate interest rate parity, consider the case of a U.S. investor who can buy default-free 180-day Swiss bonds that promise a 4% nominal annual return. The 180-day foreign (Swiss) interest rate, r_f, is 4% ÷ 2 = 2% because 180 days is one-half of a 360-day year. Assume also that the indirect quotation for the spot exchange rate is 0.8816 Swiss francs per dollar, as shown in Table 27-3. Finally, assume that the 180-day forward exchange rate is 0.8802 Swiss francs per dollar, which means that in 180 days the investor can exchange 1 dollar for 0.8802 Swiss francs.

The U.S. investor could receive a 4% annualized return denominated in Swiss francs, but if he ultimately wants to consume goods in the United States, then those

Swiss francs must be converted to dollars. The dollar return on the investment depends, therefore, on what happens to exchange rates over the next 6 months. However, the investor can lock in the dollar return by selling the foreign currency in the forward market. For example, the investor could simultaneously do the following:

1. Convert $1,000 to 881.60 Swiss francs in the spot market: $1,000(0.8816 Swiss francs per dollar) = 881.60 Swiss francs.
2. Invest the Swiss francs in a 180-day Swiss bond that has a 4% annual return, or a 2% semiannual return. This investment will pay 881.60(1.02) = 899.23 Swiss francs in 180 days.
3. Agree today to exchange the Swiss francs in 180 days at the forward rate of 0.8802 Swiss francs per dollar, for a total of (899.23 Swiss francs) ÷ (0.8802 Swiss francs per dollar) = $1,021.620.

Hence this investment has an expected 180-day return in dollars of $21.62/$1,000 = 2.162%, which translates into a nominal annual return of 2(2.162%) = 4.324%. In this case, the expected 4.324% return consists of 4% from the Swiss bond itself plus 0.324% because the market believes that the Swiss franc will strengthen relative to the dollar. Observe that, by locking in the forward rate today, the investor has eliminated all exchange rate risk. And because the Swiss bond is assumed to be default-free, the investor is certain to earn a 4.324% annual dollar return.

Interest rate parity implies that an investment in the United States with the same risk as the Swiss bond should also have a return of 4.324%. When we express interest rates as periodic rates, we can express interest rate parity by the following equation (later in the chapter we will use a slightly different version of interest rate parity when we consider multi-year cash flows):

$$\frac{\text{Forward exchange rate}}{\text{Spot exchange rate}} = \frac{1 + r_h}{1 + r_f} \qquad \text{(27–1)}$$

Here r_h is the periodic interest rate in the home country, r_f is the periodic interest rate in the foreign country, and the forward and spot exchange rates are expressed as direct quotations (that is, units of home currency per unit of foreign currency).

Using Table 27-3, the direct spot quotation is 1.13430 dollars per Swiss franc = (1/0.8816 Swiss francs per dollar), and the direct 180-day forward quotation is 1.13611 = (1/0.8802). Using Equation 27-1, we can solve for the equivalent home rate, r_h:

$$\frac{\text{Forward exchange rate}}{\text{Spot exchange rate}} = \frac{1 + r_h}{1 + r_f} = \frac{1 + r_h}{1 + 0.02} = \frac{1.13611}{1.13430} \qquad \text{(27–1a)}$$

$$1 + r_h = \left(\frac{1.13611}{1.13430}\right)(1 + 0.02) = 1.021628$$

The periodic home interest rate is 2.1628%, and the annualized home interest rate is (2.1628%)(2) = 4.326%, the same value we found before except for a slight difference due to rounding.

After accounting for exchange rates, interest rate parity states that bonds in the home country and the foreign country must have the same actual rate of return in the investor's currency. In this example, the U.S. bond must yield 4.326% to provide the same return as the 4% Swiss bond. If one bond provides a higher return, then investors will sell their low-return bond and flock to the high-return bond. This activity will cause the price of the low-return bond to fall (which pushes up its yield) and the price of the high-return bond to increase (driving down its yield). These effects will continue until the two bonds again have the same returns after accounting for exchange rates.

In other words, interest rate parity implies that an investment in the United States with the same risk as a Swiss bond should have a dollar value return of 4.326%. Solving for r_h in Equation 27-1, we indeed find that the predicted interest rate in the United States is 4.326%, the same return except for the slight rounding difference.

Interest rate parity shows why a particular currency might be at a forward premium or discount. Note that a currency is at a forward premium whenever domestic interest rates are higher than foreign interest rates. Discounts prevail if domestic interest rates are lower than foreign interest rates. If these conditions do not hold, then arbitrage will soon force interest rates and exchange rates back to parity.

SELF TEST

What is interest rate parity?

Assume that interest rate parity holds. When a currency trades at a forward premium, what does that imply about domestic rates relative to foreign interest rates? What does it imply when a currency trades at a forward discount?

Assume that 90-day U.S. securities have a 4.5% annualized interest rate whereas 90-day Swiss securities have a 5% annualized interest rate. In the spot market, 1 U.S. dollar can be exchanged for 1.2 Swiss francs. If interest rate parity holds, what is the 90-day forward rate exchange between U.S. and Swiss francs? **(0.8323 $/SFr or 1.2015 SFr/$)**

On the basis of your answer to the previous question, is the Swiss franc selling at a premium or discount on the forward rate? **(Discount)**

27-8 **Purchasing Power Parity**

We have discussed exchange rates in some detail, and we have considered the relationship between spot and forward exchange rates. However, we have not yet addressed the fundamental question: What determines the spot level of exchange rates in each country? Although exchange rates are influenced by a multitude of factors that are difficult to predict, particularly on a day-to-day basis, market forces over the long run work to ensure that similar goods sell for similar prices in different countries after taking exchange rates into account. This relationship is known as "purchasing power parity."

Purchasing power parity (PPP), sometimes referred to as the *law of one price*, implies that the levels of exchange rates and prices adjust so as to cause identical goods to cost the same amount in different countries. For instance, if a pair of tennis shoes costs $150 in the United States and 100 pounds in Britain, then PPP implies that the exchange rate must be $1.50 per pound. Consumers could purchase the shoes in Britain for 100 pounds, or they could exchange their 100 pounds for $150 and then purchase the same shoes in the United States at the same effective cost (assuming no transaction or transportation costs). Here is the equation for purchasing power parity:

$$P_h = (P_f)(\text{Spot rate}) \qquad \textbf{(27–2)}$$

or

$$\text{Spot rate} = \frac{P_h}{P_f} \qquad \textbf{(27–3)}$$

Here

P_h = The price of the good in the home country ($150 in our example, assuming the United States is the home country).

P_f = The price of the good in the foreign country (100 pounds).

Note that the spot market exchange rate is expressed as the number of units of home currency that can be exchanged for one unit of foreign currency ($1.50 per pound).

Purchasing power parity assumes that market forces will eliminate situations in which the same product sells at a different price overseas. For example, if the shoes cost $140 in the United States then importers/exporters could purchase them in the United States for $140, sell them for 100 pounds in Britain, exchange the 100 pounds for $150 in the foreign exchange market, and earn a profit of $10 on every pair of shoes. Ultimately, this trading activity would increase the demand for shoes in the United States and thus raise P_h, increase the supply of shoes in Britain and thus reduce P_f, and increase the demand for dollars in the foreign exchange market and thus reduce the spot rate. Each of these actions works to restore PPP.

Note that PPP assumes that there are no transportation or transaction costs and no import restrictions, all of which limit the ability to ship goods between countries. In many cases, these assumptions are incorrect, which explains why PPP is often violated. An additional problem for empirical tests of the PPP theorem is that products in different countries are rarely identical. There are frequently real or perceived differences in quality that can lead to price differences in different countries.

Still, the concepts of interest rate parity and purchasing power parity are vitally important to those engaged in international activities. Companies and investors must anticipate changes in interest rates, inflation, and exchange rates, and they often try to hedge the risks of adverse movements in these factors. The parity relationships are extremely useful when anticipating future conditions.

What is meant by purchasing power parity?

A computer sells for $1,500 U.S. dollars. In the spot market, $1 = 115 Japanese yen. If purchasing power parity holds, what should be the price (in yen) of the same computer in Japan? **(¥172,500)**

HUNGRY FOR A BIG MAC? GO TO UKRAINE!

Purchasing power parity (PPP) implies that the same product will sell for the same price in every country after adjusting for current exchange rates. One problem when testing to see if PPP holds is that it assumes that goods consumed in different countries are of the same quality. For example, if you find that a product is more expensive in Switzerland than it is in Canada, one explanation is that PPP fails to hold, but another explanation is that the product sold in Switzerland is of a higher quality and therefore deserves a higher price.

One way to test for PPP is to find goods that have the same quality worldwide. With this in mind, *The Economist* magazine occasionally compares the prices of a well-known good whose quality is the same in nearly 120 different countries: the McDonald's Big Mac hamburger.

In early 2014, a Big Mac cost about $4.62 in the United States but could be purchased for about $2.27 in Ukraine after converting dollars to the Ukrainian hryvnia. *The Economist* "backed out" the exchange rate implied by the purchasing power parity relationship and calculated that the hryvnia was undervalued by about 51%. In other words, the hryvnia would have to appreciate against the dollar by about 51% for the PPP relationship to hold. At the other extreme, a Big Mac sold for the equivalent of $7.14 in Switzerland and for even more in Norway. If the PPP relationship holds, then these currencies are overvalued relative to the dollar by about 55%.

If the PPP relationship holds, then the Big Mac test suggests that there is an opportunity for investors to profit by shorting the Swiss franc and going long in the hryvnia. We don't suggest that you do this, but we do recommend that you avoid Big Macs if you travel in Switzerland.

Source: The Economist, online edition, **www.economist.com/content/big-mac-index**.

27-9 Inflation, Interest Rates, and Exchange Rates

www

For current international interest rates, go to **www.bloomberg.com** and select Market Data. Then select Rates and Bonds.

Relative inflation rates, or the rates of inflation in foreign countries compared with that in the home country, have many implications for multinational financial decisions. Obviously, relative inflation rates will greatly influence future production costs at home and abroad. Equally important, inflation has a dominant influence on relative interest rates and exchange rates. Both of these factors influence decisions by multinational corporations for financing their foreign investments, and both have an important effect on the profitability of foreign investments.

The currencies of countries with higher inflation rates than that of the United States will by definition *depreciate* over time against the dollar. Countries where this has occurred include Mexico and all the South American nations. On the other hand, the currencies of Switzerland and Japan, which have had less inflation than the United States, have generally *appreciated* against the dollar. In fact, *a foreign currency will, on average, depreciate or appreciate against the U.S. dollar at a percentage rate approximately equal to the amount by which its inflation rate exceeds or is less than the U.S. rate.*

Relative inflation rates also affect interest rates. The interest rate in any country is largely determined by its inflation rate. Therefore, countries currently experiencing higher rates of inflation than the United States also tend to have higher interest rates. The reverse is true for countries with lower inflation rates.

It is tempting for a multinational corporation to borrow in countries with the lowest interest rates. However, this is not always a good strategy. Suppose, for example, that interest rates in Switzerland are lower than those in the United States because of Switzerland's lower inflation rate. A U.S. multinational firm could therefore save interest by borrowing in Switzerland. However, because of relative inflation rates, the Swiss franc will probably appreciate in the future, causing the dollar cost of annual interest and principal payments on Swiss debt to rise over time. Thus, *the lower interest rate could be more than offset by losses from currency appreciation.* Similarly, multinational corporations should not necessarily avoid borrowing in a country such as Brazil, where interest rates have been very high, because future depreciation of the Brazilian real could make such borrowing end up being relatively inexpensive.

SELF TEST

What effects do relative inflation rates have on relative interest rates?

What happens over time to the currencies of countries with higher inflation rates than that of the United States? To those with lower inflation rates?

Why might a multinational corporation decide to borrow in a country such as Brazil, where interest rates are high, rather than in a country like Switzerland, where interest rates are low?

27-10 International Money and Capital Markets

From World War II through the 1960s, the U.S. capital markets dominated world markets. Today, however, the value of U.S. securities represents less than one-fourth the value of all securities. Many corporations are finding that international markets often offer better opportunities for raising or investing capital than are available domestically. The growth of the international markets has also opened up opportunities for investors. One way for U.S. citizens to invest in world markets is to buy the stocks of U.S. multinational corporations that invest directly in foreign countries. Another way is to purchase foreign securities—stocks, bonds, or money market instruments issued by foreign companies. Security investments are known as *portfolio investments*, and they are distinguished from *direct investments* in physical assets by U.S. corporations.

GREASING THE WHEELS OF INTERNATIONAL BUSINESS

What do bribery and tax shelters have in common? Both are targets of international regulation.

Thirty-seven countries have now signed the Organization for Economic Cooperation and Development's Anti-Bribery Convention. This requires each country to pass legislation making it a crime for companies to bribe public officials. The United States, which signed the convention, has been the most aggressive in prosecuting violators. It is interesting that this prosecution has not been limited to U.S. companies but also has extended to foreign companies whose stocks are listed in the United States. For example, Statoil, a Norwegian firm, was fined $10.5 million in 2006 for bribing Iranian officials. Subsidiaries of Vetco International, headquartered in the United Kingdom, were fined $26 million in 2007 for bribing Nigerian officials. Siemens, a German company, holds the record for the largest fine paid to date (2012), with over *$1.6 billion* paid to regulatory agencies in the United States and Germany.

Among the international organizations striving to reform global taxation and eliminate tax-shelter abuse are the Joint International Tax Shelter Information Centre, the Seven Country Working Group, and the Leeds Castle Group. Their goals include improving transparency, eliminating double taxation, and abolishing tax havens.

What does the reformation of tax havens have in common with the elimination of bribery? First, both of these problems distract companies from focusing on their core business issues, and both create uneven playing fields where providing the best product at the best price isn't as important as who you know (and bribe!) or how clever your lawyers are. Second, these problems reduce transparency in capital markets, making it harder for investors to identify the best firms. When investors are uncertain about a company, the cost of capital goes up. Thus, there is a direct link between transparency and a company's ability to raise capital at a fair price.

Sources: Janet Kersnar, "View from Europe," *CFO,* June 2007, p. 25; and Kayleigh Karutis, *CFO,* "Global Norming," May 2007, p. 22.

27-10a **Eurodollar Market**

A **Eurodollar** is a U.S. dollar deposited in a bank outside the United States. (Although they are called Eurodollars because they originated in Europe, Eurodollars are actually any dollars deposited in any part of the world other than the United States.) The bank in which the deposit is made may be a non-U.S. bank, such as Barclays Bank in London; the foreign branch of a U.S. bank, such as Citibank's Paris branch; or even a foreign branch of a third-country bank, such as Barclays' Munich branch. Most Eurodollar deposits are for $500,000 or more, and they have maturities ranging from overnight to about 1 year.

The major difference between Eurodollar deposits and regular U.S. time deposits is their geographic locations. The two types of deposits do not involve different currencies—in both cases, dollars are on deposit. However, Eurodollars are outside the direct control of the U.S. monetary authorities, so U.S. banking regulations, including reserve requirements and FDIC insurance premiums, do not apply. The absence of these costs means that the interest rate paid on Eurodollar deposits can be higher than domestic U.S. rates on equivalent instruments.

The dollar is the leading international currency. However, British pounds, euros, Swiss francs, Japanese yen, and other currencies are also deposited outside their home countries; these *Eurocurrencies* are handled in exactly the same way as Eurodollars.

Eurodollars are borrowed by U.S. and foreign corporations for various purposes but especially to pay for goods imported from the United States and to invest in U.S. security markets. Also, U.S. dollars are used as an international currency or medium of exchange, and many Eurodollars are also used for this purpose. It is interesting to note that Eurodollars were actually "invented" by the Soviets in 1946. International merchants did not trust the Soviets or their rubles, so the Soviets bought some dollars (for gold), deposited them in a Paris bank, and then used these dollars to buy goods in the world markets. Others found it convenient to use dollars this same way, and soon the Eurodollar market was in full swing.

Eurodollars are usually held in interest-bearing accounts. The interest rate paid on these deposits depends: (1) on the bank's lending rate, because the interest a bank earns on loans determines its willingness and ability to pay interest on deposits, and (2) on rates of return available on U.S. money market instruments. If money market rates in the United States were above Eurodollar deposit rates, then these dollars would be sent back and invested in the United States; if U.S. rates were lower than Eurodollar deposit, which is more often the case, then more dollars would be sent out of the United States to become Eurodollars. Given the existence of the Eurodollar market and the electronic flow of dollars to and from the United States, it is easy to see why interest rates in the United States cannot be insulated from those in other parts of the world.

Interest rates on Eurodollar deposits (and loans) are tied to a standard rate known by the acronym **LIBOR**, which stands for **London Interbank Offered Rate**. LIBOR is the rate of interest offered by the largest and strongest London banks on dollar deposits of significant size. On May 30, 2014, LIBOR rates were just a little above domestic U.S. bank rates on time deposits of the same maturity—0.15% for 3-month CDs versus 0.23% for LIBOR CDs. The Eurodollar market is essentially a short-term market; most loans and deposits are for less than 1 year.

27-10b **International Bond Markets**

Any bond sold outside the country of the borrower is called an *international bond*. However, there are two important types of international bonds: foreign bonds and Eurobonds. **Foreign bonds** are bonds sold by a foreign borrower but denominated in the currency of the country in which the issue is sold. For instance, Nortel Networks (a Canadian company) may need U.S. dollars to finance the operations of its subsidiaries in the United States. If it decides to raise the needed capital in the United States, then the bond would be underwritten by a syndicate of U.S. investment bankers, denominated in U.S. dollars, and sold to U.S. investors in accordance with SEC and applicable state regulations. Except for the foreign origin of the borrower, this bond would be indistinguishable from those issued by equivalent U.S. corporations. However, because Nortel is a foreign corporation, the bond would be a foreign bond. Furthermore, because it is denominated in dollars and sold in the United States under SEC regulations, it is also called a **Yankee bond**. In contrast, if Nortel issued bonds in Mexico that were denominated in pesos, then they would be foreign bonds, not Yankee bonds.

The term **Eurobond** is used to designate any bond issued in one country but denominated in the currency of some other country. Examples include a Ford Motor Company issue denominated in dollars and sold in Germany and a British firm's sale of euro-denominated bonds in Switzerland. The institutional arrangements by which Eurobonds are marketed are different from those for most other bond issues, with the most important distinction being a far lower level of required disclosure than is usually found for bonds issued in domestic markets, particularly in the United States. Governments tend to be less strict when regulating securities denominated in foreign currencies, because the bonds' purchasers are generally more "sophisticated." The lower disclosure requirements result in lower total transaction costs for Eurobonds.

Eurobonds appeal to investors for several reasons. Generally, they are issued in bearer form rather than as registered bonds, so the names and nationalities of investors are not recorded. Individuals who desire anonymity, whether for privacy reasons or for tax avoidance, like Eurobonds. Similarly, most governments do not withhold taxes on interest payments associated with Eurobonds. If the investor requires an effective yield of 10%, then a Eurobond that is exempt from tax withholding would simply need a coupon rate of 10%. Another type of bond—for instance, a domestic issue subject to a 30% withholding tax on interest paid to foreigners—would need a coupon rate of 14.3% to yield an after-withholding rate of 10%. Investors who desire secrecy would not want to file for a refund of the tax, so they would prefer to hold the Eurobond.

The Bank for International Settlements reports that of the roughly $22 trillion in foreign bonds outstanding 36% are denominated in dollars, 45% in euros, with British pounds, Japanese yen, Swiss francs, and Australian dollars accounting for most of the rest. Although centered in Europe, Eurobonds are truly international. Their underwriting syndicates include investment bankers from all parts of the world, and the bonds are sold to investors not only in Europe but also in such faraway places as Bahrain and Singapore. Up to a few years ago, Eurobonds were issued solely by multinational firms, by international financial institutions, or by national governments. Today, however, the Eurobond market is also being tapped by purely domestic U.S. firms, which often find they can lower their debt costs by borrowing overseas.

27-10c **International Stock Markets**

New issues of stock are sold in international markets for a variety of reasons. For example, a non-U.S. firm might sell an equity issue in the United States because it can tap a much larger source of capital than in its home country. Also, a U.S. firm might tap a foreign market because it wants to create an equity market presence to accompany its operations in that country. Large multinational companies also occasionally issue new stock simultaneously in multiple countries. For example, Alcan Aluminum, a Canadian company, issued new stock in Canada, Europe, and the United States simultaneously, using different underwriting syndicates in each market.

In addition to new issues, outstanding stocks of large multinational companies are increasingly being listed on multiple international exchanges. For example, Coca-Cola's stock is traded on six stock exchanges in the United States, four stock exchanges in Switzerland, the Frankfurt stock exchange in Germany, the Lima stock exchange in Peru, and the Mexican stock exchange in Mexico City. Some 500 foreign stocks are listed in the United States—an example here is Royal Dutch Petroleum, which is listed on the New York Stock Exchange. U.S. investors can also invest in foreign companies through American Depository Receipts (ADRs), which are certificates representing ownership of foreign stock held in trust. About 1,700 ADRs are now available in the United States, with most of them traded on the over-the-counter (OTC) market. However, more and more ADRs are being listed on the NYSE, including England's British Airways, Japan's Honda Motors, and Italy's Fiat Group.[6]

27-10d **Sovereign Debt**

Sovereign debt is the total amount that a government owes. Economics courses on public finance cover government debt in detail, but government debt also has an enormous impact on the topics we address in this book, including interest rates, risk, credit availability to nonfinancial corporations, and corporate valuation. Following is a brief overview of sovereign debt along with some key insights that managers should keep in mind.

Countries with well-developed economies usually issue debt denominated in their own currencies, but lesser developed countries often issue debt denominated in a foreign currency. Some government debt offerings are governed only by the issuing country's judicial system, which often does not provide much protection for lenders. However, most government debt is issued under the auspices of international law (or the laws of the borrowing country) and we focus only on this type of sovereign debt.

Most government debt is held by financial institutions, pension funds, mutual funds, hedge funds, and individual investors. However, a few governments, such as China, actually own significant amounts of other governments' debt. Let's take a look at some facts, and then draw some implications for managers and investors.

First, how much sovereign debt are we talking about? The Organization for Economic Co-Operation and Development (OECD) reported about $49 trillion in total government debt for 31 developed countries for 2013.[7] The United States owes about 36% of this total, and Japan owes about 21% of the total, followed by Germany and Italy, and then France, the United Kingdom, Germany, and Spain (each of which owes between 3% and 7% of the total).

In terms of the United States, the total federal debt as of mid-year 2014 is about $17.5 trillion, with about $12.5 trillion called public debt because it is owed to investors; the rest is owed to other U.S. government entities, such as the Social Security Trust fund.[8] Foreign investors own about $5.9 trillion in U.S. treasury securities. Of this, China alone owns over $1.2 trillion, or about 10% of the U.S. public debt.

Government debt can be used to invest in infrastructure, such as the highways, which are expected to "pay off" in the future with higher productivity, higher gross domestic product (GDP), and higher tax collections. However, governments can also

---

6. For an interesting discussion of ADRs and the costs faced by listing companies when the ADR is underwritten by investment banks, see Hsuen-Chi Chen, Larry Fauver, and Pei-Ching Yang, "What Do Investment Banks Charge to Underwrite American Depository Receipts?" *Journal of Banking and Finance,* April 2009, pp. 609–618.

7. See **www.oecd-ilibrary.org/economics/economics-key-tables-from-oecd_2074384x** for the raw data for GDP and public debt as a percentage of GDP.

8. This total does not include debt issued by government-sponsored agencies, for which the U.S. government provides an implicit guarantee.

use debt to finance deficit spending on items that aren't really investments. Such stimulus spending can help an economy avoid a recession, but it dampens economic growth in the long run.

How much debt is too much? To put it another way, how much debt is likely to lead to missed payment to lenders, default, or restructuring? One indicator is the ratio of a country's debt to its GDP. Table 27-4 reports estimated ratios for the end of 2013 for 48 highest of the 160 countries reported by the *CIA World Factbook*. Several of the Eurozone countries involved in debt or banking crises as we write this in mid-2014 are highlighted. The median ratio of all reported countries is 45.6%. While no particular level of debt/GDP guarantees a problem, it is no coincidence that several of the Eurozone countries facing problems (Greece, Italy, Ireland, and Portugal) have high ratios.

Even more telling is the change in the ratio over time. Greece went from a ratio of around 110% in 2004 to 165% by 2012. With a ratio that high, it should be no surprise that in late 2009 Greece began facing the possibility of defaulting on its debt. Because the debt is denominated in euros, Greece's problem was also the European Monetary Union's (EMU) problem. In addition to bailout loans from the EMU far exceeding €100 billion, Greek bond investors agreed in 2012 to

TABLE 27-4	Government Debt: Public Debt as a Percentage of Gross Domestic Product				
Country	Public debt / GDP (%)	Country	Public debt / GDP (%)	Country	Public debt / GDP (%)
Japan	226.1	Spain	93.7	Malta	75.3
Zimbabwe	202.4	France	93.4	Belize	75.1
Greece	175	Egypt	92.2	Netherlands	73.3
Italy	133	United Kingdom	91.1	United States	71.8
Iceland	130.5	Barbados	90.5	Slovenia	71.7
Portugal	127.8	Antigua and Barbuda	89	Albania	70.5
Ireland	124.2	Canada	86.3	Dominica	70
Jamaica	123.6	Cabo Verde	86.2	Saint Vincent and the Grenadines	68
Lebanon	120	Saint Kitts and Nevis	83	Israel	67.1
Cyprus	113.1	Germany	79.9	Aruba	67
Sudan	111	Hungary	79.8	Croatia	66.2
Grenada	110	Jordan	79.1	Sao Tome and Principe	65.5
Singapore	105.5	Sri Lanka	78.4	Uruguay	62.8
Eritrea	104.7	Saint Lucia	77	El Salvador	62
Belgium	102.4	Morocco	76.9	Serbia	61.2
Puerto Rico	96.5	Austria	75.7	Bahrain	61.2

Source: CIA Factbook, **https://www.cia.gov/library/publications/the-world-factbook/rankorder/2186rank.html**.

restructure the debt, which essentially reduced the value of the debt by a little over 50% of its original face value.

The Eurozone crisis was not over when we wrote this in mid-2014. Greek citizens were angrily protesting budget cuts and austerity measures imposed as conditions of the bailouts. At this point in time it is not even sure that Greece will continue to use the euro, which would have enormous consequences for the rest of the EMU and the world. Greece is not the only country having problems. Major Spanish banks needed over €41 billion in bailouts in 2012, and analysts worry that similar problems loom in Italy, Portugal, and Ireland.

Interconnected global economies and financial markets mean that one country's problems often affect the rest of the world. For example, the bleak short-term economic outlook in the Eurozone is likely to drag down growth in China and other exporters to Europe, including the United States.

STOCK MARKET INDICES AROUND THE WORLD

In the United States, the Dow Jones Industrial Average (^DJI) is the most well-known stock market index. Similar indices also exist for each major world financial center. As shown in the accompanying table, India's market has had the strongest performance during the past 10 years while Japan's has had the weakest.

Hong Kong (^HSI)
In Hong Kong, the primary stock index is the Hang Seng. Created by HSI Services Limited, the Hang Seng index is composed of 33 large stocks.

Great Britain (^FTSE)
The FT-SE 100 Index (pronounced "footsie") is the most widely followed indicator of equity investments in Great Britain. It is a value-weighted index composed of the 100 largest companies on the London Stock Exchange.

Japan (^N225)
In Japan, the principal barometer of stock performance is the Nikkei 225 Index. The index consists of highly liquid equity issues thought to be representative of the Japanese economy.

Germany (^GDAXI)
The Deutscher Aktienindex, commonly called the DAX, is an index composed of the 30 largest companies trading on the Frankfurt Stock Exchange.

India (^BSESN)
Of the 22 stock exchanges in India, the Bombay Stock Exchange (BSE) is the largest, with more than 6,000 listed stocks and approximately two-thirds of the country's total trading volume. Established in 1875, the exchange is also the oldest in Asia. Its yardstick is the BSE Sensex, an index of 30 publicly traded Indian stocks that account for one-fifth of the BSE's market capitalization.

Note: For easy access to world indices, see **http://finance.yahoo.com/m2** and use the ticker symbols shown above in parentheses.

Relative 10-Year Performance (Starting Values = 100)

	United States	Germany	Great Britain	Hong Kong	India	Japan
April 2004	100	100	100	100	100	100
April 2014	167	245	151	177	391	127

Differentiate between foreign portfolio investments and direct foreign investments.

What are Eurodollars?

Has the development of the Eurodollar market made it easier or more difficult for the Federal Reserve to control U.S. interest rates?

Differentiate between foreign bonds and Eurobonds.

Why do Eurobonds appeal to investors?

27-11 Multinational Capital Budgeting

Until now we've discussed the general environment in which multinational firms operate. In the remainder of the chapter, we see how international factors affect key corporate decisions, beginning with capital budgeting. Although the same basic principles apply to capital budgeting for both foreign and domestic operations, there are some key differences. These include the types of risks faced by the firm, cash flow estimation, and project analysis.[9]

27-11a Risk Exposure

Foreign projects may be more or less risky than equivalent domestic projects, and that can lead to differences in the cost of capital. Higher risk for foreign projects tends to result from two primary sources: (1) exchange rate risk and (2) political risk. However, international diversification might result in a lower risk.

Exchange rate risk concerns the value of the basic cash flows in the parent company's home currency. Foreign currency cash flows turned over to the parent must be converted into U.S. dollars, so projected cash flows must be translated to dollars at the expected future exchange rates. An analysis should be conducted to ascertain the effects of exchange rate variations on dollar cash flows; then, on the basis of this analysis, an exchange rate risk premium should be added to the domestic cost of capital. It is sometimes possible to hedge against exchange rate risk, but it may not be possible to hedge completely, especially on long-term projects. If hedging is used, then the costs of doing so must be subtracted from the project's operating cash flows.

---

9. Many domestic companies form joint ventures with foreign companies; see Insup Lee and Steve B. Wyatt, "The Effects of International Joint Ventures on Shareholder Wealth," *Financial Review,* November 1990, pp. 641–649. For a discussion of the Japanese cost of capital, see Jeffrey A. Frankel, "The Japanese Cost of Finance," *Financial Management,* Spring 1991, pp. 95–127. For a discussion of financial practices in the Pacific basin, see George W. Kester, Rosita P. Chang, and Kai-Chong Tsui, "Corporate Financial Policy in the Pacific Basin: Hong Kong and Singapore," *Financial Practice and Education,* Spring/Summer 1994, pp. 117–127.

CONSUMER FINANCE IN CHINA

The financial frontier for consumer finance is in China, where applicants must often wait more than a month to get a credit card and even longer for car loans or home mortgages. But that is changing quickly, as GE Money (formerly known as GE Capital) is among a host of financial players looking to partner with or become part owners of Chinese banks. Other foreign investors include financial institutions from all over the world, such as Citigroup (United States), ING Group (Netherlands), Hang Seng Bank (Hong Kong), and the Royal Bank of Scotland. Even investment banks (Goldman Sachs) and private equity firms (Newbridge Capital) are in the hunt.

What makes Chinese banks attractive? First, China is now allowing foreign-owned banks to make direct loans to Chinese customers. Second, China has a huge consumer base with a growing middle class that is purchasing homes, cars, and other consumer goods. Third, many Chinese banks might be considered "fixer-uppers" because they hold too many uncollectible loans (up to

9.2% of their loan portfolios), have weak information technology systems, and provide poor customer service. GE Money, which brings considerable business expertise (in addition to cash) to the partnership, views these problems as opportunities. For example, GE Money helped Shenzhen Development Bank (SDB) introduce a Walmart credit card, an Auchen credit card (Auchen is a large French retailer), and various mortgage services. All the results aren't yet in, but GE has helped SDB reduce the time to get a credit card from over a month to just 5 days.

Investing in China isn't without risks, with an estimated 60% of partnerships not providing the return that was anticipated at the deal's inception. Problems include insufficient pre-deal planning, a lack of focus and traction in the immediate post-deal period, a failure to integrate cultures, and a lack of flexibility in adapting to local conditions. Still, the potential rewards are enormous, so you should expect to see more foreign investment in China.

Source: Don Durfee, "Give Them Credit," *CFO,* July 2007, pp. 50–57.

Political risk refers to potential actions by a host government that would reduce the value of a company's investment. It includes at one extreme expropriation of the subsidiary's assets without compensation, but it also includes less drastic actions that reduce the value of the parent firm's investment in the foreign subsidiary.[10] These actions include higher taxes, tighter repatriation or currency controls, and restrictions on prices charged. The risk of expropriation is small in traditionally friendly and stable countries such as Great Britain or Switzerland. However, in Latin America, Africa, the Far East, and Eastern Europe, the risk may be substantial. Past expropriations include those of ITT and Anaconda Copper in Chile; Gulf Oil in Bolivia; Occidental Petroleum in Libya; Enron Corporation in Peru; BP, ConocoPhillips, ExxonMobil, and Chevron in Venezuela; and the assets of many companies in Iraq, Iran, and Cuba.

Note that companies can take steps to reduce the potential loss from expropriation, including one or more of the following:

1. Finance the subsidiary with local capital.
2. Structure operations so that the subsidiary has value only as a part of the integrated corporate system.

---

10. For an interesting article on expropriation, see Arvind Mahajan, "Pricing Expropriation Risk," *Financial Management*, Winter 1990, pp. 77–86.

TABLE 27-5	The 2013 Transparency International Corruption Perceptions Index (CPI)					
Top-Ranked Countries			**Bottom-Ranked Countries**		
Rank	**Country**	**2013 CPI Score**	**Rank**	**Country**	**2013 CPI Score**
1 (tie)	Denmark	91	111 (tie)	Kosovo	33
	New Zealand	91		Tanzania	33
3 (tie)	Finland	89	116 (tie)	Albania	31
	Sweden	89		Nepal	31
9 (tie)	Australia	81		Vietnam	31
	Canada	81	160 (tie)	Cambodia	20
11	Luxembourg	80		Eritrea	20
12 (tie)	Germany	78		Venezuela	20
	Iceland	78	171	Iraq	16
18	Japan	74	174	Sudan	11
19 (tie)	United States of America	73	175 (tie)	Afghanistan	8
	Uruguay	73		North Korea	8
				Somalia	8

Source: www.transparency.org.

3. Obtain insurance against economic losses from expropriation from a source such as the Overseas Private Investment Corporation (OPIC).

If OPIC insurance is purchased, then the premiums paid must be added to the project's cost.

Several organizations rate countries according to different aspects of risk. For example, Transparency International (TI) ranks countries based on perceived corruption, which is an important part of political risk. Table 27-5 shows selected countries. New Zealand and Denmark are rated by TI as the most honest countries, while Somalia is the most dishonest. The United States is ranked nineteenth.

27-11b **Cash Flow Estimation**

Cash flow estimation is more complex for foreign than domestic investments. Most multinational firms set up separate subsidiaries in each foreign country in which they operate, and the relevant cash flows for the parent company are the dividends and royalties paid by the subsidiaries to the parent, translated into dollars. Dividends and royalties are normally taxed by both foreign and home country governments, although the home country may allow credits for some or all of the foreign taxes paid. Furthermore, a foreign government may restrict the amount of the cash that may be **repatriated** to the parent company. For example, some governments place a ceiling, stated as a percentage of the company's net worth, on the amount of cash dividends that a subsidiary can pay to its parent. Such restrictions normally are intended to force multinational firms to reinvest earnings in the foreign country, although restrictions are sometimes imposed to prevent large currency outflows, which might disrupt the exchange rate.

Whatever the host country's motivation for blocking repatriation of profits, the result is that the parent corporation cannot use cash flows blocked in the foreign country to pay dividends to its shareholders or to invest elsewhere in the business. Hence, from the perspective of the parent organization, the cash flows relevant for foreign investment analysis are the cash flows that the subsidiary is actually expected to send back to the parent. Note, though, that if returns on investments in the foreign country are attractive and if blockages are expected to be lifted in the future, then current blockages may not be bad; however, dealing with this situation does complicate the process of cash flow estimation.

Some companies attempt to circumvent repatriation restrictions (and to lower their taxes) through transfer pricing. For example, a foreign subsidiary might obtain raw materials or other input components from the parent. The price the subsidiary pays the parent is called a **transfer price**. If the transfer price is high then the foreign subsidiary's costs will be high, leaving little or no profit to repatriate. However, the parent's profit will be higher because it sold to the subsidiary at an inflated transfer price. The net result is that the parent receives cash flows from the subsidiary via transfer pricing rather than as repatriated dividends. Transfer pricing also can be used to shift profits from high-tax to low-tax jurisdictions. Of course, governments are well aware of these possibilities, so governmental auditors are on guard to prevent abusive transfer pricing.

DOUBLE IRISH WITH A DUTCH TWIST

Untapped consumer markets, access to natural resources, and low production costs in foreign countries aren't the only reason U.S. corporations open foreign subsidiaries. Consider the case of the search engine and online advertising company, Google Inc. In 2010, Google reported $29.3 billion in sales on its consolidated income statement. Out of this total, about $12.5 billion were from Google's wholly owned international subsidiaries. Had these sales been realized by Google's domestic operations, they would have been subject to U.S. taxes at rates up to 35%. However, through the use of a complicated tax haven known as the "Double Irish" and the "Dutch Sandwich," Google managed to pay only 2.7%. Here's how it works.

First, Google establishes an Irish subsidiary that operates in the Bahamas (we'll call this the Irish/Bahamas subsidiary). The Bahamas have no corporate income taxes, and Ireland has special tax laws that make tax havens possible. Google transfers the licensing rights to use its search engine technology to this subsidiary, and this is where all the profits from international sales will end up. Next, the Bahamas subsidiary establishes a subsidiary that operates in the Netherlands. The Netherlands is special because even though it requires corporate taxes to be paid, it allows easy transfers to the Bahamas. The Netherlands subsidiary then establishes an Irish subsidiary that operates in Ireland and is assigned all the revenues from advertising sales. The Bahamas and Netherlands subsidiaries may even have zero employees while the Irish subsidiary has some employees, but not very many, because virtually all of the services are provided by U.S. employees.

Complicated? You bet! Google owns the Irish/Bahamas subsidiary, which owns the Netherlands subsidiary, which owns the Irish subsidiary. When advertising revenue from sales made in, say, Britain comes in, the Irish subsidiary receives these. However, it makes very little profit and therefore pays very little tax to Ireland because it pays a huge licensing fee to its parent, the Netherlands subsidiary, which, in turn makes little profit because it pays a huge licensing fee to its parent, the Irish/Bahamas subsidiary. And because the Bahamas has no corporate income tax, no tax is due on these profits.

So how might Google's shareholders ultimately benefit if profits remain in the Bahamas? The Bahamas subsidiary might someday pay a dividend to Google, at which point the profits would be taxed at Google's U.S. corporate tax rate. At that point, Google might pay a dividend to stockholders. In the interim, though, Google uses these profits, which have been taxed at almost a zero tax rate, to invest in international operations. And if, at some future point in time, Congress passes a law like it did in 2004 allowing corporations a one-time opportunity to repatriate earnings at a reduced tax rate, then that money will end up back in U.S. Google's hands.

Google's tax deferral strategy is legal, and many companies use it, including Oracle Corp., Facebook, Eli Lilly, and Pfizer. Whether it is good public policy for Congress to allow these shelters to exist is another matter entirely. Even though the Bahamas subsidiary earns higher profits because its net tax rate is almost zero, these profits don't help U.S. employment or other U.S. businesses because they aren't used for investment in the United States. It is estimated that these shelters reduce U.S. tax revenues by roughly $60 billion per year, an amount that would make a significant dent in the government deficit. The U.S. Treasury and Congress considered restricting them in 2009, but heavy lobbying from such companies as GE, Hewlett-Packard, and Starbucks convinced Congress not to make the changes.

Sources: Joseph B. Darby III and Kelsey Lemaster, "Double Irish More than Doubles the Tax Savings," *Practical US/International Tax Strategies*, May 15, 2007, Volume 11, no. 9, pp. 2, 11–16; Jesse Drucker, "U.S. Companies Dodge $60 Billion in Taxes With Global Odyssey," **www.bloomberg.com/news/2010-05-13/american-companies-dodge-60-billion-in-taxes-even-tea-party-would-condemn.html**, May 13, 2010; and Jesse Drucker, "The Tax Haven That's Saving Google Billions," Bloomberg Businessweek, October 21, 2010, **www.businessweek.com/magazine/content/10_44/b4201043146825.htm**.

27-11c Project Analysis

Consider a domestic project that requires foreign raw materials, or one where the finished product will be sold in a foreign market. Because the operation is based in the United States, any projected nondollar cash flows—costs of raw materials and revenues of the finished product—should be converted into dollars. This conversion does not present much of a problem for cash flows to be paid or received in the short run, but there is a significant problem in estimating exchange rates for converting long-term foreign cash flows into dollars because forward exchange rates are usually not available for more than 180 days into the future. However, long-term expected forward exchange rates can be estimated using the idea behind the interest rate parity relationship. For example, if a foreign cash flow is expected to occur in 1 year, then the 1-year forward exchange rate can be estimated using domestic and foreign government bonds maturing in 1 year. Similarly, the 2-year exchange rate can be estimated using 2-year bonds. Thus, foreign cash flows can be converted into dollars and added to the project's other projected cash flows, and then the project's NPV can be calculated based on its cost of capital.

Now consider a project to be based overseas, so that most expected future cash flows will be denominated in a foreign currency. Two approaches can be used to estimate such a project's NPV. Both begin by forecasting the future cash flows denominated in the foreign currency and then determining the annual repatriations to the United States, denominated in the foreign currency. Under the first approach, we convert the expected future repatriations to dollars (as described earlier) and then find the NPV using the project's cost of capital. Under the second approach, we take the projected repatriations (denominated in the foreign currency) and then discount them at the foreign cost of capital, which reflects foreign interest rates and relevant risk premiums. This produces an NPV denominated in the foreign currency, which can be converted into a dollar-denominated NPV using the spot exchange rate.

The following example illustrates the first approach. A U.S. company has the opportunity to lease a manufacturing facility in Great Britain for 3 years. The company must spend £20 million initially to refurbish the plant. The expected net cash flows from the plant for the next 3 years, in millions, are $CF_1 = £7$, $CF_2 = £9$, and $CF_3 = £11$. A similar project in the United States would have a risk-adjusted cost of capital of 10%. The first step is to estimate the expected exchange rates at the end of 1, 2, and 3 years using the multi-year interest rate parity equation:

$$\text{Expected t-year forward exchange rate} = (\text{Spot exchange rate})\left(\frac{1 + r_h}{1 + r_f}\right)^t \quad \text{(27–4)}$$

where the exchange rates are expressed in direct quotations and the interest rates are expressed as annual rates, not periodic rates. (Recall that the direct quote is for units of home currency per unit of foreign currency.) We are using the interest rate parity equation to estimate expected forward rates because market-based forward rates for maturities longer than a year are generally not available.

Suppose the spot exchange rate is 1.8000 dollars per pound. Interest rates on U.S. and U.K. government bonds are shown below, along with the expected forward rate implied by the multi-year interest rate parity relationship in Equation 27-4:

	Maturity (Years)		
	1	**2**	**3**
r_h (annualized)	2.0%	2.8%	3.5%
r_f (annualized)	4.6%	5.0%	5.2%
Spot rate ($/£)	1.8000	1.8000	1.8000
Expected forward rate based on Equation 27-4 ($/£)	1.7553	1.7254	1.7141

The current dollar cost of the project is £20(1.8000 $/£) = $36 million. The Year-1 cash flow in dollars is £7(1.7553 $/£) = $12.29 million. Table 27-6 shows the complete time line and the net present value of $2.18 million.

TABLE 27-6	Net Present Value of International Investment (Cash Flows in Millions)			
	Year			
	0	**1**	**2**	**3**
Cash flows in pounds	−£20	£7	£9	£11
Expected exchange rates (dollars/pound)	1.8000	1.7553	1.7254	1.7141
Cash flows in dollars	−$36.00	$12.29	$15.53	$18.86
Project cost of capital	10%			
NPV	$2.18			

SELF TEST

List some key differences in capital budgeting as applied to foreign versus domestic operations.

What are the relevant cash flows for an international investment: the cash flow produced by the subsidiary in the country where it operates, or the cash flows in dollars that it sends to its parent company?

Why might the cost of capital for a foreign project differ from that of an equivalent domestic project? Could it be lower?

What adjustments might be made due to exchange rate risk and political risk to the domestic cost of capital for a foreign investment?

27-12 International Capital Structures

Companies' capital structures vary among countries. For example, the Organization for Economic Cooperation and Development (OECD) reported that, on average, Japanese firms use 85% debt to total assets (in book value terms), German firms use 64%, and U.S. firms use 55%. One problem when interpreting these numbers is that different countries often use different accounting conventions with regard to: (1) reporting assets on the basis of historical versus replacement cost, (2) the treatment of leased assets, (3) pension plan funding, and (4) capitalizing versus expensing R&D costs. These differences make it difficult to compare capital structures.

A study by Raghuram Rajan and Luigi Zingales of the University of Chicago attempted to account for differences in accounting practices. In their study, Rajan and Zingales used a database that covered fewer firms than the OECD but that provided a more complete breakdown of balance sheet data. They concluded that differences in accounting practices can explain much of the cross-country variation in capital structures.

For example, when Rajan and Zingales measure capital structure as interest-bearing debt to total assets, German firms use less leverage than U.S. firms, a different result compared to the OECD report. What explains these conflicting results? Rajan and Zingales argue that much of the difference is explained by the way German firms account for pension liabilities. German firms generally include all pension liabilities (and their offsetting assets) on the balance sheet, whereas firms in other countries (including the United States) generally "net out" pension assets and liabilities on their balance sheets. To see the importance of this difference, consider a firm with $10 million in liabilities (not including pension liabilities) and $20 million in assets (not including pension assets). Assume that the firm has $10 million in pension liabilities that are fully funded by $10 million in pension assets. Therefore, net pension liabilities are zero. If this firm were in the United States, it would report a ratio of total liabilities to total assets equal to 50% ($10 million/$20 million). By contrast, if this firm operated in Germany, both its pension assets and liabilities would be reported on the balance sheet. The firm would have $20 million in liabilities and $30 million in assets—or a 67% ($20 million/$30 million) ratio of total liabilities to total assets. Total debt is the sum of short-term debt and long-term debt and *excludes* other liabilities, including pension liabilities. Therefore, the measure of total debt to total assets provides a more comparable measure of leverage across different countries.

Rajan and Zingales also make a variety of adjustments that attempt to control for other differences in accounting practices. The effects of these adjustments suggest that companies in Germany and the United Kingdom tend to have less leverage, and that firms in Canada appear to have more leverage, than firms in the United States, France, Italy, and Japan. This conclusion is supported by the average times-interest-earned ratio for firms in a number of different countries. Recall from Chapter 7 that the times-interest-earned ratio is the ratio of operating income (EBIT) to interest expense. This measure indicates how much cash the firm has available to service its interest expense. In general, firms with more leverage have a lower times-interest-earned ratio. The data indicate that this ratio is highest in the United Kingdom and Germany and lowest in Canada.

Are there international differences in firms' financial leverage? Explain.   **SELF TEST**

27-13 Multinational Working Capital Management

Working capital management in a multinational setting involves more complexity than purely domestic working capital management. We discuss some of these differences in this section.

27-13a Cash Management

The goals of cash management in a multinational corporation are similar to those in a purely domestic corporation: (1) to speed up collections, slow down disbursements, and thus maximize net float; (2) to shift cash as rapidly as possible from those parts of the business where it is not needed to those parts where it is needed; and (3) to maximize the risk-adjusted, after-tax rate of return on temporary cash balances. Multinational companies use the same general procedures for achieving these goals as domestic firms, but the longer distances and more serious mail delays make such devices as lockbox systems and electronic funds transfers especially important.

Although multinational and domestic corporations have the same objectives and use similar procedures, multinational corporations face a far more complex task. As noted earlier in our discussion of political risk, foreign governments often place restrictions on transfers of funds out of the country. So even though IBM can transfer money from its Salt Lake City office to its New York concentration bank just by pressing a few buttons, a similar transfer from its Buenos Aires office is far more complex. Buenos Aires funds must be converted to dollars before the transfer. If there is a shortage of dollars in Argentina or if the Argentinean government wants to conserve dollars so they will be available for the purchase of strategic materials, then conversion, and hence the transfer, may be blocked. Even if no dollar shortage exists in Argentina, the government may still restrict funds outflows if those funds represent profits or depreciation rather than payments for purchased materials or equipment, because many countries—especially those that are less developed—want profits reinvested in the country in order to stimulate economic growth.

Once it has been determined what funds can be transferred, the next task is to get those funds to locations where they will earn the highest returns. Whereas domestic corporations tend to think in terms of domestic securities, multinationals are more likely to be aware of investment opportunities around the world. Most multinational corporations use one or more global concentration banks, located in money centers such as London, New York, Tokyo, Zurich, or Singapore, and their staffs in those cities, working with international bankers, are able to take advantage of the best rates available anywhere in the world.

27-13b Credit Management

Consider the international cash conversion cycle for a foreign company importing from the United States: The order is placed, the goods are shipped, an account payable is created for the importer and an account receivable is created for the exporter, the goods arrive in the foreign country, the importer sells them, and the importer collects on the sales. At some point in this process, the importer pays off the account payable, which is usually before the importer collects on its own sales. Notice that the importer must finance the transaction from the time it pays the account payable until it collects on its sales. In many poorer, less developed nations, the capital markets are not adequate to enable the importer to finance the cash conversion cycle. Even when foreign capital markets are available, the additional shipping time might lengthen the cash conversion cycle to such an extent that the importer can't afford the financing costs. Thus, there is enormous pressure on the exporter to grant credit, often with very long payment periods.

But now consider the situation from the exporter's point of view. First, it is much more difficult for the exporter to perform a credit analysis on a foreign customer. Second, the exporter also must worry about exchange-rate fluctuations between the time of the sale and the time the receivable is collected. For example, if IBM sold a computer to a Japanese customer for 90 million yen when the exchange rate was 90 yen to the dollar, IBM would obtain 90,000,000/90 = $1,000,000 for the computer. However, if it sold the computer on terms of net/6 months and if the yen then fell against the dollar, so that 1 dollar would now buy 112.5 yen, IBM would end up realizing only 90,000,000/112.5 = $800,000 when it collected the receivable. Hedging with forward contracts can reduce this exchange rate risk, but what about the credit risk?

One possibility is for the importer to obtain a letter of credit from its bank whereby the bank certifies that the importer will meet the terms of the account payable or else the bank will pay. However, the importer often must pay the bank a relatively large fee for the letter of credit, and letters of credit might not be available to companies in developing countries.

A second option is for the importer essentially to write a check to the exporter at the time of the purchase, but to postdate the check so that it cannot be cashed until the account payable's due date. If the importer's bank promises that it will "accept" the check even if there are insufficient funds in the importer's account, then the check becomes a financial instrument called a **banker's acceptance**. If the bank is strong, then this virtually eliminates the credit risk. In addition, the exporter can then sell this banker's acceptance in the secondary market if it needs funds immediately. Of course, it must sell the banker's acceptance at a discount to reflect the time value of money, because the banker's acceptance is essentially a short-term financial security that pays no interest, similar to a T-bill. Financing an international transaction via a banker's acceptance has many benefits for the exporter, but the importer often must pay the bank a relatively large fee, and this service might not be available to companies in developing countries.

A third alternative is for the exporter to purchase export credit insurance, in which an insurer makes a commitment to pay the exporter even if the importer defaults. Sometimes the "insurer" is a government agency, such as the Japanese Ministry of International Trade and Industry (MITI) or the United States Export-Import Bank. Other times, the insurer is a private insurance company. These large insurance companies have developed expertise in international credit analysis, and they can spread the risk over a large number of customers. These advantages allow them to offer credit insurance at rates that often make it less costly than either letters of credit or bankers' acceptances. In fact, export credit insurance has been so successful that it has virtually killed the market for bankers' acceptances and has become the primary way in which companies manage the credit risk of international sales.

27-13c **Inventory Management**

As with most other aspects of finance, inventory management for a firm in a multinational setting is similar to but more complex than for a purely domestic firm. First, there is the matter of the physical location of inventories. For example, where should ExxonMobil keep its stockpiles of crude oil and refined products? It has refineries and marketing centers located worldwide, and one alternative is to keep items concentrated in a few strategic spots from which they can then be shipped as needs arise. Such a strategy might minimize the total amount of inventories needed and thus might minimize the investment in inventories. Note, though, that consideration will have to be given to potential delays in getting goods from central storage locations to user locations all around the world. Both working stocks and safety stocks would have to be maintained at each user location as well as at the strategic storage centers. Problems like the Iraqi occupation of Kuwait in 1990 and the subsequent trade embargo, which brought with it the potential for a shutdown of production of about 25% of the world's oil supply, complicate matters further.

Exchange rates also influence inventory policy. If a local currency—say, the Danish krone—were expected to rise in value against the dollar, then a U.S. company operating in Denmark would want to increase stocks of local products before the rise in the krone, and vice versa if the krone were expected to fall.

Another factor that must be considered is the possibility of import or export quotas or tariffs. For example, Apple was buying certain memory chips from Japanese suppliers at a bargain price. Then U.S. chipmakers accused the Japanese of dumping chips in the U.S. market at prices below cost, and they sought to force the Japanese to raise their prices.[11] This led Apple to increase its chip inventory. Then computer sales slacked off, and Apple ended up with an oversupply of obsolete computer chips. As a result, Apple's profits were hurt and its stock price fell, demonstrating once more the importance of careful inventory management.

As mentioned earlier, another danger in certain countries is the threat of expropriation. If that threat is large, then inventory holdings will be minimized and goods will be brought in only as needed. Similarly, if the operation involves extraction of raw materials such as oil or bauxite, processing plants may be moved offshore rather than located close to the production site.

Taxes have two effects on multinational inventory management. First, countries often impose property taxes on assets, including inventories; when this is done, the tax is based on holdings as of a specific date, such as January 1 or March 1. Such rules make it advantageous for a multinational firm: (1) to schedule production so that inventories are low on the assessment date, and (2) if assessment dates vary among countries in a region, to hold safety stocks in different countries at different times during the year.

Finally, multinational firms may consider the possibility of at-sea storage. Oil, chemical, grain, and other companies that deal in a bulk commodity that must be stored in some type of tank can often buy tankers at a cost not much greater—or perhaps even less, considering land cost—than land-based facilities. Loaded tankers can then be kept at sea or at anchor in some strategic location. This eliminates the danger of expropriation, minimizes the property tax problem, and maximizes flexibility with regard to shipping to areas where needs are greatest or prices highest.

This discussion has only scratched the surface of inventory management in the multinational corporation—the task is much more complex than for a purely domestic firm. However, the greater the degree of complexity, the greater the rewards from superior performance, so if you are willing to take challenges along with potentially high rewards then look to the international arena.

SELF TEST

What are some factors that make cash management more complicated in a multinational corporation than in a purely domestic corporation?

Why is granting credit riskier in an international context?

Why is inventory management especially important for a multinational firm?

---

11. The term "dumping" warrants explanation, because the practice can be so important in international markets. Suppose Japanese chipmakers have excess capacity. A particular chip has a variable cost of $25, and its "fully allocated cost," which is the $25 plus total fixed cost per unit of output, is $40. Now suppose the Japanese firm can sell chips in the United States at $35 per unit, but if it charges $40 then it won't make any sales because U.S. chipmakers sell for $35.50. If the Japanese firm sells at $35, it will cover variable costs plus make a contribution to fixed overhead, so selling at $35 makes sense. Continuing, if the Japanese firm can sell in Japan at $40 but U.S. firms are excluded from Japanese markets by import duties or other barriers, then the Japanese will have a huge advantage over U.S. manufacturers. This practice of selling goods at lower prices in foreign markets than at home is called "dumping." U.S. firms are required by antitrust laws to offer the same price to all customers and, therefore, cannot engage in dumping.

Summary

Multinational companies have more opportunities, but they also face more risks than do companies that operate only in their home market. This chapter discussed many of the key trends affecting the global markets today, and it described the most important differences between multinational and domestic financial management. The key concepts are listed below.

- **International operations** are becoming increasingly important to individual firms and to the national economy. A multinational, transnational, or **global corporation** is a firm that operates in an integrated fashion in a number of countries.
- Companies "go global" for these reasons: (1) to expand their markets, (2) to obtain raw materials, (3) to seek new technology, (4) to lower production costs, (5) to avoid trade barriers, and (6) to diversify.
- Several major factors distinguish financial management as practiced by domestic firms from that practiced by multinational corporations: (1) different currency denominations, (2) different economic and legal structures, (3) languages, (4) cultural differences, (5) role of governments, and (6) political risk.
- When discussing **exchange rates**, the number of U.S. dollars required to purchase one unit of a foreign currency is called a **direct quotation**, while the number of units of foreign currency that can be purchased for one U.S. dollar is an **indirect quotation**.
- **Exchange rate fluctuations** make it difficult to estimate the dollars that overseas operations will produce.
- Prior to August 1971, the world was on a **fixed exchange rate system** whereby the U.S. dollar was linked to gold and other currencies were then tied to the dollar. After August 1971, the world monetary system changed to a **floating system** under which major world currency rates float with market forces, largely unrestricted by governmental intervention. The central bank of each country does operate in the foreign exchange market, buying and selling currencies to smooth out exchange rate fluctuations, but only to a limited extent.
- **Pegged exchange rates** occur when a country establishes a fixed exchange rate with a major currency. Consequently, the values of pegged currencies move together over time.
- A **convertible currency** is one that may be readily exchanged for other currencies.
- **Spot rates** are the rates paid for delivery of currency "on the spot," whereas the **forward exchange rate** is the rate paid for delivery at some agreed-upon future date—usually 30, 90, or 180 days from the day the transaction is negotiated. The forward rate can be at either a **premium** or a **discount** to the spot rate.
- **Interest rate parity** holds that investors should expect to earn the same risk-free return in all countries after adjusting for exchange rates.
- **Purchasing power parity**, sometimes referred to as the *law of one price*, implies that the level of exchange rates adjusts so that identical goods cost the same in different countries.

- Granting credit is more risky in an international context because, in addition to the normal risks of default, the multinational firm must worry about **exchange rate changes** between the time a sale is made and the time a receivable is collected.
- Credit policy is important for a multinational firm for two reasons: (1) Much trade is with less-developed nations, and in such situations granting credit is a necessary condition for doing business. (2) The governments of nations such as Japan, whose economic health depends on exports, often help their firms compete by granting credit to foreign customers.
- Foreign investments are similar to domestic investments, but political risk and exchange rate risk must be considered. **Political risk** is the risk that the foreign government will take some action that will decrease the value of the investment; **exchange rate risk** is the risk of losses due to fluctuations in the value of the dollar relative to the values of foreign currencies.
- Investments in **international capital projects** expose firms to exchange rate risk and political risk. The relevant cash flows in international capital budgeting are the dollars that can be **repatriated** to the parent company.
- **Eurodollars** are U.S. dollars deposited in banks outside the United States. Interest rates on Eurodollars are tied to **LIBOR**, the **London Interbank Offered Rate**.
- U.S. firms often find that they can raise long-term capital at a lower cost outside the United States by selling bonds in the **international capital markets**. International bonds may be either **foreign bonds**, which are exactly like regular domestic bonds except that the issuer is a foreign company, or **Eurobonds**, which are bonds sold in a foreign country but denominated in the currency of the issuing company's home country.

Questions

27-1 Define each of the following terms:
   a. Multinational corporation
   b. Exchange rate; fixed exchange rate system; floating exchange rate
   c. Trade deficit; devaluation; revaluation
   d. Exchange rate risk; convertible currency; pegged exchange rate
   e. Interest rate parity; purchasing power parity
   f. Spot rate; forward exchange rate; discount on forward rate; premium on forward rate
   g. Repatriation of earnings; political risk
   h. Eurodollar; Eurobond; international bond; foreign bond
   i. The euro

27-2 Under the fixed exchange rate system, what was the currency against which all other currency values were defined? Why?

27-3 Exchange rates fluctuate under both the fixed exchange rate and floating exchange rate systems. What, then, is the difference between the two systems?

27-4 If the Swiss franc depreciates against the U.S. dollar, can a dollar buy more or fewer Swiss francs as a result?

27-5 If the United States imports more goods from abroad than it exports, then foreigners will tend to have a surplus of U.S. dollars. What will this do to the value of the dollar with respect to foreign currencies? What is the corresponding effect on foreign investments in the United States?

27-6 Why do U.S. corporations build manufacturing plants abroad when they could build them at home?

27-7 Should firms require higher rates of return on foreign projects than on identical projects located at home? Explain.

27-8 What is a Eurodollar? If a French citizen deposits $10,000 in Chase Bank in New York, have Eurodollars been created? What if the deposit is made in Barclays Bank in London? Chase's Paris branch? Does the existence of the Eurodollar market make the Federal Reserve's job of controlling U.S. interest rates easier or more difficult? Explain.

27-9 Does interest rate parity imply that interest rates are the same in all countries?

27-10 Why might purchasing power parity fail to hold?

Problems
Answers Appear in Appendix B

Easy Problems 1–4

27-1 Cross Rates
At today's spot exchange rates 1 U.S. dollar can be exchanged for 9 Mexican pesos or for 111.23 Japanese yen. You have pesos that you would like to exchange for yen. What is the cross rate between the yen and the peso; that is, how many yen would you receive for every peso exchanged?

27-2 Interest Rate Parity
The nominal yield on 6-month T-bills is 7%, while default-free Japanese bonds that mature in 6 months have a nominal rate of 5.5%. In the spot exchange market, 1 yen equals $0.009. If interest rate parity holds, what is the 6-month forward exchange rate?

27-3 Purchasing Power Parity
A computer costs $500 in the United States. The same model costs 550 euros in France. If purchasing power parity holds, what is the spot exchange rate between the euro and the dollar?

27-4 Exchange Rate
If euros sell for $1.50 (U.S.) per euro, what should dollars sell for in euros per dollar?

Intermediate Problems 5–8

27-5 Currency Appreciation
Suppose that the exchange rate is 0.60 dollars per Swiss franc. If the franc appreciates 10% against the dollar, how many francs would a dollar buy tomorrow?

27–6 Cross Rates

Suppose the exchange rate between U.S. dollars and the Swiss franc is SFr1.6 = $1 and the exchange rate between the dollar and the British pound is £1 = $1.50. What then is the cross rate between francs and pounds?

27–7 Interest Rate Parity

Assume that interest rate parity holds. In both the spot market and the 90-day forward market, 1 Japanese yen equals 0.0086 dollar. In Japan, 90-day risk-free securities yield 4.6%. What is the yield on 90-day risk-free securities in the United States?

27–8 Purchasing Power Parity

In the spot market, 7.8 pesos can be exchanged for 1 U.S. dollar. A pair of headphones costs $15 in the United States. If purchasing power parity holds, what should be the price of the same headphones in Mexico?

Challenging Problems 9–14

27–9 Exchange Gains and Losses

Your Boston-headquartered manufacturing company, Wruck Enterprises, obtained a 50 million-peso loan from a Mexico City bank last month to fund the expansion of your Monterrey, Mexico plant. When you took out the loan, the exchange rate was 10 U.S. cents per peso, but since then, the exchange rate has dropped to 9 U.S. cents per peso. Has Wruck Enterprises made a gain or a loss due to the exchange rate change, and how much? Note that your shareholders live in the United States.

27–10 Results of Exchange Rate Changes

In 1983, the Japanese yen-U.S. dollar exchange rate was 245 yen per dollar, and the dollar cost of a compact Japanese-manufactured car was $8,000. Suppose that now the exchange rate is 80 yen per dollar. Assume there has been no inflation in the yen cost of an automobile so that all price changes are due to exchange rate changes. What would the dollar price of the car be now, assuming the car's price changes only with exchange rates?

27–11 Spot and Forward Rates

Boisjoly Watch Imports has agreed to purchase 15,000 Swiss watches for 1 million francs at today's spot rate. The firm's financial manager, James Desreumaux, has noted the following current spot and forward rates:

	U.S. Dollar/Swiss Franc	Swiss Franc/U.S. Dollar
Spot	1.6590	0.6028
30-day forward	1.6540	0.6046
90-day forward	1.6460	0.6075
180-day forward	1.6400	0.6098

On the same day, Desreumaux agrees to purchase 15,000 more watches in 3 months at the same price of 1 million Swiss francs.

a. What is the cost of the watches in U.S. dollars, if purchased at today's spot rate?

b. What is the cost in dollars of the second 15,000 batch if payment is made in 90 days and the spot rate at that time equals today's 90-day forward rate?

c. If the exchange rate for is 0.50 Swiss francs per dollar in 90 days, how much will Desreumaux have to pay (in dollars) for the watches?

27–12 Interest Rate Parity
Assume that interest rate parity holds and that 90-day risk-free securities yield 5% in the United States and 5.3% in Germany. In the spot market, 1 euro equals $1.40. What is the 90-day forward rate? Is the 90-day forward rate trading at a premium or a discount relative to the spot rate?

27–13 Foreign Investment Analysis
Chapman Inc.'s Mexican subsidiary, V. Gomez Corporation, is expected to pay to Chapman 50 pesos in dividends in 1 year after all foreign and U.S. taxes have been subtracted. The exchange rate in 1 year is expected to be 0.10 dollars per peso. After this, the peso is expected to depreciate against the dollar at a rate of 4% a year forever due to the different inflation rates in the United States and Mexico. The peso-denominated dividend is expected to grow at a rate of 8% a year indefinitely. Chapman owns 10 million shares of V. Gomez. What is the present value of the dividend stream, in dollars, assuming V. Gomez's cost of equity is 13%?

27–14 Foreign Capital Budgeting
The South Korean multinational manufacturing firm, Nam Sung Industries, is debating whether to invest in a 2-year project in the United States. The project's expected dollar cash flows consist of an initial investment of $1 million with cash inflows of $700,000 in Year 1 and $600,000 in Year 2. The risk-adjusted cost of capital for this project is 13%. The current exchange rate is 1,050 won per U.S. dollar. Risk-free interest rates in the United States and S. Korea are:

	1-year	2-year
U.S.	4.0%	4.25%
S. Korea	3.0%	3.25%

a. If this project were instead undertaken by a similar U.S.-based company with the same risk-adjusted cost of capital, what would be the net present value and rate of return generated by this project?

b. What is the expected forward exchange rate 1 year from now and 2 years from now? (*Hint:* Take the perspective of the Korean company when identifying home and foreign currencies and direct quotes of exchange rates.)

c. If Nam Sung undertakes the project, what is the net present value and rate of return of the project for Nam Sung?

Spreadsheet Problem

27–15 Build a Model: Multinational Financial Management
Start with the partial model in the file *Ch27 P15 Build a Model.xls* on the textbook's Web site. Mark Collins, luthier and businessman, builds and sells

custom-made acoustic and electric stringed instruments. Although located in Maryville, Tennessee, he purchases raw materials from around the globe. For example, he constructs his top-of-the line acoustic guitar with onboard electronics, the MC-28, from rosewood and mahogany imported from a distributor in Mexico, spruce harvested in and imported from Canada, and ebony and the electronics imported from a Japanese distributor. He obtains other parts in the United States. When broken down on a per-guitar basis, the component and finishing costs are as follows:

Rosewood and mahogany: 2,750 Mexican pesos
Spruce: 200 Canadian dollars
Ebony and electronics: 12,400 Japanese yen
Other parts plus woodworking labor: $600

Collins sells some of this model in the United States, but the majority of the units are sold in England, where he has developed a loyal following and the guitars have become something of a cult symbol. There, his guitars fetch £1,600, excluding shipping. Mark is concerned about the effect of exchange rates on his materials costs and profit.

You will find Tables 27-1, 27-2, and 27-3 useful for this problem.

a. How much, in dollars, does it cost for Collins to produce his MC-28? What is the dollar sale price of the MC-28 sold in England?
b. What is the dollar profit that Collins makes on the sale of the MC-28? What is the percentage profit?
c. If the U.S. dollar were to depreciate by 10% against all foreign currencies, what would be the dollar profit for the MC-28?
d. If the U.S. dollar were to depreciate by 10% only against the pound and remain constant relative to all other foreign currencies, what would be the dollar and percentage profits for the MC-28?
e. Using the forward exchange information from Table 27-3, calculate the return on 90-day securities in England if the rate of return on 90-day securities in the United States is 3.9%.
f. Assuming that purchasing power parity (PPP) holds, what would be the sale price of the MC-28 if it were sold in France rather than in England? (*Hint:* Assume England is the home country.)

MINI CASE

With the growth in demand for exotic foods, Possum Products' CEO Michael Munger is considering expanding the geographic footprint of its line of dried and smoked low-fat opossum, ostrich, and venison jerky snack packs. Historically, jerky products have performed well in the southern United States, but there are indications of a growing demand for these unusual delicacies in Europe. Munger recognizes that the expansion carries some risk. Europeans may not be as accepting of opossum jerky as initial research suggests, so the expansion will proceed in steps. The first step will be to set up sales subsidiaries in France and Sweden (the two countries with the highest indicated demand), and the second is to set up a production plant in France with the ultimate goal of product distribution throughout Europe.

Possum Products' CFO, Kevin Uram, although enthusiastic about the plan, is nonetheless concerned about how an international expansion and the additional risk that entails will affect the firm's financial management process. He has asked you, the firm's most recently hired financial analyst, to develop a 1-hour tutorial package that explains the basics of multinational financial management. The tutorial will be presented at the next board of directors meeting. To get you started, Uram has supplied you with the following list of questions:

a. What is a multinational corporation? Why do firms expand into other countries?

b. What are the six major factors that distinguish multinational financial management from financial management as practiced by a purely domestic firm?

c. Consider the following illustrative exchange rates.

U.S. Dollars Required to Buy One Unit of Foreign Currency	
Euro	1.2500
Swedish krona	—

Units of Foreign Currency Required to Buy One U.S. Dollar	
Euro	—
Swedish krona	7.0000

(1) What is a direct quotation? What is the direct quote for euros?

(2) What is an indirect quotation? What is the indirect quotation for kronor (the plural of krona is kronor)?

(3) The euro and British pound usually are quoted as direct quotes. Most other currencies are quoted as indirect quotes. How would you calculate the indirect quote for a euro? How would you calculate the direct quote for a krona?

(4) What is a cross rate? Calculate the two cross rates between euros and kronor.

(5) Assume Possum Products can produce a package of jerky and ship it to France for $1.75. If the firm wants a 50% markup on the product, what should the jerky sell for in France?

(6) Now assume that Possum Products begins producing the same package of jerky in France. The product costs 2 euros to produce and ship to Sweden, where it can be sold for 20 kronor. What is the dollar profit on the sale?

(7) What is exchange rate risk?

d. Briefly describe the current international monetary system. How does the current system differ from the system that was in place prior to August 1971?

e. What is a convertible currency? What problems arise when a multinational company operates in a country whose currency is not convertible?

f. What is the difference between spot rates and forward rates? When is the forward rate at a premium to the spot rate? At a discount?

g. What is interest rate parity? Currently, you can exchange 1 euro for 1.25 dollars in the 180-day forward market, and the risk-free rate on 180-day securities is 6% in the United States and 4% in France. Does interest rate parity hold? If not, which securities offer the highest expected return?

h. What is purchasing power parity? If a package of jerky costs $2 in the United States and purchasing power parity holds, what should be the price of the jerky package in France?

i. What effect does relative inflation have on interest rates and exchange rates?

j. Briefly discuss the international capital markets.

k. To what extent do average capital structures vary across different countries?

l. Briefly describe special problems that occur in multinational capital budgeting, and describe the process for evaluating a foreign project. Now consider the following project: A U.S. company has the opportunity to lease a manufacturing facility in Japan for 2 years. The company must spend ¥1 billion initially to refurbish the plant. The expected net cash flows from the plant for the next 2 years, in millions, are CF_1 = ¥500 and CF_2 = ¥800. A similar project in the United

States would have a risk-adjusted cost of capital of 10%. In the United States, a 1-year government bond pays 2% interest and a 2-year bond pays 2.8%. In Japan, a 1-year bond pays 0.05% and a 2-year bond pays 0.26%. What is the project's NPV?

m. Briefly discuss special factors associated with the following areas of multinational working capital management:
(1) Cash management
(2) Credit management
(3) Inventory management

SELECTED ADDITIONAL CASE

The following case from CengageCompose covers many of the concepts discussed in this chapter and is available at http://compose.cengage.com.

Klein-Brigham Series:

Case 18, "Alaska Oil Corporation."

Values of the Areas under the Standard Normal Distribution Function

TABLE A-1	Values of the Areas under the Standard Normal Distribution Function

Z	0.00	0.01	0.02	0.03	0.04	0.05	0.06	0.07	0.08	0.09
0.0	.0000	.0040	.0080	.0120	.0160	.0199	.0239	.0279	.0319	.0359
0.1	.0398	.0438	.0478	.0517	.0557	.0596	.0636	.0675	.0714	.0753
0.2	.0793	.0832	.0871	.0910	.0948	.0987	.1026	.1064	.1103	.1141
0.3	.1179	.1217	.1255	.1293	.1331	.1368	.1406	.1443	.1480	.1517
0.4	.1554	.1591	.1628	.1664	.1700	.1736	.1772	.1808	.1844	.1879
0.5	.1915	.1950	.1985	.2019	.2054	.2088	.2123	.2157	.2190	.2224
0.6	.2257	.2291	.2324	.2357	.2389	.2422	.2454	.2486	.2517	.2549
0.7	.2580	.2611	.2642	.2673	.2704	.2734	.2764	.2794	.2823	.2852
0.8	.2881	.2910	.2939	.2967	.2995	.3023	.3051	.3078	.3106	.3133
0.9	.3159	.3186	.3212	.3238	.3264	.3289	.3315	.3340	.3365	.3389
1.0	.3413	.3438	.3461	.3485	.3508	.3531	.3554	.3577	.3599	.3621
1.1	.3643	.3665	.3686	.3708	.3729	.3749	.3770	.3790	.3810	.3830
1.2	.3849	.3869	.3888	.3907	.3925	.3944	.3962	.3980	.3997	.4015
1.3	.4032	.4049	.4066	.4082	.4099	.4115	.4131	.4147	.4162	.4177
1.4	.4192	.4207	.4222	.4236	.4251	.4265	.4279	.4292	.4306	.4319
1.5	.4332	.4345	.4357	.4370	.4382	.4394	.4406	.4418	.4429	.4441

(Continued)

Z	0.00	0.01	0.02	0.03	0.04	0.05	0.06	0.07	0.08	0.09
1.6	.4452	.4463	.4474	.4484	.4495	.4505	.4515	.4525	.4535	.4545
1.7	.4554	.4564	.4573	.4582	.4591	.4599	.4608	.4616	.4625	.4633
1.8	.4641	.4649	.4656	.4664	.4671	.4678	.4686	.4693	.4699	.4706
1.9	.4713	.4719	.4726	.4732	.4738	.4744	.4750	.4756	.4761	.4767
2.0	.4773	.4778	.4783	.4788	.4793	.4798	.4803	.4808	.4812	.4817
2.1	.4821	.4826	.4830	.4834	.4838	.4842	.4846	.4850	.4854	.4857
2.2	.4861	.4864	.4868	.4871	.4875	.4878	.4881	.4884	.4887	.4890
2.3	.4893	.4896	.4898	.4901	.4904	.4906	.4909	.4911	.4913	.4916
2.4	.4918	.4920	.4922	.4925	.4927	.4929	.4931	.4932	.4934	.4936
2.5	.4938	.4940	.4941	.4943	.4945	.4946	.4948	.4949	.4951	.4952
2.6	.4953	.4955	.4956	.4957	.4959	.4960	.4961	.4962	.4963	.4964
2.7	.4965	.4966	.4967	.4968	.4969	.4970	.4971	.4972	.4973	.4974
2.8	.4974	.4975	.4976	.4977	.4977	.4978	.4979	.4979	.4980	.4981
2.9	.4981	.4982	.4982	.4982	.4984	.4984	.4985	.4985	.4986	.4986
3.0	.4987	.4987	.4987	.4988	.4988	.4989	.4989	.4989	.4990	.4990

Answers to End-of-Chapter Problems

We present here some intermediate steps and final answers to selected end-of-chapter problems. Please note that your answer may differ slightly from ours because of rounding differences. Also, although we hope not, some of the problems may have more than one correct solution, depending on what assumptions are made when working the problem. Finally, many of the problems involve some verbal discussion as well as numerical calculations; this verbal material is not presented here.

2-1 $b = 1.08$.

2-2 $r_s = 10.40\%$.

2-3 $r_M = 12\%$; $r_{sB} = 16.9\%$.

2-4 15.96%.

2-5 $\hat{r} = 11.40\%$; $\sigma = 26.69\%$.

2-6 a. $\hat{r}_M = 13.5\%$; $\hat{r}_j = 11.6\%$.
   b. $\sigma_M = 3.85\%$; $\sigma_j = 6.22\%$.

2-7 a. $b_A = 1.40$.
   b. $r_A = 15\%$.

2-8 a. $r_i = 14.8\%$.
   b. (1) $r_M = 13\%$; $r_i = 15.8\%$.
      (2) $r_M = 11\%$; $r_i = 13.8\%$.
   c. (1) $r_i = 17.6\%$.
      (2) $r_i = 13.4\%$.

2-9 $b_N = 1.25$.

2-10 $b_p = 0.7625$; $r_p = 12.1\%$.

2-11 $b_N = 1.1250$.

2-12 4.5%.

2-13 a. $\bar{r}_A = 11.80\%$; $\bar{r}_B = 11.80\%$.
   b. $\bar{r}_p = 11.80\%$.
   c. $\sigma_A = 25.3\%$; $\sigma_B = 24.3\%$;
      $\sigma_p = 16.3\%$.

2-14 a. $b_X = 1.3471$; $b_Y = 0.6508$.
   b. $r_X = 12.7355\%$; $r_Y = 9.254\%$.
   c. $r_p = 12.04\%$.

3-1 1.4.

3-2 12%.

3-3 16.2%; 45.9%.

3-4 a. Alternative SML: $r_i = r_{RF} + \left(\dfrac{r_M - r_{RF}}{\sigma_M}\right)\rho_{iM}\sigma_i$

3-5 a. $b = 0.56$.
   b. X: 10.6%; 13.1%.
      M: 12.1%; 22.6%.
   c. 8.6%.

3-6 a. $b = 0.62$.

4-1 $928.39.

4-2 12.48%.

4-3 8.55%.

4-4 7%; 7.33%.

4-5 2.5%.

4-6 0.3%.

4-7 $1,085.80.

4-8 YTM = 6.62%; YTC = 6.49%.

4-9 a. 5%: $V_L = \$1,518.98$;
             $V_S = \$1,047.62$.
         8%: $V_L = \$1,171.19$;
             $V_S = \$1,018.52$.
        12%: $V_L = \$863.78$;
             $V_S = \$982.14$.

4-10 a. YTM at $829 = 13.98%;
       YTM at $1,104 = 6.50%.

4-11 14.82%.

4-12 a. 10.37%.
  b. 10.91%.
  c. −0.54%.
  d. 10.15%.

4-13 8.65%.

4-14 10.78%.

4-15 YTC = 6.47%.

4-16 a. 10-year, 10% coupon = 6.75%;
      10-year zero = 9.75%;
      5-year zero = 4.76%;
      30-year zero = 32.19%;
      $100 perpetuity = 14.29%.

4-17 C_0 = $1,012.79; Z_0 = $693.04;
     C_1 = $1,010.02; Z_1 = $759.57;
     C_2 = $1,006.98; Z_2 = $832.49;
     C_3 = $1,003.65; Z_3 = $912.41;
     C_4 = $1,000.00; Z_4 = $1,000.00.

4-18 5.8%.

4-19 1.5%.

4-20 6.0%.

4-21 a. $1,251.22.
  b. $898.94.

4-22 a. 8.02%.
  b. 7.59%.

4-23 a. r_1 = 9.20%; r_5 = 7.20%.

5-1 $5; $2.

5-2 $27.00; $37.00.

5-3 $1.67.

5-4 $3.70.

5-5 $1.90.

5-6 $2.39.

5-7 $1.91.

6-1 5.8%.

6-2 25%.

6-3 $3,000,000.

6-4 $2,000,000.

6-5 $3,600,000.

6-6 $25,000,000.

6-7 Tax = $107,855;
    NI = $222,145;
    Marginal tax rate = 39%;
    Average tax rate = 33.8%.

6-8 a. Tax = $3,575,000.
  b. Tax = $350,000.
  c. Tax = $105,000.

6-9 AT&T bond = 4.875%;
    AT&T preferred stock = 5.37%;
    Florida bond = 5%.

6-10 NI = $450,000;
     NCF = $650,000.

6-11 a. $2,400,000.
  b. NI = $0;
     NCF = $3,000,000.
  c. NI = $1,350,000;
     NCF = $2,100,000.

6-12 a. NOPAT = $756 million.
  b. $NOWC_{14}$ = $3.0 billion;
     $NOWC_{15}$ = $3.3 billion.
  c. Op. capital$_{14}$ = $6.5 billion;
     Op. capital$_{15}$ = $7.15 billion.
  d. FCF = $106 million.
  e. ROIC = 10.57%.
  f. Answers in millions:
     A-T int. = $72.
     Inc. in debt = −$284.
     Div. = $220.
     Rep. stock = $88.
     Purch. ST inv. = $10.

6-13 Refund = $120,000.
     Future taxes = $0; $0;
     $40,000; $60,000; $60,000.

7-1 AR = $400,000.

7-2 Debt ratio = Debt-to-assets ratio = 15%.

7-3 M/B = 10.

7-4 P/E = 16.0.

7-5 ROE = 12%.

7-6 S/TA = 2.4; TA/E = 1.67.

7-7 CL = $2,000,000;
    Inv = $1,000,000.

7-8 Net profit margin = 3.33%;
    L/A = 42.86%.
    Debt ratio = 21.43%.

7-9 $262,500; 1.19.

7-10 TIE = 4.13.

7-11 Sales = $600,000;
    COGS = $450,000;
    Cash = $28,000;
    AR = $60,000;
    Inv. = $120,000;
    FA = $192,000;
    AP = $110,000;
    Common stock = $140,000;

7-12 Sales = $2,580,000.

7-13 a. Current ratio = 2.01;
    DSO = 77 days;
    Inv TO = 5.67;
    FA turnover = 5.56;
    TA turnover = 1.75;
    PM = 1.5%;
    ROA = 2.6%;
    ROE = 6.4%;
    Debt ratio = 33%;
    L/TA = 59%.

7-14 Quick ratio = 0.8;
    CA/CL = 2.3;
    Inv. TO = 4.2;
    DSO = 37 days;
    FA TO = 10.0;
    TA TO = 2.3;
    ROA = 5.9%;
    ROE = 13.1%;
    PM = 2.5%;
    Debt ratio = 27.5%;
    L/TA = 54.8%;
    PE ratio = 5.0;
    P/CF ratio = 2.0;
    M/B ratio = 0.65.

8-1 D_1 = $1.5750; D_3 = $1.7364;
    D_5 = $2.1011.

8-2 $\hat{P}_0$ = $21.43.

8-3 $\hat{P}_1$ = $24.20; $\hat{r}_s$ = 16.00%.

8-4 r_{ps} = 10%.

8-5 $50.50.

8-6 V_{op} = $6,000,000.

8-7 V_{op} at 2018 = $15,000 (millions).

8-8 g = 9%.

8-9 $\hat{P}_3$ = $43.08.

8-10 a. 11.67%.
    b. 8.75%.
    c. 7.00%.
    d. 5.00%.

8-11 $32.00.

8-12 $25.03.

8-13 $\hat{P}_0$ = $10.76.

8-14 a. $125.
    b. $83.33.

8-15 a. 7%.
    b. 5%.
    c. 12%.

8-16 a. (1) $15.83.
    (2) $23.08.
    (3) $39.38.
    (4) $110.00.
    b. (1) Undefined.

8-17 a. HV_2 = $2,700,000.
    b. $2,303,571.43.

8-18 a. $713.33 million.
    b. $527.89 million.
    c. $43.79.

8-19 a. $1.79
    b. PV = $3.97.
    c. $18.74.
    d. $22.71.

8-20 a. $2.01, $2.31, $2.66, $3.06, $3.52.
    b. $\hat{P}_0$ = $39.42.
    c. D_1/P_0 = 5.10%;
        D_6/P_5 = 7.00%.

8-21 $\hat{P}_0$ = $78.35.

9-1 AFN = $283,800.

9-2 AFN = $583,800.

9-3 AFN = $63,000.

9-4 ΔS = $202,312.

9-5 a. $590,000; $1,150,000.
    b. $238,563.

9-6 AFN = $360.

9-7 a. $13.44 million.
   b. 6.38%.
   c. LOC = $13.44 million.

9-8 a. Total assets = $33,534 (thousands);
       Deficit = $2,128 (thousands).
   b. LOC = $2,128 (thousands).

9-9 LOC = $128,783.

11-1 a. 13%.
    b. 10.4%.
    c. 8.45%.

11-2 5.2%.

11-3 9%.

11-4 5.41%.

11-5 13.33%.

11-6 10.4%.

11-7 9.17%.

11-8 13%.

11-9 7.2%.

11-10 a. 16.3%.
     b. 15.4%.
     c. 16%.

11-11 a. 8%.
     b. $2.81.
     c. 15.81%.

11-12 a. $g = 3\%$.
     b. $EPS_1 = \$5.562$.

11-13 16.1%.

11-14 $(1 - T)r_d = 5.57\%$.

11-15 a. $15,000,000.
     b. 8.4%.

11-16 Short-term debt = 11.14%;
      Long-term debt = 22.03%;
      Common equity = 66.83%.

11-17 $w_{std} = 0\%$; $w_d = 20\%$;
      $w_{ps} = 4\%$; $w_s = 76\%$;
      r_d(After-tax) = 7.2%;
      $r_{ps} = 11.6\%$; $r_s \approx 17.5\%$.

12-1 NPV = $2,409.77.

12-2 IRR = 12.84%.

12-3 MIRR = 11.93%.

12-4 PI = 1.06.

12-5 4.44 years.

12-6 6.44 years.

12-7 a. 5%: $NPV_A = \$16,108,952$;
               $NPV_B = \$18,300,939$.
       10%: $NPV_A = \$12,836,213$;
               $NPV_B = \$15,954,170$.
       15%: $NPV_A = \$10,059,587$;
               $NPV_B = \$13,897,838$.
    b. $IRR_A = 43.97\%$; $IRR_B = 82.03\%$

12-8 $NPV_T = \$409$; $IRR_T = 15\%$;
     $MIRR_T = 14.54\%$; Accept.
     $NPV_P = \$3,318$; $IRR_P = 20\%$;
     $MIRR_P = 17.19\%$; Accept.

12-9 $NPV_E = \$3,861$; $IRR_E = 18\%$;
     $NPV_G = \$3,057$; $IRR_G = 18\%$;
     Purchase electric-powered forklift because
     it has a higher NPV.

12-10 $NPV_S = \$814.33$;
      $NPV_L = \$1,675.34$;
      $IRR_S = 15.24\%$;
      $IRR_L = 14.67\%$;
      $MIRR_S = 13.77\%$;
      $MIRR_L = 13.46\%$;
      $PI_S = 1.081$;
      $PI_L = 1.067$.

12-11 $MIRR_X = 17.49\%$;
      $MIRR_Y = 18.39\%$.

12-12 a. NPV = $136,578;
        IRR = 19.22%.

12-13 b. $IRR_A = 20.7\%$;
        $IRR_B = 25.8\%$.
     c. 10%: $NPV_A = \$478.83$;
               $NPV_B = \$372.37$.
        17%: $NPV_A = \$133.76$;
               $NPV_B = \$173.70$.

d. (1) MIRR_A = 14.91%;
   MIRR_B = 17.35%.
   (2) MIRR_A = 18.76%;
   MIRR_B = 21.03%.
e. Crossover rate = 14.76%.

12-14 a. $0; −$10,250,000;
   $1,750,000.
   b. 16.07%.

12-15 a. NPV_A = $18,108,510;
   NPV_B = $13,946,117;
   IRR_A = 15.03%; IRR_B = 22.26%.
   b. NPV_Δ = $4,162,393;
   IRR_Δ = 11.71%.

12-16 Extended NPV_A = $12.76 million;
   Extended NPV_B = $9.26 million.
   EAA_A = $2.26 million;
   EAA_B = $1.64 million.

12-17 Extended NPV_A = $4.51 million.
   EAA_A = $0.85 million;
   EAA_B = $0.69 million.

12-18 NPV of 360-6 = $22,256.
   Extended NPV of 190-3 = $20,070.
   EAA of 360-6 = $5,723.30;
   EAA of 190-3 = $5,161.02.

12-19 d. 7.61%; 15.58%.

12-20 a. Undefined.
   b. NPV_C = −$911,067;
   NPV_F = −$838,834.

12-21 a. A = 2.67 years;
   B = 1.5 years.
   b. A = 3.07 years;
   B = 1.825 years.
   c. NPV_A = $12,739,908; IRR_A = 27.27%;
   NPV_B = $11,554,880; IRR_B = 36.15%;
   Choose both.
   d. NPV_A = $18,243,813;
   NPV_B = $14,964,829;
   Choose A.
   e. NPV_A = $8,207,071; NPV_B = $8,643,390;
   Choose B.
   f. 13.53%.
   g. MIRR_A = 21.93%;
   MIRR_B = 20.96%.

12-22 a. 3 years; NPV_3 = $1,307.
   b. No.

13-1 a. $22,000,000.
   b. No.
   c. Charge it against project and add
   $1.5 million to initial investment outlay.

13-2 $7,000,000.

13-3 $3,600,000.

13-4 NPV = $6,746.78
13-5 a. Straight Line: $425,000 per year.
   MACRS: $566,610; $755,650; $251,770;
   $125,970.
   b. MACRS, $27,043.62 higher.

13-6 a. −$1,118,000.
   b. $375,612; $418,521; $304,148.
   c. $437,343.
   d. NPV = $78,790; Purchase.

13-7 a. −$89,000
   b. $26,332; $30,113; $20,035.
   c. $24,519.
   d. NPV = −$6,700;
   Don't purchase.

13-8 a. NPV = $106,520.

13-9 NPV of replace = $2,083.51.

13-10 NPV of replace = $11,468.48.

13-11 E(NPV) = $3 million;
   σ_{NPV} = $23.622 million;
   CV_{NPV} = 7.874.

13-12 a. NPV = $15,732;
   IRR = 11.64%;
   MIRR = 10.88%; Payback = 3.75 years.
   b. $65,770; −$34,307.
   c. E(NPV) = $13,041;
   σ_{NPV} = $43,289;
   CV = 3.32.

13-13 a. −$87,625.
   b. $31,574; $36,244; $23,795; $20,687;
   $4,575.
   c. −$4,623.

13-14 a. −$529,750.
   b. New depreciation: $155,000; $248,000;
   $148,800; $89,280; $89,280.
   c. Net incremental cash flows: $143,000;
   $175,550; $140,830; $119,998; $203,872.

d. NPV = $30,059.

13-15 a. Expected CF_A = $6,750;
Expected CF_B = $7,650;
CV_A = 0.0703.
b. NPV_A = $10,036;
NPV_B = $11,624.

13-16 a. E(IRR) ≈ 15.3%.
b. $38,589.

13-17 a. $117,779.
b. σ_{NPV} = $445,060;
CV_{NPV} = 3.78.

14-1 a. $1.074 million.
b. $2.96 million.

14-2 a. $4.6795 million.
b. $3.208 million.

14-3 a. −$19 million.
b. $9.0981 million.

14-4 a. −$2.113 million.
b. $1.973 million.
c. −$70,222.
d. $565,090.
e. $1.116 million.

14-5 a. $2,562.
b. E[NPV] = $9,786; Value of growth
option = $7,224.

14-6 P = $18.646 million;
X = $20 million; t = 1;
r_{RF} = 0.08; σ^2 = 0.0687;
V = $2.028 million.

14-7 P = $10.479 million;
X = $9 million; t = 2;
r_{RF} = 0.06; σ^2 = 0.0111;
V = $2.514 million.

14-8 P = $18,646;
X = $20,000; t = 2;
V = $5,009.

15-1 Payout = 33.33%.

15-2 Payout = 20%.

15-3 Payout = 52%.

15-4 V_{op} = $175 million;
n = 8.75 million.

15-5 P_0 = $80.

15-6 $6,900,000.

15-7 n = 4,000; EPS = $5.00;
DPS = $1.50; P = $40.00.

15-8 D_0 = $4.25.

15-9 Payout = 17.89%.

15-10 a. (1) $2,808,000.
(2) $3.34 Million.
(3) $7,855,000.
(4) Regular = $2,808,000;
Extra = $5,047,000.

15-11 a. $10,500,000.
b. DPS = $0.50; Payout = 4.55%.
c. $9,000,000.
d. No.
e. 40%.
f. $1,500,000.
g. $12,875,143.

15-12 a. $848 million.
b. $450 million.
c. $30.
d. 1 million; 14 million.
e. $420 million; $30.

16-1 20,000.

16-2 1.0.

16-3 3.6%.

16-4 $300 million.

16-5 $30.

16-6 40 million.

16-7 a. ΔProfit = $850,000;
Return = 21.25% > r_s = 15%.
b. $Q_{BE,Old}$ = 40;
$Q_{BE,New}$ = 45.45.

16-8 a. V = $3,348,214.
b. $16.74.
c. $1.84.
d. 10%.

16-9 30% debt:
WACC = 11.14%;
V = $101.023 million.
50% debt:
WACC = 11.25%;

V = $100 million.
70% debt:
WACC = 11.94%;
V = $94.255 million.

16-10 a. 0.870.
   b. b = 1.218; r_s = 10.872%.
   c. WACC = 8.683%;
      V = $103.188 million.

16-11 WACC at optimal debt level: 8.89%.

17-1 $500 million.

17-2 $821 million.

17-3 $620.68 million.

17-4 $813.125 million.

17-5 a. b_U = 1.125.
   b. r_{sU} = 15.625%.
   c. 16.62%; 18.04%; 20.23%.
   d. 20.23%.

17-6 a. V_U = V_L = $20 million.
   b. r_{sU} = 10%; r_{sL} = 15%.
   c. S_L = $10 million.
   d. $WACC_U$ = 10%;
      $WACC_L$ = 10%.

17-7 a. V_U = $12 million;
      V_L = $16 million.
   b. r_{sU} = 10%; r_{sL} = 15%.
   c. S_L = $6 million.
   d. $WACC_U$ = 10%;
      $WACC_L$ = 7.5%.

17-8 a. V_U = $12 million;
      V_L = $15.33 million;
      $3.33 million.
   b. V_L = V_U = $20 million; $0.
   c. V_U = $12 million;
      V_L = $16 million;
      $4 million.
   d. V_U = $12 million;
      V_L = $16 million;
      $4 million.

17-9 a. V_U = $12.5 million.
   b. V_L = $16 million; r_{sL} = 15.7%.
   c. V_L = $14.5 million; r_{sL} = 14.9%.

17-10 a. V_U = V_L = $14,545,455.
   b. At D = $6 million:

r_{sL} = 14.51%;
      WACC = 11.0%.
   c. V_U = $8,727,273;
      V_L = $11,127,273.
   d. At D = $6 million:
      r_{sL} = 14.51%;
      WACC = 8.63%.
   e. D = V = $14,545,455.

17-11 a. V = $3.29 million.
   b. D = $1.71 million; Yield = 8.1%.
   c. V = $3.23 million; D = $1.77 million;
      Yield = 6.3%.

17-12 a. $713.33 million.
   b. $563.29 million.
   c. $71.33 million.
   d. $57.86 million.
   e. $621.15 million.

18-1 a. $700,000.
   b. $3,700,000.
   c. −$2,300,000.

18-2 964,115 shares.

18-3 10,000 shares at $20 per share.

18-4 a. $$22,016,893; $40.03 per share.
   b. (1) Abercrombe: D/A 30.43%; P/E 15.91;
          M/B 2.19; ROE 13.8%; P/FCF 21.47.
      (2) Gunter: D/A 20.00%; P/E 15.02; M/B
          2.35; ROE 15.7%; P/FCF 18.50.
      (3) B&C: D/A 18.18%; P/E 15.40; M/B 2.22;
          ROE 14.4%; P/FCF 20.02.
   c. (1) Price based on: Abercrombe P/E $41.36;
          Gunter P/E $39.04.
      (2) Price based on: Abercrombe M/B
          $39.38; Gunter M/B $42.30.
      (3) Price based on: Abercrombe P/FCF
          $42.94; Gunter P/FCF $37.01.

18-5 $14.74; $13.708 million.

18-6 a. After-tax call cost = $2,640,000.
   b. Flotation cost = $1,600,000.
   c. $1,920,000; $768,000.
   d. $3,472,000.
   e. New tax savings = $16,000;
      Lost tax savings = $19,200.
   f. $360,000.
   g. PV = $9,109,413.

h. $5,637,413.

18-7 a. NPV = $2,717,128.

19-1 a. (1) 50%.
(2) 60%.
(3) 50%.

19-2 Cost of owning = −$127;
Cost of leasing = −$128;
NAL = −$1.

19-3 a. Energen: Debt/TA = 50%;
Hastings: Debt/TA = 33%.
b. TA = $200.

19-4 a. NAL = $108,147.

19-5 a. PV of leasing = −667,261;
PV of owning = −$713,300;
NAL = $46,039
b. $245,703.

20-1 $182.16.

20-2 20 shares.

20-3 a. (1) $0.
(2) $0.
(3) $5.
(4) $75.
b. 10%; $100.

20-4 Premium = 10%: $46.20;
Premium = 30%: $54.60.

20-5 a. 14.1%.
b. $12 million before tax.
c. $331.89.
d. Value as a straight bond = $699.25;
Value in conversion = $521.91.
f. Value as a straight bond = $1,000.00;
Value in conversion = $521.91.

20-6 b. Plan 1, 49%; Plan 2, 53%;
Plan 3, 53%.
c. Plan 1, $0.59; Plan 2, $0.64;
Plan 3, $0.88.
d. Plan 1, 19%; Plan 2, 19%;
Plan 3, 50%.

20-7 a. Year = 7;
CV_7 = $1,210.422;
CF_7 = $1,290.422.
b. 10.20%.

21-1 $3,000,000.

21-2 AR = $59,500.

21-3 r_{NOM} = 75.26%; EAR = 109.84%.

21-4 EAR = 8.49%.

21-5 $7,500,000.

21-6 a. DSO = 38 days.
b. AR = $156,164.
c. AR = $141,781.

21-7 a. 73.74%.
b. 14.90%.
c. 32.25%.
d. 21.28%.
e. 29.80%.

21-8 a. 45.15%.

21-9 Nominal cost = 14.90%;
Effective cost = 15.89%.

21-10 14.91%.

21-11 a. 60 days.
b. $420,000.
c. 7.3.

21-12 a. 56.8 days.
b. (1) 2.7082.
(2) 18.96%.
c. (1) 36.6 days.
(2) 2.95.
(3) 20.68%.

21-13 a. ROE_T = 11.75%;
ROE_M = 10.80%;
ROE_R = 9.16%.

21-14 a. Feb. surplus = $2,000.
b. $164,400.

21-15 a. $100,000.
c. (1) $300,000.
(2) Nominal cost = 37.24%;
Effective cost = 44.59%.
d. Nominal cost = 24.83%;
Effective cost = 27.86%.

21-16 a. 14.35%.

21-17 a. $300,000.
b. $2,000.
c. (1) $322,500.
(2) $26,875.

(3) 13.57%.
(4) 14.44%.

22-1 $233.56.

22-2 EAR = 21.60%.

22-3 a. 12%.
     b. 11.25%.
     c. 11.48%.
     d. 14.47%. Alternative b has the lowest interest rate.

22-4 a. 11.73%.
     b. 12.09%.
     c. 13.45%.

22-5 ΔNI = $-$$3,381.

22-6 ΔNI = +$27,577.

22-7 d. 8.3723%.

22-8 a. March: $146,000; June: $198,000.
     b. Q1: ADS = $3,000; DSO = 48.7 days.
         Q2: ADS = $4,500; DSO = 44.0 days.
         Cumulative: ADS = $3,750;
         DSO = 52.8 days.
     c. 0$-$30 days: 65%; 31$-$60 days: 35%.
     d. Receivables/Sales = 130%.

22-9 a. With discount = $83.33.
         Without discount = $250.
     b. With discount = $641.03.
         Without discount = $384.62.
     c. Nominal cost of trade credit = 18.18%. Effective cost of trade credit = 19.83%. Bank cost = 23.08%.
     d. Cash = $126.90; NP = $434.60.

22-10 a. (1) $27,500.
          (3) $25,833.

23-1 a. 3,000 bags.
     b. 4,000 bags.
     c. 2,500 bags.
     d. Every 12 days.

23-2 b. $22,500.
     c. 100 transfers per year

24-1 Net payment = LIBOR + 0.2%.

24-2 r_d = 7.01%.

24-3 r_d = 5.96%;
     Futures = $89,748.42.

24-4 Net to Carter = 9.95% fixed;
     Net to Brence = LIBOR + 3.05% floating.

24-5 a. Sell 105 contracts.
     b. Bond = $-$$1,414,552.69;
         Futures = $1,951,497.45;
         Net = +$536,944.76.

25-1 AP = $375,000; NP = $750,000;
     SD = $750,000; Stockholders = $343,750.

25-2 a. Total assets: $327 million.
     b. Income: $7 million.
     c. Before, $15.6 million;
         After, $13.0 million.
     d. Before, 35.7%;
         After, 64.2%.

25-3 a. $0.
     b. First mortgage holders, $300,000; Second mortgage holders, $100,000 plus $12,700 as a general claimant.
     c. Trustee's expenses, $50,000;
         Wages due, $30,000;
         Taxes due, $40,000.
     d. *Before subordination*
         Accounts payable = $6,350;
         Notes payable = $22,860;
         Second mortgage = $12,700 + $100,000;
         Debentures = $25,400;
         Sub. debentures = $12,700.
         After subordination
         Notes payable = $35,560;
         Sub. debentures = $0.

25-4 a. $0 for stockholders.
     b. AP = 24%; NP = 100%; WP = 100%;
         TP = 100%; Mortgage = 85%;
         Subordinated debentures = 9%;
         Trustee = 100%.

26-1 P_0 = $25.26.

26-2 P_0 = $41.54.

26-3 $25.26 to $41.54.

26-4 Value of equity = $46.30 million.

26-5 a. $V_{op\ Unlevered}$ = $32.02 million;
         $V_{Tax\ shields}$ = $11.50 million.

b. V_{op} = $43.52 million;
  max = $33.52 million.

26-6 a. 10.96%.
  b. (All in millions)
    FCF_1 = $23.12,
    TS_1 = $14.00;
    FCF_3 = $12.26,
    TS_3 = $16.45;
    FCF_5 = $23.83,
    TS_5 = $18.90.
  c. HV_{TS} = $510.68 million;
    HV_U = $643.89 million.
  d. Value of equity = $508.57 million.

27-1 12.358 yen per peso.

27-2 f_t = $0.00907.

27-3 1 euro = $0.9091 or
    $1 = 1.1 euros.

27-4 0.6667 euros per dollar.

27-5 1.5152 SFr.

27-6 2.4 Swiss francs per pound.

27-7 $r_{NOM-U.S.}$ = 4.6%.

27-8 117 pesos.

27-9 +$500,000.

27-10 $24,500.

27-11 a. $1,658,925.
   b. $$1,646,091.
   c. $2,000,000.

27-12 b. f_t = 1.3990 dollars per Swiss franc; discount.

27-13 $322 million.

27-14 a. $89,357; 20%.
   b. 1,039.90 won per U.S. dollar and 1029.95
     won per U.S. dollar.
   c. 78,150,661 won; 18.85%.

28-1 FV_5 = $16,105.10.

28-2 PV = $1,292.10.

28-3 I/YR = 8.01%.

28-4 N = 11.01 years.

28-5 N = 11 years.

28-6 FVA_5 = $1,725.22;
    $FVA_{5\,Due}$ = $1,845.99.

28-7 PV = $923.98;
    FV = $1,466.24.

28-8 PMT = $444.89;
    EAR = 12.6825%.

28-9 a. $530.
   b. $561.80.
   c. $471.70.
   d. $445.00.

28-10 a. $895.42.
    b. $1,552.92.
    c. $279.20.
    d. $160.99.

28-11 a. N = 10.24 ≈ 10 years.
    b. N = 7.27 ≈ 7 years.
    c. N = 4.19 ≈ 4 years.
    d. N = 1.00 ≈ 1 year.

28-12 a. $6,374.97.
    b. $1,105.13.
    c. $2,000.00.
    d. (1) $7,012.46.
      (2) $1,160.38.
      (3) $2,000.00.

28-13 a. $2,457.83.
    b. $865.90.
    c. $2,000.00.
    d. (1) $2,703.61.
      (2) $909.19.
      (3) $2,000.00.

28-14 a. PV_A = $1,251.25;
      PV_B = $1,300.32.
    b. PV_A = $1,600;
      PV_B = $1,600.

28-15 a. 7%.
    b. 7%.
    c. 9%.
    d. 15%.

28-16 a. $881.17.
    b. $895.42.
    c. $903.06.
    d. $908.35.

28-17 a. $279.20.

b. $276.84.

c. $443.72.

28-18 a. $5,272.32.

b. $5,374.07.

28-19 a. Universal, EAR = 7%;
Regional, EAR = 6.14%.

28-20 a. PMT = $6,594.94;
Interest$_1$ = $2,500;
Interest$_2$ = $2,090.51.

b. $13,189.87.

c. $8,137.27.

28-21 a. I = 14.87% ≈ 15%.

28-22 I = 7.18%.

28-23 I = 9%.

28-24 a. $33,872.11.

b. (1) $26,243.16.

(2) $0.

28-25 N = 14.77 ≈ 15 years.

28-26 6 years; $1,106.01.

28-27 (1) $1,428.57.

(2) $714.29.

28-28 $893.26.

28-29 $984.88.

28-30 57.18%.

28-31 a. $1,432.02.

b. $93.07.

28-32 I$_{NOM}$ = 15.19%.

28-33 PMT = $36,949.61.

28-34 First PMT = $9,736.96.

Selected Equations

Chapter 1

$$\text{Value} = \frac{FCF_1}{(1 + WACC)^1} + \frac{FCF_2}{(1 + WACC)^2} + \frac{FCF_3}{(1 + WACC)^3} + \cdots + \frac{FCF_\infty}{(1 + WACC)^\infty}$$

Chapter 2

$$\text{Expected rate of return} = \hat{r} = \sum_{i=1}^{n} P_i r_i$$

$$\text{Historical average, } \bar{r}_{Avg} = \frac{\sum_{t=1}^{T} \bar{r}_t}{T}$$

$$\text{Variance} = \sigma^2 = \sum_{i=1}^{n} (r_i - \hat{r})^2 P_i$$

$$\text{Standard deviation} = \sigma = \sqrt{\sum_{i=1}^{n} (r_i - \hat{r})^2 P_i}$$

$$\text{Historical estimated } \sigma = S = \sqrt{\frac{\sum_{t=1}^{T} (\bar{r}_t - \bar{r}_{Avg})^2}{T - 1}}$$

$$\hat{r}_p = \sum_{i=1}^{n} w_i \hat{r}_i$$

$$\sigma_p = \sqrt{\sum_{i=1}^{n} (r_{pi} - \hat{r}_p)^2 P_i}$$

$$\text{Estimated } \rho = R = \frac{\sum_{t=1}^{T} (\bar{r}_{i,t} - \bar{r}_{i,Avg})(\bar{r}_{j,t} - \bar{r}_{j,Avg})}{\sqrt{\sum_{t=1}^{T} (\bar{r}_{i,t} - \bar{r}_{i,Avg})^2 \sum_{t=1}^{T} (\bar{r}_{j,t} - \bar{r}_{j,Avg})^2}}$$

$$COV_{iM} = \rho_{iM}\sigma_i\sigma_M$$

$$b_i = \left(\frac{\sigma_i}{\sigma_M}\right)\rho_{iM} = \frac{COV_{iM}}{\sigma_M^2}$$

$$b_p = \sum_{i=1}^{n} w_i b_i$$

Required return on stock market $= r_M$

Market risk premium $= RP_M = r_M - r_{RF}$

$$RP_i = (r_M - r_{RF})b_i = (RP_M)b_i$$

$$SML = r_i = r_{RF} + (r_M - r_{RF})b_i = r_{RF} + RP_M b_i$$

Fama-French 3-Factor Model: $(\bar{r}_{i,t} - \bar{r}_{RF,t}) = a_i + b_i(\bar{r}_{M,t} - \bar{r}_{RF,t}) + c_i(\bar{r}_{SMB,t}) + d_i(\bar{r}_{HML,t}) + e_{i,t}$

Chapter 3

$$\hat{r}_p = w_A\hat{r}_A + (1 - w_A)\hat{r}_B$$

Portfolio SD $= \sigma_p = \sqrt{w_A^2\sigma_A^2 + (1 - w_A)^2\sigma_B^2 + 2w_A(1 - w_A)\rho_{AB}\sigma_A\sigma_B}$

Minimum-risk portfolio: $w_A = \dfrac{\sigma_B(\sigma_B - \rho_{AB}\sigma_A)}{\sigma_A^2 + \sigma_B^2 - 2\rho_{AB}\sigma_A\sigma_B}$

$$\hat{r}_p = \sum_{i=1}^{N} (w_i\hat{r}_i)$$

$$\sigma_p^2 = \sum_{i=1}^{N}\sum_{j=1}^{N} (w_i w_j \sigma_i \sigma_j \rho_{ij})$$

$$\sigma_p^2 = \sum_{i=1}^{N} w_i^2\sigma_i^2 + \sum_{i=1}^{N}\sum_{\substack{j=1 \\ j\neq i}}^{N} w_i\sigma_i w_j\sigma_j\rho_{ij}$$

$$\sigma_p = \sqrt{(1 - w_{RF})^2\sigma_M^2} = (1 - w_{RF})\sigma_M$$

CML: $\hat{r}_p = r_{RF} + \left(\dfrac{\hat{r}_M - r_{RF}}{\sigma_M}\right)\sigma_p$

$$r_i = r_{RF} + \frac{(r_M - r_{RF})}{\sigma_M}\left(\frac{Cov(r_i, r_M)}{\sigma_M}\right) = r_{RF} + (r_M - r_{RF})\left(\frac{Cov(r_i, r_M)}{\sigma_M^2}\right)$$

$$b_i = \frac{\text{Covariance between Stock i and the market}}{\text{Variance of market returns}} = \frac{\text{Cov}(r_i, r_M)}{\sigma_M^2} = \frac{\rho_{iM}\sigma_i\sigma_M}{\sigma_M^2}$$

$$= \rho_{iM}\left(\frac{\sigma_i}{\sigma_M}\right)$$

$$\text{SML} = r_i = r_{RF} + (r_M - r_{RF})b_i = r_{RF} + (RP_M)b_i$$

$$\sigma_i^2 = b_i^2\sigma_M^2 + \sigma_{e_i}^2$$

$$\text{APT: } r_i = r_{RF} + (r_1 - r_{RF})b_{i1} + \cdots + (r_j - r_{RF})b_{ij}$$

Chapter 4

$$V_B = \sum_{t=1}^{N}\frac{\text{INT}}{(1 + r_d)^t} + \frac{M}{(1 + r_d)^N}$$

$$\text{Semiannual payments: } V_B = \sum_{t=1}^{2N}\frac{\text{INT}/2}{(1 + r_d/2)^t} + \frac{M}{(1 + r_d/2)^{2N}}$$

$$\text{Yield to maturity: Bond price} = \sum_{t=1}^{N}\frac{\text{INT}}{(1 + \text{YTM})^t} + \frac{M}{(1 + \text{YTM})^N}$$

$$\text{Price of callable bond (if called at N)} = \sum_{t=1}^{N}\frac{\text{INT}}{(1 + r_d)^t} + \frac{\text{Call price}}{(1 + r_d)^N}$$

$$\text{Current yield} = \frac{\text{Annual interest}}{\text{Bond's current price}}$$

$$\text{Current yield} + \text{Capital gains yield} = \text{Yield to maturity}$$

$$r_d = r^* + \text{IP} + \text{DRP} + \text{LP} + \text{MRP}$$

$$r_{RF} = r^* + \text{IP}$$

$$r_d = r_{RF} + \text{DRP} + \text{LP} + \text{MRP}$$

$$\text{IP}_N = \frac{I_1 + I_2 + \cdots + I_N}{N}$$

Chapter 5

$$\text{Exercise value} = \text{MAX}[\text{Current price of stock} - \text{Strike price, 0}]$$

$$\text{Number of stock shares in hedged portfolio} = N = \frac{C_u - C_d}{P_u - P_d}$$

$$V_C = P[N(d_1)] - Xe^{-r_{RF}t}[N(d_2)]$$

$$d_1 = \frac{\ln(P/X) + [r_{RF} + (\sigma^2/2)]t}{\sigma\sqrt{t}}$$

$$d_2 = d_1 - \sigma\sqrt{t}$$

Put–call parity: Put option $= V_C - P + Xe^{-r_{RF}t}$

Value of put $= P[N(d_1) - 1] - Xe^{-r_{RF}t}[N(d_2) - 1]$

Chapter 6

EBIT = Earnings before interest and taxes = Sales revenues − Operating costs

EBITDA = Earnings before interest, taxes, depreciation, and amortization
$\qquad$ = EBIT + Depreciation + Amortization

Net cash flow = Net income + Depreciation and amortization

NOWC = Net operating working capital

$\qquad$ = Operating current assets − Operating current liabilities

$$= \left(\begin{matrix} \text{Cash + Accounts receivable} \\ \text{+Inventories} \end{matrix}\right) - \left(\begin{matrix} \text{Accounts payable} \\ \text{+Accruals} \end{matrix}\right)$$

Total net operating capital = Net operating working capital

$\qquad\qquad$ + Operating long-term assets

NOPAT = Net operating profit after taxes = EBIT(1 − Tax rate)

Free cash flow (FCF) = NOPAT − Net investment in operating capital

$$= \text{NOPAT} - \left(\begin{matrix} \text{Current year's total} \\ \text{net operating capital} \end{matrix} - \begin{matrix} \text{Previous year's total} \\ \text{net operating capital} \end{matrix}\right)$$

$$\text{FCF} = \text{Operating cash flow} - \frac{\text{Gross investment}}{\text{in operating capital}}$$

$$\text{Return on invested capital (ROIC)} = \frac{\text{NOPAT}}{\text{Total net operating capital}}$$

MVA = Market value of stock − Equity capital supplied by shareholders

$\qquad$ = (Shares outstanding)(Stock price) − Total common equity

$$\text{MVA} = \text{Total market value} - \text{Total investor-supplied capital}$$

$$= \left(\begin{array}{c} \text{Market value of stock} \\ +\text{Market value of debt} \end{array}\right) - \text{Total investor-supplied capital}$$

$$\text{EVA} = \left(\begin{array}{c} \text{Net operating profit} \\ \text{after taxes(NOPAT)} \end{array}\right) - \left(\begin{array}{c} \text{After-tax dollar cost of capital} \\ \text{used to support operations} \end{array}\right)$$

$$= \text{EBIT}(1 - \text{Tax rate}) - (\text{Total net operating capital})(\text{WACC})$$

$$\text{EVA} = (\text{Total net operating capital})(\text{ROIC} - \text{WACC})$$

Chapter 7

$$\text{Current ratio} = \frac{\text{Current assets}}{\text{Current liabilities}}$$

$$\text{Quick, or acid test, ratio} = \frac{\text{Current assets} - \text{Inventories}}{\text{Current liabilities}}$$

$$\text{Inventory turnover ratio} = \frac{\text{Cost of goods sold}}{\text{Inventories}}$$

$$\text{DSO} = \text{Days sales outstanding} = \frac{\text{Receivables}}{\text{Average sales per day}} = \frac{\text{Receivables}}{\text{Annual sales}/365}$$

$$\text{Fixed assets turnover ratio} = \frac{\text{Sales}}{\text{Net fixed assets}}$$

$$\text{Total assets turnover ratio} = \frac{\text{Sales}}{\text{Total assets}}$$

$$\text{Debt ratio} = \frac{\text{Total debt}}{\text{Total assets}}$$

$$\text{Liabilities-to-assets ratio} = \frac{\text{Total liabilities}}{\text{Total assets}}$$

$$\text{Market debt ratio} = \frac{\text{Total debt}}{\text{Total debt} + \text{Market value of equity}}$$

$$\text{Debt-to-equity ratio} = \frac{\text{Total debt}}{\text{Total common equity}}$$

$$\text{Equity multiplier} = \frac{\text{Total assets}}{\text{Common equity}}$$

$$\text{Times-interest-earned (TIE) ratio} = \frac{\text{EBIT}}{\text{Interest charges}}$$

$$\text{EBITDA coverage ratio} = \frac{\text{EBITDA} + \text{Lease payments}}{\text{Interest} + \text{Principal payments} + \text{Lease payments}}$$

$$\text{Net profit margin} = \frac{\text{Net income available to common stockholders}}{\text{Sales}}$$

$$\text{Operating profit margin} = \frac{\text{EBIT}}{\text{Sales}}$$

$$\text{Gross profit margin} = \frac{\text{Sales} - \text{Cost of goods sold}}{\text{Sales}}$$

$$\text{Return on total assets (ROA)} = \frac{\text{Net income available to common stockholders}}{\text{Total assets}}$$

$$\text{Basic earning power (BEP) ratio} = \frac{\text{EBIT}}{\text{Total assets}}$$

$$\text{ROA} = \text{Profit margin} \times \text{Total assets turnover} = \frac{\text{Net income}}{\text{Sales}} \times \frac{\text{Sales}}{\text{Total assets}}$$

$$\text{Return on common equity (ROE)} = \frac{\text{Net income available to common stockholders}}{\text{Common equity}}$$

$$\text{ROE} = \text{ROA} \times \text{Equity multiplier}$$

$$= \text{Profit margin} \times \text{Total assets turnover} \times \text{Equity multiplier}$$

$$= \frac{\text{Net income}}{\text{Sales}} \times \frac{\text{Sales}}{\text{Total assets}} \times \frac{\text{Total assets}}{\text{Common equity}}$$

$$\text{Price/earnings (P/E) ratio} = \frac{\text{Price per share}}{\text{Earnings per share}}$$

$$\text{Price/cash flow ratio} = \frac{\text{Price per share}}{\text{Cash flow per share}}$$

$$\text{Book value per share} = \frac{\text{Common equity}}{\text{Shares outstanding}}$$

$$\text{Market/book (M/B) ratio} = \frac{\text{Market price per share}}{\text{Book value per share}}$$

Chapter 8

V_{op} = Value of operations

$\quad$ = PV of expected future free cash flows

$$= \frac{\text{FCF}_1}{(1 + \text{WACC})^1} + \frac{\text{FCF}_2}{(1 + \text{WACC})^2} + \cdots + \frac{\text{FCF}_\infty}{(1 + \text{WACC})^\infty}$$

$$= \sum_{t=1}^{\infty} \frac{\text{FCF}_t}{(1 + \text{WACC})^t}$$

$$V_{op} \text{ (for a perpetuity)} = \frac{FCF}{WACC}$$

Total intrinsic value = Value of operations + Short-term investments

Intrinsic value of equity = Total intrinsic value − All debt − Preferred stock

Intrinsic stock price = Intrinsic value of equity/Number of shares

During constant growth, $FCF_t = FCF_{t-1}(1 + g_L)$

$$V_{op}\text{(constant growth)} = \frac{FCF_1}{WACC - g_L}$$

Horizon value of operations: $HV_t = \dfrac{FCF_t(1 + g_L)}{WACC - g_L}$

$$V_{op,0} = \sum_{t=1}^{T} \frac{FCF_t}{(1 + WACC)^t} + \frac{HV_T}{(1 + WACC)^T}$$

$$V_{op(\text{at Horizon Year T})} = OpCap_T \left[1 + \frac{\left((1 + g_L)\dfrac{OP_T}{CR_T} - WACC \right)}{WACC - g_L} \right]$$

$$\frac{OP_T}{CR_T} = \frac{(NOPAT_T/Sales_T)}{(OpCap_T/Sales_T)} = \frac{NOPAT_T}{OpCap_T} = ROIC_T$$

$$Vop_{(\text{at Horizon Year T})} = OpCap_T \left[1 + \frac{(1 + g_L)ROIC_T - WACC}{WACC - g_L} \right]$$

$$\hat{P}_0 = \text{PV of expected future dividends} = \sum_{t=1}^{\infty} \frac{D_t}{(1 + r_s)^t}$$

Constant growth: $\hat{P}_0 = \dfrac{D_0(1 + g)}{r_s - g_L} = \dfrac{D_1}{r_s - g_L}$

$$\hat{r}_s = \frac{D_1}{P_0} + g$$

Capital gains yield $= \dfrac{\hat{P}_1 - P_0}{P_0}$

Dividend yield $= \dfrac{D_1}{P_0}$

For a zero growth stock, $\hat{P}_0 = \dfrac{D}{r_s}$

$$\bar{r}_s = \text{Actual dividend yield} + \text{Actual capital gains yield}$$

$$\text{Horizon value of stock} = \hat{P}_T = \frac{D_{T+1}}{r_s - g_L} = \frac{D_T(1 + g_L)}{r_s - g_L}$$

$$\hat{P}_0 = \left[\frac{D_1}{(1 + r_s)^1} + \frac{D_2}{(1 + r_s)^2} + \cdots + \frac{D_T}{(1 + r_s)^T}\right] + \frac{\hat{P}_T}{(1 + r_s)^T}$$

$$= \left[\frac{D_1}{(1 + r_s)^1} + \frac{D_2}{(1 + r_s)^2} + \cdots + \frac{D_T}{(1 + r_s)^T}\right] + \frac{[(D_{T+1})/(r_s - g_L)]}{(1 + r_s)^T}$$

$$V_{ps} = \frac{D_{ps}}{r_{ps}}$$

$$\hat{r}_{ps} = \frac{D_{ps}}{V_{ps}}$$

Chapter 9

$$\begin{matrix} \text{Additional} \\ \text{funds} \\ \text{needed} \end{matrix} = \begin{matrix} \text{Required} \\ \text{asset} \\ \text{increase} \end{matrix} - \begin{matrix} \text{Spontaneous} \\ \text{liability} \\ \text{increase} \end{matrix} - \begin{matrix} \text{Increase in} \\ \text{retained} \\ \text{earnings} \end{matrix}$$

$$\text{AFN} = (A^*/S_0)\Delta S - (L^*/S_0)\Delta S - MS_1(1 - \text{Payout ratio})$$

$$\text{Self-supporting g} = \frac{M(1 - \text{POR})(S_0)}{A_0^* - L_0^* - M(1 - \text{POR})(S_0)}$$

$$\begin{matrix} \text{Full-} \\ \text{capacity} \\ \text{sales} \end{matrix} = \frac{\text{Actual sales}}{\begin{matrix} \text{Percentage of capacity} \\ \text{at which fixed assets} \\ \text{were operated} \end{matrix}}$$

$$\text{Target fixed assets/Sales} = \frac{\text{Actual fixed assets}}{\text{Full-capacity sales}}$$

$$\begin{matrix} \text{Required level} \\ \text{of fixed assets} \end{matrix} = (\text{Target fixed assets/Sales})(\text{Projected sales})$$

Chapter 11

$$\text{After-tax component cost of debt} = r_d(1 - T)$$

$$M(1 - F) = \sum_{t=1}^{N} \frac{\text{INT}(1 - T)}{[1 + r_d(1 - T)]^t} + \frac{M}{[1 + r_d(1 - T)]^N}$$

$$r_{ps} = \frac{D_{ps}}{P_{ps}(1 - F)}$$

Market equilibrium: $= \dfrac{\text{Expected}}{\text{rate of return}} = \hat{r}_M = \dfrac{D_1}{P_0} + g = r_{RF} + RP_M = r_M$

$\qquad\qquad\qquad = $ Required rate of return

Note: D_1, P_0, and g are for the market, not an individual company.

$$r_M = \hat{r}_M = \frac{D_1}{P_0} + g$$

Note: g is long-term growth rate in dividends for the market and D_1 and P_0 are for the market, not an individual company.

CAPM: $r_s = r_{RF} + b_i(RP_M)$

DCF: $r_s = \hat{r}_s = \dfrac{D_1}{P_0} + $ Expected g in dividends per share

Own-bond-yield-plus-judgmental-risk-premium:

$$r_s = \frac{\text{Company's own}}{\text{bond yield}} + \frac{\text{Judgmental}}{\text{risk premium}}$$

g = (Retention rate)(ROE) = (1.0 − Payout rate)(ROE)

$$r_e = \hat{r}_e = \frac{D_1}{P_0(1 - F)} + g$$

WACC $= w_d r_d(1 - T) + w_{ps}r_{ps} + w_s r_s$

Chapter 12

$$NPV = CF_0 + \frac{CF_1}{(1 + r)^1} + \frac{CF_2}{(1 + r)^2} + \cdots + \frac{CF_N}{(1 + r)^N}$$

$$= \sum_{t=0}^{N} \frac{CF_t}{(1 + r)^t}$$

IRR: $\quad CF_0 + \dfrac{CF_1}{(1 + IRR)^1} + \dfrac{CF_2}{(1 + IRR)^2} + \cdots + \dfrac{CF_N}{(1 + IRR)^N} = 0$

$$NPV = \sum_{t=0}^{N} \frac{CF_t}{(1 + IRR)^t} = 0$$

MIRR: PV of costs = PV of terminal value

$$\sum_{t=0}^{N} \frac{COF_t}{(1+r)^t} = \frac{\sum_{t=0}^{N} CIF_t(1+r)^{N-t}}{(1+MIRR)^N}$$

$$PV \text{ of costs} = \frac{\text{Terminal value}}{(1+MIRR)^N}$$

$$PI = \frac{PV \text{ of future cash flows}}{\text{Initial cost}} = \frac{\sum_{t=1}^{N} \frac{CF_t}{(1+r)^t}}{CF_0}$$

$$\text{Payback} = \begin{array}{c} \text{Number of} \\ \text{years prior to} \\ \text{full recovery} \end{array} + \frac{\begin{array}{c} \text{Unrecovered cost} \\ \text{at start of year} \end{array}}{\begin{array}{c} \text{Cash flow during} \\ \text{full recovery year} \end{array}}$$

Chapter 13

$$\text{Project cash flow} = FCF = \begin{array}{c} \text{Investment outlay} \\ \text{cash flow} \end{array} + \begin{array}{c} \text{Operating} \\ \text{cash flow} \end{array} + \begin{array}{c} \text{NOWC} \\ \text{cash flow} \end{array}$$
$$+ \begin{array}{c} \text{Salvage} \\ \text{cash flow} \end{array}$$

$$\text{Expected NPV} = \sum_{i=1}^{n} P_i(NPV_i)$$

$$\sigma_{NPV} = \sqrt{\sum_{i=1}^{n} P_i(NPV_i - \text{Expected NPV})^2}$$

$$CV_{NPV} = \frac{\sigma_{NPV}}{E(NPV)}$$

Chapter 14

$$CV = \frac{\sigma(\text{PV of future CF})}{E(\text{PV of future CF})}$$

$$\text{Variance of project's rate of return: } \sigma^2 = \frac{\ln(CV^2 + 1)}{t}$$

Chapter 15

Residual distribution = Net income − [(Target equity ratio)(Total capital budget)]

Number of shares repurchased $= n_{Prior} - n_{Post} = \dfrac{Cash_{Rep}}{P_{Prior}}$

$$n_{Post} = n_{Prior} - \frac{Cash_{Rep}}{P_{Prior}} = n_{Prior} - \frac{Cash_{Rep}}{S_{Prior}/n_{Prior}} = n_{Prior}\left(1 - \frac{Cash_{Rep}}{S_{Prior}}\right)$$

Chapter 16

$$V_{op} = \sum_{t=1}^{\infty} \frac{FCF_t}{(1 + WACC)^t}$$

$$WACC = w_d(1 - T)r_d + w_s r_s$$

$$ROIC = \frac{NOPAT}{Capital} = \frac{EBIT(1 - T)}{Capital}$$

$$EBIT = PQ - VQ - F$$

$$Q_{BE} = \frac{F}{P - V}$$

$$V_L = S_L + D$$

MM, no taxes: $V_L = V_U$

MM, corporate taxes: $V_L = V_U + TD$

Miller, corporate and personal taxes: $V_L = V_U + \left[1 - \dfrac{(1 - T_c)(1 - T_s)}{(1 - T_d)}\right]D$

$$b = b_U[1 + (1 - T)(D/S)] = b_U[1 + (1 - T)(w_d/w_s)]$$

$$b_U = b/[1 + (1 - T)(D/S)] = b/[1 + (1 - T)(w_d/w_s)]$$

$$r_s = r_{RF} + RP_M(b)$$

$$r_s = r_{RF} + \text{Premium for business risk} + \text{Premium for financial risk}$$

$$\text{If } g = 0: V_{op} = \frac{FCF}{WACC} = \frac{NOPAT}{WACC} = \frac{EBIT(1 - T)}{WACC}$$

$$\text{Total corporate value} = V_{op} + \text{Value of short-term investments}$$

$$S = \text{Total corporate value} - \text{Value of all debt}$$

$$D = w_d V_{op}$$

$$S = (1 - w_d) V_{op}$$

$$\text{Cash raised by issuing debt} = D - D_0$$

$$P_{Prior} = S_{Prior}/n_{Prior}$$

$$P_{Post} = P_{Prior}$$

$$n_{Post} = n_{Prior} \left[\frac{V_{opNew} - D_{New}}{V_{opNew} - D_{Old}} \right]$$

$$n_{Post} = n_{Prior} - (D_{New} - D_{Old})/P_{Prior}$$

$$p_{Post} = \frac{V_{opNew} - D_{Old}}{n_{Prior}}$$

$$NI = (EBIT - r_d D)(1 - T)$$

$$EPS = NI/n$$

Chapter 17

Adjusted present value approach (g = constant):

$$\text{Tax savings} = (\text{Interest expense})(\text{Tax rate})$$

$$\text{Value of operations} = V_{op} = V_{Unlevered} + V_{Tax\ shield}$$

$$V_L = V_U + V_{Tax\ shield}$$

$$V_{Tax\ shield} = \frac{r_d TD}{r_{TS} - g}$$

$$V_L = V_U + \left(\frac{r_d}{r_{TS} - g}\right)TD$$

MM, no taxes (T = 0 and g = 0):

$$V_L = V_U = \frac{EBIT}{WACC} = \frac{EBIT}{r_{sU}}$$

$$r_{sL} = r_{sU} + \text{Risk premium} = r_{sU} + (r_{sU} - r_d)(D/S)$$

MM, corporate taxes ($r_{TS} = r_d$ and g = 0):

$$V_L = V_U + TD$$

$$V_U = S = \frac{EBIT(1 - T)}{r_{sU}}$$

$$r_{sL} = r_{sU} + (r_{sU} - r_d)(1 - T)(D/S)$$

Miller, personal taxes ($r_{TS} = r_d$ and g = 0):

$$V_U = \frac{EBIT(1 - T_c)}{r_{sU}} = \frac{EBIT(1 - T_c)(1 - T_s)}{r_{sU}(1 - T_s)}$$

$$CF_L = (EBIT - I)(1 - T_c)(1 - T_s) + I(1 - T_d)$$

$$V_L = V_U + \left[1 - \frac{(1 - T_c)(1 - T_s)}{(1 - T_d)}\right]D$$

Compressed adjusted present value approach ($r_{TS} = r_{sU}$ and g = constant):

$$V_L = V_U + \left(\frac{r_d TD}{r_{sU} - g}\right)$$

$$r_{sL} = r_{sU} + (r_{sU} - r_d)\frac{D}{S}$$

$$r_{sU} = w_s r_{sL} + w_d r_d$$

$$b = b_U + (b_U - b_D)\frac{D}{S}$$

Compressed adjusted present value approach ($r_{TS} = r_{sU}$):

$$\begin{array}{l} \text{Horizon value of} \\ \text{unlevered firm} \end{array} = HV_{U,N} = \frac{FCF_{N+1}}{r_{sU} - g} = \frac{FCF_N(1 + g)}{r_{sU} - g}$$

$$\text{Horizon value of tax shield} = \text{HV}_{\text{TS,N}} = \frac{\text{TS}_{N+1}}{r_{sU} - g} = \frac{\text{TS}_N(1+g)}{r_{sU} - g}$$

$$V_{\text{Unlevered}} = \sum_{t=1}^{N} \frac{\text{FCF}_t}{(1 + r_{sU})^t} + \frac{\text{HV}_{\text{U,N}}}{(1 + r_{sU})^N}$$

$$V_{\text{Tax shield}} = \sum_{t=1}^{N} \frac{\text{TS}_t}{(1 + r_{sU})^t} + \frac{\text{HV}_{\text{TS,N}}}{(1 + r_{sU})^N}$$

Chapter 18

Amount left on table = (Closing price − Offer price)(Number of shares)

Chapter 19

NAL = PV of leasing − PV of owning

Chapter 20

$$\text{Price paid for bond with warrants} = \text{Straight-debt value of bond} + \text{value of warrants}$$

$$\text{Conversion price} = P_c = \frac{\text{Par value of bond given up}}{\text{Shares received}}$$

$$= \frac{\text{Par value of bond given up}}{\text{CR}}$$

$$\text{Conversion ratio} = \text{CR} = \frac{\text{Par value of bond given up}}{P_c}$$

Chapter 21

$$\text{Inventory conversion period} = \frac{\text{Inventory}}{(\text{Cost of goods sold})/365}$$

$$\text{Receivables collection period} = \text{DSO} = \frac{\text{Receivables}}{\text{Sales}/365}$$

$$\text{Payables deferral period} = \frac{\text{Payables}}{(\text{Cost of goods sold})/365}$$

Appendix C   Selected Equations   **1117**

$$\begin{matrix} \text{Cash} \\ \text{conversion} \\ \text{cycle} \end{matrix} = \begin{matrix} \text{Inventory} \\ \text{conversion} \\ \text{period} \end{matrix} + \begin{matrix} \text{Average} \\ \text{collection} \\ \text{period} \end{matrix} - \begin{matrix} \text{Payables} \\ \text{deferral} \\ \text{period} \end{matrix}$$

$$\begin{matrix} \text{Accounts} \\ \text{receivable} \end{matrix} = \begin{matrix} \text{Credit sales} \\ \text{per day} \end{matrix} \times \begin{matrix} \text{Length of} \\ \text{collection period} \end{matrix}$$

$$\text{ADS} = \frac{(\text{Units sold})(\text{Sales price})}{365} = \frac{\text{Annual sales}}{365}$$

$$\text{Receivables} = (\text{ADS})(\text{DSO})$$

$$\begin{matrix} \text{Nominal annual cost} \\ \text{of trade credit} \end{matrix} = \frac{\text{Discount percentage}}{100 - \dfrac{\text{Discount}}{\text{percentage}}} \times \frac{365}{\dfrac{\text{Days credit is}}{\text{outstanding}} - \dfrac{\text{Discount}}{\text{period}}}$$

Chapter 22

$$\Delta I \text{ for increase in sales} = [(DSO_N - DSO_0)(S_0/365)] + V[(DSO_N)(S_N - S_0)/365]$$

$$\Delta I \text{ for decrease in sales} = [(DSO_N - DSO_0)(S_N/365)] + V[(DSO_0)(S_N - S_0)/365]$$

$$\Delta P = (S_N - S_0)(1 - V) - r(\Delta I) - (B_N S_N - B_0 S_0) - (D_N S_N P_N - D_0 S_0 P_0)$$

$$\text{Cost of carrying receivables} = (DSO)\left(\frac{\text{Sales}}{\text{per day}}\right)\left(\frac{\text{Variable}}{\text{cost ratio}}\right)\left(\frac{\text{Cost of}}{\text{funds}}\right)$$

$$\text{Simple interest rate per day} = \frac{\text{Nominal rate}}{\text{Days in year}}$$

$$\text{Simple interest charge for period} = (\text{Days in period})(\text{Rate per day})(\text{Amount of loan})$$

$$\text{Face value}_{\text{Discount}} = \frac{\text{Funds received}}{1.0 - \text{Nominal rate(decimal)}}$$

$$\text{APR rate} = (\text{Periods per year})(\text{Rate per period})$$

Chapter 23

$$\text{Total cost} = \text{Holding cost} + \text{Transactions cost}$$

$$= \frac{C}{2}(r) + \frac{T}{C}(F)$$

$$C^* = \sqrt{\frac{2(F)(T)}{r}}$$

$$A = \frac{\text{Units per order}}{2} = \frac{S/N}{2}$$

$$TCC = (C)(P)(A)$$

$$TOC = (F)(N)$$

$$TIC = TCC + TOC$$

$$= (C)(P)(A) + F\left(\frac{S}{2A}\right)$$

$$= (C)(P)(Q/2) + (F)(S/Q)$$

$$EOQ = \sqrt{\frac{2(F)(S)}{(C)(P)}}$$

Chapter 26

$$FCFE = \frac{\text{Free}}{\text{cash flow}} - \frac{\text{After-tax}}{\text{interest expense}} - \frac{\text{Principal}}{\text{payments}} + \frac{\text{Newly issued}}{\text{debt}}$$

$$= \frac{\text{Free}}{\text{cash flow}} - \frac{\text{Interest}}{\text{expense}} + \frac{\text{Interest}}{\text{tax shield}} + \frac{\text{Net change}}{\text{in debt}}$$

$$FCFE = \text{Net income} - \frac{\text{Net investment in}}{\text{operating capital}} + \frac{\text{Net change}}{\text{in debt}}$$

$$HV_{FCFE,N} = \frac{FCFE_{N+1}}{r_{sL} - g} = \frac{FCFE_N(1 + g)}{r_{sL} - g}$$

$$V_{FCFE} = \sum_{t=1}^{N} \frac{FCFE_t}{(1 + r_{sL})^t} + \frac{HV_{FCFE,N}}{(1 + r_{sL})^N}$$

$$S = V_{FCFE} + \text{Nonoperating assets}$$

$$\frac{\text{Total value of shares to target shareholders}}{\text{Total post-merger value of equity}} = \frac{\text{Percent required by}}{\text{target stockholders}} = \frac{n_{New}}{n_{New} + n_{Old}}$$

Chapter 27

$$\text{Single-period interest rate parity}: \frac{\text{Forward exchange rate}}{\text{Spot exchange rate}} = \frac{1 + r_h}{1 + r_f}$$

$$\frac{\text{Expected t-year}}{\text{forward exchange rate}} = (\text{Spot rate})\left(\frac{1 + r_h}{1 + r_f}\right)^t$$

$$P_h = (P_f)(\text{Spot rate})$$

$$\text{Spot rate} = \frac{P_h}{P_f}$$

Chapter 28

$$FV_N = PV(1 + I)^N$$

$$PV = \frac{FV_N}{(1 + I)^N}$$

$$\text{PV of a perpetuity} = \frac{PMT}{I}$$

$$FVA_N = PMT\left[\frac{(1 + I)^N}{I} - \frac{1}{I}\right] = PMT\left[\frac{(1 + I)^N - 1}{I}\right]$$

$$FVA_{due} = FVA_{ordinary}(1 + I)$$

$$PVA_N = PMT\left[\frac{1}{I} - \frac{1}{I(1 + I)^N}\right] = PMT\left[\frac{1 - \dfrac{1}{(1 + I)^N}}{I}\right]$$

$$PVA_{Due} = PVA_{Ordinary}(1 + I)$$

$$PV_{Uneven\ stream} = \sum_{t=1}^{N} \frac{CF_t}{(1 + I)^t}$$

$$FV_{Uneven\ stream} = \sum_{t=1}^{N} CF_t(1 + I)^{N-t}$$

$$I_{PER} = \frac{I_{NOM}}{M}$$

$$APR = (I_{PER})M$$

Number of periods $= NM$

$$FV_N = PV(1 + I_{PER})^{\text{Number of periods}} = PV\left(1 + \frac{I_{NOM}}{M}\right)^{MN}$$

$$EFF\% = (1 + I_{PER})^M - 1.0 = \left(1 + \frac{I_{NOM}}{M}\right)^M - 1.0$$

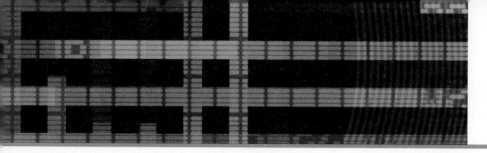

501(c)(3) corporation A charitable organization that meets the IRS requirements for tax-exempt status under the tax code section 501(c)(3).

abandonment option Allows a company to reduce its output in response to changing market conditions. This includes the option to contract production or abandon a project if market conditions deteriorate too much.

absolute priority doctrine States that claims must be paid in strict accordance with the priority of each claim, regardless of the consequence to other claimants.

account receivable Created when a good is shipped or a service is performed and payment for that good is made on a credit basis, not on a cash basis.

accounting income Income as defined by Generally Accepted Accounting Principles (GAAP).

accounting profit A firm's net income as reported on its income statement.

acquiring company A company that seeks to acquire another firm.

actual, or realized, rate of return, $\bar{r}_s$ The rate of return that was actually realized at the end of some holding period.

actuarial rate of return The discount rate used to determine the present value of future benefits under a defined benefits pension plan.

additional funds needed (AFN) Those funds required from external sources to increase the firm's assets to support a sales increase. A sales increase will normally require an increase in assets. However, some of this increase is usually offset by a spontaneous increase in liabilities as well as by earnings retained in the firm. Those funds that are required but not generated internally must be obtained from external sources.

add-on basis installment loan Interest is calculated over the life of the loan and then added on to the loan amount. This total amount is paid in equal installments. This raises the effective cost of the loan.

adjusted beta A beta calculated to reflect a tendency to trend toward the value of 1.0.

agency cost or problem An expense, either direct or indirect, that is borne by a principal as a result of having delegated authority to an agent. An example is the costs borne by shareholders to encourage managers to maximize a firm's stock price rather than act in their own self-interests. These costs may also arise from lost efficiency and the expense of monitoring management to ensure that debtholders' rights are protected.

agency debt Debt issued by federal agencies. Agency debt is not officially backed by the full faith and credit of the U.S. government, but investors assume that the government implicitly guarantees this debt, so these bonds carry interest rates only slightly higher than Treasury bonds.

aggressive short-term financing policy Refers to a policy in which a firm finances all of its fixed assets with long-term capital but part of its permanent current assets with short-term, nonspontaneous credit.

aging schedule Breaks down accounts receivable according to how long they have been outstanding. This gives the firm a more complete picture of the structure of accounts receivable than that provided by days sales outstanding.

alternative minimum tax (AMT) A provision of the U.S. Tax Code that requires profitable firms to pay at least some taxes if such taxes are greater than the amount due under standard tax accounting.

American option An option that may be exercised any time up until its expiration date.

amortization A noncash charge against intangible assets, such as goodwill.

amortization schedule A table that breaks down the periodic fixed payment of an installment loan into its principal and interest components.

amortized loan A loan that is repaid in equal periodic amounts (or "killed off") over time.

anchoring bias Occurs when predictions of future events are influenced too heavily by recent events.

annual report A report issued annually by a corporation to its stockholders. It contains basic financial statements as well as management's opinion of the past year's operations and the firm's future prospects.

annual vesting A certain percentage of the options in a grant vest each year. For example, one-third of the options in the grant might vest each year.

annuity A series of payments of a fixed amount for a specified number of periods.

annuity due An annuity with payments occurring at the beginning of each period.

APR The nominal annual interest rate is also called the annual percentage rate, or APR.

arbitrage The simultaneous buying and selling of the same commodity or security in two different markets at different prices, thus yielding a risk-free return.

Arbitrage Pricing Theory (APT) An approach to measuring the equilibrium risk–return relationship for a given stock as a function of multiple factors, rather than the single factor (the market return) used by the CAPM. The APT is based on complex mathematical and statistical theory, and it can account for several factors (such as GNP and the level of inflation) in determining the required return for a particular stock.

arrearages Preferred dividends that have not been paid and hence are "in arrears."

asset allocation models Used by pension fund managers to make funding and investment decisions; these models use computer simulations to examine the risk/return characteristics of portfolios with various mixes of assets.

asset management ratios A set of ratios that measure how effectively a firm is managing its assets.

assignment An informal procedure for liquidating debts that transfers title to a debtor's assets to a third person, known as an assignee or trustee.

asymmetric information theory Assumes managers have more complete information than investors and leads to a preferred "pecking order" of financing: (1) retained earnings, followed by (2) debt, and then (3) new common stock. Also known as signaling theory.

at-the-money option An option for which the strike price is equal to the stock price.

average tax rate Calculated by taking the total amount of tax paid divided by taxable income.

balance sheet A statement of the firm's financial position at a specific point in time. The firm's assets are listed on the left-hand side of the balance sheet; the right-hand side shows its liabilities and equity, or the claims against these assets.

banker's acceptance Created when an importer's bank promises to accept a postdated check written to an exporter even if there are insufficient funds in the importer's account. If the bank is strong, then this financial instrument virtually eliminates credit risk.

Bankruptcy Reform Act of 1978 Enacted to speed up and streamline bankruptcy proceedings. This law represented a shift to a relative priority doctrine of creditors' claims.

basic earning power (BEP) ratio Calculated by dividing earnings before interest and taxes by total assets. This ratio shows the raw earning power of the firm's assets before the influence of taxes and leverage.

Baumol model A model for establishing the firm's target cash balance that closely resembles the economic ordering quantity model used for inventory. The model assumes: (1) that the firm uses cash at a steady, predictable rate, (2) that the firm's cash inflows from operations also occur at a steady, predictable rate, and (3) that its net cash outflows therefore also occur at a steady rate. The model balances the opportunity cost of holding cash against the transactions costs associated with replenishing the cash account.

behavioral finance A field of study that analyzes investor behavior as a result of psychological traits. It does not assume that investors necessarily behave rationally.

benchmarking When a firm compares its ratios to other leading companies in the same industry.

best efforts arrangement A type of contract with an investment banker when issuing stock. In a best efforts sale, the investment banker is only committed to making every effort to sell the stock at the offering price. In this case, the issuing firm bears the risk that the new issue will not be fully subscribed.

beta coefficient, b A measure of the amount of risk that an individual stock contributes to a well-diversified portfolio.

binomial approach A way to price options that assumes that the underlying stock can only increase or decrease a certain amount each period.

binomial lattice A graph of the stock price and payoffs in a binomial options pricing model.

bird-in-the-hand theory Assumes that investors value a dollar of dividends more highly than a dollar of expected capital gains, because a certain dividend is less risky than a possible capital gain. This theory implies that a high-dividend stock has a higher price and lower required return, all else held equal.

Black-Scholes option pricing model A model to estimate the value of a call option. It is widely used by options traders.

board of trustees Group of community leaders who control a tax-exempt, charitable organization. Members of the board of trustees must have no direct economic interest in the organization.

bond A promissory note issued by a business or a governmental unit.

bond insurance Protects investors against default by the issuer and provides credit enhancement to the bond issue.

bond rating A bond's quality rating. This is issued by one of the bond rating agencies like S&P, Fitch, or Moodys. A high rating means the bond is safe, and a low rating means it is very risky.

book value per share Common equity divided by the number of shares outstanding.

break-even point The level of unit sales at which costs equal revenues.

breakup value A firm's value if its assets are sold off in pieces.

business risk The risk inherent in the operations of the firm, prior to the financing decision. Thus, business risk is the uncertainty inherent in future operating income or earnings before interest and taxes. Business risk is caused by many factors; two of the most important are sales variability and operating leverage.

bylaws A set of rules drawn up by a company's founders that specify such things as election of directors, stockholder rights, and procedures for changing the bylaws.

call option An option that allows the holder to buy the asset at some predetermined price within a specified period of time.

call premium The sum over and above the bond's par value a bond issuer must pay to the bondholder when it is called.

call protection A bond with a deferred call is said to have call protection. It cannot be called for several years after it was issued.

call provision Gives the issuing corporation the right to call the bonds for redemption. The call provision generally states that if the bonds are called then the company must pay the bondholders an amount greater than the par value, or a call premium. Most bonds contain a call provision.

capacity option Allows a company to change the capacity of its output in response to changing market conditions. This includes the option to contract or expand production. It also includes the option to abandon a project if market conditions deteriorate too much.

Capital Asset Pricing Model (CAPM) A model based on the proposition that any stock's required rate of return is equal to the risk-free rate of return plus a risk premium reflecting only the risk remaining after diversification. The CAPM equation is $r_i = r_{RF} + b_i(r_M - r_{RF})$.

capital budget Outlines the planned expenditures on fixed assets.

capital budgeting The whole process of analyzing projects and deciding whether they should be included in the capital budget.

capital gain (loss) The profit (loss) from the sale of a capital asset for more (less) than its purchase price.

capital gains yield Results from changing prices and is calculated as $(P_1 - P_0)/P_0$, where P_0 is the beginning-of-period price and P_1 is the end-of-period price.

capital intensity ratio The dollar amount of assets required to produce a dollar of sales. The capital intensity ratio is the reciprocal of the total assets turnover ratio.

capital market Capital markets are the financial markets for long-term debt and corporate stocks. The New York Stock Exchange is an example of a capital market.

capital rationing Occurs when management places a constraint on the size of the firm's capital budget during a particular period.

capital structure The manner in which a firm's assets are financed; that is, the right side of the balance sheet. Capital structure is normally expressed as the percentage of each type of capital used by the firm such as debt, preferred stock, and common equity.

capitalizing Incorporating the lease provisions into the balance sheet by reporting the leased asset under fixed assets and reporting the present value of future lease payments as debt.

cash balance plan A type of defined benefits plan in which benefits are defined in terms of the cash balance in the employee's account rather than monthly salary.

cash budget A schedule showing cash flows (receipts, disbursements, and cash balances) for a firm over a specified period.

cash conversion cycle The length of time between the firm's actual cash expenditures on productive resources (materials and labor) and its own cash receipts from the sale of products (that is, the length of time between paying for labor and materials and collecting on receivables). Thus, the cash conversion cycle equals the length of time the firm has funds tied up in current assets.

cash discounts The amount by which a seller is willing to reduce the invoice price in order to be paid immediately, rather than in the future. A cash discount might be 2/10, net 30, which means a 2% discount if the bill is paid within 10 days and otherwise the entire amount is due within 30 days.

CDO, collateralized debt obligation Created when large numbers of mortgages are bundled into pools to create new securities that are then sliced into tranches; the tranches are recombined and re-divided into securities called CDOs.

CDS, credit default swap Derivative in which a counterparty pays if a specified debt instrument goes into default; similar to insurance on a bond.

Chapter 11 bankruptcy The 11th chapter of the bankruptcy statutes, regulates reorganization in a bankruptcy.

Chapter 7 bankruptcy The 7th chapter of the bankruptcy statutes, regulates liquidation in a bankruptcy.

characteristic line Obtained by regressing the historical returns on a particular stock against the historical returns on the general stock market. The slope of the characteristic line is the stock's beta, which measures the amount by which the stock's expected return increases for a given increase in the expected return on the market.

charitable contributions One way that not-for-profit businesses raise equity capital. Individuals and firms make these contributions for a variety of reasons including concern for the well-being of others, the recognition that accompanies large donations, and tax deductibility.

charter The legal document that is filed with the state to incorporate a company.

check-clearing process When a customer's check is written upon one bank and a company deposits the check in its own bank, the company's bank must verify that the check is valid before the company can use those funds. Checks are generally cleared through the Federal Reserve System or through a clearinghouse set up by the banks in a particular city.

classified boards A board of directors with staggered terms. For example, a board with one-third of the seats filled each year and directors serving 3-year terms.

classified stock Sometimes created by a firm to meet special needs and circumstances. Generally, when special classifications of stock are used, one type is designated "Class A," another as "Class B," and so on. For example, Class A might be entitled to receive dividends before dividends can be paid on Class B stock. Class B might have the exclusive right to vote.

cleanup clause A clause in a line of credit that requires the borrower to reduce the loan balance to zero at least once a year.

clientele effect The attraction of companies with specific dividend policies to those investors whose needs are best served by those policies. Thus, companies with high dividends will have a clientele of investors with low marginal tax rates and strong desires for current income. Conversely, companies with low dividends will have a clientele of investors with high marginal tax rates and little need for current income.

cliff vesting All the options in a grant vest on the same date.

closely held corporation Refers to companies that are so small that their common stocks are not actively traded; they are owned by only a few people, usually the companies' managers.

coefficient of variation, CV Equal to the standard deviation divided by the expected return; it is a standardized risk measure that allows comparisons between investments having different expected returns and standard deviations.

collection policy The procedure for collecting accounts receivable. A change in collection policy will affect sales, days sales outstanding, bad debt losses, and the percentage of customers taking discounts.

collections float Float created while funds from customers' checks are being deposited and cleared through the check collection process.

combination lease Combines some aspects of both operating and financial leases. For example, a financial lease that contains a cancellation clause—normally associated with operating leases—is a combination lease.

commercial paper Unsecured, short-term promissory notes of large firms, usually issued in denominations of $100,000 or more and having an interest rate somewhat below the prime rate.

commodity futures Futures contracts that involve the sale or purchase of various commodities, including grains, oilseeds, livestock, meats, fiber, metals, and wood.

common stockholders' equity (net worth) The capital supplied by common stockholders—capital stock, paid-in capital, retained earnings, and (occasionally) certain reserves. Paid-in capital is the difference between the stock's par value and what stockholders paid when they bought newly issued shares.

comparative ratio analysis Compares a firm's own ratios to other leading companies in the same industry. This technique is also known as benchmarking.

compensating balance (CB) A minimum checking account balance that a firm must maintain with a bank to compensate the bank for services rendered or for making a loan; generally equal to 10%–20% of the loans outstanding.

composition Creditors voluntarily reduce their fixed claims on the debtor by accepting a lower principal amount, reducing the interest rate on the debt, accepting equity in place of debt, or some combination of these changes.

compounding The process of finding the future value of a single payment or series of payments.

computer/telephone network A computer/telephone network, such as NASDAQ, consists of all the facilities that provide for security transactions not conducted at a physical location exchange. These facilities are, basically, the communications networks that link buyers and sellers.

conditional value at risk (CVaR) The average portfolio value (or loss) conditional upon the portfolio value being less than a specified threshold value (or threshold percentile). It can also be defined as the average NPV, conditional upon the NPV being less than a specified threshold value (or threshold percentile). It is also called the expected shortfall (ES).

congeneric merger Involves firms that are interrelated but do not have identical lines of business. One example is Prudential's acquisition of Bache & Company.

conglomerate merger Occurs when unrelated enterprises combine, such as Mobil Oil and Montgomery Ward.

conservative short-term financing policy Refers to using permanent capital to finance all permanent asset requirements as well as to meet some or all of the seasonal demands.

consol A type of perpetuity. Consols were originally bonds issued by England in the mid-1700s to consolidate past debt.

constant growth model Valuation assuming constant growth in free cash flow or in dividends.

continuous probability distribution Contains an infinite number of outcomes and is graphed from $-\infty$ and $+\infty$.

conversion price The effective price per share of stock if conversion occurs; the par value of the convertible security divided by the conversion ratio.

conversion ratio The number of shares of common stock received upon conversion of one convertible security.

conversion value The value of the stock that the investor would receive if conversion occurred; the market price per share times the conversion ratio.

convertible bond Security that is convertible into shares of common stock, at a fixed price, at the option of the bondholder.

convertible currency A currency that can be traded in the currency markets and can be redeemed at current market rates.

convertible security Bonds or preferred stocks that can be exchanged for (converted into) common stock, under specific terms, at the option of the holder. Unlike the exercise of warrants, conversion of a convertible security does not provide additional capital to the issuer.

corporate alliance A cooperative deal that stops short of a merger; also called a strategic alliance.

corporate bond Debt issued by corporations and exposed to default risk. Different corporate bonds have different levels of default risk, depending on the issuing company's characteristics and on the terms of the specific bond.

corporate governance The set of rules that controls a company's behavior toward its directors, managers, employees, shareholders, creditors, customers, competitors, and community.

corporate valuation model Defines the total value of a company as the present value of its expected free cash flows discounted at the weighted average cost of capital (i.e., the value of operations) plus the value of nonoperating assets such as T-bills.

corporation A corporation is a legal entity created by a state. The corporation is separate and distinct from its owners and managers.

correlation The tendency of two variables to move together.

correlation coefficient, ρ (rho) A standardized measure of how two random variables covary. A correlation coefficient (ρ) of $+1.0$ means that the two variables move up and down in perfect synchronization, whereas a coefficient of -1.0 means the variables always move in opposite directions. A correlation coefficient of zero suggests that the two variables are not related to one another; that is, they are independent.

cost of common stock, r_s The return required by the firm's common stockholders. It is usually calculated using Capital Asset Pricing Model or the dividend growth model.

cost of equity The price of using equity capital.

cost of new external common equity, r_e A project financed with external equity must earn a higher rate of return because it must cover the flotation costs. Thus, the cost of new common equity is higher than that of common equity raised internally by reinvesting earnings.

cost of preferred stock, r_{ps} The return required by the firm's preferred stockholders. The cost of preferred stock, r_{ps}, is the cost to the firm of issuing new preferred stock. For perpetual preferred, it is the preferred dividend, D_{ps}, divided by the net issuing price, P_n.

costly trade credit Credit taken (in excess of free trade credit) whose cost is equal to the discount lost.

country risk Risk that arises from investing or doing business in a particular country.

coupon interest rate Stated rate of interest on a bond; defined as the coupon payment divided by the par value.

coupon payment Dollar amount of interest paid to each bondholder on the interest payment dates.

covariance between Stock i and the market, COV_{iM} Covariance is the degree to which random variables move together. The covariance between a stock and the market is the degree to which the stock return moves with the market's return.

covenant (for a bond), or restrictive covenant A requirement placed on the company issuing the bond. Usually to protect the bondholders.

coverage ratio Similar to the times-interest-earned ratio, but it recognizes that many firms lease assets and also must make sinking fund payments. It is found by adding earnings before interest, taxes, depreciation, amortization (EBITDA), and lease payments and then dividing this total by interest charges, lease payments, and sinking fund payments over $1 - T$ (where T is the tax rate).

covered call option A call option written when the writer has the stock to back up the call if it is exercised.

cramdown Reorganization plans that are mandated by the bankruptcy court and binding on all parties.

credit enhancement Enables a bond's rating to be upgraded to AAA when the issuer purchases bond insurance. The bond insurance company guarantees that bondholders will receive the promised interest and principal payments. Therefore, the bond carries the credit rating of the insurance company rather than that of the issuer.

credit period The length of time for which credit is extended. If the credit period is lengthened, then sales will generally increase, as will accounts receivable. This will increase the firm's financing needs and possibly increase bad debt losses. A shortening of the credit period will have the opposite effect.

credit policy The firm's policy on granting and collecting credit. There are four elements of credit policy, or credit policy variables: credit period, credit standards, collection policy, and discounts.

credit standards The financial strength and creditworthiness that qualifies a customer for a firm's regular credit terms.

credit terms Statements of the credit period and any discounts offered—for example, 2/10, net 30.

cross rate The exchange rate between two non-U.S. currencies.

crossover rate The cost of capital at which the NPV profiles for two projects intersect.

cumulative preferred dividends A protective feature on preferred stock that requires all past preferred dividends to be paid before any common dividends can be paid.

currency appreciation Occurs to a particular currency when it increases in value relative to another particular currency. For example, if the exchange rate of 1.0 dollar per euro changes to 1.1 dollars per euro, then euro has appreciated against the dollar by 10%.

currency depreciation Occurs to a particular currency when it decreases in value relative to another particular currency. For example, if the exchange rate of 1.0 dollar per euro changes to 0.9 dollars per euro, then euro has depreciated against the dollar by 10%.

current ratio Indicates the extent to which current liabilities are covered by those assets expected to be converted to cash in the near future; it is found by dividing current assets by current liabilities.

current yield (on a bond) The annual coupon payment divided by the current market price.

days sales outstanding (DSO) Used to appraise accounts receivable and indicates the length of time the firm must wait to receive cash after making a sale. It is found by dividing receivables by average sales per day.

DCF (discounted cash flow) techniques The net present value (NPV) and internal rate of return (IRR) techniques are discounted cash flow (DCF) evaluation techniques. These are called DCF methods because they explicitly recognize the time value of money.

dealer market In a dealer market, a dealer holds an inventory of the security and makes a market by offering to buy or sell. Others who wish to buy or sell can see the offers made by the dealers and can contact the dealer of their choice to arrange a transaction.

debenture An unsecured bond; as such, it provides no lien against specific property as security for the obligation. Debenture holders are therefore general creditors whose claims are protected by property not otherwise pledged.

debt ratio The ratio of total debt to total assets, it measures the percentage of funds provided by investors other than preferred or common shareholders.

debt service requirements The total amount of principal and interest that must be paid on a bond issue.

debt-to-equity ratio Ratio of debt divided by equity.

decision trees A form of scenario analysis in which different actions are taken in different scenarios.

declaration date The date on which a firm's directors issue a statement declaring a dividend.

default risk The risk that a borrower may not pay the interest and/or principal on a loan when it becomes due. If the issuer defaults, investors receive less than the promised return on the bond. Default risk is influenced by the financial strength of the issuer and also by the terms of the bond contract, especially whether collateral has been pledged to secure the bond. The greater the default risk, the higher the bond's yield to maturity.

default risk premium (DRP) The premium added to the real risk-free rate to compensate investors for the risk that a borrower may fail to pay the interest and/or principal on a loan when they become due.

defensive merger Occurs when one company acquires another to help ward off a hostile merger attempt.

deferred call A provision on a callable bond that prevents it from being called until several years after issue.

defined benefit plan Under this type of pension plan, employers agree to give retirees a specifically defined benefit.

defined contribution plan Under this type of pension plan, employers agree to make specific payments into a retirement fund and retirees receive benefits that depend on the plan's investment success.

depreciation A noncash charge against tangible assets, such as buildings or machines. It is taken for the purpose of showing an asset's estimated dollar cost of the capital equipment used up in the production process.

derivatives Claims whose value depends on what happens to the value of some other asset. Futures and options are two important types of derivatives, and their values depend on what happens to the prices of other assets. Therefore, the value of a derivative security is derived from the value of an underlying real asset or other security.

detachable warrant A warrant that can be detached and traded separately from the underlying security. Most warrants are detachable.

devaluation The lowering, by governmental action, of the price of its currency relative to another currency. For example, in 2013 the Argentinian bolivar was devalued from $0.23 per bolivar to $0.16 per bolivar.

development bond A tax-exempt bond sold by state and local governments whose proceeds are made available to corporations for specific uses deemed (by Congress) to be in the public interest.

direct quotation When discussing exchange rates, the number of units of home currency required to purchase one unit of a foreign currency.

disbursement float Float created before checks written by a firm have cleared and been deducted from the firm's account; disbursement float causes the firm's own checkbook balance to be smaller than the balance on the bank's records.

discount bond Bond prices and interest rates are inversely related; that is, they tend to move in the opposite direction from one another. A fixed-rate bond will sell at par when its coupon interest rate is equal to the going rate of interest, r_d. When the going rate of interest is above the coupon rate, a fixed-rate bond will sell at a "discount" below its par value. If current interest rates are below the coupon rate, a fixed-rate bond will sell at a "premium" above its par value.

discount interest Interest that is calculated on the face amount of a loan but is paid in advance.

discount on forward rate Occurs when the forward exchange rate differs from the spot rate. When the forward rate is below the spot rate, the forward rate is said to be at a discount.

discounted cash flow (DCF) approach A method of valuing a business that involves the application of capital budgeting procedures to an entire firm rather than to a single project.

discounted payback period The number of years it takes a firm to recover its project investment based on discounted cash flows.

discounting The process of finding the present value of a single payment or series of payments.

distribution policy The policy that sets the level of distributions and the form of the distributions (dividends and stock repurchases).

diversifiable risk Refers to that part of a security's total risk associated with random events not affecting the market as a whole. This risk can be eliminated by proper diversification. Also known as company-specific risk.

divestiture The opposite of an acquisition. That is, a company sells a portion of its assets—often a whole division—to another firm or individual.

dividend irrelevance theory Holds that dividend policy has no effect on either the price of a firm's stock or its cost of capital.

dividend reinvestment plan (DRIP) Allows stockholders to automatically purchase shares of common stock of the paying corporation in lieu of receiving cash dividends. There are two types of plans: one involves only stock that is already outstanding; the other involves newly issued stock. In the first type, the dividends of all participants are pooled and the stock is purchased on the open market. Participants benefit from lower transaction costs. In the second type, the company issues new shares to the participants. Thus, the company issues stock in lieu of the cash dividend.

dividend yield Defined as either the end-of-period dividend divided by the beginning-of-period price or as the ratio of the current dividend to the current price. Valuation formulas use the former definition.

DuPont equation A formula showing that the rate of return on equity can be found as the profit margin multiplied by the product of total assets turnover and the equity multiplier.

EBITDA Earnings before interest, taxes, depreciation, and amortization.

ECN In an ECN (electronic communications network), orders from potential buyers and sellers are automatically matched and the transaction is automatically completed.

economic life The number of years a project should be operated to maximize its net present value; often less than the maximum potential life.

economic ordering quantity (EOQ) The order quantity that minimizes the costs of ordering and carrying inventories.

Economic Value Added (EVA) A method used to measure a firm's true profitability. EVA is found by taking the firm's after-tax operating profit and subtracting the annual cost of all the capital a firm uses. If the firm generates a positive EVA, its management has created value for its shareholders. If the EVA is negative, management has destroyed shareholder value.

effective (or equivalent) annual rate (EAR or EFF%) The effective annual rate is the rate that, under annual compounding, would have produced the same future value at the end of 1 year as was produced by more frequent compounding, say quarterly. If the compounding occurs annually, then the effective annual rate and the nominal rate are the same. If compounding occurs more frequently, then the effective annual rate is greater than the nominal rate.

efficient frontier The set of efficient portfolios out of the full set of potential portfolios. On a graph, the efficient frontier constitutes the boundary line of the set of potential portfolios.

Efficient Markets Hypothesis (EMH) States: (1) that stocks are always in equilibrium and (2) that it is impossible for an investor to consistently "beat the market." The EMH assumes that all important information regarding a stock is reflected in the price of that stock.

efficient portfolio Provides the highest expected return for any degree of risk. The efficient portfolio also provides the lowest degree of risk for any expected return.

embedded options Options that are a part of another project. Also called real options, managerial options, and strategic options.

Employee Retirement Income Security Act (ERISA) The basic federal law governing the structure and administration of corporate pension plans.

enterprise risk management (ERM) A process that includes risk identification, risk assessment, and risk responses. ERM requires the participation of all levels within an organization.

entity multiple A type of market multiple that calculates the entity value of a company by multiplying EBITDA by an EBITDA market multiple. It is called an entity multiple because it is used to value the entire company, not just the stock.

entity valuation model The free cash flow valuation model because it values the entire company, not just its common stock.

entrenchment Occurs when a company has such a weak board of directors and has such strong anti-takeover provisions in its corporate charter that senior managers feel there is little chance of being removed.

EOQ model The equation used to find the economic ordering quantity.

EOQ range The range around the optimal ordering quantity that may be ordered without significantly affecting total inventory costs.

equilibrium The condition under which the intrinsic value of a security is equal to its price; also, when a security's expected return is equal to its required return.

equity risk premium, RP_M Expected market return minus the risk-free rate; also called market risk premium or equity premium

ESOP (employee stock ownership plan) A type of retirement plan in which employees own stock in the company.

euro The currency used by nations in the European Monetary Union.

Eurobond Any bond sold in some country other than the one in whose currency the bond is denominated. Thus, a U.S. firm selling dollar bonds in Switzerland is selling Eurobonds.

Eurodollar A U.S. dollar on deposit in a foreign bank or a foreign branch of a U.S. bank. Eurodollars are used to conduct transactions throughout Europe and the rest of the world.

European option An option that may only be exercised on its expiration date.

event risk The chance that some sudden event will occur and increase the credit risk of a company, thereby lowering the firm's credit rating and value of its outstanding bonds.

exchange rate Specifies the number of units of a given currency that can be purchased for one unit of another currency.

exchange rate risk Refers to the fluctuation in exchange rates between currencies over time.

ex-dividend date The date when the right to the dividend leaves the stock. This date was established by stockbrokers to avoid confusion, and it is 2 business days prior to the holder-of-record date. If the stock sale is made prior to the ex-dividend date, then the dividend is paid to the buyer; if the stock is bought on or after the ex-dividend date, the dividend is paid to the seller.

exercise price The price stated in the option contract at which the security can be bought (or sold). Also called the strike price.

exercise value Equal to the current price of the stock (underlying the option) minus the strike price of the option.

expectations theory States that the slope of the yield curve depends on expectations about future inflation rates and interest rates. Thus, if the annual rate of inflation and future interest rates are expected to increase, then the yield curve will be upward sloping; the curve will be downward sloping if the annual rates are expected to decrease.

expected rate of return, $\hat{r}_s$ The rate of return expected on a stock given its current price and expected future cash flows. If the stock is in equilibrium, the required rate of return will equal the expected rate of return.

expected return on a portfolio, $\hat{r}_p$ The weighted average of the expected returns on the individual stocks comprising the portfolio.

expected shortfall (ES) The average portfolio value conditional upon the portfolio value being less than a specified threshold value (or threshold percentile). It can also be defined as the average NPV conditional upon the NPV being less than a specified threshold value (or threshold percentile). It is also called the conditional value at risk (CVaR).

expiration date The date after which an option may no longer be exercised. In the U.S. many options expire on the Saturday following the third Friday of the expiration month.

extension A form of debt restructuring in which creditors postpone the dates of required interest or principal payments, or both.

extra dividend A dividend paid, in addition to the regular dividend, when earnings permit. Firms with volatile earnings may have a low regular dividend that can be maintained even in years of low profit (or high capital investment) but is supplemented by an extra dividend when excess funds are available.

factor analysis A statistical procedure used to extract Arbitrage Pricing Theory parameters from a large sample of stocks. It identifies common factors that explain stock returns.

fairness The standard of fairness states that claims must be recognized in the order of their legal and contractual priority. In simpler terms, the reorganization must be fair to all parties.

Fama-French three-factor model Includes one factor for the excess market return (the market return minus the risk-free rate), a second factor for size (defined as the return on a portfolio of small firms minus the return on a portfolio of big firms), and a third factor for the book-to-market effect (defined as the return on a portfolio of firms with a high book-to-market ratio minus the return on a portfolio of firms with a low book-to-market ratio).

FASB Financial Accounting Standards Board Promulgates standards for issues pertaining to private organizations.

FASB Statement 13 The Financial Accounting Standards Board statement that spells out the conditions under which a lease must be capitalized and the specific procedures to follow.

feasibility The standard of feasibility states that there must be a reasonably high probability of successful rehabilitation and profitable future operations.

feasible set Represents all portfolios that can be constructed from a given set of stocks; also known as the attainable set.

financial distress costs Incurred when a leveraged firm facing a decline in earnings is forced to take actions to avoid bankruptcy. These costs may be the result of delays in the liquidation of assets, legal fees, the effects on product quality from cutting costs, and evasive actions by suppliers and customers.

financial futures Provide for the purchase or sale of a financial asset at some time in the future, but at a price that is established today. Financial futures exist for Treasury bills, Treasury notes and bonds, certificates of deposit, Eurodollar deposits, foreign currencies, and stock indexes.

financial intermediary Intermediary that buys securities with funds that it obtains by issuing its own securities. An example is a common stock mutual fund that buys common stocks with funds obtained by issuing shares in the mutual fund.

financial lease Covers the entire expected life of the equipment; does not provide for maintenance service, is not cancellable, and is fully amortized.

financial leverage The extent to which fixed-income securities (debt and preferred stock) are used in a firm's capital structure. If a high percentage of a firm's capital structure is in the form of debt and preferred stock, then the firm is said to have a high degree of financial leverage.

financial merger A merger in which the companies will not be operated as a single unit and for which no operating economies are expected.

financial risk The risk added by the use of debt financing. Debt financing increases the variability of earnings before taxes (but after interest); thus, along with business risk, it contributes to the uncertainty of net income and earnings per share. Business risk plus financial risk equals total corporate risk.

financial service corporation A corporation that offers a wide range of financial services such as brokerage operations, insurance, and commercial banking.

financing deficit The shortfall of spontaneous liabilities, planned change in external financing (total changes of debt, preferred stock, and common stock from the preliminary financing plan), and internal funds (net income less planned dividends) relative to additional assets required by the operating plan.

financing feedback Circularity created when additional debt causes additional interest expense, which reduces the addition to retained earnings, which in turn requires a higher level of debt, which causes still more interest expense, causing the cycle to be repeated.

financing surplus The excess of spontaneous liabilities, planned change in external financing (total changes of debt, preferred stock, and common stock from the preliminary financing plan), and internal funds (net income less planned dividends) relative to additional assets required by the operating plan.

fixed assets turnover ratio The ratio of sales to net fixed assets; it measures how effectively the firm uses its plant and equipment.

fixed exchange rate system The system in effect from the end of World War II until August 1971. Under the system, the U.S. dollar was linked to gold at the rate of $35 per ounce, and other currencies were then tied to the dollar.

floating exchange rates The system currently in effect, where the forces of supply and demand are allowed to determine currency prices with little government intervention.

floating-rate bond A bond whose coupon payment may vary over time. The coupon rate is usually linked to the rate on some other security, such as a Treasury security, or to some other rate, such as the prime rate or LIBOR.

flotation cost, F Those costs occurring when a company issues a new security, including fees to an investment banker and legal fees.

forecast horizon or horizon date or terminal date The last year of the forecast.

forecasted financial statements approach A method of forecasting financial statements to determine the additional funds needed. Many items on the income statement and balance sheets are assumed to increase proportionally with sales. As sales increase, these items that are tied to sales also increase, and the values of these items for a particular year are estimated as percentages of the forecasted sales for that year.

foreign bond A bond sold by a foreign borrower but denominated in the currency of the country in which the issue is sold. Thus, a U.S. firm selling bonds denominated in Swiss francs in Switzerland is selling foreign bonds.

foreign exchange (FX) risk The risk that a change in a currency exchange rate might adversely affect a company.

foreign trade deficit A deficit that occurs when businesses and individuals in the United States import more goods from foreign countries than are exported.

forward contract A contract to buy or sell some item at some time in the future at a price established when the contract is entered into.

forward exchange rate The prevailing exchange rate for exchange (delivery) at some agreed-upon future date, which is usually 30, 90, or 180 days from the day the transaction is negotiated.

founders' shares Stock owned by the firm's founders that have sole voting rights but restricted dividends for a specified number of years.

free cash flow (FCF) The cash flow actually available for distribution to all investors after the company has made all investments in fixed assets and working capital necessary to sustain ongoing operations.

free cash flow valuation model Defines the total value of a company as the present value of its expected free cash flows discounted at the weighted average cost of capital (i.e., the value of operations) plus the value of nonoperating assets such as T-bills.

free trade credit Credit received during the discount period.

friendly merger Occurs when the target company's management agrees to the merger and recommends that shareholders approve the deal.

fully funded pension plan A pension plan in which the present value of all expected retirement benefits is equal to assets on hand.

fund capital Not-for-profit business equivalent of equity capital. It consists of retained profits and charitable contributions.

fundamental beta A beta adjusted for such fundamental risk variables as financial leverage or sales volatility.

fundamental value or price Value or price that incorporates all relevant information regarding expected future cash flows and risk.

funding strategy Necessary for a defined benefit plan and involves two decisions: how fast should any unfunded liability be reduced and what rate of return should be assumed in the actuarial calculations.

FVA_N The future value of a stream of annuity payments, where N is the number of payments of the annuity.

$FVIFA_{I,N}$ The future value interest factor for an ordinary annuity of N periodic payments paying I percent interest per period.

$FVIF_{I,N}$ The future value interest factor for a lump sum left in an account for N periods paying I percent interest per period.

FV_N The future value of an initial single cash flow, where N is the number of periods the initial cash flow is compounded.

GAAP, Generally Accepted Accounting Principles A set of standards for financial reporting established by the accounting profession.

GASB, Government Accounting Standards Board Promulgates standards for issues pertaining to governmental entities.

general obligation bonds Type of municipal bonds which are secured by the full faith and credit of a government unit; that is, backed by the full taxing authority of the issuer.

general partner Partner in a partnership who has unlimited liability.

going public The act of selling stock to the public at large by a closely held corporation or its principal stockholders.

golden parachute A payment made to executives who are forced out when a merger takes place.

greenmail Targeted share repurchases that occur when a company buys back stock from a potential acquirer at a higher than fair-market price. In return, the potential acquirer agrees not to attempt to take over the company.

gross profit margin Ratio of gross profit (sales minus cost of goods sold) divided by sales.

growth option Occurs if an investment creates the opportunity to make other potentially profitable investments that would not otherwise be possible, including options to expand output, to enter a new geographical market, and to introduce complementary products or successive generations of products.

GSE (government-sponsored entity) debt Debt issued by government-sponsored entities (GSEs) such as the Tennessee Valley Authority or the Small Business Administration; not officially backed by the full faith and credit of the U.S. government.

guideline lease Meets all of the Internal Revenue Service (IRS) requirements for a genuine lease. If a lease meets the IRS guidelines, the IRS allows the lessor to deduct the asset's depreciation and allows the lessee to deduct the lease payments. Also called a tax-oriented lease.

Hamada equation Shows the effect of debt on the beta coefficient—increases in debt increase beta, and decreases in debt reduce beta.

hard currencies Currencies considered to be convertible because the nation that issues them allows them to be traded in the currency markets and is willing to redeem them at market rates.

hedge portfolio (in options pricing) A portfolio consisting of stock and options that is instantaneously risk-free. In a binomial model, this means the portfolio payoffs are the same in the up and the down states.

hedging A transaction that lowers a firm's risk of damage due to fluctuating commodity prices, interest rates, and exchange rates.

herding behavior When one group of investors does well, other investors begin to emulate them, acting like a herd of sheep.

historical rate of return The realized rate of return over some past time interval.

holder-of-record date If a company lists the stockholder as an owner on the holder-of-record date, then the stockholder receives the dividend.

holding company A corporation formed for the sole purpose of owning stocks in other companies. A holding company differs from a stock mutual fund in that holding companies own sufficient stock in their operating companies to exercise effective working control.

holdout A problematic characteristic of informal reorganizations whereby all of the involved parties do not agree to the voluntary plan. Holdouts are usually made by creditors in an effort to receive full payment on claims.

horizon value of operations The value of operations at the end of the explicit forecast period. It is equal to the present value of all free cash flows beyond the forecast period, discounted back to the end of the forecast period at the weighted average cost of capital.

horizontal merger A merger between two companies in the same line of business.

hostile merger Occurs when the management of the target company resists the offer.

hurdle rate The project cost of capital, or discount rate. It is the rate used to discount future cash flows in the net present value method or to compare with the internal rate of return.

improper accumulation The retention of earnings by a business for the purpose of enabling stockholders to avoid personal income taxes on dividends.

income bond Pays interest only if the interest is earned. These securities cannot bankrupt a company, but from an investor's standpoint, they are riskier than "regular" bonds.

income statement Summarizes the firm's revenues and expenses over an accounting period. Net sales are shown at the top of each statement, after which various costs, including income taxes, are subtracted to obtain the net income available to common stockholders. The bottom of the statement reports earnings and dividends per share.

incremental cash flow Those cash flows that arise solely from the asset that is being evaluated.

indentures A legal document that spells out the rights of both bondholders and the issuing corporation.

independent projects Projects that can be accepted or rejected individually.

indexed, or purchasing power, bond The interest rate of such a bond is based on an inflation index such as the consumer price index (CPI), so the interest paid rises automatically when the inflation rate rises, thus protecting the bondholders against inflation.

indifference curve The risk–return trade-off function for a particular investor; reflects that investor's attitude toward risk. An investor would be indifferent between any pair of assets on the same indifference curve. In risk–return space, the greater the slope of the indifference curve, the greater is the investor's risk aversion.

indirect quotation When discussing exchange rates, the number of units of foreign currency that can be purchased for one unit of home currency.

inflation Increase in the price level.

inflation premium (IP) The premium added to the real risk-free rate of interest to compensate for the expected loss of purchasing power. The inflation premium is the average rate of inflation expected over the life of the security.

informal debt restructuring An agreement between a troubled firm and its creditors to change existing debt terms. An extension postpones the required payment date; a composition is a reduction in creditor claims.

information content, or signaling, hypothesis A theory that holds that investors regard dividend changes as "signals" of management forecasts. Thus, when dividends are raised, this is viewed by investors as recognition by management of future earnings increases. Therefore, if a firm's stock price increases with a dividend increase, the reason may not be investor preference for dividends but rather expectations of higher future earnings. Conversely, a dividend reduction may signal that management is forecasting poor earnings in the future.

initial public offering (IPO) Occurs when a closely held corporation or its principal stockholders sell stock to the public at large.

initial public offering (IPO) market Going public is the act of selling stock to the public at large by a closely held corporation or its principal stockholders, and this market is often termed the initial public offering market.

I_{NOM} The nominal, or quoted, interest rate.

insiders The officers, directors, and major stockholders of a firm.

interest coverage ratio Also called the times-interest-earned (TIE) ratio; determined by dividing earnings before interest and taxes by the interest expense.

interest rate The price of using debt.

interest rate parity Holds that investors should expect to earn the same return in all countries after adjusting for risk.

interest rate risk Arises from the fact that bond prices decline when interest rates rise. Under these circumstances, selling a bond prior to maturity will result in a capital loss; the longer the term to maturity, the larger the loss.

interlocking boards of directors Occur when the CEO of Company A sits on the board of Company B while B's CEO sits on A's board.

internal rate of return (IRR) method The discount rate that equates the present value of the expected future cash inflows and outflows. IRR measures the rate of return on a project, but it assumes that all cash flows can be reinvested at the IRR rate.

international bond Any bond sold outside of the country of the borrower. There are two types of international bonds: Eurobonds and foreign bonds.

in-the-money option An option that, if exercised immediately, would be exercised profitably. For a call, this is when the stock price exceeds the strike price. For a put, when the stock price is less than the put price.

intrinsic stock price Intrinsic value of equity divided by the shares outstanding.

intrinsic value of equity The estimated value of operations plus nonoperating assets minus the value of debt and the value of preferred stock.

intrinsic value or price Value or price that incorporates all relevant information regarding expected future cash flows and risk.

inventory conversion period The average length of time to convert materials into finished goods and then to sell them; calculated by dividing total inventory by daily costs of goods sold.

inventory turnover ratio Cost of goods sold divided by inventories.

inverted (abnormal) yield curve A downward-sloping yield curve.

investment bank A firm that assists in the design of an issuing firm's corporate securities and in the sale of the new securities to investors in the primary market.

investment strategy Deals with the question of how the pension assets portfolio should be structured given the assumed actuarial rate of return.

investment timing option Gives companies the option to delay a project rather than implement it immediately. This option to wait allows a company to reduce the uncertainty of market conditions before it decides to implement the project.

investment-grade bond Securities with ratings of Baa/BBB or above.

investor-supplied capital Total amount of short-term debt, long-term debt, preferred stock, and total common equity shown on a balance sheet. It is the amount of financing that investors have provided to a company. It also called total investor-supplied capital.

investor-supplied operating capital The total amount of short-term debt, long-term debt, preferred stock, and total common equity shown on a balance sheet, less the amount of short-term investments shown on the balance sheet. It is the amount of financing used in operations that investors have provided to a company. It is also called total investor-supplied operating capital.

Jensen's alpha Measures the vertical distance of a portfolio's return above or below the Security Market Line; first suggested by Professor Michael Jensen, it became popular because of its ease of calculation.

joint venture Involves the joining together of parts of companies to accomplish specific, limited objectives. Joint ventures are controlled by the combined management of the two (or more) parent companies.

junk bond High-risk, high-yield bond issued to finance leveraged buyouts, mergers, or troubled companies.

lessee The party leasing the property.

lessee's analysis Involves determining whether leasing an asset is less costly than buying the asset. The lessee will compare the present value cost of leasing the asset with the present value cost of purchasing the asset (assuming the funds to purchase the asset are obtained through a loan). If the present value cost of the lease is less than the present value cost of purchasing, then the asset should be leased. The lessee can also analyze the lease using the IRR approach or the equivalent loan method.

lessor The party receiving the payments from the lease (that is, the owner of the property).

lessor's analysis Involves determining the rate of return on the proposed lease. If the internal rate of return of the lease cash flows exceeds the lessor's opportunity cost of capital, then the lease is a good investment. This is equivalent to analyzing whether the net present value of the lease is positive.

leveraged buyout (LBO) A transaction in which a firm's publicly owned stock is acquired in a mostly debt-financed tender offer, resulting in a privately owned, highly leveraged firm. Often, the firm's own management initiates the LBO.

leveraged lease The lessor borrows a portion of the funds needed to buy the equipment to be leased.

liabilities to assets ratio The ratio of total liabilities to total assets, it measures the percentage of funds provided by creditors.

LIBOR London Interbank Offered Rate; the rate that U.K. banks charge one another.

limited liability company See limited liability partnership

limited liability partnership A limited liability partnership (LLP), sometimes called a limited liability company (LLC), combines the limited liability advantage of a corporation with the tax advantages of a partnership.

limited partner Partner in a partnership whose liability is limited to the amount of the investment.

limited partnership A partnership in which limited partners' liabilities, investment returns, and control are limited; general partners have unlimited liability and control.

line of credit An arrangement in which a bank agrees to lend up to a specified maximum amount of funds during a designated period.

liquidation in bankruptcy The sale of the assets of a firm and the distribution of the proceeds to the creditors and owners in a specific priority.

liquidity Liquidity refers to a firm's cash and marketable securities position and to its ability to meet maturing obligations. A liquid asset is any asset that can be quickly sold and converted to cash at its "fair" value. Active markets provide liquidity.

liquidity premium (LP) A liquidity premium is added to the real risk-free rate of interest, in addition to other premiums, if a security is not liquid.

liquidity ratio A ratio that shows the relationship of a firm's cash and other current assets to its current liabilities.

lockbox plan A cash management tool in which incoming checks for a firm are sent to post office boxes rather than to corporate headquarters. Several times a day, a local bank will collect the contents of the lockbox and deposit the checks into the company's local account.

long hedges Occur when futures contracts are bought in anticipation of (or to guard against) price increases.

Long-Term Equity AnticiPation Security (LEAPS) A long-term option.

low-regular-dividend-plus-extras policy Dividend policy in which a company announces a low regular dividend that it is sure can be maintained; if extra funds are available, the company pays a specially designated extra dividend or repurchases shares of stock.

lumpy assets Those assets that cannot be acquired smoothly and instead require large, discrete additions. For example, an electric utility that is operating at full capacity cannot add a small amount of generating capacity, at least not economically.

make-whole call provision A bond call feature in which the company has to pay a call price that is essentially the same as the market value of a similar non-callable bond.

managerial options Options that give opportunities to managers to respond to changing market conditions. Also called real options.

margin requirement The margin is the percentage of a stock's price that an investor has borrowed in order to purchase the stock. The Securities and Exchange Commission sets margin requirements, which is the maximum percentage of debt that can be used to purchase a stock.

marginal tax rate The tax rate on the last unit of income.

market equilibrium The condition in which expected return = required return. In terms of prices, market price = intrinsic value.

market multiple method Multiplies a market-determined ratio (called a multiple) to some value of the target firm to estimate the target's value. The market multiple can be based on net income, earnings per share, sales, book value, or number of subscribers.

market portfolio A portfolio consisting of all stocks.

market price Stock price observed in the financial markets.

market risk That part of a security's total risk that cannot be eliminated by diversification; measured by the beta coefficient.

market risk premium, RP_M The difference between the expected return on the market and the risk-free rate.

Market Value Added (MVA) The difference between the market value of the firm (that is, the sum of the market value of common equity, the market value of debt, and the market value of preferred stock) and the book value of the firm's common equity, debt, and preferred stock. If the book values of debt and preferred stock are equal to their market values, then MVA is also equal to the difference between the market value of equity and the amount of equity capital that investors supplied.

market value ratios Relate the firm's stock price to its earnings and book value per share.

marketable securities Can be converted to cash on very short notice and provide at least a modest return.

maturity date The date when the bond's par value is repaid to the bondholder. Maturity dates generally range from 10 to 40 years from the time of issue.

maturity matching short-term financing policy A policy that matches asset and liability maturities. It is also referred to as the moderate, or self-liquidating, approach.

maturity risk premium (MRP) The premium that must be added to the real risk-free rate of interest to compensate for interest rate risk, which depends on a bond's maturity. Interest rate risk arises from the fact that bond prices decline when interest rates rise. Under these circumstances, selling a bond prior to maturity will result in a capital loss; the longer the term to maturity, the larger the loss.

merger The joining of two firms to form a single firm.

Miller model Introduces the effect of personal taxes into the valuation of a levered firm, which reduces the advantage of corporate debt financing.

MM Proposition I with corporate taxes $V_L = V_U + TD$. Thus, firm value increases with leverage and the optimal capital structure is virtually all debt.

MM Proposition I without taxes $V_L = V_U = EBIT/r_{sU}$. Since both EBIT and r_{sU} are constant, firm value is also constant and capital structure is irrelevant.

MM Proposition II with corporate taxes $r_{sL} = r_{sU} + (r_{sU} - r_d)(1 - T)(D/S)$. Here the increase in equity costs is less than the zero-tax case, and the increasing use of lower-cost debt causes the firm's cost of capital to decrease. In this case, the optimal capital structure is virtually all debt.

MM Proposition II without taxes $r_{sL} = r_{sU} + (r_{sU} - r_d)(D/S)$. Thus, r_s increases in a precise way as leverage increases. In fact, this increase is just sufficient to offset the increased use of lower-cost debt.

moderate net operating working capital policy A policy that matches asset and liability maturities. It is also referred to as maturity matching or the self-liquidating approach.

Modified Internal Rate of Return (MIRR) method Assumes that cash flows from all projects are reinvested at the cost of capital, not at the project's own IRR. This makes the modified internal rate of return a better indicator of a project's true profitability.

money market A financial market for debt securities with maturities of less than 1 year (short-term). The New York money market is the world's largest.

money market fund A mutual fund that invests in short-term debt instruments and offers investors check-writing privileges; thus, it amounts to an interest-bearing checking account.

Monte Carlo simulation analysis A risk analysis technique in which a computer is used to simulate probable future events and thus to estimate the likely profitability and risk of a project.

mortgage bond A bond for which a corporation pledges certain assets as security. All such bonds are written subject to an indenture.

multinational (or global) corporation A corporation that operates in two or more countries.

municipal bond Issued by state and local governments. The interest earned on most municipal bonds is exempt from federal taxes and also from state taxes if the holder is a resident of the issuing state.

municipal bond insurance An insurance company guarantees to pay the coupon and principal payments should the issuer of the bond (the municipality) default. This reduces the risk to investors who are willing to accept a lower coupon rate for an insured bond issue compared to an uninsured issue.

mutual fund A corporation that sells shares in the fund and uses the proceeds to buy stocks, long-term bonds, or short-term debt instruments. The resulting dividends, interest, and capital gains are distributed to the fund's shareholders after the deduction of operating expenses. Some funds specialize in certain types of securities, such as growth stocks, international stocks, or municipal bonds.

mutually exclusive projects Projects that cannot be performed at the same time. A company could choose either Project 1 or Project 2, or it can reject both, but it cannot accept both projects.

naked call option A call option written when the writer does not have the underlying stock in his or her portfolio to back up the option if it is exercised.

National Association of Securities Dealers (NASD) An industry group primarily concerned with the operation of the over-the-counter (OTC) market.

natural hedge A transaction between two counterparties where both parties' risks are reduced.

net advantage to leasing (NAL) The dollar value of the lease to the lessee. It is the net present value of leasing minus the net present value of owning.

net cash flow The sum of net income plus noncash adjustments.

net float The difference between a firm's disbursement float and collections float.

net operating working capital (NOWC) Operating current assets minus operating current liabilities. Operating current assets are the current assets used to support operations, such as cash, accounts receivable, and inventory. They do not include short-term investments. Operating current liabilities are the current liabilities that are a natural consequence of the firm's operations, such as accounts payable and accruals. They do not include notes payable or any other short-term debt that charges interest.

net present value (NPV) method The present value of the project's expected future cash flows, discounted at the appropriate cost of capital. NPV is a direct measure of the value of the project to shareholders.

net working capital Current assets minus current liabilities.

new issue market The market for stock of companies that go public.

nominal (quoted) interest rate, I_{NOM} The rate of interest stated in a contract. If the compounding occurs annually, the effective annual rate and the nominal rate are the same. If compounding occurs more frequently, the effective annual rate is greater than the nominal rate. The nominal annual interest rate is also called the annual percentage rate, or APR.

nominal rate of return, r_n Includes an inflation adjustment (premium). Thus, if nominal rates of return are used in the capital budgeting process, then the net cash flows must also be nominal.

nominal risk-free rate of interest, r_{RF} The real risk-free rate plus a premium for expected inflation. The short-term nominal risk-free rate is usually approximated by the U.S. Treasury bill rate, and the long-term nominal risk-free rate is approximated by the rate on U.S. Treasury bonds.

nondiversifiable risk Risk that cannot be diversified away.

nonnormal cash flow projects Projects with a large cash outflow either sometime during or at the end of their lives. A common problem encountered when evaluating projects with nonnormal cash flows is multiple internal rates of return.

nonoperating assets Include investments in marketable securities and noncontrolling interests in the stock of other companies.

nonpecuniary benefits Perks that are not actual cash payments, such as lavish offices, memberships at country clubs, corporate jets, and excessively large staffs.

NOPAT (net operating profit after taxes) The amount of profit a company would generate if it had no debt and no financial assets.

normal cash flow project A project with one or more cash outflows (costs) followed by a series of cash inflows.

normal distribution A widely used probability distribution. One feature is that the actual value will be within ±1 standard deviation of the *expected* return 68.26% of the time.

normal yield curve When the yield curve slopes upward it is said to be "normal," because it is like this most of the time.

not-for-profit corporation A tax-exempt charitable organization. The tax code defines a charitable organization as any corporation, community chest, fund, or foundation that is organized and operated exclusively for religious, charitable, scientific, public safety, literary, or educational purposes. This standard may be expanded to include an organization that provides health care services provided other requirements are met.

off–balance sheet financing A financing technique in which a firm uses partnerships and other arrangements to (in effect) borrow money while not reporting the liability on its balance sheet. For example, for many years neither leased assets nor the liabilities under lease contracts appeared on the lessees' balance sheets. To correct this problem, the Financial Accounting Standards Board issued FASB Statement 13.

official statement Contains information about municipal bond issues. It is prepared before the issue is brought to market.

open outcry auction A method of matching buyers and sellers in which the buyers and sellers are face to face, all stating a price at which they will buy or sell.

operating capital The sum of net operating working capital and operating long-term assets, such as net plant and equipment. Operating capital also is equal to the net amount of capital raised from investors. This is the amount of interest-bearing debt plus preferred stock plus common equity minus short-term investments. Also called total net operating capital, net operating capital, or net operating assets.

operating company A company controlled by a holding company.

operating current assets The current assets used to support operations, such as cash, accounts receivable, and inventory. It does not include short-term investments.

operating current liabilities The current liabilities that are a natural consequence of the firm's operations, such as accounts payable and accruals. It does not include notes payable or any other short-term debt that charges interest.

operating lease Provides for both financing and maintenance. Generally, the operating lease contract is written for a period considerably shorter than the expected life of the leased equipment and contains a cancellation clause; sometimes called a service lease.

operating leverage The extent to which fixed costs are used in a firm's operations. If a high percentage of a firm's total costs are fixed costs, then the firm is said to have a high degree of operating leverage. Operating leverage is a measure of one element of business risk but does not include the second major element, sales variability.

operating merger Occurs when the operations of two companies are integrated with the expectation of obtaining synergistic gains. These may occur in response to economies of scale, management efficiency, or a host of other factors.

operating profit margin Ratio of earnings before interest and taxes divided by sales.

opportunity cost A cash flow that a firm must forgo in order to accept a project. For example, if the project requires the use of a building that could otherwise be sold, then the market value of the building is an opportunity cost of the project.

opportunity cost rate The rate of return available on the best alternative investment of similar risk.

optimal distribution policy The distribution policy that maximizes the value of the firm by choosing the optimal level and form of distributions (dividends and stock repurchases).

optimal dividend policy The dividend policy that strikes a balance between current dividends and future growth and maximizes the firm's stock price.

optimal portfolio The point at which the efficient set of portfolios—the efficient frontier—is just tangent to the investor's indifference curve. This point marks the highest level of satisfaction an investor can attain given the set of potential portfolios.

option A contract that gives its holder the right to buy or sell an asset at some predetermined price within a specified period of time.

ordinary (deferred) annuity An annuity with a fixed number of equal payments occurring at the end of each period.

original issue discount (OID) bond In general, any bond originally offered at a price that is significantly below its par value.

original maturity The maturity of a bond when it was issued.

out-of-the-money option An option that, if exercised immediately, could not be exercised profitably. For a call, the stock price is less than the strike price. For a put, the stock price is greater than the strike price.

overfunded pension plan A pension plan in which the assets on hand exceed the present value of all expected retirement benefits.

par value The nominal or face value of a stock or bond. The par value of a bond generally represents the amount of money that the firm borrows and promises to repay at some future date. The par value of a bond is often $1,000, but it can be $5,000 or more.

parent company Another name for a holding company. A parent company will often have control over many subsidiaries.

partnership A partnership exists when two or more persons associate to conduct a business.

payables deferral period The average length of time between a firm's purchase of materials and labor and the payment of cash for them. It is calculated by dividing accounts payable by credit purchases per day (i.e., cost of goods sold ÷ 365).

payback period The number of years it takes a firm to recover its project investment. Payback does not capture a project's entire cash flow stream and is thus not the preferred evaluation method. Note, however, that the payback does measure a project's liquidity, so many firms use it as a risk measure.

payment date The date on which a firm actually mails dividend checks.

payment, PMT Equal to the dollar amount of an equal or constant cash flow (an annuity).

payment-in-kind bond (PIK bond) A bond that doesn't pay cash coupons but, instead, pays out a percentage of additional bonds.

payments pattern approach A method of monitoring accounts receivable that looks for changes in a customers' payment pattern. This takes into account the seasonal nature of customer orders.

pegged exchange rates Rates that are fixed against a major currency such as the U.S. dollar. Consequently, the values of the pegged currencies move together over time.

Pension Benefit Guarantee Corporation Established by ERISA to insure corporate defined benefits plans; PBGC steps in and takes over payments to retirees of bankrupt companies with underfunded pension plans.

perfect hedge A hedge in which the gain or loss on the hedged transaction exactly offsets the loss or gain on the unhedged position.

periodic rate, I$_{PER}$ The rate charged by a lender or paid by a borrower each period. It can be a rate per year, per 6-month period, per quarter, per month, per day, or per any other time interval (usually 1 year or less).

permanent net operating working capital The NOWC required when the economy is weak and seasonal sales are at their low point. Thus, this level of NOWC always requires financing and can be regarded as permanent.

perpetuity A series of payments of a fixed amount that continue indefinitely.

physical location exchanges Exchanges, such as the New York Stock Exchange, that facilitate trading of securities at a particular location.

plug technique Technique used in financial forecasting to "plug" in enough new liabilities or assets to make the balance sheets balance.

poison pills Shareholder rights provisions that allow existing shareholders in a company to purchase additional shares of stock at a lower-than-market value if a potential acquirer purchases a controlling stake in the company.

political risk Refers to the possibility of expropriation and the unanticipated restriction of cash flows to the parent by a foreign government.

pooling of interests A method of accounting for a merger in which the consolidated balance sheet is constructed by simply adding together the balance sheets of the merged companies. This is no longer allowed.

portability A portable pension plan is one that the employee can carry from one employer to another.

portfolio A group of individual assets held in combination. An asset that would be relatively risky if held in isolation may have little or no risk if held in a well-diversified portfolio.

post-audit The final aspect of the capital budgeting process. The post-audit is a feedback process in which the actual results are compared with those predicted in the original capital budgeting analysis. The post-audit has several purposes, of which the most important are to improve forecasts and operations.

precautionary balance A cash balance held in reserve for random, unforeseen fluctuations in cash inflows and outflows.

preemptive right Gives the current shareholders the right to purchase any new shares issued in proportion to their current holdings. The preemptive right enables current owners to maintain their proportionate share of ownership and control of the business.

preferred stock A hybrid security that is similar to bonds in some respects and to common stock in other respects. Preferred dividends are similar to interest payments on bonds in that they are fixed in amount and generally must be paid before common stock dividends can be paid. If the preferred dividend is not earned, the directors can omit it without throwing the company into bankruptcy.

premium bond Bond prices and interest rates are inversely related; that is, they tend to move in the opposite direction from one another. A fixed-rate bond will sell at par when its coupon interest rate is equal to the going rate of interest, r_d. When the going rate of interest is above the coupon rate, a fixed-rate bond will sell at a "discount" below its par value. If current interest rates are below the coupon rate, a fixed-rate bond will sell at a "premium" above its par value.

premium on forward rate Occurs when the forward exchange rate differs from the spot rate. When the forward rate is above the spot rate, it is said to be at a premium.

prepackaged bankruptcy (or pre-pack) A type of reorganization that combines the advantages of informal workouts and formal Chapter 11 reorganization.

pre-tax earnings or income The amount of earnings (or income) that is subject to taxes. It is also equal to earnings before interest and taxes (EBIT) less the interest expense. It is sometimes called earnings before taxes (EBT)

price/cash flow ratio Calculated by dividing price per share by cash flow per share. This shows how much investors are willing to pay per dollar of cash flow.

price/earnings (P/E) ratio Calculated by dividing price per share by earnings per share. This shows how much investors are willing to pay per dollar of reported profits.

price/EBITDA ratio The ratio of price per share divided by per share earnings before interest, depreciation, and amortization.

primary market Markets in which newly issued securities are sold for the first time.

priority of claims in liquidation Established in Chapter 7 of the Bankruptcy Act. It specifies the order in which the debtor's assets are distributed among the creditors.

private markets Markets in which transactions are worked out directly between two parties and structured in any manner that appeals to them. Bank loans and private placements of debt with insurance companies are examples of private market transactions.

private placement The sale of stock to only one or a few investors, usually institutional investors. The advantages of private placements are lower flotation costs and greater speed, since the shares issued are not subject to Securities and Exchange Commission registration.

probability distribution A listing, chart, or graph of all possible outcomes, such as expected rates of return, with a probability assigned to each outcome.

production opportunities One of the factors affecting the cost of money. Represents the ability to turn capital into benefits.

professional association See professional corporation.

professional corporation (PC) Has most of the benefits of incorporation, but the participants are not relieved of professional (malpractice) liability; known in some states as a professional association (PA).

profit margin on sales Calculated by dividing net income by sales; gives the profit per dollar of sales.

profit sharing plan Under this type of pension plan, employers make payments into the retirement fund but the payments to retirees vary with the level of corporate profits.

profitability index Found by dividing the project's present value of future cash flows by its initial cost. A profitability index greater than 1 is equivalent to a project's having positive net present value.

profitability ratios Ratios that show the combined effects of liquidity, asset management, and debt on operations.

progressive tax A tax system in which the higher one's income, the larger the percentage paid in taxes.

project cash flows The incremental cash flows of a proposed project.

project cost of capital The risk-adjusted discount rate for that project.

project financing Financing method in which the project's creditors do not have full recourse against the borrowers; the lenders and lessors must be paid from the project's cash flows and equity.

projected (pro forma) financial statement Shows how an actual statement would look if certain assumptions are realized.

promissory note A document specifying the terms and conditions of a loan, including the amount, interest rate, and repayment schedule.

proprietorship A business owned by one individual.

prospectus Summarizes information about a new security issue and the issuing company.

proxy A document giving one person the authority to act for another, typically the power to vote shares of common stock.

proxy fight An attempt to take over a company in which an outside group solicits existing shareholders' proxies, which are authorizations to vote shares in a shareholders' meeting, in an effort to overthrow management and take control of the business.

public markets Markets in which standardized contracts are traded on organized exchanges. Securities that are issued in public markets, such as common stock and corporate bonds, are ultimately held by a large number of individuals.

public offering An offer of new common stock to the general public.

publicly owned corporation Corporation in which the stock is owned by a large number of investors, most of whom are not active in management.

purchase accounting A method of accounting for a merger in which the merger is handled as a purchase. In this method, the acquiring firm is assumed to have "bought" the acquired company in much the same way it would buy any capital asset.

purchasing power parity Implies that the level of exchange rates adjusts so that identical goods cost the same in different countries. Sometimes referred to as the "law of one price."

put option Allows the holder to sell the asset at some predetermined price within a specified period of time.

put—call parity A relationship between call and put option prices.

PV The value today of a future payment, or stream of payments, discounted at the appropriate rate of interest. PV is also the beginning amount that will grow to some future value.

PVA$_N$ The value today of a future stream of N equal payments at the end of each period (an ordinary annuity).

PVIFA$_{I,N}$ The present value interest factor for an ordinary annuity of N periodic payments discounted at I percent interest per period.

PVIF$_{I,N}$ The present value interest factor for a lump sum received N periods in the future discounted at I percent per period.

quick, or acid test, ratio Found by taking current assets less inventories and then dividing by current liabilities.

real options Occur when managers can influence the size and risk of a project's cash flows by taking different actions during the project's life. They are referred to as real options because they deal with real as opposed to financial assets. They are also called managerial options because they give opportunities to managers to respond to changing market conditions. Sometimes they are called strategic options because they often deal with strategic issues. Finally, they are also called embedded options because they are a part of another project.

real rate of return, r$_r$ Contains no adjustment for expected inflation. If net cash flows from a project do not include inflation adjustments, then the cash flows should be discounted at the real cost of capital. In a similar manner, the internal rate of return resulting from real net cash flows should be compared with the real cost of capital.

real risk-free rate of interest, r* The interest rate on a risk-free security in an economy with zero inflation. The real risk-free rate could also be called the pure rate of interest since it is the rate of interest that would exist on very short-term, default-free U.S. Treasury securities if the expected rate of inflation were zero.

realized rate of return, r̄ The actual return an investor receives on his or her investment. It can be quite different from the expected return.

receivables collection period The average length of time required to convert a firm's receivables into cash. It is calculated by dividing accounts receivable by sales per day.

red herring (preliminary) prospectus A preliminary prospectus that may be distributed to potential buyers prior to approval of the registration statement by the Securities and Exchange Commission. After the registration has become effective, the securities—accompanied by the prospectus—may be offered for sale.

redeemable bond Gives investors the right to sell the bonds back to the corporation at a price that is usually close to the par value. If interest rates rise, then investors can redeem the bonds and reinvest at the higher rates.

refunding Occurs when a company issues debt at current low rates and uses the proceeds to repurchase one of its existing high–coupon rate debt issues. Often these are callable issues, which means the company can purchase the debt at a call price lower than the market price.

registration statement Required by the Securities and Exchange Commission before a company's securities can be offered to the public. This statement is used to summarize various financial and legal information about the company.

reinvestment rate risk Occurs when a short-term debt security must be "rolled over." If interest rates have fallen then the reinvestment of principal will be at a lower rate, with correspondingly lower interest payments and ending value.

relative priority doctrine More flexible than absolute priority. Gives a more balanced consideration to all claimants in a bankruptcy reorganization than does the absolute priority doctrine.

relaxed net operating working capital policy A policy under which relatively large amounts of cash, marketable securities, and inventories are carried and under which sales are stimulated by a liberal credit policy, resulting in a high level of receivables.

relevant risk The stock's contribution to the risk of a well-diversified portfolio.

reorder point The inventory level at which a new order is placed.

reorganization in bankruptcy A court-approved attempt to keep a company alive by changing its capital structure in lieu of liquidation. A reorganization must adhere to the standards of fairness and feasibility.

repatriation of earnings The cash flow, usually in the form of dividends or royalties, from the foreign branch or subsidiary to the parent company. These cash flows must be converted to the currency of the parent and thus are subject to future exchange rate changes. A foreign government may restrict the amount of cash that may be repatriated.

replacement chain (common life) approach A method of comparing mutually exclusive projects that have unequal lives. Each project is replicated so that they will both terminate in a common year. If projects with lives of 3 years and 5 years are being evaluated, then the 3-year project would be replicated 5 times and the 5-year project replicated three times; thus, both projects would terminate in 15 years.

replicating portfolio A combination of the underlying stock and a risk-free investment that instantaneously replicates the payoffs of an option.

required rate of return, r_s The minimum acceptable rate of return, considering both its risk and the returns available on other investments.

required return on a portfolio, r_p The weighted average of the required returns on the individual stocks comprising the portfolio.

reserve borrowing capacity Exists when a firm uses less debt under "normal" conditions than called for by the trade-off theory. This allows the firm some flexibility to use debt in the future when additional capital is needed.

residual distribution model In this model, firms should pay dividends only when more earnings are available than needed to support the optimal capital budget.

residual value The market value of the leased property at the expiration of the lease. The estimate of the residual value is one of the key elements in lease analysis.

restricted charitable contributions Donations that can be used only for designated purposes.

restricted net operating working capital policy A policy under which holdings of cash, securities, inventories, and receivables are minimized.

restricted voting rights A provision that automatically deprives a shareholder of voting rights if the shareholder owns more than a specified amount of stock.

retained earnings The portion of the firm's earnings that have been saved rather than paid out as dividends.

retiree health benefits Companies must accrue the retiree health care liability and show the accrued liability on the balance sheets rather than expense the cash flows as they occur.

return on common equity (ROE) Found by dividing net income by common equity.

return on invested capital (ROIC) Net operating profit after taxes divided by the operating capital.

return on total assets (ROA) The ratio of net income to total assets.

revaluation Occurs when the relative price of a currency is increased. It is the opposite of devaluation.

revenue bonds Type of municipal bonds that are secured by the revenues derived from projects such as roads and bridges, airports, water and sewage systems, and not-for-profit health care facilities.

reverse split Situation in which shareholders exchange a particular number of shares of stock for a smaller number of new shares.

revolving credit agreement A formal, committed line of credit extended by a bank or other lending institution.

rights offering Occurs when a corporation sells a new issue of common stock to its existing stockholders. Each stockholder receives a certificate, called a stock purchase right, giving the stockholder the option to purchase a specified number of the new shares. The rights are issued in proportion to the amount of stock that each shareholder currently owns.

risk arbitrage The practice of purchasing stock in companies (in the context of mergers) that may become takeover targets.

risk aversion A risk-averse investor dislikes risk and requires a higher rate of return as an inducement to buy riskier securities.

risk in a portfolio context The risk that a stock adds to a portfolio, as opposed to the risk of the stock if it is held by itself.

risk premium for Stock i, RP_i The extra return that an investor requires to hold risky Stock i instead of a risk-free asset.

risk-adjusted discount rate Incorporates the risk of the project's cash flows. The cost of capital to the firm reflects the average risk of the firm's existing projects. Thus, new projects that are riskier than existing projects should have a higher risk-adjusted discount rate. Conversely, projects with less risk should have a lower risk-adjusted discount rate.

risky event An uncertain outcome that adversely affects a company's objectives.

roadshow Before an IPO, the senior management team and the investment banker make presentations to potential investors. They make three to five presentations daily over a 2-week period in 10 to 20 cities.

S corporation A small corporation that, under Subchapter S of the Internal Revenue Code, elects to be taxed as a proprietorship or a partnership yet retains limited liability and other benefits of the corporate form of organization.

safety stock Inventory held to guard against larger-than-normal sales and/or shipping delays.

sale-and-leaseback A type of financial lease in which the firm owning the property sells it to another firm, often a financial institution, while simultaneously entering into an agreement to lease the property back from the firm.

salvage value The market value of an asset after its useful life.

savings and loan associations (S&Ls) Financial institutions that take in most of their deposits from members of their community.

scenario analysis A shorter version of simulation analysis that uses only a few outcomes. Often the outcomes are for three scenarios: optimistic, pessimistic, and most likely.

seasonal effects on ratios Seasonal factors can distort ratio analysis. At certain times of the year, a firm may have excessive inventories in preparation of a "season" of high demand. Therefore, an inventory turnover ratio taken at this time will be radically different than one taken after the season.

seasoned issue A bond that has been on the market for a while

secondary market Markets in which securities are resold after initial issue in the primary market. The New York Stock Exchange is an example.

secured loan A loan backed by collateral, which is often in the form of inventories or receivables.

Securities and Exchange Commission (SEC) A government agency that regulates the sales of new securities and the operations of securities exchanges. The SEC, along with other government agencies and self-regulation, helps ensure stable markets, sound brokerage firms, and the absence of stock manipulation.

securitization The process whereby financial instruments that were previously thinly traded are converted to a form that creates greater liquidity. Securitization also applies to the situation where specific assets are pledged as collateral for securities, thus creating asset-backed securities. One example of the former is junk bonds; an example of the latter is mortgage-backed securities.

Security Market Line (SML) Represents, in a graphical form, the relationship between the risk of an asset as measured by its beta and the required rates of return for individual securities. The SML equation is one of the key results of the CAPM: $r_i = r_{RF} + b_i(r_M - r_{RF})$.

semistrong form of market efficiency States that current market prices reflect all publicly available information. Therefore, the only way to gain abnormal returns on a stock is to possess inside information about the company's stock.

sensitivity analysis Indicates exactly how much net present value will change in response to a given change in an input variable, other things held constant. Sensitivity analysis is sometimes called "what if" analysis because it answers this type of question.

shareholder rights provision Also known as a poison pill, it allows existing shareholders to purchase additional shares of stock at a price that is lower than the market value if a potential acquirer purchases a controlling stake in the company.

Sharpe's reward-to-variability ratio A portfolio's average return in excess of the risk-free rate divided by its standard deviation. It is a measure of how much extra return a portfolio offers over the risk-free rate for a unit of stand-alone risk.

shelf registration Frequently, companies will file a master registration statement and then update it with a shortform statement just before an offering. This procedure is termed shelf registration because companies put new securities "on the shelf" and then later sell them when the market is right.

short hedges Occur when futures contracts are sold to guard against price declines.

simple interest The situation when interest is not compounded; that is, interest is not earned on interest. Also called regular interest. Divide the nominal interest rate by 365 and multiply by the number of days the funds are borrowed to find the interest for the term borrowed.

sinking fund Facilitates the orderly retirement of a bond issue. This can be achieved in one of two ways: (1) the company can call in for redemption (at par value) a certain percentage of bonds each year, or (2) the company may buy the required amount of bonds on the open market.

social value Projects of not-for-profit businesses are expected to provide a social value in addition to an economic value.

soft currencies Currencies of countries that set the exchange rate but do not allow their currencies to be traded on world markets.

special dividend A dividend paid, in addition to the regular dividend, when earnings permit. Firms with volatile earnings may have a low regular dividend that can be maintained even in years of low profit (or high capital investment) but is supplemented by an extra dividend when excess funds are available.

special tax bonds Type of municipal bonds that are secured by a specified tax, such as a tax on utility services.

speculative balances Funds held by a firm in order to have cash for taking advantage of bargain purchases or growth opportunities.

spin-off Occurs when a holding company distributes the stock of one of the operating companies to its shareholders, thus passing control from the holding company to the shareholders directly.

spontaneous liabilities Liabilities that grow with sales, such as accounts payable and accruals.

spot rate The exchange rate that applies to "on the spot" trades or, more precisely, to exchanges that occur 2 days following the day of trade (in other words, current exchanges).

spread, underwriting The difference between the price at which an underwriter sells the stock in an initial public offering and the proceeds that the underwriter passes on to the issuing firm; the fee collected by the underwriter. It is often about 7% of the offering price.

spread, yield The difference between the yield of a bond relative to another bond with less risk.

stakeholders All parties that have an interest, financial or otherwise, in a not-for-profit business.

stand-alone risk The risk an investor takes by holding only one asset.

standard deviation, σ A statistical measure of the variability of a set of observations. It is the square root of the variance.

statement of cash flows Reports the impact of a firm's operating, investing, and financing activities on cash flows over an accounting period.

statement of stockholders' equity Statement showing the beginning stockholders' equity, any changes due to stock issues/repurchases, the amount of net income that is retained, and the ending stockholders' equity.

stepped-up strike (or exercise) price A provision in a warrant that increases the strike price over time. This provision is included to encourage owners to exercise their warrants.

stock dividend Increases the number of shares outstanding but at a slower rate than splits. Current shareholders receive additional shares on some proportional basis. Thus, a holder of 100 shares would receive 5 additional shares at no cost if a 5% stock dividend were declared.

stock option Allows its owner to purchase a share of stock at a fixed price, called the strike price or the exercise price, no matter what the actual price of the stock is. Stock options always have an expiration date, after which they cannot be exercised.

stock repurchase Occurs when a firm repurchases its own stock. These shares of stock are then referred to as treasury stock.

stock split Current shareholders are given some number (or fraction) of shares for each stock share owned. Thus, in a 3-for-1 split, each shareholder would receive three new shares in exchange for each old share, thereby tripling the number of shares outstanding. Stock splits usually occur when the stock price is outside of the optimal trading range.

strategic options Options that often deal with strategic issues. Also called real options, embedded options, and managerial options.

stretching accounts payable The practice of deliberately paying accounts late.

strike (or exercise) price The price stated in the option contract at which the security can be bought (or sold).

strong form of market efficiency Assumes that all information pertaining to a stock, whether public or inside information, is reflected in current market prices. Thus, no investors would be able to earn abnormal returns in the stock market.

structured note A debt obligation derived from another debt obligation. Permits a partitioning of risks to give investors what they want.

subordinated debenture Debentures that have claims on assets, in the event of bankruptcy, only after senior debt (as named in the subordinated debt's indenture) has been paid off. Subordinated debentures may be subordinated to designated notes payable or to all other debt.

sunk cost A cost that has already occurred and is not affected by the capital project decision. Sunk costs are not relevant to capital budgeting decisions.

super poison put A provision in a bond covenant which enables a bondholder to turn in, or "put," a bond back to the issuer at par in the event of a takeover, merger, or major recapitalization.

swap An exchange of cash payment obligations. Usually occurs because the parties involved prefer someone else's payment pattern or type.

sweetener A feature that makes a security more attractive to some investors, thereby inducing them to accept a lower current yield. Convertible features and warrants are examples of sweeteners.

synchronization of cash flows Occurs when firms are able to time cash receipts to coincide with cash requirements.

synergy Occurs when the whole is greater than the sum of its parts. When applied to mergers, a synergistic merger occurs when the post-merger earnings exceed the sum of the separate companies' pre-merger earnings.

takeover An action whereby a person or group succeeds in ousting a firm's management and taking control of the company.

tapping fund assets Deals with the issue of allowing a corporation to invest its pension fund assets to the corporation's own advantage.

target capital structure The relative amount of debt, preferred stock, and common equity that the firm desires. The weighted average cost of capital should be based on these target weights.

target cash balance The desired cash balance that a firm plans to maintain in order to conduct business.

target company A firm that another company seeks to acquire.

target distribution ratio Percentage of net income distributed to shareholders through cash dividends or stock repurchases.

target payout ratio Percentage of net income paid as a cash dividend.

targeted share repurchases Also known as greenmail, occurs when a company buys back stock from a potential acquirer at a price that is higher than the market price. In return, the potential acquirer agrees not to attempt to take over the company.

tax loss carryback and carryforward Ordinary corporate operating losses can be carried backward for 2 years or forward for 20 years to offset taxable income in a given year.

tax preference theory Proposes that investors prefer capital gains over dividends, because capital gains taxes can be deferred into the future but taxes on dividends must be paid as the dividends are received.

taxable income Gross income less a set of exemptions and deductions that are spelled out in the instructions to the tax forms that individuals must file.

technical analysts Stock analysts who believe that past trends or patterns in stock prices can be used to predict future stock prices.

TED spread The 3-month LIBOR rate minus the 3-month T-bill rate. It is a measure of risk aversion and measures the extra compensation that banks require to induce them to lend to one another.

temporary net operating working capital The NOWC required above the permanent level when the economy is strong and/or seasonal sales are high.

tender offer The offer of one firm to buy the stock of another by going directly to the stockholders, frequently over the opposition of the target company's management.

term structure of interest rates The relationship between yield to maturity and term to maturity for bonds of a single risk class.

terminal value Value of operations at the end of the explicit forecast period; equal to the present value of all free cash flows beyond the forecast period, discounted back to the end of the forecast period at the weighted average cost of capital.

time line A graphical representation used to show the timing of cash flows.

time preferences for consumption One of the factors affecting the cost of money. Consumers would, everything else equal, prefer to consume now over consuming later.

time value (of an option) The price of an option minus its exercise value.

times-interest-earned (TIE) ratio Determined by dividing earnings before interest and taxes by the interest charges. This ratio measures the extent to which operating income can decline before the firm is unable to meet its annual interest costs.

total assets turnover ratio Measures the turnover of all the firm's assets; it is calculated by dividing sales by total assets.

total carrying cost The costs of carrying inventory.

total inventory costs The sum of ordering and carrying costs.

total net present value (TNPV) Equal to net present value plus net present social value in a not-for-profit business.

total ordering cost The costs of ordering inventory.

tracking (or target) stock Stock whose dividends are tied to a particular part of a company.

trade credit Debt arising from credit sales and recorded as an account receivable by the seller and as an account payable by the buyer.

trade deficit Occurs when a country imports more goods from abroad than it exports.

trade discounts Price reductions that suppliers offer customers for early payment of bills.

trade-off model The addition of financial distress and agency costs to either the MM tax model or the Miller model. In this model, the optimal capital structure can be visualized as a trade-off between the benefit of debt (the interest tax shelter) and the costs of debt (financial distress and agency costs).

transactions balance The cash balance associated with payments and collections; the balance necessary for day-to-day operations.

Treasury bond Bonds issued by the federal government; sometimes called T-bonds or government bonds. Treasury bonds have no default risk.

Treasury Inflation-Protected Securities (TIPS) A bond issued by the U.S. Treasury indexed to the inflation rate.

trend analysis An analysis of a firm's financial ratios over time. It is used to estimate the likelihood of improvement or deterioration in its financial situation.

Treynor's reward-to-volatility ratio A portfolio's average return in excess of the risk-free rate divided by its beta. This measures the extra return a portfolio offers over the risk-free rate for a unit of beta risk.

trustee (for a bond) An official who represents the bondholders and makes sure the indentures are carried out.

uncollected balances schedule Helps a firm monitor its receivables better and also forecast future receivables balances; an integral part of the payments pattern approach.

underfunded pension plan A pension plan in which the present value of expected retirement benefits exceeds the assets on hand.

underinvestment problem A type of agency problem in which high debt can cause managers to forgo positive NPV projects unless they are extremely safe.

underwritten arrangement Contract between a firm and an investment banker when stock is issued. An investment banker agrees to buy the entire issue at a set price and then resells the stock at the offering price. Thus, the risk of selling the issue rests with the investment banker.

value at risk (VaR) The dollar value that defines a specified percentile in the probability distribution of portfolio's loss or a project's NPV. For example, if the specified percentile is 5%, a VaR of −$1 million means that there is a 5% probability that the portfolio will lose $1 million or more.

value of operations (V_{op}) The present value of all expected future free cash flows when discounted at the weighted average cost of capital.

variance, σ^2 A measure of the distribution's variability. It is the sum of the squared deviations about the expected value.

venture capitalist The manager of a venture capital fund. The fund raises most of its capital from institutional investors and invests in start-up companies in exchange for equity.

vertical merger Occurs when a company acquires another firm that is "upstream" or "downstream"; for example, an automobile manufacturer acquires a steel producer.

vesting If employees have the rights to receive pension benefits even if they leave the company prior to retirement, their rights are said to be vested.

vesting period Period during which employee stock options cannot be exercised.

warrant A call option, issued by a company, that allows the holder to buy a stated number of shares of stock from the company at a specified price. Warrants are generally distributed with debt, or preferred stock, to induce investors to buy those securities at lower cost.

weak form of market efficiency Assumes that all information contained in past price movements is fully reflected in current market prices. Thus, information about recent trends in a stock's price is of no use in selecting a stock.

weighted average cost of capital (WACC) The weighted average of the after-tax component costs of capital—debt, preferred stock, and common equity. Each weighting factor is the proportion of that type of capital in the optimal, or target, capital structure.

white knight A friendly competing bidder that a target management likes better than the company making a hostile offer; the target solicits a merger with the white knight as a preferable alternative.

window dressing Techniques employed by firms to make their financial statements look better than they really are.

working capital A firm's investment in short-term assets—cash, marketable securities, inventory, and accounts receivable.

workout Voluntary reorganization plans arranged between creditors and generally sound companies experiencing temporary financial difficulties. Workouts typically require some restructuring of the firm's debt.

Yankee bonds Bond issued by a foreign borrower denominated in dollars and sold in the United States under SEC regulations.

yield curve The curve that results when yield to maturity is plotted on the y-axis with term to maturity on the x-axis.

yield to call (YTC) The rate of interest earned on a bond if it is called. If current interest rates are well below an outstanding callable bond's coupon rate, then the YTC may be a more relevant estimate of expected return than the YTM because the bond is likely to be called.

yield to maturity (YTM) The rate of interest earned on a bond if it is held to maturity.

zero coupon bond Pays no coupons at all but is offered at a substantial discount below its par value and hence provides capital appreciation rather than interest income.

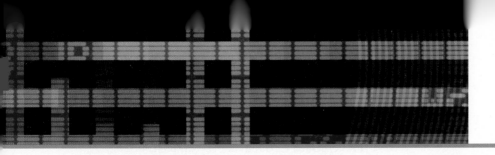

A

Abreo, Leslie, 730
Adams, Paul D., 828n
Agrawal, A., 396n
Ainina, M. Fall, 1004n
Alderson, Michael J., 775n
Allen, Jeffrey W., 1031n
Altman, Edward I., 962n, 968n
Amram, Martha, 563n
Anderson, Kenneth E., 1019n
Andrade, Gregor, 633n
Appleton, Elaine L., 827
Ashcraft, Adam B., 30
Asquith, P., 581n, 791n

B

Baker, H. Kent, 603n, 709n, 1004n
Baker, Malcolm, 630n, 633n
Bansal, Vipul K., 949n
Barberis, Nicholas, 78, 78n
Barclay, Michael J., 630n
Baskin, Jonathon, 629n
Bauguess, Scott, 713n, 716n
Baumol, William, 896, 896n
Benartzi, Shlomo, 581n
Beranek, William, 971n
Berger, Philip, 998n
Berk, Jonathan B., 81n
Bernanke, Ben, 39, 629n
Berra, Yogi, 347, 624
Betker, Brian L., 976n
Bhagwat, Yatin, 438n
Bielinski, Daniel W., 1004n
Billingsley, Randall S., 791n
Black, Fischer, 198
Blake, Marshall, 924n
Blume, Marshall E., 113n, 115, 115n
Bodnar, Gordon M., 927n
Boehmer, Robert, 971n
Bonker, Dick, 880n

B (continued)

Born, Jeffrey A., 582n
Brav, Alon, 601n
Brennan, Michael, 563n
Brick, I. E., 392n
Brook, Yaron, 581n
Brooks, Robert, 176n, 325n
Brown, Keith C., 949n
Bruner, Robert E., 424n
Bubnys, Edward L., 121n
Buffett, Warren, 604n
Burman, Leonard, 578n, 625n
Burns, N., 396n

C

Campbell, John Y., 51n, 77n
Carbaugh, Robert, 1051n
Carhart, Mark, 75n
Castelino, Mark G., 945n
Chadha, S., 396n
Chan, Louis K. C., 51n
Chan, Su Han, 1030n
Chance, Don M., 176n, 198
Chang, Rosita P., 579n, 1070n
Charlton, William, Jr., 581n
Chatterjee, Sris, 976n
Chen, Hsuen-Chi, 1067n
Chen, Yehning, 968n
Cherney, Mike, 717
Chiang, Raymond C., 732n
Choi, Jongmoo Jay, 1049n
Christensen, Clayton M., 506
Clements, Jonathan, 73
Colbert, Stephen, 834
Constantinides, George, 78n, 713n
Cooley, Philip L., 679n
Cooney, John W., 713n
Copeland, Thomas E., 120n
Corman, Linda, 759n
Cruise, Tom, 23
Crum, Roy, 1040n

Subject Index

determinants of, 148–149, 148n
global economic crisis, 25
inflation premium, 150–152, 151n
multinational corporations, 1062–1063
nominal risk-free rate, 152
real risk-free rate of interest, 149–150, 149n
term structure of, 163–164
Interest tax shield, 656
Interest-only loans, 875
Interlocking boards of directors, 392
Intermediate Financial Management, 3
Internal control systems, 397
Internal expansion, 995
Internal rate of return (IRR), 459–465
  calculating, 459–460
  as evaluation measure, 465
  multiple, 460–462
  mutually exclusive projects and, 462–465
International Accounting Standards Board (IASB),
  220, 266, 750
International bond markets, 1065–1066
International business, 1064
International corporate governance,
  400–401
International country risk, 22
International Financial Reporting Standards
  (IFRS), 266
International Monetary Fund (IMF), 1051
International stock markets, 1066–1067
International Swaps and Derivatives
  Association, 27
Interstate public offerings, 701
In-the-money, 177
Intrinsic (fundamental) price, 9, 12
Intrinsic stock price, 302–303, 318, 591–595
Intrinsic (fundamental) value
  cash distributions on, 590–595
  corporations, 32, 33f
  cost of debt, 128, 147
  financial statements, 208, 253
  managerial behaviors and, 388–389
  risk and return, 38, 92
  stock options, 176
  stock prices, 301–302, 318
  stocks, 10, **302**
Intrinsic value of equity, 302
Inventory control systems
  accounting for, 902–905
  computerized systems, 901

just-in-time systems, 901–902
  outsourcing, 902
Inventory conversion period, 812
Inventory management, 826–827
  multinational corporation, 1079–1080
Inventory turnover ratio, 259–260, 270t
Inverse floaters, 949
Inverted ("abnormal") yield curve, 164
Investing activities, 218
Investment bankers
  mergers and, 1026–1027
Investment banking house, 13
Investment banks/underwriters, 700
  role of, 720–721
Investment policy, 436
Investment tax credit (ITC), 760
Investment timing option
  real options, 546–556
Investment timing options, 522
Investment-grade bonds, 155
Investors
  capital and, 412
  global economic crisis, 28
  indifference curve and, 103n
  optimal portfolio for, 100–101
  securitization of mortgages, 24
Involuntary petition, 968
IP (inflation premium), 150–152, 151n
IPOs. *See* **Initial public offerings (IPOs)**
IRR. *See* **Internal rate of return (IRR)**
ITC (investment tax credit), 760

J

Japan
  corporate governance in, 400–401
  stock index, 1069
J.C. Penney, 392
Jensen's alpha, 112
JIT (just-in-time) system, 901–902
Jobs and Growth Act, 578
Johnson & Johnson, 158
Joint venture, 1029
JPMorgan Chase, 29, 394, 583, 721, 963
Junior mortgages, 153
Junk bonds, 155, 165
"Just vote no" campaign, 391
Just-in-time (JIT) system, 901–902